stephanie alexander

ran the acclaimed Stephanie's Restaurant for twenty-one years before closing on New Year's Eve in 1997. The restaurant was the recipient of many national and international awards and accolades, and was regarded as an essential Melbourne experience. Stephanie made the momentous decision to close the restaurant in order to concentrate on her writing and to find the time to explore new ventures. In partnership with her daughter Lisa Montague, longtime friend Angela Clemens and cheese expert Will Studd, Stephanie opened the Richmond Hill Cafe and Larder in the autumn of 1997.

Stephanie was awarded an Order of Australia in 1994 for her services to the hospitality industry and to tourism, and for encouraging young apprentices. In 1995 she received an Australian Achiever award, which was presented to her by the Prime Minister.

Stephanie cooks from the heart but is always practical and understands very well the interests of the home cook. Through her writing and teaching, Stephanie continues to be an outspoken champion of the quality and diversity of Australian produce and the importance of good food in our lives. Her favourite pastimes are travelling and sharing a table with friends and family. Stephanie is a regular contributor to various national food publications. Her previous books include *Stephanie's Feasts and Stories*, *Stephanie's Seasons* and *Recipes My Mother Gave Me*. A series of cooking schools conducted near Siena, Italy, in 1997, in collaboration with Maggie Beer, led to *Stephanie Alexander & Maggie Beer's Tuscan Cookbook*, released in 1998.

the cook's

stephanie alexander

companion

Photography by Earl Carter

VIKING

Viking
Penguin Books Australia Ltd
487 Maroondah Highway, PO Box 257
Ringwood, Victoria 3134, Australia
Penguin Books Ltd
Harmondsworth, Middlesex, England
Penguin Putnam Inc.
375 Hudson Street, New York, New York 10014, USA
Penguin Books Canada Limited
10 Alcorn Avenue, Toronto, Ontario, Canada M4V 3B2
Penguin Books (N.Z.) Ltd
Cnr Rosedale and Airborne Roads, Albany, Auckland, New Zealand
Penguin Books (South Africa) (Pty) Ltd
4 Pallinghurst Road, Parktown 2193, South Africa

First published by Penguin Books Australia Ltd, 1996

20 19 18 17 16 15 14 13 12
Text copyright © Stephanie Alexander, 1996
Photographs copyright © Earl Carter, 1996

Designed by Sandy Cull
Photography by Earl Carter
Cover illustration by Rossana Vecchio
Text illustrations by Jacqui Young
Typeset in Sabon and Gill Sans by Midland Typesetters,
Maryborough, Victoria
Printed by South China Printing Co Ltd, Hong Kong

National Library of Australia
Cataloguing-in-Publication data:

Alexander Stephanie, 1940– .
    Stephanie Alexander: the cook's companion.

    Bibliography.
    Includes index.
    ISBN 0 670 86373 4.

    1. Cookery, Australian – Dictionaries. 2. Food – Dictionaries.
    3. Nutrition – Dictionaries. I. Title.

641.300994

contents

IN MEMORY OF MY MOTHER, MARY BURCHETT

i n t r o d u c t i o n This book is an attempt to encapsulate the experiences and wisdom gained during more than 25 years in professional kitchens and more than 40 years of enthusiastic cooking. I learnt to cook at my mother's side, and the images of her that have stayed with me (and that still bring a feeling of loss more than 10 years after her death) include Mum bent in front of the Aga oven scooping baked potatoes into her apron, shaping bread rolls for dinner, forking rough troughs in the mashed potato on top of the shepherd's pie, slipping a slice of butter under the crust of Grandma's bramble cake, or in full beekeeper's outfit setting out to gather the honey from the hive. | Many young people no longer learn to cook at home. Some have little experience of the family table. I hope this book might help to fill this gap. While writing it, I have pretended that you, the reader, have been at my side as I shop and select, store, chop, laugh, taste and, above all, enjoy the heady world of great food. I want it to be the essential book for all those who love good food, and my aim has been to provide reliable information and inspiration for every busy food lover. Before you can cook with confidence you need to understand the raw materials. Here I give advice on how to choose a supple fresh bean rather than a tired bean. Preparing and storing those beans is also covered. Quick ideas to start you off are accompanied by recipes (all delicious!), most of which do not take a long time to prepare, although many will cook slowly without special attention.   *The Cook's Companion* does not claim to be encyclopedic. Rather I have considered what you are likely to have on hand in the cupboard or refrigerator or kitchen fruit bowl, or can easily obtain from the neighbourhood shopping centre. Do not look here for entries on asparagus peas, pignuts, bung kwangs, cardoons, cape gooseberries, riberries, guavas, mallow leaves, wild boar, partridge or other such exotic delicacies, and I apologise to lovers of kiwi fruit, pomegranates and persimmons. Space was my problem.   Nonetheless, *The Cook's Companion* includes an alphabetical listing of an extraordinary array of ingredients, many of which have been introduced to Australian kitchens over the last 20 years, some far more recently. I urge interested cooks to experiment with new ingredients and to ask the shopkeeper the best way of using unfamiliar foods. See a new shellfish, a new vegetable or a new cheese and try it as soon as possible.   A feature of Australia's food industry is the different climatic regions that not only permit us to enjoy freshly harvested fruit and vegetables for extended periods but also have the effect of blurring the seasons. It is not so easy to state with authority that an item is in season, for example, from April to June. Somewhere else in the country an early crop is probably being grown, while somewhere else a late crop will be going in. New research continues to find ways of permitting a second crop to be planted. Where possible, I have included national availability, but in general the seasonal information I give is from the perspective of the south-eastern States and can only be a guide. However, the over-riding principles of choosing fresh rather than frozen, local rather than long-travelled and premium rather than tired produce should result in the food with the best flavour being selected and enjoyed wherever you live. | It has been a deliberate decision *not* to describe foods in terms of their nutritional makeup. Nutrition is an important science and has contributed extremely valuable insights into the way foods affect our bodies. Recent research that has established the healthy consequences of following a Mediterranean diet is an outstanding example of this. Nutritional research has also been vital in reinforcing the importance of balance, variety and moderation in the diet and in debunking myths such as the belief that bread makes you fat. But knowing how many grams of fat or what vitamins a food contains or whether it includes anti-oxidants seems to be almost immaterial to the way the food choices of most people are made. I believe that noticing differences in depth of flavour, texture and juiciness, and appreciating, for example, the smell of warm strawberries produces more food lovers and fewer fast-food addicts than attempts to convince the latter to abandon 'bad' foods because of their nutritional paucity. | *The Cook's Companion* has been an enormous project and will, by the time of publication, have been with me for nearly 4 years. It will all have been worthwhile if this book encourages young people to cook and experienced cooks to enjoy cooking more.

a c k n o w l e d g e m e n t s *As always in a project of this size there are many individuals who deserve special thanks. First and foremost, thanks go to Caroline Pizzey for her tireless editing and support. Caroline sustained me whenever I felt overwhelmed by the size of the task I had set myself. I thank Julie Gibbs, Viking publisher, for her belief in this book, and her team at Penguin: Katie Purvis for coordinating the production and Sandy Cull for her design.* | *Various industry experts read or discussed sections of the manuscript and I found their comments very helpful. They include, in alphabetical order, Allan Bellman, Cobden Smokehouse; Richard Bennett, Australian Horticultural Corporation; Michael Canals, Canals Seafoods; Bronwyn and Geoff Dobson, potato growers extraordinaire; Susan Dodds, Sydney Market Authority; Vince Gareffa, Mondo di Carne in Perth; Chris Joyce, tree nut expert; Geoff Linton, wine and vinegar maker from Yalumba vineyards; Jim Mendolia, Mendolia Seafoods; Ian Milburn, Glenloth Game; John Millington, Luv-a-Duck; Max and Michael Redlich, Redlich's Meats; Elisabeth Seaton, chestnut grower; Will Studd, cheese expert of William Wild; John Sussman, food consultant, and Peter Wall, wine and vinegar maker from Yalumba vineyards. Assistance also came from Chris Pip in the initial research stage.* | *Cookery has always been reliant on sharing and osmosis for growth and development, and all cooks rely on the work of others for inspiration. In particular, Elizabeth David, Jane Grigson and Claudia Roden have long been a source of wisdom. Australian colleagues who were turned to for advice and recipes for* The Cook's Companion *include Maggie Beer, George Biron, Marieke Brugman, Robert Castellani, Dany Chouet, Jill Dupleix, Mogens Bay Esbensen, Meera Freeman, Catherine Kerry, Janni Kyritsis, Christine Manfield, Steve Manfredi, Mietta O'Donnell, Damien Pignolet, Charmaine Solomon and David Thompson. A special thank you goes to Louis Glowinski, whose amazing book* The Complete Book of Fruit Growing in Australia *demonstrates how lively as well as authoritative a reference work can be – particularly cheering given the paucity of comprehensive reference books on Australian food cultivation and production. Despite all this help there will be errors and I take full responsibility for them.*

e q u i p m e n t This section lists the utensils that I use regularly in my kitchen and includes definitions of the less-familiar items you may come across in this book. Not every kitchen needs every item, and a planned, well-balanced range needn't break the bank. To help you plan any future purchases, I discuss the materials from which saucepans and the like are made, and their benefits or otherwise, in the entry 'Raw Materials'. | There are, however, essential items that I certainly would not be without. These include metric measuring spoons and cups, a set of electronic scales, stainless steel mixing bowls (large, medium and small) and wire cake racks. Spatulas, both rubber and the long flexible variety, get a lot of work in my kitchen, as do large lifting spoons (one of which should be slotted), ladles of varying sizes, tongs, a range of wooden spoons and whisks (I have a variety, from a small one for whisking 1–2 eggs to a large, flexible balloon whisk). I keep 2 pepper mills at the ready, one for black pepper and the other for white. I also have a coffee grinder that is only ever used for grinding spices. | Cross-references to other entries in this section appear here in inverted commas (as in *see also* 'Frying Pan').

BAIN-MARIE	A bain-marie is used for cooking custards, terrines and some puddings. There is no need for special equipment. Use a baking or gratin dish lined with a cloth to stop small custard moulds moving about. The dish should be deep enough so that hot water can be poured two-thirds to half the way up the sides of the moulds.
BAKING DISH	Apart from 2 all-purpose aluminium baking dishes of different sizes, I have 2 porcelain gratin dishes that can be carried from oven to table.
BAKING TRAY	The best baking trays are made from pressed steel and are very heavy. They never buckle but they will rust unless coated with a fine film of oil before storage. Inexpensive baking trays are fine, but discard them if they become rusted or badly scratched. Invest in a rolled sheet of baking fibreglass from a specialist kitchen supplier. With this spread on a baking tray no biscuit will ever stick. *See also* 'Raw Materials'.
BAMBOO SKEWERS	*see* 'Skewers, Soaking'
BREAD TIN	If you enjoy making bread, buy heavy tins; these are usually painted black on the outside. Bread tins should never be washed as the build-up of flour protects the next batch from sticking. Simply dislodge any stuck-on bits of dough and sharply rap the tin to rid it of excess residue.
CAKE TIN	I have a couple of cake tins with a shiny non-stick finish that have been very successful, especially with things like nut-based sponge cakes that want to stick. All the others I own are aluminium. I have a 22 cm × 5 cm all-purpose round tin, a 20 cm × 6 cm square tin for fruit cake, 2 different sizes of springform tin (22 cm and 24 cm), a couple of 20 cm × 4 cm sponge tins and a 22 cm × 5 cm ring tin. *See also* 'Flan Tin'.
CASSEROLE	I prefer **enamelled cast-iron** (*see* 'Raw Materials') casseroles in round and oval shapes (these are referred to as *cocottes* by the French). I like the fact that I can brown the meat or vegetables first on top of the stove and continue the preparation in the same pot in the oven and even present it at the table. Enamelled cast-iron casseroles are expensive but they last almost forever and are a great gift for anyone starting a household. **Pottery** casseroles are ideal for slow-cooked oven dishes. Food also looks good presented in them.
CHARGRILL PAN	The chargrill pan is a quick and easy alternative to the barbecue. There are small, inexpensive ridged cast-iron pans that are perfect for 2 chicken breasts or 2 fish cutlets, or there is the much more expensive but undeniably superior Le Creuset cast-iron grill that fits across 2 burners on the usual domestic stove. Australia's own Furphy makes a chargrill pan, too, but it requires

oiling to prevent rusting. Cooking in this way requires efficient ventilation to cope with the smoke and fumes.

see 'Sauce Dishes, Chinese'	**CHINESE SAUCE DISHES**

Inspired by the Chinese, I now have a stock of white facewashers that can be dampened, rolled and steamed hot or heated in the microwave. Guests really appreciate these towels after a platter of barbecued quail, prawns or chicken wings.

	CLOTH, HOT, DAMP

see 'Casserole'	**COCOTTE**

see 'Sieves and Strainers'	**COLANDER**

This specialist saucepan is used for making couscous (although it is not essential). It comes in 2 parts and is usually made from lightweight aluminium. The bottom half bellies outwards a little and holds broth, vegetables, poultry and meat. The top half has a perforated base that sits tightly over the bottom half. The dampened couscous grain is placed in the top half and is then tightly covered with the lid and steamed.

COUSCOUSIER

see 'Frying Pan'	**CRÊPE PAN**

Most freestanding electric mixers are equipped with a dough hook, intended for the effective kneading of bread or brioche. All bread can be kneaded by hand but brioche especially needs long, slow kneading with a dough hook.

DOUGH HOOK

A blender has a flask and, usually, adjustable speeds. It is ideal for whipping sauces perfectly smooth and numerous other tasks. It takes over where a food processor stops. Sauces whizzed in the blender will change colour as they absorb quantities of air.

ELECTRIC BLENDER

I have never been a fan of the hand-held mixer – it seems to lack power, and it also keeps the cook immobile. Depending on the task, I prefer to use a whisk, a rotary beater or a large freestanding electric mixer. However, many cooks swear by a hand-held mixer. If buying a large electric mixer, make sure you buy one with a dough hook – essential for making brioche and labour-saving when making bread. Some mixers have optional mincer and blender attachments too.

ELECTRIC MIXER

This specialist and fancy piece of equipment has been designed to make turning fish on a grill foolproof. It is excellent if you grill fish regularly. The

FISH GRILL, HINGED

old-fashioned hinged grill used to cook sausages over a camp-fire will do the same job, as long as the fish is not too thick. There are even more specialised grills designed just to cook sardines!

FISH KETTLE	This long, rectangular pan has been designed specifically for poaching a whole fish. The fish sits on a perforated rack that is easily lifted out, so that the fish can be drained and served. One of the nicest of all fish to poach whole is a salmon. Many of the fish kettles I have seen would not hold a salmon, so do be certain that you have bought the right size.
FLAN TIN, LOOSE-BOTTOMED	Loose-bottomed flan tins can be made from tin or aluminium or have a non-stick surface. These tins come in different depths as well as different diameters. I find 10 cm, 22 cm, 24 cm and 26 cm tins the most useful sizes, and I have a 24 cm × 5 cm deep tin that I use for quiches.
FOOD MILL	The wonderful Mouli is used every day in my kitchen – to purée tomato sauce (cooked with skins on for extra flavour), to purée vegetable soup, to mill potatoes for making gnocchi, and so on. There is a very small one sold as a Baby-Mouli. This is just frustrating. Get a bigger one that will balance well over a largish basin.
FOOD PROCESSOR	What did we do without one? I have 2, a standard one and a smaller machine that is ideal for nuts, spices and garlic, all of which can get lost in a larger processor bowl.
FRYING PAN	The average household needs 2 frying pans of different sizes. One should have a lid, preferably domed to permit a large volume of, say, mushrooms or spinach to be sautéd. Also invest in at least 1 non-stick frying pan, preferably 2, and save one for omelettes and scrambled eggs and the other for fish. A special pan used for cooking pancakes (usually sold as a crêpe pan) isn't essential but is certainly useful if you make pancakes frequently. *See also* 'Raw Materials'.
GRATIN DISH	A gratin dish is usually rectangular or oval and of ovenproof porcelain or other ceramic that will withstand oven temperatures of around 200°C (I find a 30 cm gratin dish a good size). Gratin dishes are used to make potato gratins, of course, but are extemely useful for other vegetable dishes, especially those with crumbs on top, or baked pasta or shepherd's pie. Gratin dishes can also be placed under a hot griller without cracking. They can be as large as a baking dish, and used in the same way, or much smaller.
ICE-CREAM MACHINE	If you love making your own ice-cream and sorbet, you will need one of these. Most machines will churn the product very well but the ice-cream will

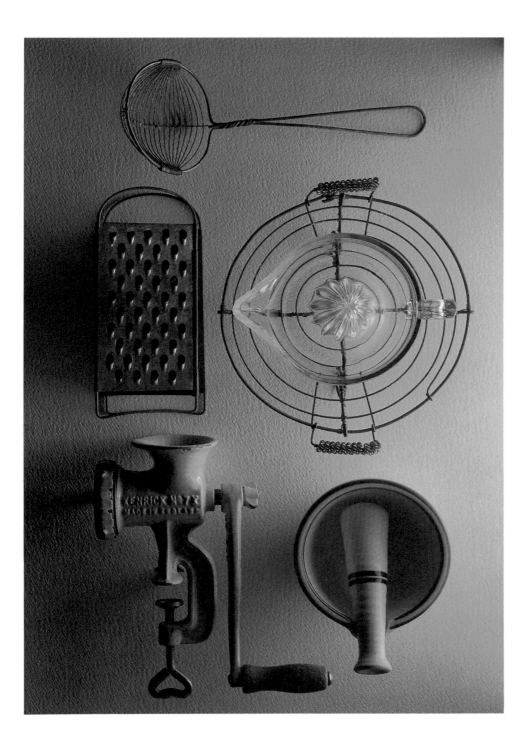

still need time in the freezer to firm to the consistency you wish for serving, so plan accordingly.

**JAPANESE
VEGETABLE
SLICER AND
SHREDDER**

This simple and ingenious plastic box is fitted with a lid that holds interchangeable blades and permits fast, safe slicing or shredding of carrots, celeriac, cucumber, and so on. You will find it in Asian food stores and some hardware stores.

KNIVES

Buy the best knives you can or ask for a knife for a Christmas gift, as they are expensive. Properly designed knives have a balance and an edge that are entirely absent from cheap knives. It is impossible to chop parsley or slice effectively without a good all-purpose *cook's* knife. Your own height and size will dictate the size of knife you are most comfortable with. I use a cook's knife with a 25 cm blade for all-purpose chopping. I also use one with a 20 cm blade. Next in importance is a good *paring* or vegetable knife. Then a strong *serrated* knife that is not flexible. Then a curved, pointed *boning* knife. Then a strong, sharp *cleaver*. There is also an endless array of *specialist* knives, some more useful than others. There are filleting knives, turning knives (for shaping chunks of carrot), grapefruit knives, salmon-slicing knives, and so on. A parmesan knife has a small dagger-like blade in a round, chunky wooden handle and is specifically designed to gouge chunks from parmesan cheese. You will also need a *steel* for sharpening your knives, and a long-handled kitchen *fork*.

LARDING NEEDLE

Available from kitchenware suppliers, a larding needle is used to thread lardons (small cubes or pieces of belly pork or fat) through meat before cooking, especially meat that is particularly lean. I have rarely used a larding needle, although it is useful for all cooks to know of its existence.

LOG MOULD

A log mould can be made either from enamelled cast-iron or aluminium. The enamelled cast-iron Le Creuset pâté or terrine mould is ideal for setting ice-cream as well as its original use.

MANDOLINE

The mandoline is a stainless steel item that does the same thing as a Japanese slicer/shredder. It is very expensive and much more dangerous than the Japanese version. I do not recommend it for the home kitchen unless you enjoy living dangerously. *See also* 'Japanese Vegetable Slicer and Shredder'.

**MARBLE PASTRY
SLAB**

As maintaining a cool temperature is vital when making pastry, a marble slab is a good investment, though not essential. While marble can be inserted into a workbench when building a kitchen, a slab can be bought from a kitchenware supplier.

MORTAR AND PESTLE	Spices and the like are ground in a mortar (a solid bowl) with a pestle (a small, heavy truncheon-like implement). Usually made from porcelain, marble or stone, a mortar and pestle are sold as a pair by kitchenware suppliers. Granite mortar and pestles are also available very reasonably from some Asian food stores. Choose a large mortar and pestle for grinding spices, herbs and aromatics for curries – a 20 cm mortar will come with a suitably heavy pestle. Held just above the mortar by its narrower end, the pestle is dropped onto the ingredients, with the force of the fall and the weight of the pestle doing all the work for you.
PARMESAN KNIFE	*see* 'Knives'
PASTA MACHINE	An inexpensive Italian pasta machine clamps to a kitchen bench and kneads, rolls and cuts flat pasta sheets. Easy and satisfying to use, a pasta machine, like a bread tin, should not be washed. Remove any trapped dough and dust away any flour residue before storing.
PASTRY BRUSH	Choose a pastry brush with natural rather than nylon bristles to avoid melted bristles when working with hot ingredients. A useful item to have on hand for glazing pastry or buttering dishes and the like.
PASTRY SCRAPER	Used when making shortcrust pastry to cut the butter into the flour, a pastry scraper is available from kitchenware suppliers.
PEELERS	The Australian-designed plastic **vegetable** peeler is justly renowned. It is sharper and altogether more efficient than other models made elsewhere. *Asparagus* peelers have the blade set crosswise rather than vertically and are designed to be pulled down the asparagus spear. They are also essential if you wish to peel peppers or tomatoes.
PIE DISH	A much more prosaic item than a pie plate, the pie dish is often made from aluminium or enamelled aluminium. It is used for all-purpose baking and roasting. Traditionally a pie dish sat underneath the roast beef and batter for a Yorkshire pudding was poured in.
PIE PLATE	Usually made of vitreous china or porcelain that is often dark brown and highly glazed, pie plates vary in diameter but are rarely more than 5–6 cm deep. They have sloping sides and are ideal for double-crust fruit pies or a lemon meringue pie. They also look good enough to be taken to the table from the oven. I use a large 22 cm × 4 cm pie plate, and have a couple of 14 cm × 3 cm pie plates for individual serves.
POULTRY SHEARS	*see* 'Scissors'

The raw materials used to manufacture saucepans, frying pans and casseroles include aluminium, stainless steel, enamelled cast-iron, pressed steel and copper. Non-stick coatings are also used. Each material has its benefits.

Aluminium is a very good conductor of heat. Aluminium pans can be bought in many different qualities (the heavier the better) and are easy to clean. However, they are no good for delicate, pale sauces as aluminium gives a grey colouration. Food left standing in aluminium pans can also develop a metallic taste.

On its own *stainless steel* is a poor conductor of heat. The best stainless steel pans have a heavy base in which there is a layer of aluminium or copper. These are excellent pans for making sauces and stock, since they conduct heat well but do not cause discoloration or give off flavours.

The main feature of *enamelled cast-iron* kitchenware is versatility. As long as a good-quality pan with a heavy base is bought, enamelled cast-iron is hard to beat. It heats well (holding the heat exceptionally well), looks good and is easy to clean. Some of these pans have a matt-black finish and are designed to be used on higher heat than those with white-glazed interiors. Enamelled cast-iron pans are made in a very large range of shapes and sizes, from small saucepans to large casseroles. The main disadvantage is that they are very heavy.

Pressed steel is used almost exclusively to make frying pans and woks and is often sold with a sticky protective coating. To remove this, wash the pan well in hot soapy water, then dry thoroughly. To temper the pan, heat it with 1 cm vegetable oil to very hot, then cool the oil and heat it again. Discard the oil and wipe the pan with kitchen paper before storing it. The pan must always be wiped with oily paper before being put away as pressed steel is very prone to rust.

For most of us *copper* pans are of academic interest only. Copper is a magnificent conductor of heat but it is dreadful to keep clean and is frighteningly expensive. Cheap copper pans are a waste of money. The only practical variety are those made for restaurants, which have a stainless steel or nickel lining in place of the easily worn tin lining of old.

Several brand names are associated with tough *non-stick coatings* on pans and cake tins. Some of the best frying pans have a non-stick and slightly dimpled surface. Choose a good-quality pan and do not use it if the surface has become scratched and is at all flaky. Metal tongs and harsh scouring pads will quickly damage the surface.

An electric rice cooker provides a foolproof way of guaranteeing perfect rice. I wish a smaller one was made as mine takes up too much room on my bench at home and is too large for the cupboard. But it does its job wonderfully well. While rice cookers are widely available, check Asian food stores for a good range at competitive prices.

SALAD SPINNER	The salad spinner dries salad leaves with a minimum of fuss. Washed salad leaves or herbs are placed in the inner basket. The lid is put on and one spins the inner basket, forcing the water into the outer basket. The spinner works very well as long as one is not too violent. The leaves still need to be rolled in a clean tea towel to absorb the last traces of moisture.
SAUCE DISHES, CHINESE	These inexpensive little dishes are available from Asian food stores and perform a multitude of tasks, from their original purpose of holding dipping sauces to keeping herbs and spices under control during preparation.
SAUCEPANS	Do not buy saucepans in a set as rarely does one want all the sizes. Buy the best you can afford, after having read the entry 'Raw Materials'. A starter set might be a *stockpot*, 2 saucepans that are *20 cm diameter*, a *16 cm diameter stainless steel* saucepan for making sauces or custards and a *small non-stick* saucepan for heating milk. Add to this a couple of casseroles and a lidded frying pan and you're in business. Other more specialised pieces can be added later if necessary. *See also* 'Casserole', 'Frying Pan', 'Stockpot'.
SCISSORS	Buy a strong pair of kitchen scissors that will cut poultry and trim fish fins as well as cutting baking paper!
SIEVES AND STRAINERS	Sieves and strainers vary from the simplest *aluminium strainer* to extremely expensive, conical *fine-mesh stainless steel sieves* intended for saucemaking. Buy one or two that fit the bowls or jugs you use. Buy a *nylon sieve* for straining raspberries or similar, as an aluminium strainer will discolour the fruit. A *stainless steel colander* with a long handle is invaluable for straining vegetables or pasta over the sink.
SIMMER MAT	Slip a simmer mat under any saucepan in which you have a thick mixture that is liable to catch, such as chutney, jams and curry sauces. Simmer mats are more necessary when using a gas stove.
SKEWERS, SOAKING	Bundles of bamboo skewers are readily available from supermarkets or hardware or Asian food stores. They should be soaked in water for 30 minutes before being threaded with meat, poultry, seafood, vegetables or fruit for grilling. They are also useful for testing whether a cake is cooked! And I have sometimes used them to skewer a rolled shoulder of lamb or, cut in half, rolls of fish stuffed with a fish mousse.
SPRINGFORM TIN	*see* 'Cake Tin'
STEAMER, CHINESE BAMBOO	Inexpensive and widely available at all Asian food stores, these stackable bamboo steamer baskets fit on top of a saucepan. Take either your saucepan

or its measured diameter to the store to ensure you buy the right size. Remember to buy a lid as well.

STOCKPOT

A stockpot is essential for making stock and soup and for cooking a reasonable amount of pasta. I have a 10 litre and a 20 litre stockpot – a 10 litre stockpot is the smallest you should consider buying.

STRAINERS

see 'Sieves and Strainers'

TERRACOTTA DISHES, SPANISH

Terracotta dishes are used in Spain to cook almost everything. They are flameproof and ovenproof. They also chip very easily, but are quite inexpensive. I like the 12 cm diameter shallow dishes and use them for individual gratins – in Spain they would be used to bake eggs. Look for them in Spanish or Portuguese food stores, or kitchenware shops.

TERRINE MOULD

Confusion results from the word 'terrine', since it means both the container and its contents. A chopped or minced mix of meat, poultry and flavourings is baked in a terrine mould, either cast-iron or earthenware, in a bain-marie. Once cooked, the terrine is lightly weighted before being cut into slices to serve cold.

THERMOMETERS

It is a good idea to own a meat thermometer, a general thermometer (useful for custards) and a candy thermometer. The candy thermometer is only relevant over boiling point as it registers the various stages of sugar syrup leading to caramel (106–160°C). It can also be used when making jams and jellies and for deep-frying.

WOK

A wok is an essential cooking utensil for all Asian food and stir-frying. A new wok must be seasoned like any *pressed steel* item and will frequently have a sticky coating when you buy it in an Asian food store. Also buy a *wok sang*, the shovel-like implement for moving and tossing the food. Sophisticated woks are also available with *non-stick* coatings or made from *cast-iron.* They are useful but not necessary. A little practice is all that is required to manage a traditional wok. *See also* 'Raw Materials'.

b a s i c s This section includes definitions of some of the less-familiar ingredients and terms you may encounter in this book. It also includes frequently used preparations, such as stock, pastry and batter. The symbol ✓ that appears in the main part of the book indicates that you should turn to this, the Basics section, for more information or a recipe. | Cross-references to other entries in Basics appear here in inverted commas (as in *see also* 'Acidulated Water'). Cross-references to other sections in this book appear in small capital letters (as in *see* TOMATOES).

Certain fruit (apples, pears) or vegetables (artichokes) are steeped in acidulated water (water to which lemon juice, vinegar or salt has been added) while they are being prepared or waiting to be cooked to prevent any cut surfaces darkening. Allow 1 tablespoon salt, the juice of 1 lemon or 1 tablespoon vinegar to 1 litre water.

ACIDULATED WATER

This Italian term literally means 'to the tooth' and describes correctly cooked pasta and, sometimes, vegetables, implying a little resistance to the bite.

AL DENTE

Almost all tarts benefit from the pastry shell being cooked before it is filled. Roll out the pastry, then wrap it around the rolling pin and let it unroll over the flan tin or pie plate. Press it into the edges of the tin well and trim the pastry. (It is usual to roll the pin over the top of the tin to give a very clean edge. With very short pastry, such as the shortcrust pastry I use, I prefer to cut the edge 1 cm higher than the edge of the tin and fold it over as it is inclined to shrink during baking, even after chilling.) Chill or freeze the pastry case for at least 20 minutes before baking. (It can be baked when frozen.) Line the pastry with foil and fill this with dried beans or chick peas or buy some pastry weights that you keep for this purpose. Bake at 200°C for 15 minutes, then remove the foil and weights and bake for another 5 minutes. If the tart is to be filled with a liquid, have the filling warm or hot and pour it into the pastry case while the pastry is still hot. This prevents any liquid seeping. *See also* 'Pastry'.

BAKE BLIND

beer batter

This batter produces a very crisp coating for most deep-fried food. This quantity is sufficient for 4 pieces of fish.

BATTER

250 g self-raising flour
½ cup beer
1 cup cold water

Whisk ingredients until smooth. Add ground spices (pepper, turmeric, cumin) or substitute 2–3 tablespoons chickpea flour or ground rice for an equivalent quantity of self-raising flour for a change.

cornflour batter

This very transparent batter is ideal for zucchini or pumpkin flowers – the quantity given here is sufficient for 8–10 flowers.

250 g cornflour
1 cup cold water
2 egg whites, lightly whisked
  to break the gel

Mix ingredients together. The batter should drip from your fingers and appear translucent.

BATTER
continued

batter with egg white
Another classic batter for deep-fried food. This quantity coats 10 fritters.

250 g plain flour
1 teaspoon salt
6 tablespoons olive *or*
  vegetable oil
1½ cups warm water
2 egg whites, stiffly beaten

Put flour and salt into a bowl and make a well. Mix oil with warm water and tip into bowl. Work batter until smooth. Leave for at least 1 hour before folding in egg whites, then use immediately.

BÉARNAISE SAUCE *see* 'Hollandaise Sauce'

BÉCHAMEL SAUCE *see* 'Roux'

BEER BATTER *see* 'Batter'

BEURRE BLANC

Making beurre blanc *causes a lot of needless anxiety. It is simplicity itself once it is understood that the butter has to be added to the reduction quite quickly, so that the first lot remains as a creamy emulsion and doesn't overheat and turn to oil. When made with Australian butter (from grass-fed cows)* beurre blanc *will be distinctly yellow. Made from the butters of Normandy and the Loire, where the butter is a pale cream, it is a white butter sauce. Variations are achieved by varying the ingredients of the reduction (fish stock, cider, vermouth) or by finishing the sauce with a spoonful of a warm vegetable purée (tomato, red pepper, sorrel) or chopped herbs.*

1 tablespoon finely chopped
  shallots
½ cup dry white wine
coarsely ground white pepper
100 g unsalted butter
few drops of lemon juice
salt
freshly ground black pepper

Simmer shallots, wine and pepper in a small heavy-based saucepan until mixture is a mush without obvious liquid. Cut butter into 6 chunks and, over a moderate heat, start whisking it in, a chunk at a time, until all is incorporated. Season with lemon juice, salt and pepper. Take off stove and rest in a warm place.

BEURRE MANIÉ

Literally meaning 'worked butter', this paste of roughly two-thirds flour and a third softened butter can be added at the last minute to simmering sauces or casseroles to thicken juices quickly. *Beurre manié* is ideal to use to thicken a sauce or juices lightly when the flavour is perfect and further reduction would intensify the flavour too much. The *beurre manié* is always added just before you are ready to serve. Divide *beurre manié* into pieces the size of a cannellini bean and scatter all at once over the surface of the simmering liquid. Shake the pan or agitate the contents with a wooden spoon until thickened, and then do not boil again.

BLACK BEANS, FERMENTED

Also known as salted soy beans or pounded black beans, these small black beans have been preserved by being fermented with salt and spices. They are usually used chopped in Chinese dishes and add a pungency and saltiness. Black beans are often combined with ginger and garlic (crab with black beans and ginger is one of my favourites). Best rinsed before use to avoid excessive saltiness, the beans are quite soft and easy to crush. They are available in Asian food stores and can be stored in a cool place for months.

BLANC

Vegetables that discolour on contact with air, such as artichoke hearts, celeriac or silverbeet stalks, are often cooked in a *blanc* to preserve their colour. To make a *blanc*, whisk 2 tablespoons flour into 1 litre water flavoured with salt, lemon juice and, maybe, herbs. The *blanc* is brought to a boil before the vegetables (which ought to be waiting in a bowl of acidulated water) are added. The vegetables should be cooked until tender when tested with a skewer or the point of a knife. *See* 'Acidulated Water'.

BLANCH

Blanching involves plunging ingredients into a large quantity of boiling water and then draining and refreshing them under cold water. This method is used to set the colour and to parcook vegetables. It is not a method I usually use as I dislike the taste of cold water that often remains, in beans or asparagus, for example. The method is also used to loosen skins from tomatoes, almonds, garlic, and so on.

BRIOCHE

This quantity is sufficient for 1 × 500 g loaf or 8 individual brioches. Brioche dough needs lots of energetic working. It is best to beat this sticky mass in an electric mixer fitted with a dough hook.

250 g plain flour
pinch of salt
1 teaspoon instant dried yeast
½ cup milk
1 tablespoon sugar
3 egg yolks, lightly beaten
75 g softened butter

Mix flour, salt and yeast. Warm milk and sugar slightly until sugar has dissolved. Combine egg yolks and warm milk mixture. Make a well in flour, then pour in liquid and mix to a dough. Work in an electric mixer fitted with a dough hook until dough forms a smooth ball, about 10 minutes. Continue beating while adding butter in 2 lots. The dough should be shiny and smooth and will come away cleanly from sides of bowl.

Cover bowl with a clean cloth and leave dough to double in size in a draught-free place for about 2 hours. Knock back dough and briefly knead again. Shape into a loaf or divide into individual buns. Allow to

BRIOCHE
continued

rise again, covered, for 1 hour. Bake at 180°C for 30 minutes (15 minutes for individual brioches) or until well risen and golden. Tip out of tin onto a baking tray and return to oven for a further 10 minutes (5 minutes for individual brioches) to brown. Cool before using.

sultana brioche Soak 50 g sultanas in 1 tablespoon brandy, if desired, and scatter over the dough once it has been knocked back after the first rising. Briefly knead again and continue with the recipe.

bread-and-butter pudding Slices from sultana brioche make a luxurious bread-and-butter pudding. Mix 3 eggs, 3 tablespoons sugar, 2 cups cream and additional dried fruit or peel and pour over and around toasted and buttered brioche. Sprinkle with castor sugar and bake at 180°C for 25 minutes or until firm.

BUTTER

Butter is made by churning cream and is required to have a minimum of 80 per cent milk fat. (There is also an increasing range of dairy products that have lower levels of milk fat and are blended with vegetable oils and water. These composite *spreads* remain softer than butter at refrigerated temperatures but cannot compare in flavour.) There are both *salted* and *unsalted* butters on the market. Unsalted butter is also known as sweet butter and is preferred by many cooks for making desserts and pastry. A *lactobacillus* culture is added to cream several hours before churning to make *cultured* butter. Such butter has extra flavour and is somewhat reminiscent of European butters made with whole (unpasteurised) milk. It is also possible to buy *ghee*, the Indian word for *clarified* butter. The milk solids and any salt have been removed, and the ghee can be heated to a higher temperature than butter before burning.

clarified butter Clarifying butter is simple to do yourself: melt and simmer butter until the solids fall to the bottom of the saucepan, then ladle the liquid butter through a damp muslin cloth into a bowl. The clarified butter in the bowl will set solid and can be refrigerated for weeks without fear of rancidity. **noisette butter** Noisette butter carries the cooking process used to make clarified butter a step further. Cook the butter until it is a golden brown and begins to smell nutty. The milk solids will appear as golden specks at the bottom of the saucepan. Stop the cooking quickly by putting the pan into a basin of cold water. Noisette butter can be frozen successfully. Hot noisette butter, literally 'hazelnut' butter, can be spooned over pasta, brains, fish, liver or whatever.

**CAKE TESTS
CLEAN**

Test if a cake is cooked by inserting a very fine skewer (it used to be a straw from the straw broom) in the centre to see if there is any stickiness. If there is, cook a further 5 minutes before checking again. Some cakes are meant to be fudgy in the centre, even though they are sufficiently cooked. The recipe should say so.

see 'Sugar Syrup'	**CARAMEL**

Caul fat is the peritoneum, a fatty veil that encases the guts of a pig. Caul is without equal for wrapping small patties of meat or a stuffed pig's trotter, or to line a dish in which a pâté or terrine mixture is to be baked. It crisps and browns beautifully in the oven or under the grill. It also freezes well, so buy more than you need (you will need to order it from your butcher). To prepare caul fat, soak it in lightly salted water overnight to remove all blood, then dry well. Divide between small bags and freeze. Thaw caul fat directly in warm water and dry well before use. *See* PORK for more details.

CAUL FAT

see 'Pepper'	**CAYENNE PEPPER**
see 'Stock'	**CHICKEN STOCK**
see 'Butter'	**CLARIFIED BUTTER**
see 'Stock'	**CLARIFIED STOCK**

While coconut milk can be bought in liquid and dried forms from super-markets and Asian food stores, it can also be made at home. Charmaine Solomon gives a detailed explanation of how to make coconut milk in her monumental *Complete Asian Cookbook*. *See* NUTS for instructions.

COCONUT MILK

The food to be cooked in a court-bouillon, literally meaning 'short boil', cooks very briefly (fish, brains, shellfish), therefore the liquid must be well-flavoured before one starts. This quantity is sufficient for cooking 10 sets of brains or 2 × 300 g trout.

COURT-BOUILLON

1 litre water
4 tablespoons white-wine
    vinegar
1 carrot, sliced
1 onion, sliced
1 sprig thyme
1 bay leaf
a few parsley stalks
2 teaspoons salt
10 black peppercorns

Simmer all ingredients for 30 minutes, then strain and proceed with recipe. Individual recipes will specify required cooking times.

Literally 'cream' in French, this term leads to crème anglaise (egg custard), crème pâtissière (pastry cream), crème caramel (baked caramel custard) and

CRÈME

crème fraîche (naturally soured cream). It can be very confusing for English-speaking cooks. *See also* 'Egg Custard', 'Pastry Cream'.

CRÊPES	*see* 'Pancakes'

CRUMBLE TOPPING

Resist the temptation to process the crumble ingredients in a food processor: you will end up with very fine crumbs that quickly become a ball of dough. It is the lumpy character of the topping that gives it crunch. This quantity is sufficient for 6 serves.

The fruit to which you are adding the crumble will determine the cooking time, as will the size of the dish used. This recipe is for a large crumble of substantial fruit, such as apples or apricots; a berry crumble will need only 15–20 minutes (I might even cook it at 200°C for 15 minutes to ensure the crumble is crunchy but the berries have not collapsed). If you are making individual crumbles, allow about 15 minutes' cooking time.

100 g brown sugar
1 teaspoon baking powder
1½ teaspoons ground ginger
60 g unsalted butter
150 g plain flour
2 cups drained poached *or* puréed fruit

Mix sugar, baking powder and ground ginger. Crumble butter into flour with your fingers to form pea-sized pieces, then toss flour mixture with sugar mixture. Spoon fruit into a buttered 1 litre ovenproof dish and strew with topping. Bake at 180°C for 40 minutes until topping is golden brown and bubbling at the edges.

CURRY PASTES AND POWDERS

Indian, Thai and Indonesian cuisines all include curried dishes, each dramatically different from the next because of the subtle combinations of spices and aromatics. The selection, grinding and combining of spices is an art refined by years of practice. Specialist books give instructions on what to buy and how to combine, roast, pound and prepare these pastes and powders. Excellent spice combinations are sold in Indian food stores, and specialist ranges of prepared South-East Asian pastes are available in most supermarkets and all Asian food stores. I often add freshly chopped appropriate herbs to such products to give them a lift.

CUSTARD	*see* 'Egg Custard'

DRESSED WEIGHT

The weight of a bird once plucked, gutted and trimmed is described as the 'dressed weight', a term that is usually restricted to poultry.

DRIED SHRIMP PASTE	*see* 'Shrimp Paste, Dried'

see 'Spices'	**DRY-ROASTED SPICES**

EGG CUSTARD

This is the basic stirred custard that one serves with steamed puddings. My version uses half milk, half cream. Make it with all milk, if you prefer. It is also the base for vanilla ice-cream, with a slight modification. This quantity makes 3 cups custard.

1 cup milk
1 cup cream
1 vanilla bean, split
5 egg yolks
125 g castor sugar

Bring milk, cream and vanilla bean to simmering point in a heavy-based saucepan. Whisk egg yolks with sugar until light and foamy, then whisk in warm milk and cream. Return to rinsed-out pan and cook over a moderate heat, stirring constantly with a wooden spoon, until mixture thickens and coats back of spoon. Strain into a cold bowl, then scrape some vanilla seeds from the split pod into the cooling custard. Serve warm or cold.

vanilla ice-cream If using the custard as the base for ice-cream, alter the proportions to 1½ cups milk to ½ cup cream. Churn the mixture in an ice-cream machine according to the manufacturer's instructions.

see 'Roux'	**ESPAGNOLE SAUCE**
see 'Pastry'	**FILO PASTRY**

FISH SAUCE

Also known as *nam pla*, *nuoc man* or *patis*, fish sauce is a thin, light-brown, very salty and aromatic liquid that is made from fermented fish and shrimps and is essential in South-East Asian cookery. A little goes a long way and brands vary in strength. Be cautious at first. Fish sauce is available from Asian food stores and most supermarkets.

see 'Stock'	**FISH STOCK**

FRANGIPANE

To a pastry cook, a frangipane is a mixture of ground almonds, butter, sugar and eggs that is sometimes flavoured with a liqueur. It is a quick and delicious filling for a tart. If the tart is only half-filled with the mixture, it makes an ideal base on which to bake a layer of halved stone fruit, such as apricots, peaches or plums. *See* Almond Frangipane Tart in NUTS.

FRITTATA

Essentially a thick omelette that includes quite a lot of vegetables and sometimes cheese, a frittata is usually served warm, cut into wedges. *See* BROCCOLI, POTATOES and SILVER BEET for recipes.

GELATINE

Gelatine *leaves* produce a superior result to gelatine *powder* as they dissolve instantly without the worry of lumps of undissolved powder remaining. Note that 3 teaspoons gelatine powder is the equivalent of 6 leaves. This quantity will set 2 cups liquid to a light jelly, while 1 rounded tablespoon powder or 9 leaves will set 2 cups liquid to a firm, moulded jelly. To dissolve gelatine leaves, soak them in cold water for 5 minutes, then remove them and squeeze well. Drop the squeezed leaves into a little of the mixture you are preparing (if the mixture is hot – if not, drop the leaves into 2 tablespoons boiling water) and stir to dissolve. Tip this back into the main preparation and continue with the recipe.

GHEE

see 'Butter'

GROUND RICE

Ground rice is used to make cakes and sweets in Asia and in the West to thicken sauces and to add to batters or biscuits (such as traditional Scottish shortbread), where it contributes a nice crunch. Ground rice is available from supermarkets. Also available is rice flour, a more finely ground version.

HALOUMI CHEESE

This hard Cypriot goat's milk cheese is made with a stretched curd and is often folded over dried mint. It is delicious cut into chunks and grilled on the barbecue and then seasoned with a few drops of lemon juice. Look for haloumi cheese in delicatessens and at fresh food markets.

HOLLANDAISE SAUCE

A classic hollandaise sauce is not built upon a reduction as in this recipe but on eggs and lemon juice alone. Try it this way, but I find it a bit flat. As I have suggested using unsalted butter, make sure your finished sauce is well seasoned. An extra flake of sea salt can make all the difference to the lift and balance of your sauce.

Hollandaise sauce is the traditional partner for asparagus, artichokes and eggs Bénédict. This quantity is sufficient for 4 artichokes, 4 serves of asparagus or 6 eggs Bénédict. Hollandaise sauce is also the basis for a number of equally famous sauces: béarnaise, mousseline and Maltese sauce.

200 g unsalted butter
3 tablespoons white-wine vinegar
pinch of coarsely ground white pepper
2 tablespoons water
3 egg yolks
juice of ½ lemon

Melt butter gently and allow to cool a little. Place vinegar, pepper and water in a small saucepan and reduce to 1 tablespoon liquid. Transfer liquid to a small bowl that fits comfortably over a stable small saucepan half-filled with hot water. Add egg yolks and whisk well over moderate heat until thick and foamy. Whisk in butter a little at a time, still over heat. When all butter is incorporated you should have a bowl of thick creamy sauce. Add lemon juice to taste. Herbs can be added, too, if you like.

béarnaise sauce The classic sauce to serve with a fillet of beef. Use tarragon vinegar in place of white-wine vinegar and add 2 finely chopped shallots and 2 tablespoons freshly chopped tarragon to the reduction. Stir 1 tablespoon very finely chopped fresh tarragon into the finished, strained sauce. **mousseline sauce** This sauce is lovely with asparagus and artichokes and delicious with freshly boiled prawns and picked crab meat. Allow the hollandaise sauce to cool until barely warm, then whisk into it a quarter of its volume of firmly whipped cream. **maltese sauce** Substitute the juice of a blood orange for the lemon juice. This sauce is good with asparagus.

HOLLANDAISE SAUCE continued

---

see 'Meat, Refrigerating', 'Safe Food-Handling'

HYGIENE

---

see 'Yeast, Instant Dried'

INSTANT DRIED YEAST

---

see 'Setting Stage'

JELLY STAGE

A lardon is a small cube or rectangle (about 2 cm × 1 cm) of belly pork, pork fat or bacon used as a crisp garnish in a salad or to thread through a lean cut of veal or beef intended for slow cooking. In the latter case, belly pork or pork fat is pulled through slits in the meat with a larding needle.

LARDON

---

see 'Pastry'

LARD PASTRY

Lemongrass is a furled, strap-leafed herb used extensively in South-East Asian cooking. It is available fresh in most greengrocers these days and in all Asian food stores. Only the tender pale leaves and the inner part of the root are used. Sometimes the herb is cut into quite large sections to flavour a broth – one is not expected to eat these large bits.

LEMONGRASS

Fruit, biscuit or cake is 'macerated' when it is soaked in some flavouring liquid, usually a wine or liqueur.

MACERATE

---

see 'Hollandaise Sauce'

MALTESE SAUCE

Maltose, a heavy malt sugar, is used to coat the skins of duck, squab pigeons, chicken and quail so that they brown beautifully when roasted or fried. Look for maltose in health food shops or speciality food stores. Honey can be used as a substitute, using the same quantity.

MALTOSE

MATZO CRACKERS	A thin, crisp unleavened bread, matzo crackers are traditionally eaten during the Jewish Passover holiday.

MAYONNAISE	*This is one of the most versatile sauces there is. Together with hollandaise, it illustrates how an emulsion occurs when egg yolks absorb a relatively large amount of fat; in this case oil but in the case of hollandaise, butter. Each sauce has many variations, including the garlic-enriched Provençal speciality Aïoli (see GARLIC).*

Mayonnaise can be made well in a food processor or blender. However, it absorbs a lot more air and will never have the same 'glop' or yellow sheen to it as when made by hand. The food processor method is particularly useful if making a large amount or if you are adding another ingredient to the sauce, making its colour or its perfect texture not so important.

Mayonnaise that curdles during preparation can be saved by taking a clean bowl, working an extra egg yolk to a smooth paste and slowly adding the failed sauce, beating well after each spoonful.

3 egg yolks

pinch of salt

lemon juice *or* white-wine
   vinegar

300 ml olive oil

white pepper *or* Tabasco

Choose a comfortable basin and rest it on a damp cloth, so it cannot slip around. Work egg yolks with salt and 1 tablespoon lemon juice for a minute until smooth. Gradually beat in oil using a wooden spoon and adding the first few tablespoons one at a time and beating very well after each. After a third of the oil has been added, the rest can be added in a thin, steady stream, beating all the while. (This is easiest to do if you have a helper to pour while you beat.) Taste for acidity and adjust with drops of lemon juice, salt and pepper. Refrigerate with plastic film pressed on the surface to prevent a skin forming. Allow it to return to room temperature and then stir the sauce to ensure it is smooth and skin-free.

mustard mayonnaise Add 1 tablespoon (or more) Dijon mustard to the bowl with the egg yolks in the initial stage and continue with the recipe. Add freshly cut herbs, too, if you like. This sauce is required for Celeriac Rémoulade (*see* CELERY AND CELERIAC) and can also be used with other vegetable salads.   **tartare sauce** Tartare sauce is used with fried fish, cold tongue and brain fritters. Make the mayonnaise as above and stir in quantities of chopped pickled cucumber, drained capers, freshly chopped parsley and chives and a smaller amount of very finely chopped onion or shallot.

MEAT, REFRIGERATING	Harmful bacteria breed faster at warmer temperatures. If meat or poultry is held at 0°C it should be perfect for 14 days. If held at 4°C (a commercial coolroom, more or less) it will be fine for 5–6 days. If held at 10°C (a

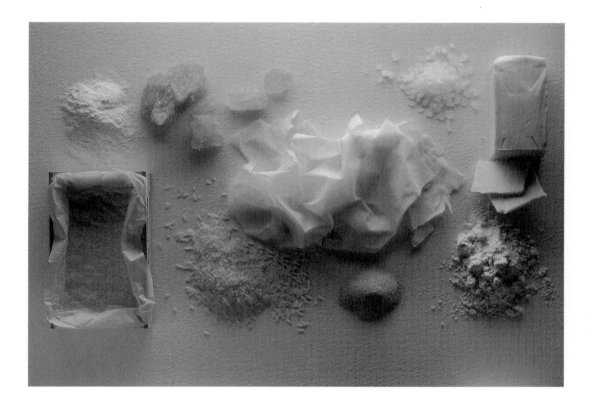

domestic refrigerator with normal daily opening and closing), the shelf life of the same product is 3 days. We cannot know for certain how a product has been handled by a retailer. Has it been supplied fresh 2 days previously? Has it been supplied fresh and then been frozen, maybe at the end of its useful life? Has it been supplied frozen and thawed at room temperature? Or at coolroom temperature? For all these reasons one should never thaw poultry or meat on the side of the sink. *See also* 'Safe Food-Handling'.

MEAT AND POULTRY, TEST FOR DONENESS

To test whether a large roasting cut is cooked, insert a skewer into the centre of the *meat* for 1 minute at the end of the cooking time, then remove it and put it on your bottom lip. The meat is ready when the skewer is quite hot and the juices are a rosy-pink. To test whether a *chicken* is cooked, at the end of the cooking time insert a skewer into the thickest part of the bird (usually the thigh); the juices should run clear rather than pink. For specific cooking instructions, turn to the entry for the type of meat or bird you wish to cook.

MIRIN

The wine used in Japanese cookery is called mirin. It is used to add a mild sweetness to sauces and to glaze grilled food. Some recipes advise cooks to warm the mirin and to light it with a match to burn off its alcohol content before using. I don't do this, except when making Ponzu Sauce (*see* p. 30).

MOUSSELINE SAUCE

see 'Hollandaise Sauce'

MUSTARD MAYONNAISE

see 'Mayonnaise'

NOISETTE BUTTER

see 'Butter'

NUTS, OVEN-TOASTED

Nuts are often toasted to bring out their flavour (hazelnuts) or to give an intense nuttiness (almonds). Spread the nuts on a baking tray, oiled or not depending on the eventual use of the nuts, and toast at 150°C for about 10 minutes. Check once or twice and shake the tray, so that the nuts toast evenly. Some nuts, especially pine nuts, toast very fast.

PALM SUGAR

see 'Sugar'

PANCAKES

This quantity of batter will make about 15 thin, lacy pancakes or crêpes. Stack the pancakes one on top of the other when cold and wrap them in plastic film. They will keep overnight in the refrigerator if they are not needed straightaway. The batter will also keep overnight in a covered container. Just stir any risen butter back into the batter and bring the batter to room temperature before using. >

PANCAKES
continued

250 g plain flour
60 g butter
pinch of salt
1½ cups milk
3 eggs

Put flour into a basin and make a well. Warm butter, salt and milk until butter has melted. Break eggs into well and work in some flour. Add warm milk mixture and whisk until quite smooth. Refrigerate for 2 hours before cooking. The consistency should be like thin cream. If not, thin with more milk.

Heat a frying pan (preferably one designed for cooking pancakes). Wipe pan with a piece of buttered paper for the first pancake. Lift pan from heat, then ladle in batter and swirl to spread it to edges of pan. Set pan back over heat. After 1 minute, lift thin outer edge of pancake with a fine spatula and flip pancake using your fingers or spatula. Repeat process. You will get better – and so will the pancakes!

PASTRY

filo pastry

This very fine pastry dough is used, layered, for sweet and savoury dishes in Greek and Middle Eastern cookery. Although not the same as North African *warka* dough or Austrian strudel dough, filo (or phyllo) makes an excellent substitute. Filo pastry is often sold frozen. Leave it in the refrigerator overnight to thaw. Unwrap the package and carefully unfold the stacked sheets of dough. As the dough dries out quickly, cover the stack at all times with a sheet of foil and cover this with a slightly damp tea towel, so that the damp towel does not come into contact with the pastry. Only peel off a sheet of pastry as you need it. Each sheet needs to be lightly brushed with oil or melted butter before being covered with another. Rewrapped unused filo will keep in the refrigerator for up to a week.

lard pastry

This traditional pastry is from the north of England. It is very flexible and rather biscuit-like when cooked. My mother always used it when making a double-crust apple pie, and so do I. It is essential for Grandma's Bramble Cake (see BERRIES AND CURRANTS) and good for Rhubarb Pie (see RHUBARB). It makes enough for a double-crust pie in a 24 cm or 26 cm pie plate. Lard, clarified pork fat, is available from supermarkets and butcher shops.

200 g plain flour
200 g self-raising flour
½ teaspoon salt
200 g lard (at room
    temperature)
180 ml cold water

Sift flours and salt together, then rub lard in quickly. Make a well in the centre and work in water. Knead for 2–3 minutes until you have a springy, elastic dough. Form into a ball and chill for 20 minutes before rolling out. There is no need to chill the pastry once the pie plate has been lined, nor is lard pastry ever baked blind.

puff pastry

This preparation is long and fairly complicated. Cooks who enjoy mastering technique should take comfort from the fact that the more one makes puff pastry, the better it becomes. Impatient cooks, like me, will either buy it or look for a recipe that doesn't need it! Good home-made puff pastry is sublime and a labour of love, so be properly appreciative. At Stephanie's Restaurant we use salted butter, but many cooks prefer unsalted. Quantities given will make a rectangle of rolled-out dough about 30 cm × 20 cm.

Puff pastry is rarely baked blind in the usual sense. You may, however, wish to use it to make an onion tart or a cream-layered mille-feuille, both of which require cooked pastry that is subsequently filled. To prevent it rising, the pastry is 'docked' before it is baked (that is, pricked all over with a fork) or pressed flat with a heavy baking tray during cooking (this is the method used to make flaky sheets for mille-feuille). See also 'Bake Blind'.

250 g plain flour
pinch of salt
150 ml water
juice of ½ lemon
250 g cold butter

Mix flour, salt, water and lemon juice into a dough. Knead quickly until it feels elastic. Put dough on a plate, then cover with plastic film and refrigerate for at least 30 minutes (or overnight).

Unwrap butter and pound it to a pliable square with a rolling pin. Remove dough from refrigerator and roll out to a long rectangle the same width as the block of butter with the centre third twice the thickness of the ends. Place butter on this thicker section and envelop it with the 2 ends. Rotate dough so that an open end is facing you. Flatten middle of dough with rolling pin, at the same time rolling a little towards each end. Using your fingers, force butter into the corners of dough, then close ends over, completely covering butter. Gently flatten the ends with your hand.

Begin first roll. Lightly flour top and bottom to prevent pastry from sticking. Roll pin rapidly, extending the pastry as you go. The rolling movement is a firm, even push away from you. Do not roll dough back and forth relentlessly. If you have any breaks, sprinkle dough with flour. Fold top and bottom ends to meet at the centre, then fold one end on another, like closing a book. This is the first roll completed. Wrap pastry in foil and refrigerate for 30 minutes. Repeat this process another 3 times, resting the pastry for 30 minutes each time. (The pastry is rested between the rolls to firm the butter and relax the gluten in the flour. The butter must be firm, otherwise the layers will break down and merge. The gluten must be relaxed, otherwise the pastry may retract severely and distort when rolled and baked.)

After the fourth and last roll, refrigerate pastry for at least 1 hour before rolling and cutting it. Cut shapes should be rested again for

PASTRY
continued

30 minutes before baking. Always cut puff pastry with a sharp knife. If the edges are dragged at all they will not rise evenly and the layers will appear pressed together.

shortcrust pastry

This quantity will line a 22 cm, 24 cm or 26 cm loose-bottomed flan tin, with varying amounts left over. I use it for both sweet and savoury tarts as I prefer its crispness to the 'shortbready' character of sweet shortcrust pastries. I refer to this pastry as Damien's pâte brisée, *since the recipe comes from my friend Damien Pignolet.*

180 g unsalted butter
240 g plain flour
pinch of salt
3 tablespoons water

Remove butter from refrigerator 30 minutes before making pastry. Sieve flour and salt onto a marble pastry slab or workbench. Chop butter into smallish pieces and toss lightly in flour. Lightly rub to combine partly. Make a well in centre and pour in water. Using a pastry scraper (and being mindful of the technique you have observed of mixing cement), work paste to a very rough heap of buttery lumps of dough. Using the heel of your hand, quickly smear pastry away from you across the workbench. It will combine lightly. Gather together, then press quickly into a flat cake and dust with a little flour. Wrap pastry in plastic film and refrigerate for 20–30 minutes. When required, roll out pastry, dusting generously with flour as necessary. Line tin as described under 'Bake Blind' and proceed as indicated.

PASTRY CREAM

Also known as crème pâtissière, *this is the traditional filling for fresh fruit tarts. It is also used to fill choux puffs. This quantity makes sufficient to line 6 individual fruit tarts or 1 × 24 cm or 26 cm pastry case.*

2 cups milk
1 vanilla bean, split
6 egg yolks
175 g castor sugar
50 g cornflour

Scald milk with vanilla bean. Beat egg yolks with sugar and cornflour until thick. Pour in milk and whisk until quite smooth. Return mixture to rinsed-out saucepan and stir continuously over moderate heat until pastry cream has thickened, is smooth and has come to a boil. Beat vigorously for 1 minute. Pour through a coarse strainer resting over a bowl. Wash and dry vanilla bean and reserve for another use. Press plastic film onto pastry cream to prevent a skin forming. Use pastry cream when it is cold. I prefer to lighten it by incorporating about a quarter to a third its volume of unsweetened firmly whipped cream. >

variations Crushed macaroons, crushed Praline (*see* NUTS) or liqueurs can be added to the pastry cream.

PASTRY CREAM
continued

PEPPER

Black and white pepper and green peppercorns are all produced from the berries of *Piper nigrum*, a vine native to Asia. To make **black** pepper, the peppercorns, picked green, are left to ferment for a few days and are then sun-dried until shrivelled and black–brown in colour. For **white** pepper they are picked mature and soaked until soft, when they are rubbed to remove their outer skin. The peppercorns are then washed and sun-dried until bleached white. White peppercorns are hotter and less aromatic than black peppercorns. **Green** peppercorns are picked when immature and marketed undried, either fresh, freeze-dried or canned in natural juices. Keep separate grinders for black and white peppercorns, and use white pepper when making a pale sauce in which ground black pepper would be obvious.

P. *nigrum* has been grown in Queensland since 1987 by the Campagnolo family at Silkwood and its peppercorns can be bought fresh June–December. **Pink** peppercorns (from a type of rose and available in brine or freeze-dried), **Szechuan** peppercorns (from the prickly ash and used in Chinese cookery) and **cayenne** pepper (produced by grinding cayenne chillies, *see* PEPPERS AND CHILLIES) do not come from *P. nigrum*.

PITA BREAD

Unleavened, flat, Middle Eastern pita bread is available in all supermarkets. It can be opened out and stuffed with fillings to make satisfying sandwiches. It can also be opened out, then toasted for 10 minutes at 200°C in the oven and served with dips or, as in the Middle East, the toasted pieces can be crumbled and used to line the bottom of the salad bowl or platter before other ingredients are added. Pieces of fresh pita can also be torn or cut, then deep-fried and scattered with a little roasted spice, such as roasted cumin, to offer with drinks. Pita bread freezes perfectly.

PIZZA DOUGH

Authentic pizza alla Romana *has less yeast than other pizza doughs and a long proving time, and is then stretched to incredible lengths before baking. This simplified version makes enough for 2 × 26 cm pizza trays.*

1 tablespoon instant dried yeast	Mix yeast and salt with flour. Mix 1 tablespoon olive oil with the water and beat into dry ingredients using a dough hook.
1 teaspoon salt	
400 g plain flour	Knead until mixture is smooth and elastic, about 8 minutes. (This can be done by hand
olive oil	but will need 10–15 minutes' kneading.)
1 cup lukewarm water	Grease bowl with 1 tablespoon olive oil.

Transfer dough to bowl, then cover with plastic film or a tea towel and allow to rise in a draught-free place until doubled in size (about

**PIZZA
DOUGH**
continued

1½ hours). Knock back dough, then fold gently in 4 and allow to rise again, covered, for 30–45 minutes. Proceed immediately with recipe (*see* ONIONS, OREGANO AND MARJORAM and ROSEMARY for recipes).

POACH

The boiling point for water is 100°C. Poaching takes place at 94°C. It is important when instructed to poach that the surface of the water only ever shivers – it should not break (as when simmering or boiling), otherwise the ingredient being poached may toughen.

PONZU SAUCE

This sauce lasts for years! I warm it and spoon a little onto seared scallops and serve slivers of Pickled Ginger (see GINGER) alongside. It is also excellent with warmed or cold oysters or grilled fish. The recipe uses 2 important ingredients in Japanese cooking: bonito, a member of the mackerel family which is sold dried and flaked, and konbu seaweed, a variety of kelp also sold dried. Both are available from Asian food stores.

80 ml mirin or rice wine
600 ml light soy sauce
¾ cup white rice vinegar
1 cup lemon juice
20 g flaked bonito
2 × 5 cm pieces konbu
    seaweed

Heat mirin in a saucepan, then remove from heat and touch surface with a lighted match to burn off alcohol. Combine all ingredients in a glass jar or stainless steel container and allow to stand for 24 hours. Strain sauce into a sterilised bottle, discarding debris, and store. Use at full strength or dilute with a little water.

PUFF PASTRY

see 'Pastry'

RED-COOKED

In Chinese cookery meat and poultry are often steeped in dark soy sauce to produce a deep-red, glazed exterior. Such meat is described as being red-cooked, of which Cha Siu-style Pork (*see* PORK) is an example.

RICE FLOUR

see 'Ground Rice'

RICE VINEGAR

There are many varieties of Chinese rice vinegars, all of which are sweet to a degree. *White* rice vinegar is clear and mild and used for sweet and sour dishes. *Black* rice or Chenkong rice vinegar is very dark and very mellow. It is used for braised dishes and sauces. *Red* rice vinegar is sweet and spicy and is used most frequently in dipping sauces. Rice vinegars are available from Asian food stores.

ROCK SALT

see 'Salt'

ROCK SUGAR

see 'Sugar'

A *roux* is made by cooking a paste of butter and flour and then slowly
adding hot liquid (stock or milk) to make a sauce. One can either have a
blond *roux*, where the flour does not brown at all, or a brown *roux*, where
the butter and flour are cooked more thoroughly. Flour-thickened brown
sauces have gone out of fashion, many modern chefs preferring to reduce
their basic stocks to sauce consistency. However, for home cooks making a
roux is still an essential technique to understand. Use equal quantities of
flour and butter, although some cooks add a little extra butter, and 2 cups
hot liquid per 20 g butter to produce a sauce of medium thickness suitable
for most needs. To make a **blond roux**, melt butter, then stir in plain flour
and cook, stirring, for about 3 minutes before gradually adding hot liquid.
Bring to simmering point, stirring all the time. Once this point has been
reached, reduce the heat to the lowest setting and allow the sauce to murmur
along for another 15–20 minutes to ensure that all traces of flour have
disappeared. To make a **brown roux**, melt the butter, then stir in the flour
and cook, stirring, until the flour is an even nut-brown colour. Then proceed
as for a blond *roux*.
velouté sauce Hot stock added to a blond *roux* produces a velouté
sauce. **béchamel sauce** Hot milk is added to a blond *roux* to produce a béchamel sauce. Cheese is also often added. *See* Fennel with Simple
Cheese Sauce in FENNEL or Lasagne in PASTA AND NOODLES for recipes.
espagnole sauce Veal stock is added to a brown *roux* to make a
brown or espagnole sauce.

ROUX

The safest rule to avoid food poisoning is to buy small quantities of fresh
food frequently and to cook and eat what you have bought without delay.
Most food poisoning is caused either by reheating food without boiling it,
or leaving food around at room temperature for hours. Bacteria multiply
when they are warm: not when they are too hot or too cold.
　A few rules. ***Don't*** thaw food by putting it in hot water. ***Don't*** add cold
food to warm food without immediately reheating to boiling point. ***Reheat***
food right through until it is too hot to touch. ***Don't*** wrap hot food in plastic
wrap, thereby creating the perfect steamy environment for bacterial growth.
Don't store raw and cooked food together. ***Don't*** use the same knife or
cutting board for raw and cooked food without thoroughly washing both
between jobs. ***Cool*** large quantities of food quickly – stand it in cold or iced
water, stirring frequently, and then refrigerate it. ***Don't*** leave food out of
the refrigerator for hours and hours (a maximum of 2 hours is recommended). And ***remember***: take a chiller in the boot of the car when you go
shopping and on picnics for all meat, fish, poultry and dairy products. *See
also* 'Meat, Refrigerating'.

**SAFE
FOOD-HANDLING**

SALT

Our bodies need salt to survive, but far less than many people ingest, as salt occurs naturally in almost all foods. Salt imparts flavour to food and also combats bacteria by drawing out moisture within food, as happens when food is cured with salt. My preference is for sea salt, particularly the flaked variety when making salads. *Rock* salt is mined and often coloured by other minerals. It is produced and marketed in different grades, some coarser than others. It can be used as a bed on which to bake potatoes or to display oysters and for sprinkling on snow or ice in old-fashioned ice-cream churns. Red rock salt is used in important ceremonies and feasts in Hawaii. *Sea* salt (*gros* salt in French) is evaporated sea water, which, once it has become crystallised through the action of wind and sun, is harvested, washed and processed. Sea salt can be coarse for the salt mill or can be intended to be crumbled between the fingers (as with Maldon sea salt). *Kosher* salt is a variety of sea salt produced in accordance with orthodox Jewish faith. *Refined* or table salt is fine sea salt to which other substances have been added to ensure that it is free-flowing. Iodine is added to some refined salt. *Seasoned* or spiced salt is salt that has been pounded with garlic, onion, celery seeds or citrus peel, or some other combination.

SEA SALT

see 'Salt'

SETTING STAGE

To test whether a jam, jelly or marmalade has reached setting or jelly stage, place a tablespoon of the preserve on a cold saucer and chill it for a few minutes. Push your finger through the middle of the blob – if it remains in 2 distinct halves, the setting stage has been reached.

SHORTCRUST PASTRY

see 'Pastry'

SHRIMP PASTE, DRIED

Trasi, terasi, balachan or *blachan* all refer to a dark paste made from dried shrimps that is used in Indonesian, South-East Asian and Malaysian cooking. It is very pungent and is usually fried in a wok with other spices as an initial preparation for a dish. It can be bought as a paste or in a block from Asian food stores.

SOY BEANS

see 'Black Beans, Fermented'

SOY SAUCE

Different types of soy sauce are available at all Asian food stores and some supermarkets. Soy sauce is made from fermented black (soy) beans, wheat, yeast, salt and sugar. *Dark soy* is thicker and sweeter and altogether more powerful than *soy* or *light soy* sauces. Dark soy is used whenever a deep colour is wanted and thus for all red-cooked dishes. *See also* 'Red-cooked'.

Throughout this book mention is made of many different spices that add **SPICES** excitement and subtle flavours to dishes. Always buy a small quantity of each spice and store it in a cool, dry place in a tightly sealed jar. Do not buy packaged sets of spices. Apart from the obvious fact that there will be some you never use, it is impossible to know how long ago they were packed. Buy spices from an appropriate shop: an Indian shop for curry spices and an Asian food store for Asian spices. These are likely to have knowing customers who will insist on freshness. Many spices are dry-roasted before being ground to achieve their fullest flavour.

to dry-roast spices Heat a heavy-based frying pan and toss each spice separately over moderate heat until aromatic and darker in colour. Cool, then grind in a coffee grinder reserved for the purpose, or use a mortar and pestle.

This topping can be used with all manner of stewed or poached fruit. The **SPONGE TOPPING** *quantity given is sufficient for 6 serves.*

60 g butter

4 tablespoons castor sugar

2 eggs

150 g self-raising flour, sifted

¼ cup milk

2 cups drained poached or
  puréed fruit

Preheat oven to 180°C. Cream butter and sugar until light and fluffy. Add eggs, one at a time, beating well after each. Fold flour and milk alternately into egg mixture to make a soft batter. Put fruit into a 1 litre buttered pie dish and cover with topping. Bake for 30 minutes until well risen, firm and golden brown.

Jars and bottles that are to be filled with jam, pickles, sauces and the like **STERILISE** must be sterilised beforehand. (It is not necessary to sterilise bottles or jars that are later processed in a water bath, as the jars will be sterilised during the processing time.) Wash the jars in hot soapy water and then rinse them in hot water. Place in a stockpot of boiling water for 10 minutes and then drain upside down on a clean tea towel. Dry thoroughly in an oven set at 150°C. Remove the jars from the oven to fill them while still hot.

This technique gives Chinese vegetable cooking its crunchy, shiny, slippery **STIR-FRY** and delectable character. You will need a *wok* and a *wok sang*, the utensil used to scrape and toss food in the wok. Remember to keep the heat high – the food should cook quickly, not stew.

Heat the wok. Add sufficient vegetable oil to the hot wok to generously coat the food you are about to add. Splash hot oil up the sides of the wok to coat the entire surface. Add the vegetables in the order in which they will take to cook. The thickest stems go in first, the leaves last of all. There should be a loud hiss, which indicates that the wok is hot enough. Toss the contents. When all the pieces are shiny and hissing and sizzling, add a little water or light stock and a pinch of salt or a splash of soy sauce and slap on the lid. Try not to lift the lid until the food is cooked – allow about 3 minutes for bok choy, for example. If necessary, make a cornflour slurry (see below) and add it at the end of the cooking time to thicken the sauce. Many delicious dishes result from adding meat, fish, mushrooms, sausage, fermented black beans or all manner of spicy bits and pieces to the basic vegetables. My advice is to master the basic technique first, then turn to the experts for specific instruction and inspiration.

cornflour slurry To thicken ½ cup liquid, mix 2 teaspoons cornflour with 2 teaspoons water or light soy sauce. Stir in a little of the juice from the wok, then pour the mixture back into the wok and stir over heat until the sauce has thickened and is smooth.

STOCK

Stocks of all kinds – fish, meat, poultry and vegetable – are handy to have in the freezer. A meal of risotto, a soup or a sauce can then be prepared with very little fuss. Make use of any bones, whether the carcass of a roast chicken or the bones the butcher has removed for you when preparing a cut for stuffing.

Meat and fish stocks can be *clarified* to remove all particles of fat and other impurities to produce a clear and sparkling stock. Clarified stock is used to make consommé and can be set with gelatine to make a savoury jelly or layered over cold foods to give a flavoursome, shiny finish and exclude any air that might oxidise the dish (a duck or chicken liver parfait, for example). Ensure that the stock you intend to clarify is full flavoured, as the process draws some of the flavour from it.

clarified stock Whisk 2 egg whites, ½ cup finely chopped vegetables and your chosen stock together and tip the mixture into a saucepan. Stir over moderate heat until the liquid just reaches simmering point. Simmer undisturbed for 1 hour. Turn off the heat and remove the 'raft' of egg white and vegetables. Strain the stock through a damp muslin cloth into a clean bowl and taste for seasoning.

---

chicken stock

This quantity makes about 2 litres. If a deeper-coloured stock is required, lightly oil the bones and vegetables and bake at 180°C for about 20 minutes until lightly browned, then proceed with the recipe.

1–2 fresh chicken carcasses, chopped 500 g chicken wings *(continued next page)*	Place chicken bones, wings and gizzards in a stockpot and cover generously with cold water. Bring to simmering point and skim well. Add remaining ingredients. Adjust heat

2 chicken gizzards, cleaned
  (if available)
I onion, sliced
I carrot, sliced
I leek, sliced
I stick celery, sliced
6 mushrooms
I piece lemon zest
I tomato, peeled, halved and
  seeded
I bay leaf
I sprig thyme
a few parsley stalks
6 black peppercorns

to maintain a very gentle simmer and simmer for 4 hours. Strain stock and allow to get cold. Remove any fat that has risen. Reduce stock to concentrate its flavour, if desired. Refrigerate for 2–3 days, or freeze.

---

fish stock

This quantity makes about 2 litres. The character of the stock can be changed by adding fennel seeds or stalks, mushrooms, saffron, tomatoes, and so on.

heads and bones of 2 flathead
2 tablespoons olive oil
I onion, sliced
I carrot, sliced
I leek, sliced
I stalk celery, sliced
3 stalks parsley
I bay leaf
I generous sprig thyme
6 black peppercorns
150 ml dry white wine

Wash bones well, scraping away any blood, and cut out and discard gills. Chop bones into a few pieces. Drain well. Warm oil in a stockpot. Add bones and cook for 5 minutes, then add all other ingredients and stir. Cover well with cold water and bring slowly to simmering point, then skim. Simmer for 20 minutes. Have ready a strainer lined with damp muslin over a large basin. Ladle stock through muslin, then allow to cool. Refrigerate for 2 days, or freeze.

---

veal stock

Ask the butcher to saw the meat into small pieces. Any other meaty bones are fine to use, too. This quantity makes about 3 litres.

I kg veal shanks, sawn into
  small pieces
I kg beef brisket, sawn into
  small pieces
(continued next page)

Preheat oven to 200°C. Place all meat in a baking dish and sprinkle with oil. Roast for 20 minutes, then turn meat over. Roast for another 20 minutes – during this time meat will become golden brown. Slice 2 of the

STOCK
continued

1 pig's trotter, sawn in half
2 tablespoons olive oil
3 onions
6 cloves garlic, crushed
2 carrots, sliced
2 leeks, sliced
2 sticks celery, sliced
6 mushrooms, chopped
2 large tomatoes, unpeeled
    and halved crosswise
1 bay leaf
1 sprig thyme
a few black peppercorns

onions and add to baking dish with garlic and all vegetables except tomatoes. While vegetables and meat are browning, cut remaining unpeeled onion in half crosswise. Fry onion and tomato halves, cut-side down, in a lightly oiled heavy-based frying pan until cut sides are very dark.

Remove bones, meat and vegetables from baking dish, put in a stockpot and add onion and tomato. Cover generously with cold water, then bring to simmering point and skim very well. When no more scum rises, add herbs and peppercorns and maintain a bare simmer for 8 hours. Strain and allow to cool, then remove any fat that has risen. Boil to reduce or concentrate the flavour, if desired, and refrigerate for 2–3 days, or freeze.

---

vegetable stock
This recipe will result in a fairly neutral stock suitable for all-purpose poaching and saucemaking. More specific character can be added by using different spices or vegetables. This quantity makes about 3 litres.

3 onions
2 tomatoes, unpeeled and
    halved crosswise
3 tablespoons olive oil
2 leeks, sliced
2 carrots, sliced
2 celery stalks, sliced
125 g mushrooms, sliced
6 cloves garlic, peeled
6 black peppercorns
a few parsley stalks
1 generous sprig thyme
1 bay leaf
4 litres water

Preheat chargrill pan or griller. Dice 2 of the onions and halve the other crosswise. Drizzle onion and tomato halves with 1 tablespoon of the oil and grill until the surface is quite black. Heat rest of oil in a stockpot and sweat remaining vegetables and garlic for 5 minutes. Add all other ingredients, including grilled vegetables, and bring slowly to simmering point, then skim. Simmer for 3 hours. Allow to cool, then strain, pressing hard on vegetables to extract maximum flavour. Refrigerate for 2–3 days, or freeze.

SUGAR

Australian sugar (sucrose) is derived from sugar cane. (Exactly the same product results by refining juice from sugar beets.) The refining process extracts the molasses from the sugar-cane juice and crystallises the remainder to become sugar as we know it. The crystallisation process is undertaken in stages, producing different types of sugar along the way. ***Raw*** sugar is the name given to the crystals before they have been fully refined. *Demerara* and *muscovado* sugars are specific types of raw sugar with varying amounts of molasses. ***White*** sugar, the most refined of all sugars, is sold by the size of its granules. ***Granulated*** white sugar is the all-purpose sugar we use most often. ***Castor*** sugar has smaller granules than granulated sugar and is particularly suited to baking, as the smaller granules make creaming easier. ***Icing*** sugar is the finest of all white sugars and feels like powder. It is labelled 'pure icing sugar' or 'icing mixture'. In the latter case, a very small amount of anti-caking compound has been added. Most cooks prefer to use pure icing sugar and to press it through a sieve to extract any small lumps. In modern manufacture ***light-brown*** and ***dark-brown*** sugars are usually made by adding clarified molasses to white sugar. In this way the consumer is assured that the sugar contains no impurities. The darker the sugar, the higher the molasses content.

There are specialist sugars that are worth knowing about, especially if you enjoy cooking Asian food. They can be bought from Asian food stores. ***Rock*** sugar, chunks of crystallised raw sugar from sugar cane, is used in the Chinese kitchen when red-cooking meat or poultry. It has the same subtle difference of flavour as brown sugar has over white sugar. To break off chunks, wrap the rock sugar in a towel and smash it with a meat mallet. ***Palm*** sugar, also known as *gula jawa* or *nam tan peep*, is not made from sugar cane but from the boiled-down sap of coconut and palmyrah palms. It is usually sold in discs that you can chop, crush or grate. Some varieties are much darker than others. Dark-brown sugar is an acceptable substitute, but do try to find palm sugar as its flavour is unique.

SUGAR SYRUP

Sugar syrup is either light or heavy, depending on its final purpose, and can also be caramelised. Flavourings, such as vanilla bean, lemon or orange zest, cinnamon sticks or aromatic herbs, are often added to sugar syrup. Very dense sugar syrups are needed for specialist confectionery work, which is outside the scope of this book, other than to mention making caramel for Orange Caramel Syrup (*see* ORANGES, MANDARINS AND GRAPEFRUIT) and Caramel Custard (*see* EGGS). **light sugar syrup** Heat 2 parts water to 1 part sugar and stir until the sugar has dissolved. Light sugar syrup is used to poach fruit. The syrup should barely move during this process. Some fruit poaches in 5 minutes (cherries), while others may take an hour or more (pears). **heavy sugar syrup** Heat 1 part water to 1 part sugar and stir until the sugar has dissolved. Heavy sugar syrup is used for making fruit sorbets. To make simple fruit sorbets, take an equal volume of cold heavy sugar syrup and strained fruit purée and add a few drops of lemon juice. Churn in an ice-cream machine following the manufacturer's instructions. **caramel** Heat 1 part water to 4 parts sugar and stir until the sugar has dissolved. Wipe any stray drops of syrup on the sides of the saucepan with a pastry brush dipped in cold water. Stop stirring once the syrup is quite clear. Have a bowl of cold water ready near by. When the syrup has cooked to the colour you want, remove the pan from the heat and set it in the cold water to stop the cooking. Use as soon as possible to coat a mould or add other ingredients, such as orange juice.

SZECHUAN PEPPERCORNS	*see* 'Pepper'

TAMARIND	The tamarind tree produces a seed pod that is used extensively in Indian and South-East Asian cookery. The seeds are embedded in dense, sticky *pulp*, the aromatic sweet–sourness of which is very appealing. Tamarind pulp is available seeded and also as a paste from Asian food stores. Tamarind pulp is soaked to produce tamarind *water* – it is this rather than the pulp itself that is used in cooking.

tamarind water Soak 40 g tamarind pulp in ½ cup hot water for at least 30 minutes, then squeeze the pulp and press it and the liquid through a coarse strainer. The somewhat unappetising-looking dark liquid is then measured and the desired quantity is added to the recipe.

TARTARE SAUCE	*see* 'Mayonnaise'

TEST FOR DONENESS	*see* 'Meat and Poultry, Test for Doneness'

TESTS CLEAN	*see* 'Cake Tests Clean'

THAWING MEAT	*see* 'Meat, Refrigerating'

TOMATO SAUCE	References in this book are to home-made preparations rather than shop-bought ones. Such sauce is easy to make and a joy when tomatoes are at their peak in summer. *See* Fresh Tomato Sauce in TOMATOES.

VANILLA	Vanilla is the best-loved flavouring for ice-cream, and is essential in the pastry kitchen. It intensifies the flavours of the foods with which it is combined, as well as contributing its own perfume. True vanilla is from the bean or pod of the wild orchid *Vanilla planifolia* that grows in the tropics. The long, thin beans are cured in the sun in an involved process that leaves them very dark and shrivelled. The finest vanilla is said to be from Mexico, then Madagascar, then Tahiti and then the West Indies. A *vanilla bean* should be stored in a screw-top jar in the refrigerator. Vanilla

beans, split or not, can be dried and re-used. Pieces can also be buried in a jar of castor sugar, which will become deliciously perfumed. Some cooks split the bean and scrape out the tiny soft seeds. This gives a characteristic speckled look to custards and ice-creams and is a guarantee that real vanilla has been used. *Pure vanilla*, made by macerating chopped beans, should not be confused with vanillin, which is a synthetic and harsh-flavoured liquid sold as *imitation vanilla essence*. Pure vanilla is very powerful and a drop may well be sufficient – the flavour of imitation vanilla essence doesn't compare.

see 'Egg Custard'	**VANILLA CUSTARD**
see 'Stock'	**VEAL STOCK**
see 'Stock'	**VEGETABLE STOCK**
see 'Roux'	**VELOUTÉ SAUCE**

YEAST, INSTANT DRIED

Instant dried yeast can be mixed directly with dried ingredients when making bread. Formerly dried yeast had to be mixed with a little sugar and liquid to start it working before adding it to the dry ingredients. Always check your packet of dried yeast to be sure which sort you have. Instant dried yeast is available from supermarkets and delicatessens. *See* BREAD for more information about yeast and breadmaking.

anchovies

Many people dismiss anchovies from their diet because they are so salty. It is not always understood that anchovies can be considered as a *condiment*. A very little adds piquancy or excitement to a dish, stuffing or sauce. It is only the true anchovy lovers (I am one) who enjoy a whole salted anchovy on toast! │ Most anchovies caught in Australia are used as fishing bait or processed to fish paste. But in Fremantle the enterprising Mendolia family has pioneered an Australian industry of high-quality anchovies that are cured in salt, then skinned and filleted and packed in olive oil. This excellent product is marketed under the brand name of Bella del Tindari. In seasons when the anchovies are too small to process, which happens from time to time (and is the case at the time of writing), the Mendolia family processes sardines the same way. Marketed as Auschovies, this product is an Australian first. │ It is worth noting that Jim Mendolia has not only developed and promoted an entire industry, but has designed machines that efficiently skin and fillet these tiny fish and has created a 120 g package (a round tin with a resealable plastic lid) that is far more user-friendly than the traditional long sardine or anchovy tin one used to wrestle with.

VARIETIES AND SEASON

The Australian anchovy (*Engraulis australis*) is similar to the European species. It is about 3 cm long and often confused with the sardine or whitebait. It is purplish green on the back and upper sides and silvery-white below, and is found from Cape Capicorn in Queensland, through the southern waters and around to Shark Bay in Western Australia.

Anchovies are fished all year, with the majority of the catch available March–September in eastern and southern States and September–June (for both anchovies and sardines) in the west. Processing involves packing the just-caught fish in ice slurries on the boat. At Jim Mendolia's factory the fish are deheaded and gutted and layered in salt for 24 hours to draw out all the blood. The fish are washed in clear brine, then layered and salted and left under weights to cure for 4–6 months. They are washed in more brine, then skinned and filleted and packed in olive oil.

Australian anchovies and Auschovies are sold as fillets packed in olive oil in 60 g, 120 g and 500 g cans. Auschovies are also available cooked in spring water or tomato sauce. It is possible to buy imported headed and gutted sardines and, sometimes, anchovies packed in layers of salt in 4 kg tins. These fillets must be soaked before use.

SELECTION AND STORAGE

When buying **canned** anchovies, look for the Australian fish from Fremantle as they are packed in superior oil and the fillets are firmer and less salty than many imported brands. For home use, the 120 g can with the resealable plastic lid from Bella del Tindari is an ideal choice.

If you are fortunate enough to catch or be given **fresh** anchovies, which deteriorate very quickly, eat them no more than 8 hours out of the water, or else gut and wash well in lightly salted water to remove all slime and refrigerate for a day or two.

PREPARATION AND COOKING

The flesh of the anchovy is soft and slightly oily. Fresh anchovies are enjoyed in Mediterranean countries, either marinated and eaten raw, or grilled. Salting firms the fish, which is why the most popular way of preparing them is as cured fillets. The cured fillets dissolve readily into hot cooking juices, sauces and casseroles.

SALTED Cured Australian fillets packed in olive oil require no preparation other than to drain them of any excess oil. However, if you have purchased whole fish that are packed in salt, soak them in water or milk for a few hours before rinsing, drying and stripping off the fillets. There is a knack to this and until you are proficient you may well end up with very raggy fish.

FRESH

To eat raw Slit the raw fish open along the belly, then gut them and rub off the scales with a cloth. Rinse and pat them dry, then marinate them for 1–2 hours in red wine, lemon juice or red-wine vinegar. Drain the fish, then put them in a dish with the best olive oil and some finely chopped garlic and parsley and leave overnight. Next day, lift out the fish, grind over pepper and eat on fresh bread. **To grill** Slit the raw fish open along the belly, then gut them and rub off the scales with a cloth. Rinse and pat them dry. Lightly oil the gutted fish and sizzle them on a barbecue hotplate for 2 minutes only.

anchovy butter

MAKES ½ CUP

This butter is delicious on grilled fish (sublime with tuna or red mullet), new potatoes boiled in their skins (work in freshly chopped parsley too) and on grilled or toasted bread.

3 anchovies
juice of I lemon
100 g softened unsalted butter
freshly ground black pepper or
   Tabasco

Mash anchovies with lemon juice and mix well with butter. Add pepper to taste. Pack into small pots, cover and refrigerate for up to a week, or roll in a doubled sheet of foil and freeze.

anchovy vinaigrette

Use this warm or cold with barbecued kangaroo or a platter of grilled vegetables (especially onion, eggplant or zucchini), or even spooned over a poached or fried egg nestled on puréed spinach on top of a slice of toast.

4–5 parts fruity olive oil
I part red-wine vinegar
finely chopped anchovies
freshly ground black pepper
freshly chopped parsley

Mix oil and vinegar (over gentle heat if intending to serve it warm) and add chopped anchovies and pepper to taste. Stir in enough parsley to make a thick sauce and serve either warm or cold.

anchovy and puff pastry rolls

MAKES 18–24

These rolls are easy to put together if you love making puff pastry or have some scrappy bits in the freezer.

20 anchovies, drained
I quantity Puff Pastry
I egg, beaten

Preheat oven to 220°C. Halve anchovies lengthwise. Roll pastry thinly to a rectangle and arrange lines of anchovies at intervals

anchovy bites
Combine fresh breadcrumbs and freshly grated parmesan cheese and moisten with olive oil. Press crumbs onto raw, cleaned anchovies (fold a filleted fish in half, if desired, or 'sandwich' 2 fillets together) and bake at 220°C for 5 minutes until crusty and brown. Serve scattered with capers.

anchovy scrambled eggs
Melt 2 chopped anchovies in a bowl over simmering water, then stir into whisked eggs and scramble.

of 6 cm. Cut pastry between anchovies with a very sharp knife. Fold pastry over and press edges together to encase anchovies, then cut into rolls 3 cm long. Brush with egg and bake for 10 minutes. (Uncooked anchovy rolls freeze perfectly; brush with egg and bake, still frozen, for 12 minutes.) Serve hot.

anchovy won tons
Roll an anchovy in a won ton wrapper and deep-fry in clean, hot oil at 175°C until golden and blistered.

jansson's temptation
Include anchovies in a gratin of potato, onion and cream to make this classic Scandinavian dish.

anchovy toast
Serve anchovies on hot fingers of toast (no butter) to offer with a drink. For fancier versions, add strips of roasted red pepper (see p. 538) or Smoky Eggplant Purée (see EGGPLANTS).

bagna cauda sauce

MAKES 1½ CUPS

Usually served with raw vegetables for dipping, this sauce is also a luxurious accompaniment for a boiled artichoke, grilled fish or poached egg. There are many other versions, the best-known of which consists simply of olive oil, garlic, butter and anchovies.

400 ml cream
1 teaspoon softened butter
8 anchovies, finely chopped
1 teaspoon chopped garlic
freshly chopped parsley
   (optional)

Boil cream in a heavy-based saucepan for 5 minutes, stirring often, until lightly thickened. Melt butter in a heavy-based pan and add anchovies and garlic. Cook briefly without browning. Pour on cream and stir, then stir in parsley, if using. Serve warm.

pissaladière

SERVES 6

This is the Niçoise classic. I sometimes combine well-cooked tomato with the onion, or spread mustard over the pastry before adding the onion.

3–4 onions, thickly sliced
olive oil
1 quantity Puff Pastry
16 anchovies, halved
   lengthwise
12 black olives, stoned

Slowly cook onion in 2 tablespoons olive oil until very soft. Preheat oven to 220°C. Roll pastry out to make a 30 cm × 20 cm rectangle and transfer to a baking tray. Leaving a 1 cm rim, prick pastry all over with a fork and add a thick layer of onion. Arrange anchovy strips in rows to form large diamonds. Put an olive in centre of each diamond and drizzle over a little oil. Bake for 20 minutes until pastry is brown and crisp. Serve warm.

other recipes

cabbage salad with anchovy sauce *see* CABBAGES AND BRUSSELS SPROUTS
goat's cheese on salad leaves with an anchovy dressing *see* CHEESE
jenny's caesar salad *see* EGGS
maggie beer's barbecued kangaroo with anchovy vinaigrette and soft polenta *see* KANGAROO
vitello tonnato *see* VEAL

a p p l e s   The original apple was most probably the fruit of the *Malus pumila*, a crabapple. As apples do not grow true to seed, and some develop 'sports' or mutations, new varieties constantly appear, including those developed by scientists. There have been in excess of 7000 varieties of apples, with more than 100 currently grown commercially throughout the world. Many of these are excellent apples, but so are (or were) many older varieties that are becoming rare, or have disappeared.   Commercial considerations determine the apples we are offered. Varieties that transport, store and yield well and are resistant to disease take preference over varieties that do none of these things. It is up to us, the consumers, to indicate which apples we enjoy most. If we buy mediocre or tasteless apples, the industry will continue to believe they are popular and will continue to produce them.   The Australian Horticultural Corporation proudly claims that Australia is the world's healthiest apple-growing environment, protected from the acid rain and industrial pollution that threatens much of European agriculture. We also lack a number of the world's worst pests and diseases because of our isolation. Apples are grown in all States, with Victoria being the leading producer.

apples
go
with
butter
sugar
cinnamon
dried fruit
cheese
cream
pastry
pork
shellfish
vanilla
Calvados
brandy
honey
golden syrup
eggs
duck

VARIETIES AND SEASON

The following list includes some familiar apples available in Australia. Most greengrocers sell apples by variety, unlike many other fruit, and are happy to discuss varietal differences. The suggested seasonal availability of different varieties can be confusing. Varying growing conditions around the country can mean different harvesting seasons, and often the months specified include the time the fruit is expected to remain edible under controlled-atmosphere storage.

BOGLE This miniature variety was developed in Australia. It has golden, red-blushed skin and is sweet but not exciting to eat raw (I find it tastes both of apple and plum). It is most delicious baked slowly until its skin wrinkles. I like it especially in an upside-down apple tart. Harvested in April, the bogle is available from cool storage until September–October.

BONZA This crisp, red apple is harvested April–May and keeps well. A Jonathan 'sport' with some of the character of a Jonathan, this fine eating apple originated in Batlow, New South Wales.

COX'S ORANGE PIPPIN Raised in 1825 by Richard Cox at Slough, England, this apple symbolises the issues surrounding the decline of old varieties in favour of new: looks being more important than flavour and commercial considerations taking precedence over quality. Golden yellow and flushed brownish red to russet, the Cox cooks beautifully and is wonderful to eat – dense, juicy and well balanced in its acidity. It keeps well and develops a mellow character, reminding us that apples were once stored in draughty barns, so that their full flavour might develop. Grown mainly in Tasmania, it is harvested in March.

GALA The original gala, often called a golden gala, is a cross between a Kidd's orange (a derivative of Cox's orange pippin) and a golden delicious and originated in New Zealand. It has golden, red-striped skin and is crisp and rather sweet, making it a fine eating apple. Strains – the royal, imperial and regal galas – are generally better coloured than the original.

GOLDEN DELICIOUS This was developed in the late 1800s in the United States. It has pale-green skin that becomes gold-freckled and has juicy, aromatic flesh. It is excellent to eat and cooks well, as it keeps its shape and develops a beautiful golden translucence.

This apple is my favourite all-rounder and the one I choose for sautéing or making apple tarts. It is harvested March–August.

GRANNY SMITH   This familiar apple has glossy, green, greasy skin. The crisp, firm white flesh has a tart flavour. It is a popular cooking apple, especially if a collapsed purée is required. The Granny Smith is harvested March–May.

The Granny Smith was grown as a chance seedling in New South Wales by Maria Ann Smith in 1860, and is now popular all over the world. Australians take their green apple for granted, but I have watched as foreigners have expressed serious doubts about the wisdom of eating a green apple, finding it hard to believe that such a fruit could be ready to eat!

GRAVENSTEIN   This apple originated 300 years ago in Germany or Denmark. First on the market, it is medium to large and striped in green, yellow or red. It has a flattened shape with creamy-white, crisp and rather aromatic flesh. A lovely eating apple when freshly harvested late January–March, it doesn't keep well.

JONATHAN   Small to medium, round and bright to dull deep red with some green, the Jonathan is a very popular eating apple. Its flesh is white, crisp and juicy with medium acidity and has a wonderful flavour when eaten straight from the tree. It does not store particularly well. The Jonathan, which originated in the United States, is harvested February–mid-April.

LADY WILLIAM   An old variety from a chance cross between a Granny Smith and a rokewood apple, the Lady William was developed in the 1960s in Western Australia. A deep-red apple with crisp, tart flesh when freshly picked, it mellows with storage and is both good for eating and cooking (particularly the latter). Harvested May–July, stored apples are available until well after August.

PINK LADY   This new cross between a golden delicious and a Lady William originated in Western Australia. It has dense, firm flesh with a flavour reminiscent of its golden delicious parent and is an excellent eating apple. It is harvested April–May.

RED DELICIOUS   The 5 bumps ('crown') around the 'eye' distinguish this apple from other varieties. There are many strains, ranging from striped to dark blackish red and elongated. The flesh has moderate to low acidity and is aromatic and sweet. The red delicious is harvested March–May. It is the most widely grown dessert apple in the world and originated in the United States. However, it is my least favourite apple in the world. I find it flat in flavour and boring.

RED FUJI | Bred in Japan, where it is a major variety, and grown in Australia mainly for the export market, this apple is sometimes grown to an enormous size and is round and dull red with a crisp texture and sweet flavour. It often has a translucent, 'honey' core, which indicates a concentration of sugars rather than a disorder. It is a good eating apple and is harvested April–May.

SUNDOWNER | This apple is a cross between a golden delicious and a Lady William and originated in Western Australia. It looks similar to a pink lady but has darker skin. Rather tart when freshly picked, it mellows with storage. It is harvested in May.

SELECTION AND STORAGE

Apples taste best picked ripe from the tree but fruit picked fully ripe does not keep well. It is impossible to pick all apples on the day they are at their prime. Those apples harvested earlier than ideal are best for longer storage; those that are harvested later than ideal are usually marketed first. It is freely admitted that apples kept in controlled-atmosphere storage gradually lose their flavour and crisp texture. In general, early apples keep less well than the later-picked varieties.

Some varieties are better for eating than for cooking, and vice versa. Those with a higher sugar content will hold their shape better when cooked. Refer to 'Varieties and Season', ask your greengrocer and experiment.

Choose fruit that is true to the variety colour. Large apples do not keep as well as smaller fruit and all apples lose their crispness 10 times faster at room temperature than if refrigerated in a ventilated plastic bag.

PREPARATION

No preparation other than washing is required when eating an apple as a snack. Many recipes require apples to be peeled before being cooked. To stop a peeled apple browning, brush it with lemon juice.

apple toast
Grate an unpeeled, juicy eating apple, then mix with a generous teaspoon of ground cinnamon and pile on hot, hard buttered toast. This is one of my favourite breakfast dishes. (Don't bother with this if you favour sliced white bread. The soggy mixture will soak instantly into the unsatisfactory bread and all you will have is a pappy mess.)

recipes

buttered apple

SERVES 4

This apple can be enjoyed just as it is, or can be folded inside a pancake. Slip the filled pancake back into the pan and warm it through in the juices.

60 g butter

2 tablespoons castor *or* brown sugar

3 eating apples, cut into chunks

1 vanilla bean, split

1 small piece cinnamon stick or 1 lemon verbena leaf

Melt butter and sugar gently in a wide-based frying pan. Add apple and spices and cover pan tightly for 5 minutes until fruit has softened. Remove lid and watch closely. Don't shake and disturb the pieces too much – they only need to be turned once and should become a deep gold. Once tender, increase heat and shake gently as the apple becomes lightly caramelised.

quick apple cake

2 cups peeled and chopped eating apple

2 tablespoons Kellybrook Winery apple brandy, brandy *or* rum

140 g unsalted butter

160 g plain flour

1 teaspoon baking powder

3 eggs

120 g castor sugar

Soak fruit in chosen spirit for 30 minutes. Preheat oven to 200°C. Butter a 24 cm ring tin or 22 cm round cake tin. Melt butter and allow to cool. Sift flour and baking powder. Beat eggs and sugar until thick and fluffy and fold in flour mixture gently. Drizzle in melted butter, then fold it in. Fold in apple and any juice. Spoon into prepared tin and bake for 40 minutes until cake is golden brown and tests clean. Serve warm or cold with cream.

simple apple tart

1 quantity Shortcrust Pastry

4 tablespoons sieved Apricot Jam (see p. 53)

3 eating apples, peeled and thinly sliced

Line an 18 cm or 20 cm loose-bottomed flan tin with pastry. Bake blind at 200°C for 20 minutes until golden. Remove pastry case from oven and reduce temperature to 180°C. Remove weights and foil and allow pastry case to cool a few minutes. Warm jam and brush some over case. Arrange apple in slightly overlapping concentric circles. Bake for 15 minutes. Baste with remaining jam and cook 15–20 minutes until apple looks a little caramelised on the edges. **apple purée** Line the pastry case with apple purée mixed with a few drops of brandy before adding the apple. **cream glaze** Glaze the tart twice during cooking with thick cream rather than more jam. The cream will bubble and thicken and be absorbed by the apple.

scorched apple
Grill oiled chunks of apple on a hotplate or on a sheet of foil under the griller, or fry in a little oil in a heavy-based, cast-iron frying pan, until scorched a deep golden brown but not burnt. Serve alongside some good-quality pork sausages or a roast duckling.

pork and apple
Bake halved and cored apples with roast pork for the last hour of the cooking time.

apple crumble
Top stewed or Buttered Apple (see p. 48) with Crumble Topping and bake at 180°C for 25 minutes until golden and bubbling.

apple yeast sugar tart

250 g plain flour
pinch of salt
1 tablespoon sugar
1 teaspoon instant dried yeast
1 egg
½ cup warm milk
30 g softened butter
2 eating apples
½ cup brown sugar
3 tablespoons thick cream

Sift flour, salt, sugar and yeast into a bowl. Whisk egg with milk and mix into flour mixture. Work in butter and knead to a smooth, thick batter. Sprinkle with extra flour, cover and leave to rise in a draught-free place for 30 minutes. Knock back dough, then press it into a 22 cm buttered pie plate or loose-bottomed flan tin and allow to recover for 30 minutes (it will have puffed slightly). Preheat oven to 225°C. Peel apples and cut into eighths. Arrange apple on dough and cover with brown sugar. Bake 10 minutes, then reduce heat to 200°C. Spoon cream over apple and bake 20 minutes. The top should be slightly caramelised and the tart light and spongy. Eat warm.

baked apples
Stuff apples with honey and dried fruit and bake in a buttered dish with a little water drizzled around at 200°C for 1 hour.

apple and cheese
Offer a sliced Granny Smith apple with a cheese selection.

apple charlotte   SERVES 4

125 g softened butter
½ cup sugar
5 golden delicious apples, peeled and thickly sliced
½ stick cinnamon
8 thin slices white bread, crusts removed

FOR THE MOULD
20 g softened butter
sugar
ground cinnamon

Preheat oven to 180°C. To prepare the mould, butter a 500 ml pudding basin or charlotte mould. Combine 2 tablespoons sugar and 1 teaspoon ground cinnamon and scatter over mould, turning to coat.

Heat 50 g of the butter with sugar until sugar has dissolved and has just started to colour. Add apple and cinnamon stick, then cover tightly and reduce heat. Stir or shake occasionally to prevent sticking. Melt rest of butter in another saucepan. Trim each slice of bread to fit base and sides of mould. Brush one side of each slice with butter and line mould, overlapping slices slightly, buttered side to the outside. Remove cinnamon stick and crush apple roughly (there should still be some texture). Pile apple into lined mould and press down to fill well. Top with bread, buttered-side uppermost. Sprinkle with extra cinnamon and sugar and bake for 1 hour. Serve warm, unmoulded, with thick cream.

other recipes

erna's red cabbage with apple *see* CABBAGES AND BRUSSELS SPROUTS
waldorf salad *see* CELERY AND CELERIAC

apricots   I once lived in a house with a very old garden that boasted a magnificent apricot tree. The tree was smothered with rose-blushed fruit every January. I believe it was a moorpark. I made jam, I made chutney, I made and froze apricot purée and I ate many a perfect apricot. There was so much fruit I did not ever resent the birds helping themselves too.   Known in China as early as 2500 BC, the apricot (*Prunus armeniaca*) is a stone fruit of the rose family. It was brought to Europe from China via the Silk Road through the Far East and then through the Mediterranean. As a result of this journeying, both Moroccan and Persian cuisines have exotic recipes for stews and rice dishes combining meat (usually lamb or chicken) with spices and dried fruit, including apricots (Claudia Roden has a good selection of these in her wonderful *New Book of Middle Eastern Food*).   The apricots we know in Australia are all orange in colour and their flesh is firmer, drier and less sweet than varieties still grown in Asia. Apparently many Asian apricots have sweet kernels; although we might crack one or two to add aroma to a jam or syrup, the kernels of our apricots contain small amounts of prussic acid and are bitter and poisonous if eaten in any quantity. >

apricots
go
with
pistachios
almonds
vanilla
lamb
rice
barley
dried fruit
cardamom
cinnamon
chicken
brandy
honey
cream
yoghurt
sugar

Most of the world's apricots are produced in California, Iran, Turkey and Australia. Our main areas of commercial cultivation are Victoria's Goulburn and Murray valleys, the Derwent Valley in Tasmania and the coastal plains and tablelands of New South Wales. The Californians developed the art of drying apricots, and now Australia has its own most important dried fruit industry. Fruit is dampened and then stacked on racks in sulphur houses (the sulphur helps retain the flavour and colour). The sun does the rest of the work. It takes no fewer than 6 kg of fresh apricots to produce 1 kg of dried, which may help to explain their relatively high price.

VARIETIES AND SEASON

Apricots are rarely identified by variety in greengrocers' shops in my experience. Owners of backyard trees may recognise their own variety, but the names I read in my reference bible (*The Complete Book of Fruit Growing in Australia* by Louis Glowinski) are quite unfamiliar, other than the moorpark. Tree-ripened fruit is available mid-November–February, with the peak supplies in December and January, but the crop is very perishable. Glowinski lists, among others, glengarry and divinity as early varieties, goldrich and trevatt as mid-season varieties and moorpark and Morocco as late-season varieties. Dried apricots are available throughout the year.

SELECTION AND STORAGE

Apricots must be chosen on flavour alone. Quite pale fruit may have surprising juiciness and flavour and some richly coloured fruit can be hard and disappointing. Many varieties develop full flavour after they have become highly coloured. Ripe fruit will feel a little yielding when cupped in the hand. Like all stone fruit, tree-ripened fruit is the ultimate pleasure but it can be difficult to achieve, even if one has a tree in the garden. Allow under-ripe fruit to ripen at room temperature. Some advise leaving it in a brown paper bag away from direct sunlight to hasten the process. Under-ripe fruit can be refrigerated for a week, but give it several days at room temperature to develop flavour before eating.

Dried apricots stored in an airtight glass jar at a low temperature to prevent further drying out will keep for up to a year. They can also be frozen, and in humid climates should be refrigerated.

PREPARATION

Fresh apricots are not usually peeled as the skin is thin and has no unpleasant furriness. However, they are usually stoned before being cooked. Halve the fruit along the natural groove and remove the stone. If desired, wrap the stone in a cloth and crack it with a heavy mallet to extract the kernel to add its faintly bitter almond flavour to a syrup or jam. (Apricot kernels give the distinctive flavour to the liqueur Amaretto di Saronno and the popular Italian amaretti biscuits.) **Dried** apricots can be used as they are or soaked overnight in water or wine to plump them.

apricot jam

MAKES 1.5 LITRES

Home-made apricot jam on buttered brown bread is a favourite of mine. And sieved apricot jam warmed with a spoonful of liqueur makes the best glaze for light-coloured fruit tarts, such as pear or apple. Some cooks chop the fruit for the jam very small, others prefer it whole.

1.5 kg fresh apricots, firm-ripe
    rather than soft
1.5 kg sugar
1 cup water
2 tablespoons lemon juice

Preheat oven to 160°C. Wash the apricots, then halve or quarter them and remove stones. Wrap half the stones in a napkin and crack them with a meat mallet. Extract kernels and set aside. Discard debris.

Place sugar in a clean cast-iron casserole or baking dish and warm it in oven. Put fruit, water and lemon juice into a stainless steel saucepan (or a copper preserving pan, if you have one) and bring slowly to a boil. Simmer until fruit is tender, about 20 minutes, or longer if you prefer your jam not to have chunks of fruit in it. Add warmed sugar and reserved kernels to pan, stirring until sugar has dissolved, then boil rapidly for about 15 minutes or until setting point is reached. Ladle into hot, sterilised jars, distributing the kernels evenly, and seal.

stuffed apricots
Stuff halved ripe apricots with soft, fresh cheese (cow's or goat's) as a delicious and sustaining snack.

apricot crumble
Pile Crumble Topping over stewed apricots and bake for 40 minutes at 180°C until topping is golden and bubbling.

poached apricots

SERVES 4

1 cup water
1 cup white wine
1 cup sugar
1 vanilla bean
8 fresh apricots, halved
brandy, Amaretto di Saronno
    or sweet vermouth

Combine all ingredients except apricots and liqueur. Stir over heat until sugar has dissolved, then simmer for 5 minutes. Add apricots and allow syrup to return to a simmer, then reduce heat so syrup is barely moving. Press baking paper down on fruit to prevent excessive evaporation. The fruit should be tender in 5 minutes. Remove apricots with a slotted spoon to a wide dish and boil syrup for 5 minutes to concentrate flavour. Cool for a few minutes, then add liqueur. Return apricots to syrup and serve cold with thick cream, mascarpone, yoghurt, Simple Lemon Syllabub (*see* LEMONS AND LIMES), ice-cream or Olive Oil and Dessert Wine Cake (*see* OLIVES AND OLIVE OIL).
c u s t a r d Drain poached fruit and serve surrounded by a moat of

delicious Egg Custard ✐ (reserve the syrup for glazing a tart). **crumble or sponge topping** Arrange poached fruit in a buttered dish and add a crumble ✐ or sponge ✐ topping and bake at 200°C for 25–30 minutes until golden and bubbling.

middle eastern fruit salad   SERVES 4

This fruit salad can be varied infinitely, so do not worry if you only have some of the ingredients. It keeps for days and can also be enjoyed at breakfast with cereal or yoghurt. It becomes a very special dessert if combined with Orange and Cardamom Ice-cream (see ORANGES, MANDA-RINS AND GRAPEFRUIT). At Stephanie's we serve this salad with Marieke's Saffron Pears (see PEARS) sprinkled with chopped pistachios.

½ stick cinnamon

2 cloves

30 g dried apples

50 g dried apricots

30 g dried figs

30 g dried pears

30 g dried peaches

I teaspoon honey

I tiny pinch ground saffron

½ vanilla bean, split

I strip lemon zest

20 g flaked almonds

20 g shelled pistachios

few drops of orange-flower
   water

Tie cinnamon and cloves in muslin and put with the fruit, honey, saffron, vanilla bean and zest into a stainless steel pot and barely cover with cold water. Bring slowly to simmering point and cook for 15 minutes. Cool, then stir in nuts and add orange-flower water to taste.

fresh apricot tart

I quantity Shortcrust Pastry ✐

½ cup lightly toasted ground
   almonds

18 fresh apricots, halved or
   quartered

½ cup castor sugar

¼ cup Poached Apricots syrup
   (see p. 53) or warm Apricot
   Jam (see p. 53)

Line a 22 cm loose-bottomed flan tin with pastry and bake blind ✐ at 200°C for 20 minutes. Remove pastry case but leave oven on. Scatter almonds over pastry case and fill with apricots, cut-side up. Sprinkle sugar into cavities of fruit. Bake for 10 minutes, then brush with syrup. Bake a further 10 minutes then remove from oven. The fruit will have started to brown around edges and will subside as the tart cools.

---

apricot fool
Purée cooked dried apricots and their juices and fold purée through half its volume of sweetened whipped cream. Heighten the flavour with a little lemon juice.

apricots in wine
Sprinkle sugar and a glass of the best dessert wine you have over freshly sliced, perfectly ripe apricots. Press plastic film down on the fruit and leave to macerate for an hour.

apricot glaze
Use apricot stewing liquid as a glaze for brushing over a simple apple tart as it cooks.

artichokes

The dull-green, purple or bronze globe artichoke (*Cynara scolymus*) is a member of the thistle family. The part one eats is in fact the flower-bud, which is inedible when opened. In mature artichokes, the hairy 'choke' that lines the prized heart is the beginning of this development. The largest bud sits at the top of this huge plant and can weigh upwards of 500 g. Those lowest on the main stem are lateral buds, often culled while small to encourage development of the remaining buds. While they may be tender and should be enjoyed, they are not the same as the very small, fully formed artichokes one sees in Europe produced from specific varieties. These artichokes are not widely planted in Australia as yet. | Artichokes have a reputation of being tricky to prepare and fiddly to eat. As a result, many food lovers have yet to tackle their first boiled artichoke. The flavour is quite unlike anything else (except cardoons, and most of us will never taste a cardoon unless we grow them). They contain cynarin, a sweet-tasting chemical that sweetens the flavour of the thing you eat next, making wine taste pretty nasty. (Interestingly, this phenomenon is much less pronounced if the artichokes have been crumbed and fried.) >

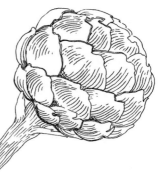

The thistly point of each leaf is inedible, and in mature artichokes the hairy choke is discarded. To eat boiled artichoke, one scrapes the fleshy side of the leaf against the teeth and then discards the leaf. It is important to judge properly the amount of sauce, so that you still have some when you reach the tender heart.

It all sounds like a lot of work for very little. Try one and see why artichoke devotees feast on these thistles each spring with such enthusiasm. The French are not as keen on all the hard work as the Italians, who work away happily surrounded by fingerbowls and mountains of leaves. French recipes tend to concentrate on fancy ways of cooking and serving the heart, or *fond*. In European markets one can buy already pared-down hearts sold in buckets of acidulated water – a wonderful convenience food. We cannot.

VARIETIES AND SEASON

Green globe artichokes are usually available by late June, while purple globes arrive a little later. The season is June–November, with the peak being August–October. Size does not indicate quality. Varieties grown here do not have hearts as large as the great Breton artichokes sold in France. Ours are not inferior in flavour, but it can be mystifying to see photographs in European books of artichoke hearts stuffed with poached eggs or mounds of asparagus tips when one is staring at a trimmed heart that might hold a poached quail's egg, if lucky! Incidentally, the Jerusalem artichoke, a tuber, bears no relation to the globe artichoke (*see* JERUSALEM ARTICHOKES).

SELECTION AND STORAGE

Choose plump, heavy artichokes with tightly closed leaves and a firm stem. Never buy a limp-stalked artichoke with partially opened leaves that curl backwards from the plant; this indicates that the artichoke was picked some time ago and is starting to deteriorate. Tiny artichokes may have a looser leaf formation but they should still feel firm and springy; when a leaf is pulled away there should be a definite squeak. Artichokes start to lose condition as soon as they have been harvested. They can be refrigerated in the vegetable crisper for a few days in a vegetable storage bag.

PREPARATION AND COOKING

Cut or trimmed artichokes discolour very quickly, so have a lemon at hand to rub on any exposed surface. Standing trimmed artichokes in acidulated water ✔ will also prevent discoloration.

TO BOIL | Have ready a stainless steel or enamelled cast-iron stockpot of boiling, salted water (aluminium tends to discolour artichokes). Trim each stalk, leaving 6 cm attached. (The artichokes will sit more neatly in a serving bowl without their

stalks, but the inner part of the stalk is very tender and tastes just like the heart. One can always cook the artichokes, stem on, and serve the stems alongside.) Snap off the first few layers of leaves until you start to see a yellow–green base to the leaves. Rub all exposed surfaces with lemon. If the leaves are pointy and prickly, snip off the tops, then trim the whole globe by a third. Rub the cut surfaces with the lemon.

Drop the artichokes into the boiling water, keeping them submerged with an upturned plate. Boil for 15 minutes. Lift an artichoke out and run a thin skewer through the thickest part. If there is only slight resistance, your artichokes are cooked. If there is a hard centre, cook a further 5 minutes. Remove and drain upside down on a plate for a few minutes. Turn the right way up and spread the leaves a little with your fingers. If serving a vinaigrette sauce with the artichoke, spoon a little over and into the leaves while they are still warm. Arrange on a serving platter, stalks in the air, spoon over a little more vinaigrette and provide each diner with a large plate, a separate bowl of vinaigrette and either a fingerbowl, an extra napkin or, best of all, a hot, damp cloth, as offered in Chinese restaurants.

fried artichoke hearts

Dip boiled artichoke hearts in beaten egg and then fine breadcrumbs mixed with one-third freshly grated parmesan cheese and fry in olive oil until crisp and golden. I have successfully partnered these with quickly seared scallops.

TO FRY

If the artichokes are being boiled before being fried, boiling them in a *blanc* helps to keep the colour. (I also refrigerate the cooked artichokes in this liquid for up to 3 days before frying them.) Prepare the artichokes as for boiling but add a handful of plain flour to 4 litres water and whisk it smooth. The water will become slightly viscous – this is the *blanc*. Drop in the artichokes and boil as above. When three-quarters cooked, allow the artichokes to cool in the liquid off the heat. Refrigerate the artichokes and their liquid in a non-reactive container. Drain well before use. Fry the artichokes in butter (or butter and oil) as they are, or dip in egg and then breadcrumbs or polenta (add parmesan cheese to the breadcrumbs, if desired) before frying until golden.

stewed artichoke

Stew quartered prepared artichokes in a wide frying pan with cracked peppercorns and equal quantities of water and olive oil until tender and water has evaporated. Squeeze over lemon juice and scatter with fresh herbs.

TO STUFF OR BRAISE

Cut through the leaves about halfway from the bottom of the artichoke. Snap off the outside leaves until you reach the pale-yellow leaves and rub well with lemon. Using a melon baller, hollow out the artichoke, discarding any purple-tinged leaves and the choke. Divide the stuffing between the leaves and the hollowed-out centre. Cook with the minimum delay. Stuffed artichoke dishes are delicious served warm rather than hot, so don't be concerned about starting this process early.

FOR A SALAD

When preparing baby artichokes for a salad, speed is the thing. Trim off any dark outside leaves and cut away the top third of each artichoke. Cut the artichokes in half from top to bottom and rub with lemon. Drop into a bowl of acidulated water 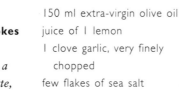. Remove and dry well before use. Cut each trimmed artichoke into sixths, quarters or thin slices and quickly toss with the very best olive oil to prevent oxidisation. Combine with salad ingredients and serve at once.

THE HEART | If you are only planning to use the hearts (or 'bottoms'), snap off all the leaves and discard the choke. Rub the hearts with lemon and drop into acidulated water 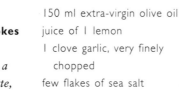. Sauté in olive oil or boil and then sauté quickly, or fill and bake.

recipes

artichokes with tomato vinaigrette

SERVES 2–4

boiled artichokes
Serve boiled artichokes with a simple vinaigrette, Hollandaise Sauce ✎, Béarnaise Sauce ✎ or a bowl of melted butter thick with chopped parsley and thyme.

150 ml extra-virgin olive oil
juice of 1 lemon
1 clove garlic, very finely
  chopped
few flakes of sea salt
freshly ground black pepper
2 ripe tomatoes, peeled,
  seeded and finely chopped
1 tablespoon freshly chopped
  parsley
4 artichokes, freshly boiled

Mix all ingredients, except artichokes, and check seasoning. Spoon vinaigrette over and into warm artichokes and serve.

gratin of artichokes

SERVES 3–6

artichoke salad
Toss raw, sliced small artichoke with inner sticks of celery, witlof, watercress, shaved parmesan, sliced radish, wine vinegar and olive oil and grind over black pepper.

4 cloves garlic
2 large onions, finely sliced
  into rings
olive oil
1 bay leaf
1 sprig thyme
6 artichokes
1 cup fresh breadcrumbs
3 anchovies
3 tablespoons freshly chopped
  parsley
freshly ground black pepper

Preheat oven to 180°C. Finely slice 3 of the garlic cloves and mix with onion. Pour a generous film of oil into a shallow gratin dish that will hold artichokes and onion in 1 layer and pile in garlic and onion. Add bay leaf and thyme, cover with foil and bake for 30 minutes. Meanwhile, prepare artichokes for stuffing, then stand in acidulated water ✎ until required. Blend breadcrumbs, 2 tablespoons olive oil, remaining garlic clove and anchovies in a food processor, then stir in parsley. Drain artichokes, pat dry and fill with two-thirds of the crumb mixture. Remove gratin dish from oven. Invert artichokes into dish, grind on pepper and scatter remaining crumbs over entire surface. Drizzle with more oil. Return to oven, uncovered, and bake for 1 hour until artichokes test tender and crumbs are golden. >

vegetables Fresh Tomato Sauce (*see* TOMATOES) or a spoonful of wine vinegar and a handful of seeded raisins can also be added to the onion. The onion can also be enriched with or replaced by any other vegetable dish, Ratatouille (*see* ZUCCHINI AND SQUASH), for example.

artichokes and peas with sage   SERVES 2–4

This delicious first course or accompaniment is based on a recipe from Deborah Madison's The Savory Way.

2 large artichokes
juice of 1 lemon
3 tablespoons extra-virgin
 olive oil
6–8 fresh sage leaves
1 onion, sliced
¾ cup water
1 cup freshly shelled peas
salt
freshly ground black pepper
20 g unsalted butter
freshly chopped parsley

Trim each artichoke back to its heart, then quarter it and rub with lemon juice. Warm oil with sage in an enamelled cast-iron saucepan. Add onion and artichoke and stir to coat. Add water and cook over moderate heat – dribbling in a little more water as it evaporates – for 20 minutes, after which artichoke should be nearly tender. Add a little more water, then drop in peas and cook until done, about 5 minutes. There should be only syrupy liquid left. Season, add butter and parsley and shake to mix.

artichoke stew   SERVES 6

½ cup olive oil
6 artichokes, trimmed
6 small new potatoes, washed
12 pickling onions, peeled
6 small carrots, peeled
2 cloves garlic, peeled
juice of 1 lemon
1 tablespoon plain flour
1 cup water *or* light Chicken
 Stock
salt
freshly ground black pepper
½ cup freshly chopped parsley

Warm oil in a shallow heatproof gratin dish large enough to take all vegetables. Add vegetables, garlic and lemon juice. Mix flour and water to a paste and pour over vegetables. The vegetables should be barely covered with water – if not, add a little more. Season well. Cover dish with greased baking paper and then a lid and simmer for 45 minutes, then check vegetables are tender. Increase heat and boil to thicken sauce, then check seasoning. Serve warm or hot, scattered with parsley.

artichoke heart salad
Toss sliced boiled artichoke hearts with cooked and peeled broad beans. To make a fancier salad, add cooked small prawns or yabby tails and dress with fruity olive oil and wine vinegar or Mousseline Sauce. (In Summer Cooking *Elizabeth David whisks a cupful of the beans' cooking water with 2 egg yolks and the juice of a lemon over a gentle heat until slightly thickened and then pours it over this salad.)*

other recipes

brains and artichoke hearts with browned butter *see* BRAINS
robert's beans *see* BEANS, DRIED

a s p a r a g u s   A member of the Liliaceae family, asparagus (*Asparagus officinalis*) is believed to have originated in the eastern Mediterranean and Asia Minor. It appeals to nearly all the senses – smell, taste, sight and feel – and has a distinctive earthy and leafy flavour. | Popular folklore suggests that eating asparagus can cure bee stings (or does one rub asparagus onto the painful part?), ease toothache and restore eyesight. Asparagus also has a reputation as being 'a real stinker' as far as wine enthusiasts are concerned. The sulphurous flavour provides a difficult challenge for the winemaster seeking a complementary marriage (a herbaceous fresh wine is its best companion). | In Australia green and white asparagus are available, with the green being the most popular variety for eating. White asparagus is predominantly used in the canning industry here, although in the last few seasons it has been possible to buy some very fine fresh white asparagus. The biggest production areas are on Queensland's south coast and Atherton Tableland, and in Victoria's lower Murray Valley.

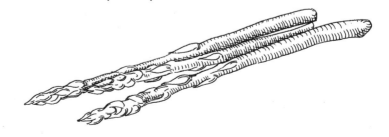

VARIETIES AND SEASON

Asparagus means spring just as surely as the first wisteria or cherry blossom. It is a temperate crop requiring a definite cold season for growing. It is available September–December, with some earlier and later pickings. Green and white asparagus are the same variety but the white is harvested while the spear is still below the ground; green asparagus is cut when the tips are 20 cm above the ground. It takes 5 years to develop a good asparagus and the spears are still cut by hand.

Be wary of imported asparagus and think how much moisture it has lost on its 20-hour minimum trip from wherever it was harvested. And ask yourself why you must have asparagus in the autumn or the winter.

SELECTION AND STORAGE

Asparagus is very perishable. Perfection is to eat it the same day it is picked. For most of us that means taking note of where the asparagus was grown. Select that which has travelled the shortest distance, and then look at it critically. The cut end should not look dried out, split or, worse still, wrinkled. The spears should be clean, smooth and bright green, the tips unblemished and dark green, with maybe a hint of purple. (Mould and mildew starts on the tips when asparagus has been stored too long.) The woody inedible portion should not be too long or there will be too much waste.

Both thin spears and thicker spears are delicious. It makes sense to select asparagus all much the same thickness for even cooking. Buy what you need for the next day or so, but not for the next week. Avoid bundles held together with rubber bands, which are frequently quite tight and damage or weaken the asparagus spears. Also, unscrupulous wholesalers or retailers can hide poor-quality or damaged spears in the centre of the bunch. Refrigerate asparagus in a vegetable storage bag in the crisper for up to 2 days.

PREPARATION AND COOKING

Wash the asparagus. Exert gentle pressure on the bottom of each spear until it breaks where it is tender. Discard the woody ends, unless you want to make a vegetable stock. For **green** asparagus, peel the last 3–4 cm, if desired, to make sure every bit is edible. (I usually do not, preferring to be a little more extravagant when I snap off the ends.) **White** asparagus needs peeling from tip to bottom, as the skin is thick and tough. In some French restaurants in Australia our delectable, tender green asparagus is peeled from stem to tip. In my opinion this is ignorant, pretentious and totally unnecessary.

Cooks differ about asparagus cooking. I believe it should be possible to bite through the cooked stem without meeting any resistance and there should be no crunch. The stem, however, should bend only slightly if you are holding it in your fingers. It should not droop!

asparagus
goes
with
olive oil
butter
raclette cheese
gruyère cheese
parmesan cheese
eggs
breadcrumbs
mustard
parsley
chives
tarragon
ham
bacon
potatoes
cream
mushrooms
smoked salmon
oranges
light soy sauce
walnuts

TO BOIL

Bundle asparagus into portions of equal size and tie with string. Bring a large saucepan of lightly salted water to a boil. Throw in the bundles and boil, uncovered, for 4–6 minutes. Fish out a bundle and test a spear at its thickest point with the tip of a sharp knife. The knife should just slip through and the asparagus should still be bright green, not grey. Remove the asparagus, drain quickly, discard string and rest spears on a clean, dry cloth for a minute. Do *not* refresh the asparagus under cold water unless you want it to taste of cold water! Proceed with the recipe. If serving asparagus as is, roll it while warm in a spoonful of extra-virgin olive oil, a teaspoon of walnut oil or some barely melted butter. Do not add vinegar or lemon juice to cooked asparagus as it will stain the perfect green colour and cause the skin to wrinkle.

recipes

asparagus with coddled eggs

SERVES 6

asparagus rolls
Make proper asparagus rolls – delicious! Trim crusts from good-quality wholemeal, multigrain or rye bread, then butter. Lie a cooked asparagus spear diagonally across the bread with its tip protruding, and roll up. For a change, mash hardboiled egg and parsley into the butter for spreading, or parsley and tarragon.

80 g butter, melted
6 large eggs (preferably newly laid free-range eggs)
salt
freshly ground black pepper
2 tablespoons freshly chopped parsley
1 tablespoon freshly chopped chervil
1 tablespoon freshly chopped chives
1 tablespoon freshly chopped tarragon
1 cup fine white breadcrumbs
24 asparagus spears of even size, freshly boiled
3 tablespoons cream

Brush inside of 6 porcelain egg coddlers with 1 tablespoon of the melted butter. Break an egg into each and lightly season. Mix herbs and divide between 6 small dishes (Chinese sauce dishes are an ideal size). Put remaining butter in a small saucepan with breadcrumbs. Over gentle heat, spoon crumbs over and over until they are a lovely, toasted biscuit colour. Tip them onto kitchen paper for a few minutes, then divide between another 6 small plates.

To coddle eggs, fill a saucepan large enough to take coddlers with water to a depth of 2–3 cm and bring to a simmer. Screw on lids and put coddlers in pan. The water should come two-thirds up sides of coddlers. Cook for 4 minutes.

Drain hot asparagus for a moment on a clean cloth and discard string. Roll asparagus in a buttered dish and divide between 6 serving plates. Remove coddlers from pan, carefully unscrew lids (they will be *hot*) and pour 2 teaspoons cream into each coddler. Arrange dishes of herbs and crumbs on each plate or on side plates. To enjoy this delicious dish, dip asparagus in egg, roll in herbs and crumbs – and bite!

asparagus soup

SERVES 6

500 g asparagus spears
60 g butter
I tablespoon fresh chervil *or*
  I large sprig thyme
I small onion, sliced
2 cloves garlic, sliced
2 potatoes, peeled and chopped
I litre water
salt
white pepper
whipped cream
extra chervil *or* thyme, finely
  chopped

Snap woody ends off asparagus and discard. Cut tips from half the spears and slice rest of asparagus very thinly. Cook asparagus tips until tender in lightly salted boiling water. Drain and leave aside.

Melt butter in a large saucepan and sweat chervil, onion, garlic and potato for 5 minutes. Add water, then cover and simmer for 15 minutes until vegetables are tender and potato is starting to break up. Remove lid and increase heat, so that liquid boils rapidly, then add sliced asparagus and boil for 5 minutes.

Purée contents of pan and pass soup through a strainer. Taste for seasoning and texture. If soup is at all 'hairy', strain it again. It should be quite smooth and a beautiful spring green. Serve topped with a dollop of whipped cream, the cooked tips warmed in butter or by dipping in boiling water for a few seconds, and finely chopped chervil.

asparagus custards

SERVES 6

As the asparagus is not cooked for very long, each spear must be trimmed thoroughly of its woody end – there should be no trace of stringiness and the total weight of the tender spears should not exceed 200 g.

200 g trimmed best-quality
  asparagus spears
400 ml cream
I teaspoon very finely
  chopped garlic
2 teaspoons finely chopped
  fresh chervil *or* tarragon
4 eggs, lightly whisked
salt
white pepper

Preheat oven to 160°C. Butter 6 × 100 ml soufflé dishes. Slice asparagus spears very thinly. Drop spears into lightly salted boiling water for 2 minutes, then drain well.

Simmer cream with garlic until reduced to 300 ml. Purée asparagus, hot garlic cream and herbs in a food processor until smooth. Pour purée onto eggs and mix, then pass through a coarse strainer. Taste for seasoning. Pour mixture into prepared soufflé dishes, then stand them in a baking dish lined with a tea towel and pour in water to come two-thirds up their sides. Bake for 25–30 minutes until just set. Allow to stand for 5 minutes before unmoulding to serve. Nap with Beurre Blanc ✓ and garnish with extra asparagus tips or scatter around herbs or tiny spring peas.

asparagus platter
Serve a platter of boiled asparagus with a dipping sauce of extra-virgin oil, Hollandaise Sauce ✓, barely melted butter, a lightly poached egg and freshly cut herbs, or lemony mayonnaise. Don't forget the sea salt, pepper mill, lemons and wine vinegar.

bbq asparagus
Grill raw or lightly boiled asparagus on the barbecue until well marked and crisp–tender. Dip asparagus into light soy sauce mixed with melted butter or a few drops of sesame oil.

a v o c a d o s The avocado or avocado pear (*Persea americana*) is native to Mexico and Central America and was introduced to the West Indies in the early sixteenth century. When visiting the West Indies many years ago I was intrigued to see avocado served at most meals. A very large fruit would be brought to the table and everyone would carve themselves a 'peg' of pear, as it was known. One peeled one's piece and the fruit was left until the next meal. (I don't recall it turning brown, nor do I remember seeing lemon juice squeezed on the unused portion, but maybe it was done without my noticing.) The avocado now flourishes in Australia and has been popular here since the 1960s. The pear-shaped fruit range in length from 5–30 cm, and the tree can grow to over 18 m. Avocados mature on the tree but ripen 1–2 weeks after harvest. Maturity is assessed for commercial crops by testing the fat content of the fruit. The avocado is the only fruit that contains fat, with mono-unsaturated fat comprising up to 25 per cent of the fruit when mature. The Australian commercial avocado crop is concentrated in southern Queensland's coastal districts, the Atherton Tableland in North Queensland and northern New South Wales.

VARIETIES AND SEASON

I can remember when avocados had a short season during the autumn and winter only and were considered very exotic. They were also very expensive. Now they are available all year round, with May–November the peak season, and are reasonably priced. There are more than 700 varieties of avocado worldwide, and 70 are known to be grown in Australia, of which the fuerte, hass and sharwill are the main varieties. Other commercial varieties are the hazzard, zutano, rincon, edranol, nabal and reed. Some authorities give the maturity dates for these latter varieties as up to 2 months later than the main varieties, so there is clearly considerable difference between growing areas.

The pear-shaped *fuerte* avocado is rich in flavour with a buttery texture. It is easy to peel, and has a smooth dull-green skin. It matures March–June. The *hass* can be pear-shaped or roundish and has a pebbly skin and a small seed. It is the only variety that changes colour with maturity, from dark green to a purplish black. The yellow, creamy flesh has a nutty, buttery flavour. This avocado matures July–November. Slightly rounder than the fuerte, the *sharwill* has knobbly green skin and is rich and creamy. It matures May–July.

In Far North Queensland at the Sunday market in Port Douglas I have bought *reed* avocados in July and September that were memorable for their glorious meaty texture and buttery flavour and their enormous size. They were as large and almost as round as a small beach ball. The attractive *salad* or *cocktail* avocados are not another variety but unfertilised fruit. They are small and seedless with excellent flavour.

SELECTION AND STORAGE

Buy avocados for use on the day or up to 2 weeks ahead. Most greengrocers will have fruit ready for dinner tonight as well as for a few days hence. Ask, and if you do not receive fruit in the condition you want it, go back and protest. Skin colour does not indicate ripeness, although a green hass avocado will certainly not be ripe! Ripeness can only be judged by cradling the fruit, which should feel supple. A ripe hass avocado will have some give at the stem end and the skin will be purple–black.

Avocados should be ripened in an airy spot, not in the refrigerator. Very hard fruit can take 4–5 days to ripen. To hasten ripening, place avocados in a brown paper bag with a ripe banana or apple (these give off ethylene gas, which aids ripening). Once ripe, eat them without delay. A ripe avocado can be stored in the vegetable crisper for a few days but will start to deteriorate almost straightaway.

avocados go with
chillies
lemons
coriander leaves
parsley
limes
oranges
bacon
chicken
salt
pepper
salted codfish
spring onions
crab
prawns
cos lettuce
grapefruit
mint
tomatoes
tuna
cumin
fetta cheese

avocado spread
Squash avocado onto wholemeal bread and top with tuna or sliced chicken breast, salt and pepper for a wonderful sandwich.

PREPARATION

Cut the avocado lengthwise into halves and twist to separate. Insert a sharp knife into the seed, twist and lift out the seed. (Avocados will discolour once cut, but this can be delayed by brushing the exposed flesh with lemon juice.) Turn the fruit upside down on the cutting board to remove the skin, if required. Strip the skin from the fruit starting from the narrow end. Alternatively, hold the avocado half in the palm of your hand and slip a large tablespoon between the fruit and the skin and ease the flesh away. Once peeled, avocado flesh can be cubed, balled, sliced, cut into wedges or mashed. If it is to be added to a hot dish, do so right at the end as cooked avocado flesh can taste bitter and rather unpleasant.

recipes

avocado mousse   SERVES 4

avocado salad
Toss cubed avocado, fetta cheese, tomato and spring onion in a bowl with a thick, herby vinaigrette or olive oil and wine vinegar and serve in cos lettuce leaves as a first course.

2 gelatine leaves
2 perfectly ripe avocados
juice of 1 lemon
red-wine vinegar
salt
Tabasco
1 tablespoon finely chopped
    fresh parsley
1 tablespoon finely chopped
    watercress

Soften gelatine leaves in cold water for 5 minutes. Halve avocados, reserving skins, and scoop flesh into a food-processor bowl. Brush skins liberally with lemon juice and set aside. Purée avocado and add vinegar (up to 1 teaspoon), salt and Tabasco to taste. Bring 1 tablespoon water to a simmer in a small saucepan, then squeeze gelatine leaves and drop into pan. They should dissolve instantly, but stir to make sure.

With food-processor motor running, add gelatine solution to avocado. Scoop mixture into a bowl and fold in herbs. Spoon mousse into avocado skins, then smooth and leave to set for a few hours. The texture will be deliciously creamy and the colour bright green. **to turn out** This mousse can be set in small ceramic pots brushed with walnut oil, then turned out. Surround with peeled prawns or crab for an elegant first course. **dip** Serve mousse with celery and cucumber sticks as a soft dip. **sandwiches** If kept covered and refrigerated, this mousse makes a great sandwich spread in place of butter.

avocado and citrus
Combine orange and grapefruit segments with chunks of avocado, chopped coriander leaves and freshly cooked prawns or crab meat and dress with citrus juice and olive oil for an excellent first course or simple lunch.

guacamole   SERVES 4

Everybody has their own version of guacamole. Mine is pared down to the essentials, just as I was served it at Rosa Mexicana, a fine restaurant in New York, where it came with freshly made tortilla (toasted triangles of pita bread will do!). Guacamole can also be a fancy garnish for a crab salad or a filling for a hollowed-out baked potato to accompany grilled chicken. I don't add tomato, but many cooks do.

2 perfectly ripe avocados,
    peeled and chopped

juice of 2 limes *or* 1 lemon

2 tablespoons freshly chopped
    coriander leaves

½ teaspoon finely chopped
    fresh chilli

salt

3 spring onions, finely
    chopped

Toss avocado in lime juice. Add coriander, chilli, salt and spring onion. Serve as soon as possible – immediately is best.

saltfish and avocado

SERVES 4–6

Saltfish and ackee is the national dish of Jamaica, or it certainly was when I was there in the mid-1960s. The ackee is a curious tree, and the flavour of its edible parts is reminiscent of the buttery character of avocado. This delicious substitute dish is great for brunch – but apologies should go to Monty and all lovers of saltfish and ackee.

500 g salted codfish

2 tablespoons olive oil

1 large onion, finely chopped

125 g smoked streaky bacon,
    diced

1 red pepper, diced

1 small fresh chilli, seeded and
    finely sliced

2 avocados, peeled and diced

Soak codfish overnight in a large bucket of cold water. Drain codfish. Place in an enamelled or stainless steel saucepan, cover with cold water and bring very slowly to simmering point. Remove from heat and allow fish to rest for 10 minutes in cooking water. Drain, then flake fish, discarding skin and bone. Cover and keep warm.

Heat oil and sauté onion until quite soft and starting to colour. Add bacon and red pepper and sauté, stirring, until pepper is soft and bacon has started to crisp. Stir in fish and chilli. When thoroughly hot, tip in avocado. Stir to mix and serve for brunch on a wide platter with hot toast.

chicken breasts with almond sauce and guacamole

SERVES 6

Guacamole is the perfect garnish for this unusual dish of poached chicken breasts with a sauce of pounded almonds and green leaves. The sauce can be made in advance and refrigerated until needed.

avocado dressing
Whizz lots of herbs into a vinaigrette in the food processor and add chopped spring onion. Spoon this thick green dressing into the hollow of half an avocado or, for a change, present the avocado upside down with the green sauce sliding over its curved back.

avocado pita
Fill pita bread with cubed avocado, fetta cheese, tomato and spring onion and season with lots of pepper.

avocado and cumin
Flavour mashed avocado with roasted cumin seeds and spoon onto soft Indian-style bread.

6 medium Pontiac potatoes

1 litre Chicken Stock

6 chicken breast fillets, skin
  removed

2 tablespoons butter

1 cup Guacamole (see p. 66)

2 tablespoons flaked almonds,
  toasted

few sprigs of coriander

SAUCE

1 onion, finely diced

6 large cos *or* iceberg lettuce
  leaves, shredded

1 cup roughly chopped fresh
  coriander leaves

1 cup roughly chopped flat-
  leaf parsley

2 cloves garlic, finely chopped

1–2 fresh hot chillies, seeded
  and finely chopped

1 cup finely ground blanched
  almonds

½ cup Chicken Stock

salt

Preheat oven to 200°C. Bake potatoes in their jackets for 1 hour until cooked. Remove from oven and set aside to cool. Reset oven to 180°C.

To make the sauce, place onion, lettuce, coriander leaves, parsley, garlic and chilli in a food processor and process to a reasonably smooth purée. Mix in almonds and ½ cup chicken stock, then taste for salt. Tip into a heavy-based frying pan and cook gently for 5 minutes, stirring all the time to prevent the mixture sticking. Set aside.

In a wide saucepan, bring 1 litre chicken stock to a bare simmer, slip in breast fillets and cover. Turn after 3 minutes. After a further 3 minutes the breasts should be cooked (they will feel slightly springy when pressed with your fingertip). Remove to a plate with a slotted spoon, cover and keep warm. Reserve 1½ cups poaching liquid.

Cut off tops of potatoes and carefully scoop out flesh. Reserve shells. Roughly mash potato flesh with butter and return to empty shells.

Bring reserved poaching liquid to a boil. Stir in green sauce until well blended and thoroughly hot. Return potatoes to oven for 5 minutes to warm through. Remove from oven and top with a generous portion of guacamole. To serve, place a filled potato in the centre of each warmed plate. Slice chicken breasts, arrange on plates and spoon over hot sauce. Scatter with toasted almonds and coriander sprigs.

b *a c o n*

'Better beans and bacon in peace, than cakes and ale in fear.' Country mouse to town mouse, *Aesop's Fables*, 550 BC.

For centuries bacon has been a staple food for the worker. Pigs were trouble-free to raise as they roamed at leisure and ate whatever they found. Bacon was made from the inexpensive part of the pig (the belly), it was produced in the household, it kept well and it was highly flavoured, so a little went a long way, and, of course, it was delicious. | Almost two-thirds of Australia's pig meat is processed as ham, bacon or other speciality smallgoods. Bacon is the cured (that is, salted) smoked or unsmoked meat from the sides and belly of a 'baconer' pig. A baconer tends to be larger and fatter than a 'porker', 'superporker' or 'finisher', a pig destined for the fresh-meat industry. Baconers are sold at 24 weeks and weigh 70–100 kg. Most pigs for fresh meat are sold at around 60 kg. | Traditionally bacon is cured by being rubbed with dry salt. The meat is turned in this salt for up to 2 weeks and is then either air-dried, cold-smoked or hot-smoked. Air-dried or cold-smoked bacon is raw meat, in the same way as prosciutto crudo is 'raw' ham compared with the slice of ham you might buy for a sandwich. Hot-smoked bacon is thoroughly cooked. >

Here and there specialist butchers and smallgoods manufacturers continue to produce raw or 'green' bacon. They are likely to be German, Austrian or Italian. The product may be called raw kaiserfleisch, green bacon or pancetta. However, most bacon these days is injected with brine and then hot-smoked using atomised 'smoke' dissolved in water. The entire process takes a matter of days. This mechanised 'smoking' can produce well-textured and flavoursome bacon when it is carefully done. When carelessly done, the meat absorbs too much liquid and watery, tough bacon that oozes moisture in the pan is the result.

Bacon is still a product much loved by most people and a major supermarket item. However, it is perceived as costly, so the mass manufacturers are intent on reducing this perception. Modern technology allows manufacturers to increase the weight of their product using water, phosphates and other components by up to 70 per cent. In Australia, bacon that has a higher moisture content can be sold legally for less than bacon that is pure meat.

I dislike the usual packaged sliced bacon. It is wet and flabby and the slices are too thin to use for the initial aromatic seasoning for a beef, chicken or rabbit casserole. It is more versatile, and cheaper, to buy a chunk of smoked or unsmoked streaky bacon that can be cut as needed, either into slices for an occasional fry-up or into lardons for Beef Bourguignon (*see* BEEF). Streaky bacon in the piece is readily available from delicatessens, some butchers, and all our fresh food markets.

VARIETIES AND SEASON

Bacon is available all year and comes in various guises. ***Middle rashers*** have a round 'eye' of lean meat. ***Streaky bacon*** is the tail end of the loin (it does not contain the eye) and is often known as belly bacon or kaiserfleisch. ***Breakfast rashers*** or picnic rashers are made from the trimmings of older pigs and shaped to resemble bacon. ***Gammon*** is popular and widely available in the United Kingdom but not here. Gammon is a joint of pork that has been cured as for bacon and that may or may not have been cold-smoked and which is ready for boiling or frying (*see* HAM).

SELECTION AND STORAGE

Lean bacon should be a clear pinky-red and the fat should be white. The lean should not have a brownish tinge, nor should the fat be at all yellow. My favourite is smoked streaky or belly bacon. Buy a large piece and refrigerate it for up to 2 weeks. It will keep quite well unwrapped, or you can wrap the cut end in foil. White crystals that appear on the surface are only salt – just wipe them off. (Streaky bacon bought in the piece will take a long time to deteriorate, although it may become quite hard after a month in storage.) Or you can ask for your bacon to be sliced, but twice the thickness of the packaged variety. Any good delicatessen will do this for you. Wrap the parcel in plastic film and then in foil; the bacon will keep for 5 days or so in the refrigerator. Do not use any sliced bacon that has become at all slimy as this indicates bacteria are at work on the exposed surfaces.

If buying vacuum-packed bacon, ensure that the vacuum-pack is absolutely tight around the slices. If it is at all loose there will be air inside and the bacon will have started to deteriorate. Beware of bubbles in vacuum-packed meat as these indicate the product might be off. Once you have opened packaged bacon discard the packaging and wrap the bacon in grease-proof paper or plastic film and then in foil.

If you wish to freeze a quantity of sliced bacon, wrap it in a double layer of foil. It will still dry out a little. Streaky bacon freezes much better than middle rashers, the eye of which becomes very brittle.

PREPARATION AND COOKING

Cut the rind off a piece of streaky bacon only as you need to. The rind is very flavoursome and can be dropped into a casserole or into a soup pot. Discard it before serving.

TO FRY OR GRILL

Fry Bacon fat is very soft and melts easily, so it can easily stick to the frying pan. To avoid this when frying, either heat a film of oil in the pan before putting in the rashers or add 5 mm water with the bacon. The water will have evaporated by the time the bacon's own fat has started to run.   **Grill** Place the rashers on a sheet of foil under a hot griller. Bacon rashers can also be barbecued or cooked on a chargrill pan.

LARDONS

Some recipes require lardons; these are small cubes or rectangles of belly pork (*see* PORK). In France home cooks would use fresh (that is, unsalted) belly pork. If you are using cubes cut from a piece of bacon, cover them with cold water, bring to a boil and discard the water before proceeding with the recipe.

TO LARD OR BARD

French recipes often instruct one to *lard* a piece of meat with long strips of pork fat (a larding needle is sometimes used). Similarly, you might be instructed to *bard* something, which means you put a layer of pork fat over a piece of meat without fat of its own. In both cases, bacon fat can be used, but be aware that as it will almost certainly be smoked it will add quite a distinctive flavour to the food.

recipes

warm bean salad with a bacon garnish   SERVES 4

This garnish is also great with broad beans or broccoli.

250 g green beans
1 tablespoon olive oil
3 rashers thickly sliced streaky
  bacon
1 onion, finely diced
1 clove garlic, finely sliced
2 tablespoons freshly chopped
  parsley
freshly ground black pepper

Cook beans, drain and keep warm. Warm oil in a frying pan and fry bacon over a moderate heat until crisp. Remove bacon to a plate. Sauté onion in oil and bacon fat until soft and starting to colour. Add garlic and sauté for 1 minute more. Crumble or cut bacon into small pieces. Return to pan, add parsley and pepper and tip the lot over the warm beans.

bacon muffins   MAKES 12

2 rashers streaky bacon, rind
  removed
1 tablespoon olive oil
1 egg
1 cup milk
250 g self-raising flour
pinch of salt

Grease 12 muffin tins well and preheat oven to 180°C. Gently sauté bacon in oil until crisp, then remove to a plate, reserving 3 tablespoons oil and bacon fat. Whisk egg with milk and reserved bacon fat. Sift flour and salt, then mix in crumbled bacon and make a well. Quickly work in liquid. The mixture will not look smooth because of the bacon. Spoon into prepared tins, filling each two-thirds full. Bake for 20 minutes until well puffed and golden brown. Serve warm.

egg and bacon pie   SERVES 6

1 quantity Shortcrust Pastry
6 rashers thickly sliced smoked
  streaky bacon, rind removed
2 tablespoons freshly chopped
  parsley
1 teaspoon freshly chopped
  chives
11 eggs
salt
freshly ground black pepper

Preheat oven to 180°C. Line a loose-bottomed 22 cm flan tin with just over half the pastry and chill for 30 minutes. Roll out rest of pastry to make a lid and set aside.

Lightly fry bacon and cut into pieces. Scatter two-thirds of the bacon over base of pastry case. Scatter with half the herbs. Break 10 of the eggs, one at a time, into a cup and slip each into pastry case, being careful not to break yolks. Season and add rest of herbs. Carefully add remaining bacon, then cover with pastry lid. Let pastry settle over the hump of each egg, then trim it and seal edges carefully. Whisk remaining egg and a

potatoes and bacon
Boil new potatoes and toss with chives and crisply fried and crumbled bacon.

bacon and beans
Save any chunky scraps or the ends from a piece of streaky bacon to cook with beans or potatoes or to add to a stew.

bacon and tomatoes
Serve grilled tomatoes on toast with crisp bacon rashers.

bacon flavouring
Add minced bacon to stuffings or meatloaves.

pinch of salt together and brush over pastry. Bake for 35 minutes until a rich gold. Allow to cool before removing from tin. Serve warm or cold.

quiche lorraine   SERVES 6

A quiche lorraine is basically a custard, so it must not cook too quickly or it will curdle and result in a tough filling that has large holes in it. The nicest quiches are those at least 4 cm deep. Choose your tin accordingly.

1 quantity Shortcrust Pastry
4 rashers thickly sliced streaky
   bacon, rind removed
4 egg yolks
2 eggs
1½ cups cream
freshly grated nutmeg
salt
freshly ground black pepper

Line a 20 cm loose-bottomed flan tin with pastry and bake blind on a baking tray at 200°C for 20 minutes. Remove pastry case from oven and reset oven to 180°C.

Fry bacon gently until crisp, turning it once. Cut bacon into small pieces and scatter over pastry case. Whisk together egg yolks, eggs, cream and seasonings. Taste and adjust seasoning, if necessary. Pour egg mixture over bacon and cook for 20–35 minutes until firm and golden. Cool quiche to lukewarm before eating.
cheese Add a handful of diced best-quality gruyère cheese to the mixture. **potato and onion** Before baking, add a scattering of thickly sliced, boiled new potatoes with or without 2–3 tablespoons sautéed chopped onion.

bacon omelette
Add crisp, crumbled bacon and parsley to an omelette.

bacon sandwich
Make a sandwich of crisp bacon rashers and wholemeal bread.

other recipes

bacon and mustard dressing for 'bitey' greens *see* SALAD GREENS
chestnut and bacon salad *see* CHESTNUTS
english lamb's liver and bacon *see* LIVER
pea and ham soup *see* PEAS
potato salad with bacon and sour cream *see* POTATOES
pumpkin and bacon soup *see* PUMPKINS
salad of softboiled egg with bacon *see* EGGS
veal chops in red wine with bacon and mushrooms *see* VEAL
warm spinach salad *see* SPINACH

b a n a n a s A native of South-East Asia, the banana (*Musa* species) is not a palm or a tree at all. Its 'trunk' is made up of tightly furled leaves produced by an underground rhizome or corm that only open out at the top of the plant. Once fully grown the plant produces a single flower-stem that bends under its own weight as bananas develop from the female flowers. Male flowers hang down to form the 'bell', which is eaten in some countries. (It is bitter and requires lengthy soaking before becoming palatable.) | Each banana is known as a finger, a number of fingers (around 15) form a hand and several hands (around 8) become the bunch, weighing about 20 kg. It takes 9 months to produce fruit after planting in the tropics, and double that in subtropical climates. After harvesting the plant is cut to the ground and a new plant grows from suckers produced by the rhizome. | We tend to be fairly conservative in our use of bananas. When I visited the West Indies in the 1960s I discovered it was commonplace to eat bananas as part of the savoury course. Boiled green bananas were always served with fish and goat curries, and sliced fried plantains were often on the breakfast table or served alongside meat and fish. And everywhere bananas are grown, locals wrap food in the leaves to cook on the grill or on hot coals.

VARIETIES AND SEASON

There are hundreds of banana varieties, but in Australia we only know the cavendish, lady finger and, to a far smaller extent, plantain, available only in tropical banana-growing areas and occasionally in the fresh-produce section of Asian food stores. *Cavendish* varieties, small or large, are the bananas we eat every day. The *lady finger* has a sweet lemony flavour that is most distinctive. The *plantain* is intended for cooking and is too astringent to enjoy fresh. Bananas are available all year round, with heaviest supplies in summer and autumn. They are grown along the northern New South Wales and Queensland coast and the central coast of Western Australia.

SELECTION AND STORAGE

Bananas mature off the plant, so there is no harm in choosing green fruit. As bananas ripen starch is converted to sugars, the fruit softens and the colour changes from yellow–green to yellow, to gold with brown splashes and eventually to almost brown. When stored in cool conditions the ripening of mature fruit is suspended. To ripen, the temperature is raised and the fruit is exposed to ethylene gas. (At home you can do this by putting unripe bananas into a brown paper bag with a ripe banana or an apple.)

Fruit should be free of bruising and should not be split. To eat immediately, select fruit with a few brown splashes. To eat in a few days' time, select bananas with bright-yellow skins and green tips. To make ice-cream or banana cake, select fruit that is heavily marked with brown or use fruit that has become too ripe for eating fresh. Ripe fruit can be refrigerated but the extreme cold will cause the skin to blacken. This does not harm the flavour but does look strange. The effect of the low temperature can be reduced by wrapping the fruit in several layers of newspaper.

If you live in the tropics and can harvest your own bananas, it is recommended to cut the entire bunch once the bananas have lost their angular look. The bunch should then be hung in a cool place to continue ripening. (Alternatively, pick 1–2 hands from the top of the bunch at the first sign of colour change and ripen those first.) If you allow the bananas to ripen fully on the bunch it is certain they will be attacked by both fruit bats and green ants, leaving one with the urgent problem of what to do with more than a hundred ripe bananas.

PREPARATION

Peel and eat! Or peel and bake or fry, either whole, sliced or mashed. Use a stainless steel knife when cutting bananas to avoid discoloration, and toss the banana in lemon juice to prevent it darkening. For recipes requiring a good quantity of banana purée, a food processor is ideal, although a ripe banana can be squashed very simply in a bowl, as every parent knows.

bananas
go
with
cream
sugar
brown sugar
maple syrup
bacon
breakfast cereals
raisins
rum
kirsch
lemons
coconut
fish
nutmeg
cinnamon
honey
nuts
vanilla
yoghurt
fruit salad
chillies
pork
onions
cumin
curry spices
chicken

Plantain are peeled, sliced and fried to serve as a vegetable. At the High Falls banana farm in Miallo, Far North Queensland, fried plantain and bacon is one of the special luncheon dishes.

recipes

baked bananas with meatloaf

SERVES 4

I love baked bananas – my children think they are awful. When I was a child my mother fed a household of 7 on a very slender budget. One of the favourite family dinners was a simple meatloaf with baked bananas, potatoes baked in their jackets and copious amounts of gravy.

This recipe is a perfect example of the nostalgia associated with childhood pleasures. In writing this down I cannot believe how I suddenly want to cook this dish tonight, and yet I haven't thought about it for years.

The quantities can easily be doubled, in which case the meatloaf should be made longer rather than fatter or the cooking time will need to be increased.

banana smoothie
Make a banana smoothie by whizzing 1 banana, 1 cup cold milk, 1 teaspoon honey and a grating of nutmeg in the blender.

500 g minced beef topside
½ cup fresh white
   breadcrumbs
I egg
I small onion, very finely
   chopped
I clove garlic, finely chopped
salt
freshly ground black pepper
olive oil
4 large potatoes, washed and
   cut in half
4 rashers smoked streaky
   bacon, rind removed
4 bananas, peeled

GRAVY
I tablespoon plain flour
I tablespoon tomato paste
½ cup dry white wine
1½ cups vegetable cooking
   water *or* stock
salt
freshly ground black pepper
2 tablespoons freshly chopped
   parsley

Preheat oven to 200°C. Make meatloaf by mixing all ingredients other than oil, potato, bacon and bananas. Form into a fat sausage shape and roll in oil.

Place potatoes directly on oven rack. Put meatloaf in a baking dish just big enough to hold it with room for bananas. Bake for 45 minutes. Remove from oven, then drape bacon over loaf and place bananas around it. Return to oven for 30 minutes.

Transfer meatloaf, bacon and bananas to a warm serving plate and tip any excess fat from baking dish, being careful to retain juices. To make the gravy, place baking dish over moderate heat and scatter in flour. Stir, scrape and cook flour for 2 minutes. Add tomato paste and wine. Stir again, then add vegetable cooking water gradually, stirring until you have a smooth gravy. Bring to a boil. If gravy is too thick, add more water. Check seasoning. Strain into a serving jug and stir in parsley. Slice the hot meatloaf and serve with a banana, a potato and a slice of bacon alongside and pass the gravy.

simple banana cake

125 g softened unsalted butter

1½ cups sugar

2 eggs

1 cup mashed ripe banana

few drops of pure vanilla

250 g plain flour

1 teaspoon bicarbonate of soda

½ teaspoon salt

½ teaspoon ground cinnamon

⅛ teaspoon ground allspice

½ cup buttermilk or ½ cup
    milk and 1 teaspoon lemon
    juice

Butter and flour a 20 cm square cake tin, then line base with baking paper. Preheat oven to 180°C.

Cream butter and sugar until pale and fluffy. Beat in eggs, banana and vanilla. Sift dry ingredients and add to mixture, alternating with buttermilk. Spoon into tin and bake for 45 minutes or until cake tests clean. Cool cake in its tin on a wire rack for a few minutes before turning out. Cool completely before cutting or storing in an airtight tin.

walnut and brown sugar topping
Combine 3 tablespoons coarsely chopped walnuts, 3 tablespoons self-raising flour, 1½ teaspoons ground cinnamon, 100 g softened butter and 3 tablespoons brown sugar. Scatter over the uncooked banana cake and bake as above.

baked flaming bananas with butterscotch sauce

SERVES 4

This sauce is so good that I have given quantities for twice as much as you need. The leftovers can be refrigerated in a covered container for up to a week. The sauce becomes very thick when cold, so warm it in a microwave oven or over a low heat for a moment or two before serving.

4 bananas, skins on

4 tablespoons dark rum

BUTTERSCOTCH SAUCE

¾ cup sugar

¼ cup boiling water

50 g unsalted butter

¾ cup brown sugar

few drops of pure vanilla

100 ml thick cream

To make the sauce, dissolve sugar in a saucepan over gentle heat until a deep gold. Carefully pour on boiling water and stir until smooth. Remove from heat and stir in butter and brown sugar. Return to heat and stir until mixture is smooth and brown sugar has dissolved. Stir in vanilla and cream. Set aside.

Bake bananas in their skins on a hot barbecue. Turn after 10 minutes; after a further 10 minutes the skins should be black and the bananas soft and very hot. Transfer to a serving dish, carefully slit skins and peel back one side. Warm rum in a saucepan, light with a match and pour flaming rum over exposed banana. Serve with warm butterscotch sauce.

chocolate bananas
Slit the skin of a banana, cutting into the flesh, and push in pieces of dark chocolate. Wrap the banana in a double layer of foil and bake in hot coals.

banana passion
Spoon passionfruit over sliced banana and serve with thick cream or coconut cream.

banana icy-pole
Peel a banana and insert an icy-pole stick in one end and freeze. An instant treat for the young.

banana ice-cream

SERVES 6

*I use this ice-cream in a favourite lunchtime dessert at Stephanie's – the banana split. I am not sure whether it is the delicious ice-cream, the luscious chocolate sauce or the passionfruit that makes it **so** good.*

350 g peeled, chopped ripe
  banana
juice of ½ lemon
100 ml light Sugar Syrup
white rum
300 ml cream

Blend banana and lemon juice in a food processor until smooth. Add sugar syrup and rum to taste, then add cream. Taste to check there is sufficient rum. Churn in an ice-cream machine according to the manufacturer's instructions – but do not overchurn. The ice-cream must stay creamy.

Serve as it is, with a tropical fruit salad or with Fast Chocolate Sauce (*see* CHOCOLATE).

other recipes

papaya and banana smoothie *see* TROPICAL FRUIT
sabee sabee kumala *see* SWEET POTATOES

see also TROPICAL FRUIT

b a s i l   The herb basil (*Ocimum* species) originated in India and was introduced to Europe in the sixteenth century. Basil is a tender annual much loved by snails, and young plants also need protection from frosts. Once basil is growing strongly, pinching out the flower-heads keeps the plant producing leaves. | Basil has an aniseed flavour. Its most famous partnership is with a ripe tomato and olive oil, although some might argue that pesto deserves that accolade. I have one Italian friend who tells me that he only ever eats his pesto the next season and that he makes, bottles and leaves his pesto topped with a film of olive oil to mature. On the other hand, in Rome and other Italian towns where I have shopped, brilliant green, just-made pesto is on sale in every *salumeria* each day throughout the summer months. | Basil is also a favourite flavouring in South-East Asian cookery, appearing in curries, soup and noodle dishes.

basil

goes

with

tomatoes

extra-virgin olive oil

fresh white cheese

lamb

eggplants

potatoes

pine nuts

parmesan cheese

walnuts

zucchini

sardines

prawns

rock lobsters

scallops

VARIETIES AND SEASON

There are more than 40 varieties of basil, with 3 commonly available in Australia: sweet, bush and red basil. Asian basil is another variety we should all know; it is available from Asian fresh food stores. I have also grown licorice basil and cinnamon basil. They have curiosity value but none of the power of the more usual varieties. Basil is available December–April.

The most common variety, *sweet* basil (*Ocimum basilicum*), has large, shiny green leaves and a strong, sweet aroma. (Sometimes a variety with huge, floppy leaves and a similar fragrance to sweet basil is sold as **elephant** basil.) Carrying smaller leaves and having a more compact form than sweet basil, **bush** basil (*O. minimum*) also has a milder flavour. It bears white flowers in autumn. *Red* or opal-leafed basil (*O. basilicum purpurascens*) has dark-purple, shiny medium-sized leaves. It bears lavender flowers in summer and autumn. *Asian* basil (*O. sanctum*), also known as Thai or holy basil, has small green leaves that are slightly hairy. The flavour is strongly aniseed with a hint of cloves.

SELECTION AND STORAGE

Dried basil is not a patch on the fresh herb, which is now readily available. Basil is usually sold as a bunch with its roots attached. Buy good-looking basil without blackened leaves (the leaves blacken when they are wet or damaged). It is best stored with the roots in a jug of cold water and a plastic bag pulled over the leaves, preferably in the refrigerator. If you buy basil as a cut bunch, do not wash it but refrigerate it in a plastic bag lined with kitchen paper. Either way it will last for a week.

PREPARATION

In most cases, the leaves should be stripped from the stems. Basil darkens when bruised and for this reason one is often counselled to tear the leaves into small pieces if making a quick pasta sauce or a dressing for sliced tomato rather than using a knife. The flavour does not change with either method.

recipes

basil butter

MAKES 1 CUP

A slice of this butter floated on a fresh tomato soup is delicious. A little can be added to any cooked tomato dish, too.

250 g butter
1 cup basil leaves, torn into
  small pieces
freshly ground black pepper

Blend all ingredients in a food processor until bright green. Scrape butter onto baking paper and form into a sausage shape. Roll up and wrap in foil, then freeze.

basil stuffing for lamb

This stuffing is suitable for a boned leg of lamb – ask your butcher to do the boning.

100 g streaky bacon, finely
   chopped
15 basil leaves, torn into pieces
3 cloves garlic, finely chopped
1 tablespoon freshly chopped
   parsley
2 tablespoons roasted pine nuts

Combine bacon, basil, garlic and parsley in a food processor or pound with a mortar and pestle, then mix in pine nuts. Press this paste into boned leg and skewer opening closed. Roast lamb immediately.

bocconcini, tomato and basil salad   SERVES 4

Bocconcini are small white cheeses sold in a tray of brine. Sometimes they are very tiny indeed and are called milk cherries. I prefer the next size up for this salad as the oil and pepper penetrate better if the cheeses are cut.

1 cup basil leaves, torn into
   small pieces
½ cup olive oil
freshly ground black pepper
12 bocconcini, cut into 3–4
   pieces
2 punnets yellow pear
   tomatoes, halved
½ cup black olives
2 teaspoons red-wine vinegar
   (optional)
salt
2 cups washed and dried baby
   spinach leaves

Place basil and two-thirds of the oil in a large bowl and add a generous grinding of pepper. Add tomato and olives. Put cheese and remaining oil in another bowl and add pepper. Allow ingredients in both bowls to macerate for at least 30 minutes. Taste and decide if you need vinegar to sharpen your salad. (This will depend on how acidic the tomato is.) Add salt to taste.

To serve, drain the cheese (the whey that oozes from the macerating cheese will spoil the dressing). Pile spinach leaves on a beautiful platter and tip the tomato, cheese and dressing on top. (If the leaves are mixed in the bowl they will become limp.)

variations Surround salad with garlic-rubbed toasted breadstick slices, maybe spread with sun-dried tomato paste, or add chunks of avocado to the salad with the olives and tomato.

pesto   SERVES 4–6

I enjoy the performance at a bistro I know in Rome where steaming spaghetti is brought to the table in a large bowl and the elderly maître d'hôtel adds the amount of pesto he deems suitable, lifts and tosses and then

basil sauce
Mix a large quantity of torn basil leaves with enough richly flavoured extra-virgin olive oil to make a thick sauce and toss through good-quality spaghetti or spoon over a grilled cutlet or thick fillet of fish or barbecued squid.

fried basil
Deep-fry basil leaves for a garnish.

expertly serves each diner with nary a strand of spaghetti out of place. Proper ceremony for a culinary classic!

I do not agree with bistro cooks who think that pesto goes well with all chargrilled meats, although I have used pesto with lamb, and I do like it with grilled eggplant. Pesto, which originated in Genoa, has a powerful flavour that works best when combined with a much larger mass of something delicate and starchy. It is sublime when stirred into hot spaghetti, allowed to melt among delicate dumplings of potato gnocchi or tossed with small bocconcini cheeses.

pesto sardines
Spread Pesto (see p. 81) in the belly cavities of sardines before grilling or frying.

basil on pizza
Scatter torn basil leaves over a pizza before baking.

basil bocconcini
Marinate halved tiny bocconcini in olive oil and pepper and spear on toothpicks with basil leaves and halved cherry tomatoes.

1 cup well-packed basil leaves
½ cup extra-virgin olive oil
30 g pine nuts
2 cloves garlic, crushed
salt
60 g freshly grated best-quality
    parmesan cheese

Blend basil, oil, pine nuts, garlic and salt until smooth. This can be done most easily in a blender (stop once or twice to stir contents), food processor or large mortar and pestle. When evenly blended, scrape into a bowl and stir in cheese. Store, covered with a film of olive oil, in a screw-top jar. If using pesto as a pasta sauce, thin the desired quantity with a spoonful of pasta cooking water. The sauce will combine much more readily with the pasta.

coriander peanut pesto

MAKES 1 CUP

This exciting condiment is from Chris Manfield's Paramount Cooking and illustrates the versatility of basil when combined with Asian flavours. Stir this delicious pesto through noodles, add it to broths or use it with Asian vegetables or when making won tons or spring rolls. It is also marvellous in chicken sandwiches! I have successfully substituted sweet basil when I have been unable to buy Asian basil.

200 ml peanut oil
40 g blanched raw peanuts
2 small fresh green chillies,
    minced
1 tablespoon minced ginger
8 cloves garlic, minced
100 g Asian basil leaves
25 g Vietnamese mint leaves
100 g coriander leaves
1 teaspoon shaved palm sugar
2 teaspoons fish sauce
1 tablespoon strained fresh
    lime juice

Heat oil and roast peanuts in a frying pan over medium heat until golden. Strain peanuts from oil and cool. Reserve oil. Blend peanuts in a food processor with chilli, ginger and garlic. Add herbs and half the reserved oil and blend to form a smooth paste. Add sugar, fish sauce and lime juice and blend until herbs are finely minced. Gradually pour in remaining oil to make a smooth paste. Store pesto, covered with a film of oil, in a glass container in the refrigerator.

soupe au pistou

SERVES 4–6

In the south of France pistou, a near-relative of pesto, is stirred into a rich vegetable soup. I have also been offered a gratin (or a tian, *as such dishes are known in Provence) of layers of fried eggplant mixed with tomato sauce and pistou and topped with grated gruyère.*

1 onion, sliced

3 tablespoons olive oil

2 large tomatoes, peeled and chopped

1.5 litres cold water

2 potatoes, peeled and cut into 1 cm dice

2 leeks, finely sliced

2 carrots, peeled and diced

1 cup cooked cannellini or haricot beans

1 zucchini, cut into 1 cm dice

250 g green beans, cut into 5 cm lengths

salt

freshly ground black pepper

freshly grated gruyère cheese

PISTOU

3 cloves garlic

1 cup loosely packed basil leaves

3 tablespoons extra-virgin olive oil

To make the pistou, crush garlic and basil to a paste in a mortar and pestle. Slowly add oil and work it in well. (Pistou can be made successfully in a *small* food processor or blender, in which case the oil is added before the garlic and basil.)

In a large saucepan sauté onion in oil until softened. Add tomato and sauté for 5 minutes, then add water and bring to simmering point. Add potato, leek, carrot and cannellini beans and simmer for 15 minutes. Add zucchini and green beans and simmer for 10 minutes. Taste for seasoning, remembering that the pistou will add extra excitement. Ladle soup into bowls and pass the pistou and grated cheese (a heaped teaspoonful of pistou is about the right amount for my taste).

pesto and vegetables
Serve Pesto (see p. 81) with boiled potatoes, sliced or grilled tomato, grilled eggplant or a fritto misto of eggplant, zucchini and broccoli.

pesto toast
Spread Pesto (see p. 81) on toast, top with a melting cheese (mozzarella, fontina or raclette) and grill.

other recipes

tomato soup with basil and croutons *see* TOMATOES

bay leaves *Laurus nobilis* is correctly known as the sweet bay tree rather than the bay laurel, which is unrelated and poisonous. Confusion has existed for centuries. Poets were crowned with 'laurel' (hence poet laureate) and in the Middle Ages those passing their first university exams were *bacca laureatus*, similar to the title of the university qualifying examination in France today (*baccalauréat*). | Originating in the Mediterranean, the sweet bay is a dense evergreen with glossy leaves about 5 cm long that grows slowly to its full 15 m height. It can also be trimmed and grown as a decorative and useful standard in a large pot. Rich in symbolism and aroma, it is an appropriate gift for those moving to a new home or starting life together. | Bay leaves have aromatic oil glands in both the bark and the shiny green leaves. The leaves are used to flavour stews, soups and braised dishes. A bay leaf is essential in a bouquet garni, the bundle of flavour we slip into the stockpot that usually comprises a bay leaf, a sprig of thyme and parsley stalks.

VARIETIES AND SEASON

Bay leaves are available all year round.

SELECTION AND STORAGE

Bay leaves can be used straight from the tree or bought dried. They are more pungent fresh than dried, so a little goes a long way. It is customary to hang *fresh* leaves in a bunch or on a branch until quite dry and then to store the leaves in an airtight container. Bunches of leaves left hanging in the kitchen for months may look romantic but the leaves will become dusty and greasy.

If buying **dried** bay leaves, look for unbroken leaves and some remnant of colour. Bronze–green leaves are fresher than those that are the colour of cardboard. Even the oldest bay leaves will still carry some memory of the original flavour. Use an extra leaf if they are not very aromatic.

PREPARATION

Usually bay leaves are left whole for easy retrieval; however, if crushed, the flavours meld faster. A piece of crushed bay leaf is hard to swallow, so I think it better either to completely pulverise the bay leaves or to tear them into a maximum of 4 pieces that are still recognisable.

**bay leaves
go
with**
stocks
vegetable soups
dried beans
lentils
broad beans
pork
quail
sweet peppers
veal
potatoes
garlic
onions
rabbit
bacon
milk
cream

bread sauce to serve with roast chicken SERVES 6

recipes

Nothing could be more English than bread sauce. The first time I was offered it was in a stone farmhouse in Somerset in the 1960s. With a fat well-roasted chicken and plenty of vegetables it has an undeniable charm (made with rich chicken stock instead of milk it becomes even more fla- voursome, but I don't think this would please the traditionally minded).

425 ml milk or rich Chicken
   Stock
1 shallot, very finely diced
1 bay leaf
5 black peppercorns
pinch of cayenne pepper
pinch of ground mace
pinch of freshly grated nutmeg
4 cloves
salt
white pepper
50 g fresh white breadcrumbs
3 tablespoons thick cream

Simmer milk with shallot, bay leaf, peppercorns, spices, salt and pepper for 15 minutes. Remove peppercorns if you wish, stir in breadcrumbs, then remove from heat and allow to steep until breadcrumbs have absorbed liquid. When ready to serve, reheat sauce, stirring well with a wooden spoon, then adjust seasoning and stir in cream. Serve a good spoonful on each plate and pass any extra sauce in a separate bowl.

peppers and bay
Stew sweet peppers slowly with whole, fresh bay leaves, sliced garlic and a generous amount of olive oil until meltingly soft, stirring once or twice. I like the look of the drab olive leaves against the rich sunset yellows, oranges and reds.

barbecued skewers of bay leaves and pork

MAKES 1

This quantity fills a skewer. Multiply the ingredients according to how many you are feeding and how hungry they are. This combination is mentioned by Elizabeth David.

beans and bay
Warm a torn bay leaf in extra-virgin olive oil, toss through just-cooked green beans for a few minutes and season.

½ pork fillet, cut into 2 cm thick slices
8 squares streaky bacon, 1 cm thick
4 slices breadstick, 1 cm thick
2 bay leaves, torn in half
freshly ground black pepper
olive oil

Flatten pork slices slightly by thumping them with your hand. Thread bacon, bread, ½ bay leaf and pork on skewer until filled. Grind over pepper and brush with oil. Barbecue for about 10 minutes, turning 2–3 times, brushing with oil at each turn. The bread, bacon and pork will look crusty and charred but will be soft and succulent and imbued with the aroma of bay leaves.

potatoes with bay
Slip a bay leaf into the pan when you boil new potatoes.

queen mab's puddings

SERVES 8

Mab was the deliverer of dreams, 'the fairies' midwife', so maybe these unusual and ethereal puddings imply fantasy, other-worldliness.

braised vegetables
Place several bay leaves in the bottom of an oiled gratin dish before braising onions, turnips, witlof or artichokes.

bay leaf custard
Use a bay leaf instead of a vanilla bean when making a hot Egg Custard to serve with a steamed pudding.

1 litre milk
150 g castor sugar
3 bay leaves
2 vanilla beans, split
2 strips lemon zest
4 eggs, separated
7 gelatine leaves
100 g glacé fruit (angelica, quince, citron, orange, apricot and marrons glacés, for example), diced
sweet almond oil

Stir milk, sugar, bay leaves, vanilla beans and zest in a large saucepan over gentle heat until sugar dissolves, then bring slowly to scalding point. Leave to infuse for 1 hour.

Beat egg yolks until pale and pour in milk, bay leaves and vanilla beans. Return to rinsed-out pan and cook over moderate heat until custard coats back of a spoon. Strain custard into a large bowl standing in a larger bowl half-filled with ice. Soak gelatine leaves in cold water for a few minutes. Squeeze, then dissolve in a few spoonfuls of hot water and stir into custard. Whisk cooling custard very gently from time to time. Leave to get cold.

Beat egg whites to soft peaks and fold into cooled custard. Whisk gently until custard thickens. When practically set, fold in glacé fruit and ladle mixture into 8 × 150 ml soufflé dishes brushed with sweet almond oil. Refrigerate for a few hours. Unmould and serve with poached fruit.

other recipes

rosemary and bay leaf savoury custards *see* ROSEMARY

beans, dried

Dried beans are known collectively as pulses, together with LENTILS and CHICK PEAS. There are hundreds of varieties and many have different names in different parts of the world. This can be confusing for a cook reading a recipe from another country. However, as the differences in taste and texture tend to be subtle, varieties are interchangeable in most recipes. │ A basic diet of grains supplemented with pulses supplies all the forms of protein needed in the human diet. Dried beans are also filling and inexpensive, which is why they feature so prominently in peasant cooking, especially in the Middle East, Latin America and the Mediterranean region. When preparing dried beans I am reminded of a balmy autumn evening in the courtyard of a simple restaurant in Florence (well known as the city of the bean-eaters), where I enjoyed *pasta e fagioli*, a terracotta-coloured bean soup shining under a ribbon of fine olive oil and served warm rather than piping hot. And every year I cook a cassoulet, a masterpiece of French regional cookery, where layers of creamy beans are studded with preserved duck and chunks of pork under a deep-gold crust. These and all dried bean dishes look at their best served in rustic pottery or stoneware, the browns, creams and rust colours echoing the hues of the beans. >

dried beans

go

with

olive oil

butter

onions

carrots

celery

garlic

chillies

coriander

cream

lemon juice

cumin

paprika

tomatoes

tomato paste

maple syrup

sweet peppers

minced beef

artichokes

rosemary

parmesan cheese

bacon

duck

thyme

goose

ham

lamb

sausages

parsley

savoury

pork

Beans are ideal where long, slow cooking is desired, and their mealy, creamy texture combines well with other ingredients in soups, salads, patties, stews, casseroles and purées. Of these, the best-known bean dishes are the cassoulet and the more homely chilli con carne.

The indigestible sugars raffinose and stachyose in dried beans can create intestinal gas when they meet the bacteria in the human gut. Since these sugars leach out of the beans into the cooking water, discarding the first water in which the beans come to a boil may make them less gassy.

VARIETIES AND SEASON

Dried beans are available all year round. Ideally, they should be from the previous year's crop and therefore be all sold before the end of autumn when a new crop should be freshly harvested and dried. The following varieties are those most widely available in Australia.

Adzuki This tiny, reddish-brown bean has a cream-coloured seam and sweetish flavour. **Black-eyed** Also known as the cornfield or black-eyed pea in America's southern states, this small, kidney-shaped bean is creamy-white with a black 'eye'. It is similar in flavour to a cannellini bean. **Borlotti** Also called a cranberry bean, the borlotti is large and kidney-shaped, and has beige and claret markings, a smooth texture and a ham-like, nutty flavour when cooked. **Broad** This large, broad and flat bean, also known as the fava or shell bean, can be green, brown or beige and is smooth and creamy with a tough skin and mealy texture. **Butter** The white butter or Lima bean is available large or small and is similar in shape to the broad bean. It has a mild flavour and smooth texture. **Cannellini** This white, kidney-shaped bean is larger than the haricot, mild in flavour and has a fluffy texture when cooked. **Haricot** Used to make baked beans, haricot or navy beans are small and white with a mild flavour and lots of fibre. **Mung** Available black or green, the slightly sweet mung bean is the seed used for bean sprouts. **Pinto** This bean is beige speckled with brown and similar in flavour and texture to the red kidney bean. **Red kidney** This kidney-shaped, dark-red bean is full flavoured and mealy. **Soya** The most nutritious of all beans and the most easily digested, the soya bean is small, very hard, beige and oval and has a mild flavour.

SELECTION AND STORAGE

It is impossible to tell whether dried beans are 1 or 4 years old just by looking at them. I prefer to buy them where they are weighed for me rather than from the supermarket, where the little packets may well have been packaged a long time ago. Best of all is to buy from a specialist Greek or

Middle Eastern food store where you suspect the turnover is high. If buying beans from a loose sack, run a handful through your fingers to ensure there are no tiny holes in the beans, indicating burrowing insects.

Store dried beans in a covered container away from direct sunlight and in a dry place. In humid climates store the beans in the freezer.

PREPARATION AND COOKING

Most dried beans require some soaking, mostly overnight. (Some cooks also add a pinch of bicarbonate of soda to assist in softening the beans. I do not do this. It is certainly not necessary if the beans are only a season out of the pod.) There is a school of thought that believes it is never necessary to soak overnight, advocating instead a quick-soak method as yielding superior texture and flavour. I have not found this. Beans that are insufficiently hydrated are more likely to break up in the cooking process.

TO SOAK Most dried beans need to be soaked overnight in plenty of cold water. (*Adzuki* and *mung beans* only need to be soaked for an hour or so. Italian, Greek and Middle Eastern cooks soak *broad beans* for up to 48 hours with frequent changes of water and then pop the beans out of the very tough skins. Dried broad beans are often sold already skinned.) Discard any beans that are discoloured or that float to the top when the soaking water and beans are agitated. Discard the soaking water. **Quick method** If you have forgotten to soak the beans overnight, pour boiling water over them and leave for 3 hours. Discard this water and continue as if the beans had been soaked overnight.

TO COOK Cover the soaked beans generously with fresh cold water and bring to a boil. Simmer gently for 1–2 hours or until the beans are tender (test the beans by tasting them). Avoid stirring the beans as they tend to break up and do not salt the cooking water as this toughens the skins, causing the beans to split.

robert's beans   SERVES 4   recipes

One of my former employees has quite a way with dried beans! This dish is always creamy and soothing, seasoned beautifully and comes with a freshly shaved layer of parmesan. A generous, delicious first course.

Robert sometimes uses other beans than cannellini, such as giant butter or broad beans. He also uses parmesan oil in place of olive oil (he soaks parmesan rind in olive oil for a month).

250 g dried cannellini beans,
  soaked
I carrot, diced
I stick celery, diced
I small onion, diced
2 cloves garlic, crushed *or*
  finely chopped
I bay leaf
a few parsley stalks
I sprig thyme
2 tablespoons olive oil
2 artichokes, cooked in a
  Blanc ✐ and cut in half
pinch of saffron threads
½ cup Chicken Stock ✐
freshly ground black pepper
parmesan cheese
I tablespoon extra-virgin
  olive oil

quick minestrone
*Use cooked beans as
the basis for a quick
minestrone soup.*

Rinse soaked beans and put in a large
saucepan with carrot, celery, onion, garlic
and herbs. Simmer, uncovered, for 1½ hours
until beans are just tender. Drain.

Heat olive oil in a heavy-based frying pan
and warm artichokes through. Add saffron,
stock and 2 cups beans and their cooking
vegetables. Stir frequently until liquid has
nearly all evaporated and the beans and
artichokes look creamy. Season with pepper
and stir in 1 tablespoon freshly grated
parmesan cheese. Spoon into heated pasta
bowls, drizzle over extra-virgin olive oil and
shave a little more parmesan directly onto
the beans.

white bean purée

MAKES 2 CUPS

*This Italian recipe is a great favourite. I use it as a topping for sourdough
toast brushed with olive oil; the topping becomes golden after 10 minutes
or so in a hot oven. The purée is also very good alongside a grilled quail or
grilled vegetables.*

175 g dried cannellini or
  haricot beans, soaked
3 cups cold water
I tablespoon tomato paste
salt
I teaspoon chopped garlic
I teaspoon finely chopped
  rosemary
extra-virgin olive oil
¾ cup hot Chicken Stock ✐
juice of ½ lemon
freshly ground black pepper

Rinse soaked beans, put in a large saucepan
with water and add tomato paste and a
scant pinch of salt. Bring to a boil, lower
heat and simmer, uncovered, for 2 hours.
The beans should be covered with water for
the first 1½ hours. When beans are tender
almost all the water should have been
absorbed. Purée in a food processor.

Sauté garlic and rosemary in a little oil.
Add purée and mix well. Pour in stock and
stir well over heat until thoroughly
absorbed. The purée should now be smooth,
thick and shiny. Add extra oil, lemon juice,
salt and pepper to taste. This purée keeps well, refrigerated in a covered
container, for several days.

haricot beans in cream sauce SERVES 6

Serve these beans as the vegetable accompaniment to a roasted leg of lamb or a baked veal chop.

1 onion
2 cloves
1 bay leaf
1 sprig thyme
6 sprigs parsley
.500 g dried haricot beans, soaked
2 sticks celery, sliced
1 carrot, diced
2 cloves garlic, finely chopped
1 cup thick cream
30 g unsalted butter
salt
freshly ground black pepper
freshly grated nutmeg

Peel onion and stud with cloves. Tie herbs with string to make a bouquet garni. Rinse soaked beans and put into a large saucepan and cover with cold water. Add vegetables, garlic and bouquet garni and bring to a boil. Cook over moderate heat at a steady simmer for 1½ hours until beans are tender. Drain, discarding bouquet garni and onion.

Boil cream in a wide, heavy-based saucepan. Add butter, salt, pepper, nutmeg and beans. Simmer briskly, stirring, until beans have absorbed most of the cream. Check seasoning and serve at once.

beans with spinach
Toss cooked beans with finely diced raw onion, extra-virgin olive oil and parsley and add diced ham or sausage, fried bacon and a handful of cooked spinach or silver beet.

chilli con carne SERVES 8

500 g dried beans (for example, borlotti, black-eyed, red kidney)
1 kg chuck steak, cut into 2 cm cubes
2 bay leaves
2 onions, diced
2 cloves garlic, chopped
2 tablespoons olive oil
1 kg tomatoes, peeled, seeded and roughly chopped
salt
1½ teaspoons freshly ground black pepper
1 teaspoon cayenne pepper
2 teaspoons paprika
½ teaspoon ground cumin
2 tablespoons polenta

Soak beans overnight, then drain and rinse. Put beans into an enamelled cast-iron casserole with meat, bay leaves, onion and garlic and barely cover with cold water. Bring to a simmer and cook until beans are just tender (check after 1½ hours).

Preheat oven to 180°C. Heat oil in a large frying pan or cast-iron casserole. Stir in tomato, seasonings and polenta. Simmer for 10 minutes until tomato has collapsed. Tip sauce over meat and beans, stir well, then check and adjust seasonings. Transfer pot to oven and cook for 1 hour. Serve it as is – chilli con carne is a complete meal in its own right.

baked beans

SERVES 4

The best-selling, mass-market item of this name is characterless beside my version! This quantity makes a sustaining meal for 4 and can be doubled or tripled easily. Smaller quantities are good alongside smoked pork loin (kassler) or meaty pork sausages.

bean jaffle

Make a jaffle using wholemeal or rye bread, home-made Baked Beans (see p. 92) and grated cheese or leftover lamb.

375 g dried borlotti or red kidney beans, soaked

2 tablespoons olive oil

1 large onion, diced

3 cloves garlic, chopped

2 carrots, diced

2 rashers thickly sliced streaky bacon, cut into 1 cm wide strips

2 red peppers, seeded and cut into 2 cm squares

1 green pepper, seeded and cut into 2 cm squares

1 x 400 g can peeled tomatoes in juice

1 bay leaf

1 sprig thyme

1 teaspoon paprika

½ teaspoon crushed coriander seeds

salt

freshly ground black pepper

3 tablespoons maple syrup, treacle, golden syrup *or* honey

Preheat oven to 160°C. Rinse soaked beans, then put into a saucepan and cover with cold water. Bring to a boil, then strain and rinse with cold water. Heat oil in a large enamelled cast-iron casserole and sauté onion, garlic, carrot and bacon. After 5 minutes, when onion has softened and bacon is sizzling, add red and green peppers. Purée tomatoes and juice in a food processor and add to casserole with beans and remaining ingredients, except maple syrup. Mix well. Add sufficient cold water to cover beans by 4 cm. Transfer casserole, tightly sealed, to oven and bake for at least 4 hours. Stir well after 2 hours, checking that it is still reasonably sloppy (if it is too dry, add a little water and reduce oven temperature). After 4 hours, stir in maple syrup, extra salt and plenty of freshly ground black pepper. The beans should now be in a rich sauce. If too thick, add a little extra water; if too runny and the beans are tender, increase oven temperature and continue to cook. Serve with a green salad.

other recipes

bok choy with fermented black beans *see* BOK CHOY

slow-roasted leg of lamb with dried beans *see* LAMB

soupe au pistou *see* BASIL

b e a n s ,   f r e s h   Before the fifteenth century 'beans' meant 'broad beans' to Europeans. The broad bean is the only bean native to Europe and evidence of its place in the diet dates from the Bronze Age. All the others came from the New World and were introduced to Europe by Christopher Columbus. | Fresh beans are one of my all-time favourites. Nothing beats a dish of slender young beans quickly boiled and tossed with a nut of butter or a slurp of olive oil. Instead of priding themselves on the size their beans can attain, home gardeners should pick beans while they are tiny to experience the flavour explosion and exquisite tenderness of green beans eaten in their immature state. Occasionally in Australia one finds commercial growers prepared to pick their beans smaller than the average. These smaller beans are marketed by the dreadful name of 'beanettes'. Consumers must understand why these beans cost more. The grower has been prepared to give up crop weight for superior quality. He or she cannot be expected to lose money. It is also much more labour intensive to search for smaller beans among the bushes. In the middle of summer it is sometimes necessary to pick twice a day. Be delighted that the grower is prepared to try for higher quality and pay the extra cheerfully!

fresh beans

go

with

butter

olive oil

garlic

fermented black

 beans

almonds

peanuts

parmesan cheese

ham

prawns

parsley

chives

chillies

cream

celery

spring onions

cashews

turmeric

onion

Chinese roast pork

potatoes

sweet peppers

mushrooms

beetroots

pine nuts

bacon

walnuts

fetta cheese

olives

sea salt

mint

VARIETIES AND SEASON

The most common beans in our markets are broad, green, runner and wax beans, while snake beans, available from Asian greengrocers and food stores, are becoming more widely available.

BROAD | *Vicia faba* has a large, flat green pod with a pale 'cottony' lining in which nestle large seeds. The pod is usually discarded. Available June–October/November, broad beans are one of the delights of spring. By the end of the season they become mealy rather than sweet and should be used in purées or dips rather than as a fresh bean. The broad bean is also known as the fava or shell bean.

In his marvellous newsletter *Kitchen Talk*, Michael Boddy recalls that some people – most notably, and oddly, those with Greek or Armenian ancestry – have an inherited allergy to toxins found in raw broad beans. These toxins are rendered harmless by cooking. Bear this in mind when serving raw broad beans.

GREEN | Also known as French beans, the green bean (*Phaseolus vulgaris*) grows on a small bush, although some varieties are climbers. There are a great many varieties available but the main distinctions are between stringed or stringless, dwarf or large, flat or round and pale-yellow or green beans. There are also purple varieties that turn green when cooked. The green bean is sometimes still referred to as the string bean because of the tough string that one once had to remove. Nowadays the string has been bred out of most varieties. Home gardeners who collect their own seed may need to string their beans and some commercial varieties, notably the large flat beans, can still have strings too. The many varieties are lumped together in the market. The peak season in the southern States is November–March (in Victoria the first delicate, pencil-slim, stringless beans from Mildura are available by 1 December, in time for our summer menu). Queensland and Western Australian green beans are available April–November.

RUNNER | *P. coccineus*, also known as the scarlet runner, is a climbing green bean, larger and coarser than the green bean. Most varieties have scarlet flowers. These beans are often grown to scandalous proportions. The peak season is summer.

SNAKE | *Vigna sesquipedalis* or the Chinese bean is grown throughout tropical Australia and South-East Asia. The thin green beans grow to 40 cm, are sold in bundles and are available December–May.

WAX Sometimes called yellow or butter beans, wax beans have yellow pods and black seeds and are, in fact, a pale-yellow variety of the green bean. This bean is less common than other varieties and is available December–May. It can be superb when home-grown but seems to deteriorate much faster than other varieties. Too often looks deceive and the beans have overmature seeds and tough pods.

SELECTION AND STORAGE

Freshness is all. (When purchasing beans outside the local season, remember that they will have travelled a considerable distance, so be especially vigilant about their quality and condition.) Never be fooled into thinking that a bean that bends will ever taste worthwhile. Beans should not be wrinkled, the ends should be undamaged and there should be no sign of dampness or discoloured patches. *Green, runner, wax* and *snake* beans must be crisp, brightly coloured and, most of all, young (usually this means small, although with runners and snake beans this is not the case). The beans should not have noticeable swellings where the seeds are – those that do are overmature.

Broad beans should look moist and crisp, never collapsed and flabby. If you can select your own broad beans, choose smaller pods. The beans inside will also be smaller and more delicate in flavour.

Refrigerate beans in the crisper in a vegetable storage bag for 2–3 days. Podded broad beans freeze well and should be transferred directly from the freezer to the pot.

PREPARATION AND COOKING

Check any bean to be cooked whole (*green, runner* or *wax* beans) for strings (note that snake beans are stringless). Cut off the end where the bean was attached to the bush, and cut off the little tail at the other end, if you wish. If the beans are home-grown or bought at the peak of condition leave this little curved tail as it will be quite tender. Because of their extraordinary length, *snake* beans are usually chopped into smaller pieces before cooking. While they can be cooked as a green bean is, snake beans are often stir-fried. *Broad* beans are shelled before cooking.

Some cookbooks advise you to run your perfectly cooked beans under cold water to stop the cooking instantly. I disapprove of this practice. The beans may be brilliantly coloured but they will taste of cold water rather than young sweet bean melded with the suave note of butter or the excitement of olive oil.

TO COOK **Green, wax, runner or snake** The chlorophyll in green beans reacts with acids in the cooking water, causing the beans to become a drab olive-green. To prevent this happening, use masses of water to dilute the acids and leave the

bean dressings
Dress warm beans with olive oil, salt, pepper and a few drops of wine vinegar or balsamic vinegar, mayonnaise, boiled cream, parsley, chives, salt and pepper, or Bagna Cauda Sauce (see ANCHOVIES).

beans and . . .
Combine warm beans with one of the following: small boiled potatoes, warm boiled beetroots, quickly sautéd bacon or pancetta, a handful of toasted walnut halves or pine nuts, sautéd mushrooms or onion, strips of roasted red pepper, chunks of fried or grilled eggplant, water chestnuts and light soy sauce, or butter-crisped breadcrumbs.

saucepan uncovered, so that the volatile acids can disperse. There should be sufficient lightly salted water so that it does not go off the boil for more than a few moments when you drop in the beans. Boil rapidly, uncovered, for 5–8 minutes (depending on the size of the beans) and then test a bean. Cook beans until they are bite-tender, not squeaky against the tooth. Tip the beans quickly into a colander, shake to drain away the last drops of water and then toss the beans with a nut of unsalted butter or a spoonful of the best olive or walnut oil and serve at once. **Broad** Blanch the shelled beans rapidly in lots of boiling water for 3 minutes, drain quickly under cold water, so that the beans can be handled, and then slip each bean out of its tough skin. The startlingly emerald-green kernels can be rewarmed in a little melted butter or boiling water for a minute only. With very young, home-grown broad beans, there is no need to remove the outer skin of each bean. Simply boil, drain, butter, season and serve.

recipes

byessar – moroccan broad bean dip

*Serve this purée with fresh or toasted pita bread and a plate of fat black olives. It can also be used as a dip for raw vegetables or spread on sourdough bread and bubbled under the griller, just as described for the White Bean Purée (*see* BEANS, DRIED*). As these beans are to be puréed, they are cooked for much longer than if they were to be served freshly boiled and removed from their skins. A kilogram of broad beans in their pods will yield about 300 g beans when shelled.*

herring and beans
Toss chunks of matjes herring and potato with sour cream, then add warm green beans, mild onion, parsley and chives.

parmesan beans
Shell home-grown raw broad beans, dip in the best extra-virgin olive oil or walnut oil, add a flake of sea salt and a shaving of fresh parmesan cheese and enjoy on or with crusty bread.

1 kg broad beans, shelled
2 cloves garlic, chopped to a paste
1 teaspoon freshly chopped oregano
1 teaspoon ground cumin
150 ml extra-virgin olive oil
salt
freshly ground black pepper

GARNISH
1 teaspoon paprika
½ teaspoon chilli powder
½ teaspoon ground cumin
1 tablespoon extra-virgin olive oil
3 spring onions, finely chopped

Boil beans in lightly salted water for 15 minutes until quite tender. Drain through a colander set over a bowl and reserve the cooking water. Tip ½ cup cooking water into a blender. Add beans, garlic, oregano, cumin, oil, salt and pepper and blend. If too thick, pour in a further ½ cup cooking water and blend again to a smooth purée, stopping and scraping mixture once or twice. Taste and adjust seasonings. Transfer purée to a flat, rustic-looking bowl. To garnish, mix paprika, chilli powder and cumin with oil and dribble a pattern onto the purée. Scatter with spring onion.

green beans with fermented black beans

SERVES 4

Fermented black beans are in fact soy beans and are widely used in Chinese cooking. Serve this dish with boiled rice or as it is.

250 g green or snake beans
1 teaspoon fermented black beans
1 teaspoon finely chopped garlic
1 tablespoon olive oil
½ teaspoon freshly sliced chilli or chilli paste
1 teaspoon sugar
3 tablespoons water

If using snake beans, cut into manageable lengths. Mash black beans with garlic. Heat oil in a wok or frying pan and sauté garlic and black bean paste for 30 seconds over a high heat. Tip in the beans and stir to coat. Add chilli and sugar, stir quickly and pour in water. Cover, reduce heat to moderate and cook for 4 minutes.

chinese sausage Sauté slices of lap cheong sausage (*see* SAUSAGES) in the wok before adding the garlic and black bean paste.

andalusian broad beans

SERVES 4

This recipe is for home-grown broad beans only. The pods must be no longer than 12 cm and are eaten as well as the beans.

1 kg home-grown young broad beans
½ cup extra-virgin olive oil
1 onion, finely chopped
3 cloves garlic, finely chopped
100 g raw ham, cut into 1 cm squares
3 tablespoons fino sherry
1 cup water
salt
freshly ground black pepper
2 tablespoons fresh breadcrumbs
1 tablespoon freshly chopped parsley
2 hardboiled eggs, roughly chopped

Preheat oven to 180°C. Remove strings from bean pods and top and tail pods. Chop into short pieces, following the swell of each bean. Warm oil in a heatproof and ovenproof dish (in Spain it would be terracotta). Sauté onion and garlic until they soften but do not colour. Add raw ham and sauté another few minutes. Add beans, sherry, water, salt and pepper and bring to simmering point. Cover and bake in oven for 1 hour. At the end of the cooking time, the beans should be completely tender and there should not be an excess of liquid. If there is, boil hard on the stove for a few minutes. The finished dish should be moist and juicy, not sloppy. Stir in breadcrumbs and parsley and scatter over egg. Adjust seasoning and serve.

beans with fetta and mint
Toss shelled (but unpeeled), raw young broad beans lightly with cubes of fetta cheese, oily black olives, shredded mint leaves, olive oil, lemon juice and freshly ground black pepper. Serve on a flat platter with good bread and a jug of olive oil alongside.

yabbies and beans
Make Yabby Salad with Walnuts and Potatoes (see YABBIES*) but use 250 g small green or yellow beans instead of potatoes and forget the salad leaves.*

salade niçoise

SERVES 4

There are many versions of this salad. This is the one I prefer. It is closest to the salads I am usually offered in the south of France.

Some cooks prefer to add grilled fresh tuna. I have never been served a salade niçoise made with fresh tuna in Nice but there is no reason to stick slavishly to tradition. For that reason, sometimes I add garlic croutons or a few brilliant nasturtium blossoms, which are usually rioting in the garden during the summer when this salad or one very like it takes centre stage any day I am able to eat at home.

almond beans
Fry a handful of flaked almonds or sliced water chestnuts in olive oil, add a tiny touch of fresh chilli or chilli paste and toss through warm beans. Add shellfish or fish for a more elaborate first course.

warm bean salad
Add 1 tablespoon finely chopped mild salad onion or cooked, crispy onion, or quickly sautéd bacon or pancetta to a warm salad of beans.

1 mignonette lettuce or 2
  large handfuls soft-leafed
  salad selection
200 g beans, freshly boiled
2 ripe tomatoes, cut into
  wedges
1 x 200 g can tuna in olive oil
2 hardboiled eggs (preferably
  free-range), quartered
2–4 potatoes, freshly boiled
  and cut into chunks *or*
  halved
2 tablespoons olive oil
1 teaspoon wine vinegar
  (optional)
salt
freshly ground black pepper
16 small black olives
8 anchovies, split lengthwise

Cover a platter with washed, dried salad leaves. Gently mix warm beans, tomato, drained tuna, egg and potato with olive oil, vinegar (if the tomatoes are not too acidic), salt and pepper and tumble onto salad leaves. Scatter olives and anchovies over.

other recipes

curried beans with cashews *see* NUTS

warm bean salad with a bacon garnish *see* BACON

b e e f   The Australian meat industry offers high-quality meat to the domestic market and increasingly to export markets. Beef quality is determined largely by the breed, age and sex of the animal and also depends on the methods of feeding, fattening, slaughtering and the treatment post-slaughter. | If one eats meat, beef is likely to be a favourite. After 20 years in my restaurant I have dared to offer a menu without beef only half a dozen times. The public seems to love best of all roasted or grilled prime cuts of beef served with a luscious sauce. However, flavour is not mentioned nearly as often as tenderness. The most tender cuts seem to be preferred for special occasions over those that have more flavour but also more muscle fibre. | At the time of writing we are being told that soon much of the meat in our supermarkets will be graded and labelled accordingly. I hope it will not be labelled for tenderness only, as I want to know the age of my beef and whether it comes from a grain- or grass-fed beast, as a guide to depth of flavour.

VARIETIES AND SEASON

Three categories of beef are available: yearling, prime and mature. *Yearling* beef is 1–2 years old, has a small amount of creamy fat and light-red, fairly floppy flesh with no fat marbling and a mild flavour. *Prime* beef is 2–4 years old, has firm creamy fat and bright-red, fairly firm flesh with some marbling and good flavour. Most beef sold in Australia is prime. *Mature* beef is more than 4 years old, has creamy-yellow fat and dark-red, firm flesh with pronounced marbling and a very full and 'beefy' flavour.

Consumers are also able to choose between grain-fed and grass-fed beef. *Grain-fed* or lot-fed beasts are fed grain-dominated rations for a minimum of 3 months in controlled conditions. Such beef has maximum marbling. *Grass-fed* beasts are raised and fattened on pasture. The majority of beef in Australia is grass-fed. Advocates of grain-fed beef suggest that climatic variations and seasonal differences can lead to an inconsistency of quality in grass-fed beef. (Certainly in a drought year the condition of beef cattle deteriorates.) Advocates of grass-fed beef feel that the best animals give a 'beefier' flavour. There is also concern about the environmental implications of growing so much grain to sustain the grain-fed beef industry.

Whether it's grain- or grass-fed, all beef is aged, to some degree. Ageing gives tenderness by allowing naturally occurring enzymes in the meat to break down muscle fibre. It is achieved by hanging the carcass for a certain length of time – a process increasingly taking place inside vacuum-packaging.

Good-quality beef is available throughout the year in Australia. I prefer the full flavour of grass-fed beef from a larger animal. This 'heavy beef', as it is known in the trade, is much harder to locate than the younger yearling beef that many cooks seem to prefer. Make friends with a good butcher and enjoy the benefits.

SELECTION AND STORAGE

Beef cuts are described as being from the *hindquarter* or the *forequarter*. The tender cuts with little connective tissue can be roasted, fried or grilled but the tougher cuts should be stewed or braised, which softens the connective tissue. Each of these cuts has a specific name and should be asked for as such in your butcher shop. Request the appropriate cut for the appropriate cooking procedure – do not try to save money and purchase a cheaper cut and then try to grill it rather than stew it. Some cuts that are more expensive per kilogram may not have as much waste as other cheaper cuts.

FOR ROASTING For memorable roast beef that evokes Empire and largesse one cannot do better than splurge on a *wing-rib sirloin* from the hindquarter or a *standing-rib roast* from the forequarter. These magnificent cuts are expensive as one is paying for a lot of bulky bone, but the flavour is incomparable. Both can also be ordered as boneless joints – sirloin or porterhouse – which are easier to carve, but the meat lacks the special sweetness that comes from being cooked on the bone and is less dramatic in presentation. A large piece of *rump* can also be roasted, although my preference for choice rump is to barbecue or grill. *Fillet* is everyone's favourite, and is delicious and easy to handle.

I would never roast *cornercut topside* or *bolar blade*, or certainly not by my preferred method of roasting, which relies on a high oven temperature and long resting time. However, both are well suited to pot-roasting. In this method, the meat is seared at a high temperature in a covered pot on top of the stove; the temperature is then lowered and a little liquid is added during the cooking time to moisten the dish and provide a small amount of concentrated juice.

FOR GRILLING OR FRYING | All the prime cuts are sold sliced ready for grilling or frying; however, these are often cut too thinly. Ask your butcher to slice *sirloin* or *porterhouse*, *T-bone*, *fillet* or *rump* at least 5 cm thick. This is essential if you like your beef rare or medium–rare. A large cut (for example, a T-bone steak) will then serve 2 people; simply slice the meat off the bone on the diagonal. *Oyster blade* should be cut thinner and is better fried than grilled.

FOR BRAISING | Braising beef offers infinite variation of flavour and style. The *round, topside, fresh silverside* and *skirt steak* from the hindquarter can all be braised, while the forequarter provides *bolar blade*, *blade steak* and *spareribs.* All cuts recommended for braising can be cooked in a piece or cut into small or large cubes or slices for some very famous preparations (beef bourguignon, beef à la mode, beef goulash and beef olives, for example).

FOR STEWING | *Shin beef* (also known as gravy beef) makes superb pies and beef broth. *Chuck steak* is my choice for beef curries. The *round, topside, fresh silverside, skirt steak, bolar blade, blade steak* and *brisket* can also be stewed.

MINCED BEEF | Minced beef is available in several grades. To make successful hamburgers you need a percentage of fat (maybe 20 per cent), so do not feel you must only buy the leanest (and most expensive) minced topside.

SALTED MEAT | Corned beef has a definite place in our history and has sustained many a country family for generations. It is usual to buy meat already salted from the butcher, either boned and rolled *brisket* or *silverside* in the piece.

MARROW BONES | Marrow bones are from the leg of the animal and the butcher can supply them sawn into neat pieces. Reject the ends of the marrow bone (unless buying the bone for stock only) as it is impossible to extract the tiny piece of marrow from them. The ends are also very heavy, so you pay more for no reward.

VACUUM-PACKED | Cuts available vacuum-packed tend to be whole muscles (fillet, for example), rather than slices or with the bone in. Vacuum-packed meat looks different in the bag from unpackaged fresh meat. It is a purple–red colour caused by an oxygen-carrying protein known as myoglobin. On exposure to air this protein absorbs oxygen and within a short time the meat regains its natural colour. A common comment about vacuum-packed meat is that there is a bad smell when the bag is opened. Provided the vacuum has not been broken (and if it has the bag will leak), this smell is not a concern and, again, after a short time in fresh air, this 'confinement' odour will disappear.

Refrigerate raw beef immediately you get it home. The ideal way to store fresh meat is to put it on a rack in a container and cover it with a damp cotton cloth (this keeps the meat moist, while the juices, which can sour meat, collect under the rack). Next best is to wrap the meat in greaseproof paper. Note that frost-free refrigerators dry out food quickly – so protect and check your meat.

Large joints of meat should be used within 5 days. Cubed meat should be used within 2–3 days, while minced beef should be used within 48 hours. Frozen meat should be thawed in the refrigerator.

Long-term storage of vacuum-packed meat is not recommended for home refrigeration (note that all vacuum-packed meat must be refrigerated). Always store this meat with the fat surface uppermost to prevent juices seeping into the fat and causing discoloration. Beware of any bubbles that appear in vacuum-packed beef as they indicate the meat might be off. The shelf life of vacuum-packed meat after it has been removed from the bag is less than for fresh meat. Use as soon as possible, certainly within 2 days.

PREPARATION AND COOKING

When roasting or grilling meat, remove it from the refrigerator a good hour before cooking. This is especially important if you like rare meat. You do not want a grilled exterior and a frigid interior. Trim off most of the visible fat from beef cuts before roasting, grilling or braising. Most, not all!

TO ROAST | When roasting a prime cut of beef, such as *wing-rib sirloin*, leave a 1 cm cap of fat to melt and baste the roast as it cooks. Your butcher should have chined the beef joint (that is, removed the upper spinal bones), so that you can slice through the ribs easily when carving the meat. If this has not been done you will have to carve the whole piece of meat away from the bone frame, turn it on its side and then slice it as for a boneless roast.

Remove any silver membrane from a *fillet of beef*, as it shrinks during cooking. Your butcher will probably have done this for you. There is also a thin piece of meat attached to the side of the fillet that is heavily marbled and gristly. Known as the 'chain', this needs to be removed (heavily trimmed, it is perfect to use for the Fast Red-wine Sauce, p. 105).

I prefer to roast beef at a higher heat for a shorter time than at a lower temperature for longer. Do allow plenty of resting time – the meat will sit happily, wrapped loosely in a double layer of foil, in a warm spot (a plate-warming drawer is perfect) for up to 1 hour. Cutting into unrested meat will see all the precious juices on the serving platter rather than in the roast.

Cook roasting joints on the bone in a preheated oven at 240°C for the first 15 minutes, then reduce the heat to 180°C. For a boneless roast, roast at 220°C for the required time. Refer to the roasting table below for an approximate cooking time to allow per 500 g. (If you use a meat thermometer, your meat will be rare when the internal temperature reaches 60°C; medium meat is achieved at 70°C and well-done meat at 75°C. The temperature of cooked meat continues to rise 2–3 degrees while resting, so remember to remove the meat from the oven just short of the desired internal temperature.) Be aware that the shape and thickness of the joint will also influence cooking time. A fillet of beef will cook in a shorter time (up to half the time if long and thin) than the same weight of topside.

	On the bone (per 500 g)	Boneless (per 500 g)
Rare	15 minutes	10 minutes
Medium	20 minutes	15 minutes
Well done	25 minutes	20 minutes

TO GRILL OR FRY If you are grilling a T-bone or other *steak* that has an edge of fat, snip this fat right through to the meat in several places, so that the membrane that lies between the fat and the lean does not curl and pucker the edges of the steak as it grills. Remove all membrane and connective tissue from cuts such as *chuck* or *blade* before grilling.

Always have your griller, chargrill pan or frying pan hot before you paint a film of oil on it and add the lightly oiled meat. Allow the meat to seal well before turning it to cook the other side. A rare 5 cm thick steak on the bone will take about 10 minutes to cook; off the bone, allow about 7 minutes. Rest, wrapped loosely in foil, for 5–10 minutes before serving.

TO BRAISE
OR STEW When cutting meat for a braise or stew, follow the natural separations of the meat as far as possible, then cut across individual muscles. Meat that is cut willy-nilly across several different muscles can twist and bend in very strange ways in the cooking pot and can be tough. The connective tissue on such cuts as chuck or blade will melt to tenderness when braised slowly.

Whether a dish is a stew or a braise, the result will be better if it is cooked gently for longer. **Braise** Braising is discussed in detail in OXTAIL. Essentially, braising involves cooking a piece or pieces of meat at a low-to-moderate temperature in a covered cast-iron or earthenware casserole for a long time in just enough liquid to ensure a succulent result. The meat may or may not be floured and sealed in hot oil before cooking. Aromatic vegetables and other ingredients are usually added. Expect a cut suitable for braising, for example cornercut topside or bolar blade, that will feed 4–6 people to take about 2 hours at 180°C. **Stew** Stewing is an imprecise term for a technique that is very similar to braising with rather more liquid involved, and more likely to be done on top of the stove than in the oven.

MARROW BONES Pieces of marrow bone should be soaked overnight to extract all the blood. The soft marrow can then be pushed out firmly. Simmer in water for 3–4 minutes and serve with poached meats, such as pot-au-feu, or on top of fillet steaks.

recipes

roasted fillet of beef for a party

SERVES 6

1 x 2 kg fillet of beef
olive oil
freshly ground black pepper
1 quantity Fast Red-wine
  Sauce (see p. 105)
1 bunch spinach
water
20 g Parsley Butter (see
  p. 494)
12 cloves garlic, unpeeled
12 flat mushrooms
40 g butter
scant pinch of salt
6 medium–large pontiac or
  desiree potatoes

In the evening before or on the morning of the party, trim fillet (or ask the butcher to do this) and reserve any scraps for sauce. Trim last 4 cm from skinny end of tail, dice and reserve for sauce. Paint fillet with oil. Tuck thin end of tail underneath to even out thickness. Tie with string in 4–5 places to bind it to a firm 'log'. Grind over pepper and refrigerate.

Make the red-wine sauce. Refrigerate until needed. Tear stems from spinach leaves and discard. Drop leaves into a bowl of water as you go. When all leaves are prepared, swish them around and then transfer to sink draining board. Repeat process with clean water. Transfer dripping leaves to a stockpot and cook, covered, over moderate heat for 5 minutes, stirring

once or twice, until leaves have wilted. Drain in a colander and rinse with cold water to cool quickly. Squeeze dry and either refrigerate, covered, until needed or put into a small saucepan with parsley butter ready for a fast reheat.

Drop garlic into a saucepan, cover with cold water and bring to a boil. Tip off water. Repeat twice. Slip garlic from skins and reserve.

Put mushrooms into a wide frying pan with butter, 1 cup water, salt and a grinding of pepper. Cover and simmer for 10 minutes. Set aside.

Two hours before dinner, remove meat from refrigerator. An hour and a half before dinner, roll potatoes onto oven rack and heat oven to 220°C. One hour before dinner, put meat into oven and cook for 20 minutes for rare meat or 30 minutes for medium. Remove meat, roll in a double sheet of foil and keep warm. Reheat mushrooms. Reheat sauce, then drop in mushrooms and reserved garlic. Have a pre-dinner glass of wine, serve the olives or whatever.

To serve, unwrap meat and tip collected juices into sauce. Retrieve crusty potatoes. Reheat spinach (add parsley butter if prepared ahead). Carve meat onto plates. Ladle over sauce, mushrooms and garlic and add the spinach. Easy, wasn't it?

no sauce Forget the sauce. Reheat the garlic with the mushrooms. Offer Parsley Butter and mustard or make Béarnaise Sauce.

fast red-wine sauce

The way we make our red-wine sauce is a useful technique for the home cook to learn. The sauce will be much richer if stock is used, but I have constructed excellent sauces using fortified wine or table wine and water. This sauce freezes perfectly.

1 cup red wine
½ bay leaf
1 shallot, sliced
1 tablespoon olive oil
1 cup finely chopped lean meat trimmings
1 cup finely chopped aromatic vegetables (celery, onion, carrot)
2 cups Veal, Chicken or Vegetable Stock or water
20 g softened unsalted butter
freshly ground black pepper

Heat red wine with bay leaf and shallot and reduce to make ¾ cup, then set aside. Film a heavy-based frying pan with oil and sear meat to brown it extremely well. Scatter over vegetables. The pan should be hot enough so that the pieces brown rather than stew, and not so hot that they burn. Pour over a third of the stock and stir to release any piece of meat or vegetable that has stuck. The liquid should bubble up furiously and almost evaporate in a minute. While there is still a little liquid, add half remaining stock. This time it should settle to a simmer and there will be the beginnings of a sauce in the pan.

sliced beef
Slice chilled raw beef paper-fine and serve with olive oil, salt, freshly ground black pepper and shaved parmesan, roasted red peppers and anchovies or raw mushroom salad.

Stir again so nothing sticks. After 1–2 minutes add remaining stock and reduced red wine. The liquid should be a reddish brown and start to smell very pleasant. Adjust heat and simmer for 5–10 minutes until reduced a little. Strain into a small saucepan, pressing on contents of sieve. Taste. The sauce will taste of wine but should be more complex. Return to rinsed-out pan and boil hard to increase intensity and mature flavours, then drop in butter while still boiling. This will give your sauce 'eyes' or shine. Taste for pepper. There will be no need for salt as the natural salts from the meat and vegetables will have seasoned the sauce.

variations Use white wine or vermouth instead of red wine. Add a spoonful of puréed vegetable, such as onion, turnip or tomato, to the finished sauce. Leeks, mushrooms and garlic can be included with the aromatic vegetables. Bone marrow used in place of butter will result in a simple bordelaise sauce.

yorkshire puddings   MAKES 12

If cooking either a bone-in joint or boneless piece of sirloin, Yorkshire pudding will turn it into the traditional British roast beef. If you remember to leave the oven on when you remove the meat to rest, these puddings can go straight in.

150 g plain flour
pinch of salt
1 egg
1¼ cups milk
1 tablespoon vegetable oil

Sift flour and salt into a bowl. Break egg into centre of flour, then gradually add milk, beating well. Set aside 1 hour. When meat is resting, oil a muffin tray or small metal cake tins standing on a tray (or use some hot fat rendered by the roasting beef).

Heat tins in oven for a few minutes. Pour in batter to come halfway up tins. Bake on top shelf for 25 minutes at 180°C till puffed and crisp.

beef bourguignon   SERVES 6

In the 1960s this dish was one of the favourite choices for dinner parties. And why not for now, too? It is delicious, yields lots of rich juices that complement Australia's great red wines, requires no last-minute attention and simmers away in the oven while the cook does other things. It can be made the day before it is needed and will only improve in the reheating. The classic garnish of small onions or shallots, bacon lardons and mushrooms appears in the French repertoire in many other dishes (with rabbit and chicken, for instance).

Ask your butcher to cut the steaks 5 cm thick.

2 tablespoons olive oil

200 g streaky bacon, cut into
    1 cm cubes

12 small onions *or* 24 shallots,
    peeled

1.5 kg blade *or* chuck steak,
    cut into 5 cm cubes

freshly ground black pepper

plain flour

2 tablespoons brandy
    (optional)

2 cups red wine

1 bay leaf

1 sprig thyme

2–3 stalks parsley

small piece of orange zest

3 cloves garlic, finely chopped

2 cups well-flavoured meat
    stock

18 small flat mushrooms

40 g softened butter

Preheat oven to 180°C. In an enamelled cast-iron casserole that will hold all the beef comfortably, heat half the oil and brown bacon gently. Remove with a slotted spoon and leave aside. Add onions and allow them to become golden all over, then set aside with bacon.

Season beef with pepper and brown in oil and bacon fat in the casserole, adding remaining oil if needed. Do not brown too many cubes at once. (The most common mistake of learner cooks is to crowd the pan at this stage, so that the meat stews rather than seals.) As each piece becomes a rich brown, remove it from the casserole. When beef is browned, tip off any fat, replace meat and scatter over 2 tablespoons flour. Keep heat quite high as you turn and stir meat with a wooden spoon to allow flour to cook a little.

Warm brandy in a small saucepan, touch with a lighted match and pour flaming spirit over beef. Shake casserole until flames die out. Still keeping heat high, slowly pour in wine. Stir and lift again, so that the wine bubbles and reduces somewhat as it hits the hot pan.

To make a bouquet garni, tie herbs and orange zest with string. Add to meat with garlic and reserved onions and bacon, along with their juices. Pour on sufficient stock to barely cover contents. Press a piece of baking paper down on liquid and cover with a well-fitting lid. Transfer to oven and cook for 2 hours. If meat is tender, add mushrooms and return to oven for 30 minutes. If meat is still chewy, cook a further hour before adding mushrooms. (At this stage the dish can be allowed to cool, then refrigerated overnight and gently reheated when needed.)

To finish the dish, ladle off 1 cup juices. Work butter and 2 tablespoons flour to a smooth paste (this is a *beurre manié*). Add paste to juices and mash quickly using a fork until quite smooth. Tip this liquid into the casserole and lift and stir to distribute. Bring casserole to a boil on top of the stove to thicken slightly. Remove the bouquet garni. Serve with small boiled potatoes generously sprinkled with freshly chopped parsley.

vegetables If you prefer to eat more vegetables and less meat, brown small peeled turnips or chunks of carrot after the onions and add them at the same time.

asian beef salad
Combine light soy sauce, fresh lime juice, fish sauce, garlic, chilli and sugar and toss through finely sliced rare beef and lots of freshly chopped coriander leaves.

steak marinade
Marinate rump steaks in 1 cup Fresh Tomato Sauce (see TOMATOES), ½ cup Worcestershire sauce, 2 tablespoons chutney and the juice of a lemon. Barbecue and grind over plenty of black pepper to serve.

cold beef salad

SERVES 2–3

This delicious salad came about the evening after I had entertained friends on roasted fillet of beef and potatoes baked in their jackets. Some of both remained and the fillet was quite rare. I also had an eggplant and some tomatoes and there was basil in the garden.

parsley steaks

Chargrill 2 cm thick fillet steaks for 2 minutes a side and top with Parsley Butter (see PARSLEY).

hamburger surprise

Slip a nugget of garlic butter or blue cheese worked with butter into a hamburger before cooking to provide a delicious surprise.

I eggplant, cubed
salt
2 onions, sliced
olive oil
I clove garlic, finely sliced
I tablespoon Satay Sauce
  (see p. 446) or chutney
I teaspoon sambal oelek
2 cold baked or boiled
  potatoes, chopped
200 g leftover rare roast beef,
  finely sliced
2 tomatoes, chopped
6 fresh basil leaves, torn
sea salt
freshly ground black pepper
2 tablespoons extra-virgin
  olive oil

Sprinkle eggplant with salt and leave to sweat for 30 minutes. Fry onion in 2 tablespoons oil until starting to caramelise, then add garlic.

Put satay sauce and sambal oelek into a salad bowl and tip in onion and garlic. Add potato and beef. Rinse eggplant and pat dry, then fry in oil until golden brown. Add eggplant to bowl. Turn everything slowly and carefully, so every piece of meat and vegetable receives its share of sauce.

Put tomato into a different bowl, then scatter over basil and add a few flakes of sea salt and a grinding of pepper. Splash over extra-virgin olive oil and leave to soak up flavours. Transfer beef salad to a flat platter and scatter with basil fragments on chopping board. Serve tomato salad alongside.

stephanie's famous steak sandwich

SERVES I

Often imitated but never equalled, much less bettered, this sandwich has been a best-seller at Stephanie's Restaurant for nearly a decade. It is so popular that we cannot take it from the lunch menu.

I slice sourdough bread
olive oil
4–6 flat mushrooms
20 g softened butter
½ cup water
salt
freshly ground black pepper
2 x 80 g slices fillet steak
¼ cup Fast Red-wine Sauce
  (see p. 105)
(continued next page)

Toast bread on one side. Paint untoasted side with oil and set aside. Cook mushrooms in a small frying pan with butter and water until juices run and mushrooms look shiny. Keep warm.

Season steak and grill quickly, turning once (about 3 minutes each side for medium, 2 minutes each side for medium–rare). Keep warm. Heat sauce and drop in mushrooms. Remove from heat.

Quickly grill or toast oiled side of bread.

¼ cup Caramelised Onions
    (see p. 465)
½ cup well-squeezed cooked
    spinach

Warm caramelised onion. Reheat spinach and pile on toast. Place meat on top and mushrooms around. Top with onion and spoon remaining sauce on and around.

aunt nora's steak and kidney pudding   SERVES 4–6

If you need to feed the masses, double this quantity and make 2 puddings.

1 kg blade steak, cut into
    2 cm cubes
250 g ox kidney, trimmed and
    cut into small pieces
1½ tablespoons plain flour
125 g flat mushrooms, roughly
    chopped
1 small onion, very finely
    chopped
1 teaspoon salt
freshly ground black pepper
½ cup rich stock *or* water

SUET CRUST
500 g plain flour
250 g coarsely grated suet
2 teaspoons baking powder
1 teaspoon salt
1 cup water

Grease a 1 litre basin. To make the suet crust, mix ingredients and knead lightly. The dough should not be too stiff. Roll two-thirds of dough quite thinly into a round and line basin.

Combine steak and kidney with flour, mushrooms, onion, salt and pepper. Pack into basin. Roll out remaining dough to make lid. Wet edges and press to seal very well. Stand basin on a steamer rack in a stockpot and pour in boiling water to come two-thirds of the way up its sides. Cover and steam for 4 hours (you may need to top up water from time to time).

To serve, heat stock to boiling. Remove basin from water very carefully (wrap it with a napkin to prevent being burnt). Cut a small hole in the lid and carefully pour in stock. Wait 10 minutes before serving. The pudding is traditionally served at the table from the basin still wrapped in the napkin. I like serving a purée of buttery parsnip with this and a big dish of beans or crisply sautéed cabbage.

simplest beef stew   SERVES 4–6

This stew is a good example of how you can fling everything together in 15 minutes and forget about it while it's cooking. Experiment with ingredients: you may want to include caraway seeds or chilli paste or chutney, for example. The variations are endless.

1.5 kg chuck *or* blade steak,
    cut into large cubes
2 tablespoons plain flour
(continued next page)

Preheat oven to 180°C. Roll beef in flour mixed with paprika. Place in an enamelled cast-iron casserole that will hold ingredients comfortably with not too much extra space.

2 teaspoons paprika

1 x 425 g can peeled tomatoes

2 onions, diced

2 cloves garlic, sliced

1 stick celery, finely sliced

3 carrots, peeled and cut into chunks

3 potatoes, cut into chunks

1 cup red wine

salt

freshly ground black pepper

Whizz tomatoes and their juice in a food processor, or crush roughly with a wooden spoon, and add to meat. Add remaining ingredients to casserole and stir. Press a piece of baking paper over contents and cover with lid. Cook in oven, undisturbed, for 1½ hours. Taste for seasoning. Check if meat is tender and cook longer if necessary. Offer a bowl of yoghurt and maybe a small bowl of sliced pickled dill cucumbers.

other recipes

baked bananas with meatloaf *see* BANANAS

bolognese sauce *see* PASTA AND NOODLES

chilli con carne *see* BEANS, DRIED

cock-a-leekie *see* LEEKS

grilled spiced beef on rosemary skewers *see* ROSEMARY

middle eastern meatballs with coriander leaves *see* CORIANDER

mum's steak and kidney pie *see* KIDNEYS

pine nut and meat pastries *see* NUTS

satay marinade and sauce *see* NUTS

simple ginger marinade for rump steak *see* GINGER

stuffed bush marrow with yoghurt sauce *see* ZUCCHINI AND SQUASH

winemerchant's sauce for a grilled steak *see* ONIONS

see also KIDNEYS; LIVER; OXTAIL; TONGUE; TRIPE

b e e t r o o t s   *Beta vulgaris* is a native of the Mediterranean region. The early Romans ate only the leaves, a reminder to modern cooks that the whole plant is edible.   The beetroot (or beet as it is known in the United States) struggles for popularity. Is it because many of us are reminded of ugly salad sandwiches, where purple beetroot juice stained awful white bread, or bowls of sliced beetroot floating in throat-grabbing vinegar served up for Sunday tea? Or is it because beetroots take a long time to cook, and are therefore not a likely impulse buy? Or maybe it's because they can be messy to prepare (Jane Grigson called beetroot 'the bossy vegetable' because its colour can take over the kitchen).   Its lack of popularity is a pity, as beetroot properly prepared is a sophisticated vegetable that contributes glamour and satisfaction via its glorious colour and lovely, suave sweetness. (Its smooth texture and sweet flavour partners game particularly well.) Having said that, the small hybrid beetroots have become very popular. Their startling colours look wonderful in all manner of salads, both cooked and raw.   All this aside, beetroot is wonderfully versatile – it can be steamed, boiled, baked or grated and eaten hot, cold or raw – and well worth the effort.

VARIETIES AND SEASON

Standard large red varieties are not identified by name in the shops (home gardeners will be familiar with Detroit dark red and Darwin globe). These beetroots range in colour from deep purple to pale red. Mature beetroots are the size of a tennis ball, while baby or mini beets are picked when the size of a golf ball. There is also a rarely encountered red, long oval variety, the cylindra. Newer beetroot hybrids can be gold, white or red-and-white striped and are picked at golf-ball size. These smaller varieties do not bleed in the same way as the standard form. Beetroots are available all year, with the peak season being June–November.

SELECTION AND STORAGE

Fresh beetroots should be smooth-skinned, with no splitting or scars around the tops. (Red beets, if faded, have probably been subjected to high temperatures while growing, when they are actually a temperate crop.) The leaves can look floppy, especially in warm weather, but should be intact. Do not buy a beetroot if the stems have been cut level with the root as the colour will start to leach from it as soon as it is put into water.

Beetroots can be stored in an airy cupboard or in the refrigerator crisper in a vegetable storage bag for up to 2 weeks. The leaves and stems should be used within 2 days of purchase.

PREPARATION AND COOKING

The preparation for both large and small beetroots is the same. Cut the stems and leaves away from the beetroot, leaving 2–3 cm attached. The leaves will revive after a good soak in cold water. Wash well as the closely packed stems are a good hiding place for insects. Wash the beetroot to remove any surface soil. Do *not* cut off the long tapering root. Beetroots should never be peeled before cooking unless you wish the colour to run (if making a soup, for example).

TO BOIL, BAKE OR STEAM | **Boil** Boil medium-sized beetroots in plenty of lightly salted water for 1½ hours or until tender. Small beetroots will only take 30 minutes. **Bake** Wrap medium-sized beetroots in foil and bake them at 180°C for 2 hours or until tender. **Steam** Larger beetroots will take 1 hour to become tender when steamed, while small beetroots will take 15–20 minutes (keep an eye on the water level in the steamer!).

Whether boiling, baking or steaming beetroots, the final steps are the same. To test for doneness, insert a fine skewer. It should slip right through the beetroot. Rub skins off beetroots under running water (wear rubber gloves to avoid purple-stained hands). Allow the beetroots to cool a little before slicing and dressing. (The flavour will blend better, however, if the dressing hits the beetroot while it is still warm.) The chopping board will need a good scrub – coarse kitchen salt will help. If serving plain, toss butter or a little oil through the cooked beetroot. Serve beetroot salads warm or at room temperature. Boiled or steamed beetroots can be blended with thick cream to make an exotic purée that is marvellous served with game dishes.

THE LEAVES | Blanch the washed leaves and stems in lightly salted boiling water for 5 minutes. Chop the leaves into smaller pieces and add to soups, stuffings, salads or pasta sauces or stew them with olive oil in a covered pan.

FOR SOUPS AND SAUCES | Soups and consommés made with beetroot can take on a less attractive rust-red or brownish colour through overcooking or boiling. Add a small amount of raw or cooked, grated or diced beetroot to the dish moments before serving to restore the colour.

beetroot dip
Purée roasted beetroots with olive oil, finely chopped garlic and chilli to a consistency suitable for dipping. Stir in ground roasted cumin and coriander seeds and salt to taste. Serve with toasted pita bread.

simple clear beetroot soup
SERVES 4

As already mentioned, when cooking beetroots in broth the lovely ruby colour changes to brownish red after boiling. A final garnish of either shredded cooked beetroot or a little freshly infused beetroot stock improves the colour.

3 beetroots, boiled and peeled
1.5 litres well-flavoured beef,
    Veal or Chicken Stock
salt
freshly ground black pepper
juice of 1 lemon
1 tablespoon freshly chopped
    parsley
2 teaspoons freshly chopped
    chives
sour cream

If beetroot leaves are not too bruised or wilted, wash well, slice finely and leave aside. Cut beetroots into small neat dice. Leave aside 2–3 tablespoons for garnish and put rest into a large saucepan with stock. Bring to simmering point. Simmer very gently for 30 minutes.

Blanch leaves in lightly salted water for 2–3 minutes. Drain very well and chop into bite-sized pieces. Just before serving, drop reserved beetroot and blanched leaves into soup and season with salt, pepper and lemon juice. Mix herbs with sour cream and offer separately. The soup can also be served cold.

grated beetroot
Mix grated raw beetroot with grated carrot, finely sliced celery, toasted walnuts, cider vinegar and honey for a crunchy salad.

tossed beetroot
Give refrigerated beetroot a lift by tossing it with warm olive oil or adding warm potato or hardboiled egg.

very simple cold borscht

SERVES 4

4 medium–large beetroots
2 large white onions, very
    finely chopped
2 sticks celery, very finely
    chopped
1 tablespoon olive oil
1 tablespoon best-quality red-
    wine or sherry vinegar
2 tablespoons freshly chopped
    parsley
salt
freshly ground black pepper
200 ml cream

Simmer trimmed beetroots for 2 hours until tender. Rub off and discard skins. Cut beetroots into chunks and blend with sufficient cooking water to make a thickish soup. Do not aim for a super-smooth purée. Texture is desirable!

Sauté onion and celery in oil until well softened (about 10 minutes), stirring occasionally. Drain very well and add to soup with vinegar, parsley, salt and pepper. Lastly, whisk in cream. Serve chilled.

beetroot crisps
Shave strips of beetroot and other root vegetables with a potato peeler and deep-fry at 160°C to make exotic crisps to go with drinks.

stewed beetroots
Stew parboiled, peeled small beetroots in olive oil or butter, grind over pepper and scatter with chives and parsley.

buttered grated beetroot

SERVES 4

Serve this as a luxury vegetable with a grilled steak or, even better, a grilled squab pigeon.

2 cups grated raw beetroot
60 g unsalted butter
1 tablespoon water
2 teaspoons red-wine vinegar
salt
freshly ground black pepper

Place beetroot, butter, water and vinegar in a small saucepan and cook, covered, for 8 minutes, stirring once or twice. Uncover and check beetroot is just tender. Raise heat and boil off any extra liquid, if necessary, and season. The beetroot should still be a little crisp and look shiny from the butter.

capers Scatter over a teaspoon of drained, deep-fried capers as an unusual and delicious garnish. The tiny buds open like minuscule flowers.

other recipes **raw beetroot and yoghurt salad** *see* YOGHURT

berries and currants

When I was a child, gathering blackberries was a seasonal adventure, enjoyed in the same way as gathering mushrooms is. One returned with purple mouth and hands and any exposed limbs scratched and streaked with a mix of blood and purple fruit juice. The buckets of fruit were turned into blackberry jam, eaten with clotted cream, or spread on buttered wholemeal bread. In my home we always had Grandma's bramble cake for dinner that night! │ Today Australian markets offer a wonderful array of berries from spring through to autumn (and year round, in the case of strawberries), with new varieties extending the once much shorter fresh seasons. The popularity of English summer pudding as an alternative to the traditional boiled plum pudding in Australia surely owes something to this and, of course, to the reality of a hot Christmas. │ It is easy to be bountiful with berries. I love a mix of crimson raspberries, scarlet strawberries and dark-purple blackberries tossed together and heaped in a shallow bowl lined with strawberry leaves. I have an old-fashioned powdered-sugar castor that I bring out at berry time, and enjoy offering soft white cheese, mascarpone or thick cream that stands in peaks, too. >

berries

go

with

cream

sour cream

crème fraîche

fresh white cheese

sugar

honey

lemon juice

pastry

butter

balsamic vinegar

Cointreau

Grand Marnier

kirsch

Amaretto di
 Saronno

brandy

light red wine

port

tokay

Many berries cook magnificently – especially raspberries and blackberries. As we all know, berries make wonderful jams, jellies and sauces. Strawberries are delicious sliced and warmed very briefly in a liqueur before being folded in a pancake, piled onto a waffle or used to fill a shortcake. And you should cultivate anyone who has a prolific mulberry tree!

VARIETIES AND SEASON

Home gardeners and professional growers will be familiar with the varietal names of raspberries, strawberries and other berries. The general public, however, is rarely introduced to these names. Few of us could recognise a willamette raspberry from a fairview, or a shasta strawberry from a tioga. Be assured that there are significant differences in flavour, scent, size, colour, texture and season. It is because growers plant different varieties that we are able to enjoy berry fruits for such a long season.

Incidentally, the blackberry and its hybrids (including the loganberry, youngberry and boysenberry) and the raspberry are members of the *Rubus* genus. Occasionally in advertisements for pick-your-own berry farms one reads of 'rubus' growers. Now you know what they grow!

BLACKBERRY | *Rubus fruticosus* is the luscious fruit of the thorny bramble bush and a member of the rose family. It is claimed that Baron Ferdinand von Mueller, the designer of Melbourne's Botanic Gardens, sprinkled seed of the common bramble along country byways to offer nourishing nibbles to bushwalkers. Blackberry canes spread quickly and form dense and impenetrable barriers. The blackberry is classified as a noxious weed in Australia and farmers do all they can to eradicate it from their properties. That said, there are often stands of blackberries along country roads.

The many blackberry hybrids, in which the spreading habit of the wild plant has been controlled more or less, have extended the season from early summer to mid-autumn. Some of the best known are the loganberry, youngberry and boysenberry. The *loganberry* looks like a large raspberry but is a distinctive pink–burgundy colour and ripens in mid-summer (late December–January). The *youngberry* is black–purple when ripe and is harvested just after the loganberry. A large berry with very fine hairs, the *boysenberry* is exceptionally juicy and is harvested just after the youngberry.

BLUEBERRY | Native to North America and part of the *Vaccinium* genus, blueberries have white or pale-green flesh, insignificant seeds and deep-blue skin with a waxy gloss. Varieties vary a great deal in size and shape. Blueberries are a new crop to Australia, with the first research plantings in the late 1960s. We now have a thriving industry established in the coastal and cooler regions of the east coast from Queensland to Tasmania and in the south-west of Western Australia. Blueberries are available September–March, the peak season being November–February.

CURRANT

Red, black and white currants are not grapes, despite the confusion with the name of the dried grape. They are the fruit of the *Ribes* species, along with the gooseberry. Currants grow wild across the whole of Europe and north Asia to Siberia. The modern improved varieties have larger berries. The small, shiny berries are exquisite to look upon and unique in flavour. **Red** and ***white*** currants are tart, delicate and intense. They are almost always cooked, either as a jam or jelly, or combined with other fruit to create jewel-like fruit tarts. White currants are sweeter than redcurrants. ***Blackcurrants*** have the most intense colour and flavour of all and are used to make blackcurrant juice, jam and crème de cassis, the liqueur used to make a kir when mixed with white wine and a kir royale when mixed with sparkling wine. Once cooked with sugar their almost medicinal flavour makes a rich, powerfully flavoured tart filling. The leaves of the blackcurrant bush have a distinctive scent and are sometimes used to add flavour to pickling vinegars for fruit pickles (plums, for example). Currants are available briefly in December and occasionally in January.

GOOSEBERRY

Ribes grossularia still grows wild in northern regions of Europe and Africa. Cultivated gooseberries do best when allowed to ripen slowly in climates with cold winters and cool summers. Scotland and Tasmania both produce excellent gooseberries. There are more than a hundred varieties but they are usually described as the red, green and yellow types. All have finely veined and transparent skin. In Australia the roaring lion gooseberry, which becomes red when ripe, is the variety almost always grown. Its fruit is often picked green when at its most sour and acidic and marketed as being good for making pies and tarts. The flavour develops in cooking with the addition of sugar. Gooseberries are most plentiful December–January, and are only available in the summer months.

MULBERRY

Morus nigra, the black mulberry, is a large tree, not a bush. Botanically its fruit are not true berries but 'collective fruit'. The fruit is first green, then pink and finally becomes a purple–red. When ripe, black mulberries have a rich, winey flavour. Stains from mulberry juice are impossible to remove from clothing. *M. alba* and *M. rubra* bear white and red fruit, respectively.

Mulberry trees, once valued for both their fruit and leaves, which were used to feed silkworms, can be found in established Australian gardens but their commercial production is still small. Mulberries are available October–February, depending on climatic conditions.

RASPBERRY

The raspberry (*Rubus idaeus*) is a member of the rose family and still grows wild all over Europe. Raspberries are the most heavenly of fruits. I can think of few taste experiences so pure and satisfying. One swallows a perfect berry and the flavour wells around the mouth like the finest wine. Raspberries need protection from heat and drying winds and do best in Tasmania and elevated parts of the mainland. There are red, black and yellow raspberries but only the red is grown widely in Australia. In the last few years, however, delicious, velvety golden raspberries, as well as a black variety, have appeared in some specialised markets. Buy them if you are lucky enough to see them.

There are 2 main types of raspberry grown commercially – those that fruit once a year in summer and those that fruit twice a year, in summer and autumn. The season for summer raspberries extends from late November to February, with peak supplies in January. The autumn-bearing raspberries produce their second crop March–April.

STRAWBERRY

The fruit of the genus *Fragaria*, a member of the rose family, is practically everyone's favourite. The exquisite true wild or wood strawberry – *F. vesca* – has been known and highly esteemed in Europe for centuries but is rarely seen in Australia. Today's commercial varieties are all descended from quite different species introduced to Europe from North and South America in the seventeenth and eighteenth centuries. Other related tiny strawberries, sold as alpine strawberries, are sometimes available at plant nurseries.

Strawberries are harvested in southern Australia during summer and in Queensland in winter, making them available all year round. The peak season is September–January. Although varieties now grown have improved in flavour and juiciness and are more likely to have been picked fully ripe, it is still wise to remember that some strawberries appearing in the southern States during winter may not be worth eating. Beware of varieties grown for their durability rather than flavour.

SELECTION AND STORAGE

Most berries are at their best picked from the bush while still warm from the sun. Most ought to be picked so ripe that they will only last the next day or so. If you do not grow any berries, the next best thing is to visit a pick-your-own farm. (Go early in the day, before you and the fruit wilt under the hot sun.) When buying fruit in punnets, inspect the container carefully and turn it upside down. Refuse any fruit that is squashed and any punnet that is oozing juice or that smells even faintly fermented. Once home, discard any berries that are at all damaged. Most berries should be refrigerated, unwashed, on a plate lined with kitchen paper and covered with plastic film.

Blackberry The best wild blackberries are those gathered a week or so after they have achieved full colour. This is usually in early autumn. When picking blackberries to make jam or jelly, also pick some not-so-ripe fruit. These berries have a higher percentage of pectin, which is necessary to help the jam or jelly set quickly. **Blueberry** These berries do not ripen further after picking and the first of the season are not necessarily the sweetest. If you grow a blueberry bush you will know that the clusters of berries do not ripen simultaneously. Leave the berries on the bush for a few days after they turn blue as the flavour will improve. Do not store blueberries in a metal container as pigments in the berries can cause a reaction with the metal and dark, unattractive stains can be transferred to both the berries and the container. These fruit last very well under refrigeration for at least a week. **Currant** All currants will hang on the bush for several weeks once fully ripe. Redcurrants should be brilliantly coloured in the punnet. Store, refrigerated, for up to a week. **Gooseberry** In my opinion gooseberry tarts and pies are best made with fruit that has been allowed to ripen to a gold–green at least. The acidity of fully green fruit can be overwhelming. The fruit will continue to ripen off the bushes and keeps for weeks in a cool, dark place. **Mulberry** These berries are often picked underripe and can taste bland or sour. Unripe fruit will continue to ripen if stored in a warm place for a day or so. If picked ripe but too long ago, mulberries quickly develop a 'beery' smell. These are to be avoided. Ripe fruit often falls from the tree and can then be gathered from the ground. Mulberries keep for a few days, refrigerated. **Raspberry** Even one mouldy raspberry in a punnet will taint the rest. Raspberries should be picked fully ripe and eaten within 2 days of purchase. **Strawberry** Strawberries should be picked with their stems and calyces (green 'crowns') intact. Avoid berries displaying white or, worse still, green coloration around the top of the berry. Check that there are no soft spots or bruises. Avoid underdeveloped strawberries with patches of prominent seeds. Ripe strawberries have glossy skins. Store in the refrigerator and use as soon as possible.

PREPARATION

One of the delights of using berry fruits is the minimal preparation they require. If berries have been stored in the refrigerator, remove them at least 30 minutes before you wish to serve them. Their true flavour is revealed at room temperature.

Avoid washing berries unless they are very muddy. (***Mulberries*** are the exception to this rule as often they have been gathered from the ground.) If berries do need washing, do it very briefly and drain and dry them well. (Do not remove the stems and calyces from *strawberries* before washing them, otherwise the fruit will absorb water.) Place the fruit in a colander and either spray with a fine hose or dip the colander in and out of a sink half-filled with water. Allow the fruit to drain in the colander and then tip it onto a tray lined with lots of kitchen paper.

Before cooking, pull *currants* from their stalks unless making jelly, cut the tops and tails off *gooseberries*, and hull *strawberries* (remove stems and calyces). Always use non-reactive (enamelled cast-iron or stainless steel) pans to cook berries. Aluminium pans can alter the colour of the fruit.

recipes

strawberry salmon

Partner smoked salmon with ripe strawberries and freshly ground black pepper.

old-fashioned raspberry vinegar

MAKES I LITRE

Use whenever a light, fruity vinegar is required or as a cordial with soda for a fancy summer drink.

500 g raspberries
2 cups white-wine vinegar *or* red-wine vinegar
2 cups castor sugar

Lightly crush berries in a food processor, then tip into a glass, china or stainless steel bowl and pour over vinegar. Stand bowl overnight. Next day, strain through a fine sieve into a preserving jar or thick, clean jar of any sort. Add sugar and stir well. Stand jar in a preserving pan and add cold water until it comes two-thirds up sides of jar. Bring to a boil slowly, stirring occasionally. Simmer for 1 hour. Strain into hot, sterilised bottles, then seal and keep in a cool, dark place.

quick strawberry jam

MAKES 3 CUPS

This is my grandmother's recipe. The jam is very lightly set and is a glorious clear red, through which one can see whole berries.

500 g ripe small strawberries
750 g sugar
¼ teaspoon tartaric acid

Hull strawberries and halve if large. Put berries into a stainless steel or enamelled cast-iron saucepan. Cook gently, uncovered, for 15 minutes (no water is needed for this). Add sugar and tartaric acid, stirring until sugar has dissolved. Increase heat and boil rapidly for 10–15 minutes until setting stage is reached. Remove from heat and stir as jam cools a little. Divide fruit and liquid between hot, sterilised jars and seal.

simple redcurrant jelly

MAKES 2 CUPS

There is no need to strip the redcurrants from their stems when making this simple preserve, which can also be made from blackcurrants.

500 g redcurrants
500 g sugar

Combine currants and sugar in a stainless steel or enamelled cast-iron saucepan and crush fruit against sides. Bring to a boil, stirring once to ensure there is no undissolved sugar, then boil hard for 8 minutes. Skim and strain mixture, then quickly pour into hot, sterilised jars and seal.

gooseberry butter

MAKES I LITRE

An unusual and lovely filling for tartlets or sponge cakes.

1 kg gooseberries
2 tablespoons water
500 g castor sugar
100 g unsalted butter
4 eggs, lightly beaten

Put fruit and water into an enamelled cast-iron or stainless steel saucepan, then cover and simmer for 10 minutes or until fruit is tender. Press fruit through a sieve and return to rinsed-out pan. Add sugar to purée and stir over moderate heat until sugar has dissolved. Add butter a lump at a time and stir until combined. Beat in eggs well with a wooden spoon over a low heat until mixture thickens, about 10 minutes. Do not allow mixture to boil or it will curdle. Pour into warm, sterilised jars and seal.

raspberry sauce

MAKES I CUP

This sauce is often called a raspberry coulis, a French word that means a thick purée of fruit or vegetable. Use it with other fruit (its most famous use is in a peach Melba), chocolate cake or ice-cream. Exactly the same method will make a blackberry, mulberry or strawberry sauce, all of which will keep for a few days under refrigeration and freeze perfectly.

250 g raspberries
juice of 1 lemon
½ cup castor sugar
1 tablespoon brandy or other liqueur (optional)

Blend ingredients in a food processor until shiny and sugar crystals have disappeared. Press through a coarse sieve to extract raspberry seeds. Taste for sweetness.

berry tart Toss whole strawberries in a spoonful of this sauce when making the Fresh Berry Tart on p. 122 (if you do this, omit the redcurrant glaze).

berry toast
Make French toast by dipping a slice of bread in egg whisked with a little milk and fry until crisp in butter, then top with warmed raspberries.

berry syrup
Toss strawberries or mulberries with castor sugar and a few spoonfuls of balsamic vinegar and allow to form a syrup at room temperature for 30 minutes. Serve with sponge-finger biscuits for dunking in the juices.

berry sponge
Fold mashed strawberries and/or raspberries into firmly whipped cream and fill a plain sponge cake. Dust with icing sugar.

strawberry shortcake

SERVES 4

Red, ripe strawberries are superb sliced and piled into a hot, buttered shortcake and eaten with thick cream.

250 g self-raising flour
pinch of salt
60 g sugar
80 g softened unsalted butter
2 egg yolks
50 ml milk
250 g strawberries, sliced
a little extra sugar
extra softened butter
icing sugar

Preheat oven to 180°C. Mix flour, salt and sugar in a large basin. Rub butter into flour mixture until it resembles breadcrumbs. Mix egg yolks lightly with milk. Make a well in dry ingredients and add liquid. Work together quickly to make a soft dough. Turn onto a baking tray and form into a round 4 cm thick × 15 cm diameter. Bake for 15 minutes until golden. Allow to cool a little.

Mix berries with a little sugar. Split shortcake into 2 layers and while still warm spread base with additional butter. Pile on sliced berries, lightly place on lid, dust with icing sugar and cut into wedges. Pass thick cream separately.

berry crumble
Strew Crumble Topping over raspberries, loganberries or blackberries, add a thin slice of butter and bake at 180°C for 15 minutes.

brandy berries
Warm blackberries or blueberries with sugar and brandy and serve over vanilla ice-cream or in a pancake.

fresh berry tart

SERVES 6–8

I cannot resist a well-made berry tart. For my taste the crust should be a well-baked shortcrust pastry rather than the more usual sweet shortcrust.

I quantity Shortcrust Pastry
I cup Pastry Cream
250 g berries
100 g red or white currants
   (optional)
3 tablespoons redcurrant or
   blackcurrant jelly, warmed

Line an 18 cm loose-bottomed flan tin with pastry and bake blind at 200°C for 20 minutes. Remove foil and weights and allow to cool.

Spread pastry cream over pastry case. Arrange berries (and currants, if using) thickly over cream, either in tightly fitting concentric circles or piled on for a more random effect. With a large spoon, glaze tart with melted jelly. Eat within an hour or two before the pastry cream softens the base of the tart.

cream cheese Replace the pastry cream with cream cheese processed with an equal quantity of cream. This is delicious but super-rich!

grandma's bramble cake

This is my family's heirloom dish. It has the same appeal as a berry crumble – lots of hot juices – but in this case the berries are piled into a rich lard pastry. Very rich, very indulgent but a truly wonderful dish. I use

*blackberries for tradition but I have also made this dessert with mulberries,
raspberries or gooseberries.*

1 quantity Lard Pastry
2 cups blackberries
1 egg
pinch of salt
1 tablespoon cold water
⅓–½ cup sugar (depending on
   sweetness of fruit)
60 g softened unsalted butter

Preheat oven to 200°C. Roll two-thirds of
pastry into a round 26 cm in diameter.
Transfer to a slightly larger ovenproof pie
plate. (The cake will be presented on this
plate.) Roll remaining dough into a 12 cm
round. The pastry should be 6 mm thick.

   Tip fruit into lined pie plate. Pleat pastry
around fruit, so that it resembles an old-
fashioned mob cap. The edges should lean
in, containing the fruit like a wall. Rest the smaller pastry round on top.
Do not seal the lid or press it down heavily as it has to be removed after
baking. Put pie plate on a baking tray with a rim in case juices run.
Whisk egg, salt and cold water together. Brush pastry with this eggwash.

   Bake for 25 minutes until pastry is cooked and golden brown. Take
cake from oven and, using a spatula, carefully lever off lid. Tip in sugar
and butter. Replace lid and leave cake in a warm place for at least 15
minutes and up to 30 minutes before cutting and serving in wedges. Be
prepared – use a spoon as well as a knife and a pie lifter to serve. There
will be plenty of delicious juices. Serve with clotted or thick cream.

blueberry muffins

MAKES 12

200 g blueberries
220 g plain flour
2 teaspoons baking powder
125 g sugar
¾ cup milk or buttermilk
1 egg
¾ cup vegetable oil

Preheat oven to 180°C and thoroughly
grease 12 muffin tins with a little oil. Halve
berries. Sift flour and baking powder and
stir in sugar. Mix milk, egg and oil together.
Make a well in centre of flour and beat in
liquid. Mix in berries. Spoon batter into
muffin tins until two-thirds full. Bake for
20–25 minutes. Cool muffins on a wire
rack. Serve slightly warm, split, with butter and jam or just jam.

summer pudding

SERVES 4

*It is possible to make a good summer pudding using some frozen fruit. It is
not, however, possible to make a good summer pudding using all frozen
fruit, as the quality of the juice is diminished. Strawberries are not good,
and too many blackberries or blackcurrants will result in purple juice rather
than rich crimson.*

gooseberry tart
*Substitute 1 cup
gooseberries for the
apples in Apple
Yeast Sugar Tart
(see APPLES).*

**strawberries and
amaretti**
*Sprinkle strawberries
with Grand Marnier
or Cointreau and a
little castor sugar
and crumble a few
amaretti biscuits
among the juices.
Offer sour or thick
cream or crème
fraîche separately.*

**berries and
cheese**
*Serve strawberries
and/or raspberries
with a fresh white
cheese, such as
Whitelaw or
whipped ricotta,
and offer a jug of
pouring cream.*

1 loaf thinly sliced bread,
    crusts removed
½ cup water
125 g sugar
125 g redcurrants stripped
    from their stalks
125 g loganberries *or*
    mulberries
375 g raspberries

Cut sufficient triangles of bread to line the bottom of a 1 litre basin. The lining should be a good fit to prevent premature or excessive loss of juice. Cut slices to line sides. Reserve 2–3 slices to form the lid.

Place water and sugar in a large saucepan. Cover and simmer until sugar has dissolved. Add any frozen fruit now and allow it to thaw. Tip in fresh fruit and give a good stir. Cover and allow fruit to return to a boil, then remove from heat. Stand a colander or muslin-lined strainer over a bowl and tip in fruit and liquid. Leave until juice has drained into bowl. Reserve juice. Allow fruit to cool completely.

Place bread-lined basin on a tray with a rim or on a large, rimmed plate. Spoon in fruit right to top. Level fruit, then pour over a little reserved juice, so that filling looks wet but is not swimming in liquid (keep any remaining juice for serving). Cover with reserved bread. Place a double sheet of foil over pudding, then press in a saucer that just fits inside rim of basin. Weight saucer with tins and refrigerate pudding overnight or up to 2 days.

To serve, remove weights, saucer and foil. Place a deep serving plate over basin and invert carefully. The pudding should be a deep crimson and some juice will ooze and seep onto the serving plate. If the colour is not as rich as you would like, spoon over some of the extra juice. Offer the remaining juice when the pudding is cut, along with thick cream.

other recipes

fig and raspberry tart *see* FIGS
fig won tons *see* FIGS
honey wafers with bruised raspberries *see* HONEY
rhubarb and red fruit sago sauce *see* RHUBARB

b o k   c h o y

bok choy A bowl of rice, some stir-fried greens and at least a quarter of the world's population is satisfied every day! The Asian fresh-produce stores in all Australian capital cities have introduced interested shoppers to a world of different foods, especially green vegetables. Shops displaying vegetables arranged in shining green mounds seduce food lovers with the undeniable freshness of the produce and the enthusiasm with which these goods are selected by our Vietnamese and Chinese migrants. Bok choy is included here not only because it is one of my favourite green vegetables, but as a reminder that alongside it will be *gai laan* (Chinese broccoli, *see* BROCCOLI), with its fleshy stem and white flowers, and the more slender, yellow-flowered *choi sum* (Chinese flowering cabbage) and many more delicious vegetables. The small bundles of bok choy deserve star treatment. Also known as bak choy, bak choi, baak choi and pak choi, bok choy or Chinese white cabbage (*Brassica chinensis*) has a number of pale-green, broad, fleshy stems joined at the base. Each stem has a rounded dark-green leaf and the stems and leaves are folded fatly like a flower-bud. >

Bok choy is very versatile and equally delicious in Western and Asian cooking. It has a mild but distinct cabbage flavour and its leaf stalks are succulent and crisp when correctly cooked. It is stir-frying that gives Asian vegetables their crunchy, shiny, slippery and delectable character.

VARIETIES AND SEASON

There are many varieties of bok choy, including larger plants with fleshy white stems and crisp, olive-coloured leaves. Bok choy is at its best in the cooler months, April–October.

SELECTION AND STORAGE

If you are able to, purchase bok choy from an Asian food store. The turnover is huge and the produce has to be very fresh to satisfy the discerning customers. Only buy fresh-looking, supple greens without any trace of insect damage or yellow or withered leaves.

Like all members of the *Brassica* genus (which includes cabbages, Brussels sprouts, cauliflower and broccoli), this vegetable yellows after a few days and develops rank flavours. Refrigerate for no more than 2–3 days in vegetable storage bags in the crisper.

PREPARATION AND COOKING

Bok choy (and all other Asian greens) should be washed in lots of cold water to flush out any insects lurking inside the folded leaves. Swish the vegetables around quite vigorously. If the vegetables are to be split in half or cut into chunks, trim them before washing them. Bok choy needs little trimming if it is to be stir-fried or braised whole. An occasional insect-damaged leaf may need to be removed and the root end trimmed. If you prefer to stir-fry the leaves separately, cut through the root end to free the leaves and pay special attention to the ends of the leaves when washing.

While bok choy is often stir-fried ✓, it can also be boiled to produce a delicate vegetable accompaniment.

TO BOIL Cook whole or halved bok choy briefly in plenty of salted water. Drain extremely well in a colander to avoid diluting any accompanying sauce.

bok choy with fermented black beans   SERVES 2

The saltiness of fermented black beans is the perfect foil to bok choy's subtle flavour. For a change, try the recipe for Green Beans with Fermented Black Beans (see BEANS, FRESH) but use bok choy instead. Sweet roast pork (cha siu) can be bought from Asian food stores but is also easy to prepare at home (see p. 565).

I tablespoon vegetable oil
I clove garlic, crushed
I tablespoon fermented black
  beans
100 g Chinese sweet roast
  pork, diced
2 small bok choy, quartered
pinch of sugar
2 tablespoons water

Heat oil in a wok and stir-fry garlic, black beans and pork for 1–2 minutes. Add bok choy and toss to coat. Scatter on sugar and add water. Reduce heat, then cover and cook for 2 minutes. Serve with rice.

**chicken broth
with bok choy**
Stir-fry sliced bok choy with a couple of drops of light soy sauce and add to clear chicken broth with sliced chicken breast, slivers of mushroom and rice or egg noodles.

bok choy in hot and sour sauce   SERVES 2

I tablespoon vegetable oil
I dried chilli
2 small bok choy, quartered
pinch of salt
2 tablespoons sugar
I teaspoon cornflour
2 tablespoons cider vinegar
2 tablespoons light soy sauce
I tablespoon rice wine

Heat oil in a wok and toss chilli over a low heat for 1–2 minutes. Increase heat and add bok choy. Toss for 2 minutes until shiny. Combine remaining ingredients and stir into wok, mixing well. Turn into a dish and serve hot or cold with rice.

ginger bok choy
Boil bok choy stalks for 1 minute, then toss in a wok with oil and shredded ginger for 2 minutes. Season with sesame oil and serve.

b r a i n s   I consider brains a delicacy. They are delicate in flavour, tender of texture and combine well with sharp flavours and crisp textures. People from some cultures believe that eating brains will improve their own intelligence, while people from others believe the opposite and will not touch them. | Brains, like tripe, are remarkably popular in my restaurant, leading me to wonder how often one partner loves them while the other cannot bear either preparing or seeing them, so that the offal lover pounces on a dish when offered one. | While perhaps most associated with French cookery, brains are also enjoyed in Chinese cuisine, where texture is much appreciated. One of the most delicious brain preparations I have tasted is the steamed cucumber and lamb's brains in a spicy tomato sauce that is a speciality of Cheong Liew, Adelaide's master chef and the author of the wonderful *My Food*. Inspired by his Chinese grandmother but most definitely his own, this dish shows how East and West can meet in perfect harmony.

VARIETIES AND SEASON

Lamb's brains are inexpensive and available all year. Each brain is described and sold as a 'set'. There are many recipes in French classical cookery requiring *calf's* brains, which are the equivalent of 3 sets of lamb's brains and similar in flavour and texture. One might as well forget about these dishes. Restaurant owners can sometimes manage to divert calf's brains from an export order but I have never seen them in a suburban butcher's shop.

SELECTION AND STORAGE

The brains that I buy are usually frozen, packed in boxes of 6 and stamped for export. (Someone somewhere appreciates them.) Do not thaw frozen brains earlier than the evening before you intend to serve them. If brains are purchased fresh they must be refrigerated at once and used within a day or so as they are very perishable. Do *not* carry fresh brains around for hours in a shopping bag or hot car.

PREPARATION AND COOKING

Brains must be properly prepared – soaked, peeled and poached – to be palatable. Soak the brains in lightly salted cold water overnight in the refrigerator; this makes the removal of the membrane easier. Carefully peel off the membrane, removing all the bloody parts. Soak the brains again in clean salted water for an hour in the refrigerator.

Sometimes, and my butcher cannot explain why this is so, I receive brains that are pale and flabby and do not have any clear signs of blood vessels or membranes. These brains are devilish to peel and will never slip out of their membrane coating. When I have no alternative but to use brains such as these I prepare them differently. Using an ordinary potato peeler, peel the brains while still frozen and then soak them in salted water. Check each set again to ensure there are no traces of blood.

TO POACH | Poach the brains very gently in Court-bouillon ✑ for 5 minutes. Lift a set from the saucepan with a slotted spoon. It should feel just firm when pressed. Drain the brains on a clean cloth. Allow to cool and then cover until needed.

**brains
go
with**
capers
browned butter
lemons
walnuts
bacon
wine vinegar
balsamic vinegar
parsley
watercress
paprika
olive oil
spinach
green peas
spring onions
mushrooms
breadcrumbs
anchovies
tomatoes

recipes

brain salad with celery and mustard cream sauce

SERVES 4

When preparing the brains for this salad, keep any uneven bits to use when making the sauce.

brain bites
Deep-fry bite-sized pieces of poached brain in Beer Batter at 175°C until golden and crisp. Serve as a cocktail nibble with grilled pancetta and a spicy home-made relish.

bacon and brains
Combine crumbled crisp bacon with bite-sized pieces of crumbed brain as a filling for a wholemeal sandwich.

4 handfuls rocket or other green leaves of character, washed and dried
4 sets of brains, poached
salt
freshly ground black pepper
I tablespoon Dijon mustard
I teaspoon red-wine vinegar
2 tablespoons very finely chopped inner stalks celery
2 tablespoons freshly chopped parsley
200 ml cream, firmly whipped
I handful walnut halves, toasted

Arrange salad leaves on 4 plates. Cut brains into thin, even slices. (Reserve end slices and any irregular bits.) Overlap slices in centre of salad leaves and season.

In a food processor, blend reserved brain trimmings, mustard and vinegar to a cream. Scrape mixture into a bowl and fold in celery, parsley and whipped cream. Taste for seasoning and spoon over sliced brains. Scatter walnuts over and serve.

brains and artichoke hearts with browned butter

SERVES 4

2 tablespoons olive oil
100 g cold unsalted butter
4 artichoke hearts, cooked and quartered
4 sets of brains, poached
salt
white pepper
8 fresh sage leaves
½ lemon, peeled, diced and seeded
juice of ½ lemon
2 tablespoons freshly chopped parsley

Heat oil and 40 g of the butter and sauté artichoke for several minutes. Add brains and sauté until lightly coloured on both sides and warmed through. Remove artichoke and brains to a warm plate or oven set at 150°C. Season lightly.

Wipe out pan and return it to heat with sage and diced lemon. Wait a moment, then stir in remaining butter and allow to colour to a rich brown. Instantly stop butter cooking by adding lemon juice. Replace brains and artichoke, then add parsley and spoon at once onto a hot serving dish. **broad beans or peas** Instead of artichoke hearts, add a handful of blanched, peeled broad beans or freshly cooked, shelled green peas with the second quantity of butter. **salad leaves** Serve on soft salad leaves dressed with the lemony sage butter from the pan.

brain fritters

SERVES 4

4 sets of brains, poached
salt
freshly ground black pepper
1 egg
2 tablespoons milk
1 cup fine breadcrumbs
100 g butter, clarified ✓

Separate the 2 lobes of each set of brains. Cut each lobe in half lengthwise and season. Whisk egg with milk. Dip each piece of brain in egg mixture and then coat well with breadcrumbs. Refrigerate for up to 1 hour. Fry until golden in clarified butter until golden and crunchy, about 3 minutes a side. Serve with Tartare Sauce ✓.

mayonnaise Try Mayonnaise ✓ mixed with sambal oelek and a teaspoonful of tomato purée instead of tartare sauce, or mix a little smooth Dijon and some grain mustard into the mayonnaise for a change, or horseradish. **seasonings** Replace a third of the breadcrumbs with freshly grated parmesan cheese. Or add chopped capers to the breadcrumbs. Or stir a generous quantity of chopped herbs into the whisked egg.

b r e a d

The essential ingredients of almost all bread are flour, water and salt. Most breads have a leavening agent, either yeast or an active starter, such as is used in the making of sourdough breads. | Bread was first made thousands of years ago by harvesting grains from wild plants, grinding the grains with stones, mixing this coarse flour with water, forming it into cakes and baking them in the sun. From these early beginnings came improved varieties of grain, the understanding that fermentation lightened bread and the use of ovens in which the breads were baked. | The 'simplification' of breadmaking was developed by commercial bakeries during the 1960s in Britain. A few minutes of intense mechanical agitation in high-speed mixers and the addition of 'emulsifiers' and 'improvers' replaced the conventional method of allowing the dough to prove and mature. By using the 'simplified' method the dough does not have a chance to ripen and develop naturally. Yeast is added more or less as a flavouring. At this time 95 per cent of the Australian public purchased white bread, of which 60 per cent was sliced and wrapped. The sliced and wrapped loaves were all produced by the simplified breadmaking method. >

From the 1970s onwards, however, demand increased for more varied breads. In addition to the spread of suburban hot-bread bakeries, which still produce more or less simplified breads, the specialist bakeries established to service the needs of Australia's ethnic populations found their clientele included those dissatisfied with simplified bread. Thanks to these communities we can now buy chewy Lebanese breads baked in wood-fired ovens, crusty French baguettes and country-style round loaves, satisfying white Italian pane duro loaves or ciabatta and focaccia, and Jewish challah and caraway rye breads, to name a few.

The bread industry illustrates well the problem I have with describing foods solely in terms of nutritional makeup. There is no doubt that all bread is low in fat and sugar and high in complex carbohydrates and dietary fibre. All bread also contains protein, vitamins and minerals. But what about texture and flavour! The best that can be said of sliced white bread is that it is nutritionally acceptable, convenient, universally available and easy to chew. By giving such lifeless examples the nutritional stamp of approval nutritionists are not helping to encourage young palates away from the bland and mediocre. I urge you to experiment with tasting and making different breads. Many people already enjoy making their own, not only for its flavour but also for the satisfaction gained from slow rhythmic kneading and the fragrance the rising or cooking loaf gives the kitchen. There are dozens of books on breadmaking; if you get involved, you will have a lifetime of discovery ahead of you.

VARIETIES

The following breads are those most commonly encountered in our bakeries.

Brown This bread contains a minimum of 50 per cent wholemeal flour.
Flat These breads can be leavened (pita bread, for example) or unleavened (mountain bread) and are common throughout the Middle East. Both are excellent as wrappers for food, as well as being useful toasted for salads or soups or to dip into sauces. **Mixed-grain** A mix of wholemeal and white flour, rye meal and rye flour, this bread can also include wheatgerm, cracked wheat and other cereals, and non-fat milk solids. **Rye** Dark rye bread has a higher proportion of rye flour than light rye, which must contain at least 30 per cent rye meal or flour. **Soda** Damper is a type of soda or quick bread, where flour, salt and water are mixed with bicarbonate of soda or baking powder. Other soda breads are often mixed with buttermilk or sour milk to add lightness to the mixture. **Sourdough** Rather than using yeast, sourdough bread is usually made from unbleached white flour and uses a 'starter', flour and water that is 'fed' with additional flour and water and allowed to ferment until judged ripe and ready to use. The characteristic sour taste of this bread is due to the presence of lactic acid.

Sourdough takes longer to ferment and rise (days, sometimes, rather than an hour or so) and produces a much more compact crumb and a chewier texture. **Sweetened** Also known as fancy breads, there is an almost infinite variety of these breads and pastries, which include croissants, brioches, muffins and crumpets. Some are now mainstream, others are baked by specialists. **White** Simplified or traditional methods can be used to make white bread, as can bleached or unbleached flour. Styles vary widely – from sliced, wrapped bread and crusty Italian or French loaves to dense, chewy substantial breads. **Wholemeal** This bread is also called wholegrain, wholewheat or wheatmeal, and has a minimum of 90 per cent wholemeal flour.

SELECTION AND STORAGE

It is not enough to know whether bread is made from white or rye flour to make an informed choice. You must also know *how* it is made to be sure that you are buying or making the style of bread you want. Whether bread is classifed as white, wholemeal, mixed-grain or rye it can be made by the 'simplified' method, with conventional yeast-sponge and dough, or sour-dough technique, or by other specialised methods.

When making your own bread you need to choose your yeast and flour carefully, as each is available in different forms with their own peculiarities.

YEAST Yeast can be bought fresh as a compressed block or dried as granules. One uses half the quantity of dried yeast to fresh. Recipes vary, but 1 tablespoon dried yeast will leaven 1 kg flour. *Fresh* yeast can become stale and lose its potency. Only buy fresh yeast that smells sweet and is creamy in colour, not dry, grey or at all crumbly. Store fresh yeast unwrapped in a small screw-top jar in the refrigerator, where it will be fine for a fortnight. *Dried* yeast comes in 2 forms – in small sachets, the contents of which usually need to be dissolved in a little lukewarm water before being added to the dry ingredients, or as instant granules that are added directly to the dry ingredients. I always use instant dried yeast for convenience. Store all dried yeast in the refrigerator.

FLOUR Look for flour sold as *strong, bread* or *pizza* flour. Such flours are milled from wheat that has a high gluten content. A gluten content of 12–15 per cent is necessary to trap the gas produced by the rising loaf, thereby assuring a well-aerated bread. Normal household flour is made from low-gluten soft wheat, with most of the bran extracted, and is bleached. Strong flours can have more or less of the bran left in them during the milling process. Some mills produce specialised flours, such as stone-ground wholemeal flour. Unbleached strong flour is widely available and will give a lovely creamy colour to your loaves.

Strong flours made from grains other than wheat can also be obtained. Each has its own characteristics that will enable the enthusiastic breadmaker to vary the flavour of breads *ad infinitum*.

Most breads should be stored at room temperature in a well-ventilated crock or bin, where it should keep for several days. Sourdough breads keep particularly well. Always keep the bread crock free of stale scraps of bread as these can turn your fresh bread mouldy. Wipe the crock out at least once a week and dry it in the sunshine. Bread, whole or sliced, can also be frozen, wrapped well, where it will keep for several weeks. As flat breads dry out quickly, store them in the freezer and warm them in the oven before use. Revive dry flat bread by sprinkling it with water and warming it in the oven.

PREPARATION AND COOKING

Bought bread requires no preparation, unless given in a particular recipe. There are, however, a number of steps that are required when making bread, and all home breadmakers should become familiar with them. And once the bread is cooked, never succumb to temptation and cut into it while still hot. You will compress the crumb of the bread, and hot bread is indigestible!

SPONGING Some recipes instruct you to mix the yeast with a small amount of the flour and water and leave it to 'sponge'. This sponge is later incorporated into the larger mass of flour. This is old-fashioned breadmaking, largely unnecessary these days due to our stronger and faster commercial yeasts. I ignore these instructions and add the total water to the total flour in a single operation.

KNEADING Kneading is the essential action of working the dough to develop the gluten and transform a sticky mix into a smooth and elastic dough. It can be done in an electric mixer fitted with a dough hook quite satisfactorily, but new breadmakers should knead a few loaves by hand until they can easily recognise the moment at which their bread is fully kneaded. **To knead by hand** Kneading by hand should be a slow, gentle process. Start by lightly flouring your workbench. Curl your fingers over the back of the piece of dough, then lift and fold the dough towards you. With the heel of your hand, push the dough away from you. Repeat this process, giving the dough a quarter turn after every 2 kneads, until the dough is smooth and elastic. It takes about 15 minutes to knead 1 kg bread dough by hand.

PROVING Proving bread dough is usually described in terms of the dough 'doubling' in size, which it will do in widely varying times, depending on variables such as the type and quantity of yeast used and the temperature of the day and the area where the bread is being made. Standard bread doughs will double in size in about 1½ hours in a draught-free place, best in a covered, greased bowl.

KNOCKING BACK

This instruction refers to dough that has proved. It usually means to tip the risen dough onto the workbench and fold or punch it to collapse it; the dough is then kneaded again. The dough is then usually left to prove a second time. Knocking back dough slows down the rising. The slower the rising process or processes before the bread is baked, the better the flavour and aeration.

CRUSTINESS

The crust of a bread is affected by such things as the shape of the loaf, the character of the dough, the heat of the oven, the cooking time and whether the bread is misted with water during baking. Cook bread at a high temperature and ensure that the oven is preheated. The baking trays should also be heated if the loaf is free-form and to be rolled from a floured cloth directly onto the tray. A water spray is an essential kitchen gadget for the dedicated bread-maker. Both the sides of the oven as well as the loaves should be sprayed quickly several times during the baking process to increase the finished crust.

TESTING HOLLOW

A thoroughly cooked loaf will sound hollow when the bottom crust is rapped with the knuckles. Most breads, including loaves cooked in tins, are best returned to the oven for 5 minutes at the end of the cooking time out of their tins or removed from their trays to crisp the undersides. All bread should be cooled on a wire rack.

BREADCRUMBS

When you come to the end of a loaf, turn it into breadcrumbs using the food processor. Put the crumbs in 2 plastic bags, one inside the other, then date and freeze them. Breadcrumbs can be used straight from the freezer to crumble on gratins. Frozen breadcrumbs can also provide subtle thickening for a stew or soup and are an important ingredient in some puddings. Allow frozen breadcrumbs to thaw completely on kitchen paper before coating food that is to be fried.

recipes

country-style crusty bread   MAKES 2

Here is a simple all-purpose loaf that keeps well (in fact I prefer it a day old) and makes superb crunchy toast.

800 g unbleached strong flour

200 g wholemeal strong flour

1 tablespoon instant dried
yeast

1 tablespoon salt

2 tablespoons olive oil

2 tablespoons unprocessed
bran (optional)

600 ml lukewarm water

Using an electric mixer fitted with a dough hook, mix and knead all ingredients on lowest speed for 10–15 minutes until dough is smooth but not sticky. Divide dough in half and put each half in a lightly oiled bowl. Cover bowls with tea towels and leave in a draught-free place until doubled in size (about 1 hour). Knock back dough and knead each piece by hand for a few minutes. Allow to rise again for about 30 minutes. Form each piece into a loaf like a fat cigar. Place loaves on a liberally floured tea towel and allow to rise again for 30 minutes.

Preheat oven to 220°C with a heavy baking tray in it. Roll each loaf onto hot baking tray. Bake about 15 minutes, turn loaves over and bake another 5 minutes. Tap base of each loaf and remove from oven if it sounds hollow. Allow to cool completely on a wire rack before cutting.

fast sourdough If you like a sour character to your bread, tear off a piece of kneaded dough before letting it rise and store the piece at room temperature in a bowl covered with a damp cloth for 3 days. Next time you make bread, incorporate this dough in your mix. Tear off some of this new batch and keep it for another 3 days. And so on. This is the simplest way of imparting the flavour of sourdough to your loaves.

sabrina's breadsticks
MAKES 2

These breadsticks are made twice a day in my restaurant. The small amount of yeast and the slow rising time contributes to their character. By doubling the yeast, the rising times can be halved, however.

1 teaspoon instant dried yeast
or 2 teaspoons fresh yeast

300 ml lukewarm water

500 g unbleached strong flour

2 teaspoons salt

fine semolina *or* polenta

If using fresh yeast, place in a cup, squash with a few spoons of warm water and leave until it froths. Add to bowl of an electric mixer fitted with a dough hook with flour, salt and balance of water. If using dried yeast, mix yeast with flour and salt, then place in bowl of mixer and on lowest speed beat in water. Whether you are using fresh or dried yeast, beat well for at least 5 minutes until dough is very smooth. (This will take 10–15 minutes of firm kneading by hand.) Place dough in a lightly oiled bowl and cover with a tea towel. Put bowl in a draught-free place and allow to rise until doubled for about 3 hours.

Gently ease risen dough onto workbench. Fold in 4, return to bowl and allow to rise a second time for 1½ hours. Remove from bowl as before and divide into 2 portions. Keep dough covered with a clean, dry cloth while working with each piece. Roll each piece of dough into a long log and place on a floured tea towel. Leave, covered, for 45 minutes.

Preheat oven to 250°C with a baking tray in it. Sprinkle hot baking tray with semolina and roll breadsticks from cloth onto it. Slash top of each loaf a few times with a razor blade. Quickly put baking tray into oven and spray sides of oven with a fine mist of water. Bake for 25 minutes, spraying oven and bread every 10 minutes. Push sticks off tray for last 5 minutes to crisp bottoms. Cool completely before cutting.

quick pizza base After the first rising, tear off a small piece of dough. With well-oiled hands, and on a well-oiled pizza tray, spread out the dough, patting and prodding it as thin as possible. Allow it to recover for 30 minutes, then poke it down firmly again. Spread the base with your desired topping and bake at 250°C for 10 minutes. Slip the pizza from the tray onto the oven rack to brown for 5 minutes.

olive bread

MAKES I

This is a very versatile bread. It can be formed into a conventional cigar-shaped loaf after its first rise and allowed to rise again. It can be pressed out onto an oiled baking tray after its first rise, and then baked in the style of a focaccia. Or it can be torn into small pieces and baked as flattened individual olive breads. All ways it is delicious.

600 g strong flour
150 g stoned black olives, halved
2 teaspoons salt
1 tablespoon instant dried yeast
2 teaspoons finely chopped
  fresh rosemary
4 tablespoons olive oil
300 ml warm water
sea salt

Mix flour, olives, salt, yeast and rosemary in a large bowl. Add oil to water. Make a well in flour and tip in liquid, then stir to mix well. Tip onto an oiled workbench and knead with oiled hands for 15 minutes (or transfer to an electric mixer fitted with a dough hook) until dough is springy and elastic. Place dough in a lightly oiled bowl, cover with a clean tea towel and leave in a draught-free place to double in size (about 45 minutes).

Tip dough *gently* onto workbench. Do not knock back. Work into a cigar-shaped loaf with oiled hands, then place on a floured tea towel and allow to rise again for 30 minutes.

Preheat oven to 220°C with a baking tray in it. Roll loaf onto tray, scatter with flakes of sea salt and bake for 20 minutes (there is no need to mist oven with water). This bread is particularly good served slightly warm. **flavourings** Substitute green olives for black. Add chopped semi-dried tomatoes or lightly crisped bacon. **olive focaccia** After the first rising, transfer the dough to an oiled baking tray and flatten with oiled

croutons
Make croutons to toss through salads by chargrilling sliced breadstick brushed with olive oil or frying day-old cubes of bread.

chive bread
Work chopped chives into bread dough and form into small rolls to bake and offer with soup.

herring on rye
Top a slice of dark rye bread or pumpernickel with herring salad.

tomato on toast
Have a tomato on toast for breakfast.

hands until a rectangle 2–3 cm thick. Scatter with flakes of sea-salt and drizzle with a little olive oil. Allow to recover for 30 minutes, then bake at 250°C until browned and crisp.

pappa al pomodoro

SERVES 4

Bread is used to thicken soup and add nourishment to broths. This Italian soup requires first-class ingredients to bring out its charm.

2 cloves garlic, finely chopped
extra-virgin olive oil
500 g ripe tomatoes, seeded
  and chopped
small handful of fresh basil leaves,
  coarsely chopped *or* torn
freshly ground black pepper
salt
1 litre Chicken Stock ✐ or meat
  broth
500 g crustless day-old bread,
  cut into 1 cm cubes
freshly grated parmesan cheese

Briefly sauté garlic in a little oil and add tomato, basil and pepper. Cook for 5 minutes. Add salt and stock and bring gently to simmering point. Add bread and cook for a few minutes more, stirring. Cover and cook on lowest heat for 30 minutes. Adjust seasoning, then ladle into bowls, pour over 2 tablespoons extra-virgin olive oil and serve hot, warm or cold. Offer the cheese separately.

walnut bread
Try goat's cheese on walnut and raisin bread.

smoked salmon bagel
Spread a poppyseed bagel with cream cheese and fill it with smoked salmon.

panzanella

SERVES 4

This Tuscan salad is made and presented in many ways. Some cooks add anchovies or tuna or hardboiled eggs; sometimes cucumber and hot peppers are included. This is a simple version, achievable in minutes.

2 thick slices coarse bread at
  least a day old
6 ripe tomatoes, cubed
1 small red onion, finely diced
½ cucumber, diced
1 stick celery, finely sliced
2 cloves garlic, crushed
½ cup fresh basil leaves, torn
  into small pieces
⅓ cup extra-virgin olive oil
2 tablespoons red-wine vinegar
salt
freshly ground black pepper

Remove crusts and cut or tear bread into small pieces. Put into a bowl and sprinkle with cold water. The bread should be moist but not soggy. Add vegetables, garlic and basil. Dress with oil and vinegar, toss well and adjust seasoning. Allow to stand for 30 minutes, so that the flavours blend.

patafla from provence

SERVES 4–8

Mentioned by Elizabeth David in A Book of Mediterranean Food, *this simple but delicious appetiser or picnic food should be made the day before you wish to enjoy it.*

1 baguette
4 ripe tomatoes, cubed
1 small red onion, diced
2 green peppers, seeded and
    diced
10 juicy black olives, stoned
    and roughly chopped
10 large green olives, stoned
    and roughly chopped
1 tablespoon capers
1 tablespoon diced pickled
    cucumbers
⅓ cup extra-virgin olive oil
salt
freshly ground black pepper

Slice baguette lengthwise, pull out the crumb and tear into small pieces. Combine with other ingredients and mix very well, so that oil and bread bind. Fill baguette halves with mixture, press together and roll tightly in plastic film. Refrigerate overnight. Cut into thick slices to serve.

other recipes

bread sauce to serve with roast chicken *see* BAY LEAVES
buttered parsnip with toasted crumbs *see* PARSNIPS
cheese rarebit *see* CHEESE
fennel-seed breadsticks *see* FENNEL
gazpacho *see* TOMATOES
parsley and breadcrumb crust *see* PARSLEY
summer pudding *see* BERRIES AND CURRANTS
tomato soup with basil and croutons *see* TOMATOES
turnip leaves sautéd with anchovies and breadcrumbs *see* TURNIPS AND
    SWEDES

broccoli

My first broccoli was bought from the Cincotta greengrocery in Rosebud in about 1960. I remember it being presented with much ceremony at the family table. It was the vegetable that heralded The Change! There was Before Broccoli and there is now After Broccoli. The vegetable shop has never been the same again. | A member of the cabbage and cauliflower family, *Brassica oleracea* was cultivated by the Venetians as early as the sixteenth century. It has clusters of green flower-buds that form a head atop branching small stalks. When the main head is harvested, smaller clusters sprout from the central stalk. The leaves, stalk and flower-heads are all edible, although the stalk needs to be peeled of its tough skin. The stalks of very young broccoli can be peeled and eaten raw in a mixed salad, but on the whole I think broccoli is better cooked and dressed while warm. | Practically every way one serves asparagus or artichokes will be successful with broccoli. I consider it a luxury vegetable and therefore suitable to be served as a course on its own.

VARIETIES AND SEASON

The most common type of broccoli available in Australia is the green-sprouting calabrese. There is also a purple-flowering variety that turns green when cooked, and the attractive lime-green romanesca, which has triangular florets, as well as a variety known as Chinese broccoli or *gai laan*, which has small white flowers. The latter has longer, more slender stalks, larger leaves and a less significant flower-head than the more common variety. It is ideally suited to stir-frying. Broccoli is available all year, with the peak season being June–November.

SELECTION AND STORAGE

Select heads that are blue–green and very compact. The flower-buds should not have started to separate or to flower, nor should there be any tinge of yellow. Avoid any strong-smelling broccoli. If buying Chinese broccoli, look for unblemished plants with more flowers in bud than in bloom.

Refrigerate broccoli in vegetable storage bags in the crisper for a couple of days. It can also be stood in a jug of water and lightly covered with a plastic bag in the refrigerator for several days.

PREPARATION AND COOKING

Broccoli is notorious for harbouring small caterpillars. Separate the florets from the stems and leaves and soak the lot in lightly salted water for 10 minutes. Peel the stalks (this is tedious but the flesh within is so sweet and delicate it is worth the effort) and cook separately from the florets. Boil, steam or stir-fry the stalks until the tip of a knife will just penetrate. The florets can also be steamed, although I prefer to boil them.

TO BOIL   Plunge the florets or stems into plenty of lightly salted water – the chlorophyll in the vegetable normally reacts with the acids in the cooking water, causing the broccoli to become a drab green, but using lots of water dilutes the acids. Cook, uncovered (cooking it uncovered also allows the acids to disperse), until the water has returned to a boil (2–3 minutes). Drain very well and transfer to a hot dish (broccoli becomes cold very quickly, so do not delay). Combine the stems and florets and toss. Serve warm with melted butter or at room temperature dressed with olive oil. Do not add vinegar or lemon juice as it will darken the vegetable and cause it to wrinkle unattractively.

recipes **broccoli as a sauce for pasta**   SERVES 2–4

This sauce is often served with oriecchette, small ear-shaped pasta. The broccoli and pasta must be cooked in the same water for this dish, although not at the same time. Oriecchette is a very specialised pasta, not always easy to find, but the sauce is so good it is worth making the dish with small pasta shells, which are universally available.

500 g broccoli florets
extra-virgin olive oil
400 g oriecchette *or* small
   pasta shells
½ cup fresh breadcrumbs
1 clove garlic
6 anchovies, chopped
16 large black *or* green olives,
   stoned
freshly ground black pepper

Bring a large saucepan of lightly salted water to a boil. Drop in broccoli and simmer for 4–5 minutes. Remove broccoli, reserving water, and drain well in a colander. Splash extra-virgin olive oil over broccoli and set aside.

Bring water back to a boil and cook pasta until just tender (10–15 minutes). While pasta is cooking, toss breadcrumbs in a frying pan with some oil until golden. Set aside. In the same pan, add another spoonful of oil and gently sauté garlic with anchovies. Add olives. Tip broccoli into this pan and toss to reheat.

Drain pasta well and return it to pasta pot. Tip in broccoli mixture, drizzle with oil and grind in pepper. Serve in bowls and scatter over toasted breadcrumbs.

broccoli frittata

SERVES 4

If using sausage, choose a Polish style and skin it.

500 g broccoli
olive oil
1 onion, finely chopped
1 clove garlic, finely chopped
½ small fresh chilli, seeded
   and very finely chopped
½ cup diced ham *or* mild
   sausage
½–1 cup cooked pasta
6 eggs, lightly whisked
freshly grated parmesan
   cheese

Separate broccoli florets from stem and wash well. Peel stalk and cut into sticks. Cook broccoli in plenty of lightly salted water for 3 minutes. Drain well.

Heat 2 tablespoons oil in a heavy-based frying pan and sauté onion for 2 minutes. Add garlic and chilli and sauté 1 minute, then add broccoli, ham and pasta. Sauté a minute longer, then tip into a bowl. Add eggs to bowl.

Preheat griller. Put wiped-out frying pan over high heat and add a slurp of oil. When hot, quickly tip in contents of bowl. Allow mixture to sizzle and set for a minute without disturbing it. Lower heat to moderate and cook until bottom is brown and crusty and top looks moist but not liquid. Scatter over parmesan and place pan under griller to brown quickly. Using a wide-bladed, flexible metal spatula, loosen frittata and slip it onto a warm dish. Serve cut into wedges with a salad. >

broccoli and beans
Mix cooked broccoli with perfect green and yellow beans and toss with extra-virgin olive oil.

broccoli pesto
Purée lightly cooked broccoli with basil, parsley, pine nuts, parmesan and olive oil and toss through hot pasta as a variation on pesto.

broccoli gratin
Make a simple broccoli gratin by following the recipe for Fennel with Simple Cheese Sauce (see FENNEL*).*

tossed broccoli
Toss hot broccoli with toasted almonds and crisp bacon.

tomato sauce Add a little Fresh Tomato Sauce (*see* TOMATOES) to the bowl with the other ingredients.

warm broccoli and cauliflower salad

SERVES 6

stir-fried broccoli
Stir-fry broccoli stems and florets with sliced chilli, garlic and a little oyster sauce.

broccoli cream
Mix puréed warm broccoli with a spoonful of cream and serve with grilled fish or chicken.

1 head broccoli, separated into florets
1 cauliflower, separated into florets
3 tablespoons extra-virgin olive oil
1 teaspoon dried oregano
1 tablespoon freshly chopped parsley
3 teaspoons lemon juice
salt
freshly ground black pepper

Boil broccoli and cauliflower in separate saucepans of lightly salted water until cooked, about 8 minutes. Drain very well, then combine in a warmed salad bowl. Mix oil, oregano, parsley and lemon juice together and pour over vegetables. Season. Lift and turn the pieces with your fingers to mix properly.

variations Add 1 tablespoon toasted pine nuts, roasted red pepper strips or black olives at the last minute and toss.

b u g s   Visitors to Australia must wonder what they are about to receive when they are told that there are bugs for dinner! 'Bugs on the barbie' seems a more truly Australian dish than 'prawns on the barbie', although bugs are, in fact, found all over the world. Many countries ignore them or use them exclusively in fish stews.   Barbecued Moreton Bay bugs say 'holiday' to me, as they are a favourite meal when I spend a week each year with dear friends in North Queensland. We sit in bathers, sarongs or shorts sipping iced white wine and feasting on barbecued bugs and a huge platter of wok-tossed Asian greens bought from the Sunday market. The spicy smell from the mosquito coil is also part of this memory.   In shape, bugs resemble a fossil with insignificant legs. They vary in size (the largest are the size of a small rock lobster), markings and colour, but they are all delicious. The edible flesh is only in the tail section and the carapace (shell) is exceptionally hard. (Bugs shed their shells as they grow and from time to time one finds a soft-shelled bug, evidence of a recent moult. This soft shell is still far too hard to eat.)

VARIETIES AND SEASON

These crustaceans have many other names around the world – bay lobster, shovel-nosed lobster, slipper lobster, flathead lobster and *cigale de mer* being just a few – but I must say I prefer the vernacular. Reference works usually refer to bay or shovel-nosed lobsters, and the bugs found in our waters are considered to belong to one or the other group. Our most commonly available bugs are Balmain and Moreton Bay bugs. Other species are marketed, somewhat confusingly, as plain 'bugs'. A shovel-nosed lobster, the **Balmain bug** (*Ibacus peronii*) is found south of Brisbane and along the southern coast of Western Australia. It is broader around the head than the **Moreton Bay bug** (*Thenus orientalis*). A bay lobster, the Moreton Bay bug is found along the entire northern Australian coast in muddy inshore coastal waters, hence its other common name of mud bug. It often has a 'weedy' aroma due to the seagrass beds in which it lives.

Those who live in the far north will be familiar with *reef bugs*, the members of the *Thenus* genus that are also known as sand bugs and are found in deeper offshore waters. Reef bugs are longer and narrower than Balmain and Moreton Bay bugs and are rarely seen in our markets.

Bugs are most readily caught during a full moon when they rise to the surface. They are available all year frozen, either whole or as tails only.

SELECTION AND STORAGE

Allow 3–4 bugs per person if serving them plain with dipping sauces. Live Moreton Bay bugs are now sold at the Sydney fish market. However, bugs are rarely available live in the southern States, although a friend in East Gippsland, Victoria, has bought Balmain bugs locally. Bugs are very perishable and are mostly frozen at sea. Moreton Bay and the rarer reef bugs are shipped frozen, whole and green (uncooked) or tails only, to southern markets. It is more economical – but less dramatic – to buy frozen bug tail meat rather than whole bugs, as much of the weight is in the inedible head. Bugs are also sold cooked, though be wary of these if you cannot be guaranteed that they have been cooked within the last 12 hours, preferably more recently. Stale bugs (sometimes the case if one buys cooked bugs) may smell of ammonia or rancid garlic.

If you do see live bugs, buy those that are liveliest and whose tails are still snapping. Avoid those that are sluggish and feel light in weight as they may have been kept without food in a tank or they may have recently moulted (in which case their new soft shells may be filled with very soft flesh).

Store frozen bugs in plastic bags in a separate freezer compartment, not the ice-cream section of an older-style refrigerator, and use within a month. Thaw in the refrigerator on a layer of kitchen paper. If you have bought thawed bugs, remove the meat from the tails before refrigerating. Use fresh bugs as soon as possible after purchase, certainly within 24 hours.

PREPARATION AND COOKING

Most of us will only ever handle frozen bugs. However, should you obtain *live* bugs I suggest chilling them in the refrigerator or freezer to slow them right down before boiling them as instructed below. They will die instantly on being tipped into the boiling water. (If you have live bugs but wish to prepare a dish for which raw bug meat is required, quickly dip the bugs in and out of boiling water to kill them.) *Frozen* bugs require very little preparation: buy them, thaw them, wash them and then cook them. The intestinal thread that runs down the centre of the tail must be removed before serving. It is easy to identify if you have split the bugs. As with all crustaceans, do not cook bugs if you have bought them cooked.

TO BOIL	Cook live or frozen green bugs whole in sea water or Court-bouillon until the shells turn

a brilliant red, about 10 minutes (this depends on their size). This method is suitable for bugs requiring no further cooking.

TO ROAST, GRILL OR BARBECUE	**Roast** Cook whole bugs in a very hot oven (240°C) for 15 minutes, then split them and

flick out the intestinal threads. **Grill or barbecue** Cook whole or halved bugs for 10–15 minutes, depending on their size, until the shells are a brilliant red.

TO SHELL	Turn the bug so that the shell is facing down. With heavy kitchen scissors cut along each

side of the softer underbelly skin. Peel it back then pull the meat away from the hard shell. The intestinal thread should stay with the shell and you should have a clean piece of shellfish in your hand.

yam goong – salad of bug meat with mint and lemongrass

SERVES 2–4

recipes

This delicious salad is from Mogens Bay Esbensen's book, Thai Cuisine.

1 stalk lemongrass, finely
  sliced
juice of 6 limes *or* 2 lemons
2–3 fresh red chillies, chopped
1 cup fresh mint leaves
1 tablespoon fish sauce
500 g raw bug meat, sliced
sprigs of mint

Combine all ingredients, except bug meat and mint sprigs. Place bug meat in a strainer and dip quickly into and out of boiling water. While still warm, add bug meat to dressing and marinate for 30 minutes. Garnish with mint sprigs.

bugs and . . .
Pan-fry, grill or barbecue bug meat and include it in a tomato-based pasta sauce or shellfish stew.

bug meat coconut curry

SERVES 4

This curry is based on a recipe of Mogens Bay Esbensen's that was originally intended for chicken. If you live in Far North Queensland, look out for the fresh green peppercorns available there.

roasted bugs
Spoon chilli oil or melted butter thick with freshly chopped basil, or Fresh Tomato Sauce (see TOMATOES*), over roasted bugs and squeeze over lemon juice.*

fried bugs
Deep-fry chunks of raw bug meat in Beer Batter at 175°C and serve with Tartare Sauce or Fresh Tomato Sauce (see TOMATOES*) or chutney.*

bugs and spinach
Drizzle chilli oil and squeeze lemon juice over roasted bugs served on a platter of fresh spinach leaves.

1 teaspoon crushed green peppercorns
750 g raw bug meat, cut into bite-sized pieces
50 g plain flour
100 ml vegetable oil
50 g red Thai curry paste
1 cup coconut cream
25 g brown sugar
2 tablespoons fish sauce
60 g chopped roasted peanuts
1 cup chopped fresh basil

Rub peppercorns into bug meat and roll pieces in flour. Heat oil in a wok or heavy-based frying pan and quickly seal bug meat. Remove it to a plate and set aside. Pour off almost all the oil, then add curry paste and stir for 2 minutes. Stir in coconut cream, sugar, fish sauce and peanuts. Simmer for 5 minutes, then return bug meat to sauce and cook for 5 minutes. Turn onto a serving platter and garnish with basil. Serve with jasmine rice or plain boiled rice and a stir-fried green vegetable.

fettuccine with bug meat and roasted tomato sauce

SERVES 2–4

8 ripe tomatoes, peeled and roughly chopped
1 onion, chopped
3 cloves garlic, chopped
1 teaspoon fresh thyme leaves
1 bay leaf
1 small fresh chilli, seeded but whole
extra-virgin olive oil
salt
500 g raw bug meat, cut into bite-sized pieces
grated zest of 1 lemon
juice of ½ lemon
500 g fresh fettuccine
1 cup shelled clams or mussels (optional)
2 tablespoons freshly chopped parsley

Preheat oven to 180°C. Place tomato, onion, garlic, thyme, bay leaf, chilli and 100 ml oil into a baking dish that will hold ingredients in a 4 cm thick layer. Roast for about 1 hour until tomato looks a bit scorched, onion is quite soft and there are plenty of juices. Remove chilli and discard. Taste for salt. Set roasted tomato sauce aside.

In a frying pan, quickly sauté bug meat in a spoonful of oil. Scatter over zest and lemon juice. Add tomato sauce to bug meat and simmer over a brisk heat while you cook the fettuccine. Add clams, if using, and parsley. Toss the sauce with the drained pasta and serve.

Cabbages and brussels sprouts

I have had to work at learning to understand and like, much less love, cabbage and Brussels sprouts. In my second year of secondary school I had my first and last practical lessons in cookery. These classes were guaranteed to turn most off cooking: lesson 1 was white stew; lesson 2 was brown stew. Both were accompanied by smelly, watery, overcooked cabbage. | It was years before I realised that cabbage could be lightly cooked and butter and parsley did wonders for it, that Brussels sprouts were best with some crispness left in them (as opposed to being cooked to the texture of wet blotting paper), that cabbage was delicious raw and that red cabbage could be braised with apple. | Cabbage and Brussels sprouts belong to the *Brassica* genus, as do cauliflower, broccoli, kohlrabi, kale, Chinese cabbage, *choi sum* and *gai laan*. They originated in northern Europe – cultivated cabbages in Germany in the 1100s and Brussels sprouts, not surprisingly, in Belgium in the 1700s. >

Cabbage is important in the cookery of most European, African and Asian cuisines. It is cooked with potatoes in Ireland, with a variety of pork products and pork and goose fat in France, and it is salted and fermented to make sauerkraut in Germany. Asian countries have their own cabbages that can be stir-fried or used in place of Western varieties. Cabbage can be sautéd, boiled and buttered, stir-fried, stuffed (either whole or as individual leaves) or made into rich one-pot soups, and it is the basis for coleslaw and other salads that are either dressed raw or wilted by applying heat or adding an acidic ingredient. Brussels sprouts can be boiled and buttered, and that is about as far as I go with them. While I cannot abide stewed Brussels sprouts, the 'buttering' can include other ingredients, such as lots of fresh herbs, toasted almonds or sautéd chestnuts.

VARIETIES AND SEASON

Australian greengrocers offer unnamed firm, round, white, green or red varieties of cabbage with very compact leaves; the less compact, crinkly-leafed Savoy, with its brilliantly green outer leaves; and other varieties that are more or less tightly packed, round or flattened. Many these days also sell the longer, broad-ribbed Chinese or Peking cabbage. Only the Savoy or the Chinese seems to be requested by variety. We do not tend to grow the small, loose-hearted, spring greens that I enjoy very much when visiting England.

There is a cabbage available for all seasons. Tight-hearted, white to green varieties are available through the winter. My favourite cabbage, the crinkly Savoy, is at its best in the spring. Dramatic red cabbage is best in the autumn. Brussels sprouts, which again are not sold by variety, are regarded principally as a winter vegetable.

SELECTION AND STORAGE

Cabbages should be heavy for their size. Loose-leafed varieties should look crisp and brightly coloured with perky leaves – avoid any cabbages with drooping leaves. Tight cabbages should not have outer leaves falling away from the rest of the cabbage. The outer leaves should have a slight sheen and there should be no obvious sign of insect damage. The cabbage should smell good with no trace of that tell-tale odour of overcooked greens. The stalk end should be moist. *Brussels sprouts* should be small, bright green (with never a trace of yellow) and firm and the leaves should be tightly furled. Avoid those that are floppy. They also should smell good.

Tight-hearted cabbages are best for storage. Kept in a cool place where air can circulate around them (the coolroom at your greengrocer's, for example), they will keep well for weeks. All tight-hearted varieties will also keep well for a week in the crisper section of the refrigerator in a vegetable storage bag. Loose-leafed cabbages should be eaten within a few days of being bought. If you are cooking for one or two and only need a quarter of cabbage, buy it on the day you intend to cook it and ensure that it is cut from a *whole* cabbage at the greengrocer's. Slicing tears cabbage cells and releases the enzymes that hasten its oxidisation and deterioration – a good reason not to buy sections of cabbage tightly wrapped in plastic film. Brussels sprouts will keep, refrigerated, for a few days in a vegetable storage bag in the crisper.

PREPARATION AND COOKING

The cardinal rules for cooking cabbage and Brussels sprouts are not to overcook either and to drain them very well. That said, there are many European recipes where cabbage is cooked for hours in a slow oven with smoked pork or preserved meats and other vegetables. These dishes end up smelling good and mellow, not at all like overcooked boiled cabbage.

TO BOIL | **Cabbage** Cut the cabbage before washing it, otherwise you are simply rinsing the outside leaves. Discard any coarse outside leaves. Cabbage can be cut in manageable wedges or it can be sliced. If serving cabbage in wedges, do not cut out the edible stalk that holds the wedge together. If slicing cabbage, slice the stalk finely too and cook it with the sliced leaves. Place the washed cabbage wedges or slices in a heavy saucepan (do not fill the pan more than half full), cover tightly and cook over a moderate heat in the water clinging to the leaves for 5 minutes. Stir once or twice. Drain the cooked cabbage well in a colander and return it to the hot pan. If serving as is, add a spoonful of freshly chopped herbs and a nut of butter and season. **Brussels sprouts** Remove any loose leaves but leave the stem intact. (Some cooks cut a cross on the stem end to aid cooking but I have never found it makes any difference.) Wash the sprouts well. In order to retain their bright-green colour, boil the sprouts in plenty of water with the lid off, for no more than 8 minutes (the chlorophyll in the vegetables reacts with the acids in the cooking water, causing the sprouts to become a drab green – using lots of water dilutes the acids and cooking the sprouts uncovered allows the acids to disperse). Drain well and toss with butter and herbs.

FOR SALADS | Cut a wedge of cabbage, then wash and drain it in a colander. Turn it out onto a chopping board, so that the flat side provides a stable base. Holding the wedge firmly in one hand, slice thinly and evenly with the other. Many food processors have cutting blades designed to shred cabbage. If you are happy with yours, use it by all means. Some brands deliver a bruised and scrappy shred.

FOR STUFFING | **A whole cabbage** In this preparation the washing and blanching takes place at the same time. Select a loose-leafed cabbage and cut a slice from the top of it to expose more of the leaves. Immerse the entire cabbage in a large pot of boiling water for 5 minutes. Lift it out using a wide skimmer or tip it gently into a colander. Leave the cabbage for a few minutes to cool. Spread the leaves away from the heart. Proceed with the recipe and simmer for at least 2 hours. **Individual leaves** If using a loose-leafed Savoy cabbage, proceed as above and after blanching cut the leaves away from the stalk and leave them to drain. If you have a tightly packed variety, turn the raw cabbage upside down, cut out the stalk and ease off as many leaves as possible. To obtain more leaves, immerse the cabbage in boiling water as described above, drain and ease away more leaves. Leaves that were eased off raw will now need to be dipped into boiling water, so that all are equally pliable. Stuffed leaves are simmered for 45 minutes.

SAUERKRAUT Sauerkraut can be bought in tins or plastic bags from delicatessens or supermarkets, and can sometimes be bought loose from fresh food markets. It is almost always shredded. I prefer to rinse it in cold water to remove any excess salt. Squeeze it with your hands and then drain for 1 hour before using.

recipes

one-pot cabbage soup

SERVES 6

sauerkraut

Serve sauerkraut with a ham hock, a smoked frankfurter, good potatoes and mustard.

Variations on this recipe are traditional fare in south-west France. Sometimes they are known as la potée, *sometimes* la garbure.

500 g piece smoked streaky
   bacon, rind removed
12 small potatoes, halved
12 baby carrots, halved
6 golf-ball-sized turnips, halved
6 pickling onions, quartered
500 g green beans, cut into
   3 cm pieces
250 g shelled green peas
½ Savoy or other green,
   loose-leafed cabbage, sliced
freshly ground black pepper
freshly grated nutmeg

Put bacon, potato, carrot, turnip and onion in a heavy saucepan. Cover with cold water, bring to a boil and simmer very gently for 45 minutes. Raise heat to a bubbling boil and add beans. After 5 minutes add peas. After another 5 minutes add cabbage. Reduce heat and simmer a further 10 minutes. Lift out bacon, cut into small pieces and return to pot. Taste for salt (almost certainly none will be needed because of the bacon) and season with pepper and nutmeg. Serve with good sourdough bread.

red cabbage salad

SERVES 4

This wilted salad can accompany duck or pork. The Chinese use this technique with many vegetable dishes. A wok is the perfect implement.

2 tablespoons pine nuts

olive oil

2 tablespoons duck fat, pork
 fat *or* olive oil

2 cloves garlic, finely chopped

½ red cabbage, shredded

6 anchovies, roughly chopped

I teaspoon red-wine vinegar

freshly ground black pepper

Fry pine nuts in a film of oil until golden, then remove and reserve. Wipe out pan, then melt fat and sauté garlic for a moment. Add cabbage and anchovies and toss for 1–2 minutes until cabbage is shiny and starting to soften. Sprinkle over vinegar, toss again and grind on pepper. Scatter pine nuts over and serve at once on hot plates.

potato Before adding the cabbage, toss small cubes of cooked potato in oil until crusty – you will probably need to double the amount of oil or fat or else add cubes of bacon to render more fat. When the potato has browned and the bacon (if using it) is smelling wonderful, proceed with the cabbage, anchovies (optional), pepper and pine nuts.   **onion** Before adding the cabbage, toss finely sliced onion and slices of Chinese lap cheong or other firm sausage in oil and add chopped ginger with the garlic. Forget about the pine nuts and anchovies.   **greens** Omit the anchovies, add Chinese broccoli (*gai laan*) and/or peeled stems of conventional broccoli, chunks of asparagus and green beans and splash with soy sauce instead of wine vinegar and – hey presto! – you have changed the character of your dish. Now all it needs is a bowl of fragrant rice.

cabbage salad with anchovy sauce   SERVES 4

In many preparations salt is used to soften vegetables and draw out juices as a preliminary to pickling them. One should only toss delicate salad leaves in a dressing that contains acidic ingredients (salt, lemon juice or vinegar) at the very last moment in order to avoid fibre breakdown and soggy greens. However, the breaking down of fibres can be used to advantage when the leaves are particularly tough and resistant. Cabbage coleslaw relies on this technique, as does this salad, which can be eaten as a first course, as a salad course or as a vegetable bed for a grilled fish steak or chicken breast.

I clove garlic, finely chopped

1–2 anchovies, finely chopped

pinch of salt

freshly ground black pepper

I teaspoon red-wine vinegar

2 tablespoons extra-virgin
 olive oil

I tablespoon freshly chopped
 parsley

2 cups sliced green cabbage

Whisk all ingredients except cabbage. In a large bowl, toss dressing and cabbage very well and leave for at least 30 minutes. The cabbage salad can be made up to 2 hours ahead of dinner.

variations Add sautéd sliced mushrooms, sautéd cooked potato or tiny pieces of salted herring. (Matjes herring fillets are particularly delicious. If using herring, substitute chopped dill for the parsley.)

bubble-and-squeak

Make bubble-and-squeak by frying a sliced onion in lots of olive oil until limp and golden. Add equal quantities of seasoned and lightly cooked cabbage and potato and press firmly over the onion. Cook until brown and crusty underneath. Divide into quarters and turn to brown the other side.

whole cabbage stuffed with pork, liver and capers

SERVES 6

A great dish for a winter evening. If you prefer to stuff individual leaves, the cooking time is 45 minutes (see Cabbage Leaves Stuffed with Pork, Sausage and Rice *on p. 155 for instructions for dealing with single leaves).*

stir-fried cabbage

Stir-fry sliced cabbage in hot olive oil with garlic and cook, covered, until crisp–tender. Add fresh herbs and crushed coriander and toss with sliced sausage or a grilled hamburger, allowing the flavours to mingle for a minute or two. Offer Dijon mustard on the side.

1 cabbage, blanched and
   drained
stock, water or tomato juice
1 bay leaf
1 sprig thyme
2 cloves garlic
1 carrot, sliced (optional)
1 onion, sliced (optional)

STUFFING
500 g minced pork
8 chicken livers, finely
   chopped
1 tablespoon well-drained
   capers
½ cup fresh breadcrumbs
2 tablespoons freshly chopped
   parsley
1 teaspoon freshly chopped
   thyme
½ teaspoon ground allspice
salt
freshly ground black pepper
1 egg

Mix stuffing ingredients together. Fry a small ball of stuffing gently, then allow to cool and taste for seasoning. Adjust seasoning of remaining stuffing if necessary.

Open leaves of cabbage out like a flower and, starting from centre, add a little filling, folding leaves over as you go. Continue until cabbage is re-formed. Wrap cabbage in a piece of muslin and tie with string. Place cabbage in a heavy casserole and add stock to come two-thirds up sides of cabbage. Tuck in bay leaf, thyme and garlic. If using water, add carrot and onion to add flavour. Cover tightly and simmer for 2 hours.

To serve, lift out cabbage and taste juices. Boil to reduce if they are not savoury and delicious. Untie muslin and present your stuffed cabbage whole. Cut into wedges to serve as you would a Christmas pudding. Spoon over juices. Serve a bowl of creamy mashed potato or parsnip alongside.

chestnuts If you have access to cooked chestnuts, they are marvellous added to the stuffing. I would then leave out the capers.

erna's red cabbage with apple

SERVES 6

There are many versions of this German or Flemish way with red cabbage, often known as choux flamande. *This one was shown to me by a German 'aunt' by marriage and can be reheated once or twice, so make plenty. It is perfect with sausages, pork chops, a casserole of rabbit or roasted quail.*

3 tablespoons water
1 red cabbage, sliced, washed
   and drained
(continued next page)

Place water, cabbage, sugar and salt in a heavy-based saucepan. Add apple, cover tightly and cook very gently (using a simmer mat) for about 1 hour. Lift lid and stir

2 tablespoons brown sugar

pinch of salt

2 Granny Smith apples, peeled
and sliced

¼ cup cider vinegar

60 g butter

apple into softened cabbage. Tip in vinegar
and butter. Cook, covered, a further
15 minutes. Stir once more. The cabbage
should look shiny from the melted butter.
There should still be some evidence of apple
slices – not just a mush.

cabbage leaves stuffed with pork, sausage and rice

SERVES 8

*This stuffing can also be used for a whole cabbage, which will need to be
simmered for 2 hours (see Whole Cabbage Stuffed with Pork, Liver and
Capers on p. 154 for instructions for dealing with a whole cabbage).*

leaves of 1 cabbage, blanched

1 carrot, diced

1 onion, diced

1 bay leaf

1 clove garlic

1 sprig thyme

stock, water or tomato juice

freshly ground black pepper

STUFFING

2 large onions, finely chopped

1 tablespoon olive oil

200 g salted belly pork,
minced

1 large clove garlic, chopped

100 g long-grained rice

400 g flavoursome sausages
(Spanish fresh chorizo,
North African merguez *or*
Italian pure pork)

2 tomatoes, peeled, seeded
and finely chopped

1 tablespoon tomato paste

salt

freshly ground black pepper

Preheat oven to 180°C. To make stuffing,
sauté onion in oil for a few minutes. Add
pork, garlic and rice. Stew for 10 minutes,
stirring from time to time. Skin sausages
and crumble into a bowl and add pork
mixture and remaining ingredients. Mix
well, then taste for seasoning.

Spread cabbage leaves out on workbench.
Divide stuffing between them and fold up,
tucking ends in as well as you can, and tie
with cotton wound around and around each
roll. Don't bother to tie a bow – the rolls
will be easier to unravel if you have left a
string dangling.

Place rolls in a large, enamelled cast-iron
casserole in a tight layer, seam underneath,
and scatter over carrot and onion. Add bay
leaf, garlic and thyme. Barely cover with
stock and grind over some pepper. Place a
plate on rolls to prevent them moving too
much and cover with a lid. Bake for
45 minutes (or cook on the stove on a
simmer mat). Serve rolls and their juices
with mashed potato or a vegetable purée.

leftovers In place of sausages you could
use the minced remains of a roasted leg of lamb or braised beef. Include
any juices that have set around the leftover meat.

coleslaw

*Make a mixed
coleslaw of red,
green and crinkly
leafed cabbage and
dress with a
mustardy
vinaigrette. Make a
fancier version by
adding crumbled
bacon, fried capers
or finely sliced
fennel and inner
stalks of celery.*

**sprouts and
cheese**

*Toss hot Brussels
sprouts with butter
and freshly grated
parmesan cheese.*

sauerkraut with juniper berries and sparkling wine

SERVES 8

This special sauerkraut dish goes very well with roast pork. Some of the meat juices can be added at the end to mellow the flavour even more.

sprouts and nuts
Toss hot Brussels sprouts with butter, herbs, sautéd chestnuts or slivered or flaked toasted almonds and season with plenty of pepper.

½ cup pork fat, duck fat or lard
3 onions, sliced
1 sprig thyme
1 bay leaf
1 teaspoon black peppercorns
10 juniper berries, lightly crushed
1 x 750 ml bottle méthode champenoise sparkling wine
1.5 kg sauerkraut, rinsed and drained
2 large potatoes, grated
2 tablespoons kirsch

Heat fat and sauté onion in a large saucepan until quite soft but not browned. Add thyme, bay leaf, peppercorns, juniper berries, sparkling wine and sauerkraut and mix well. Place pan on a simmer mat and cook very gently, uncovered, for about 1½ hours. Stir from time to time to ensure mixture is not sticking. Stir in potato and simmer a further 20 minutes. Taste for seasoning, add kirsch and serve.

other recipes

southern-style greens and ham *see* HAM

c a r r o t s   Actually a biennial herb of the parsley family (as are parsnip and celery), the carrot (*Daucus carota*) has changed a great deal since the Moors brought a purple root from North Africa to Spain around the twelfth century AD. These early carrots spread to Holland, where the orange carrot was first developed, and from there to the rest of Europe. So exotic were carrots considered in Elizabethan England that carrot fronds were worn as decoration on hats and vests as one might have worn feathers. | Carrots are cheap and probably one of the most frequently bought vegetables, but one cannot say that they have an exciting image. And yet cooking without carrots is unthinkable. Their sweetness and unique flavour is essential in all stocks and, for me, carrot is the vegetable that is in almost every stew or braise I prepare. There are hundreds of ways to cook carrot, from the plainest to the most exotic. It would be possible (though not a good idea) to eat carrot at every stage of the meal – raw carrots with Bagna Cauda Sauce as an appetiser (*see* ANCHOVIES), followed by Carrot Soup with Orange (*see* p. 160), beef with glazed carrots, and a Carrot and Nutmeg Tart (*see* p. 162).

VARIETIES AND SEASON

Carrots come large and small, tapering, stumpy or round, and are pale to deep orange in colour. The deeper the orange colour of the carrot, the more carotene it contains (carotene is converted to Vitamin A in the body). Some varieties are naturally deeper in colour than others, while carrots grown at low temperatures during winter tend to be paler.

Carrots are not sold by varietal type, although one can choose between 'baby' carrots and mature carrots. Baby carrots are usually thinnings of a main crop but they may also be a fast-maturing variety intended to be harvested small. Carrots are available all year.

SELECTION AND STORAGE

Select *baby* carrots that are firm with sweet-smelling, fresh-looking tops and inspect the bunch critically. The carrots should not be *too* infantile. Flavour develops as the carrot grows, so avoid bunches with lots of very pale, spindly carrots. If you grow your own carrots, the dainty leaves of freshly pulled young carrots can be added to the salad or soup bowl. They have a definite and spicy flavour that is pleasant when the leaves are just picked but not so pleasant after a few days at the greengrocer's. Remove the tops for better storage, unless using them, as they become slimy after a few days. Baby carrots are best eaten within 3 days of purchase.

Select *mature* carrots that are firm with no signs of soft patches, split ends or discoloured skin. Very large carrots are suspect as they may be overmature and have inedible woody centres. Mature carrots keep well for 5–6 days in a vegetable storage bag in the refrigerator crisper.

PREPARATION AND COOKING

Full-flavoured *baby* carrots may only need rinsing if you are including them on a platter of raw vegetables or in a school lunch or are boiling and buttering them. Some cooks like to rinse and then scrub carrots with a firm-bristled brush rather than peel them. However, I always peel *mature* carrots as I find that the skin can taste bitter.

If the carrots are to be *boiled* as a separate vegetable they can be left whole or cut any way you please – into chunks, julienne, thin or thick slices or batons. If the carrots are to simmer with a *stew*, use mature carrots and leave them in larger chunks. Also select larger carrots to bake beside a *roast*. If carrots are to be *stir-fried* with other vegetables, the carrots selected should be smaller and/or finely sliced (it is not pleasant to have hard carrots and perfect asparagus spears in the same stir-fry).

TO BOIL | When cooking carrots with water, only use the bare minimum so that any remaining liquid will be well flavoured. This liquid can then be thickened with cream or *beurre manié* to become a sauce. Carrots are nicest if cooked to the barely tender stage but definitely past the hard and crunchy point. For finely cut or shredded carrots, this will mean around 5 minutes. For larger chunks or thick slices, it may mean up to 15 minutes.

TO ROAST | Roasted carrots will take at least 1 hour to become tender, a bit wrinkled and caramelised. Simply add to the baking dish at the appropriate time and turn once or twice during the cooking time.

caramelised carrot

recipes

Carrot caramelises beautifully without extra sugar. Marcella Hazan inspired me to add chopped mortadella sausage to carrot cooked this way. The combination is very good and goes extremely well with meat that is plainly sautéd, such as a veal scaloppine, or with grilled pork sausages.

carrots, sliced	Sauté carrot and sausage, if using, for about
olive oil	20 minutes in 5 mm oil, turning frequently.
mortadella sausage, chopped	The carrot will develop dark-brown, crispy
(optional)	edges and look quite shiny by the time it is
freshly ground black pepper	tender. Grind on pepper before serving.

glazed carrots

This fancy way of presenting vegetables has the advantage that the initial cooking can be done several hours ahead. More sophisticated flavours are possible if the glazing is done using chicken or veal stock and if more than one type of vegetable is glazed (turnips and small onions work well). Mixed glazed vegetables look lovely when presented in a shallow dish for self-service.

carrots, peeled	If using baby carrots, leave them whole.
salt	Chop mature carrots into chunks. Cook
butter	carrots in very lightly salted water until
freshly chopped parsley,	barely tender (they have a further 5 minutes
chervil *or* tarragon	of cooking later on). Drain but reserve
freshly ground black pepper	1 cup cooking water. Spread carrots out
	on a tray lined with kitchen paper.

When ready to serve, select a wide saucepan that will hold carrots very comfortably in a single layer and tip in reserved cooking water, a walnut-

creamy carrot
Cook 2 cups sliced carrot in a covered, heavy-based saucepan over moderate heat with 1 tablespoon butter, 2 tablespoons water and a tiny pinch of salt for 8 minutes. Uncover, increase heat to evaporate any extra water and serve. Add 1 tablespoon thick cream or sour cream and cook for 2 minutes before stirring in freshly chopped parsley, chives, savoury or tarragon.

sized piece of butter and carrots. Shake gently over moderate heat until liquid has evaporated and carrots are shiny. Scatter over parsley and check seasoning. Be careful if adding any salt as the lightly salted cooking water will have concentrated.

carrot juice
Peel and juice 2–3 carrots for a marvellous start to the day.

carrot soup with orange   SERVES 6

This interesting soup is a variation of a basic carrot soup and can be served hot or chilled. Experiment with the base recipe by omitting the orange juice and using milk or water instead of the stock. The flavourings can include a bay leaf or a spice such as paprika, turmeric or nutmeg.

carrot fritters
Deep-fry carrot shavings at 160°C for 3 minutes. Drain on kitchen paper and serve lightly salted or dusted with ground cumin.

500 g carrots, chopped
I onion, sliced
I leek, finely sliced (white part only)
2 tablespoons olive oil
I litre Chicken Stock
juice of 2 oranges
I clove garlic
I tablespoon sherry vinegar
salt
freshly ground black pepper
2 tablespoons finely chopped young carrot tops
grated zest of I orange
extra-virgin olive oil

Sweat vegetables in oil, tightly covered, for 5 minutes. Add stock, orange juice, garlic and vinegar. Simmer until carrot is very tender, then purée, holding back 1 cup liquid. Adjust consistency of soup with reserved liquid and taste for seasoning. Reheat or chill to serve. Finish each serving with the carrot tops, zest and a swirl of extra-virgin olive oil.

carrot and peas
Boil sliced carrot in a little lightly salted water until nearly cooked, then add peas and simmer until tender. Over heat, drop in a piece of Beurre Manié and shake to blend – add another piece when the first has disappeared and so on, until mixture has thickened sufficiently. Season and stir in freshly chopped parsley.

indian-style carrot fritters   MAKES 25

I teaspoon salt
I½ teaspoons ground cumin
I½ teaspoons ground coriander
½ teaspoon ground turmeric
¼ teaspoon cayenne pepper
150 g plain flour
½ cup beer
I large egg, lightly beaten
I cup well-packed grated carrot
6 spring onions, finely chopped (including greens)
vegetable oil for deep-frying
I bunch fresh coriander

Sift salt, spices and flour into a bowl. Add beer and egg, mixing well. Stir in carrot and spring onion.

Heat oil to a depth of 1 cm in a heavy-based frying pan and fry fritter mixture by the spoonful until golden brown, about 3–4 minutes. Turn fritters to cook other side. Drain well on crumpled kitchen paper. Serve on a platter lined with fresh coriander.

carrot salad with thai seasoning   SERVES 4–6

2 cups finely grated carrot

2 cloves garlic, finely chopped

1 fresh red chilli, seeded and finely chopped

3 cm piece ginger, finely chopped

1 teaspoon brown sugar

1 stalk lemongrass

juice of 3 limes *or* 1 lemon

2 teaspoons fish sauce

2 tablespoons freshly torn coriander leaves and finely chopped stems

2 tablespoons roughly chopped raw peanuts

Mix ingredients well and leave to marinate for several hours in the refrigerator. This salad is excellent as a bed for yabbies or barbecued prawns and can also be part of a series of salads. Serve at room temperature.

green papaya salad Substitute 2 cups grated green papaya for the carrot. Omit the ginger, lemongrass and coriander and add 2 finely sliced shallots and 1 roughly chopped tomato. Pound all ingredients except lime juice, fish sauce and papaya to a paste in a large mortar or combine briefly in a food processor. Mix in remaining ingredients and adjust lime juice and fish sauce to taste. Serve with shellfish or on dry biscuits or croutons with drinks.

simple carrot cake

125 g self-raising flour

¾ cup brown sugar

½ teaspoon ground cinnamon

½ teaspoon freshly grated nutmeg

⅔ cup olive oil

2 eggs, lightly beaten

2 cups finely grated carrot

½ cup roughly chopped walnuts

Preheat oven to 180°C. Mix together flour, sugar and spices. Add oil and eggs and beat in a food processor or electric mixer for 1 minute. Stir in carrot and walnuts. Pour into an 18 cm springform tin and bake for about 1 hour. Cool in tin before turning out. When cold, dust with icing sugar mixed with ground cinnamon or ice with a simple lemon icing.

creamy topping In a food processor, blend 125 g cream cheese or mascarpone, 250 g pure icing sugar and 60 g softened butter. Add a few drops of pure vanilla, then spread over the top of the cake.

carrot and mustard seeds
Mix grated raw carrot with plenty of lemon juice and arrange on a flat dish. Heat a tablespoon each of vegetable oil and clarified butter and fry some black mustard seeds until they pop. (This takes only a few seconds.) Pour oil and seeds over the carrot.

carrot spaghetti
Make carrot 'spaghetti' using the appropriate food processor disc or a Japanese vegetable shredder and cook in lightly salted water for 5 minutes, then drain and toss with herbs and butter.

carrot and nutmeg tart

SERVES 6

This tart is based on a recipe in The Art of Cookery, *written by an English cook, Hannah Glasse, in the eighteenth century.*

simple carrot salad

Dress grated carrot with olive oil, lemon juice and freshly chopped parsley or chervil and decorate with fat black olives.

½ quantity Shortcrust Pastry
100 g carrot, finely grated
60 g ground almonds
2 egg yolks
1 egg white
150 ml cream
60 g cooled, melted butter
½ teaspoon freshly grated nutmeg
2 tablespoons castor sugar

Line a 4 cm deep pie plate with pastry and bake blind at 200°C for 20 minutes. Remove foil and beans and lower oven temperature to 180°C. Mix remaining ingredients together and pour into pastry case. Bake for 15–20 minutes until filling has set and developed a golden crust. Good warm or cold.

cauliflowers

cauliflowers Mark Twain described cauliflower as 'cabbage with a college education', and a well-grown cauliflower is certainly a very handsome sight. | Cauliflower (*Brassica oleracea*) is another vegetable introduced to Europe by the Spanish Moors, who brought this vegetable from the Arab world. Cauliflower is similar in structure to broccoli, to which it is related. Its swollen head consists of tiny white flowers known as the 'curd'. This compact white mass is surrounded by green leaves that encase and protect the developing head. Modern varieties have increased the size of the flowering head. | Cauliflower contains mustard oils, which are natural chemicals that give the vegetable its flavour but also break down into a variety of smelly sulphur compounds when the cauliflower is heated. Therefore, the longer cauliflower is cooked the worse it will smell. And the smell of long-cooked cauliflower is certainly very pervasive! If I am planning a dish of cauliflower cheese I try to cook the cauliflower hours beforehand to allow the smell to be forgotten by dinner.

cauliflowers

go

with

gruyère cheese

cheddar cheese

parmesan cheese

mozzarella

breadcrumbs

butter

parsley

anchovies

olives

broccoli

capers

olive oil

lemon juice

oregano

turmeric

cumin

garlic

coriander

ham

VARIETIES AND SEASON

Cauliflowers grow best in cool or temperate climates and are available all year, with the peak season being during winter. Different varieties produce heads of different sizes. In the last few years several new forms of cauliflower have appeared, including a miniature cauliflower suitable for serving as a single portion. It has a fine flavour and looks most attractive, with its pale-green inner leaves framing the baby-faced flower-head. This miniature variety is very popular for home gardeners, as it matures in just 10 weeks from seedling transplant. The dreadfully named 'broccoflower' is another newcomer. This cauliflower has green curds and resembles broccoli. A cross between a cauliflower and a romanesca broccoli is also available. This vegetable is bright yellowy-green and has pointed florets.

SELECTION AND STORAGE

Size has no relationship to quality or to flavour. The curds should be tightly packed and very white (or green, in the case of broccoflower). They darken with age, so avoid any cauliflower that has deep-cream or, worse still, brownish curds. There should be no suggestion of separation of the florets or of a 'ricey', granular texture. This last indicates that the head was over-mature when it was cut from the plant. The leaves should look fresh and green without any yellow tinge. Like other members of the *Brassica* genus (cabbage, broccoli), cauliflower should be avoided if it has an unpleasant smell. Inspect all cauliflowers carefully for any tell-tale burrowing holes.

Remove all but the innermost leaves and refrigerate cauliflower in a vegetable storage bag in the crisper. It will be fine for a few days, but do not expect the best results if you allow your cauliflower to become limp and rank-smelling.

PREPARATION AND COOKING

There is endless contradiction among the authorities about how to prepare and cook cauliflower. I was most amused – and rather confused – to read the experts and to be told emphatically to soak, not to soak, to cook head down, to cook head uppermost, never to separate into florets, to separate into florets, to blanch first, never to blanch first, and to add bread, milk, lemon juice or vinegar to the cooking water. So, my advice is to follow a few sensible guidelines and then please yourself!

Until recently I had never washed a cauliflower. But now I sometimes find that miniature cauliflowers are infested with tiny brown specks that are alive. I wash these under a strong spray of water; if that doesn't dislodge the bugs, I soak the cauliflower for 10 minutes in lightly salted water. It may also be a good idea to soak home-grown, unsprayed cauliflowers for 10 minutes in lightly salted water. If I am dealing with a standard-sized cauli I usually break it into large florets.

Cauliflower is best cooked in a non-aluminium saucepan as aluminium reacts with the chemical makeup of the cauliflower and can change its creamy-white colour to yellow.

TO COOK Cook pieces of cauliflower or a whole miniature cauliflower in lots of lightly salted water for about 8 minutes until just tender. Drain very well and either sauce, butter or dress it. If the cauliflower has been cooked until just tender and very well drained, I do not rinse it in cold water to stop further cooking as I believe that often this 'refreshing' leaves a vegetable tasting of cold water rather than of itself. **A whole cauliflower** Several of the authorities I consulted mentioned a liking for cooking a standard cauliflower whole, so that it can be presented intact. To do this, trim the cauliflower of all extraneous leaves and stalk. Cut the core out of the central stem, so that the head will cook more evenly. Stand the cauliflower, head uppermost, in a deep saucepan filled with 6 cm of water. Cover the pan tightly (with foil if the cauliflower is sticking out of the pan) and cook over a moderate heat for about 10 minutes.

sautéd cauliflower

recipes

SERVES 6

Make this with either a large cauliflower or single-serve caulis. For a beautiful result, try mixing bright-green broccoflower with the cauliflower.

6 miniature or 1 large
  cauliflower
½ cup olive oil
½ cup fresh breadcrumbs
3 anchovies, finely chopped
2 cloves garlic, finely sliced
2 tablespoons freshly chopped
  parsley
1 tablespoon extra-virgin olive
  oil
freshly ground black pepper

Select a deep, heavy-based saucepan with a lid. If using miniature caulis, halve them if larger than an egg and cut stems level. If using a standard cauliflower, separate into quite large florets. Heat olive oil and add cauliflower. Cover and cook for 5 minutes. Remove lid and scatter over crumbs. Cook uncovered over moderate heat, carefully turning from time to time, until cauliflower is just tender and crumbs have browned, a further 5 minutes or so.

Place anchovies with garlic in a small bowl over boiling water until anchovies melt. Stir in parsley and extra-virgin oil. Transfer cauliflower and crumb mixture to a serving dish, spoon over anchovy oil and grind on pepper. Serve warm or hot.

cauliflower bites
Dip florets of young cauliflower into Beer Batter and deep-fry at 175°C. Serve with spicy tomato relish or home-made chutney or sprinkle with Sesame and Coriander Dukkah (see CORIANDER).

cauliflower polonaise

SERVES 4

This classic garnish is delicious scattered over broccoli, green beans or asparagus but is best-known with cauliflower.

dips and crudités
Arrange tiny, raw cauliflower florets, carrot sticks, crisp radishes, slices of raw zucchini and raw fennel, cherry tomatoes and inner stalks of celery on an attractive platter, with a bowl of Hummus (see CHICK PEAS)*, Smoky Eggplant Purée (see* EGGPLANTS) *or Bagna Cauda Sauce (see* ANCHOVIES) *in the centre.*

½ cauliflower, separated into florets
2 hardboiled eggs
2 tablespoons fresh breadcrumbs
40 g butter
I tablespoon freshly chopped parsley
salt
freshly ground black pepper

Cook cauliflower, then drain well and keep warm. Shell eggs and separate yolks from whites. Press yolks through a coarse strainer onto a plate using the back of a spoon. Chop whites finely. In a frying pan, brown crumbs in butter, tossing them to avoid burning. Mix eggs, crumbs, parsley and seasoning lightly and scatter over hot cauliflower.

capers Add 1 tablespoon well-drained, fried capers. When capers are fried, the tiny heads open out like a miniature rose.

middle eastern cauliflower fritters

MAKES 20

Do not grate the cauliflower in advance as it will become too wet.

I large cauliflower
½ cup chickpea flour
I teaspoon freshly ground roasted cumin seeds
I teaspoon freshly ground roasted coriander seeds
I teaspoon salt
I teaspoon ground turmeric
pinch of ground ginger
pinch of cayenne pepper
I egg, lightly beaten
vegetable oil for deep-frying

Grate cauliflower into a bowl and add remaining ingredients except oil. Mix well. Squeeze into walnut-sized balls and fry in 1 cm hot oil until dark brown. Serve hot.

muff's soup

SERVES 6

This recipe was given to me by a friend who described it as the perfect dieter's dinner. She had no need to lose weight. But the soup is delicious.

1 cauliflower, cut into pieces, including stem
1 litre fat-free Chicken Stock
1 teaspoon Vegemite
freshly ground black pepper
freshly chopped parsley
freshly grated parmesan cheese

Cook cauliflower in stock until tender. Add Vegemite and stir until dissolved. Purée cauliflower and stock, then check seasoning. Stir in parsley. Serve, and pass the grated parmesan (be generous with it).

cauliflower cheese
For a weekend lunch, cloak just-tender cauliflower with the sauce used to make Fennel with Simple Cheese Sauce (see FENNEL), top with best-quality grated parmesan and breadcrumbs and bake at 180°C until golden and bubbling.

cauliflower and potato pie

SERVES 4

This recipe is based on one in Lynda Brown's The Cook's Garden.

1 cauliflower, separated into florets
1½ cups leftover mashed potato *or* 3–4 cooked potatoes
3 tablespoons cream *or* sour cream
freshly grated nutmeg
salt
freshly ground black pepper
2 tablespoons olive oil
3 tablespoons freshly grated parmesan cheese

Preheat oven to 180°C. Cook cauliflower in plenty of lightly salted water for 5 minutes. Drain very well. Process for 30 seconds in a food processor or chop by hand. Mix cauliflower with potato (crush the cooked potatoes, if using). Add cream and seasonings. Use half the oil to grease an ovenproof pie plate or gratin dish. Press cauliflower mixture into dish, then drizzle with remaining oil and sprinkle with parmesan. Bake for 30 minutes until golden brown. Serve with a juicy braise or stew.

celery and celeriac

The most well-known forms of *Apium graveolens*, celery and celeriac belong to the parsley family, as do the parsnip and carrot. | Celery has a long history and was prized by the ancient Egyptians, Greeks and Romans who believed that it could cure many ills, ranging from impotence to constipation. Nowadays most celery is consumed raw as a snack and in salads. It is also indispensable in the stockpot and when finely chopped and sautéd with onion, garlic and carrot forms the base for countless Mediterranean stews, while Chinese cooks stir-fry celery with all manner of other ingredients. It is less well known that celery can also be cooked and served as a vegetable in its own right, an exquisite dish of great delicacy. | Too often cooks lop off and discard the last 10 cm of the bunch; by doing this they are ignoring the prize within. The base of celery is considered a delicacy in France, where a dish of braised hearts of celery is offered with ceremony to accompany simply cooked poultry, meat or fish. (In France and Asia a bunch of celery is often much smaller than those in our markets, so the heart would serve one. The base of an Australian bunch of celery can be quartered lengthwise to serve four.) >

The bulbous celeriac, though root-like in appearance, is a corm and has brown warty skin and white flesh that tastes like celery. Sometimes called celery root, it was introduced to Britain from Egypt in the eighteenth century, although it is still something of a rarity in British cookery. Thanks to Australia's European migrants, celeriac is becoming more widely available here. A bit like the big, bad banksia men of *Snugglepot and Cuddlepie* fame in appearance, this knobbly vegetable becomes one of the staples of French charcuterie, celeriac rémoulade, when thickly peeled and grated and mixed with mustardy mayonnaise. Make it yourself and you will understand why this pungent, crunchy salad is such a favourite. Thick slices of celeriac can also be baked, just as parsnip and pumpkin are; the sweetness of these works well with rabbit or game birds. Celeriac also makes a delicious purée and great chips and is much more versatile than it first appears.

VARIETIES AND SEASON

Most celery is 'blanched' to prevent the stalks becoming too dark in colour, too tough and too strongly flavoured. Nowadays market gardeners blanch celery during the last few weeks before harvest by wrapping the stems in black polythene. When books caution you to wash celery very, very well to rid it of all the dirt trapped between the leaves, they are probably referring to the earlier method of blanching, where the celery was grown in a trench and soil was heaped around it.

Celery is available all year, with the peak season January–August. Celeriac is available in autumn and winter and sometimes through spring.

SELECTION AND STORAGE

Select bunches of *celery* that look crisp, not limp, and have fresh-looking leaves. Avoid bunches with cracks in the outer stalks. Prefer buying an entire bunch to half a bunch if you suspect the bunch was halved more than a day ago. Celery should be refrigerated in the crisper in a vegetable storage bag for a few days only.

Select *celeriac* that are baseball-sized, not enormous. Some very large specimens can be hollow and cottony in the centre. The celeriac should feel heavy and look fresh, not sunken, soft or withered. Freshly harvested celeriac will have a greenish look at the base of its leaves. As there is always a lot of waste with celeriac, choose the freshest first and then the smoothest. Celeriac will keep well in the refrigerator for at least a week.

PREPARATION AND COOKING

CELERY Separate the number of stalks required from the base and wash. Remove any strings from the outside of the stalk by making a small cut at the wide end (but not more

**celery
and
celeriac
go
with**
sea salt
olive oil
parsley
blue cheese
goat's cheese
olives
oranges
eggs
potatoes
apples
butter
cream
mustard
walnuts
squid
chicken
fish
ham
anchovies
chives
witlof
mayonnaise
game birds
rabbit

than a third through) and pulling the strings away and down the stalk with a knife. (With modern stringless varieties this is largely unnecessary except for the very outside stalks, and often they are reserved for the stockpot where the strings do not matter at all.) Soak the celery in a bowl of cold water to crisp it if serving it raw. Leave the pale tufts of leaves attached to the inner stalks. (They are delicious deep-fried!) Cut as desired.

CELERY HEART Discard the outer stalks (set them aside for making stocks or soups). Trim the root end free of any muddy bits and cut the thinnest slice possible from the bottom and discard it. Cut through the bunch about 10 cm from the end and quarter the heart lengthwise.

CELERIAC Cut celeriac discolours on contact with air, although the flavour does not change. When preparing celeriac, have a basin of acidulated water ✎ ready into which all peeled pieces can be dropped. Peel the celeriac thickly to remove all knobs and warts, then cut it into quarters and drop them into the water. Slice each quarter further, as desired, returning the celeriac to the water as you go.

TO COOK CELERIAC To avoid discoloration, chunks or slices of celeriac are often cooked in a *blanc* ✎. To make a *blanc*, whisk 2 tablespoons plain flour into 1 litre cold water and bring to a boil, whisking from time to time. Cook the celeriac in the *blanc* until barely tender (about 10 minutes). The celeriac can be refrigerated in this liquid in a stainless steel or china basin or a plastic container for several days. When needed, the celeriac is extracted from the liquid, dried with kitchen paper and baked or sautéed. **To bake** Dry pieces of celeriac that have been cooked in a *blanc*, roll them in a little oil and drop into a baking dish when roasting meat, as you would with a piece of pumpkin. The celeriac may take up to 20 minutes to develop a golden colour. Serve with chicken, or whatever. **To sauté** Dry pieces of celeriac that have been cooked in a *blanc* and fry in a little oil for 10 minutes or so until golden on both sides. Raw pieces of celeriac will take 15–20 minutes to sauté. **To purée** Peel the celeriac and cut it into chunks, immersing each into a bowl of acidulated water ✎ as you go. Cook the celeriac in lightly salted water in a non-reactive saucepan until tender, 10–15 minutes. Drain and mash as for potato (*see* p. 573). Beat in seasonings, butter, cream or olive oil – all or some – and serve hot.

braised celery

SERVES 4

In the 1960s I visited a French restaurant in a lane off George Street in Sydney. I ate John Dory fillets surrounded by delicious buttery braised celery. I have never forgotten the experience.

As with other vegetable dishes to accompany fish, I prefer to use a light chicken stock rather than fish stock as reduced fish stock can dominate. You can delay the final reduction of the juices for an hour or so. In this case, ensure that the celery has time to become thoroughly hot again before you increase the heat.

40 g butter
1 or 2 bunches celery,
   trimmed and quartered
1 clove garlic, sliced
2 cups Chicken Stock
salt
freshly ground black pepper

Preheat oven to 180°C. Select an ovenproof and flameproof dish that will hold the celery quite snugly (a cast-iron gratin dish is ideal). On stove top, melt butter and turn celery in it, then add garlic. Pour over just enough stock to nearly cover celery and press a piece of buttered baking paper over it. Bake for about 30 minutes, turning once. Remove from oven when celery is tender. If you are ready to serve, return dish to top of stove and reduce over a moderate to high heat until remaining liquid is syrupy, turning celery occasionally. Season and serve.

potato and celeriac purée

SERVES 4–6

Serve this delicious dish with braised beef or oxtail or grilled lamb chops.

2 cloves garlic, unpeeled
1 cup cream
4 potatoes, peeled
1 celeriac, cooked in a *blanc*
hot milk (optional)
salt
freshly ground black pepper

Cover garlic with cold water in a small saucepan and bring to a boil. Tip off water and repeat process twice. Slip garlic cloves from skins and simmer gently in cream until quite soft, then purée. Cook potatoes until tender, then drain and mash. Pour over garlic cream and mix well.

Pass celeriac through the medium disc of a food mill and mix with potato and garlic cream. Beat in a little boiling milk with a wooden spoon if purée is too stiff. If purée is not quite smooth, pass it through the medium disc of the food mill again. Adjust seasoning. Reheat purée in a covered bowl in a microwave oven or in a steamer and serve.

celeriac crisps
Deep-fry thinly sliced or shaved raw celeriac at 160°C and serve as a nibble with drinks.

celery and blue cheese
Mash equal quantities of creamy blue cheese and butter and fill the channels of celery sticks, then cut them into cocktail-sized pieces.

celery salad
Toss sliced celery with warm potatoes and hardboiled eggs – or fennel, mint and fat olives – and dress with olive oil and lemon juice.

waldorf salad

This classic salad is often tossed with sour cream, but I prefer to use mayonnaise. I also prefer to use red-skinned apples, perhaps Jonathans or even gravensteins. With sustaining bread, this is a great lunch, achievable in 10 minutes.

pinzimonio

Pile choice raw vegetables, including young inner leaves of celery, on a plate and offer the very finest extra-virgin olive oil, sea salt and ground pepper.

apples, cut into bite-sized
    chunks
celery, sliced
orange segments
walnuts, toasted
Mayonnaise ✐
cos lettuce leaves (optional)

Toss all ingredients except lettuce together and spoon into lettuce leaves, if using. Serve at once.

celeriac sautéd with lentils and walnut oil
SERVES 4

This dish is based on a recipe of Deborah Madison's that appeared in The Savory Way.

celeriac chips

Dip finely sliced raw celeriac in melted clarified butter ✐ and bake at 200°C on a baking tray lined with baking paper until tender and golden at the edges, about 10 minutes. These chips can be returned to a hot oven for 5 minutes for further crisping and browning if prepared ahead.

1 tablespoon olive oil
½ onion, finely chopped
½ carrot, finely chopped
2 inner sticks celery, sliced
1 clove garlic, finely chopped
1 bay leaf
1 cup brown lentils, washed
½ celeriac, peeled and cut
    into 1 cm cubes
pinch of salt
1 cup Chicken Stock ✐ or
    water
2 tablespoons freshly chopped
    parsley
1 tablespoon walnut oil
1 teaspoon sherry vinegar
freshly ground black pepper

Heat olive oil in a heavy frying pan and sauté onion, carrot, celery, garlic and bay leaf for 5 minutes. Tip in lentils and celeriac and add salt. Pour in stock and bring to a boil. Cook over a moderate heat, stirring every couple of minutes, until there is no noticeable liquid left (about 20 minutes). The lentils should still taste nutty and the celeriac should be barely tender. If there is still some liquid, increase heat and boil hard, stirring continuously. Stir in parsley, walnut oil and vinegar and add pepper to taste. Serve with sausages, chops or a ham steak or enjoy it just on its own.

stir-fried squid and celery   SERVES 4

Ask your fishmonger to clean your squid for you, or turn to SQUID, CALAMARI, CUTTLEFISH AND OCTOPUS *for instructions. The trick when stir-frying is to ensure your wok is hot before you start cooking and that a high temperature is maintained.*

6 small squid, cleaned
3 tablespoons vegetable oil
4 sticks celery, cut into 2 cm diagonal pieces
3 thin slices ginger, peeled
3 tablespoons rice wine
100 ml Chicken Stock
few drops of sesame oil

Slit each cleaned squid tube open. With a sharp knife, score squid in a close diagonal pattern, cutting only halfway into flesh. Cut squid into small pieces about 3 cm square.

Heat half the vegetable oil in a wok. Stir-fry celery over a high heat until shiny and transparent. Remove celery and wipe out wok. Heat remaining oil and add ginger, pressing and tossing it. Add squid and toss for 1 minute until it is curled and white. Add rice wine, celery, stock and sesame oil. Cover and cook over high heat for 3 minutes, then serve.

celeriac rémoulade   SERVES 2–4

This delicious starter is very addictive. With a bowl of fat olives and some good bread, and maybe a platter of thinly sliced salami, I wouldn't need anything more for lunch on a sunny autumn or winter's day.

1 celeriac
1 lemon
½ cup Mustard Mayonnaise
1 tablespoon freshly chopped parsley

Peel celeriac thickly and rub exposed surfaces with lemon. Chop into quarters and drop into a bowl of acidulated water. Shred celeriac, using the shredding disc of your food processor or Japanese vegetable slicer, and allow it to fall directly into the mayonnaise. Stir well to mix and add parsley.

leftovers Partner rémoulade with other raw vegetables or toss with small cooked prawns or mussels or both as a fancy beginning to dinner.

brain salad with celery and mustard cream sauce *see* BRAINS

fried celery leaves
Deep-fry pale-green or yellow celery leaves dipped in Cornflour Batter and serve with fillets of delicate fish or platters of grilled vegetables or as part of a fritto misto.

sauce for celery
Serve sticks of celery with Bagna Cauda Sauce (see ANCHOVIES).

celeriac coleslaw
Shred celeriac and add it to a cabbage coleslaw.

other recipes

cheese

c h e e s e   The fascination of cheese lies largely in the infinite variety that result from one basic product: milk. Cheese is made from the curds or solids of cow's, goat's, sheep's or buffalo's milk, which are separated from the whey and suitably ripened. The milk may be skimmed, partly skimmed, left whole or enriched with cream to produce an endless variety of flavours and styles. The diversification and marketing of cheese to the Australian domestic market began in earnest in the mid-1980s when export sales of milk slumped. There were very few farmhouse or speciality cheeses produced in Australia then. Today Australia has a flourishing cheese industry and in Victoria alone more than 50 types of speciality cheeses are made. However, not all specialist cheeses are farmhouse cheeses. 'Farmhouse cheese' means that the cheese has been made on a farm with milk from that farm alone. >

Standards in cheesemaking have been set by classic European cheese types. Some of these cheeses are available in Australia, although our health regulations prohibit the importation of any cheese made with whole (unpasteurised) milk. Neither can our own cheesemakers use unpasteurised milk. There is a strong belief among many of our cheesemakers that this requirement is detrimental to the production of optimum-quality cheese, and the recently formed Australian Specialist Cheesemakers' Association is preparing to challenge the National Food Authority on this issue.

For those fascinated by cheese it is important to experience European cheese as well as the local version. One would expect local cheeses to display their own characters, given the peculiarities of our pastures and our climate. It would be a mistake, however, if local cheesemakers did not recognise that in many cases they are still learning. We should not expect *uniformity* from specialist cheeses but we should be able to expect *consistency*. Our cheesemakers are working on it.

For a cheese lover it is an exciting time. Australia is producing some fine cheeses and there is no doubt that the industry will continue to progress and expand.

VARIETIES AND SEASON

Cheese can be categorised in a variety of ways. I find that the categories suggested by Will Studd, Australia's sole member of France's Guilde des Fromagers, are most helpful of all. (It needs to be remembered that the cheeses falling within categories such as 'goat's milk' or 'blue' vary enormously in style. Some cheeses may also belong to more than one category.)

Some cheeses are best made with spring milk (blue and harder varieties), some with autumn milk (surface-ripened cheeses) and some cheeses are made using only morning or evening milk or a mixture of both (parmesan cheese). For most of us these differences are things to marvel at as further examples of the mysterious art of cheesemaking.

As far as seasonal availability goes, most Australian specialist cheeses I know of are available all year. However, the best milk comes from late-spring, early summer and early autumn pastures, which in turn leads to fine-flavoured cheeses at this time. Will Studd would like to think that one day retailers and consumers will appreciate this.

BLUE | Blue cheeses ripen from the inside out and moulds are injected into the body of the curd. This category includes a wide range of styles, from creamy to crumbly and from mild to sharp-flavoured. The best-known European models include *roquefort* (from sheep's milk) and *gorgonzola* (from cow's milk). Australian examples of this style of cheese include Tarago River Cheese Co.'s Gippsland

hard
cheeses
go
with
bread
oatmeal biscuits
apples
grapes
pears
salad leaves
ham
pasta
walnuts
almonds
olives
celery
dates
raisins
chutney
pickles

Blue, Timboon Farmhouse Cheese's Farmhouse Blue and the Milawa Cheese Co.'s Milawa Blue.

COOKED

To make a cooked cheese, the milk is heated to temperatures exceeding 48°C and the curd is pressed and then matured. Such cheeses – *gruyère, parmesan, emmental*, and so on – have the lowest moisture content of all and keep for the longest time. Heidi Gruyère and Swissfield Emmental are some Australian examples. Parmigiano–Reggiano, the finest of Italy's parmesan cheeses, is imported into Australia. Appellation considerations mean we cannot hope to make a true parmesan here (dependent as it is on having the region around Parma as its origin). However, Will Studd feels there is a definite niche market available for the development of good hard cheeses in Australia.

FRESH

These cheeses are uncured and unripened and usually uncooked. They may or may not be salted. This category includes *cottage cheese, cream cheese, ricotta, bocconcini, mozzarella, mascarpone* and *fromage blanc*. Australian examples are Top Paddock's Whitelaw, Mamma Lucia's Bocconcini and Purrumbete Mozzarella (which is made from buffalo's milk, as mozzarella should be).

GOAT'S

Goat's cheeses have a very distinctive flavour. Some are fresh and some are surface-ripened with a soft white mould that is often sprinkled with fine black ash. The ash inhibits crust development and keeps the cheese inside very white. Kervella (Farmhouse Cheese) produces Fromage Fermier Chèvre and Milawa Cheese Co. makes Milawa Chèvre.

PROCESSED

The ripening action in processed cheese is stopped at a given point by heat treatment and the cheese remains constant and uniform in texture throughout its life. These are the cheeses you find most readily in your supermarket.

SEMI-HARD

For semi-hard cheese the milk is treated at a lower temperature than for cooked cheeses and the resulting cheese is matured, the best from 4 months to a year. This group includes *cheddars* as well as specialised cheeses, such as *raclette*, which is intended for melting. Local examples include Swissfield Raclette, Top Paddock Cheddar and the Tarago River Cheese Co.'s Hillcrest Mature.

SHEEP'S

This category includes traditional ethnic cheeses (*fetta*) as well as more experimental cheeses modelled after famous European cheeses such as *roquefort*. The

Milawa Cheese Co.'s Milawa Roc is an example of the latter, while Mount Emu Creek Fetta illustrates the former.

soft **cheeses go with**
bread
herbs
cream
paprika
cumin
olive oil
pepper
grilled sweet
* peppers*
olives
sultanas soaked in
* white wine*
raspberries
quince paste
salad leaves
anchovies

SURFACE-RIPENED WASHED RIND | To make a washed-rind cheese, the curd is gently pressed and then dipped in brine both to salt the cheese and to form the crust. The cheese is regularly washed with more brine and/or wine and/or liqueur. The flavours achieved range from mild and nutty to very spicy and aromatic. The cheese ripens from the inside. A good washed-rind cheese should have a smooth crust, look a bit swollen and not have a sagging middle or hardened crusty edges. The Milawa Cheese Co. produces King River Gold in this style, Mungabareena comes from Swissfield and Top Paddock makes Wine Washed Rind.

SURFACE-RIPENED WHITE MOULD | The cheeses in this group include triple-cream and brie styles. Mould grows on the surface of the cheese and develops inwards. **Bries** and **camemberts** are only mature when the cheese is soft right through to the centre. In **triple-cream** cheese the changing texture only occurs for about a third of the way into the cheese, so that 2 textures result. Local examples include Jindi Brie, Jindi Supreme and Timboon Farmhouse Cheese Camembert.

SELECTION AND STORAGE

Specialist cheese shops are appearing in the suburbs and almost every shopping strip now has a 'gourmet' shop that sells a range of cheeses. Ask if the brie or camembert you are buying is ready to eat and if there is a particular cheese that is in perfect condition. Note that market forces have led to almost all hard cheeses being waxed rather than sold as a cloth-encased, whole cheese. This is regrettable as cheese is a living thing and cannot 'breathe' in a wax coat. For this reason, too, Will Studd counsels cheese lovers against buying hard cheese that has been vacuum-packed.

According to Will, we should store our cheese at 9–12°C wrapped in cloth in a damp place, such as a cellar or cool cupboard with good airflow. (I should add that Will is an Englishman and comes from the land of pantries and larder cupboards!) This is impossible for most of us and in our climate the refrigerator is the usual place for storing cheese. (Will recommends the vegetable crisper.)

Unwrapped cheese will dry out very rapidly, particularly the softer, high-moisture types. It is better to wrap cheese in calico cloth; greaseproof paper is next best. Failing that, foil or plastic film will do (however, avoid wrapping blue cheese in foil). Natural cheese that is wrapped for too long in an impervious film can develop harmless surface moulds and 'off' flavours that may dissipate if the cheese is unwrapped and exposed to the air for an hour or so. Therefore, make sure you unwrap your cheese well before dinner, cut away any surface mould and allow the cheese to come to room temperature before eating.

Different cheeses keep for different lengths of time, with the hard types (for example, parmesan) lasting the longest. Cottage, ricotta and cream cheeses have a short storage life. Check that they still smell sweet and appetising, not sour. Their maximum life is 5 days unless the cheese has been vacuum-packed, although sometimes it is much less.

PREPARATION AND SERVING

When preparing a *cheese platter*, if you have one perfectly ripe cheese do not bother with a wider selection. It is better to consume one perfect cheese at a meal than to end up with a motley collection of tiny pieces that will all dry up in the refrigerator over the next few days. If you are determined to offer a selection, do not have more than 3 cheeses. Remember to unwrap the cheese well before you plan to eat it, and allow it to come to room temperature.

There is no reason to serve sliced kiwifruit or unripe hard strawberries with *any* cheese in the world! Crusty bread is the best all-rounder with cheese, and apart from serving oatmeal or wheatmeal biscuits with a mature cheddar, bread is always preferable to biscuits. A sourdough loaf with a dense crumb and chewy crust is my favourite. And I prefer it grilled or toasted. Olive bread works very well with goat's cheese, and a walnut loaf can be wonderful with blue cheeses (always assuming that the nuts used in the bread are not rancid). Breads with sultanas in them are excellent with some washed-rind, 'aromatic' cheeses.

It is certainly not the case that one can only serve a dry, full-bodied red wine with cheese. One skilled winemaker suggests as a general rule that the lighter the cheese, the lighter the wine. Try a late-picked white wine or a botrytis-affected dessert wine with a creamy blue cheese. Sauvignon blanc can partner goat's cheese well, as can a light pinot noir. The floral and spicy character of a gewürztraminer is a pleasant surprise with a strongly flavoured washed-rind cheese.

When *cooking with cheese*, too high a temperature will force moisture out of the protein tissue, making the cheese stringy. Always add cheese to sauces at the last minute and cook just long enough to melt the cheese.

recipes

cheese rarebit

MAKES 1

This fancy cheese on toast is called a Welsh rarebit if Caerphilly cheese is used, and a Leicestershire rarebit if Leicestershire cheese is used. I suggest using a slice of full-bodied bread, such as sourdough.

20 g butter

100 g cheddar or other hard cheese, crumbled or grated

2 tablespoons milk

salt

freshly ground black pepper

1 teaspoon prepared English mustard

1 slice substantial bread, toasted and buttered

Melt butter and add cheese. Stir gently until cheese melts, then gradually add milk. Season to taste with salt, pepper and mustard and pour over hot buttered toast.

cheese and ale A simple variation on the rarebit. Coarsely grate 100 g mature farmhouse cheddar (or other good hard cheese) and put it into a heavy-based saucepan with 100 ml ale. Heat very gently, stirring, until smooth. Serve very hot on hot buttered toast.

raclette cheese fritters

SERVES 2

1 x 100 g slice raclette or emmental cheese, cut 5 mm thick

1 cup Beer Batter

vegetable oil for deep-frying

Cut cheese in half and freeze overnight. Dip cheese slices in batter and fry in a good depth of clean, hot oil until golden brown. Drain well on crumpled kitchen paper and serve with a small salad, pickled cucumbers and any other vegetable pickle you have in the cupboard. A fruit chutney is excellent with this, as is Green Tomato Relish (*see* TOMATOES).

gougères

MAKES 12

These cheese-flavoured, airy yet crunchy choux puffs are a speciality of Burgundy. The technique of making choux paste is so easy that you will have also mastered how to make chocolate éclairs, cream puffs and even a croquembouche, the beautiful celebration cake popular in France for first communions and weddings.

140 g plain flour

100 g gruyère, emmental or other hard cheese

½ cup milk

½ cup water

100 g butter

pinch of salt

5 eggs

1 extra egg yolk, lightly beaten

Preheat oven to 220°C. Sift flour and have it ready on a plate. Grate cheese coarsely or cut it into fine strips.

Put milk, water, butter and salt into a large heavy-based saucepan. Bring to a boil, then immediately lift pan from heat, place it on a heatproof surface and tip in flour in one quick movement. Stir vigorously with a wooden spoon until smooth. Return pan to a low heat and continue to stir vigorously until paste comes cleanly away from sides of pan (3–4 minutes). >

cucumber cream cheese

Mix grated, squeezed cucumber, finely chopped garlic, salt and pepper with cream cheese and press it into an oiled small basin for an hour. Turn it out, cover it lavishly with lumpfish roe and surround with garlic croutons or toasted pita bread for a party buffet.

parmesan oil

Save rinds from parmesan cheese and infuse in olive oil for 2–3 days. Strain and store in the refrigerator and use over pasta or baked vegetables or for drizzling in soup.

Transfer paste to bowl of a food processor and, with the motor running, add 2 eggs. Incorporate thoroughly before adding a further 2 eggs. Incorporate thoroughly before adding final egg. Add three-quarters of the cheese and blend. Transfer paste to a piping bag.

Cover a baking tray with baking paper and pipe on rounds of paste 6–8 cm in diameter. Paint top of each puff with the extra egg yolk and scatter with remaining cheese. Without delay, transfer puffs to oven for 10 minutes. Do *not* disturb them. Lower temperature to 200°C and cook for 10 minutes with oven door wedged ajar with a wooden spoon, so that steam from the rising puffs can escape. Serve at once. If you are delayed, the puffs can be held in a turned-off oven for 5–10 minutes or transferred to a warming oven.

cream puffs If making cream puffs, omit the cheese and allow the puffs to cool on a wire rack away from sudden draughts. When quite cold, split and fill with firmly whipped cream or Pastry Cream ✎ and dip each puff into melted chocolate or drizzle with golden caramel.

bocconcini pizza
Slice bocconcini lavishly over an uncooked pizza base ✎, sprinkle with olive oil, pieces of roasted sweet pepper and freshly ground black pepper and bake on a pizza tray at 220°C for 10 minutes. Slide the pizza from the tray onto the oven rack and bake a further 5 minutes to crisp the base. Eat as a snack or to accompany Gazpacho (see TOMATOES*).*

cheese straws

MAKES 25

100 g unsalted butter
100 g plain flour
100 g mature cheddar, grated
salt
cayenne pepper

Briefly blend butter with flour in a food processor until mixture resembles breadcrumbs. Add cheese and season and process quickly until dough forms a ball. Wrap dough in greaseproof paper and chill for 1 hour or so.

Preheat oven to 200°C. Roll pastry out 5 cm thick and cut into straws (or small triangles). Place pastries well apart on a baking tray lined with baking paper. Bake for 15 minutes until golden brown. Cool briefly on tray, then cool completely on a wire rack. Store in an airtight tin.

spicy biscuits Omit 1 tablespoon grated cheese and add 2 teaspoons chilli sauce. Scatter the biscuits with sesame seeds before baking.

flaky goat's cheese biscuits

MAKES 30

100 g fresh goat's cheese
1½ tablespoons freshly grated parmesan cheese
150 g softened unsalted butter
scant pinch of salt
¼ teaspoon cayenne pepper
175 g plain flour, sifted

Blend cheeses, butter, salt and cayenne pepper quickly in a food processor until smooth. Remove to a bowl and fold in flour. Spoon mixture onto baking paper and roll into a log about 5 cm in diameter. Refrigerate for several hours until firm. Slice thinly and bake at 180°C for 10 minutes. Cool, then store in an airtight tin.

goat's cheese on salad leaves with an anchovy dressing

SERVES 4

8 slices breadstick

4 tablespoons extra-virgin
    olive oil

2 cloves garlic

80 g butter

8 slices fresh goat's cheese

1 cup fine fresh breadcrumbs

2 anchovies, finely chopped

2 cups small salad leaves,
    washed and dried

2 tablespoons freshly chopped
    parsley

2 teaspoons freshly chopped
    chives

freshly ground black pepper

Brush breadstick slices with 1 tablespoon of the oil. Bake or grill quickly until golden on both sides, then wipe with 1 cut garlic clove. Set aside. Melt half the butter and roll each slice of goat's cheese in it. Press a generous layer of breadcrumbs onto each slice of cheese and refrigerate until needed. Place anchovies in a small bowl resting over a saucepan of simmering water. The anchovies will melt into a cream. Remove and keep aside. Roll salad leaves in a clean cloth. Refrigerate until needed.

When ready to serve, divide salad leaves between 4 warmed plates. Divide breadstick croutons between salads. Heat remaining butter in a non-stick frying pan and cook crumbed slices of cheese on both sides until golden, turning very gently with a wide spatula. Slip cheeses onto salad leaves. Finely chop remaining garlic clove, add to frying pan and sauté for 1 minute. Stir in anchovies, remaining oil and herbs. Remove at once from heat and spoon over salad leaves and cheese. Grind pepper over and serve as a first course.

greek country salad

SERVES 4

4 tomatoes, cut into chunks

2 Lebanese cucumbers, peeled
    and cut into chunks

4 spring onions, chopped

1 green pepper, seeded and
    diced

extra-virgin olive oil

few drops of red-wine vinegar

12 kalamata olives

salt

freshly ground black pepper

1 thick slice fetta cheese,
    cubed

Put tomato into a wide salad bowl and add cucumber, spring onion and green pepper. Pour over a good slurp of oil and allow to stand for 30 minutes. Add vinegar and olives. Season, being careful with salt as some fetta cheese is very salty, and mix well. Scatter fetta over and serve.

parmesan and ...
Buy good parmesan cheese (the very best is Parmigiano–Reggiano) and grate it freshly onto pasta or into soups or enjoy a chunk of it with a crisp pear. If a recipe calls for shaved parmesan, use a conventional vegetable peeler.

blue cheese sauce
Add crumbled blue cheese to Béchamel Sauce before coating just-tender cauliflower or fennel or cooked macaroni. Bake in a hot oven until golden and bubbling.

classic cheese soufflé

SERVES 4

Soufflés are not nearly as fraught with danger as some cookery books would have you believe. The cheese sauce for this one can sit at room temperature for 1 hour before the egg whites are added. Cover the sauce with a piece of buttered baking paper to prevent a hard skin forming.

marinated cheese

Marinate chunks of goat's cheese in olive oil with a bay leaf, sprigs of thyme, a small sprig of rosemary and freshly cracked pepper. Use after a week. Also use the oil!

grilled haloumi

Oil slices of haloumi and grill on the barbecue or fry in a little oil. Eat on toast or in a salad or serve alongside grilled sausages.

butter
3 tablespoons freshly grated
  parmesan cheese
2 tablespoons plain flour
1 cup warm milk
3 tablespoons freshly grated
  gruyère cheese
4 egg yolks
salt
freshly ground black pepper
5 egg whites

Preheat oven to 200°C. Butter a 1 litre soufflé dish well, then tip in 1 tablespoon of the parmesan cheese and coat sides and base. Melt 30 g butter in a small heavy-based saucepan. Stir in flour and cook over moderate heat, stirring, for 2 minutes. Gradually add milk, stirring all the while. Bring to a boil, then reduce heat and allow sauce to simmer for 5 minutes. Stir in gruyère and remaining parmesan cheese and then the egg yolks, one at a time. Taste for seasoning. Transfer to a large mixing bowl.

Whisk egg whites until creamy and firm. Tip half on top of the cheese sauce, and, using a metal spoon, lift and fold whites through mixture. Continue with remaining egg whites. The soufflé mixture should look spongy and frothy. Transfer mixture to prepared dish and run your thumb around edge of soufflé mixture. It will rise within this flattened edge. Place soufflé in oven and do not disturb for 25 minutes. Open the door gently and peep at it. The centre should be well risen and browned. Touch gently: the soufflé should yield but not feel liquid.

Remove soufflé from oven and take it straight to the table. Allow a moment for all to admire it before serving each guest with some of the crusty top and some of the creamy, saucy middle. The best way to cut a soufflé is with 2 large serving spoons dipped in boiling water.

gruyère tart

1 quantity Shortcrust Pastry
250 g gruyère or emmental
  cheese, cut into tiny dice
1 cup cream
salt
freshly ground black pepper
freshly grated nutmeg
2 eggs
1 egg yolk

Line a 22 cm loose-bottomed flan tin with pastry and bake blind at 200°C for 20 minutes. Allow to cool.

Scatter cheese over pastry case. Warm cream and season it with salt, pepper and nutmeg. Mix eggs and egg yolk into cream and pour gently into pastry case. Bake at 200°C for 20 minutes. Allow to cool for a few minutes before cutting. >

variations Tiny dice of a mild sausage such as mortadella or a mild cured ham can be scattered among the cheese cubes, as can fresh herbs.

stephanie's twice-baked goat's cheese soufflés

SERVES 6

This soufflé has been on the menu at Stephanie's for a very long time. It is so popular that we cannot remove it. The soufflés are not served in their dishes, so it is possible to use aluminium moulds or even teacups of approximately 150 ml capacity.

80 g butter
60 g plain flour
350 ml warm milk
75 g fresh goat's cheese
1 tablespoon freshly grated parmesan cheese
2 tablespoons freshly chopped parsley or parsley and other herbs
3 egg yolks
salt
freshly ground black pepper
4 egg whites
2 cups cream

cheese omelette
Add cubes of fetta or other sharp cheese to an omelette.

garlic cheese
Season fresh cheese with a little garlic paste, freshly ground pepper and lots of herbs and offer with hot toast.

Preheat oven to 180°C. Melt 20 g of the butter and grease 6–8 soufflé dishes. Melt remaining butter in a small heavy-based saucepan. Stir in flour and cook over moderate heat, stirring, for 2 minutes. Gradually add milk, stirring all the while. Bring to a boil, then reduce heat and simmer for 5 minutes.

Mash goat's cheese until soft and add to hot sauce with parmesan and parsley. Allow to cool for a few minutes. Fold yolks in thoroughly and taste for seasoning. Beat egg whites until creamy and fold quickly and lightly into cheese mixture. Divide mixture between prepared moulds and smooth surface of each. Stand moulds in a baking dish lined with a tea towel and pour in boiling water to come two-thirds up their sides. Bake for about 20 minutes until firm to the touch and well puffed. Remove soufflés from oven – they will deflate and look wrinkled. Allow to rest for a minute or so, then gently ease them out of moulds. Invert onto a plate covered with plastic film and leave until needed.

To serve, preheat oven to 180°C. Place soufflés in a buttered ovenproof gratin dish, so that they are not touching. Pour over cream (⅓ cup per soufflé) to moisten them thoroughly. Return to oven for 15 minutes. The soufflés will look swollen and golden. Serve with cream from the dish or with Fresh Tomato Sauce (*see* TOMATOES) spooned around them or with a small green salad.

honey cheesecake

SERVES 8

This is a traditional cheesecake rather than the fluffy decorated cakes that one can buy. Use a distinctively flavoured honey for preference.

1 quantity Shortcrust Pastry
200 g full-cream cottage
    cheese
4 tablespoons honey
100 g castor sugar
1 level teaspoon ground
    cinnamon
4 eggs
extra ground cinnamon
extra castor sugar

Line a 4–6 cm deep 22 cm pie plate with pastry and bake blind at 200°C for 20 minutes. Remove from oven and lower temperature to 180°C.

Work cottage cheese, honey, castor sugar, cinnamon and eggs together in a food processor to make a smooth cream. Pour into pastry case. Sprinkle thickly with a mixture of cinnamon and castor sugar and bake for 30 minutes or until set. Allow to cool before serving.

english curd tart

SERVES 8

This curiously textured tart was a speciality of my Yorkshire grandmother, who died when I was 9 years old.

The English plate pies are much less grand than a French tart. Although traditionally the pastry is not baked blind, I recommend that it is, as one of the least attractive features of some English tarts and pies is their white uncooked crusts.

1 quantity Shortcrust Pastry
90 g softened butter
60 g castor sugar
250 g cottage cheese
1 tablespoon fine breadcrumbs
pinch of salt
freshly grated nutmeg
2 eggs
60 g currants

Line a 4–6 cm deep 20 cm pie plate with pastry and bake blind at 200°C for 20 minutes. Remove from oven.

Cream butter and sugar in a food processor. Add cottage cheese, breadcrumbs, salt and nutmeg and blend well. Briefly blend in eggs, then stir in currants. The mixture may look curdled at this stage. Pour mixture into pastry case and bake at 200°C for 10 minutes, then lower heat to 180°C and cook until tart is firm, about 20 minutes. Serve warm or cool.

zabaglione with mascarpone

SERVES 6

8 egg yolks
150 g castor sugar
1 cup marsala
300 g mascarpone
½ cup crushed amaretti
    biscuits

Whisk egg yolks and sugar in a bowl over simmering water until thick and pale. Add marsala gradually, whisking constantly for 15 minutes. Remove from heat and whisk mixture until it cools, then refrigerate until thoroughly chilled. Fold in mascarpone and amaretti and divide between glass bowls.

blue cheese butter
Mash blue cheese with butter and use instead of butter on a baked potato or a grilled steak.

cheesy potato patties
Grate a cheese such as raclette or gruyère into cold mashed potato, roll into patties, flour lightly, fry in oil and butter until golden and serve with grilled sausages.

grate your own
Give up buying processed cheese slices and buy a simple cheese grater instead.

'devonshires'
Serve triple-cream cheese and berry jam on scones.

other recipes

bocconcini, tomato and basil salad *see* BASIL

braised fennel in meat juices with cheese *see* FENNEL

fennel with simple cheese sauce *see* FENNEL

fettuccine with gorgonzola *see* PASTA AND NOODLES

ham and ricotta stuffing for lamb *see* LAMB

garlic and goat's cheese custards *see* GARLIC

gratin of silverbeet stems *see* SILVER BEET

jenny's caesar salad *see* EGGS

labna – yoghurt cheese *see* YOGHURT

lyn's cherry cheesecake *see* CHERRIES

mushroom caps stuffed with goat's cheese on vine leaves
  see MUSHROOMS

onion and blue cheese pizza *see* ONIONS

onion and cheese tart *see* ONIONS

radicchio braised with blue cheese *see* SALAD GREENS

spanakopita *see* SPINACH

spinach and ricotta gnocchi *see* SPINACH

spinach ricotta terrine with pear dressing *see* SPINACH

sweet marjoram and mozzarella fritters *see* OREGANO AND MARJORAM

twice-cooked zucchini soufflés *see* ZUCCHINI AND SQUASH

witlof in cheese sauce *see* WITLOF

cherries

With their glowing, smouldering crimson or scarlet skins and high gloss, cherries seem too good to be true. I have a platter of deep-blue apothecary's glass and in cherry season it has pride of place on my wooden table piled with cherries (with a small bowl placed discreetly beside it for the pips). Add to this the exquisite beauty of a cherry tree in full frothy blossom and the satiny markings of cherry wood and it is not surprising that cherries are celebrated all over the world wherever they grow. | Modern cherries are divided into 3 main groups: the sweet cherries (*Prunus avium*), the sour cherries (*P. cerasus*) and the in-betweens. There has been extensive hybridisation within the main species, resulting in subdivisions that are made according to the shape of the fruit and colour of the skin, the colour and character of the flesh and the colour of the juice. | Cherries are an ancient fruit and originated in south-eastern Europe and western Asia. There are still many cherry recipes that are closely linked to these areas, especially from Russia, Hungary, Turkey and Germany, the latter of which is home to the fabulous Black Forest cake. Kirsch and other cherry liqueurs are also produced in central and eastern Europe. >

European cherry recipes are all intended for the sour cherry, which develops far greater complexity and depth of flavour than a sweet cherry when cooked. Inevitably, sweet cherries will have to be substituted most of the time. It should be noted, however, that there are a few growers of sour cherries in South Australia and central Victoria who are trying hard to produce enough fruit to satisfy those clamouring to buy it. I am one of them!

VARIETIES AND SEASON

In Australia the Young and Orange districts of New South Wales produce more than 80 per cent of the nation's cherry crop. Victoria and South Australia also have important plantings. Sweet cherries are not usually sold by varietal name, but a few varieties are worth special comment. Some sweet cherries are light red or deep red when at their best, such as burgsdorf or Henderson's seedling. These varieties taste over-ripe when they have become black. Other sweet cherries, such as Stella, Bing, Sam, Ron's seedling, St Margaret and black boy, are at their best *only* when the fruit has become very dark. Napoleon, Florence and Rainier have yellow skins with a red or pink blush when fully ripe.

In mid-January for the last few years some lucky people have been able to buy sour morello cherries. From a group of sour cherries with dark fruit and juice, this is the cherry used in the luscious Black Forest cake.

Cherries are available October–February, with the peak season being mid-summer. They range in colour from creamy-yellow with red splashes to almost black.

SELECTION AND STORAGE

All cherries are susceptible to rain and hail. Should either occur just before harvest the fruit will split and quickly rot.

Cherries keep far better with the stalks intact. Select cherries that are full and very shiny with green stems; dull cherries are usually over-ripe. Do not buy undersized fruit (cherries gain up to a third of their volume and flavour in the last week before harvesting; if the fruit has been picked early you will miss out on both size and taste).

Sweet cherries keep well for several days in a vegetable storage bag in the refrigerator. *Sour* cherries will keep for several weeks under refrigeration. All cherries can be frozen, with or without stones. Before freezing cherries, ensure the fruit is dry, then pack it into rigid containers, pour in enough light Sugar Syrup ✓ to cover it and add a squeeze of lemon juice.

One can also buy sun-dried cherries in some food stores. I have yet to be convinced of their advantages. I ate a dried cherry pie in New Orleans that had a very concentrated flavour (more raisiny than cherry, I thought) and the texture remained chewy and dense even after cooking.

**cherries
go
with**
*brandy
almonds
goat's cheese
cream cheeses
yoghurt
white wine
rosé wine
port
sago
duck
squab pigeons
tongue
ham
sour cream
thick cream
vanilla ice-cream
butter
citrus juices
cinnamon
chocolate
pastry
cloves*

PREPARATION

Do not remove stalks before storing or preparing cherries, and wash cherries just before eating. Use first any cherries that have lost their stalks on the trip home from the shop. Cook cherries in a non-aluminium saucepan to preserve the colour better.

The kernels inside the cherry pips add a subtle almond flavour to the cooked fruit. Tie a few cracked pips in a piece of muslin whenever you poach cherries and when making jam. Cherries contain little pectin, so if you are making jam you will need redcurrant juice, apple juice or powdered pectin to ensure a good set. Some European recipes do not add any of these. These recipes use sour cherries, which have more pectin, and the preserve made is often meant to be quite runny.

Cherries were never stoned in our house. I am still reluctant to stone cherries for many preparations because of the subsequent loss of juice and the damage one does to the shape of the cherry and, the real reason, because sucking on the cherry pip seems to be part of the pleasure. However, I am always over-ruled in the restaurant by those who tell me that a customer may choke or break a tooth!

TO STONE Buy a cherry stoner if you are planning to do this often (it's a very tedious task). Otherwise, make a small slit near the top of the cherry and gouge out the pip with your finger or a small knife. Do not delay the poaching or cooking as precious juice will start to seep from the wound at once. (When you bruise or slice a cherry you also release an enzyme that turns the fruit brown. The browning can be delayed by dipping the fruit in lemon juice.)

preserved cherries

cherries with cheese

Eat cherries with crusty bread and goat's cheese.

I kg cherries, rinsed
2 cups sugar
I litre water

Stone cherries and crush 6 pips by wrapping them in a cloth and tapping them with a hammer. Tie pips in a piece of muslin. Dissolve sugar in water in a large saucepan. Add cracked pips and simmer for 5 minutes. Tip in cherries and simmer for 1–2 minutes only. Drain, reserving syrup. Pack hot, sterilised jars with cherries. Simmer syrup for 5 minutes to thicken it slightly. Pour syrup into jars and seal.

To ensure safe keeping, it is wise to simmer the sealed jars in boiling water for 15 minutes. Turn off the heat and allow the jars to cool completely before drying, labelling and storing.

pickled cherries

Cherries, sweet or sour, are delicious pickled. The cherries keep well and although they can become progressively wrinkled, the flavour is still good after a year. I like pickled cherries with Pork Rillettes (see PORK), one of the easiest and most satisfying examples of traditional French charcuterie.

700 g sugar

850 ml white-wine vinegar

24 black peppercorns

12 cloves

6 bay leaves

1 clove garlic, unpeeled (optional)

1 kg sweet *or* sour cherries, rinsed

Dissolve sugar in vinegar in a large saucepan. Add all other ingredients except cherries and simmer for 10 minutes. Allow syrup to cool completely. Check cherries and discard any that are bruised or split. Trim stalks to 1 cm and pack fruit into hot, sterilised ✐ preserving jars. Pour cold vinegar syrup over fruit and seal. Leave for a few weeks before eating.

cherry pancakes
Mix chopped cherries with cream cheese, sugar and cinnamon for a pancake filling. Warm the filled, folded pancakes in butter until crisp on the outside and the filling is almost oozing.

sour cherries in brandy

In autumn I often partner sour cherries prepared this way with Victorian venison. A few of these cherries warmed in their own syrup can also be spooned over ice-cream as a simple sauce. Three months after preparing them the cherries are quite wonderful.

1 kg sour cherries, rinsed and stems trimmed to 1 cm

1 stick cinnamon, 3 lemon myrtle leaves *or* 3–4 crushed cherry pips

300 g sugar

3 cups brandy

Pack cherries into hot, sterilised ✐ preserving jars. Divide cinnamon stick or lemon myrtle leaves between jars (or add a muslin bag of crushed pips to each). Dissolve sugar in a little of the brandy. Add remaining brandy and divide between jars, ensuring fruit is covered. Seal and leave undisturbed for at least 8 weeks.

poached cherries

SERVES 4

500 g cherries, stems removed

½ cup sugar

juice of 1 lemon

1 tablespoon brandy, kirsch *or* port (optional)

Rinse cherries and put in a saucepan with sugar and lemon juice. Cover and simmer gently for 10 minutes until cherries are tender and have given up a lot of juice. Remove fruit with a slotted spoon. Boil juice rapidly for 2 minutes and pour over fruit. Add liqueur if using. These cherries are for immediate eating.

russian sour cherry soup

SERVES 6

This 'soup' is served as a dessert course and comes from Please to the Table: the Russian Cookbook *by Anya von Bremzen and John Welchman.*

1 kg sour cherries, rinsed
2 cloves
½ stick cinnamon
300 ml water
2 cups late-picked white wine
  or rosé wine
½ cup sugar
juice of 1 orange
1 tablespoon lemon juice
grated zest of 1 orange

Stone cherries and reserve pips. Set aside 1 cup cherries. Crack a handful of pips and tie them in a piece of muslin with cloves and cinnamon. Put muslin bag, reserved cherries, water, wine and sugar in a large saucepan. Bring to a boil, stirring, and simmer, covered, until cherries are very soft (about 20 minutes).

Transfer cherries and 1 cup cooking liquid to a food processor and blend until smooth. Stir purée back into pan. Add citrus juices, zest and reserved cherries. Simmer until cherries just start to soften. Taste for sugar. Remove muslin bag and refrigerate soup until ready to serve. Offer a bowl of sour cream or crème fraîche with the soup.

---

chocolate cherries
Dip Sour Cherries in Brandy (see p. 189) in melted bittersweet chocolate for an explosive after-dinner treat.

cherry sauce
Heat stoned cherries in butter with a little sugar and serve on top of a sweet omelette or with ice-cream.

---

mum's cherry sago

SERVES 6

My childhood memory of cherries is of cherry sago. Mum would make a big pot of it and we children kept a very close check on how many pips each of us left on our plate.

2 tablespoons sago
½ cup sugar
400 ml water, red wine or
  port
½ stick cinnamon
500 g cherries, rinsed and
  stems removed

Gently simmer sago in a saucepan with sugar, water and cinnamon, stirring until sago is nearly transparent. Add cherries, stir well, then cover and simmer for 10 minutes until cherries are tender and juice is pink. Tip into a basin and chill.

lyn's cherry cheesecake

SERVES 8

The charm of this recipe is the contrast between the smooth creamy filling and the fresh juicy cherries. The filling is equally delicious used as a pastry cream for tartlets. The cherries can be stewed or preserved but I love it best when they are uncooked but very juicy. The pips must *be removed.*

200 g butter, melted

1 teaspoon ground ginger

350 g wheatmeal biscuit
   crumbs

250 g cream cheese

2 tablespoons kirsch

½ cup sifted pure icing sugar

300 ml crème fraîche

300 ml cream, stiffly whipped

500 g stoned cherries

Combine melted butter with ginger and biscuit crumbs. Press into a 22 cm springform tin and even out base and sides using a straight-sided glass. Chill until firm.

Work cream cheese, 1 tablespoon of the kirsch and icing sugar in a food processor until a smooth cream. Add crème fraîche. Scrape into a bowl and fold in cream. Pile into chilled biscuit case and smooth down evenly. Chill for at least 1 hour.

When ready to serve, remove cheesecake from tin and transfer to a serving plate. Sprinkle cherries with remaining kirsch and pile on top of cake. Cut with a knife dipped in hot water.

glaze Some of my friends have made this using Poached Cherries (*see* p. 189) and have then used the cherry juice thickened with arrowroot as a glaze. If you want this more stable look, the proportions are 1 tablespoon arrowroot to 1½ cups fruit juice. (Arrowroot is a starch derived from a West Indian tuber and is used mostly to thicken soups, sauces and desserts. It is useful in fruit glazes as it thickens without causing cloudiness.)

cherry tartlets
Fill tartlets with Pastry Cream or sweetened whipped cream cheese and pile high with stoned cherries. Glaze with gently melted redcurrant jelly.

cherry and almond tart

This recipe is a simplified version of one from Jane Grigson's Fruit Book. *The tart base can also be brushed with jam, and often the tart is iced or scattered with more of the nuts at the end of the cooking time.*

1 quantity Shortcrust Pastry

90 g butter

90 g castor sugar

1 egg

1 extra egg yolk

3 tablespoons plain flour

125 g ground almonds

1 cup Preserved Cherries (see
   p. 188), drained but syrup
   reserved

100 g icing sugar

Line a 20 cm loose-bottomed flan tin with pastry and bake blind at 200°C for 20 minutes. Reserve remaining pastry for making lattice top.

Reduce oven temperature to 180°C. Cream butter and castor sugar until pale. Add egg, extra egg yolk, flour and ground almonds to make a paste. Spread a thin layer of paste over pastry case. Scatter cherries over evenly. Dab on remaining paste and smooth as well as you can with a flexible knife. Cover paste with a lattice of pastry strips. Bake for 25 minutes until tart feels springy and firm. Cool for a few minutes, then brush all over with icing sugar mixed with a few drops of reserved syrup. Return to oven for a further 5 minutes. Serve warm or cold.

chervil

Originating in ancient Rome, chervil (*Anthriscus cerefolium*) has long been valued for its medicinal properties (it was thought to be a blood purifier). It is a delicate herb with soft fern-like leaves. Many gardeners experience difficulty with chervil in our hot summers, as the leaves often turn a reddish colour and then wither. Because of this, although it is a biennial, chervil is best treated as an annual in Australia. Chervil has a delicate aniseed flavour. When mixed with tarragon, chives and parsley, it becomes the classic *fines herbes* combination. It is used to complement delicately flavoured ingredients: scrambled eggs is fine, but roast beef would be a disaster!

VARIETIES AND SEASON

Chervil prefers shade, drowns in heavy rain and burns in very hot sun. It is available in the shops most of the year but its peak season in mild climates is spring.

SELECTION AND STORAGE

Choose chervil with clear green rather than brownish or reddish leaves. Store washed chervil in a paper-lined plastic bag in the refrigerator, where it will keep for a week. It will not keep for more than a day if it is stored wet.

PREPARATION

Chervil, which grows close to the ground, often has a lot of dirt trapped in its leaves. To wash, float the chervil in a large bowl of water, swish it a few times, then lift it from the water and dry very well on a clean cloth or kitchen paper. To use, pull each little leaf from its stem and then pull its sections apart. This is preferred to chopping as the tiny triangular pieces are so pretty. However, it must be carefully done as if whole leaves are left intact diners can choke! The tiny pieces are called *pluches* in French, which refers to their feathery quality.

When a mixture of *fines herbes* is scattered on a fillet of fine fish, part of the charm for me, apart from the delicious flavour, is the recognisable triangular scraps of chervil, the pieces of tarragon leaf, the tiny hollow beads of cut chives and the chopped parsley. So much more aesthetic than merely chopping everything to green dust.

chervil goes with
eggs
potatoes
soft white cheeses
fish
cream sauces
peas
young carrots
chicken
zucchini
raw salmon

chervil tart

SERVES 6

1 quantity Shortcrust Pastry
1 bunch chervil, washed
½ small onion, finely chopped
600 ml cream
3 eggs
2 extra egg yolks
salt
freshly ground black pepper
freshly grated nutmeg

Line a 22 cm loose-bottomed flan tin with pastry and bake blind at 200°C for 20 minutes.

Tear chervil leaves into tiny pieces, reserving stems. Set aside 1 tablespoon leaves for garnish. Place chervil stems, onion and cream in a saucepan. Bring slowly to simmering point, then turn off heat, cover and allow to infuse for 1 hour. Strain cream, pressing well on onion and chervil stems, then reheat to simmering point. Drop in chervil leaves (not garnish) and blend hot cream to a delicate pale green in a food processor. Whisk eggs and egg yolks to combine, then whisk in chervil cream. Season with salt, pepper and nutmeg and pour warm filling into pastry case. Bake at

cheese and fines herbes
Offer a bowl of fines herbes, a jug of pure cream and a pepper mill with a soft fresh cheese.

180°C until just set (about 20 minutes). Allow to cool before serving. Scatter reserved chervil leaves over each portion.

herbs This is a master recipe and can be used with other herbs, alone or in combination. A *fines herbes* tart is delicious, as is a parsley tart.

chervil on soup
Scatter chervil onto cold cream soups, such as green pea, cucumber or potato and leek soup.

peas and chervil
Drain cooked young peas or carrots, warm through in butter and chervil and season.

zucchini with chervil
Cook sliced, washed baby zucchini in just the water clinging to them, a little butter and chervil or fines herbes *and season.*

carpaccio of salmon with fines herbes   SERVES 4

A very simple, fresh first course.

4 thin slices raw salmon
I tablespoon fresh chervil
    leaves
I teaspoon very finely
    chopped chives
I teaspoon very finely
    chopped parsley
I teaspoon very finely
    chopped tarragon
2 tablespoons finely diced
    ripe tomato
I tablespoon extra-virgin
    olive oil
freshly ground black pepper
sea salt
lime wedges

Divide salmon between chilled plates, then scatter with herbs and tomato, drizzle with oil and season. Serve with wedges of lime.

chestnuts

The chestnut we know is the edible fruit of the European chestnut tree, *Castanea sativa*, although Chinese and American species also bear nuts. French and Italian mountain folk have long relied on chestnuts as a staple food. In some areas of Europe chestnuts are still associated with extreme poverty. Before the introduction of the potato from the New World chestnut flour was used to make a rough bread and was the principal part of the diet. | Today chestnuts are of great interest gastronomically as they are equally splendid in savoury or sweet dishes. They make a delicious soup, can be added to stuffings and tarts, can dress up Brussels sprouts and cabbage, can be made into dumplings and gnocchi and combine equally well with sausages and game or chocolate and cream. Bees are attracted to chestnut flowers, and in Italy I have sampled chestnut honey that was exquisite. | Once, not so long ago, one tasted fresh chestnuts in Australia only if one knew someone who had a chestnut tree. Few arrived in the marketplace. Like so many other hedgerow gatherings, the crop was mostly appreciated by European migrants. >

chestnuts
go
with
brandy
sugar
chocolate
vanilla
rum
coffee
cream
sea salt
cabbage
Brussels sprouts
pine nuts
sausages
pheasant
guinea fowl
turkey
quail
mushrooms
bacon
fennel seeds
orange zest
port
Madeira
red wine
celery
bitter salad leaves

Harvesting chestnuts, however, can be agonising. The nut is encased in a husk or 'burr' with very sharp prickles that penetrate most gardening gloves. On top of this, chestnuts are one of the most time-consuming of all foods to prepare. The most convincing recommendation of their delicious flavour is that food lovers are prepared to endure the prickles and the hours of shelling and digging away at the inner skins to get at them. One of my suppliers has developed a way to peel chestnuts and she sells me kilos of beautifully peeled nuts that have been blanched and snap-frozen. They thaw with no appreciable change in texture or flavour and are instantly ready for braising with poultry or game, or to turn into a rich and creamy soup.

When cooked, chestnuts have an earthy, sweet nutty taste and a starchy consistency. They are the only nut treated as a vegetable and must be boiled or roasted before eating.

VARIETIES AND SEASON

There are several types of chestnut. In Europe the important distinction is between the marron, which produces a large single nut inside each prickly husk, and the domestic chestnut (*chataigne* in French), which has 2–3 nuts inside each husk. In Australia it is the domestic variety that is grown. Chestnuts are grown mainly in the highland areas of Victoria, with scattered plantings throughout the rest of Australia. Plantings are increasing and there is an active Chestnut Growers of Australia association, based in Myrtleford, north-east Victoria. Fresh chestnuts are available March–June.

SELECTION AND STORAGE

If you have access to a chestnut tree, gather the nuts as soon as they fall to the ground. *Fresh* chestnuts need to be dried a little to reduce their moisture content before being at their best for eating and to avoid mould developing. Either spread the nuts out in the sunshine until there is no moisture visible on the skin, or rub the nuts with a soft cloth before storing them. These dried nuts should give a little when squeezed. Like many nuts, chestnuts are best stored in the refrigerator and will keep in an airtight container for several weeks. (It is useful to know that 1 kg chestnuts will yield about 500 g when shelled.)

Dehydrated chestnuts are also available. Store these in an airtight container. Many recipes specify tinned *chestnut purée*, which is available from delicatessens and some supermarkets. Some food writers are careless and do not differentiate between the sweetened product and the natural product. Read the label carefully to be sure you are buying the correct sort. The sweetened purée lists corn syrup among its ingredients. The unsweetened purée includes salt and is labelled 'natural' or unsweetened. One can also buy *canned* or bottled whole chestnuts; again, these are usually packed in water and labelled 'natural', but sometimes come in a heavy vanilla corn syrup. The canned or bottled whole natural chestnuts are a great product; in fact, I have had more success with them than with dried chestnuts.

Specialist Italian food stores sometimes sell imported chestnut flour that is used to make a traditional Italian cake called *castagnaccio*. This flour must be very fresh and is prone to weevil infestation.

PREPARATION AND COOKING

Whatever method is planned to remove the outer and inner skins of a fresh chestnut, the outer skin or shell *must* be pierced to relieve the heat and pressure that builds up during cooking. If the shell is not cut, the chestnut may explode. The best implement for slitting chestnuts is the very sharp Stanley knife, available at hardware and craft stores. Hold the nut down flat on a board to score it. If you need **whole** chestnuts, you can boil, roast, deep-fry or microwave slit nuts before removing the outer and inner skins. If the flesh is to be used for **soup** or a **purée**, where looks do not matter, process the nut by boiling, roasting, frying or microwaving it, and then cut it in half and scoop the flesh out with a small, sharp spoon.

TO PEEL | **Boil** Score outer skins and simmer the nuts for 15 minutes. Only remove one chestnut at a time from the hot water: this will make it much easier to remove the outer and inner skins. It is impossible to remove the inner skin if the nut is cold. **Roast** Score outer skins and roast the chestnuts at 180°C or barbecue them for 20 minutes. Remove the nuts from the heat and wrap them in a towel for 5 minutes before attempting to remove the outer and inner skins. **Deep-fry** A colleague of mine swears that he has better results by deep-frying scored chestnuts, a few at a time, at 180°C for about 1 minute. The skin comes off more easily if the nuts are hot, so only do a few at a time. **Microwave** Place scored chestnuts in a single layer on a glass plate and microwave on high for 5–6 minutes, stirring several times, until the chestnuts are soft. Leave them to stand for 5 minutes before peeling them while still warm.

TO COOK | Simmer peeled chestnuts in milk or water, depending on the intended use, until tender, 10–15 minutes. There is no need to cook peeled chestnuts further if they are to be cooked with other ingredients later.

DEHYDRATED CHESTNUTS | Dehydrated chestnuts must be soaked in plenty of water overnight, then rinsed and simmered in water, milk or stock, depending on the intended use. They take a long time to become tender (at least 1 hour) and can break up before this stage is reached.

chestnuts and rich juices
Put 100 g peeled chestnuts, 125 g diced streaky bacon, ½ cup roasting juices or well-flavoured stock (or water) and a grinding of pepper into a cast-iron casserole and bake, covered, at 180°C for 45 minutes. Tip the chestnuts around a roasted chicken, game bird, turkey or joint of venison and serve.

cabbage with chestnuts
Add peeled chestnuts with the apple when cooking Erna's Red Cabbage with Apple (see CABBAGES AND BRUSSELS SPROUTS*).*

TO PURÉE

Chestnut purée is used to make desserts and gnocchi or to accompany meat dishes. Place the peeled nuts in a saucepan, cover with water (and sugar, if for a sweet purée) and simmer until tender. Drain, then pass through a food mill or process briefly in a food processor. You can also use half milk and half water or stock to vary the flavour of the purée.

recipes

chestnuts and mushrooms

SERVES 4

roasted chestnuts
Roast scored chestnuts over coals, then peel them, one at a time, and eat with a few flakes of sea salt.

hot wine chestnuts
Do as they do in the mountainous Auvergne region of France: place a napkin soaked in red wine over a plate of hot roasted chestnuts and keep warm for 30 minutes before eating these super-charged morsels!

16 chestnuts, peeled
1 cup Chicken Stock or water
4 large flat mushrooms
2 cloves garlic, finely chopped
4 tablespoons freshly chopped parsley
2 tablespoons fresh breadcrumbs
olive oil
sea salt
freshly ground black pepper

Preheat oven to 200°C. Simmer chestnuts in stock for 10 minutes, then drain, reserving stock. Remove stalks from mushrooms. Chop stalks, mix with garlic, parsley and breadcrumbs in a bowl and set aside.

Film a shallow gratin dish with oil. Place mushrooms in gratin dish, stalk-side up, and season. Coarsely chop chestnuts and arrange on mushrooms. Scatter over parsley mixture and drizzle with reserved stock. Bake for 30 minutes. Serve as a first course or as a special vegetable dish with a plain grill.

chestnut soup

SERVES 8

1 potato, diced
1 stick celery, finely sliced
1 onion, finely chopped
1 clove garlic, finely chopped
40 g butter
1 kg chestnuts, peeled (to yield 500 g)
1 litre Chicken Stock
100 ml cream
salt
freshly ground black pepper
1 tablespoon muscat, sherry or tokay (optional)

In a heavy-based stockpot sweat vegetables and garlic in butter over a gentle heat for 5 minutes. Add chestnuts and stock and simmer, covered, for 25 minutes until nuts are quite tender. Purée contents of pot, then pass through a fine sieve and return purée to pot. Add cream and simmer soup for 15 minutes to allow it to reduce slightly. If still too thin, simmer a further 15 minutes, uncovered. If too thick, adjust with extra stock or water. Season to taste. Before serving, add fortified wine to hot soup.
duck or squab pigeon A very grand soup can be made if you add chopped breast meat from a duck or squab pigeon to the finished soup. Simmer the carcass gently in the chicken stock beforehand to emphasise the flavour.

chestnut and walnut pastries   MAKES 30

These are delicious served alongside Chestnut Soup (see p. 198) and the rest can be frozen uncooked to reappear as freshly baked treats to serve with drinks. You can make the pastry in a food processor, if you like.

1 small onion, finely chopped
½ stick celery, very finely
  chopped
1 clove garlic, finely chopped
olive oil
400 g chestnuts, cooked and
  peeled (to yield 200 g)
50 g walnuts, toasted
50 g unsalted cashew nuts
2 eggs
2 teaspoons muscat, tokay or
  sherry
1 teaspoon grated orange zest
1 tablespoon freshly chopped
  parsley
salt
freshly ground black pepper
SOUR CREAM PASTRY
1 cup plain flour
pinch of salt
125 g unsalted butter
2 tablespoons sour cream

To make the pastry, sift flour and salt, then rub in butter until crumbly. Add sour cream and work together lightly. Chill for 30 minutes. Roll out thinly and cut rounds of 8 cm diameter.

Preheat oven to 200°C. Sweat onion, celery and garlic in 1 teaspoon oil for a few minutes, then tip into a bowl. In a little more oil, sauté chestnuts, walnuts and cashews briefly. Chop roughly and add to vegetables. Mix 1 of the eggs and the remaining ingredients into nuts and taste for seasoning. Beat remaining egg. Brush edges of each pastry round with water, place 1 teaspoon filling on each and pinch edges together to form a Cornish pasty shape. Chill for 30 minutes. Brush pastries with beaten egg and bake for 15 minutes or until golden brown.

quick chestnut soup
Make a quick chestnut soup by sautéing onion, carrot and celery, then add unsweetened chestnut purée, dilute with chicken stock or water and top with a dollop of cream. Season with salt and pepper and add a splash of sherry or other fortified wine.

sprouts and chestnuts
Add excitement to lightly cooked Brussels sprouts by tossing them with cooked chestnuts.

chestnut purée
Top a tiny portion of tinned sweetened chestnut purée with brandy-flavoured whipped cream.

chestnut and bacon salad   SERVES 4

Use curly endive, radicchio and other salad leaves that have a bit of bite.

4 handfuls salad leaves,
  washed and dried
4 rashers smoked streaky
  bacon cut 5 mm thick
500 g chestnuts, peeled
  (to yield 250 g)
2 teaspoons Dijon mustard
⅓ cup walnut oil
few drops of red-wine vinegar
freshly ground black pepper

Place salad leaves in a wide, shallow bowl or on a platter. Sauté bacon gently in a heavy-based frying pan until it starts to render some fat. Cook until crisp, then break into pieces and add to salad. Toss chestnuts in hot bacon fat for 2–3 minutes, remove and add to salad. Add mustard to pan with oil. Stir to mix, then add vinegar. Pour hot dressing over salad immediately and toss to mix. Serve at once.

chestnut mont blanc

SERVES 4

When I was 12 years old there was a Hungarian restaurant called the Topsy on the first floor of a very unprepossessing building in a back lane in Melbourne. The elderly couple who owned and operated this establishment introduced me to one of life's most glorious desserts, a proper Mont Blanc. Years later, after many sessions in my restaurant kitchens with sharp knives, boiling water and sore fingers, I remain astonished that this sweet was offered autumn after autumn at the Topsy.

chestnuts in wine
Simmer peeled chestnuts, covered, in 3 parts marsala to 1 part red wine sweetened with a little sugar until tender and the syrup is thick (about 15 minutes). Serve with cream.

1 kg chestnuts, cooked and peeled (to yield 500 g)
2 cups milk
1 vanilla bean, split
1 cup castor sugar
2 tablespoons best brandy
2 cups cream, lightly whipped

Simmer chestnuts in milk with vanilla bean, uncovered, until tender and milk has been absorbed (about 20 minutes). Press chestnuts and any liquid through a food mill. Beat in sugar with a wooden spoon. Return purée to pan and cook, stirring constantly, until it comes together (a bit like choux pastry). Allow to cool completely.

Press cooled purée through coarsest hole of a food mill or potato ricer over a serving platter, letting 'worms' form a loose 'mountain'. Sprinkle with brandy. Spoon cream over peak of mountain just before serving.

other recipes

crépinettes and chestnuts *see* SAUSAGES

chick peas The chick pea (*Cicer arietinum*) has been cultivated since Neolithic times and remains an important food in the Middle East, India, Italy, France and most Spanish-speaking countries, where it is used in stews, to make pastes and as a flour. Primarily dried and used as a pulse, chick peas have a wonderful nutty flavour and are rich in protein, inexpensive and very sustaining. │ Chickpea flour is used a great deal in Indian cooking, where it is known as Bengal gram or besan flour. In Europe, chickpea flour is used to make *socca*, a thin, moist pancake sold in the markets of Nice, where it is also used to make a type of polenta that is sliced and fried in olive oil. These little cakes are known as *panisses* and *panizza* in northern-Italian markets. │ Most of us know chick peas only in their dried form but they can be eaten fresh in the late spring when they are briefly brilliantly green. I have watched villagers on a Greek island snacking on fresh green chick peas and wondered what it was they were relishing. │ One can also buy tinned chick peas, which do quite well for an emergency salad, but the cost is high compared with cooking dried chick peas yourself.

chick peas
go
with
olive oil
pepper
lemon juice
preserved lemons
chillies
spinach
parsley
capers
onions
cumin
turmeric
paprika
coriander
garlic
anchovies
almonds
pine nuts
ham
mint
salt codfish
tomatoes
olives

VARIETIES AND SEASON

There are 2 main types of chick pea available: the large, creamy garbanzo and the smaller, darker desi chick pea. The garbanzo is the most commonly seen variety in Australia.

SELECTION AND STORAGE

As with all pulses, it is difficult to know how long chick peas have been dried and stored. One would like to think one is buying the dried pulses of the immediate past growing season. As this is impossible to know, I prefer to buy chick peas from a stall at the market that I know has a large turnover. Always check closely that there are no signs of burrowing insects. If buying chickpea flour, available from health food stores or Indian groceries, check carefully for weevil infestation.

Store chick peas in an airtight container and discard any that are discoloured. Store chickpea flour as you would ordinary flour.

PREPARATION AND COOKING

As with all pulses, dried chick peas need to be soaked and cooked before further preparation is possible.

TO SOAK AND COOK   Soak dried chick peas overnight, generously covered with cold water. There is no need to add bicarbonate of soda to the soaking chick peas (it was once thought it helped soften them). Next day, pour away the soaking water and cook the chick peas in fresh water with other aromatics according to the recipe. The chick peas will take about 2 hours to become tender. (It is best to add salt at the end of the cooking process as adding it earlier can delay the cooking time; more importantly, the liquid will reduce substantially over the long cooking time, concentrating any seasonings.) When tender, allow the chick peas to cool in their cooking water. They will swell a little more as they cool and can then be drained. **Quick method** The soaking process can be hurried by pouring boiling water over dried chick peas and leaving them to stand for 3–4 hours before cooking them as above in fresh water.

recipes **falafel**   MAKES 40

A well-known Middle Eastern speciality that is surprisingly easy to make at home. While falafel are made with chick peas in Israel, Syria, Lebanon and Jordan, the Egyptians use dried white broad beans. Eat falafel just as they are with drinks or, better still, dipped into Smoky Eggplant Purée (see EGGPLANTS*), Hummus (see p. 203) or Teradot Sauce (see* NUTS*), a blend of walnuts and tahina.*

450 g chick peas, soaked

½ onion, chopped finely

I clove garlic, chopped

1½ cups coarsely chopped
  parsley

I cup coarsely chopped
  coriander leaves

½ cup coarsely chopped mint
  leaves

pinch of cayenne pepper

I tablespoon salt

½ teaspoon freshly ground
  black pepper

I teaspoon baking powder

2 teaspoons ground coriander

3 tablespoons cumin seeds

vegetable oil for deep-frying

Drain chick peas, rinse thoroughly and drain again. In a large bowl mix all ingredients, except oil. Transfer mixture to a food processor in batches and blend until a rough chop of mostly green with specks of white chick peas. The mixture should start to hold together. Continue until all the mixture has been processed. Form mixture into 4 cm diameter balls, squeezing gently, then flatten and shallow-fry in 1 cm oil until crisp and golden, about 3 minutes a side. Drain on crumpled kitchen paper. Serve hot.

tossed chick peas
Toss cooked chick peas in the remains of a soup or stew. Present them spread out on a flat plate rimmed with fresh coriander and drizzled generously with fruity olive oil for an interesting first course.

hummus

MAKES 4–6

The word for chick pea in Arabic is hummus, *and so well loved is the creamy purée made from this pulse that the purée itself has taken its name. Here is Claudia Roden's version of hummus.*

At a conference I attended in Tunisia this purée appeared on the breakfast table next to a platter of the softest, creamiest sheep's milk ricotta cheese and alongside thinly sliced red onions and green-shouldered, pleasantly acidic tomatoes.

chickpea dukkah
Mix roughly chopped, salted cooked chick peas with roasted cumin seeds and a piece of finely ground cinnamon stick. Eat as is or sprinkle on warm pita bread, vegetable salads, hot boiled potatoes or fish.

250 g chick peas, soaked

salt

freshly ground black pepper

2 teaspoons ground cumin

2 large cloves garlic, crushed

3 tablespoons lemon juice

I good pinch cayenne pepper
  (optional)

sprigs of parsley

3 tablespoons olive oil

Cook chick peas until very soft and add salt towards end of cooking time. Cool a little in the cooking water. Transfer chick peas to a blender and season with pepper and cumin. Process, gradually adding remaining flavourings (except oil) until your preferred balance is achieved (remember, though, that the flavour should be sharp). Add a little cooking water and blend again to make a soft purée. Spoon onto a rustic flat plate, garnish with parsley and drizzle over oil.

Serve as an appetiser with fresh or pickled vegetables and pita bread.

tahina This paste made from sesame seeds is often mixed with hummus – a delicious variation correctly called *hummus bi tahina*. Halve the above quantity of chick peas and add 150 ml tahina to the purée.

chickpea batter

MAKES 2 CUPS

Try this batter when making vegetable fritters. The quantity is sufficient for 30 fritters. The batter will keep 3–4 days, refrigerated, although it may need to be thinned with a little water.

garlic chick peas
Fry cooked chick peas in a little oil for 3–4 minutes and then toast them in the oven at 160°C until browned and slightly shrunken, about 20 minutes. Mix the chick peas with finely chopped garlic and salt. Serve hot as a snack.

200 g chickpea flour
1½ cups water
2 teaspoons very finely chopped garlic
2 tablespoons olive oil
2 teaspoons freshly ground cumin seeds
½ teaspoon freshly ground black pepper
½ teaspoon ground turmeric
¾ teaspoon baking powder
pinch of salt

Mix ingredients together. Dip vegetables such as thin ribbons of zucchini or cauliflower florets into batter and deep-fry at 175°C until crisp and golden. Drain on crumpled kitchen paper and serve hot.

lablabi

SERVES 4

chickpea salad
Toss cooked chick peas with rich olive oil and chopped chives and parsley from the garden and serve with a plate of ripe tomatoes for a much-appreciated, simple lunch.

In Tunisia I was introduced to a soupy breakfast or snack dish called lablabi that was absolutely delicious. Back home I turned it into a soup that has become one of my favourite dishes.

1 litre Chicken Stock
1½ cups cooked chick peas
2 teaspoons Harissa (see p. 539)
2 teaspoons ground cumin
1 teaspoon salt
2 slices sourdough *or* unleavened bread, broken into small pieces
4 tablespoons chopped fresh flat-leaf parsley
4 tablespoons freshly chopped coriander leaves
1 tablespoon chopped capers
4 softboiled eggs
olive oil

Simmer stock, chick peas, harissa, cumin and salt for 15 minutes, then check seasoning. Divide bread, herbs and capers between 4 heated soup bowls. Scoop an egg from its shell into each bowl, then ladle soup over and drizzle with olive oil. Serve at once.

chick peas with spinach

SERVES 4

Versions of this dish are cooked all over the Mediterranean. Sometimes meatballs are added at the end.

225 g chick peas, soaked
1 large bunch spinach
2 tablespoons olive oil
1 large onion, finely chopped
sea salt
150 ml yoghurt
2 cloves garlic, finely chopped
freshly ground black pepper
1 teaspoon finely chopped
   fresh mint
paprika

Drain chick peas, rinse and cook in fresh water until soft. Set aside in cooking water. Wash spinach, discarding tough ribs and stems and any damaged or discoloured leaves, then chop finely.

Heat oil, add onion and cook gently for 15 minutes until soft. Add spinach and stew for 5 minutes. Tip chick peas and a few spoonfuls of cooking water into spinach and onion, then add salt to taste and cook over a brisk heat for 5 minutes until liquid has evaporated.

Whisk yoghurt with garlic, a little salt, pepper and mint. Arrange chickpea mixture on a shallow plate, then pour over yoghurt and sprinkle with paprika. Serve hot or cold with pita bread and something crunchy and sharp, such as Pickled Turnips (*see* TURNIPS AND SWEDES) or fresh radishes.

catalonian chick peas and almonds Sauté the onion with 2 large, peeled and roughly chopped tomatoes. Add the spinach and cook as above, then add the chick peas with a spoonful of cooking water and some pepper. A Spanish *picada* is then added and the dish is simmered for 10 minutes. To make the *picada*, grind 8 blanched almonds, a few pine nuts, salt, 3 tablespoons freshly chopped parsley and 2 garlic cloves in a mortar. **andalusian chick peas and salt cod** Soak 200 g dried cod for 24 hours, changing the water at least twice. Cook soaked chick peas with a bay leaf, diced carrot and diced onion. Drain and flake the fish. Sauté another onion with the spinach in olive oil, as in the original recipe, and add the cod. Add the cooked chick peas and quite a lot of cooking water to make a soupy stew.

chickpea salad with the remains of roast lamb

SERVES 4

This recipe is included as a model. The roast lamb can be replaced with any other meat or fish.

spiced chick peas
Cook chick peas with a little turmeric until tender, then drain and sprinkle with cumin, chilli powder and lemon juice.

chickpea and broccoli salad
Toss lightly cooked broccoli with cooked chick peas and dress with warm olive oil, lemon juice and a scattering of parsley.

250 g chick peas, soaked
1 bay leaf
1 onion, diced
1 carrot, diced
2 cloves garlic, finely chopped
2 tablespoons extra-virgin
   olive oil
½ cup Caramelised Onions
   (see p. 465)
½ cup freshly chopped parsley
½ cup finely chopped spring
   onions
salt
freshly ground black pepper *or*
   finely chopped chilli
roast lamb, cut into chunks

chick peas and ...
Add darkly fried onion, cooked silverbeet stems, spinach or chicory, garlic or snippets of fried ham, bacon or sausage to cooked chick peas dressed with oil and herbs.

Drain chick peas and rinse. Place in a deep saucepan, generously cover with cold water and add bay leaf. Bring to a boil, skim, lower heat to a simmer and add onion, carrot and garlic. Simmer until tender, uncovered. (This whole process will take at least 1½ hours.) When tender, drain chick peas, then stir in oil, caramelised onion, parsley and spring onion and season. Toss through roast lamb or arrange meat around the chick peas.

other recipes

lamb shanks with couscous *see* LAMB

chicken and the christmas turkey

I could cook chicken a different way each night for a long time without becoming bored, and I am never unmoved by the sight of a roasted chicken. In the restaurant, however, my chicken dishes are never best-sellers. It seems the public equates chicken these days with the ordinary, the everyday and the cut-price. | How times change. I remember when a large, home-reared roasted bird was an absolute treat for Sunday lunch. We held our breath as it was brought to the table. Grandpa stropped his knife and slice after snowy slice curled from the breast, each one rimmed with golden crisp skin. One chicken fed all 7 of us, with leftovers. | In ancient Rome it was noticed that what hens were fed influenced the eventual flavour of the bird. Fattened chicken became a delicacy, and there are many recipes for chicken in the work of Apicius, a celebrated Roman cook. The French king Henri IV guaranteed, in the sixteenth century, that chicken would be regarded forever as a powerful symbol of European democracy and domestic harmony when he announced that he hoped 'to make France so prosperous that every peasant will have a chicken in his pot on Sundays'. >

Nowadays the production of chicken in Australia and other Western countries is a highly commercial and mechanised process. The overwhelming majority of chicken available is produced by medium-to-large corporations that provide chicks and grain to growers, and then transport and prepare the birds before delivering them to supermarkets. The growers rear thousands of chicks under cover in a thermally controlled, artificially lit environment on carefully monitored food. This large-scale, automated production has made chicken cheap and accessible. As a result, there has been a huge jump in chicken consumption in Australia since the 1960s. Before 1963, 4.4 kg of poultry per person were consumed each year. By 1995 Australians were eating 27.2 kg of poultry per person annually.

Sadly, most consumers only know these standardised birds, bred for maximum tenderness (rather than flavour), speed of development and/or to produce as many eggs as possible in the shortest possible time. To quote myself, when discussing the benefits of raising chickens in *Stephanie's Australia*, 'the principles are surprisingly the same for a chicken as for an adolescent! If either one sits around all day, removed from all stimuli, eating large quantities of junk food with a high sugar and salt content, they very soon become listless, spotty, saggy and pretty dreary'. In comparison, the free-range bird presents a taut breast and thick, plump thighs – and a rich, wonderful flavour.

In real terms the price of chicken is lower now than it was 5 years ago, and some specialist producers offering free-range birds have been forced out of business. Today less than 1 per cent of the nation's chicken production is classed as free-range. I urge you to support those farmers producing free-range chickens – for your own delight and to sustain the industry.

As turkey – originally a native of the United States, Mexico and Central America – is rarely cooked at any other time of year than Christmas (or Thanksgiving) I discuss all aspects of dealing with that bird in the recipe for Christmas Turkey on p. 216.

VARIETIES AND SEASON

All breeds of chicken are descended from the wild, red jungle fowl of India that was tamed around 2000 BC. There are only a few varieties of chicken (*Gallus gallus domestica*) grown commercially for their meat and eggs in Australia – the white leghorn, light Sussex, New Hampshire, white rock and australorp. There are enthusiasts who breed their own small flocks, but almost all growers are dependent on the large companies for a supply of day-old chicks.

Chicken is available all year, although seasonal differences may occasionally restrict the supply of free-range birds. Chicken is described and sold in terms of its age and size rather than with any reference to its breed. Within each broad category of chicken (for example, poussin) the bird is further described by a number that corresponds to its weight (a no. 16 chicken weighs no less than 1.6 kg). A *poussin* is a young bird aged 3–4 weeks weighing 400–500 g. It is best suited to grilling. **Chicken** can be as young as 6 weeks (1.4 kg) and as old as 10 weeks (2.7 kg). (I have no idea where one would obtain a no. 27 chicken other than from my own supplier, who is prepared to grow free-range birds to this size. Such birds are never seen in the supermarket.) Chicken can be roasted, grilled, poached or casseroled. It is sold whole, or portioned into breast fillets, wings, drumsticks, thighs, chicken chops, 'drumettes' or 'winglets'. Chicken livers, feet and carcasses are all available, as are minced, cooked, marinated or smoked chicken and other processed products.

A hen that has stopped laying is known as a **boiler**. Boilers are always very tough and need long, moist cooking to tenderise the flesh. However, they can be used to produce a superior chicken stock. (Do not confuse a 'boiler' with the American 'broiler', a young chicken intended for grilling.)

SELECTION AND STORAGE

If possible choose a *free-range*, *grain-fed* chicken. Check for a label guaranteeing its place of origin and that it has been genuinely free-ranged. As any chicken can develop a yellow tinge if fed on maize (corn), including battery birds, if the choice is between a yellow commercial chicken or a paler free-range bird, opt for the latter. Freedom to move around, grow more slowly and put on muscle rather than fat is more important than skin colour.

Next choice would be a *fresh mass-produced* chicken to avoid the watery, flabby skin often present in a frozen battery chicken. If a *frozen* bird is your only option, take the chicken out of its plastic bag, sit it on a thick wad of kitchen paper on a plate in the refrigerator, not the sink draining board, and allow it to thaw slowly, uncovered. Dry it inside and out before seasoning and cooking. Firm, dry skin will crisp and brown better than wet skin.

When selecting chicken *livers*, reject any that have a greenish stain (this can also be cut away before cooking), as it imparts a bitter flavour.

All chicken should be removed from its wrappings and refrigerated as soon as you bring it home. Transfer it to a clean plate and cover with plastic film. A whole fresh chicken should be used within 4 days of purchase (2 days for a thawed whole chicken). Portioned fresh or thawed chicken, minced chicken and chicken livers should be cooked within 2 days of purchase. Chicken stock should be boiled again after 2 days' refrigeration and should then be used within 24 hours or frozen.

Always thaw chicken under refrigeration. Never cook chicken that is partially frozen. While the outer layers cook and crisp, a frozen or icy interior may prevent a temperature high enough to kill potentially dangerous microorganisms such as salmonella from being reached.

PREPARATION AND COOKING

TO JOINT Place the chicken, breast uppermost, on a board. Pull each leg out and away from the breast and carefully cut the skin low down to preserve as much skin cover for the delicate breast meat as possible. Twist the leg backwards, cut around the exposed ball joint and sever the leg. Divide the leg into a drumstick and thigh. Press the wing joint back towards the chopping board and cut between the ball and socket joint at the shoulder to sever the wing. Cut straight through the breastbone to divide the breast section and cut away the backbone. Remove the 2 little cushions of flesh on either side of the backbone (the 'oysters') and add to the jointed chicken. If making a casserole, the backbone can be cooked with the other pieces to add extra flavour, or it can be reserved for stock.

TO BONE Stuffed boned chicken can either be roasted and served hot or poached and served cold. First remove the wishbone, located at the neck cavity embedded in the breast fillet. Next, cut the skin down the spine to the parson's nose (the base of the spine). With a small, sharp knife, release the skin and flesh from one side of the chicken, being careful to free the knuckle from the socket of the leg and wing joint (the legs and wings are to remain in place), and continue until you reach the thick breast meat. Repeat on the other side. Now free the 2 breast fillets, being careful not to pierce the skin that adheres closely to the breast bone. Remove the carcass. Stuff the boned bird according to the recipe and sew up or wrap in foil like a bolster. Poached in stock, a stuffed boned bird will take about 45 minutes.

TO STUFF **Under the skin** Remove the wishbone and gently insert your first 2 fingers under the breast skin and ease it from the flesh. Ensure the stuffing is at room temperature and insert a spoonful under the skin. Pull the skin back into place and smooth the stuffing evenly by spreading it with the palm of your hand. **The cavity** Prepare the bird for roasting, ensuring the cavity is dry, and pack in the stuffing just prior to cooking (do not let the stuffed bird stand as the stuffing will absorb the juices, providing a breeding ground for micro-organisms).

TO ROAST Remove the neck and, if present, giblets from inside the bird. (The neck and gizzard can be put into the baking dish and the liver can be sautéd separately or they can be added to the quick stock I suggest making with the cooked carcass on page 215.) Remove all loose fat and wipe the chicken dry inside and out.

Using your fingers and a small knife, ease out the wishbone (this will make carving much easier). Season and roast according to the recipe. If you are not following a recipe, brush the chicken with melted butter, oil or lemon juice and cook at 220°C for 1 hour, turning it from side to side every 20 minutes, finishing breast uppermost. To test for doneness, insert a skewer into the thigh – the juices should run clear, not pink. A stuffed boned bird will take 45 minutes–1 hour. Allow the cooked chicken to settle for 10 minutes before carving it.

TO GRILL | Cut a *poussin* or 1.4–1.8 kg *chicken* down the back, either side of the backbone, and press on the breastbone to flatten the bird out. Wipe both sides dry, season and proceed with the recipe. If using *portions*, wipe the pieces dry. Slash the thickest part on any drumsticks, so that the heat can penetrate evenly. Season and proceed with the recipe. If you are not using a recipe, brush the chicken with olive oil, then grind on pepper and grill on both sides until the skin crisps and the flesh is firm – about 15 minutes for a poussin or 25 minutes for a small chicken. A chicken breast fillet, skin on, will take 10 minutes all up; its underfillet will only take 1 minute a side. Any juices should run clear, not pink – test by inserting a skewer into the thickest part.

TO STEAM | Use breast meat for the best results. Remove and discard the skin. Remove the sinew from the underfillet and proceed with the recipe. If you are not using a recipe, put the chicken on a plate, cover it tightly with foil and steam in a bamboo steamer for about 6 minutes until springy to the fingertips. Steamed chicken is often marinated first – allow 15 minutes for the flavours to be absorbed.

chicken liver pâté

MAKES 1 CUP

600 g chicken livers (to make
    500 g cleaned)
100 g softened butter
2 tablespoons brandy
salt
freshly ground black pepper
freshly grated nutmeg

Cut away any greenish stained liver, as even a scrap will make the pâté bitter, and pull each lobe away from its connecting threads.

Heat 1 tablespoon of the butter in a non-stick frying pan until just foaming. Add half the livers and sauté quickly until golden brown on each side and still quite soft in the middle. (In my experience the cooking livers spit and jump, so stand well back.) Remove livers to a plate. Add another tablespoon of butter and sauté remaining livers the same way until golden brown. >

Return first batch of livers to pan with second batch, increase heat and tip on brandy. Ignite brandy with a match, tilting pan to spread flames. Add a little salt, pepper and grated nutmeg. Transfer livers to a food mill or food processor and sieve or blend. (If you use a processor, you will also need to press the pâté through a coarse sieve to extract any sinews that remain.) Return liver mixture to food processor and incorporate remaining butter. Check seasoning. Press pâté into a small pot or pots and chill well.

The surface of the pâté will oxidise, that is, it will darken in contact with the air. If you wish to stop this, cover the finished pâté with a thin layer of clarified butter ✦. Serve with hot toast.

barbecued chicken wings

MAKES 12

Another favourite, hot or cold, to cook on the barbecue or in the oven, as here. The seasonings can vary according to whim! Drumsticks can be used, too, but take up to an hour to cook.

I tablespoon vegetable oil
I tablespoon honey *or* hoisin sauce
2 tablespoons light *or* dark soy sauce
I teaspoon sambal oelek *or* chilli sauce
I tablespoon tomato paste *or* Fresh Tomato Sauce (see p. 709)
2 cloves garlic, smashed *or* roughly chopped
freshly chopped ginger
½ cup Chicken Stock ✦ *or* water
12 chicken wings *or* 20 drumettes

Preheat oven to 200°C. Select a baking dish into which the wings will fit easily. Add oil and seasonings, including stock. Toss wings to coat and bake for 30 minutes until tender, shaking dish from time to time. Increase heat to evaporate liquid and so wings become dark and shiny. This may only take 10 minutes, so keep a close watch on them.

steamed chicken breast

SERVES I

Sometimes when I am feeling delicate I cook some fragrant jasmine rice and while it is cooking I marinate a chicken breast. If making this dish for 2, put the plate with the marinated chicken inside a bamboo steamer basket and set it over hot water.

fried chicken

Dip a skinned, flattened chicken breast fillet in egg and fresh, seasoned breadcrumbs, or in a mixture of 2 parts breadcrumbs to 1 part finely grated parmesan cheese, and fry until golden in clarified butter ✦.

chicken kebabs

Marinate diced chicken breast fillets in soy sauce, sherry and fresh ginger or in yoghurt, oil and lemon zest and grill on bamboo skewers.

1 chicken breast fillet, skin
   removed
1 tablespoon light soy sauce
2 teaspoons dry sherry *or*
   mirin
1 clove garlic, chopped
1 teaspoon chopped ginger
1 cup jasmine rice
pinch of salt
1½ cups water
1 spring onion, very finely
   sliced

Briefly marinate chicken in soy sauce, sherry, garlic and ginger on a plate. Put rice and salt into a saucepan slightly larger than the plate and add water. Bring to a boil over moderate heat, then reduce to lowest setting and simmer, covered. When cooked, scatter spring onion over chicken, position plate over steaming rice and cover plate very tightly with foil. Check chicken after 6 minutes – it may need another few minutes (it should be springy to the fingertips when cooked). Transfer a portion of rice to a heated bowl, pour juices from plate over rice and add thinly sliced chicken. Serve with steamed or stir-fried ✎ Chinese vegetables, bok choy, for example. The remaining rice can be reheated or fried.

cold chinese white-cooked chicken with seared spring onion sauce

SERVES 6

This is absolutely delicious and a family favourite for my Boxing Day buffet table. The sauce is just as good with plain egg noodles, steamed rice or grilled chicken breast as it is with this poached chicken.

2 spring onions, sliced
5 cm knob ginger, sliced
1 x 2 kg free-range chicken
ice

SEARED SPRING ONION SAUCE

4 spring onions, finely
   chopped
1 teaspoon finely chopped
   ginger
1 teaspoon finely chopped
   garlic
3 tablespoons light vegetable
   oil
3 tablespoons light soy sauce
1 tablespoon rice wine *or* dry
   sherry
1 teaspoon sesame oil

Select a stockpot large enough to submerge chicken. Fill with water, add spring onion and ginger and bring to a boil. Plunge in chicken, breast down. Allow liquid to return to boiling point and skim surface carefully, then adjust heat to a gentle simmer, put on lid tightly and cook for 10 minutes. Turn off heat – do not lift lid – and leave for 45 minutes.

Have ready a large tub of cold water into which you empty a whole tray of ice cubes. (The aim is to chill the chicken quickly, so that the juices solidify in a thin layer under the taut, shiny skin.) Lift chicken from pot very carefully using a strong egg slice – avoid tearing the delicate breast skin at all costs. Drain liquid from cavity and plunge

orange chicken
Squeeze orange or cumquat juice over a roasting chicken and add the citrus skins to the baking dish.

chicken and grapes
Add a handful of seeded grapes to the final juices of a roasting chicken and deglaze with verjuice (see GRAPES AND VINE LEAVES*) instead of wine.*

bird into iced water and leave for 1 hour. Remove chicken to a plate and refrigerate. The chicken will be sensational any time over the next 4 days.

Separate legs from bird, cutting through the bone in the Chinese manner with a heavy cleaver. (The cleaver must be sharp and you must be bold and decisive. Keep your other hand right out of the way and sharply and firmly bring the blade down.) The bone will be red in the centre and the meat will be pearly-pink. Alternatively, slice skin and meat from thighs and drumsticks and discard bones. Remove each breast fillet, keeping skin and layer of jellied juice intact. Slice neatly across the grain.

To make the sauce, mix spring onion, ginger and garlic in a bowl. Heat vegetable oil until smoking hot and pour it over contents of bowl. Stir, then add remaining ingredients.

To serve, arrange meat on a platter and spoon over sauce. I like to serve a bowl of juicy honeydew melon chunks alongside.

roast chicken – the all-time favourite   SERVES 4

This is the way I roast my chicken – with the vegetables around the bird. Chunks of parsnip, pumpkin, turnip and carrot and small onions are all good to add with the potato.

1 x 1.8 kg chicken
1 lemon, halved
2–3 cloves garlic
salt
freshly ground black pepper
1 large sprig rosemary
walnut-sized piece of butter
2–3 red-skinned potatoes,
    quartered
mixed vegetables, cut into
    chunks
extra fresh rosemary
¼ cup olive oil
white wine, vermouth, stock *or*
    water

An hour and a quarter before dinner, preheat oven to 220°C. Rub chicken vigorously inside and out with lemon. Crush garlic with the back of a knife, roll in salt and pepper and insert in cavity with lemon halves, rosemary sprig and butter. Put chicken into a large baking dish.

Put vegetables into a bowl and season. Add a few rosemary leaves and oil and toss to coat. Scatter vegetables around chicken and massage its skin with the seasoned olive oil. Turn chicken on its side.

Place baking dish in centre of oven. After 20 minutes, turn chicken over onto its other side and carefully turn vegetables. After a further 20 minutes, turn chicken breast-side up, baste with juices, loosen vegetables and roast for another 20 minutes. (During this final cooking time, dry and dress a large green salad.)

Reduce oven temperature to 160°C. Transfer chicken and vegetables to a heatproof plate and rest in oven. Discard all fat from baking dish and deglaze over heat with wine. Stir vigorously to dislodge all the cooked-on good bits, and lengthen with either a little more wine or add some home-

middle eastern chicken

Toss sliced hot chicken breast fillet with diced Preserved Lemon (see LEMONS AND LIMES*) and couscous or hot chick peas. Add plenty of freshly chopped coriander and parsley leaves and roasted ground cumin.*

chicken salad

Dress hot sliced chicken breast fillet with Pesto (see BASIL*), add to a salad and sprinkle with toasted pine nuts.*

made stock or tomato sauce or cream. Joint chicken, arrange on a serving platter with vegetables and pour over juices.

short cut If you only have 45 minutes before dinner, cut the chicken in half down either side of the backbone using heavy scissors. (Reserve the backbone for the stock.) Season and massage chicken as above. Put the garlic and lemon halves underneath the chicken in the baking dish. The vegetables will need to be cut smaller to cook in time (or forget roast vegetables and serve a salad and grilled eggplant or green beans). There will be no need to turn the chicken, although it should be basted with juices after the first 20 minutes.   **gravy** If you believe that chicken must have gravy, stir 1 tablespoon plain flour into the baking dish before deglazing. Wait until the flour is a good brown colour before adding 1 cup deglazing liquid and stirring very vigorously with a wooden spoon to avoid lumps. As an alternative to plain flour, mix 2 teaspoons flour to a paste with 2 teaspoons Dijon mustard.   **roast chicken stock** While you are clearing up, put the chicken carcass (together with neck, giblets and backbone, if reserved) in a saucepan with a sliced onion, carrot and bay leaf and barely cover with cold water. Add parsley stalks and celery if you have them. Simmer for an hour or so, then strain and chill overnight. Pour the stock into ice-cream or ice-cube trays and freeze. The next time you roast a chicken you will have some light stock to add flavour to the juices.

stephanie's chicken provençale   SERVES 4

There are so many classic and impromptu ways to casserole a chicken that I hesitate to mention any for fear of being confusing. And yet a cut-up chicken combined with vegetables, seasonings and some liquid is so easy and satisfying – 10 minutes' preparation and then feet up and out with the newspaper while dinner cooks itself.

Casseroled chicken includes all wet curries, Moroccan tagines, Chinese one-pot dishes, French regional classics (such as this one from Provence, chicken in vinegar sauce from the Beaujolais, and chicken with cider, cream and apples from Normandy) and thousands more. I recommend you read up on regional techniques and experiment.

I believe that a casserole of chicken is best eaten as soon as it is ready. Contrary to many food writers, I do not enjoy reheated chicken casseroles very much. The pieces seem to lose their plumpness and succulence and very quickly are transformed into rags.

1 x 1.8 kg chicken

salt

(continued next page)

Preheat oven to 200°C. Joint chicken into thighs, drumsticks and wings and cut each breast fillet in half, keeping it on the bone.

chicken and pasta
Toss sliced hot chicken breast fillet and Parsley Butter (see PARSLEY) with fettuccine.

tandoori drumsticks
Marinate skinned, slashed drumsticks in tandoori paste mixed with yoghurt and lemon juice and bake at 200°C for about an hour. Serve with rice.

freshly ground black pepper

2 red peppers, halved

2 yellow peppers, halved

4 large ripe tomatoes, peeled
or 1 × 410 g can peeled
tomatoes

2 anchovies, chopped

2 tablespoons very freshly
chopped parsley

18 large black olives, stoned
and halved

2 tablespoons olive oil

1 onion, sliced into rings

4 cloves garlic, finely chopped

½ cup dry white wine or half
wine, half vermouth

1 bay leaf

1 large sprig thyme

4 small zucchini, cut into
chunks

---

thai drumsticks
*Marinate drumsticks
in a Thai curry
paste and cook in
stock and coconut
milk with finely
chopped lemongrass
and fresh coriander.*

chilli chicken
*Mix a little chilli
sauce through sliced
steamed chicken
breast fillet and
serve with egg
noodles and stir-
fried greens.*

**chicken with
chive sauce**
*Reduce chicken
stock to a strong
glaze and add a
tablespoon each of
cream and chopped
onion chives at the
last minute for a
sauce to serve with
a grilled or poached
chicken breast.*

You should have 10 pieces. Season.

Grill peppers, skin-side up, until black. Wrap in a cloth for 10 minutes, then remove skin, cores and seeds. Slice thickly and set aside. Chop tomatoes roughly and set aside. Put anchovies into a bowl and stand bowl over simmering water to melt. Stir in parsley and olives and set aside.

Select a large, enamelled cast-iron casserole that will hold the chicken and vegetables and can be used both for the initial browning and the completed dish. Heat oil and brown chicken in batches, so that the heat remains high and there is a good sizzle. Transfer browned pieces to a plate. Pour off most of the fat and lightly sauté onion for 5 minutes. Add garlic and replace chicken, with drumsticks and thighs on the bottom. Add any juices that have collected on the plate. Reheat until there is a sizzle from the casserole. Pour over wine and allow to sizzle up the sides and quickly reduce. Add tomato and any juice, bay leaf and thyme. Cover with foil and a lid and bake in oven for 45 minutes. Stir gently and add sliced peppers and zucchini. Replace lid and cook a further 20 minutes. The chicken should be tender but not collapsed and the zucchini should still be a little firm.

When ready to serve, rebubble, uncovered, on top of stove and scatter with parsley, olive and anchovy mixture. Serve with a green salad and small waxy potatoes boiled in their jackets.

pasta sauce Chop leftovers – be careful of bone fragments – and reheat as a quick pasta sauce.

christmas turkey

SERVES 8–10

Everyone seems to have a horror story of cooking their first turkey. My own was arriving in London on Christmas Eve looking forward to cooking the turkey bought by my beloved to find a bird that was barely contained in a large enamelled washbasin, which, of course, did not fit in the ancient stove. My partner roped the oven door more or less shut. My memory about whether we ever ate this bird is quite vague, although I do remember making a chestnut stuffing.

Turkey is usually sold frozen. It can be bought whole or as a 'buffe', the marketing name for the breast fillets on the bone. Avoid any turkey that is labelled 'prebasted' as it will have been injected with nameless substances: you can do better with butter and lemon yourself. A whole turkey weighing 4–5 kg will feed 8–10 people, as will a 3 kg buffe breast. Thaw a frozen turkey in the refrigerator, freed of all wrappings and sitting on a wad of kitchen paper on a platter. Be warned: a whole bird can take up to 2 days to thaw completely.

The biggest problem when cooking a turkey is that the breast meat is always done before the legs are tender. The solutions are either to buy a buffe or to carve the legs away from the bird once the breast is tender and return them to the oven to finish cooking. If you like, the leg meat can be served tossed through a large green salad as a second course once you have enjoyed the breast meat, stuffing and juices.

There is rarely room to roast vegetables in the baking dish with the turkey. If you have a second oven a selection of vegetables can be baked separately – allow 1½ hours at 180°C for oiled chunks to be tender and crisp. The vegetables can also be cooked in advance and returned to the oven with the turkey legs for a further 30 minutes to reheat and crisp. Otherwise braise vegetables on the stove.

Accompaniments to roast turkey are traditional, and each family has its own traditions, so serve what you like best! Tinned cranberry sauce seems to appear regularly but better than this would be home-made spiced fruits, either offered separately or dropped into the sauce for the last few minutes.

asian chicken

Roast a chicken rubbed with light soy sauce and honey and add freshly sliced ginger to the baking dish.

turkey breast

Pan-fry thin slices of raw turkey breast, as they do in Italy, or roll them around a stuffing and sauté them. Any recipe for veal scaloppine can be adapted to use raw sliced turkey breast, which will cook in just a few minutes.

1 x 4–5 kg turkey
salt
freshly ground black pepper
1 lemon, halved
2 cloves garlic, crushed
generous sprig of thyme *or*
   rosemary
butter

BREAD STUFFING
80 g butter
turkey liver (if present)
200 g smoked streaky bacon,
   diced
1 large onion, finely diced
200 g minced pork
1 tablespoon marsala, port *or*
   muscat
300 g fresh white
   breadcrumbs

(continued next page)

Allow turkey to come to room temperature before cooking it. To prepare the stuffing, heat butter in a frying pan until foaming, then sauté liver until lightly browned. Removed liver from pan. Add bacon and onion to pan and sauté gently until onion has softened. Add pork and sauté until it just changes colour. Tip in marsala. Chop liver and combine in a bowl with contents of pan and remaining ingredients.

Preheat oven to 220°C. Wipe and dry bird inside and out with kitchen paper and remove giblets and neck, if present (use these to make a stock or add them to the baking dish to ensure a well-flavoured sauce). Transfer turkey to a baking dish and season very well. Rub inside and out with cut lemon and put garlic and thyme into cavity. Stuff bird loosely, since all stuffings swell when cooking. Rub bird generously

2 tablespoons freshly chopped
   parsley
1 teaspoon freshly chopped
   lemon thyme
1 teaspoon freshly chopped
   sage
2 eggs
salt
freshly ground black pepper

with butter and cover an entire baking dish with a well-buttered doubled sheet of foil.

Allow 20 minutes per 500 g for cooked breast meat and slightly underdone legs (the total cooking time for a 4 kg turkey will be about 2 hours 40 minutes). Remove foil every 20 minutes and baste bird with cooking juices, then replace foil. Reset oven to 180°C after first 40 minutes. Discard foil for final 30 minutes to brown breast. When cooking time has finished, test for doneness by inserting a fine skewer into the thickest part of the breast: the juices should run clear, not pink. Carve off legs, then wrap turkey loosely in a doubled sheet of foil and set aside on a platter in a warm place. Increase oven temperature to 200°C and return legs to oven for a further 30 minutes. While the legs are finishing, scoop out the stuffing, prepare a sauce and finish any vegetables.
other stuffings Make a chestnut and barley stuffing by substituting 1½ cups peeled chestnuts for the dried fruit used in Janni's Barley Stuffing (*see* QUAIL AND SQUAB PIGEONS) – it can be made a day ahead. Try Traditional Sage Stuffing for Goose, Duck or Turkey (*see* SAGE), too. **sauce** To make a simple sauce, pour the juices in the baking dish into a tall jug. Allow the fat to rise, then discard it. Over moderate heat, scatter 2 tablespoons plain flour into the baking dish and stir and scrape until it browns. Add 1 cup white wine and stir and scrape some more. Add the juices from the jug and simmer. Add herbs to complement those in the stuffing and any juices that have seeped onto the platter or some chicken stock. Season well.

other recipes

bread sauce to serve with roast chicken *see* BAY LEAVES

chicken breasts with almond sauce and guacamole *see* AVOCADOS

chicken breasts with sage *see* SAGE

chicken congee *see* RICE

chicken in the pot with tarragon cream sauce *see* TARRAGON

chicken noodle soup (as it should be) *see* PASTA AND NOODLES

cock-a-leekie *see* LEEKS

panang gai – dry chicken curry *see* NUTS

quick yoghurt marinade for chicken or lamb *see* YOGHURT

satay marinade and sauce *see* NUTS

southern chicken, ham and okra gumbo *see* OKRA

traditional sage stuffing for goose, duck or turkey *see* SAGE

vietnamese chicken and mint salad *see* MINT

see also LIVER

c h i v e s Resembling a small clump of grass, chives are a member of the lily (*Allium*) family, as are onions and garlic. The stems, which are in fact leaves, are faintly onion- or garlic-scented, depending on the variety. | This herb is easy to grow and is perennial, the plants dying down at the end of autumn and returning in the spring. (In my garden the chives often remain throughout the winter, although they are usually rather straggly.) As the clump grows back thicker each spring, it is a good idea to separate it after 2 years. The clump should be cut frequently during the spring and summer to encourage regrowth, but don't cut it to the ground and don't pull at it. Cut the amount you need with scissors. | To get the most out of chives, the fine leaves must be cut to release the flavour and to make them edible. They should be warmed (as in an omelette), not cooked, or snipped with scissors and added to a dish at the last minute. Chives are the herb par excellence to use with eggs. Deciding whether to serve scrambled eggs with chives or parsley poses a real dilemma for me. Both seem perfect marriages. >

onion

chives

go

with

chicken

eggs

fish

potatoes

cucumber

celery

beetroots

butter

garlic

chives

go

with

eggs

prawns

fish

beef

shallots

garlic

pork

chives and . . .
*Snip onion chives
onto boiled,
buttered potatoes,
a salad of wilted
cucumber slices or
scrambled eggs on
toast.*

One of the silliest garnishes introduced during the days of nouvelle cuisine was a pair of long chive stems crossed over food. What was one supposed to do with them? Swallow the chives and choke? Or push them aside? The latter, I imagine, and this sums up the stupidity and wastefulness of such unnecessary garnishing.

VARIETIES AND SEASON

Two varieties of chives are available widely and all year round in Australia – onion chives and garlic chives. **Onion** chives (*Allium schoeno-prasum*) have hollow, thin leaves about 30 cm long that produce pink–mauve puffball-like flowers, which are edible but very strong. **Garlic** chives (*A. tuberosum*) have flat leaves like blades of grass and are strongly garlic-scented. They produce a starry head of small, individual white flowers, which are edible (as are the flower-buds). Garlic chives are used a great deal in Asian cooking, where they are known as *gau choi*, or *gau choi fa* if including the flower-bud.

SELECTION AND STORAGE

Choose **onion** chives that are brightly coloured, fresh and not slimy, nor should they have more than a faintly onion-like smell. **Garlic** chives should have a small, tight flower-bud at the end of each stalk. If the flower-bud has opened the garlic chives are considered too old to eat (although the flower can be separated and scattered over, for example, a grilled chicken breast). Garlic chives should not be wilting, nor should they be slimy or smell at all rank.

Chives become slimy if stored in water. The best solution is to cut what you need from the garden and use them at once. If you have bought a bunch, refrigerate it, unwashed, in the crisper in a paper-lined plastic bag for up to 2 days.

PREPARATION

Wash only what you need and dry the chives thoroughly before cutting them or you will squeeze the juices out onto the cutting surface with your knife. Discard the lowest portions of the stems, which are the toughest. **Garlic** chives and their flower-buds are usually cut into lengths for stir-frying; **onion** chives are finely sliced.

chinese stir-fry of garlic chives and bean sprouts

SERVES 2–4

vegetable oil

1 handful garlic chives, cut into 2.5 cm pieces

1 cup bean sprouts

1 tablespoon light soy sauce

few drops of sesame oil

2 tablespoons Chicken Stock ✎

2 teaspoons cornflour

Heat a wok, then add a little vegetable oil and heat. Stir-fry ✎ chives and bean sprouts for 30 seconds. Add soy sauce and sesame oil. Mix stock and cornflour, then tip into wok and stir until slightly thickened. Serve with chicken dishes and rice.

chive pancakes

Add snipped onion chives to Pancake Batter ✎ intended for savoury pancakes.

potato and chive cake

SERVES 4

500 g floury potatoes

60 g unsalted butter

2 egg yolks

sea salt

freshly ground black pepper

¼ cup freshly snipped chives

clarified butter ✎ or olive oil

Preheat oven to 180°C. Boil potatoes until tender, then drain and peel. Pass potatoes through the medium disc of a food mill. Beat butter and egg yolks into potato, then season and stir in chives. Grease an ovenproof frying pan with clarified butter and press in mixture (or form 4 cakes inside hamburger rings on a greased baking tray) and bake for 45 minutes until firm (or 20–25 minutes for individual cake). Invert potato cake and cut into wedges, or remove small cakes from rings. Brush with a little more butter and sprinkle with extra chives. Serve with a green salad and tomato or Tomatoes Provençale (*see* TOMATOES) for a delicious lunch, or as an accompaniment to a simple grill.

garlic chives

Substitute garlic chives for spring onions in most Chinese recipes.

chive batter

Add chives to Beer Batter ✎ before dipping and deep-frying fish or prawns.

other recipes

carpaccio of salmon with fines herbes *see* CHERVIL

herb and pumpkin soup *see* PUMPKINS

c h o c o l a t e

chocolate I am not a chocoholic – I can take it or leave it. However, people have been passionate about chocolate for at least 1200 years, when the first cacao trees (*Theobroma cacao*) arrived in Mexico from South America. | The word 'chocolate' comes from the Central American Indian for 'warm beverage', which reminds us that even after chocolate was introduced to Europe from the New World in the 1500s it was used until the mid-1800s only as a drink. | I once watched a woman making her breakfast chocolate on a Primus stove in an old French film. She grated a block of chocolate into a small saucepan of hot milk. I thought this looked such a special drink that, when holidaying at an Austrian ski resort a year or so later, I eagerly ordered hot chocolate after a particularly nose-tingling walk. What arrived was a mug filled with whipped cream. The waitress poured molten chocolate into the cream in a thin, shining stream from a silver pot. The cream collapsed as quickly as melting snow. It was the richest concoction I have ever been faced with, and quite undrinkable as far as I was concerned. >

Like my hot chocolate, many chocolate combinations are impossibly rich and frequently too sweet. Inexperienced or generous cooks need to remember to hold back when serving chocolate. Not too much, not too often and the very best quality should always be the motto. While chocolate is used to make everything from cakes to sauces for meat dishes (in Spain and Mexico), my favourite chocolate experiences all tend to centre around bitter and very dark chocolate, roasted almonds, deep caramel and orange peel!

One needs to understand a few basic facts about how chocolate is made not only to rid it of its mystique, but also to understand why the best chocolate is much more costly than other varieties. Chocolate is made from the seeds of cacao beans, the fruit of the cacao tree, which is grown commercially in Africa, South America, New Guinea, the West Indies and Vanuatu. (Most of the chocolate produced in Australia is made from beans from Africa and New Guinea.) The cacao beans are fermented, dried, roasted and hulled to separate the shells from the meat or nibs. The nibs are then ground and melted to make a paste called chocolate liquor.

If allowed to harden, chocolate liquor, made up of half cocoa butter and half cocoa solids, becomes unsweetened cooking chocolate. Cocoa solids when crushed and sieved become cocoa powder. Cocoa butter, unique among vegetable fats in that it is solid at room temperature but melts in the mouth, is added to unsweetened cooking chocolate to contribute melting qualities and lushness. Other ingredients, such as sugar, vanilla and milk products and sometimes emulsifiers that are cheaper than pure cocoa butter, are added to unsweetened cooking chocolate and determine the character and quality of the chocolate. The chocolate is then 'conched' (kneaded) to make it sensuously smooth. The longer it is conched, the smoother the texture. Cheaper products are worked by simpler methods and can feel gritty on the tongue. The temperature of the chocolate is slowly lowered in a process known as tempering. Tempered chocolate hardens with a shiny gloss and breaks with a snap. Quality chocolate is then aged 60–90 days.

VARIETIES AND SEASON

Chocolate is categorised by its chocolate liquor and cocoa butter content as *unsweetened, bittersweet, semi-sweet, milk* or *white*.

Bittersweet and semi-sweet chocolate have less sugar than milk chocolate, which has less chocolate liquor, and white chocolate has no chocolate liquor at all. The more bitter the chocolate, the more intense the chocolate flavour. The less bitter, the more sugar and less intense flavour. Prefer bittersweet varieties for general cooking.

The supermarket may describe its cooking chocolate as *dark, milk* or *white*. Prefer dark chocolate for cakes, puddings and sauces. Specific recipes may require milk or white chocolate. Avoid any products sold as *compound*

chocolate

goes

with

almonds

walnuts

hazelnuts

pecans

macadamias

pistachios

figs

prunes

butter

honey

cream

rum

Cognac

muscat

sugar

oranges

raisins

chestnuts

Amaretto di
*   Saronno*

caramel

coffee

coconut

marzipan

sour cream

eggs

vanilla

chocolate. These have a lower percentage of chocolate liquor and other fats, such as soya, palm kernel or coconut oils, have been added. These fats melt at higher temperatures than cocoa butter, but the taste and texture of compound chocolate does not compare with better-quality products.

Speciality food stores, cookware suppliers and cookery schools sell high-quality **couverture** chocolate, which is designed to provide a thin, even coating with a high gloss. Couverture has a high level of cocoa butter and is also recommended for more general cooking uses because of its quality and flavour. It is widely available in bittersweet, semi-sweet and milk.

Cocoa is available unsweetened and sweetened (the latter is usually sold as drinking chocolate). The rich, dark, unsweetened Dutch cocoa, to which bicarbonate of soda has been added to neutralise the cocoa's acidity, is considered the Rolls-Royce of all cocoas used in cooking.

SELECTION AND STORAGE

Chocolate is one of life's luxuries. Buy the best and enjoy it from time to time. Do not eat so much chocolate that you move past pleasure into sensory and stomach overload.

Chocolate keeps better in a thick slab or chunks rather than in tiny pieces. Avoid buying chocolate 'bits' because of this. **Dark** chocolate has a shelf life of about a year. **Milk** chocolate has a shelf life of about 6 months.

To store chocolate, wrap it well in foil and keep in a cool, dry place away from strong odours and with good air circulation (15–20°C is ideal). Warmer temperatures cause the cocoa butter to rise to the surface, forming a greyish 'bloom'. This bloom does not affect chocolate that is to be melted and used in baking, but it does alter its texture. If chocolate is stored under refrigeration (essential in tropical areas), it will sweat when brought to room temperature and will shatter rather than snap when broken. Allow the chocolate to recover from the cold before breaking.

Chocolate can also be frozen. Pack it in a moisture-proof container and thaw it in the same package to allow the chocolate to reabsorb the moisture it gave off while frozen.

PREPARATION

When used in cakes and puddings, *cocoa* is usually sifted with the other dry ingredients. For sauces and some desserts, cocoa is usually mixed to a smooth paste with liquid, as its high starch content causes it to form lumps if added directly to hot liquid. In order to cook the starch and to improve its digestibility, all cocoa-based products should be heated to boiling point.

Most recipes using *chocolate* require that it be melted. There are several ways to melt chocolate: in a double boiler, in a bowl over hot water, in the microwave oven or with other ingredients over direct heat. Before commencing, remember the following.

- Chop or grate chocolate before melting it.
- Your spoon and bowl must be completely dry. If water or steam find their way into melting chocolate, the chocolate will seize and tighten, ruining the consistency. (If this happens, a spoonful of vegetable oil will remedy the situation. Butter will *not* help as it also contains moisture, which will cause the chocolate to stiffen even more.)
- Never melt chocolate alone over direct heat.
- High heat is chocolate's worst enemy – it causes melting chocolate to become dry and grainy.
- Chocolate burns very easily. Burnt or scorched chocolate must be thrown away.
- Do not melt more than 500 g chocolate at any one time as it is too difficult to keep the temperature even with a larger quantity.
- Never use a pan or bowl that contains chocolate residue to melt another batch.

TO MELT

Double boiler Bring water to a full boil in the bottom of a double boiler, then turn off the heat. Place grated chocolate in the top of the double boiler and settle the pan in the bottom half. The water in the bottom pan should come right up to the level of the chocolate in the smaller pan. Allow the chocolate to stand undisturbed for 5 minutes, then stir it until completely melted. **Over hot water** Bring a saucepan of water to a full boil, then turn the heat very low. Put the grated chocolate into a bowl wide enough to be suspended by the saucepan and stand it over the water. Cover the bowl tightly with a lid or foil, so that neither water nor steam will spoil the chocolate. Allow the chocolate to stand undisturbed for 5 minutes, then stir it until completely melted. **Microwave oven** Put the chocolate, broken into small pieces or grated, into a microwave-safe bowl. Do not cover the bowl as moisture may form, causing the chocolate to seize. Microwave on medium for 1–2 minutes. The chocolate will retain its shape but will have changed from a dull brown to glossy. Stir the melted chocolate until smooth. **With other ingredients** To melt chocolate with milk, cream, coffee or water, add chocolate to cool rather than hot liquid and melt gently over direct heat. Stir. The chocolate must melt slowly.

fast chocolate sauce

MAKES 1½ CUPS

125 g bittersweet chocolate, grated
½ cup cream
½ cup milk
1 teaspoon honey

Combine all ingredients in a saucepan and heat gently, stirring until smooth. Serve with vanilla ice-cream or poached figs or pears.

chocolate hedgehog

375 g wheatmeal biscuits

¾ cup chopped walnuts

125 g unsalted butter

¾ cup castor sugar

4 tablespoons Dutch cocoa

2 eggs, lightly beaten

ICING

125 g bittersweet chocolate, chopped

1 tablespoon dark rum

60 g butter

Lightly butter a 20 cm square tin. Break biscuits into small pieces and place in a large mixing bowl with walnuts. Melt butter with castor sugar and stir until sugar has dissolved. Mix in cocoa, then stir over heat until smooth. Allow to cool.

Stir eggs into butter mixture, then pour this over biscuit and walnuts. Mix very well. Press into prepared tin in a 2 cm deep layer. Chill while you make the icing.

Put chocolate, rum and butter in a bowl over hot water and stir until melted. Pour onto hedgehog and tilt tin to achieve a smooth, even layer. Refrigerate briefly to set icing before cutting into fingers or squares.

chocolate curls
Spread bittersweet chocolate melted with one-sixth its weight of butter directly onto a baking tray and allow to set. Dip a large knife into hot water and dry it, then scrape down the chocolate to create curls for decorating cakes or desserts. Store any unused curls in an airtight container.

mum's red devil's cake

This was the cake that was often packed in my school lunch-box. I love its chewy texture and deep reddish brown colour. Mum never iced this cake but I suppose you could. The recipe comes from my grandmother's handwritten collection. A note beside the rather odd method advises that this cake will keep indefinitely! That is quite a claim.

125 g butter

200 g brown sugar

2 eggs, separated

½ cup milk

250 g plain flour

1 teaspoon bicarbonate of soda

1 tablespoon warm water

CHOCOLATE MIXTURE

150 g bittersweet chocolate, chopped

150 g brown sugar

½ cup milk or buttermilk

few drops of pure vanilla

1 egg yolk, lightly beaten

Preheat oven to 180°C and butter a 24 cm round springform or square cake tin.

To make the chocolate mixture, gently melt chocolate with sugar, milk and vanilla in a saucepan. When smooth, add egg yolk and cook over gentle heat until mixture thickens slightly. Pour through a strainer into a large mixing bowl and allow to cool.

Cream butter and sugar until light. Beat egg yolks lightly and mix with milk, then add to butter mixture alternately with flour. Add cooled chocolate mixture, combine well and return all to large mixing bowl.

Dissolve bicarbonate of soda in the warm water and stir into mixture. Whisk egg whites until creamy, then fold into mixture.

Pour into prepared tin and bake for 1 hour or until cake tests clean. Cool cake completely before cutting.

rum and macadamia brownies

125 g unsalted butter
100 g bittersweet chocolate, chopped
2 eggs
1 cup castor sugar
2 tablespoons dark rum *or* honey
100 g plain flour, sifted
scant pinch of salt
125 g macadamias, chopped

Preheat oven to 180°C. Butter a 20 cm square tin. Put butter in a saucepan over low heat. When half-melted, add chocolate and stir until it has melted and mixture is smooth. Remove from heat and cool.

Beat eggs and castor sugar until thick and creamy. Stir in cooled chocolate mixture and rum, then flour, salt and macadamias. Pour into prepared tin and bake for 30 minutes. Cool and cut into squares.

chocolate and almond cake

This well-known recipe is based on the French classic reine de Saba *or* Queen of Sheba's *cake, made particularly famous by Elizabeth David. It is for those who love rich chocolate cakes that are not too sweet and are easy to make on a whim. I prefer this cake served as a dessert with thick cream and maybe some raspberries.*

125 g bittersweet chocolate, chopped
1 tablespoon brandy
1 tablespoon black coffee
100 g unsalted butter
100 g castor sugar
100 g ground almonds
3 eggs, separated
icing sugar

Preheat oven to 160°C. Butter an 18 cm round cake tin and line it with baking paper. (If you are sure your springform tin does not leak you might prefer to use it, as this cake is very fragile and often cracks when turned out.)

Combine chocolate, brandy and coffee in a bowl over water or in a double boiler. Stir when melted and add butter and sugar. Mix well. Add ground almonds and stir very well. Lightly beat egg yolks and stir into bowl off the heat. Beat egg whites until firm. Lighten chocolate mixture with a spoonful of egg white, then fold in rest of whites and spoon into prepared tin. Bake for 40–45 minutes. The cake will still test a little gooey in the centre. It will have developed a crust and be very fragile. Cool completely in the tin, then carefully invert onto a serving plate. Dust with icing sugar.

mietta's chocolate cake

Mietta O'Donnell and partner Tony Knox operated Mietta's restaurant and literary salon in Melbourne for more than 20 years. Mietta served this cake covered with chocolate and brandy butter cream.

chocolate prunes
Soak stoned prunes in muscat or tokay, insert roasted almonds in place of the stones and dip each in melted bittersweet couverture.

chocolate and muscat
Serve chunks of the very best couverture on a bread board with a heavy knife, coffee, muscatel raisins and a glass of liqueur muscat instead of dessert.

250 g butter
200 g castor sugar
4 eggs, separated
250 g drinking chocolate
4 tablespoons milk
125 g self-raising flour
60 g ground rice

BUTTER CREAM

250 g bittersweet chocolate,
    melted and cooled
250 g softened butter
brandy

Preheat oven to 180°C. Butter a 22 cm square cake tin and line it with baking paper. Cream butter and sugar until pale and fluffy. Add egg yolks, drinking chocolate and milk and beat well. Mix flour with ground rice and add to chocolate mixture, beating well. Whip egg whites until soft peaks form, then fold into mixture. Pour into prepared tin and bake for 1–1½ hours. Halfway through baking, cover tin with foil to prevent it getting too brown on top. Cool completely before icing.

To make the butter cream, beat cooled chocolate with butter until fluffy and spreadable, then beat in brandy to taste. Spread generously over top and sides of cake and refrigerate until set. Serve cake not too cold in small portions and offer thick cream.

marieke's chocolate cake

Marieke Brugman and her partner Sarah Stegley have pioneered the field of gourmet country retreats at their memorable property, Howqua Dale, in north-eastern Victoria. Marieke serves this very dense and delectable cake covered with a layer of chocolate ganache. Tiny portions, please!

150 g bittersweet chocolate,
    grated
150 g ground almonds
130 g unsalted butter
130 g castor sugar
7 egg yolks
9 egg whites

CHOCOLATE GANACHE

375 g bittersweet chocolate,
    chopped
1 cup cream

Preheat oven to 180°C. Butter a 20 cm round cake tin and line with baking paper. Combine chocolate and almonds. Cream butter and sugar until pale, then add yolks one at a time and beat well (this can be done in the food processor). Add chocolate mixture. Beat whites to creamy peaks and fold into mixture. Pour into prepared tin. Stand tin in a baking dish and fill dish with hot water to come two-thirds up sides of tin. Bake for 45–60 minutes until cake tests clean. Cool in tin before turning out.

To make the ganache, put chocolate and cream into a saucepan and heat gently, stirring until chocolate has melted and mixture is quite smooth. Transfer to bowl of an electric mixer and beat until cool and thick. Spread over cake and allow to set before cutting.

---

eugénies

Blanch 2–3 cm wide strips of orange zest to remove all bitterness, then simmer in light Sugar Syrup until transparent. Drain and dry the zest thoroughly for several hours on a wire cake rack, then dip each piece in melted chocolate (the very best) and roll it in Dutch cocoa. An after-dinner treat from Michel Guérard.

chocolate self-saucing pudding

SERVES 4

125 g plain flour
scant pinch of salt
60 g castor sugar
2 teaspoons baking powder
2 tablespoons Dutch cocoa
½ cup chopped walnuts
½ cup milk
40 g butter, melted
1 egg
few drops of pure vanilla

TOPPING

180 g brown sugar
2 tablespoons Dutch cocoa
1 cup boiling water

Preheat oven to 180°C and butter a 750 ml pie dish. Sift flour, salt, castor sugar, baking powder and cocoa into a bowl, then stir in nuts. Combine milk, melted butter, egg and vanilla and mix into dry ingredients. Pour into pie dish.

To make the topping, mix brown sugar and cocoa and sprinkle over pudding batter. Pour boiling water carefully over all ingredients. Bake for 40–45 minutes until puffed in centre and pudding feels firm when pressed lightly with your fingertips. To serve, spoon out cake and its sauce while hot.

chocolate truffles
Dip small balls of chilled ganache (see p. 228) in melted bittersweet chocolate and roll in cocoa. Add glacé ginger or chopped nuts to the ganache, if desired.

chocolate amaretti puddings

SERVES 10

½ cup crumbled amaretti
    biscuits
1 cup milk
3 tablespoons cream
3 eggs, separated
45 g butter
100 g sugar
4 tablespoons Dutch cocoa

CARAMEL

¼ cup water
1 cup sugar

Preheat oven to 180°C. To make the caramel, stir water and sugar over heat until sugar has dissolved. Stop stirring and cook until a deep caramel colour. Remove from heat and immediately dip base of pan into cold water to stop cooking. Pour caramel into 10 × 150 ml pudding moulds, tilting to spread caramel. Butter any exposed surfaces.

Soak crumbled biscuits in milk and cream. Cream butter and sugar in a food processor, then add egg yolks, one at a time. Add cocoa and soaked biscuits but do not over-process. Whisk egg whites until snowy peaks form, then fold gently into pudding mixture.

Fill moulds with mixture, then stand them in a baking dish lined with a tea towel and pour in hot water to come two-thirds up their sides. Cover baking dish with foil and bake for 25–30 minutes until puddings feel springy but not solid when pressed lightly. Remove baking dish and puddings from oven but leave foil in place for 5 minutes to minimise 'falling'. Serve warm.

chocolate fig roll
Finely chop 2 cups dried figs and ½ cup blanched almonds and blend to a sticky paste in a food processor with ½ cup grated dark chocolate. With lightly oiled hands, roll the mixture into a sausage shape, then dust with 1 tablespoon icing sugar, wrap in baking paper and refrigerate. Serve thin slices with coffee.

chocolate sorbet

SERVES 8

This sorbet is a great favourite of mine as it is so refreshing. Do not decide to churn the mixture without boiling it first. As mentioned earlier, cocoa needs to be brought to boiling point to cook the starch in it.

chocolate figs
Slice dried figs dipped in melted couverture to show off their seeds.

250 g castor sugar
60 g Dutch cocoa
1 tablespoon instant coffee
pinch of ground cinnamon
3 cups water

Mix dry ingredients in a bowl. Gradually mix to a smooth paste with some of the water. Add balance of water, then transfer to a saucepan and bring mixture to boiling point, stirring until sugar has dissolved. Simmer for 5 minutes and then strain into a jug and allow to cool. Churn in an ice-cream machine according to the manufacturer's instructions. The sorbet can be made and stored in the freezer the morning of the day it is required but loses texture if prepared any further ahead.

fudgy chocolate mousse

SERVES 8–10

200 g bittersweet chocolate, chopped
4 eggs, separated
100 g softened unsalted butter
2 teaspoons castor sugar

Melt chocolate gently in a large bowl over hot water. Remove bowl from heat, then beat in egg yolks, one at a time. Add butter, beating well until mixture is glossy and smooth.

Whip egg whites until soft peaks form. Sprinkle sugar over and continue to whip until whites are satiny. Fold quickly but thoroughly into chocolate mixture. Transfer mixture to a serving bowl or individual bowls and chill.

Allow mousse to come to room temperature before serving. If in a large bowl, a tablespoon dipped into boiling water will enable you to spoon out perfectly shaped quenelles of mousse, if desired.

other recipes

chocolate-dipped prunes with brandy cream *see* PLUMS AND PRUNES
date and chocolate cake *see* DATES
prune fritters *see* PLUMS AND PRUNES

coriander

coriander The botanical name of coriander – *Coriandrum sativum* – comes from the Greek *koris*, meaning 'bug'. I was interested to read this in Rosemary Hemphill's *Herbs for All Seasons* as one of my cooks used to refer disparagingly to coriander leaves as smelling like squashed ants. The aroma is certainly very distinctive! | Coriander is a native of the Mediterranean region and was used in Eygpt as early as 1550 BC. Its feathery green leaves superficially resemble parsley, but the similarity ends there, even though it is sometimes called Chinese parsley. In the United States it is known as cilantro. Some Australian cooks have been known to describe sauces as being made with cilantro. This is a silly practice guaranteed to confuse the public rather than expand culinary understanding. >

**fresh
coriander
goes
with**
prawns
garlic
chillies
pork
beef
scallops
avocados
fish
ginger
coconut
noodles
fish sauce
soy sauce
mint
parsley
chicken
yoghurt

**coriander
seeds
go
with**
beef
lamb
lentils
mushrooms
sesame seeds
hazelnuts
caraway seeds
olives
chicken
chick peas
eggplants

It would be difficult to imagine the cuisines of South-East Asia or the Middle East without this herb. The fragrant seeds have a faintly citrus flavour that is totally different from that of the leaves, stems and roots. The seeds are a common flavouring in the Middle East. The leaves, stems and roots of coriander are used in Asia to flavour curries and seafood or with vegetables and fruit to make simple accompaniments. Coriander is also fried with garlic and other spices to add pungency to a wide range of dishes. I cannot do more than hint at the wondrous and complex dishes of South-East Asia, where so many flavours, including coriander, intermingle to create some of the most exciting food on earth.

Coriander leaves are an acquired taste for some. If you are unsure of your guests' palates, do not overload dishes with fresh coriander.

VARIETIES AND SEASON

Coriander is easy to grow but sets seed quickly. Plant several seeds at a time in succession to keep the leaves coming along. Coriander is available all year.

SELECTION AND STORAGE

Frequently one serves or is served food arranged on a bed of coriander leaves or topped with a handful of coriander leaves. The leaves for such presentation must be the very youngest and freshest. The youngest and freshest coriander is always available by the bunch from Asian food stores. Supermarkets are increasingly stocking coriander, too. Do not buy bunches that are wilted or have damaged, blackened, water-logged leaves. The bunch should smell sweet, not acrid.

Stand the bunch with its roots in cold water, with a plastic bag over the leaves, in the refrigerator for 4–5 days. Once washed and used, any remaining coriander should be dried well, stored in a paper-lined plastic bag in the refrigerator and used within 2 days.

PREPARATION

As coriander is notorious for trapping grit among its tightly closed inner leaves, always wash it very well in lots of cold water. Rub the dirt from the roots, as your recipe may instruct you to use these as well as the leaves and stems. Inspect the leaves carefully before drying them gently in a spinner, tea towel or kitchen paper. Ensure that the leaves are thoroughly dry before chopping them.

recipes

sesame and coriander dukkah

MAKES 1–1½ CUPS

Dukkah makes an interesting change from peanuts when serving drinks. It can also be sprinkled over vegetable fritters or grilled fish. The texture should be coarse, certainly not a powder. You can use a food processor for the nuts and a coffee grinder for the seeds. Serve the dukkah in a shallow bowl surrounded by triangles of toasted pita bread brushed with olive oil. Any extra can be kept in a screw-top jar for another day.

175 g sesame seeds
50 g coriander seeds
50 g hazelnuts
sea salt
coarsely ground black pepper

Place sesame seeds on a sheet of foil and grill for a few moments. Be careful not to burn them. Grind briefly. Dry-fry coriander seeds in a frying pan until fragrant, then grind coarsely. Roast hazelnuts at 180°C until brown, then rub in a cloth to remove as much skin as possible. Crush roughly. Mix ground nuts and seeds together and season with salt and pepper.

middle eastern meatballs with coriander leaves

SERVES 4

These meatballs can be served with drinks or as part of a selection of cold or warm dishes with Fresh Tomato Sauce (see TOMATOES*) or Smoky Eggplant Purée (see* EGGPLANTS*). Make smaller meatballs if serving them with drinks (the mixture will yield about 40 cocktail-sized meatballs and about 25 larger ones to serve as part of meal).*

Ask the butcher to mince the meat for you on the finest hole of his mincer, or to pass it through the mincer twice.

500 g finely minced lean lamb
  or beef
pinch of salt
1 onion, finely chopped
2 teaspoons ground cumin
1 teaspoon ground allspice
pinch of cayenne pepper
1 cup coarsely chopped fresh
  coriander leaves
olive oil

Blend all ingredients except oil in a food processor until smooth and pasty. Wet your hands to stop mixture sticking and form small balls. Heat oil in a frying pan and brown meatballs. Drain well on crumpled kitchen paper. The meatballs can also be partially cooked and finished in the oven when required.

coriander sauce
Finely chop 1–2 slices ginger with 1–2 garlic cloves and some coriander stems and mix with warmed light soy sauce. Serve as a sauce for roasted scallops or freshly opened oysters.

coriander yoghurt
Mix drained thick yoghurt (see p. 776) with chopped coriander leaves and an equal quantity of chopped spring onion, then season with salt and eat with crispbread and bean sprouts for breakfast.

coriander olives
Mix your favourite olives with coriander seeds crushed in a mortar, some finely chopped garlic and a little olive oil and marinate for at least a day.

thai steamed fish with coriander root, chilli and lime juice
SERVES 4

This recipe is based on one from David Thompson's book Classic Thai Cuisine. *David's recipe specifies 4–10 chillies. The larger quantity is for chilli aficionados only! You need a whole fish for this dish – for instructions on steaming fish, an easy task, turn to* FISH.

coriander paste
Blend a large handful of coriander leaves and stems with a small handful of mint leaves, a fresh, seeded green chilli and enough lemon juice and a little water to make a green paste, and stir into creamy yoghurt, adding salt to taste. Serve with curries or use as a dip for raw vegetables or toasted pita bread.

1 coriander root
1 teaspoon salt
4 cloves garlic
4 fresh green chillies
3 tablespoons fresh lime juice
1 tablespoon castor sugar
2 tablespoons fish sauce
1 × 800 g firm-fleshed sea fish
  (snapper, bream,
  coral trout)

In a food processor, blend coriander root with salt and garlic to make a paste. Add chillies, lime juice, sugar and fish sauce. Blend until sugar dissolves. Score fish through its thickest part, then spoon over sauce and steam until cooked (about 10 minutes).

hot spicy fish
SERVES 6

This dish is of Middle Eastern origin, where it is called samak harra, *and is from Claudia Roden's* A New Book of Middle Eastern Food.

lentil salad
Season a salad of cooked brown lentils with olive oil, lemon juice, crushed garlic, salt, pepper, ground coriander seeds and lots of freshly chopped parsley.

1 × 1.5–2 kg firm-fleshed sea
  fish (snapper, blue eye,
  coral trout, red emperor)
375 g walnuts, coarsely
  chopped
1 bunch coriander, finely
  chopped
7–10 cloves garlic, crushed
½ cup olive oil
juice of 2–3 lemons
salt
1 teaspoon ground cinnamon
½ teaspoon cayenne pepper

Preheat oven to 180°C. Wash fish inside and out and dry thoroughly. Place in a lightly oiled baking dish. Combine remaining ingredients to a sauce-like consistency, adding a little water if necessary. Spoon some sauce into cavity of fish and pour rest on top. Bake for 40 minutes or until fish is done. Serve hot or cold.

other recipes

coriander peanut pesto *see* BASIL
green herb pilaf *see* RICE

c o r n The seed of a type of grass, sweetcorn, maize, Indian corn, corn on the cob or simply corn (*Zea mays*) is the only cereal crop native to the Americas, having originated in prehistoric Mexico. It was one of the 'magic plants' that sustained the Mayans, Aztecs, Inca and North American Indians (the others being chillies, beans and squash). Within 50 years of Columbus bringing corn back to Spain it was grown all over Europe. │ There has long been considerable confusion in the English language over the word 'corn', since it was originally used to describe the staple grain of any country. Our use of the term 'cornflour' is a remnant of this. The cornflour we buy (known as cornstarch in America) is made from wheat, not corn, and now is usually labelled as 'wheaten cornflour' or 'wheaten starch'. │ Sweetcorn is much loved and revered in the United States, where it is always known as 'corn'. Some of the finest regional recipes and folk stories feature this vegetable and remind me of Li'l Abner – dishes such as corn pone, hominy grits, succotash and hoe cakes. >

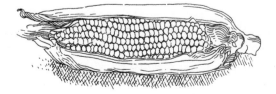

Those who have lived in the United States wax lyrical about roadside stalls selling just-picked corn ready to be rushed to a waiting pot of simmering water. Apparently there is more understanding there than here that sweetcorn begins to deteriorate the moment it is picked. Each little kernel of sweetness begins to convert into starch within hours (40 per cent of the sugar content can be lost in 6 hours at room temperature), so that of all vegetables this is one that is a revelation when home-grown.

Sweetcorn is a warm-climate crop, suitable for Australia. My grandfather grew the sweetcorn in our family and I enjoyed many a breakfast of cob after cob of just-picked ears. My brothers and sister and I would all play the games that I imagine all corn eaters play of who has most left, and as the eldest I would bossily dictate how many rows to eat at once, or decide to chomp on one row only and then quickly revert to the beginning, just like the returning carriage of an old-style typewriter, I used to think.

Corn has an extraordinary range of uses around the world, aside from the universally loved corn on the cob. In Mexico and Central America corn flour is used to make tortillas, the popular flatbread of that region. The husks of corn cobs are used in Mexican cooking to make tamales, which are packages of food usually first wrapped in tortillas and then in corn husks before being steamed or grilled, much as one uses banana leaves in South-East Asia. Polenta, as most cornmeal is known here, is a northern-Italian speciality that is currently very popular on restaurant menus. A porridge of water, salt and cornmeal, it is eaten as is or else is allowed to cool before being cut into shapes and fried or grilled until crisp.

Anyone intrigued by corn should read the relevant chapter in Margaret Visser's extraordinary book *Much Depends on Dinner*. She writes that one cannot buy anything in a North American supermarket (except fresh fish) that has been untouched by corn, either as animal feed, food colouring, carton coatings, corn oil (used in soap, insecticides, commercial mayonnaise and salad dressings), corn syrup (used in processed meats, sweets, sauces and ice-cream) or cornstarch (found in all baby foods, jams, pickles, commercial vinegars, headache tablets, toothpaste and detergents).

VARIETIES AND SEASON

The main types of corn grown around the world are dent corn, flint corn, flour corn, popcorn and sweetcorn. Each is grown for a particular purpose – don't think that corn is just corn! Only sweetcorn is grown to be eaten fresh. All other corns are able to be dried and reconstituted years later.

DENT This is the most widely grown corn in the world. The kernels are sweet and starchy with softer skins (hulls). They are ground to make cornmeal, which is sold as *maize meal* and *maize flour* to avoid confusion with wheaten cornflour. It is possible to buy stone-ground maize flour and meal made from soft dent corn (if used to make polenta, a more pasty, less textured product results).

FLINT | The kernels of this corn have very hard hulls. Most of the *polenta* available in Australia is made from yellow flint corn and we can choose between medium or fine grind. In Italy one can also choose between white and yellow polenta. It is possible to buy imported Italian polenta, the very best of which is from stone-ground, naturally dried corn kernels.

FLOUR | This corn is grown almost exclusively in South and Central America, where it is ground by hand. The flour is treated with lime and kneaded into a dough known as *masa*, which is then dried and ground and sold as *masa harina* to be fried or baked as tortillas.

POPCORN | This variety of corn is grown specifically to be sold as *popcorn* and the kernels have very hard outer skins. When heated, the starch inside each kernel fills with steam until the kernel bursts. American Indians have been popping corn for thousands of years!

SWEETCORN | This is the corn with which we are all familiar and which we eat as *corn on the cob*. It has been bred to be cooked and eaten immediately rather than dried and ground into meal or flour. It is not sold by variety, but new varieties have been bred that are sweeter and retain their sweetness longer after picking. (Home gardeners should look out for honeysweet, miracle and lochief cultivars.) There are white as well as yellow varieties of sweetcorn but I have only seen white corn once or twice in Australia. American cookbooks are full of recipes for blue corn, fashionable in establishments specialising in the cookery of the South-West. At the time of writing blue corn is not grown commercially in Australia. One also sometimes sees cobs of multi-coloured corn. These are grown as novelties or animal feed and are not suitable to eat. Fresh *'baby'* corn is growing in popularity as a convenient vegetable for stir-frying. It is not the immature fruit of a conventional plant but a special variety (snowpop is the name of one cultivar). Fresh sweetcorn is available all year, the peak season being September–March.

SELECTION AND STORAGE

CORNFLOUR | The term cornflour, as mentioned earlier, has long been the cause of confusion, since the product most of us know is actually made from wheat. Now that 100 per cent corn cornflour is available in Australia, the term 'wheaten cornflour' has been adopted by the manufacturers of the wheat-based product to mini-mise that confusion. Known as cornstarch in the United States, true corn-flour produces a smoother, more transparent thickened liquid than can be made using wheaten cornflour. It has twice the thickening power of wheaten cornflour (true cornflour is almost 100 per cent starch whereas wheaten cornflour is about 70 per cent starch) and is especially recommended for fruit pie fillings, sauces and Chinese stir-fries. Always make a paste with some of the liquid to be thickened (and the sugar, if relevant) and add some of the hot liquid to the paste before tipping the thickening agent back into the pot. Store cornflour in an airtight container.

MAIZE FLOUR AND MEAL

Stone-ground maize flour and meal are readily obtainable in health food stores. Both are ground from softer corn and are distinctly 'floury' when compared with the grittiness of polenta. They are suitable for baking, but as corn has no gluten it can only be added as a flavouring to flour used for breadmaking. Store maize flour and meal as you would ordinary flour.

POLENTA

In Australia we have a good local medium-grind polenta, and a fine-grind polenta which I suspect is made from imported dent corn. It is also possible to buy instant polenta, which I do not recommend at all. It produces a soft, claggy paste with none of the gritty texture one expects from good polenta. There are also imported products made from buckwheat, or a mixture of grains. The final texture of polenta is affected by the coarseness of the corn grind and also by the amount of water used. Once familiar with the process cooks will vary the amount of water for a denser or less dense polenta. I prefer to use coarse polenta for all dishes and vary the water depending on whether I want to slice and grill or barbecue it or serve soft polenta. Fine polenta is more difficult to handle as it lumps more easily. Polenta keeps well in an airtight container.

SWEETCORN

Just-picked corn may be best, but most of us have to buy our sweetcorn. Never buy corn that has been stripped of its husk and wrapped in plastic. Buy it in its husk with a tassel of pale 'silk' visible. The husk should be grassy-green, not yellowing at all, and with a suggestion of coolness when touched. If the silk – a collection of hair-like fibres – is brittle and dark brown and the leaves of the husk do not feel soft and supple, you are handling old corn.

If you grow your own or if the greengrocer is obliging, peel back the husk a little and inspect the kernels. They should be round and full and very lustrous, not squared off and dull. The rows should be evenly full. If you pierce a kernel with your fingernail, it should ooze milky juice. If the juice is clear, the corn is immature (and the kernels will be small and not fully coloured); if the juice is thick and sticky, the corn is past its prime.

Always store sweetcorn protected by its husk and only strip it as the water boils. Use within 2 days for the finest flavour and accept with regret that, if shop bought, it will still not taste like home-grown corn. (A friend with a bumper crop froze sweetcorn, husk, silk and all, in freezer bags and tells me that it yielded better-quality kernels than those that had been cut from the cob and frozen in small containers.) One can also buy sweetcorn kernels in a can and I have found them quite satisfactory, but they lack the sweetness and creaminess of freshly cut kernels.

PREPARATION AND COOKING

The American chef Bert Greene said in his book *Greene on Greens*, 'You may stroll to the garden to cut the corn but you had darn well better run back to the kitchen to cook it.' Again, a counsel of perfection that only home gardeners will experience. There are several schools of thought of how best to cook sweetcorn. Bert Greene has more advice for dealing with just-picked corn.

> Shaker cooks place ears of husked and desilked corn in a large pot of cold water seasoned with the barest pinch of sugar until the water boils. At that point they cover it and cook it one minute more or as long as it takes to say the Lord's Prayer *fast*. Then they drain it and serve the ears as quickly as possible with butter, salt and pepper on the side.

My advice is more prosaic. Unless it is being barbecued, all sweetcorn should be stripped of its husk and silk before cooking. Leave the stems on for easy eating. When boiling corn, do not salt the water as salt delays the softening of the kernels. Home-grown or freshly picked corn cooks faster than sweetcorn bought from your greengrocer.

TO BOIL **Just-picked corn** Bring a large saucepan of unsalted water to a boil. Slide the cobs in one by one, then cover the pan and simmer for 5–10 minutes, then drain. **Shop-bought corn** Cook the cobs in unsalted boiling water only until tender, maybe as long as 15 minutes. Alternatively, bring a large saucepan of half water and half milk to a boil. Slip in the cobs, simmer for 10–15 minutes until a kernel tests tender, then drain. (The milk is supposed to add a milky taste to the kernels, thereby approximating more closely the flavour of home-grown corn.)

TO BARBECUE Peel back the husk, but do not remove it, and then strip away the silk. Fold the leaves back into position and tie with string (which will burn away in time). Dip the cob briefly in water and roast over hot coals, turning every 5 minutes. It will be ready in 15 minutes or so. Pull back the charred husk and test the kernels are tender. (Foil can be used to wrap sweetcorn ready for the barbecue but the romance will be lost. Barbecued corn will also not be as good without its husk.)

cheesy polenta
Make polenta for 4 serves using 100 g polenta and 2 cups water. When cooked, stir in 125 g thinly sliced fontina or raclette cheese. Turn the polenta into a hot serving dish and dribble over 3 tablespoons noisette butter. Serve at once, topped with shavings of parmesan, alongside a full-flavoured stew.

TO REMOVE KERNELS

Whole Stand the cob on its end on a large flat plate. Using a sharp knife and cutting downwards, cut the kernels as close to the cob as possible. With the back of the knife, scrape down the cob to ensure that there is no milky juice left behind. **Grated** Stand the cob on its end on a large flat plate. Using a sharp knife and working down the cob, slice halfway through the kernels. With the back of the knife, rake down the cob, 'grating' the remnants of the kernels as you go, until you have extracted as much of the corn and milky juice as possible. The grated corn will resemble scrambled eggs.

TO DRY-ROAST KERNELS

Cut whole kernels from the cob and dry-roast them in a single layer in a heavy-based frying pan, stirring until the kernels are coloured a deep golden brown. Roasted kernels add a deep smoky taste to dishes that may otherwise seem too sweet and bland.

TO MAKE TRADITIONAL POLENTA

To make polenta the traditional way you will need a very large, heavy saucepan – and patience. Not only patience to stir the mixture, but patience to clean the saucepan. Polenta leaves a fine layer of cooked-on paste on the bottom of the pan, which even after long soaking in hot water is still difficult to remove. (A non-stick pan might be a good idea but these are usually lightweight or not deep enough.) You will need a whisk for the initial stirring in of the grain and a long-handled wooden spoon for the cooking, as polenta spits. Stock can be used instead of all or some of the water, and in some recipes butter, cheese, mushrooms or other ingredients are stirred in at the end of cooking.

To make polenta for 8–10 serves, bring 2 litres water to a boil in a large saucepan. Add 350 g polenta (or 500 g for a stiffer paste) in a constant stream with one hand, whisking vigorously with the other until the mixture starts to boil. Stir the polenta with a wooden spoon more or less constantly until the mixture forms a solid mass and breaks cleanly away from the sides of the pan. This will take about 20 minutes. Add salt. Either tip the polenta onto a flat serving dish (traditionally a wooden board) and serve at once with or without a sauce, or turn it into a wet or oiled, shallow baking dish, then smooth the surface and allow it to cool and set. **To bake or chargrill** When the polenta is cold and has set, cut it into wedges, rectangles or rounds with a wet knife and dip these in olive oil. Place on an oiled baking tray and bake at 200°C until a golden crust forms. If grilling or barbecuing, put the oiled pieces of polenta onto the lightly oiled, preheated surface and leave them alone. Polenta releases itself from the cooking surface once it has formed an adequate crust and can then be readily turned. Poking at it or trying to turn it too soon will always mean that the forming crust is left on the grill.

popcorn

SERVES 4

recipes

You must use a heavy-based frying pan with a well-fitting lid when making popcorn.

1 tablespoon vegetable oil
½ cup popping corn kernels
½ teaspoon salt
3 tablespoons olive oil *or* 60 g butter, melted
tiny pinch of cayenne pepper *or* 1 teaspoon ground roasted cumin seeds

Heat oil until hot in frying pan. Add kernels in a single layer, then cover pan. When you hear kernels start to pop, turn down heat and shake pan gently. When popping noise stops, take pan from heat and tip popped corn into a serving dish. Mix with salt, oil and seasoning.

steamed baby corn

Steam fresh baby corn for 5 minutes and toss with unsalted butter and chopped tarragon, parsley and chives. Serve on its own for a luxurious first course or as a side dish.

sweetcorn brunch fritters

MAKES 20

3 corn cobs
1½ cups coarse polenta
¼ cup plain flour
1 teaspoon bicarbonate of soda
½ teaspoon salt
2 cups buttermilk
40 g unsalted butter, melted
1 egg, separated
vegetable oil

Grate kernels from cobs to achieve 1¼ cups. Combine polenta, flour, bicarbonate of soda and salt. Make a well and add buttermilk, butter and egg yolk. Stir briefly to combine and add grated corn. Beat egg white until stiff and fold into batter.

Lightly oil a heavy-based frying pan. Fry spoonfuls of batter, well spaced, until bubbles form on surface of fritters, which should be about 10 cm in diameter. Turn and cook other side. Transfer fritters to a

bbq corn

Barbecue corn and enjoy with garlic butter, olive oil or just plain butter. Dust corn with paprika after cooking for a warm, spicy flavour.

warm oven until all are cooked. Serve as they are or as a stack layered with a little unsalted butter. Offer maple syrup and crisp bacon for a wonderful brunch.

polenta pancakes

MAKES 20

These are easier to make than yeast blini and are delicious with such delicacies as herrings, smoked salmon, smoked eel or smoked salmon roe. They are also great with honey or maple syrup or, for a complete change of character, Melita's Skordalia (see GARLIC) or Tzatziki (see YOGHURT). Do not mix the batter until you are ready to cook as the polenta will absorb all the liquid, making it necessary to add more and more milk.

corn and onion
Cut kernels from boiled corn. Sauté a chopped onion in a little butter, then stir in the kernels, a big spoonful of sour cream and a generous amount of parsley and chives and bubble over fierce heat for 1 minute. Serve on a muffin or substantial slice of toast or alongside grilled meat or poultry.

½ cup polenta
pinch of salt
175 ml boiling water
1 egg
½ cup milk
30 g plain flour
30 g butter, melted
extra butter or oil

Combine polenta with salt in a bowl and pour boiling water over. Fork through and leave for 10 minutes. Add egg, beating very well, then gradually stir in milk. Add flour and butter and beat until quite smooth. The mixture should have the consistency of thin cream – adjust with milk if necessary.

Brush a non-stick frying pan with melted butter or oil and cook pancakes, using 1 tablespoon batter for each (they should be about 8 cm in diameter). Turn and brown other side when bubbles appear on surface of pancakes. Keep warm in a low oven until all pancakes are ready. Stack and serve with a bowl of your preferred garnish, or top with smoked fish.

sweetcorn soup with spiced butter

SERVES 4

This recipe is a reminder of the simple principles discussed in detail in the recipe for Leek and Potato Soup (see LEEKS). The quality of the finished product reflects the quality of the vegetables and the character of the liquid chosen.

grilled polenta
Grill wedges of polenta until crusty, then top with blue cheese and grill again to melt the cheese. Serve with sausages, mushrooms or roasted quail.

40 g butter
1 clove garlic, chopped
1 large onion, chopped
1 litre water
kernels from 4 corn cobs
salt

SPICED BUTTER
¼ teaspoon toasted cumin
  seeds
2 tablespoons finely chopped
  fresh parsley
½ teaspoon freshly ground
  black pepper
40 g softened unsalted butter

Melt butter in a stockpot or saucepan and sweat garlic and onion for 5 minutes. Add water and bring to a boil. Simmer for 10 minutes, then add corn kernels. Simmer a further 10 minutes. Taste a kernel for tenderness. Purée soup in a food processor and pass each batch through a coarse strainer resting over a large bowl. Return soup to pan and taste for salt.

To prepare the spiced butter, grind cumin seeds to a powder in a mortar and pestle. Mix parsley with cumin and ground pepper, then blend well with butter. Serve the soup with some spiced butter in each bowl.

no mess polenta (after tony's birthday dinner)

SERVES 8–10

Just after writing about making polenta the traditional way I dined with fellow polenta lovers. They shared with me their discovery of how to make trouble-free but good polenta with no difficult saucepans to wash. They read about the technique in Lynne Rossetto Kasper's The Splendid Table *(she in turn credits Carlo Middione, who wrote of the method in* The Food of Southern Italy*). I tried it, was thrilled with the method and pass it on to those who have not read either of the above works. It may not please the purists, but what a breakthrough!*

2 litres boiling water
2 teaspoons salt
2 cups polenta

Select a basin that will hold 3 litres and fits well over a large stockpot. Fill stockpot two-thirds with water and bring to a boil. Pour the 2 litres boiling water into the basin and add salt. Add polenta and whisk thoroughly for 4–5 minutes until grain thickens evenly. Tuck a large sheet of foil over basin and seal edges well. Fit basin over boiling water in stockpot and adjust heat, so that it maintains a steady boil. Set timer for 1½ hours. Every 20 minutes lift basin off pot (be careful of steam), remove foil and give polenta a good stir, lifting and scooping right to the bottom. Reseal and continue cooking. At the end of the cooking time the polenta can be served soft with a saucy stew or tipped into a wet tray and allowed to set.

rosemary and polenta pan bread

SERVES 6–8

This bread can accompany antipasto, roasted vegetables or a composed salad or, made without rosemary, can be spread with butter and a flowery honey for afternoon tea.

1 cup coarse polenta
½ teaspoon salt
½ teaspoon bicarbonate of soda
1 egg
1 cup buttermilk
1 teaspoon very finely
   chopped fresh rosemary
2 teaspoons extra-virgin
   olive oil
½ cup cream

Preheat oven to 220°C. In a bowl, combine polenta, salt and bicarbonate of soda. In a smaller bowl, whisk egg, buttermilk and rosemary together. Pour buttermilk mixture into polenta and stir only until combined. Heat a 20 cm cast-iron frying pan in oven for 5 minutes. Swirl oil into pan and spoon in batter, spreading it evenly. Pour cream evenly over top and return pan to oven. Bake until a knife inserted in centre comes out dry and clean, about 15 minutes. Cool

polenta chips
Slice cooked, set polenta thinly and deep-fry at 160°C. Serve these chips alongside a rich rabbit, chicken or veal stew.

corn on the cob
Serve a platter of fresh corn on the cob with plenty of butter and salt and pepper. Offer toothpicks!

prawns and corn
Mix chopped prawns, roasted sweetcorn kernels and chilli with an egg. Wrap in lightly oiled corn husks and barbecue quickly while the main event is still cooking.

in pan for 5 minutes before turning out onto a wire rack. Serve at room temperature for a sustaining lunch.

variations Substitute half yoghurt and half milk for buttermilk. Chopped, grilled sweet peppers can be added to the batter, too.

stir-fried corn
Add roasted corn kernels to any vegetable stir-fry.

cantonese-style sweetcorn and crab meat soup

SERVES 4

This delicious soup is adapted from a recipe in Irene Kuo's The Key to Chinese Cooking.

5 corn cobs
vegetable oil
2 tablespoons finely chopped
    spring onions
1 teaspoon very finely
    chopped ginger
250 g picked crab meat
salt
1 tablespoon mirin, rice wine
    or dry sherry
600 ml Chicken Stock
2 tablespoons light soy sauce
1 tablespoon cornflour
2 tablespoons water
2 teaspoons sesame oil
1 egg
1 tablespoon black or red rice
    vinegar

Grate corn to achieve 2 cups. Heat 2 tablespoons vegetable oil in a heavy-based saucepan or wok. Sear spring onion and ginger for 30 seconds. Add crab meat, then sprinkle with salt and mirin and stir lightly. Pour in stock, corn and soy sauce, stirring until soup comes to a boil. Reduce heat and simmer for 2–3 minutes. Mix cornflour, water and sesame oil and stir until quite smooth, then add a little hot soup and stir to blend. Tip mixture back into soup, swirling it in evenly. Turn off heat and trail egg whisked with a pinch of salt and 1 teaspoon vegetable oil over surface, stirring slowly to break up strands. Add vinegar and taste for salt. Adjust with soy sauce. Serve immediately.

other recipes

maggie beer's barbecued kangaroo with anchovy vinaigrette and soft polenta *see* KANGAROO

sweet potato cornbread or corn pone *see* SWEET POTATOES

c r a b s   I adore crab and will often sally forth with the precise aim of eating it. Usually I head for Victoria Street or Little Bourke Street in Melbourne, where the Vietnamese, Chinese and Malaysian cooks handle these handsome crustaceans with the skill and understanding that comes from long cultural familiarity. | Asian restaurants specialise in a wide range of dishes featuring sectioned crabs seared at high heat in woks. My favourites include Cantonese mud crab with ginger, or crab in black bean sauce. Malaysian and Vietnamese cooks also specialise in delicious crab rolls, *poh pia* and *goi cuon* respectively, for which thin omelettes or rice-flour wrappers are rolled around crab meat, pork, fresh mint, shredded lettuce and all manner of subtle and interesting ingredients. Crab also features in many Thai soups and salads. | Crabs are designed in such a way that to separate and extract the body meat from each nook and cranny has to be regarded as a labour of love. This is why a picked salad of absolutely fresh crab meat has to be one of the greatest treats for all crustacean lovers. One should do as little as possible to such a luxury.

crabs
go
with
lemon juice
olive oil
salt
pepper
parsley
chervil
tarragon
chillies
light soy sauce
fish sauce
onions
spring onions
garlic
ginger
breadcrumbs
coconut
grapefruit
mango
limes
mint
coriander leaves
avocados
Tabasco
eggs
mayonnaise
butter

VARIETIES AND SEASON

Australia is lucky to have a wide variety of crabs. The crabs most likely to be seen in our markets are the blue swimmer, mud, king and sand crabs.

TO IDENTIFY | **Blue swimmer** *Portunus pelagicus* is the most common edible crab in the world and is found in all Australian and Asian waters. The legs, paddles and claws are tinted a vibrant cobalt to light blue but all turn red when cooked. The average blue swimmer weighs 300–700 g. Known as the blue manna crab in Western Australia, the blue swimmer is not the same crab as the American blue crab (*Callinectes sapidus*). **King** *Pseudocarcinus gigas* is the largest crab in Australia and perhaps the largest crab in the world. It is also known as the Bass Strait, giant, Tasmanian king or deep-sea crab and is plentiful in southern waters. Its unusual shell is scarlet mottled with cream before cooking, after which it turns red. While an average crab weighs about 5 kg, large specimens can weigh up to 15 kg. The meat in the pincer claws is sometimes served as a steak in Tasmanian restaurants. **Mud** Also known as the mangrove crab, *Scylla serrata* is regarded as the best culinary crab in Australia. It is widely distributed in the tropics but particularly off Queensland. The mud crab is a dull bronze–green that changes to fiery red when cooked. The average weight of a mud crab is 1.5 kg. **Sand** Known also as the red spot or ghost crab, *Ovalipes australiensis* is a small pale crab with a relatively soft shell that has 2 large dark spots. It is prolific in South Australia's Spencer and St Vincent's gulfs but does not travel well. Those that make it to Victorian fish markets are sold dead but uncooked. I use uncooked sand crabs for fish soups and stocks but only when they smell absolutely fresh. **Spanner** *Ranina ranina* is found along the eastern and western coasts of Australia and is most plentiful July–October. Known as a frog crab in Western Australia, the fiery red spanner crab has a large, shield-shaped carapace and large claws that appear out of proportion with its insignificant legs. An average spanner crab weighs 500 g.

Experiments are continuing with blue swimmer crab aquaculture, but at the time of writing there were no commercial crab farms in Australia. Availability depends on various seasonal factors. There are closed seasons for crabs in midsummer, and as crabs are commonly caught by rock lobster fishermen, who have to observe a closed season for rock lobsters, supply can be affected at other times of the year too.

It is notable that since an Asian export market has been established for king and mud crabs, the price of each has escalated on the home market. This is what has also happened, sadly, to our rock lobster industry.

SELECTION AND STORAGE

Like all crustaceans, crabs are very perishable as they contain amino acids that encourage bacterial growth. If you are on the coast and there are crabs to be caught, seek local knowledge whether the habitat is known to be polluted or not. The best protection is to buy a *live* crab from a reputable fishmonger or fish market, cook it yourself and eat it without delay.

Crustaceans such as rock lobsters, bugs and crabs have a hard, jointed external skeleton or shell that they shed periodically and replace as they grow. In some places crabs are in demand just after moulting, when they are sold as *soft-shelled* crabs. They are so tender that every part other than the gills can be eaten. Such crabs are a delicacy in Louisiana in the United States. Occasionally these crabs are caught in South Australia by those who fish for their own crabs, but they are never sold commercially.

Crabs are sold live or cooked. Select a crab that feels heavy, as it means it will have grown into its latest shell. It should not feel light or have liquid sloshing around inside the body. *Live* crabs will have their pincer claws firmly tied to prevent any crab attack! *Cooked* crab should smell pleasant and there should be no cracks or holes in the shell. Some cooked crabs will have been *frozen*. Allow a frozen cooked crab to thaw in the refrigerator, then extract the meat and eat it as soon as possible.

Picked crab meat is available fresh and frozen. 'Picked' simply means that all the meat from a cooked crab has been extracted from every crevice, and all fragments of cartilage have been removed. Freshly picked crab meat (from blue swimmer, spanner or mud crabs) is becoming more readily available. It is highly perishable and it should be stored in its bag unopened on ice and used within 36 hours. Frozen, picked crab meat can be quite satisfactory, especially for crab cakes, sauces or adding to soups or omelettes. It should be thawed in the refrigerator and used very quickly. In my experience frozen, green (uncooked) crab meat is not successful. Picking crab meat is a slow, therefore costly, process.

PREPARATION AND COOKING

If you have ordered a crab from your fishmonger, make sure he or she knows whether you want a live or cooked crab. A cooked crab should never be cooked again. A live crab is required for any dish where the crab is to be sautéd. There are several ways to dispatch a live crab, a practice that causes many cooks some angst.

TO KILL | A live crab will be brought home from the market or fishmonger's with its claws tied. If needed for *sautéing*, best of all is to ask the fishmonger to cut the crab into quarters for you and hurry home, then refrigerate it and cook it that day. If needed *whole* or for *picked crab meat*, either refrigerate the crab for a couple of hours to put it to sleep, drown it first in cold water in the laundry tub or freeze it for a few hours before cooking or chopping it (these methods are also suitable for a crab to be sautéd). The king crab is almost always too large for a domestic pot and is thus best cooked by the fishmonger.

TO BOIL

A crab is boiled when the meat is to be eaten as is (picked crab meat, for example). Bring salted water to a boil in a large stockpot (allow 150 g rock salt per 1 litre water). Plunge the sleepy, drowned or frozen crab into the boiling water and cook for 8 minutes per 500 g. Allow the crab to cool in its cooking water for 10 minutes, then drain. Cool it rapidly under cold running water before refrigerating it.

PICKED CRAB MEAT

A boiled crab is required when preparing picked crab meat. Prepare the work area by putting a large tea towel under your chopping board to catch all the liquid. Have ready 2 bowls – one for shell and cartilage, one for meat – and a meat mallet, pair of scissors, metal skewer and heavy knife.

Twist off the legs as close to the body as possible. Prise off the top shell. (The top shell or carapace can be washed and dried and looks decorative with the crab meat returned to it.) Discard the feathery grey gills. Discard the bony section at the head. Rinse away the yellow or brown 'mustard' unless you want to save a little to flavour a mayonnaise or sauce. (It is delicious but very strong. A tablespoon will be plenty for flavouring.) Cut the body of the crab into quarters.

Crack the large claws with a hard mallet. Extract the meat, pulling it away from the tough membrane if you are handling a king crab. Cut along the small legs with scissors, then break them in half and extract the meat. Using the skewer and your heavy knife to expose the body meat, carefully slip the body meat from each piece of the body, being careful not to include fragments of cartilage. When all the meat has been recovered, discard all shell and cartilage fragments or reserve them to make stock or to enrich fish stock. Cover the crab meat with plastic and refrigerate until required. Wash the work area and chopping board very well and soak the tea towel before laundering it.

TO SAUTÉ

Drop the chopped, sleepy, drowned or frozen crab into boiling water for 5 minutes. Drain it well and cool rapidly under cold running water. With a sharp, heavy cleaver, chop into pieces, if whole. Remove the head sac and feathery gills.

Use a wok or a large frying pan that has a lid and have all the ingredients ready (refer to your favourite Asian cookbook for specific recipes). The following is a suggestion for how you might proceed.

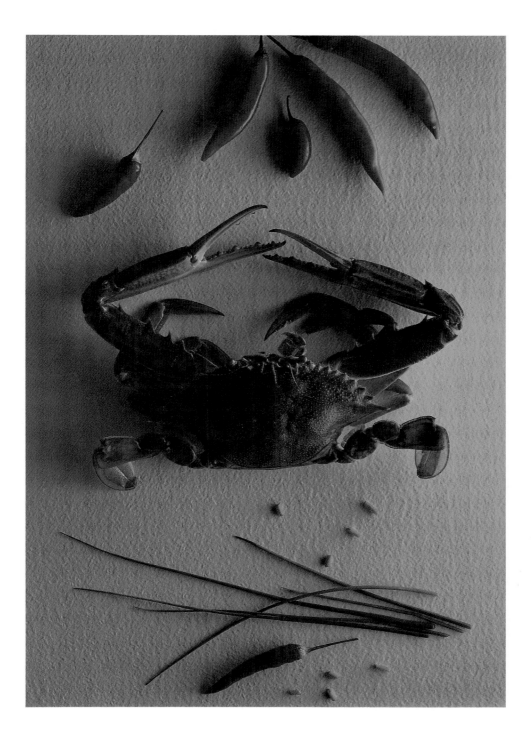

Sear slices of ginger and garlic in hot oil. Add pieces of crab and any other solid ingredients, such as sliced chillies, fermented black beans and pieces of spring onion. Toss to mix over high heat until the crab shell turns red. Add stock (or stock and soy, or water, tomato sauce or coconut milk), then cover the wok and reduce the heat. Simmer for 10 minutes, then taste for seasoning. Stir in any 'finishings' – chopped herbs, lightly whisked egg, coconut cream – and serve.

fried blue swimmer crab shells

SERVES 4

30 g cellophane noodles

500 g picked crab meat

1 fresh chilli, seeded and finely chopped

2 spring onions, very finely chopped

2 tablespoons coconut cream

2 teaspoons fish sauce

1 tablespoon finely chopped fresh coriander leaves and stems

4 blue swimmer crab shells, cleaned

2 egg whites, stiffly beaten

vegetable oil for deep-frying

Pour boiling water over noodles and allow to stand for 3–4 minutes. Drain well and cut noodles with scissors into 2 cm pieces. Mix noodles in a bowl with all the other ingredients except crab shells, egg white and oil. Pack mixture into crab shells. Spoon egg white over each shell. Fry filled crab shells in plenty of hot oil until egg white is golden brown. Serve hot and offer lime or lemon wedges and a small saucer of chilli sauce.

crab with mayonnaise

Mix creamy crab 'mustard' with Mayonnaise and extend it with softly whipped cream, a teaspoon of tomato purée and a few drops of Tabasco. Pile picked crab meat on top of finely shredded iceberg lettuce and surround it with a ring of the sauce.

vietnamese mang cua soup

SERVES 4

This soup is based on an idea in Alan Davidson's lovely book Seafood.

1 litre light Chicken Stock

6 spears asparagus, cut diagonally into thin slices

1 cup picked crab meat

3 tablespoons tapioca flour

2 eggs, beaten

fish sauce

finely chopped fresh chilli

1 tablespoon freshly chopped coriander leaves

1 tablespoon finely chopped spring onions

Bring stock to a boil, throw in asparagus and simmer 4 minutes. Add crab meat. Mix tapioca flour to a paste with some stock. Add a little more stock, then stir mixture back into pan. Lower heat and slowly pour in eggs, mixing gently with a fork. Season to taste with fish sauce and chilli. Divide soup between bowls and scatter with fresh greens.

crabby soup

SERVES 4–6

Small sand crabs add richness and flavour to fish soups. There ought to be no big deal about what goes into fish soup – the catch of the day and the state of the vegetable garden will determine that – although there is no question that some fish have a more robust character than others. Flathead, gurnard, red mullet and snapper are ideal.

crab salad
Extend a small amount of picked crab meat with choice salad leaves and chunks of ripe avocado and season with a few drops of olive oil and a generous squeeze of lemon or lime juice.

chilli crab
Substitute crab for rock lobster in Violet Oon's Chilli Lobster (see ROCK LOBSTERS*).*

asian crab
Season picked crab meat with a few drops of fish sauce, very finely chopped fresh chilli and some coriander leaves and garnish with finely sliced crisp-fried onion and garlic.

2–3 small flathead *or* similar rock fish
4–6 small crabs, cleaned and quartered (but uncooked)
handful of wild fennel tops, chopped
3 tablespoons olive oil
4 large ripe tomatoes *or* 1 × 410 g can peeled tomatoes
2 onions, diced
4 cloves garlic, sliced
2 carrots, peeled and sliced
parsley stalks
1 bay leaf
large sprig of thyme
1 small fresh chilli *or* 1 teaspoon sambal oelek
pinch of saffron *or* ½ teaspoon ground turmeric
1 tablespoon tomato paste
1 cup dry white wine
salt
freshly ground black pepper

GARNISH
4–6 slices day-old bread
1 clove garlic, halved
2 tablespoons freshly chopped parsley

Chop fish into chunks, retaining heads. Place fish, crab and fennel in a bowl with 1 tablespoon of the olive oil and marinate for 1 hour. If using fresh tomatoes, halve them and grill until skin is blistered and cut surface is black, then chop. If using canned tomatoes, chop them, reserving all juice.

Heat remaining oil in a stockpot and sauté onion, garlic, carrot and parsley stalks until onion is well coloured. Remove vegetables and set aside. Tip crab into pot and cook over high heat, stirring, until shells are red. Return sautéd vegetables to pot with fish and fennel and all other ingredients. Cover with water by 12–14 cm. Bring slowly to simmering point and cook, uncovered, for 30 minutes.

Press contents of pot through largest disc of a food mill into a clean saucepan. (If you do not have a food mill, strain liquid and set aside, then purée vegetables, fish and crab solids in a food processor using a little reserved stock to assist.) Simmer strained liquid (and debris from food processor) for 10 minutes. Strain a second time, pressing well on debris. Check seasoning.

Grill bread and rub with garlic. Put a slice into each bowl and ladle over soup. Scatter with parsley and serve immediately.
variations Steamed mussels or clams or both can be slipped into the soup just before serving, as can pieces of fish separately simmered in a little of the soup. Add boiled potatoes as well to make a main meal.

crab cakes

MAKES 4

These crab cakes, based on a recipe from Paul Bertolli and Alice Waters's Chez Panisse Cooking, *are a very simple and popular way of using crab. If you don't have quite enough crab, make up the weight with some delicately flavoured fresh fish.*

250 g picked crab meat

I tablespoon sour cream

I egg

I tablespoon very finely
chopped spring onions

I tablespoon freshly chopped
coriander leaves

I teaspoon lemon *or* lime
juice *or* a few drops of fish
sauce

salt

Tabasco

⅓ cup fresh breadcrumbs

½ cup clarified butter

Mix all ingredients other than breadcrumbs and clarified butter and taste for seasoning. Form mixture into 4 cakes. Spread breadcrumbs on a plate and coat each cake generously. Refrigerate until needed.

Melt clarified butter in a frying pan. Fry cakes about 3 minutes a side and transfer to a heated platter lined with kitchen paper. Offer a mayonnaise flavoured with chopped herbs, or a tomato or red pepper sauce, and serve with lemon wedges.

crab and fruit
Combine picked crab meat on a flat platter with sliced mango or pink grapefruit segments.

other recipes

cantaloupe sauce for rock lobster or crab *see* MELONS

cantonese-style sweetcorn and crab meat soup *see* CORN

pea shoots with crab meat *see* PEAS

cucumbers A member of the gourd or melon genus, cucumbers (*Cucumis sativus*) have mild-flavoured flesh and an exceptionally high water content, making them one of the most refreshing summer vegetables. | Once on a stony Greek beach a small girl came to stare at me. We did not share any language. She had shiny black hair, pink cheeks and was a picture of health and happiness. She was rapturously crunching on a cucumber. At the time I mused on the cultural differences that made one child ecstatic about a cucumber, whereas in our own community the treat probably would have been a frozen confection on a stick. | Everyone remembers Lady Bracknell from Oscar Wilde's play *The Importance of Being Earnest* and her liking for cucumber sandwiches. Apart from cucumber sandwiches, cucumbers are used by most of us as a salad ingredient. But they are more versatile than this. They make delicious cold soups, combine brilliantly with yoghurt to accompany curries or Middle Eastern dishes, are elegant sautéd in butter, and they make excellent sweet or crunchy pickles. Despite the abundant evidence of their international culinary appeal, cucumbers still have a faint echo of upper-class English hothouses to me. But then, I do love cucumber sandwiches!

VARIETIES AND SEASON

The main types of cucumber available to Australians are the apple, burpless, gherkin, green ridge and Lebanese. Cucumbers are available all year, with the peak season being November–March.

Apple This rounded cucumber has cream to white to light-green skin that is tough and must be peeled. The flesh is very juicy and has larger seeds than other varieties. **Burpless** Also known as the telegraph or continental cucumber, this cucumber is usually picked when it is 15–20 cm long. It is slender, dark green and has fewer and smaller seeds than a green ridge cucumber. **Gherkin** This is a group of short, slim, rough-skinned cucumbers grown just for pickling. (It is also possible for home gardeners to pick immature fruit from the long green varieties when they are 5–10 cm long to use for pickling.) **Green ridge** This cucumber is probably the most well-known variety, although it has been superseded in popularity by the long green burpless variety. It is smooth-skinned and dark green and usually picked when about 20 cm long. **Lebanese** This cucumber has dark-green, tender skin and is picked and eaten when around 10 cm in length. It is very sweet, the flesh is pale green and drips with juice and the seeds are tiny.

SELECTION AND STORAGE

Cucumbers must be crisp. Feel a cucumber before buying it to ensure it is tight and bursting with health. It should not have any dark or, worse still, soft patches. The green varieties should be green and glowing. Never buy a green cucumber that looks at all yellow.

Cucumbers do not like excessive cold. In mild weather there is no need to refrigerate them. As they are such a popular summer vegetable, and our summers are rarely mild, those cucumbers with the most tender skins are usually bought wrapped in plastic film to better help them withstand the cold of the crisper. They will keep well for at least 5 days.

PREPARATION

Always taste a slice of cucumber before you cut up the whole thing as every now and then you come across one that is horribly bitter. Tough cucumber skin is not very pleasant either, so taste a piece and decide whether it needs to be discarded. I do not peel either Lebanese or the long burpless varieties, although I do peel apple and green ridge cucumbers. Similarly, some cooks prefer to seed cucumbers. I do this only if the seeds are big and hard (as in an apple cucumber) or if I don't want the seeds to float around in a sauce. Sliced cucumber left to stand will lose a lot of water, so it makes sense to discard this liquid if you plan to combine the cucumber with yoghurt or sour cream.

cucumbers go with

sour cream
cream
yoghurt
chives
parsley
paprika
cumin
garlic
coriander
borage
mint
dill
peas
butter
lemons
olive oil
cider vinegar
salmon
trout
chicken
soft white cheese
spring onions
strawberries
crab
fish
pears
tomatoes
fetta cheese
olives
ginger

Some cooks also salt their cucumbers to remove any bitterness and allow them to stand and drain for 30 minutes before rinsing, drying and dressing them. The cucumber loses its crispness but it does develop an appealing slippery character prepared in this manner. I prepare salads both ways – salted and unsalted. The Japanese soak sliced cucumber in lightly salted, very cold water, which increases the crispness.

recipes

cucumber and olives

Drizzle cucumber chunks with extra-virgin olive oil and offer with olives as an appetiser while the barbecue is heating up.

cucumber garnish

Dice fresh pear and cucumber, stir in chopped tarragon, parsley or chives and dress with olive oil and cider vinegar for a pretty garnish to serve with smoked salmon, trout or eel.

pickled cornichons

These crunchy small cucumbers – the smaller the better – are an indispensable accompaniment to rustic Pork Rillettes (see PORK*), pâtés and terrines. Nora Carey includes this recipe in her book* Perfect Preserves.

1.5 kg small pickling
    cucumbers, washed
1 cup butcher's salt
1.5 litres white-wine vinegar
2 cups water
6 bay leaves
1 tablespoon whole allspice
1 tablespoon black peppercorns
1 tablespoon white peppercorns

Dry cucumbers and mix with salt in a large bowl. Allow to stand overnight, then drain.

Combine 2 cups of the vinegar with water in a large bowl and tip in cucumbers. Drain again at once and arrange in sterilised jars, dividing bay leaves and spices between them. Cover cucumbers with remaining vinegar and seal. Store in a cool place for at least 6 weeks before eating. Refrigerate after opening.

cucumber as a cooked vegetable   SERVES 2

Cucumber is very pleasant as a cooked vegetable, especially with fish or chicken.

1 long cucumber, peeled and
    cut into chunks
walnut-sized piece of butter
juice of ½ lemon
1 tablespoon freshly chopped
    chives, dill or parsley

Steam cucumber until tender (about 5 minutes), then drain. In a small non-stick frying pan, melt butter and toss with cucumber over heat until butter is golden brown. Quickly stop butter cooking by adding lemon juice and chives and tip over grilled fish or chicken breast.

beurre blanc Toss steamed cucumber with Beurre Blanc flavoured with tarragon or dill. Drop in boiled peas, if you like. **cream** Bring 3 tablespoons thick cream to a boil and drop in well-drained, steamed cucumber chunks and toss over moderate heat. Add a few drops of lemon juice and a herb of your choice when the cream has all but reduced to a glaze. Grind on some pepper.

thai cucumber salad

SERVES 4

Serve this salad with barbecued prawns or Cold Chinese White-cooked Chicken with Seared Spring Onion Sauce (see CHICKEN AND THE CHRISTMAS TURKEY*).*

4 shallots, very finely sliced
I tablespoon vegetable oil
2 long cucumbers, peeled and
    seeded
I tablespoon brown sugar
2 tablespoons rice vinegar *or*
    white-wine vinegar
I fresh chilli, seeded and finely
    chopped
50 g peanuts, roasted and
    chopped
2 tablespoons freshly chopped
    coriander leaves and stems
fish sauce

Sauté shallots gently and slowly in oil until brown but not burnt. Drain on kitchen paper. Cut cucumber into 1 cm cubes. Dissolve sugar in vinegar. Toss vinegar mixture through cucumber, then add all other ingredients, seasoning to taste with fish sauce.

filled cucumber
Make cucumber cases by cutting a peeled, long cucumber into 4 cm long chunks, then, using the small end of a melon baller, hollow out most of the inside, leaving a base and the sides intact. Turn the little barrels upside down and drain for 1 hour, then fill with crab or crayfish mixed with Mayonnaise, Guacamole (see AVOCADOS*) or Tabbouleh (see* PARSLEY*).*

wilted cucumber salad

This sort of salad can accompany a wide range of dishes from cold poached salmon to curries and beef goulash, or be part of a Middle Eastern buffet or a light first course. Vary the quantities of the basic ingredients as desired, and try using different herbs. It is said that young borage leaves taste like cucumber – I find that the hairy texture turns me off the leaves before I register the flavour. But, then, I do think that the blue flowers, which look wonderful with wilted cucumber, taste like oysters if one closes one's eyes while swallowing (another bit of folklore).

cucumber, sliced
salt
yoghurt, sour cream *or*
    fromage frais
freshly ground black pepper
freshly chopped herbs (optional)
borage flowers (optional)

Scatter cucumber lightly with salt and place in a colander standing on a plate. Leave for 1 hour. Rinse cucumber lightly and pat dry with a clean cloth. Transfer to a bowl, stir in yoghurt and season. Add a generous quantity of fresh herbs and/or borage flowers.

variations Add finely crushed garlic and freshly chopped mint, freshly chopped dill and sultanas, fresh coriander, or ground cumin and paprika.

cucumber and oysters
Serve wedges of Lebanese cucumber and watercress sandwiches with freshly opened oysters (as does my friend Damien Pignolet).

cold cucumber soup

SERVES 4–6

cucumber sandwiches
Cut peeled cucumber into thin slices and fill well-buttered wholemeal sandwiches for afternoon tea.

1 small onion, finely chopped
2 tablespoons olive oil
2 long cucumbers *or*
  6 Lebanese cucumbers
1 cup freshly chopped dill
  leaves
800 ml Chicken Stock
salt
freshly ground black pepper
1 cup sour cream
3 egg yolks
2 tablespoons dry sherry
grated zest of 1 lemon
extra dill leaves

Sauté onion in oil in a saucepan. Peel, seed and grate cucumbers. Add cucumber and dill to onion and simmer for 5 minutes. Add stock and bring to a boil, then reduce heat to low. Season, then simmer for 5 minutes. Blend in a food processor or blender until smooth.

Whisk sour cream with egg yolks and sherry. Stir 1 cup hot soup into egg yolk mixture, then whisk it back into the main quantity. Add lemon zest and adjust seasoning. Refrigerate for several hours. Garnish with extra chopped dill before serving.

accompaniment Top fingers of hot toast with caviar or lumpfish roe or a scraping of Anchovy Butter (*see* ANCHOVIES) for a super-luxurious accompaniment.

other recipes

dill pickles *see* DILL
gazpacho *see* TOMATOES
greek country salad *see* CHEESE
tzatziki *see* YOGHURT

c u m q u a t s Even though it resembles a perfect miniature orange, the cumquat is not a true citrus fruit. True citrus have 8–15 sections, while the cumquat has 3–6 sections. | A native of China, the cumquat (*Fortunella* species) is widely grown in Australia as an ornamental tree. Most people keep their cumquats in tubs on verandahs but grown in the open ground the trees flourish and can provide a most beautiful screen or windbreak, as well as many jars of marmalade. The fruit and blossom are highly perfumed and there is almost always some of either to be seen. The flavour of the cumquat fruit is complex: sweet and bitter and scented all at once. For most palates the fruit is too tart for eating fresh, although the fruit is eaten in its entirety when it is cooked, pickled or preserved. | I have written a great deal about cumquats over the years. Cumquat marmalade is the best of all breakfast preserves, with a scented sharpness and a golden glow all its own. I pickle cumquats with spices and vinegar and also preserve cumquats in brandy. As I discovered a few years ago, 3-year-old brandied cumquats are sublime. The fruit of this batch had almost candied and its dark liquor was very luscious indeed.

cumquats
go
with
butter
sugar
wine vinegar
parsley
duck
pork
calf's liver
kidneys
sausages
raisins
currants
apples
brandy
pudding batters
ice-cream

VARIETIES AND SEASON

The varieties of cumquat we can buy as a tree or as fruit from some greengrocers are *Fortunella japonica* (marumi) and *F. margarita* (nagami). *F. japonica* has round fruit that has sweeter skin and flesh than the oval *F. margarita*. A healthy cumquat tree produces fruit from autumn to spring.

SELECTION AND STORAGE

If you have a cumquat tree, snip the fruit rather than pull them off, as pulling will tear away some of the skin and for some uses the fruit should be intact. Pick the fruit when it is dry, just before you require it. Fruit tipped into a bucket must be carefully examined for bruised, mouldy or squashed cumquats. Inspect shop-bought cumquats thoroughly as they begin to deteriorate as soon as they are picked. For marmalade, select ripe but still firm cumquats. Blowsy, over-ripe or sodden fruit makes poor marmalade. Store cumquats in a single layer in a cool place for no more than 24 hours. Do not wash the fruit more than an hour before processing it.

PREPARATION

Cumquats require little preparation other than a good wash and do not need to be peeled before use.

recipes

pickled cumquats

cumquat chicken
or fish
*Tuck Cumquat
Butter (see p. 259)
into a foil parcel
with a chicken
breast or piece of
fish and bake it in
the oven, then tip
onto a plate heaped
with tender salad
leaves drizzled with
a little olive oil. Be
generous with the
pepper mill.*

These fruit flavour a roast chicken or duck beautifully. Crush one inside the cavity of the bird and, when it is cooked, use a tablespoon of the vinegar to deglaze the baking dish before adding a glass of wine or stock.

1 teaspoon salt
600 ml water
500 g cumquats, washed
150 g castor sugar
½ stick cinnamon
1 teaspoon cloves
600 ml white-wine vinegar

Dissolve salt in water in a saucepan and bring to a boil. Pour over cumquats in a bowl and stand for 12 hours. Drain.

Simmer sugar and spices in vinegar until sugar has dissolved. Simmer a further 5 minutes. Carefully pack cumquats into a hot, sterilised jar, then pour in boiling vinegar syrup and seal. Store in a cool place. Leave for several weeks before using. Both the pickling syrup and the cumquats can be used.

brandied cumquats

MAKES 1 LITRE

Chop these delicious cumquats and add with or without the syrup to steamed puddings or ice-cream or other fruit to give interest to a crumble

*or pie. Served with coffee they make a very sophisticated ending to a meal,
in the tradition of the 'spoon' sweets of Greece and Turkey.*

500 g cumquats, washed
500 g sugar
600 ml brandy
1 vanilla bean

Place cumquats in a large, sterilised
preserving jar. Add sugar and brandy and
cover. Stir contents every few days with a
clean skewer until sugar has dissolved, then
leave to mature for 2 months before using.

cumquat stuffing
*Chop Pickled
Cumquats (see
p. 258) into stuffing
for poultry, game,
lamb or pork.*

my mother's cumquat marmalade   MAKES 3 LITRES

*There are many, many versions of this marmalade. Here is the one used by
my mother. Sometimes I slice the fruit instead of quartering it.*

2 kg cumquats, washed
sugar

Discard any stems and cut cumquats into
quarters, flicking out and reserving pips.
Tie pips in muslin or a clean handkerchief.
Put fruit and pips into a ceramic, glass or stainless steel bowl and barely
cover with cold water (about 1.5 litres). Leave overnight.

Next day, measure fruit and soaking water into cups, noting the number
(my last batch measured 13 cups). Cook fruit in its soaking water with
pips, until tender, then add 1 cup sugar to each previously measured cup.
Boil briskly until marmalade reaches setting point (about 25 minutes).
Allow to cool until a skin starts to form, then stir gently to distribute
fruit. Discard pips and bottle in hot, sterilised jars, sealing while hot.

**pork and
cumquats**
*Scatter Pickled
Cumquats (see
p. 258) into the
baking dish with
a loin of pork.*

cumquat butter   MAKES 1 CUP

250 g softened unsalted butter
1 tablespoon seeded and
   finely chopped Pickled
   Cumquats (see p. 258)
2 teaspoons cumquat pickling
   juices
2 tablespoons very well-
   reduced Chicken Stock
   (optional)
freshly ground black pepper
½ teaspoon very finely
   chopped garlic
1 tablespoon freshly chopped
   parsley

Whizz all ingredients in a food processor
until well combined. Scrape onto a large
doubled sheet of foil and form into a roll by
twisting the ends in opposite directions.
Freeze, and slice as required.

cumquat sauce
*Melt a slice of
Cumquat Butter (see
p. 259) over a
grilled chicken or
duck breast, pork
chop or liver or
sautéd kidneys for a
very fast and good
sauce.*

sussex pond puddings

SERVES 8

I remember with pleasure eating a version of this pudding at Gay Bilson's Berowra Waters Inn several years ago. Traditionally, this pudding is made in a large pudding basin with a whole lemon, pricked all over, in the middle. Suet is available from your butcher.

christmas cumquats

Add Brandied Cumquats (see p. 258) to your Christmas cake or fruit mince mixture for a very Australian touch.

500 g self-raising flour
pinch of salt
250 g suet, grated
125 ml milk
125 ml water
butter
16 cumquats, halved
8 teaspoons Seville orange marmalade
8 heaped teaspoons dark brown sugar
8 walnut-sized knobs unsalted butter

Preheat oven to 160°C. Sift flour with salt and rub in suet lightly with fingertips. Tip in milk and water and combine to form a dough. Knead briefly, then roll out pastry and cut into 8 × 16 cm circles. Cut a quarter from each circle for pudding lids.

Butter 8 × 150 ml pudding moulds. For each mould, fit larger piece of pastry in mould, pressing the 2 cut edges together. Work pastry well into moulds. It should come slightly above the rim.

Flick out seeds from cumquat halves with a small knife. Place 1 teaspoon marmalade, 1 heaped teaspoon brown sugar, 1 knob unsalted butter and 4 cumquat halves in each mould. Shape reserved pieces of pastry into balls and then roll to form lids. Brush pastry rims with water, lay on lids and firmly pinch edges together. Completely enclose each mould in buttered aluminium foil, pleating the top to allow for expansion of crust. Place moulds in a baking dish lined with a tea towel and pour in enough hot water to come two-thirds up sides of moulds. Bake for 1½ hours.

Unmould the puddings and serve with a hot Egg Custard ✓ or a custard made from fruit syrup and egg yolks, such as Eliza Acton's Quince Custard (*see* p. 612).

 **d a t e s** The date palm (*Phoenix dactylifera*) is thought to have originated in Mesopotamia in about 3500 BC. Dates have been an essential food for all Arab peoples for thousands of years and today date palms are still treated with reverence in the Middle East. One date palm takes 5–6 years to produce, but it is then capable of producing up to 70 kg of fruit annually for 80 years. It is easy to understand how important date palms were to nomadic people. In 1993 I was invited to a date-tasting in an oasis in Tunisia. More than 10 varieties of date were spread on tables for the visitors to enjoy. We walked on hand-woven carpets spread one on top of the other to protect us from the hot sand. These sun-warmed dates were magnificent. It is to the Middle East that cooks should look for the widest repertoire of date dishes. Claudia Roden includes some exotic combinations in her classic work *A New Book of Middle Eastern Food*, mouth-watering dishes such as pigeons simmered with ginger, saffron, cinnamon, dates and honey, or turnips sautéd in butter with sliced dates. Anglo-Saxon cooks, brought up on packets of semi-dried dates, are more inclined to make date loaves, scones or slices. >

dates

go

with

cream cheese

thick cream

brown sugar

pistachios

almonds

walnuts

raisins

bacon

lamb

chicken

honey

saffron

cinnamon

bananas

cloves

fresh ginger

grated orange zest

date balls

Work equal quantities of stoned, chopped semi-dried dates and walnut pieces to a paste in a food processor, then roll mixture into small balls and coat with icing sugar for a sweet snack to serve with coffee.

Most of the 'fresh' dates available in Australia have, in fact, been imported frozen from Israel or California. Their high sugar content (55 per cent) makes dates suitable for freezing as it keeps them moist.

Australia's sole date farm – the Meccah Date Farm in Alice Springs – produces only enough dates to supply a steady stream of tourists and a few local clients. Crops are being experimented with elsewhere in the Centre and in Western Australia.

VARIETIES AND SEASON

Dates range in colour from golden brown to black, but rarely would a consumer know the variety of date he or she were eating. At the Meccah Date Farm I have tasted the dark medjool and a creamy-coloured deglet noor.

Fresh dates are available all year round from greengrocers and some supermarkets. Semi-dried dates are often sold pressed into blocks in supermarkets and delicatessens. It can be difficult to separate one date from another.

SELECTION AND STORAGE

Either fresh or semi-dried dates can be used when dates are required, although sometimes one is better than the other.

'Fresh' (frozen) dates have an excellent shelf life. I have dipped into a bowl of these dates over a month without noticing any significant deterioration. There is no need to store fresh dates in the refrigerator. They are meant to be eaten as they are and warmed by the sun, so room temperature is just fine.

Semi-dried dates are best used chopped into pies and puddings or other baked goods. They are not nearly as appealing as fresh dates for snacking on, as the skins are tough and 'crackly'. Store semi-dried dates in an airtight glass container once the packet has been opened. Kept this way, they will last for months.

PREPARATION

Each date has a long, thin seed and a hard bit where the date was joined to the plant that must be removed before cooking. As a rule of thumb, 500 g fresh dates will yield 2¼ cups whole, 2 cups when stoned, 1¾ cups when roughly chopped and 1½ cups when finely chopped. Recipes may specify that semi-dried dates be soaked to soften them before use.

If you are cutting dates into pieces it is easier to do this with scissors dipped in hot water than with a knife, as they are so sticky. Similarly, it is easier to cut up a lot of dates if you have chilled them for a few hours.

When adding dates to a cake or pudding batter, coat them with flour first to prevent them from sinking to the bottom of the tin or basin.

date and walnut biscuits

MAKES 30

250 g dates, stoned
½ cup chopped walnuts
75 g butter
½ cup brown sugar
2 eggs, beaten
3 tablespoons sour cream
175 g plain flour
½ teaspoon baking powder
½ teaspoon ground cinnamon
¼ teaspoon bicarbonate of
   soda

Preheat oven to 180°C and grease baking trays, or line them with baking paper.

Cut dates into pieces using scissors and mix with walnuts. Cream butter and sugar and beat in eggs until light, then beat in sour cream. Mix a third of the flour into the dates and nuts to coat them well. Combine remaining ingredients and stir into egg mixture with dates and nuts.

Drop spoonfuls of batter onto baking trays. Bake about 10 minutes until browned. Cool on a wire rack.

date scones

MAKES 10

This recipe is from Katherine de Pury at Yeringberg vineyard at Coldstream in Victoria's Yarra Valley.

250 g self-raising flour
½ teaspoon freshly grated
   nutmeg
pinch of salt
20 g butter
2 tablespoons sugar
250 g dates, stoned and
   chopped
3 tablespoons milk
3 tablespoons water

Preheat oven to 210°C and grease a baking tray. Sift flour, nutmeg and salt together, then rub in butter. Add sugar and dates. Combine milk and water and mix into flour to form a soft but firm dough. Knead together quickly, then press out on a floured surface and cut into squares. Bake for 7 minutes, then reduce heat to 180°C and cook a further 8 minutes until golden.

savoury stuffed dates
Serve savoury stuffed dates with drinks: try crisped bacon mixed with cream cheese, herbs and pepper, or minced cold lamb or chicken mixed with chutney, herbs and pepper.

indian dates
Make an Indian sweet by frying stoned fresh dates in clarified butter for less than a minute and serving them with thick cream mixed with a generous quantity of chopped pistachios.

date and chocolate cake

SERVES 8–10

This dessert – more torte than cake – is superb and very easy to make.

6 egg whites
200 g castor sugar
200 g dates, stoned and
   chopped
200 g dark chocolate, chopped

Preheat oven to 180°C and grease a 24 cm springform tin well.

Beat egg whites until stiff, then slowly beat in sugar to form a soft meringue. Fold in dates and chocolate. Tip mixture into prepared tin and bake for 1 hour. Turn off oven but leave cake in until oven is cold. Leave cold cake in tin overnight to soften before serving covered with whipped cream or mascarpone.

sticky toffee pudding

SERVES 8

This pudding has everything going for it: it is delicious, easy to make, requires no fancy equipment and everyone loves it.

sweet stuffed dates

Stuff stoned fresh dates with any of the following and serve with coffee: a blanched roasted almond; 2 parts ground almonds to 1 part castor sugar moistened with rosewater or orange-flower water; cream cheese mixed with a liqueur (Cointreau, Grand Marnier or Amaretto di Saronno), liqueur-soaked raisins or chopped glacé ginger; or marzipan combined with soaked fruits, chopped nuts, grated chocolate and liqueur.

170 g dates, stoned and chopped
1 teaspoon bicarbonate of soda
300 ml boiling water
60 g butter
170 g castor sugar
2 eggs
170 g self-raising flour
½ teaspoon pure vanilla

SAUCE
400 g brown sugar
1 cup thick cream
250 g butter
1 vanilla bean, split

Preheat oven to 180°C and butter an 18 cm square cake tin. Mix dates and bicarbonate of soda. Pour over water and leave to stand.

Cream butter and sugar, then add eggs, one at a time, beating well after each. Fold flour in gently, then stir in date mixture and vanilla and pour into prepared tin. Bake in centre of oven for 30–40 minutes until cooked when tested with a skewer.

To make the sauce, bring all ingredients to a boil. Reduce heat and simmer for 5 minutes. Remove vanilla bean. Pour a little sauce over warm pudding and return it to oven for 2–3 minutes so sauce soaks in. Cut pudding into squares and pass extra sauce.

dill   A hardy annual, dill (*Anethum graveolens*) is native to India, China and western Asia and related to parsley and the carrot. The herb is considered to have soothing qualities, as its name *dilla* from the Norse for 'to lull' implies. Dill water has long been used by mothers to attempt to relieve colic in babies. (Speaking for myself I did not find it helped much. My baby spat out the dill water and kept on screaming!) This pretty, feathery herb is often confused with fennel as the leaves are very similar. However, dill leaves are a blueish green, while fennel leaves are yellowish green. Fennel grows to a height of 2 metres; dill is never more than 1 metre in height and is often picked before the plant has developed a flower-head. While wild fennel has a strong aniseed flavour, dill resembles caraway more closely. Both the leaves and the seeds of dill are used in cooking. Dill seeds are almost identical in appearance to aniseed, caraway and fennel seeds, so it is most important that the jars in your pantry are clearly labelled. The leaves are often used in salads and with fish or eggs; dill seeds are an important ingredient when seasoning vinegar, especially for pickling. >

dill
goes
with
potatoes
cucumbers
eggs
green beans
dried beans
zucchini
sour cream
beetroots
herrings
salmon
tomatoes
cabbages
sauerkraut
rice
fresh white cheese

Dill leaves go well with fresh as well as pickled cucumber and with all members of the squash and zucchini family. Fresh dill is a classic flavouring in Scandinavian gravlax (cured marinated salmon), while the seeds are frequently used to flavour sauerkraut. Dill is also very popular in Russian cooking.

The common name of 'dill weed' is a reminder that, if not chopped finely, dill leaves can look very ragged and unwanted when draped over food.

VARIETIES AND SEASON

Dill is an annual and grows easily from seed. In our climate it is available all year round.

SELECTION AND STORAGE

Select fresh-looking dill with green not yellow leaves. Store unwashed fresh dill in a paper-lined plastic bag in the refrigerator for up to a week.

PREPARATION

Wash fresh dill just before use. It is usually chopped quite finely and scattered over food. Sprigs are preferred for layering with pickles. The decorative flower-heads are well flavoured and are used in pickling mixtures.

recipes

dill pickles

Choose the smallest pickling cucumbers from the greengrocer in late summer.

cucumber and dill
Toss blanched cucumber chunks, freshly chopped dill and melted unsalted butter over heat until the cucumber is hot and the butter is a nutty brown.

12 small cucumbers, scrubbed and chilled
4 large sprigs dill
2 or more grapevine leaves
1 sprig tarragon
4 cloves garlic
1 bay leaf
1 small dried chilli
4 black peppercorns, coarsely crushed
pinch of dill seeds
250 g salt

Place all ingredients in a saucepan and cover with boiling water. Jam lid on pan and leave to cool completely. When cold, pour contents into a hot, sterilised jar, ensuring that brine covers cucumbers. Leave for 2 weeks before using and refrigerate once opened. (Any white scum that forms on top is harmless and can be removed with a small spoon.)
variation For a crunchier and sharper pickle, *see* Pickled Cornichons in CUCUMBER.

gravlax

SERVES 8

Fresh salmon is the traditional fish to use for gravlax, but a fillet of tuna is also excellent. If the fish fillet is much larger than a kilogram, allow an additional 24 hours in the marinade.

1 large salmon *or* tuna fillet
(at least 1 kg)
4 cloves garlic
400 g sugar
500 g rock salt
1 bunch dill, roughly chopped
¼ cup dry vermouth *or* vodka

Remove small bones in thickest part of fillet using tweezers. Crush garlic with back of a knife and combine with sugar, salt, dill and vermouth, then rub fish well with mixture. Pack fish in mixture in a glass, stainless steel or ceramic dish. Cover with plastic film and place weights on the fish. Refrigerate overnight (or for 12 hours), then turn and leave a further 12 hours. Brush off excess salt and herbs and pat fish dry with kitchen paper. Slice thinly and serve with rye bread, horseradish cream, plain sour cream and freshly snipped dill or Mustard Sauce (see below).

mustard sauce

SERVES 8

The traditional sauce to serve with gravlax in Scandinavia, this is also good with smoked eel and herring fillets.

2 tablespoons Dijon mustard
3 teaspoons red-wine vinegar
1 teaspoon sugar
4–6 tablespoons olive oil
salt
freshly ground black pepper
2 tablespoons freshly chopped
dill leaves

Combine mustard, vinegar and sugar. Vigorously whisk in oil to create an emulsion. Season to taste and add dill.

herring fillets with potatoes and dill

SERVES 4

The contrast between the hot potatoes and cold herrings is part of the charm of this first course, so don't be tempted to cook the potatoes beforehand and serve them cold.

4 matjes herring fillets, drained
½ small red onion, finely sliced
1 tablespoon freshly chopped
dill leaves
8 small new potatoes
sour cream *or* Mustard Sauce
(see p. 267)

Arrange herring fillets on 4 plates. Scatter onion rings and dill over herring. Cook potatoes until tender, then drain and serve alongside herring. Spoon a generous dollop of sour cream onto each plate.

dill cream
Stir freshly chopped dill leaves into plain sour cream, or prepared horseradish mixed with sour cream, and serve with fillets of hot-smoked trout as a speedy and delicious first course.

dill frittata
Make a frittata using eggs, grated zucchini, chopped spring onions and freshly chopped dill.

dill mayonnaise
Stir freshly chopped dill into mayonnaise with drained and chopped capers and serve with fish or mix with small, steamed beetroots, or cooked or raw button mushrooms.

other recipes

cold cucumber soup *see* CUCUMBER
yabbies with dill butter sauce *see* YABBIES

d u c k The next-most popular main course in my restaurant after beef, duck is considered luxury or 'special occasion' food. It seems that few people buy duck to prepare at home as a duck will only feed 2 people, and chicken is considered better value for the dollar. | Although a duck has a big frame, it also has a higher fat content, thicker skin and less meat than other poultry, but its rich flavour is very delicious. That said, duck in Australia are nowhere near the quality of many birds available to the French, who have a far wider range from which to choose. (The French and the Chinese are the greatest duck cooks.) We can provide commercially produced birds that are deep-breasted and often chewy (muscovy) or shallow-breasted and tender (pekin). Here and there enterprising growers are attempting to put the flavour back into duck by concentrating on what they eat and how they are reared. | The flavour of wild duck is not as widely known here as it is in Europe and Britain, although each State has its own duck-shooting season. The practice is controversial as conservationists claim that endangered species are shot along with the approved species of wild duck. | Wild duck can vary in texture and flavour from tender and delicious to tough and fishy. Roasted at a high temperature and served underdone, a good wild duck will taste superb, while an old bird will be extremely disappointing.

VARIETIES AND SEASON

There are at least 60 species of domesticated duck, but the variety most commonly bred for the Australian table is the *pekin* (also known as the Peking), which originated in China. Pekin duck are ready for the table at 8 weeks of age, when they weigh 1.5–2 kg. Pekin duck develop unsightly and hard-to-remove pin feathers at this age and if not killed before the feathers appear must be held (and fed) for a further 4–5 weeks before killing. Most of this time is spent growing feathers, so there is little inducement for growers to grow the birds to 12 weeks. Growers who are prepared to wait until the bird is 13–14 weeks old before killing it will have an exceptionally well-defined duck to sell and consumers should be overjoyed to find a meaty duckling weighing 2.3 kg. We have to be prepared to pay a premium price for such a bird.

The *muscovy* duck (originally from South America), a larger bird than the pekin, is slower to mature and has a richer flavour but more textured flesh. Experts I have spoken to have said that the public has not warmed to the muscovy, probably because of its size and correspondingly high price. Consequently, there are fewer muscovy being produced commercially, although they are still popular with smaller growers. A muscovy drake can weigh 3 kg dressed (plucked and gutted and head, neck and feet removed) at 14 weeks, while the female weighs about 1.5 kg at 12 weeks of age. Older birds are correspondingly larger.

The '*mule*' duck, a cross between a muscovy drake and a pekin duck, is very popular in Asia but experiments in Australia have not been continued with. The duck dressed out at around 2.8 kg but were perceived by the public to be too expensive. These birds sound most exciting, with the best characteristics of both breeds: meatiness, tenderness and a good size.

Khaki Campbell duck are another popular variety but are produced as egg-layers, not for meat. (I discuss the uses of duck eggs in EGGS.)

Production on large commercial duck farms is year round. As with intensive chicken farming, the light is manipulated, so that the duck continue to lay. Free-ranged birds are reluctant to lay once the weather is cold and wet when their instincts tell them the conditions are poor for rearing young. The best season for free-range ducks is November–April.

SELECTION AND STORAGE

Duck is available whole (head on or off), portioned, fresh or frozen. The neck, giblets and livers are also available. In my opinion a whole duck weighing less than 1.9 kg is not worth buying. The breast meat is very thin compared to the size of the skeleton.

Most duck are supplied *fresh* to the marketplace as the public perception is that 'fresh' equals 'young' and 'new'. I prefer to buy fresh duck whenever possible as one is able to give the breast a good squeeze to see if there is an

duck goes with
olives
cherries
oranges
turnips
cumquats
limes
eggplants
carrots
garlic
hoisin sauce
spring onions
salad leaves
sea salt
pistachios
honey
walnuts
red cabbage
curry paste
celery

adequate layer of meat underneath the thick skin. A young fresh duck will also have a pliable beak and feet and the skin will be pearly, creamy-white. However, it is important to understand that a properly **blast-frozen**, well-wrapped bird is always preferable to buying a fresh duck that is then stuffed into a crowded home freezer, where it may well take days to freeze solid, losing condition all the time. As frozen duck is usually sold without head or feet, one's best guide is to buy from a reliable source.

When selecting duck livers, reject any that have a greenish stain (which can also be cut away) as it imparts a bitter flavour.

Refrigerate *fresh* duck and livers, freed of all wrappings, on separate plates and cover with plastic film. Use a whole fresh duck within 3 days and portioned fresh duck and duck livers within 2 days. Reboil duck stock after 2 days and use within 24 hours, or freeze.

Always thaw *frozen* poultry in the refrigerator, freed of all wrappings, on a pad of kitchen paper. Once thawed, cover lightly with a clean cloth to stop it drying out and use within 2 days. Never cook poultry that is partially frozen. While the outer layers cook and crisp, a frozen or icy interior may prevent a temperature high enough to kill potentially dangerous micro-organisms such as salmonella from being reached.

PREPARATION AND COOKING

FOR ROASTING FRENCH-STYLE | Remove any loose fat, neck and giblets from inside the bird. Wipe inside and out with kitchen paper. Cut off the first wing joint and reserve for stock or the baking dish. Rub the duck all over with a little olive oil and season inside and out. Tuck some extra flavouring inside the bird that connects with its ultimate flavour, for example, a thick slice of orange, cherries, pickled cumquats, olives, crushed garlic cloves or a thick slice of onion, and so on. Prick the skin around the legs and neck cavity with a fork and remove the wishbone for easier carving. Proceed with the recipe (*see* p. 273).

TO JOINT A ROASTED DUCK | Slice the legs away from the body where they join the breast. Bend the legs backwards to expose the ball joint and cut between this joint to release them. Sever the wings in the same manner. Slice off one breast and cut the meat crosswise into thick strips. Do the same with the other breast.

TO COOK DUCK LEGS | **To roast** Slash each leg twice through the thickest part of the thigh. Roast at 180°C for at least 1 hour. **To confit** Season duck legs with rock salt and leave overnight. Brush off all salt and gently roast in melted duck or pork fat at 160°C for at least 1 hour until tender. Cool and refrigerate the legs in enough of the rendered fat to cover them. To serve, remove the required number of legs (do not scrape off any fat clinging to them) and reheat on a cake-cooling rack placed over a baking sheet in a 180°C oven until the skin is crisp. Drain the fat away.

TO GRILL DUCK BREASTS | Score the fat side with a sharp knife in a rough criss-cross (this helps render the fat). Season the duck breasts with salt and pepper and paint the flesh side with a trace of olive oil. Preheat the griller and put plates in a low oven.

Place the duck breasts skin-side up and grill for 8 minutes. Pour the accumulated fat from the drip pan to avoid it catching fire, and turn the breasts. Grill a further 2 minutes. Transfer the duck breasts to the warm plates, cover and allow to rest for 5 minutes.

roasted duck legs with eggplant

SERVES 4 **recipes**

This recipe is based on one that appears in Stephanie's Seasons *but here I use legs rather than a whole bird. The legs are meant to be black and shiny when cooked – so don't be alarmed!*

8 duck legs
salt
2 eggplants, cut into wedges
2 tablespoons hoisin sauce
2 tablespoons oil
5 cloves garlic
2 cm piece ginger, peeled and finely chopped
½ cup well-flavoured stock
2 tablespoons light soy sauce
freshly ground black pepper

Preheat oven to 200°C. Slash duck legs twice through thickest part of thigh. Lightly salt eggplant and drain in a colander while legs are cooking.

Rub duck legs with hoisin sauce and 1 tablespoon of the oil and place in an oiled baking dish with 3 of the garlic cloves, unpeeled and flattened with the back of a knife. Roast in oven for 1 hour, turning every 20 minutes. Pour away rendered fat when you turn legs. When tender, drain off any additional fat and keep legs warm.

Rinse eggplant and dry well. Finely chop remaining garlic. Heat remaining oil in a wok or frying pan and scatter in ginger and garlic. Add eggplant and brown well. Lower heat, pour in stock and soy sauce and cover. Cook for 5 minutes until eggplant is very tender. Grind over pepper and serve eggplant wedges and juices with the roasted duck legs.

duck liver pâté
Substitute duck livers for chicken livers in Chicken Liver Pâté (see CHICKEN*) to make a country-style pâté.*

cath's sugar-cured duck legs

This is a speciality of South Australian caterer Cath Kerry's.

duck salad
Serve sliced grilled duck breasts on salad leaves, dress with the cooking juices and a few drops of good vinegar and scatter with oven-toasted walnuts.

sugar
coarse salt
duck legs
cracked black pepper
fresh bay leaves

Rub equal quantities of sugar and coarse salt into duck legs with a generous amount of cracked black pepper. Arrange in a dish, tuck in a couple of fresh bay leaves and refrigerate for 2–3 days.

Wipe off excess salt and roast duck legs in a dry baking dish at 180°C for 1 hour or until golden brown and tender when tested with a fine skewer. The legs will give off quite a bit of fat, which can be used to sauté potatoes. The legs can also be reheated, either as they are or on a bed of cabbage, for example.

duck liver parfait   SERVES 8

This is a particularly delicious and rich duck liver preparation (it can also be made with chicken or squab pigeon livers). Any unused parfait will keep for 2–3 days.

cumquat duck
Squeeze cumquats over a roasting duck and then add the cumquat skins to the baking dish.

600 g duck livers (to make
    500 g cleaned)
2 eggs
300 ml cream
2 teaspoons Cognac, Madeira
    or sweet vermouth
scant pinch of salt
scant pinch of ground white
    pepper
125 g unsalted butter, gently
    melted and cooled

Preheat oven to 180°C. Inspect livers to ensure there are no greenish specks of bile – even a trace will make the parfait bitter. Pull livers away from connecting threads very carefully. Rinse and tip onto a clean cloth to dry well.

Purée livers in a food processor. Add eggs, cream, Cognac, salt, pepper and cooled melted butter. Pass mixture through a sieve lined with a large, doubled piece of muslin. (The easiest way to achieve this is to have an assistant. You each gather up one end of muslin and twist and squeeze in opposite directions, forcing the liquid into a basin beneath the sieve. You will have a very pure liver custard in the basin and lots of specks of liver in the muslin at the end of this important straining process.)

Oil an ovenproof 1 litre gratin dish. Pour custard into dish and bake for just 12 minutes until barely firm in centre. Refrigerate overnight.

To serve, dip a tablespoon into boiling water and scoop out a portion of parfait. Turn it upside-down on the plate to expose its delicate pink colour. Serve with hot toast. (The parfait will darken on contact with the air, so press a piece of plastic film right up against any unused portion.)

french-style roast duck

SERVES 2

This method of cooking will result in a well-cooked, tender duck with a sauce made from the pan juices, its specific character coming from the garnish chosen. I have given vegetables as the garnish here, and list other suggestions, such as cherries, below.

Even if you intend to serve both the leg and breast to each person it may be easier to roast them separately rather than wrestle with the carving of the duck.

1 duck
12 small turnips, peeled
12 small carrots, peeled
12 small potatoes, peeled
1 cup well-flavoured stock
salt
freshly ground black pepper
ROASTING *MIREPOIX*
1 small onion, cut into 5 mm
   dice
1 carrot, cut into 5 mm dice
1 stick celery, sliced
2 cloves garlic, unpeeled and
   lightly crushed
1 large sprig thyme
1 bay leaf
6 black peppercorns
½ cup white wine (dry, sweet,
   fortified – you choose)
1 slice lemon
wing tips
duck neck (optional)
duck gizzard (optional)
duck heart (optional)

Preheat oven to 220°C and prepare duck for roasting French-style (*see* p. 270).

Distribute *mirepoix* ingredients over baking dish. Put duck in dish on its side. Roast for 20 minutes. Tip off accumulated fat and baste bird. Turn duck to other side. Roast for 20 minutes. Tip off accumulated fat and baste bird. Turn duck breast-side up. Add garnishing vegetables. Reduce oven temperature to 200°C. Roast for 30 minutes, then tip off accumulated fat.

To make the sauce, remove duck and vegetables from baking dish and keep warm on a plate loosely covered with foil. Tip off any remaining fat and add stock to baking dish and boil hard on top of stove, scraping and stirring. Strain sauce into a small saucepan, pressing very well on the *mirepoix* debris. (This is where you add flavourings if not using vegetables.) Taste for salt and pepper. Spoon a little sauce over duck and return to oven for 10 minutes to crisp skin. Carve duck at the table with sauce on the side, or joint and present bathed in sauce.

duck and melon
Roast a duck, allow it to cool to room temperature and cut the meat and skin into bite-sized pieces. Toss with cubes of peeled honeydew melon at the last minute and dress with lemon juice.

sauce variations Omit garnishing vegetables and instead add ingredients to the strained sauce to impart a flavour of your choice. Try a handful of stoned sour or sweet cherries or Pickled Cumquats (*see* CUMQUATS), or the blanched zest of 1 orange or 1 lemon or 2 limes, or the flesh from large green olives. **quick duck stock** Instead of discarding the bones of a roasted duck, lightly roast them with 1 carrot, 1 stick celery and 1 onion. Tip off the fat and deglaze the baking dish with wine, port or the liquid from Pickled Cumquats (*see* CUMQUATS). Transfer the deglazed liquid to a saucepan, then add 1 litre water or light stock and simmer 2–3 hours. Use another day or freeze or make a delicious soup by simmering brown lentils or chestnuts in the stock and then puréeing the lot.

chinese-style roast duck

SERVES 2

This is a simplified version of pekin duck served in restaurants with pancakes. Usually the separating of the skin from the flesh is done using a bicycle pump. One can also buy Chinese-style roast duck, so this recipe is for those who are determined to work through the very satisfying process.

Any duck bought in Chinatown will have its head and feet attached, which is essential for this recipe. A suburban poultry supplier will need to be given notice if you want an entire bird.

Squab pigeon and quail are also delicious scalded, dried, coated and roasted in the same way.

1 pekin duck, head attached
COATING MIXTURE
1 cup water
½ cup rice vinegar
½ cup maltose *or* honey
½ teaspoon bicarbonate of
    soda

Remove any loose fat and giblets from cavity and rinse inside and out, then close vent by either sewing it shut or skewering it firmly. Chop off head, if still present, leaving neck. Push neck skin right down neck bone to where neck joins body. Chop off exposed neck bone (freeze this for making stock another day). Very carefully ease breast skin away from breast meat through neck opening (the skin is *very* fragile), using your fingers or the back of a rounded spoon. If you find this impossible, make a small cut in the neck skin to give yourself a little more room (like opening a tuck, in dressmaker's language). Or do as the Chinese do and insert the nozzle of a bicycle pump between skin and meat, and pump to inflate skin. Tie off neck with a long piece of string.

Bring a deep pot of water to a boil. Hold duck by its string and dip it in and out of boiling water 3 times. Hang duck to dry over a plate in front of a fan for 30 minutes. Bring coating ingredients to a boil, then ladle over duck repeatedly until skin is well coated. Dry for 2–3 hours in front of a fan. The duck can now wait in a cool, dry spot until you are ready to roast it. (In a restaurant rows of duck hang in the coolroom. At home the refrigerator is the only alternative and the air is too humid for anything but short-term storage. Remember, the duck skin should be dry.)

Preheat oven to 250°C. Place a baking dish full of water in bottom of oven. Place duck directly on oven rack above dish, breast-side down, for 10 minutes. Reduce temperature to 200°C. Turn duck, then roast for

quick chinese duck
Buy a chopped duck and a serve of egg noodles in Chinatown. Once home, scatter the noodles with freshly chopped spring onions and a few drops of sesame oil, and add any juices from the duck and arrange the meat on top.

10 minutes and turn again. Continue to roast, turning frequently, for a further 45 minutes until duck is golden brown and very crispy.

To serve, slice skin away first and then the meat, or chop through both skin and meat. Eat with noodles or spring onions, hoisin sauce and Chinese pancakes bought from a takeaway food shop.

black satin duck with egg noodles SERVES 2–4

6 shiitake mushrooms

6 slices peeled ginger

1 cup dark soy sauce

4 tablespoons light soy sauce

1 cup water

1 tablespoon sesame oil

80 g brown or rock sugar

2 tablespoons honey

4 points star anise

1 duck, cut into pieces
  (drumsticks, thighs, breast)

3 tablespoons spring onions,
  finely chopped

EGG NOODLES

250 g yellow egg noodles,
  boiled and drained

2 teaspoons sesame oil

2 tablespoons light soy sauce

1 tablespoon rice vinegar

½ teaspoon sugar

Soak mushrooms in plenty of warm water for 2 hours. Drain and discard stems. Put mushrooms, ginger, soy sauce, water, sesame oil, sugar, honey and star anise into a heavy-based stockpot and bring to the boil. Add duck pieces. Cover and simmer very gently for about 1 hour until duck is quite tender. It is ready when a fine skewer will slip through a duck leg without resistance.

Remove duck pieces from pot and arrange attractively on a deep serving dish. Spoon juices over and refrigerate. The dish will set to a light jelly. Chill egg noodles and mix with sesame oil, soy sauce, rice vinegar and sugar. Scatter duck with spring onion and serve alongside chilled, seasoned egg noodles.

black satin chicken This dish is also excellent when made with chicken wings instead of duck.

duck breast salad with sherry and soy sauce SERVES 2

2 duck breasts

2 tablespoons light soy sauce

4 tablespoons water

2 tablespoons Fino sherry

2 handfuls salad leaves,
  washed

1 teaspoon sherry vinegar

2 teaspoons extra-virgin
  olive oil

freshly ground black pepper

Strip skin from duck breasts and reserve skin. Marinate duck breasts overnight in soy sauce.

Next day, cut skin into strips and place in a heavy-based pan with water. Cook gently over low heat until strips have shrivelled to crisp little morsels (cracklings) and liquid fat is clear. Lift out cracklings with a slotted spoon and drain on kitchen paper. Strain fat into a clean container, cool and refrigerate. >

In a heavy-based frying pan, heat 2 tablespoons cold duck fat to very hot. Remove duck breasts from soy sauce and sear for 2 minutes a side. Lower heat and pour over sherry and any soy sauce remaining in the bowl. Turn breasts in juices and quickly transfer both duck and juices to a warm plate. Cover and rest for 5 minutes.

Warm 1 teaspoon cold duck fat and mix with sherry vinegar and olive oil. Dress salad leaves with this mixture and divide between 2 plates. Slice duck breast thinly and drape over greens. Drizzle juices over meat. Grind over pepper and scatter with a few cracklings. Serve immediately.

other recipes

chinese-style glazed liver *see* LIVER

traditional sage stuffing for goose, duck or turkey *see* SAGE

see also LIVER

eggplants

Originating in tropical Asia, eggplants are now best-known in Asian, Middle Eastern and Balkan cooking but are appreciated the world over, as demonstrated by their collection of common names: aubergine, eggfruit and brinjal. | Eggplants (*Solanum melongena*) are named for the shape of the best-known varieties, while other varieties are oblong, round or sausage-shaped. They can be white, green, purple, purple–black, violet, yellowish white, pink-and-white striped or even bright orange. Eggplants vary considerably in size from pea-sized to about the size of a butternut pumpkin. | The versatility of the eggplant is astonishing. Eggplants can be fried, battered, layered in a gratin, grilled, stuffed, stewed, puréed or baked. Some of the best-known vegetable dishes in the world feature eggplant, including Greece's moussaka, Italy's eggplant parmigiana, France's ratatouille and the Middle East's baba ghanoush. | I could not exist for more than a few days without cooking some eggplant. And yet for many cooks this is one of the most mysterious of vegetables. They may admire its good looks but have no idea of how to handle it. I recommend to new enthusiasts the work of food writers who specialise in the cuisines of India, the Middle East or the Mediterranean.

VARIETIES AND SEASON

Eggplants need a long, hot season for growing and are not recommended for home gardeners in the south. Australian markets provide year-round supplies of the best-known oval, egg-shaped and oblong, deep-purple varieties of eggplant. The small, slender eggplants that are sometimes called Japanese eggplants are available from Asian food stores and are becoming more widely available in supermarkets and greengrocers. The tiny pea-shaped and very seedy eggplants used in Thai and Indonesian dishes are an acquired taste as they are quite bitter. They are sold in Asian food stores and markets. The peak season for all eggplants is November–March.

SELECTION AND STORAGE

Become comfortable with the regular, more versatile variety of eggplant and a few simple preparations before experimenting with pea-sized or long varieties, which have specific uses.

Always choose medium-sized eggplants (unless otherwise directed) that are smooth, very shiny and heavy for their size. Reject any that are wrinkled, bruised, scarred or have dull skins. Check for any holes that could suggest worm entry, especially near the stem end. The flesh should give a little under gentle pressure. Eggplants refrigerate well in the crisper for several days.

PREPARATION AND COOKING

Eggplants are not usually peeled, but most authorities recommend salting the flesh before cooking it to extract bitter juices. The green calyx is always removed. Be careful – it can give you a painful jab. Some cooks believe that by peeling the eggplant they remove more of the bitterness. With garden-picked young eggplants I would not bother. If you find, having cut the eggplant, that the seeds are very hard and too pronounced, the eggplant is overmature and the seeds will taste hard and unpleasant. I discard such eggplants or use them for a purée and then sieve out the seeds.

TO SALT Slice, cube or wedge the eggplant, scatter it with kitchen salt and leave for 30 minutes–1 hour. If it is covered with a weighted plate or tray the juices will be extracted in the shorter time. Rinse and pat dry with kitchen paper. (I lay my salted eggplant on the clean draining board of the sink and top it with a baking tray filled with tins and packets from the pantry cupboard. When ready, I remove the groceries and the tray and slide the eggplant into the sink, which is half-full of cold water, swish them around and drain them in the colander before patting them dry. All the mess is thus contained on the sink.) The prior salting also helps to rid the eggplant of extra liquid and reduces the amount of oil it soaks up during frying or sautéing. Middle Eastern recipes often recommend to soak a halved or cut-up eggplant in salted water for an hour before cooking to achieve the same effect. Which-ever method you use, dry the eggplant pieces very well before proceeding.

**TO GRILL
OR ROAST**

To grill Brush prepared sliced eggplant with olive oil and grill under an overhead griller or on a chargrill pan for 3–5 minutes each side. **To roast** Roast the eggplant over a flame, turning it frequently until the skin is quite black and the flesh is soft. Allow to cool. Remove every bit of skin, rinsing your fingers in cold water as you go. Rinse the eggplant quickly. This gives an irresistible smoky flavour to the flesh that cannot be achieved by roasting the eggplant in the oven.

**TO FRY
OR BAKE**

To fry Dip prepared sliced eggplant in your favourite batter and deep-fry in clean vegetable oil at 175°C, or coat in flour mixed with herbs, spices or cheese and shallow-fry in clean vegetable oil until golden. **To bake** Eggplant soaks up oil like a sponge. Eggplant slices fried in olive oil are delicious but much the same flavour can result using a method that dramatically reduces the quantity of oil absorbed. After salting, rinsing and drying, arrange the pieces in a single layer in a baking dish and add water to come two-thirds up the sides of the slices. Bake at 180°C for 45 minutes. The eggplant will be soft but not mushy and will look pretty unappetising. Brush the slices with the best olive oil you have and grill for a few minutes on each side – lo and behold, richly browned tender eggplant with a fraction of the oil!

smoky eggplant purée

MAKES 1½ CUPS

This classic preparation occurs in the cuisines of the Mediterranean, the Middle East and India. Roasting the eggplant over a flame gives an incom-parable smoky flavour. Baking it in the oven will produce a pleasant purée but without the haunting memory of the Middle East and oriental braziers and camp-fires. This basic purée of smoky eggplant is the sort of dish I would like to see more cooks attempting because it is so good and so versatile.

Puréed eggplant can be served as it is with toasted pita bread or aug-mented by any number of flavourings, including yoghurt, or can be mixed with other cooked vegetables to stuff chickpea or buckwheat flour pancakes or a small baked pumpkin. At a recent cooking class, I rubbed toasted slices of breadstick with garlic, piled each crouton with eggplant purée and then added quickly sautéed pine forest mushrooms. The firm, meaty mushrooms contrasted nicely with the soft purée.

As this purée keeps for several days in the refrigerator, I always roast at least 3 eggplants, preferably more.

3 eggplants, roasted and
  peeled
2 cloves garlic
salt
½ cup finely chopped flat-leaf
  parsley *or* ¼ cup finely
  chopped flat-leaf parsley and
  ¼ cup finely chopped basil
juice of 1 lemon
olive oil
freshly ground black pepper

Press each roasted eggplant in your hands or with the back of a spoon to extract as much moisture as possible.

Mash garlic to a paste with a scrap of salt. Chop eggplant pulp finely and add garlic paste and herbs, or purée in a food processor, depending on how smooth or chunky you want it. Incorporate lemon juice and add olive oil to taste. Season. **baba ghanoush** Beat 180 ml tahina paste into the purée with the juice of 3 lemons and a pinch of cumin to make the famous baba ghanoush. **mustard seeds** Heat mustard seeds in a little oil until they pop, then add the chopped eggplant to evaporate more moisture and achieve a drier purée. **tomato and onion** Fry a sliced onion until deep gold, stir in 1 tablespoon tomato paste and another crushed garlic clove and cook for a minute. Add a few spoonfuls of water and stir in the eggplant purée. **pickle** Chop 1–2 pieces Indian lime pickle finely and add to the purée or, my favourite, use Preserved Lemons (*see* LEMONS AND LIMES) for a delightfully piquant note.

caponata

SERVES 4

This Sicilian dish keeps very well. In her wonderful account of life in Sicily, Pomp and Sustenance, *Mary Taylor Simetti notes that some Sicilian cooks add cocoa to this preparation, although she does not. This recipe is based on hers. I have served caponata piled on an oval platter and surrounded by chopped hardboiled eggs as the main dish for a simple lunch.*

2 eggplants, cut into 2 cm
  cubes
salt
6 inner sticks celery, cut into
  2 cm pieces
1 cup olive oil
1 onion, sliced
1 cup stoned green olives
½ cup well-drained capers
1½ cups Fresh Tomato Sauce
  (see p. 709)
½ cup white-wine vinegar
2 tablespoons sugar
¾ cup toasted almond slivers

Sprinkle eggplant with salt and drain for 1 hour. In the meantime, blanch celery for 1 minute in boiling water.

Rinse eggplant well, drain, dry and fry in two-thirds of the oil until golden. Drain on kitchen paper. Sauté onion in remaining oil until it begins to colour. Add celery and cook a minute longer, then add olives, capers, tomato sauce, vinegar and sugar. Simmer for 5 minutes. Stir in eggplant and simmer for 10 minutes. Check seasoning and refrigerate for 24 hours.

Bring back to room temperature and serve sprinkled with almond slivers.

eggplant and ginger
Serve sour cream, finely chopped fresh ginger, and freshly chopped coriander and mint leaves spiced with fresh chilli in separate bowls alongside Smoky Eggplant Purée (see p. 279).

eggplant salad
Sprinkle grilled eggplant with balsamic vinegar and torn basil leaves and leave to serve cold, even the next day.

fried eggplant
Dip prepared, sliced eggplant in plain flour mixed with ground cumin or paprika or one-third parmesan cheese and shallow-fry in clean vegetable oil until golden.

japanese eggplant slices SERVES 2–6

These 'stuffed' eggplant slices make a hearty first course and are equally good as a snack.

6 x 2 cm thick slices eggplant
1 teaspoon salt
100 g chicken mince
2 teaspoons dark soy sauce
2 teaspoons mirin
1 tablespoon finely chopped
   spring onion
2 teaspoons finely chopped *or*
   grated ginger
olive oil

Score one side of each eggplant slice twice in opposite directions. Sprinkle salt on scored side and allow to stand for 30 minutes, then rinse and dry well. Blend chicken, soy sauce and mirin to a smooth paste in a food processor. Spread meat mixture on eggplant on scored side. Fry eggplant in plenty of oil over medium heat, stuffing-side down first, for 3–4 minutes. Turn carefully and fry other side for another few minutes. Sprinkle with ginger and spring onion. If preferred, the chicken mixture can be sandwiched between 2 slices of eggplant.

imam bayildi SERVES 3–6

A classic Turkish recipe for stuffed eggplants. Folklore claims that a Turkish priest, the imam, *fainted with pleasure on being served this dish by his wife.*

3 eggplants, halved lengthwise
1 large onion, finely sliced
½ cup olive oil
2 cloves garlic, finely chopped
4 large ripe tomatoes, peeled,
   seeded and chopped
1 bay leaf
pinch of ground cinnamon
3 tablespoons freshly chopped
   parsley
salt
freshly ground black pepper
juice of 1 large lemon

Scoop out eggplant flesh, then chop and lightly salt it and set aside. Lightly salt eggplant shells and leave upside down for 30 minutes. Rinse and dry shells.

Preheat oven to 180°C. Cook onion slowly in 2 tablespoons of the oil. Add garlic and sauté for 1 minute, then add tomato, bay leaf, cinnamon and parsley and cook another 5 minutes. Tip into a bowl.

Rinse and dry eggplant flesh. Heat 3 tablespoons of the oil and sauté eggplant. Add to bowl, mix and check seasoning.

Pile filling into eggplant shells and brush with a little oil. Pack shells into an oiled baking or gratin dish. Pour in enough water mixed with lemon juice and remaining oil to barely cover eggplant. Bake for 30–45 minutes until soft. Allow to cool and serve at room temperature or cold.

meat and rice Briefly sautéed minced beef or lamb can be mixed with the vegetables, as can currants, nuts or rice.

eggplant parmigiana
Layer slices of fried eggplant in a deep dish with Fresh Tomato Sauce (see TOMATOES) *and parmesan cheese. Bake at 180°C until cheese is golden and the dish is bubbling. Sprinkle currants and toasted pine nuts on each layer and use provolone cheese rather than parmesan for a Sicilian speciality.*

eggplant and pesto
Spoon a little Pesto (see BASIL) *onto grilled eggplant slices, then reheat until bubbling.*

thai-style eggplant salad

SERVES 4

8 Japanese eggplants, sliced
   and grilled
2 hardboiled eggs, sliced
4 shallots, very thinly sliced
1 tablespoon fish sauce
1 teaspoon dried shrimp paste
1 teaspoon brown sugar
1 teaspoon fresh lemon juice
1 tablespoon fresh coriander
   leaves

Arrange eggplant on a platter. Garnish with eggs and shallots. Combine fish sauce, shrimp paste, sugar and lemon juice and spoon over salad. Decorate with coriander leaves and serve.

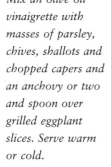

eggplant vinaigrette
Mix an olive oil vinaigrette with masses of parsley, chives, shallots and chopped capers and an anchovy or two and spoon over grilled eggplant slices. Serve warm or cold.

eggplant sandwich
Sandwich prepared eggplant slices with grated haloumi or mozzarella cheese mixed with an egg and shallow-fry in clean vegetable oil until golden.

eggplant curry

SERVES 4

A vital ingredient in this dish is tamarind, the seedpod of a large tree used extensively in Indian cookery. Its aromatic sweet–acrid flavour is unique and worth discovering. This curry can also be made with the slender Japanese eggplants.

40 g tamarind pulp
½ cup hot water
500 g small–medium eggplants
salt
125 g desiccated coconut
2 teaspoons hot Indian-style
   curry paste
½ teaspoon mustard seeds
4 tablespoons vegetable oil
1 teaspoon freshly chopped
   ginger
1 teaspoon chopped garlic
8–10 curry leaves
2 large onions, chopped
pinch of ground turmeric
2 cups cold water
juice of 2 limes
fresh coriander leaves

Soak tamarind in hot water for 30 minutes. Slash eggplants deeply on each side, then soak in lightly salted water for 15 minutes. Drain, dry and set aside.

In a heavy-based frying pan large enough to take all ingredients, dry-roast coconut until golden, then mix with curry paste.

Sauté mustard seeds in oil for 1 minute. Add ginger, garlic and curry leaves, then sauté for a few minutes and add onion, turmeric and coconut curry paste. Cook until onion has softened. Add cold water and eggplant, then add salt to taste.

Squeeze soaked tamarind and push through a sieve resting over a bowl. Add tamarind water to eggplant. Cook until eggplant is tender and sauce has reduced, about 20 minutes. Sprinkle with lime juice and coriander leaves before serving.

other recipes

ratatouille *see* ZUCCHINI AND SQUASH
roasted duck legs with eggplant *see* DUCK

e g g s

eggs An egg is the perfect protein pack and a meal in minutes. No refrigerator should be without them. Many of us still regard a softboiled egg with fingers of buttered toast as a lifeline, yearned for when one feels full of aches and pains or seen by many as an essential part of the Sunday-night ritual. │ As always, fresh is best and eggs laid by birds allowed to roam and peck at dirt and worms are a revelation. I remember with great pleasure egg dishes I enjoyed during a holiday in Bali. The eggs were richly coloured and full of the flavours I remembered from my childhood when Grandpa tended our hens. Nowadays, I purchase my eggs from one of the farms where the hens range freely and enjoy a varied diet. The yolks are sunset-orange, the whites hump thickly around the yolks and the flavour is magnificent. │ The chemistry of the extraordinary egg is fascinating and complex, and even a rudimentary understanding of how and why certain things happen when eggs are whipped, heated, stirred and cooked is of great help to all cooks. >

Many of the cooking properties of eggs hinge on their ability to trap air (soufflés, meringues) or liquid (custards) and then be 'set' by heat. Egg proteins are naturally coiled and linked. Heating or beating breaks these links and enables the proteins to attach themselves to each other in a mesh that traps air bubbles or liquid. When heated, the air and liquid trapped in the egg-protein mesh swell until they reach the temperature at which egg protein becomes solid or coagulates.

The temperature at which an egg coagulates, 'sets' or cooks varies according to a number of factors, including how quickly the egg is heated. The chemical chain of events speeds up when the temperature is increased. A stirred custard heated slowly starts thickening at a lower temperature than if heated quickly and takes longer to coagulate, thereby providing a wider safety margin. A stirred custard cooked fast will curdle very fast also. (I encourage all cooks to cook a custard to curdling point deliberately once in order to appreciate just how thick a custard can become before it curdles. In my experience, most cooks are nervous about making custards and do not cook them long enough.)

When an egg-based dish is heated beyond the coagulation temperature or is held too long at this temperature the bonded proteins force out the water they have trapped. Most cooks will have seen a curdled sauce or a baked custard that has possibly shrunk from the sides of the mould and has holes in it filled with a watery substance.

The ability of egg whites to foam is marvellous and miraculous. It is made possible by the action of 3 proteins: globulin, which contributes to the quality of the foam (duck eggs are deficient in this protein), and ovumucin and conalbumin, which contribute to the stability of the foam. The air trapped in the protein mesh of the beaten egg whites continues to expand when heated. This is why egg whites to be cooked are whisked or whipped to soft (elastic) peaks rather than dry, 'rocky' whites, which will be stiff, lumpy and inelastic. However, the addition of sugar prevents stiffly whipped whites from becoming too dry.

Most professional chefs feel that egg whites whisked in a copper bowl have greater stability than whites beaten in other containers and also believe that their soufflés rise to greater heights. This is perhaps because copper ions combine with the protein conalbumin to make a very stable foam. The resultant film surrounding the air bubbles expands *more* before coagulating than is the case with egg whites beaten in other containers.

The astonishing egg has many uses, quite apart from in batters, cakes, puddings, stuffing, biscuits, breads and so on and so on. Lipoproteins in egg yolks surround and coat a tiny drop of oil or butter and hold it in suspension, making possible such wonderful emulsified products as mayonnaise and hollandaise and béarnaise sauce. Eggs can be used as an enriching liaison and thickener in soups, sauces or stews; as a coating for fried foods, where the set egg prevents fat soaking into the food; or as a binding agent when mixing raw poultry or fish to make quenelles or other mousse-like stuffings. An egg yolk lightly beaten with a spoonful of water and a tiny pinch of salt gives the shiniest and best-looking glaze to baked breads or pastries, while an egg white lightly beaten and brushed over a baked pastry case that is then returned to the oven for a minute or two will prevent the case becoming soggy when filled. Egg white is an effective clarifying agent used in wine and vinegar-making, as well as in the preparation of jellies and consommés.

VARIETIES AND SEASON

Fresh eggs are available all year round. *Hen* eggs are the eggs we all buy. They are sold by size (note that the larger the egg, the more egg white present). Most recipes use medium (55 g) eggs, though some may use 61 g eggs. *Bantam* eggs, sometimes available from farms, are an ideal size for setting in well-flavoured savoury jelly. *Quail* eggs are popular for garnishing and for pickling. They are delicate in flavour and have the most beautiful speckled shells. *Duck* eggs are larger and stronger in flavour than hen eggs. Cooks enjoy the extra richness that duck eggs give to custards, pasta and cakes. Duck eggs are deficient in globulin, however, one of the proteins that contributes to the ability of hen egg whites to trap and hold air when whisked. Duck eggs, therefore, are unsuitable for making soufflés or meringues. Fresh food markets and some delicatessens carry different types of eggs.

SELECTION AND STORAGE

When possible, buy *free-range* eggs. There is no nutritional difference between a free-range or commercially farmed egg, or a brown or white egg, for that matter. However, there is an enormous difference in the flavour of a naturally farmed egg compared with one produced commercially.

The majority of eggs sold in Australia (more than 90 per cent) are infertile eggs produced by hens farmed intensively. The most popular crossbreed, from a white leghorn male and black australorp female, produces white eggs. Other crosses produce brown hens that lay brown eggs.

The colour of the yolk depends on what the hen has eaten. A free-range hen tends to produce eggs with deep-yellow yolks. However, some birds farmed intensively are fed pigments that deepen yolk colour.

Eggs are best stored in their carton in the refrigerator as they can lose as much quality in one day at room temperature as 4–5 days in the refrigerator. (Do not store eggs in the moulded racks in the refrigerator as they absorb odours from other foods.) Keep eggs with the pointed end down, as this keeps the yolk centred and prevents damage to the air cell at the blunt end of the egg.

Unbroken egg yolks can be refrigerated covered with a little water for up to 3 days. Broken egg yolks can be refrigerated for the same length of time if plastic film is pressed onto the surface. Egg whites can be stored in an airtight container for a week and can also be successfully frozen. (An average egg white measures 30 ml or 1½ tablespoons, which is handy to know when you are faced with a container of stored egg whites!)

TO TEST FOR FRESHNESS As an egg ages, moisture lost through the shell is replaced by air, which enlarges the air cell at the blunt end of the egg. **Water test** A fresh egg placed in a bowl of water will generally lie at the bottom, while a stale egg will float, blunt-end up. (A weak shell or a hairline crack in the shell can also cause a fresh egg to float. Discard any egg that floats, just to be safe.) **Saucer test** A fresh egg broken into a saucer will have a bright, unbroken yolk surrounded closely by thick, viscous white that settles firmly around the yolk. There will be some thin egg white that settles in an irregular pattern. The yolk of a stale egg becomes larger and is easily broken. The thick white becomes less gelatinous. Such eggs will slump on the saucer. Very liquid whites are unsuitable for beating as they give a very poor foam.

PREPARATION AND COOKING

TO SEPARATE Have 2 dry bowls ready. It is wise to break each egg over a cup just in case you break the yolk. A scrap of yolk or shell is best removed using a piece of egg shell. To separate, crack the egg on the edge of the cup, then gently tip the white and yolk from one shell to the other, allowing the white to slip into the bowl below as you go. Be careful not to break the yolk! Tip the yolk into the second bowl.

TO WHISK EGG WHITES Discard any egg white with even the tiniest trace of egg yolk when preparing to whisk, as yolk hinders foaming. Egg whites will foam better if they are at room temperature. All utensils must be clean and dry when beating egg whites. (Even a drop of moisture will prevent them foaming properly.) Beat the egg whites until soft peaks form. Avoid under- or overbeating as the foam will exude liquid, as will whipped egg whites left standing.

TO BOIL Allow eggs to come to room temperature to reduce the risk of cracking. Bring sufficient lightly salted water to a boil to cover generously the number of eggs that are to be boiled. Using a spoon, slip the eggs into the water and boil them gently for 3–5 minutes: allow 3 minutes for very soft yolks and barely set whites, 4 minutes for still-runny yolks but well-set whites and 5 minutes for firm yolks.   **To hardboil** Put eggs in a saucepan of cold water and bring to the boil. Boil eggs for 8 minutes, then pour off the water and run plenty of cold water over the eggs to stop the cooking process. Tap the egg shells to break the membrane to allow for easier peeling.

TO FRY | Fried eggs can be either shallow-fried or deep-fried. The first method is the most usual and the fat used can be oil, bacon fat or butter. Deep-fried eggs are cooked in oil until the egg white puffs up to enclose the yolk and becomes very crisp.

Using a non-stick frying pan is a good idea. You will use much less fat and the eggs will not break when they are lifted out. Break each egg into a cup to ensure that the yolk is intact. If frying with bacon fat, add a trace of oil to the frying pan and fry the bacon first. When crisp, remove the bacon and keep it warm, then slip the egg into the hot fat. Otherwise, heat a film of vegetable oil, oil and a little butter or just butter and fry the eggs gently until cooked to your liking. Baste the yolk with a little of the hot fat.

TO SCRAMBLE | Some cooks make a huge production of scrambled eggs and advise double saucepans and that the process should take a very long time. I find this quite unnecessary. However, it is a good idea to use a non-stick pot or frying pan as it minimises the soaking and scraping.

Whisk the eggs with a little milk or cream and salt and pepper. Have ready any additional flavouring – herbs, smoked fish, puréed or cooked vegetables, and so on. Gently melt a good knob of butter (20 g to 3 eggs) and when it is just starting to sizzle, tip in the well-beaten eggs. Stir gently and continuously with a wooden spoon until the eggs have formed into creamy curds. Add the chopped herbs just as the last curds are forming. Stir once more and tip onto waiting buttered toast.

TO POACH | There are many theories on poaching eggs and in desperation some have resorted to using poaching pans that deliver solid egg puddings, quite unlike the delicate nature of a properly poached egg.

Break each egg into a cup to ensure the yolk is intact. Have ready a deep frying pan with at least 10 cm of simmering, lightly salted water. Stir the water with a spoon until you have created a whirlpool. Drop an egg into the centre of this and wait for 3–4 minutes. The water will settle and the egg will have formed itself into a neatish oval. Remove the egg with a slotted spoon, drain for a moment on a folded cloth and then slide onto hot toast or into a pan of cold water, if you are poaching many eggs. To reheat poached eggs, slip each egg onto a slotted spoon and hold for 1 minute in simmering water. Drain as before.

OMELETTES | Have ready a well-seasoned frying pan, preferably non-stick, that is reserved for omelette-making. Prepare any filling and heat the plate before cooking the omelette.

Break 2 eggs into a bowl and season with salt, pepper and herbs, if using. Beat the eggs lightly with a fork and melt a walnut-sized lump of butter in the pan. As soon as the butter starts to foam, tip in the beaten egg, tilting the pan so that the egg covers the base. Using a wooden spoon, drag the cooked egg to the centre allowing the uncooked mixture to flow to the edges. Repeat once more. This will only take 2 minutes. Spoon in any filling and fold the furthest third of the omelette over the filling, encouraging it with the wooden spoon, and then fold the remaining third over the filling as the omelette slides out onto the heated plate. Skim the cooked surface with a tiny piece of butter and eat at once.

BUTTERED EGGS | Butter a 250 ml porcelain dish, slip in an egg and season. Pour over a spoonful of cream and bake at 180°C for 8 minutes until the white has just set. Sprinkle over finely chopped herbs before serving. A Spanish flameproof terracotta dish can be used to cook the eggs directly over a medium heat. If the little dishes are covered, either with a lid or foil, the eggs will emerge with what Elizabeth David has so aptly called a 'mirrored appearance'.

CUSTARDS | **Baked** A bain-marie or water bath in which a custard or mousse is baked must never reach simmering point or else the custard will toughen and be full of holes. The optimum oven temperature for a water bath is 150–170°C. **Stirred** Before commencing, have ready a cold basin with a strainer sitting over it. Once the custard has thickened properly it will coat the back of a wooden spoon and a finger drawn through the custard will leave a clean path. Pour the thickened custard through the strainer without delay.

SAUCES | Butter sauces that include eggs must be cooked gently, below the coagulation temperature of the yolk (75°C), or the sauce will curdle. For this reason never boil a sauce once the egg has been added.

QUAIL EGGS | Quail eggs have a very tough shell and inner membrane and are difficult to peel neatly. They are usually fried or poached to garnish a salad or crouton, or hard-boiled to set in a terrine or savoury jelly or for pickling. **To boil** Bring lightly salted water to a boil. Lower in eggs, then stir gently to keep the eggs moving for 1–2 minutes to 'centre' the yolks. Cook the eggs for 4 minutes if they are to be used as a terrine garnish or if they are to be set in jelly;

6 minutes is recommended if the eggs are to be pickled.   **To shell** To shell boiled eggs, tap the shell all over. Peel the crumpled shell away from the rounded end first. (Plunging the cooked eggs into iced water for 3 minutes can make peeling them easier.) If boiled eggs are to be pickled, soak them in a solution of half white-wine vinegar and half water, which will partially dissolve the shell and soften the membrane, making peeling easier. It will also contribute a slight vinegar flavour to the eggs, so is only suitable for eggs to be pickled.   **To fry** Cut the top from each egg and slip the eggs onto a saucer. Film a non-stick frying pan with olive oil or clarified butter and cook the eggs briefly. If the whites have coalesced, you can cut individual eggs out with a round cutter. This is not a good thing to do to a non-stick pan, however!   **To poach** Cut the top from each egg and slip the eggs onto a saucer. Slide the eggs into barely simmering lightly salted water. Poach for 2 minutes, then lift the eggs out with a slotted spoon. Drain briefly over a cloth or folded kitchen paper, then serve.

miniature omelettes   MAKES 20

Tiny omelettes fried in oil so that they puff and have frilled edges are very good served with drinks. Cumin, one of the favourite spices of the Middle East, goes particularly well with eggs, as does mint. Tiny omelettes will cook instantly, so they must not have fillings or additions that do not.

3 eggs

good pinch of ground cumin

finely chopped fresh mint

finely chopped fresh parsley

3 spring onions, very finely
   chopped

salt

freshly ground black pepper

olive oil

Mix eggs with cumin in a bowl. Stir in mint and rather more parsley. Add spring onion and season. Mix well.

Heat oil to a depth of 5 mm in a heavy-based frying pan. Using a teaspoon, quickly slip spoonfuls of mixture into hot oil. Allow omelettes to puff up and brown around edges (there's no need to turn them). Remove with a slotted spoon to a hot plate covered with crumpled kitchen paper and keep warm. When all omelettes are cooked, serve at once, sprinkled if you like with a little more cumin mixed with sea salt.

stuffed eggs

This is a quick party dish that can be more or less substantial depending on the filling.

eggs
Mayonnaise ✎ or sour cream
freshly chopped herbs
rollmop herrings, anchovies or
canned tuna, drained and
chopped

Hardboil number of eggs required. Halve, then remove egg yolks to a bowl. Slip egg whites into a bowl of cold water until needed.

In a food processor, work yolks to a creamy paste with some mayonnaise, herbs and rollmop herrings, tasting as you go. Drain egg whites on a clean cloth. Fill cavities with creamed mixture using a piping bag and settle eggs on a bed of lettuce leaves.

filling Use ham or spinach, sorrel or watercress instead of fish, or anything else you like particularly.

pickled eggs

1 tablespoon black
    peppercorns
1 tablespoon whole allspice
3 slices peeled ginger
1 litre white-wine vinegar or
    cider vinegar
10 hen or 20 quail eggs,
    hardboiled and peeled

Simmer all ingredients except eggs in a non-reactive saucepan for 5 minutes. Put eggs into a sterilised ✎ jar and pour in hot pickling solution to cover them completely. Leave eggs for at least a week before using. The eggs keep for a month or more.

tea eggs The Chinese have a wonderful variation on these savoury eggs. The shells of the hardboiled eggs are not removed but are tapped all over to crack them. Instead of using the above pickling solution, simmer the eggs for 1½ hours in a mixture of 2 tablespoons salt, 2 tablespoons soy sauce, 1 star anise, 2 tablespoons Chinese oolong tea and enough water to cover them. Allow the eggs to cool in the sauce, which will have seeped under the cracked shells, adding both flavour and beautiful markings. To serve, shell and halve the eggs and offer the strained sauce for dipping. Note that as these eggs are not pickled they should be eaten as soon as possible.

son-in-law eggs

SERVES 4

walnut-sized piece of tamarind
    pulp
½ cup hot water
125 g palm sugar
3 tablespoons fish sauce
juice of 1 lime
vegetable oil for deep-frying
4 hardboiled eggs, peeled
1 tablespoon fried sliced garlic
fresh coriander leaves

Soak tamarind in water for 30 minutes. Mix well, then squeeze and press through a strainer into a bowl. Combine palm sugar, fish sauce and 1 tablespoon tamarind water in a saucepan and simmer, stirring, until sugar has dissolved. Stir in lime juice and taste for a good balance of sweet, salty and sour. Adjust to suit your taste.

Heat a good quantity of oil and deep-fry eggs until golden brown, about 5 minutes. ➢

---

eggs mayonnaise
Hardboil best-quality eggs, then halve and arrange them cut-side down on a bed of soft butter lettuce, nap with a soft blanket of Mayonnaise ✎ and sprinkle with baby capers.

prawns and eggs
Sauté shelled prawns until glassy, pour over beaten, seasoned eggs and lightly scramble.

Drain, cut eggs into quarters, dip into sauce and eat as an appetiser with fried garlic and coriander as accompaniments.

jenny's caesar salad

SERVES 4

This ever-popular salad depends on eggs and anchovies and parmesan cheese – what an irresistible combination.

3 eggs

1 rasher streaky bacon, sliced
　or cubed

olive oil

2–3 slices sourdough bread,
　crusts removed

2 cos lettuce hearts, washed
　and well dried

6 anchovies, cut into strips

2 tablespoons freshly grated
　parmesan cheese

2 tablespoons freshly chopped
　parsley

DRESSING

1 teaspoon sea salt

¾ teaspoon freshly ground
　black pepper

1 clove garlic, crushed to a
　fine paste

¼ teaspoon mustard powder

1 teaspoon Dijon mustard

1 teaspoon lemon juice

2 tablespoons tarragon *or*
　red-wine vinegar

½ cup extra-virgin olive oil

1 egg

Mix all dressing ingredients together in a screw-top jar. Shake well and set aside. Bring a saucepan of water to a boil and boil eggs for 4 minutes exactly.

In a frying pan, fry bacon in a little oil. Remove from pan. Cut bread into 1 cm cubes and fry in bacon fat, tossing to crisp. Remove from pan and drain on kitchen paper.

Peel eggs and cut into large chunks or quarters. Arrange lettuce leaves on a platter. Drizzle with dressing. Turn leaves in dressing and scatter on egg, anchovies, bacon, croutons, cheese and parsley. Eat at once.

boiled egg
Serve a boiled egg with toast 'soldiers' spread with Anchovy Butter (see ANCHOVIES) *or topped with grilled cheese, or use asparagus spears as 'soldiers' instead.*

chervil and eggs
Scatter chervil onto scrambled eggs or into an omelette.

salad of softboiled egg with bacon

SERVES 2

2 handfuls soft salad leaves

2 eggs

1 rasher smoked streaky
　bacon, cut into 1 cm cubes

(continued next page)

Wash and dry greens, then wrap them in a dry cloth and refrigerate until needed. Heat a salad bowl by filling it with very hot water, and warm 2 dinner plates. >

1 thick slice bread from a
dense loaf, cut into 2 cm
cubes

1 tablespoon good-quality
olive oil

few drops of red-wine vinegar

1 tablespoon freshly chopped
parsley

1 teaspoon freshly chopped
chives

freshly ground black pepper

Bring a saucepan of water to a boil and boil eggs for exactly 3 minutes. Remove eggs to a plate. Sauté bacon over moderate heat in a frying pan until fat starts to run. Remove with a slotted spoon and keep warm. Sauté bread cubes in bacon fat. Return bacon to pan, remove from heat and push to one side.

Tip water from salad bowl, then quickly dry it and pour in oil and vinegar, salad leaves and contents of pan. Mix all together with your hands.

Arrange as attractive heaps on heated plates. Crack an egg over each salad and scoop out contents using a teaspoon. Scatter over herbs and a grinding of pepper. Eat at once.

additions Include other ingredients and sauté appropriately: chunks of cooked potato, chicken or duck livers, a slice of tuna (grilled or sautéd rare), slices of pork sausage, toasted walnuts, or leftover cooked lamb or chicken. **dressing** Vary the dressing by including mustard, a special vinegar, sour cream or home-made relish or chutney.

quail eggs in coconut sauce   SERVES 6

2 teaspoons ground turmeric

4 cloves garlic, finely chopped

2 teaspoons ground coriander

1 teaspoon ground ginger

1 teaspoon ground cumin

400 g onions, finely chopped

1 stalk lemongrass, finely
chopped

400 g tomatoes, peeled,
seeded and chopped

1 cup coconut milk

1 tablespoon lemon juice

1 tablespoon Fried Coconut
(see p. 605)

12 hardboiled quail eggs,
peeled

Cook all ingredients, except eggs, over moderate heat for 20 minutes. Stir from time to time to prevent mixture sticking. Add eggs and cook for 10 minutes. This dish can be made the day before and gently reheated. It is also good cold.

oeufs à la neige – floating islands

SERVES 6

This classic French sweet of poached meringues surrounded by a moat of custard is very easy and very impressive. Sometimes a little raspberry purée is flicked into the custard, or sliced peaches or berries are added. Crushed Praline (see NUTS) is sometimes scattered over the meringues at the last minute. This dessert can be made 3 hours in advance and be kept in a cool place (the laundry rather than the refrigerator).

2 litres water
5 egg whites
pinch of salt
30 g castor sugar
CUSTARD
2 cups milk
1 vanilla bean
5 egg yolks
100 g castor sugar

To make the custard, bring milk to scalding point with vanilla bean, remove from heat and leave aside to infuse. Beat egg yolks and 100 g sugar until pale, then strain on milk. Wash and dry vanilla bean and reserve. Transfer custard to a saucepan and heat gently, stirring with a wooden spoon until custard thickens. The custard is ready when you can create a channel in the custard on the back of the spoon with your finger. Pour custard into a bowl and chill.

Bring water and washed vanilla bean to simmering point in a wide saucepan. Hold water at a bare simmer. Whisk egg whites with salt until soft peaks form. Scatter over castor sugar and continue to whisk until firm and shiny. Dip a serving spoon in the hot water, then use it to scoop a ball of meringue into the barely simmering water. Scoop 5 more balls, wiping the spoon clean each time. Poach gently for 5 minutes, turning halfway through. Remove meringues with a slotted spoon and leave to cool on a clean, folded tea towel.

To serve, pour cold custard into a large serving platter or individual bowls and float meringues on top.

pavlova

SERVES 6–8

Every Australian family has its pavlova tradition. In mine the crisp baked shell was always turned upside down to be spread with cream and passionfruit. In this way the marshmallow middle melded with the cream and the sides and base stayed crisp.

Pavlova can be difficult to cook as the meringue needs a short period of high heat to set and crisp the exterior and then a long period of cooling heat to set but not dry out the marshmallowy interior. Experiment with your own oven. If syrupy droplets form on the surface of the meringue, you'll know you have overcooked it; liquid oozing from the meringue is a sign of undercooking.

omelette fillings
Fill an omelette with smoked fish in a cream and chive sauce, ham scraps heated in a spoonful of cream with a teaspoon of Dijon mustard added, a purée of sorrel, leftover Ratatouille (see ZUCCHINI AND SQUASH), or sliced mushrooms sautéd with a touch of garlic and reduced to a thick mass with a spoonful of sour cream.

4 egg whites (at room
    temperature)
pinch of salt
250 g castor sugar
2 teaspoons cornflour
1 teaspoon white-wine vinegar
few drops of pure vanilla
300 ml cream, firmly whipped
pulp of 10 passionfruit

Preheat oven to 180°C. Line a baking tray with baking paper. Draw a 20 cm circle on the paper. Beat egg whites and salt until satiny peaks form. Beat in sugar, a third at a time, until meringue is stiff and shiny. Sprinkle over cornflour, vinegar and vanilla and fold in lightly. Mound onto paper-lined baking tray within circle and flatten top and smooth sides. Place in oven, immediately reduce heat to 150°C and cook for 1¼ hours. Turn off oven and leave pavlova in it to cool completely. Invert pavlova onto a platter, pile on cream and spoon over passionfruit pulp.

sue's meringues   MAKES 24

Meringues, I admit, can be tricky; some say their success can even depend on the weather (they are not meant to like the damp!). But with practice, and knowing the peculiarities of your own oven, you can turn leftover egg whites into a wonderful treat that stores well and turns simple berries into a special dessert.

I mention a few cooking tips in the recipe for Pavlova above that are perfect here, too. To reduce or increase the quantities given here, simply allow 60 g castor sugar to an egg white.

2 egg whites (at room
    temperature)
120 g castor sugar
¼ teaspoon pure vanilla

Preheat oven to 150°C and line a baking tray with baking paper. Beat egg whites until stiff peaks form, then add sugar, a little at a time, still beating. Beat in vanilla. Place small spoonfuls of meringue on baking tray and bake for 45 minutes. Turn oven off, leave door slightly ajar and allow meringues to cool completely in oven. Store in an airtight container lined with greaseproof paper.

caramel custard   SERVES 4

2 eggs
2 egg yolks
2 tablespoons castor sugar
350 ml milk
CARAMEL
1 cup castor sugar
½ cup water

To make the caramel, dissolve sugar in water in a small saucepan over moderate heat. Bring to a boil, brushing sides of pan clean with a pastry brush dipped in cold water to prevent crystals of sugar syrup sticking to the sides. Increase heat and boil syrup steadily until a deep-golden caramel. >

egg and chives
Scoop a softboiled egg into a bowl with 1 teaspoon butter, 1 teaspoon breadcrumbs, salt, pepper, onion chives and parsley.

egg and spinach
Slip a poached egg onto buttered spinach on hot toast, shave over parmesan cheese and drizzle on olive oil or spoon on Hollandaise Sauce for eggs Florentine.

fishy scrambled eggs
Fold some smoked trout, salmon or eel into scrambled eggs.

Remove pan from heat and allow any bubbles to subside, then pour caramel into a 500 ml ovenproof porcelain dish. Turn bowl carefully to coat sides evenly. (I use a straight-sided soufflé dish for this, but any shape will do.)

Lightly whisk eggs, egg yolks and sugar together, then pour on milk. Whisk, then strain into caramel-lined dish. Place dish in a baking dish and pour in hot water to come just over halfway up sides. Bake at 160°C for 45 minutes until just set. Remove custard immediately from baking dish and refrigerate overnight. To serve, place a deep plate over custard and carefully invert. The custard should be surrounded by dark caramel.

orange I love infusing orange zest in the hot milk for 1 hour before making the custard, and in the winter I accompany this custard with fresh slices of orange.

amaretti and coffee semifreddo

12 amaretti biscuits, roughly crumbled

4 tablespoons strong black coffee

2 tablespoons Amaretto di Saronno liqueur

6 egg yolks

few drops of pure vanilla

¾ cup milk

250 g castor sugar

3¾ cups cream, softly whipped

almond oil

chocolate-coated coffee beans

Soak biscuits in coffee and liqueur while you prepare custard. In an electric mixer, beat egg yolks and vanilla until very thick and lemon-coloured. Heat milk and sugar to simmering point in a saucepan and stir until sugar has dissolved. Simmer for 2 minutes, then pour onto beaten egg yolks with the mixer motor running and continue to beat until cold. Fold in the cream lightly but thoroughly. Swirl in the soaked biscuits with any remaining liqueur. Do not blend completely, as the lumps of biscuit and veins of liqueur are part of the charm.

Brush a 1.5 litre log mould with almond oil and line it with a doubled strap of foil. Pour mixture into mould and freeze. Cut into thick slices to serve and scater with chocolate-coated coffee beans.

baked custard tart

The custard tart was always a favourite of mine at the school tuckshop. This home-made version is even more delicious!

1 quantity Shortcrust Pastry
1 egg white, lightly beaten
2 eggs
2 egg yolks
2 cups cream
1 cup milk
3 tablespoons castor sugar
freshly grated nutmeg

Line a 24 cm × 4 cm deep loose-bottomed flan tin with pastry and bake blind at 200°C for 20 minutes until golden. Remove pastry case from oven and remove foil and weights. Brush baked shell liberally with egg white and return to oven for 5 mintues to seal crust. Reduce oven temperature to 160°C.

Whisk eggs and egg yolks together. Warm cream and milk and stir in sugar until dissolved. Strain liquid over eggs and mix gently. Pour into pastry case and bake for about 1 hour until just set (check after 50 minutes). Generously grate nutmeg over the top while tart is still warm. Serve cold.

other recipes

asparagus custards *see* ASPARAGUS

asparagus with coddled eggs *see* ASPARAGUS

avgolemono – greek egg and lemon soup *see* LEMONS AND LIMES

broccoli frittata *see* BROCCOLI

classic cheese soufflé *see* CHEESE

egg and bacon pie *see* BACON

eggs in tarragon jelly *see* TARRAGON

eliza acton's quince custard *see* QUINCES

garlic and goat's cheese custards *see* GARLIC

ham soufflé *see* HAM

kitchen garden soup with tiny herb omelettes *see* PEAS

lemon curd *see* LEMONS AND LIMES

mushroom custards *see* MUSHROOMS

passionfruit curd *see* PASSIONFRUIT

poached eggs with yoghurt and garlic sauce *see* YOGHURT

potato and sorrel omelette *see* POTATOES

potato frittata *see* POTATOES

quiche lorraine *see* BACON

rosemary and bay leaf savoury custards *see* ROSEMARY

silverbeet frittata *see* SILVER BEET

softboiled-egg vinaigrette *see* ROCK LOBSTERS

spanish ham and eggs *see* HAM

springtime pea custards *see* PEAS

stephanie's twice-baked goat's cheese soufflés *see* CHEESE

twice-cooked zucchini soufflés *see* ZUCCHINI AND SQUASH

zabaglione with mascarpone *see* CHEESE

f e n n e l   'For I am he who hunted out the source of fire, and stole it, packed in pith of a dry fennel stalk.' Aeschylus, *Prometheus Bound*. | Fennel is native to Europe and is much loved in Italy, where it is often eaten raw at the finish of a meal instead of fruit to clear the palate and aid digestion. Fennel seeds are said to have the same effect. | Bulb or Florence fennel (*Foeniculum vulgare* var. *azoricum*), sometimes sold as 'finocchio', is a variety of common fennel – a declared noxious weed in several Australian States. It is important to recognise the difference between the common or wild fennel, which romps over vacant land and sets seed easily, and Florence fennel, which develops a distinctive, aromatic fleshy bulb of overlapping celery-like stalks. Common fennel grows about 2 metres high, has thin, strong flower-stems, feathery yellow–green leaves and tiny yellow flowers arranged in flat clusters. | Both common and bulb fennel have an intense aniseed flavour for which many do not care. I did not like it when I was a teenager and viewed with distaste the platter of raw fennel that my mother offered as a salad in the autumn. But I grew to love it as I now love chervil and tarragon and ouzo and sambucca, all of which taste more or less of aniseed. >

fennel
goes
with
olive oil
sea salt
lemon juice
parmesan cheese
goat's cheese
butter
pepper
chicken stock
pasta
olives
tomatoes
almonds
walnuts
fish
garlic
chillies
mushrooms
potatoes
chicken
ham
Pernod
eggs
cream
anchovies
rocket
watercress
radicchio
capers

The seeds, leaves and young stalks of common fennel are very useful for fish stuffings and flavouring fish stews. The stalks are often used to flame grilled fish in the Mediterranean region. On the Greek islands, where 'eating weeds' is a well-established spring pastime, the young shoots and leaves of common fennel are boiled and eaten with olive oil and lemon juice. However, a little goes a long way and nobody needs to plant common fennel!

Bulb fennel is very versatile. The sharp and surprising tang of its stalks combines well with other salad ingredients. When cooked, its flavour is much mellowed and marries brilliantly with the richness of stock, butter and parmesan cheese, or olive oil and parmesan, or richly flavoured tomato sauce. It can be the star performer in soups and purées if passed through a food mill to remove any trace of the stringy stalks. And fennel seeds added to a simple bread dough is one of my favourite things – at Stephanie's Restaurant we make tiny fennel-seed breadsticks and balance them on a bowl of mussels cooked with saffron and tomatoes.

VARIETIES AND SEASON

Bulb fennel is available fresh May–October. Recently I have also bought very small fennel bulbs directly from the grower all through spring and into midsummer. Some specialist greengrocers also stock this delicate vegetable. *Common* fennel is available all year, although it is at its most tender and luxuriant in the spring.

SELECTION AND STORAGE

It is very important to be certain that any *common* fennel you pick has not been sprayed. Many gardens have unwanted common fennel, so prefer this source to plants growing along the roadside.

It is best to choose *bulb* fennel that still has its tops on, if possible, as freshness is the best guide to quality. Tops that are green and sweet-smelling will indicate recent picking. Tops that are slimy, brown and collapsed tell a different story. Muddiness or lack of mud is no guide to how recently the bulb was picked. Avoid fennel that smells stale or sour or that shows any sign of bruising.

Refrigerate unwashed *bulb* fennel tightly wrapped in plastic film in the crisper and use within 4–5 days. Pick and use *common* fennel without delay. If you must store it, tightly enclose it in a vegetable storage bag, so that its strong odour does not taint other food in the refrigerator.

PREPARATION AND COOKING

The only preparation *common* fennel requires is thorough washing. Almost all *bulb* fennel will need the outer stalks removed as they are often damaged or tough and stringy (they are fine for stock or soup, but not for salads or cooking as a special vegetable). Trim the base of the bulb. The bulb can be left whole, with the feathery foliage and any minor stalks removed, or halved, quartered, sliced or diced. For a salad, separate the stalks and slice very finely. Stalks intended to be eaten raw can be soaked in iced water for an hour to improve their crispness, if necessary. The feathery leaves can be chopped and added to a sauce or dressing at the last minute. They can also be added to mixtures of herbs for flavouring omelettes or to garnish other dishes.

TO BLANCH | Many dishes require that whole or portioned bulb fennel be simmered first in lightly salted water until tender (this takes 15–20 minutes for a whole bulb). The tender bulb needs to be drained very well in a colander before being cooked further. The cooking water can be used to cook pasta to serve with the fennel or it can be the start of a lovely vegetable and fennel or fish soup.

fennel with simple cheese sauce   SERVES 2

A simple cheese sauce was the first recipe I suggested my children learn. They certainly would not have added cooked fennel to it, but they might have used cauliflower or macaroni and dotted the top of the dish with bread-crumbs and more grated cheese.

40 g butter
2 tablespoons plain flour
1½ cups warm milk
1 cup freshly grated gruyère
  or mozzarella cheese
salt
white pepper
freshly grated nutmeg (optional)
1 bulb fennel, blanched and
  drained
4 tablespoons fine white
  breadcrumbs (optional)
extra 2 tablespoons grated
  cheese

Preheat oven to 180°C and butter or oil a gratin dish. Melt butter in a saucepan, then stir in flour and cook for 2 minutes over a gentle heat, stirring with a wooden spoon. Gradually stir in milk and bring to a boil, stirring continuously. Add gruyère cheese and stir until melted. Taste for seasoning and adjust. Add a little nutmeg, if using.

Arrange fennel in gratin dish and spoon over sauce. Scatter with breadcrumbs, if using, and extra cheese. Bake until well browned and bubbling at the edges, about 30 minutes.

braised fennel in meat juices
with cheese   SERVES 2

Vegetable dishes with as much character as this one can stand alone. But a small portion would be brilliant alongside a scaloppine of veal in its own syrupy sauce and perhaps a fried sage leaf or two!

1 bulb fennel, thickly sliced
1 tablespoon olive oil
1 cup Veal or Chicken Stock
½ cup freshly grated pecorino
or parmesan cheese
freshly ground black pepper
1 tablespoon roughly chopped
fresh parsley
1 tablespoon roughly chopped
feathery fennel tops

fried fennel

Dip slices of blanched fennel into egg and then into fine breadcrumbs (or a mixture of one-third parmesan cheese to two-thirds breadcrumbs) and fry in hot, clean oil or a mixture of butter and oil. Serve with lemon quarters or Mayonnaise into which you have stirred lots of chopped fennel leaves.

fennel gratin

Boil sliced fennel in enough seasoned water to cover barely until tender, then tip into a buttered gratin dish, scatter with freshly grated parmesan cheese and bake at 180°C until golden.

Place fennel in a heatproof shallow dish or a heavy-based frying pan in which it can be served and drizzle with oil. Heat for a minute or two to start oil sizzling. Turn fennel over. Add stock, cover with foil to delay its evaporation, and adjust heat to maintain a steady simmer. When fennel is tender and there is still some liquid left (about 15 minutes), increase heat, remove lid and scatter on cheese. (The cheese and stock will combine to make an instant sticky glaze – shake pan vigorously to prevent contents sticking badly.) Place dish under a heated griller for a minute to develop an appetising crust. Grind over pepper and scatter on herbs and serve warm.

fennel and potato fry-up   SERVES 2

1 bulb fennel, blanched and
drained
1 red-skinned potato, boiled
and drained
2 tablespoons olive oil
2 rashers smoked streaky
bacon
1 teaspoon fennel seeds
(optional)
salt
freshly ground black pepper
½ onion, finely chopped
1 clove garlic, finely chopped
1 tablespoon freshly chopped
parsley

Chop fennel and potato into 2 cm pieces and combine in a bowl. Heat a trace of the oil in a frying pan and cook bacon until crisp. Remove bacon and break or chop into small pieces. Add bacon and fennel seeds, if using, to bowl and season.

Add remaining oil to bacon fat in pan and sauté onion for 3 minutes. Add garlic and fennel mixture. Cook over a moderate heat, turning contents of pan frequently. The aim is to achieve lots of crispy brown bits but no burnt bits. This should take about 15 minutes. When ready, tip into a hot serving dish and scatter with parsley.

fennel and tomato fish soup   SERVES 4

By increasing the amount of fish, this could become a meal! (Hapuku, snapper, rock ling or blue eye are good varieties of fish to use – either on their own or as a mixture.)

pinch of saffron threads

2 tablespoons warm water
   or stock

1 bulb fennel

1 onion, chopped

3 cloves garlic, chopped

2 tablespoons olive oil

4 large tomatoes, peeled and
   chopped

piece of orange zest

salt

freshly ground black pepper

1.5 litres water *or* Fish Stock

500 g fish, cut into bite-sized
   chunks

2 parboiled potatoes, cut into
   1 cm cubes

Infuse saffron in the 2 tablespoons warm water. Chop fennel, reserving tops for garnish.

Sauté onion, garlic and fennel in oil in a large saucepan for 5 minutes, stirring. Add tomato, zest, salt, pepper and saffron mixture, then simmer for 5 minutes. Generously cover vegetables with water and simmer until tender. Purée or, for a coarser texture, pass through coarse disc of a food mill. Adjust seasoning. Return soup to rinsed-out pan. Slip in fish and potato and simmer for 5–10 minutes until cooked. Serve garnished with chopped fennel tops.

fennel sauce

Combine equal quantities of finely chopped capers, dill and spring onions with twice the quantity of finely chopped fennel. Stir in extra-virgin olive oil, season to taste and serve with poached or grilled fish, or as a dressing for raw fish.

fennel-marinated fish

SERVES 2–4

This marinade is ideal for small fish, such as sardines, herring, sand whiting or red mullet, that are to be grilled quickly on the hotplate or over the coals of a barbecue. For a very Mediterranean touch, throw common fennel onto the barbecue to add its aroma.

½ bulb fennel, very finely
   chopped

2 cloves garlic, finely chopped

1 small fresh chilli, seeded and
   finely chopped

2 tablespoons freshly chopped
   parsley

1 teaspoon grated lemon zest

3 tablespoons olive oil

1 teaspoon sea salt

fresh *or* preserved vine leaves,
   rinsed and dried

4 small fish *or* 12 sardines

lemon wedges

Work all ingredients except vine leaves, fish and lemon wedges to a smooth paste in a mortar or food processor. Rub fish inside and outside with paste. Wrap each fish in lightly oiled vine leaves. Grill on barbecue, turning once only. (Sardines will need 2 minutes a side; red mullet and other small fish will need 5 minutes a side.) Serve with lemon wedges. The charred vine leaves are delicious but should probably not be swallowed.

fennel and walnuts

Toss toasted walnuts, semi-dried tomatoes and shavings of parmesan cheese through a lightly dressed fennel salad.

fennel salad

Tuck tiny warm potatoes, anchovies and quartered hardboiled eggs into a fennel salad.

fennel-seed breadsticks

MAKES 4

This bread is delicious with shellfish and fish soups. The dough can also be used to make 20 very small sticks like grissini. If you need any reassurances about making bread, turn to BREAD.

oiled fennel
Dress sliced fennel and some of the inner feathery leaves with the best olive oil and serve with sea salt, freshly ground pepper and a cheese platter or other raw vegetables.

baked fennel
Bake a blanched, quartered bulb of fennel in a tangy home-made tomato sauce and serve with a green salad.

tiny pinch of ground saffron or
   saffron threads
2 cups warm water
1 tablespoon instant dried
   yeast
1 tablespoon salt
500 g plain flour
250 g semolina flour
1 tablespoon finely ground
   fennel seeds
extra semolina flour (optional)

Infuse saffron in warm water for a few minutes. Mix yeast, salt, flours and fennel seeds together in bowl of an electric mixer.

Using a dough hook, and with machine on low speed, add saffron mixture to dry ingredients. Mix and knead for 10 minutes until dough is smooth. Turn out onto bench and knead for a few more minutes. Tip dough into an oiled bowl, cover with plastic film and allow to double in size in a draught-free place (about 1½ hours).

Gently knock back dough and divide into 4 pieces. Roll each piece of dough into a stick shape and place in breadstick tins or on a tray lined with a clean cloth dusted with semolina flour to prevent the dough from sticking. Allow to rise again, covered lightly with plastic film, for 30 minutes or until doubled in size.

Preheat oven to 220°C. Transfer tins to oven (if the sticks are on the cloth-lined tray, gently roll them onto a preheated baking tray) and spray inside of oven and dough with a fine mist of water. Reduce heat to 200°C and bake about 20 minutes until the breadsticks sound hollow when tapped and are crusty.

other recipes

slow-roasted loin of pork with garlic, rosemary and fennel *see* PORK

f i g s

f i g s   A fully ripe fig eaten warm from the tree is an emotional experience. A basket of freshly picked figs brought to the table with a soft white cheese or a plate of just-sliced curls of palest pink ham has to be the perfect beginning to a late-summer lunch.   The fig tree, most likely a native of Syria, is one of the most ancient plants in civilisation. To ancient travellers, the fruit of the fig was of special value as it could be dried, and drying meant that it could be carried long distances and could be stored. Figs were brought to the West by the Phoenician caravan trade along the old Silk Route, and were spread across Europe by the Romans.   The fig features in the mythology of the ancient world. The fig tree was the Tree of Life to the ancient Egyptians and figs have been found in Egyptian tombs (as dried as their owners, says my favourite horticulturist, Louis Glowinski); it sheltered Romulus and Remus in Roman mythology; and it was regarded by the Greeks as a symbol of fertility. In the Bible we read that all's right with the world when we have 'everyman under his vine and under his fig tree'. And, of course, Adam and Eve's use of its leaves ensured eternal notoriety for the fig tree. >

figs
go
with

raw ham
goat's cheese
fresh white cheese
rocket
late-picked wine
dessert wine
kassler ham
honey
raspberries
brown sugar
butter
cream
Cognac
Armagnac
Cointreau
hazelnut liqueur
almonds
walnuts
candied orange peel
fennel seeds
lemons
orange-flower water
cinnamon
ginger
bay leaves

The domesticated fig tree (*Ficus carica*) is hardy and will flourish in a range of climates. It prefers a hot summer for growing and ripening the main crop of fruit, which appears in late summer and continues throughout autumn. In Australia commercial plantings of fig trees have increased in importance, especially in the irrigated inland areas along the Murray River.

Fig trees can attain venerable size and seem to be amazingly tolerant of neglect. My friend and colleague Maggie Beer writes of a fig tree on Kangaroo Island, South Australia, that is so large that its owner has cut steps in its branches and holds picnics in the tree itself! At my restaurant we have a magnificent tree that bears generously each year and seems to be growing directly out of the asphalted car park.

VARIETIES AND SEASON

There are 4 main types of fig: the common or Adriatic fig and the Smyrna, San Pedro and wild figs. Each type has different pollination requirements and within each type there are many, many varieties. Tim Low points out in his *Wild Food Plants of Australia* that Australia has more than 40 native figs that produce fruit ranging from sweet and delicious to dry and tasteless (he also says that Aborigines 'probably ate most kinds of figs, and used the bark from some to make nets').

Figs grown commercially in Australia belong to the common fig group and are not sold by their variety. They mature their fruit without pollination and are classified according to the colour of their skin – white, purple, black and red. Some common figs produce 2 crops, a light crop in the summer and a heavier crop in the autumn. Many do not – my tree, for example, produces only one crop.

It is very confusing attempting to name one's favourite variety or varieties of fig as the names change from place to place and what I might think of as a green fig might be considered a white fig by someone else. According to Louis Glowinski's *The Complete Book of Fruit Growing in Australia*, the **black Genoa** (a large purple fig with very sweet crimson flesh), **brown Turkey** (a purple–brown fig with sweet pink–brown flesh), **white Adriatic** (a bright-green fig with well-flavoured red flesh) and **white Genoa** (a yellow–green fig with mildly flavoured amber flesh) are the main varieties available to us. March is the optimum month for figs, although the season stretches from late December through to the end of April.

SELECTION AND STORAGE

If you own a fig tree the biggest problem is beating the birds to the ripe fruit! Pick figs as soon as they have gained full skin colour for their variety and they begin to droop a little with their weight. If the tree is enormous and there is plenty for you and the birds, leave the fruit another day until the skin just starts to split. These figs will have attained optimum sweetness.

Figs picked fully ripe are very perishable and ferment very quickly. If buying fresh figs, it is best to eat them that same day. However, they will keep for 2–3 days in the refrigerator but will probably start to ooze juice. Store *fresh* figs in a single layer on a plate lined with their own leaves, if possible. *Dried* figs can be bought in pressed blocks, or loose from some health food and gourmet shops. They are also sold preserved in sugar as glacé figs. Stored in an airtight glass container they seem to last forever.

PREPARATION AND COOKING

Most *fresh* figs are peeled before eating or cooking, although you may prefer to serve those varieties with very thin skins as they are. (In Italy I was served fresh quartered figs with the skin pulled away from the flesh to resemble a flower.) Always cut off the stems. The sap that oozes from the stem ends, and to a lesser extent from the skin, is a common skin irritant. In some cultures this sap is used to curdle milk for simple cheesemaking in place of rennet. Fresh figs can be served whole or sliced or can be poached, baked, grilled or made into preserves. *Dried* figs are sometimes steamed for 10 minutes before being chopped and added to pudding batters and the like.

TO DRY   **Oven-dried** Arrange whole or halved fresh figs on a rack and leave them overnight in an oven with the pilot light on or the thermostat set at 60°C. If still not completely dry the next morning, leave the figs to dry a little longer. **Sun-dried** Fresh figs can also be dried in the sun, either hung in strings or spread out on a tray, although this method is trickier. The fruit must be turned regularly and must be brought in before any evening mist descends. The figs will take several days to become quite dry.

quail with dried figs and olives   SERVES 4   recipes

4 large dried figs, quartered
1½ cups dry red wine
½ cup stoned black olives
4 large or 8 small quail
salt
freshly ground black pepper
80 g butter
2 tablespoons olive oil
1 small onion, finely chopped
2 cloves garlic, finely chopped
2 tablespoons freshly chopped
    parsley

Soak figs overnight in wine. Next day add olives to figs. Open each quail by cutting either side of the backbone and pressing bird flat (discard backbones). Dry very well, then season.

Heat butter and oil in a heavy frying pan or casserole large enough to take all the quail. Brown quail, skin-side down, very thoroughly. (You don't need to turn them.) Lower heat, scatter on onion and garlic and sauté for a minute or so. Add wine, olives and figs, then cover and simmer for 10

fish on fig leaves
Grill a piece of firm fish on a couple of washed fig leaves to impart a curious aromatic flavour – a little like coconut, to my palate.

minutes until quail are tender. Transfer birds to a platter in a warm oven and bubble up the sauce. Taste for seasoning. Spoon over and around birds and scatter over parsley.

Serve with boiled potatoes on a large platter of salad leaves drizzled with olive oil. The sauce will be all the extra dressing the salad requires.

poached figs in alcoholic syrup SERVES 6

Some people don't like the texture of uncooked figs yet love the flavour. They might like these poached figs.

1 cup sugar
1½ cups water
juice of ½ lemon
½ vanilla bean, split
12 large or 18 small ripe figs, peeled
100 ml Cognac or Armagnac
3 tablespoons thick cream

Put sugar, water, lemon juice and vanilla bean in a large saucepan and heat gently until sugar has dissolved. Add figs and cover. Gently simmer for 5 minutes until figs are tender, then allow to cool in syrup.

Add spirit and leave for 30 minutes. Serve figs and their juice on a flattish plate and drizzle with cream.

liqueur Use 60 ml Cointreau or green Chartreuse – or your preferred liqueur – instead of the Cognac. You can also use Stone's ginger wine instead of the water.

fig and raspberry tart SERVES 8

1 quantity Shortcrust Pastry
1 egg white, lightly beaten
1 cup Pastry Cream
¼ cup whipped cream
1 punnet raspberries
4 ripe red-fleshed figs, peeled and cut crosswise into 5 mm slices
½ cup redcurrant jelly
1 tablespoon water

Line a 22 cm loose-bottomed flan tin with pastry and bake blind at 200°C for 20 minutes. Brush pastry case with egg white and return to hot oven for 5 minutes to seal. Cool completely.

Mix pastry cream with whipped cream and spread over base of pastry case. Arrange a band of 2–3 raspberries around edge of tart and fill in middle with fig slices. Fill any holes where fig slices meet with raspberries.

Melt redcurrant jelly with water and stir until smooth. Cool a little, then spoon over fruit. Eat tart within an hour as it will soften quickly.

figs in ham
Wrap whole, peeled small figs in trimmed raw ham and skewer with a toothpick for a treat with drinks. (Be careful that the ham has been well trimmed of fat and is not more than one layer thick or your guests could choke!)

fig and rocket salad
Toss rocket leaves, quartered ripe figs and goat's cheese with olive oil and a mild red-wine vinegar.

grilled figs
Halve unpeeled ripe figs, place on a washed fig leaf, dot with butter, grind over pepper and grill until warmed through. Serve with a ham steak, pork chop, duck breast or grilled bacon.

fig won tons

MAKES 12

*To keep the filo pastry from drying out, stack the pieces and cover with a
sheet of foil and top with a damp cloth.*

500 g sugar

3 cups water

ground aniseed

1 cup fresh orange juice

15 ripe figs

6 sheets filo pastry, cut into
   quarters

100 g unsalted butter, melted

2 tablespoons crushed,
   strained raspberries

juice of ½ lemon

WALNUT FILLING

¼ teaspoon ground aniseed

½ teaspoon ground cinnamon

1 tablespoon brandy

3 strips lemon zest

¼ cup sugar

¼ cup water

1 cup finely ground walnuts

To make the walnut filling, combine all
ingredients except walnuts and simmer for
5 minutes until syrupy. Remove lemon zest
and stir in walnuts. You should have a thick
paste. Allow to cool completely.

    To poach the figs, dissolve sugar in water
and simmer with ½ teaspoon ground
aniseed for 5 minutes until quite syrupy.
Add orange juice. Place figs in syrup and
simmer until tender, about 10 minutes.
Remove the 12 most shapely figs with a
slotted spoon and drain. Reserve remaining
figs and syrup for the sauce.

    Preheat oven to 200°C. Place 12 pastry
squares well apart and brush with melted
butter. Cover each square with a second
and brush with butter. Place 1 tablespoon
walnut filling in the centre of each pastry
square. Centre a fig on the walnut filling.
Press a spoonful of walnut filling into each
fig. Pull up pastry and twist to close each parcel. Bake on lightly buttered
baking trays for 10 minutes until pastry is golden.

    Make the sauce while the parcels are baking. Purée the 3 reserved figs
with 1 cup poaching syrup. Stir in strained raspberries and ¼ teaspoon
ground aniseed and flavour with lemon juice, tasting as you go. To serve,
divide baked parcels between plates and spoon some sauce around. Offer
cream or vanilla ice-cream.

caramelised figs

*Roll tender-skinned
figs in castor or
brown sugar and
arrange side by side
in a buttered pie
plate or gratin dish.
Bake at 220°C for
10–15 minutes.
Cool and serve.*

**figs and raspberry
cream**

*Spread peeled, ripe
figs with a sauce
made from crushed,
sieved raspberries
mixed with enough
whipped cream
to turn the sauce
deep pink.*

squab pigeon and fig salad *see* QUAIL AND SQUAB PIGEONS   other recipes

f i s h

I want every cook in the land to know that with a piece of fresh fish and a lemon in one hand, and a bottle of olive oil in the other, dinner is only 10 minutes away! It is a travesty that most of the fish eaten in Australia is consumed as fish fingers made from imported, minced, pressed frozen fish. | There are more than 1000 edible varieties of fish in Australian waters. And yet compared with other countries Australians eat very little fish. While many Anglo-Saxon Australians are still nervous about bones and reserve their fish-eating for fish and chips and fish fingers, our Asian and Mediterranean immigrants are appreciative and knowledgeable fish-eaters. To food-loving visitors one of the marvels of Australia is its abundance of reasonably priced seafood. For Australians travelling in Asian and European countries it comes as a surprise to note the very high prices asked for fish. Such prices reflect diminished availability due to overfishing, the distance travelled, which has implications for freshness, and the esteem with which the public regard fresh fish. >

Although Australian fishing is not as intensive as in other parts of the world, the quality of our water and the closeness of the markets in the main cities assure us abundant choice and quality. Until recently the fish industry was dependent on stocks of wild fish. However, as Australia is as guilty as the rest of the world of overfishing certain species, we have had to become used to closed seasons being declared in order to allow fishing beds the necessary recovery time. As a result, aquaculture or fish farming has become increasingly important, with Tasmanian Atlantic salmon leading the way.

The best reason to eat fish is that it tastes good. As well as this it is good for us. Fish can be eaten raw, 'cooked' with lemon or lime juice, cured, cold-smoked or hot-smoked, or pickled, and, of course, it can be cooked in thousands of wonderful ways.

VARIETIES AND SEASON

What's in a name? A great deal, when one is an ichthyologist. Although we recognise and buy our fish by their common names and by descriptions of their shape, colour, texture, fat content and flavour, it is only by referring to scientific names that fish can be properly identified all around the world. Common names are often very descriptive and add colour and character to the language. But sometimes they change from one locality to another and are not always confined to one species. For example, the blue eye (*Hyperoglyphe antarctica*) is also known as the blue-eye trevalla, deep-sea trevalla, trevalla, deep-sea trevally, sea trevally, blue-eye cod and big eye. In different parts of the country golden perch is identified as Murray perch, callop or yellowbelly, while jewfish is also called mulloway, butterfish or kingfish.

Here and there the early colonists also confused matters by ascribing European common names to fish with no connection to that particular genus. Australian salmon (*Arripis* species) is an example of this – it is no more related to the salmon family than Murray cod (*Maccullochella peelii*) is part of the cod family.

Some varieties are available all year, while others are subject to seasonal factors. Some varieties are localised, such as the westralian jewfish, and others are common throughout most Australian waters, such as flathead or snapper. Some are freshwater fish, such as the Murray cod, while others are deep-sea varieties, such as the marlin and the hapuku.

We can go through the alphabet several times listing our best-known fish varieties. We can start at albacore and go on to whiting, ticking off barramundi, blue grenadier, coral trout, the dories, the emperors, flathead, garfish, gurnard, jewfish, ling, mullet, ocean perch, redfish, shark, snapper, Spanish mackerel, tommy ruff and trevalla on the way.

SELECTION AND STORAGE

Fish has to be fresh to be sensational. It is worth saying it again – *fresh* fish is sensational! But still shoppers buy frozen fillets of fish from supermarket cabinets and wonder why it is flabby and lacking in flavour. It is nonsense to say that all fish tastes the same and reveals that the speaker is not acquainted with the flavours of truly fresh fish.

Find a good fish shop or patronise the fresh fish stalls in any of our food markets and make friends with the fishmonger. A good fishmonger will advise you about the varieties of fish for sale that day and when and where each type was caught. If you are offered an unfamiliar fish, be prepared to experiment and learn to *trust* the fishmonger. A good fishmonger can also help you to recognise freshness in a fish, will scale, gut and fillet your fish (and give you the bones if you want to make fish broth), and can advise on what cooking method suits each variety. If you find the fish to be unsatisfactory – and this usually means stale – return it promptly.

Local fish from inlets and bays are likely to be freshest of all as they have less distance to travel to the point of sale. However, even though most deep-sea fish are likely to be 2–3 days old when they arrive at the fishmonger's, if they have been carefully handled on the boat they will still be of fine quality by the time you buy them. Some farmed and trawled fish have their bloodlines removed and this dramatically increases shelf life.

Truly fresh fish should not smell. The eyes should be clear and protruding and the gills should be bright pinky-red, never brown. The body should look shiny and be firm and springy when prodded. It is preferable to select a whole fish and have it filleted than to buy fillets that have already been cut as a great number of frozen fillets are sold to fish shops. Never buy fillets that are soggy or browning at the edges – they have certainly been thawed and will taste awful.

Buy fish on the day you want to eat it, or the day before if absolutely necessary. Hurry home with it and refrigerate it at once. (If home is a long way from the shop, carry a small insulated bag or box with an ice-pack in the boot of the car.) Discard the wrapping and re-wrap the fish in aluminium foil rather than plastic film.

When bad weather delays the Tasmanian fishing fleet, the catch is usually frozen; similarly, as boats from Queensland and the Northern Territory spend so long at sea, their hauls are frozen, making fresh fish somewhat of a rarity in the north. However, fish that is frozen on board a fishing boat using a blast freezer has been very rapidly frozen. (This fish is sometimes sold as 'fresh frozen', a contradiction in terms.) A home freezer cannot do this. The texture of fish that freezes slowly will suffer considerable deterioration. If you have no option but to buy frozen fish, transfer it to the freezer as fast as possible. Thaw the fish on a wad of kitchen paper in the refrigerator. Never freeze fish with the guts intact and *never* refreeze thawed fish.

In selecting fish for dinner you must remember that not all fish is successful cooked every way, or, put more simply, not all fish can be grilled or poached. Fish with softer flesh are less suited to the barbecue. In some varieties the skin is delicate and it tears and sticks to barbecue grills or hotplates. Thick, meaty steaks or cutlets cut from deep-sea varieties are perfect for the home grill or barbecue. Some fish have soft flesh that breaks up quickly and are better steamed than poached. Thin or flat fish are not suitable for poaching or steaming as they will overcook and will not be succulent. The safest bet is to buy the best fish on offer and ask your fishmonger how to cook it. Be prepared for a few experiments. No one has all the answers!

PREPARATION AND COOKING

Any fishmonger will clean and fillet your fish, but as anglers will want to do this themselves sometimes, I include instructions below. (Note, however, that filleting in particular is an art best performed by the fishmonger as not all fish are handled the same way. Leave filleting for the breakfast flathead caught on holiday!)

Most cooks will want to steam, bake, grill, poach or fry their fish. Each of these basic methods is capable of infinite variation.

TO CLEAN AND FILLET **To clean** Clean the fish as soon as possible after catching it. Slit the fish open from the tiny hole in the belly to the head. Empty the cavity of all guts and scrape away any dark blood from the backbone. Rinse very well. Using the back of a heavy knife or a proper fish-scaling implement, scrape the scales away working from the tail to the head. Rinse and dry the fish well once cleaned. **Sardines** Slit the belly of each sardine and empty out the contents. Rinse the fish under running water and rub off the scales. Cut off the head and lift out the backbone, which will pull away quite easily. Pat the fish dry. **To fillet** Remove the head and, using a thin, flexible knife, work firmly from the tail, holding the knife parallel to the backbone. Remove the fillet, then turn the fish over and repeat the process.

TO STEAM From an Asian food store, buy a Chinese bamboo steamer basket (and lid) that fits over one of your saucepans. (In fact, buy 2, as they can be stacked on top of one another.) Take the saucepan to the shop to be sure you get the right size. (A bamboo steamer can also be balanced on crossed chopsticks in a wok filled with water.)

The fish can either be steamed on a lightly oiled plate inside the bamboo steamer or on leaves, such as bok choy, lettuce or vine leaves, spread over the base of the steamer. The fish can also be flavoured as you wish and then wrapped in blanched lettuce leaves or oiled aluminium foil. The advantage of steaming fish on a plate or in a foil package is that other ingredients can be included – for example ginger, garlic, light soy sauce and rice wine or lemon zest, bay leaves and vermouth – that form a simple sauce for the steamed fish.

Steaming is quick. A fillet that is 2 cm thick at the thickest part (flathead, for example) will cook in about 5 minutes. A 6 cm thick chunk (such as blue eye) will take 8–10 minutes to steam; a whole small fish (such as bream) will take 10–12 minutes. If any fish is wrapped, it will take a few minutes longer.

hong kong steamed fish

Steam a whole 800 g snapper or other firm-fleshed sea fish for 10 minutes or until cooked. Heat 2 tablespoons vegetable oil until smoking and pour it over the fish to crisp the skin. Serve scattered with sliced spring onion and lots of freshly chopped coriander.

TO BAKE

Whole large fish This method is suited to whole fish, especially large fish that will present dramatically and feed 4–6 people. One of Australia's most popular and most delicious fish is snapper. It is an ideal baking fish. One of my favourites is a large rock flathead, but it is unusual to find a flathead that will serve more than 2–3. Check the fish carefully for any scales. Cut off the fins and trim the tail, if you wish. Using a small sharp knife, scrape away any blood or dark-stained skin in the belly cavity. Rinse the fish under the tap and dry it very well. Rub the cavity with salt and tuck in a generous sprig of a fresh herb and 1–2 sliced garlic cloves and a slice of lemon, or fill the cavity with a savoury stuffing based on rice, breadcrumbs, couscous or cracked wheat.

Select a suitably sized baking dish and pour in a film of olive oil. (Choose a dish that can go to the table from the oven, as lifting a whole baked fish neatly onto a platter is a perilous procedure. If you do not have a suitable dish, lay a doubled strap of foil long enough to protrude from each end of the fish in a baking dish and position the fish on it. With some assistance you should be able to lift the cooked fish onto a serving platter with less risk of accident.) Transfer the fish to the baking dish and, using a sharp knife, slash through the skin twice at the thickest part on either side of the backbone. The slashes should be about 1 cm deep and will ensure that the fish cooks evenly. Rub the fish generously with olive oil and season it with salt and pepper. (Sometimes I put more of the chosen herb in the slits, along with another slice of lemon.) Pour over a glass of white wine.

Bake the fish at 180°C until the flesh exposed by the slashes is no longer translucent. For a snapper to feed 6, that is a fish of about 2.5 kg, the baking time will be 45–60 minutes. For a large flathead of approximately 1 kg, the baking time will be about 25 minutes.

The baking dish can be covered with foil for part of the cooking time. This is more suitable for a larger fish as it will hasten the cooking process and prevent the skin from becoming too hard. Baste the fish with its juices from time to time. Remove the foil for the last 15 minutes, or the fish will not have one of its great attractions – crackling golden skin. All sorts of ingredients can be added to the baking dish to vary this basic method.

Smaller fish, cutlets or fillets An attractive way of baking smaller fish, cutlets or larger fillets is *en papillote*. The fish is encased in

well-oiled or buttered baking paper or aluminium foil and the edges are folded together very tightly. (I find baking paper is trouble-free; even the best-oiled foil still sticks sometimes.) A whole small fish weighing 250 g (such as a rainbow trout) will take 15 minutes at 200°C. A single cutlet or fillet will take 8–10 minutes, depending on its thickness. Vegetables, herbs and other seasonings are often baked with the fish, making each parcel a complete meal. Because the fish cooks so quickly the vegetables must be either already cooked (such as sorrel or spinach), cut into julienne (celery, carrot and leek, for example) or be of a variety that cooks quickly (such as snowpeas). Each guest opens a parcel at the table and breathes in the lovely smells.

TO GRILL Grilling is a very primitive cooking method and therein lies its charm. The fish has to be best quality and there should be no need for fancy sauces.

Grilling is suitable for whole fish, cutlets or thick chunks of fish. It is not suitable for most skinless fillets, unless the fish is cooked on baking paper, and should be avoided with varieties known to have soft skin, such as red snapper. A hinged fish grill, in which the fish is enclosed, is useful when grilling over hot coals. It makes it easy to turn the fish, which is otherwise difficult and certain to result in burnt fingers. A picnic sausage grill makes a good substitute for the fancy imported hinged fish grills, although its bars are too wide apart to make it any use for grilling sardines.

I love grilled fish skin and almost always cook my fish skin-side to the heat source, so that the skin blisters and becomes very crisp. With a chunk of fish, I score the skin once or twice before grilling to prevent it curling.

Prepare the barbecue or preheat a chargrill pan or an overhead griller and line its tray with foil. Ensure that the surface of the fish that will be nearest the heat source is not wet and lightly oil it. (Too much oil will cause flaring on the grill.) The oil can include chopped herbs, very finely sliced chilli or a grinding of fresh pepper. Grill 2–4 minutes a side, depending on the thickness of the fish, basting it once or twice.

TO POACH Poaching is a lovely way of cooking a whole fish, such as salmon. To poach large fish successfully you really need a fish kettle, a rectangular aluminium pot that has a perforated platform on which the fish lies and on which it can be lifted out easily. To poach smaller fish, a conventional baking dish is satisfactory.

The poaching medium can be fresh water, sea water, fish broth or milk, but is most commonly Court-bouillon ✐, which is flavoured before the fish is slipped into it. Fish broth is preferred when the liquid is used again to make a sauce, or when the fish will be served in its broth, for example as a fish soup. There are many ways to make a fish broth, from a rich bouillabaisse to a simple stock ✐ using a few fish bones, vegetables, herbs and water.

fried sardines
Roll cleaned sardines in polenta and shallow-fry in hot olive oil until golden and crunchy. Serve with lemon wedges, Fresh Tomato Sauce (see TOMATOES) *or a plate of fried or battered and fried eggplant.*

grilled fish and ...
Serve a pot of Anchovy Butter (see ANCHOVIES)*, a spoonful of chilli oil, a scattering of chopped Preserved Lemon (see* LEMONS AND LIMES) *or Mayonnaise ✐ with grilled fish, along with boiled potatoes and a green salad.*

To poach a large fish, slip the fish into cold poaching liquid and bring it to a simmer (using cold liquid avoids the outside cooking much faster than the middle). The liquid should just shiver – it *must not* boil or the fish will break up. Small fish can be put directly into warm poaching liquid as they cook more quickly. For every 2.5 cm thickness, allow 10 minutes to achieve thoroughly cooked fish. A fine skewer should slip through the cooked fish with no resistance. If you prefer your salmon 'glassy' on the bone, reduce the cooking time a little. When cooked, remove the fish immediately from the poaching liquid or it will continue to cook. The fish must be drained very well before being served, otherwise liquid that oozes from the fish will spoil any accompanying sauce. It is usual to remove the skin from poached fish after cooking, as it looks rather ragged.

As it is difficult to season any food that is to be cooked in liquid, season the fish *after* cooking and prefer a highly seasoned sauce such as Herbed Mustard Sauce (*see* p. 315). Equally good served warm, poached fish is ideal to serve cold, in which case a thick herb vinaigrette or a herb mayonnaise can be spread or spooned over the fish on its serving platter.

horseradish butter sauce

Make a lovely sauce for a delicately flavoured pan-fried fish by mixing freshly grated horseradish with warm melted butter and salt and pepper.

baked salmon and witlof

Toss chunks of witlof in melted butter and scatter the chunks around a slice of raw salmon on a sheet of buttered foil or baking paper. Fold up the parcel and steam for 5 minutes or bake at 200°C for 8 minutes. Serve with a squeeze of lemon, a garnish of parsley and boiled potatoes.

TO DEEP-FRY

Fish and chips is still a great favourite and if the fish is fresh, the batter delicate and crunchy and the chips not greasy it is deservedly popular. Deep-frying is suitable for fillets that are not very thick. My favourite variety to deep-fry is garfish, followed by King George whiting, followed by tail fillets of rock flathead. The oil used, as for all deep-frying, must be clean and heated to 175°C and there should be plenty of it. Dip pieces of fish into Beer Batter ✓ and cook until golden, submerging the fish with tongs to ensure even cooking. Do not overcrowd the pan. Drain the fish on crumpled kitchen paper and serve at once.

I have never appreciated the idea of vinegar sprinkled on either fried fish or chips – is it a substitute for a squeeze of lemon, I wonder? I like Tartare Sauce ✓ with my fried fish, and as I get older and find rich food harder to digest I prefer to enjoy fried fish as a morsel or starter before dinner than as the main attraction.

TO PAN-FRY

Pan-frying is an exquisite method of cooking the most exquisite fish. Fillets of garfish or King George whiting cooked in butter with a squeeze of lemon, a generous strewing of mixed parsley, chives and tarragon is luxury comfort food. Don't spoil its special quality by piling vegetables onto the plate. Serve them beforehand or afterwards.

It is important to have a good frying pan, ideally a non-stick pan reserved for frying fish, and hot serving plates. Use the best-quality butter, preferably clarified ✓ or else mixed with olive oil to raise its burning point.

Heat the butter quickly, then add the fish and reduce the heat to moderate. Turn thin fillets (garfish) almost immediately. Whiting takes 2–3 minutes a side, while thicker fillets may take 4 minutes a side. Very thick chunks of tuna or salmon, for example, are often sealed at high heat and served rare or medium, like a steak.

TO CRUMB | Fish fillets are often crumbed before being pan-fried or deep-fried. Mix together in a shallow bowl an egg, salt, freshly ground black pepper and 1 teaspoon oil. Have ready a plate of flour and another of fresh breadcrumbs. Dust the fillet with flour, shake off any excess, dip into the egg and then into the crumbs. Shake off the extra crumbs. Deep-fry or pan-fry until golden brown, drain on kitchen paper and serve.

herbed mustard sauce

MAKES 1 CUP

120 g unsalted butter

2 tablespoons Dijon mustard

4 egg yolks

3 teaspoons wine vinegar

salt

freshly ground black pepper

2 tablespoons freshly chopped parsley

2 teaspoons freshly chopped chives

2 teaspoons freshly chopped tarragon

Melt butter gently and allow to cool. In a bowl, work mustard into egg yolks as if making Mayonnaise. Add vinegar, seasonings and herbs to bowl. Gradually beat in cooled melted butter. Use within an hour or butter will start to set. This sauce is lovely with poached fish.

simple horseradish sauce

MAKES ½ CUP

This sauce is ideally suited to poached fish and keeps for a week. A good commercially produced creamed horseradish is fine to use; if you have fresh horseradish, grate it and mix it with whipped cream and a little white-wine vinegar.

1 tablespoon creamed horseradish

2 teaspoons dill seeds

2 tablespoons finely chopped fresh dill leaves

120 ml sour cream

Stir all ingredients together and refrigerate until required.

fish with anchovy paste

Chop an anchovy with a clove of garlic and 1 teaspoon butter. Heat a non-stick frying pan for 3 minutes, then paint it with olive oil and drop in a very thin slice of firm-textured fish (tuna or marlin, for example). Count to 10, turn the fish over and count to 10 again. Spread the anchovy paste on the fish and eat with boiled potatoes or salad.

simple coconut-milk fish curry

SERVES 4

4 stalks lemongrass, outer
    leaves removed
8 spring onions, outer leaves
    removed
6 cloves garlic
750 g fish chunks (each piece
    weighing about 50 g)
4 small fresh chillies, seeded
    and finely sliced
3 cups coconut milk
4 kaffir lime leaves
fish sauce

Cut pale part of lemongrass into 5 mm pieces and discard rest. Pound lemongrass with a meat mallet to flatten and crush fibres. Cut spring onions into 1 cm slices. Crush garlic in a mortar or chop very finely. Place fish, spring onion, lemongrass, chilli and garlic in a saucepan with coconut milk. Simmer very gently, uncovered, for 10–15 minutes until cooked. Add lime leaves, then fish sauce to taste. Serve with fragrant rice.

polynesian raw fish salad

SERVES 4

This salad is served very cold and relies on lime juice to 'cook' the fish. Once dressed, the salad can be returned to the refrigerator for up to an hour to chill thoroughly. Make it with any fish with a fillet at least 1 cm thick.

juice of 3 limes *or* 2 lemons
500 g fish, skinned and cut
    into bite-sized pieces
100 ml thick coconut milk
    or coconut cream
salt
freshly ground black pepper
    or 1 fresh chilli, seeded and
    finely sliced
2 ripe tomatoes, finely diced
2 spring onions, very finely
    sliced

Pour lime juice over fish in a non-reactive bowl and refrigerate for 1–2 hours. Lift fish out of juice with a slotted spoon, drain in a strainer over a bowl and transfer to another bowl. Discard juice. Stir coconut milk into fish and season to taste. Pile fish in a mound on a serving plate, surround with tomato and scatter over spring onion. Serve very cold.

fish balls

I remember my mother turning the excess flathead brought home by my father and brothers from fishing trips into fish balls. I don't think she added the coriander leaves or fish sauce that you find in the popular Thai fish cakes but she probably added herbs from her extensive garden. This 'recipe' is very flexible – add whatever quantities you like of whatever seasonings you have on hand. To make 20 bite-sized balls, you'll need 250 g fish.

baked stuffed salmon
Stuff a whole Tasmanian Atlantic salmon with breadcrumbs or cracked wheat, lemon zest, lemon juice, parsley and toasted pine nuts mixed with an egg, then wrap it in foil and bake for about 45 minutes until medium–rare.

salmon cutlets
Pan-fry a cutlet or fillet of Tasmanian Atlantic salmon in the merest trace of oil and serve with stewed sweet peppers, olives, tomatoes and Caramelised Onions (see ONIONS).

salmon carpaccio
Serve Tasmanian Atlantic salmon raw with a dressing of olive oil, chives and a squeeze of lime.

fish scraps, skinned

fresh coriander leaves and
   stalks

garlic

fresh basil leaves

chilli paste

fish sauce

coconut milk

fresh ginger

soy sauce

rice wine

spring onions

Purée fish scraps in a food processor. Add flavourings and blend to a smooth paste. Dip a teaspoon into hot water and then scoop out a fish ball. Continue until all balls are formed. Shallow-fry or deep-fry fish balls in hot oil or poach them in fish broth or steam them. Serve with drinks, toss with noodles or settle among a platter of stir-fried vegetables.

middle eastern Use parsley, ground coriander and cumin, paprika and lemon juice instead of Asian flavourings.

sugar-coated grilled rock ling SERVES 4

This recipe is best for boneless fish that is not very thick.

8 x 80 g pieces rock ling

2 teaspoons sea salt

juice of 2 limes *or* 1 small
   lemon

8 tablespoons brown sugar

zest of 1 lime *or* lemon

Rub fish with salt and lime juice. Refrigerate for 1–2 hours. Dry very well. Light barbecue or preheat an overhead griller or a non-stick frying pan. Rub each piece of fish with 1 tablespoon sugar and a little zest and grill, turning once. Serve with Thai-style Dipping Sauce (*see* YABBIES).

pan-fried fish with browned
butter sauce SERVES 1

Garnishing pan-fried fillets of fish with browned butter is absolutely delicious but the timing is tricky. The last-minute cooking and garnishing is great if it works. It does require a bit of experience to deal with it speedily, so that the sauce doesn't burn and the fish doesn't become lukewarm. This dish is an ideal treat for the single diner.

1 fillet fish

walnut-sized piece of butter

juice of ½ lemon

a few capers

few tiny segments lemon,
   peeled

finely chopped fresh parsley

Pan-fry fish and slip onto a hot dish. Wipe pan quickly, add butter and cook until light brown. Add lemon juice to butter to halt cooking, then add capers, lemon and parsley and pour over fillet – still piping-hot, we hope. Serve immediately.

simple browned butter sauces
Cook unsalted butter (best quality) until

bbq sardines
Wrap cleaned sardines in oiled grapevine leaves and secure with a toothpick. Grill over coals for 4 minutes until the leaves are well charred. Drizzle with a squeeze of lemon and olive oil.

asian bream
Steam a small bream topped with chopped spring onion, freshly sliced ginger, a sliced garlic clove, 3 tablespoons light soy sauce and 2 tablespoons dry sherry for 10–15 minutes and eat with boiled rice.

fish mayonnaise
Tease leftover baked fish from the bones, toss lightly with Mayonnaise and serve with a green salad.

golden brown and nutty-smelling ('noisette butter'). Add a dash of lemon juice and some freshly chopped parsley to make *beurre meunière*.

blue eye cutlets with cumin

SERVES 4

1 tablespoon cumin seeds, roasted and ground

1 tablespoon very finely chopped garlic

3 tablespoons freshly chopped parsley

½ teaspoon salt

1 tablespoon olive oil

4 thick blue eye cutlets *or* chunks

Combine cumin, garlic, parsley, salt and oil in a bowl. Dry fish pieces and roll very thoroughly in cumin mixture, coating well. Grill, turning once. Serve with a salad of black olives, orange slices and very fresh and tender watercress or other greens.

other recipes

carpaccio of salmon with fines herbes *see* CHERVIL

chilli and lime sauce *see* PEPPERS AND CHILLIES

crabby soup *see* CRABS

fennel and tomato fish soup *see* FENNEL

fennel-marinated fish *see* FENNEL

flathead poached with milk and tarragon *see* TARRAGON

gravlax *see* DILL

herring fillets with potatoes and dill *see* DILL

hot spicy fish *see* CORIANDER

macadamia fish curry *see* NUTS

mexican ceviche *see* LEMONS AND LIMES

north african ginger marinade for fish *see* GINGER

padang sour–sharp fish *see* TROPICAL FRUIT

sardines in vine leaves *see* GRAPES AND VINE LEAVES

saltfish and avocado *see* AVOCADOS

thai steamed fish with coriander root, chilli and lime juice
  see CORIANDER

tuna grilled with rosemary *see* ROSEMARY

garlic

g*a r l i c* With the increasing interest in good food, the proliferation of recipes that include garlic and the everyday sight of garlic hanging in greengrocers' shops and supermarkets, I believe that this wonderful herb has finally overcome most of the prejudices once directed at it. (There are still some, however, who perceive garlic as 'exotic' and who are nervous about having it on the breath.) │ Newcomers to garlic need to know that it can be used very subtly and should not overpower. They will also be delighted to discover how mellow and sweet gently cooked whole cloves of garlic are. │ Garlic (*Allium sativum*) is a member of the lily family, along with leeks, onions, chives and shallots. Its head, made up of 12–15 cloves, grows underground. Each clove is encased in a thin, papery skin; the whole head is wrapped in several more layers of thicker skin. The clove itself encases the bud or germ. The green shoots that appear above the ground are also edible and this spring garlic (lifted before the bulbs are mature) is eagerly awaited in Greece and other garlic-loving countries. Recently Australian shoppers have also been able to buy this green garlic, sold as garlic shoots and resembling firm leeks. >

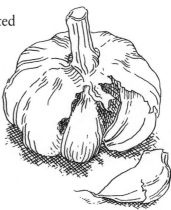

Garlic has been grown since before recorded history and probably originated in central Asia. It was important in the culinary, medicinal and religious practices of many ancient civilisations, and is said to have been fed to the Egyptian slaves building the pyramids to promote strength. There are an astonishing number of myths and beliefs concerning garlic, ranging from its ability to ward off vampires to its use as a folk remedy for high blood pressure and for fighting diseases from the common cold to cancer. Modern medical research does not discount the value of garlic.

However, my interest in garlic is how it is used in the kitchen. The flavour of garlic depends on how it is prepared. It can be used raw or fried, poached, roasted or sautéd and can be cooked peeled or unpeeled. Whole poached or roasted cloves of garlic are sweetest and mildest of all.

It is only when you cut into garlic that its distinctive smell emerges. This is because when the cell walls are damaged a powerful sulphur compound is released. The more the clove is cut, the stronger the smell! Heating destroys the compound, which is why cooked garlic is so much milder.

VARIETIES AND SEASON

There are several varieties of garlic, and they vary in size and skin colour. Australian-grown garlic tends to be the Italian type, which has pinkish skin and smallish cloves. We import a large amount of garlic from California, China and Argentina. There is also a monster variety known as elephant garlic that I have only seen for sale a few times. It is much milder.

Garlic is harvested in the late spring to midsummer when the green leaves have died down, and needs to be dried thoroughly before being stored or sold. Dried garlic is available all year round. Garlic shoots are available from midwinter to spring.

SELECTION AND STORAGE

Freshly harvested garlic, damp and crunchy, is a special treat and usually only available to home gardeners. This garlic is juicy and mild in flavour. Full pungency only develops after drying. Garlic must be dried right through to the centre, otherwise it will become mouldy.

Choose a head of dried garlic that is firm and hard without soft or discoloured patches. (Soft and discoloured garlic tastes rancid and will spoil any dish to which it is added.) Larger heads with larger cloves are less tedious to peel but have no other advantage.

Garlic should be stored in a cool, dry place where air can circulate around it. Do not refrigerate garlic as the cold, wet air will encourage mould. Do not use garlic that is visibly sprouting, and remove the indigestible green germ from the centre of each clove if the garlic is to be eaten raw. Dried garlic keeps well for several months.

PREPARATION AND COOKING

TO SEPARATE A HEAD | Place the head of garlic on your bench and bang it firmly with a heavy frying pan.

TO PEEL A CLOVE | **For chopping finely** Place the clove on a bench, flattest-side down, and thump it with the flat side of a large knife, the force coming from the fist of your other hand held steady on the top of the knife. Lift the papery skin away. (Some cooks use a garlic press to achieve the same result. I find it fiddly gouging inside the mechanism for the inevitable portion of garlic that has not been squashed through the holes.) **To be used whole** Using a small paring knife, cut away the nub at the base of the clove and peel off the skin. Alternatively, drop the clove into a saucepan of cold water, slowly bring it to simmering point, then run the garlic under cold water and peel away the skin. (The second method will cook the garlic slightly.)

TO CHOP FINELY | After peeling, sprinkle the smashed garlic with a tiny pinch of salt, which will stop the pieces flying from the bench, and chop with an up-and-down movement achieved by holding the tip of your knife firmly on the bench with one hand and moving the blade across the pile of garlic to be chopped with the other. A professional chef will also smear finely chopped garlic across the surface with the flat of the knife to achieve a super-fine garlic paste.

TO ROAST A HEAD | Remove any extra layers of papery skin. Slice the top off the entire head to expose the cloves as if you were beheading a boiled egg. Oil the garlic and bake in a moderate oven at 180°C for about 45 minutes until quite soft. The oiled head can also be wrapped and roasted in oiled aluminium foil.

TO BLANCH AND PURÉE | A cream and garlic purée is best for incorporating into well-seasoned mashed potato, while a garlic purée made with stock or meat juices makes a beautiful sauce. A purée made from sieved, cooked garlic can be spooned into a small jar, sealed with a layer of good olive oil and be kept refrigerated for a week and used to flavour all sorts of dishes.

Place unpeeled garlic cloves in a saucepan of cold water and bring slowly to simmering point. Pour off the water and repeat the process twice more. The blanched garlic cloves will slip easily from their skins and are ready to be simmered in cream, meat juices or stock until quite soft, and then puréed, or cooked in water until soft and then pressed through a fine sieve.

garlic in stews
Get into the habit of adding sliced or whole peeled garlic cloves to stews where they melt slowly into the juices and add a wonderful flavour.

TO FRY | Many French chefs will advise never to fry sliced garlic. They have obviously never watched a Chinese or Thai cook 'poaching' very thinly sliced garlic cut lengthwise from the clove in warm–hot vegetable oil until golden and absolutely crisp. These garlic wafers are a very popular garnish on Asian salads.

Garlic fried too hot or for too long, so that it becomes black, is horribly bitter and inedible. It will ruin any dish to which it is added. Throw it out and start again.

TO FLAVOUR A ROAST | Cut slivers from a peeled clove. Stick the knife point into the meat, and insert the slivers. Alternatively, tuck several unpeeled garlic cloves underneath the meat in the baking dish and maybe squash them into the juices at the end. You can also add a spoonful of garlic purée to the roasting juices whether flavouring the meat with slivered or whole cloves.

TO FLAVOUR STOCK | I use whole heads of garlic sliced crosswise to flavour all the long-simmered meat stocks I make in the restaurant. At home I add 3–4 cloves of unpeeled garlic cut crosswise with the rest of the vegetables.

recipes

aïoli

SERVES 6

garlic purée and ...
Spread garlic purée on toast for a great sandwich or to use as a crouton underneath a roast chicken or toss it through steamed vegetables or stir it into pan juices to thicken them slightly.

Raw garlic is crushed and pounded to make 2 magnificent sauces – pesto (see BASIL*) and aïoli, the superb garlicky mayonnaise eaten in the south of France with a selection of hot and cold boiled vegetables, fish and snails.*

The name aïoli refers to both the sauce and a meal. Le grand aïoli can be very grand indeed, with more than a dozen components, while aïoli can also be deliciously humble. With hot boiled potatoes, carrots and green beans and cold tomatoes, hardboiled eggs and celery, an aïoli lunch will still be a feast. Le grand aïoli would also include poached chicken, flaked, cooked salt cod, artichoke hearts or cardoons and so on.

12 cloves garlic
pinch of salt
4 egg yolks
3 cups olive oil
juice of ½ lemon

Grind garlic in a mortar with salt to form a pulp. Transfer garlic to a large bowl and work in egg yolks using the pestle. Start adding oil very gradually, a few drops at a time, building the sauce bit by bit as for Mayonnaise ✐. It will become very thick.

Towards the end, add lemon juice and taste for salt. (The aïoli will taste powerfully of garlic, but remember that one eats just a little with each bite of potato, bean or whatever.) >

As with all mayonnaise sauces, if it should curdle place an extra egg yolk into a clean bowl and slowly work in the failed sauce a little at a time. The sauce should reconstitute perfectly.

garlic butter

MAKES I CUP

Garlic butter has many uses other than as a spread for toast or bread. The butter is traditionally used to pack into snail shells. It can be spread on top of opened mussels or pipis or a thin fillet of fish before they are grilled. It can be spooned into hot pasta, and, without the breadcrumbs, can slide over a minute steak or chicken breast.

10 cloves garlic, peeled
200 g unsalted butter
2 tablespoons finely chopped
  parsley
2 tablespoons fresh
  breadcrumbs
I teaspoon green Chartreuse,
  Pernod *or* sambucca
salt
freshly ground black pepper
few drops of lemon juice
dash of Tabasco

Roughly chop garlic. In a food processor, cream butter with garlic until quite smooth. Transfer mixture to a bowl and beat in remaining ingredients. Spoon into a pot for immediate use, or roll in baking paper and then in foil and freeze. (Frozen garlic is best used within a couple of weeks or it can taste stale.)

garlic bread
Cut slashes in a breadstick and spread each side of the slash with Garlic Butter (see p. 323, but omit the breadcrumbs from the recipe). Wrap loosely in foil and bake at 180°C for 20 minutes. Leave the foil parcel open at the top so the bread is crisp, not flabby.

garlic olives
Marinate brine-packed olives in extra-virgin olive oil with thinly sliced garlic, freshly sliced chilli and some herbs for as little as an hour (a day would be better).

persian sugar-pickled garlic

This pickled garlic improves with age – for as long as 15 years! The recipe is based on one in Janet Hazen's delightful book Garlic. *Margaret Shaida in* The Legendary Cuisine of Persia *tells us that Persian vinegar can be made from dates. In view of this, I have used cider vinegar here rather than wine vinegar for a milder pickle. Enjoy pickled garlic with cold meat or as part of an antipasto platter, or chop it into vegetable or grain salads.*

4 heads garlic, cloves
  separated
2 cups cider vinegar
2 cups water
I cup sugar
6 cloves (the spice, not
  more garlic)
2 tablespoons black
  peppercorns

Place all ingredients in a large, heavy-based saucepan. Bring to a boil over high heat and cook for 10 minutes, stirring from time to time. Reduce heat to moderate and cook for 5 minutes. Remove from heat and cool to room temperature. Transfer to a hot, sterilised glass jar large enough to take all the garlic and liquid. Seal and refrigerate for at least a month before serving.

garlic and potato
Bake unpeeled garlic cloves with chunks of oiled potato scattered with sprigs of rosemary.

melita's skordalia

SERVES 6

This recipe dates from a magical week I spent on the island of Ithaca with my friend Melita, as recorded in Stephanie's Feasts and Stories. *'Melita . . . returned triumphant with a basket of* kritama *[rock samphire] picked from the water's edge. We ate some of these "weeds" (as she called them) at lunch as a salad, and the rest that evening, lightly boiled and accompanied by the Ithacan version of skordalia, a cold garlic and potato sauce.'*

Try this sauce with fish, either salted, grilled or poached, adding a little fish juice for extra flavour, or with raw or cooked vegetables.

4 cloves garlic *or more*
    to taste
pinch of salt
3 potatoes, washed
1 cup olive oil
juice of 1 lemon
¼–½ cup milk
salt
freshly ground black pepper

Crush garlic and salt in a mortar until dissolved into a creamy paste. Boil potatoes, then peel and mash them. Combine potato with creamed garlic in mortar (or pass through a food mill), then add oil and lemon juice alternately. Adjust consistency with milk, a few drops at a time. (It should be like a thick mayonnaise.) Taste for seasoning. Eat within 2 days.

garlic and saffron soup

SERVES 6

This soup, based on a recipe from Deborah Madison in The Savory Way, *is delicate, restorative in flavour and beautiful to look at. You can also cook some fine soup pasta separately in lightly salted water, then drain it and add it to the broth.*

10 large cloves garlic, peeled
2 litres Chicken Stock ✎
1 bay leaf
4–5 stalks parsley
2–3 large sprigs tarragon
2–3 sprigs thyme
2 cloves (the spice, not
    more garlic)
1 tablespoon extra-virgin
    olive oil
pinch of saffron threads
salt
freshly grated parmesan
    cheese
freshly chopped parsley

Put all ingredients except the parmesan and parsley into a stockpot and slowly bring to simmering point. Cover pot and simmer gently for 30 minutes until garlic is absolutely soft. Turn off heat and allow to stand for 15 minutes. Strain soup and adjust seasoning.

Bring soup back to a boil in rinsed-out pot and serve. Offer bowls of parmesan and chopped parsley.

---

garlic spread

Store roasted heads of garlic in olive oil in the refrigerator and use the soft, sweet garlic pulp as a spread or ingredient. The garlicky oil is delicious as well.

garlic croutons

Wipe a cut garlic clove across a slice of grilled or baked bread and serve with fish soup or grilled tomatoes or top with freshly sliced tomato. Use thinly sliced breadstick painted with oil and make croutons the same way for serving with soups or salads.

bourride

Whisk Aïoli (see p. 322) into the liquid used to poach fish to create a creamy sauce. Serve garlic-swiped croutons alongside.

garlic and goat's cheese custards

MAKES 6

12 cloves garlic, blanched
300 ml milk
1 bay leaf
1 sprig thyme
100 g soft fresh goat's cheese
1 egg
2 egg yolks
salt
freshly ground black pepper
150 ml cream

Preheat oven to 160°C and butter 6 × 150 ml soufflé dishes.

Simmer blanched garlic in milk with bay leaf and thyme until quite soft. Strain and discard herbs. Purée garlic with cheese and half the milk in a food processor. Lightly beat egg, egg yolks, seasonings, cream and remaining milk together and stir into garlic purée. Pour into prepared soufflé dishes. Stand custards in a baking dish lined with a tea towel and pour in hot water to come halfway up their sides. Bake for 25 minutes until just set. Serve warm with garlic-swiped croutons on the side.

tiny custards Tiny custards (60 ml) are a delightful garnish for roasted lamb.

roasted garlic
Serve a roasted head of garlic with a chunk of fresh goat's cheese and oiled chunks of wonderful tomatoes as an easy and fantastic luncheon dish.

other recipes

garlic and ginger dipping sauce *see* YABBIES

garlic prawns *see* PRAWNS

harissa *see* PEPPERS AND CHILLIES

lamb and garlic jus *see* LAMB

oysters with garlic butter *see* OYSTERS

parsley and garlic cream sauce *see* PARSLEY

pesto *see* BASIL

pine forest mushrooms with garlic, cream and parsley *see* MUSHROOMS

poached eggs with yoghurt and garlic sauce *see* YOGHURT

roasted leg of lamb with rosemary and garlic and all the trimmings
   see LAMB

rosemary and garlic butter *see* ROSEMARY

rosemary 'pesto' *see* ROSEMARY

scallops on the half-shell with garlic *see* SCALLOPS

slow-roasted loin of pork with garlic, rosemary and fennel *see* PORK

tzatziki *see* YOGHURT

g i n g e r   Usually described as a root, ginger (*Zingiber officinale*) is in fact a tuberous rhizome, as are its near relations turmeric and galangal. It is presumed to be a native of tropical Asia and was one of the first oriental spices known to Europe, becoming central to the spice trade. | In many Asian countries the medicinal or health-giving properties of ginger are inextricably linked with its use as an ingredient. A woman who has given birth in southern China, for example, is fed Chinese-style Trotters with Ginger and Black Rice Vinegar (*see* TROTTERS), a rich dish that includes an enormous amount of ginger. It is believed that this dish will prevent the woman catching a chill, assist her reproductive cycle to return to normal and also aid her digestion. The dish is also delicious, unlike much Western medicine! (I am indebted for this insight and for much more information regarding ginger to Bruce Cost's remarkable book, *Ginger East to West*.) >

The use of ginger in cooking and as medicine is very widespread. I find its unique combination of hot, clean and cool flavours quite irresistible. One cannot even contemplate the cooking of China, South-East Asia or Japan without ginger. It is also central to Indian cooking and important in its ground form in the Middle East and North Africa. Medieval Europe relied heavily on spice – ginger was often used to disguise the taste of rank meat, and is still used to diffuse fish, meat and shellfish odours – and the word 'spice' was often used to mean ginger. European interest in ground ginger lingers on in popular sweet dishes such as gingerbread. Ginger was introduced by the Spanish and Portuguese to their colonies, so that it also became important in the cookery of Africa, the West Indies and South America.

Ginger can be sliced, chopped, grated, juiced or minced, or mashed to a paste with other spices. It can also be dried, ground and rubbed into fish and meat; it is a vital ingredient in the pickles, sauces, relishes and chutneys of several cultures; it is used as a drink, as a spice in puddings, cakes and custards; and it is eaten as a sweetmeat when preserved in syrup.

Many of us have ornamental ginger plants that scent the garden exquisitely at evening time, as they do in Singapore, where scrupulously manicured roads are lined with stands of flaming ginger flowers. These plants (*Hedychium* species) belong to the same family as ginger but are not eaten. (However, I have a Laotian recipe where petals of the ginger flower are chopped with pork and shrimps, wrapped in banana leaves and grilled.)

Australia is one of the world's most important ginger producers. Almost all the crop is grown on cooperative farms near Buderim on Queensland's Sunshine Coast. The ginger showroom at Buderim, with its astounding range of ginger-based products, is a most successful tourist attraction.

VARIETIES AND SEASON

Ginger is harvested twice a year and is available all year round. The first harvest, in February, is when the ginger is immature and tender without a protective skin, just like early potatoes. This crop is pale gold, each 'hand' having pink fingertips. The ginger is very crisp, but has a less developed flavour. The second crop, harvested May–August, produces ginger with tougher skin. This ginger has more fibre than the immature variety. The flavour is much more pronounced and is hotter. The size of the hands and the colour of the skin in the mature crop relate to locality rather than being indicative of the quality of the ginger.

Other members of the Zingiberaceae family are favoured for their culinary usefulness, too. The Japanese pickle the spring shoots of *Z. mioga*, which they dye red and refer to as 'blushing ginger'. Australia has a native ginger (*Alpinia caerulea*); however, its gingery taste comes not from a rhizome but the seeds of its blue fruit, once eaten by Aborigines.

fresh ginger goes with
garlic
spring onions
rice vinegar
soy sauce
coriander leaves
mushrooms
fish
pork
chicken
beef
crabs
shellfish
rice wine
green beans
Chinese greens
eggplants
limes
turmeric
cumin
chillies
lemongrass
onions
coconut milk
tamarind
fish sauce
mint
basil
yoghurt

ground
ginger
goes
with
nutmeg
raisins
honey
cinnamon
almonds
cloves
treacle
brown sugar
aniseed

roast ginger
chicken
Stuff thin slices of
fresh ginger into the
cavity of a chicken,
rub the skin with
ginger or ginger
juice and then roast.

moroccan lamb
Roll lamb shanks in
ground ginger before
simmering them in
stock scented with
a cinnamon stick.
Serve with diced
Preserved Lemon
(see LEMONS AND
LIMES) *and couscous*
for an echo of
North Africa.

SELECTION AND STORAGE

Years ago, when ginger was hard to find, it was customary to store it sliced in sherry. Today ginger has become a standard item in all greengrocers, so no longer does one need to make do with withered specimens or go to great lengths to preserve it.

When buying ginger, ensure that the rhizome is fresh looking and very firm and crisp. Choose first-crop or immature ginger for preserving in syrup, candying or cooking in small chunks as a vegetable. The older the ginger the more fibrous and the hotter it will be. (Fibrous ginger is not suited to fine slicing but it can be grated.) Ginger should not look dark and wrinkled, regardless of its maturity. Nor should it bend!

Store fresh ginger in the refrigerator crisper for a week or two, especially in humid climates where cut ginger becomes mouldy quickly. (A Chinese friend tells me that she keeps ginger in a tightly closed jar in her refrigerator and that it is perfect after a month.)

Ground ginger is made from dried ginger and is available in all supermarkets. Store it in an airtight container.

PREPARATION

Ginger should be peeled unless you are adding slices to stock or plan to discard it before serving.

TO PEEL AND CHOP Cut off any knobs and peel them separately with a vegetable peeler or a small knife. Peel the main stalk. Slice the ginger across the fibres. Stack the slices and then slice into strips as finely as you want. Turn the stack at right angles and cut again if you want finely chopped ginger. A food processor is helpful for chopping a lot of ginger. The ginger should be sliced evenly before it is processed. **Paste** Once chopped, ginger can be ground to a paste in a food processor, or with other ingredients in a mortar.

TO GRATE Asian food stores sell useful plastic, bamboo or pottery ginger graters that look like miniature old-fashioned washboards – *oroshigane* in Japanese. If you make a lot of dipping sauces that include ginger, buy one of these gadgets.

TO EXTRACT ESSENCE OR JUICE **Essence** Pour enough boiling water to just cover washed ginger peelings and leave it to steep until quite cold. Squeeze the peel in a clean cloth or doubled piece of muslin and use the ginger juice to add heat to a clear broth. **Juice** If you need a few drops of ginger juice, press finely chopped ginger through a garlic press or squeeze it in a clean cloth.

simple ginger marinade for rump steak SERVES 4

1 × 800 g thick slice rump
    steak
2 bundles bok choy, washed
MARINADE
4 cm knob fresh ginger,
    peeled and finely chopped
2 cloves garlic, finely chopped
2 tablespoons vegetable oil
2 tablespoons soy sauce

Mix all ingredients for marinade together in a shallow dish and turn steak in it. Leave for 1–3 hours.

Grill steak over hot coals or under a very hot griller for 4 minutes each side. Transfer to a warm plate and pour over the rest of the marinade.

Stir-fry bok choy leaves in a wok. Slice steak diagonally and serve on top of bok choy. Spoon over remaining juices.

ginger soup
Add ginger juice to a clear chicken broth with some finely chopped spring onions.

north african ginger marinade for fish SERVES 6

2 teaspoons toasted cumin
    seeds
1 bunch coriander, washed
    and roughly chopped
1 fresh chilli
4 cloves garlic, peeled and
    crushed
4 thick slices fresh ginger,
    peeled
juice of 1 lemon
2 tablespoons water
1 tablespoon paprika
2 slices fresh turmeric *or*
    2 teaspoons ground
    turmeric
2 teaspoons salt
½ cup olive oil
1 × 2 kg snapper, cleaned

Combine all ingredients except fish in a food processor and blend to a paste. Score both sides of fish diagonally and rub paste in well. Leave for 1 hour.

Preheat oven to 180°C. Bake fish for 45–60 minutes until flesh exposed by slashes is opaque. (More trickily, barbecue fish in a hinged grill. Do not attempt to place fish directly on barbecue grill as the marinade is inclined to stick.)

fish with ginger
Strew a generous julienne of fresh ginger and spring onion and 1 teaspoon finely chopped garlic over a whole fish or a chunky fillet, pour over light soy sauce and a little rice wine, mirin or sherry and steam.

scallops with ginger
Spoon warm light soy sauce over roasted scallops on the half-shell and garnish with deep-fried shreds of ginger, leek and carrot or very finely chopped fresh ginger.

pickled ginger

As well as being offered with sushi and sashimi in Japanese restaurants, this pickle is served with salted preserved duck eggs in Hong Kong, and I sometimes serve it with a grilled sliced duck breast that has been seasoned with ginger juice before grilling. It keeps for months in the refrigerator.

250 g young, fibre-free fresh
ginger, peeled and cut into
even pieces
2 teaspoons salt
1 cup white rice vinegar
100 ml water
3 tablespoons sugar

Sprinkle ginger with salt and leave for 24 hours. Mix vinegar, water and sugar in a bowl and leave until sugar has dissolved. Lift ginger from salt and place in marinade. Refrigerate for at least 1 week before using. Cut into paper-thin slices across the grain to serve.

prawns with ginger, spring onion and tomato
SERVES 4

Fingerbowls or hot, damp cloths are a necessity for this dish (Chinese cotton facewashers are ideal).

20 prawns in the shell
3 tablespoons vegetable oil
1 tablespoon freshly chopped
ginger
2 cloves garlic, finely chopped
2 tablespoons chopped spring
onions (including green
tops)
2 teaspoons brown sugar
½ teaspoon sambal oelek
1 cup fresh tomato purée

Pull heads from prawns and discard. Slit shell of each prawn along outer curve and discard intestinal vein.

Heat 2 tablespoons of the oil in a wok or cast-iron frying pan until very hot. Sear prawns until shells are bright red on each side. (This will take less than 1 minute a side.) Remove prawns to a hot plate and wipe out wok. Heat remaining oil and sear ginger, garlic and spring onion for 1 minute. Add sugar and sambal oelek and stir, then add tomato purée. Bubble all together and replace prawns. Cook over high heat for 2–3 minutes, then serve with rice or a platter of green vegetables, or quickly tossed baby spinach leaves.

ginger mousse
SERVES 4

4 tablespoons milk
300 ml cream
4 egg yolks
75 g castor sugar
2 tablespoons very finely
chopped fresh ginger
4 tablespoons white rum
2 gelatine leaves
2 tablespoons boiling water
ice
3 egg whites
extra 30 g castor sugar

Cut strips of baking paper long enough to make collars that stand 6 cm above the rim of 4 × 150 ml soufflé dishes and fasten with elastic bands.

Bring milk and cream to scalding point. Whisk together egg yolks and 75 g castor sugar. Add ginger and rum to egg mixture and pour on hot milk and cream. Return to rinsed-out saucepan and cook over a moderate heat, stirring, until custard thickly coats back of a wooden spoon. Pour most of custard through a strainer resting over a

---

sashimi
Serve wasabi paste, Pickled Ginger (see p. 329) and slices of spanking-fresh raw fish alongside a saucer of light soy sauce with a little finely chopped fresh ginger in it.

ginger yoghurt
Stir 2 tablespoons finely chopped fresh ginger, 2 seeded and chopped fresh chillies, 2 tablespoons finely chopped fresh coriander leaves, 1 tablespoon finely chopped fresh mint leaves and 1 tablespoon lemon juice into a cup of thick yoghurt and serve with a curry.

bowl, leaving a little liquid and ginger behind. Purée this and add to custard.

Soak gelatine leaves in cold water for a few minutes. Squeeze and drop into the boiling water, then swish to dissolve completely and stir into cooling custard. Stir custard occasionally until cold, then strain once more. Stand bowl in a larger bowl filled with ice until custard starts to set.

Whip egg whites to form snowy peaks. Gradually beat in 30 g castor sugar to make a glossy meringue, then fold into custard. Spoon into prepared moulds and refrigerate.

To serve, peel paper collars away from mousse and press chopped nuts or sliced glacé ginger on the sides, if you wish. I use chopped Australian pistachios, which are gloriously green.

gingerbread

This is one of those dark, fudgy gingerbread cakes, not the chewy sort used for making gingerbread men or houses. I like a square of gingerbread with Banana Ice-cream (see BANANAS).

125 g softened unsalted butter

½ cup dark brown sugar

1 cup treacle *or* molasses

3 eggs

450 g plain flour

1 teaspoon bicarbonate of soda

2 tablespoons ground ginger

1½ teaspoons ground cinnamon

1 teaspoon ground nutmeg

¾ cup buttermilk

4 tablespoons fresh orange juice

Preheat oven to 180°C. Grease a 4 cm deep 30 cm × 22 cm tin and line it with baking paper. Cream butter and sugar in a large bowl. Stir in treacle, then beat in eggs, one at a time. Sift flour with bicarbonate of soda and spices and set aside. Combine buttermilk and orange juice. Beat flour and buttermilk alternately into creamed mixture, a third at a time, finishing with flour. Pour into prepared tin and bake for 50 minutes or until cake tests clean. Cool on a wire rack before turning out. Serve with whipped cream, poached fruit or ice-cream.

asian ginger sauce
Combine 2 tablespoons finely chopped fresh ginger, 2 tablespoons light soy sauce and 2 tablespoons black rice vinegar and add sugar to taste. Serve as a dipping sauce with steamed crab, steamed prawns, barbecued mussels, or a steamed, skinless chicken breast flavoured with equal quantities of rice wine and ginger juice.

other recipes

chinese-style trotters with ginger and black rice vinegar *see* TROTTERS

cold chinese white-cooked chicken with seared spring onion sauce
see CHICKEN AND THE CHRISTMAS TURKEY

garlic and ginger dipping sauce *see* YABBIES

red-cooked pig's tripe with ginger *see* TRIPE

grapes and vine leaves

The grapevine is one of the oldest plants in cultivation – there have been grapes for 2 million years – and both the fruit and the vine can be used in the kitchen. | Most modern varieties and cultivars are descended from the *Vitis vinifera* vine that grew wild in the Caucasus and was cultivated around 5000 BC, while other species are native to North America. For thousands of years, the *Vitis* group has provided both fresh and dried fruit and, of course, wine and its associated attractions. | Grapes are the world's largest fruit crop, and winemaking has been an important industry since the time of the ancients. (Wine was being made 6000 years ago in Egypt!) I shall not touch further on wine grapes other than to note that the Australian wine industry is a venerable one. It began with the planting of cuttings brought to the colony in 1788 with Captain Arthur Phillip and its present-day reputation is very high worldwide. (I will add, however, that winemaking is not restricted to commercial operations. One in 100 Victorian households produces its own wine and, according to a survey undertaken by the Australian Bureau of Statistics in January 1994, almost 10 per cent of the wine drunk in Victoria is made by amateurs!) >

The quality of our grapes also contributes significantly to the success of the highly regarded Australian dried-fruit industry. The superior flavour of our muscatel grape clusters sun-dried on the stem says 'Australia' to me as much as any other culinary icon I can think of.

Many a suburban garden is delightfully shaded by one or more grapevines, which means a ready supply of grapes and grapevine leaves during the summer months and grapevine prunings for the barbecue in late autumn and early winter. (I sometimes cut grapevine into small pieces, dampen a small handful and use them sprinkled over a glowing fire to hot-smoke quail or chunks of salmon. I must say I have never detected any distinctive grapey flavour, but it is rather a romantic thing to do.) Vine leaves make excellent wrappers for a variety of ingredients, including savoury rice, which results in the Greek and Turkish speciality, dolmades, or when used to protect and add flavour to foods cooked over an open flame. Fully ripe grapes add subtle sweet flavours in sauces and as garnishes, especially with poultry, and Elizabeth David has a well-known recipe for oxtail braised under a layer of grapes, which are later sieved into the sauce.

While there is no better way to enjoy grapes than fresh from the vine, sometimes one has too many. My friend and colleague Maggie Beer has been working on perfecting her verjuice for several years and is now marketing the result commercially. Verjuice (the juice of unripe green grapes) was a common ingredient in the fourteenth and fifteenth centuries. Maggie uses it to deglaze roasting pans to add a special tart character to sauces, especially those for poultry or pork, or dressings. (Maggie warns that verjuice must be stabilised or when bottled it can explode. With this in mind I prefer to buy her verjuice rather than contemplate making my own.)

grapes go with

goat's cheese
fetta cheese
mascarpone
almonds
yoghurt
sour cream
pork
chicken
squab pigeon
guinea fowl
quail
terrines
brioche
brown sugar
walnuts
oxtail

VARIETIES AND SEASON

Grapes are described by their colour, shape, juiciness, skins (tough or less tough), seeds (seeded or seedless), bunch size and flavour. Varietal names are not often used at the point of sale, other than for the best-known varieties, such as sultana. Work continues on developing new varieties, especially seedless grapes, for which there is definite market preference.

Commercially produced grapes are stored at very low temperatures (just short of freezing point) to extend their storage life, which ranges from 2 months for early varieties such as sultana and waltham cross to 4–6 months for later varieties. Climatic conditions can affect the leaf and berry (grape) size, as can the action of a spray such as gibberellic acid, routinely applied to sultana grapes to increase the size of the berries. The peak season for freshly picked grapes is late summer through to early autumn.

vine
leaves
go
with
sardines
rice
currants
dill
mint
mushrooms
lamb
tomatoes
lemon
pine nuts
garlic
red mullet
Tommy ruff

Early muscat This yellow, round, medium-sized seeded grape has a firm skin, soft and juicy pulp and a strong muscat flavour. It is an early variety. **Flame seedless** This bright-red, round, medium-sized grape has a firm, juicy texture and a pleasant flavour. Its main advantage is in being seedless. It is an early variety. **Muscat gordo blanco** Also known as muscat of Alexandria, this versatile grape is used for wine, is dried for raisins and is eaten as a table grape. The yellow–green, large, oval and seeded berries have moderately tough skin and firm and fleshy pulp that has a strong muscat flavour. It is a mid-season variety. **Muscat Hamburg** Also known as the black muscat, this variety is dried for muscatels and, after the sultana, is the most widely grown table grape. The oval berries are blue–black, large-to-medium in size and seeded. The skin is firm and the pulp soft and juicy with a pleasant and pronounced muscat flavour. It is a mid-season variety. **Nyora** This variety was bred in Leeton, New South Wales. Its berries are dark purple, large, long and oval and are seeded. The skin is tough, the pulp soft and fleshy and the berries have a pleasant vinous flavour. It is a late-season variety. **Ruby seedless** This is the latest red-skinned seedless grape to appear in the market. It has red, small-to-medium, oval berries, firm skin, firm and juicy pulp and is pleasantly flavoured. It is a mid-season variety. **Sultana** Eighty per cent of the table grapes consumed in the world are sultana grapes. The same variety is grown and marketed in the United States as Thompson seedless. It is also the main drying grape in Australia. The sultana has yellow–green, small to medium-sized berries of oval shape that are firm and juicy with a distinctive vinous flavour. It is a mid-season variety. **Waltham cross** These long berries are golden green, large, oval, and seeded. The skin is firm and the pulp is firm and juicy with a pleasant vinous flavour. It is a mid-season variety.

SELECTION AND STORAGE

Grapes do not ripen off the vine, so insist on tasting one to see if it is sweet. Examine bunches closely and do not buy any grapes that are broken, sticky or in any way withered. Good-quality grapes will look full and taut and the stems will be green and supple, not withered or dark. Some varieties have a 'bloom' on the fruit, while other varieties look quite shiny.

As they must be picked fully ripe, grapes do not store well in home conditions. Best of all is to go to the vine and cut off a bunch, wash it and eat it, but this is not possible for most of us. Buy only as many as you will eat in 2–3 days. Wash only what you intend to eat as damp grapes will quickly go mouldy. Refrigerate the rest in a plastic bag in the crisper.

Select tender *vine leaves* as you need them before the summer sun starts to crisp them. *Dried fruit* should be stored in a cool cupboard in glass or rigid plastic containers that will keep out air, moisture and insects. Do not keep dried fruit in their packages once opened. Direct exposure to heat and air will cause the fruit to become dry and hard. In humid climates it is even a good idea to refrigerate or freeze dried fruit.

When raisins are mechanically seeded the skin is punctured and air can act on the natural sugars present in the fruit and cause crystallisation. This is not harmful and does not affect the flavour of baked goods.

PREPARATION

Wash *grapes* just before using them. Nestle them on a flat platter on a layer of their own leaves, if possible, and offer scissors. (I become quite angry with my children, who pick indiscriminately at a bunch of grapes leaving what was once a thing of beauty looking undignified and violated.)

Many recipes instruct the cook to peel and seed grapes. I rarely peel grapes, but I do sometimes remove the seeds, as crushed grape seeds are very bitter and can spoil a dish. The simplest way to do this is to halve the grape and flick out the seeds with the point of a knife. Or buy seedless grapes.

In some recipes *dried fruit* is plumped in hot water before being used. Australian dried fruit is packed soft and moist, making this step rarely, if ever, necessary. However, sometimes dried fruit is steeped in wine to infuse its flavour; both the wine and the fruit are then used.

You may need to dip *vine leaves* in boiling water for a minute to make them pliable and to ensure they won't tear. It is also easy to pickle your own leaves to use when the vine is bare. Preserved vine leaves are sold quite widely in jars or vacuum-packed. In each case, the leaves are stored in brine and must be rinsed in fresh water and dried with a clean cloth before use.

sardines in vine leaves

SERVES 4

This is fiddly but fun, and fresh sardines are worth making a fuss about.

16 sardines
1 bunch coriander, finely chopped
2 cloves garlic, finely chopped
2 tablespoons toasted, finely chopped pine nuts
olive oil
freshly ground black pepper
16 fresh *or* preserved vine leaves, stems removed

Cut head from each sardine, open out body, remove guts and pull out backbone, then rinse fish, rubbing off scales under running water. Dry fish and transfer to a plate.

Mix coriander, garlic and pine nuts. Place a spoonful in each sardine and close fish over stuffing. Drizzle with olive oil and grind over pepper.

Rinse or blanch vine leaves, then spread on a bench. Roll each sardine in a leaf and secure with a toothpick. Drizzle with a little more oil. Grill over hot coals or under a gas griller, turning once. Serve with lemon wedges.

chicken with grapes
Stuff a chicken or duck with a handful of seeded, peeled grapes and roast. Deglaze the pan with verjuice and add more grapes and a spoonful of cream.

pickled vine leaves

full-sized, tender fresh vine
  leaves, stems trimmed
½ cup salt
2 litres water

Dip each leaf in boiling water for 1 minute and dry on kitchen paper. Stack leaves in bundles of about 20, then fold stack over and tie with fine string.

Dissolve salt in water in a large saucepan and bring to a boil. Dip each bundle into boiling brine and count to 10. Remove to hot, sterilised jars and pack tightly. Pour over brine to cover completely. Store in a cool place and leave at least a week before using. To use, remove a bundle with tongs, then spread out the leaves and rinse and dry them (don't return any unused leaves to the jar). The pickled vine leaves last for months.

grape and olive bread
Knead lightly crushed grapes and chopped young grapevine leaves and tendrils into risen Olive Bread dough (see BREAD). Press dough out onto a pizza tray with well-oiled hands and allow to recover for 10 minutes. Drizzle with olive oil, scatter over sea salt and bake at 250°C until crisp. Serve with fresh ricotta for lunch in the vineyard!

grilled cheese in vine leaves
Wrap a thick slice of a melting cheese such as raclette, gruyère or fontina in an oiled vine leaf and grill on the barbecue until the leaves are charred and the cheese is soft, then eat with bread, vine leaf and all.

janni's dolmades

MAKES 24

24 fresh or preserved vine
  leaves
½ onion, finely chopped
150 ml fruity olive oil
½ cup long-grain rice
1¼ cups water
¼ cup pine nuts
¼ cup freshly chopped parsley
1 tablespoon freshly chopped
  dill leaves
salt
freshly ground black pepper
1¼ cups tomato juice

If vine leaves are fresh, blanch if stiff or rinse briefly and cut off stems. If using preserved vine leaves, rinse, pat dry and spread on a clean, dry surface.

To make the stuffing, sauté onion in oil, add rice and stir well for 2 minutes. Add water and all ingredients except tomato juice and salt and pepper. Simmer very gently, stirring from time to time, until rice is cooked, approximately 10 minutes. Taste for salt and pepper, then allow to cool.

Spread leaves, smooth-side down, on bench and divide stuffing between them. Roll up each leaf tightly, tucking ends in well. Pack rolls into a saucepan that will take them in one layer. Pour over tomato juice. Put a plate on top of rolls and weight it lightly. Bring to a boil, then simmer very gently for 45 minutes until leaves are quite tender. Allow to cool in saucepan. Serve at room temperature. To store, refrigerate dolmades in a covered ceramic or glass dish.

ajo blanco – white gazpacho from malaga

SERVES 6

The very best Spanish sherry vinegar is the only product that will add the necessary zing to this soup. Despite my earlier comments about peeling grapes, it is worth stripping the peel from the grapes for this lovely dish.

125 g sourdough bread

1 cup milk

60 g blanched almonds

2 cloves garlic, crushed

pinch of salt

200 ml extra-virgin olive oil

2 tablespoons sherry vinegar

2 cups water

GARNISH

100 g sourdough bread, cut
into 1 cm cubes

2 tablespoons olive oil

125 g grapes, peeled and
seeded

Soak bread in milk. In a food processor, work almonds, garlic and salt to a paste. Add milk-soaked bread and blend well. With the motor running slowly, add oil, stopping to scrape bottom of bowl 2–3 times. The consistency should be that of thick mayonnaise. Remove to a bowl and slowly whisk in vinegar and water. Check for seasoning. Refrigerate for several hours.

Fry cubed bread in oil and drain well. Whisk soup again, ladle it into flattish bowls and drop a handful of grapes into each bowl. Garnish with croutons.

rotegrütze

The Barossa Valley has plenty of reminders of its Lutheran past and traditions – from the salty pretzels, dill cucumbers and sausages to the Polish and German speciality of rotegrütze. It was here I encountered for the first time rotegrütze made from grape juice, and realised my own similar recipe, which features raspberries and rhubarb, had taken some turnings.

Rotegrütze means 'red grain' and there are many versions, all involving red fruits and sago. I now wonder whether my mother's cherry sago had a similar derivation.

red grapes

sugar

sago

shiraz

Blend grapes in a food processor to a fine mash, then strain through wet muslin. For every 3 cups juice, take ½ cup sugar, ½ cup sago and ¾ cup wine. Boil, stirring often, until thick. Cool, then pour into a glass bowl or individual dishes and allow to set. Serve with thin cream.

grape gratin

seedless grapes, washed

sour cream *or* mascarpone

ground ginger

brown sugar

Arrange grapes in a tightly packed layer in a shallow gratin dish. Spoon over a generous amount of sour cream and refrigerate overnight.

Mix ground ginger into sugar and strew an even layer over cream. Place under a preheated griller and grill until sugar melts and caramelises. Serve at once.

bbq mullet in vine leaves
Clean red mullet but leave the richly flavoured liver and the scales, then wrap in vine leaves and grill over hot coals. The vine leaf and skin can be pulled away together, leaving the cooked flesh exposed. Serve with olive oil, pepper or butter or, best of all, Anchovy Butter (see ANCHOVIES).

grapes and . . .
Serve chilled grapes with a soft, full-fat cheese at the end of a meal, maybe with a few walnuts as well, or partner dried muscatel clusters with a selection of harder cheeses when the time for fresh grapes is past.

emily bell's christmas puddings

MAKES 2

This is my grandmother's Christmas pudding – the best in the world! I have successfully kept these puddings for a year in the refrigerator. They were even more *delicious the next year. Each pudding will serve 6 people.*

You will need to order the suet from your butcher. Packet suet is already mixed with flour and will alter the proportions.

bbq quail in vine leaves

Over hot coals grill quail wrapped in vine leaves – both seasoned and oiled – and turn frequently, brushing with a little more oil to keep the quail and leaves sizzling.

lamb dolmades

Add 200 g minced lamb to the ingredients for Janni's Dolmades (see p. 336). Sauté the lamb with the onion until lightly browned, then proceed with the recipe.

500 g suet
180 g plain flour
180 g fresh white
   breadcrumbs
360 g seedless raisins
360 g currants
180 g sultanas
125 g candied peel
180 g dark brown sugar
grated zest of 1 lemon
½ nutmeg, grated
¼ teaspoon salt
2 tablespoons lemon juice
½ teaspoon ground cinnamon
4 eggs
100 ml brandy
600 ml milk

Strip skin from suet and grate suet on the largest hole of a grater or with the grating disc of a food processor to achieve 360 g grated suet. (Measure this very carefully.)

Mix all ingredients together in a large basin. (Everyone should have a stir and a wish!) The mixture should be fairly wet. Increase milk a little, if necessary. Leave overnight.

Next day, eat a bit and see if it has enough spice for your taste and adjust, if necessary. Pack mixture into 2 × 1 litre buttered basins, then cover with a disc of greaseproof paper and a doubled sheet of foil. Tie securely under the rim with a doubled length of string. Stand each basin on a wire rack inside a stockpot and add boiling water to come two-thirds up the sides of the basins. Boil for 6 hours, topping up stockpots as needed with more boiling water. Cool and store in a cool place until Christmas Day.

The puddings will take at least 1 hour's boiling on Christmas Day to be really hot, but can boil away for a lot longer. Serve with custard or ice-cream or flame the turned-out pudding with warmed brandy.

other recipes

mushroom caps stuffed with goat's cheese on vine leaves
see MUSHROOMS

sautéd silver beet with olive oil, pine nuts and currants
see SILVER BEET

squid stuffed with rice and currants *see* SQUID, CALAMARI, CUTTLEFISH
AND OCTOPUS

h *a m*

The delicacy we know as ham is an example of necessity becoming the mother of invention. An oversupply of feral pigs in Roman Gaul (France) meant that methods had to be found to preserve this excellent food for the winter. Salting and smoking was the answer. The rest is history! │ There are many different styles of ham, countries – and regions within a country – becoming well known for a particular style. However, nowadays many names refer to the production method rather than the geographic locality. Pork products are a prohibited import in Australia, so never think that a Virginia or York ham has come from Virginia or York. (Mind you, if you happen to be in Parma or Bayonne, do not leave without tasting the local ham.) │ Ham can be cooked or not cooked, smoked or unsmoked, air-dried or dried by mechanical means, or stored in vacuum packaging. Whether it is to be a whole leg ham on the bone, a single muscle ham (such as a gypsy ham), a pressed, boneless, skinless ham (such as a virginia ham) or a so-called 'baked' ham, a ham goes through several processes. >

ham
goes
with
mustard
mustard fruits
pickled fruit
potatoes
cabbage
witlof
gruyère cheese
lentils
chick peas
spinach
olives
pistachios
parsley
cloves
brown sugar
carrots
cider
chicken

Firstly, the meat is brined. It is then hung to drain and dry for an hour or so before being smoked (if applicable), usually by an automatic process, and cooked in a thermostatically controlled, low-temperature steam-injected oven. 'Baked' hams are skinned, rubbed with various mixtures and returned to the oven at a higher temperature to glaze the outside.

Advances in technology have meant that almost all smallgoods manufacturers now use standardised brines and liquid smoke to process their goods, and they rely on accurate thermostats to control each stage of the process, rather than drawing on years of experience. Here and there traditionalists still prepare their hams in a more individual manner. The production of raw ham still remains a very artisanal industry at the time of writing.

At present Australia has no regulation controlling the water content permissible in hams, unlike Europe. All hams lose water during the cooking process, at least 25 per cent. It is considered reasonable that the ham should regain at least this amount of water or the finished product could be dry. However, some products (especially pressed ham) have considerable amounts of excess water added.

Ham is very versatile. Ham pieces can be minced to make fillings and mousses. Slices can be simmered in a separately made sauce. Chunks of ham can be set in a well-flavoured meat jelly with lots of parsley and chopped garlic to make the well-known Burgundian dish of *jambon persillé*. Small chunks of ham are cooked with pulses or greens in many countries of the world to stretch a small amount of meat. Scraps can be added to omelettes, soufflés, tarts and vegetable dishes. Spaniards have a huge variety of cooked dishes using ham, often coupled with eggs, sweet peppers and onions.

Uncooked hams, sliced paper-thin, are quite wonderful. The Italian variety is often partnered with ripe melon or fresh figs in summer and autumn. When the ham is freshly cut, so that it falls in moist rosy curls onto the plate, and the melon or figs are bursting with juice, it is hard to think of a lovelier start to a meal. (By the way, the Italian word *prosciutto* means ham, not raw ham. *Prosciutto crudo* is the correct Italian for raw ham, and *prosciutto cotto* for cooked ham. I mention this as many people asking for slices of *prosciutto* become quite affronted if the shopkeeper enquires what sort of ham they want.)

VARIETIES AND SEASON

Ham is available at all times of the year. The range is endless and different butchers and firms produce their own specialities with unique names.

One of my favourite suppliers, John Wilson of Mohr Food, gave me a 'summer barnyard' ham for Christmas 1994. It looked sensational, its skin deep brown and polished like a well-cared-for saddle. (The special gloss was achieved by rubbing the skin with pig's blood during the smoking process.)

It was nestled on a bed of sweet-smelling straw in a deep wooden box and was sweet and moist to the last slice.

The names of the world's most popular hams are used inappropriately in Australia. Where the names once referred to a location and a technique developed there, the original recipes are rarely used in this country. Here are a few styles of ham commonly available in Australian shops.

BAKED VIRGINIA Traditionally, baked virginia ham is a whole leg trimmed of fat that is heavily smoked over hickory and has a long maturing period. This style of ham is baked rather than simmered in liquid. In the United States, pigs destined for Virginia ham are supposed to be reared on peanuts.

GAMMON It is very common to see small cured (but not cooked) joints from the leg called gammon on sale in the United Kingdom, where the pig is still a more economical animal than the cow or lamb. Gammon can be smoked or unsmoked. Unsmoked gammon is what some of us know as pickled pork. To make gammon, the leg is brined as if it were to become bacon and is then drained for about a week and possibly cold-smoked before being sold, usually cut into small portions or sliced as gammon steaks. Gammon can be baked or pan-fried or cooked with vegetables or pulses (split peas or brown lentils are particularly good).

GYPSY Prepared from the forequarter of the pig, gypsy ham is a single-muscle ham that has been brined and cooked.

HOCKS The hock is the cured, smoked and cooked end of the ham leg (the shank is the equivalent joint in a lamb) used to make pea and ham soup. It is also possible to buy ham hocks that are pickled and lightly smoked but not cooked.

KASSLER Not strictly ham as it does not come from the leg, kassler is from the loin of the pig. It is cured and drained in the same manner as a ham, and is then smoked and cooked again exactly as a ham. Due to its delicate nature it cannot tolerate being tumbled or massaged in order to take up excess water and consequently remains a high-quality product. Kassler can be cooked briefly in a piece, is ideal to slice thickly and warm over sauerkraut or can be lightly glazed and baked and served with a fruit sauce, such as blackcurrant, gooseberry or apple.

LEG | **On the bone** Some hams on the bone are lightly smoked, some are heavily smoked. Some are cured with molasses, which results in a black skin and imitates the English hams of Suffolk and Bradenham. Some cures have sugar in them as well as salt, which is said to counteract the harshness of the salt and result in a sweeter, milder ham. **Boneless** Boneless leg ham is a whole or half leg that has had the bone removed and excess fat trimmed. Always prefer boneless leg ham to pressed ham.

PRESSED | Sometimes described on the label as 'manufactured meat', this product has a high water content and is made up of various mismatched trimmings that are tumbled or massaged to assist bonding and then pressed together into an improbably round or square shape before being cooked. I do not recommend it.

RAW | Raw hams (*prosciutto crudo* in Italy, *rohschinken* in Germany, *jambon de Bayonne* in France, *serrano* in Spain, and so on) are highly prized speciality products. Some are smoked, some are not. They are dry-salted and then dried by either air-drying or mechanical means. Raw hams have a high salt content – 7 per cent compared with 2 per cent in a cooked ham.

STEAKS | These slices from the forequarter of the pig are a cheaper and less satisfying alternative than a piece of kassler. They are cooked and only need frying or grilling.

SELECTION AND STORAGE

For a novice, a visit to a specialist smallgoods supplier can be daunting. Ask for one or two slices of each variety of ham and ask the shopkeeper to write the name of each variety on each parcel. Get to know what you like.

LEG | To store a ham on the bone, wrap it in a damp tea towel or pillowcase rinsed in 1 part vinegar to 5 parts water. Store the ham in the coldest part of the refrigerator and rinse the tea towel every 2–3 days. (Butchers will also advise that you refrigerate the ham, covered as above, on a wire rack set in an airtight container to ensure it stays dry.) A well-wrapped ham will keep for 2 weeks in this manner. After this time I would use the ham quickly in cooked dishes or wrap chunks in plastic film, then in foil, and freeze them.

RAW | The slicing of raw ham can only be done properly using a commercial electric slicer (talented butchers or those with experience can still cut raw ham by hand, but it is a dying art). Always order your *prosciutto crudo* sliced, but allow time for it to be done as it needs time to be done well. Each layer ought to be separated from the next with a sheet of waxed paper and each slice ought to be laid tenderly just so. This can be fraught with danger and risk if requested 5 minutes before closing time on a Saturday morning.

Store the raw ham in its shop wrappings, especially the sheets of waxed paper separating the layers, and use it by the next day. The beauty of this ham is its softness and pale-pink colour. It will harden and become dark after a day. Leftover *prosciutto crudo* can be used in cooked dishes or snipped into salads, but it will never be as glorious as when it was just sliced.

SLICED

Buy ham as required to use for salads and sandwiches. Discard the shop wrappings, rewrap in greaseproof paper and use within a few days. Do not eat sliced ham that is curled at the edges or that smells sour or is even slightly sticky.

PREPARATION

Sliced ham requires no preparation other than to trim it of fat, if desired. If using *raw ham* to wrap other foods, trim away all fat as it can catch in one's throat.

Many cooks like to decorate the fat side of a leg of ham, either by glazing it and baking on the glaze, or more simply by pressing a layer of well-browned breadcrumbs into the fat. When serving a leg of ham also serve bowls of your home preserves. Pickled plums, cherries, crabapples, pears, oranges and Italian mustard fruits are all appropriate.

**TO CARVE A HAM
ON THE BONE**

Invest in a ham knife, which is long and thin and makes slicing a ham much easier. Remove the skin but do not discard it. (It can be pressed over the unused portion of the ham before it is wrapped and refrigerated. Eventually strips of it can be cooked with dried beans or lentils or used to flavour stock for soup.) Arrange the ham so that its hock end is towards the carver. Cut a thin slice from the underside, so that the ham does not wobble. To carve, cut long slices from each side of the ham (this is the method I follow). Alternatively, cut through to the hock bone about 10 cm from its end. Make another cut at an angle to this, thus removing a small wedge. Continue to cut slices towards the knuckle, increasing the angle. Run the knife along the bone to release all the slices. Turn the ham over and do the same thing on the other side.

recipes

glaze for baked ham

1 orange
2 tablespoons Dijon mustard
3 tablespoons brown sugar
1 leg cooked ham
cloves
½ cup white wine

Preheat oven to 180°C. Grate zest from orange, then juice orange. Mix zest, juice, mustard and sugar together. Remove skin from ham and score fat in a diamond pattern. Press a clove into middle of each diamond. Spread glaze over ham. Place ham in a baking dish and pour in wine to prevent ham sticking. Bake for 20 minutes until a rich shiny colour.

southern-style greens and ham   SERVES 6

This is my version of a dish I tasted in New Orleans that was cooked by one of America's best-known exponents of soul cooking, Edna Lewis. It is served with grilled pork chops or good sausages, although I sometimes serve it with lots of crusty bread instead. Cornbread would be traditional in the southern States. Grilled triangles of polenta would be good, too, although not a bit traditional. The long-cooked greens are traditional and a crisp savoy cabbage is by far the best green to use.

1 tablespoon olive oil
3 smoked ham hocks
2 onions, diced
6 large cloves garlic, sliced
1 bay leaf
1 teaspoon fresh thyme leaves
12 black peppercorns
1 fresh red chilli, seeded
6 whole allspice
3 cloves
2.5 litres water
1 savoy cabbage, cut into 6
    wedges (attached at stem
    end)
6 red-skinned potatoes
salt
freshly ground black pepper
red-wine vinegar

Heat oil in a stockpot and brown hocks, then remove them to a plate. Reduce heat and cook onion and garlic for about 10 minutes until soft, then add bay leaf. Tie rest of herbs and spices in a square of muslin and add to pot with hocks and water. Bring to a boil, then skim and simmer, uncovered, for 1½ hours.

Remove spice bag. Add cabbage and potatoes, then cover and simmer for 30 minutes. Remove cabbage and potatoes with a skimmer and reserve. Test if hocks are quite tender. Remove hocks and cut meat and some of the skin into bite-sized pieces. Increase heat and boil liquid until well reduced and very flavoursome. Cut potatoes into quarters or chunks. Return cabbage, potato and meat to pot to reheat. Taste for salt and pepper. Sprinkle with a few drops of red-wine vinegar. Serve the meat and cabbage with some of the 'potlikker' in deep bowls. Pork chops or sausages are served on top.

ham paste
Work minced ham with Dijon mustard to taste and add about half its volume of unsalted butter to make a potted paste. Spread on hot toast and serve as hot triangles with a vegetable soup, or top with cooked mushrooms or grilled tomato halves.

ham omelette
Warm chopped ham in a spoonful of home-made tomato sauce or chutney as an omelette filling.

beans with ham
Toss warm, boiled green beans with cubes or shreds of ham, fresh herbs and crisp croutons.

ham and pistachio mousse

SERVES 6

The success of this recipe is closely related to the quality and jellied character of the stock you use. The ideal jelly results from adding 1–2 pig's trotters to the stock – either pork or chicken – and cooking them for 3–4 hours. Check that the stock has set really firmly before measuring out the quantity you need for this dish. If it has not set firmly, reduce it by boiling or add some gelatine ✐.

500 g trimmed ham
300 ml jellied stock
 (preferably chicken or pork)
150 ml cream
2 egg whites
½ cup shelled unsalted
 pistachios
Tabasco
salt

Place ham in a food processor and chop finely. Tip in melted but cold jellied stock and purée. Transfer to a bowl. Whip cream until stiff but still foldable. Whip egg whites to a firm snow. Fold nuts, cream and egg whites into ham purée. Taste for seasoning. Use drops of Tabasco and a little salt, if necessary. Spoon mousse into a mould and refrigerate until set.

Dip mould briefly into hot water and turn out onto a serving plate. Serve with hot toast and a cucumber salad as the first course for a dinner party. The mousse can also be divided between 6 × 125 ml moulds.

ham soufflé

SERVES 4

Don't worry about making a paper collar for the dish or even whether you have a proper soufflé dish. Think of this recipe as a simple ham pudding suitable for a light dinner with salad and fruit and you will make it often.

1 cup chopped ham
1 cup Simple Cheese Sauce
 (see p. 299)
2 tablespoons freshly chopped
 parsley
3 egg yolks
salt
Tabasco
4 egg whites

Preheat oven to 180°C and butter a 1 litre soufflé or gratin dish well. Combine ham and cheese sauce. Add parsley and beat in yolks one at a time. Season mixture with salt and Tabasco. Whip whites firmly, but not until rocky, and fold into mixture. Pile into prepared dish and bake for 20–25 minutes until well risen and firm in the centre when pressed lightly with your fingertip.

---

croque monsieur
Mix grated gruyère cheese with enough Dijon mustard and cream to make a thick paste. Toast a slice of bread on one side only, then lay a thick slice of ham on the untoasted side, spread with the cheesy mixture and grill until golden and bubbly.

ham and rocket
Toss rocket leaves in an olive oil vinaigrette and wrap bundles of leaves in thin slices of leg ham. Leave the rocket poking out the ends of the bundles and arrange on a flat plate.

ham salad
Mix equal quantities of ham, gruyère cheese and celery, all cut into sticks, through a green salad.

spanish ham and eggs

SERVES 1

This is a great eat-on-the-knee dish when you are alone and watching a movie on television.

The inexpensive, flameproof terracotta dishes on sale in Spanish shops are perfect for making this. How I lusted after these dishes when I was in Spain recently! Shop after shop with the most wonderful shapes and sizes, each one a few dollars only but, as is so often the case for the Australian traveller, the problem was how to get them home. And, as is also so often the case, back home in Melbourne at Casa Iberica, I bought some!

melon and ham
Arrange thin, peeled melon slices and finely sliced raw ham on a platter for a stress-free first course for a summer lunch or dinner. (Do not prepare this ahead as the ham will become soggy.)

2 tablespoons olive oil
1 thick slice ham
2 teaspoons sugar
3 tablespoons red-wine vinegar
2 eggs, broken into a cup
salt
freshly ground black pepper
freshly chopped parsley

Heat oil in a 14 cm round flameproof dish and sauté ham, turning it once. Remove ham and sprinkle sugar into dish. As it caramelises, pour on vinegar and let it bubble. Return ham to dish and carefully slide in eggs. Season and cook, either on top of the stove or in the oven, until the egg whites have just set. Scatter over parsley and eat with good bread. Be careful – the dish will be very hot!

other recipes

andalusian broad beans *see* BEANS, FRESH
ham and ricotta stuffing for lamb *see* LAMB
pea and ham soup *see* PEAS
petits pois – french-style green peas *see* PEAS
pressed tongue *see* TONGUE
saltimbocca alla romana *see* SAGE
southern chicken, ham and okra gumbo *see* OKRA

h o n e y

h **o n e y** People have used honey since long before recorded history. It was the principal form of sweetening until sugar cane reached Europe in the ninth century. Cane sugar remained a luxury for many hundreds of years while honey continued to be widely used. One cannot imagine the cakes of the Middle East without honey, or Mediterranean countries without nougat in all its varieties. Honey contains sugars, plant acids, mineral salts and other elements and many claims are made about its medicinal powers. It is universally accepted as a soother of sore throats. │ Honey is made from the nectar that the honeybee collects from flowers. The nectar itself is a liquid produced by flowering plants to attract the insects needed to ensure pollination. The nectar is collected by the bee with its tongue and is stored in the hive. Worker bees add enzymes to the nectar and transfer it to wax storage chambers, the honeycomb. During the process water is evaporated and the nectar becomes honey. │ Without the honeybee cross-pollination would not occur. Fruit growers and market gardeners welcome apiarists setting hives on their properties and in many cases employ them to do so. >

Australian Aborigines still collect honey from wild bees and 'sugarbag' is very highly prized. It is intensely flavoured and most delicious. The honeybee is not native to Australia and was introduced to Australia in 1822 not only to provide food for early settlers but to ensure the fertilisation of crops. In some quarters there is concern, however, that the presence of honeybees reduces the amount of food available to native birds and insects, thereby restricting their role in pollinating native flora.

VARIETIES AND SEASON

The flavour, colour and viscosity of honey depends on the type of plants from which it is collected. Australia produces some of the finest single-flower honeys in the world, ranging from mild-flavoured **yellow box**, **clover** or **blue-gum** honeys to the distinctively flavoured **leatherwood** honey produced in the rainforests of Tasmania. Single-flower honeys are more costly for obvious reasons. Most commercial honeys are blended, often using honey from different locations as well as different plants. There are also honeys produced from the flowers of herbs, which can be very powerfully flavoured. While **lavender** honey makes a wonderful ice-cream, **fennel** honey I find useful for glazing pork chops but cannot contemplate on my toast.

Australia is the world's ninth-biggest producer of honey and about 40 per cent of the crop is exported. Honey is collected once a year during the flowering season of each plant.

SELECTION AND STORAGE

It is possible to have a honey-tasting at some specialist stores or at honey stalls at fresh food markets. Otherwise my advice would be to buy and try and get to know several different honeys. Lighter-flavoured honeys are best for general purposes.

Store honey away from light and avoid the refrigerator. The balance between the various sugars in honey will determine whether it is a liquid or crystallised honey. Most liquid honeys become granular at low temperatures. This does not affect their quality and by gently warming the jar in hot (not boiling) water the honey will become liquid again. Crystallisation can also occur through exposure to excessive light.

PREPARATION

When measuring honey, dip the spoon in boiling water first, so that the honey will slide onto the spoon easily and slip off just as easily. Wooden honey twirlers are a favourite item for those who prefer to add honey to their tea or coffee or when serving a honey pot on the table.

When substituting honey for sugar in a cake or biscuit mixture, use the same weight of sweetener, but reduce the liquid in the recipe by a quarter. (It is so much easier to spoon honey than weigh it – 1 tablespoon honey equals 30 g.) You will need to reduce the recommended cooking temperature by 15°C, which may lengthen the baking time by a few minutes. Be aware that as honey is sweeter than sugar the final result will be different.

almond and honey slice

½ quantity Shortcrust Pastry

185 g unsalted butter

100 g castor sugar

5 tablespoons honey

50 ml cream

50 ml brandy *or any other* liqueur *or spirit*

300 g flaked almonds

Preheat oven to 200°C. Line a 30 cm × 20 cm baking tray with baking paper and then with pastry. Bake blind for 20 minutes, then remove weights and foil. Turn oven up to 220°C. Bring remaining ingredients to a boil, stirring. Spread evenly over pastry. Bake until topping is bubbling and has caramelised evenly, about 15 minutes. Cool before cutting into fingers or squares.

honey wafers with bruised raspberries SERVES 8

These fragile wafers are based on a recipe that appeared in Stephanie's Seasons, *where they were teamed with a banana cream. They can be stored in an airtight container for up to 3 days. Excess batter will store well, covered, in the refrigerator for several days.*

150 g softened unsalted butter

240 g castor sugar

6 tablespoons full-flavoured honey

120 g plain flour, sifted

1 teaspoon ground ginger

2 egg whites

500 g raspberries

2 cups cream, firmly whipped

icing sugar

Preheat oven to 180°C. In a food processor, cream butter and sugar. Add honey, flour, ginger and egg whites and blend to a spreadable consistency. Spread batter onto baking trays lined with baking paper to form 8 cm rounds (you need 24 wafers in all). Bake for 7–8 minutes until golden brown. Cool wafers for 1 minute then, using a flexible spatula, lift onto a wire rack to cool.

To serve, mix raspberries with cream, crushing berries a little to stain cream pink. Anchor a cold wafer to each plate with a tiny dob of cream. Pile on a spoonful of raspberries and cream, balance another wafer on top, pile on a second spoonful of cream and top with a third wafer biscuit. Dust with icing sugar.

recipes

honey and lemon
Soothe a sore throat by steeping freshly grated ginger in boiling water and adding a spoonful of honey and a dash of lemon juice.

honey chicken
Mix 1 part honey to 4 parts light soy sauce, then add finely chopped fresh ginger and rub over the skin of a whole chicken before roasting.

honey biscuits
Brush plain biscuit shapes with warmed honey before baking.

honey butter
Mix 2 parts butter to 1 part honey and spread on toast or crumpets.

loukoumathes – greek honey fritters

SERVES 4

1 teaspoon instant dried yeast
pinch of salt
1¼ cups plain flour
1 cup warm water
olive oil
4 tablespoons honey
1 tablespoon ground cinnamon

Mix yeast and salt with flour and work to a smooth batter with water. Heat oil in a deep saucepan and drop spoonfuls of batter into it. Cook for 2–4 minutes or until golden. Drain on kitchen paper. Drizzle with honey and sprinkle with cinnamon and serve while hot.

elderflower blossoms Elderflower blossoms can be separated and dropped into the batter before frying.

honey pancakes
Spread pancakes with warmed honey and sprinkle with lemon juice.

nougat ice-cream

SERVES 8–10

100 g castor sugar
60 g liquid glucose
5 tablespoons honey
8 egg whites
800 ml cream, softly whipped
180 g glacé fruit, chopped
90 g candied peel

ALMOND PRALINE
125 g castor sugar
90 g flaked almonds, toasted
  until pale brown

To make the praline, dissolve sugar in a heavy-based saucepan over heat. Brush sides of pan with cold water to prevent sugar crystallising. When sugar has dissolved and is golden, add almonds and pour onto an oiled baking tray to set. When cold, break praline into pieces and pulverise in a food processor or with a meat mallet.

To make the ice-cream, place sugar, glucose and honey in a saucepan. Simmer and stir once or twice until sugar has dissolved. Boil until mixture registers 116°C on a candy thermometer. When syrup is nearly ready, beat egg whites in an electric mixer until they hold stiff peaks. Pour syrup onto egg whites with mixer running and beat until mixture is quite cold. Fold cream into cooled nougat, then fold in fruit, peel and praline. Pour into a 1.5 litre enamelled cast-iron terrine mould lined with baking paper and neaten top with a spatula. Cover with a piece of baking paper cut to fit and freeze.

To serve, cut into generous slices and accompany with poached fruit.

ricotta and honey
Surround a super-fresh ricotta cheese with peeled perfect figs and serve a pot of leatherwood or other wild honey alongside with a wooden honey twirler resting in it.

honey nut spread
Mix finely chopped walnuts to a paste with thick aromatic honey (lavender, for instance) and the same quantity of thick cream. Use as a spread for sandwiches for afternoon tea, as suggested by Elizabeth David.

washday pudding

SERVES 4

This recipe comes from my mother's cookbook, Through My Kitchen Door. *In her chapter on honey she is reminded of Christopher Robin's playmate Pooh, the bear of very little brain, whose thoughts were always returning to his store of honey pots.*

200 g self-raising flour

pinch of salt

¾ cup milk

thick cream

SYRUP

2 tablespoons honey

125 g sugar

40 g butter

1 cup hot water

Make a soft dough with the flour, salt and milk. Spoon into an ungreased 1 litre basin. Mix syrup ingredients together and pour over and around pudding. Cover pudding with a doubled sheet of foil and tie in place under rim of basin. Steam for 45 minutes and serve with cream.

honey madeleines

MAKES 24

These delicate cakes look wonderful piled on a Victorian cake plate (the sort that has a pedestal). Madeleine trays, made specifically for these shell-shaped cakes, are available in specialist cookware shops. Each tray usually makes 12 cakes.

90 g unsalted butter

½ tablespoon honey

2 eggs

75 g castor sugar

1 tablespoon brown sugar

tiny pinch of salt

1 drop pure vanilla

90 g plain flour

1 teaspoon baking powder

a little extra unsalted butter

a little extra flour

pure icing sugar

In a saucepan, melt butter with honey over a low heat. Allow to cool. Combine eggs, castor sugar, brown sugar, salt and vanilla in a food processor. Add flour sifted with baking powder, then add cooled butter and honey. Allow this batter to rest for at least 1 hour, or even overnight, before baking.

Preheat oven to 180°C. Barely melt extra butter and liberally paint 2 madeleine tins. Dust with extra flour. Rap tins on edge of sink to knock off excess flour. Spoon in batter to two-thirds full and bake for 9 minutes. Cool for 1 minute and then dislodge cakes by sharply rapping edge of tray. Allow madeleines to cool completely on a wire rack – they will become crisp on the outside. Dust with icing sugar on the curved side before serving.

honey sauce

This simple sauce is delicious poured around chunks of hot apples or pears that have been cooked in butter and sugar until lightly caramelised, or it can be offered with Washday Pudding (see p. 351).

½ cup mild-flavoured honey
I vanilla bean, split
½ cup cream
I tablespoon unsalted butter

Put honey into a small saucepan and scrape in vanilla seeds. Warm gently, stirring to mix well. Add cream and butter and bring to a boil. Boil, stirring, for 3 minutes, then allow to cool (the sauce will thicken as it cools). Serve warm.

other recipes

honey cheesecake *see* CHEESE
quinces baked in honey *see* QUINCES

jerusalem artichokes

These knobbly tubers are not really artichokes at all. Nor do they have anything to do with Jerusalem. (In fact, they are a native of North America, where they were cultivated by the American Indians before the sixteenth century.) It is thought that their name is a corruption of *girasole*, the Italian for sunflower, and that the flavour resembles the heart of a globe artichoke. | Jerusalem artichokes (*Helianthus tuberosus*) have beige skins and look a little like fresh ginger. They have crisp, white flesh similar in texture to a raw potato. When crisp and newly dug the tubers are sweet and earthy and the flavour is nutty. They can be cooked as for a potato but their texture becomes softer. | Jerusalem artichokes contain no starch, so their carbohydrates are well tolerated by diabetics and hypoglycaemics. However, these same carbohydrates are of a type that cannot be broken down by any enzymes we possess. The undigested carbohydrates pass into the gut intact, where they produce great quantities of gas! Jerusalem artichokes are the subject of some ribaldry because of this side effect. | People who grow Jerusalem artichokes are usually delighted to give some away as the tubers spread rapidly.

VARIETIES AND SEASON

Newer varieties tend to be less knobbly than those of old, which makes peeling easier. Jerusalem artichokes are in season May–October.

SELECTION AND STORAGE

Select Jerusalem artichokes that are firm, not squishy, and look for those with the fewest knobs and bumps. You may need to trim the worst bumps, so buy more than you think you will need. Store in a cool, dry place away from light. They will be fine for at least a week.

PREPARATION

Jerusalem artichokes discolour once cut. For this reason, have a bowl of acidulated water ✑ handy and drop the artichokes into it as you go.

TO PEEL | Jerusalem artichokes should be trimmed of any dark stringy roots and peeled before cooking. Peeling used to be a painful task as the knobs meant a great deal of waste. Newer, smoother varieties have made the task easier. Cutting away the worst bumps first will also aid peeling.

I once made a soup and tried to save time by washing and scrubbing the tubers and leaving them unpeeled. The soup had none of the delicacy of flavour that I remembered, nor was it the usual pure cream colour.

TO SLICE | Be careful when slicing raw Jerusalem artichokes as they are small and slippery. Dry each one well and cut a thin slice from one side, so that the artichoke will sit firmly on your chopping board. Slice as required; a Japanese slicer and shredder is handy if you need fine slices.

recipes

scallops with jerusalem artichokes

SERVES 4

jerusalems and tomato

Slice raw Jerusalem artichokes thinly and toss immediately with extra-virgin olive oil, lemon juice, parsley and sliced tomatoes.

4 Jerusalem artichokes, peeled
olive oil
unsalted butter
24 scallops on the half-shell
4 tablespoons freshly chopped
    parsley
lemon wedges
freshly ground black pepper

Preheat oven to 220°C. Steam or boil Jerusalem artichokes for 3 minutes. Drain, cool and cut into small dice (about 5 mm). Heat a mixture of olive oil and butter and sauté artichoke until golden and crisp. Drain excess oil and butter and leave artichoke dice in pan until ready to serve (only leave for a few minutes or artichoke will become soggy). >

Wipe each scallop to free it of any grit. Trim away the black intestinal thread from each scallop, then paint scallops with a trace of oil and place on a baking tray. Roast for 5 minutes.

Return artichoke pan to heat, toss to reheat and add parsley. Spoon mixture over each scallop and serve with lemon wedges, passing the pepper grinder.

beurre blanc Ambitious cooks may also wish to make a *beurre blanc* and add a teaspoonful to each scallop.

jerusalem artichoke soup

SERVES 4

60 g butter

500 g Jerusalem artichokes, peeled and cut into even chunks

1 onion, sliced

1 clove garlic, lightly crushed

1 stick celery, finely sliced

1 litre Chicken or Veal Stock, milk or water

salt

freshly ground black pepper

freshly snipped chives

freshly grated nutmeg

thick cream (optional)

Melt butter in a heavy-based saucepan and sweat vegetables for 5 minutes, stirring once or twice. Add liquid and simmer until artichoke is tender. Purée, then pass through a strainer into a clean saucepan. Adjust seasoning and reheat. Serve scattered with chives and nutmeg. (You may wish to add a little cream to soup made from stock or water before serving, either stirred into the soup or floated on top of each portion.)

jerusalem artichokes provençale

SERVES 4

500 g Jerusalem artichokes, peeled and cut into walnut-sized chunks

½ cup fresh breadcrumbs

2 tablespoons olive oil

2 cloves garlic, very finely chopped

3 large ripe tomatoes, peeled and chopped

1 tablespoon freshly chopped parsley

1 tablespoon extra-virgin olive oil

Boil Jerusalem artichoke until three-quarters cooked. Drain. Toast breadcrumbs in a heavy-based frying pan in 1 tablespoon of the olive oil until golden, stirring constantly. Set aside.

Heat remaining olive oil and sauté garlic for a moment. Add tomato and artichoke. Cook over a brisk heat, shaking and stirring occasionally to prevent sticking, until tomato has given up all its moisture and pan looks fairly dry. Stir in parsley, then tip the lot into a heated serving dish, scatter over toasted crumbs and sprinkle with extra-virgin olive oil. Serve hot or warm.

jerusalem salad
Use Jerusalem artichokes in salads as you would new potatoes.

jerusalem chips
Peel Jerusalem artichokes and slice thinly at an angle, then dry well and deep-fry in clean oil at 160°C until golden. Drain the chips well, then salt lightly and serve with drinks or alongside a grilled piece of meat or as a garnish for Jerusalem Artichoke Soup (see p. 355).

jerusalem artichoke tart

1 quantity Shortcrust Pastry
8 Jerusalem artichokes, peeled
handful of cooked, chopped
    spinach or silver beet
300 ml cream
3 eggs
1 egg yolk
freshly chopped herbs
salt
freshly ground black pepper

Line a 22 cm loose-bottomed flan tin with pastry and bake blind at 200°C for 20 minutes. Reduce oven temperature to 180°C.

Boil Jerusalem artichokes in lightly salted water until tender, then slice thickly. Combine artichoke, spinach, cream, eggs, egg yolk and herbs in a bowl and season. Pour into pastry case and bake for 20 minutes until set and golden on top. Serve warm with a green salad.

Kangaroo

Kangaroo There is great media interest in what constitutes Australian cuisine and although one can argue long and hard about this concept there can be little doubt that using an indigenous product must qualify a dish as Australian. | One cannot imagine anything more Australian than kangaroo. Kangaroo is high-quality meat that is tender and richly flavoured and at its most delicious when roasted or grilled rare, or medium–rare, if you must. (Do not trust any recipe that tells you to cook kangaroo slowly and for a long time. Exactly the opposite is the case, unless you are dealing with the tail. The secondary cuts are only suited to braising and stewing and are definitely less interesting.) As a true game meat it is lean and has the lowest cholesterol level of all red meats. Its prime cuts are reminiscent of young farmed venison. Recipes for one are mostly interchangeable with the other, although one must allow a great deal less time to cook the smaller joints of kangaroo. The tail makes a wonderful soup and consommé. | Far from being a contemporary novelty only, there are many accounts of early settlers and explorers enjoying our native game. My own great-grandfather's diary records entertaining the local parson with a fine roast of kangaroo in the 1870s in Gippsland, Victoria. >

kangaroo
goes
with
red-wine sauces
anchovy butter
béarnaise sauce
pepper
olive oil
juniper berries
native peppercorns
polenta
olives
eggplants
sweet peppers
zucchini
beetroots
radicchio
caramelised onions
spicy chutneys
mushrooms
horseradish
mustard
basil
sun-dried tomatoes
parmesan cheese

In the 1990s you are most likely to encounter kangaroo on a restaurant menu, as it is our open-minded chefs who have responded most enthusiastically to this exciting and unique product. Many chefs are using kangaroo in interesting dishes, some incorporating indigenous spices and fruit in sauces or accompaniments, others adapting it to their own cuisine. Kangaroo goes well with tamarind and chilli, cardamom, cumin seed or coriander seed. Or it can be coarsely minced and used to make hamburgers. Italian cooks find it well suited to pasta sauces, and it is wonderful roasted or grilled quickly and served rare, with or without a sauce.

There has been strong opposition from some in the community to the use of kangaroo meat for human consumption. The emotional arguments range from a belief that the method of slaughter (shooting) is cruel, and meat from wild kangaroos is nasty to eat and unhygienic, to objections to eating the national symbol. Tell that to a Frenchman and advise him not to eat cockerel!

All members of the Macropodidae family are protected from random hunting by State legislation; a small number of the more populous species are culled under permit. (Since the white settlers arrived in this continent and set about changing the native habitat, some species of kangaroo have increased in numbers and are thriving on the unnaturally plentiful water and feed supplied by crops, pastures and dams.) An annual cull of kangaroos is conducted by registered shooters who work at night, and the gutted carcasses are transferred to field chillers at once. The size of each State's cull is determined annually and is based on scientific assessment that takes into account natural phenomena that might have affected numbers.

My friend Maggie Beer, who cooked so beautifully for many years at The Pheasant Farm Restaurant in South Australia's Barossa Valley, is an enthusiastic and intelligent spokesperson for using kangaroo. In an article in the *Good Weekend* magazine, she says, 'Kangaroos are, and always should be, protected wildlife. Speaking from my knowledge of the South Australian situation, I'm satisfied that the animal is treated humanely, with its culling being handled intelligently under the supervision of the National Parks and Wildlife authorities.'

Culled carefully, our kangaroos are a renewable resource of superb quality. Both the meat and the skins are in demand. Australia desperately needs exportable product. It seems short-sighted, to say the least, not to use this resource and promote the domestic and export markets for kangaroo actively.

VARIETIES AND SEASON

The species culled under licence are almost exclusively the eastern grey, the western grey and the red kangaroo. Other species are fully protected. All wildlife is fully protected in conservation reserves. Kangaroo meat is available all year through selected distributors.

SELECTION AND STORAGE

The interested home cook may find kangaroo difficult to locate as regulations vary from State to State (at the time of writing) where it can be sold: in most States it must be sold sealed (vacuum-packed or under plastic film) and in some it cannot be displayed with other meat. Try your local fresh food market or specialist delicatessen or food store.

In New South Wales kangaroo is available in some supermarkets. One of our national supermarket chains has responded to pressure from the vociferous minority group opposed to the eating of kangaroo and removed kangaroo from its shelves. I consider this a disappointing and retrograde step. Australia's largest distributor is Southern Game Meats and I would suggest ringing them for your nearest supplier.

The most usual cuts available are fillet, loin, rump, topside, tail and chopped meat (round, silverside and lean mince). The best results will occur with the prime roasting and grilling cuts – the *fillet*, *loin* and *rump*. Topside and chopped meat are for use in casseroles and pies. Kangaroo darkens quickly on contact with air (oxidises), so it is essential to buy it vacuum-packed or even frozen. Do not open the pack until a few hours before cooking.

As kangaroo has less than 2 per cent fat there is no likelihood of fat rancidity and sealed packets of meat can be refrigerated for a lot longer than other meat – distributors of kangaroo meat claim 4–6 weeks.

PREPARATION AND COOKING

Kangaroo is usually sold trimmed of all silver membrane, sinew and gristle. Once the meat has been removed from the packaging it should be wiped with kitchen paper, trimmed of any remaining silver membrane, then speedily rubbed with olive oil to protect it and cracked black pepper to flavour it. The meat should then be cooked without delay, at a very high temperature and for a very short time.

TO COOK A piece of *fillet* (the undercut of the loin) will take no more than 5 minutes in a hot frying pan or in a hot (220°C) oven. The *boned loin* will take no more than 7 minutes in a hot oven. As with all quickly cooked red meats, after removing it from the pan or oven, transfer it at once to a hot plate, cover and leave to rest for a further 5–10 minutes before carving.

recipes

kangaroo tail soup

SERVES 4

1 kangaroo tail, skinned
    and chopped
2 tablespoons olive oil
3 onions
2 carrots
4 sticks celery
1 bay leaf
1 large sprig thyme
4 stalks parsley
1 strip orange zest
water
4 tablespoons pearl barley
1 tablespoon tomato paste
salt
freshly ground black pepper
1 tablespoon medium–dry
    sherry
freshly chopped parsley

Rinse tail well and dry it thoroughly. Seal tail pieces in a heavy-based frying pan with oil. Remove tail to a stockpot.

Slice 1 onion, 1 carrot and 2 sticks celery and brown well in frying pan. Tie bay leaf, thyme, parsley stalks and zest with string and add to stockpot with browned vegetables. Pour in water to cover barely. Bring slowly to simmering point, skimming well. Adjust heat to a very gentle simmer and simmer for 4 hours. Cool overnight and remove any fat that has risen to the top.

Finely dice remaining onions and carrot and slice celery. Reheat soup, then strain and strip meat from tail. Discard cooked vegetables. Return shredded meat to pot with barley, tomato paste (diluted with some of the soup) and fresh vegetables and simmer until barley and vegetables are tender. Taste for seasoning. Just before serving add sherry. Garnish each portion generously with chopped parsley.

kangaroo steaks

Paint very thin steaks cut from the loin or diagonally from the fillet with olive oil, then scatter them with a mix of crushed peppercorns and a few juniper berries and cook on a super-hot chargrill pan for 30 seconds each side. Serve with Anchovy Butter (see ANCHOVIES*), mustard, horseradish mixed with thick cream, or home-made chutney.*

warm salad of roasted or grilled kangaroo

SERVES 4

4 kangaroo fillets or 2 boned
    loins
4 tablespoons extra-virgin
    olive oil
freshly ground black pepper
½ cup dry red wine
20 black olives, seeded and
    roughly chopped
2 large ripe tomatoes, peeled
    and diced
4 handfuls salad leaves,
    washed and dried
2 tablespoons freshly chopped
    parsley

Coat fillets with a little of the oil and pepper. Heat barbecue or oven to highest temperature possible. Heat a heavy-based frying pan on the stove and seal kangaroo for 45 seconds each side. Transfer to oven or barbecue and cook for 2 minutes each side. Leave to rest on a warm plate, loosely covered with a lid or foil, for at least 5 minutes.

Deglaze frying pan with wine and boil over high heat to reduce by two-thirds. Remove pan from heat and add olives, tomato and remaining olive oil.

Arrange salad leaves on plates. Slice

kangaroo and drop into pan with sauce. Turn to coat and arrange meat on the salad leaves. Spoon over any extra sauce, then scatter with parsley and freshly ground pepper.

polenta If you have any leftover polenta, you could serve a grilled slice on the side of the salad. **salad** Add extra ingredients to the salad, for example asparagus, baby green beans, Caramelised Onions (*see* ONIONS), boiled new potatoes or boiled baby beetroots.

maggie beer's barbecued kangaroo with anchovy vinaigrette and soft polenta SERVES 4

I have included Maggie's instructions for cooking polenta here. You may also like to try making No Mess Polenta (see CORN*).*

4 kangaroo fillets, trimmed of
   sinew
150 ml fruity extra-virgin
   olive oil
freshly ground black pepper
900 ml well-reduced Chicken
   Stock
2 cups polenta
2 teaspoons sea salt (Maldon,
   preferably)
100 g parmesan cheese, grated
walnut-sized piece of butter
1 lemon
1 clove garlic, chopped
1 tablespoon small capers
8 sprigs mint
4 anchovies (Western
   Australian, preferably),
   chopped

Coat fillets with a little of the oil and pepper. Set aside.

Bring half the stock to a simmer. Mix remaining stock with polenta in a large saucepan to make a paste and add salt. Add hot stock to polenta, stirring constantly to avoid lumps. Stir over a low heat for 20 minutes until polenta comes away from pan. Add parmesan and butter and check for seasoning. Keep warm in a shallow bowl that can be taken to the table.

Grate lemon zest, then squeeze lemon. Combine garlic, remaining oil, capers, lemon zest and juice and the stalks of the mint, chopped very finely (reserve the leaves), to make a vinaigrette.

Heat barbecue or oven to highest temperature possible. Heat a heavy-based frying pan on the stove and seal kangaroo for 45 seconds each side. Transfer to oven or barbecue and cook for 2 minutes each side. Leave to rest on a warm plate, loosely covered with a lid or foil, for at least 5 minutes.

Warm the vinaigrette and add anchovies, then drop in torn mint leaves. Slice kangaroo diagonally, arrange on hot plates and spoon over sauce. Offer polenta to spoon on the side.

bbq kangaroo
Surround serves of carved barbecued kangaroo with warm Ratatouille (see ZUCCHINI AND SQUASH*) and spoon Anchovy Vinaigrette (see* ANCHOVIES*) over the meat and the vegetables.*

kangaroo meatballs
Fry tiny meatballs made from seasoned minced kangaroo meat, then roll them in warmed chutney or home-made relish and serve with drinks.

kangaroo and sauce
Serve barbecued kangaroo with Fast Red-wine Sauce (see BEEF*).*

k i d n e y s

Leopold Bloom in James Joyce's novel *Ulysses* enjoyed everything about kidneys, but 'most of all he liked grilled mutton kidneys which gave to his palate a fine tang of faintly scented urine'. | Kidneys are the glandular excretory organs of animals. They have a strong and distinctive taste and an equally distinctive texture. Some people do not enjoy either. On the other hand, some people appreciate them as delicacies. | Kidneys are classed as offal or variety meats and are readily bought from most butchers. The French consider offal a delicacy, while Anglo-Saxons often reject such things untried – except for kidneys. Traditional cooked English breakfasts have long included devilled kidneys, and what could be more English than a steak and kidney pudding? | The French have an elaborate restaurant dish where a whole calf's kidney is baked in the oven, still encased in its own fat (suet). This dish is very rich and one has to love both fat and lots of kidney! Most people prefer the powerful flavour and rich gravy of kidney in smaller quantities, either as a small first course, on toast as a supper or breakfast dish or as an ingredient in a pie or pudding. >

Kidneys are inspected at the abattoirs as part of a quick check on the health of the animal. The inspectors are clearly not food lovers and they slash indiscriminately at the kidneys with the result that most kidneys arrive badly gashed and impossible to grill and present properly as a neat, opened-out shape. I find this very frustrating and an excellent example of lack of respect for an ingredient.

VARIETIES AND SEASON

Ox and *calf's* kidneys are multi-lobed, while *pig's* and *sheep's* kidneys are shaped like a haricot bean. The kidneys of young animals have a more delicate flavour, and milk-fed animals have paler kidneys. *Lamb's* and calf's kidneys are the most delicate in flavour and the most tender. (Many food lovers consider that calf's kidneys have the best flavour of all.) Ox kidneys have a hearty flavour, while pig's kidneys give the strongest flavour.

SELECTION AND STORAGE

Pig's kidneys add richness to pâtés and terrines, while ox kidneys are preferred for steak and kidney mixtures as they are most suited to long cooking. The more delicate calf's and lamb's kidneys are usually sliced and sautéd or grilled.

All offal should be bought fresh and used as soon as possible. Kidneys are best bought still protected by their own fat (suet) or membrane, which keeps the kidneys moist and fresh. However, it is often removed at the abattoirs. Kidneys ought to look firm and shiny without any dried edges or an unpleasant smell. (Remember, though, that a faint whiff of urine is considered normal!) Sometimes one can buy veal or pork chops with a portion of kidney attached. These are great treats and should be handled gently to keep the kidney portion attached.

Store kidneys for up to 2 days on a plate covered with plastic film in the refrigerator.

PREPARATION AND COOKING

All kidneys must be skinned and the core trimmed before cooking. The core is made up of fat that will melt as it grills, so there is no harm done if you leave bits of it intact. (Some kidney aficionados prefer to leave the core intact to moisten and baste the kidney as it grills.)

Ox kidneys are sometimes soaked in lightly salted warm water (or water with lemon juice or vinegar added) for an hour to remove any strong taste. Some soak kidneys for grilling in milk for 15 minutes.

All kidneys must either be cooked very quickly and served while still pink in the centre or be cooked for a long time, as for a pie or pudding. In-between kidneys will be hard and quite unappetising.

kidneys
go
with
butter
mustard
onions
bacon
chutney
mushrooms
sausages
rice
marsala
parsley
anchovies
lemon juice
Worcestershire sauce
paprika
beef
sage
rosemary

TO SKIN

Lamb's or pig's kidneys Remove any suet still attached, then remove the membrane by slitting the rounded side of the kidney and pulling the membrane back towards the core. Pull out as much as possible of the core and cut it away. Open out the kidney, cutting from the rounded side towards the core but leaving the kidney halves still attached. Trim away as much of the core as you can without brutalising the kidney. (Alternatively, do not open out the trimmed kidney but cut it across into 1 cm slices.) **Calf's or ox kidneys** Pull the membrane away from the lobes and cut away as much of the visible core as you can. Cut the kidneys across into 1 cm slices, removing as much of the core as possible without damaging the slices.

TO GRILL OR PAN-FRY

To grill If grilling lamb's kidneys, keep them 'butterflied' on 2 fine skewers. Paint prepared kidneys with olive oil and grill for 1–2 minutes a side on a chargrill pan or barbecue, turning them once. Remove to a warm plate and rest for 1 minute. Pour away any juices and add a little butter if desired. **To pan-fry** Heat butter until it is foaming and seal the prepared kidneys for 1–2 minutes a side for pink kidneys. Rest for 1 minute, then add sauce ingredients, if desired, and heat through quickly.

recipes

chinese kidney salad

SERVES 4

In Chinese Gastronomy *Hsiang Ju Lin and Tsuifeng Lin comment that 'the textural variation of innards is interesting to [Chinese] gourmets ... the grainy quality of liver, the unctuous intestine, the fibrous gizzard, the spongy maw and crunchy tripe all stand apart from each other, to be appreciated as delicacies, each with its unique texture'.*

kidney with butter
Top chargrilled slices of lamb's kidney with Anchovy Butter (see ANCHOVIES*) or butter fragrant with lemon juice and chopped capers.*

3 pig's kidneys, skinned, trimmed and sliced
4 tablespoons dry sherry or rice wine
1 teaspoon salt
1 cup blanched bean sprouts
SAUCE
2 tablespoons rice wine
2 teaspoons vegetable oil
1 teaspoon light soy sauce
½ teaspoon sesame oil
scant pinch of sugar

To make the sauce, combine ingredients and set aside.

Rinse kidney slices. Score each slice, using a small sharp knife, in a criss-cross fashion. Pour over sherry and salt and mix well.

Bring a large saucepan of water to a boil. Lower in kidney slices, then remove immediately. Bring fresh water to a boil and repeat process. Do this twice more.

Stir cleansed kidney slices into half the sauce and pour remaining sauce over bean sprouts in a separate bowl. Allow kidney to cool and eat as an appetiser.

devilled kidneys

SERVES 4

Constance Spry has this to say about devilled dishes: 'the bark . . . of devils is generally fiercer than their bite . . . with one or two exceptions the finished dish might be described as aromatic rather than peppery'. The principle of devilled food seems to be that it includes something hot, something piquant and something sweet. Often the dishes are intended for grilling or barbecuing, where the marinade ingredients darken to an appetising crust.

2 tablespoons Worcestershire
   sauce
2 tablespoons tomato relish
   or sauce
dash of paprika
1 teaspoon sugar
1 tablespoon dried English
   mustard
40 g butter
8 lamb's kidneys, skinned and
   sliced
1 tablespoon plain flour
1 cup stock
salt
freshly ground black pepper

Mix Worcestershire sauce, tomato relish, paprika, sugar and mustard to a paste. Melt butter in a frying pan and cook kidney quickly, then remove to a warm plate. Stir flour into pan and cook for 1 minute. Add Worcestershire sauce paste. Stir to mix and add stock, then stir until sauce is smooth and bring to a boil. Taste for salt and pepper. Return kidneys and juices to the sauce to heat through and serve at once on hot toast.

Devilled kidneys are good with crisp bacon alongside or a bunch of the freshest, crispest watercress.

kidney and mushrooms

Toss sautéed mushrooms with chargrilled slices of lamb's kidney.

grilled rosemary kidneys

Strip the leaves from 10 cm long rosemary sprigs, leaving a tuft at one end. Skewer butterflied lamb's kidneys, then grind over pepper and baste with oil and grill for 3–5 minutes a side.

calf's kidney with spinach

SERVES 2

3 cups prepared young spinach
   leaves
1 calf's kidney, skinned and
   trimmed
60 g butter
1 tablespoon olive oil
1 small onion *or* 2 shallots,
   finely chopped
100 ml marsala, sherry *or* port
3 tablespoons well-flavoured
   Chicken Stock
pinch of paprika
100 ml cream
salt
freshly ground black pepper

Blanch spinach in lightly salted water, drain and rinse in cold water to stop it cooking. Squeeze very well. Cut kidney into walnut-sized pieces.

Heat spinach in half the butter and keep warm. Heat remaining butter with oil in a frying pan. Sauté kidney quickly for 3–4 minutes. Transfer to a colander standing over a plate. Add onion to pan with marsala and reduce until barely moist. Add stock, paprika and cream and simmer for 5 minutes. Return kidney to sauce, adjust seasoning and serve with the spinach arranged in a ring around the kidney.

mum's steak and kidney pie

SERVES 6

My family's steak and kidney pie tradition uses an unusual lard pastry (also used for Grandma's Bramble Cake, see BERRIES AND CURRANTS)*, which is very short and crumbly (although Aunt Nora made hers with a suet crust, see* BEEF).

You will need to place an upturned egg cup or a proper pie funnel in the centre of the meat mixture and slit the crust above the egg cup if there is no pie funnel, so that the steam can escape and the crust crisps properly.

Don't serve potatoes with this pie, but maybe a purée of buttered carrots or swedes and a big bowl of buttered green beans or tiny Brussels sprouts instead.

grilled kidneys
Skim grilled kidneys with butter, garlic butter or herb butter.

kidneys in sauce
Add cream and mustard or wine and butter to pan-fried kidneys and heat through quickly. For a change, use wine vinegar or fresh herbs.

1.5 kg chuck steak, thickly sliced
1 ox kidney, trimmed and cut into 2 cm pieces
3 tablespoons plain flour
salt
freshly ground black pepper
1 large onion, diced
1 litre Veal Stock ✑ or water
4 large red-skinned potatoes, cubed
½ quantity Lard Pastry ✑
milk
1 egg

Trim fat from beef but leave in any connective tissue, which will melt slowly and supply gelatinous texture to the gravy. Cut beef into 4 cm cubes. Roll beef and kidney in seasoned flour and place in a saucepan with onion and extra salt and pepper. Pour over enough stock to cover meat barely. Mix well. Cover and bring very slowly to simmering point. Allow to cook, barely simmering, for 2 hours and skim once or twice.

When beef is nearly cooked but still has a little resilience, add potato. Simmer for 1 hour until potato and beef are tender. Taste gravy and adjust seasoning. Transfer meat and potato into a 2 litre china pie dish. Settle a pie funnel or upturned egg cup in centre of dish.

Preheat oven to 200°C. Roll out pastry to 1 cm thick. Brush rim of pie dish with milk and lift on crust. Press edges firmly. Whisk egg and a pinch of salt together and brush surface. Bake for 15 minutes, then lower temperature to 180°C and bake a further 30 minutes. If pastry is becoming too brown, cover with aluminium foil.

other recipes

aunt nora's steak and kidney pudding *see* BEEF

l a m b　　For centuries, lamb has been associated with religious ceremonies and festivals in many cultures over much of the world. It is important in Muslim countries of the Middle East, where a lamb is served at weddings and to mark the birth of a child. At Passover Jews gather for the ceremonial family roast of lamb, and for Christians the lamb has a special significance as a symbol of Christ and is eaten to celebrate Easter.　|　As everyone knows, sheep came to Australia with the first settlers and any history of the sheep industry is in fact a history of white exploration and expansion across the continent. In the 1950s we were even said to be riding on the sheep's back, although the most valuable commodity then was the sheep's wool, not its meat.　|　The industry is still a major one in Australia today, both for wool and meat. Australia produces some of the finest lamb in the world. It is tender, full of flavour and plentiful. Mutton was the favoured meat of the nineteenth century but today succulent pink lamb has won out as the most popular dish. >

lamb
goes
with
artichokes
anchovies
tomatoes
eggplants
zucchini
onions
garlic
sweet peppers
carrots
turnips
potatoes
mushrooms
rosemary
mint
raisins
pine nuts
almonds
spinach
green beans
broad beans
chick peas
couscous
lemons
cracked wheat
parsley
rice
lentils
dried beans
quinces
preserved lemons
saffron
olives
olive oil
breadcrumbs
parmesan cheese
salad leaves

The Australian Meat and Livestock Corporation claims research shows that many Australian cooks believe buying lamb is expensive and wasteful because of the bone and fat that remains on the plate. Their marketing arm is attempting to convince Australians to buy more lamb that has been butchered and trimmed in ways that remove the fat and bone. This is being sold as Trim Lamb. However, it is still possible to buy lamb on the bone and with its fat intact. Excess fat can easily be removed from lamb before cooking, but remember that a thin layer of fat bastes meat as it roasts or grills, keeping it moist. Trim Lamb must be cooked carefully to avoid it being dry and tough.

As lamb is enjoyed in so many countries of the world, with a change of garnish you can whirl your family from the Middle East (spices, raisins, lentils) to North Africa (prunes, olives, pickled lemons, almonds, couscous), India (saffron, rice, tamarind, curry spices) or the Mediterranean (peppers, onions, zucchini, tomatoes, yoghurt).

VARIETIES AND SEASON

Australian sheep meat is branded according to age and one determines the age of a sheep by the number of teeth it has. *Lamb* is from sheep younger than 12 months old that have no permanent teeth. It is recognised by the red brand on the flesh. *Spring lamb* is 3–10 months old. A few Australian farmers are now marketing their lamb at a very young age (generally under 8 weeks of age) as *milk-fed lamb*. A brown brand indicates an age between 15–30 months old; this meat is called *hogget* or *two-tooth*. Sheep that is not branded is *mutton*, and is at least 2 years old. The older the sheep the stronger the flavour and the coarser the texture. Milk-fed lamb is buttery and delicate. Mutton is strongest of all and is thought by some to have the aroma of the sheepyard!

Modern sheep-farming aims to produce animals for meat that have less fat than those bred exclusively for high-grade wool. Various cross-breeds using the merino crossed with British breeds create shorter more compact carcasses that are the basis of Australia's prime lamb industry. Consumers buy what they are offered and have no idea what breed of animal they are receiving.

Good-quality lamb is available all year round but the delicately flavoured spring lamb that appears at the end of winter is especially delicious.

SELECTION AND STORAGE

The texture and flavour of lamb is much improved by hanging and ageing for several days after it has been slaughtered. This process is carried out by the butcher. If any lamb you buy is tough you should ask the butcher how old it was and how long it was hung.

The meat of lamb is a clear rosy colour. As the animal ages the colour deepens to purplish red in mutton. Avoid any lamb that has a brownish tinge. Lamb fat should be creamy-white and firm and dry to the touch.

It is important that you buy a cut suitable for the use you have in mind: roasting, grilling, frying or braising. Do not try to save money and purchase a cheaper cut and then try to grill rather than braise or stew it.

FOR ROASTING The *leg* is the most popular joint for roasting, with a *boned and rolled shoulder* or *loin* not far behind. (Kept whole and on the bone, 2 loins form a very grand roasting joint known as the *saddle*.) The *rack* or best end of neck is a glamorous cut. Each rack consists of 8 ribs, but you can order the number of ribs you want (usually 4 per person) if you prefer to roast the racks individually rather than carving them at the table. Two racks tied together with their trimmed bones intertwined make a very impressive roast dinner for 4 people (this is known as a *guard of honour*). Ask the butcher to cut away the chine bone, so that it is possible to cut easily between the ribs. A *forequarter* roast from the shoulder is made up of chops; it can be slow-roasted and should be eaten with friends who enjoy chewing on bones. A *breast of lamb* or lamb flap is rarely seen in butchers' shops these days as it is fatty, but it makes a very inexpensive boned and rolled roast. *Trim Lamb* cuts are mainly derived from the leg (silverside, topside or round) or a heavily trimmed and boned loin. Trim Lamb cuts need to be painted with oil to compensate for the lack of fat and cooked at high temperatures.

FOR GRILLING OR FRYING **Grilling** Because grilling is fast, choose only the most tender cuts. Grilling cuts from the loin are sold as *chump chops* and *middle loin* or *loin chops*. (Ask the butcher to cut you double loin chops. They can be grilled until the outside is crisp and deep brown, while the inside will still be pink. Double-thickness chops are perfect for the barbecue, where it is only too easy to achieve charred and inedible chops.) *Forequarter chops* from the shoulder are usually sold as barbecue chops. (This meat is full of flavour and is more gelatinous than the meat from the loin or hind leg but it has a lot more sinew. I find these chops one of the most disappointing cuts and would much prefer to bone, cube and braise the meat or to slow-roast the whole joint.) A *'butterflied' leg of lamb* makes an impressive grill: get the butcher to prepare the meat for you. *Trim Lamb* cuts, from the leg and loin, are suitable for grilling but must be painted with oil and cooked quickly at a high temperature. **Frying** Lamb *cutlets* cut from the rack are sometimes flattened and dipped into beaten egg and fine white breadcrumbs and fried in clarified butter or oil. (If you love crunchy crumbed cutlets, ask the butcher to flatten the cutlets, but do the egging and crumbing yourself. Crumbs get soggy after a while, so the butcher always gives each cutlet a very thick coating. Also, sometimes the crumbs are 'flavoured' with horrible dusty herbs.) The small **underfillet** from the loin (sold as 'fillet') is particularly good for pan-frying or chargrilling.

FOR BRAISING The **shoulder** (including the forequarter) is often boned and chopped for use in curries and pies and all manner of braises. **Neck chops** or middle chops are becoming hard to find, but are very inexpensive. They are marbled with fat and need long, slow cooking to become succulent. This is the cut to use if you want to try a traditional French braise with turnips, carrots and potatoes. Together with the **shank** from the forequarter or hindquarter, it is the cut I go for when making a couscous dinner.

MINCED LAMB The **shoulder**, **loin** or **leg** can be minced and spiced to make great lamb burgers or tiny meatballs. Ask the butcher to mince lean lamb finely for you; sometimes a recipe requires meat that has been minced twice.

Large pieces of lamb will keep for 4–5 days in the refrigerator. The ideal way to store meat is to free it of all wrappings, set it on a wire rack over a plate or tray and cover it with a damp cotton cloth to prevent the surface drying out. Any juices, which can sour the meat, will collect under the rack. Next best is to cover the meat with greaseproof paper. Note that frost-free refrigerators dry food out quickly.

Chopped or minced lamb should be used within 24 hours. To store, remove it from the shop wrappings and refrigerate on a covered plate. Frozen meat should be thawed in the refrigerator and used within 24 hours.

PREPARATION AND COOKING

Even in cultures where lamb is prized, many do not appreciate the flavour of lamb fat. Trim off most of the visible fat, leaving just sufficient to baste the meat. If you remove every vestige of fat you must protect the exposed meat by painting it with olive oil, spreading over some oily marinating paste or wrapping the joint in a thin layer of caul fat, or the surface of the meat will be dry and leathery. This is especially true of Trim Lamb cuts.

TO BONE Awkwardly shaped pieces of lamb, such as the shoulder, neck or breast, are easier to cook and carve if they have been boned. Prime cuts such as the leg and the loin can also be boned. This is usually done so that the meat can be stuffed. My advice is to cultivate a butcher who is pleased to do this for you. Always ask that the bones be returned to make a soup or stock.

Boning is not very difficult. A sharp knife is essential, as is some patience.

Investigate the shape of the piece of meat you are dealing with and always keep the sharp edge of the knife against the bone. Fingers are useful for separating the flesh from the bone, too.

TO ROAST | Lamb can be roasted bone-in or boned. A leg or loin of lamb can be rubbed with oil and pepper and have slivers of garlic inserted in the flesh and a sprig of rosemary tucked underneath it or in the sawn-through shank. Let it rest for 30 minutes before roasting.

I prefer to roast at a high temperature (220°C), which can cause fat to sputter in the oven. I place a baking dish with 2 cm water in it on the bottom of the oven and sit the meat directly on the oven rack. The fat drops into the pan and does not burn. Baste the leg or loin several times with the collected juices or wine.

For pink lamb allow 10 minutes per 500 g. For better-done lamb allow 15 minutes per 500 g. For well-done lamb allow 20 minutes per 500 g. If you are using a meat thermometer, the internal temperature is 60°C for medium–rare, medium is 65°C, while well-done is 80°C.

Once cooked, I allow the meat to rest, covered loosely in a warm place, for at least 20 minutes (a leg) or 15 minutes (a rack or full loin). While the meat is resting, pour off the collected fat and deglaze the baking dish with a little wine or wine vinegar. Serve this as a simple 'jus' or extend it with stock, the juices from the roasting meat, garlic purée or fresh tomato sauce or follow any of the other suggestions made later in this section. **Racks of lamb** Trim all meat and fat from the exposed bones and wrap the bones in aluminium foil to prevent them burning or charring in the oven. A whole or double rack will take 20 minutes to cook at 220°C and need 15 minutes resting on a hot dish in a warm place. An individual portion of 4 cutlets may be cooked after 15 minutes. Test with a skewer pushed into the fattest part of the rack exactly as explained in the Roasted Leg of Lamb with Rosemary and Garlic and All the Trimmings (*see* p. 376).

TO GRILL | Remove any excess fat, which will flare on the grill, and rub the meat with oil to prevent it sticking. (Be especially careful when preparing to cook small patties or brochettes of lamb as they are much more likely to stick.) If using an electric or gas overhead griller, it is preferable to start the grilling at a high heat to brown and crisp the meat and then to lower the heat to complete the cooking. This is harder to regulate if grilling on a charcoal barbecue.

Single loin chops will take 7–10 minutes all up. Grill double loin chops fast initially, then reduce the heat a little; they will take 15 minutes to cook. An opened-out or 'butterflied' leg of lamb will take 30–40 minutes to grill and should then rest, loosely covered, before slicing, as if it had been roasted.

When grilling a butterflied leg of lamb it is essential that the heat be reduced or the outside will be charred and the inside still raw.

Season all meat *after* it has been cooked, otherwise the juices will be drawn out during cooking.

TO PAN-FRY | This method is ideal for small tender cuts (such as the underfillet) or thin slices from tender cuts (such as the loin) or boned and tied medallions from the loin, which might also be stuffed.

Remove all connective tissue and silver membrane, then dust the meat with seasoned flour, seal in olive oil or oil and butter and proceed with the particular recipe. The simplest way to proceed is to seal the seasoned meat as described above, then to add liquid (stock, wine, tomato sauce, water), which will thicken slightly to create a simple sauce. Infinite variations are possible by the addition of finely chopped herbs either before or after the liquid has been added, sautéd garlic, quickly blanched vegetables such as small onions or mushrooms, and so on. **Cutlets** Trim away any excess fat and dip cutlets in whisked egg or melted butter and then in breadcrumbs. Fry cutlets in plenty of hot oil or clarified butter ✐. Do not crowd the pan or the temperature will drop rapidly. (If this happens the crust will soak up the fat and the whole dish will be ruined.) **Underfillets** Trim the fillets of any silver membrane and pan-fry quickly in hot oil or butter and oil. They will only take a few minutes. Allow to rest before slicing.

TO BRAISE | This moist, gentle method of cooking is ideal when selecting a tougher cut of lamb, such as the neck, shank or shoulder, or if cooking mutton. Such cuts have plenty of gelatinous connective tissue that softens after being cooked for 1½ hours at 180°C, preferably in an enamelled cast-iron casserole.

Braised lamb is usually accompanied by a selection of vegetables. The liquid may be simply water or stock or a strained wine marinade. The meat is usually floured and seared first of all; any crusty bits left in the searing pan should be rinsed out with some of the liquid and added to the pot. Braising is discussed in more detail in OXTAIL.

TO STUFF | A boned shoulder of lamb can be stuffed and rolled before roasting or braising. A loin or leg of lamb can also be stuffed. Ask your butcher to tunnel-bone a leg for you; the butcher will extract the bones and create a neat pocket, ideal for stuffing. A rolled, stuffed joint needs to be tied firmly with string. A pocketed stuffed joint needs to be skewered closed but does not need to be tied. Do not pack too much stuffing in – most stuffings swell during the cooking.

Stuffings vary from simple breadcrumbs seasoned with an onion and fresh herbs and bound with an egg to elaborate combinations of ham, soft cheeses, rice, nuts, vegetables and fruit. Whatever combination you prefer it should be moist and well seasoned.

lamb shank broth

SERVES 6

A lamb shank is one of my favourite cuts. Shanks do not cook quickly but like most slow-cooked dishes they require little attention. With one shank you can make a delicious and filling soup; with several, a family dinner.

1 lamb shank
1 onion, diced
1 bay leaf
1 sprig thyme
2.5 litres water
20 g pearl barley, rinsed
2 carrots, peeled and diced
1 leek, sliced
1 turnip, peeled and diced
1 stick celery, strings removed
    and finely sliced
salt
freshly ground black pepper
freshly chopped parsley

Place shank, onion, bay leaf and thyme in a stockpot and add water. Bring to simmering point. Skim and simmer for 1 hour, then add barley. Simmer for 1 hour. Add remaining vegetables and simmer for 30 minutes until vegetables are tender. Remove shank and cut meat into small pieces. Return meat to pot and simmer for 30 minutes. Taste for seasoning. Serve garnished generously with parsley.

middle eastern A vaguely Middle Eastern dish results with just a few changes to the above recipe and by starting with 2 shanks. To the 2 lamb shanks and onion, add ½ teaspoon ground turmeric, ½ stick cinnamon, ½ teaspoon crushed coriander seeds, ½ teaspoon crushed black peppercorns and 2 cloves finely chopped garlic. Add water and simmer as above. Instead of the barley, add 375 g brown lentils with the rest of the vegetables and cook a further 45 minutes. Serve with plenty of freshly chopped coriander leaves and pass sambal oelek, Preserved Lemons (*see* LEMONS AND LIMES) or Harissa (*see* PEPPERS AND CHILLIES).

kibbeh

SERVES 4

Kibbeh has been eaten in the Middle East for at least 2000 years. Traditionally it is eaten raw. The lamb paste is spread on a shallow plate, drizzled with olive oil and/or lemon juice and often decorated with some or all of the following: paprika, finely chopped spring onion, chopped parsley, toasted pine nuts and mint sprigs. It is scooped up with soft pita bread or young, crisp cos lettuce leaves. Ask your butcher to mince very lean lamb twice through the finest hole of his mincer, or do it yourself at home.

120 g finely cracked wheat

500 g lamb, finely minced

salt

1 onion, very finely chopped

2 teaspoons ground cumin

1 teaspoon ground allspice

pinch of cayenne pepper

Rinse cracked wheat in a sieve with cold water and squeeze it very hard. Mix all ingredients together (a food processor is quite good for this) until you have a smooth paste.

olive cutlets
Spread cutlets with a little Italian Black Olive Paste (see OLIVES AND OLIVE OIL) *before dipping in whisked egg and breadcrumbs.*

lamb and garlic jus

This is the base for all lamb sauces I make. When cooking at home it is simple to pour off any fat from a baking dish and deglaze with a glass of wine, red or white, and add a little stock, if you have any. But sometimes you may have lamb bones left after boning a leg. Instead of giving them all to the dog, why not make some sauce and freeze it for a rainy day?

1 kg lamb bones

1 onion, chopped

1 carrot, chopped

1 leek, chopped

1 stick celery, chopped

100 g mushrooms *or*
  mushroom trimmings *or*
  50 g dried mushrooms,
  chopped

1 cup dry red *or* white wine

3 stalks parsley

1 bay leaf

1 sprig thyme

a few black peppercorns

3 cloves garlic, crushed

3 tablespoons tomato paste

GARLIC PASTE

8 cloves garlic, peeled

1 small onion, finely chopped

1 tablespoon tomato paste

Roast bones at 200°C in a lightly oiled baking dish until well browned. Transfer to stockpot. Tip off almost all fat from pan. Put vegetables into pan and roast until well coloured. Transfer vegetables to stockpot, tip off any fat remaining and place baking dish over a brisk heat. Deglaze pan with wine, stirring and scraping well. Tip deglazing juices into stockpot. Add herbs, peppercorns, garlic and tomato paste and generously cover with cold water. Bring to simmering point, skimming well, and reduce heat to maintain a gentle simmer. Cook for 6 hours, skimming every hour and replacing the volume of skimmings with cold water. Strain, pressing well on vegetables, and refrigerate stock overnight for all fat to rise. Next day, remove fat.

To make the garlic paste, cover garlic and onion with cold water, bring to a boil and pour water away. Repeat process twice. Cover blanched onion and garlic with a little lamb stock and add tomato paste. Simmer gently until garlic is soft. Sieve this sauce or purée it in a food processor. >

Bring stock to a boil and check flavour. Boil hard to concentrate flavour if it is at all insipid. When stock is strong enough, whisk in garlic paste, stirring to blend thoroughly. Adjust seasoning. Use as required or freeze in small quantities for deglazing or to create an instant sauce.

marinating paste

This paste is sufficient for marinating a leg of lamb, a whole loin or 8 thick chops.

3 tablespoons Dijon mustard
1 tablespoon light soy sauce
1 tablespoon plain flour
1 tablespoon olive oil
1 teaspoon finely chopped
   fresh rosemary leaves
freshly ground black pepper

Mix all ingredients together and smear liberally over meat. Roast or grill as usual (if grilling, allow surface to sear and seal well before attempting to turn it). The paste will cook to a dark crust.

variation Substitute a hot pepper relish or puréed chutney for the soy sauce.

pan-fried fillets
Pan-fry lamb underfillets seasoned with pepper and fresh rosemary, then deglaze pan with a little red wine and stir in some redcurrant jelly to glaze. Slice on the diagonal to serve.

slow-roasted leg of lamb with dried beans

SERVES 4–6

A roasted leg of lamb remains a very popular family dish, and rightly so. It will feed 4–6 and still leave meat for a salad or sandwiches the next day, it is difficult to cook badly and it cooks itself without any fuss. This version is a favourite in French families (and mine!). The meat will not be pink.

1 large sprig rosemary
1 leg of lamb, trimmed
salt
freshly ground black pepper
1 tablespoon olive oil
375 g cannellini *or* haricot
   beans, soaked overnight
1 onion, diced
2 carrots, diced
2 cloves garlic, chopped
2 tablespoons tomato paste
1 litre hot water *or* Lamb and
   Garlic Jus (see p. 374)

Preheat oven to 180°C. Tie rosemary to lamb and rub meat with salt and pepper, then with oil. Drain beans and bring to a boil in plenty of cold water, then drain again. Mix beans with onion, carrot and garlic. Place meat in a deep baking dish and strew beans and vegetables around it. Dissolve tomato paste in hot water and pour over vegetables. Bake for 2 hours, covered for the first hour with aluminium foil. By the end of cooking the meat should be quite soft and the beans should be tender but still moist and have developed a slight crust. Serve with a large green salad.

ham and ricotta stuffing for lamb

100 g cooked ham, finely
  chopped
1 clove garlic, finely chopped
2 tablespoons freshly chopped
  parsley
150 g ricotta
salt
freshly ground black pepper
2 eggs

Combine all ingredients except eggs. Mix in sufficient egg to make a manageable stuffing that is not too hard. Taste for salt and pepper. Stuff your selected piece of meat and cook.

mediterranean lamb
Tip Ratatouille (see ZUCCHINI AND SQUASH*) into a deglazed baking dish to reheat and serve with roast lamb.*

roasted leg of lamb with rosemary and garlic and all the trimmings   SERVES 4–6

This method will result in pink lamb. More and more Australians are appreciating their lamb cooked medium to medium–rare.

I like to offer the carved meat on a central platter with the juices spooned over it. This means that I can sit back and enjoy the spectacle of the food before it is eaten.

1 sprig rosemary
1 leg of lamb, trimmed
1 clove garlic, cut into 4
olive oil
salt
freshly ground black pepper
4 red-skinned potatoes
2 onions, unpeeled and halved
  horizontally
4 parsnips, peeled
4 carrots, peeled
1 cup water
1 cup wine, stock *or* water

Tie rosemary to lamb. Poke 4 little incisions into meat with the tip of a sharp knife and insert garlic spears. Rub meat with 1 tablespoon olive oil and season with salt and pepper. Leave at room temperature for 30 minutes.

Preheat oven to 220°C. Place potatoes directly on oven rack. Arrange remaining vegetables in a baking dish with water and a film of oil. Place lamb directly on oven rack alongside potatoes with baking dish immediately below. After 45 minutes test lamb at its thickest point by slipping in a thin skewer. Leave it in place for 1 minute and then feel it on your lower lip. The skewer should feel quite hot and the juices that ooze from the pierced spot should be rosy-pink. (If the juices are red and the skewer is only faintly warm, leave the meat for a further 10 minutes and then test it again.)

Remove meat from oven and wrap loosely in foil. Keep in a warm, draught-free spot for at least 15 minutes while vegetables continue to cook. When vegetables are tender and well coloured, remove to a warm plate. Pour excess fat from baking dish and deglaze it with wine. >

Carve lamb onto a heated serving platter, adding any juices to the sauce in the pan, and arrange the vegetables around the meat. Offer the potatoes from a basket, so that they do not lose their crunch, and serve a green salad or other accompanying vegetables.

salad of grilled lamb   SERVES 4

One of the best Trim Lamb cuts is the boned middle loin of lamb, sometimes known as rib-eye or lamb strap. This choice piece of meat can be sautéd, poached or cut into medallions and grilled, but best of all is this method of opening the piece out flat and then grilling it very quickly.

Have your garnishes ready before you start cooking. A reminder list might include washed and dried salad leaves, vinaigrette or other dressing, boiled potatoes, green beans, roasted tomatoes, parsnip chips (see PARSNIPS), *chopped sun-dried tomatoes, and so on.*

2 boned middle loins of lamb
olive oil
salt
freshly ground black pepper
4 handfuls salad leaves,
   washed and dried
4 tablespoons Pesto (see
   p. 81) or Anchovy Butter
   (see p. 43)

Ensure that meat is totally freed of fat and membrane. Using a sharp knife, and holding the blade parallel with the bench, slice through each piece of meat, but not quite through. Open out. Pound each piece of meat a little with flat of your hand, then slip it into a plastic bag and gently and evenly pound it with flat side of a meat mallet (or a rolling pin) until a little less than 5 mm thick. Paint meat with oil.

Preheat a chargrill pan. Slap meat on hot grill, then turn it 45 degrees after 1 minute. After a further minute, turn meat over and repeat on second side. Remove cooked meat to a hot plate and season.

Toss salad leaves and arrange on 4 plates. Cut meat into strips and divide between plates. Add pesto or butter, which will melt deliciously over the lamb, then add other chosen garnishes.

lamb shanks with couscous   SERVES 4

This is an example of an impressionist recipe. You need to grasp the central idea and then make it up as you go!

1 cup chick peas, soaked
   overnight
4 lamb shanks or 8 neck chops
plain flour
2 bay leaves
(continued next page)

Cook chick peas in plenty of lightly salted water for 1½ hours until tender. Drain and set aside.

Roll meat in flour. Tie herbs and zest with string to make a bouquet garni. Dice 2 of the onions. Place meat, diced onion and

crumbed cutlets
Mix one-third freshly grated parmesan cheese to two-thirds fresh breadcrumbs for a particularly delicious and golden crust for cutlets.

oregano marinade for lamb
Marinate 500 g lean lamb in 4 tablespoons olive oil, 1 tablespoon lemon juice and 1 tablespoon crumbled dried oregano, then grind over pepper and grill until charred on the outside and pink inside.

4 generous sprigs thyme

6 stalks parsley

4 pieces dried *or* fresh orange
  zest

4 large onions

2 teaspoons sambal oelek

2 teaspoons paprika

I stick cinnamon

generous pinch of saffron
  threads

stock, tomato juice *or* water

4 potatoes

4 carrots, peeled

4 chunks pumpkin, peeled

4 zucchini, cut into chunks

400 g couscous, moistened as
  directed on packet

freshly chopped parsley *or*
  coriander

roast lamb

*Slow-roast a leg of
lamb on a bed of
thickly sliced potato,
sliced onion, diced
garlic and fresh
rosemary moistened
with 1 cup water.*

**anchovy roast
lamb**

*Spike a leg of lamb
with pieces
of anchovy before
roasting.*

bouquet garni in a deep casserole or a
couscousier. Add sambal oelek, paprika,
cinnamon and saffron. Generously cover
with stock. Bring to simmering point,
uncovered, then skim and continue to
simmer for 1 hour. Add chick peas and
simmer for 30 minutes.

Start adding vegetables according to the
time they will take to cook. (Potatoes,
onions and carrots will take 30 minutes,
pumpkin 15 minutes and zucchini
5 minutes.) Test shanks are tender and taste
broth for salt.

Steam couscous in the perforated top of a
couscousier that fits over the pot, or in an
enamelled colander over a separate pot of
boiling water. Serve couscous separately
from meat, vegetables and juices. Scatter
stew with parsley and offer Harissa (*see*
PEPPERS AND CHILLIES) or Preserved Lemons
(*see* LEMONS AND LIMES). Reheat any leftovers with water and without
lamb for a great soup.

sweet and sour lamb   SERVES 6

4 tablespoons olive oil

2 onions, thinly sliced

1.5 kg lamb shoulder, cubed

I½ cups water *or* lamb stock

½ cup red-wine vinegar

3 tablespoons tomato paste

2 tablespoons sugar

3 tablespoons toasted
  pine nuts

3 tablespoons seeded raisins

½ teaspoon salt

½ teaspoon freshly ground
  black pepper

Heat 3 tablespoons of the oil and fry onion
until quite soft, stirring frequently. Drain
through a sieve over a small bowl, pressing
on onion to extract all the oil. Heat onion-
frying oil and remaining olive oil in a large
frying pan and brown lamb. Transfer lamb
and onion to an enamelled cast-iron
casserole. Pour off any fat in pan and
deglaze it with a little of the water. Add
deglazing liquid to casserole with vinegar,
tomato paste, sugar and remaining water.

Simmer for 1 hour, stirring once or twice.
Add pine nuts and raisins and cook for
30 minutes until meat is very tender. If
liquid seems too thin, increase heat and boil rapidly to reduce it. Season
and serve with rice, couscous or chunky pasta.

moroccan tagine with quince

SERVES 6

Claudia Roden gives this recipe in A New Book of Middle Eastern Food *and comments that dishes that combine the sweet and the savoury are surprising to many who have not yet encountered the brilliantly coloured and richly spiced dishes of the Middle East and North Africa.*

650 g quinces, unpeeled and sliced

40 g butter

1 kg lamb shoulder, cubed

2 onions, finely chopped

salt

freshly ground black pepper

pinch of cayenne pepper

pinch of paprika

1 bunch coriander, finely chopped

¼ teaspoon ground saffron

½ teaspoon ground ginger

Sauté quince in butter until well coloured on both sides. Remove and reserve.

Place all ingredients other than quince and 1 of the chopped onions in an enamelled cast-iron casserole and barely cover with water. Bring to simmering point, then taste for salt and peppers and adjust if necessary. Simmer, covered, for 1 hour. Add remaining chopped onion and quince and cook until quince is just tender. Stir onion and quince through the meat and serve with plain steamed rice or couscous.

lamb stock It is not traditional, but the water could be replaced with lamb stock if you had some. **fruit** The quince could be omitted and apple, pear, dates, raisins or prunes used instead, alone or in combination.

other recipes

basil stuffing for lamb *see* BASIL

chickpea salad with the remains of roast lamb *see* CHICK PEAS

devilled kidneys *see* KIDNEYS

english lamb's liver and bacon *see* LIVER

english mint sauce *see* MINT

lamb and yoghurt from a pakistani recipe *see* YOGHURT

lebanese grilled liver *see* LIVER

middle eastern meatballs with coriander leaves *see* CORIANDER

pine nut and meat pastries *see* NUTS

quick yoghurt marinade for chicken or lamb *see* YOGHURT

roman lamb stew *see* SAGE

satay marinade and sauce *see* NUTS

stuffed bush marrow with yoghurt sauce *see* ZUCCHINI AND SQUASH

see also BRAINS; KIDNEYS; LIVER; TONGUE

l e e k s   The leek (*Allium porrum*) is a member of the lily family and shares the *Allium* genus with garlic and various onions. The Sumerians cultivated leeks as early as 2500 BC, but it is with the Welsh that the leek is most closely identified. In the twelfth century the Welsh wore leeks on their hats to distinguish them from their enemies, and the leek has remained the Welsh symbol to this day. │ Leeks are sometimes referred to as poor man's asparagus. The comparison is with the European white asparagus, and when slender, tender leeks are boiled and dressed with olive oil, chopped chives, parsley and maybe finely minced hardboiled egg the similarity is surprising. │ Many dishes that feature onions can substitute leeks for a milder flavour. Leeks are perhaps best-known as a major ingredient in leek and potato soup (known as vichyssoise when served cold), and as an essential addition to the stockpot, but their culinary uses go far beyond this. Leek pies and tarts show how well leeks, butter, cream and pastry go together. The gentle sweetness of the leek is also often contrasted with something sharp or salty, such as anchovies, mustard dressings, raw ham or salt cod. Leeks are a favourite ingredient in French bourgeois dishes, such as pot-au-feu, and the Scots have their traditional cock-a-leekie.

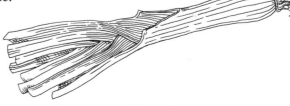

VARIETIES AND SEASON

The most widely grown variety in Australia is Welsh wonder. Leeks are available all year, the peak season being October–May. In the temperate parts of the country leeks are harvested during the spring and summer. In tropical climates leeks grow best during the cooler months.

SELECTION AND STORAGE

The edible part of the leek is the thick white stem and the palest part of the green tops. In order to maximise the development of the white stem, leeks are 'blanched': soil is 'hilled up' around each leek or sometimes the leeks are covered by tubes filled with soil. This explains why leeks are notorious harbourers of grit and why so much attention must be paid to cleaning them.

Choose medium-sized leeks rather than giants, or smaller if cooking them whole. (In my opinion leeks should only ever be cooked whole if they are *very* young and tender.) Select leeks that look crisp and white and without split, discoloured outer leaves or yellow or withered tops. Ask the greengrocer to lop off the dark-green top and then inspect the leek closely to make sure that it does not have a solid, woody core. This tends to occur at the end of winter.

Wrap leeks in a vegetable storage bag and refrigerate in the crisper for up to a week.

PREPARATION

The most important preparation when handling leeks is to remove the dirt trapped between the leaves. If the leeks are to be sliced and then steamed, stewed or sautéd, simply discard the green tops (wash and keep for a soup or stock), cut the leeks into rings and swish them well in plenty of cold water. Lift the sliced leek from the water and drain well. (Do *not* tip the washed leek through a colander, water, grit and all, or you will risk finding some of the dirt back among the leek.) One is usually instructed to boil off excess moisture when cooking leeks, so drained leeks should be patted dry with a cloth or kitchen paper before starting the cooking process.

To remove dirt from leeks that are to be left whole, remove one or two outer layers and make a crosswise slit at the leafy end and stand the leeks, leafy-end down, in a tall jug of water for 1–2 hours. (In fact, I prefer to split leeks in half lengthwise, keeping them attached at the root end, so that I can fan the leaves under cold running water like a pack of cards. The leeks can be steamed or stewed for a little less time this way than if left whole.)

Leeks can be boiled, steamed, stewed or sautéd and should be tender but not mushy. Undercooked leeks are impossible to eat and one can choke on them. Less than al dente is plain bad cooking where leeks are concerned.

leeks
go
with
butter
cream
pastry
chives
garlic
parsley
potatoes
pastry
eggs
ham
gruyère cheese
goat's cheese
olive oil
mustard
chicken
boiled beef
salt cod
anchovies
watercress

Leeks intended as a first course with a vinaigrette dressing are greatly improved if, after steaming or boiling whole, they are placed on kitchen paper on a plate, covered with plastic film and weighted for 1 hour. They will expel a large amount of water. Pour off this water and slice the leeks as you wish and then toss with or spoon over the dressing. Pressed like this the leeks will not look like some soggy vegetable floating in a watery sea.

recipes

cock-a-leekie

SERVES 8

This recipe appears in Scottish cookbooks dating from the sixteenth century. Cock-a-leekie is a soup in which the chicken and shin of beef used to make the delicious broth are sliced back into the soup, to which are added leeks and plump prunes.

I have a much-prized edition of The Cook and Housewife's Manual *by Mistress Margaret (Meg) Dods, published in* MDCCCXXXVII (1837), *in which the author firmly rejects the prunes. 'Prunes used to be put to this soup. The practice is obsolete.' I am just as convinced that the prunes are essential. They complement the sweetness of the leeks, add complexity to the broth and look sensational: dark floating shapes among the white, brown and green.*

leek scrambled eggs

Stir Buttery Leeks (see p. 383) into softly scrambled eggs and serve alongside smoked salmon or on toast for breakfast.

leek vinaigrette

Make a vinaigrette with 2 teaspoons Dijon mustard, 3 tablespoons olive oil and 1 teaspoon red-wine vinegar, then toss through steamed young leeks and decorate with minced egg.

1 kg beef shin, chopped on the bone
2 litres water
1.5 kg leeks, trimmed
18 prunes, stoned
1 × 2 kg chicken
salt
freshly ground black pepper

Place beef in a stockpot with water. Bring to a boil, skim, and simmer very gently for 3 hours, partly covered.

While beef is simmering, slice half the leeks lengthwise, then wash and drain well and tie in a bundle with a thread. Slice remaining leeks into 1 cm rings, then wash well, drain and set aside. If prunes are hard and wizened, pour boiling water over and leave for 1 hour. Drain, reserving water.

Add chicken and bundle of leeks to stockpot and simmer for 45 minutes, uncovered. Add prunes and any reserved soaking water.

Remove beef and chicken. Discard skin of chicken and bones from beef. Discard bundle of leeks. Cut chicken and beef into bite-sized pieces and return meat to pot with sliced leek. Simmer very gently for 5 minutes until leek is tender. Adjust seasoning and serve soup in wide bowls, so that the diner can enjoy the colours as well as the rising aromas.

leeks à la grecque

SERVES 4

This is a very tasty first course when young, slender leeks are available. It is also a good choice as part of a buffet selection if you are having a party as the leeks can be prepared ahead of time and brought back to room temperature. However, like all stewed vegetable dishes, they are at their most delicious when served shortly after cooking.

The method 'à la grecque' is a useful one to learn as exactly the same procedure can be used for button mushrooms, small zucchini or squash, okra or pickling onions. The cooking times will vary though.

8 medium *or* 12 very slender
   leeks, slit lengthwise
1 cup water
3 tablespoons best-quality
   olive oil
2 tablespoons tomato paste
1 bay leaf
1 sprig thyme
1 clove garlic, lightly crushed
juice of 1 lemon
a few coriander seeds, crushed
freshly ground black pepper
salt

Choose a non-reactive frying pan (that is, not an aluminium one) with a heavy base and a lid. Rinse and drain leeks. (If they are very long, halve them crosswise.) Simmer all ingredients, except leeks, for 2 minutes in frying pan. Add leeks in a single layer and bring to simmering point. Reduce heat, then cover and cook for 10 minutes until leeks are tender when pierced with a fine skewer. Remove lid and allow to cool. Taste for salt. I like to tip the leeks and all their juices into a white rectangular dish and strew over some very freshly chopped parsley.

variations A common and delicious variation is to add sultanas to the liquid at the beginning of the cooking time. Other variations are possible – what about snips of Preserved Lemon (*see* LEMONS AND LIMES), dried apricots or Pickled Plums (*see* PLUMS AND PRUNES)?

buttery leeks

SERVES 4

This essential leek preparation is sometimes called a 'fondue' of leeks by those who insist on French terminology.

6 leeks, sliced
60 g butter
salt
freshly ground black pepper
freshly grated nutmeg

Wash and drain leek, then dry well. Melt butter in a frying pan and add leek in a layer no more than 6 cm deep. Cover pan and cook leek 5–7 minutes until nearly tender. Remove lid, increase heat and stir while excess liquid evaporates. >

dressed leeks
Roll cooked young leeks in extra-virgin olive oil and plenty of chopped herbs or spoon over Anchovy Vinaigrette (see ANCHOVIES*).*

leek omelette
Add sautéd sliced mushrooms to Buttery Leeks (see p. 383) and use as an omelette filling.

leeks and seafood
Add cooked prawns or yabby tails or roasted sweet peppers cut into strips to a dressing for young leeks for a fancy first course.

When leek looks quite soft and there is nothing slopping around in the pan, season with salt, pepper and nutmeg. Serve as a separate vegetable or place underneath or on top of a grilled veal chop or chicken breast.

leek pastries Place a tablespoon of Buttery Leeks in a 10 cm round of Puff Pastry ✐ (the pastry could be lined with a slice of ham spread with mustard). Pinch together to form a pasty, brush with beaten egg and bake at 220°C until golden. **leek tarts** Mix Buttery Leeks with 3 eggs, 2 egg yolks and 600 ml cream and bake in a prebaked 20 cm Shortcrust Pastry ✐ case at 180°C for 20 minutes. Crumble some fresh goat's cheese into the above mixture to make a leek and goat's cheese tart.

leek and potato soup

SERVES 8

60 g butter
6 leeks, sliced and washed
4 potatoes, peeled and cubed
I large onion
I stick celery
2 cloves garlic
water
I bay leaf
I sprig thyme
salt
freshly ground black pepper
2 tablespoons freshly chopped
    parsley
I teaspoon freshly chopped
    chives

Melt butter in a heavy-based stockpot. Add vegetables and garlic, then cover and lower heat. Sweat together for 10 minutes, stirring from time to time, until leek is well softened. Barely cover with cold water, then add bay leaf and thyme. Simmer, uncovered, until potato is tender.

Remove bay leaf and thyme and purée or blend soup, keeping some liquid aside in case soup needs to be thinned. Season carefully (many vegetable soups of this sort suffer from being underseasoned).

To serve, reheat to boiling point and scatter with chopped herbs.

vichyssoise When served cold this soup becomes vichyssoise. Substitute olive oil for the butter, as oil does not solidify when chilled and butter will. Cold chilled butter leaves an unpleasant greasy texture in the soup. Chill, then swirl a little extra cream into the soup before serving and scatter with herbs.

leek sauce
Reduce chicken or fish stock to a near glaze and stir in Buttery Leeks (see p. 383) to make a rich sauce for fish or shellfish.

leek garnish
Make a delicious crispy garnish for fish by deep-frying a julienne of leek, carrot and fresh ginger at 160°C.

other recipes
leek and cream stew for roasted scallops *see* SCALLOPS

lemons and limes Citrus fruit have existed for a very long time and are thought to have begun with the citron (*Citrus medica*), which is now grown almost exclusively in Corsica and Sicily where its skin is candied and its essential oils are used in the perfume industry. | The lemon (*C. limon*) originated in Kashmir and by 2000 BC was in southern China, from where it moved to Persia; the Arabs took the lemon to the Mediterranean in the tenth century AD. The Crusades also helped the lemon to spread far and wide, and lemons were growing in Britain by the sixteenth century. | Originating in tropical Asia (probably Malaysia), the lime (*C. aurantifolia*) is older than the lemon and contributed to its evolution. The lime is used more widely in tropical countries than the lemon and is a great deal stronger in flavour. All Australians know that Captain James Cook warded off scurvy on board the *Endeavour* by issuing his crew with vitamin C rich lime juice. Captain Arthur Phillip arrived in Botany Bay in 1788 with citrus trees, including lemons and limes, collected in Brazil en route to Australia. >

With a lemon tree taking pride of place in so many Australian gardens it is often a question of how to use the fruit. And yet for a cook no day passes without an opportunity to appreciate its unique tang and its qualities as a tenderiser, flavour enhancer, and preserver of colour in other fruit and vegetables. It is a refreshing source of acidity for drinks and is a major ingredient in cakes, tarts, biscuits and creams. Lemon is mandatory with seafood, either as a squeeze of juice on a grilled or fried fillet or as the basis of a sauce. Both lemon and lime zest are used in making syrups in which to poach other fruit, while lemon peel can be candied for a delicious after-dinner treat. Lime juice is the base of many dipping sauces in Thai cookery that are sweetened with palm sugar and spiked with chilli, herbs and spices. And kaffir lime leaves are indispensable in South-East Asian cookery.

It is the zest, the coloured part of the lemon or lime peel, that has the aromatic perfume, while the juice carries the flavour. Tiny drops of oil are released when the zest is cut or grated. A slice of lemon or lime in tea adds an entirely different quality than a squeeze of juice. Many recipes require that the juice and zest be used, so that the full flavour is experienced. The white pith that surrounds the flesh contains pectin, which is necessary to ensure a good 'set' if you plan to make marmalade.

VARIETIES AND SEASON

Lemons are available all year. On backyard trees the lemons hang obligingly for weeks, with the heaviest crops occurring in late winter and spring. Consumers will pay more for their lemons in summer than in spring, when the less prolific summer crop is in high demand. During our summer months we also often buy imported Californian lemons.

The principal varieties of lemon available in Australia are the Lisbon, eureka and meyer. Currently it is fashionable to debunk the meyer lemon. I do not share this opinion. I have eaten a memorable meyer lemon tart in one of the finest restaurants in the world, Chez Panisse in Berkeley, California, and I also remember the meyer lemon ice-cream my mother made from our tree when I was a teenager.

The two main varieties of *lime* are the Mexican and the Tahitian; the rarely seen kaffir lime is also worth a mention. There is a flourishing Tahitian lime industry centred in northern New South Wales, with the peak season in autumn, although fruit is harvested all year round. Australians should consider using more local limes in the autumn rather than buying imported lemons while waiting for the peak local lemon crop.

Eureka This variety of lemon has thick-skinned fruit and fewer thorns than the Lisbon. It also produces more heavily during the summer months and is a popular home-garden choice. **Kaffir** The kaffir or makrut lime (*C. hystrix*), also known as the wild lime or Mauritius papeda, is an essential flavouring in Thai cooking and grows in parts of tropical Australia. The leaves are used extensively and are most distinctive, being like a figure 8 made up of 2 leaves joined end to end. The rough-skinned fruit is also used but is rarely seen fresh. The fresh leaves are available very occasionally throughout the year. **Lisbon** The Lisbon lemon has a slightly thinner skin than the eureka. The tree is more frost tolerant than the eureka lemon, has more thorns and produces fewer lemons in the summer. **Mexican** This small, roundish green fruit, considered the 'true' lime, is also known as the West Indian or key lime. It requires hot, tropical growing conditions to produce good-sized fruit and is rarely seen in Australia. **Meyer** This variety of lemon is a lemon–orange hybrid. The fruits are roundish, yellow–orange in colour, sweeter than and without the acidity of the lemon. The fruit is thin-skinned and has an interesting aromatic flavour. **Tahitian** The larger Tahitian or Persian lime is less lime-flavoured than the Mexican lime and its skin and flesh are yellowy green rather than deep green. It is a much hardier tree than the Mexican lime and is the variety grown commercially in Australia.

SELECTION AND STORAGE

Choose brightly coloured yellow *lemons* heavy for their size. Inspect closely for soft spots. Dry, juiceless lemons usually indicate that the tree has been stressed. Green fruit will not turn yellow off the tree, although it can still be used, and will not have developed its fullest flavour. As lemons store so well on the tree (and look gorgeous as well), why bother to pick fruit not yet ripe? However, fruit allowed to hang on the tree for months will eventually develop very thick rind and have a coarse flavour.

Lemons will deteriorate quickly if picked or bought damp. Wherever one damp lemon touches another, mould will form and the lemons will soften and rot. (In times past lemons were stored in boxes lined with sand or sawdust, so that they did not touch each other and all moisture was absorbed. I also remember when each lemon was wrapped in a twist of tissue paper.)

Lemons are so beautiful that they should be stored in a bowl where they can be admired. They will keep well in mild weather for more than a week. If you live in a humid climate, you may have to refrigerate lemons, where they will store well for several weeks.

Limes are ripe when green-skinned, unlike lemons. Limes stored for several weeks begin to lose their green glossiness and their skins will become yellowish. These limes are still fine to use, and in fact the juice content of the lime increases after picking and during storage. Lime flesh is always a greenish yellow and it is practically seedless. Limes can be stored in the refrigerator for up to 3 weeks.

Kaffir lime leaves used in South-East Asian cooking are available in Asian food stores fresh, frozen or dried. Dried leaves are to be avoided as they contribute none of the aromatic quality of the fresh leaf, and frozen is nowhere near as good as fresh either. The flavour and aroma of the fresh leaf is reminiscent of lemon verbena as well as lemon. I urge you to buy the fresh leaves as there is no substitute for this flavour. The zest of the rough-skinned fruit is also used. The fruit is available frozen from some Asian food stores. Substitute lime zest or juice in Thai recipes, but buy the real thing when it comes to the leaves.

PREPARATION

Lemons and limes are sometimes waxed before being stored. It is a sensible precaution to wash the fruit under warm water just before using it. Dry well before grating or zesting. Remember that the pith can impart a bitter taste in cooking, so it is advised to avoid it.

The average-sized lemon or lime will yield 2–3 tablespoons juice (40–60 ml), 1 tablespoon grated zest and about ¼ cup flesh.

TO JUICE   If using lemon juice for lime juice, double the quantity required as lime juice is much stronger. Run the fruit under a warm tap or soak it in a bowl of hot water for 30 minutes before squeezing. The juice yield will be increased considerably. Lemon or lime juice can be frozen in ice-cube trays, and then the blocks can be tipped into a freezer bag for later use.

TO ZEST OR GRATE   The oil glands are contained in the coloured part of the peel (the zest) only. Zest is usually required in very fine strips or grated. To gather zest, either use a grater (yields the finest fragments), a zester (produces long, thin shreds) or a vegetable peeler to strip slices of zest that you then cut into julienne. When using a grater, stand it over a flat plate and be prepared to give it several firm whacks with a wooden spoon to dislodge the zest. If the recipe also uses the juice, pour the juice over the grater held over the bowl of ingredients to help dislodge the zest.

If you are zesting or grating large numbers of lemons or limes and have no plans for the juice, the fruit will deteriorate very quickly if stored without its protective skin. Better to juice them and freeze the juice than find a basket or bowl of fermenting lemons or limes. Or cut up the flesh as described below and use it in a sauce.

TO SEGMENT   Remove the zest and cut a slice from one end of the lemon or lime, so it will stand on your board without wobbling. Cut the white pith away from the flesh, slicing from top to bottom following the curve of the fruit. Cut the flesh into segments by slipping a small sharp knife alongside the membrane of one section to the centre of the lemon or lime. Cut along the other side of the section, freeing it. Drop it into a bowl. Do this with the rest of the sections. Squeeze the membrane you will have left in your hand over the freed sections. Cut these sections into smaller pieces as you wish.

lemon cordial

MAKES 1.5 LITRES

Lemon cordial is an old-fashioned drink that gains added sophistication if mixed with bruised mint leaves and soda water or a measure of gin and soda. It keeps for months.

2 kg castor sugar
1 litre water
30 g citric acid
30 g tartaric acid
juice of 6 lemons, strained
finely grated zest of 2 lemons

Dissolve sugar in water over heat in a stockpot. Add citric and tartaric acids. Stir to ensure that all is completely dissolved. Cool. Stir in juice and zest, and bottle. Dilute to taste with water, lemonade, soda water or mineral water.

carpaccio dressing
Drizzle raw salmon or tuna with olive oil, then sprinkle over torn herbs and lemon or lime zest and grind over black pepper. Squeeze over lemon or lime juice just before serving.

lime lover's punch

SERVES 6

½ cup sugar
1 cup warm water
2 cups light *or* dark rum
juice of 4 limes
1 cup orange juice
crushed ice
4 slices lime
mint sprigs

Dissolve sugar in water, then tip syrup into a large jug or bowl. Add rum and lime and orange juices. Refrigerate until very cold.
  Half-fill long glasses with crushed ice. Add a slice of lime and a sprig of mint and pour over punch. Very alcoholic – beware!

lemon and lime granita

SERVES 8

This recipe is based on one given in Mary Taylor Simetti's lovely book Pomp and Sustenance.

1½ cups sugar
1 litre water
200 ml lemon juice
juice of 2 limes

Make a syrup by dissolving sugar in half the water over heat. Cool, then add lemon and lime juice and remaining water and stir. Pour into a shallow aluminium cake tin, >

then freeze. After 30 minutes scrape down sides and bottom of tin, and mix the frozen part that has solidified into that which is still liquid. Repeat every 30 minutes until granita is a firm, flaky slush. Serve as soon as possible, piled into tall glasses, or else store in a sealed plastic container.

If left too long the granita will 'burn', that is, the water will separate and form ice crystals.

candied peel

This is very easy to make and store. The best lemons for candying are those with thick skins. If you have squeezed a lemon for its juice, keep the halves. (You can also freeze juiced lemons until you have enough to candy.) Not only can the peel be added to cakes (such as Angie's Lemon Cake, see p. 394) or pressed into the top of butter biscuits before baking, but a piece of candied citrus peel is perfect with after-dinner coffee. A jar of candied citrus peel also makes a welcome Christmas present.

lemons, halved and squeezed
sugar
castor sugar

Cut lemon halves into 4–6 pieces. Leave all white pith intact. Place fruit in a heavy-based saucepan and cover generously with cold water. Bring to a boil, then pour off water. Repeat this process twice to remove bitterness from fruit, then drain well. Weigh fruit and return to pan with same weight of sugar. Cook gently until sugar has dissolved completely, then cook steadily for 1 hour until peel is translucent. Drain peel and dry on a cake rack resting over a tray somewhere out of the way of ants. The draining can take a couple of days. Turn after 12 hours. When dry, roll peel in castor sugar and store in airtight jars.

michael boddy's sweet lime pickle

In his extraordinary newsletter Kitchen Talk, *Michael Boddy included this odd recipe. No cooking needed!*

2 tablespoons salt
I cup brown sugar
I tablespoon cayenne pepper
I tablespoon ground turmeric
I tablespoon raisins
I8 limes, quartered

Combine all ingredients except limes, then pour over limes. Pack limes and pickling liquid in sterilised glass jars and store in a cupboard for 2–3 weeks. Every other day, stir mixture and stand jars in sun for 1 hour.

lemon stuffing
Mix grated lemon zest and juice with fresh herbs, an egg and either fresh breadcrumbs or cooked rice to make a stuffing for a fish, sweet peppers or hollowed-out small squash.

kaffir lime and ...
Sprinkle julienne strips of kaffir lime leaves over a fish before steaming or mix finely chopped kaffir lime leaves into a prawn salad.

preserved lemons

At Stephanie's Restaurant we preserve lemons in the Middle Eastern manner. Some may consider this a very complicated thing to do with a lemon but they cannot have tasted the finished product!

Preserved lemons last at least a year without refrigeration, and a slice of pickled lemon enlivens a stuffing or is a marvellous garnish for grilled poultry or fish. There are an infinite number of Middle Eastern recipes that include some of this exciting condiment.

250 g coarse kitchen salt

10 lemons, scrubbed and
   quartered

1 bay leaf

2–3 cloves

1 stick cinnamon

extra lemon juice

Scatter a spoonful of salt into a 1 litre sterilised jar. Tip lemons into a wide plastic tub with remaining salt and mix well. Massage fruit vigorously and pack into jar, curved-side out, inserting pieces of bay leaf, cloves and splinters of cinnamon stick at intervals. Press down hard on fruit to release as much juice as possible. Spoon salt mixture left in tub over fruit. Cover with extra lemon juice, if required. (If a wedge of lemon is not covered with lemon juice, it sometimes develops white mould. It doesn't look great but it is harmless.) With a clean cloth dipped in boiling water, wipe neck of jar free of salt and cap tightly. Let the lemons mature for at least 1 month in a cool spot (not the refrigerator) before using.

lime stuffed chicken
Put 2 kaffir lime leaves, lemongrass and the stems and roots of a bunch of coriander in the cavity of a chicken before roasting or steaming it.

lemon curd

MAKES 2 CUPS

This is delicious as a spread for toast or scones, to sandwich together a sponge cake or as the filling for small tartlets. A pot of home-made lemon curd is also a lovely gift. It keeps for weeks if well sealed and refrigerated after opening.

2 large lemons

100 g unsalted butter

175 g sugar

3 eggs, lightly whisked and
   strained

Finely grate zest and juice lemons. In a heavy-based saucepan, combine butter, lemon juice, zest and sugar. Stir constantly over heat until sugar has dissolved. Add eggs off the heat and stir to mix well. Cook over gentle heat, stirring constantly, until mixture has thickened. Do not allow it to boil or it will curdle. Pour straight into small, hot, sterilised jars or into a bowl if using immediately.

avgolemono – greek egg and lemon soup

SERVES 6

1.5 litres well-flavoured
 Chicken Stock ✐, free of fat
salt
freshly ground black pepper
100 g long-grain rice
3 large eggs
juice of 2 lemons

Bring stock to simmering point. Adjust seasoning and drop in rice. Simmer for 15 minutes until rice is cooked.

 Beat eggs and lemon juice until frothy. Add a ladleful of hot stock to egg mixture and continue to whisk. Remove stock from heat and allow to cool for 2–3 minutes. Quickly tip in egg mixture, stirring to mix well. Taste again for salt and pepper. Serve at once.

veal and lemon
Top pan-fried veal with warm slices of lemon or lime caramelised in a few drops of oil.

lemon meatballs
Copy the Sicilians and flatten small meatballs between lemon leaves before grilling them on the barbecue.

tom yam goong – sour prawn soup

SERVES 6

12 medium prawns
3 stalks lemongrass, tender
 part only
2 litres Chicken Stock ✐
5 kaffir lime leaves
roots of 1 bunch coriander,
 well washed
150 g small mushrooms,
 whole or sliced
3 shallots, sliced
2 tablespoons fish sauce
10 fresh chillies, seeded and
 very finely sliced
4 spring onions, cut into
 2.5 cm pieces
100 ml fresh lime juice
2 teaspoons chilli paste
1 cup fresh coriander leaves

Shell and de-vein prawns, leaving heads and tails intact. Crush lemongrass and cut into 5 cm pieces. Bring stock to a boil in a stockpot and add lemongrass, lime leaves, coriander roots, mushrooms, shallots, fish sauce and chilli. Simmer for 10 minutes, then add spring onion, lime juice, chilli paste and prawns. Cook until prawns just turn pink. Add coriander leaves and serve immediately.

lemon salad based on marcella's

SERVES 6

This recipe originally appeared in Marcella's Kitchen *by Marcella Hazan. I have had the privilege of watching it being prepared by Marcella herself and of eating it in her dining room in Venice!*

2–3 lemons, washed

salt

1 red pepper

2 Lebanese *or* 1 long
    cucumber

freshly ground black pepper

extra-virgin olive oil

1 tablespoon coarsely chopped
    flat-leaf parsley leaves

Slice lemons as thinly as possible and flick out all seeds. Spread slices on a tray, then sprinkle with salt and leave for 30 minutes. Rinse and drain slices, then pat dry.

Cut pepper into sections following its natural curves. With a loose-wristed zigzag action, peel with an asparagus peeler. Remove all seeds and ribs from pepper and cut lengthwise into very thin slices. Cut cucumber into paper-thin slices. On a shallow serving platter arrange a bed of overlapping cucumber slices and top with lemon. Decorate salad with red pepper slices. Grind over pepper, drizzle with oil and scatter over parsley. Lovely with Vitello Tonnato (*see* VEAL) or cold, crumbed veal scaloppine.

mexican ceviche   SERVES 4

This can be made with any fish with a fillet at least 1 cm thick.

500 g firm white-fleshed fish,
    trimmed and cut into 1 cm
    cubes

1 cup fresh lime juice

2 cloves garlic, very thinly
    sliced

2 tablespoons olive oil

500 g ripe tomatoes, seeded
    and diced

½ cup Fresh Tomato Sauce
    (see p. 709)

1 red onion, finely chopped

1 bunch coriander, coarsely
    chopped

1 tablespoon freshly chopped
    oregano

2 teaspoons sambal oelek

2 tablespoons finely chopped
    pickled mild chillies

3 tablespoons sliced green olives

½ teaspoon salt *or* to taste

Marinate fish in lime juice for 2 hours in refrigerator. Meanwhile, warm garlic in oil over low heat for 5 minutes. Tip oil and garlic into a bowl, then add remaining ingredients (except fish) and mix well.

Drain fish very well, then toss with tomato mixture. Taste for seasoning and serve immediately.

lamb marinade
Marinate lamb to be skewered and barbecued in 2 tablespoons olive oil, 1 tablespoon lemon juice and fresh oregano or rosemary for 1 hour.

lemon butter sauce
Work Dijon mustard and a few drops of lemon juice into butter for a quick sauce for grilled fish, asparagus or a chicken breast.

angie's lemon cake

This cake is made in minutes in the food processor. Jane Grigson has a very similar recipe in her Fruit Book. *She adds candied lemon peel to the cake mixture and a tablespoon of gin to the final syrup.*

lemon cleaner
*Make a paste
of lemon juice, salt
and a little egg
white for cleaning
copper saucepans.*

1 lemon
200 g castor sugar
250 g self-raising flour
pinch of salt
1 level teaspoon baking
    powder
250 g softened unsalted butter
4 large eggs
SYRUP
150 g castor sugar
juice of 1 lemon

Preheat oven to 160°C. Line an 18 cm round cake tin with baking paper.

Zest and juice lemon. Pulverise zest with sugar in a food processor. Sift flour with salt and baking powder and add with butter and eggs to food processor. Process until smooth. Tip mixture into prepared tin, then smooth top and bake for 1½ hours.

To make the syrup, mix sugar with lemon juice. Turn the hot cake out onto a serving dish and spoon syrup over. Leave to cool.

lemon delicious pudding   SERVES 8

This is a classic and in many families the ultimate pudding – the golden sponge topping hiding a creamy lemon sauce. It can be quickly prepared and then slipped into the oven to cook as soon as the main course has come out to rest.

2 lemons
60 g butter
1½ cups castor sugar
3 eggs, separated
3 tablespoons self-raising flour
1½ cups milk

Preheat oven to 180°C and butter a 1 litre ovenproof basin or serving dish. Zest 1 lemon and juice both. In a food processor, cream butter with zest and sugar, then add egg yolks. Add flour and milk alternately to make a smooth batter. Scrape mixture from sides of processor bowl and blend in lemon juice. Transfer to a basin. Whisk egg whites until creamy and firm and fold gently into batter. Pour batter into prepared basin. Stand basin in a baking dish and pour in hot water to come halfway up sides of basin. Bake for 1 hour. Allow to cool a little before serving. I like it best with pouring cream.

lemon ice-cream

MAKES 1.5 LITRES

This ice-cream can be poured directly into a basin or log mould if you do not have a churn. It will not have quite as creamy a texture but it will still be delicious.

175 ml lemon juice
6 egg yolks
finely grated zest of 3 large
   lemons
250 g castor sugar
3 cups cream, lightly whipped

Reduce lemon juice over high heat to make 75 ml, then set aside. Beat egg yolks with zest in an electric mixer.

While yolks are beating, dissolve sugar in reduced lemon juice in a small saucepan and bring to a boil. Pour simmering lemon syrup over egg yolks with mixer motor still running. Beat until cool and very thick. Fold in lightly whipped cream. Churn in an ice-cream machine according to the manufacturer's instructions.

simple lemon syllabub

SERVES 4

1 lemon
50 ml late-picked white wine
   or Sauternes
20 ml brandy
1 tablespoon castor sugar
1½ cups cream

Remove zest with a vegetable peeler, then juice lemon. Place all ingredients except cream in a basin and refrigerate overnight. Next day, remove zest. (If you prefer the texture, the lemon zest can be finely grated instead of removed in one length, and left in the sweet.) Place liquid and cream in bowl of an electric mixer and whip until quite firm. Spoon into glass bowls and serve with a crisp biscuit or berries.

trifle Syllabub is also delicious piled onto a wine trifle in place of the usual whipped cream.

lemon tart

SERVES 8–10

1 quantity Shortcrust Pastry
3 large lemons
6 eggs
250 g castor sugar
pure icing sugar
200 ml cream

Line a 24 cm loose-bottomed deep flan tin with pastry, then bake blind at 200°C for 20 minutes. Reset oven to 160°C.

Zest and juice lemons. Combine eggs and sugar until well amalgamated, then add zest and juice and stir well. Add cream and mix well using a balloon whisk. Pour into just-baked pastry case and bake for 35–45 minutes until almost set. Cool in tin for at least 30 minutes before serving. Serve dusted with icing sugar and with thick cream.

lemon roulade

SERVES 10

This delicious dessert combines an airy sponge with lemon curd and whipped cream. The exciting juxtaposition of tangy lemon with cream also features in one of Stephanie's Restaurant's most celebrated desserts, the lemon curd layer cake, in which pancakes are layered with lemon curd.

melted butter
6 eggs, separated
60 g flour
2 teaspoons lemon juice
grated zest of 1 lemon
½ cup castor sugar
extra castor sugar
1 cup Lemon Curd (see p. 391) or 300 ml cream, whipped
pure icing sugar

Preheat oven to 180°C. Line a 34 cm × 24 cm Swiss-roll tin with baking paper. Brush paper and sides of tin well with melted butter and dust with a tiny bit of flour. Beat egg yolks, flour, juice and zest with sugar until pale and thick.

Beat egg whites to form stiff peaks, then fold lightly but thoroughly into egg yolk mixture. Spoon into prepared tin and smooth top. Bake for 15–20 minutes.

When springy, remove tin to a wire rack for 10 minutes, then turn cake out onto baking paper sprinkled with castor sugar. Gently peel away backing paper. Allow cake to cool, then spread with lemon curd or whipped cream and roll up, using paper to help you. Dust with icing sugar before serving. If you have used lemon curd, offer whipped cream separately.

other recipes

chilli and lime sauce *see* PEPPERS AND CHILLIES

lemon risotto *see* RICE

pineapple and lime juice salsa *see* PINEAPPLES

polynesian raw fish salad *see* FISH

sugar-coated grilled rock ling *see* FISH

thai steamed fish with coriander root, chilli and lime juice
see CORIANDER

lentils

The lentil (*Lens culinaris*) belongs to the pulses, the edible seeds of leguminous plants. Some pulses are eaten fresh (green beans and green peas) and others are eaten dried (lentils, split peas, cannellini beans, and so on). Dried pulses have been a staple food in many parts of the world for thousands of years. | The lentil is an ancient legume, perhaps originally from northern Syria. It has been cultivated in the eastern Mediterranean for at least 10 000 years. Lentil dishes play an important part in Middle Eastern and Indian cookery, where they are collectively known as dhals. | Lentils linked with grains provide all the proteins humans need in their diet. It is interesting to see how often the traditional dishes of poor cultures have combined these elements. To name a few, in North Africa one eats couscous with chick peas, in the West Indies one enjoys rice with black-eyed peas, and in India dhal is eaten with rice and breads. | Many cultures that have relied on cooking with dried pulses during long cold winters have also had to rely on salted and preserved meats at the same time of year. Hence, there are many examples of lentils cooked with sausages, bacon and salt pork. >

**lentils
go
with**

*onions
garlic
olive oil
butter
parsley
coriander
cumin seeds
mustard seeds
ginger
chillies
carrots
bacon
salt pork
sausages
spinach
lemons
tomatoes
rabbit
hare
squab pigeon
venison
guinea fowl*

lentil salad

*Toss cooked lentils
with olive oil, finely
chopped onion,
garlic and lots of
parsley or coriander
and season with salt
and pepper and
serve as a salad,
perhaps ringed with
tomato wedges and
sliced cucumber.*

Lentils are also great with game and make excellent one-pot vegetable dishes and superb salads. Indian cooks spice their dhals by adding flavourings cooked in ghee or oil. This is a trick worth copying when serving other pulses as well. Good combinations are mustard seeds, cumin seeds or diced onion fried with freshly chopped ginger.

VARIETIES AND SEASON

Dried lentils are available all year round. They are usually identified by their colour and size and whether they have been split and skinned. (Note that green and yellow split peas are pulses but *not* lentils.)

Brown These lentils are sold whole and unskinned. They retain their shape well when cooked. Some shops and food writers call these green or Continental lentils. **Puy** This is the tiny, dark French lentil, grown in the Auvergne at Le Puy, and recently imported into Australia. These slate-coloured, tiny lentils have the best texture and flavour of all but are very expensive. **Red** Tiny red or Egyptian lentils have a spicy flavour. They are sold skinned and split. They are in fact a deep orange–red, not scarlet. They cook quickly to an orange purée.

SELECTION AND STORAGE

Split and skinned lentils are usually chosen when making a soup or purée, as they break down more readily. Whole lentils are chosen for salads or when serving as a vegetable as they hold their shape better.

I like buying lentils from Indian or Middle Eastern suppliers as I believe that they have more pressure applied to them to maintain a high quality by their knowledgeable customers than has the supermarket. There is no way of knowing, but ideally you should be buying lentils dried from the most recent crop. Inspect the lentils to see that there is no obvious insect damage. Store lentils in a dry airtight container. Do not store lentils for more than 1 year – there should be another delivery by then!

PREPARATION

Lentils do not need to be soaked overnight, but they do need careful washing and inspection. (Sometimes a recipe in which not much liquid is used will require a longer soaking time to ensure the lentils swell sufficiently.) Wash the lentils in several changes of water (they are often dusty) and then spread the drained, soaked lentils on a tea towel and check them closely for tiny stones or grit. It is quite common to find such surprises, so do not be tempted to omit this step.

Lentils can take a surprisingly short time to cook, sometimes as little as 20 minutes, so check them frequently.

basic brown lentils

SERVES 6–8

500 g brown lentils, washed
  and drained

I onion, quartered

I clove garlic

I bay leaf

I large sprig thyme

salt

freshly ground black pepper

lemon juice

butter *or* olive oil

freshly chopped parsley

Place lentils, onion, garlic, bay leaf and thyme in a saucepan and cover generously with cold water. Cover and bring slowly to a boil. Reduce heat to maintain a steady simmer and test lentils after 20 minutes. If tender, drain into a colander and discard onion, garlic, bay leaf and thyme.

Return lentils to rinsed-out pan and season with salt, pepper and lemon juice. Stir in butter and parsley.

with poultry and game Brown lentils make a delicious accompaniment to poultry and game, especially roasted squab pigeon, guinea fowl, quail or wild rabbit. Add ½ cup roasting juices or well-flavoured stock and a nut of butter to the hot lentils. A slosh of port, muscat or other fortified wine would be good bubbled with the stock and lentils, too. Bacon or ham sautéd with an onion can also be added to the lentils and stock.

tuscan lentil purée

SERVES 6

500 g brown lentils, washed
  and drained

40 g unsalted butter

I small onion, finely chopped

3 tablespoons finely chopped
  celery stalks

I carrot, finely chopped

3 tablespoons finely chopped
  parsley stalks

2 tablespoons olive oil

150 ml hot well-flavoured
  stock

juice of ½ lemon

Simmer lentils with butter and plenty of water until soft. Drain and press through a food mill.

Sauté vegetables and parsley stalks in oil until soft and well coloured. Stir into lentil purée and gradually beat in hot stock and lemon juice. The purée should not be too stiff. Adjust seasoning.

Serve hot with a braised rabbit or beef dish, sausages, a roasted bird, meatballs or a tomato salad.

brown lentil salad

SERVES 6

If you can find the French Puy lentils, this salad will be even better. This is a master recipe. You can sauté other vegetables, such as carrot, celery, celeriac or sweet peppers, with the onion. Roasted cumin or mustard seeds fried in oil or walnut oil and toasted walnuts could be added instead of the extra-virgin olive oil.

lentils and cheese
Toss cooked lentils with crumbled goat's cheese and plenty of torn basil. Dress with a vinaigrette mixed with a little finely chopped spring or red onion.

petit sale aux lentilles
Make this classic French bistro dish by poaching 1 kg skinned and boned salted belly pork gently for 1½ hours. Slice and add to a pot of cooked lentils and serve with mustard.

lentils and spinach
Stir cooked lentils and a large pinch each of ground coriander and cumin into hot, buttery spinach and season with salt and pepper.

375 g brown lentils, washed
½ cup olive oil
1 onion, finely chopped
3 cloves garlic, finely chopped
2 teaspoons salt
½ cup freshly chopped parsley
1 tablespoon red-wine vinegar
1 tablespoon extra-virgin
   olive oil
freshly ground black pepper

Soak lentils in plenty of water for 2 hours, then drain well, reserving 1 cup soaking water. Heat olive oil in a saucepan and sauté onion until golden. Add garlic and sauté for 1 minute. Add lentils, salt and reserved soaking water. Cook, stirring frequently, over moderate heat for 20–25 minutes until water has evaporated and lentils are cooked. They should not be mushy and should still have a nuttiness to them. Tip lentils into a bowl and stir in parsley, vinegar and extra-virgin olive oil. Grind on plenty of pepper. The salad could be expanded with olives, Caramelised Onions (*see* ONIONS), Preserved Lemons (*see* LEMONS AND LIMES), finely chopped spring or red onion, wedges of tomato or halved hardboiled eggs.

lentil soup

Drop 1 cup cooked lentils into 3 cups simmering chicken stock and purée to make a hearty soup. Season and serve with hot cream swirled into it, slices of crisp grilled sausage, plenty of parsley, crisp bacon or fried croutons. Add cooked chestnuts that have been tossed in olive oil and tomato paste for a more subtly flavoured soup.

sausages and lentils

Grill frankfurters, bratwurst or chorizo sausages and serve whole or cut into chunks mixed into cooked lentils.

north indian lentils

SERVES 4–6

This lentil dish is great with chicken. Or it could be one of a series of vegetable dishes for a vegetarian meal.

350 g red lentils, washed and
   drained
1 litre water
2 cloves garlic, finely chopped
2 slices fresh ginger, finely
   chopped
1 teaspoon freshly chopped
   coriander leaves
1 tablespoon ground turmeric
¼ teaspoon cayenne pepper
1½ teaspoons salt
1½ tablespoons lemon juice
5 tablespoons vegetable oil
1 teaspoon cumin seeds
1 onion, sliced into rings
lemon wedges

Put lentils and water into a saucepan and bring to a boil. Skim, then add garlic, ginger, coriander, turmeric and cayenne pepper. Cover, leaving lid very slightly ajar, then lower heat and simmer for about 1 hour. Stir occasionally, checking each time whether lentils have collapsed into a near-purée. Add salt and lemon juice. The finished dhal will be like a thick soup.

In a small frying pan, heat 3 tablespoons of the oil and cook cumin seeds gently until darkened. Pour oil and seeds over dhal. Wipe out pan, and fry onion in remaining oil until dark brown. Drain on kitchen paper.

Spoon dhal into a serving dish, scatter over onion and put lemon wedges around.

o t h e r   r e c i p e s

celeriac sautéd with lentils and walnut oil *see* CELERY AND CELERIAC

l i v e r   Another controversial ingredient. Some will shudder, others will find it hard to resist. Liver is a rich source of iron and probably the most popular offal meat of all.   The term 'offal' covers all meats found inside the carcass of an animal (liver, heart and kidneys) and also its extremities (head, feet, ears and tail). Most parts of the world have a repertoire of offal cookery, ranging from humble dishes enjoyed by the poor (tripe and onions, for example) to rather esoteric and elaborate preparations, such as stuffed pig's ears or *foie gras*. Liver is one of the most tender and luxurious offal meats and is best cooked quickly.   Livers from different animals are used in different ways in different cultures. European and Asian butchers are accustomed to liver. Anglo-Saxon butchers are learning but are still more used to orders for 'lamb's fry', as our mothers described a whole lamb's liver. The Chinese prefer pig's liver and usually blanch or marinate it to rid it of what is described as its 'mealy' texture. In the Middle East lamb's liver is more usual, although calf's liver is also favoured. Poultry livers are enjoyed universally. >

In Tuscany many meals commence with a platter of crostini topped with sautéd chicken livers that have usually been coarsely chopped with pancetta and herbs and sometimes anchovies or capers. I have twice ordered the very famous Venetian dish of calf's liver with onions in Venice and both times the liver was cut into strips and was thoroughly cooked. English cooks traditionally serve rashers of crisp bacon with lamb's liver, an excellent combination. The French are partial to calf's liver and the livers of specially fattened ducks and geese. *Pâté de foie gras* is this large liver cooked in its own fat and pressed (it contains no ingredients other than seasoning). The silky richness and melting texture of *pâté de foie gras* make it unlike any other food, and briefly pan-fried slices of raw *foie gras* also make memorable dishes. (The force-feeding of animals is not permitted in Australia and the tinned product available is a travesty of the real thing.)

Liver is a dense meat. One does not need to serve a large portion. While I prefer it cooked pink in the middle, some dishes requiring longer cooking are equally good – one should never assume that there is only one way of producing a delicious result. Serve something starchy or crispy – mashed potatoes, potatoes fried with rosemary and olive oil until crusty or grilled polenta – and don't forget the classic accompaniment, a pile of slowly cooked, melting golden onions.

VARIETIES AND SEASON

Liver is available all year, although the finest *calf's* liver will be found during peak veal season, which is in the winter and spring. Calf's liver, with its smooth texture and delicate flavour, is the finest of all livers. A very pale liver may indicate that it is from a milk-fed animal or from an animal that has had a diet relatively high in fat. The size of the liver relates to the size of the animal. *Lamb's* liver is usually much smaller and stronger in flavour than calf's liver and is very good to eat. *Pig's* liver is strongly flavoured and dark in colour. *Duck* and *chicken* livers are readily available and are often sold with the hearts attached. *Squab pigeon* livers can sometimes be ordered, while *goose* livers are very difficult to find.

SELECTION AND STORAGE

Like *lamb's* liver, *calf's* liver is usually sautéed or grilled, although it can also be gently braised or roasted whole. *Pig's* liver is often minced for pâtés and terrines or can be slowly braised. It is the liver preferred in Chinese cooking. *Poultry* livers are usually sautéed, fried or grilled or used to make pâtés or mousses.

Offal deteriorates faster than other meats and should be absolutely fresh when purchased. All liver should have a bright glossy sheen and no unpleasant smell. *Poultry* livers should look shiny and not be crushed. Each liver has a gall bladder attached to it, which is usually removed before sale. If the livers have been roughly handled, the bladder may have burst and the liver will be stained green with bile and is spoilt. Even a speck of this greenish fluid will render the livers unacceptably bitter.

It is more practical to ask the butcher to slice liver for you than to attempt to do it yourself. European butchers understand *calf's* liver very well and consider it a delicacy. They will be very respectful of your order and will slice the liver just as you want it.

Refrigerate liver, freed of all wrappings, on a plate or in a bowl, covered with plastic film. Use liver within 2 days of buying it.

PREPARATION AND COOKING

All liver is covered with a fine membrane. Before cooking *calf's*, *lamb's* or *pig's* liver it is important to remove this membrane as it will shrink in the cooking process and cause the slices to curl and buckle in the pan. This is not necessary with poultry livers.

If you have bought a larger piece of liver intending to braise or slice it yourself, the membrane will still be in place. Some butchers will skin the livers before cutting the number of slices you require. Some will not, as the membrane also protects the surface of the liver from drying out. Always check before starting to cook.

TO PREPARE **Calf's, lamb's and pig's liver** Peel away one corner of the membrane and with one hand press gently on the liver while peeling the membrane away with the other. Turn the liver over and inspect the underside of the liver for tubes that have been left in and cut them away as neatly as you can. (This is particularly pertinent to lamb livers, which are much smaller. It may be better to cut lamb's liver into strips to avoid the valves.) **Poultry livers** Inspect each liver very carefully and remove any gall bladders still present. Cut around the small dark gall bladder, removing a small section of the liver as well, so that you remove the gall bladder intact. Slice away any greenish stained sections.

TO PAN-FRY OR GRILL CALF'S OR LAMB'S LIVER For both methods the cooking should be done with medium–high heat as the outside should develop a slight crust and the middle should still be faintly pink. **Pan-frying** Liver for pan-frying should be sliced 5 mm thick. Dip each slice in seasoned flour, or flour mixed with paprika, and shake off the excess. This will prevent the liver from sticking to the pan. Choose a pan in which the slices will fit without too much extra space. Extra space can mean that the chosen fat will burn. I prefer to sauté liver in clarified butter ⚲ or in a mixture of butter and olive oil as straight butter burns too quickly. It will take 2 minutes each side. **Grilling** Liver for grilling should be sliced 1 cm thick and lightly oiled. Each slice will take about 3 minutes a side under a preheated overhead griller or on a hot char-grill pan. It should be brown on the outside and pink in the middle. Transfer the cooked slices to a warm plate and season with ground pepper and sea salt. Scatter over freshly cut herbs, if desired.

TO BRAISE | Trim away large tubes from the underside of a 1 kg piece of liver. Remove membrane. Rub all over with olive oil and transfer to a heated gratin dish in an oven set at 220°C. Baste with good stock after 10 minutes, then turn, reduce oven temperature to 160°C and braise a further 15 minutes, spooning the collected juices over the liver after another 10 minutes. Remove from the oven and allow to rest covered in a warm place for 15 minutes. Carve in thin slices and serve with a vegetable purée (potato, onion, parsnip) and maybe a dish of sautéd mushrooms. Reheat any collected juices to boiling, boost with an extra spoonful of stock or juices from the sautéd mushrooms, and spoon over the liver.

recipes

hungarian chopped chicken liver SERVES 6

liver and ...
Deep-fry capers, parsnip chips or Sweetcorn Brunch Fritters (see CORN) *to serve with a warm liver salad.*

5 eggs
1 large onion, very finely chopped
olive oil
500 g chicken livers, trimmed
paprika
salt
freshly ground black pepper
2 teaspoons Dijon mustard

Hardboil eggs and mash with a fork while still warm. Sauté onion in a little oil until very soft. Add livers to hot onion and sauté for 5 minutes until firm to touch. Sprinkle with paprika, salt and pepper to taste. Pass through coarse disc of a food mill and then lightly mix the liver mixture with egg and mustard. Taste and adjust seasoning. Serve on hot toast, with toasted pita bread or on matzo crackers.

chinese noodle soup with pig's liver SERVES 4

200 g thin rice noodles
2 teaspoons oil
2 slices ginger, finely chopped
1 fresh chilli, seeded and very finely sliced
2 spring onions, cut into 4 cm lengths
3 cups Chicken Stock
250 g pig's liver, very thinly sliced
black *or* red rice vinegar

Soak noodles in warm water for 30 minutes, then drain well. Heat oil in a wok and quickly toss ginger, chilli and spring onion. Add stock and bring to a boil, then drop in drained noodles and liver. Stir to mix. After 1 minute ladle soup into bowls and drizzle in a little vinegar to taste. Eat at once.

chinese-style glazed liver

SERVES 6–10

These make an unusual savoury to hand with drinks. I sometimes serve them on toothpicks, or else as a buffet dish for 8–10 people, gleaming like brown nuggets on a flat dish covered with stir-fried snowpeas.

500 g chicken *or* duck livers, trimmed
I tablespoon freshly chopped ginger
2 spring onions, cut into 4 cm lengths
I tablespoon dark soy sauce
boiling water

SAUCE
2 tablespoons oil
2 tablespoons dark soy sauce
2 tablespoons sugar
I tablespoon rice wine
I tablespoon sesame oil
black rice vinegar

Place livers in a frying pan with ginger, spring onion and soy sauce. Barely cover with boiling water. Bring to a boil. Simmer for 2 minutes, then drain and discard ginger and spring onion.

To make the sauce, heat oil in a wok. Toss livers in hot oil for 30 seconds. Add soy sauce, sugar and rice wine and toss and shake together. Sprinkle in sesame oil and stir once. Splash in a few drops of vinegar, shake to mix and tip onto a serving dish. Serve warm or hot.

warm liver salad
Add zing to a warm liver salad with pickled cherries, olives or sun-dried tomatoes.

liver with bacon
Deglaze a pan used to sauté poultry livers with wine vinegar or wine. Return the livers to the pan and add crispy bacon or pancetta and glazed onion or sautéd apple, grapes or mushrooms and toss to combine. Serve on salad leaves drizzled with olive oil and grind on pepper.

venetian liver and onion

SERVES 2

While liver is often cooked until just pink, this dish is traditionally served thoroughly cooked.

4 tablespoons olive oil
2 large onions, thinly sliced
salt
freshly ground black pepper
40 g butter
400 g calf's liver, skinned, trimmed and cut into I cm thick strips
2 tablespoons freshly chopped parsley

Heat oil in a frying pan and gently sauté onion, covered, until it softens and collapses. Remove lid and cook for about 20 minutes until onion is sweet and golden. Season. Remove to a strainer set over a bowl. Heat butter in pan with oil drained from onion. Quickly sauté liver until browned on all sides. Reduce heat and cook for 5 minutes until thoroughly cooked. Return onion to pan and toss to reheat. Serve sprinkled with parsley. Add extra pepper, if desired.

english lamb's liver and bacon

SERVES 4

1 tablespoon olive oil (the English would have once used dripping)
4 thickish rashers streaky bacon
4–8 slices lamb's liver, skinned
plain flour
salt
freshly ground black pepper
3 tablespoons well-flavoured stock

Brush a frying pan with oil and cook bacon until crisp. Remove bacon to a serving dish and keep warm. Dip liver in flour seasoned with salt and pepper and shake off excess. Add a little oil to pan depending on amount of bacon fat left and sauté liver until brown on both sides, 2–3 minutes per side. Remove liver to serving plate, then pour off any fat and rinse out pan with stock. Pour pan juices over liver and serve at once.

bbq liver

Wrap seasoned slices of pig's liver in caul fat with a bay leaf or sprig of rosemary and grill on the barbecue.

liver in butter

Pan-fry lamb's or calf's liver, then rinse out the pan with balsamic vinegar and add a knob of butter. Shake the butter and vinegar together and spoon over the liver.

liver and garlic

Add red wine and blanched, peeled garlic cloves to the pan after pan-frying lamb's or calf's liver. When hot and well reduced, add a nut of butter and pour over and around the liver and serve with buttered spinach.

pig's liver faggots

SERVES 4

The word 'faggot' means 'bundle' and each bundle should be wrapped in lacy caul fat, the top of which will melt and crisp during baking. Soak the caul fat for an hour before using and dry spread out on a clean tea towel.

250 g pig's liver, skinned, trimmed and cut into chunks
200 g fresh, skinned belly pork, cut into chunks
1 onion, diced
2 tablespoons freshly chopped parsley
1 tablespoon freshly chopped thyme leaves
60 g fresh breadcrumbs
salt
freshly ground black pepper
1 egg
4 pieces pig's caul fat (each about 12 cm square)

Preheat oven to 180°C. Pass liver, pork, onion and herbs through the coarsest hole of a mincer twice to achieve a good texture. Combine mince with breadcrumbs, salt, pepper and egg and form into 4 balls (faggots). Wrap each one in caul fat and place, seam-side down, in an oiled dish just big enough for the faggots, which should be nearly touching. Bake for 1 hour. Cover dish with foil if faggots are browning too fast. They should be moist but with a crisp, brown top.

Serve with a purée of potato or potatoes fried with rosemary and a purée of tart apples.

lebanese grilled liver

SERVES 4

4 cloves garlic, finely chopped

pinch of sea salt

3 tablespoons extra-virgin·
olive oil

freshly ground black pepper

1 tablespoon dried mint

4 x 1 cm thick slices lamb's
liver, cut into chunks

2 lemons

SALAD

sliced tomatoes

thinly sliced red onions

freshly picked heads of young
parsley

Work garlic to a paste with salt. Mix with oil, pepper and mint and pour over liver. Allow to rest for 1 hour. Thread liver onto skewers and grill over a hot charcoal fire for preference, or under an overhead griller, until brown and crusty on the outside but still a little pink inside. Baste with more of the marinade.

Toss salad ingredients together. Place skewers on top. Tip over any remaining marinade and squeeze lemons over.

liver with sage
Crisp sage or rosemary leaves in a tablepoon of butter, squeeze on lemon and tip over lamb's or calf's kidney.

squab pigeon liver and turnip salad

SERVES 4

This rather understated salad is very luxurious due to the wonderful richness of squab pigeon livers. If they are unobtainable, duck livers are the best substitute. I like this salad served with large pieces of sourdough toast and Walnut Spread (see NUTS). A frivolous thought – if you ever found yourself in possession of a single black truffle, it would make a sensational addition to the salad, chopped and added at the same time as the mushrooms.

1 tablespoon yellow mustard
seeds

8 golfball-sized turnips, peeled

1 cup Chicken Stock

8 button mushrooms

250 g unsalted butter

1 bay leaf

1 piece orange zest

1 generous sprig thyme

400 g squab pigeon livers

few drops of red-wine
vinegar

freshly ground black pepper

sea salt

4 handfuls rocket leaves,
washed

Cover mustard seeds with warm water and leave to swell for 30 minutes. Place turnips in a saucepan with stock and cook very gently, tightly covered, until nearly tender, about 7 minutes. Add mushrooms and simmer a further 3–4 minutes. Uncover, tip into a salad bowl and leave to cool.

Place a fine-meshed wire rack over a flat tray. Melt butter very slowly with bay leaf, orange zest and thyme in a small saucepan. It should be too hot to leave your finger in but definitely not simmering. Clean the livers of any connecting veins. Slip half the livers into the hot butter and poach until firm but still springy to the touch. Remove with a slotted spoon to the wire rack. >

Repeat with second batch of livers. (Strain seasoned butter and refrigerate for later use in other recipes.)

Drain mustard seeds. Drain turnips and mushrooms, slice thickly and return to salad bowl. Add mustard seeds and liver. Reduce chicken stock to syrupy juices by fast boiling, then add vinegar, pepper and sea salt to taste. Pour stock over contents of salad bowl and toss gently. To serve, arrange small heaps of rocket leaves on each plate and top with liver-and-turnip mixture.

other recipes

chicken liver pâté *see* CHICKEN AND THE CHRISTMAS TURKEY

duck liver parfait *see* DUCK

grilled italian-style squab with liver crostini *see* QUAIL AND SQUAB PIGEONS

simple country terrine *see* PORK

whole cabbage stuffed with pork, liver and capers *see* CABBAGES AND BRUSSELS SPROUTS

see also BEEF; CHICKEN AND THE CHRISTMAS TURKEY; DUCK

melons

Deliciously scented and full of juices, melons are the fruit of the trailing vines of the family Cucurbitaceae – this includes cucumbers and marrows as well as the cantaloupe, honeydew melon and watermelon. (All forms hybridise easily, and Alan Davidson relates in his book *Fruit* that in the nineteenth century the French took great care to cultivate melons well apart from other gourds to avoid 'incestuous intercourse' with cucumbers!) Africa seems to be the common point of origin, although melons travelled very early on: watermelon is recorded as being eaten in Egypt in 4000 BC. Cantaloupe with vanilla ice-cream was a regular treat in all the summers of my youth. Nowadays I prefer my cantaloupe at breakfast, with lemon juice and maybe a bruised mint leaf. Honeydew melon works well as a salad with rich poultry such as duck or goose, again dressed with lemon juice. Watermelon is the most refreshing of fruit on a hot summer's day. In countries where the water supply may be suspect a big slice of watermelon is a safe and delicious way of slaking one's thirst, as the flesh of the watermelon contains more than 90 per cent water. >

melons
go
with
hams
lemons
oranges
prawns
crab
rock lobster
smoked chicken
roasted duck
mint
late-picked wines
fortified wines
rum
grapes
strawberries
raspberries
pears
ground ginger
glacé ginger

Each year I pickle watermelon rind and the by-product is a huge bowl of watermelon flesh. Any not eaten is put through the juicer and drunk, straight or mixed with a quantity of orange juice. The sunset colour is heavenly, as is the flavour.

VARIETIES AND SEASON

There are 3 main groups of dessert melon (all belonging to the species *Cucumis melo*) – the cantaloupes (*C. melo cantaloupensis*), the musk or netted melons (*C. melo reticulata*) and the winter melons (*C. melo inodorus*) – and then there is the watermelon (*C. citrullus*).

In Australia it is common for the terms 'rockmelon' and 'cantaloupe' to be used interchangeably to describe all orange-fleshed melons, whether the skin is smooth, netted, scaly or ridged or the fruit is perfectly round or oval. In Europe distinction is made between smooth-skinned cantaloupes and muskmelons, most of which have 'netted' skin. But in North America, the term 'cantaloupe' is used to describe the most popular variety of muskmelon.

Melons are available all year round. Cantaloupe and muskmelons are best in the summer, as are watermelons. Winter melons are best in the autumn, confusingly. When ripe all dessert melons should be fragrant and juicy.

Cantaloupe The melon we call a cantaloupe in fact belongs to the Reticulatus group. It has a light overlay pattern that stands out from the skin and is lighter in colour than the base skin. The flesh is usually a medium orange. A true cantaloupe does not have netted skin and belongs to the Cantaloupensis group. **Cassaba** One of the Inodorus group, this melon has green or yellow ridged skin and pale-yellow flesh. **Charentais** A member of the Cantaloupensis group, this melon has a smooth yellow–green skin and is small and round. The flesh is deep orange and is said to have the finest flavour of all melons. There are infinitesimal quantities of this French aristocrat being grown in Victoria. **Gallia** One of the Reticulatus group, this green-fleshed melon has a netted skin. **Honeydew** A member of the Inodorus group, this melon has a smooth and hard creamy-green skin that ripens to creamy-yellow. Its pale-green flesh has a more cottony texture than the flesh of either Reticulatus or Cantaloupensis melons. **Ogen** This green-fleshed member of the Cantaloupensis group has a smooth, ridged creamy-yellow skin with speckled green stripes. **Watermelon** *C. citrullus* is the largest melon and is round or barrel-shaped with bright-pink flesh and black seeds. A small, sweet watermelon with dark-green markings on the skin and brilliant-yellow flesh has appeared under the name 'champagne melon' in recent years.

SELECTION AND STORAGE

As a general rule select a melon that feels heavy for its size. Check that the melon gives a little when pressed at the stem end – this is an indication of ripeness. Melons need air to circulate around them as they mature. Often a ripening melon will be lifted from the ground, still on the vine, and supported on an upturned flowerpot or similar. A brown mark may result. This is not a sign of inner damage. However, soft or sunken spots are a definite sign of spoilage. Reject such fruit.

Cantaloupes are picked at half-slip or full-slip stage – the 'slip' refers to the ease with which the stem separates from the melon. When the stem separates readily the melon is ripe. If melons are picked at half-slip the flavour is not fully developed. As cantaloupes do not ripen further after picking this is a regrettable practice and is no doubt dictated by transportation concerns. When you take a deep sniff you should be able to detect a rich, ripe aroma.

Honeydew melons should display blotched patches of yellow or have a distinctly creamy colour rather than a greenish white skin. Unripe honeydew melons are very insipid, whereas a ripe one is glorious. A honeydew, stored at room temperature for 2–3 days, will ripen after picking, unlike other melons. Cantaloupes stored in the sun will not ripen further but the flesh softens and becomes juicier. Therefore, cut melons at room temperature to enjoy the maximum juice.

Watermelons are often displayed cut as rarely does one wish to buy a whole one. Prefer richly coloured fruit – it is a good indicator of sweet flesh. The seeds should be black, not white. If you wish to buy a whole watermelon, tap the sides of the fruit. It should sound faintly hollow.

Once cut, a cantaloupe melon must be covered with plastic film or stored in a closed plastic bag in the refrigerator. Left unwrapped, its perfume will invade all other unwrapped food. Prevent a cut watermelon or honeydew from drying out by pressing plastic film against the cut surface.

PREPARATION

There is little to do to prepare a melon for instant enjoyment. Halve it, remove the seeds if dealing with a cantaloupe or honeydew variety, cut it into wedges and eat it with a spoon or from your hands. Peel the sections if you wish or if the melon is to be used in a composite salad. Cut a watermelon into slices or chunks and flick out the visible seeds with the point of a knife. It is best to eat watermelon out of doors, so that one can be cheerfully abandoned during the spitting process.

Kitchenware suppliers sell melon ballers of different sizes which will produce balls as small as a pea to as large as a marble. These spoons are sometimes referred to as 'parisienne spoons'.

coconut melon
Toss chunks of cantaloupe in coconut milk, sweetened to taste. Pieces of young jellied coconut in syrup, available from Asian food stores, are a great addition, too.

pickled watermelon rind

This old-fashioned preserve is good with most meats, particularly brawn or pâtés, and I like it as a condiment with hot, boiled salted beef or raw ham. Served in this way it is reminiscent of the mustard sweet pickles of northern Italy, sold in jars as mostarda di Cremona.

melon and prawns

Toss chunks of honeydew melon or cantaloupe with peeled prawns, finely shredded mint leaves, coriander leaves and stems, very finely chopped hot chilli and a squeeze of lemon or lime juice.

I kg watermelon rind
¼ cup salt
I litre water
PICKLING SYRUP
I kg sugar
600 ml white-wine vinegar
600 ml water
I lemon, thinly sliced
I stick cinnamon
I teaspoon cloves
I teaspoon whole allspice

Cut rind into squares of 2 cm or 6 cm × 1 cm strips, leaving a blush of pink. Soak rind overnight in salt and water.

Next day, drain rind, put it in a saucepan, cover with cold water and simmer for 30 minutes, until the head of a pin will easily pierce the skin. Drain.

Make the pickling syrup by simmering all the ingredients for 10 minutes. Add rind and boil rapidly until rind is translucent. Fill hot, sterilised ✐ jars with rind and pour over syrup, ensuring there are no air bubbles.

Leave for about a week. It is even better if you leave it for a month before eating.

melon tartlets

Bake Shortcrust Pastry ✐ tartlet cases for 20 minutes at 200°C, then spoon in Pastry Cream ✐ and cover with sliced ripe melon tossed with finely chopped fresh mint. Serve at once. (The tartlets become soggy if filled more than 30 minutes before serving.)

cantaloupe sauce for rock lobster or crab

MAKES 2 CUPS

This is a delicious starter to a summer meal: sliced rock lobster tail arranged with a large spoonful of tiny melon balls, some shredded mint leaves and pale-coral melon sauce spooned over the meat.

When making Cantaloupe Ice-cream (see p. 413), set aside some of the melon purée. Don't serve the ice-cream at the same meal though!

3 tablespoons puréed cantaloupe
½ cup Mayonnaise ✐
juice of ½ lemon
½ cup cream, softly whipped
salt
Tabasco

Combine purée with mayonnaise, lemon juice and cream. Season with salt and Tabasco and serve with sliced rock lobster tail or picked crab meat. This quantity is sufficient for a 1.5 kg rock lobster or about 1½ cups freshly picked crab meat.

cantaloupe ice-cream

SERVES 6–8

This recipe is originally from the work of Elizabeth David and it has long been a favourite at Stephanie's Restaurant. We often surround each wedge with a large spoonful of sliced summer stone fruit – peaches, nectarines, apricots and plums – all lightly sugared and soused with a late-picked wine. The fruit and juices are heavenly.

This ice-cream is also good with puréed, sweetened and strained raspberries. This sauce is known as Melba Sauce and is said to have been created to garnish the famous Peach Melba invented by Auguste Escoffier for Dame Nellie Melba at the Savoy Hotel in the late nineteenth century.

1 cantaloupe
125 g castor sugar
4 egg yolks
few drops of kirsch
juice of ½ lemon
300 ml cream

Halve melon crosswise and discard seeds. Scoop out flesh. Place emptied halves in a freezer bag and freeze until quite firm.

Purée flesh in a food processor with sugar until smooth. Cook this purée over low heat until sugar has dissolved. Beat egg yolks until pale, then pour over hot purée. Return mixture to a clean pan and cook, stirring, over low heat until lightly thickened. Pour at once into a chilled bowl, stir in kirsch and lemon juice and allow to become quite cold. Add cream, then whisk lightly to combine and pour through a coarse strainer standing over a bowl. Churn in an ice-cream machine according to the manufacturer's instructions. Pack ice-cream into frozen melon halves and smooth tops. Return to freezer in freezer bags.

When ready to serve, carefully cut each half into 3–4 wedges, using a sawing action and a serrated knife.

marinated melon
Cut a lid from a small melon, scoop out the seeds and fill with a small glass of late-picked flowery wine, then replace the lid and chill for an hour. Serve as is, or tip the wine into a decanter and serve alongside the marinated melon.

melon fruit salad
Add a squeeze of lemon juice, a slosh of rum and glacé ginger to balls of cantaloupe, watermelon and honeydew.

m i n t　A plant of mint (*Mentha* species) is forever, and it will also spread forever. All mints have a creeping root system that makes them very hardy and explains why they are so invasive and almost impossible to kill off. If you grow mint, contain it in a tub or pot or in a small self-contained garden patch. | The flavour of mint is appreciated in many cultures, not only by the English with their mint sauce, as the French like to suggest. Mint originated in ancient Greece (where they enjoyed it in their bath water as well as their food) and it is still a most popular herb in Greece today. The Greeks combine dried spearmint with hard goat's milk cheeses and sometimes also include this combination in bread. The Cypriot cheese haloumi is a stretched curd cheese that has leaves of mint embedded in it. I like to add wintermint to tabbouleh, Middle Eastern cucumber and yoghurt salads or Indian raitas. Asian and Indian cooks enjoy mint's cleansing note, too, and it is seen as a suitable foil to hot dishes in their cuisines. | The flowering tops of all mints contain traces of camphor, which adds the sharp, clean scent included in toothpastes, room deodorants and the like.

VARIETIES AND SEASON

There are many varieties of mint, maybe as many as thirty. Spearmint and wintermint are the most useful for culinary purposes, but you may also come across a few others. Mint is available all year round as it is grown in glasshouses and in the warmer parts of the continent during the southern winter. The peak season for all mints is summer.

Applemint *M. rotundifolia* has soft, velvety round leaves that are pleasant to touch, but I find the apple flavour a little sweet. **Eau-de-cologne** Also known as bergamot mint, *M. piperita citrata* is used mainly in pot-pourri as its metallic green leaves are highly scented, as its name implies. **Pennyroyal** *M. pulegium* has a very strong peppermint odour and is best used as an attractive ground cover. **Peppermint** *M. piperita* grows wild on hillsides in Provence, where it is popular as an infusion or tisane. It has smallish, purple-tinged green leaves with an obvious peppermint fragrance. **Spearmint** *M. viridis* or *M. spicata* is the most common mint grown in Australia. The leaves are long and narrow with serrated edges and have a distinctive spearmint aroma. This mint dies down in winter. **Vietnamese** The herb popularly known as Vietnamese mint, *Polygonum pulchrum*, is not a true mint. It is very hot and pungent and has long, pointed leaves that are tinged with purple. **Wintermint** *M. cordifolia* has rounder leaves than spearmint that are crinkly or 'pebbled' in appearance. It has the advantage of not dying down in the winter. I find its flavour similar to but more rounded than that of spearmint.

SELECTION AND STORAGE

If buying mint, select bunches with brightly coloured leaves that are not drooping or looking black or yellow. Mint that has been kept in water will quickly blacken. Do not wash mint before storing it. Store it in a paper-lined plastic bag in the refrigerator and use as soon as possible.

PREPARATION

Mint should be washed and dried before chopping. Strip individual leaves from the stem before chopping or if using whole. Sprigs are used whole for garnish and in hot or cold drinks.

**mint
goes
with**
*lamb
potatoes
peas
carrots
gin
tea
lime juice
garlic
chillies
rice noodles
bean shoots
pork
prawns
yoghurt
cucumbers
tomatoes
parsley
coriander
cracked wheat
lemons*

english mint sauce

MAKES 1½ CUPS

recipes

Mint sauce for roast lamb is best served in a sauce boat with a spoon, so that one spoons the solids onto the meat and does not just pour out flavoured vinegar.

large handful of small mint
  leaves
1 teaspoon sugar
1 tablespoon boiling water
3 tablespoons white-wine or
  cider vinegar

Strip mint leaves from stems and chop very finely. Mix with sugar. Add boiling water to dissolve sugar and then add vinegar.

mint gravy Add the chopped mint and sugar to the baking dish after pouring out the excess fat. Stir in 1 tablespoon plain flour over heat until a good brown colour, then add 1 cup water or stock. Stir vigorously to avoid lumps.

minted vegetables
Toss finely chopped mint with buttered new potatoes, the first of the peas in spring or buttered boiled carrots.

mint and yoghurt chutney   MAKES 1½ CUPS

There is an infinite variety of fresh chutneys that are made to accompany Indian foods. They can also be used as a dip with vegetable fritters and curry puffs or as a sauce for a grilled or baked fish.

tomato mint salad
Dress wedges of tomato with freshly chopped mint and spring onion, lemon juice, finely sliced fresh chilli and a touch of salt and sugar. Serve with steamed rice and a grilled fillet of fish.

1 cup freshly chopped
  coriander leaves
½ cup freshly chopped mint
  leaves
1 fresh chilli, seeded
1 tablespoon lemon juice
3 tablespoons water
200 ml thick yoghurt
salt

In a blender, combine all ingredients except yoghurt and salt. Whisk yoghurt until creamy and stir into paste, then taste for salt. Use within a few hours.

mint and spring onion chutney   MAKES 1 CUP

iced mint
Set mint sprigs in ice to add to punches or fruit drinks.

Garam masala is a spice mixture that can be made from a number of ingredients. Charmaine Solomon gives several recipes in her Complete Asian Cookbook. *Cinnamon and cardamom occur in all versions. Other spices include cloves, nutmeg, cumin, coriander and pepper. Garam masala can also be bought from an Indian grocery. It is best to avoid supermarket versions as the whole point of such spice mixtures is freshness.*

tomato mint soup
Add freshly chopped mint to a summer tomato soup as a change from basil.

1 cup fresh mint leaves
6 spring onions
2 fresh chillies, seeded
1 clove garlic
2 teaspoons sugar
1 teaspoon salt
1 teaspoon garam masala
juice of 2 lemons *or* 3 limes
2 tablespoons water

Blend all ingredients in a food processor, then pack into a small bowl and chill until needed.

vietnamese chicken and mint salad SERVES 4

This recipe is based on one found in Nicole Routhier's The Foods of Vietnam.

2 cooked chicken breasts, skinned and thinly sliced
4 cups finely sliced Chinese cabbage
I cup grated carrot
½ cup freshly chopped mint leaves
fresh coriander leaves
crisp-fried shallots *or* fried peanuts (optional)

DRESSING
2 fresh chillies, seeded and finely chopped
3 cloves garlic, finely chopped
2 tablespoons brown sugar
I tablespoon rice vinegar
3 tablespoons fresh lime *or* lemon juice
3 tablespoons fish sauce
3 tablespoons vegetable oil
2 spring onions, finely sliced

Combine all dressing ingredients and leave for 30 minutes. Mix salad ingredients except for coriander and shallots and toss with dressing. Arrange on a platter and garnish with coriander. Sprinkle over crisp-fried shallots, if desired.

mint gin
Slip a sprig of mint into a gin and tonic instead of the traditional lime or lemon slice, or as well as.

yoghurt mint drink
Whisk 1 part yoghurt with 3 parts iced water and add salt and a sprig of mint for a drink on a very hot and humid day.

other recipes

cracked wheat and cashew salad with mint *see* NUTS
jill's warm prawn and mint salad *see* PRAWNS
tabbouleh *see* PARSLEY
tzatziki *see* YOGHURT
yam goong – salad of bug meat with mint and lemongrass *see* BUGS

mushrooms

mushrooms Wild mushrooms have traditionally been gathered from paddocks and wooded country. The mushroom is a fungus, and its method of reproduction was discovered by the French in 1678, who began growing mushrooms in caves. Modern cultivation methods were developed over the following couple of centuries. The cultivation of the common mushroom (*Agaricus bisporus*) is a thriving industry and these high-quality graded mushrooms represent the type most of us buy regularly. | I have always been fascinated by mushrooms – they are invisible one day but by the next have pushed their way through earth and leaf mulch to emerge damp and dewy, ready for the eagle eye and eager hand of the enthusiastic mushroom gatherer. | Sumerians were using wild mushrooms in 3500 BC. The Greeks exported them to the Romans and the Egyptians served them only to the Pharaohs – they were considered food fit only for the gods. >

The Europeans are passionate gatherers of wild mushrooms and have generations of experience. Even today in Europe local pharmacists are always on hand during the autumn months to identify and distinguish the delicious from the dangerous. A visit to France or Italy during the months of September and October will offer endless opportunities to be regaled with cèpes or porcini, chanterelles or girolles, orange-capped ovoli (sliced and eaten raw in Italy with olive oil and parmesan cheese), mousserons, black trompettes de mort and many, many more. The earthy, sweet, sometimes buttery, sometimes meaty textures and flavours are magnificent.

Of all the wild mushrooms, the elusive truffle reigns supreme. In Europe truffles are 'hunted' by specially trained dogs and pigs. It is a delicacy prized for its musky, haunting flavour and its surprising crunchy texture. At the time of writing the first hazelnut trees inoculated with truffle spore have been planted in Tasmania and we are all holding our breath for the moment of truth when we will know whether the enterprising young men who have pioneered this venture will gather the first Australian black truffles. Early attempts in California and New Zealand have apparently had some success. Black truffles from the Périgord region of France command jaw-dropping prices of several thousand dollars a kilogram. The potential market for fresh truffles out of season is enormous.

Ignoring the more exotic species for the moment, genuine field mushrooms are still out there for the dedicated hunter-gatherers among us. Interestingly I have never seen what we know as a field mushroom for sale in Europe. As there are fewer and fewer opportunities for the suburban dweller to produce or handle food direct from the source, so wild mushrooms continue as a symbol of a simpler life more in tune with the seasons.

It is only recently that Australian restaurants have started to be supplied with unusual species of wild mushroom and it is proper that we should proceed with caution. Wild-mushroom supply is entirely dependent on weather conditions. A dry autumn will produce few mushrooms. A wet and cold autumn will be similarly disappointing. A wet spring will diminish the morel supply. But given a sunny day after convincing rain, a tin billy and an old trusty knife, a few hours strolling through countryside where there is a loose ground-mulch of decaying leaves or a recently ploughed paddock or a dark pine forest carpeted with pine needles and one will be rewarded by the sight of lifting mounds of soil and, beneath, the prize. Near by will be other mushrooms already fully emerged and unfurled with that fecund smell of damp earth, resinous pine and sweet mushroom odour clinging to them.

VARIETIES AND SEASON

Mushrooms are classified as cultivated and wild. In Australia we can now buy **cultivated** common, Swiss brown, oyster, shiitake and enokitake

**mushrooms
go
with**
*butter
olive oil
garlic
shallots
toast
onions
parsley
chives
nutmeg
pine nuts
ham
lemons
red-wine vinegar
coriander
cream
stock
eggs
parmesan cheese
goat's cheese
vine leaves
chillies
breadcrumbs
rice
asparagus
barley
snails
chicken
chicken livers
guinea fowl
rabbit
squab pigeon
steak
artichokes
potatoes
salt
pepper*

mushrooms all year round. The exotics have only 2 per cent of the market and are correspondingly more expensive.

COMMON

Cultivated *Agaricus bisporus* are sold in stages of development, or grades. **Button** (baby or champignon) mushrooms are small, white and tightly closed. **Cup** mushrooms have a full flavour and firm texture. They are larger than buttons and have partially opened but have not flattened out. **Flat** mushrooms are fully matured with a rich flavour, are large and have a soft texture. These are the closest to field mushrooms in taste.

ENOKITAKE

Flammulina velutipes, a long-legged, tiny-capped, slightly crunchy cream mushroom, is delicate in flavour and much appreciated in Asian cooking, especially for adding to clear broths. It is also known as the golden needle mushroom.

OYSTER

Also known as the abalone mushroom, *Pleurotus ostreatus* is a large fungus that is shaped like an oyster shell and has a very delicate flavour. It is pearly-white to beige and occasionally apricot–pink and very light.

SHIITAKE

Also known as the Japanese mushroom, *Lentinus edodes* was previously only available dried but is now cultivated in both Australia and New Zealand. More delicate in appearance than the common mushroom, the shiitake has a brown cap and a meaty flavour. Its perfume is more noticeable in the dried form.

SWISS BROWN

This is the same species as *Agaricus bisporus*, the common cultivated mushroom – in fact, it is the original form. It was around 1920 that a mutant strain with a white rather than chestnut-brown top appeared. Market preference developed for a white mushroom, so that what was the usual has now become the exotic. The Swiss brown is more robust in flavour than the white cultivated mushroom and at present is only grown to the button stage. Very recently, however, I saw fully opened Swiss browns being offered for sale at a very high price and labelled as Portobello mushrooms.

There are hundreds of **wild** mushrooms. Here I have noted only those that are commonly gathered at the time of writing. If you have Russian, Polish or Italian friends they will almost certainly enjoy additional varieties to the ones mentioned here.

In this instance 'wild' means 'gathered in the wild', making indigenous and escaped exotic mushrooms both wild. We are still learning about our native species, of which the black fellow's bread (*Polyporus mylittae*) must be among the strangest. It is rarely seen and only occurs after a bushfire has swept through an area. The large, soccer-ball-sized growth is found underground and is hard with a brown exterior and a chalky-textured, lemon-flavoured, creamy-beige interior. Apparently it produces some surface fungi but it is the underground growth that is eaten. It is strikingly primitive to look at and a culinary curiosity rather than a treat.

BOLET | Slippery Jack, Blue Mountain cèpes and other regional names usually all refer to *Suillus luteus* and *S. granulatus*, which belong to the *Boletus* genus and have come to Australia with introduced flora. They are *not* cèpes or porcini (*B. edulis*), lacking the distinctive swollen stem and rich flavour of this aristocrat. They do resemble *B. edulis*, however, in that each has a spongy mass rather than gills under the cap. The cap is slippery in texture and is usually a dark orange–brown. Once cooked, these mushrooms have a flavour somewhere between a field mushroom and poached bone marrow.

Bolets appear in the autumn, often in pine forests. Both species are found in Western Australia, South Australia, Victoria and New South Wales, while *S. granulatus* is also found in Queensland.

FIELD | *Agaricus campestris* is the mushroom we all know: creamy broad caps with liver-pink gills below. It can be found dotting paddocks in autumn.

MOREL | *Morchella conica* is shaped like a hollow, conical gnome's hat or a Christmas tree. The cap is made up of crinkled cavities (which can trap dirt) and can be as small as a strawberry or as large as an egg. To my palate the Australian morels are richly flavoured but lack the scent of the French varieties. The only commercial quantities of morels I have heard of are gathered in Victoria, although there have certainly been sightings in South Australia, Tasmania and New South Wales. Morels are very highly prized and their location is guarded by those in the know! They occur in the early spring.

PINE FOREST | Also known as the saffron milkcap, *Lactarius deliciosus* occurs most abundantly in pine forests and in other areas of introduced habitat. The cap, gills and stem of this large, fleshy mushroom are orange. When sliced it oozes an orange–red juice that turns greenish if the mushroom is not cooked and eaten at once. It is an autumn mushroom and is found in all States except Queensland.

SELECTION AND STORAGE

When gathering *wild* mushrooms avoid specimens that are badly broken or have evidence of insect infestation. Increasingly, wild mushrooms are on sale in season at fresh food markets and from speciality greengrocers. Many varieties of wild mushroom are also available dried and some are available cooked and frozen, ready for immediate use. Imported dried cèpes and morels have excellent flavour.

Choose *cultivated* buttons or caps with white tops (unless buying Swiss browns) as any discoloration means they are old. Such specimens are, however, fine for soup. Reject any mushroom that is withered.

Shiitake mushrooms should be firm and dry (the stems are useful for flavouring stocks but are otherwise forever tough). *Oyster* mushrooms should be buff-cream, taupe or salmon-pink, depending on the variety, with no darkening areas. Shiitake and oyster mushrooms should be stored in a single layer. They are usually purchased in trays arranged in such a way. If bought loose, spread them out on a plate and cover with a barely damp clean cloth.

Enokitake mushrooms should look supple but not slimy, nor should the stem ends look brown or wet. They should be cream, not beige, in colour. Store them in their original wrappings for 4–5 days.

Both fresh black and white *truffles* are sublime when handled generously but their price puts them beyond most of us. Fresh black truffles are imported into Australia in our summer, the main black truffle season in Europe, and white truffles from Italy are imported during our late spring. Canned truffles are not worth the money. Store truffles in a jar of rice or a covered bowl with eggs and use within a day or so (the truffle will scent the eggs).

Keep all mushrooms other than truffles in the refrigerator but not in a plastic bag, which makes them sweat. Wet mushrooms deteriorate rapidly. Most supermarkets and greengrocers supply paper bags for storing cultivated mushrooms.

Pine forest mushrooms, *Suillus granulatus* and morels can be **dried** or **frozen** instead of being stored fresh. They should be used within 6 months. (There is no point freezing cultivated mushrooms that are available all year. Also, very tender varieties, such as oyster and enokitake mushrooms, do not freeze satisfactorily as they turn to mush when removed from the freezer.) Pine forest mushrooms, *S. granulatus* and cultivated button mushrooms can also be **preserved** in liquid.

TO DRY

Slice large mushrooms thickly and spread them on a sheet of newspaper on a tray. Place the tray in a sunny, dry position away from domestic animals and birds until the mushrooms are completely dry (this can take several days). Turn the

garlic mushrooms
Chop the stems from large flat mushrooms with garlic and scatter over the caps, then oil generously and grill. Serve on toast.

stewed mushrooms
Cook flat mushrooms in 1 cm water with a large knob of butter in a wide frying pan. Hold mushrooms in their juices and boil vigorously just before serving alongside steak, chicken or scrambled eggs. Save the juices for deglazing a pan when next making a sauce, or freeze it.

mushrooms over after a day. Completely dried mushrooms should break, not bend. (If drying your mushrooms outside, don't forget to bring the tray inside each evening before the dew falls.)

Alternatively, sliced or whole mushrooms (such as morels) can be threaded on string and hung in festoons in a sunny window until completely dry.

Once the mushrooms are dry, store them in an airtight jar or tin. Use them as they are, rehydrate them in water or grind them to a powder for adding subtlety to sauces or stews.

TO FREEZE | Choose excellent, firm-fleshed undamaged specimens for freezing. (When freezing morels I reduce their bulk and fragility by dipping them briefly in boiling water and then in iced water before draining them thoroughly.) Place unwashed and dry mushrooms in a plastic bag, then remove all the air and freeze as quickly as possible. (In the restaurant we create a vacuum with a machine that extracts the air.) Use frozen. The texture will never be the same as using fresh mushrooms but the flavour will be excellent. It is an ideal method for adding exotic flavours to more conventional fresh mushrooms, soups or stews.

TO PRESERVE IN LIQUID | Mushrooms can be preserved in oil or their own juices. Once the mushrooms have been packed into jars, whether preserved in oil or their own juices, seal the jars, then wrap each in a sheet of paper held in place with a rubber band. Place the jars in a large stockpot. Fill the pot with cold water to the level of the lids, bring to a boil and maintain a full boil for 1½ hours. Allow the jars to cool in the water. Unwrap and dry the jars and store away from the light. **In oil** Slice mushrooms thickly, then sprinkle them with salt and leave for 1 hour. Wipe dry. Heat a thin layer of olive oil in a frying pan and quickly sauté the mushrooms to remove some of their liquid. Pack into sterilised preserving jars. Add a few peppercorns and cover with olive oil. **In their own juices** Wipe the mushrooms clean. Keep them whole unless they are very large. Bring a large pot of salted water to a boil with the juice of 2–3 lemons. Drop in the mushrooms and boil for 3 minutes. Drain and pack into sterilised preserving jars. Add extra salt and a few peppercorns. Pack the mushrooms in tightly.

PREPARATION AND COOKING

The best rule with mushrooms is to prepare them as little as possible and eat them as soon as possible. There is no need to wash or peel any mushroom, whether wild or cultivated. A damp cloth is sufficient to wipe away any dirt. Use a soft brush to remove grass from wild mushrooms. Slicing mushrooms tears the cell walls and releases an enzyme that causes the flesh

mushroom fry-up
Fry some sliced mushrooms, potato, onion and garlic in olive oil in a non-stick pan, turning carefully and frequently to preserve the golden crusty bits. Serve as is on toast or toss with fettuccine, parsley and parmesan cheese and maybe fork through a raw egg. A favourite Sunday-night treat in my house!

to darken quickly. This reaction can be delayed by brushing or tossing the mushroom slices in lemon juice or oil and lemon juice. Darkened mushroom slices still taste great.

CULTIVATED

Common and Swiss brown Remove the stems from cap mushrooms if you intend to stuff them. Chop up the stems and add them to the stuffing mixture. **Enokitake** Requiring very little cooking, enokitake are best if their crisp texture is retained. They are ideal for adding to stir-fries at the end of the cooking time or dropping into a clear soup just before serving. **Oyster** These mushrooms have a delicate flavour that can be easily lost or swamped. I like them simply brushed with oil and grilled or simmered in clear soups. Do not serve these mushrooms raw as some people have a violent allergic reaction to them when uncooked. **Shiitake** Trim off the stems before using. Shiitake can be braised, grilled or sautéd. If grilling whole, brush generously with oil beforehand. Dried shiitake need to be soaked in warm water or stock for 30 minutes. The liquid can be filtered and used in the dish too. The stems are too tough to eat but can be added to stocks.

WILD

Bolet Slice the stems across and the caps into thick slices, or keep whole if very small. Bolets are wonderful with garlic, shallots and parsley and also with sticky stocks and cream. They cook very quickly and develop a wobbly texture like poached bone marrow. If cooked too hot or too long they will taste bitter. Dried Italian porcini or French cèpes are the same mushroom and are suitable for adding to braises, soup or pasta dishes. They need to be soaked in warm water or stock for 30 minutes. The liquid can be filtered and used in the dish too. The flavour is much stronger than the fresh bolets available in Australia, or the fresh cèpe or porcini. **Field** This is one mushroom that may, rarely, need to be peeled. A damp cloth usually suffices. Slice or chop as required, and add the stem to any stuffing ingredients. **Morel** Most Victorian morels are very clean, unlike those one sees in France. Slice through the conical cap and inspect closely. Morels gathered on a wet or damp day can develop worm infestation quickly, which can be a bit alarming. Morels can be braised with stock or cream or both. They are delicious with pasta, rice or poultry. Dried morels have a more smoky perfumed flavour. They should be soaked in warm water for 15 minutes. The soaking water can be filtered and added to the dish. **Pine forest** These mushrooms can be treated as bolets are. They do not develop the velvet texture of the bolets but retain a bit of crunch. **Truffle** Scrub thoroughly just before using. Peel the truffle (reserving all peelings for the stockpot) and then slice or chop as required.

pine forest mushrooms with garlic, cream and parsley

SERVES 2–4

If gathering the mushrooms yourself, prefer the smaller ones as the larger they are, the older they are and the more likely to be battered, stained greenish and maybe even wormy. Serve this as a first course or as a light lunch or supper with a veal chop or braised rabbit. The mushrooms, once cooked, can be combined with other mushrooms.

8 pine forest mushrooms
20 g butter
1 tablespoon olive oil
2 cloves garlic, chopped
½ cup cream
3 tablespoons freshly chopped
   parsley
salt
freshly ground black pepper

Remove any grass and dirt from mushrooms with a soft brush. Thickly slice mushrooms when you are ready to cook them (but not before). Heat butter and oil and sauté mushrooms over a high heat. Add garlic, sauté a further minute and then add cream, keeping the heat high. In a few minutes the cream will have reduced to a thick sauce. Toss in parsley and season.

croustades of mushroom Flat cultivated mushrooms can be cooked using this method, perhaps with the addition of some finely chopped onion or shallot. Both varieties can also be combined and piled into a hollowed-out and crisped bread case or pastry shell, as a sandwich filling between 2 rectangles of puff pastry or, more simply, piled onto hot toast. A nice final touch is to scatter chopped bone marrow into the pan at the last moment to add a gloss and suaveness to the dish.

pickled button mushrooms

600 ml white-wine vinegar
300 ml water
2 bay leaves
1 clove garlic, unpeeled and
   bruised
12 black peppercorns
6 coriander seeds
generous sprig of thyme *or*
   fennel
1 kg button mushrooms
olive oil

Bring all ingredients other than mushrooms and oil to a boil and simmer for 10 minutes. Drop in mushrooms and simmer for 5 another minutes. Remove mushrooms with a slotted spoon to a large, hot, sterilised jar and boil liquid for a further few minutes. Cover mushrooms with liquid and add a generous slurp of oil. Seal tightly and leave for at least 3 weeks before eating. This pickle keeps for at least 6 months.

mushroom soup
Simmer sliced mushrooms in rich beef or chicken stock with a crustless slice of sourdough bread, then blend and season for a wonderful mushroom soup.

pepper mushrooms
Wrap Pickled Button Mushrooms (see p. 425) in a fat strip of roasted, skinned red pepper and skewer with a toothpick to offer with drinks.

mushroom caps stuffed with goat's cheese on vine leaves

SERVES·6

12 large flat mushrooms

1 onion, finely chopped

2 cloves garlic

olive oil

½ cup pine nuts, sautéed until golden

½ cup freshly chopped, loosely packed parsley

2 tablespoons freshly chopped oregano

150 g fresh goat's cheese (preferably Kervella)

salt

freshly ground black pepper

24 fresh large grapevine leaves

Preheat oven to 200°C. Remove stems from mushrooms and chop. Sauté onion, garlic and mushroom stems in 1 tablespoon oil until softened. Add roughly chopped pine nuts and herbs and allow to cool. Mash goat's cheese until soft and combine with herb mixture. Season to taste.

Brush vine leaves with oil and line a shallow gratin dish. Place a mushroom on top of each leaf. Spoon stuffing into mushrooms, drizzle with a few drops of oil, cover with a layer of oiled vine leaves and bake until leaves are dark and crispy and filling is bubbly, about 20 minutes. The leaves will have shrunk and made some delicious juices. Rearrange mushrooms on top of leaves and spoon over collected juices. The top leaves may be too dark and crispy to eat, but do try them. The bottom ones will be limp but very tasty.

mushrooms à la grecque

SERVES 2–4

A classic and delicious way with small button mushrooms, this is good hot or cold. Serve with bread for mopping up the delicious juices. This quantity serves 2 as a first course or 4 as part of an antipasto selection.

½ cup extra-virgin olive oil

½ cup water

2 ripe tomatoes, peeled and chopped

freshly ground black pepper

½ teaspoon crushed coriander seeds

1 bay leaf

1 sprig thyme

salt

juice of ½ lemon

250 g button mushrooms

Simmer all ingredients except mushrooms for 5 minutes. Add mushrooms and cook for another 5 minutes. Remove mushrooms with a slotted spoon and reduce sauce for a few minutes. Pour over mushrooms in a flat serving dish.

variations A handful of sultanas can be cooked at the same time as the mushrooms. A teaspoon of chilli paste will make the dish more piquant. Chopped ginger and a pinch of ground saffron will add a different character again.

---

mixed grill

Toss flats, cups, buttons and shiitake or oyster mushrooms (sliced if large) with olive oil, salt, pepper and a few slivers of fresh red chilli. Grill in a single layer on a sheet of foil, turning once. Scatter with a few ground almonds, fresh breadcrumbs or toasted pine nuts and serve as a first course.

mushrooms and …

Serve grilled mushrooms with a slice of herb butter, a spoonful of Pesto (see BASIL) or a spoonful of mascarpone melting over them.

mushroom tartlets

MAKES 8

60 g butter
1 teaspoon freshly grated
   nutmeg
1 teaspoon ground coriander
250 g Swiss brown or button
   mushrooms, sliced
2 tablespoons cream
sea salt
freshly ground black pepper
1 quantity Shortcrust Pastry
1 egg, beaten

Preheat oven to 220°C. Melt butter in a large frying pan and add spices. Sauté mushrooms gently with a lid on for 5 minutes. Remove lid, then add cream and increase heat to maximum. Allow juices to bubble and reduce completely, stirring to prevent sticking. Taste for seasoning, then allow to cool.

Cut 16 pastry rounds 8 cm in diameter. Line 8 patty tins (not loose-bottomed flan tins) with pastry and prick well with a fork. Divide cooled mushroom mixture between tins and brush edges of pastry with egg. Cover with remaining pastry and seal edges well. Using a sharp knife, mark tops of tartlets with fine lines from centre out to resemble gills of a mushroom. Brush tartlets with egg and bake for 20 minutes until golden brown and crisp. Serve warm.

tiny mushroom pasties The same mixture can be spooned onto the same rounds of pastry and the edges pinched together to form small pasties. This method yields about 16.

mushroom custards

SERVES 4

A mix of wild and cultivated mushrooms will result in a more exciting custard.

½ clove garlic, sliced
40 g butter
200 g mixed mushrooms,
   chopped
salt
freshly ground black pepper
1 cup cream
½ cup milk
3 eggs, lightly whisked

Preheat oven to 160°C and butter 4 × 150 ml custard moulds well. Soften garlic in butter in a frying pan, add mushrooms, salt and pepper and stew until all liquid has evaporated. Add cream and reduce by a third, then add milk. Purée mushrooms and juices in a blender until quite smooth. Pour purée onto eggs and season to taste. Pour into prepared moulds standing in a baking dish lined with a folded tea towel and pour in water to come halfway up their sides. Bake for 20–25 minutes or until set. Serve as a first course, perhaps accompanied by grilled mushrooms or *beurre blanc* lightened with some of the mushroom juices given off in the first sautéing.

mushroom salad
Toss sliced button mushrooms with the best extra-virgin olive oil, finely chopped shallots or mild red onion, coriander leaves and stems and lots of parsley and season with sea salt, freshly ground black pepper, freshly grated nutmeg and red-wine vinegar or lemon juice. Finely chopped inner celery stalks are a good addition.

morel pasta sauce
Stew fresh morels and a finely chopped onion in butter and cream and toss with freshly cooked fettuccine. Grate over nutmeg and pepper and scatter with plenty of parsley.

mushrooms en papillote

SERVES 2

500 g mixed mushrooms
   (wild and cultivated)
¼ cup extra-virgin olive oil
½ cup cream *or* crème fraîche
3 tablespoons freshly chopped
   parsley
1 tablespoon freshly chopped
   tarragon
2 cloves garlic, very finely
   chopped
pinch of sea salt
freshly ground black pepper
40 g unsalted butter, melted

Preheat oven to 200°C. Remove stems from mushrooms and slice stems. Leave caps whole or quarter them, depending on size. Combine all ingredients other than butter and toss through mushrooms and stems.

Cut 2 × 28 cm rounds of baking paper, then fold in half. Cut a rounded curve at one end, so that the opened paper resembles a heart. Brush melted butter over paper hearts and place on a baking tray. Pile mushrooms on one side, then fold other side over and crimp edges closed very tightly. Bake for 20 minutes.

Serve parcels sealed, and cut or rip open at the table for a magnificent gush of aroma.

potatoes Tiny cooked potatoes could be included with the mushrooms.

chestnuts and mushrooms *see* CHESTNUTS

spinach roulade *see* SPINACH

veal braised with mushrooms and wine *see* VEAL

veal chops in red wine with bacon and mushrooms *see* VEAL

mussels

mussels Fifteen years ago the major mussel fishery in Victoria was the dredged mussel from Port Phillip Bay. This industry has since closed and along with it has gone the experience of sandy and gritty mussels with heavily barnacled shells. | The majority of blue mussels consumed in Australia today are cultivated on long lines supported by buoys using 'spat' collected from natural mussel settlements. Grown on 'collector' ropes August–September, the young mussels are thinned and declumped January–February and returned to the water on new ropes for a further 7–10 months. The farmed mussels we buy are clean, plump and tasty and look very handsome in their sleek and shiny navy-blue shells. | There are mussel leases in Port Phillip and Westernport bays, and in specific sites off the coasts of southern New South Wales, Tasmania and Western Australia. (Mussels grown under the salmon enclosures in Tasmania are of exceptional quality.) Some wild mussels are still gathered by divers, principally in Jervis Bay, New South Wales, at Lakes Entrance in Victoria and in Cockburn Sound, Western Australia, but those mussels harvested wild account for less than 5 per cent of the total harvest. >

Mussels, like oysters, are indiscriminate filter feeders and can accumulate toxins from polluted waters or the notorious 'red tides' created by concentrations of certain harmful organisms and must therefore be gathered from clean habitats. It is *not* safe to gather mussels from local piers or jetties. The industry has improved dramatically over the last few years and the supply of cultivated mussels is well priced and reliable. Don't take chances! (If you are keen to collect shellfish on your next holiday, stick to pipis – *Plebidonax deltoides* – which are found under the sand at the water's edge and can be cooked the same way as mussels. Make sure you check with the locals about the cleanliness of the beach.)

VARIETIES AND SEASON

The Australian blue mussel is *Mytilus edulis planulatus*. New Zealand has the green-lipped mussel, *Perna canaliculus*, which is imported into Australia.

The main harvest of cultivated mussels is July–February, but thanks to the expansion and development of mussel farming, mussels are obtainable from somewhere almost all year. When mussels spawn they become ragged and thin. It is not possible to pinpoint the exact moment when a mussel colony will spawn as it is mostly governed by water temperature. Spawning is usually late summer but will vary from one locality to another.

Cultivated mussels get the same nutrients as wild ones but miss out on pollution, sand and grit. They also have cleaner shells.

SELECTION AND STORAGE

There should be no problem obtaining top-quality mussels in Australia providing you have a good fishmonger to advise you when the shellfish are spawning. However, as already explained, there may be times when there are no suitable mussels for a few weeks.

Mussels must be alive when bought and cooked. A dead mussel will gape open and must be discarded. A live mussel may have its shell ajar but will close when tapped firmly. It is extremely unlikely that you will come across a cultivated mussel with its shell wedged tight with sand, as I have experienced with dredged mussels. Like all shellfish, mussels should be consumed as soon as possible after harvesting. However, they will keep, refrigerated and covered with a damp cloth, for 2 days.

PREPARATION AND COOKING

Tip the mussels gently into cold water and swish them around. Remove them one at a time and pull the protruding clump of hairs (the 'beard') downwards with a sharp tug. Transfer the cleaned mussel to a bowl of water and continue. If handling wild mussels, scrub them well to remove the barnacles if you propose to serve the mussels and their shells in a soupy mixture.

The mussels will only take about 5 minutes to cook, so everything should be ready. There are countless ways to prepare mussels. They can be consumed raw and are often included this way on a shellfish platter in France but are definitely an acquired taste. Mussels can be wedged, hinge-end down, in a pan of rock salt and be opened on a barbecue, but the juices are largely lost. In Provence they have a more sophisticated way of bar-becuing mussels where one gets the barbecued smokiness and the juices. Best of all is to serve *moules à la marinière* – mussels steamed in white wine. Steaming is the first step for many elaborate dishes, where the mussels may be coated with a sauce and placed under a grill or the meat may be extracted from the shell to mix with other ingredients. Usually the cooking juices are strained for use in a sauce or dressing. The top shell is often discarded for a less rustic preparation.

Almost all authorities advise that after steaming one should discard any mussel that does not open. I find that when a mussel is reluctant to open it is often especially vigorous and has a very tight hold on its shell. I do not discard unopened mussels without removing those that have opened and giving the reluctant ones another go!

Most blue mussels in Victoria host tiny soldier crabs. These crunchy creatures are quite edible but most people prefer to flick them from the opened mussel before serving.

TO OPEN A RAW MUSSEL	Force the shells a little apart by pushing the top and bottom shell in opposite directions.

Slip in a wide-bladed knife and cut the white mussel 'foot' that keeps the shell tightly closed.

TO STEAM IN WINE	Place unopened mussels no more than 2 layers deep in a wide pan (I sometimes use a

large wok). Scatter over a finely chopped onion, a few peppercorns, a bay leaf, a sprig of thyme and enough white wine to cover the bottom of the pan by 1 cm. Jam on the lid and turn the heat to maximum. In 4–5 minutes there will be a great gush of steam from the pan and, when the lid is removed, you will see that the shells have sprung apart. Using tongs, transfer all the opened mussels to a hot dish. Place any unopened mussels back on the heat for another minute or so. Add them to the bowl but discard any that haven't opened by now. Strain the juices over the mussels and serve at once.

TO BARBECUE	The best way to barbecue mussels is to open them raw and place them shell-down to the

heat, so that as the heat penetrates the shell the mussel contracts with a hiss of its own sizzling juice. Pour the very best olive oil over, grind on some pepper and tuck in.

A simpler way, but one that will lose more of the juice, is to heat a heavy frying pan a third full of rock salt on the barbecue until very hot. Be careful – the salt will jump and crackle. Lay the cleaned – but unopened – mussels on the salt, hinge-end wedged into the salt. As they open, quickly remove them to a heated dish. Dip the hot mussels into the best olive oil flavoured with freshly ground black pepper before eating.

gratin of mussels

SERVES 4

mussel dipping sauces
Make dipping sauces for steamed mussels by mixing melted butter, crushed cardamom and coriander seeds and black pepper or warm soy sauce or Ponzu Sauce and finely chopped fresh ginger.

2 kg mussels in the shell, bearded
½ cup white wine
fresh breadcrumbs
olive oil
SAUCE
2 shallots, chopped
2 cloves garlic, finely chopped
2 tablespoons olive oil
I carrot, finely diced
500 g tomatoes, peeled, seeded and chopped
I tablespoon tomato paste
grated zest of I lemon
freshly ground black pepper

Steam mussels open in wine, then remove and discard top shells. Reserve strained juices.

Preheat oven to 220°C. To make the sauce, sauté shallots and garlic in oil until soft. Add carrot and sauté for 5 minutes. Add tomato, tomato paste and lemon zest and cook for 5 minutes. Stir in reserved juices and simmer until sauce is thick. Season with pepper.

Place mussels in a single layer on an ovenproof platter and spoon over sauce. Scatter with breadcrumbs and drizzle with oil. Bake for 10 minutes until golden and bubbling, then scatter with parsley. The dish is good hot or at room temperature.

crumbed mussels
Top steamed mussels with oily breadcrumbs with or without parsley and finely chopped garlic and brown the crumbs under a hot griller. Or top the mussels with finely diced bacon as well as the oily breadcrumbs and garlic and drizzle with Worcestershire sauce after grilling.

marinated mussels

Steamed mussels either on the half-shell or slipped from their shells can be marinated and served tucked among crisp inner cos leaves as part of a buffet or mixed in a shallow bowl with cooked prawns and pipis.

extra-virgin olive oil
cider vinegar
steamed mussels
very finely chopped shallots or spring onions
lots of coarsely chopped parsley

Mix 4 parts oil to 1 part vinegar and add remaining ingredients, ensuring there is enough parsley to make a thick dressing. Marinate mussels for 30 minutes before serving.
variation A little freshly chopped chilli and coriander leaves will add a spiciness to the dressing.

mouclade

SERVES 2

Purists may frown, but curry powder is an essential ingredient in mouclade, one of the most popular mussel dishes served on the Brittany coast.

I kg mussels in the shell, bearded

½ cup dry white wine

2 shallots, chopped

freshly ground black pepper

freshly chopped parsley

SAUCE

40 g butter

2 tablespoons flour

I clove garlic, finely chopped

I egg yolk

100 ml cream

I teaspoon curry powder

I tablespoon lemon juice

Steam mussels open in wine, shallots and pepper. Strain cooking juices and set aside. Remove and discard top shells. Reserve mussels on a hot dish and cover with plastic film to prevent them drying out.

To make the sauce, melt butter, stir in flour and cook, stirring, over moderate heat for 3 minutes. Gradually stir in reserved juices and garlic. Bring to simmering point, stirring, and simmer for 5 minutes.

Whisk egg yolk with cream, curry powder and lemon juice in a small bowl. Slowly pour egg mixture into hot sauce, stirring well, but do not allow to boil. Pour sauce over reserved mussels, scatter generously with parsley and serve immediately.

garlic mussels

Dab garlic butter on steamed mussels after discarding the top shells and place under a very hot griller for 2 minutes. Serve with a bowl of croutons for mopping up the juices.

steamed mussels

Add cream, a good pinch of saffron threads and a few crushed fennel seeds to the pan before jamming on the lid when steaming mussels.

mussels in coconut-milk curry

SERVES 4

I tablespoon peanut oil

I teaspoon Thai green curry paste

I clove garlic, very finely chopped

I tablespoon very finely chopped fresh ginger

½ teaspoon ground turmeric

2 cups coconut milk

2 kaffir lime leaves

I stalk lemongrass, tender part only, very finely chopped

32 mussels, bearded

2 teaspoons fish sauce

I teaspoon palm sugar

I tablespoon fresh lime juice

2 tablespoons freshly torn basil leaves

Heat oil and sauté curry paste, garlic and ginger for 2 minutes. Add turmeric, coconut milk, lime leaves and lemongrass and simmer, uncovered, for 5 minutes. Add mussels, cover, then increase heat and cook for 5 minutes until mussels have opened. Add fish sauce, palm sugar and lime juice and simmer for 1 minute, shaking pan to mix ingredients well. Divide between bowls and scatter over basil leaves. Serve jasmine rice alongside.

mussel salad

Toss shelled steamed mussels with boiled waxy potatoes, parsley, spring onions and a mustardy vinaigrette and pile onto salad leaves.

jean's mussels   SERVES 4

200 g walnut halves

48 mussels in the shell,
  bearded

½ cup dry white wine

I bulb fennel, finely diced

2 carrots, peeled and finely
  diced

2 sticks celery, finely diced

2 tablespoons unsalted butter

I cup water

pinch of saffron threads

2 cloves garlic, finely chopped

I tablespoon olive oil

½ cup finely chopped parsley

I cup cream

Place walnuts in a bowl and cover with boiling water. Leave for 5 minutes, then drain. Dry in a low oven. Steam mussels open in wine, then discard top shells. Reserve strained juice. Keep mussels in a warm place, covered.

Place fennel, carrot and celery in a wide pan with butter and water. Cover and bring to a boil over low heat. Drain, reserving cooking liquid. Add reserved mussel liquor to vegetable cooking liquid and return mixture to wide pan. Drop in saffron threads and simmer until reduced by one-third. Meanwhile, sauté garlic in olive oil in a non-stick frying pan. Add walnuts and toss for 2–3 minutes until lightly coloured. Process walnuts and garlic until finely ground and stir in parsley.

Heat 4 wide soup plates to very hot. Divide mussels between plates. Add cream and drained vegetables to saffron-flavoured liquid and increase heat. Boil all together, stir in walnut–parsley mixture and spoon over the waiting mussels.

n u t s   I can remember the first time I tasted toasted pine nuts. It must be 30 years ago but I still remember the surprise and delight. They were as rare and costly as jewels in those days. I also recall sipping ice-cold coconut water from a drinking coconut after a steep climb to view a temple in Java, and eating delicious cashew-nut butter spread on a thick slice of wholemeal bread at Shakahari Restaurant in Melbourne's Carlton nearly 30 years ago. I enjoy the candied walnuts sold at the Victoria Market (at the restaurant we include them with grilled apples as a small side salad to accompany a soupy stew of pork hocks and beans); I have eaten fresh green almonds, sliced very thinly, with a roquefort and puff pastry confection at a smart 3-star restaurant in France, and have savoured superb, fat dry-roasted fritz almonds served with various herb sorbets and shaved dark chocolate at the Queenscliff Hotel once long ago. And I love the fantastic peanut, cucumber, chilli and red rose-petal salad we make to accompany platters of Cold Chinese White-cooked Chicken with Seared Spring Onion Sauce (*see* CHICKEN AND THE CHRISTMAS TURKEY). >

almonds
go
with
honey
chocolate
peaches
apricots
vanilla
cream
chicken
trout

bunya
nuts
go
with
lamb
buffalo
kangaroo
spinach
garlic
barramundi
cream

cashews
go
with
coconut milk
beans
cauliflower
fish
cracked wheat
chicken
almonds
rice

Australia grows many varieties of nuts and is the home of the macadamia nut. We are particularly proud of this fact as, so far, it is the only commercially valuable crop indigenous to this country. Other home-grown nut crops that are growing in importance are cashews, pecans and pistachios, all previously fully imported into this country. Australia currently exports both macadamias and pecans. We also have small walnut and hazelnut industries, and South Australia has always been famous for its almonds and Queensland for its peanuts.

Nuts are not only eaten whole, roasted and salted or plain. They are also ground into pastes, used as thickeners in many dishes and pressed into oils; they are flaked, slivered or crushed or can be enrobed with sugar, yoghurt or chocolate. Nuts are often combined with spices, herbs and seeds to make exotic mixtures. Some cuisines use nuts far more than others – especially those of the Middle East, Asia and South-East Asia. Pine nuts are a good example of how widely some nuts can be used: they are used in the meat, vegetable and pasta stuffings of Greece, Italy and the Middle East; they can be scattered over and through salads; and they are probably best known as an essential ingredient in the Genoese sauce Pesto (*see* BASIL). Pine nuts also feature in Sicilian pastries and other sweet dishes.

As nuts are everyone's favourite nibble it is good to know that the fat in them is mostly unsaturated and often mono-unsaturated. This is the same 'healthy' fat found in olive oil that has made the Mediterranean diet, which places a greater emphasis on all foods from plant sources (which of course includes nuts), a useful guide to healthy eating. (Coconuts are the odd one out when lauding nuts for their high proportion of mono-unsaturated fats – at 94 per cent, coconut is the most saturated oil in the world!)

VARIETIES AND SEASON

ALMOND

The almond is native to the eastern Mediterranean and is grown commercially in South Australia in McLaren Vale and the Riverland and in the Sunraysia district in Victoria. (It is a glorious sight to visit McLaren Vale in the early springtime to see the almond orchards in full lacy bloom.) When fully mature the kernel of the fruit of the almond tree splits its green outer coating to reveal the brown husk within – the almond we all recognise.

In Europe fresh almonds, those picked while the green coating is fresh and the kernel within damp and a bit soft, are considered a great delicacy and often served with fresh white cheese or summer stone fruits. Some specialist fruit shops now stock these in December and January.

The sweet almond (*Prunus amygdalus* var. *dulcis*) is preferred over the bitter almond, and a number of varieties are grown. Most growers prefer what are known as paper shell ('nonpareil') nuts, which, as the name implies, are easier to peel. Almonds are harvested in Australia in early autumn.

BUNYA | This nut is in fact the seed of the bunya pine (*Araucaria bidwillii*), a large rainforest tree found in southern Queensland. The tree fruits every 3 years and the seeds or nuts are held in the bracts of a very large cone that can weigh up to 10 kg. Each seed or nut has a hard outside shell that must be slit before the edible part can be extracted. A single bunya nut is about the size and shape of a large brazil nut, and its flavour is a little reminiscent of a chestnut mixed with the resinous quality of a pine nut. Aborigines from hundreds of kilometres away used to assemble in the Bunya Mountains in Queensland every 3 years in December to feast on these delicious starchy nuts.

Bunya nuts can be braised, roasted, minced into purées or ground to make flour. At present it is difficult to locate these nuts as they are not cultivated and are only sold by a few native food suppliers.

CASHEW | Australia spends around $20 million annually importing cashews (*Anacardium occidentale*) and we are now growing some of our own, mostly on the Atherton Tableland in Queensland and some in the Northern Territory near Darwin. The cashew is native to Brazil and the West Indies. The tree produces the well-known nut attached to a juicy tropical fruit the shape and size of a small apple. The juice from the fruit is a popular drink in Brazil and the West Indies. Australian cashews are harvested in August–October.

COCONUT | The coconut palm (*Cocos nucifera*) is native to Malaya but grows widely throughout tropical countries of the world. The coconut is covered with a brown fibrous husk that in turn is covered by a large dark-green-to-brown pod.

Trees can produce up to 75 nuts a year. These nuts are produced in clusters several times a year and take up to 6 months to mature. Young coconuts (sometimes known as 'jelly' or drinking coconuts) have soft white flesh and plentiful milky liquid in the centre. It is the coconut milk squeezed from the flesh, not this coconut water, that is called for in so many Asian recipes. Mature coconuts have hard flesh ideal for grating, and the centre of the nut is hollow. Coconut oil (copha) is made from the dried coconut meat (copra).

HAZELNUT | The hazelnut (*Corylus avellana*) is native to temperate regions of North America, south-east Europe and Asia. There are experimental plantings in the cool temperate areas of our eastern and southern States, such as north-eastern Victoria.

The nuts are small and round with a pointed tip in a brown skin, itself encased in a hard brown shell, which, when picked, is protected by a greenish husk. In Europe hazelnuts are sometimes referred to as cob nuts, while 'improved' larger varieties are often called filberts.

coconut goes with
chicken
fish
beef
beans
rice
turmeric
kaffir lime leaves
lemongrass
chillies

hazelnuts go with
chocolate
almonds
pork
duck
cinnamon
oranges

macadamias go with
honey
barramundi
chicken
rice
chillies

peanuts
go
with
chillies
tamarind
pork
chicken
beef
cucumber
snake beans

pecans
go
with
blue cheese
goat's cheese
bitter greens
duck
garlic
croutons
cream
maple syrup
molasses
lemon juice

Hazelnuts are harvested in Australia in March–April and in Europe in August–September.

MACADAMIA Australian Aborigines have enjoyed macadamias (or kindal kindal or baphal nuts) for thousands of years. The nuts were 'discovered' by European settlers in the subtropical rainforests of Queensland in the mid-1800s. The trees were exported to Hawaii in the 1890s as shade for livestock and it was not long before an astute American saw the potential of the fruit: the rest is history. The nut is still known as the Hawaiian nut in the United States.

The Australian macadamia industry, mostly centred in northern New South Wales and on the Atherton Tableland in Queensland, dates from the 1960s and is growing fast. In 1995 local production outstripped American production for the first time, making Australia the world's largest producer.

Two species of macadamia tree are grown commercially in Australia (*Macadamia integrifolia* and *M. tetraphylla*), both of which are now rarities in the wild. Each nut is encased in a tough outer shell, which in turn is enclosed in a feathery green husk. The nuts fall to the ground when ripe and need special equipment to be cracked open. The nut has a delicious creamy flavour and is creamy-white in colour. It is harvested in autumn.

PEANUT Peanuts (*Arachis hypogaea*) are not a true nut but the pods of a leguminous plant. Grown on long tendrils below the ground, they are also known as ground or monkey nuts. They originated in South America and are a staple food in Africa and Asia, with India, China and the United States being the principal growers. Peanuts are also grown extensively in Queensland. Peanut oil is highly prized in the cooking of many countries. The Australian peanut harvest is in April–May.

PECAN The pecan (*Carya illinoensis*) is native to North America and closely related to the hickory nut. The nut has a structure similar to the walnut, although it is longer, rather oblong in shape, more pointed and the outer shell is easier to crack. Like walnuts, the immature nut is encased in a thick green husk that splits open when the nut is ripe.

The main plantings in Australia are in coastal New South Wales and south-western Western Australia (the value of the pecan export crop was $15 million in 1995). The Australian harvest is in April–May.

PINE NUT The pine nut is the edible seed or kernel from the cones of various *Pinus* species native to the south-west of the United States, Mexico and southern Europe. The nut is small, creamy-white and shaped rather like an elongated capsule. It is softer than most other nuts and has an oily, slightly mealy texture and a resinous flavour. It has higher levels of saturated fats than some nuts: of its total fat content, 40 per cent is mono-unsaturated. Pine nuts are imported into Australia from both China and Europe.

PISTACHIO *Pistacia vera* is indigenous to the Middle East and Asia Minor. Its startling green nut is encased in a thin brown shell, which is itself enclosed in a soft husk of miraculous colours – vivid pink, purple and green – when freshly harvested. When mature the shell encasing the nut splits. Colour and flavour in pistachios are closely related. Browny-green nuts are older than those that are a vibrant emerald.

Australia has a pistachio industry based in the Murray Valley that has the achievable aim of producing half the quantity of nuts that Australia currently imports in the next few years. (Having sampled these nuts days after they were harvested I can say with authority that they were magnificent: their outer husks were a glorious marbled kaleidoscope of vivid pink and purple splashed with green.) The pistachio crop is harvested in March.

WALNUT The walnut (*Juglans* species) is thought to have originated in ancient Persia or China. Persians used walnuts for barter and the Greeks dedicated the walnut to Diana, whose feasts were held under walnut trees. In the Mediterranean area the walnut is the classic nut, taking over the definition of the general word for nut in several languages. And there is something wonderfully contemplative about cracking fresh walnuts to accompany a fine piece of hard cheese or aged goat's cheese.

Walnuts have a smooth outer green husk, which splits open when the nuts are ripe for harvesting. A creamy-brown shell encases the oval, ridged and pungent kernel, which is formed in distinct halves. When mature the outer shells have hardened and are easily cracked. Immature nuts are sometimes picked before the outer shell has hardened and can be pickled or candied. Walnuts are also used to make the sublime roasted walnut oil of France.

The overwhelming majority of walnuts on sale in Australia have been imported, shelled, from California, while some come from India and China. Walnuts are grown in the Ovens Valley in Victoria and in river valleys in New South Wales and South Australia. There are also experimental plantings in Tasmania and in the irrigation areas of the Murray Valley.

Walnuts are harvested in April–May in Australia.

pine nuts go with
basil
parmesan cheese
veal
pasta
garlic
rice
salad leaves
quail

pistachios go with
sausages
terrines
rice
yoghurt
baklava
honey
semolina
almonds

walnuts go with
blue cheese
goat's cheese
bitter greens
pears
duck
garlic
croutons
cream

SELECTION AND STORAGE

A high percentage of imported nuts sold are stale and many are rancid (this applies especially to walnuts). Search out a specialist health food shop or a nut merchant at a fresh food market and ask to try a nut in the shell before buying any. Buy small quantities of *shelled* nuts as you need them, as they deteriorate faster out of their shells. Purchase a small sack of walnuts in the shell from a local grower in April or May! (I find that a sack, stored in an outdoor shed, provides perfect walnuts from one harvest to the next.)

As tree nuts age, their oils oxidise and become rancid. Storing nuts away from light will slow down this process but cannot stop it forever. Raw nuts *in the shell* are air-dried to discourage the growth of mould. They can then be stored for up to 9 months in a cool, dry, airy place. Most nuts keep much better in their shells or, if this is impossible, certainly in their inner skins (almonds, hazelnuts and pistachios, for example). Most *shelled* nuts should be stored in an airtight container in a cool place, such as the refrigerator, or can be frozen in an airtight container. Shelled pistachios must be stored in an airtight and lightproof container in order to retain their colour.

Shake the coconut you plan to buy to see how much liquid is in it: a young drinking coconut will slosh. The shelf life of a whole coconut is 2–3 months. Chunks of fresh coconut stay fresh in the refrigerator in water if the water is changed daily. (Have your greengrocer halve the coconut for you – a difficult task to undertake at home.) Store desiccated coconut in an airtight container in a cool, dry place.

PREPARATION AND COOKING

Most nuts are available in various forms: shelled, roasted, ground, blanched, and so on. However, to ensure freshness prepare your own nuts as often as you can. This applies particularly to blanching almonds. Supermarkets do not store nuts under refrigeration and you have no way of knowing how long those packets of blanched, slivered or ground almonds have sat on the shelves.

TO BLANCH

Almonds Place nuts in a small bowl and cover with boiling water. Leave for 5 minutes and then slip the brown skins from the nut. Dry on a clean cloth.

TO PREPARE A COCONUT

Strip the fibrous husk from the coconut. Punch a hole in each of the soft 'eyes' at the top of the nut and drain out the liquid. Crack the coconut carefully into pieces using a heavy cleaver or ask the greengrocer to do this for you (it is dangerous work – be careful).

For a drinking coconut when the nut is still green, such as one encounters in Asian markets, the merchant will slice off sufficient of the top so that you can get at the sweet water. The soft inner jelly is delicious.

In countries where *coconut milk* is part of everyday cooking, cracked coconut halves are used to make proper coconut milk. In these countries one can buy simple household gadgets that make grating the coconut flesh very easy. I have seen one shaped a little like a lemon squeezer that clamps to a kitchen bench. One holds the coconut half over the grating section and turns a handle. Coconut can also be grated using a hand-held grater. In Australia coconut milk is widely available in tins and in powdered form.

TO MAKE COCONUT MILK There are several ways to make coconut milk, the easiest of which uses desiccated coconut. Process 2 cups desiccated coconut and 2½ cups hot water in a blender for 30 seconds. Strain through a fine-meshed sieve or piece of muslin, squeezing out all moisture and catching the coconut milk in a bowl below. Repeat the process using the same coconut and 2½ cups more hot water.

TO BOIL **Peanuts** Boil nuts with shells on in salted water for 45 minutes or until the kernels are tender. Drain well before serving. Boiled peanuts will keep in the refrigerator for up to 5 days. **Bunya nuts** Boil nuts in lightly salted water for 30 minutes. Remove one at a time, then slit the pointed end with a Stanley knife or a heavy, very sharp knife and peel the brown husk away from the nut. The nuts are much easier to peel when hot, so only extract a nut at a time from the water and place the pot back on the stove if the water cools.

TO DRY-ROAST **Bunya nuts** Chop off the pointed end of each nut with a cleaver and discard. Roast the nuts at 180°C for 45 minutes. Extract the nuts and peel off the husk, as for a chestnut. **Hazelnuts** Spread the nuts on a baking tray and roast at 180°C for about 10 minutes until the nuts are golden and smell toasty. Tip the nuts into a clean tea towel and rub vigorously to remove the brown skins. Tip the nuts and skins into a wide, coarse sieve and shake, so that the skin fragments settle or sift out the bottom. **Peanuts** The nuts can be roasted with their skins on or off. Roast in one layer on a baking tray at 140°C for up to 25 minutes. Stir the nuts to prevent scorching. Cool completely before storing.

TO FRY Use peanut oil for preference. Heat the oil to 150°C and then deep-fry the nuts for 3–10 minutes, watching carefully to ensure they don't burn. Drain very well. Cool and lightly salt the nuts, if desired.

TO TOAST Toss the nuts in a little light oil and either spread them on a baking tray and place them in an oven at 180°C for 5–10 minutes or toss over a low heat in a frying pan. (If toasting pine nuts, watch closely as they burn in a flash unless they are kept moving.) Once the desired colour is achieved, tip the nuts out onto a paper-lined tray to absorb any excess oil. Cool completely before storing.

recipes

nuts in warm salads

Add toasted hazelnuts, pine nuts or walnuts to green salads tossed with a little roasted hazelnut and walnut oil, fried poultry livers or quail breasts, crispy bacon or cheesy croutons.

teradot sauce

MAKES 1 CUP

This is especially good with fried Falafel (see CHICK PEAS) and also works well as a dip for pickled vegetables.

120 g walnuts
boiling water
2 cloves garlic
4 tablespoons light tahina
    paste
juice of 1 lemon
4 tablespoons freshly chopped
    parsley
salt
freshly ground black pepper

Place walnuts in a bowl and cover with boiling water. Allow to stand for 1 hour. Drain, then rub walnuts hard in a clean cloth. Dry thoroughly in a warm oven. (This process will remove any bitterness left in the walnut skins.) Purée walnuts, garlic, tahina and lemon juice in a food processor. Scrape into a bowl and stir through parsley, salt and pepper. Add more lemon juice if too thick and maybe a little hot water. Adjust seasoning.

walnut spread

MAKES 1 CUP

This spread can be used to make an appetiser to serve with drinks or to accompany a salad using toasted walnuts.

50 g peeled garlic
sea salt
100 g walnuts, coarsely
    chopped
1 tablespoon dry white wine
100 g unsalted softened butter
1 teaspoon walnut oil
freshly ground black pepper

Crush garlic to a paste with salt in a mortar. Blend in walnuts and wine until you have a smooth paste. Gradually work in butter and oil. Season to taste with pepper.

    To serve, spread on crusty country bread or croutons.

variation Add 100 g softened blue cheese to the paste.

macadamia sambal

MAKES 1 CUP

This fiery sambal can be spooned into clear noodle soups, eaten with simply poached chicken, smeared over grilled fish or, for some chilli enthusiasts, used as a bizarre spread for breakfast toast. It can also be spread on small crackers, corn chips or pieces of toast to make fiery scoops for an avocado or chickpea dip.

½ cup macadamia *or*
   vegetable oil
2 onions, finely diced
15 macadamias
20 g dried shrimp paste
6 fresh chillies, seeded and
   finely chopped
1 tablespoon finely chopped
   fresh ginger
1 tablespoon light soy sauce
juice of ½ lime

Heat oil until very hot in a heavy-based frying pan. Add onion and fry over moderate heat, stirring frequently, until onion is deep gold. Remove onion to a bowl with a slotted spoon, pressing on it and allowing oil to fall back into the pan. Sauté nuts in oil until golden brown. Remove to bowl with onion. Fry shrimp paste for 2 minutes, then strain off and reserve any oil and add shrimp paste to onion and nuts. Stir chilli, ginger and soy sauce into onion mixture. Transfer to a food processor and blend to a paste. Scrape into a bowl and add sufficient reserved oil and lime juice to make a spreadable paste. Spoon into a small jar, add a thin layer of onion oil to protect paste, then cover and refrigerate.

spiced nuts
Toss warm toasted macadamias or almonds with sea salt, a scrap of cayenne pepper and a mixture of toasted and ground cumin, coriander and sesame seeds.

pine nut and meat pastries

MAKES 36

When handling filo pastry, keep a light, damp cloth on a sheet of foil as a cover for the unused pastry – it will stay supple this way.

1 onion, finely chopped
2 tablespoons olive oil
500 g lean lamb *or* beef, very
   finely minced
2 tablespoons pine nuts
salt
freshly ground black pepper
1 teaspoon ground cinnamon
½ teaspoon ground allspice
5 tablespoons water
6 sheets filo pastry
melted butter

Preheat oven to 200°C. Fry onion in oil until quite soft. Add meat and fry lightly until it changes colour. Stir in pine nuts and fry for 2 minutes. Season and add cinnamon and allspice, then moisten with water. Cook for a few minutes more until water has been absorbed, then allow to cool.

Position a sheet of pastry so that the longest edge runs across your workbench. Cut pastry downwards into 6 equal strips. Brush each strip with melted butter. Place a teaspoonful of nut mixture in top right corner of each strip. Fold corner down to enclose filling. Continue to fold pastry to make a tight triangle. Do the same with each strip of pastry. Brush each triangle with melted butter and bake for 15 minutes until golden brown.

variation This filling can also be used to stuff small blanched onions or hollowed-out tomatoes.

cracked wheat and cashew salad with mint
SERVES 4

1 tablespoon olive oil
225 g cracked wheat
1½ cups water
salt
125 g roasted unsalted cashews
2 tablespoons lemon juice
1 clove garlic, crushed
1 tablespoon freshly chopped mint
3 tablespoons freshly chopped parsley
freshly ground black pepper
2 tablespoons extra-virgin olive oil

Heat olive oil in a large saucepan and stir in cracked wheat. Stir to coat and then add water, salt and cashews. Bring to simmering point, then reduce heat, cover and simmer for 15 minutes until liquid has been absorbed. Tip into a large bowl. When cool, dress with lemon juice, garlic, mint and parsley. Grind over pepper and check seasoning. Mix well. Drizzle with extra-virgin olive oil. Serve with warm pita bread and other salads or with grilled chicken.

nutty fish fillets
Dip thin fish fillets in egg and then in very finely ground almonds or hazelnuts and fry quickly in a mixture of clarified butter and a little oil until golden brown.

curried beans with cashews
SERVES 4

These beans are intended to be crunchy – hence the instructions to break my golden rule of not refreshing beans under running water.

500 g green beans
1 small onion, finely chopped
1 tablespoon light vegetable oil
30 g clarified butter
1 teaspoon brown mustard seeds
60 g raw cashew nuts
1 teaspoon garam masala
pinch of cayenne pepper
½ teaspoon ground turmeric
½ teaspoon ground cumin
1 cup coconut milk
salt

Cut beans into 6 cm pieces. Blanch in plenty of boiling, salted water until still a little undercooked. Refresh quickly under running water and pat dry with kitchen paper. Fry onion in oil and butter with mustard seeds and cashews, stirring until onion is soft and golden. Add remaining spices and coconut milk and simmer for 5 minutes. Add beans and simmer for a further 5 minutes. Taste for salt. Serve immediately as a side dish as part of a curry meal.

pistachio and pork terrine

Traditionally, terrines such as this would be encased either in thin strips of back fat or in a veil of caul fat. Do this if you want to. The mixture does not really need any extra fat, though.

⅓ cup shelled pistachios
2 tablespoons Cognac
1 tablespoon salt
½ teaspoon freshly ground
    black pepper
¼ teaspoon freshly grated
    nutmeg
1 kg lean, boneless pork
    shoulder, lightly pickled
300 g hard back fat

Chop pistachios coarsely and mix with Cognac, salt, pepper and nutmeg. Cut meat and fat into 4–5 cm cubes and combine with pistachio mixture. Leave overnight.

Next day, put mixture through coarsest hole of mincer. (If you do not have a mincer do not put meat through the food processor. This will purée it. Either chop the mixture by hand or ask your friendly butcher if he will put it through his mincer for you.)

Preheat oven to 180°C. Pack the mince into a 1.5 litre cast-iron or earthenware terrine mould, then stand it in a baking dish and pour in boiling water to come halfway up sides of mould. Bake for 1 hour. Test that juices are clear by inserting a skewer. Allow terrine to cool for 1 hour and then weight it with a full bottle of oil or similar and allow to cool overnight.

Remove terrine from mould, slice quite thinly and serve with a hot potato salad and a green salad.

pistachio and pork sausage This recipe is very successful used as a sausage filling, for which you will need sausage casings. Poach the filled casings for 30 minutes in barely simmering water, then turn off the heat and allow to cool completely in the water.

beans and hazelnuts
Fry hazelnuts lightly in butter, then toss with parsley and finely chopped shallots and mix into just-cooked green beans.

panang gai – dry chicken curry   SERVES 4

I love this recipe from Mogens Bay Esbensen's book Thai Cuisine. *All the frying and chopping is done hours before dinner and the final cooking is done in 10 minutes.*

750 g skinless chicken, cut
    into bite-sized pieces
1 teaspoon fresh Queensland
    or tinned green
    peppercorns, crushed
2 tablespoons plain flour
100 ml peanut oil
2 tablespoons red curry paste
1 cup coconut milk
1 tablespoon sugar
2 tablespoons fish sauce
60 g roasted peanuts, chopped
fresh basil leaves

Rub chicken with peppercorns and toss in flour. Heat oil in a wok and stir-fry chicken until well coloured and nearly cooked. Remove chicken to a platter and set aside. (The chicken can be refrigerated for several hours at this stage. Do not wash wok – cover it with a clean cloth.)

Pour away most of the oil and reheat wok, if necessary. Add curry paste and stir-fry for 2 minutes. Add coconut milk, sugar, fish sauce and peanuts and stir well for 5 minutes. Return chicken to wok and toss in sauce until thoroughly hot. Turn out onto a platter and garnish with basil.

macadamia fish curry

SERVES 4

Many Indonesian recipes use ground candlenuts (or kemiri nuts) as a thickening in gravies and sauces, often in dishes using coconut milk. Ground macadamias work very well as a substitute.

nutty jerusalems
Toss hot, boiled Jerusalem artichokes with butter, parsley and roughly chopped, peeled and toasted hazelnuts. Delicious with a grilled chicken breast or a sautéed thin slice of veal accompanied by lemon wedges.

1 onion, diced
2 cloves garlic, crushed
1 teaspoon finely chopped
  fresh ginger
1 teaspoon salt
1 teaspoon chilli paste
½ teaspoon dried shrimp
  paste
1½ cups coconut milk
8 macadamias, roughly
  chopped
1 stalk lemongrass (tender
  part only), finely sliced
500 g firm-textured fish, cut
  into bite-sized chunks
1 teaspoon palm *or* brown sugar
4 tablespoons lemon juice

Put all ingredients other than fish, sugar and lemon juice into a saucepan and bring to simmering point. Simmer, uncovered, for a few minutes until sauce is thick. Add fish and simmer for 5 minutes. Add sugar and lemon juice and check for salt. Serve immediately.

satay marinade and sauce

SERVES 4

This recipe makes more satay sauce than you will require, but it keeps for months if refrigerated in a screw-top jar. If you do not have raw peanuts on hand for the satay sauce, substitute 250 g crunchy peanut butter and add it with the tamarind water and coconut milk.

Both the marinade and satay sauce can also be used with prawns and fish.

Always soak bamboo satay skewers for 30 minutes in cold water before threading the meat onto them. This prevents the sticks burning through before the meat or fish is cooked.

500 g cubed lamb, beef, pork
  or chicken
MARINADE
2 teaspoons red curry paste
4 cloves garlic, chopped
1 teaspoon ground turmeric
½ cup soy sauce
(continued next page)

To make the marinade, blend all ingredients in a food processor. Marinate meat for at least 1 hour before threading onto soaked bamboo skewers.

To make the satay sauce, soak tamarind pulp in boiling water for 30 minutes, then squeeze and press through a food mill or coarse strainer and reserve liquid. Crush

2 stalks lemongrass (tender
  part only)
2 tablespoons palm *or* brown
  sugar

SATAY SAUCE

2 tablespoons tamarind pulp
4 tablespoons boiling water
2 cups shelled raw peanuts,
  dry-roasted
peanut oil
5 cloves garlic, chopped
5 fresh red chillies, finely
  chopped
150 g brown *or* palm sugar
2 cups coconut milk
salt

nuts in a food processor.

Heat a wok or frying pan with a little oil and fry garlic until pale gold. Immediately add chilli, peanuts and sugar. Stir in tamarind water and coconut milk. Mix well and add salt to taste. Cook, stirring, until oil separates and floats to top. Turn off heat and allow to cool. Spoon into a jar and refrigerate until required.

To serve, grill marinated meat on all sides, then spoon over satay sauce and offer extra sauce at the table.

pistachio ice-cream
Add finely ground pistachios to the hot custard when making vanilla ice-cream and stir from time to time as it cools before churning.

praline
MAKES 1½–2 CUPS

This nut toffee is a useful standby to sprinkle over or stir through ice-cream or to add to other desserts. It keeps well in a screw-top jar.

250 g blanched *or* skinned
  nuts, toasted
1 cup sugar
½ cup water

Spread nuts over a lightly oiled baking tray. Dissolve sugar in water over heat and cook until a deep amber. Pour over nuts and let harden. Break into pieces and store in a screw-top jar. A finer praline is obtained by processing small pieces in a food processor (a terrible noise!) or wrapping the pieces in a clean tea towel and crushing them with a meat mallet.

spicy hazelnut fingers
MAKES 36

2 eggs
200 g castor sugar
few drops of pure vanilla
1 teaspoon ground cinnamon
60 g candied peel, finely
  chopped
180 g ground almonds
120 g ground hazelnuts
½ teaspoon baking powder
1 cup pure icing sugar
juice of 1 lemon

Preheat oven to 140°C and line 2 baking trays with baking paper. Beat eggs, castor sugar and vanilla until pale and thick. Fold in cinnamon, peel, nuts and baking powder. Using a plain nozzle, pipe mixture in fingers onto baking trays. Bake for 30 minutes.

Mix icing sugar with drops of lemon juice until you have a thinnish mixture. Dribble icing over biscuits as soon as they come from oven.

almond frangipane tart

SERVES 6–8

Almond frangipane will keep for a week in a covered container in the refrigerator. It can also be used to fill tartlets.

**macadamia
meringue**
*Fold some
roughly chopped
macadamias into a
meringue mixture
before baking.*

christmas pudding
*Substitute
macadamias for
almonds in your
Christmas pudding.*

1 quantity Shortcrust Pastry
2 tablespoons apricot jam
3 tablespoons flaked almonds

ALMOND FRANGIPANE
120 g unsalted butter
150 g castor sugar
200 g ground blanched
    almonds
2 eggs
3 tablespoons brandy or rum
    (optional)

Line a 22 cm loose-bottomed flan tin with pastry and bake blind at 200°C for 20 minutes until golden.

To make the frangipane, cream butter and sugar in a food processor. Add almonds, eggs and brandy and blend well. Warm jam, then spread over pastry case and spoon in frangipane. Cook at 180°C for 15 minutes. Open oven and scatter flaked almonds over surface of tart. Cook a further 10 minutes until tart is brown, almonds are golden and centre feels springy to touch.

variations You can construct fancier tarts by topping the frangipane with fruit, such as poached pears, cherries or soaked dried apricots. Or you can fold some chopped glacé or dried fruit into the frangipane before filling the pastry case.

walnut afternoon tea cake

This cake does not look spectacular but it tastes wonderful. Try it with berries and cream. For a change, make it with pecans, almonds or hazelnuts.

5 eggs, separated
5 tablespoons castor sugar
2 teaspoons lemon juice
grated zest of 1 lemon
3 teaspoons rum
175 g walnuts, finely ground
icing sugar
extra lemon juice

Preheat oven to 200°C. Butter a 20 cm round cake tin and line its base with baking paper. Beat egg yolks with sugar until pale and thick. Add lemon juice, zest, rum and walnuts. Whisk whites to a creamy snow and fold into nut mixture. Spoon into prepared tin and bake until cake feels springy to touch, about 20 minutes. Cool slightly in tin before allowing to cool completely on a wire rack. This cake is fragile owing to its complete lack of flour. Ice with a thin lemon icing and serve with thick cream.

old-fashioned almond bread

Almond bread is not very sweet and therefore goes well with sweeter desserts, such as creams or ice-creams.

3 egg whites

90 g castor sugar

90 g plain flour

90 g unblanched almonds

Preheat oven to 180°C. Oil a log tin and line it with baking paper. Whip egg whites until stiff. Beat in sugar and then fold in flour and almonds. Tip into prepared tin and bake for 45–55 minutes until golden brown and firm to touch. Cool on a wire rack. When cold, cut carefully into thin slices with a serrated knife. Spread slices on a tray and return to oven set at 140°C for 15 minutes. Turn slices when light gold and repeat process. Cool completely before storing in an airtight tin, where it will keep for a long time.

pecan pie

SERVES 8

I quantity Shortcrust Pastry

I cup pecans, shelled and roughly chopped

½ cup sugar

¾ cup maple syrup

juice of I large lemon

60 g butter, melted and cooled

3 eggs

extra 8 perfect pecan halves

Line a 24 cm loose-bottomed flan tin with pastry and bake blind for 20 minutes at 200°C.

To make the filling, whisk together remaining ingredients, except extra pecans, and pour into pastry case. Carefully place 8 pecans around edge. Bake at 180°C until firm (about 25 minutes). Cool and serve warm or cold with unsweetened cream.

ground nuts in cakes

Replace some of the flour in a cake with an equal quantity of finely ground almonds, hazelnuts or walnuts to add a subtle flavour and texture.

brutti ma buoni

MAKES 24

Brutti ma buoni *means 'ugly but good'. These chunky biscuits are a great Italian favourite.*

200 g hazelnuts

8 egg whites

240 g castor sugar

few drops of pure vanilla

Preheat oven to 180°C. Dry-roast hazelnuts and remove skins (*see* p. 441). Chop hazelnuts roughly. Reset oven to 150°C.

Beat egg whites to soft peaks, then gradually beat in sugar until you have a shiny meringue. Stir in vanilla and nuts. Transfer to a saucepan and cook, stirring, over a low heat for 10 minutes. The mixture will slacken first and then combine and become a light-brown colour and start to pull away from the pan.

Place well-spaced spoonfuls of the mixture on a baking tray lined with kitchen paper. Bake for about 30 minutes until golden brown. Cool on wire racks. When biscuits are quite cold, store in an airtight container.

coconut ice

MAKES 20

125 g copha
250 g desiccated coconut
500 g pure icing sugar, sifted
2 drops pure vanilla
2 egg whites
few drops of pink food
   colouring

Melt copha until it is just warm to the touch. Mix coconut, icing sugar, vanilla, copha and egg whites in a bowl. Divide in half and tint one half pale pink. Quickly press plain half into a 20 cm square tin and smooth evenly with a piece of plastic wrap and something flat, such as a wrapped block of hard butter. Remove plastic and top with pink half. Press evenly. Cut into generous squares to serve.

other recipes

almond and honey slice *see* HONEY

bug meat coconut curry *see* BUGS

cherry and almond tart *see* CHERRIES

chicken breasts with almond sauce and guacamole *see* AVOCADOS

chocolate and almond cake *see* CHOCOLATE

chocolate hedgehog *see* CHOCOLATE

coriander peanut pesto *see* BASIL

damien's toasted almond rice *see* RICE

date and walnut biscuits *see* DATES

fig won tons *see* FIGS

fried coconut *see* QUAIL AND SQUAB PIGEONS

ham and pistachio mousse *see* HAM

jean's mussels *see* MUSSELS

mussels in coconut-milk curry *see* MUSSELS

nougat ice-cream *see* HONEY

pear and walnut salad *see* PEARS

pesto *see* BASIL

quail eggs in coconut sauce *see* EGGS

quince and nut cake *see* QUINCE

rosemary 'pesto' *see* ROSEMARY

rum and macadamia brownies *see* CHOCOLATE

sautéd silver beet with olive oil, pine nuts and currants
   see SILVER BEET

simple coconut-milk fish curry *see* FISH

waldorf salad *see* CELERY AND CELERIAC

yabby salad with walnuts and potatoes *see* YABBIES

yoghurt and pistachio cake *see* YOGHURT

Okra   Often called lady's fingers, okra (*Hibiscus esculentus*) are known as bhendi in India, bamia in the Middle East and gumbo in southern American States. │ Okra is native to Africa, although some give India that credit. Whichever, the slave trade saw the arrival of okra in the United States, where it became important in the cooking of the Caribbean and the southern States. Slave traders also introduced okra to Egypt and other Arab countries. │ Intriguingly shaped, this 5-sided, tapering vegetable has a neat cap and stalk at one end and is in fact the immature pod or fruit of a member of the mallow family and a cousin of the cotton plant. When sliced and then cooked for a long time each pod exudes a mucilaginous glue that thickens stews. Jane Grigson rather wonderfully describes this texture as 'jellied smoothness'. In fact, the stickiness and sliminess of okra has made it a vegetable with limited appeal to the Anglo-Saxon palate. Other cultures view it differently. It is this slimy characteristic that is prized in the making of gumbo, a stew of okra, tomato, chilli and seafood, chicken or other meats that is ubiquitous in the restaurants of New Orleans. >

okra
goes
with
garlic
onions
tomatoes
mustard seeds
turmeric
lemons
potatoes
olive oil
coriander
mint
cumin seeds
chillies
parsley
mushrooms
ham
chicken
lamb
prawns
chick peas
yoghurt

Okra is very popular in regional Indian cookery, where recipes for stuffed and sautéd okra with a rainbow of spices are magical. Middle Eastern cookbooks have many recipes that combine okra with tomatoes, onions, garlic, coriander seed, lamb or chicken and lemon juice. The texture of these dishes is largely the result of the melding of the okra with the other ingredients over a long cooking time.

The slimy character is lessened when okra is eaten cold. Okra can be boiled or steamed, cooled and served as part of a buffet selection accompanied by a spicy tomato sauce as a dip, or briefly sautéd and combined with spices and yoghurt. My contribution is to remind cooks that okra can also be cooked quickly, so that it remains a little crunchy.

VARIETIES AND SEASON

Okra is almost always olive-green but recently purplish red okra has been available too. Okra is in the markets in summer and autumn.

SELECTION AND STORAGE

Choose the smallest okra, preferably as small as your little finger. Larger okra are likely to be stringy. Young okra will look velvety, be bright olive-green and should snap rather than bend, just like a good green bean. Inspect closely and reject any okra with brownish patches or soft spots. The tip should not be shrivelled and the stem at the cap end should look perky, not collapsed. Refrigerate for several days in a vegetable storage bag in the crisper.

PREPARATION

The preparation method depends on the dish you are making, but all okra should be washed and dried before it is trimmed or sliced. If it is as young as it should be, you can merely cut off the tip of the stem and peel the cap rather than slicing it off, thus retaining the attractive conical shape and minimising the stickiness. It can also be cut into thick slices and quickly fried or steamed; the stickiness will be minimal because of the fast cooking.

Some Turkish recipes begin with instructions to 'prepare' okra by pouring white-wine vinegar over the trimmed pods and sprinkling them with salt. The vinegar and salt are rubbed into the okra and left for 30 minutes. The okra is then rinsed and dried before being used. The okra is said to be 'bleached' and will not lose its texture, even when simmered for a long time. (To 500 g okra use 50 ml vinegar and 2 tablespoons salt.) A similar result is achieved by soaking the trimmed okra in 1 part vinegar to 4 parts water for an hour before cooking.

Cook okra in stainless steel or enamelled cast-iron saucepans as aluminium will turn it rather grey. The flavour is the same, the eye appeal is not.

pickled okra

MAKES 2 CUPS

500 g young okra, washed,
    dried and trimmed

2 cloves garlic, peeled

2 fresh chillies, seeded

2 cups cider *or* white-wine
    vinegar

¼ cup water

¼ cup salt

1 teaspoon celery seeds

1 teaspoon mustard seeds

Sterilise a 500 ml jar or 2 smaller jars.
Pack jar with okra, garlic and chillies. Place
all other ingredients in a stainless steel
saucepan and bring to a boil. Pour over
okra and seal jar. Leave for at least 2 weeks
before using. The pickle keeps well for 6
months, but must be refrigerated after
opening. Serve it with cold poultry or meat
or as a side dish with meat or fish curries.

fried okra
*Sauté trimmed
whole okra in hot
oil for 3–4 minutes,
then cool and roll in
a lightly beaten egg
and polenta and
deep-fry. Serve with
drinks with a spicy
tomato sauce or
home-made tomato
relish.*

okra with tomatoes

SERVES 4–6

*This is a master recipe and can be varied with additional or alternative spices
and ingredients (sliced button mushrooms could be added as could sultanas,
and so on). Sautéd cubes of lamb could be cooked separately in a fresh
tomato sauce and then combined with this dish to make a main meal to be
partnered with rice.*

4 tablespoons olive oil

1 large onion, finely chopped

3 cloves garlic, finely chopped

500 g young okra, washed,
    dried and trimmed

2 tomatoes, peeled and
    roughly chopped

1 teaspoon ground coriander
    seeds

1 teaspoon salt

juice of ½ lemon

freshly ground black pepper

water

Heat oil and sauté onion in a deep saucepan
or frying pan until soft and golden. Add
garlic and sauté a further minute. Add okra
and sauté for several minutes, turning once.
Stir in remaining ingredients and a few
spoonfuls of water. Cover pan, reduce heat
and simmer for 10–15 minutes until okra is
just tender. Remove lid, check seasoning
and boil hard for 2 minutes if sauce seems
at all watery. Serve hot or cold.

okra stew
*Sauté whole
trimmed okra in
oil for 5 minutes.
Sprinkle with sugar,
salt, pepper, lemon
juice and water,
then cover and
simmer for 5
minutes. Strew with
freshly chopped
parsley or coriander
and serve warm or
cold.*

southern chicken, ham and okra gumbo

SERVES 6–8

*The following recipe is based on one given by the late American Bert Greene
in his enjoyable book* Greene on Greens. *The making of a 'proper' gumbo
assumes mythic status in Louisiana. Australian cooks do not have ready
access to filé powder or powdered sassafras, which apparently imparts a*

faintly pine-scented flavour to the gumbo when a pinch is sprinkled into each bowl at the very last moment.

4 tablespoons vegetable oil
¼ cup plain flour
salt
freshly ground black pepper
500 g boneless chicken
  (including thigh meat)
60 g unsalted butter
500 g diced leg ham
2 onions, chopped
2 cloves garlic, finely chopped
2 sticks celery, finely sliced
1 green pepper, diced
3 ripe tomatoes, peeled,
  seeded and chopped
1 litre Chicken Stock ✎
1 tablespoon chilli sauce
1 bay leaf
1 sprig fresh thyme
½ teaspoon ground allspice
400 g okra, washed and dried,
  cut into 5 mm slices
2 spring onions, chopped
freshly chopped parsley

Heat 3 tablespoons of the oil and stir in flour over a low heat to make a very dark *roux*. This will take about 1 hour, with lots of stirring. (This step is essential and the *roux* that is used must be dark, dark brown and very silky.) Set aside.

Season chicken and sauté in a frying pan in half the butter and remaining oil until deep golden. Set aside. Sauté ham in same pan and transfer to plate with chicken, together with any juices. Sauté onion, garlic, celery and green pepper in remaining butter, then transfer to a deep casserole. Stir in tomato and *roux* and gradually work in stock and chilli sauce to taste. Add herbs and allspice and bring to a boil, stirring constantly. Add chicken and ham and cook, uncovered, for 1 hour. Add okra and cook for a further 30 minutes. Discard bay leaf and divide gumbo between deep bowls. Serve sprinkled with spring onion and parsley.

okra dip
Stir sautéd sliced okra into yoghurt whisked with ground mustard seeds and finely chopped green chilli and fresh ginger and serve with pita bread as a dip.

okra and mint
Sauté trimmed whole okra and sliced onion gently in olive oil until barely tender, then strew with freshly chopped mint and season with salt and freshly ground black pepper.

okra pancakes
Mix finely sliced okra into spicy Chickpea Batter (see CHICK PEAS*) and shallow-fry as tiny pancakes.*

stir-fried okra and prawns

SERVES 4

2 tablespoons vegetable oil
1 fresh chilli, seeded
4 spring onions, cut into
  4 cm pieces
2 cloves garlic, finely sliced
12 prawns, shelled and
  deveined
12 small okra, washed, dried
  and cut into 5 mm pieces
2 tablespoons Chicken Stock ✎
light soy sauce

Heat oil with chilli in a wok. Toss in spring onion, turning and flipping constantly for 1 minute. Add garlic, prawns and okra and toss for 3 minutes, then pour on stock and cover wok. Cook for 1 minute, then remove lid. Discard chilli, then splash in soy sauce and serve at once with steamed rice.

Olives and olive oil

Olive trees (*Olea europaea*) originated in Africa and Asia Minor but have been grown all over the Mediterranean for 6000 years, making them the oldest cultivated tree in existence. | You can grow your own olive tree. It will not fruit for 5 years but it will outlast you and your grandchildren, as the tree will live for hundreds of years. The olive tree symbolises tenacity as well as longevity, flourishing in many harsh and exposed places. And an olive branch is still a powerful symbol of peace. | The major bounty of the tens of millions of trees growing worldwide is the oil extracted from their fruit. This oil is the great medium for Mediterranean cooking and is enjoying wonderful press at the moment, as it has been shown to have approximately 77 per cent mono-unsaturated fat. These fats are the 'goodies' in the nutritional debate, compared with the 'baddies', the saturated fats (butter, lard and fatty meat). It is wise to remember that moderation in all things is a sensible rule. Large consumption of olive oil may keep you healthy but not necessarily thin. It still contains the same kilojoules as any other oil! >

olives
go
with
bread
garlic
onions
pepper
chillies
tomatoes
anchovies
capers
cheese
walnuts
almonds
salad leaves
lemons
cumin
coriander
fennel
rabbit
chicken
lamb
oranges
potatoes
salted fish
fish
herbs

The first olive trees came to South Australia in 1844 from Marseilles, France. Several enterprising people are now producing olive oil in Australia. Some very good oil is coming from the Grampians in western Victoria, the Clare and Barossa valleys and McLaren Vale in South Australia, and the Benedictine monastery at New Norcia, Western Australia.

How can I encapsulate the central place that olive oil has in all things culinary? It is the finest oil to use for sautéing and grilling. It provides the important final touch in a vegetable minestrone or a cold gazpacho; it emulsifies mayonnaise and aïoli; it binds pesto and tapenade; it sauces tomatoes and carpaccio of beef; it gives cakes a characteristic moist, fine texture. Above all, olive oil is the essential ingredient in a good green salad. The better the oil, the more memorable the salad.

Olives come in a wide variety of shapes, sizes, colours and styles. All are inedible straight from the tree. A bitter glucoside, oleuropein, has to be leached from the olive before it can be enjoyed. At present, there are plenty of home-cured olives in Australian–Mediterranean households, but very few are prepared commercially. In contrast, to visit an olive stall in a French market town in the south is an unforgettable experience. There are pink olives, violet olives, greenish bronze olives, green olives and black olives; some are split, some wrinkled, some dried, some tiny, some huge; some are marinated with preserved lemons, some with fennel stalks and cracked coriander seeds and some with chillies. One can select a different olive every day for a month, and I did just that in October 1992. Every lunch and dinner on that holiday started with a plate of olives and a glass of rosé. And that was just in France. Olives are also important in the cultures and cuisines of Turkey, Syria, Lebanon, Egypt, Spain, Italy and North Africa, where they are added to breads, rice dishes, stuffings, pasta sauces, soups, game and classic beef casseroles.

VARIETIES AND SEASON

Olive experts recognise innumerable varieties. A few of the most important commercial varieties are the Spanish manzanillo, sevillano, gordal, picual and verdillo olives; the rosciolo, biancolilla and frantoio from Italy; the picholine and pigalle from France and, from the United States, the mission. Not every one is suitable for oil production.

Commercial olive trees are produced by grafting. In Australia most fresh olives available are wild and a result of haphazard seed propagation. These trees always revert to the original small-fruited variety.

Fresh olives are sold only by colour and this is determined by when they are picked. In Australia green olives are available March–August and black olives April–August. Olives for oil are usually picked when fully ripe and black. The sooner the olives are pressed after picking, the better the oil.

SELECTION AND STORAGE

OLIVES Olives can be bought fresh from markets during the season in southern Australia. You can also often pick olives from trees on the side of the road in South Australia. Pick green olives for pickling when they are pale green or yellow, and black olives for pickling when dark purplish in colour. Do not gather olives from the ground as bruised olives have off flavours.

Prepared olives can be found in delicatessens – try any new olive you see. (The exception, and the one to beware at all costs, is the sliced, 'black' stoned olive, sold in bottles and frequently found on pizzas. This olive is a fraud! It is an unripe green olive, soaked in a bath of lye and then pumped with oxygen, which turns it an unlikely solid black.)

As a pickled product, olives do not need to be stored under refrigeration although many of us find it convenient to do so. Don't serve olives straight from the refrigerator. They are much better at room temperature.

OLIVE OIL Olive oils have a wide variety of flavours ranging from light and buttery to very fruity. The colour also varies from a deep green–gold to light gold. The deeper the colour, the fuller the flavour. The flavour and colour depend on the quality and variety of the olive, the climate and soil in which the tree grew, the care with which the tree was cultivated, how the oil was extracted and how well it was stored.

The labelling of olive oil is very precise. Once it was common to refer to 'cold-pressed' and 'first-pressed' olive oils. Technology has advanced and these terms are largely meaningless today. Most olive oil is now produced with only one pressing but more powerful presses are used. The final acidity of the oil varies from year to year and crop to crop. It is this measurement that distinguishes an oil that may be sold as extra-virgin and one that may be sold as virgin olive oil.

Extra-virgin olive oil is a virgin olive oil of outstanding flavour, colour and aroma that has a maximum acidity of no more than 1 per cent. (Acidity is perceived as sharpness at the back of the mouth.) *Virgin olive oil* indicates an oil with a good but slightly subdued 'fruity' flavour; its acidity may not exceed 1.5 per cent. *Olive oil* (once labelled as pure olive oil) is blended from refined, lesser-quality virgin olive oil and unrefined virgin olive oil, for additional flavour.

For general-purpose cooking it is best to use olive oil. Much of the flavour of the finest extra-virgin olive oil is lost when heated. Reserve the finest (and most expensive) extra-virgin olive oil for adding to dishes at the last minute or to use as a condiment on salad leaves for example. Develop the habit, too, of setting a glass cruet or a bottle of extra-virgin olive oil on the table

fetta and olives
Sprinkle the finest sheep's milk fetta cheese with extra-virgin olive oil mixed with some very finely chopped garlic and thyme leaves and enjoy with fat, oily black olives.

marinated olives
Marinate black olives in olive oil and add toasted cumin seeds and tiny dice of raw fennel or celery; finely chopped chilli and garlic and a fresh bay leaf; or thyme leaves, coarsely chopped fresh parsley and tiny dice of Preserved Lemon (see LEMONS AND LIMES).

at every mealtime. Some diners will become addicted to this delicious condiment and will prefer to moisten their bread with oil, not butter.

Olive oil should be stored away from light in a cool cupboard, where it should stay fresh for at least a year. Rancid oil will spoil a dish. Taste a newly purchased bottle of oil before using it. Oil does not improve with age, unlike good wine. It is a sensible and economic idea to buy an excellent oil in bulk and decant it into well-stoppered bottles.

PREPARATION

It is easy to pickle your own olives but it does require patience. I give recipes for preserving olives later in this chapter. It is much simpler, however, to buy olives in brine and marinate them yourself.

Always taste olives before adding them to stews. If they are exceptionally salty, cover them with cold water, bring to a boil and drain before using.

Where recipes call for stoned or pitted olives I find it easier to cut the flesh from the stone, certainly if I am using green olives. Some varieties of black olive are very soft and one can easily press them open and lift out the stone. (Don't try to stone the tiny Ligurian olives, though.) When chopping olives in the food processor pay special attention to removing every stone.

Olives should be added towards the end of slow-cooked dishes, so that they perfume and flavour but still retain all their texture.

As a rule of thumb, 500 g fleshy olives will yield 2¼ cups whole, 2 cups when stoned, 1¾ cups when roughly chopped and 1½ cups when finely chopped.

recipes

avocado and olive dip
Purée a ripe avocado with chopped black olives, garlic and olive oil and season with salt, pepper and lemon juice. Serve as a dip with raw vegetables.

cracked green olives

5 kg green olives
water
1 kg rock salt
several bay leaves (preferably fresh)
orange zest
fennel leaves (including a couple of seed heads)
1 handful coriander seeds

Tap each olive firmly with a wooden mallet to split flesh without cracking stone, or slit to stone with a small knife. Soak olives in water for 9 days, changing water daily. Taste, and if still bitter continue to soak for another 2–3 days. Drain olives.

Boil 10 litres water with rock salt and flavourings for 5 minutes. Allow to cool completely. Pour cold brine over olives packed into clean, sterilised containers (a glazed earthenware container is traditional, glass jars are fine) and leave for a further 6–8 days. These olives are best eaten within a month or so. They darken when exposed to the air, so they are always served in a small bowl with some of the juice.

melita's black olives

fresh black olives
rock salt
pieces of lemon *or* Preserved
   Lemon (see p. 391)
slivers of garlic
sprigs of thyme *or* rosemary
olive oil (optional)
red-wine vinegar (optional)

Put olives in a bucket of water. Leave for 40 days, changing the water every 2 days.

After 40 days, drain olives and cover with rock salt. Leave for 2 days, then wash olives well in cold water and pack them into clean, sterilised jars with lemon, garlic and thyme. Cover with oil or vinegar or half and half. Seal and leave for 2 weeks before eating. These olives will keep for at least 6 months.

italian black olive paste

MAKES 1½ CUPS

This paste is delicious on chewy bread and hot toast, underneath the tomato on a bruschetta and as a stuffing for hardboiled eggs when worked to a paste with the yolks. It can also be served alongside grilled fish as one might serve mustard with steak.

1 cup big, oily black olives,
   stoned and chopped
2 cloves garlic, very finely
   chopped
½ cup freshly chopped flat-
   leaf parsley
2 large sprigs rosemary, leaves
   stripped and finely chopped
2 large sprigs thyme, leaves
   stripped
⅓ cup olive oil
freshly ground black pepper
extra-virgin olive oil

In a food processor blend all ingredients except extra-virgin olive oil until fairly smooth. Taste for pepper and pack into a small pot. Cover with 5 mm extra-virgin olive oil and refrigerate. This paste keeps for weeks.

veal Spread a thin layer of olive paste on a veal scaloppine or lamb cutlet before dipping in egg and breadcrumbs and shallow-frying. **tapenade** The French tapenade is very similar but includes chopped anchovies, drained tuna, rinsed capers and lemon juice.

bruschetta
Cut a thick slice of sourdough bread, toast it on both sides, rub with a cut clove of garlic, top with thickly sliced ripe tomato, salt and pepper and generously anoint with extra-virgin olive oil.

olive pasta sauce
Chop parsley, basil, garlic and olive flesh together. Make into a thick paste with extra-virgin olive oil and pepper and toss through spaghetti. Add chopped anchovies and lemon zest for a change.

olive oil and dessert wine cake

SERVES 10

This recipe is a slightly modified version of one given in Chez Panisse Menu Cookbook, *a modified version again of an earlier recipe that appeared in Alice Waters's* Chez Panisse Cooking. *It is the perfect accompaniment to poached or fresh peaches or nectarines and is a revelation when served with a fine dessert wine. I use an Australian dessert wine when making (and eating!) this cake.*

5 eggs, separated

¾ cup sugar

½ cup dessert wine

6 tablespoons extra-virgin olive oil

150 g plain flour

pinch of salt

2 egg whites

½ teaspoon cream of tartar

pure icing sugar

Preheat oven to 180°C. Butter a 22 cm springform cake tin and line base with baking paper. Beat egg yolks with half the sugar until pale and thick, then add wine and oil. Fold in flour and salt and transfer to a large bowl. Wash and dry mixer bowl and beat egg whites with cream of tartar until they hold soft peaks. Beat in remaining sugar until you have a soft meringue. Fold lightly but thoroughly into yolk mixture.

Spoon into prepared tin and bake for 20 minutes. Lower temperature to 160°C and bake for 20 minutes. Turn off oven, cover cake with a buttered round of baking paper and leave to cool slowly. Remove from oven after 15 minutes. (The cake tends to deflate as it cools, so it needs to be protected from sudden changes of temperature.) Dust with icing sugar before serving.

sautéd olives
Sauté olives in olive oil until just warm, grind pepper over or stir in tiny specks of fresh chilli and serve warm.

other recipes

aïoli *see* GARLIC

ajo blanco – white gazpacho from malaga *see* GRAPES AND VINE LEAVES

caponata *see* EGGPLANTS

greek country salad *see* CHEESE

olive bread *see* BREAD

oxtail braised with black olives *see* OXTAIL

pissaladière *see* ANCHOVIES

quail with dried figs and olives *see* FIGS

roasted yabbies with thyme oil *see* YABBIES

rock lobster oil *see* ROCK LOBSTERS

sautéd silver beet with olive oil, pine nuts and currants *see* SILVER BEET

stephanie's chicken provençale *see* CHICKEN AND THE CHRISTMAS TURKEY

veal brisket stuffed with olives *see* VEAL

O n i o n s The onion (*Allium* species) is native to central and western Asia and has been used for more than 6000 years. Like garlic, to which it is related, onion is credited with healing powers, ranging from curing the common cold, a bad complexion or baldness to improving poor sight, not to mention warding off evil. │ Throughout any book on food, onions play an essential supporting role in stocks, soups, stews and stuffings. But they can also assume star status. They are simple yet sophisticated. They can be cooked quickly or baked slowly. They are inexpensive, always available and admired in every cuisine of the world. │ Onions are prized for their pungency and for the intense sweetness they assume after long gentle cooking, during which heat converts their volatile oils into sugars. Of all the ways I love them – large, small, red, brown, yellow, white; boiled, baked, stuffed, creamed – perhaps my favourite is caramelised. My least favourite is raw, although very thinly sliced raw onion is marvellous interleaved with ripe red tomatoes and olive oil, as it is with a salad of sliced oranges and black olives or with capers and smoked salmon. I can only watch in fascination when someone eats a large, fiery pickled onion – although I do enjoy mild pickled shallots.

VARIETIES AND SEASON

There are hundreds of onion varieties but only a few are grown for marketing. An initial distinction is made between *dry* onions, which are left in the ground to mature until the tops die down, and *green* onions, which are pulled while still young and before the bulb has fully formed.

The main *dry* onions available are the white, brown, yellow Spanish, red and pickling onions and shallots. Within Australia we have difficulties with the names of *green* onions, which may be called spring onions, scallions or salad onions. Although recognised individually, they are in fact the same thing: an immature onion.

A wide variety of onions is available all year, although some of the larger-bulbed spring onions are best in spring and summer. Cooler climates produce pungent onions, while warmer growing conditions produce milder onions that are larger in size.

BROWN | Freely available, this dry onion has firm, crackling golden-brown skin.

PICKLING | Also known as 'small whites', these dry onions can be any variety. The size is a consequence of close planting and early harvesting. The really tiny *pearl* onions are never seen in Australian markets. They are rightly considered a delicacy in France. Market demand could easily change this.

RED | This dry onion looks very decorative. Some varieties are more pungent than others and all sizes and shapes, from spherical to flattened to oval, are available. In some varieties the red pigment stops after the first layer or so. In other varieties it penetrates to the centre of the onion. Red onions are often sold in bunches with their tops still attached. Locally grown red onions are available from summer to midwinter, while onions are imported from California at other times.

SALAD | This green onion is simply a spring onion that has been grown a little further until the bulb starts to swell. Onions picked at this stage, when the bulb is the size of a cherry, or even later (when the bulb can be the size of a table-tennis ball), are variously described as salad, spring or new onions. They are generally widely available.

SHALLOT | This dry variety (*Allium ascalonicum*) produces several small bulbs together in a single plant. They are milder than onions and much used in French and Asian cooking. They are considered essential for French sauce-making, where they are often reduced with wine or wine vinegar, and are very tedious to peel. Both golden shallots with crackling skins and pinky-grey shallots are now available in Australia. They are known as eschallots in New South Wales.

SPRING | Known as scallions in New South Wales, spring onions are immature onions pulled when the top is still green and before the bulb has swollen at all. This green onion is evenly slim from root to top. The tops are hollow and are used as well as the white bulb end. They are used extensively in Asian cooking and are available universally.

WHITE | More pungent than a brown onion, the dry white onion is universally available and has firm, papery white skin.

YELLOW SPANISH | Sometimes called an odourless onion, this dry variety is not in fact odourless but is less pungent than the white or brown onion. It has a softer, flakier creamy-yellow skin and stores less well than the white or brown onion.

SELECTION AND STORAGE

I find little difference between a well-dried brown or white onion for general-purpose cooking. The sweeter, softer yellow Spanish onions are ideal for baking, stuffing or boiling. Mild red onions are ideal to use raw in a salad. Some also like salad onions served this way, while they can also be braised, steamed or simmered. Spring onions are most often used as a garnish, although they can also be stir-fried. The sweeter the onion the sooner it should be used.

Dry onions should be just that – dry! Avoid any onion that feels damp or spongy. White and brown onions of any size should have firm, dry crackling skins and yellow and red onions should feel firm. All onions should smell sweet without any trace of a tell-tale, acrid, damp 'off' odour. Do not buy sprouting onions. Store dry onions where air can circulate freely around them. Hanging a bunch of red onions is both decorative and sensible. Dry onions stored appropriately should last for at least a month. An onion that has been peeled will deteriorate fast. Wrap it in plastic film or store it in a bowl of water in the refrigerator and use it the next day.

Green onions should be trimmed of unnecessary tops; the roots can be trimmed, too, if you like. Remove any rubber bands, which will damage the bunch. Wrap the bunch in kitchen paper and refrigerate in a vegetable storage bag in the crisper. Use within a few days before the green tops start to deteriorate. Do not use green onions if the green tops have become yellow or slimy, as this is a sign of age, poor storage or both.

green onions go with

noodles
pork
beef
soy sauce
rice
ginger
garlic
fish
bean curd
asparagus
chicken
shellfish

PREPARATION

Onions can be sliced, chopped, fried or sautéed or used raw. They can also be baked and barbecued whole, still in their skins. They can be boiled, with or without skins, and then halved and the centres carefully hollowed out for stuffing. (The scooped-out centres should be chopped and added to the stuffing.) The beauty of the onion is that it requires very little preparation.

dark roasted onions

Halve unpeeled onions and lightly oil, then roast cut-side down on a flat griddle or in a heavy-based frying pan until deep brown to black. Add to beef, game and veal stocks for wonderful colour and intensity.

DRY ONIONS

When dry onions are chopped a volatile sulphur-rich oil is released that causes one's eyes to water. (Known as the lachrymator, this substance actually creates sulphuric acid when it mingles with the moisture in the eye!) Many theories are advanced on how to reduce this effect. The best by far is to peel onions in the draught of a strong exhaust fan – preferably under the exhaust hood. The next best idea is to chill the onions for a while, which slows the release of the volatile oil. Or, some say, you can chop the onion under water. (This always sounds very, very dangerous to me, especially if you are using as sharp a knife as I would hope!) Or wear glasses. Or just get on with the job as fast as possible and don't worry. Be wary of chopping onions in a food processor. It is easy to overprocess them and end up with a wet mixture that will not sauté properly. The food processor tends to crush the onion rather than chop the pieces cleanly. **Large dry onions** Strip off the skin, cut the onion from top to root for slices or leave whole for rings. Discard a slice from the root end of the onion, which never softens. Place the onion cut-side down on the chopping board. Cut thin slices lengthwise for crescents. To dice, cut lengthwise and then crosswise at right angles. For finer dice, slice the onion twice horizontally before cutting it lengthwise. Cut a whole onion crosswise to achieve rings. Thicker slices should be cut for baking or grilling. **Shallots and pickling onions** Dip pickling onions or shallots in boiling water for 5 minutes, then transfer to cold water. They will then be easier to peel. Slice the peeled onions into fine rings or else cut from the root to the tip and crosswise if a fine dice is required. A small and very sharp knife is required for shallot dicing.

GREEN ONIONS

Spring onions Strip off any damaged outer green leaves and cut away roots. Wash and dry, then slice according to the recipe. Many Asian recipes require spring onion sections 4–6 cm long. As a garnish, the spring onions are best finely sliced. By slitting each spring onion lengthwise and cutting on an angle, one creates elliptical shapes also popular as a garnish. Longer pieces of spring onion are sometimes finely cut at each end and soaked in cold water to make 'brushes' to serve with the pancakes that accompany Peking duck. **Salad onions** Trim off the green tops and trim the root end. The green tops are very strong in flavour; a small amount can be added to stocks.

caramelised onions

MAKES 2 CUPS

This is my favourite way to eat onion. If you have a jar of caramelised onions in the refrigerator a fry-up of mushrooms and onions is halfway there. You can also add them to pasta sauces (they are marvellous on their own with shell pasta), use them in frittatas, as a topping for a quick pizza, on a steak or a piece of grilled tuna, or in a warm salad of chick peas, or to add instant depth of flavour to a stew.

20 small or pickling onions,
   peeled
½ cup olive oil
1 bay leaf
1 sprig rosemary

Quarter or slice onions. Tip all ingredients into a heavy-based frying pan and put over moderate heat. (A non-stick pan does a very good job also. Be careful to use a non-scratching implement for stirring.) Cover pan and cook for 15 minutes until onion has begun to soften, stirring frequently. Remove cover and continue to cook, stirring, until onion has separated and started to turn a rich caramel brown. It doesn't matter if sections look very dark. This adds flavour. The important thing is to stir frequently to prevent sticking. (If this looks likely, add an extra spoonful or so of oil. The onions can be drained of any excess oil before using.)

These onions and their oil keep well in a covered container in the refrigerator for several days. The oil is just as delicious as the onions!

glazed onions

SERVES 4

These onions are delicious with all meat and poultry. They can also be added to a stew 10 minutes before serving it.

500 g pickling onions, peeled
40 g butter
1 tablespoon castor sugar
1 cup stock or water from
   blanching onions

Simmer onions in lightly salted water for 10 minutes. Drain, keeping some of the water if you do not have any stock. Melt butter in a frying pan that will just hold onions in a single layer. Add onions and roll to coat in butter. Scatter over sugar and stock. Cover with buttered baking paper and cook at a moderate pace until liquid has nearly evaporated. Shake to prevent sticking. The onions should be shiny and there should only be drops of liquid left.

sweet-and-sour onions Dilute 1 tablespoon tomato paste with ⅓ cup good-quality red-wine vinegar. Tip this onto the cooked onions and cook for a further 5–10 minutes to reduce. Finish with toasted pine nuts and freshly chopped parsley or stripped thyme leaves.

onion fritters
Soak thinly sliced onion in milk for 20 minutes, then pat dry, dip in batter and fry in medium–hot (but not smoking) olive oil until crisp and dark. Drain on kitchen paper, salt lightly and serve with drinks.

stuffed onions
Chop the centres from some halved, parboiled yellow Spanish onions and mix with other savoury ingredients (ham, fresh herbs, olives, anchovies) and moisten with olive oil. Stuff the onion halves and bake at 180°C for 45 minutes.

winemerchant's sauce for a grilled steak

SERVES 2

4 shallots, finely chopped
½ cup dry red wine
1 tablespoon freshly chopped
   parsley
squeeze of lemon juice
80 g unsalted butter
freshly ground black pepper

Reduce shallots with wine to a moist purée. Stir in parsley and lemon juice and beat in butter using a whisk or wooden spoon. Season with pepper and spoon over a quickly grilled and very rare steak.

onion purée
Cook sliced onion very slowly in butter in a covered non-aluminium pan on the stove for at least 1 hour until a rich yellow and completely tender. Add a spoonful of chicken stock, a small handful of cooked rice, a spoonful of cream or a sliced garlic clove and purée and season. Serve with a grilled chicken breast, pan-fried veal or grilled calf's liver.

french onion soup from stephanie's

SERVES 6–8

80 g butter
9 white or brown onions,
   sliced into rings
1 litre dry white wine
freshly ground black pepper
2 tablespoons Cognac
6 x 3 cm thick slices
   sourdough bread
1 cup firmly packed grated
   gruyère cheese
1.5 litres well-flavoured
   Chicken or Veal Stock
salt

Preheat oven to 180°C. Select an ovenproof gratin dish (approximately 6 cm deep) in which the onion will form a well-packed layer. Grease dish with half the butter and add onion. Dot onion with remaining butter. Pour over wine and grind over pepper. Bake, uncovered, for at least 2 hours, stirring once or twice, until onion is very soft.

Increase heat to 220°C and cook for 1 hour until top layer of onion has started to caramelise. Sprinkle surface with Cognac.

Select ovenproof soup bowls. Break each bread slice in half. Place a spoonful of onion in each bowl, then cover with a piece of bread and top with cheese. Repeat with another layer of onion, bread and cheese. Ladle over stock and taste for seasoning.

Bake in oven until soup is bubbling hot and top crust is golden. Submerge crust in each bowl just before serving to soften it.

champ
Make a hollow in a dollop of creamy mashed potato, then fill with melted butter and a large spoonful of finely chopped spring onion to make this Irish speciality.

onion and blue cheese pizza

MAKES 2

This quantity is for 16 generous pieces – enough to start a party!

200 g blue cheese, crumbled
1 heaped cup Caramelised
   Onions (see p. 465)
1 quantity Pizza Dough

Preheat oven to 220°C. Knock back dough, divide and press thinly onto 2 large pizza trays with well-oiled hands. Allow dough to recover for 5 minutes, then scatter over cheese and spread on onions. Bake for 15 minutes.

Slide pizzas off trays onto oven racks for 5 minutes to crisp bases. >

variations Strew rocket leaves on top of the cheese before adding the onion. You could add oily stewed peppers and stoned olives for another combination.

onion and cheese tart

SERVES 6

There are many, many ways to make an onion tart: with or without cheese, with different styles of cheese, with stock instead of cream, with sliced, diced or even puréed onions, with strips of bacon or ham, and so on. Here is one version.

1 quantity Shortcrust Pastry
1 kg onions, chopped or finely
   sliced
80 g butter
1 tablespoon plain flour
3 eggs
150 ml cream
100 g cheese (preferably
   crumbled blue cheese *or*
   grated gruyère *or* good
   cheddar)
salt
freshly ground black pepper
¼ teaspoon crushed caraway
   seeds *or* freshly grated
   nutmeg (optional)

Preheat oven to 200°C. Line a 22 cm loose-bottomed flan tin with pastry, then bake blind at 200°C for 20 minutes. Remove foil and weights and allow to cool.

Cook onion slowly in butter in a heavy-based, non-aluminium frying pan, covered, until golden and tender (about 25 minutes). Drain. Stir in flour off heat. Whisk eggs with cream and add onion mixture and cheese. Taste for seasoning and add caraway seeds, if using.

Pour mixture into pastry case and bake at 180°C for 20 minutes until filling is set. Serve warm.

baked onions
Bake whole large brown, yellow or white onions in the coals of a barbecue or in the oven until tender (at least 50 minutes). Cut in half with a serrated knife and serve with a cruet of extra-virgin olive oil or butter, sea salt and pepper and maybe some freshly cut herbs.

other recipes

cold chinese white-cooked chicken with seared spring onion sauce
  see CHICKEN AND THE CHRISTMAS TURKEY
green herb pilaf *see* RICE
mint and spring onion chutney *see* MINT
pissaladière *see* ANCHOVIES
venetian liver and onion *see* LIVER

Oranges, mandarins and grapefruit

Oranges, mandarins and grapefruit For many of us life would not be the same if we could not start the day with a glass of freshly squeezed sweet orange juice and a scraping of Seville marmalade on our toast! The bitter orange (*Citrus aurantium*) originated in China and perhaps India some 4000 years ago and was taken to Spain by the Arabs, which is why it is known today as the Seville orange. The formal plantings of Seville oranges in Moorish town squares are still one of the delights of southern Spain. The evening air is scented with orange blossom at the same time as the trees display glowing mature fruit. The Spanish Seville orange crop is mostly sold to the United Kingdom to manufacture its famous bitter marmalades. It is also the orange used in the manufacture of liqueurs such as Grand Marnier, curaçao, Cointreau and triple sec. Its tart juice is much appreciated in Caribbean and Central American fish and chicken dishes. >

The sweet orange (*C. sinensis*) came to the Mediterranean much later, in the late fifteenth century, brought by traders from the east. Both sweet and bitter oranges were first prized for the fragrance of their peel and blossom, and orange trees in tubs have remained a symbol of luxury in Europe. Orange-flower water is a traditional and much-loved flavouring in eastern European, Middle Eastern and Indian cookery.

Orange seeds were planted in New South Wales by Captain Arthur Phillip in 1788. Today oranges are grown in the irrigation areas of the Murray and Murrumbidgee rivers, on the plains in New South Wales and in the hills near Perth in Western Australia. The citrus industry is an extremely important one for Australia and also includes mandarins, grapefruit and some new cultivars, as well as lemons and limes (*see* LEMONS AND LIMES). Over half Australia's annual orange crop goes into juice and the market winner is single-strength fresh, 100 per cent locally processed juice.

The politics of tariffs, subsidies and accurate labelling is beyond the scope of this book but they are life and death to the local industry. Sufficient to say that if juice is labelled '100 per cent Australian orange juice' it cannot include any reconstituted juice derived from imported frozen concentrate. The nationally adopted orange squeezer symbol guarantees no concentrate, no artificial colouring, no added water and no imported fruit.

While used less extensively in the kitchen than the orange, the mandarin (*C. reticulata*) and grapefruit (*C. paradisi*) are included here as they are nevertheless important members of that family cooks worldwide couldn't live without: the citrus family.

VARIETIES AND SEASON

The most common varieties of **orange** grown in Australia are navels and valencias, while the Seville and blood orange are enjoyed in far smaller quantities. The most common varieties of **mandarin** are the imperial and ellendale. In the United States certain mandarins are known as tangerines. In the United Kingdom one variety at least is called a clementine. Some crosses are also gaining popularity. Most **grapefruit**, which are not sold by variety, are medium-to-large, yellow-fleshed fruit with smooth rind and few seeds. The flavour ranges between extremely tart and quite sweet. Carnarvon in Western Australia produces one of the best pink grapefruit in the world. The flesh is sweet and juicy and orange–pink. Yellow grapefruit are available all year. Pink grapefruit are available August–October.

BLOOD Different varieties of blood orange have differing amounts of red pigment in the flesh and skin. These oranges have more red pigment when grown in colder climates. The flavour is rich and sweet. Some people have likened it to orange

**oranges
and
mandarins
go
with**
butter
cream
brandy
liqueurs
nuts
honey
vanilla
yoghurt
cinnamon
cardamom
ham
onion
olives
rice
salad leaves
parsley
mint
paprika
cloves
pork
beetroots
chicken
beef
trotters
mustard
duck
trout
prawns
crab

with raspberry or cherry overtones. This exotic fruit is starting to interest some local growers, especially in New South Wales, where Maltese blood is one variety being grown. It is virtually seedless. Italy and Spain are the world's largest producers and consumers. Blood oranges are available July–September at specialist greengrocers.

ELLENDALE | This is a cross between a mandarin and an orange and is sometimes known as a tangor. It is larger than the imperial mandarin and the skin is a firmer fit. Ellendales are available June–October.

IMPERIAL | This small to medium-sized mandarin has smooth glossy skin that is quite thin, fairly loose and easy to peel. Imperials are the first of the mandarins and are available April–July.

MINNEALO TANGELO | The mandarin and grapefruit were crossed to produce this very juicy, easy-to-peel fruit with few seeds. It has the tangy acidity of the grapefruit with the perfume of the mandarin. This most attractive newcomer is available July–October.

NAVEL | The *Washington* navel is recognised by the dimpled navel shape at its base and its slightly pebbly skin, which is a rich orange colour. It is practically seedless and easy to peel and section. The Washington navel is available late May–September and is a winter orange. The *Lane late* navel was first developed in Mildura in 1950 from a navel sport. The fruit has paler skin but all the flavour of the Washington navel. Lane late navels or spring oranges are available late September–late December.

SEVILLE | A winter orange, the Seville is a large fruit with a thick rind, tough membrane and many seeds. It has a pronounced bitter flavour and is most suited to cooking. One still sees a few Seville oranges from June to September. Those I buy come from the Riverina.

VALENCIA | The valencia orange has smoother, thicker skin than a navel and more seeds. It is the best of all juicing oranges. The skin is often green-tinged; bright-orange coloration is a result of cold, crisp weather at ripening time, not of ripeness itself. Valencias are available August/September–March/April. It is interesting to note that the valencia orange is not grown in Valencia, Spain.

SELECTION AND STORAGE

All citrus fruit is picked ripe. Once picked it will not ripen further. It should feel heavy for its size and smell good, with no hint of fermented aromas. Avoid soft, bruised or wrinkled citrus fruit. However, fruit with some 'give' (not softness) will yield more juice than hard fruit.

Most mandarins should have tight-fitting skins – puffy skins can indicate that the fruit has been kept too long on the tree and is dry. An imperial mandarin with a tight-fitting skin, however, is immature.

It is important that consumers understand that the greenish skins of summer valencia oranges is because they are ripened in warmer temperatures. In this case green does *not* mean unripe.

Citrus fruit will stay fresh for up to 2 weeks at room temperature but their life will be extended in the refrigerator. The vitamin content is not diminished by refrigeration providing the fruit has not been peeled or sliced. Seville oranges can be frozen whole. They will collapse on thawing but will be fine for marmalade.

PREPARATION

The vitamin content of citrus fruit is best retained by peeling, zesting or slicing just before eating it. It is useful to know that a medium orange will yield 5 teaspoons grated zest, $\frac{1}{3}$–$\frac{1}{2}$ cup juice and 1 cup bite-sized pieces.

TO JUICE Stand the fruit in hot water for 15 minutes to extract the maximum juice if you refrigerate your citrus fruit or if the weather is very cold. Squeeze citrus fruit as required: stored juice loses vitamins rapidly. As blood oranges can be difficult to come by, freeze their juice whenever you can.

TO ZEST OR GRATE The oil glands are contained in the coloured part of the peel (the zest) only. Zest is usually required in very fine strips or grated. To gather zest, either use a grater (yields the finest fragments), a zester (produces long, thin shreds) or a vegetable peeler (strips slices of zest that you can then cut into julienne).

If your recipe calls for grated zest, knock the grater sharply against the mixing bowl to dislodge as much of the zest as possible. Hold the grater over the bowl and then rinse it with the juice or other liquid from the recipe. Eat the grated fruit as soon as possible, as it will quickly deteriorate without its protective oily rind.

TO SEGMENT **Oranges and mandarins** Cut a slice from the top and bottom of an orange. With a sharp knife, carve away the peel, following the curve of the fruit and slicing deep enough to remove all pith, leaving the flesh exposed. If peeling a mandarin, simply remove the skin. It is easiest now to cut thick, crosswise slices through the fruit, flicking out any seeds. The more difficult technique is to cut a peeled orange or mandarin into segments. Using a small, sharp knife, slide it down the side of a segment and then down the other side, freeing it from its enclosing membrane. When all segments have been released, squeeze the 'skeleton' over the segments to catch all the juice.

Grapefruit The ultimate luxury is to be presented with a halved grapefruit where each half segment has been loosened from its membrane. The technique to section a halved grapefruit is the same as above – use a small sharp knife and cut inside each enclosing membrane, leaving the fruit in place.

TO DRY ORANGE AND MANDARIN PEEL Dried orange peel gives a wonderful flavour to beef and game stews and is an essential ingredient in bouquet garni in Provence. Dried orange and mandarin peel are important in Chinese cookery also.

Wash and dry the orange or mandarin. Peel a long coil from the orange using a vegetable peeler and hang it in an airy spot until quite dry and brittle (this may take several days). Pieces of mandarin peel can be dried on a rack. Store in an airtight container and use within a month.

SUGARED PEEL I have described how to candy citrus peel in LEMONS AND LIMES. The method is ideal for grapefruit peel but less useful for orange peel, which is usually much thinner. Use it for thick-skinned oranges by all means. Thin-skinned oranges are better preserved in sugar.

Small sticks of orange peel, cut as thinly and with as little white pith as possible, can be layered with granulated or castor sugar in a wide-necked jar. Shake the jar each day for a week and turn it upside down now and then. This peel is excellent chopped into cakes or puddings or used to decorate small iced cakes. The sugar will also have a wonderful flavour as it will have absorbed some of the aromatic oil from the cut peel.

recipes

quick orange cordial

MAKES 1 LITRE

600 ml water
grated zest of 2 oranges
⅓ cup sugar
1¼ cups fresh orange juice

Bring water and zest slowly to a boil. Remove from heat and add sugar, stirring to dissolve. Leave to stand 15 minutes, then add juice. Strain or not as you prefer. Bottle, refrigerate and use within 1 week.

pink grapefruit and campari granita   SERVES 4–6

2 cups pink grapefruit juice
2 cups orange juice
1 tablespoon Campari
4–6 tablespoons sugar

Mix ingredients and taste for sweetness. Pour into an ice-cream tray and freeze. When frozen, cut ice into chunks and process in a food processor to a fine texture. Scrape into a bowl, cover and return to freezer until you are ready to serve. Pile into tall glasses, with or without sliced fruit on the side.

seville marmalade from a competent western-district cook

This recipe came to me from a woman who read of my failure with my first-ever Seville marmalade. She reminded me that it is most important to use fresh fruit – straight from the tree is ideal.

Seville oranges
water
salt
sugar

Thinly slice fruit, having first removed all pips and central membrane. For every 500 g prepared fruit, allow 1.8 litres water and ¼ teaspoon salt. Simmer fruit, salt and water until peel is soft and easily squashed. Allow to rest for 24 hours in a ceramic or stainless steel bowl.

Next day, measure fruit and water into a preserving pan or large stockpot using a cup. Bring to a boil and for every cup of fruit and water allow an equal measure of sugar. Return to a boil and cook for 25–30 minutes until setting or jelly stage. Bottle into hot, sterilised jars.

orange caramel syrup

The easiest way to use this syrup is to pour it over sliced oranges for a quick dessert. But the possibilities are endless. Caramel oranges can accompany pancakes warmed in brown sugar or syrup, waffles, Claudia Roden's Middle Eastern Orange Cake (see p. 474) or Middle Eastern Fruit Salad (see APRICOTS) or be served with a refreshing orange sorbet or a bowl of slightly sweetened mascarpone cheese lightened with lightly whipped egg white.

1 cup sugar
½ cup water
½ cup fresh orange juice

Stir sugar and water over heat until sugar has dissolved, then leave alone until a rich golden amber. Stand well back and pour in orange juice. When the spluttering has died down, stir gently until you have a smooth syrup. This syrup can be stored

grapefruit and crab
Add pink grapefruit segments to a crab salad.

blood orange juice
Freeze the juice of blood oranges for up to 6 months and use to make Maltese sauce, a hollandaise intended for asparagus or fine grilled fish.

orange sauce
Warm 1 tablespoon quince or redcurrant jelly and mix it with 2 tablespoons freshly grated horseradish, the juice of 2 oranges and grated orange zest and set aside for 1 hour before serving with cold pork, duck or goose.

in a screw-top jar in the refrigerator until you need it. If it becomes too thick to ladle or pour, just stand the jar in hot water for a few minutes.

caramel mandarins Whole peeled mandarins can be soaked in this caramel syrup for 30 minutes–1 hour. Strip off every scrap of pith before immersing them.

orange salad
Toss sliced orange with black olives, paper-thin slices of red onion, torn mint and rocket leaves for a great salad to accompany grilled fish or prawns or barbecued bug tails.

afternoon tea orange cake

1 large orange or mandarin
2 eggs
125 g unsalted butter, softened
¾ cup castor sugar
225 g self-raising flour

ICING
2 cups pure icing sugar
1 teaspoon melted butter
1 tablespoon fresh orange or mandarin juice
1 tablespoon Grand Marnier or Mandarin Napoleon liqueur
1 tablespoon chopped candied or sugared citrus peel

Preheat oven to 190°C and butter a 20 cm ring tin. Zest and juice orange. Combine all cake ingredients in a food processor and blend for 2 minutes until smooth and creamy. Pour into prepared tin and bake for 30–35 minutes. Cool for 5 minutes in tin before turning out onto a wire rack. Cool completely before icing.

Beat all icing ingredients except peel until quite smooth. Stir in peel. Warm icing over hot water until it thins a little and pour or spread over cake.

fairy cakes Small cakes in paper cases will take 10–15 minutes to bake. Ice as above or dust with icing sugar.

carrot and orange
Combine grated carrot, orange segments and coriander leaves and dress with olive oil and orange juice.

orange pepper
Grind well-dried orange peel in a spice grinder with black or white peppercorns and use to season a chicken breast or veal chop before grilling or sautéing.

claudia roden's middle eastern orange cake

There does not seem to be a café that does not serve its own version of this marvellous cake. It is dense and moist and the cooked peel gives it a tart and intriguing flavour that is very seductive.

I have amended Claudia Roden's method slightly by using a food processor. You may have to process the mixture in batches. The tin selected should be big enough so that the batter is no deeper than 6 cm or the cake will take much longer to cook.

Serve this cake with a pile of citrus segments and the best thick cream.

2 large oranges, washed
6 eggs, beaten
250 g ground almonds
250 g sugar
1 teaspoon baking powder

Boil oranges in a little water in a covered saucepan for 2 hours. Allow to cool, then cut open, remove pips and chop roughly.

Preheat oven to 190°C and butter and flour a springform tin. Blend oranges and remaining ingredients thoroughly in a food processor. Pour batter into prepared tin. Bake for 1 hour. If cake is still very wet, cook a little longer. Cool in tin before gently turning out.

orange and cardamom ice-cream

SERVES 8

This recipe originally appeared in Jane Grigson's Fruit Book, *where she in turn credited it to Josceline Dimbleby. Like all good recipes it has travelled widely, receiving a tweak here and a fiddle there. It is important to use a concentrated orange juice to obtain the correct flavour. This ice-cream is magic when served with Middle Eastern Fruit Salad (see* APRICOTS*).*

175 g castor sugar
½ cup water
4 eggs
½ cup concentrated orange juice
seeds from 5 cardamom pods, crushed
300 ml cream

Bring sugar and water to a boil, stirring until sugar has dissolved. Lightly beat eggs in an electric mixer. Pour on boiling syrup, beating until volume has doubled. Beat in orange juice and cardamom seeds. When well blended, stir in cream. Churn in an ice-cream machine according to the manufacturer's instructions. Freeze until needed.

orange segments
Serve slices of perfectly peeled orange at the end of a rich dinner. It is amazing how many people refuse to peel oranges but love them when the hard work has been done for them.

mandarin cream pots

SERVES 6

2 large mandarins *or* tangelos
½ cup light Sugar Syrup
2 cups cream
1 tablespoon Mandarin Napoleon liqueur
½ cup castor sugar
2 eggs
2 egg yolks

Preheat oven to 160°C. Remove zest from mandarins with a vegetable peeler and cut into fine julienne. Place in a saucepan of cold water and bring to a boil. Repeat this process. Drain and simmer zest in sugar syrup for 5 minutes. Drain. Add zest to cream and slowly bring to scalding point. Cover and set aside to infuse.

Juice mandarins and measure. You need 4 tablespoons. Whisk juice, liqueur, sugar, eggs and egg yolks together. Whisk in cooled cream. Strain, pressing well to extract every drop of flavour from zest. Pour mixture into 6 × 100 ml porcelain moulds and stand in a baking dish lined with a tea towel. Pour in hot water to come halfway up sides of moulds and bake for 20 minutes until just set. Allow to rest a few minutes in the water bath, then remove and cool completely.

When serving, float a little mandarin liqueur on each cream pot for a very extravagant effect.

other recipes

carrot soup with orange *see* CARROTS
orange and quince jelly *see* QUINCES

see also CUMQUATS; LEMONS AND LIMES

Oregano and marjoram

'Indeed Sir, she was the sweet marjoram of the Salad, or rather the herb of grace.' William Shakespeare, *All's Well that Ends Well.*

The very first thing to get straight is what oregano and marjoram are. The names are very confusing. Some say oregano and some say marjoram and maybe they mean the same herb, and then again maybe they don't. Both herbs are from the genus *Origanum,* belonging to the mint family. There are at least 25 *Origanum* species, so it is not surprising confusion abounds. | Put simply, oregano is the wild form of marjoram, of which there are a number of species, including pot and sweet marjoram. *Origanum* means 'joy of the mountains', which is apt since in France, Italy and Greece, where herbs are so well loved, hillsides are covered in these fragrant plants. (It is interesting to note that the depth of flavour can vary not only between different species but between examples of the same species, according to the soil and the amount of sunshine and water they receive.) >

Oregano is an integral part of *herbes de Provence* in France. The white-flowering pot marjoram that grows wild in Greece is picked in full flower and then dried. It is this herb that gives the distinctive flavour to many barbecued Greek dishes. Dried marjoram, thyme and sage comprise the traditional mixed herbs called for in English recipes for sausages, pork-pie fillings and the like.

I have a rampant plant of oregano that throws up long flower-stalks with pinkish purple flowers. I enjoy adding it to a posy of garden flowers for my desk, but I find that used fresh it has little culinary value. It is interesting that European writers claim that oregano is much more strongly flavoured than sweet marjoram, but the New Zealand author Gilian Painter (*The Herb Garden Displayed*) agrees with me that the leaves have little flavour. I can only suspect that it is habitat that has made the difference. When I dry the flower-heads at the end of summer they do have the distinctive pungent and slightly medicinal flavour I associate with pizza and tomato-based Italian sauces.

VARIETIES AND SEASON

The species you are most likely to encounter are oregano, sweet marjoram, pot marjoram and golden marjoram. All plants are perennial, but they do not like cold, wet winters; in colder States the plants die back almost completely during the winter.

GOLDEN MARJORAM | *O. aureum* is grown mainly for its attractive gold-and-green-dappled foliage and looks lovely in a rockery or as a ground cover. It colours more in hot weather. The tiny flowers are pink in summer. The plant has little flavour.

OREGANO | *O. vulgare* forms a dense mat of dark-green, heart-shaped leaves and in summer throws up long flower-stalks that are a reddish brown topped with pink–purple flowers. The fresh leaves taste faintly medicinal. The dried flower-heads, in particular, develop a rich and slightly resinous flavour.

POT MARJORAM | *O. onites* looks like a dainty form of oregano, with similar but smaller leaves. It is more strongly flavoured than oregano. There are both pink-flowering and white-flowering varieties. The white-flowering variety is the plant prized by Greeks, who know it as *rígani*.

SWEET MARJORAM | *O. marjorana* has small, rounded green leaves that are very fragrant. They are softer as well as smaller than those of oregano. The flower-heads are grey–green knots around which are the tiny white flowers. Sweet marjoram, also known as knot

oregano and marjoram go with

tomatoes
white cheeses
eggs
dried beans
rice
grilled fish
lamb
kid
sweetcorn
sweet peppers
chicken
lemons
olives
eggplants

onion with oregano

Slice the tops off onions and poke a sprig of marjoram or oregano into each, then wrap in well-oiled foil. Bake at 180°C or, better still, barbecue until soft (45 minutes), turning twice. Unwrap onions and drizzle 1 tablespoon melted butter into each, then season. Add extra herbs, if you desire.

marjoram, flowers in late summer to autumn. This herb has been described as having a flavour at once sharp, bitter and with a hint of camphor.

SELECTION AND STORAGE

If someone gives you a present of freshly cut sweet marjoram or oregano, store it in a paper-lined plastic bag in the refrigerator where it will keep well for a week. I have rarely seen sweet marjoram or oregano sold in bunches, as one buys other herbs. I suspect that the reason is that Australians with Italian or Greek heritage prefer the more concentrated flavour of dried oregano for their cooking and, as the herbs are so easy to grow, they grow and dry their own. One can readily buy bunches of dried pot marjoram in any Greek delicatessen, where it is sold as *rígani*. Transfer it to a clean jar and use within a few months. Do not bother buying dried oregano in a small glass jar or packet. It will inevitably have little flavour and smell dusty.

PREPARATION

Oregano is used fresh or dried, either chopped or crumbled over pizzas, meat, vegetables, poultry or fish destined for the barbecue. It is also a common ingredient in hearty soups, bean casseroles, pasta sauces and anything to do with tomatoes. The leaves and flowers of sweet marjoram can be used fresh or dried. To use fresh, strip the leaves from the stalks and add whole or chopped to omelettes, cheese dishes, creamy onion tarts, sauces or buttered vegetables a few minutes before serving. Most cooks feel that its flavour is best if it is not cooked but warmed through.

TO DRY OREGANO OR SWEET MARJORAM Pick the stalks when in flower, preferably early in the day. Tie loosely in bunches and hang upside down in the kitchen until thoroughly dried. This should only take a few days in summer. Either leave the dried bunches whole or rub the flower-heads and leaves from the stalks. Store in a clean, dry jar out of direct light and use before the next flowering season.

marjoram omelette

Scatter a spoonful of marjoram leaves onto an omelette with shavings of fetta or parmesan cheese before folding and sliding it onto the plate.

marjoram and anchovy tartlets

Line cooked tartlets with a well-reduced purée of tomato and onion, then add strips of anchovy and a generous amount of freshly chopped marjoram.

recipes

salmoriglio – oregano sauce   SERVES 6

This recipe comes from The River Cafe Cookbook *by Rose Gray and Ruth Rogers, a wonderful collection of the dishes they serve in their London restaurant. Lemon thyme or sweet marjoram can also be used.*

4 tablespoons fresh oregano
   leaves
(continued next page)

In a food processor or mortar and pestle, work oregano and salt to a paste. Add lemon juice. Slowly work in oil and season

1 teaspoon Maldon sea salt
flakes

2 tablespoons lemon juice

8 tablespoons extra-virgin
olive oil

freshly ground black pepper

with pepper. Serve with grilled fish or lamb.
The 'sauce' is very powerful, so just smear a
little over the cooked food.

sweet marjoram and mozzarella fritters   MAKES 10

1 egg

250 g fresh mozzarella,
drained, dried and grated

200 g freshly grated parmesan
cheese

2 tablespoons plain flour

1 tablespoon finely chopped
fresh sweet marjoram leaves

1 small clove garlic, finely
chopped

salt

freshly ground black pepper

olive oil

Whisk egg lightly and add all remaining
ingredients except salt, pepper and oil. Taste
and adjust seasoning. Form mixture into
small balls the size of a walnut and
refrigerate for 1 hour. Heat oil to a depth
of 1 cm in a heavy-based frying pan and fry
fritters, turning once, until golden. Drain
well and serve with drinks.

rocket and oregano pizza   MAKES 1

extra-virgin olive oil

½ quantity Pizza Dough

1 red onion, very finely sliced

1 cup torn rocket leaves *or*
other peppery greens
(mustard leaves, beetroot
tops, turnip tops)

1 cup Fresh Tomato Sauce
(see p. 709)

2 tablespoons crumbled dried
oregano leaves and flowers
or Greek *rígani*

sea salt

freshly ground black pepper

Preheat oven to 220°C and oil a large pizza
tray. Pat dough over tray with well-oiled
hands, stretching and pulling it to keep it
thin. Allow dough to recover for 5 minutes,
then cover it with onion, then rocket, then
tomato sauce and oregano and lastly drizzle
on ⅓ cup oil and season. Bake for
15 minutes until edges are very crisp, then
slide pizza from tray onto oven rack and
cook a further 5 minutes to crisp base.

oregano chicken
*Stuff large sprigs
of dried or fresh
oregano or
marjoram into the
cavity of a chicken.
Tuck more sprigs
underneath the bird
with some garlic
cloves and roast for
1 hour at 200°C,
drizzling it with
white wine and olive
oil every 20 minutes.*

**marjoram, pepper
and corn salad**
*Toss marjoram
leaves in a salad
with strips of
roasted red peppers,
kernels of barbecued
sweetcorn and
rocket leaves.*

marjoram rice
*Stir a handful
of freshly chopped
marjoram into
cooked rice or
risotto.*

O *xtail* The skinned tail of all categories of beef, oxtail has a high percentage of bone running through the middle. It is usually sold jointed into 5 cm pieces. Oxtail is flavoursome and economical but requires long, slow cooking to extract the best flavour. It is very high in fat but careful trimming can modify this. | A favourite winter choice of mine is oxtail braised with red wine and olives and served with creamy mashed potato. A friend once commented after eating this dish that he would extol its virtues at greater lengths if his lips were not stuck together! It is this sticky gelatinous quality as much as the superb dark juices that makes braised oxtail such a memorable and comforting dish. Cooked to perfection, the meat just about slips from the bones, the knobbly ends of which are golden and shiny, and the plentiful, dark sticky sauce flows in rivers into the mash. | Braising is a technique worth mastering and oxtail an ingredient that demonstrates the technique to perfection. The ingredients chosen for a braise, whether meat, poultry or vegetables, should require lengthy cooking, so that there is adequate time for an exchange of flavour to take place between the food and the liquid. >

Meat and poultry pieces can be rolled in flour and sealed in butter or oil before braising. This adds to the colour of the finished sauce but, as Harold McGee rightly points out in his book *On Food and Cooking*, the notion of sealing *in* juices and then immersing the piece of food in liquid is nonsense. Of course, the juices ooze out – and we want them to!

The pot chosen should be heavy – cast-iron, ideally – with a well-fitting lid and, most important of all, the food should fit snugly. There should be enough liquid, but not too much – it should just cover the main ingredient. The sauce will be richest if made from veal or chicken stock, but vegetable stock, a mixture of water and wine or tomato juice or plain water can all give good results. Be generous with fresh herbs; often whole garlic cloves, unpeeled or peeled, are added, too. I press buttered baking paper over the top of the braise before adding the lid to stop the surface drying out.

The oven should be turned down low, so that the cooking process is as lengthy as possible to ensure maximum extraction and exchange of flavours. (A braise can be achieved on top of the stove but there will always be the danger of food sticking to the bottom of the pot – in this case, a simmer mat and a tiny flame are essential.) A well-timed braise will be tender with just enough liquid that has reduced to sauce consistency.

oxtail goes with
carrots
onions
celery
turnips
garlic
wine
olives
orange zest
thyme
ginger
soy sauce
star anise
grapes
pickled cherries
pickled plums
potatoes
fortified wine

VARIETIES AND SEASON

Oxtail is available all year, although demand is greatest in the colder months. In hot weather the butcher may have frozen oxtail, which is satisfactory.

SELECTION AND STORAGE

The older the animal the meatier the tail and the larger the pieces. Most butchers display cut oxtail with the pieces held firm by a rubber band. Inspect the meat to see how large the large pieces are and how many tiny pieces there are. The very tiniest pieces are only suitable for the stockpot or for making oxtail soup. You will need at least 4 good-sized pieces per person. This probably means a whole tail per serve (with some leftovers).

Like all fresh meat, discard the wrappings when you get home. Store the oxtail on a plate and refrigerate, covered with plastic film, for up to 2 days.

PREPARATION

Some cooks soak oxtail overnight in salted water. This is not a good thing to do. You want the blood to enrich your sauce, not to be leached away by salted water. If the oxtail has been frozen, thaw it completely in the refrigerator and pat dry before proceeding. Cut away the excess fat from large pieces of oxtail and then follow the recipe.

recipes

oxtail consommé

SERVES 8

Because of its gelatinous character oxtail makes a particularly rich soup. When clarified and served as consommé, the soup is a magnificent orange-bronze colour. A small portion accompanied by a glass of north-east Victorian tokay or muscat is a wonderful start to a winter dinner.

The technique of clarifying broth sounds terrifying but is really quite easy. It is also a bit like magic and very satisfying.

The removed oxtail can be used to make a savoury spread. Shred the meat from the bones, whirl it in a food processor with a little mustard, some butter and seasonings – parsley and capers, for example – and use it as a sandwich filling or to make tiny pasties or pies to serve alongside the consommé.

oxtail rillettes
Mix shredded leftover braised oxtail and any jellied juices with small capers, chopped pickled cucumber and parsley and sharpen with vinegar. Serve on hot buttered toast.

3 oxtails, sawn into sections
   and trimmed of fat
1 kg chopped veal brisket
2 onions
olive oil
1 leek, sliced
1 carrot, diced
½ cup tokay or muscat
1 stick celery, chopped
2 tablespoons tomato paste
1 teaspoon peppercorns
2 cloves garlic, peeled
1 bay leaf
1 piece fresh *or* dried
   orange zest
1 large sprig thyme
3 litres Veal *or* Chicken Stock
2 stalks parsley

CLARIFICATION

4 egg whites
½ carrot, sliced
½ onion, diced
½ stick celery, diced
1 stalk parsley

Preheat oven to 200°C. Brown oxtail and veal in oven for 1 hour, turning once or twice.

Dice 1 of the onions and halve the other, unpeeled. Heat 2 tablespoons olive oil in a heavy-based frying pan and sauté diced onion, leek and carrot until starting to colour. Deglaze with tokay and tip contents into a stockpot. Heat a little more oil in frying pan and cook halved onion, cut-side down, until deep brown. Transfer scorched onion to stockpot. Add meat, discarding any rendered fat, then add remaining ingredients. Bring slowly to simmering point and skim. Adjust heat to maintain a simmer and cook for 3–4 hours. Strain soup and cool overnight. Next day, remove fat.

To clarify the consommé, combine ingredients for clarification in a food processor and process until light and frothy. Tip into cold soup and stir continuously over a moderate heat until just about to boil. Reduce heat and allow to simmer for 1 hour. Turn off heat and leave undisturbed for 5 minutes.

Line a colander or large strainer with a dampened clean cloth (doubled muslin is best) and suspend over a large bowl. With a large spoon, lift away part of the congealed 'raft' of coagulated egg white and vegetable and discard. Carefully ladle the sparkling broth into the colander, disturbing the 'raft' as little as possible. Remove colander, then taste consommé and adjust seasoning. A few drops of tokay could be added at this time. Serve hot or cold.

oxtail braised with black olives SERVES 6–8

This is the deliciously sticky braise mentioned at the beginning of this section. One must suck the bones when eating this dish, so I advise steaming or microwaving some rolled-up, wet cotton face-washers as the Chinese do for fast effective clean-ups.

6 oxtails, sawn into sections and trimmed of fat
salt
freshly ground black pepper
plain flour
butter
olive oil
100 ml brandy
1 large onion, diced
4 carrots, diced
½ bottle dry red wine
1 bay leaf
1 sprig thyme
6 cloves garlic, peeled
6 cm piece fresh or dried orange zest
1 litre stock, tomato juice or water
1 cup stoned black olives

Preheat oven to 160°C. Roll oxtail in seasoned flour and brown well in batches in a frying pan in butter and oil. Transfer browned meat to a cast-iron casserole. Place dish over a low heat and cook for 2–3 minutes. Flame with warmed brandy, shaking dish until flames have died down.

Wipe out browning pan and sauté onion and carrot in 1 tablespoon oil for 10 minutes. Pour over wine and bubble fiercely. Stir to ensure deglazing is complete and tip contents of pan over oxtail. Add herbs, garlic, zest and liquid, which should barely cover meat. Cover with buttered baking paper, then place lid on firmly and cook in oven for 2½ hours.

Strain sauce from meat into a tall jug and allow fat to rise. Protect meat from drying out by covering it again with the baking paper. Remove fat from sauce. Pour sauce back over meat, then add olives and continue to cook until oxtail is about to drop from bones, about 45 minutes. Alternatively, refrigerate braise overnight without degreasing it. The next day, or the day after, remove fat, which will have solidified, add olives and reheat as above.

elizabeth david's grapes Elizabeth David has an unusual and excellent recipe for an oxtail braise with grapes that one can make in autumn. The method is the same as the above but I use white wine instead of red and the pieces of meat in the casserole are covered with quite a thick layer of grapes pulled from their stalks. When the meat is tender, the grapes and sauce are pressed through a food mill before being returned to the pot for the final reheat. **additions** One can ignore the carrots in the initial cooking and add big chunks of carrots and turnips an hour before the end of the cooking time. Glazed pickling

oxtail brawn
Make oxtail brawn when you have lots of leftovers by packing the shredded meat into a basin with perhaps a handful of toasted pine nuts, cooked diced carrot or mushrooms, grated orange zest and parsley. Melt the jellied juices and strain over the meat, which will set quite solid. Slice and serve with a salad and home-made preserves.

onions, bacon lardons and button mushrooms can be added as for a
Beef Bourguignon (*see* BEEF).

chinese red-cooked oxtail

SERVES 4

oxtail pasta sauce
*Use the juicy
leftovers from
braised oxtail as
a delicious and
original pasta sauce.*

*Chinese 'red-cooking' results in a rich and succulent sauce. Red-cooked
dishes are often prepared in clay pots and are ideal for winter dining.*

3 tablespoons vegetable oil

2 cloves garlic, smashed but
　unpeeled

3 oxtails, sawn into sections
　and trimmed of fat

I litre water

½ teaspoon salt

3 tablespoons dry sherry or
　rice wine

I piece dried orange *or*
　mandarin zest

6 tablespoons dark soy sauce

3 teaspoons brown sugar

I star anise

2 spring onions, cut into 5 cm
　pieces

4 slices peeled fresh ginger

12 small turnips, peeled *or* 4
　medium turnips, peeled and
　quartered

Heat oil in an enamelled cast-iron casserole
and sauté garlic for 3 minutes. Remove and
reserve garlic, then brown oxtail. Remove
oxtail, then wipe out pan and return garlic
and all other ingredients except turnips.
Bring to simmering point, then cover meat
with baking paper and a lid and simmer for
2 hours, either on top of stove or in a
180°C oven. Add turnips and simmer a
further 30 minutes or until tender.

see also BEEF

Oysters

Piles of ancient shells, now part of sand dunes and coastal foreshores, are evidence that Aboriginal Australians and Torres Strait Islanders enjoyed oysters long before white settlement. A plate of freshly opened oysters, preferably swimming in natural juices, remains a favourite beginning to a meal today. | All oysters thrive in brackish water, living in bays, estuaries and rivers. The tidal flow ensures a constant supply of food for the growing oysters; as oysters, like other molluscs, are filter feeders, it is imperative that the water be free of pollutants. The subtle differences of taste and colour that occur between oysters of the same species is partly a result of the location of the oyster bed. | Many of our oysters are washed after opening. Usually they are then also cut from the shell and flipped to present the customary 'humped' look. Many of us consider this practice reprehensible: not only does the oyster die and deterioration start but the precious oyster liquor is lost. Where restaurateurs open oysters to order and serve them uncut with liquor intact, it is not uncommon for customers to complain the oysters are too salty. Much of the market has become acclimatised to washed oysters. >

oysters

go

with

lemons

limes

wine vinegar

olive oil

parsley

shallots

mild onions

spring onions

pepper

mussels

pipis

cream

butter

garlic

wholemeal bread

rye bread

soy sauce

fish sauce

leeks

carrots

The saltiness of oysters can vary from mild to strong depending on habitat. The flavour spectrum runs from full (fat or oily) through sweet to flinty. There is now a growing movement among produce-conscious retailers and restaurateurs to market oysters according to type and harvesting location. This encourages awareness of where the best oysters come from at different times of the year and educates oyster lovers about the quite different characteristics of the different species. Experiment at home by combining the 3 species of oyster available in Australia on a plate and inviting friends to taste and notice the differences, just as one might do in a wine-tasting. Incidentally, the reason that oyster forks have one side thicker than the other is that the best way to enjoy an oyster is to slide the thick edge of the oyster fork down the side to sever the muscle joining the oyster to the lower shell, before slipping the oyster and its muscle (the foot) down your throat and drinking the juice!

VARIETIES AND SEASON

Three species of oyster are available: the native flat oyster, the Pacific oyster and the Sydney rock oyster.

NATIVE FLAT | *Ostrea angasi*, also known as the southern belon or mud oyster, is grown commercially in South Australia, Tasmania and southern New South Wales. It requires high salinity to flourish. The native flat oyster has golden-tinged flesh and a rounded flaky shell. A big-flavoured oyster, it has a clean, flinty flavour with a tannic grip on the mouth. This variety is much prized in Europe (it is a close cousin of the revered belon oyster from France) but is still finding its market niche with Australian oyster lovers.

PACIFIC | *Crassostrea gigas* is also called the Japanese oyster and is a larger and faster-growing species than the Sydney rock oyster. It is native to Japan and was first introduced to Western Australia, South Australia and Tasmania around 1950. The Pacific oyster, now cultivated all over the world, is farmed commercially in Tasmania and several areas of South Australia. Port Stephens is the only area permitted for its cultivation in New South Wales. This oyster has a thin shell, the exterior of which is rough with spiky lobes and long protrusions. The flesh is steely-grey to silvery-white in colour and has noticeable iodine and briny flavours with a clean finish. Pacific oysters spawn in summer.

SYDNEY ROCK | *Saccostrea commercialis* is found along the east coast of Australia from Hervey Bay in Queensland to Lakes Entrance in eastern Victoria. Sydney rock oysters are farmed most extensively in Queensland, from Hervey Bay to Southport, and in New South Wales at Wallis Lake and Port Stephens and in the Hawkesbury and Georges rivers. Rock oysters have a thick shell with a smooth exterior. In general they are smaller than Pacific oysters. The flesh is creamy-golden to gold–green in colour and is rich and oily with a full after-taste. These oysters have 2 spawning periods, the main one in summer and the second in spring. Rock oysters are required to spend 2 days in a depuration tank (a sterile water bath) to remove any dangerous bio-toxins.

SELECTION AND STORAGE

Although eating a plate of oysters is often regarded as a summer treat, oysters are tastier in the colder months. Most are in their reproductive season sometime during the summer; the flesh becomes milky and soft and the sharp tang of the sea is diminished. As spawning is determined by water temperature, oysters from one location may spawn at a different time from oysters of the same species from a different location. A good fishmonger should be able to tell if an oyster is spawning and recommend oysters from somewhere else. Try all varieties at least once to notice the differences in appearance, flavour, texture and after-taste. Both the flesh and the liquor should be appreciated.

Buying oysters the day you want them and opening them yourself is perfection. More practically, order unopened oysters (any fishmonger can buy oysters unopened) and ask the fishmonger to open them for you. Request that each oyster is opened from the hinge and that the muscle is not cut or the oyster washed! Use opened oysters within 24 hours. Store them in the refrigerator covered with foil or plastic film. Oysters bought unopened will keep well for several days in a cool place (cellar temperature is ideal, or outside in Victoria or Tasmania in the cooler months) with a damp wad of newspaper or a damp hessian bag over them. They can also be refrigerated the same way in the crisper for a day or so. Store the oysters layered, curved-side down, so that the precious juice does not seep away.

PREPARATION

Little needs to be done to oysters other than opening them, but they can also be added to hot dishes. Even then, the preparation required is minimal. Oysters are usually only warmed through in butter, cream or a sauce, or are dropped into soups and so on at the very last moment. They should still be plump with frilly edges, not hard. However, some chowders and stews instruct one to cook oysters well and to purée them with other ingredients. Chinese cooks also prefer their oysters well cooked. Oysters Kilpatrick (oysters scattered with diced bacon and soused in Worcestershire sauce) was a much-favoured dish in the 1970s. The oysters were grilled and served bubbling. I find the flavours in the dish too aggressive unless the sauce is very discreet.

oysters with onion
Mix finely chopped shallot or red onion with very good wine vinegar, coarsely cracked pepper, a little oil and some finely chopped spring onion greens or watercress leaves and spoon over freshly opened oysters. Serve with the tiniest bread-and-butter sandwiches.

oysters and . . .
Garnish freshly opened oysters with grated horseradish, or dress with Ponzu Sauce.

TO OPEN | With a stiff nail brush, scrub each shell under running water to remove all sand and mud. Do not soak the oysters as they may open a little and lose their precious liquor. Have ready a tray thickly spread with coarse rock salt, so that the opened oysters can be balanced without spilling any juice. Place the oyster on a firm surface with the flatter shell uppermost and the hinged end towards you. Wrap your non-opening hand in a tea towel or slip on a thick, protective glove (a gardening glove, for example). Insert an oyster knife where the shell is hinged and work it into the join with a sliding, twisting and levering action. You will need to exert quite a bit of force. When you feel that the muscle has been released, lever off the top shell and discard it. Carefully place the opened oyster on the tray and wipe away any fragments of shell. The oyster will be spread flat in the shell with a wavy frill at the edges. This is what a freshly opened oyster should look like.

TO PREPARE FOR COOKING | Place a fine strainer over a bowl. Slit the muscle holding the oyster to the bottom shell and slip the oyster into the strainer. Ensure that you are not slipping in fragments of shell. The precious oyster juice will collect in the bowl. Wash the shells very well in hot water if the oysters are to be returned to them for serving. The shells can be kept warm in the bottom of an oven.

recipes **chinese batter-fried oysters** SERVES 6

dipping sauce for oysters
Mix light soy sauce and finely chopped fresh ginger for a delicious dipping sauce for cold or warm oysters.

24 freshly opened oysters
1 teaspoon salt
freshly ground black pepper
peanut oil for deep-frying
BATTER
1 cup plain flour
2 teaspoons baking powder
1 teaspoon salt
⅔ cup water
1 egg, beaten
1 tablespoon oil

Tip oysters from their shells into a bowl. Rub gently with salt for 1 minute. Rinse under cold water. Drain and set aside. Bring water to a boil in a saucepan. Dip oysters in and out of water for about 10 seconds until frilly and firm. Drain on kitchen paper and sprinkle with pepper.

To make the batter, mix flour, baking powder and salt in a bowl. Make a well and stir in water. Add egg and oil and stir until batter is smooth. Heat oil for deep-frying to 175°C. Dip each oyster in batter, drain excess and deep-fry, several at a time, until a medium brown, about 3 minutes. Drain on crumpled kitchen paper. Serve immediately with Cantonese Spiced Salt (*see* PRAWNS) or chilli sauce.

oysters with garlic butter

SERVES 6

The sensations of this first course are delightful: hot pastry, cold oyster, warm garlicky juices. Commercial puff pastry is fine to use.

Puff Pastry ✓
36 oysters, freshly opened
I egg
tiny pinch of salt
rock salt

GARLIC BUTTER

200 g softened unsalted butter
2 cloves garlic, chopped to a
   fine paste
3 tablespoons finely chopped
   fresh parsley
2 teaspoons lemon juice *or*
   oyster liquor

Preheat oven to 220°C. To make the garlic butter, blend all ingredients in a food processor, then scrape into a bowl.

Roll puff pastry *very* thinly. Cut small rounds that will fit over oyster shells. Place a dab of garlic butter on each oyster. Beat egg with salt, then brush around rim of shell and press on puff pastry. Trim excess with a sharp knife. Arrange pastry-lidded shells on rock salt on a baking tray, well apart. Lightly brush pastry with egg. Bake for 8 minutes until pastry is brown and cooked. The oysters should have just started to frill at the edges and the butter should have melted by the time the pastry is cooked.

seasoned oysters
Toss oysters, their juices, a few drops of Tabasco or chilli sauce, chopped spring onion and a rough julienne of rocket or spinach leaves, then moisten with olive oil and spoon back into the shells. Alternatively, wrap 2 or 3 of these seasoned oysters in won ton wrappers like a small cigar. Seal the ends with a little beaten egg and deep-fry in hot vegetable oil at 175°C. Serve with a bowl of hot tomato relish.

oyster soup

SERVES 6

Every chef seems to have his or her favourite recipe for oyster soup. Here is mine.

36 oysters, unopened
I cup dry white wine
2 medium potatoes, peeled
   and cut into small dice
2 leeks, sliced and well
   washed
2 tablespoons unsalted butter
generous sprig of thyme
I litre Fish Stock ✓
3 tablespoons small (I cm)
   croutons, cut from day-old
   bread
2 tablespoons clarified butter ✓
freshly ground white pepper
I cup cream
4 tablespoons finely chopped
   parsley

Open oysters over a bowl to catch all the juices. Strain juices and reserve. Place oysters in a ceramic or stainless steel dish. Add reserved juices and wine and refrigerate.

In a heavy-based pan, sweat potato and leek in butter with thyme for 10 minutes, stirring from time to time. Tip on fish stock and simmer until vegetables are tender. Discard thyme sprig and purée soup in a blender.

Fry croutons in clarified butter until golden. Drain on kitchen paper. Put oysters and the juices in which they are swimming into a wide pan and warm them briefly, just until the edges of the oysters start to frill. Strain juices into soup and taste for seasoning. >

Heat cream to boiling point. Remove from heat and slip in oysters. Tip cream-and-oyster mixture into soup and ladle into hot bowls. Sprinkle generously with parsley and croutons and serve.

oyster spring rolls

MAKES 12

Try to find fresh water chestnuts for this recipe (they are sometimes available from Asian food markets), but canned ones will do.

3 large spring roll wrappers

6 water chestnuts, finely chopped

1 slice ginger, finely chopped

3 spring onions, finely chopped (including green tops)

few drops of sesame oil

1 teaspoon light soy sauce

24 oysters, slipped from their shells

vegetable oil

Cut each spring roll wrapper into quarters. Combine water chestnuts, ginger and spring onion with sesame oil and soy sauce. Stir in oysters, turning well in seasonings. Divide mixture evenly between spring roll squares. Roll up carefully, folding in sides to enclose filling. Brush edges with water to seal. Fry for 2–3 minutes in plenty of clean oil. Drain on crumpled kitchen paper and serve at once.

Parsley

P **a r s l e y** Another herb from the rocky shores of the Mediterranean, parsley is a native of Sardinia. Renowned for its medicinal qualities among the ancients, parsley is mentioned in the *Odyssey*, where the author also noted that warriors fed their chariot horses with the herb. (The wearing of parsley wreaths to ward off drunkenness is also recorded, but not by Homer this time.) Parsley is the all-time favourite in the herb garden and the one most cooks would find hardest to do without. Imagine garlic butter or egg and bacon pie or chicken and mayonnaise or any one of a thousand warm vegetable dishes without the fresh flavour of parsley. Newly picked young sprigs of parsley have the scent of a garden just after rain and can be tossed in the salad bowl along with other choice leaves. Finely chopped parsley combined with the same quantity again of a mix of chives, tarragon and chervil becomes *fines herbes*. A delicate fish scattered with *fines herbes* and then simply sauced with a slick of melted butter and maybe a squeeze of lemon defines perfection for me. And parsley stalks are a necessary part of a bouquet garni in stocks, soup and stews.

VARIETIES AND SEASON

The 2 main varieties of parsley are curly and flat-leaf. *Curly* parsley (*Petroselinum crispum*) is probably the most familiar. Its leaves are very crinkly. *Flat-leaf* parsley (*P. hortense filicinum*) is sometimes called Italian or continental parsley. I find it stronger in flavour than the curly variety but some authorities find it milder. It has deeply divided leaves.

The rarely seen *Hamburg* parsley (*P. crispum* var. *tuberosum*) has a long, white tap root like a parsnip and is sometimes cooked like a vegetable. I have not yet tasted Hamburg parsley, which apparently has a delicious parsley–celery–parsnip flavour.

Parsley is slow to germinate and although it will self-sow it is a good idea to plant a few seedlings each year, so that you have fresh young plants coming along when the mature plants are going to seed. Curly and flat-leaf parsley are available all year (summer plantings ensure a winter crop). Hamburg parsley is not widely available but can be grown with ease. It is harvested in early summer.

SELECTION AND STORAGE

Although the varieties have a distinct character of their own, I believe it is more important that parsley is young and freshly picked than of one variety or another. That said, when deep-frying, curly parsley is preferable. For a parsley salad, when the leaves are to be torn and mixed with other ingredients, flat-leaf parsley is better suited. Do not buy parsley if the leaves feel papery rather than soft, if the leaves are brittle or discoloured or if the entire bunch is limp or smells bad.

Store a bunch of parsley in the refrigerator for a day or so with its stalks in water and a plastic bag over the leaves. If wanting to store parsley for several days, pick the leaves from the bunch, wash them, dry them gently in a salad spinner and store them in a paper-lined plastic bag in the refrigerator. The stalks can be stored in a separate bag.

Freshly chopped parsley is quite wonderful. Stale chopped parsley is detestable. And chopped parsley starts to smell and taste stale after a few hours, especially if it has sat around at room temperature. Don't be tempted to keep leftover chopped parsley for tomorrow!

PREPARATION

Over the years I have found myself at odds with the training colleges regarding the method of preparing parsley for chopping. I instruct my apprentices to proceed in the following manner. Never chop the parsley and then wash it after chopping. And never wring the chopped parsley in a tea towel, so that its precious green juice goes down the sink!

TO CHOP

Nip off just the leaves from the bunch (keep the stalks for making stock – wrap a thread around them for easy retrieval). Swish the leaves in a bowl of cold water. Next lift the leaves from the water to a colander (never tip the water through the colander or the deposited sand and dirt will redeposit among the leaves) and allow to drain. Spin the leaves gently in a salad spinner or pat them dry in a clean cloth. I find a heavy cook's knife best for chopping. Some cooks prefer to use 2 similar knives, one in each hand. I find this difficult myself. Don't use a food processor as it tends to bruise the parsley.

parsley salad

recipes

SERVES 4

This is more an idea than a specific recipe and the list of ingredients is simply to suggest what you might include. I had a version of this once at Berowra Waters Inn on the Hawkesbury River, north of Sydney. I have made my own versions, too, sometimes as a filling for a loose roll of smoked kangaroo prosciutto or smoked salmon or sometimes served on top of silky-smooth sheep's milk fetta cheese. On one occasion I served it to accompany quickly sautéd rabbit fillets and liver.

2 cups torn, young parsley
   leaves
roasted peppers
tender salad leaves (rocket,
   lamb's lettuce, watercress)
crisp-fried mushroom slices
croutons
toasted pine nuts
chopped olives
anchovies
radishes
sautéd diced red onion
chopped sun-dried tomatoes
shavings of parmesan cheese
cubes of fetta cheese
best-quality extra-virgin
   olive oil
lemon juice *or* red-wine
   vinegar

Wash and dry parsley gently but thoroughly.

Toss in a bowl with your selected ingredients and dress with oil and a few drops of lemon juice or vinegar. Serve immediately.

fried parsley
Deep-fry thoroughly washed and dried tender sprigs of parsley for 30 seconds in clean oil at 175°C, then drain on crumpled kitchen paper on a warm plate.

beans and parsley butter
Stir Parsley Butter (see p. 494) or Garlic Butter (see GARLIC*) into warm cooked cannellini beans.*

tabbouleh

SERVES 4

Tabbouleh becomes watery if refrigerated for more than a day or so. It is so simple to make it is best made and eaten as soon as possible.

vegetable salads
Make a warm vegetable salad by cooking any of the following: beetroots, baby zucchini, new potatoes, young carrots, artichoke hearts, asparagus or green beans until just tender and tossing them with plenty of parsley, salt, freshly ground black pepper and extra-virgin olive oil.

1 cup cracked wheat, soaked for 10 minutes in cold water
2 large ripe tomatoes, diced
1 small cucumber, diced
3 spring onions, finely sliced
large handful of flat-leaf parsley, coarsely chopped
large handful of mint leaves, coarsely chopped
juice of 1 lemon
1 tablespoon olive oil
salt
freshly ground black pepper

Drain cracked wheat and squeeze hard. Tip into a bowl and add other ingredients. Taste for salt and pepper.

parsley butter

Known traditionally as maître d'hôtel *butter, this is wonderful on a quickly grilled fillet steak or lamb chop or a baked potato.*

garlic and parsley garnish
Warm a crushed garlic clove in extra-virgin olive oil with parsley and perhaps an anchovy and toss through just-cooked vegetables.

60 g softened unsalted butter
1 clove garlic, finely chopped
scant pinch of salt
freshly ground black pepper
few drops of lemon juice
2 tablespoons freshly chopped parsley

Work all ingredients together and use as required. Roll any unused butter in baking paper and then in foil and freeze. A slice can be cut with a hot knife whenever you need it.

gremolata

This is a classic Italian garnish for Osso Buco (see VEAL). *It is equally good on any sticky braised veal dish, baked fish or braised artichokes or witlof.*

2 cloves garlic, very finely chopped
1/2 cup freshly chopped parsley
grated zest of 2 lemons

Mix all ingredients together lightly and scatter over dish just before serving.

parsley and garlic cream sauce

MAKES 2½ CUPS

This cream sauce can accompany Stephanie's Twice-baked Goat's Cheese Soufflés (see CHEESE). I have also turned small boiled potatoes in it with cubes of gruyère cheese and served it alongside thick slices of hot pork and pistachio sausage (see Pistachio and Pork Terrine in NUTS).

2 cups loosely packed young
    parsley leaves
5 cloves garlic
2 cups cream
salt
white pepper

Wash and dry parsley. Place unpeeled garlic in a small saucepan and cover with cold water. Bring slowly to a boil, then pour off water. Repeat this twice more to rid garlic of any bitterness. Slip garlic cloves from their skins. Bring garlic and cream slowly to simmering point in rinsed-out pan. Remove pan from heat. Check garlic is quite soft – if not, simmer cream a further 5 minutes. Add parsley to hot cream and immediately blend in a food processor, a small quantity at a time, to a smooth green sauce. Taste for seasoning. The sauce can be used at once or stored and reheated.
parsley tart Refer to the recipe for Chervil Tart (*see* CHERVIL) and use Parsley and Garlic Cream Sauce instead of the chervil preparation. Just add the eggs to the cream and cook the tart as directed.

parsley and breadcrumb crust

This is a delightful way to finish a butterflied leg of lamb, a rack of lamb, a veal roast or a thick cutlet or fillet of fish.

1 cup fresh white
    breadcrumbs
1 clove garlic, finely chopped
½ cup freshly chopped parsley
salt
freshly ground black pepper
2 teaspoons olive oil

Blend all ingredients in a food processor. Press pale-green crumbs onto meat or fish and roast in the usual manner, basting crumbs carefully with the roasting juices every 20 minutes.

parsley pesto
Toss hot spaghetti in a 'pesto' of parsley made by mixing lots of parsley with a little lemon juice, crushed garlic, crushed pine nuts and olive oil.

parsley pesto and . . .
Use parsley 'pesto' (see above) as a dip for pale inner sticks of celery and strips of fresh fennel or toss it through sliced radishes or hot, drained chick peas or lentils.

other recipes

green herb pilaf *see* RICE
herb and pumpkin soup *see* PUMPKINS
pine forest mushrooms with garlic, cream and parsley *see* MUSHROOMS
tripe with tomato and lots of parsley *see* TRIPE

P **a r s n i p s**   Originating in eastern Europe, the parsnip (*Pastinaca sativa*) is yet another member of the numerous Umbelliferae family, as are carrots, fennel, parsley, celery, celeriac and chervil. | The fleshy root, known to the Greeks and cultivated since the Middle Ages, is still a popular food in Britain, unlike the rest of Europe where its popularity waned with the introduction of potatoes from the New World. Parsnips are still used to make country wines in England. | As parsnips mature their starch turns to sugar, resulting in the characteristic sweet but pungent flavour that parsnip lovers adore. The flavour develops best in cold weather – roast weather! To my mind one of the best parts of a traditional roast dinner is the vegetables that go with it. Offered a plate of roasted pumpkin and parsnips, especially with well-browned skinny ends, and tender onions and potatoes baked in their jackets, I could happily forgo the leg of lamb. >

There is a well-known proverb that 'kind words butter no parsnips', which reminds us that parsnips need enriching with butter, oil or cream to show them at their best. They can be mashed, baked whole or sliced, glazed, turned into deep-fried chips, fried as chunky chips, turned into creamy mousses or tart fillings, or formed into croquettes. Parsnips also marry very well with Indian spices, and Jane Grigson made famous a simple recipe for soup with these flavourings.

VARIETIES AND SEASON

Parsnips are available all year, with the peak season April–October. They are not sold by variety.

SELECTION AND STORAGE

Select even-shaped, medium parsnips that do not trail off into spindly unusable roots. Avoid the giant specimens, which are more likely to have woody centres that are quite inedible. Fresh parsnips should be creamy beige in colour and firm. They should not have soft spots or smell unpleasant.

Parsnips keep well for a week refrigerated in a vegetable storage bag in the crisper. Do not wrap parsnips in plastic film, where they will sweat and rapidly deteriorate. For this reason, too, remove parsnips from any plastic wrapping before storing.

PREPARATION AND COOKING

Peel parsnips with a vegetable peeler and cut a slice from the top. If roasting the parsnips, trim any root ends that spindle to nothing, as these will burn before the rest bakes. If, despite your vigilance, the core of the parsnip is woody and fibrous, cut it out before attempting to boil or roast the parsnip.

TO PURÉE | A luxurious purée results if sliced parsnip is simmered in Veal Stock ✻ rather than water. (Extra richness results if the parsnip is sweated in a little butter for 5–10 minutes before adding the stock.) Barely cover sliced parsnip with stock and simmer until tender, then pass through a food mill, adding a spoonful of stock now and then. The purée should be 'flowing' rather than 'dolloping' as far as consistency goes. Adjust the final texture with more stock, if necessary, and season well. The purée will be very silky and a deep-beige colour.

TO ROAST | Parsnips should be roasted in the baking dish with the meat, or underneath the meat if it is roasting on the top oven rack. Drippings from the roast add succulence to the browned parsnips. Parsnips take 30–45 minutes to roast, depending on their size. I prefer to leave them whole or halved lengthwise if really big.

parsnips
go
with
butter
olive oil
cream
nutmeg
cinnamon
cumin seeds
coriander seeds
turmeric
pepper
meat stock
chicken stock
beef
pork sausages
lamb
bacon
carrots
onions
scallops
crab

recipes

buttered parsnip with toasted crumbs   SERVES 4

3 parsnips, peeled and
   trimmed
60 g butter
3 tablespoons fresh white
   breadcrumbs
freshly ground black pepper
sea salt
2 tablespoons freshly chopped
   parsley

Cut parsnips into even pieces and steam or boil until tender, then drain. Melt butter and pour over parsnip. Put buttered parsnip and breadcrumbs into a non-stick frying pan and cook for 5–10 minutes, tossing frequently until crumbs and parsnip have started to brown. Season and add parsley. Delicious with a veal chop or scaloppine.

parsnip croquettes   SERVES 6

Colin Spencer has a long-established column in Britain's Guardian *newspaper where he extols the delights of vegetables. This is one of his recipes, included in his book* Vegetable Pleasures. *I like these delicious croquettes with crispy bacon as a luxurious breakfast or brunch.*

900 g parsnips, peeled and
   trimmed
butter
1 teaspoon ground cumin
2 eggs, separated
1 tablespoon chickpea flour
sea salt
freshly ground black pepper
50 g fresh wholemeal
   breadcrumbs
olive oil

Cut parsnips into chunks. Boil until tender, then drain well. Melt 50 g butter, then add cumin and sweat for 1–2 minutes. Mash parsnip and add butter and egg yolks. Sift in chickpea flour and mix well. Season to taste. Mix thoroughly (there shouldn't be any lumps) and chill for 1 hour.

Lightly whisk egg whites. Spread breadcrumbs on a plate. Roll spoonfuls of parsnip mixture into sausage shapes or flattish cakes. Dip first in egg white and then in crumbs and refrigerate until needed. Fry in butter and oil until crisp and brown.

roasted parsnip
Toss thickly sliced peeled parsnip, carrot, turnip and potato with a slosh of olive oil, then grind over some pepper, add 2–3 unpeeled garlic cloves and roast in a baking dish at 200°C for 45 minutes, shaking the dish occasionally, until the vegetables are tender and well browned. Serve with a large salad or alongside grilled chops or sausages or a meatloaf.

parsnip and curry soup

SERVES 4

Parsnip soups are often flavoured with curry spices. The one I give here is very simple. A pinch of turmeric added at the beginning will result in a warm gold-coloured soup.

2 large parsnips, peeled
  and chopped
I onion, chopped
20 g butter
2–3 curry leaves
I teaspoon mustard seeds
I teaspoon good-quality
  Indian curry paste
pinch of ground turmeric
  (optional)
salt
freshly ground black pepper
freshly chopped coriander
  leaves

Sweat parsnip and onion with butter and spices over moderate heat for 5 minutes. Add water to cover and simmer until parsnip is quite tender, about 20 minutes. Blend in a food processor and adjust seasoning. Reheat, if required, and add a generous spoonful of coriander leaves to each bowl before serving.

parsnip chips
Deep-fry 2 mm thick slices or shavings of parsnip in clean oil at 160°C for 2–3 minutes until golden brown. Drain on crumpled kitchen paper, sprinkle with salt and serve hot or cold on their own or with grilled meat, a crab or yabby salad or grilled scallops.

parsnip tart

I quantity Shortcrust Pastry
600 ml cream
½ small onion, very finely
  chopped
I cup cooked parsnip
3 eggs
2 egg yolks
salt
freshly ground black pepper
freshly grated nutmeg
2 teaspoons freshly chopped
  chervil
I tablespoon freshly chopped
  parsley

Line a 22 cm loose-bottomed flan tin with pastry and bake blind at 200°C for 20 minutes. Reset oven to 180°C.

Bring cream and onion to simmering point and simmer for 5 minutes. Blend in a food processor or blender, then add parsnip, eggs and egg yolks. Season and stir in nutmeg and herbs. Pour mixture into baked pastry case while still warm and bake 15–20 minutes until just set. Allow to cool a little before cutting.

p a s s i o n f r u i t

The common passionfruit (*Passiflora edulis*) is grown extensively in Australian and New Zealand gardens as well as commercially and we are inclined to take it for granted. Its fruit is the most important produced by the 350 *Passiflora* species, and its heavenly fragrance can fill a room. Australians need to ensure that European and American visitors taste this sublime fruit, as it is likely to be prohibitively costly in their own countries, where it is a delicacy. | The passionfruit is native to Brazil. The Jesuit missionaries who accompanied the conquistadores to South America saw in its striking flower a means of illustrating the Crucifixion: the 10 petals and sepals represented the apostles; the crown of thorns was seen in the filaments; the 5 anthers represented the 5 wounds, while the 3 stigmas were allied with the nails used to pierce the hands and feet; and the vine's tendrils were equated with the whips. >

Passionfruit seem to bring on nostalgic longings. The memory of eating fresh passionfruit – warm sweet pulp, a summer's afternoon and probably a sunburnt nose – transports me straight back to being 10 years old and living in a seaside town. Maybe it is selective memory, but my adolescent recollections of a carbonated drink that managed to capture the refreshing acidity and perfume of this fruit are of something altogether more wonderful than the drink I can still buy. (I have heard that Mr Cottee bequeathed the brand Passiona to the Wesleyan Mission, so that the proceeds could be used to further the cause!) That long-time favourite, pavlova filled with unsweetened whipped cream and smothered with passionfruit, is still one of the best desserts in the world and the most-requested birthday treat in many Australian families.

passionfruit
go
with
tropical fruit
bananas
cream
ice-cream
yoghurt
orange juice
rum
nashi fruit

VARIETIES AND SEASON

In hotter climates a passionfruit vine may produce lightly all year, with peak crops in late summer and late winter. In southern and south-eastern Australia one expects one main crop from summer through to early autumn. Of the many species of *Passiflora*, only a handful bearing good fruit are available here.

BANANA | *P. mollissima* is a vigorous, untidy vine that crops heavily. The long yellow fruit has more pulp than common passionfruit but lacks the intensity and acid sweetness.

COMMON | *P. edulis* is a handsome evergreen vine and its fruit has deep-purple skin. The cultivar grown almost exclusively in southern and south-eastern Australia is Nellie Kelly. The fruit has deep-orange pulp with masses of small, softish black seeds, which are usually enjoyed along with the pulp.

YELLOW | Occasionally one can buy a yellow-skinned passionfruit (*P. edulis* var. *flavicarpa*) that is slightly larger and less wrinkled in appearance than the common passion-fruit. This variety grows better in tropical areas, but its pulp is not quite as perfumed as that of the common variety.

SELECTION AND STORAGE

The skin of the common passionfruit is hard and not easily damaged. Fruit is often left on the vine until it drops to the ground. In hot climates par-ticularly it should be gathered without delay as it can burn in the sun. The best passionfruit are slightly wrinkled. However, passionfruit that are too thin-skinned and wrinkly should be avoided as they will probably be slightly fermented and definitely past their prime. Fruit with an unyielding, hard shell will be inedibly sour. Passionfruit do not ripen after picking.

Passionfruit store well for at least a week at room temperature and for weeks under refrigeration. If you have a prolific garden vine and are overwhelmed with ripe fruit, passionfruit can be frozen whole. Or you can mix 2 parts pulp to 1 part sugar (the sugar prevents the pulp breaking down) and freeze it in small containers (an ice-cube tray is good).

PREPARATION

The most immediate way of enjoying passionfruit is to cut or tear off a portion of skin and squeeze the fruit directly into one's mouth. The same pleasure can be achieved more elegantly by halving the fruit and offering it with a sharp teaspoon and a bowl of castor sugar. Use a serrated knife to cut the fruit – the teeth provide grip on the sometimes tough skin.

Passionfruit is an intensely flavoured fruit, so a little goes a very long way. Its acidity brings out the flavour of other fruit in the same way that lemon juice does. The pulp of just a few fruit will flavour a large fruit salad.

Recipes for ice-cream, creams and custards often require *passionfruit juice*. As passionfruit juice is too acidic to be cooked with milk or cream, it should be added once the custard has cooled to avoid any danger of curdling. It takes a great number of passionfruit to obtain a small amount of strained pure juice. One passionfruit will yield about 2 tablespoons pulp and juice. Sieved, the pulp will yield slightly less than half its volume of pure juice. More simply, 10 passionfruit will yield about ½ cup strained juice. Where a lot of passionfruit juice is required, the juice can be diluted with an equal quantity (or sometimes more) of orange juice. The passionfruit flavour will still dominate.

TO COLLECT PASSIONFRUIT JUICE

Small quantities Scoop the pulp into a coarse strainer set over a bowl, then force the pulp and seeds against the mesh using the back of a spoon. If other liquid is required in the recipe (water or liqueur, for example), add it to the strainer to assist separating the juice from the jellied pulp. (Remember to take any liquid added into account when measuring the juice.) In a recipe where sugar is required, I often mix a little of the sugar vigorously with the pulp before pushing it through the strainer. The sugar is very effective in separating the juice from the rest. The amount of sugar taken from the recipe is not of great consequence. **Larger quantities** Scoop the pulp into an electric juice extractor and collect the pure intense juice. I often open the machine after the first extraction and collect the seeds and put them through again, adding sufficient orange juice to match the volume of passionfruit juice already collected.

recipes

passionfruit curd

MAKES 1 CUP

This mixture can be used to fill small tartlets, scones or a sponge cake.

½ cup sugar
60 g butter
2 eggs, well beaten
pulp of 6 passionfruit

Stir sugar and butter in a small saucepan over moderate heat until butter has melted and sugar has dissolved. Add egg and passionfruit pulp and stir continuously over a lower heat until mixture thickens. Pour into a hot, sterilised jar and store for up to 2 weeks until needed.

passionfruit shortbread biscuits

MAKES 40–50

These biscuits store well and taste better if freshly iced. Ice only the number you need and keep the rest in an airtight biscuit tin.

180 g softened butter
1 teaspoon finely grated
   lemon zest
100 g pure icing sugar
pulp of 3 passionfruit
100 g cornflour, sifted
180 g self-raising flour, sifted
ICING
50 g butter
1 cup pure icing sugar
pulp of 2 passionfruit

Preheat oven to 220°C. Briefly cream butter, zest and icing sugar in a food processor (be careful not to overprocess). Mix in passionfruit pulp, cornflour and flour. Scrape mixture into a bowl and chill for 20 minutes. Pipe rounds or fingers onto baking trays lined with baking paper and bake until golden brown, 5–8 minutes. Cool on a wire rack before icing.

To make the icing, melt butter. Place icing sugar in a small bowl. Add passionfruit pulp to melted butter and stir into icing sugar. Beat hard for 1–2 minutes over hot water until icing is really shiny. Dip each biscuit into icing, or else spoon icing over biscuits on wire rack with paper beneath to catch any drips. Allow to set.

passionfruit bavarois

SERVES 6

vegetable oil
3 gelatine leaves
200 ml milk
125 g castor sugar
4 egg yolks, lightly beaten
60 ml strained passionfruit juice
30 ml passionfruit pulp
1 cup cream, softly whipped

Lightly brush 6 × 150 ml moulds with oil. Soak gelatine leaves in cold water until softened. Warm milk and sugar until sugar has dissolved. Pour warm milk mixture into egg yolks and return to moderate heat in rinsed-out pan. Cook, stirring, until mixture coats back of a spoon. Strain into bowl of an electric mixer. Squeeze softened gelatine

passionfruit salad
Toss sliced banana and chunks of custard apple and papaya with passionfruit for a luxurious tropical breakfast.

passionfruit honey yoghurt
Mix the pulp of 2–3 passionfruit with icing sugar to taste and combine it with equal quantities of best-quality honey yoghurt and whipped cream. (Both Meredith Dairy and Mt Emu Creek make sensational yoghurt flavoured with wild honey.) Pile into pretty glasses and serve with a biscuit.

leaves and drop into mixer bowl. Stir until dissolved (maybe 1 minute). Beat mixture until quite cold. Add passionfruit juice and pulp and gently fold in cream. Pour into prepared moulds and refrigerate until set. Turn out to serve and spoon a little freshly scooped pulp over the top or place a halved passionfruit alongside, if desired.

banana passion

Slice a banana and top with passionfruit for a delicious dessert. Add a scoop of vanilla ice-cream and some cream for a luscious sundae.

pavlova

Pile a Pavlova (see EGGS) with unsweetened whipped cream and top with lots of passionfruit just before serving.

passionfruit sorbet

SERVES 8

10 passionfruit
1 cup strained fresh orange juice
200 ml light Sugar Syrup
50 g pure icing sugar

Halve passionfruit, then scoop out pulp, place shells on a tray and freeze. Push pulp through a fine-meshed sieve to extract ½ cup juice (or use a juice extractor and add orange juice to seeds for a second extraction). Combine juices with sugar syrup and stir in icing sugar until quite smooth. Churn in an ice-cream machine according to manufacturer's instructions. Freeze until required.

elena's passionfruit semifreddo

SERVES 8

8 egg yolks
1 cup sugar
½ cup strained passionfruit juice
2 cups cream, lightly whipped
30 ml passionfruit pulp
extra 5 passionfruit

In an electric mixer, whip egg yolks until light and creamy. Dissolve sugar in passionfruit juice over moderate heat and simmer for 2–3 minutes, stirring. Pour hot syrup onto egg yolks in a slow, steady stream, then beat mixture until cool. Carefully but thoroughly fold in cream and passionfruit pulp. Pour into 8 × 150 ml moulds and freeze for at least 5 hours until hard. Dip moulds into hot water for 30 seconds and turn out carefully onto plates. Serve with fresh passionfruit spooned over.

pasta and noodles

Popular folklore has it that Marco Polo brought the secrets of pasta back to Italy from China. In fact, there is plenty of evidence that both the Chinese and the Italians were familiar with pasta and noodles long before his time. Some Italian historians claim that the Etruscans made pasta, which puts them well ahead of the Chinese, who, it is thought, began preparing noodles in the first century AD. Whatever the case, pasta and noodles are essentially the same ingredient, many examples employing similar components and techniques in their production. It is their provenance that has determined from what grain or pulse each is prepared and how each is served. This similarity makes overlap possible, as witnessed today in the increasing use of Asian-style sauces and ingredients with pasta; on more than one occasion I have also tossed Chinese egg noodles with tomato, olive oil and basil. >

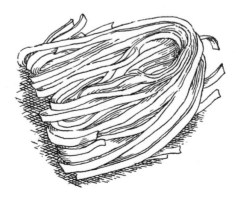

pasta

goes

with

olive oil

butter

garlic

pepper

parmesan cheese

parsley

tomatoes

capers

anchovies

sweet peppers

ham

bacon

basil

pine nuts

mushrooms

chillies

fennel

mussels

Here in Australia we can experience pasta and noodles prepared by Asian Australians and Italian Australians in their homes and restaurants, and increasingly we cook both for ourselves. Thanks to our Italian immigrants the shops are full of dried pasta (*pasta secca*) with or without eggs, both locally made and imported, and in many towns we now have shops selling fresh pasta (*pasta fresca*), which cooks in just a few minutes. Asian food stores have a huge range of fresh egg and rice noodles as well as dried noodles of every shape and type, and today it is an unusual supermarket that doesn't at least stock dried egg noodles, even in regional areas.

As with so much food, pasta and noodles display regional characteristics. The shape, texture, basic ingredients and how each is prepared and served depends on locally grown ingredients and local preferences. Soft wheat, durum wheat, buckwheat, rice, soya beans and mung beans are all used to make types of pasta and noodles.

While in Italy pasta is usually eaten as a precursor to the main meal, and then with only just enough sauce to cling to it, in Asia noodles are enjoyed for breakfast, lunch and dinner and as a snack right through the day. Each Asian country seasons and serves its noodles quite differently and the choice is enormous. My home town of Melbourne has many fine Italian restaurants and my favourite pasta dishes come from different establishments: I have ravioli filled with pumpkin and flavoured with crushed amaretti biscuits at Marchetti's Latin, tagliatelle with butter and rocket at Cafe Di Stasio, and vermicelli with bottarga (dried pressed mullet roe) at Caffe Grossi. I find it difficult to choose between the rice-noodle dish *kway teow*, a bowl of laksa with thin rice noodles or fried mee goreng with egg noodles from the nearby Penang Coffee House, and a good won ton soup is the dish I must have when I am feeling that I may have overdone things a bit.

VARIETIES AND SEASON

PASTA Italians have invented more than 300 different pasta shapes. Some shapes are only sold *dried* (tubular varieties), others are sold both dried and *fresh* (linguine, tagliatelle, fettuccine, lasagne). Commercially produced pasta is mixed and kneaded by machine and the paste is shaped or extruded by huge metal rollers. If the rollers are stainless steel or Teflon, the pasta will have a smooth finish. If the rollers are bronze, the pasta will be more textured and will look duller. Bronze-extruded pasta is considered superior, as the rougher texture enables more sauce to cling to each piece of pasta. Home-made pasta requires a machine that clamps to the kitchen bench. The dough can be made in a food processor.

Durum wheat, which grinds down into semolina, is the grain preferred in the south of Italy and is particularly suited to dried pasta, which requires longer cooking. In the north of Italy it is traditional to make pasta such as fettuccine, tagliatelle and linguine with softer wheat flours mixed with egg. This produces a faster-cooking pasta. Australian dried pasta is excellent due to the quality of the durum wheat grown in north-western New South Wales and on the Darling Downs, Queensland. In 1996 Australia sold 12 million tonnes of durum wheat to Italy.

NOODLES Asian noodles are initially described by the type of grain used to make them: wheat, rice, mung beans and buckwheat. **Wheat** *Yellow egg noodles* of varying thicknesses are sold fresh (as are squares of dough for stuffing) and are found in the refrigerated cabinets in Asian food stores. They are also sold dried in most supermarkets. *Somen* is a Japanese variety of very fine wheatflour noodle made from a hard-wheat dough slightly moistened with oil. It sometimes has egg yolk added and can be flavoured with green tea. It is hard to find other than in Japanese food stores. *Udon* is another Japanese wheat-flour noodle. It is thick and white and can be round or flat. It is also difficult to find other than in Japanese food stores. **Rice** *Rice vermicelli* are sold in various widths and are dried. They look like a skein of white wire. *Soft rice noodles* or river rice noodles are made from a paste of water and ground rice that is steamed and cut into strips. These noodles are sold fresh, either already cut or ready to be cut to whatever size the cook fancies. *Rice-stick noodles* are made from rice and tapioca flours and are sold dried. **Mung bean** Known variously as *cellophane, bean thread* and *glass noodles*, these fine noodles are extremely tough when dried and are very difficult to break. For this reason they are sold in small bundles. Interestingly, cellophane noodles are known as 'harusame' in Japan, which means 'spring rain'. **Buckwheat** Buckwheat noodles are known as *soba noodles* in Japan. They are thin and brownish grey. There is a special variety that is flavoured with green tea. Buckwheat noodles are eaten mostly in northern Japan, whereas udon and other wheat noodles are more typical of the southern part of the country.

noodles go with
soy sauce
spring onions
garlic
ginger
pork
mushrooms
seafood
chillies
poultry
rice vinegar
bean sprouts
coriander

SELECTION AND STORAGE

PASTA There are no hard-and-fast rules for selecting one pasta rather than another. It is generally agreed that thick chunky sauces are best with angular, tubular or twists of pasta, and that creamy sauces or simple oil and herb dressings are best with long strands. But experiment, and if all you have in the cupboard is spaghetti then use spaghetti!

Pasta for *soup* includes the smaller shapes, twists and circles, with names such as pastini and risone. Pasta for *saucing* includes all the long pastas, such as spaghetti and fettuccine, as well as the ribbed, angular and tubular pastas, such as rigatoni, penne and fusilli. Pasta for *baking* includes flat sheets for lasagne and cannelloni, and other shapes, such as macaroni. (Macaroni is often also used as a pasta for saucing.) Pasta for *stuffing* includes ravioli, tortellini, agnolotti and other pouches and pockets.

Buy good-quality pasta. The best dried pasta is made from durum wheat and remains firm and al dente when cooked for the correct time. Poor-quality dried pasta, and any pasta cooked in insufficient water, will become soft, flabby and sticky. As a main dish allow about 150 g fresh pasta or 100 g dried pasta per person.

The grated cheese you serve with your pasta must be of good quality, too, and have been grated recently. (Remember, though, that pasta with a seafood sauce does not need cheese.) Patronise a fresh food market or an Italian grocer and buy cheese in small quantities. Best of all is a piece of Parmigiana-Reggiano, Italy's finest parmesan cheese. Pecorino is another excellent, hard grating cheese for pasta.

There seems little sense to me in making fresh pasta and then freezing it. It is far better to enjoy fresh pasta on the day you have made it. Fresh pasta will, however, keep refrigerated for 3–4 days, covered with a sheet of foil. Dried pasta will keep indefinitely in a cool, dry place.

NOODLES

Asian noodles are also categorised as being for soup, saucing or stuffing. And, of course, noodles are also for stir-frying. Some types are used in more ways than one. In general, fresh noodles should be used as soon as possible, though some can be stored longer than others. All dried noodles will keep indefinitely in a cool, dry place.

Yellow egg noodles are cooked and then used in soup or stir-fries. Fresh egg noodles should be stored in the refrigerator and used within 3 days. *Somen* and *udon* noodles are cooked and then eaten in soup or enjoyed plain with a dipping sauce on the side. *Rice vermicelli* are eaten in soup or fried into crispy cakes (which are mixed with meat, fish and seasonings), are steamed and seasoned (maybe with oil, spring onions, fried onions and roasted peanuts) or are served cold and mixed with other ingredients as a salad. For use in soup or for stir-frying, the rice vermicelli need to be soaked and cooked first. Vermicelli can also be deep-fried without any initial cooking to create a crispy garnish. *Soft rice noodles* are used in soup or stir-fries and are also folded around savoury fillings to be dipped into sweet and hot sauces. For use in soup, the rice noodles are first dipped into hot water for 10 seconds just to heat them. These noodles do not refrigerate well as they become hard and can stick together. It is best to keep the packet at room temperature and use the noodles the same day you purchase them. *Rice-stick noodles* are used in soup and stir-fries. The noodles need to be soaked before they can be cut. They then need to be cooked for no more than a minute in boiling water. *Cellophane noodles* need to be soaked before use, when they become translucent. They can then be dropped into soup, cut and mixed into stuffings or stir-fried. They can also be deep-fried straight from the packet, when they will puff up and become very crisp. *Buckwheat noodles* are cooked and dropped into soup or are eaten cold with a dipping sauce.

PREPARATION AND COOKING

Preparing to cook pasta is simple and quick. Your sauce, or the ingredients you plan to toss through the pasta, should be ready and your serving bowls very hot by the time the pasta is cooked.

TO COOK PASTA You need a pot capable of holding at least 8 litres water to cook pasta. There should be 1 litre water for each portion of pasta and 1 litre for the pot, and the water should boil fast while the pasta is cooking. Add salt to the boiling water at the rate of 1 tablespoon per 4 litres water. Some cooks add a little olive oil; I do myself when cooking lasagne sheets, which seem to want to stick together. I tend not to when cooking other pasta. *Fresh* pasta cooks very quickly – only 2–3 minutes. *Dried* pasta can take 5–12 minutes, depending on its shape and thickness. Al dente ('to the tooth') pasta should feel firm, not soft, and not have a hard or chalky centre. Drain the cooked pasta in an enamelled colander sitting in the sink. Do not rinse it – the precious sauce-catching starch will disappear down the sink. Keep back a few tablespoons of the cooking water to thin down a too-thick sauce, such as pesto.

TO COOK NOODLES **Egg noodles** Rinse dried egg noodles in cold water to rid them of excess starch, then boil for 4 minutes in plenty of salted water until tender. Drain, rinse well in cold water and drain once again. **Somen, udon and buckwheat noodles** Bring plenty of unsalted water to a boil in a large pot. Add noodles gradually and stir slowly to prevent the noodles sticking as the water returns to a boil. Add 1 cup cold water and stir. As the water returns to a boil, add a further cup of cold water. (This process encourages the noodles to throw off excess starch.) Repeat twice more. Cook until tender. Drain the noodles in a colander, rinse them under cold running water and drain again. To reheat, place a portion of noodles in a wire basket and dip it into boiling water for an instant. Shake the basket to separate the noodles and then drop them into a heated bowl. **Rice vermicelli and rice-stick noodles** Soak the noodles in warm water for 15 minutes, then drain. Bring plenty of unsalted water to a boil and lower in the noodles in a wire basket. Stir with chopsticks or shake to separate the noodles. Remove rice vermicelli after 2 minutes, then rinse well with cold water and drain. Remove rice-stick noodles as soon as the water returns to a boil, then rinse under cold water and drain. **Cellophane noodles** Soak cellophane noodles for 15 minutes in warm water, then cut them to the length you want. Bring plenty of unsalted water to a rolling boil and cook the noodles for 15 minutes until tender. Rinse under cold water and drain.

recipes

pasta and ...
Drain pasta and quickly add olive oil and garlic to the hot cooking pot, then tip the pasta back in and toss with a big handful of freshly chopped herbs. Next time add a slosh of Fresh Tomato Sauce (see TOMATOES), cooked mussels and fish, olives and capers, or a medley of hot steamed vegetables.

garlic pasta sauce
Toss a sliced garlic clove, the best quality parmesan cheese, rocket leaves or garden-fresh parsley and good extra-virgin olive oil with hot pasta for one of the best of all pasta dishes.

home-made pasta

SERVES 4

Making fresh pasta is enjoyable and fast. You will need an Italian pasta machine that clamps to the table. These inexpensive clever machines knead, roll and cut the dough. The pasta machine should never be washed or the rollers may lose their super-smoothness. Simply brush away all flour and any dough that has stuck to the rollers.

As egg sizes vary and some flours are more absorbent than others, you may need to hold back a little of the egg when making the original dough. If it seems that you may have added too much egg, you must knead in a little more flour, either in the food processor or on your workbench. If at any time the dough feels sticky, dust it with a little flour and smooth the flour over the dough with the palm of your hand.

400 g plain flour
3 teaspoons salt
4 eggs, lightly beaten

Combine flour and salt in a food processor. With motor running add eggs. Process for a few minutes until dough clings together and feels springy (it should not feel sticky).
Tip dough onto workbench, knead it for a few minutes, then wrap it in plastic film and let it rest for 1 hour at room temperature.

Clear a large space on your workbench and have a bowl of plain flour near by. All surfaces must be quite dry. Have a pot of water on and boiling, if serving pasta immediately. Divide dough in half. Press each piece into a rectangle about 8 cm wide. Pass this piece of dough through rollers on pasta machine set to widest setting. If dough comes through raggy at edges, fold it in 3, then turn it 90 degrees and roll it through again. Change to next widest setting and pass dough through 3–4 times. Continue in this manner until dough has passed through thinnest setting. If dough gets too long to handle comfortably, cut into 2–3 pieces, then pass each piece over cutting rollers, if not making lasagne, ravioli or other filled pasta. You have a choice of 2 widths, linguine or fettuccine.

Lay cut pasta on a flour-dusted bench or clean tea towel and roll and cut remaining dough. Use as soon as possible, or hang over a length of dowelling or the back of a chair to dry. It will take 10 minutes or so for the pasta to dry in a well-ventilated room.

lasagne If you are making lasagne, your pasta sheets do not need cutting other than to be trimmed to a size suitable for lining a baking dish (don't make them too big or they won't fit in the saucepan). Don't forget that lasagne sheets will swell in size after their initial cooking. Cook the pasta a few sheets at a time in plenty of salted water for 2–3 minutes. Float the cooked sheets in a large bowl of cold water with a spoonful of oil added to prevent them sticking together. Before assembling, drain the pasta, well spaced, on a clean dry tea towel. **flavoured pasta** Cooked spinach, beetroot or pumpkin and so on can be added to the dough. The vegetable purée must be very dry. Remove 1 egg white from the basic mixture and add the purée to the flour and salt before the egg is worked in. **filled pasta** To make ravioli, place half a sheet of pasta dough rolled to the thinnest setting of the pasta machine over a ravioli tray, leaving the rest hanging off the end. Brush the surface with egg white. Pipe the chosen filling into the indentations, or spoon it in if it is a non-pipeable meat mixture, then fold the dough over the filling. Press the edges firmly between each little bump before cutting with a ravioli cutting-wheel. Refer to specialist Italian books for instructions on making tortellini, tortelloni, agnolotti, and so on. Essentially you want to enclose the filling tightly, so as not to have too much empty space nor too thick an edge of dough to avoid uneven cooking. Make up a new shape yourself! Unless ravioli and other filled pasta are to be cooked within an hour it is best to snap-freeze them on a tray lined with baking paper, so that they do not become sticky. Transfer the frozen pasta to a freezer bag for storage. Frozen ravioli can be dropped directly into rapidly boiling water and should be ready in about 5 minutes.

lasagne

SERVES 6

olive oil

4 cooked home-made lasagne
   sheets

I quantity Bolognese Sauce
   (see p. 512)

freshly grated parmesan
   cheese

BÉCHAMEL SAUCE

600 ml milk

60 g butter

60 g flour

salt

white pepper

freshly grated nutmeg

To make the béchamel sauce, heat milk to scalding point and set aside. Melt butter in another saucepan and stir in flour. Cook, stirring, until you have a smooth golden paste (known as a *roux*). Gradually work in hot milk and stir until sauce thickens and is very smooth. Continue stirring until sauce boils. Cook a further 10 minutes with pan on a simmer mat over a gentle heat. Season to taste.

Preheat oven to 180°C. Oil an oval or oblong baking dish and line with a sheet of pasta. Cover pasta with a quarter of the béchamel, then cover this with a third of the bolognese. Add a second layer of pasta, another portion of béchamel, more bolognese and then a third sheet of

pasta and sage
Stir butter- or oil-crisped sage leaves into just-cooked pasta and offer freshly grated parmesan and a pepper mill.

leftovers lasagne
Layer lasagne sheets with sautéd vegetables, béchamel sauce and chopped leftovers from last night's beef or lamb roast or stew. Top with grated cheese and bake at 180°C until bubbling and golden.

pasta. Cover with the last of the béchamel, the last of the bolognese and the remaining pasta sheet. Top with the grated parmesan and drizzle with oil. Bake until bubbling and golden, about 45 minutes.

cheese sauce By adding ½ cup grated mozzarella and 2 tablespoons freshly grated parmesan cheese to the béchamel you have made a simple cheese sauce. **vegetarian lasagne** Use fried eggplant and mushrooms instead of bolognese.

bolognese sauce

SERVES 6

This is one version – there must be thousands!

1 onion, finely chopped
1 stick celery, finely sliced
2 cloves garlic, finely chopped
2 tablespoons olive oil
400 g minced beef *or* veal
100 g pancetta or smoked
    streaky bacon, cut into small
    pieces
2 teaspoons plain flour
½ cup dry white wine
salt
freshly ground black pepper
freshly grated nutmeg
2 cups Veal *or* Chicken Stock
    or tomato juice
4 ripe tomatoes, peeled,
    seeded and chopped *or*
    1 × 375 g can peeled
    tomatoes and juice, puréed
2 tablespoons tomato paste
1 large sprig thyme
1 bay leaf

Sauté onion, celery and garlic in oil in a large saucepan until softened. Add minced meat and pancetta and fry until meat breaks up into small lumps. Sprinkle in flour, then stir well. Add wine, salt, pepper and nutmeg. Mix well, then increase heat and boil to evaporate liquid. Add stock, tomato, tomato paste and herbs. Reduce heat again and simmer for 1 hour, stirring from time to time. Taste for seasoning.

pumpkin and amaretto filling for ravioli SERVES 4

This unusual combination of sweet, savoury and perfumed has always seemed very medieval to me. The pasta is sauced with browned butter in which one has crisped fresh sage leaves. Mustard fruit are sold as mostarda di Cremona *in Italian food shops.*

creamy fettuccine
Toss cooked fettuccine with hot cream, grated lemon zest, pepper and parmesan cheese (and maybe sautéd sliced mushrooms as well).

spaghetti with pesto
Stir Pesto (see BASIL*) through hot spaghetti (thin the pesto with a couple of spoonfuls of the pasta cooking water).*

seafood linguine
Heat pipis and chopped cooked prawns in Fresh Tomato Sauce (see TOMATOES*) with lightly fried garlic, parsley and extra-virgin olive oil and toss through hot linguine.*

500 g peeled and seeded
butternut pumpkin

50 g mustard fruit, puréed

50 g fresh breadcrumbs

2 teaspoons Amaretto di
Saronno liqueur

salt

freshly ground black pepper

freshly grated nutmeg

½ quantity Home-made Pasta
dough (see p. 510)

12 fresh sage leaves

4 tablespoons unsalted butter

best-quality parmesan cheese

Cut pumpkin into even pieces and steam until tender. Dry off in a low oven for 5 minutes. Purée pumpkin and add mustard fruit, breadcrumbs and liqueur. Season with salt, pepper and nutmeg and chill thoroughly.

Roll pasta dough to thinnest setting of pasta machine. Make ravioli with pumpkin filling and cook in plenty of salted boiling water for 6 minutes. Drain well and transfer to a heated bowl. Have ready a large bowl of cold water. Drop sage leaves and butter into a small heated frying pan and swirl until butter is foaming and leaves are crisp. Remove leaves to kitchen paper to drain and dip base of pan into cold water to stop butter cooking. Spoon butter and leaves over pasta. Serve at once, offering the parmesan at table.

autumn buckwheat noodle salad

SERVES 4

If this rather spartan (but delicious) first course does not appeal, it can be made more sumptuous by adding freshly picked crab meat or thinly sliced chicken breast. Fresh bean curd can also be added.

2 tablespoons light soy sauce

4 tablespoons red rice vinegar

1 tablespoon sesame oil

1 tablespoon mirin *or* dry
sherry

½ teaspoon finely chopped
ginger

½ teaspoon finely chopped
garlic

¼ teaspoon finely chopped
fresh chilli

225 g buckwheat noodles,
cooked

2 tablespoons finely chopped
spring onion

Mix all ingredients other than cold noodles and spring onion in a bowl. Drop in noodles and toss thoroughly. Divide between plates and scatter with spring onion.

spaghetti with bacon and pine nuts
Sauté snips of bacon or pancetta and toss through hot spaghetti with toasted pine nuts, olive oil, garlic and parsley.

quick vietnamese pho
Drop boiled rice vermicelli, rice-stick or yellow egg noodles into a heated bowl. Add sliced cooked pork, chicken or seafood and bean sprouts and slivered greens. Ladle over hot chicken stock and spice with chilli and torn Vietnamese mint leaves.

fettuccine with gorgonzola   SERVES 4

This wonderfully rich dish comes from Allegro al Dente *by Rinaldo Di Stasio, Jill Dupleix and Terry Durack.*

125 g gorgonzola cheese
½ cup milk
20 g butter
salt
freshly ground black pepper
2 tablespoons cream
500 g fettuccine
2 tablespoons freshly grated
  parmesan cheese

Combine gorgonzola, milk, butter, salt and pepper in a heavy-based frying pan over a gentle heat and cook, stirring with a wooden spoon, until thick and creamy. Add cream, then raise heat a little and cook, stirring, until sauce starts to thicken, about 5 minutes. Cook pasta in boiling salted water until al dente. Drain well and tip into a warmed serving platter with sauce and parmesan. Toss quickly and serve.

chicken noodle soup (as it should be)   SERVES 4

4 large dried shiitake
  mushrooms
½ cup shredded snowpeas
1 tablespoon vegetable oil
1 tablespoon light soy sauce
1 tablespoon rice wine
1 litre well-flavoured Chicken
  Stock
1½ cups shredded, skinless
  cooked chicken breast
1 slice leg ham, shredded
250 g egg noodles, boiled and
  drained

Soak mushrooms in warm water for 30 minutes. Discard stems and finely slice caps. Toss snowpeas in boiling water for 30 seconds, then run under cold water to stop cooking. Set aside.

Heat oil in a heavy-based saucepan large enough to hold all ingredients and sauté mushrooms for 1 minute. Add soy sauce and rice wine and stir. Add stock and bring to a boil. Drop in noodles, chicken and ham and stir gently to mix well. Drop in snowpeas and taste for seasoning. Adjust with extra drops of soy sauce, if necessary.

To serve, lift noodles out first and divide between heated bowls, then ladle in the soup.

variations Substitute or add sliced cooked pork or seafood. Alternative seasonings might include chilli and Vietnamese mint. Bean sprouts can also be added.

chicken noodle salad

Chill cooked yellow egg noodles, then toss them with 2 teaspoons sesame oil, 1 tablespoon rice vinegar, 2 tablespoons soy sauce, a sprinkle of sugar and sliced chicken breast fillet. Scatter with chopped spring onion to serve.

prawns and noodles

Stir-fry prawns with slivered fresh ginger and chopped spring onion and serve with stir-fried rice-stick noodles.

stir-fried cellophane noodles with prawns

SERVES 2

125 g cellophane noodles, soaked

3 tablespoons vegetable oil

4 shallots, thinly sliced

2 cloves garlic, thinly sliced

250 g green prawns, shelled and de-veined

1 cup Chicken Stock

1 tablespoon fish sauce

2 spring onions, finely sliced

1 tablespoon freshly shredded coriander leaves

6 slices fresh chilli

Cut noodles with scissors into pieces about 8 cm long. Heat oil in a wok and sauté shallots and garlic until just starting to colour. Add prawns and toss for 1 minute, then add noodles and stir and toss. Stir in stock and fish sauce. The noodles will absorb most of the liquid. Toss through spring onions and tip onto a serving plate. Scatter with coriander leaves and chilli.

beetroot leaves and pasta
Toss beetroot leaves stewed with a little olive oil, onion, garlic and pepper through pasta.

other recipes

black satin duck with egg noodles *see* DUCK

broccoli as a sauce for pasta *see* BROCCOLI

chinese noodle soup with pig's liver *see* LIVER

fast pasta sauce with rosemary and meat juices *see* ROSEMARY

fettuccine with bug meat and roasted tomato sauce *see* BUGS

pesto *see* BASIL

salsa verde *see* TONGUE

vermouth and rock lobster fettuccine *see* ROCK LOBSTERS

peaches and nectarines

The peach (*Prunus persica*) originated in China and was mentioned in literature there as early as 551 BC. Today in China the peach tree is considered to be the tree of life and its fruit symbols of immortality and unity. A Chinese birthday seldom passes without reference to the peach, and peach blossom is carried by Chinese brides. │ In Hong Kong several years ago for the Food and Wine Festival, I watched the skilled pastry chefs fashioning tiny 'peaches' from a flour and lard pastry. These were rubbed in coloured sugar and offered as a final taste of the evening. Some time later when we hosted two of the prize-winning chefs they were delighted by my dessert of a whole poached white peach, stained rose-pink from the skin, floating in a sauce of puréed plum alongside jade-coloured ice-cream made from green tea and garnished with a wisp of jasmine blossom. >

Peaches are one of the most delectable of all fruit and should be enjoyed as often as possible during the summer and early autumn. Some shoppers seem reluctant to buy, held back perhaps by some feeling that peaches are an unaffordable luxury or that because they are so perishable they might prove disappointing. These same shoppers seem more inclined to buy a can of processed sliced peaches, nowadays canned in natural pear juice rather than the super-sweet syrup of old. I urge everyone to try the real thing and to read on for all the simple ways fresh peaches can be enjoyed.

Peach leaves have their own fragrance and are sometimes used to flavour a custard. Peach leaf ice-cream with poached peaches sounds pretty irresistible to me. And imagine if the poached peaches were covered with fine slivers of freshly picked, still damp almond kernels, as I once heard about. I have yet to coordinate all these treats at once.

Nectarines are a variety of peach (*P. persica* var. *nectarina*), not a cross between a peach and a plum, as often supposed. The best-tasting peaches and nectarines are those ripened to full softness and picked from the tree when warmed by the sun, but these must be consumed on the spot. My Aunt Molly had a white nectarine tree of massive size and I took these nectarines for granted through all those childhood summers. It is the fortunate few who have access to a backyard tree. In peach-growing country it is common to find roadside stalls selling perfectly ripe peaches at harvest time at very reasonable prices. They are a wonderful treat, and warmed from the sun too! However, most of us are at the mercy of our greengrocers, who in turn can only buy what is sent to market. Fortunately, more growers are becoming convinced of the marketing benefits of picking fruit as ripe as possible, and for the last few years I have been very pleased with the quality and ripeness of peaches and nectarines available from my local shop.

VARIETIES AND SEASON

There are both clingstone and freestone varieties of peaches and nectarines. ('Clingstone' indicates that the flesh will cling to the stone. 'Freestone' fruit slips or twists away from the stone readily.) Similarly, there are white and yellow clingstone and freestone varieties. Modern production methods and market demand favour the yellow varieties, although most peach lovers would agree that a perfectly ripe white peach or nectarine is superior in flavour, perfume and juiciness to its yellow cousin. Having said that, it is important to note that there are hundreds of varieties (160 varieties of peach are grown in Australia, for example), with new ones appearing each season. Some of the newest yellow peaches and nectarines bred in California are very delicious.

Peaches and nectarines are not sold by variety, but each variety has its season, often only a week long. The small pointy peach you enjoy so much

**peaches
and
nectarines
go
with**
*almonds
red wine
champagne
brandy
Amaretto di
   Saronno
pure vanilla
cream
lemon
brown sugar
honey
butter
raspberries
strawberries
ginger
cloves
cinnamon
macadamias*

in early December will give way to another variety a few weeks later. If you buy a peach or nectarine that is especially delicious, return to the shop and note the name of the variety printed on its box. While you won't find them identified as such, early peach varieties include flordagold (a freestone) and desert red (a clingstone). Mid-to-late-season varieties include flordastar and June lady (clingstones), and flavorcrest, flamecrest and loring (freestones). Early-season nectarines include sunblaze and maygrande (clingstones) and sunwright (a freestone). Mid-to-late-season varieties include sundollar and fairlane (clingstones), and flavortop and fantasia (freestones).

There is an unusual variety of peach that appears briefly at the very end of the season. In France it is known as the *pêche de vigne*; my greengrocer describes this special beauty as a red peach. The fruit is deep crimson right to the stone, and the skin is a deep crimson with bluish grey background tones. It is a rarity, but should you see it buy it.

Peaches and nectarines are available November–April. New low-chill varieties planted in northern New South Wales and Queensland ripen earlier and are extending the season. In general, the early varieties do not match later varieties for flavour and size.

SELECTION AND STORAGE

I prefer freestone fruit whenever possible, but clingstone fruit can be used when a recipe calls for peeled, poached whole peaches or for pieces or a purée. It is very difficult to obtain perfect peach or nectarine halves from poached clingstone fruit.

Although some growers pick their peaches and nectarines as ripe as possible, too much fruit still comes to market green and unyielding. Fruit that is picked when ripe but firm will only keep for a week at the most at room temperature, so the risk is greater for the grower, retailer and consumer (for whom the rewards are also greater!). White peaches are more fragile than yellow peaches, which is why they are harder to find in our shops.

No retailer will allow you to squeeze every peach or nectarine in the shop. Ask him or her to select ripe fruit for you. The fruit should be highly coloured, smell fragrant and, when cradled in the hand, have some 'give'. The red blush on the skin is not in itself an indicator of ripeness, as the change in colour occurs before the fruit is mature. On the other hand, you do not want fruit with green skin. If the peaches or nectarines you have bought are not ripe, return to the shop and complain.

Do not buy peaches and nectarines that have been stored in controlled atmosphere storage. Ask your retailer! This occurs late in the season as unscrupulous wholesalers try to extend the season. These peaches are horrible, with flesh that is woolly and without juice. Sometimes this disappointing fruit has been imported. As local peaches and nectarines improve, there will be fewer imports.

Ripe but firm peaches and nectarines will soften at room temperature. They will not become sweeter, however, as once picked the sugar content cannot increase. Eat the fruit once fully softened, or refrigerate it for a day or two in a ventilated plastic bag or a paper bag. Do not store peaches or nectarines sitting on top of one another, as this encourages bruising.

PREPARATION

A perfectly ripe peach or nectarine deserves to be eaten just as it is, maybe leaning over the kitchen sink to avoid the rush of juice. Nectarines are more difficult to peel than peaches but as their skins do not have the downy character of the peach I usually leave them intact. Freestone peaches peel more easily than clingstone fruit. Choose clingstone peaches if you require peeled, cooked peaches.

TO PEEL FREESTONE PEACHES Run a knife down the natural groove of each peach to the stone. Pour over boiling water and leave for a minute. Transfer the peach to a bowl of cold water, using a large spoon or lifter that will not damage the fruit. The skin should peel readily. Twist the halves away from the stone, if desired, and serve or slice. If peeled fruit has to wait for any length of time, brush it with lemon juice.

peach or nectarine chutney

MAKES 1.5–2 KG

Should you own a peach tree or ever have too many peaches, this is a delicious chutney.

1.5 kg peaches or nectarines, peeled
1.5 kg brown sugar
2 teaspoons ground ginger
1 stick cinnamon
½ teaspoon ground cloves
2 teaspoons salt
2 fresh red chillies, seeded and finely chopped
3 cups cider vinegar
2 apples, unpeeled and grated
3 onions, finely chopped

Cut peaches into thick slices or chunks. Put all ingredients into a heavy-based stockpot and stir over heat until sugar has dissolved and chutney has come to boiling point. Boil steadily for 1 hour until chutney is thick. Remove cinnamon stick before bottling into clean, dry, sterilised jars. Seal and store in a cool place away from sunlight.

spiced peaches
Top poached peach or nectarine halves with a tiny sprinkle of cayenne pepper, a clove, a fragment of cinnamon stick, butter and brown sugar and grill until bubbling. Serve with a grilled duck breast or pork chop.

peach leaf ratafia

MAKES 2 LITRES

Also for those who have their own peach tree. This style of apéritif is very common in the south-west of France, where it is served in a small glass or over ice. It can also be made with grated quinces or sliced oranges.

grilled peaches
Top poached peach or nectarine halves with butter and brown sugar and grill until bubbling.

120 peach leaves, washed and dried
1 stick cinnamon
4 cloves
2 bottles white wine
200 g sugar
1 cup vodka, eau de vie or brandy

Place leaves in a stainless steel, glass or glazed earthenware container. Add spices and wine. Stir to mix, then cover to stop insects or dust falling in and leave for 4 days. Strain, then add sugar and vodka, stirring to dissolve. Leave for 7 days, then bottle.

peaches and . . .
Serve poached peaches with vanilla ice-cream and a spoonful of chopped preserved ginger and some of its syrup; a spoonful of sweetened, strained Raspberry Sauce (see BERRIES AND CURRANTS*); whipped cream tinted deep pink with a raspberry purée; or a slosh of kirsch added to the syrup, through which some raspberry purée has been swirled.*

poached peaches or nectarines

SERVES 4–6

If the cooking of the fruit has been carefully judged and the flavour of the syrup is wonderful, poached fruit is an exquisite dessert. It deserves a better reputation. The skins give the poaching syrup its sunset colour, and the cooking makes the fruit easy to peel. It is better to poach several small batches rather than have an enormous quantity of syrup. The flavour and colour of the syrup will be much improved by successive poachings.

1 litre light Sugar Syrup
1 strip lemon zest or 1 vanilla bean, split
6–8 peaches or nectarines, washed
liqueur (optional)

Bring sugar syrup and zest to simmering point. Lightly score fruit along natural groove and lower into syrup in batches. The syrup should cover the fruit. Return to simmering point, then lower heat, so that fruit poaches rather than boils. Test fruit after 5 minutes with a fine skewer. It should be under rather than overcooked, as it may cook further in cooling syrup. Lift out with a slotted spoon onto a tray. Repeat until all fruit is poached. Increase heat and boil syrup rapidly to reduce by a third to half, depending on its flavour, then cool. Remove zest.

Skin fruit and place in a serving bowl and pour over syrup. A little liqueur can be added to the syrup at this stage – Amaretto di Saronno, kirsch or Cognac, or a fortified wine such as vermouth, tokay or port.

red-wine poaching syrup Dissolve 1 cup sugar in 1 cup fruity red wine and 600 ml water and poach the fruit as described above. Sliced raw peaches and hulled strawberries are a lovely combination with some of this red-wine syrup spooned over them.

stuffed peaches or nectarines

SERVES 4

This is a very well known Italian dish. Easy and impressive.

6 peaches or nectarines, halved
150 g crumbled amaretti
  biscuits
1 egg
2 tablespoons roughly
  chopped unblanched
  almonds
2 tablespoons brown sugar
butter
1 cup fresh orange juice

Preheat oven to 180°C. Stone fruit, then gouge out a little extra flesh and chop. Mix fruit flesh with amaretti crumbs, egg, almonds and sugar and pile into cavities. Generously butter ovenproof dish just large enough to hold fruit neatly. Arrange fruit in dish and pour over juice. Bake for 30 minutes until fruit is tender but still holding its shape. Serve hot, warm or cold with the orange syrup spooned around.

peach or nectarine iced tortoni

SERVES 6

This is a very simple iced dessert that is best eaten the day it is made or, at the latest, the next day.

3 large ripe peaches or
  nectarines, poached and
  peeled
2 tablespoons lemon juice
3 egg whites
pinch of cream of tartar
⅓ cup castor sugar
350 ml cream, firmly whipped

Line a 23 cm × 8 cm × 10 cm log tin with baking paper. Cut fruit from stones and purée with lemon juice in a food processor. Beat egg whites with cream of tartar to form soft peaks. Add sugar in 2 lots, beating after each addition, until you have a shiny meringue. Fold cream into peach purée, then fold in meringue. Pour into prepared tin, then cover with foil and freeze until firm. Remove from freezer 10–15 minutes before serving. Cut into thick slices and serve with a sliced peach or nectarine alongside.

peach bavarois

SERVES 8

If you have white or yellow peaches or nectarines that have started to look bruised and will definitely not last another day it may be the moment to make a peach bavarois. Prepare it as speedily as possible, as the peaches will discolour otherwise. If you wish, you can make individual bavarois – this quantity is sufficient for 8 × 150 ml moulds.

sugared peaches
Toss sliced, peeled white peaches with castor sugar, then press plastic film over peaches to exclude as much air as possible and leave for 1 hour. Before serving, pour over sparkling wine.

marinated peaches
Sprinkle sliced, peeled peach or unpeeled nectarine generously with sugar and fortified wine or brandy and press plastic film down tightly. Allow to macerate for 1 hour and serve with tiny Italian amaretti biscuits alongside.

6–8 peaches or nectarines,
    peeled and chopped
juice of 1 lemon
6 gelatine leaves
3 tablespoons water
pure icing sugar
600 ml cream, softly whipped
vegetable oil

Purée fruit with lemon juice – you should have 2 cups purée – and force through a coarse strainer into a bowl. Soak gelatine leaves in cold water for 2 minutes. Heat the 3 tablespoons water to simmering point, then drop in squeezed gelatine leaves and swish to dissolve. Stir gelatine into purée. Add sifted icing sugar to purée until it tastes sweet enough (remember you still have to add cream). Lightly but thoroughly fold in cream and taste for sweetness. Pour into a lightly oiled 1.5 litre pudding basin and refrigerate until set. To serve, dip basin in warm water and invert onto a serving plate, or spoon bavarois directly from basin.

peach crumble
Sprinkle chopped poached peaches with Crumble Topping✎ and cook for 25 minutes at 200°C.

peaches in syrup
Combine sliced fresh or poached peaches, nectarines, plums and apricots and serve with a red-wine syrup. The wine can be a light, fruity red wine for a change of style.

peach semifreddo
Substitute ½ cup peach or nectarine purée for the passionfruit juice and pulp in Elena's Passionfruit Semifreddo (see PASSIONFRUIT*) and add ½ cup heavy Sugar Syrup✎.*

marieke's nectarine or peach tart

SERVES 6–8

Marieke Brugman cooks this and many other delicious treats for her guests at Howqua Dale Gourmet Retreat, which she owns with Sarah Stegley in Victoria's north-east near the snowfields and fabled High Plains.

1 quantity Shortcrust Pastry✎
1 egg white
4 nectarines or peeled
    peaches, thickly sliced
150 g butter
200 g castor sugar
200 g unsalted macadamias
3 eggs
75 ml Cognac or Cointreau

Preheat oven to 200°C. Line a 22 cm loose-bottomed flan tin with pastry and bake blind✎ at 200°C for 20 minutes. Remove foil, then paint base of pastry case with egg white and return to oven for a further 5 minutes. Allow to cool. Reduce oven temperature to 160°C.

Arrange fruit in cooled pastry case. Cream butter and sugar until fluffy. Pulverise 150 g of the macadamias in a food processor and add to creamed mixture. Add eggs to mixture, one at a time, beating well after each addition, then liqueur. Chop remaining nuts roughly and fold into mixture. Pour batter over fruit and bake for 1 hour until set. Turn off heat and allow tart to cool in oven. Serve warm or at room temperature with thick cream.

p e a r s   The pears we are familiar with (*Pyrus communis*) probably originated in the Caucasus, and spread across the temperate regions of Europe with the assistance of the ancient Greeks. Pears have been cultivated since ancient times but it was not until the eighteenth century that the French and Belgians developed the buttery, melting fruit we know today.   │   In Australia pears have been grown since the arrival of the First Fleet. During the gold rushes of the 1850s pear trees were planted by the diggers along creeks, and wild pear trees can still be found today in old mining districts.   │   Pears are considered one of the most elegant and sensuous fruits by chefs, capable of infinite changes of mood and flavour, and yet pears don't seem to rate highly as a daily treat alongside the apple, for example. It needs to be mentioned that truly ripe and sublime pears have a fleeting moment of perfection. As a result the crisp and durable varieties, which may have less flavour and aroma, are seen as more reliable commercially. A ripe pear literally bursts with juice; maybe there have been too many 'burst' pears in lunch bags for them to be considered trustworthy. >

pears
go
with
cinnamon
cloves
ginger
cardamom
lemons
orange juice
honey
passionfruit
blackcurrants
raspberries
wine
port
cream
butter
vanilla beans
quinces
pistachios
almonds
olive oil
salad leaves
spinach
raw ham
blue cheese
goat's cheese
parmesan cheese
duck
walnuts
pecans
watercress
chives

I wonder if canned pears could be responsible for the lack of interest in pears for dessert. These lifeless, colourless examples have little in common with the subtle flavours and deep, glowing, gold, bronze or red translucence achieved by poaching or baking pears in red wine, spiced orange juice or saffron syrup.

VARIETIES AND SEASON

Pears are available all year in Australia, with the peak supply in autumn. The big names are undoubtedly the Packham, Williams and beurre bosc. But nowadays there is also the corella pear, the brilliant red sensation, the hard-to-find doyenné du comice, the winter nelis and the blushing cocktail pears, which are known by many names. Add to this the Asian nashi pears – the yellow–green nijisseiki and the many russet-brown cultivars – and it can be seen that the Australian pear lover has plenty to choose from.

BEURRE BOSC This elongated pear has a tapering neck, greenish brown to cinnamon-brown skin and juicy flesh. A beurre bosc will take 3–8 days to ripen at room temperature and is the preferred choice for long cooking, poaching in red wine or baking with a duck as one might do with a potato. Beurre bosc pears are available March–October.

COCKTAIL This miniature variety originated and is cultivated in several Mediterranean countries. Introduced, shall we say, 'informally' by Mediterranean migrants more than 25 years ago, this tiny greeny-gold pear is very popular. It is a perfect size for pickling and can be eaten when crunchy. Cocktail pears are available in the summer.

CORELLA This pear was developed from seed imported to South Australia's Barossa Valley by German Lutheran settlers and is small and firm with noticeable lush tropical fruit flavours. The skin is green streaked with red and gold. It can be eaten hard or soft and can be stored in the refrigerator for several weeks. The fruit is harvested in February and is then ripened further in storage. Corella pears are available April–September.

DOYENNÉ DU COMICE This broad-bottomed pear has greenish yellow skin with a red blush. Its texture and flavour is unequalled, being sweet, buttery and juicy without any grittiness. Some people detect a hint of cinnamon in its flesh. This pear bruises easily and is in grave danger of being relegated to the museum. Like most of the less common varieties, it is still grown mainly in Tasmania, where pears seem to be better understood. Doyenné du comice pears are available February–May.

NASHI Not a cross between an apple and a pear but a unique species, this Asian pear (*P. pyriformis*) was originally brought to Australia by Chinese goldminers in the 1850s and has been grown commercially here since the mid-1980s. The nashi has an appealing crisp texture and is juicy. Unlike European pears, it is picked when ripe and ready to eat. There are many, many varieties, most of which are round and resemble a small apple. The yellow-skinned nijisseiki is grown extensively in Australia, along with various russet-skinned cultivars. Nashi will store well for a week in the refrigerator. Nijisseiki will keep for 3 weeks in the refrigerator. The sweeter but slightly less crisp hosui and kosui varieties can be refrigerated for 1–2 weeks. Nashi are available February–August, with the peak season February–April.

PACKHAM'S TRIUMPH This Australian variety is the result of a cross between a Williams pear and a Uvedale St Germain (or Bell) pear by Charles Henry Packham in 1896. It is still one of the principal cultivated pears grown in Australia and the best-selling variety in the world. Its skin colour is green changing to light yellow when ripening, with white juicy flesh. This pear can be quite large and is often bumpy. It is a slow-ripening pear and purchased hard and green will take 3–8 days to ripen at room temperature. Packham's triumphs are available April–December.

RED SENSATION Formerly marketed as red Williams, crimson beauty and red duchess, this pear is in fact a red-skinned Williams pear that was originally found as a 'sport' on a green Williams tree. It is maroon when harvested and the skin changes to a bright red as the pear ripens. The creamy-white flesh has a buttery texture and is very juicy, as with the standard Williams. Red sensation pears are available January–May.

WILLIAMS Also known as the duchess, Williams bon chrétien or Bartlett pear, this medium-to-large pear has green changing to light, clear yellow skin when ripe (sometimes with a red blush) and buttery flesh. It is not suitable for long storage. A bright-yellow Williams pear is almost certainly overmature. It is a quick-ripening variety, and if bought hard will soften in 1–3 days at room temperature. Williams pears are available January–April.

sautéd pears
Sauté sliced pear in butter until lightly coloured, then scatter over sugar and toss until the sugar has melted and the pears have given off a little juice. Fill crêpes or serve on top of waffles or spoon into a pie dish and finish off with Crumble Topping or Sponge Topping.

WINTER NELIS An attractive, rounded medium-sized pear, this is ideal for poaching or baking. It is sometimes known as the quail pear, presumably because of its rather 'pouty' shape. The skin changes from yellow–green to yellow–brown when ripe and is rather tough. The flesh is a rich cream and very juicy. Winter nelis pears are available during the winter months.

SELECTION AND STORAGE

Pears are unusual in that they ripen from the inside out. They develop their finest flavour if picked hard but fully mature and then stored at a cool temperature, where they will continue to ripen slowly. Cool-stored pears are sold still needing further ripening at room temperature. The time it takes for a pear to soften depends on the variety. Pears allowed to soften on the tree survive only a matter of days after picking and their flesh quickly becomes mealy. Overripe pears, or pears allowed to ripen fully on the tree, are known as 'sleepy' pears, a charming expression that aptly evokes the fuzziness of such fruit.

Select pears that are free of cuts and bruises. Not all pears change skin colour when ripe. To test for ripeness, press gently near the stem. If it gives under moderate pressure, it's ready to eat. At this stage pears should be refrigerated in a ventilated plastic bag or a paper bag and will last for a few days. Pears need oxygen circulating around them or they will start to rot from the core out. Do not store pears one on top of the other for the same reason. (Remember when pears were sold each wrapped in its own protective tissue paper?) You can hasten the ripening of pears by putting them in a brown paper bag with a banana or apple.

For cooking, choose pears (preferably beurre bosc or Packham's) that are just ripe. Overripe pears will disintegrate very quickly.

PREPARATION

Pears can be peeled or not to eat fresh. For salads I prefer pears peeled, although I leave the skin on when offering a ripe pear to enjoy with fine cheese, which is illogical and merely shows that it is fine to do as you like.

To prepare pears for use in a salad, halve, core and slice them, then brush the slices with lemon juice or toss in a few drops of olive oil to discourage the slices from browning. Sliced nashi does not brown as quickly as conventional pear does. Always use a stainless steel or silver knife to cut fruit to prevent discolouring.

To poach pears, prepare the syrup before peeling the pears. Brush whole or quartered pears with lemon juice before dunking in the simmering syrup.

pear and parmesan

Serve a ripe pear with the best parmesan cheese.

pear and melon salad

Toss cubes or slices of ripe pear with chunks of melon, olive oil or hazelnut oil and wine vinegar. Add mint leaves and finely sliced shallot or other mild onion and season with freshly ground black pepper.

pear and spinach

Toss a chopped poached pear with butter and wilted baby spinach leaves and serve with a sautéd chicken breast fillet or grilled fish fillet.

recipes

pear and walnut salad

SERVES 2

1 ripe pear
walnut oil
1 teaspoon pear *or* cider
    vinegar
freshly ground black pepper
1 witlof
1 handful special salad leaves
    (curly frisée, rocket, lamb's
    lettuce)
2 tablespoons walnut pieces
80 g Gippsland Blue cheese
2 slices walnut *or* sourdough
    bread
1 teaspoon freshly chopped
    parsley

Peel and halve pear and remove core and stem. Slice thickly into a large bowl with 2 tablespoons walnut oil and vinegar. Grind over pepper and marinate for 30 minutes.

Preheat oven to 180°C. Cut a thin slice from root end of witlof and pull away leaves. Wash witlof and salad leaves and dry carefully. Toss walnut pieces in a few drops of walnut oil and toast on a baking tray until deep gold and crunchy. Allow to cool (do not refrigerate). Using a knife dipped in hot water, cut rind from cheese, then cut cheese into fat cubes. Leave to soften at room temperature.

When ready to serve, brush bread with walnut oil and toast. Keep warm. Gently toss witlof, salad leaves, walnuts, cheese and parsley with pear and its juices. Arrange in pyramids on plates and serve with the hot toast.

pear toast
Spread multigrain toast with mustard, then add thin slices of pear and top with blue cheese. Grill, cut into quarters and serve with a salad of watercress tossed with fruity olive oil.

pear and ham pizza
Top a pizza with strips of raw ham and thinly sliced poached pear. When just about cooked, sprinkle on blue cheese and return the pizza to the oven until the cheese browns and bubbles.

poached pears

SERVES 4

Many elegant desserts start with poached pears. One of the best known is pears belle-Hélène, a recipe from Escoffier, the creator of peach Melba. The pears are poached in vanilla syrup and served with vanilla ice-cream, candied violets and a rich chocolate sauce (see CHOCOLATE*).*

1 litre light Sugar Syrup
juice of 1 lemon
4 cloves
½ stick cinnamon *or* vanilla
    bean
4 pears

In a saucepan, bring syrup to simmering point with lemon juice and spices. Peel pears, leaving stems on for assistance in handling and for their finishing effect, but cut out the hard core end. Stand pears upright in syrup, then cover with a round of baking paper nicked with scissors, so that the stems can be poked through, and cover saucepan with a lid. Simmer extremely slowly until pears are tender – this can vary from 30 minutes– 2 hours, depending on variety and ripeness of pears. (The longer pears take to poach the more delicious the end result. Some pears take on a delightful pinkish colour through long, gentle cooking.) Leave to cool in the syrup and serve at room temperature.

to vary the syrup Use half red or white wine and half water, or half orange or apple juice and water. Add fresh ginger, or a handful of frozen raspberries or blackcurrants or scented herbs, instead of the cloves and cinnamon or vanilla bean. To make a passionfruit syrup, reduce the syrup by a third by boiling it fast, then cool and add passionfruit pulp.

caramel red-wine syrup Make a deep caramel by dissolving 1 cup sugar in 1 cup water over heat. When medium-brown, stand well back and pour on 1½ cups full-bodied red wine, then stir until the lumps of caramel have dissolved. Poach the pears in this syrup until tender, then remove the pears and reduce the syrup by a third. Pour over pears in a shallow dish and turn the pears several times as the syrup cools.

marieke's saffron pears
SERVES 6

2 cups water
2 cups white wine
2 cups sugar
I vanilla bean
6 pears
½ teaspoon saffron threads
chopped pistachios

Combine water, wine, sugar and vanilla bean in a saucepan and stir over heat until sugar has dissolved. Peel pears, leaving stem but cutting away hard core end, then add with saffron to syrup. Simmer very slowly until tender, at least 1½ hours. Roll pears in syrup every 20 minutes or so, so that they are evenly coated. Allow pears to cool in syrup, turning them as syrup cools. Serve sprinkled with pistachios.

pears baked as in savoy
SERVES 4

This magnificent dessert, inspired by the Savoy region in France, is an exercise in simplicity: pears, butter, sugar, vanilla and nothing else. Open your best bottle of dessert wine with this.

butter
4 pears
8 tablespoons castor sugar
I vanilla bean, split and
  broken into pieces
2 tablespoons water
4 tablespoons thick cream

Preheat oven to 160°C. Choose an ovenproof dish in which the halved pears will fit well with no extra space. Butter dish well and peel, halve and core pears. Place pear halves in dish, hollow-side uppermost. Scatter castor sugar over (1 tablespoon per pear half), then dot with butter. Place vanilla bean pieces in dish, then pour in water. Cover dish tightly with foil and bake for at least 1½ hours. When pears are tender and smell superb, remove foil and spoon 1 teaspoon thick cream into each pear hollow. Increase oven temperature to 200°C. Return dish, uncovered, to hotter oven for 15 minutes until cream has melted and mingled with buttery juices. Allow to cool a little before serving.

---

pork and pear

Toss peeled, halved Packham's pears into the baking dish for an hour or so when roasting pork or a duck.

pear sauce

Blend a ripe pear with ½ cup walnut oil, some olive oil and enough red-wine vinegar to sharpen it, then add pepper and serve with pork sausages.

P **p e a s** The pea is one of the oldest cultivated vegetables, although for many centuries it was only eaten dried. Dried peas are still popular as the basis for one of the most comforting of all dishes – pea and ham soup – and in the north of England pease pudding (of nursery-rhyme fame), a purée of yellow split peas, is a traditional dish: *'some like it hot, some like it cold, some like it in the pot, nine days old'*. │ It was not until the late seventeenth century that fresh green peas from Italy were introduced to the court of Louis XIV. (Green peas had been known in Italy a century earlier. The exotic snowpea or *mangetout* – literally 'eat all' – developed by Dutch market gardeners had arrived in France some 60 years before this.) The fresh peas were a sensation. │ The English are loyal to their peas plainly boiled with a sprig of mint, while the French prefer theirs stewed with butter, strips of ham and maybe a few shredded lettuce leaves to form a sauce. Cooked well, both versions can be delicious. These national preferences may explain why for convenience frozen peas are preferred in England and canned soupy peas are bought in France. >

peas
go
with
ham
bacon
poultry
onions
leeks
butter
sage
ginger
green peppercorns
carrots
parsley
mint
asparagus
celery
cream
rice
eggs
crab meat
prawns

asian soupy peas
*Simmer 1 cup
shelled peas in 1 cup
light Chicken Stock
with 1 teaspoon
mirin or other rice
wine, 1 teaspoon
Japanese soy sauce
and a pinch of sugar
until just cooked.
Divide peas between
2 small bowls,
including a little of
the cooking liquid,
and add ½ teaspoon
freshly grated ginger
to each bowl.*

Frozen peas mimic the taste of freshly picked, quickly cooked green peas, but as so few members of the public seem to be interested or prepared to grow or pod fresh peas the flavour of the frozen product has become the standard. Recently in France I was served a small copper dish brimming with perfectly cooked, freshly podded green peas, each shining like an emerald pearl. Perfect English-style peas in a classically French restaurant. The peas were unadorned save for a tiny amount of butter, and they were rightly offered as a special course. I also pod peas in my own restaurant, just before lunch, and cook them to order to accompany a roasted chicken. I often wonder how many customers recognise the fresh flavour.

Fresh peas make delicate soups and custards and are included in many vegetable, pasta and grain dishes, such as Cornish pasties, Indian samosas, risottos and vegetable omelettes. Snowpeas and snap peas, immature pods that are eaten whole, are usually stir-fried. Young shoots of the pea plant are also stir-fried, often with luxury foods such as crab meat or snake!

VARIETIES AND SEASON

The 3 main types of pea are the green pea, the snowpea and the snap pea. Also known as the garden pea or common green pea, the **green pea** (*Pisum sativum*) is the pea we all know. The **snap pea** (*P. sativum* var. *sativum*) is a rounded, full-blown smaller edible pod with peas larger than the snowpea but smaller than the green pea. The **snowpea** (*P. sativum* var. *macrocarpon*), also called the *mange-tout*, sugar pea and Chinese pea, is a flattened pea with an edible pod and immature peas. Fresh peas are marketed all year, with the peak season October–December. The best green peas in the south-eastern part of the continent are picked in the spring and early summer.

Cantonese cooks also prize **pea shoots** (*dau miu*). Because pea shoots are the growing tips of the plant, the fruiting flowers of which are removed to encourage more leaf growth at the expense of the pods, they are always expensive and considered a great delicacy. Pea shoots are available only during the early growing season of the plant, in winter and early spring.

Yellow or green **dried** peas are usually sold split. They taste the same and are used to make soups and purées and are available all year.

SELECTION AND STORAGE

Peas, like sweetcorn, are rich in sugars that turn to starch a few hours after picking. In an ideal and admittedly unattainable world peas would be rushed from the plant to the pot. The advantage of eating fresh rather than frozen peas is lost if one buys shelled peas from the greengrocer, as they may have been shelled 2 days beforehand.

Green peas should be eaten as young as possible. The pods should be bright green and waxy to the touch and they may even squeak when rubbed.

They should look fullish but there should be no bulges, which indicate that the peas are overmature. Avoid any that are yellowish or split or look dry. Buy green peas to eat as a vegetable on the same day. If they are stored in the crisper they may still be pleasant after 1 day, but don't try them the next. Make pea soup instead. Dried peas can be bought at any supermarket or health food store. Check the packet for any sign of weevils and store, once opened, in an airtight container for up to a year.

The smaller the snap pea or snowpea pod the younger and more tender it will be. Refrigerate snowpeas and snap peas for a few days in a vegetable storage bag in the crisper. Pea shoots, which should be green and very fresh looking without any sign of yellowing, wilt very quickly. They should be used on the day of picking.

As a guide when buying or picking peas, 500 g green pea pods will yield approximately 200 g (or 1 cup) shelled peas, sufficient for 2 pea lovers – just! You will need 500 g snowpeas or snap peas to feed 4–6.

PREPARATION AND COOKING

TO PREPARE | **Green peas** Pod and cook green peas as close to eating as possible. When podding, discard any that are hard as marbles, and look out for small green grubs that sometimes invade even the youngest and best-looking pods. **Snowpeas and snap peas** The strings that run lengthwise on both edges of the pod must be removed. Snap off the stem end and pull the string downward on one side, then, with a small knife, release the string on the other side and pull it back. **Dried peas** Wash them well to remove any dust. Discard any discoloured peas and check for any foreign objects, such as stones. If making a purée, it is a good idea to soak dried peas overnight, as it is then easier to estimate the amount of cooking liquid required. The soaked peas will take about an hour to cook. It is not necessary to soak peas when making soup that is to be cooked for a good length of time.

TO BOIL GREEN PEAS | Bring a small amount of lightly salted water to a boil in a saucepan with a sprig of mint, if desired. Drop in the peas, then cover the pan tightly and boil for 5 minutes or until just tender. Drain well, then shake a small piece of butter into the pan and serve at once.

TO STIR-FRY SNOWPEAS | Heat a little oil in a wok and tumble and toss trimmed peas over highest heat with any aromatics (ginger, garlic) until glossy. Add a splash of liquid (stock, soy sauce or a combination), then reduce heat, cover and cook for 2 minutes.

peas in stocks
Add a few bright-green young pea pods to flavour stocks.

peas in cream
Drain buttered boiled peas and return to the saucepan, then quickly boil for 2 minutes with 1 tablespoon thick cream for each cup of peas. Add a generous amount of freshly chopped parsley (or parsley and chives or chervil), then shake and serve. A tiny amount of Dijon mustard can also be added with the cream.

recipes

petits pois – french-style green peas

SERVES 2

pea sauce

Press boiled peas through a fine sieve and adjust to a sauce consistency with a little chicken stock and a few drops of sherry vinegar or other good wine or fruit vinegar. Season carefully and serve with vegetable fritters (artichoke hearts, for example), as a hot dipping sauce for asparagus or as a sauce for sautéd lamb's brains.

2 shallots, 1 spring onion or ½ small onion, finely sliced

2 outside leaves of an iceberg or cos lettuce, finely sliced

20 g butter

500 g pea pods, shelled

4 tablespoons water

1 thin slice ham, finely chopped

salt

freshly ground black pepper

Place shallot, lettuce and butter in a saucepan, then cover and stew over gentle heat for 5 minutes to soften but not brown. Add peas, water and ham. Season lightly. Cover pan and simmer for 5–8 minutes. The peas should be tender and surrounded by a sauce that is not too liquid. Boil rapidly if it looks sloppy.

variations Omit the ham, or add a very finely diced carrot with the onion.

kitchen garden soup with tiny herb omelettes

SERVES 8

steamed pea pods

Steam freshly picked pea pods for 5 minutes and serve with a bowl of melted butter. One dips the tender pod into the butter, chews and sucks and eventually spits out the inedible fibre. Not delicate, but delicious.

1 onion, diced

3 sticks celery, chopped

2 potatoes, peeled and diced

100 g butter

1 bay leaf

1 large sprig thyme

2 litres Chicken Stock

750 g snap peas, washed and strung

salt

white pepper

1 cup shelled peas

HERB OMELETTES

40 g sourdough breadcrumbs

1 tablespoon freshly chopped parsley

1 teaspoon freshly chopped chives

1 clove garlic, finely chopped

2 eggs

3 tablespoons duck fat *or* olive oil

Sweat onion, celery and potato in butter with herbs in a large saucepan for 10 minutes. Add stock and bring to simmering point. Simmer for 10 minutes until potato is tender. Drop in snap peas and boil vigorously for 3 minutes only. Blend at once in a food processor, then strain through a coarse strainer and season. Set aside.

To make the omelettes, blend crumbs, herbs and garlic in a food processor. Add eggs and process briefly. Heat duck fat and fry teaspoonfuls of mixture until crisp and a little puffed at the edges. Drain on kitchen paper and keep warm.

Boil peas in lightly salted water until tender, then drain. Reheat soup gently. Serve with a spoonful of peas and a couple of herb omelettes as garnishes.

pea and ham soup

SERVES 8–10

Use yellow or green split peas, whichever you prefer. Make a large pot and keep it in the refrigerator. It won't last long!

400 g split peas
1 large onion, diced
2 carrots, peeled and diced
500 g bacon bones *or* 1 small
    smoked ham hock
3 litres cold water
3 cloves garlic, peeled
1 bay leaf
1 generous sprig thyme
freshly ground black pepper

Place all ingredients in a large pot and bring slowly to simmering point. Set lid of pot a little ajar and continue to simmer for about 1½ hours until peas are quite tender. Remove bones or hock. Discard bones (reserve hock). Purée soup in a food processor or blender, then adjust seasoning. If too thick, add water. If using a hock, discard skin, then dice meat and return to soup. Reheat and serve with sippets – small cubes of bread fried crisp in olive oil.

springtime pea custards

SERVES 6

This is a bit fiddly, but it makes an exquisite start to a spring dinner party. Served with a light butter sauce and maybe a handful of quickly sautéed pea shoots, one of these custards leaves you ready to move on to a weightier dish. It could be made even more luxurious by warming perfectly trimmed and blanched asparagus tips in the sauce. It is also an interesting master recipe and the custard can be made with other choice ingredients – asparagus, mushrooms or young leeks, for example.

butter
175 g young pea pods *or* snap
    peas, washed and strung
400 ml cream
1 clove garlic, peeled
1 tablespoon chervil leaves
100 ml milk
4 eggs
salt
white pepper

Preheat oven to 160°C and thoroughly grease 6 × 150 ml soufflé dishes. Trim ends off each pea pod. Simmer cream with garlic and chervil until reduced to 300 ml. Purée in a blender and set aside.

Bring a large saucepan of water to a boil. In another saucepan, heat milk to scalding. Drop pea pods into boiling water and cook for 4 minutes. Remove and immediately purée pea pods in a food processor or blender with hot milk. Press purée through a fairly coarse strainer set over a bowl. Add reduced cream mixture to bowl. Whisk eggs well and combine with cream mixture. Strain again through a finer strainer and season. Pour custard into prepared dishes, put in a baking dish lined with a tea towel and pour in boiling water to come two-thirds up sides of dishes. Bake for 30 minutes until custards are just

zucchini and pea pasta sauce
Sauté sliced zucchini in olive oil until lightly coloured, then toss in a handful of torn basil leaves and add a generous quantity of buttered peas and cream (allow 1–2 tablespoons cream for each cup of peas). Grind on pepper, toss with freshly cooked pasta and serve with best-quality parmesan cheese.

peas with sage
Crisp a handful of sage leaves in butter in a hot frying pan for 3–4 minutes, then pour, sizzling, over hot boiled peas. Delicious with a chicken breast fillet, veal scaloppine or sweet fish fillet.

set. Allow to settle for 5 minutes before turning out. Scatter around a garnish, if any, and nap with Beurre Blanc.

pea shoots with crab meat

SERVES 2

peas and basil

Add freshly chopped basil to hot, cooked peas and toss with warmed extra-virgin olive oil instead of butter.

3 cups pea shoots
1 tablespoon vegetable oil
1 tablespoon cornflour
1 cup Chicken Stock
1 cup freshly picked crab meat
1 tablespoon rice wine
1 teaspoon sesame oil
1 egg white
white pepper (optional)

Stir-fry pea shoots in oil in a hot wok for 2 minutes. Pile onto a hot serving dish. Wipe out wok. Mix cornflour with stock and tip into hot wok. Allow to thicken smoothly, stirring. Add crab meat, rice wine and sesame oil. Stir well to combine. Whisk egg white lightly to break gel. Tip into wok and stir, so that egg white sets in fine shreds. Check seasoning and pour over pea shoots. Eat at once.

other recipes

artichokes and peas with sage *see* ARTICHOKES

jamaican rice and 'peas' *see* RICE

Peppers and chillies

Columbus took the fiery chilli (*Capsicum frutescens*) to Europe from the New World and confusingly called it a pepper, thinking he had discovered a relative of the highly prized *Piper nigrum*. He also returned with *C. annuum* plants, sweet peppers or capsicums. Confusion with the names for these plants and their fruit continues. Many American cookbooks link sweet peppers and hot chillies as chillies and then describe each variety in terms of its hotness on a scale from 1 to 10. │ Common to all *Capsicum* species is the volatile oil capsaicin, which is found in the membrane and seeds of chillies and sweet peppers in varying degrees and which gives chillies especially their characteristic 'burning' quality. Some suggest that endorphins, the body's built-in painkillers, are released when a chilli-hot dish is eaten, providing a sense of relief and pleasure when the after-effects cease! >

sweet
peppers
go
with
tomatoes
eggplants
olive oil
olives
garlic
onions
capers
anchovies
sausages
chicken
fish
bread
preserved lemons

Members of the *Capsicum* genus have been used in cooking since around 6000 BC; the Mayans cultivated these plants some 5000 years later. The Spanish introduced *Capsicum* species to Europe as early as 1493; within a century they had spread from the Americas right around the world and by the eighteenth century sweet peppers were a basic ingredient in the cooking of southern Europe. Today the chilli is the most widely used seasoning in the world. Only the British were tentative with these new plants and, apart from using them in pickles, chillies and sweet peppers became mainstream in British markets only with the advent of Caribbean and Asian migration over the last few decades.

In Australia the story is similar. Our love affair with chillies and sweet peppers started with post-war southern-European migration and has continued with more recent Asian migration. Sweet peppers are a mainstay of Mediterranean cooking and it is hard to imagine a summer meal in France, Italy, Greece or Spain without peppers in some form or other.

Today cooks in the United States, especially in the South-West, and Mexico are familiar with and distinguish between an amazingly wide range of peppers and chillies unknown to Australians. There are more than 150 varieties of pepper (both sweet and hot). Mark Miller, American chef and author of *The Great Chile Book*, claims to use 20 fresh and 20 dried types in his Coyote Cafe. Our education will no doubt continue as more and more of these exotic varieties are imported dried and are being grown by chilli enthusiasts to satisfy a market ever-eager for the new.

VARIETIES AND SEASON

In our markets the term 'chilli' is reserved for those varieties that are fiery, while 'sweet peppers' refer to all those that are not. ***Sweet peppers*** are also known as capsicums, peppers, chiles, bell peppers, pimiento, pimento, *poivrons* (French) and *peperoni* (Italian). ***Chillies*** are known as chiles, chilis and hot peppers, and by the names of individual varieties, such as bird's-eye or Scotch bonnet. Identifying a particular variety of sweet pepper or chilli can be confusing, as many have different names in different localities. Some take on different names when dried. American recipes may specify ancho, poblano, habanero, fresno, jalapeño, Scotch bonnet or other chillies and peppers, each one offering different flavour nuances and heat intensity.

In our fresh food markets the Asian cooks are most knowledgeable about different types of chillies. Those interested in learning more should investigate specialist books from Mexico, the Caribbean and the American South-West, as well as any cookery book from Asia. As I write, many Mexican and South-West varieties of chillies and sweet peppers are beginning to appear in our fresh food markets and specialist food outlets. More are being imported dried, and the packaging includes comprehensive notes referring to flavour, heat and directions on how to use them. Look out for these.

CHILLIES

Chillies come fresh or dried, usually red and green, long and pointy, but sometimes purple or chocolate and tiny and/or round. Chillies are green before they ripen to red. A ripe (red) chilli has a different flavour from a green chilli, just as we recognise the difference in flavour between a green and a red sweet pepper. Their size and colour are not a reliable guide to their strength, although the smaller the chilli, the hotter it will be usually. On a scale of 1–10, the most usual type of chilli available here scores 6–8. Chillies are also available dried and chopped (referred to as 'chilli flakes' in American books), as well as dried and ground. The cayenne chilli is dried and ground to produce *cayenne pepper*, while several varieties of dried chillies are used to make *chilli powder*. Fresh and dried chillies are available all year.

SWEET PEPPERS

Sweet peppers always start life green and then change colour as they ripen. There are red, yellow, orange, brown, purple and lime-green varieties. They are sold fresh, identified by colour almost exclusively. The lime-green sweet pepper is longer and narrower than other varieties and can be quite hot (say, 4–5 on a scale of 10). Sweet peppers continue to ripen after picking, but they may also start to wrinkle. Sweet peppers are available all year, the peak period being November–March. Various sweet peppers are used to create spices now used all over the world. *Paprika* (also known as sweet paprika) is made by grinding dried sweet peppers and can be rather spicy!

**chillies
go
with**
*tomatoes
shellfish
fish
chicken
ginger
garlic
tamarind
coconut
lime juice
cumin
coriander
fish sauce
palm sugar*

SELECTION AND STORAGE

If you are unsure whether the chilli referred to in a recipe is a sweet pepper or a hot chilli (confusion may arise if using an American book) look for clues, such as the quantity that is recommended and whether it is to be cut up small or served in large strips or pieces. The greater the quantity the more likely sweet peppers are required.

Always select sweet peppers and fresh chillies that are glossy and taut-skinned without any soft spots. Any pepper that is wrinkled was picked a long time ago, as sweet peppers last very well. The red, orange and yellow sweet peppers are the sweetest.

Sweet peppers grown hydroponically have extended the season. Hydroponic fruit is grown in water rather than soil and often in greenhouses. As a result, the fruit is evenly shaped and without blemishes. However, I have found that sun-ripened sweet peppers grown in the soil are far sweeter, even if they have a bump or two. Most retailers will probably not know for certain whether the product they sell is hydroponically grown, as there is no requirement to label fruit.

Refrigerate sweet peppers for a week in the crisper. Do not store them wrapped in an ordinary plastic bag as they will sweat. Hang fresh chillies to dry if you wish – string them using a needle and thread – or leave them in the open air and use as required. Drying chillies will shrink, and their hotness will be concentrated. I freeze fresh chillies, too, in small plastic bags. They can be slit and seeded while still frozen. The flesh will be soft on thawing but will have lost none of its pungency.

PREPARATION AND COOKING

Chillies need to be treated with caution – avoid touching your face and rubbing your eyes after handling them, since the capsaicin can burn the skin for hours. It is best to wear disposable food-preparation gloves if cutting up lots of chillies. (These are readily obtainable at pharmacies.) Never cut chillies on a surface that cannot be thoroughly washed for the same reason, and wash all knives, boards and blenders before using them again. Remember that the seeds and inner membranes are hotter than the fleshy part, which is why many recipes suggest using seeded sweet peppers and chillies.

The skin of sweet peppers can be bitter and indigestible. Unless using sweet pepper raw in salads or stuffing and baking a whole pepper, it is a good idea to remove the skin. I often don't peel peppers that are to be stewed with other foods. You may find scraps of rolled-up skin in the finished stew, as the skin sheds after long cooking, but I don't find these particularly offensive. Sweet peppers are peeled using an asparagus peeler or by roasting or grilling. The former method results in a still-raw pepper ideal for long, slow stewing or for quick sautés. The latter method results in a soft, melting pepper ready to eat or combine in thousands of preparations. If the pepper has been grilled over an open flame it will have a smokier flavour than if it has been charred under a domestic griller or baked in the oven. Wipe rather than wash or soak roasted or grilled peppers to remove the last fragments of skin, as this will retain maximum flavour.

TO ROAST OR GRILL SWEET PEPPERS If using an electric griller or an oven, halve the pepper and remove the seeds and white ribs. Brush the halved pepper lightly with oil and grill on a foil-lined tray or roast in a hot oven until the skin has blackened. If using an open flame (a gas jet or barbecue), turn a whole pepper over the flame until the skin has blackened evenly. Put the pepper in a plastic bag or wrap it in a cloth for at least 10 minutes, when it will be cool enough to handle. The skin will slip off quite easily. If there are still a lot of black specks left, wash your hands and then wipe the pepper with a damp cloth. Split open the whole pepper and remove the ribs and seeds.

Use the roasted pepper as desired or store, cut into pieces, in the very best olive oil, with or without a sprig of rosemary or a few slices of garlic, where it will keep for at least a week, providing the pieces of pepper are submerged in the oil and there are no tell-tale air bubbles.

TO BAKE STUFFED SWEET PEPPERS Choose evenly shaped sweet peppers with flat bottoms. Cut off a lid and scoop out the seeds. Rinse and dry the peppers. Choose a baking dish that will hold the peppers without too much extra space. Oil the outside of the peppers and place in position. Stuff the peppers, but not too tightly as some fillings swell (especially if they include rice). Place the lids in position and pour over and around sufficient tomato juice or stock to come halfway up the peppers. Tuck a bay leaf and a large sprig of thyme into the dish, then cover with foil and bake at 180°C for 1 hour. Remove the foil and return the dish to the oven to brown the tops of the peppers.

unpeeled sweet pepper salad

SERVES 4 recipes

A quick dish for the summer lunch table.

boiling water
1 green pepper, sliced and
    seeded
1 red pepper, sliced and
    seeded
1 teaspoon coriander seeds
1 small red onion, sliced
    paper-thin
2 cloves garlic (or less if you
    prefer), sliced paper-thin
salt
freshly ground black pepper
3 tablespoons extra-virgin
    olive oil
2 teaspoons red-wine vinegar

Pour boiling water over sliced pepper and leave for 30 minutes. Drain and pat dry on kitchen paper. Crush coriander seeds in a mortar and pestle or in a folded tea towel using a heavy meat mallet or a rolling pin. Combine pepper, onion, garlic and coriander seeds, then season and dress with oil and vinegar. Toss to mix well and serve.

spicy stuffed peppers
Cook spinach, mushrooms, pumpkin and potato with mustard seeds, turmeric, cumin and garam masala and stuff sweet peppers ready for baking.

chilli in the pot
Add a whole fresh chilli to a sauce or stew for 30 minutes, then taste to see if you have added just the right amount of piquancy.

harissa

MAKES 1 CUP

This fiery paste was seemingly eaten at every meal when I visited Tunisia in 1993! When we sat down to eat, flat earthenware dishes were placed in front of us with a healthy blob of harissa ringed with the rich, buttery olive oil of the region and a basket of flat bread. I quickly discovered the pleasure of puddling the bread in just enough harissa and then allowing it to soak up some of the delicious oil. Harissa is an essential ingredient in the wonderful chickpea soup LabLabi (see CHICK PEAS), accompanies Lamb Shanks with Couscous (see LAMB) and adds excitement to dried bean salads and slow-cooked casseroles.

250 g fresh chillies, finely
chopped
1 medium head garlic
1 tablespoon ground coriander
1 tablespoon ground caraway
seeds
1 tablespoon dried mint
3 tablespoons fresh coriander
leaves
1 tablespoon salt
olive oil

Blend all ingredients in a food processor using enough oil to make a stiffish paste. Store in a jar, covered with a thin film of oil, for several months. It is very hot!

fiery sauce Dilute Harissa with a little water or Fresh Tomato Sauce (*see* TOMATOES) to make a fiery sauce for meat.

roasted peppers and ...
Serve roasted peppers with Smoky Eggplant Purée (see EGGPLANTS) or grilled goat's cheese on croutons, or pile them on a grilled chicken breast fillet.

anchovy peppers
Cut roasted red peppers into strips 2 cm wide and trim. Put anchovies end-to-end along each pepper strip, then roll up and secure with a toothpick. Drizzle with the best olive oil you have and serve with drinks.

peperonata

SERVES 4

There are many, many recipes for sweet peppers stewed with tomatoes and other vegetables. Probably the best known is Ratatouille (see ZUCCHINI AND SQUASH). This is another useful one. It can be an accompaniment – hot or cold – to grilled sausages, lamb chops, barbecued steaks or fish.

3 tablespoons extra-virgin
olive oil
1 small onion, sliced paper-
thin
2 cloves garlic, thinly sliced
1 red pepper, cut into rings or
strips and seeded
1 yellow pepper, cut into rings
or strips and seeded
3 large ripe tomatoes, peeled
and roughly chopped
freshly ground black pepper
2 teaspoons red-wine vinegar
sea salt

Heat half the oil and cook onion until it starts to brown. Add garlic and cook a minute more. Add sweet pepper, then cover and simmer for 15 minutes. Add tomato and pepper and cook, covered, for 5 minutes. Uncover, raise heat and bubble, watching mixture does not stick, until sauce is thick. Add vinegar and boil a moment longer, then season well and stir in remaining oil.

chilli To add extra piquancy, drop in a small fresh chilli for the last 15 minutes.

with eggs Spoon peperonata into an oiled gratin dish, then make hollows with the back of a spoon and slip a raw egg into each. Drizzle the eggs with olive oil and a grinding of pepper and bake until the whites are just set. Serve as a simple lunch with a green salad.

chilli and lime sauce

MAKES 1 CUP

Ideal for serving with steamed or grilled fish, this sauce is also useful as a dipping sauce for other seafood. I have adapted David Thompson's recipe, in which he includes more garlic and chilli.

1 coriander plant (including root), well washed

1 teaspoon salt

2 cloves garlic

4 fresh small green chillies, chopped

1 tablespoon castor sugar

3 tablespoons fresh lime juice

2 tablespoons fish sauce

Chop coriander leaves coarsely and set aside. In a food processor, combine coriander root, salt and garlic with chillies to make a paste. Add sugar, lime juice and fish sauce and process until sugar has dissolved.

mechouia – tunisian roasted vegetable salad

SERVES 6

Enjoy this pepper salad as a first course or a side dish with fish.

4 green peppers, roasted and peeled

4 lime-green peppers, roasted and peeled

3 cloves garlic

3 ripe tomatoes

2 tablespoons fruity extra-virgin olive oil

salt

juice of 1 lemon

1 teaspoon capers, soaked and drained

Preheat oven to 250°C. Remove seeds from peppers, then chop flesh finely. Roast garlic and tomatoes in oven for 30 minutes until garlic is soft and tomato skins have blackened. Skin tomatoes and garlic, then drain tomatoes to rid them of excess liquid. Chop tomatoes and garlic together or blend in a food processor, then combine with sweet pepper. Stir in oil and season with salt and lemon juice. Spread in a dish and scatter capers over to serve.

sweet and sour sweet peppers

SERVES 6–8

Serve these peppers as an antipasto dish or with toasted pita bread as a snack.

3 red peppers

3 yellow peppers

1 lime-green pepper

100 ml extra-virgin olive oil

3 tablespoons balsamic vinegar

2 tablespoons sugar

1 bay leaf

2 cloves garlic, finely sliced

salt

freshly ground black pepper

Cut sweet peppers along natural grooves, then remove all seeds and membrane. Peel using an asparagus or vegetable peeler and cut flesh into strips. Heat oil in a heavy-based frying pan and add all ingredients. Cook, stirring gently, for 30 minutes until soft. Taste and adjust with drops of balsamic vinegar or a little more sugar or salt. Serve warm or cold. Store for 3–4 days in a covered dish in the refrigerator.

peppers, anchovies and cheese

Mix sliced roasted peppers with anchovies and freshly chopped parsley or cubes of soft creamy cheese, such as fontina, and use as a salad, a topping for toast or to toss with pasta.

baked stuffed peppers

Bake sweet peppers stuffed with the mixture used to make Middle Eastern Meatballs with Coriander Leaves (see CORIANDER) – include raw rice, if desired – or seasoned, minced, cooked lamb or beef mixed with chutney, home-made tomato sauce or Peperonata (see p. 540).

salsa of mixed peppers

Try this on natural oysters or grilled scallops on the half-shell or scatter over steamed mussels, or anything else that takes your fancy. This quantity of salsa is sufficient for 24 oysters or scallops.

chilli oil
Place 2 small fresh chillies in a bottle of extra-virgin olive oil with some dry-roasted rosemary leaves, then seal and leave for a week or so. Drizzle on grilled fish, barbecued seafood or hot boiled potatoes.

½ cup finely diced red pepper
½ cup finely diced yellow
  pepper
1 small fresh chilli, seeded and
  finely chopped
⅓ cup red-wine vinegar or
  cider vinegar
1 handful fresh coriander
  leaves, finely chopped
2 tablespoons very finely
  chopped shallot or mild red
  onion
juice of 1 lime or ½ lemon
¼ cup extra-virgin olive oil

Mix ingredients together and allow to mellow for 30 minutes.

other recipes

chilli con carne *see* BEANS, DRIED
rock lobster oil *see* ROCK LOBSTERS
smoked tongue with red pepper sauce *see* TONGUE
thai steamed fish with coriander root, chilli and lime juice
  see CORIANDER

p i n e a p p l e s *Ananas comosus* originated in South America, and legend has it that Columbus was welcomed with the fruit when he stepped ashore at Guadeloupe, an island in the French West Indies. Lutheran missionaries introduced the plant to Australia in 1838, and it is now grown along the Queensland coast and the northern coasts of Western Australia and New South Wales. The overwhelming majority of the crop is canned. | The pineapple grows upright from a small, spiny-leafed bush. A single pineapple is actually a multiple fruit formed by the coalescence of more than a hundred flowers, resulting in skin with a repetitive ridged pattern. The leaves of the pineapple have more or less spiny edges, which can make handling uncomfortable, and varieties are classified by these as either rough-edged or smooth-edged. | Pineapple contains the enzyme bromelin, which breaks down protein. Not only does this mean that one cannot attempt to make gelatine-based desserts using raw pineapple, but, much more macabre, I have read that plantation workers must wear gloves, so that the bromelin does not eat away their hands! >

pineapples
go
with
sugar
kirsch
brandy
rum
coriander
limes
tropical fruit
bananas
almonds
pistachios
rice
ham
pork
yoghurt
sour cream
cream
cloves
nutmeg
prawns
garlic
ginger

Bromelin is destroyed on heating, so cooked pineapple can be used to make custards or jellies quite satisfactorily. This same enzyme is thought to have positive value for the digestion: a plate of fresh pineapple is, then, the perfect finish to a rich meal.

A childhood treat used to be thick slices of ham fried quickly and then topped with slices of canned pineapple, the whole thing glazed with a tablespoon of melted and caramelised honey. This nostalgic dish was always cooked in a rickety frying pan over a campfire on family camping holidays. I remembered the dish many years later when embarking on a drive in rural New South Wales. I had a car breakdown and as rescue seemed nowhere in sight I proceeded to replicate Mum's ham steak with canned pineapple on the verge of the Mitchell Highway, somewhere back of Bourke. By the time lunch was over we were rescued by a farmer who nonchalantly improvised a tow rope from a nearby wire fence.

VARIETIES AND SEASON

Pineapples are not sold by named variety and are available all year. In summer the smaller, golden-fleshed 'roughies', named for their leaves, are prized for their sweetness, although they have less juice than other varieties. As sweetness is not as important as size for pineapples that are to be canned in heavy syrup, the larger, paler-fleshed pineapples are best for canning.

SELECTION AND STORAGE

The pineapple is one of the most popular of all tropical fruit, yet it can also be one of the most disappointing. Too often the fruit is not just sweet–sour but unpleasantly tart with only a faint echo of the rich aroma and flavour of which it is capable. Can this be because the varieties grown in Australia are best suited to canning in sweet syrup rather than for the fresh fruit market? I don't know the answer, but I have found that the smaller 'roughies' have the best flavour for eating fresh.

Pineapples do not ripen after picking, as they do not have a reserve of starch to convert to sugar. Skin colour or softness are not indicators of ripeness. Different varieties develop different skin colours when mature, ranging from green–yellow in some to red–orange in others. The colour develops at the base and spreads to the top. A soft skin is an indication of overripe or bruised fruit. Various authorities use different tests to gauge the ripeness of a pineapple. Some prefer to pull out a leaf from the top-knot: if it comes away easily, the fruit is thought to be ripe. Others, including me, believe that maturity is gauged most reliably by the smell of ripe fruit. Over-ripe fruit smells distinctly 'beery'. Still others believe that a ripe pineapple should have some 'give' and when tapped should give back a dull, thumping sound. Pineapples start to deteriorate after picking, so check that the fruit you select has no soft spots or dark bruises.

Store a pineapple in the fruit bowl for no more than a day before using it, or in the refrigerator for 2–3 days. The whole fruit should be stored in a plastic bag, if refrigerated, with the leaves left exposed. If you remove the flesh from the shell and store it in an airtight container it will refrigerate well for several days.

PREPARATION

Fresh pineapple need only be peeled, cored and sliced before serving. Remember the presence of the protein-destroying enzyme bromelin in fresh pineapple, however: not only does it prevent gelatine from setting but it will very quickly turn a meat or poultry salad mushy. It will also cause sour cream or yoghurt to 'weep', so do not mix such a dressing or salad with fresh pineapple until just before serving.

TO SLICE | Cut off the top, with the leaves, then stand the pineapple on end and slice the skin away. Turn the pineapple on its side and, using a sharp small knife, cut a small, V-shaped diagonal channel from top to bottom that traps all the 'eyes' in its path. Continue to do this right around the pineapple. The trimmed fruit will have a spiral of channelling around it and not a trace of an eye. The first time you achieve this you will feel pretty pleased with yourself! The fruit is now ready for cutting into thick or thin slices, rounds or wedges. Cut away the woody core as you go.

TO PRESERVE THE SHELL | Either slice the fruit in half lengthwise right through the crown of leaves and hollow out the flesh to leave 2 'containers', or slice off a generous lid, including the leaves, and hollow out the base using a sharp spoon. Chop the reserved pineapple, making sure you remove all the eyes and all trace of the core.

pineapple and rum pickle

MAKES 2 CUPS

This is not a very long-lasting pickle and should be used within a month. It is delicious served with smoked ham.

½ cup brown sugar
½ cup white-wine vinegar
½ cup dark rum
2 teaspoons yellow mustard
    seeds
6 cloves
2 cups fresh pineapple chunks

In a heavy-based saucepan combine sugar, vinegar, 4 tablespoons of the rum, mustard seeds and cloves. Bring slowly to a boil, stirring to ensure sugar has dissolved, then simmer for 5 minutes. Add pineapple and cook, stirring occasionally, until syrup has reduced somewhat (10–15 minutes). >

Remove from heat and stir in remaining rum. Bottle in sterilised ✒, hot jars and store for a week before using.

pineapple and lime juice salsa

SERVES 4

Try this as a side dish with barbecued pork or prawns, or with marlin or swordfish steaks.

2 cups fresh pineapple chunks
½ red pepper, finely diced
2 teaspoons sambal oelek
I tablespoon fresh lime juice
I tablespoon brown sugar
I tablespoon finely chopped
　fresh coriander leaves

Sauté pineapple in a hot, dry, non-stick frying pan until lightly caramelised. Mix all ingredients in a bowl and taste for balance. Adjust with more lime juice, sambal oelek or sugar if necessary.

golden pineapple and caramel cake

While the tin can be lined with caramel and pineapple a day in advance, this cake is most successful if it is baked and eaten within a few hours.

40 g softened butter
150 g sugar
3 tablespoons water
2 pineapples, skin and eyes
　removed
BATTER
175 g softened butter
150 g castor sugar
175 g self-raising flour
½ level teaspoon baking
　powder
I heaped tablespoon ground
　almonds
3 eggs, lightly beaten

Grease a 25 cm round cake tin (preferably non-stick) with softened butter. Dissolve sugar in water over heat and cook until a medium brown. Pour caramel over base and sides of tin, twisting to coat as evenly as possible. Halve pineapples and cut out cores. Slice fruit thickly (3–4 cm) and pack firmly into base of tin. You should have enough fruit to fill in the small spaces.

Preheat oven to 180°C. To make the batter, cream butter and castor sugar in a food processor. Combine remaining dry ingredients in a bowl, then add alternately with eggs to butter mixture in food processor. Spoon batter into prepared tin and bake for about 50 minutes until centre of cake feels firm and top has browned. When cooked, allow to cool for a few minutes in tin, then run a sharp knife around edges. Place a large plate over cake and quickly invert it. Wait for a minute or so, then ease off tin, hopefully with pineapple in place and just the right amount of moist caramel sauce. (If any pieces of pineapple remain in the tin, scoop them out with a spoon and fill in the gaps.) Serve warm with thick cream.

pineapple and prawn noodles
Toss hot or cold egg noodles with cooked prawns, fresh pineapple, garlic and ginger and dress with Chilli and Lime Sauce (see PEPPERS AND CHILLIES*).*

sugared pineapple
Sprinkle freshly sliced pineapple with sugar to sweeten and soften the flesh and leave it to macerate for an hour or so. Spoon on some coconut cream to serve.

marinated pineapple
Bathe some fresh pineapple pieces in a glass of kirsch and leave for an hour. Turn the fruit once or twice, so that all the pieces are equally flavoured. If the pineapple is very acidic you may need to add sugar.

port douglas fruit salad   SERVES 4

1 soft drinking coconut
  (optional)
1 cup fresh pineapple chunks
1 cup fresh mango chunks
1 cup fresh rose papaya
  chunks
grated zest of 2 limes
1 tablespoon finely chopped
  preserved ginger in syrup

SYRUP
juice of 2 limes
1–2 tablespoons dark rum
2 tablespoons castor sugar
½ cup orange juice

Stir all syrup ingredients together. Split open coconut, if using, and scoop out flesh in spoonfuls. Lightly toss fruit, zest, ginger and coconut in a bowl and pour over syrup. Chill for 1 hour before serving.

variation Soft coconut in a sweet syrup, available at Asian food stores, can be used instead of fresh coconut, but omit the sugar from the syrup ingredients given here.

see also TROPICAL FRUIT

plums and prunes

The plum used to be a very popular backyard fruit tree and there are many prolific trees in the gardens of older homes. Non-fruiting varieties are our best-loved trees for street plantings because of the beauty of the spring blossom and the rich autumn colour of the foliage. | As many of the recipes for plums come from Europe, the home of the plum, it is confusing for an Australian to read in cookery books such as *Jane Grigson's Fruit Book* that the finest eating plums all have yellow or green skins and that the gages are the very finest plums to buy. They might well be, but apart from a few trees in the gardens of enthusiasts, the gage group of plums is not grown widely in Australia. Nor is another European favourite available here, the small, very sweet and yellow-skinned mirabelle plum used to make the glowing, golden–green tarts seen in every French pastry shop in summer. Our country lanes do not yield sloes, a wild member of the family used to make a wonderful gin, nor do many of us come in contact with damson plums, so named for their place of origin, Damascus. >

But we are not without our own treats. The varieties of plums commonly grown in Australia belong to the Japanese plums (*Prunus salicina*) and the European plums (*P. domestica*), while there are also some plantings of myrobalan or cherry plums (*P. cerasifera*). Each has its own advantages. My favourite of the Japanese varieties is the satsuma, one of the blood plums and one of the longest lasting of the stone fruit. I love them in tarts, and puréed stewed satsumas make a delicious addition to vanilla ice-cream before it goes into the churn or to a bowl of Cornflakes.

Prune desserts still seem to provoke lots of nudging and uneasy jokes. The Anglo-Saxon preoccupation with the mild laxative effect of prunes seems to prevent much culinary appreciation of the delicious combinations possible: prunes and Armagnac or brandy, prunes and orange zest, prunes and puff pastry, or prunes, almonds and chocolate.

I once lived in Tours in France's Loire Valley for a year where every confectioner proudly displayed his or her version of the town's speciality, prunes stuffed with variously flavoured and tinted almond pastes. Each prune was dipped in syrup so that it shone and was displayed nestled in its own paper case, the split side uppermost showing its discreet bulge of luscious filling. True appreciation of a wonderful product.

VARIETIES AND SEASON

Plums can be roughly divided into plums for cooking and plums for eating fresh. Dessert plums, those for eating fresh, have a higher sugar content and are juicier. Cooking plums, particularly the blood plums, can be very acid and frequently have dry flesh and sometimes very tough skins. However, I have sometimes poached a dessert plum and eaten a cooking plum raw!

Japanese varieties are grown more extensively in Australia than European plums and usually have larger fruit with predominantly red skin tones, although some have yellow skins. The Japanese varieties include all plums collectively known as blood plums. Of these dark-fleshed, spicy plums, the best known are the satsuma and mariposa. Most Japanese plums are classed as cooking plums, but they can also be eaten fresh as dessert plums.

Australian-grown *European* plums tend to be smaller than the Japanese, with skin colours ranging from green–yellow to deep blue. Mostly they have yellow flesh and are sweet. European plums also include the aforementioned gages and the prunes, as well as the Angelina Burdett, which has yellow flesh and purple skin with a distinct bloom. Most European yellow-fleshed plums are best treated as dessert plums, but, again, they can also be cooked (and make lovely tarts). The d'Agen plum, the 'prune plum', is a well-known European variety that is ideal for drying because of its high sugar content.

Plums are available in the summer months, with the Japanese varieties appearing a good month before the European plums.

**plums
and
prunes
go
with**
*almonds
cream
stone fruit
walnuts
apples
kirsch
brandy
plum brandy
cinnamon
cloves
nutmeg
cardamom
vanilla
orange zest
red wine
pork
rabbit
game birds
lamb
soft cheeses
marzipan
chocolate*

SELECTION AND STORAGE

As with all stone fruit, plums are best picked tree-ripened for full aroma and colour. However, most are not, which is understandable as plums are the most perishable of all stone fruits. The fruit will continue to ripen after picking. Plums quickly progress from perfectly ripe to soft and squashy. When picked nearly ripe, plums will have a life of a week at room temperature, and a week longer if refrigerated.

Select fruit with the whitish bloom intact and with no sign of wrinkled or split skin. Sunburn affects plums and is indicated by a brownish patch on the cheek of the fruit. Such fruit will taste nasty and should be avoided. Most recipes merely list 'plums'. Use whatever variety you have that is ripe and of good flavour. Some varieties will become more mushy than others with cooking, but mostly this doesn't seem to matter.

When buying prunes for eating fresh, choose the largest and softest. This is not so important for prunes you intend to cook.

TO FREEZE | Ask your greengrocer for a fruit tray, complete with its inner lining, in which fruit comes nestled in its own compartment. Egg cartons will do if you are only dealing with a few plums. Wash and dry the plums, then halve them and remove the stones. Place a halved plum, cut-side down, in each depression in the tray. Cover the plum with brown sugar and top with another halved plum, then sprinkle with more brown sugar. Cover with foil and secure the lid, then slip the box into the freezer. These plums can be cooked frozen.

PREPARATION

While plums can be peeled, many cooks prefer to cook them with the skins and stones intact. The skins will loosen in the cooking and the stones are too big to swallow by accident. Sweet plums, skin intact, can be sliced away from the stone to be eaten fresh.

Check whether the prunes you have bought have been stoned – if not, stone them. There is no need to soak prunes, unless a recipe requires the soaking juices.

TO PEEL PLUMS | Slit along the natural groove of the fruit right through to the stone, or halve the fruit completely by twisting the halves away from the stone. Pour boiling water over. Leave for a few minutes, pour water away and remove the skin. Most plum stones are hard to remove and will need to be gouged out with the help of a small knife.

recipes

pickled plums

I find the blood plum varieties best for this pickle as they hold their shape well. They can be served whole or sliced. These are perfect with cold lamb or, when segmented, as part of an antipasto platter.

750 g sugar
450 ml white-wine vinegar
1 small piece cinnamon stick
6 cloves
2 small fresh red chillies (optional)
1 teaspoon whole allspice
6 cardamom pods
1.5 kg blood plums, washed and stems removed

Bring all ingredients except plums to a boil in a preserving pan, stirring until sugar has dissolved. Simmer for 5 minutes. Gently add fruit and cook until just tender (test with a fine skewer or a needle). This may only take 5 minutes, so do not go too far away. Remove fruit and pack into sterilised, hot, dry jars. Boil syrup for 5 minutes, then pour over fruit, ensuring it is covered. Seal and leave for a month before using.

plum sauce

MAKES 2 LITRES

This old-fashioned preserve is good with cold lamb, sausages or hamburgers, and a slosh of it will add piquancy to a beef, rabbit or lamb casserole. Mixed with a little oil, this sauce makes a delicious marinade. It can also be used as a dip for barbecued seafood.

1.5 kg plums, halved
1½ teaspoons cloves
1 teaspoon whole allspice
1 teaspoon black peppercorns
500 g brown sugar
2 teaspoons salt
1 tablespoon very finely chopped fresh ginger
3 cups white-wine vinegar .

Stone plums, then crack half the stones and tie them in a piece of muslin. Tie spices in another piece of muslin. Put muslin bags, plums, sugar, salt, ginger and vinegar into a large preserving pan and bring to a boil, stirring until sugar has dissolved. Cook steadily for 20 minutes until plums have collapsed. Remove muslin bags and press all juices back into sauce.

Pass sauce through the coarse disc of a food mill and return to rinsed-out pan. Boil steadily for a few minutes until sauce is as thick as you would like it. (Remember it will thicken further when it is cold and it ought to be pourable.) Pour into hot, sterilised bottles or jars, seal and label. Leave at least a week before using. This sauce keeps for months.
chillies Two small, hot dried chillies could be added to the muslin bag instead of the black peppercorns if you prefer a spicier sauce.

plum sauce for roasts
Stir stewed, puréed plums into the baking dish 15 minutes before finishing a roast of lamb or pork. Deglaze with red or white wine and a spoonful of red-wine or balsamic vinegar for a tart and interesting sauce.

spiced plum pilaf
Sauté sliced blood plums in butter with cinnamon, cloves and cardamom and toss with a pilaf of brown rice, barley or couscous. Sauté chicken livers to accompany this dish.

poached plums

SERVES 4

1½ cups water
1 cup white *or* red wine *or* port
¾ cup sugar
½ vanilla bean, split *or* ½ stick cinnamon *or* a few cardamom pods
12–15 plums, halved

Bring all ingredients except plums to a simmer, stirring to dissolve sugar. Cook for 5 minutes. Slip in plum halves and simmer for 10 minutes, then allow to cool in liquid. Refrigerate in an airtight container for up to a week.

plum soup
Dilute stewed, puréed plums with half late-picked white wine and half light Sugar Syrup to taste, then add a slosh of plum brandy and serve chilled as a cold soup. Or dilute puréed plums with fat-free chicken or beef stock for a hot or cold soup.

devils on horseback
Wrap prunes in bacon and grill until the bacon is crisp. Serve with drinks.

mieze's plum cake

SERVES 12

Here is my favourite plum recipe, a long-time classic in the restaurant's summer repertoire and guaranteed to bring rave responses. It is named for a very charming German friend of my parents who introduced this plum cake to our family nearly 40 years ago. If you are not feeding a crowd, you can halve this recipe and use a smaller springform tin. It is important that there not be too thick a layer of cake.

275 g softened butter
250 g sugar
200 g plain flour
200 g self-raising flour
pinch of salt
3 eggs, lightly beaten
100 ml milk
1 cup ground almonds *or* fresh breadcrumbs
20 ripe blood plums, halved and stoned

TOPPING
125 g butter
200 g sugar
2 teaspoons ground cinnamon
4 eggs

Preheat oven to 180°C and lightly grease a 28 cm springform tin. Cream butter and sugar until light and fluffy, then mix in flours and salt. Add eggs and milk to make a soft dough (the mixture should drop easily from the spoon). Spoon batter into prepared tin (it should not fill more than a quarter of the depth as the cake rises a great deal) then sprinkle over ground almonds. Arrange plums, cut-side up, on top, starting around outside edge and working towards centre.

To make the topping, melt butter and stir in sugar and cinnamon, then allow to cool. Whisk eggs well and stir into cooled butter mixture. Spoon over and around plums on cake. Bake for 1 hour until cake tests cooked in the centre. Serve warm with cream or ice-cream. Any leftover cake can be warmed, wrapped in foil, in the oven at 180°C for 15 minutes.

plum and plum kernel tart

I quantity Shortcrust Pastry
½ cup cake crumbs *or*
    breadcrumbs *or either*
    mixed with ground almonds
15 plums, halved and stoned
redcurrant jelly

Line a 22 cm loose-bottomed flan tin with pastry and bake blind at 200°C for 20 minutes. Increase oven temperature to 220°C. Spread a layer of cake crumbs over base of pastry case (these will absorb plum juice and avoid sogginess). Arrange halved plums in circles from outside edge in, cut-side up. Crack a few plum kernels and scatter over. Bake for 15 minutes. The fruit will swell up but will settle down after being removed from the oven. Brush tart with warmed redcurrant jelly and serve warm.

variation Beat 2 eggs with ½ cup cream, sour cream or crème fraîche and spoon over the plums before baking in the same way.

chocolate-dipped prunes with brandy cream

SERVES 6

24 large prunes, stoned
½ bottle good red wine
60 ml brandy
300 g dark couverture
    chocolate
100 g unsalted butter

BRANDY CREAM

2 egg yolks
25 g castor sugar
60 ml brandy
300 ml cream, whipped

Soak prunes in wine and brandy for at least 8 hours or up to a month, refrigerated in an airtight glass container. Drain prunes well on a wire rack resting over a tray. Line another tray with baking paper. Melt chocolate and butter in a basin resting over a saucepan of hot water, then remove from heat. Using a skewer, impale a prune, then dip it into the chocolate and allow any excess to drip off. Slip each dipped prune onto the paper-lined tray. Allow to set in a cool place.

Make the brandy cream just before serving as it deflates quickly. Beat egg yolks and sugar until fluffy, then whisk in brandy and gently fold in cream. Spoon sauce onto plates and float a prune or 4 on top.

leftover liquid Any liquid left over from soaking the prunes can be used to soak more prunes, or can be stirred into Egg Custard to make a wonderful ice-cream. A little can also be added to an egg and cream mixture when baking a plum tart. Or you can drink it!

plums in brandy

Place a snug layer of frozen plum halves into a baking dish with a good lump of butter and a slosh of brandy. Cook gently on top of the stove and serve just as they are with thick cream.

prunes in red wine

Simmer prunes in red-wine syrup (see p. 528) and allow to cool in the syrup. Serve with syrup and offer thick cream or rich yoghurt. As an alternative, add a small amount of Cognac or Armagnac and forget the cream or yoghurt.

prune fritters

SERVES 4

If you prefer, you can prepare the prunes and batter for these wonderfully indulgent fritters in advance, leaving only the deep-frying to do before serving.

plum and almond tart
Swirl some stewed, puréed plums or prunes into the filling before baking Almond Frangipane Tart (see NUTS*).*

24 prunes, stoned
½ bottle good red wine
60 ml brandy
24 blanched almonds, roasted
vegetable oil for deep-frying
100 g dark couverture
   chocolate, shaved

BATTER
150 g plain flour
tiny pinch of salt
1 tablespoon olive oil
2 tablespoons dry white wine
175 ml water
3 egg whites

Soak prunes in wine and brandy for at least 8 hours or up to a month, refrigerated in an airtight glass container. Insert a roasted almond in each prune, then impale on a skewer and allow to drain well on a wire rack resting over a tray.

To make the batter, mix flour and salt in a food processor. Combine oil, wine and water and add to food processor with motor running until you have a smooth batter. Stop machine once and check there is not a trapped layer of flour under the blade. Transfer batter to a bowl and refrigerate for an hour or so (while you eat the first part of your meal, if you like).

When ready for dessert, heat a good quantity of vegetable oil to 175°C. Firmly whisk egg whites and fold delicately into batter. Dip each prune in batter and lower skewers into hot oil in batches until batter is golden. Drain fritters on kitchen paper for a minute. Serve at once accompanied by shavings of chocolate.

other recipes

cock-a-leekie *see* LEEKS
pork with prunes *see* PORK
rabbit with prunes *see* RABBIT

pork It is thought that the ancestors of the modern pig roamed the earth as far back as 40 million years ago. The pig became a farm animal as soon as humans ceased to be nomadic and began to cultivate the first crops. Today there are more than 10 000 pig farms in Australia, which have almost entirely replaced the mixed farms of past years that reared pigs along with other animals. | Pigs are not dependent on pasture and will eat anything and everything. It is probably partly for this reason that in some religions pork is considered unclean and is forbidden. Conversely, pork is highly regarded in some parts of the world, notably in China and other Asian cultures and in the Pacific. The Chinese excel in the art of pork cookery and their repertoire of braised, stir-fried, red-cooked and roasted pork is incomparable and almost limitless. | The pig has also been of major importance in many European communities for centuries, and today every part of the animal is still used by the likes of the French *charcutier*, whose sausages, pâtés, roasts, jellied morsels and so on are awe-inspiring. Anyone interested in exploring this aspect of pork cookery must read the late Jane Grigson's astonishing book *Charcuterie and French Pork Cookery.* >

pork
goes
with
garlic
onions
olive oil
sour cream
tomatoes
maple syrup
chillies
star anise
soy sauce
ginger
spring onions
rosemary
sage
thyme
fennel
salad leaves
watercress
potatoes
red cabbage
sauerkraut
turnips
mushrooms
celery
cherries
apples
pears
prunes
mustard
lentils
pickled cucumbers

In Australia today close to 20 per cent of the meat we eat is from the pig, either as pork, ham, bacon or sausages and preserved sausages, such as salami and frankfurters. (The various by-products of the pig are so varied that I have dealt with each separately. Please turn to BACON, HAM, TROTTERS and SAUSAGES to learn more about the wonders of the pig.) Farmers have responded to nutritional messages and now pigs are often bred to have less fat and more lean meat. The Australian Pork Corporation markets its lean meat as New-Fashioned Pork and has developed new cuts requiring quick and easy cooking. There are some cooks who find that this lean pork is less juicy and without the sweetness they remember. Farmers will sometimes agree, but market forces are something else again. It is intriguing to wonder what will happen to the production of fine hams if the move to lean pork continues. I would guess that the food-loving populations of Italy, Spain and France would reject attempts to overturn centuries of tradition in the husbandry of the pigs that become their unrivalled hams and sausages. In Australia we appear to have little choice.

VARIETIES AND SEASON

Pig farming in Australia includes large and small farms but, whatever the size, the aim of most is to produce lean meat in the shortest time at the least cost to satisfy market demand. Pig farming has become a specialised and mechanised industry. The principal breeds in Australia are the large white, landrace and duroc, but breeds are constantly crossed for improved strains. The consumer, as with beef and lamb, is not sold pork by breed but by cut.

Pork from male pigs (barrows or boars) can be very strongly flavoured, while pork from a sow is generally regarded as the sweetest. Pigs are classed by their weight and all types are available all year. *Suckling* pig is a very young pig under 14 kg that can be roasted whole. Bill Marchetti of Melbourne's Marchetti's Latin is able to obtain piglets of 4 kg from a secret supplier for his delectable dish of roast suckling pig. A suckling pig has soft, sweet meat that is very succulent. A *porker* weighs up to 50 kg and is usually aged 16 weeks, while *super porkers* weigh 55–65 kg. *Baconers* weigh 70–100 kg. Over the last 15 years the super porkers, which have short legs and less fat, have been bred to create the lean 'new' pork. I do not detect any difference between the flavour or texture of pork cut from a porker or super porker. I am concerned at the loss of juiciness that appears to be a consequence of the market demand for lean pork. Unless you are very fortunate you will be supplied lean pork with a fat cover of no more than 15 mm.

However, there are a few farmers rearing pigs with a good covering of fat, but they are probably small producers. Their animals are likely to be fed skim milk and grain as opposed to the pellets (and growth promoters) included in the diet of most pigs intended to produce leaner meat.

Butchers who pride themselves on the quality of their product still prefer female pigs. They have to pay a premium to receive only sows rather than mixed. Apparently today's pig farmers believe that by slaughtering male super porkers younger than used to be the case (they are larger for their age than they used to be under older methods of pig rearing) there is no need for the pigs to be castrated; the objectionable smell and hardness in meat associated with boars is thereby avoided, they say. Butchers and smallgoods manufacturers I have spoken to are not entirely convinced. They urge consumers to ask their butchers if the pork they buy is from female pigs only. (One said to me that special attention is given to any customer who asks questions. Another reason to cultivate a good relationship with your butcher.)

The Chinese and Vietnamese communities insist that their pork has a greater covering of fat than is usual for lean pork, so it makes sense to visit a Chinese or Vietnamese butcher if wanting to buy meat of this quality. You will also be assured that the pork you buy is from a sow.

SELECTION AND STORAGE

The colour of fresh pork varies from pale pink to pinky-red according to the size of the animal and the part of the carcass from which the meat is cut. It should not look wet and the fat should be white and medium-firm in texture. It is important that you buy a cut suitable for the use you have in mind. Remember to request pork from a sow, and for maximum succulence purchase pork from a Chinese or Vietnamese butcher.

Various forms of *pork fat* can be ordered from your butcher, but allow a day or two for it to arrive. *Soft flare fat* or *hard back fat* are used when making terrines and sausages or are rendered when cooking preserved meats or 'confits'. Rendered pork fat is known as *lard* and is an important medium in many regions and cuisines, including in Creole cooking in the United States, for pastry-making in the north of England and for many uses throughout eastern and central Europe. *Caul fat*, the lacy membrane that encloses the internal organs, is wonderfully useful as a wrap for small patties of minced meat, pork or otherwise, and for lining terrines. The caul bastes the mixture it is wrapped around and becomes crisp and appetisingly brown where it is directly exposed to heat. Caul fat needs preparation before it can be used. It is sensible to buy a good quantity (at least 500 g), then prepare and freeze it.

FOR ROASTING   The most luxurious pork roasts are from the *leg* or the *loin*. The *leg* is a very large joint and is often divided into the *fillet* and *knuckle* ends and is available bone-in or boned. Alternatively, the leg is seamed into its various muscles and sold this way, as a *rump roast* for example. The skin will usually be scored by the butcher to make crackling. The *loin* can be bought bone-in or boned and is often cut into 2 pieces. ***Boned loin*** roasts are often stuffed and rolled. The shoulder end of the loin has a cap of fat on top of the eye of the loin; the middle loin has the strip of underfillet attached. The middle loin can also be trimmed on the bone (the skin will be removed along with most of the fat) to create a ***rack*** of pork. The butcher will need to remove the chine bone, so that the rack can be cut between the ribs. The ***shoulder*** of pork can also be roasted. It will normally be boned and stuffed before being rolled and tied. The ***fillet*** can be roasted whole, but because it is fat-free it needs to be basted well to prevent dryness; it only requires 15–20 minutes' cooking.

FOR BRAISING, STEWING OR POT-ROASTING All these methods, which use different amounts of liquid, are suited to the cuts of pork that benefit from moist cooking to make them tender. Pork ***neck*** (sometimes called the foreloin) can be pot-roasted or braised. If pot-roasting (in a covered container), baste with wine or stock and turn frequently. Skinned, trimmed muscles from the leg such as ***topside***, ***rump*** and ***silverside*** are also good braised or stewed, as is the ***boned shoulder***. These cuts are frequently cut into chunks and combined with an infinite variety of flavours, depending on the tradition the cook is following. Boned shoulder is also often sold salted (pickled) for use in terrines, pies and sausage-making. The ***hock*** (the lower portion of the leg) is sold fresh, salted (pickled) or smoked. A pork hock adds gelatine and delicious flavours to long-simmered stews and casseroles and the liquid it cooks in will always set to a firm jelly. The meat can be cut from the bone, seasoned and set in its own jelly as a simple brawn, or it can be boned after cooking, coated in the same sticky flavours as for ribs and baked or barbecued.

FOR GRILLING OR FRYING New-Fashioned Pork is ideal for quick cooking. The various ***steaks***, ***chops***, ***slices*** and ***strips*** are all suited to quick grilling, stir-frying, barbecuing or sautéing. As most of these cuts are heavily trimmed of fat, the meat must be painted with a little oil before cooking. Ask the butcher to cut double-thickness chops for extra juiciness.

There are a few specialised pork cuts that deserve special mention. Succulent ***belly pork*** has a mix of fat and lean and can be bought either fresh or salted (pickled), skinned or unskinned. Salted, it can be boiled to make *petit salé* to serve with lentils or dried beans; fresh it can be boiled, painted with a barbecue or devilled sauce (*see* Devilled Kidneys in KIDNEYS) and roasted or barbecued to develop a great crust. It can also be cut up and is used to make the easiest of all charcuterie, rillettes (*see* p. 561).

Ribs, an American and Chinese speciality, are cut from inside the thick end of the pork belly. They are coated in spicy flavours and then either baked or simmered until they are absolutely tender, then barbecued, deep-fried or stir-fried.

The *fillet* or *underfillet*, a long, tapering piece of fat-free meat, is tender and sweet and can be cooked whole or cut up. It usually weighs around 400 g. It cooks very quickly, making it ideal for skewering and grilling or stir-frying. I also cut thick escalopes from it, sauté them gently and finish the dish with wine and cream or prunes (*see* p. 566).

MINCED PORK | Pork mince is an invaluable resource for fast pâtés and terrines or for quick family meals. Savoury pork meatballs are great with drinks, and larger ones can be braised. As with all minced meat it is essential that mince be freshly prepared.

The ideal way to store meat is to free it of any shop wrappings, set it on a wire rack over a plate or tray and cover it with a damp cotton cloth to prevent the surface drying out. Any juices, which sour the meat, will collect under the rack. Next best is to cover the meat with greaseproof paper. (Note that frost-free refrigerators dry food out quickly.) Pickled pork should be stored in a bowl or on a deep plate, so that the brine cannot drip onto other foods, and should be used within 5 days of purchase.

Most cuts of pork should be used within 2–3 days of purchase. Use minced pork within 24 hours, however. (The relatively large number of air pockets in minced meat make it a prime candidate for rapid bacterial growth.) To store, remove it from the shop wrappings and refrigerate on a plate covered with plastic film. If you need to store meat longer, freeze it. Chops, cutlets or similar should be frozen with a layer of plastic film between each, so that the meat does not stick together and the fibres tear during the thawing process. Always thaw meat in the refrigerator overnight, *not* on the sink draining board. Pork fat can be stored for up to 5 days and also freezes perfectly. Use rind within 2–3 days or cut it into strips or smaller pieces and freeze. Cooked pork should be refrigerated as soon as it has cooled down a little. Wrap the meat in foil and use within a few days.

PREPARATION AND COOKING

Trim away excess fat before cooking pork. Save the fat and either render it to make a superb medium for frying potatoes or turnips, or freeze it to mince or chop and add to pies, terrines or stuffings to add succulence. Remember, however, that meat without any covering of fat can be very dry. As most of the New-Fashioned Pork cuts are fat-free, they must be brushed with a little oil or rendered pork fat before cooking.

It has been a common instruction to cook pork for a very long time to avoid the danger of trichinosis, a parasitic infection acquired by eating raw or insufficiently cooked food. Trichinosis has not been officially recorded in Australia but is still scrupulously guarded against and is one of the reasons imported processed pork products are forbidden. However, one does *not* have to cook pork until it is dry and splintery as a precaution. The safe internal temperature for pork is in fact 76°C. At this temperature the meat is both safe and juicy.

The following remarks are very general and should be read in conjunction with suggested flavour combinations.

TO ROAST

To prepare a roasting joint, simply season, marinate or stuff it according to your recipe. Leave a 5 mm layer of fat on a skinned piece of pork that is to be roasted. Even if intending to roast a boned piece of pork, request a few pork bones. Roasted alongside the meat, they will brown nicely and ensure good colour and flavour in the deglazed juices.

Calculate the cooking time by allowing 30 minutes per 500 g. If the meat is to be stuffed, weigh it after stuffing. If you want crackling, rub a little kitchen salt and olive oil into the score marks in the rind. Start the meat at 200°C for the first 20 minutes to ensure that the fat crisps properly, then reduce the heat to 180°C. If you have requested a skinned piece of loin or leg, the meat can be cooked more gently, at 160°C or 180°C. (By basting a skinned joint with the pan juices every 20 minutes, a wonderful glaze develops on the meat.) Test the meat near the end of the cooking time. A fine skewer should slip through without resistance and the juices should run clear. Transfer the meat to a warm place to rest, loosely covered with foil. Tip any excess fat from the baking dish and deglaze with white wine, cider, red wine or port, then add any garnishes and bubble until the flavour is as you want it.

TO BRAISE, STEW OR POT-ROAST

I have included general instructions on braising under OXTAIL. To braise, stew or pot-roast a piece of pork, tie the meat into a neat shape that will snugly fit into a cast-iron casserole with a tight-fitting lid. Seal the meat in a little hot pork fat or olive oil, then add aromatics, such as garlic cloves, bay leaves, a sprig of thyme, salt and pepper, vegetables (onions, carrots, celery and turnips), stock and/or wine. Bring to a boil, then turn the heat down low or transfer to an oven set at 160°C and cook for 30 minutes per 500 g. Turn the meat several times during cooking. At the end of the cooking time, the meat can be removed to a warm plate and the juices boiled fiercely to concentrate the flavour. It is usual practice to add fresh vegetables to the casserole about 30 minutes before the meat is cooked. Alternatively, you can prepare a separate dish of vegetables, polenta or rice and accompany the sliced meat and juices with a large salad.

**TO GRILL
OR FRY**
Brush small pieces of pork with seasoned olive oil or seasoned rendered pork fat before sautéing or grilling and do not overcook them. They can also be crumbed, marinated or wrapped in a thin veil of caul fat before grilling or sautéing. Any of these methods will protect the meat as it cooks. Medallions, butterfly chops, loin chops and noisettes will only take 4–5 minutes each side to be thoroughly cooked.

TO STIR-FRY
The selected meat should be thinly cut, so that it cooks almost the instant it hits the hot wok. The fillet is ideal for this. If you wish to include any vegetables, stir-fry these before the meat and set aside. There is no point attempting a stir-fry without a wok heated to maximum. Pour in a film of oil and splash up the sides of the hot wok. Add sliced garlic and fresh ginger, if desired, then, moments later, toss in the meat. It will change colour instantly. Add the stir-fried vegetables and any liquid, then maybe a swirl of cornflour and water mixed to a paste (slurry) – and the dish is ready.

**TO RENDER
PORK FAT**
Cut the fat into 5 cm cubes, then place in a heavy-based saucepan and pour in water to a depth of 2 cm. Simmer until the pieces of fat have disappeared. The water will have evaporated. Strain the pork fat into a container and store in the refrigerator for up to a month or else freeze it. If the fat you are rendering has skin attached, the skin will end up as little shrivelled pieces of cracklings. When you strain the fat, save these cracklings and scatter them over a green salad. This method can also be used to render duck fat.

**TO PREPARE
CAUL FAT**
Soak the caul fat overnight in the refrigerator in a bowl of lightly salted water to remove any trace of blood. The caul fat can then be frozen in small freezer bags. To thaw, soak the caul fat in warm salted water, then spread it on a clean cloth to dry before cutting and shaping it as required.

pork rillettes

SERVES 8

I always store my rillettes in a brown-glazed pot in remembrance of times past. Rillettes were another discovery of mine during the 1960s in Tours, France. This classic country dish has been the standard starter in small country restaurants of the Loire region since time immemorial, always spread on coarse country bread, always accompanied by crunchy pickled cucumbers.

1.5 kg fresh belly pork,
  skinned and boned
salt
1 bay leaf
1 large sprig thyme
2 cloves garlic
freshly ground black pepper
½ cup water

Cut meat into small pieces and rub in 1 tablespoon salt, then refrigerate for a few hours or even overnight.

Preheat oven to 160°C. Place meat in a cast-iron casserole that will hold it reasonably snugly and add herbs. Bury garlic in centre. Grind over pepper and add water. Cover with lid and cook for about 3 hours until pork is swimming in its own juices and fat and is completely tender. Tip into a colander resting over a basin. Discard thyme and bay leaf. Using your fingers or 2 forks, shred meat and fat and pack into a small pot. Spoon over fatty juice in bowl. (The garlic will have just about dissolved into the juice. Use it too.) Mix lightly and taste for seasoning – rillettes should be very well seasoned. Refrigerate until required.

modern method Tip cooked meat into a food processor and give the mixture 2–3 quick pulses. Tip the mixture into a bowl, spoon over the fat and juices and season in the same way as above.

traditional roast leg of pork   SERVES 6

I keep a cup of stock beside the oven and dribble it into the baking dish during the roasting process. By the end of the cooking time I always have a wonderful sauce.

1 × 1.5–2 kg joint of pork
  from leg, rind scored
sea salt
olive oil
freshly ground black pepper
12 pickling onions, peeled
1 bay leaf
1 large sprig thyme
stock
6 potatoes, peeled
2 golden delicious apples,
  peeled and sliced
1 tablespoon water
½ cup white wine *or* cider

Preheat oven to 200°C. Rub scored rind with a little sea salt and oil. Grind pepper over meat. Place in baking dish with onions, bay leaf and thyme and pour in water to a depth of 1 cm. Rub potatoes with oil and place around meat. Bake for 30 minutes, then pour a little stock over and around meat. Reset oven to 180°C and bake for 1½ hours, basting every 20 minutes with the juices. Dribble in a little more stock. At end of cooking time, pierce thickest part of roast with a fine skewer. If juices ooze clear, remove baking dish from oven, then lift meat, onions and potatoes to a platter and return to turned-off oven.

Pour juice from baking dish into a tall jug. Allow to settle for 10 minutes, then spoon off all fat. (While the fat is settling, cook apple in water until soft and set aside.) Stand baking dish over a medium heat

pork with onions
Dip 2 pork medallions, butterfly steaks or loin steaks in seasoned flour, then sauté for 2 minutes each side in clarified butter or olive oil. Remove from pan and replace with a cup of Caramelised Onions (see ONIONS*) or sautéd mushrooms. Heat through, then replace pork and serve.*

and pour in wine. Scrape and stir to loosen any cooked-on bits and add degreased cooking juices. Bubble to reduce. Add any juices that have collected on the plate where the meat and vegetables are resting. Pour into a heated serving jug.

Warm apple purée through in a small saucepan and carve meat. (A green vegetable such as fresh peas or beans will cook in the 5 minutes or so it takes to carve and portion the meat.) Carve off the crackling in a single piece and portion it.

simple country terrine

Pâtés and terrines frighten many cooks needlessly. They are no more complicated than making a meatloaf. The important difference is that a pork terrine is usually very thoughtfully seasoned with spices and fresh herbs, and can include small amounts of exotic ingredients, such as breast of pheasant or pigeon. Some terrines are complex to assemble but once you have the hang of it they can be fun and satisfying to make. All terrines are best made a few days before they are required. For this terrine, choose pork that has quite a lot of fat to lean.

250 g chicken livers
40 g butter
1 small onion, chopped
1 thick slice wholemeal *or* sourdough bread, crusts removed
500 g minced fat pork (shoulder, neck or belly)
250 g minced skinless poultry or rabbit
2 cloves garlic, very finely chopped
1 generous sprig thyme, leaves stripped from stalk
2 teaspoons freshly grated nutmeg
¼ teaspoon ground allspice
1 teaspoon freshly ground black pepper
2 teaspoons salt
3 eggs
50 ml brandy
1 bay leaf

Preheat oven to 180°C. Cook livers quickly in half the butter until just stiffened, then remove and cut into chunks. Add remaining butter and stew onion until soft. Process bread in a food processor to form crumbs. Mix all ingredients except bay leaf very well and pack into a 1.5 litre earthenware or cast-iron terrine mould. Mound slightly and press bay leaf on top, then cover with terrine lid. Stand terrine in a baking dish and pour in water to come halfway up sides of mould. Bake for 1 hour or until a skewer inserted in the centre comes out hot when you touch it to your bottom lip. Place a light weight on the terrine itself when it comes out of the oven (such as a full bottle of oil on its side) and allow to cool overnight. Serve with crunchy cucumbers and radishes.

lined terrines It is traditional to line a terrine mould with either thin strips of hard back fat or caul fat. It is quite a simple technique and it makes the finished pressed

crumbed pork
Coat thin, small pieces of pork (medallions, schnitzels) in oil or melted butter, then dip in seasoned breadcrumbs (or two-thirds breadcrumbs mixed with one-third parmesan cheese) and sauté.

pork and rabbit meatballs
Mix half rabbit mince and half pork mince, then season and make tiny meatballs. Fry in olive oil and serve with prunes that have been soaked for an hour in a little brandy and puréed with some grain mustard (this is one of Maggie Beer's clever ideas).

terrine easier to cut, but do not avoid making a terrine simply because you do not have any back fat or caul fat!

slow-roasted loin of pork with garlic, rosemary and fennel

SERVES 6

All over Italy one sees vans parked on country roads selling delicious roast pork stuffed into country panini. The pork is seasoned with rosemary and garlic, and often with chopped fennel as well. I have adopted this Italian seasoning as my preferred method for slow-roasting a loin of pork. Buy half a loin to feed at least 6 people. You should still have enough for a sandwich the next day! I prefer to buy the shoulder end of the loin, although be warned that it is fattier. I ask the butcher to skin and bone the loin but to give me the bones.

3 tablespoons olive oil

2 cloves garlic, very finely chopped

2 × 6 cm sprigs rosemary, finely chopped

1 tablespoon finely chopped fresh fennel leaves

freshly ground black pepper

½ loin of pork, skinned and boned

salt

3–4 pork rib bones

1 onion, diced

1 carrot, diced

1 stick celery, sliced

½ cup dry white wine

½ cup water

chunks of potato and bulb fennel *or* small, peeled turnips and onions

Preheat oven to 160°C. In a small bowl combine 2 tablespoons of the oil with garlic, rosemary, fennel leaves and a generous quantity of pepper. Open out meat and rub flesh side all over with this mixture. Roll meat into a bolster shape and tie it firmly at intervals with string. Rub any remaining mixture over fat and sprinkle with salt. Place pork bones and onion, carrot and celery in a baking dish with remaining oil. Position a wire roasting rack on top and settle meat on this. Pour wine and water into baking dish. Cook for 2 hours, basting every 30 minutes. Drain off juice and diced vegetables, strain and set aside. Discard fat that rises to the top. Remove bones and add remaining vegetables to baking dish. Increase heat to 180°C. Return meat and vegetables to oven for 1 hour. At this stage the meat should be perfectly tender and the vegetables cooked.

Remove meat and vegetables to a plate and keep warm. Pour off all additional juices into a tall jug. Allow to stand for 10 minutes, then skim off all fat and add to strained juice. Transfer baking dish to medium heat on stove. Pour all juice back into baking dish and allow to bubble up. Scrape and stir vigorously to remove any cooked-on bits and strain this simple 'jus' into a warm serving jug. Carve meat thickly, moisten with

roast pork with bay
Add a few bay leaves along with unpeeled garlic cloves to the baking dish when roasting pork or veal.

marinated pork
Marinate thin, small pieces of pork (such as medallions or butterfly steaks) in oil and lemon juice or Tomato and Maple Syrup Glaze (see p. 567) before grilling.

juice and share out the vegetables. Follow these with a large bowl of green salad.

marinade This same paste of rosemary, fennel, garlic, olive oil and pepper is great rubbed on medallions or steaks of New-Fashioned Pork intended to be sautéd, or on pork chops.

cha siu-style pork

SERVES 6–8

The delicious, red-rimmed slices of barbecued pork enjoyed in Chinese restaurants are easy to produce at home. The pork is good hot or cold and can be refrigerated, covered, for up to a week.

1 cup dark soy sauce
½ cup red rice vinegar
½ cup mirin
1 tablespoon maltose or honey
1 tablespoon hoisin sauce
1 teaspoon sesame oil
2 cloves garlic, finely chopped
1 tablespoon finely chopped ginger
1 teaspoon ground cinnamon
scant pinch of five-spice powder
1 kg pork fillet *or* belly pork

Combine all ingredients except pork. Cut pork into chunks or thick strips and marinate for 3 hours. Remove meat from marinade and allow to drip-dry on a wire rack set over a tray.

Preheat oven to 200°C. Place meat directly on oven rack and position a baking dish filled with water to a depth of 4 cm beneath it to catch any fat. Roast for 30 minutes or until cooked (belly pork may take up to 1 hour). Slice and serve with rice and wok-tossed vegetables.

spare ribs Pork spare ribs can be prepared this way, too, although they may take a little longer to become quite tender. Once roasted, finish the ribs at 220°C (or under a preheated griller) for 5–10 minutes to crisp them. **barbecue** Instead of roasting the marinated pork, try barbecuing it.

tung po pork

SERVES 3–6

There are many versions of this dish, named after poet Su Tungpo who was also famed for his culinary skills. Chinese writers on gastronomy stress that the texture of the finished pork should be custard-like. This recipe is from Ken Hom's The Taste of China.

According to Hsiang Ju Lin and Tsuifeng Lin in their marvellous book Chinese Gastronomy, *'tungpo pork is customarily served at the end of a meal with bowls of rice. People sigh, shout and groan with happiness when they see it. This is one of the pinnacles of gastronomy, and shows up the appreciation of fat in Chinese cuisine'.*

pork with cumquats
Cook Pickled Cumquats (see CUMQUATS) *with a roast leg or loin of pork and squash well when making the sauce. Serve with Sauerkraut with Juniper Berries and Sparkling Wine (see* CABBAGES AND BRUSSELS SPROUTS).

900 g fresh belly pork, boned
but not skinned
3 tablespoons peanut oil
6 spring onions, cut into
7 cm pieces
6 slices fresh ginger
125 g rock sugar or
4 tablespoons sugar
½ cup dark soy sauce
2 tablespoons light soy sauce
½ cup rice wine
½ cup water

asian pork
Seal finely sliced pork fillet tossed with 1 tablespoon light soy sauce, 1 tablespoon vegetable oil and 1 teaspoon finely chopped fresh ginger in a hot wok, then add washed watercress and any remaining marinade and cook for 2 minutes. Serve with steamed rice.

Blanch meat in a large saucepan of boiling water for 10 minutes. Remove and dry with kitchen paper. Heat a wok, then add oil and lower heat. Add meat skin-side down, and brown skin slowly until golden and crispy (10–15 minutes). Lift meat from wok and wipe off any excess fat from the meat with kitchen paper.

Put spring onion, ginger, sugar, soy sauces, rice wine, water and meat into a large cast-iron casserole. Bring to a simmer, cover tightly, and cook slowly over a very low heat for 3 hours or until meat is tender and much of the fat has been rendered. Drain liquid and discard spring onion and ginger. Pour strained liquid into a tall jug and allow to settle for 10 minutes, then spoon off all fat. Slice meat thinly and arrange on a platter. Pour sauce over and serve at room temperature.

pork with prunes

SERVES 4

This is an adaptation of a regional speciality from the French town of Tours, where I spent a very happy year in the 1960s.

12 large prunes, stoned
1½ cups dry white wine
2 pork fillets
flour
salt
freshly ground black pepper
olive oil
butter
1 tablespoon redcurrant jelly
4 tablespoons thick cream
juice of 1 lemon
2 handfuls watercress sprigs,
washed and crisped

Soak prunes in wine overnight. Next day, cut each fillet on the diagonal into 6 pieces. Flatten each piece a little with the palm of your hand and set aside. Preheat oven to low with a plate in it. Strain prunes from wine and reserve. Bring wine to simmering point, then set aside. Dust each piece of pork with seasoned flour. Heat a little oil and butter in a heavy-based frying pan until butter foams. Immediately slip in a few pieces of pork and brown over moderate heat, 3 minutes per side. Do not crowd pan. Remove cooked pork to oven and continue.

Wipe out pan with kitchen paper and reheat. Tip in warm wine and allow it to bubble fiercely. Add redcurrant jelly and cream, then stir to blend. Return meat to pan and add prunes. >

Lower heat a little. Turn meat in sauce as it reduces. Add a few drops of
lemon juice and adjust seasoning. The sauce should be toffee-coloured and
quite thick. If it is too thin, remove meat to a warm plate and boil more
fiercely. If it is too thick, add a few drops of water or an extra tablespoon
of wine. Spoon pork medallions onto plates, top with prunes, spoon over
sauce and garnish with a clump of tender watercress.

barbecued belly pork with tomato and maple syrup glaze

SERVES 6

*Ask the butcher for as lean a belly as possible for this wonderful, super-rich
dish. You will need a litre of the glaze. Any leftover glaze will keep for
weeks in a jar in the refrigerator, and can be used to make sticky pork ribs
and the like.*

1.5 kg fresh belly pork,
   skinned and boned
1 teaspoon chilli sauce
   (optional)
12 baby bok choy, washed
vegetable oil

**TOMATO AND MAPLE SYRUP
GLAZE**

1 kg tomatoes, peeled, seeded
   and roughly chopped
1 large onion, chopped
3 cloves garlic, chopped
salt
freshly ground black pepper
1 bay leaf
1 sprig thyme
maple syrup
light soy sauce

To make the glaze, cook all ingredients
except maple syrup and soy sauce over
moderate heat until soft and well reduced.
Blend in a food processor and measure. For
every 1½ cups sauce, add 1 tablespoon light
soy sauce and ½ cup maple syrup.

Preheat oven to 180°C. Brush meat
liberally with glaze mixed with chilli sauce
(if using) and put directly on oven rack.
Position a similarly sized baking dish with
a little water in it underneath meat to catch
any drips. Cook for about 1½ hours,
depending on thickness of meat. Paint meat
every 20 minutes with more glaze. Remove
meat and allow to cool and firm on a
board. (This procedure can be done hours
before the barbecue, even the day before.)

Cut cooled meat into 2.5 cm wide slices.
Brush with a little more glaze and sear over
hot coals. The glaze will become quite dark on the outside but will have
flavoured the meat quite wonderfully. Stir-fry bok choy with a few drops
of oil and water until bright green, shiny and still crisp. Top bok choy
with barbecued pork and serve immediately.

belly pork in a piquant cream sauce
SERVES 4

750 g chunk fresh *or* salted belly pork

3 tablespoons Dijon mustard

1½ cups cream

1½ tablespoons red-wine vinegar

¾ cup sliced small pickled cucumbers

1½ teaspoons crushed green peppercorns

3 tablespoons freshly chopped parsley

Simmer meat in a large saucepan of water for 1 hour, then test for doneness with a skewer. Remove meat, then dry with kitchen paper and cut into 1 cm slices. Mix mustard, cream and vinegar together. Sauté pork in a non-stick frying pan until golden and crispy, about 2 minutes a side. Tip in cream mixture and allow to bubble and reduce, then add cucumber, peppercorns and parsley. Serve piled on top of washed and dried salad leaves.

other recipes

barbecued skewers of bay leaves and pork *see* BAY LEAVES

cabbage leaves stuffed with pork, sausage and rice *see* CABBAGES AND BRUSSELS SPROUTS

chinese kidney salad *see* KIDNEYS

chinese noodle soup with pig's liver *see* LIVER

pig's liver faggots *see* LIVER

pistachio and pork terrine *see* NUTS

pork sausages with sage and tomato *see* SAUSAGES

satay marinade and sauce *see* NUTS

squid stuffed with pork and prawns *see* SQUID, CALAMARI, CUTTLEFISH AND OCTOPUS

whole cabbage stuffed with pork, liver and capers *see* CABBAGES AND BRUSSELS SPROUTS

see also BACON; HAM; KIDNEYS; LIVER; SAUSAGES; TONGUE; TROTTERS

P o t a t o e s   Our much-loved and indispensable potato (*Solanum tuberosum*), cultivated in Central and South America 4000 years ago, was brought back from the New World in the sixteenth century by the Spanish conquistadores and Sir Francis Drake and Sir Walter Raleigh. But it took 200 years for the potato to become a popular food in Europe. Its pretty flower was admired, but the plant was, after all, related to deadly nightshade, and it was rumoured that one caught leprosy from eating the tubers! │ Famine hastened its acceptance. Immediately after the French Revolution it was decreed that the rose bushes in the Tuileries gardens in Paris be uprooted to plant potatoes to feed the starving population. Potatoes brought to Prussia by Spanish mercenaries during the Thirty Years War were fed to prisoners in Prussian prison camps in the first half of the eighteenth century. It was there that they were eaten by Antoine Parmentier, a French army pharmacist. Parmentier was so convinced of the nutritional value of the potato he wrote an entire treatise promoting it. Wherever his name appears on a menu or in a recipe today, potatoes will feature largely in the dish. >

potatoes

go

with

butter

olive oil

parsley

chives

rosemary

sage

garlic

onions

cream

milk

melting cheeses

cumin

coriander

yoghurt

saffron

fish stock

salad leaves

spinach

bacon

mushrooms

beef

lamb

sausages

chicken

By the middle of the nineteenth century the Irish economy was dependent on the potato. The tragedy of the potato blight that decimated both the Irish potato crop and the population from 1845–49 changed the face of the world, as impoverished and desperate Irish migrated to the United States and Australia in large numbers.

By the beginning of the twentieth century there were more than 1000 varieties of potato known and grown. Today there are fewer than 100 varieties cultivated commercially, and most of us have access to no more than a dozen of these. Potatoes were planted in New South Wales in the earliest days of the settlement and now account for the largest tonnage of vegetables grown in Australia. We are very fortunate that our wide range of climatic regions allows potatoes to be harvested all year round.

The popularity of the potato increased rapidly once it got together with butter and oil, still an unbeatable combination. After all the potato gratins, tarts and fritters I have cooked and tasted, the dish most guaranteed to please and comfort is a bowl of new potatoes tossed with butter and parsley, or maincrop potatoes mashed with butter, milk and cream.

VARIETIES AND SEASON

Before discussing specific varieties of potato it is important to understand that there are different types of potato. A potato low in moisture and sugar and high in starch is termed *floury*. Floury specimens **bake** and **mash** perfectly and when **fried** will render golden chips or roast potatoes. Because of their low sugar content they tend to collapse when boiled. On the other hand, a *waxy* potato is high in moisture and low in starch and holds its shape and remains firm when **boiled**. Such varieties when cooked are ideal for salads or for eating just as they are with butter and parsley, or for adding raw to casseroles. Waxy potatoes are not suited to mashing or for making chips. That said, some of the newer potatoes have been bred to be all-purpose varieties – and they are more difficult to categorise.

Potatoes are also sold by stages of maturity. Every variety of potato can yield both new and maincrop potatoes. Newly dug potatoes, sold as *new* potatoes, are crisp and waxy with thin wispy skins that rub off easily. Their sugars have not yet converted to starch. The smaller new potatoes are sometimes known as chats. Be aware that many tiny potatoes are simply undersized older potatoes and do not taste like proper new potatoes. Remember, too, that new potatoes are not necessarily small. *Maincrop* potatoes are harvested fully grown and can be floury or waxy, depending on variety.

There has been renewed interest in potato varieties over the last few years, largely due to the research and marketing efforts of a few enterprising growers and the work of scientists at the Potato Research Station at Toolangi, Victoria. As a result, more and more shopkeepers are labelling their potatoes and are becoming used to customers requesting specific varieties. If you are unsure what variety is being sold in your local shop, ask.

Potatoes are available all year round and are divided into early (new) and late (mature) crops. Potatoes are frost tender, so the potatoes available in a given locality at a specific time will vary according to climatic conditions. As all varieties of potato are kept in controlled-atmosphere storage to extend the season, the consumer rarely knows when the potato he or she is buying was harvested.

Bintje This waxy, oval potato has brown skin and pale-yellow flesh. A Dutch variety, it is ideal for boiling but not mashing. **Bison** This round potato has dark-red or purple skin with shallow eyes and white flesh. It is an all-purpose potato particularly suited to boiling and baking and is also good for mashing. **Coliban** Bred by the Potato Research Station, Victoria, this round, white potato has a smooth skin that washes well. It is the most common type sold packed in supermarkets. A floury variety, it bakes and mashes well, but can disintegrate with boiling, although it can be steamed successfully. **Desiree** This waxy, long, oval, pink-skinned potato has creamy-yellow flesh. It is not suitable for deep-frying but can be boiled or baked and makes superb gnocchi. **Kennebec** An irregular white floury potato, this variety makes up 40 per cent of the crop grown in Australia and is used to make processed chips. It can be boiled, baked, fried or mashed. **Kipfler** Sometimes called the 'peanut' or 'finger' potato because of its distinctive shape, this small, long or oval variety has buff–yellow skin and yellow flesh. A waxy potato of German origin, it makes excellent eating and is best steamed. It is marvellous used in salads. **Patrone** From Holland and new to the market, this small, oval potato has creamy skin and yellow flesh. It is excellent for boiling, frying and baking. A waxy potato, it is not good for mashing. **Purple Congo** This curious oval potato is as sweet as a sweet potato, is very mealy and remains a stunning purple when cooked. It is best for boiling. **Red pontiac** Round, red-skinned with deep eyes and white flesh, this waxy, all-purpose potato is good for purées, grating, baking and boiling. **Sebago** This all-purpose, round-to-oval, white potato occupies 60 per cent of the New South Wales acreage. It can be boiled, baked, mashed or fried. **Spunta** This large potato has creamy skin and floury, yellow flesh. It breaks up easily when boiled but mashes beautifully, and is also good fried. **Tasmanian pink-eye** A small, round, buff-coloured, sweet waxy potato, this variety is distinguished by its deep-pink or purple-stained eyes. It is best boiled but not mashed. It is also sold as 'southern gold'. **Toolangi delight** This round potato has white flesh and purple skin and was bred at the Potato Research Station, Victoria. It is suitable for most types of cooking (not frying), and is recommended for making gnocchi.

SELECTION AND STORAGE

Choose potatoes that are firm and dry with unbroken skin and no sign of sprouting. Potatoes that have been stored too long will be soft and can taste sweet. Do not buy potatoes showing any green patches. (Greening occurs when potatoes suffer prolonged exposure to light, making them taste nasty and bitter. The green indicates chlorophyll, which can mean that the potato has quantities of the toxin solanine, which can cause illness. Small green patches can be cut out; more than this and the potato should be discarded.) Prefer unwashed potatoes: washed potatoes may be convenient but washing does nothing for the keeping quality of the potato. Dirt protects potatoes from bruising, deterioration and greening.

Store potatoes away from light in a well-ventilated cupboard. They can be left in the paper bag in which they were bought, but never in a plastic bag, which will make them sweat and deteriorate. Mature potatoes, especially those that are unwashed, will be fine for several weeks. New potatoes need to be cooked within a few days of purchase.

PREPARATION AND COOKING

Avoid peeling potatoes before cooking whenever possible as you will also peel away much of their food value. If you do peel potatoes, peel them very thinly. Australia's own single-bladed, plastic-handled vegetable peeler does an excellent job. Peeled potatoes are also more likely to disintegrate when boiled than unpeeled potatoes. Potatoes for salads, such as patrones or kipflers, merely need to be brushed free of any dirt before boiling or steaming. And new potatoes are never peeled.

Dress potato salads immediately the potatoes are cooked, so that the potato can absorb the oil or butter more readily. You will also use less oil or butter this way. If using mayonnaise to dress a salad, allow the potato to cool until warm or the heat will break the emulsion in the mayonnaise.

TO STEAM | Small waxy varieties are best steamed and need not be peeled beforehand. Depending on their size, potatoes take 10–15 minutes to steam. Test with a fine skewer or the point of a sharp knife. There must be no resistance. If you wish to peel the cooked potatoes, do so as soon as you can handle them.

TO BOIL | Place the whole unpeeled potatoes in lightly salted cold water, then bring them to a boil and simmer gently for 15–20 minutes until tender. Very large potatoes are often peeled and cut into chunks before cooking. Never leave cooked potatoes in their water – drain them as soon as they are tender.

TO MASH | The English prefer stiff mashed potato, while the French prefer a more flowing purée. The English usually mash their potato with butter and cold milk. The French always use hot milk and often butter as well. In the south of France olive oil is added rather than butter. Whichever consistency you prefer, drain the peeled, cooked potato well, return the saucepan to the heat for a minute or so to drive off any remaining moisture and then crush the potato with a masher, or pass it through the coarse disc of a food mill or a potato ricer. Never use a food processor or your mashed potato will have the texture of glue. Using a wooden spoon, beat in sufficient butter and milk, hot or cold, to achieve the texture you prefer. Adjust the seasoning.

TO BAKE | My favourite baking method is to wash and dry the potatoes, then stab them once or twice with a skewer and place them on the rack of the oven, preheated to 200°C. They will be tender in 1 hour, but better after 1½ hours, when the skin will be very crusty. If the potatoes are very large, halve them. The cut side of the potato will puff up and develop a crackling brown skin. (Never bake potatoes wrapped in foil as they will be flabby.) This is my standard method for cooking pontiacs or sebago potatoes. I learnt it from my mother. I can see her now, bent in front of the oven scooping the baked potatoes into her apron before bringing them to the table.

TO ROAST | Some cooks like to parboil peeled potatoes before baking them in the fatty juices around the family roast. To do this, ensure the parboiled potatoes are dry, so that they do not stick and leave their crusts in the baking dish. Turn the potatoes every 15 minutes. They will take at least 1 hour to become golden and crunchy. It is really only sensible to cook potatoes like this when you are cooking a roast of chicken, lamb or pork that will yield lots of rich juices. Otherwise if it is crusty fried potatoes you want, sauté them instead.

TO SAUTÉ | This is the potato dish served in most Italian cafés. (A large sprig of rosemary and half a dozen unpeeled garlic cloves added to the potato before you start cooking give an authentic Italian touch.) Leftover cooked potato is excellent to sauté. If you do not have leftover potato, parboil a floury variety, peel it when cool and then cut into chunky bite-sized pieces. Sauté the potato in oil, duck fat or pork fat, tossing frequently until the pieces are a deep gold and crusty. Expect to spend 15 minutes at least tossing and lifting. The trick is to cook the potato halfway, then drain and return it to the pan with a little extra oil or fat and continue to crisp. Serve at once.

TO DEEP-FRY Not many home kitchens are really set up for the safe deep-frying of chips. The oil must be thermostatically controlled, there must be plenty of it, there must be enough room in the container for the water in the potatoes to boil up without the oil overflowing, and there must be excellent ventilation to prevent the entire house smelling of frying oil. Oh, and the oil must be *very* clean, the chips must be twice-cooked – once at 160°C, and once at 175°C – and they shouldn't wait around, which means it is not much fun for the chip-fryer, who cannot move from his or her station – and people eat a lot of chips! Most people seem to compromise and buy blanched frozen chips. They are not as good as the real thing. My advice is to enjoy chips at a restaurant that does them well and forget them at home.

recipes

potato gnocchi

SERVES 6–8

olive mashed potato

Work a spoonful of olive oil and a spoonful of chopped olives into mashed potato to serve alongside grilled fish or sautéd rabbit or lamb fillets.

These potato dumplings should be light and velvety. They are absolutely delicious tossed with blue cheese and parmesan, a thin purée of well-cooked onion flecked with anchovy, a flavoursome tomato sauce, or pesto. Gnocchi are also often served with a meat sauce or ragù, but I think the meat sauce detracts from the delicate purity of these little dumplings.

Every Italian food writer has the one 'true' recipe for gnocchi. I agree with Marcella Hazan, who says absolutely no eggs; other writers almost all add eggs. As little flour as possible says one, a stiff dough says another. It is important to choose a potato that mashes well, and to cook the potatoes with their skins on. Do not delay the shaping and cooking of the gnocchi as the dough will become sticky, then need more flour and thus be heavier. The sauce for the gnocchi should be ready before you start cooking.

butter
1 kg potatoes (Toolangi delight are excellent; desiree are good too)
salt
325 g plain flour

Preheat oven to 160°C and butter a gratin dish. Bring a large saucepan of lightly salted water (at least 3 litres) to the boil in preparation for cooking gnocchi. Boil potatoes in another saucepan until tender, 15–20 minutes, then drain and peel. Pass potatoes through a food mill or a potato ricer directly onto a work surface, then sprinkle with salt. With one hand sprinkle potato with some flour and, using the heel of the other hand, work it in. The skill is to be as deft and quick as possible. Continue until all flour is incorporated. When the cooking water is at a fast boil, roll potato mixture into a long rope and cut into 1 cm pieces. Traditionally each piece is rolled across the curved side of a fork using one finger. This makes the distinctive ridges to which the sauce is said to cling more readily. (This is a knack and can take a bit of practice. Gnocchi cut into small pieces with a knife will still taste good.)

Adjust heat, so that water is simmering. Drop in some gnocchi, allowing room to swell. As gnocchi rise to surface (this takes a few minutes), lift them out with a perforated skimmer, drain for a moment over pot, tip into buttered dish and put in warm oven. Repeat with remaining gnocchi. Your chosen sauce should be hot on the stove. Pour it over the gnocchi, shake gently and serve at once.

potato frittata

SERVES 4–6

4 tablespoons olive oil
2 potatoes, sliced
2 cloves garlic, sliced
1 handful cooked spinach
    or 1 cup raw small
    spinach leaves
salt
freshly ground black pepper
2 tablespoons freshly chopped
    parsley
2 teaspoons freshly snipped
    chives
6 free-range eggs, lightly
    whisked

Heat half the oil in a heavy-based frying pan and add potato. Cover and allow to soften for 5 minutes over medium heat. Remove lid, turn potato, then add garlic and spinach and turn every few minutes until potato is tender. Transfer to a bowl and season with salt, pepper and herbs.

Wipe out pan. Pour eggs over potato and eggs. Heat remaining oil over a moderate to high heat and tip in potato mixture. The edges should frill and puff up at once. Lower heat and cook until underside is golden brown – check by lifting edge with a flexible spatula. Slide spatula around edges to ensure omelette is not

sticking. Place pan in a hot oven or under a griller to cook top. Place a warmed plate over pan and quickly invert. Eat at once.

variations Middle Eastern spices can transport this dish to Egypt, where it becomes an *eggah*. Sheep's milk cheese or a melting cheese such as raclette or gruyère can be shaved over the top before the omelette goes into the oven. The spinach can be replaced by a cup of any other cooked greens – beans, peas, zucchini, and so on.

potato and sorrel omelette

SERVES 1

Sorrel is a delicate herb that has all the sharpness and freshness of lemon. It combines particularly well with potatoes and eggs. If you grow your own sorrel – and it's very easy to do so – choose tender young leaves over larger leaves, which can be strongly flavoured. Snails adore sorrel, so check well when washing this vegetable, whether it is home-grown or bought.

sautéd potatoes
Add small pieces of smoked bacon, chopped raw witlof, sautéd onion rings, mushrooms or plenty of parsley to sautéing potatoes.

potatoes with chive cream
Infuse hot cream with a generous handful of chives and toss through boiled potatoes.

30 leaves sorrel
60 g unsalted butter
1 potato, cut into 1 cm dice
salt
freshly ground black pepper
2 eggs, lightly whisked
2 tablespoons freshly chopped
   parsley

**garlic mashed
potato**
*Add a cream and
garlic purée (see
p. 321), allowing a
clove per person, to
mashed potato
instead of, or as
well as, boiling milk,
and season to taste.
If you like, add
coarsely chopped
olives to serve with
full-flavoured fish or
a rabbit stew.*

Tear each sorrel leaf away from its central rib and discard rib. Wash and dry sorrel. Heat half the butter in a small heavy-based saucepan and add sorrel. Cover pan and cook for 2 minutes. Remove lid, then stir, cover again and leave for a further 2 minutes. The sorrel will have melted into an olive-green purée. Tip into a strainer and set aside in a warm place.

Cover potato with water and bring slowly to a boil. Simmer until just tender (5 minutes), then drain well. Mix potato with sorrel, season lightly and keep warm. Season eggs and add parsley. Heat remaining butter in a non-stick frying pan until foaming, then pour in eggs, shaking to spread. With a wooden spoon, drag cooked egg to centre, tilting pan to spread runny part again. This will take less than a minute. Tilt pan, so that omelette slides away from you. Quickly add potato and sorrel filling to centre of omelette. Fold down top third and slide omelette onto a heated plate, turning it over on itself. Skim omelette with a tiny slice of butter and eat at once.

potato cakes from grated raw potato   SERVES 4

Serve these crisp potato cakes topped with scrambled eggs, a grilled tomato or smoked fish with sour cream or horseradish. Don't let the grated potato stand for any length of time as it will discolour. It will still taste fine, but the colour will be an unappetising bluish grey.

3 large all-purpose potatoes
salt
freshly ground black pepper
60 g butter, melted
olive oil

Preheat oven to 150°C. Grate potatoes coarsely into a bowl of cold water. Rinse potato, then drain and dry carefully. Tip potato into a basin, then season and stir in melted butter. Heat a heavy-based, cast-iron frying pan and film it with oil. Drop spoonfuls of potato mixture into pan and fry until golden brown and crisp on both sides. Drain on kitchen paper and keep warm in oven until all cakes are fried.

variations Lightly sautéed onion and garlic and/or fresh herbs can also be added to the grated potato. I have also added tiny cubes of fontina or taleggio cheese to the grated potato with success. Crisped sage leaves are also lovely to stir in, as are a few crumbled, oven-crisped rosemary leaves.

curried vegetables

SERVES 4

Sometimes when the cupboard is very bare I make a simple coconut curry from any vegetables I have on hand – but it must include potato.

1 eggplant, cut into bite-sized pieces
salt
2 unpeeled waxy potatoes (pontiacs work well)
2 carrots, peeled
1 chunk butternut pumpkin, peeled
1 red pepper
3 tablespoons vegetable oil
2 cloves garlic, chopped
1 small piece fresh ginger
1 onion, chopped
½ teaspoon ground turmeric
2 teaspoons curry paste
1 teaspoon mustard seeds
½ stick cinnamon
3 curry leaves
1 x 375 ml can peeled tomatoes
1 cup coconut milk

Sprinkle eggplant with salt and set aside for 30 minutes, then rinse and dry well. Cut potatoes, carrots, pumpkin and red pepper into bite-sized pieces. Heat oil in an enamelled cast-iron casserole. Sauté garlic, ginger, onion, turmeric, curry paste, mustard seeds and cinnamon stick for 5 minutes. Stir well and add curry leaves. Add all vegetables except tomatoes to casserole and stir well to coat. Blend tomatoes and their juice in a food processor and add to casserole, then cover and simmer until the vegetables are tender, about 20 minutes. Add coconut milk and season to taste with salt. Simmer a further 10 minutes, uncovered, and serve with rice or lentils and chutney.

potato cakes
Mix leftover mashed potato with an egg and just enough plain flour to make a firm mixture, then season with herbs, salt and pepper and form into flattish cakes. Dip lightly in plain flour and fry until golden in a mixture of butter and oil and serve with fried eggs, bacon, grilled tomatoes or sausages.

potatoes in paper parcels

This dish is for the very finest small new potatoes. Serve it with a simple fish dish, poached salmon, for example.

best-quality small new potatoes
barely melted unsalted butter
sea salt
freshly ground black pepper
unpeeled garlic cloves

Preheat oven to 200°C. Wash and dry potatoes carefully, then roll them in butter. Sprinkle with salt and pepper and toss with garlic. Make individual parcels of buttery potatoes and garlic using baking paper and fold edges firmly a couple of times. Bake for 40 minutes. The paper parcels will be browned and puffed up. Serve the potatoes in their parcels – your guests or family members will enjoy tearing open the parcels and inhaling the delicious aroma.

potato drop scones

MAKES 12–15

Don't leave the batter for these drop scones for too long as it will discolour, although the flavour will still be fine. These cakes can be served with maple syrup or instead of toast under a poached or fried egg or smoked salmon.

roesti

Grate parboiled cold potatoes coarsely, then season and pack the mixture into a frying pan in which butter and oil have been heated. As the edges start to crisp and turn golden, turn the potato cake onto a plate, then return it to the hot pan to cook the second side. Serve cut into wedges.

1 potato, peeled and diced
1 egg
1 tablespoon plain flour
1½ tablespoons cream
1½ tablespoons freshly
   chopped parsley
salt
freshly ground black pepper
olive oil

In a food processor, blend potato, egg and flour to a smooth batter. Transfer to a bowl and stir in cream and parsley and season. Heat a heavy-based, cast-iron frying pan, film it with oil and cook a drop scone until lightly browned on each side. Taste for seasoning and adjust the rest of the batter if necessary. Proceed to cook drop scones.

potato gratin

SERVES 8

There are many versions of the potato gratin: with and without cheese, with and without onion, with mushrooms, with cream, with stock, with milk and cream, and so on. Sometimes the potato is blanched in milk first, sometimes not. It can become so confusing that an inexperienced cook doesn't even try! But what a treat to miss out on. A potato gratin plus a green salad makes a delicious lunch.

The essentials are to have a deep gratin dish and plenty of time. Potato gratins need to cook for a long time to become deliciously creamy inside and have a deep-golden crust on the top. This is a simple version. The flour prevents the curdled, cheesy appearance of some gratins.

potato croquettes

Mix leftover mashed potato with an egg and season. Roll the mixture into small cork shapes to make croquettes, then dip them in beaten egg and breadcrumbs before frying.

8 waxy potatoes, peeled
40 g butter
2 cloves garlic, very thinly
   sliced
salt
freshly ground black pepper
freshly grated nutmeg
   (optional)
1 teaspoon plain flour
200 ml cream
400 ml boiling milk

Preheat oven to 200°C. Slice potatoes thinly (but not too thinly). Using half the butter, grease gratin dish. Arrange potato in overlapping rows in dish, adding a little garlic from time to time. Season as you go with salt and pepper and a grating of nutmeg, if desired. Mix flour into cream and combine with milk. Pour over gratin evenly and carefully, so that potato is not disturbed. Bake for 1 hour. If the gratin seems to be browning too quickly, put it lower in oven, cover it with foil or both.

potato salad with bacon and sour cream   SERVES 4

I like to use my red-wine mustard in this delicious salad (we make this mustard commercially at the moment but a recipe also appears in Stephanie's Feasts and Stories*).*

500 g waxy potatoes (desirees are ideal)
125 g bacon, diced
2 tablespoons sour cream
1 teaspoon Dijon mustard
2 teaspoons seeded mustard
1 tablespoon red-wine vinegar
pinch of salt
1 tablespoon finely snipped fresh chives

Boil potatoes until tender, then peel and cut into 3 cm cubes and set aside. Fry bacon gently until crisp and retain bacon fat. Combine sour cream, mustards, vinegar and salt, then tip into pan with bacon and bacon fat, stirring to mix. Quickly pour over potato, lifting and stirring, and scatter with chives. Season with freshly ground black pepper, if you wish. Serve at room temperature.

potatoes with olive oil
Toss steamed or boiled potatoes with the very best extra-virgin olive oil and herbs instead of butter.

spanish potato with chorizo   SERVES 4

200 g semi-dried chorizo sausage
1 kg waxy potatoes, peeled
3 cloves garlic, finely chopped
½ onion, finely chopped
olive oil
1 bay leaf
1 teaspoon paprika
salt

Cut chorizo and potatoes into bite-sized pieces. Sauté chorizo, garlic and onion in olive oil in a cast-iron casserole or heatproof gratin dish for 5 minutes. Add potato, bay leaf and paprika, then stir and toss for 5 minutes. Add water to barely cover and simmer, uncovered, for 20 minutes until potato is tender and liquid is lightly thickened. Taste for salt. Excellent with stewed sweet peppers.

fish soup with potato
Drop sliced potato into soup made with fish stock, saffron and garlic to thicken it lightly. Serve with lots of parsley and garlic croutons.

other recipes

cauliflower and potato pie *see* CAULIFLOWERS
fennel and potato fry-up *see* FENNEL
herring fillets with potatoes and dill *see* DILL
leek and potato soup *see* LEEK
melita's skordalia *see* GARLIC
pizza rustica with potato and rosemary *see* ROSEMARY
polish sausage and potato salad *see* SAUSAGES
potato and celeriac purée *see* CELERY AND CELERIAC
potato and chive cake *see* CHIVES
roasted rosemary potatoes *see* ROSEMARY
spinach and ricotta gnocchi *see* SPINACH
yabby salad with walnuts and potatoes *see* YABBIES

P *p r a w n s* Abundant in the tropical and temperate regions of Australia, prawns are highly regarded in all Asian cuisines, and in Australia many delectable preparations can be sampled in Chinese and Thai restaurants. | We all know that 'throwing a prawn on the barbie' has been adopted by our image-makers as the quintessential Australian culinary masterpiece, but it's not a practice restricted to this continent. Throwing a prawn on the barbie is, after all, just another version of grilling prawns *a la plancha* as witnessed in every seaside bar in southern Spain. In that country grilled prawns come accompanied by a large slice of toasted white bread spread with the powerful *all-i-oli*, the Spanish version of the garlic mayonnaise popular in the south of France. This simplicity is the key to serving good prawns. I have cooked many sophisticated and clever dishes using prawns in my time, but my most memorable prawn was one enjoyed at a wooden table in Garrucha, 50 m from the Mediterranean in Andalusia, the air rich with the smell of sizzling seafood and my mouth full of fresh and garlicky flavours. >

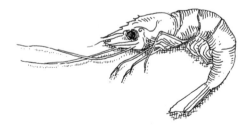

Our prawns are fished by trawlers that roam the vast areas of Australia's northern waters, including the tidal lakes and estuaries. On board these large factory trawlers some prawns may be held in chilled sea water between 0°C and 0.5°C. Fresh prawns are being held in ice slurries more and more frequently. Provided the temperature is correctly maintained, such prawns will remain in pristine condition for 3–5 days. Some are also boiled in sea water and stored in coolrooms on board, but the bulk of the catch, boiled or not, is snap-frozen and processed into bulk packs.

Prawn aquaculture is a new development that is growing rapidly in size, efficiency and importance. The farms are found mainly along the coasts of New South Wales and Queensland, while there are also experimental farms in the Northern Territory. Prawns harvested from the farms are packed in ice and delivered chilled to markets within 24–48 hours. Frozen prawns are also available.

VARIETIES AND SEASON

There are 25 or more species of prawn found in Australian waters but only a third of these are exploited commercially. In the wild prawns are fished in the summer and spring. Northern prawn farmers can harvest 2 crops a year, so farmed prawns are available fresh all year. As the bulk of the prawn catch is frozen, frozen prawns are available all year round.

BANANA | *Penaeus merguiensis* is a large, smooth-shelled prawn that is creamy-yellow and sometimes tinged with red or speckled blue. It has been recorded as growing up to 24 cm long. It is found in northern waters from Shark Bay, Western Australia, to the Tweed River, New South Wales.

BLACK TIGER | *P. monodon*, also known as the giant tiger, blue tiger, jumbo tiger, leader or panda prawn, is very large with distinctive black and white stripes across the abdomen. It is distributed from Shark Bay, Western Australia, north to Sydney and throughout the Pacific and is the species used in 95 per cent of the aquaculture in Australia.

EASTERN KING | Marketed with other species as a king prawn, *P. plebejus* is the largest and best-known prawn, grows up to 30 cm in length and is a light, reddish brown colour with bright-yellow appendages. It is found down the east coast from Mackay, Queensland, to Bass Strait.

prawns
go
with
garlic
olive oil
chillies
fish sauce
soy sauce
Worcestershire sauce
mint
coriander
basil
onions
ginger
rice wine
spring onions
chives
noodles
cumin
tomatoes
mayonnaise
lemons
limes
rice

GREASYBACK | *Metapenaeus bennettae*, also called the greentail or river prawn, is similar to the school prawn but has a rough shell that feels greasy when rubbed. It is being marketed, somewhat confusingly, with a number of *Metapenaeus* species as a school prawn. It is found down the east coast from Rockhampton, Queensland, to Victoria's Gippsland Lakes.

ROYAL RED | *Haliporoides sibogae*, a small-to-medium prawn (it grows to 20 cm in length), has a strong flavour and a very loose shell. Found in very deep waters off the Western Australian coast, off the east coast from Rockhampton, Queensland, to the eastern tip of Victoria and off the Great Barrier Reef, this prawn oxidises very quickly and must be separated from its shell as soon as possible. It is usually sold green with the shell removed and may shrink and curl up more than other varieties when cooked.

SCHOOL | *M. macleayi* is a smooth-shelled prawn up to 16 cm long, with a pale-grey body and blue tail-fan tip. It is found north of Noosa, Queensland, down to Corner Inlet, Victoria.

TIGER | *P. esculentus* is also known as the brown tiger prawn. It is smooth-shelled and can be up to 30 cm long. The head and body are striped with alternate bands of buff and dark brown or rusty orange. It is found off the west, north and east coasts of Australia, from Shark Bay, Western Australia, around to northern New South Wales.

WESTERN KING | *P. latisulcatus*, also known as the blue-legged prawn, is similar in appearance to the eastern king prawn except that its walking legs are blue and the tail fan is tipped with blue. Marketed as a king prawn, it is widely distributed along the Australian coastline, from South Australia to northern New South Wales, taking in the north and west coasts along the way.

SELECTION AND STORAGE

Only buy Australian prawns. It is rare to be offered a choice of varieties. Instead, we are offered large or small prawns that are green (uncooked) or cooked, fresh or frozen (green or cooked) and that have their shells on or off (if green). (Note that the 'green' does not refer to their colour, but their raw state.) Differences in flavour and texture between varieties are noticeable to experts but not to most consumers. Freshness is considered the most important characteristic. Frozen blocks of very small shelled prawns are imported from South-East Asia and offered for sale in Asian food stores, where they are often thawed before being sold. In my experience these prawns are tasteless.

As many prawn-fishing grounds are remote, and prawn trawlers remain at sea for weeks at a time, frozen prawns are frequently a sensible choice. This statement may appear to contradict my usual insistence on using fresh ingredients, but raw prawns deteriorate rapidly, which is why it is necessary to freeze, chill or cook them at sea. Freshly harvested, snap-frozen prawns, or fresh prawns that have been held in an ice slurry at a constant temperature, are vastly superior to prawns that have been 2–3 days out of the water and not frozen. However, since the advent of prawn-farming, it is becoming increasingly easy to find *fresh green* prawns.

Green prawns should have a pleasant sea smell and not look sweaty. Never buy green prawns with black heads or oozing black juices. While they can be bought fresh or frozen, it is far preferable to buy *frozen green* prawns if fresh farmed prawns are not available. When a recipe calls for green prawns it is not possible to substitute cooked prawns. Most prawns are bright red when cooked and may have been frozen for up to 3 months. If cooked again, these prawns will become dry, woody and unappetising.

I never buy *frozen cooked* prawns, as once thawed I find them icy-cold, flabby and depressing. Prawns cooked 2–3 days before you buy them can taste horrible and smell of ammonia. If you want to eat *freshly boiled* prawns, start with fresh green prawns and cook them yourself. Or if you are lucky enough to live near where freshly caught prawns are boiled on the spot (the Sydney Fish Market, for example), buy some and eat them from the paper, preferably in sight of the sea. From time to time fresh western king prawns are available in markets in Victoria and South Australia. These wonderful wild prawns are very special. Buy them and eat them that night!

Store frozen green prawns in the freezer compartment of your refrigerator. When needed, thaw them on a plate in the refrigerator and cook them without delay.

PREPARATION AND COOKING

Allow 4–6 average-sized prawns per person if there are other dishes on a buffet table, fewer if the prawn dish is a first course, and maybe 6 or more if dinner is barbecued prawns and nothing else. Note that 1 kg prawns in the shell yields 500 g prawn meat (heads and shells removed).

The basic preparation varies according to whether one wants the prawns with or without the shells left on, although the heads are usually removed and the intestinal vein is *always* removed. Do not cut the head from a prawn as you will lose some of the tail flesh. Instead, pull the head away from the tail. Prawns look more interesting with their tails left on. The tails also make a convenient handle if one is to dip raw prawns in batter or cooked prawns into a seasoning or dipping sauce.

The Chinese technique of massaging shelled prawns with cornflour and bicarbonate of soda is worth learning as it results in silky prawns that are never woody. This technique is called 'velveting' (*see* p. 584). Velveted prawns can be simmered in water, broth or a rich sauce for 2–4 minutes depending on size, or can be sautéed, steamed or stir-fried.

butterflied prawns
Cut shelled prawns nearly in half, so that they open out like a butterfly, then season them and dip into egg and fine breadcrumbs and shallow-fry in oil or clarified butter.
Serve with mayonnaise mixed with chutney or a dipping sauce.

TO PREPARE | **Shell on** Pull the head away from the tail section and discard it. Using scissors, cut the shell along the outer curve. With a small knife, pull out the black intestinal thread. (With practice and by applying firm pressure to the head as you pull it away from the flesh, it is possible to pull the intestinal thread out with the head. It is also possible to hook out the intestinal vein using a thin skewer without slitting open the back.) Roll prawns in a light oil. To **back-split** a prawn, remove the head as above. Using a small knife, cut into the flesh (but not all the way through) and press the 'halves' apart. Both sides should be the same thickness. Remove the vein. With the heel of your hand press down gently to further open the prawn. You should now have a flattish surface, the flesh held in place by the shell. Brush the flesh and the shell with olive oil. **Shell off** Remove head and intestinal vein as above. Peel off the shell, leaving the tail intact. 'Velvet' the prawns or roll them in oil.

prawn rolls
Stir velveted, boiled prawns into a little mayonnaise or sour cream and stuff a wholemeal roll with them for a great picnic lunch.

TO 'VELVET' | Mix ½ cup cornflour with 1 tablespoon bicarbonate of soda for every 1 kg shelled prawns. Tip the de-veined prawns into a bowl and massage the cornflour mixture quite firmly through them, working it in for 2–3 minutes. Transfer the prawns to a colander and, with the cold tap running at full pace, massage them again for a further 5 minutes. Drain well and simmer, sauté, steam or stir-fry the prawns.

TO BOIL | Thawed green prawns in the shell, head left on but de-veined, are used when boiled prawns are required. (If you wish to boil shelled prawns, you must velvet them first.) Use a large saucepan, so that the water will not go off the boil for more than a minute when the prawns are added, and add 200 g salt for every 2 litres water. Drop in the prawns when the water is boiling and simmer until they change colour, 3–4 minutes. Test one – it should not be soft, nor too hard. Remove the cooked prawns from the water immediately and allow to drain. Serve the prawns warm or at room temperature.

TO STEAM | Arrange a Chinese bamboo steamer over a saucepan half-filled with simmering water.

Line the basket with the outside leaves of a lettuce and arrange de-veined, velveted prawns on this. If you have no lettuce leaves, place the prawns on a small plate inside the basket (make sure that there is room for the steam to rise around the plate). Cover the basket and steam for about 4 minutes. Check that the prawns are no longer glassy and remove them to a warm serving dish. Steamed prawns are often served with a simple stir-fried vegetable, such as broccoli or snowpeas.

| **TO BARBECUE OR GRILL** | I do not advise barbecuing or grilling shelled prawns, although many people do. The flesh |

inevitably hardens without the protection of the shell. If barbecuing, wait until all flames have died down and the coals are white-hot. If grilling, heat your griller as high as possible and line the tray with lightly oiled foil. Place the prepared prawns on the barbie or under the griller and turn once when the shells are bright red. The prawns can also be threaded onto soaked bamboo skewers to make turning easier. When back-split, the prawns need to be skewered crosswise onto 2 skewers, so that the prawns are arranged like the rungs of a ladder. As prawns cook very fast it is a mistake to cook them through completely, especially without the protection of their shells, as they will be dry and cottony.

| **TO DEEP-FRY** | Dip shelled and de-veined prawns in cornflour and then Beer Batter ✐; the batter will cling in |

a thin, even film and one will use less of it. Deep-fry in clean olive oil at 175°C until golden (3–5 minutes). There does not need to be a bath of oil, although there must be a depth of at least 3 cm, so that the prawns can float. Like all deep-fried food, the crisp prawns must be very well drained. I enjoy Tartare Sauce ✐ with deep-fried prawns or Thai-style Dipping Sauce (*see* YABBIES), which is just as delicious but not as rich.

prawn olive oil
Wash and dry prawn heads, then sauté them over a high heat in a little oil until bright red. Pour in light olive oil, so that the prawn heads are well covered, and simmer for 5 minutes. Allow to cool, then strain the oil and bottle it. Kept refrigerated for a month, this oil is useful for drizzling on pasta or into stir-fries or shellfish salads or for making mayonnaise or vinaigrette.

cantonese spiced salt

This seasoning is served with deep-fried or barbecued food, such as prawns, or roasted, crispy chicken or duck.

| I teaspoon Szechuan peppercorns
3 tablespoons salt | Place peppercorns in a small frying pan and cover with salt. Heat very gently, shaking and stirring until peppercorns begin to smoke and smell fragrant and salt becomes |

light brown. Remove from heat and allow mixture to become quite cold. Grind in a spice grinder and store in an airtight jar. Use the spiced salt within 1–2 weeks. >

five-spice powder Add 3 teaspoons five-spice powder to this mixture for a different flavour.

chinese soy dipping sauce

MAKES ½ CUP

This sauce can be used with freshly steamed or stir-fried prawns.

2 tablespoons sugar

2 tablespoons red or white rice vinegar

2 tablespoons finely chopped fresh ginger

2 tablespoons light soy sauce

Dissolve sugar in vinegar, then add ginger and soy sauce. Store in an airtight jar and use within a few days.

prawn cakes

MAKES 10

Tiny prawn cakes can be handed around with drinks: impale them on toothpicks and have a bowl of dipping sauce on the serving tray. Larger cakes can be tossed with noodles and vegetables as a main meal.

500 g green prawns, shelled and de-veined (to yield 250 g)

1 teaspoon fish sauce

1 slice fresh ginger, finely chopped

1 clove garlic

1 tablespoon freshly chopped coriander root and fine leaves

2 tablespoons finely chopped spring onion

1 teaspoon sugar

¼ teaspoon freshly chopped chilli or sambal oelek

vegetable oil

Process all ingredients except oil to a smooth paste. Taste for saltiness and adjust with fish sauce. With wet hands, form into small balls or flattish cakes. Shallow-fry in hot oil for 2 minutes each side until golden. Drain well on kitchen paper. Decorate with young coriander leaves, if desired, and serve warm.

steamed cakes These cakes can be steamed instead of fried. A basil leaf can be pressed onto each cake before steaming.

---

grilled prawns
Back-split and de-vein green prawns, then rub them with oil and grill. Drizzle with extra-virgin olive oil and serve with lemon or lime wedges, sea salt and rye bread. Sprinkle the prawns with finely sliced fresh chilli, if desired.

prawn scrambled eggs
Add chopped green prawn meat to scrambled eggs when the first curds start to set and stir in 1 teaspoon light soy sauce and some finely chopped spring onions.

boiled prawns
Boil green prawns still in the shell and serve warm with a bowl of Mayonnaise and good bread.

middle eastern sautéd prawns SERVES 2–4

These prawns can be presented as one in a series of dishes or can be enjoyed for lunch with an orange and watercress salad or Smoky Eggplant Purée (see EGGPLANTS*). They can also be served alongside small potatoes tossed in roasted cumin seeds and olive oil.*

12 velveted prawns
2 tablespoons olive oil
1 small red onion, very finely
  chopped
2 cloves garlic, finely chopped
1 teaspoon cumin seeds,
  lightly crushed
pinch of cayenne pepper
pinch of sugar
freshly ground black pepper
juice of 1 lemon
2 tablespoons finely chopped
  parsley

Sauté prawns in half the oil in a frying pan for 1 minute each side, then remove and keep warm in an oven set at 150°C (they will still need a little more cooking). Add remaining oil and sauté onion and garlic over moderate heat until onion has softened. Add cumin, cayenne and sugar and generously grind over black pepper, then stir. Return prawns to pan and shake to mix well. Cook for 2 minutes, then add lemon juice and parsley and serve at once.

spicy prawns
Sauté shelled, velveted prawns for 2 minutes, then toss with chilli sauce, satay sauce, tomato sauce or home-made fruity relish or chutney and serve with Chinese egg noodles sprinkled with a few drops of sesame oil. Scatter with finely sliced spring onion and coriander leaves.

jill's warm prawn and mint salad SERVES 2

This first course comes from an article by Jill Dupleix that appeared in the Age *and* Sydney Morning Herald's *'Good Weekend' magazine.*

1–2 tablespoons fish sauce
juice of 1 lime *or* lemon
3 tablespoons coconut milk
1 tablespoon sugar
1 clove garlic, crushed
1 teaspoon freshly grated
  ginger
1 fresh red chilli, finely sliced
freshly ground black pepper
12 green tiger prawns, peeled
  and de-veined
2 tablespoons finely sliced
  fresh mint leaves

Mix fish sauce, lime juice, coconut milk, sugar, garlic, ginger, chilli and pepper in a bowl. Cook prawns in simmering, salted water for 1–2 minutes until pink. Toss prawns in dressing, then add mint leaves. Serve warm.

battered prawns
Dip shelled, de-veined green prawns into Beer Batter ✑ *and deep-fry in clean oil at 175°C. Serve with Ponzu Sauce* ✑ *or warmed light soy sauce into which you have stirred 1 finely chopped garlic clove, 1 teaspoon finely chopped fresh ginger and the juice of a lemon.*

garlic prawns

SERVES 4

This is one of the most popular ways of enjoying prawns. There are dozens of versions. This recipe has been adapted from the one given by Grant Blackman in The Great Australian Shellfish Cookbook.

dipping sauce for prawns
Offer the dressing for Autumn Buckwheat Noodle Salad (see PASTA AND NOODLES*) as a dipping sauce for prawns.*

8 cloves garlic, finely chopped
1 cup olive oil
24 green prawns, velveted or back-split
1 cup white wine
2 tablespoons lemon juice
1 teaspoon salt
4 tablespoons freshly chopped parsley

Mix garlic and oil in a screw-top jar and refrigerate overnight. Next day, preheat oven to 220°C. Put prawns in a single layer in an appropriately sized ovenproof gratin dish. Pour over oil and garlic to taste, add wine, lemon juice and salt and mix well. Cover loosely with foil and cook in oven for 5–8 minutes. Check that prawns are ready – they should be firm and pink. Sprinkle with parsley. Serve straight from the dish and offer good crusty bread for mopping and large napkins.

basil Bake a handful of basil leaves with the prawns to give a wonderful aroma to the dish.

other recipes

prawns with ginger, spring onion and tomato *see* GINGER
squid stuffed with pork and prawns *see* SQUID, CALAMARI, CUTTLEFISH AND OCTOPUS
stir-fried cellophane noodles with prawns *see* PASTA AND NOODLES
stir-fried okra and prawns *see* OKRA
sweet potato and prawn fritters *see* SWEET POTATOES
tom yam goong – sour prawn soup *see* LEMONS AND LIMES

pumpkins

Pumpkins The pumpkin is an everyday sort of vegetable. If one asked an Australian to nominate the vegetables referred to when we speak of 'meat and three veg', pumpkin would probably be there, along with potatoes and peas or maybe beans. It is popular but has not much social prestige. Perhaps it is because we don't tend to look past the 'everyday' varieties of pumpkin. Thinking I knew a fair bit about this vegetable and its cousins the squash, I became more and more confused the more I read. This 'everyday' vegetable is much more complex than I thought. | Pumpkins, along with bush marrows, pattipan squash, zucchini and chokos, belong to the *Cucurbita* genus, the edible gourds or squash. This group includes hundreds of varieties displaying a wide range of colours, sizes and shapes. Some authorities divide the lot into 'summer squash' (zucchini, pattipan squash, bush marrows) and 'winter squash' (pumpkin, gramma, acorn squash). 'Summer squash' are said not to need peeling, whereas winter squash do. Other authorities ignore all varieties other than pumpkin and zucchini. Still others hesitate and decide that pumpkin is a pre-winter squash. In Australia we refer to the most common varieties as pumpkin, not winter squash. I discuss summer squash in ZUCCHINI AND SQUASH. >

pumpkins
go
with
butter
olive oil
black pepper
nutmeg
soft cheese
parmesan cheese
tomato sauce
paprika
rosemary
sage
tarragon
garlic
onion
parsley
lamb
bacon
beef casseroles
cinnamon
raisins
maple syrup
cream
brown sugar

The most accurate general name for the whole lot is 'squash', the name adapted by the early pilgrims in the United States from various American Indian words for this gourd. (There is archaeological evidence that squash was a staple in the Indian diet throughout the Americas from 3000 BC.) The word 'pumpkin' was adopted in seventeenth-century Europe and derives from the Greek for melon ('pepon'), which originally meant 'cooked by the sun' or 'ripe'.

VARIETIES AND SEASON

Pumpkin varieties have improved. It is a long time since I encountered a thin-flavoured, stringy specimen, or one of those butternuts that had unexplained white lumps in the flesh. Pumpkins are available all year round.

Baby blue This small, spherical version of the Queensland blue weighs up to 2 kg. It has the same hard skin and excellent, dry deep-orange flesh of its larger namesake. **Butter** This spherical pumpkin has a flattened top, orange–pink skin and deep-yellow flesh. The skin is easy to cut and the flavour is good. It weighs 6–11 kg. **Butternut** Developed from the gramma, this pumpkin is shaped like a pear, has buff to golden brown skin and bright-orange, very sweet, dry flesh, and weighs up to 2 kg. **Crown prince** This pumpkin is a flattened drum shape and has thick grey skin and deep-orange flesh. It has excellent flavour and weighs up to 6 kg. **Dumpling** Sometimes described as a little or sweet dumpling, this small pumpkin has light-green skin striped with green that is easy to cut. It is a convenient size for stuffing but its pale-yellow flesh does not have outstanding flavour. It is not as seedy as the golden nugget. **Golden nugget** This small variety has orange skin with deep-yellow flesh. Although it can weigh up to 500 g, it is usually sold much smaller. It is a useful variety for stuffing and cuts readily but it has an indifferent flavour and a higher ratio of seeds to flesh than most other pumpkins. **Gramma** An old-fashioned variety that is long and curved like a horseshoe, the gramma has golden brown skin and excellent yellow flesh, is easy to cut and varies a great deal in size. It is also known as a trombone pumpkin. **Hubbard** A pear-shaped pumpkin with a dark-green, warty skin that is very hard to cut, this is a popular variety in the home garden. It weighs about 5 kg but can be much larger. The flavour of the orange flesh is very good. **Jarrahdale** This large round pumpkin has a ribbed grey skin that is not too difficult to cut and sweet orange flesh. It weighs 5–7 kg and keeps well. **Kent** One of the best of the newer varieties, the Kent is also known as the jap pumpkin. The skin has yellow splashes with greenish brown stripes and is very easy to peel. The flesh is deep yellow and sweet. This pumpkin weighs 2–3 kg. **Queensland blue** This well-known variety has green–grey, deeply ribbed skin and full-flavoured orange flesh. It keeps well and weighs 5–7 kg. **Spaghetti squash** Football-shaped with bright-gold skin, this squash has yellow, rathery watery flesh that unravels like spaghetti strands when cooked. It weighs 500–750 g. It is known mainly for its curiosity value as its texture is less appealing than other varieties.

Windsor black A round, flat and multi-ribbed pumpkin with dark-green–black skin, the Windsor black has good flavour and deep-orange flesh. It can weigh 8–9 kg.

SELECTION AND STORAGE

Pumpkins for storage must have firm, thick, unbroken skin and should not be harvested until fully mature. It is essential to leave 5–10 cm of stalk attached as diseases and insects can enter through the top if the stalk is removed. Whole pumpkins keep very well for weeks or even months in an airy spot, such as on a back verandah or in an old shed. Inspect whole stored pumpkins from time to time to ensure there are no splits or soft patches. If there are, cut those bits away and use the pumpkin at once.

When buying a piece of pumpkin, prefer a pumpkin that is split open in front of you or one that still has a moist-looking interior, indicating that it has been broached only a few hours previously. All cottony, stringy fibres and seeds should be removed before storing cut pumpkin in a vegetable storage bag in the crisper section of the refrigerator. Cut pumpkin should be used within a day or two as it is very susceptible to mould.

PREPARATION AND COOKING

Unless you have a good heavy knife, do not cut into a whole pumpkin. Ask your greengrocer to cut the pumpkin into manageable slices or chunks before you take it home.

Butternut pumpkins have edible skin and need only be washed or wiped before being baked. (I like the texture and flavour of the skin on a roasted butternut pumpkin, so I rarely peel it. I have noticed that many guests leave the skin on their plate. Maybe they think I am being lazy.) Other varieties can be baked in their skin, if desired, and the flesh cut away from it. However, most people peel all pumpkin.

As pumpkin can absorb large amounts of water, the trick is to cook it without turning it to mush. (For this reason I prefer steaming or baking pumpkin to boiling it.)

TO PEEL Smooth-skinned varieties can be dangerous to peel, as the knife can easily skid. Turn the pumpkin chunk so that the broadest surface of flesh is flat on your cutting board, and cut away from your hand. If the skin is really hard it may be safer to cut the pumpkin into chunks for cooking and then peel each chunk separately. An Australian-designed wooden pumpkin peeler now on the market claims to make pumpkin-peeling safe and simple.

TO BOIL Cook chunks of peeled pumpkin in a minimum of water (about 2 cm) in a tightly covered saucepan. In 15 minutes large chunks will be tender. After draining, return the pan to the stove for a few minutes, shaking it gently, to drive off any remaining moisture. Then add butter, olive oil or cream, nutmeg and herbs and season to taste. **Spaghetti squash** Boil spaghetti squash intact, for 45 minutes. Halve and discard the seeds. With a fork, carefully ease out the flesh into a hot dish, allowing the strands to separate. Season and top with Garlic Butter (*see* GARLIC), butter or Pesto (*see* BASIL).

TO STEAM Cook chunks of pumpkin, covered, over rapidly boiling water in a steamer for 10–15 minutes. Proceed with recipe or finish as for boiled pumpkin.

TO PURÉE Dry off chunks of boiled or steamed pumpkin in an oven set at 180°C for 5–10 minutes. Purée the pumpkin by using a food processor or by pushing it through a food mill. Season as for boiled pumpkin. To obtain 1 cup puréed pumpkin you will require 500 g peeled and seeded pumpkin.

TO BAKE This is the favourite cooking method of most pumpkin lovers. Cut chunks about the size of a small potato, then rub them with olive oil. Place the pumpkin alongside a roasting leg of lamb or on a separate tray with other vegetables to be baked 40 minutes before the roast will be ready. The high sugar content in pumpkin ensures that it starts to colour much faster than potatoes, so it must be added later than the potatoes when timing the traditional Sunday roast. Sometimes I want the pleasure of roast pumpkin with something other than a roast dinner and I don't want to wait 40 minutes. Then I cut pieces about 4 cm square, toss them with a little olive oil, spread them on a baking tray and put them into a hot oven (220°C). They are golden and tender in about 20 minutes. A sprig of rosemary on the tray scents the pieces deliciously.

TO STUFF Golden nugget and dumpling pumpkins are suitable for stuffing, as are small butternuts. Slice a lid off nuggets and dumplings and scoop out the seeds (keep the top slice as a lid); halve a butternut lengthwise and scrape out the seeds. I have stuffed pumpkins with various things: butter and cream mixed with pepper and chives; fresh ricotta cheese mixed with nutmeg and a little chopped spinach; Curried Vegetables (*see* POTATOES); buttered spinach; or well-seasoned minced beef or pork. Bake the small varieties for 30 minutes at 180°C and the larger butternut for at least 45 minutes. Stuffed pumpkins

pumpkin wedges
Cut peeled pumpkin into 5 mm thick slices, wedges or triangles. Dust with flour and fry in olive oil. When browned on both sides and tender, scatter with crisped sage leaves or minced garlic and plenty of freshly chopped parsley and serve.

pumpkin patties
Mix baked or mashed pumpkin with salt, pepper and an egg and form into cakes. Dust with flour and fry in oil, clarified butter or bacon fat and serve at breakfast or brunch with crisp bacon and maple syrup.

can be reheated from cold but will need about 20 minutes. Remember to bake the lid at the same time as the base!

TO COOK PUMPKIN FLOWERS | Home gardeners know the pleasures of fried zucchini flowers, but it is less well known that one can also use male pumpkin flowers in the same way. (Like the zucchini, the male flowers grow from central stems, while female flowers develop in front of the growing vegetables. It is less wasteful to use male flowers, as fertilisation will have taken place if the vegetables have set.) Remove the stem, if desired, and then remove the pistil and stamen from the centre of the flower. Dip the flower in batter and deep-fry in hot, clean oil at 175°C until golden. The flower can be stuffed with a soft melting cheese or cooked rice pilaf or risotto before being dipped in batter or rolled in beaten egg and then breadcrumbs before frying. You can also sauté chopped pumpkin flowers and add them to risottos, soups or softly scrambled eggs.

pumpkin and bacon soup

recipes

SERVES 10

Pumpkin soup exists in various Mediterranean cuisines, often combined at the last minute with cooked dried beans or chick peas, and sometimes garnished with tiny rice-shaped pasta (risi) or wild greens, such as nettles.

If I am sure that my guests are meat eaters, I usually start my pumpkin soup with bacon bones. If unsure, I omit this step and the chorizo sausage garnish and start by sweating the vegetables in olive oil and butter. I also always hold back about 2 cups of liquid during the puréeing process to avoid ending up with a soup that is too thin. This is prudent for all vegetable purée soups and especially so with pumpkin, as different varieties are more or less watery.

500 g bacon bones
1 onion, sliced
1 bay leaf
2 cloves garlic
1 teaspoon whole allspice
3 litres cold water
3 large potatoes, peeled and
    cut into chunks
1 tablespoon paprika
1 kg pumpkin, peeled and cut
    into chunks
salt
freshly ground black pepper
2 fresh chorizo sausages

Place bacon bones, onion, bay leaf, garlic and allspice in a large stockpot and add water. Bring slowly to a boil and simmer for 2 hours. Strain, pressing well on debris. Add potato, paprika and pumpkin and simmer, uncovered, until vegetables are collapsing. Purée, holding back some liquid, and adjust seasoning. Cook sausages in a frying pan over moderate heat until well browned and cooked through. Cool a little and cut into small pieces. Divide the sausage between heated soup bowls, then ladle in the soup.

pumpkin in antipasto
Sprinkle sliced, cold baked pumpkin with good olive oil and drops of red-wine vinegar and add to a plate of antipasto.

pumpkin chips
Cut very thin slices of peeled pumpkin and deep-fry until tender in plenty of hot, clean oil at 175°C. Drain well on crumpled kitchen paper and scatter with sea salt or parmesan cheese.

herb and pumpkin soup

SERVES 10–12

40 g butter

2 tablespoons olive oil

2 onions, sliced

1 leek, washed and sliced

3 cloves garlic

6 stalks parsley, washed and chopped

1 stick celery, sliced

1 bay leaf

3 litres cold water

3 potatoes, peeled and cut into chunks

1 kg pumpkin, peeled and cut into chunks

salt

freshly ground black pepper

1 cup roughly chopped flat-leaf parsley

2 tablespoons freshly snipped chives

2 tablespoons freshly chopped borage leaves (optional)

sour cream

tiny croutons

Heat butter and oil in a large stockpot and sweat onion, leek, garlic, parsley stalks, celery and bay leaf, covered, for 10 minutes, stirring frequently. Add water, potato and pumpkin and simmer until vegetables are tender. Purée, holding back some liquid, and adjust seasoning. Stir in herbs just before serving and offer sour cream and croutons separately.

pumpkin pizza
Squash a little baked pumpkin onto a pizza base with Fresh Tomato Sauce (see TOMATOES*) and top with thin slices of a melting cheese, such as mozzarella, taleggio or fontina, and bake at 240°C for 10–12 minutes.*

spicy pumpkin seeds
Wash the seeds left over from trimming pumpkin and scrape off any fibre. Dry the seeds overnight in the oven with the pilot light on or with the oven on the very lowest setting, then roast them at 200°C for 15 minutes until they are a deep gold. Scatter over a pinch of sea salt and 1 teaspoon ground toasted cumin seeds.

gratin of pumpkin

SERVES 4

500 g cubed, peeled pumpkin

2 tablespoons olive oil

salt

freshly ground black pepper

1 clove garlic, sliced paper-thin

1 large sprig rosemary or 8 fresh sage leaves

½ cup fresh breadcrumbs

Preheat oven to 180°C. Toss pumpkin with oil, salt, pepper, garlic and rosemary. Tip into a spacious oiled gratin dish and bake for about 45 minutes. Stir pieces around once or twice. Scatter breadcrumbs mixed with a little oil over surface and bake for a further 15 minutes, by which time the crumbs should be golden and the pumpkin beautifully soft.

variations If you had some leftover Fresh Tomato Sauce (*see* TOMATOES) it could be stirred into the pumpkin at the beginning of the cooking time, as could a cup of slowly stewed onion, or some chopped olives.

pumpkin scones

MAKES 10–12

250 g pumpkin, peeled and
cut into chunks
2 cups self-raising flour
salt
20 g butter
1 egg, lightly beaten
milk

Preheat oven to 200°C. Steam pumpkin until soft, then dry off in oven and purée. Sift flour with salt and rub in butter and pumpkin purée. Add egg and up to 3 tablespoons milk, if necessary, to make a soft dough, then turn out onto a floured baking tray. With floured hands, pat into a round 3 cm thick. Using the back of a knife, mark into wedges or squares. Brush dough with milk and bake for 15–20 minutes until golden brown and firm when tapped. Cool, then split and butter.

australian old-fashioned gramma pie

SERVES 4–6

Although this recipe specifies gramma, I have made this pie successfully with butternut and Kent pumpkins.

½ quantity Shortcrust Pastry
1 kg gramma, peeled
2 lemons
10 g butter
2 eggs, lightly beaten
1 egg yolk
1 cup brown sugar
½ teaspoon freshly grated
nutmeg
1 teaspoon ground cloves
2 teaspoons ground cinnamon
½ cup currants

Line an 18 cm pie plate or loose-bottomed flan tin with pastry and bake blind at 200°C for 20 minutes. Remove pastry case from oven and increase oven temperature to 220°C. Steam pumpkin, then mash. Juice and zest lemons and, with remaining ingredients, mix with pumpkin. Pour into prepared pastry case and smooth top. Bake for 10 minutes, then reduce heat to 180°C and bake a further 10–15 minutes. Serve warm or cold.

pumpkin gratin
Toss chunks of leftover cooked pumpkin with chopped garlic, salt and pepper in a shallow, oiled gratin dish. Mix enough cream, grated cheese and fresh herbs to make a thickish sauce and spoon over the pumpkin. Bake at 200°C until a richly golden crust has formed, about 15 minutes.

pumpkin and amaretto tart

SERVES 4–8

This delicious and unusual recipe, reminiscent of the pasta filling served in several Melbourne Italian restaurants (see PASTA AND NOODLES), is one of the most exciting ways to use mashed pumpkin. Serve wedges of the tart alongside a scaloppine of veal or a grilled chicken breast, or as part of an antipasto platter. It is also a wonderful first course when accompanied by a rocket and roasted pumpkin seed salad.

½ quantity Shortcrust Pastry
2 eggs, lightly beaten
1 quantity Pumpkin and
  Amaretto Filling (see
  p. 512)
6 fresh sage leaves
50 g butter
olive oil

Line an 18 cm loose-bottomed flan tin or a pie plate with pastry and bake blind at 200°C for 20 minutes. Remove pastry case from oven and reduce oven temperature to 180°C. Mix eggs into pumpkin filling. Drop sage leaves and butter into a small heated frying pan and swirl until butter is foaming and leaves are crisp. Drain on kitchen paper, then chop and add to filling. Tip mixture into prepared pastry case and level surface. Drizzle with oil and bake for 25–30 minutes until firm. Cool a little before serving.

other recipes

pumpkin and amaretto filling for ravioli *see* PASTA AND NOODLES
sabee sabee kumala *see* SWEET POTATOES

quail and squab pigeons

There are recipes for all sorts of small birds in the cuisines of most of the world. In Australia we are lucky indeed to have available to us commercially bred quail and squab pigeons of wonderful quality. | The quail is a small, plump, ground-dwelling game bird found in Europe, Asia, Africa and Australia. It has always been easily caught, preferring to run rather than fly. In Europe in the autumn game season it is common to see pairs of quail in full feather hanging in game provedores next to a brace of pheasant or grouse. All these birds can be very richly flavoured. They can also be tough, and benefit from marinades that soften the meat or slow pot-roasting. But do not be confused – the European recipes for these birds are not at all suitable for the quail that we can buy here in Australia, unless you know a farmer who shoots wild quail that live in his wheat stubble. | Commercially available quail (mostly *Coturnix japonica*) are produced on speciality poultry farms, and are as tender as butter. They are becoming a popular option as they cook quickly (taking as little as 10–15 minutes), have a delicate flavour and are inexpensive. >

quail
and
squab
pigeons
go
with
rice
barley
couscous
lentils
polenta
cracked wheat
pickled plums
pickled quinces
relishes
chutneys
caramelised onions
olive oil
bay leaves
rosemary
olives
chestnuts
shallots
spinach
soy sauce
honey
ginger
star anise
fortified wines
mushrooms
bacon
dried fruit
pine nuts
garlic
juniper
cardamom
cumin
coriander seeds

Quail can be roasted, stuffed, grilled, barbecued, fried, poached or braised. The worst sin is to overcook quail, when the flesh becomes hard. A correctly cooked quail must be pale pink on the breast, and some like it quite pinky-red. These little birds are also improved with extra seasoning. A salad of roasted quail provides the perfect moment to open a jar of home-made chutney or spiced quinces.

Quail eggs have wonderfully speckled shells. A fried quail egg on a small crouton with a wisp of crisp bacon makes a delicious and witty appetiser. The same crouton looks and tastes wonderful served alongside a roasted or grilled quail, or as the final flourish on a salad made from lettuce leaves and hot grilled quail.

A squab pigeon is a specially bred pigeon that is killed just before it is ready to leave the nest. Such birds are also known as fledglings or squeakers and weigh 300–600 g dressed weight. A squab is very tender and a delicious bird. In French cookery books it is known as a *pigeonneau*, as opposed to *pigeon de bois*. The pigeons that coo and roost on public buildings or those raised by pigeon fanciers are another matter entirely. They are edible but very tough. English cookery books that speak of wood pigeons and give recipes where the birds cook slowly for several hours refer to these birds.

I remember buying some old pigeons many years ago before I knew any better. I made a delicious stuffing with raisins plumped in muscat, crushed berries from my myrtle bush and some wild rice. I wrapped the birds in bacon and slowly braised them in stock for about 1½ hours, if I remember correctly. The stuffing and juices were delicious, but the birds were grey, with stretched goose-bump skin, and the flesh was without any moisture at all. The birds even smelt like old boots! I would never try again. I also find that birds cooked in a pressure cooker in an attempt to soften them risk tasting of powdered bones.

The success of the Australian squab industry is largely due to the enthusiasm, hard work and intelligence of Ian Milburn of Glenloth Game. Together with a group of like-minded farmers from the Victorian Mallee, he has set up a co-operative breeding and marketing project that delivers high-class birds to the marketplace. The initial decision of this group was to produce for the top of the market and to reject rigorously all but the very best birds. My restaurant has supported his efforts from the very beginning and we have never received anything other than superb birds.

A pair of breeding pigeons produces only 10–12 young a year, compared with 100 chickens a year for a laying hen, which makes squab expensive to breed and expensive to buy. It is possible to select breeding pigeons that will produce as few as 3 squab a year or as many as 20 a year. The larger number means small and scrawny birds, the smaller number would no doubt produce superb birds that would be in the Rolls-Royce price range (I wouldn't mind trying one though).

One squab pigeon is the perfect portion for a person: it cooks in less than 20 minutes and its rich buttery flesh goes beautifully with the very finest red wine (pinot noir is always my choice). Squab can be partnered with combinations such as little potatoes and onions, soft roasted garlic and creamed spinach, juniper berries and cabbage, or wild mushrooms. They can be stuffed with wild rice or barley, or steamed and then deep-fried until crisp in the Chinese manner, just like quail (*see* p. 606). Squab pigeons also have exceptionally delicious livers.

VARIETIES AND SEASON

Commercially produced *quail* are not distinguished by species. They are sold fresh or frozen (mostly frozen), usually packed in trays of 4–6, depending on size.

Australia's **squab pigeons** are collectively *Columba livia domestica* but they are identified more usually by their common names: large white, Swiss mondaine and carnot. The majority of Australian birds are cross-bred. The most advanced work on breeding squab pigeons is carried out in the United States and France. At present Australia's quarantine regulations do not permit the importation of breeding stock from these countries, so those interested in breeding squab have limited genetic material available. For the home cook this is probably only of mild interest, except to say that inbreeding eventually leads to weakened stock, which will in turn mean fewer birds.

We have an Australian native pigeon, the wonga pigeon, that is fully protected. My colleague Maggie Beer raised an interesting point when she wondered why we do not try to farm this species, such as is done with emu, with a view to improving the quality of its flesh for the table and creating our very own squab pigeon.

Squab pigeons and quail are available all year fresh or frozen. Look for them in specialist food stores and in the poultry stores at our fresh food markets. Some butchers will be able to order squab for you, while others may regularly stock quail.

SELECTION AND STORAGE

QUAIL

It is now common to be offered large or jumbo quail, ranging from 200 g upwards, while medium-sized quail are 160–200 g. One quail per person is a suitable first course. If being presented as a main meal, I would offer 2, even of the larger size. As most quail are available *frozen* it is difficult to inspect them closely. They should have been plucked carefully, so that the fine skin is not torn or otherwise damaged, especially the skin on the breast, which protects the meat and stops it drying out during the cooking process. If buying *fresh* quail, do not select any bird with ripped skin and for preference buy birds that still have their necks, heads and feet attached (frozen birds sometimes come with necks and feet intact, too). If the neck is still present, the cook can always be sure that there will be enough skin left to protect the breast. The neckbone, head and feet are also valuable for making a small amount of flavourful sauce.

One can sometimes buy **boned**, opened-out quail, which saves all the work but you are left without the bones to make a sauce. Boned quail are suitable for sautéing but need special care if grilling or barbecuing. Without the ribcage and breastbone the flesh can dry out very quickly.

SQUAB PIGEONS | When choosing squab pigeons, the Glenloth label is a guarantee of high quality. There are other quality birds available, so ask your poultry supplier for recommendations. Expect to pay more than the price of a large chicken for a quality squab pigeon. Do not buy bargain-priced birds as they will be old and tough.

Squab tend to come in 2 sizes: 300 g and 400–450 g. A 300 g bird is fine to serve per person as a first course or to combine with poultry livers or sausages or something else to create a main dish. If serving 1 squab per person as a main dish, you should purchase the larger size. One bird is small compared with half a chicken, but its breast meat is rich and dense. Even so, if you know you are feeding huge meat eaters I would buy an extra couple. On the principle of Jack Sprat and his wife, those who eat lots of meat are often not into picking at succulent small bones, whereas there will be others who will happily gnaw away and be less interested in a large portion of breast meat.

Fresh quail or squab pigeon should be freed of store wrappings and refrigerated on kitchen paper on a plate loosely covered with plastic film, and used within 2 days. If *frozen*, thaw birds overnight on a plate lined with kitchen paper in the refrigerator, freed of all plastic wrappings. Once thawed, wash them briefly, then dry well and cover with plastic film. Use thawed birds within 36 hours. While a certain containment odour may be noticed after removing a bird from its original wrappings, after washing and drying there should be no unpleasant odour. *Squab livers* should be refrigerated, covered with plastic film, on a plate and used within 24 hours.

PREPARATION AND COOKING

Preparing quail and squab may sound fiddly but, once you get the hang of it, it takes no time at all. You will note that I reserve any bones and the head, neck and feet, if present; these can be used to make Simple Quail or Squab Sauce (*see* p. 603).

As quail and squab meat is very tender there is no need to use rich marinades to tenderise the flesh. Both birds benefit, however, from being rubbed with olive oil and being closed up with herbs and seasonings.

FOR ROASTING | Cut off the first wing joint and drop it into a bowl. Cut off the head and neck, if still attached, and add to the bowl. Remember, do not cut the neck skin too close to the body as the skin will shrink on contact with the heat, exposing some of the breast meat, which will dry quickly. Gently push the neck skin back from the breast and remove the wishbone, which is embedded in the breast flesh. Work around each curve of the wishbone with a small sharp knife, especially around the join of the 2 arcs. Feel the shape of the wishbone with your fingers and ease it out and drop it into the bowl. Cut off the feet (if still present) and add to the bowl. Poke inside the bird and remove the heart and liver, if still present, and drop them into the bowl with the other trimmings. Rinse the bird under cold water, then pat it dry with kitchen paper and put it on a plate. Season as desired and then either refrigerate it covered, or leave at room temperature for up to 1 hour before roasting it.

FOR SEASONING UNDER THE SKIN | Loosen the skin over the breast by carefully sliding your fingertips under it. (Please – no long fingernails! It is impossible to do this without tearing the skin if you have long fingernails.) You have now created a space for your seasoning – a spice paste, herb butter, pesto or whatever – which will be held in place by the tucked-under neck skin.

FOR GRILLING OR BARBECUING | Follow the instructions for preparing birds for roasting through to removing the feet. Using kitchen scissors, cut up the back of the bird either side of the backbone right through to the neck opening. Drop the backbone into the bowl. Open out the bird, skin-side down, and remove the heart and liver (if still present) and add to the bowl. Rinse the bird under cold water, then pat it dry with kitchen paper and put it on a plate. Wash and dry your chopping board well and return the bird to the board, skin uppermost. Press firmly on the breastbone of the bird to flatten it further. Season as desired (the same seasonings suggested for a bird to be roasted can be used here) and either refrigerate or leave it at room temperature for up to 1 hour until you are ready to cook it.

TO BONE | You can bone quail or squab raw if you wish to stuff them, or you can bone them after grilling in order to make them more approachable for your family and friends. I wouldn't bother boning cooked birds at an informal barbecue, but I probably would if my guests were at a sit-down dinner and risked splashing juices onto silk shirts and the like. The technique is the same for both but it is more difficult with cooked birds as they will be very hot. Protect your hand with a cloth. If you are boning several, transfer each one to a very hot

fried quail
Dip halved quail in egg and then breadcrumbs, or a mixture of crumbs and parmesan, and gently shallow-fry in olive oil.

spicy quail
Moisten a mix of 3 parts freshly chopped parsley and 1 part each of ground roasted cumin seeds and finely chopped garlic with olive oil and roll boned quail in this before grilling. Serve with couscous.

plate as you finish with it as the birds will cool quickly. Keep the bones for a stock some other day (label and freeze them).

Follow the instructions for preparing the birds for roasting through to removing the feet, then cut out the backbone as for grilling. Using your fingers, pull away the fine rib bones and drop them into the bowl. Work down either side of the breast shield using a small, sharp knife until the breast meat falls away from the breastbone. Place your fingers either side of the breastbone and pull firmly upwards to remove it. Drop the breastbone into the bowl. The bird will still have leg and wing bones intact.

bbq squab

Spoon a crushed anchovy, freshly chopped parsley and crushed garlic moistened with olive oil over a freshly barbecued squab.

TO STUFF

It is possible to stuff and roast an unboned bird but it is much more accessible and pleasurable to eat if it has been boned. Place well-seasoned stuffing inside a boned bird just before cooking. Do not stuff it too tightly; as the bird will only be in the oven for about 15 minutes (quail) or 20–25 minutes (squab), the centre of the stuffing may not become thoroughly hot if there is too much of it. For the same reason, only use cooked stuffing – no raw rice, please! Pull the stuffed bird back into shape and secure it with toothpicks or by using a needle and thread (leave a long thread dangling to assist with speedy removal).

TO ROAST

Prepare birds for roasting (*see* p. 601). Season the prepared birds very well with salt and pepper, inside and out. Lightly crush an unpeeled clove of garlic and slip it into the cavity with half a bay leaf, a nut of butter, generous sprigs of thyme and rosemary and a piece of lemon zest. (The prepared birds can be refrigerated overnight or for a few hours at this stage to allow the flavours of the herbs to permeate. Allow the birds to return to room temperature before cooking. Coarsely crushed juniper berries and whole allspice can also be added.) Place the birds in a baking dish of an appropriate size (not too big), each one resting on its side on a buttered or oiled slice of breadstick, and brush with olive oil. Roast at 200° C, turning from one side to the other after 6 minutes (quail) or 8 minutes (squab). Roast for the same time on this second side. These times will result in pink breast meat. Increase times by 2 minutes a side for more well-done birds. Prick the thigh with a fine skewer: the juices should be palest pink to clear when the bird is done. Allow to rest in a warm place in the baking dish for 5 minutes or transfer to a warm plate, breast down, then cover with an upturned bowl and deglaze the baking dish to make your finishing sauce.

TO GRILL OR BARBECUE

Prepare birds for grilling (*see* p. 601). Brush both sides with a little oil and season. Heat an electric griller, chargrill pan or barbecue, then place the birds flesh-side to the heat and cook for 6 minutes (quail) or 8 minutes (squab). Turn and seal the skin for no more than 2 minutes (both birds). Rest in a warm place, skin-side down, for a few minutes before splitting, boning or serving.

TO PAN-FRY | **Whole** Prepare the bird as for grilling (*see* p. 601) and season. Heat a little olive oil in a heavy-based frying pan and cook for 4 minutes per side (quail) or 5–6 minutes per side (squab). Drain quickly on kitchen paper, then wipe out the pan and proceed to cook or heat a garnish or sauce. Cut the bird in half or joint it, if desired. **Cut-up or boned** Breast fillets and legs are sometimes cooked separately, especially as part of a salad, when they may be added whole or sliced. Boned breast fillets of quail will take 1 minute each side and 2–3 minutes to rest between warm plates. Boned squab breast fillets will take 2–3 minutes per side and then 5 minutes to rest. Legs cooked on their own will take 8 minutes (quail) and 10–12 minutes (squab).

simple quail or squab sauce

MAKES 2 CUPS

This sauce is made from the various bits of quail or squab discarded when preparing birds for roasting or grilling (see p. 601). Freeze what you don't use.

1 cup quail *or* squab trimmings
olive oil
½ carrot, diced
½ small onion, diced
1 bay leaf
1 large sprig thyme
3 tablespoons fortified wine
1 tablespoon tomato paste
1 teaspoon crushed black peppercorns
4 mushrooms, sliced
1 litre Chicken Stock

Toss quail trimmings with a few drops of oil in a baking dish and roast at 200°C until a deep gold. Remove bones to a saucepan. Add carrot, onion, bay leaf and thyme to baking dish, then sprinkle with more oil and roast for 20 minutes or so until vegetables have softened and are starting to colour.

Remove dish from oven and transfer to a moderate heat on top of stove. Tip off any visible fat. Pour in wine and stir and scrape until vegetables have loosened. Add tomato paste, peppercorns, mushrooms and half the stock. Bring to simmering point, stirring and scraping to dislodge as much as possible. Transfer contents of baking dish to saucepan and add remaining stock. Bring to simmering point, then skim and lower heat. Simmer for 1 hour, then strain, pressing well on debris. Allow stock to stand until cool. Skim off any fat that rises. When ready to use, return sauce to a boil and reduce to strengthen flavour.
variations Add a spoonful of crabapple jelly or thick cream to the reduced sauce.

quail egg salad
Fry quail eggs in a drop of olive oil in a non-stick frying pan and serve perched on top of a leafy salad to which has been added grilled or roasted quail, roasted sweet peppers and grilled eggplant chunks.

janni's barley stuffing

This mixture can be made hours before it is needed (remember, though, that the birds should be stuffed just before cooking) and any extra stuffing can be frozen for another day. This quantity is sufficient for 10–12 quail or 8 squab pigeons.

1 large onion, chopped
125 g butter
1 cup pearl barley
1 teaspoon cumin seeds
juice and zest of 1 small lemon
1 cup currants
salt
freshly ground black pepper
3 cups water

Preheat oven to 150°C. Select a cast-iron casserole with a tight-fitting lid. Sauté onion in butter until soft, then add barley and cumin seeds and stir to coat. Add lemon juice and zest with remaining ingredients to casserole. Bring to a boil, then cover tightly and cook in oven for 2 hours. By this time the water should have been absorbed and the barley should be tender. Stuff quail or squab and roast.

variations The barley could be omitted and rice used instead. Try brown rice or wild rice, or a mixture. Dried fruit, especially seeded raisins, are good, as are toasted pine nuts or almonds.

marinated quail
Halve or joint 4 quail and marinate in 1 tablespoon each hoisin sauce, soy sauce and tomato paste mixed with 1 teaspoon sambal oelek, 1 teaspoon freshly chopped ginger and a little water. Grill, barbecue or roast the quail and serve with plenty of paper napkins for sticky fingers.

squab pigeon and fig salad   SERVES 6

This fabulous first course comes from one of Australia's best chefs, Steve Manfredi, and appears in his book Fresh from Italy. *When I make this salad, I sometimes include slices of sheep's milk fetta cheese.*

3 squab pigeons
extra-virgin olive oil
freshly ground black pepper
1 head endive *or* other salad
  leaves, washed and dried
red-wine vinegar
6 ripe, soft purple figs, halved
a little Veal Stock
salt

Preheat oven to 240°C. Rub squab with oil and pepper and roast for 10–12 minutes (the squab will be quite pink). Rest for 10 minutes. Tear greens into pieces and divide between 6 plates. Cut squab breast fillets from breastbone and cut away legs, then toss meat with greens and dress with oil and vinegar. Warm figs in stock, then sprinkle in a few drops of oil and season. Arrange figs on greens, then pour over hot stock and serve.

grilled spiced indian quail with fried coconut

SERVES 6

I serve these spicy birds with Quail Eggs in Coconut Sauce (see EGGS*).*

6 quail
1 tablespoon coriander seeds
20 black peppercorns
12 cardamom pods
1 teaspoon cloves
1 teaspoon cumin seeds
1 teaspoon curry powder
1 teaspoon salt
60 g butter, melted
30 g finely chopped fresh ginger
olive oil
½ quantity Fried Coconut (see p. 605)

Prepare quail for grilling (*see* p. 601). Grind all spices to a powder and mix with salt, butter and ginger. Work 1 teaspoon spice paste under skin over entire breast surface of each bird. Smooth skin back into place, tucking it over neck edge. Rub a little paste over legs and bony inside of each bird. Reserve remaining paste for later use. Brush birds with a little oil.

To grill, place birds flesh side to heat and grill for 8 minutes. Turn and briefly seal skin side for no more than 1 minute or spice paste will burst through skin. Prick thickest part of thigh to see if juice runs clear. If undercooked, return to grill, flesh-side to heat source, for 2 minutes. Remove quail to a heated plate for 5 minutes, then bone them. Spoon over a little spice paste and turn quails in it. Serve scattered with fried coconut. I like to offer Indian pickled limes or a wedge of fresh lime also.

fried coconut

MAKES 1 CUP

This is delicious scattered on Grilled Spiced Indian Quail (see p. 605) or sprinkled over fried cauliflower or other vegetable fritters.

2 tablespoons light vegetable oil
4 cloves garlic, finely chopped
4 spring onions, finely chopped (including green tops)
1 teaspoon ground coriander
1 teaspoon ground cumin
125 g desiccated coconut
pinch of salt

Heat oil in a heavy-based frying pan. Fry garlic and spring onion for 1–2 minutes. Add spices, then coconut and salt. Lift and stir really well to mix flavours and cook until coconut is a rich brown. Allow to cool completely, then store for up to a week in a screw-top jar. To freshen, tip required quantity into a dry frying pan and stir until warmed through.

warm squab salad
Toss sliced roasted squab meat and the legs with a little oil and serve on salad leaves as a warm salad with some Caramelised Onions (see ONIONS*), roasted garlic or crisply fried slices of pancetta or smoked streaky bacon and then dress.*

squab and sweetcorn
Make a substantial salad by serving roasted squab meat on dressed greens with Sweetcorn Brunch Fritters (see CORN*), for a witty reference to the diet of these plump little birds, or croutons spread with apple, redcurrant or quince jelly.*

chinese-style fried quail or squab

For this recipe the heads and necks should not be removed from the birds. Each bird has to hang up to dry on a hook, and it is difficult to do this if there is no neck! There is no need to remove the feet either, unless you find them very worrying. If the whole idea of leaving head, neck and feet on puts you off this recipe, it would be a pity as birds are truly delicious cooked in this manner.

I do not think it would matter if the birds were dropped into the stock rather than being suspended in it. However, it is difficult to hang them to dry without using hooks, as suggested. (Drying them on a cake rack over a tray might produce something of the same effect. I have not tried it, however.) I use a wire coathanger suspended from the window lock in front of the open kitchen window. The birds thus drain into the sink. If you cannot manage this, remember to place a tray under them to catch the drips.

This quantity of stock and sauce is sufficient for 6–8 quail or 4 squab pigeons.

6–8 quail or 4 squab pigeons
vegetable oil for deep-frying
1 quantity Cantonese Spiced
   Salt (see p. 585)

SIMMERING STOCK
3 litres Chicken Stock
1 stick cinnamon, splintered
3 star anise
5 cm piece fresh ginger

COATING SAUCE
1 cup water
½ cup rice vinegar
½ cup maltose, malt extract or
   honey
½ teaspoon bicarbonate of
   soda

Bring all ingredients for coating sauce to a boil and set aside. Simmer all stock ingredients for 30 minutes in a deep but narrow pot. Pierce neck of each bird with a butcher's hook and lower birds into simmering stock, hanging hooks on edge of pot, or drop them into the stock. The birds should be totally immersed. Simmer for 5 minutes for quail or 8–10 minutes for squab (8 minutes will give a pinkish breast). Lift birds out and hang them in a draughty place, still held by the hooks, for 5 minutes to drain and dry out. Roll each bird thoroughly in coating sauce and hang and dry for 2 hours.

Preheat oven to 160°C. Heat 5 cm vegetable oil in a wok. Remove birds from hooks and carefully lower into oil. Spoon oil over and over birds. Be careful, it will spit! You may need to do this in batches. When birds are a rich brown, transfer to a plate lined with kitchen paper in oven. Serve at once with the spiced salt for dipping.

squab and apple salad
Sauté squab or chicken livers in butter and deglaze with a spoonful of muscat or sherry. Combine with grilled squab or quail in a salad with wedges of golden delicious apple that have been oiled and grilled until a deep golden brown.

roast quail
Roast quail with garlic and rosemary and serve halved on top of salad leaves dressed with olive oil, red-wine vinegar and the cooking juices.

grilled italian-style squab with liver crostini

SERVES 4

4 squab pigeons
olive oil
extra-virgin olive oil

MARINADE

1 cup dry marsala or Madeira
½ onion, very finely diced
8 juniper berries, crushed
8 black peppercorns, crushed
3 stalks parsley, very finely
   chopped

LIVER CROSTINI

150 g smoked streaky bacon,
   finely diced
12 squab livers, trimmed
olive oil
1 onion, finely chopped
2 cloves garlic, finely chopped
2 tablespoons freshly chopped
   parsley
salt
freshly ground black pepper
4 slices crusty breadstick

Prepare squab for grilling (*see* p. 601). Combine marinade ingredients in a baking dish and add squab. Refrigerate for several hours or overnight, turning squab in marinade occasionally. Next day, drain birds on a wire rack over a plate, reserving marinade.

To prepare the liver crostini, cook bacon in a heavy-based frying pan until crisp. Remove with a slotted spoon, leaving fat in pan. Sauté livers quickly for 2–3 minutes, turning once. Remove to a plate. Add a few drops of oil to pan, then add onion and garlic. Cook for 1–2 minutes over high heat, then lower heat, cover, and cook, stirring from time to time, until onion is very soft and golden brown. Return bacon to pan, increase heat and add 2 tablespoons of the marinade and any juice from livers and boil vigorously for a minute. Chop livers quite finely and return to pan, then stir in parsley and season to taste. Brush breadstick slices with oil and grill on both sides.

squab with fruit and nuts

Add pickled quinces (see QUINCES*) or cherries (see* CHERRIES*), grilled apple wedges, parsnip chips (see* PARSNIPS*), or peas, asparagus and/or artichoke hearts to a warm salad of squab. Dress the salad with hazelnut or walnut oil and add nuts to match.*

To finish, preheat oven to 160°C and heat an overhead griller or chargrill pan. Pat squab dry, then brush with oil and grill for 8 minutes a side. Bone birds or not as you prefer. Rest squab, skin-side down, for 10 minutes. Pile liver mixture onto toasted bread, drizzle with a few drops of oil and reheat in oven for 5 minutes (this can be done while squab are resting). Place a hot crostini on each plate with a squab alongside, then drizzle with extra-virgin olive oil mixed with any remaining marinade and serve immediately.

other recipes

quail eggs in coconut sauce *see* EGGS
quail with dried figs and olives *see* FIGS
squab pigeon liver and turnip salad *see* LIVER

see also LIVER

q u i n c e s   The quince (*Cydonia oblonga*) was sacred to Aphrodite and Venus, the goddesses of love, and a symbol of love, happiness and fertility in Greek and Roman times. │ It is easy to understand why so many people have been so enthusiastic about this fruit for so many centuries. The tree has exquisite pale-pink blossom and its fruit smells heavenly and has a subtle flavour and an unusual grainy texture when cooked. Quinces obligingly hang on the tree, looking decorative, until you are ready to pick them, and their high pectin content makes them ideal for jellies, jams and other preserves. One company in South Australia produces glacéd quince slices, a product I have never seen or heard of anywhere else in the world. │ While not grown commercially in any quantity, quince trees are a common sight in the gardens of old Australian country homes. Sometimes the owners of those trees are very happy to give away some fruit. However, each year there are more quinces in greengrocers and fresh food markets. As food writers comment on foods they particularly enjoy, the market responds and availability increases. We should all be encouraged by this to make our requests and comments known. >

The various names for the quince in different parts of Europe are interesting as they all refer to quince preparations. In Portuguese the quince is *marmelos*, and *marmelado* is a quince paste. These names came from the Roman name *melimelum* (honey apple) – and quinces are wonderful cooked with honey. The Greek *cydonia* (possibly referring to Cydon on Crete, where fine quinces were said to grow) became *cotognata* in Italian (also the name for Italian quince paste), which became *coing* in French and *coines* in Chaucerian English, which later became 'quince'.

English writers are mournful that quinces in their country often rot rather than ripen, preferring a sunnier climate. Their recipes always mention adding quince to apple pies but often leave it at that. Yet the quince is a most exotic ingredient and can appear at many points in a meal. Both sweet and savoury quince recipes are common in the Middle East, and while in France a few years ago I was intrigued by a Provençal speciality, *pan-coudoun*, a whole quince baked in bread dough.

Some new cooks are put off by the cooking times indicated. Quinces take a long time to cook but they can often be left in a low oven to murmur overnight. The reward is not only a panful of deep-red fruit but a kitchen that smells wonderful for hours after the cooking has finished.

quinces go with
soft white cheese
honey
apples
pears
cream
cinnamon
vanilla
lamb
chicken
quail
almonds
walnuts
pecans
ginger
butter

VARIETIES AND SEASON

Different quinces do exist, some bearing rounder fruit (*C. oblonga malformis*, commonly described as the Smyrna quince), some with more oblong-shaped fruit (*C. oblonga lusitanica*, the pineapple quince), but they do not tend to be identified by variety in the shops. We have no choice, and buy what we can get. I have found that the first quinces are usually in the markets by mid-March, with the bulk of the supply available until mid-June. Some coolstore fruit is available until the end of July or mid-August.

SELECTION AND STORAGE

If you have a quince tree, start to pick the fruit when it changes colour from bright green to pale yellow and then to bright yellow. Ripeness is also indicated by the presence of the characteristic scent. The sharper the yellow, the younger the quince; the more golden, the older. If picked when still a greenish yellow, the quinces will be exceptionally high in pectin and will make superb jelly. Check fruit for insect damage. A small hole or brown spot on the skin often indicates the presence of a tunnelling grub.

Quinces have very hard skin and do not soften at all when they are ripe. If a quince is soft it is damaged and will be rotten inside. Despite the hardness of the skin, quinces bruise easily and should be stored or displayed in a single layer in a basket. They will keep this way for months but the pectin level will diminish until the fruit is unsuitable for jelly-making. This fruit will still be fine for baking or poaching. Picked fruit that has been stored for some time will become yellowish brown.

Do not refrigerate raw quinces as the aroma is very pervasive and will penetrate other foods. As this aroma is one of the great charms of the quince, why imprison it when it could be scenting your kitchen? Having said that, quinces picked yellow–green can be frozen whole or cored in freezer bags. The cut fruit will change colour a little, but the texture will not be altered.

PREPARATION

When picked the fruit will be covered in a film of rather sticky greyish down. This needs to be washed off before proceeding to peel or cut. As quince flesh is very hard you will need a heavy knife. Take great care with the first cut in case the fruit, which can be greasy, slips. Drop peeled slices of fruit into water acidulated with lemon juice to delay browning. Mostly one cooks quinces for a very long time and the colour will darken anyway from pale yellow to pink to ruby red, so the question of discoloration is not that important. It is more relevant if frying raw slices.

Much of the pectin is contained in the skin and pips, so one is often instructed to cook quinces unpeeled or to include the skin and cores in a muslin bag in the preserving pan. When making quince jelly or any recipe where the pulp is discarded after cooking, consider making a Quince and Nut Cake (*see* p. 614) to use some of the pulp.

recipes

orange and quince jelly

MAKES 1.5 LITRES

As Seville oranges appear in early winter, just when quinces are finishing, you will have to make this beautifully coloured preserve without delay! Delicious on breakfast toast, or useful as a glaze for ham or to add to pork roasting juices.

15 quinces
6 large oranges (preferably Seville)
sugar

Wash half the quinces and quarter them. Chop coarsely, including cores (a food processor does this most efficiently). Put quince into a non-reactive saucepan, barely cover with water and simmer for 1 hour.

Strain liquid into a clean saucepan and discard pulp. Peel remaining quinces, and peel and slice oranges, removing all white pith. Chop both roughly and cook gently in quince liquid for 1 hour.

Stand a colander lined with a large doubled piece of dampened muslin over a bowl and pour in quince liquid and fruit. Do not press or squeeze or the preserve will be cloudy. Leave colander over bowl for several hours or overnight, then discard fruit. >

Measure strained liquid and add an equal quantity of sugar. Bring sugar and liquid slowly to a boil in a non-reactive saucepan, stirring once or twice until sugar has dissolved. Skim off any foam that rises. Increase heat and boil briskly. Test for setting ✓ after 10 minutes by placing a little jelly on a cold saucer. Pour finished jelly into hot, sterilised ✓ jars and seal.

george's quince paste

There are numerous versions of this wonderful preserve and, as already noted, each Mediterranean country has its own name for it. When properly made it should be thick and sliceable (it is best made with young, sharply yellow quinces that are high in pectin). I recently tasted some freshly made sheep's milk cheese with this quince paste and recognised a marriage made in heaven. The following recipe comes from George Biron, owner–chef of one of Victoria's most delightful country restaurants, Sunnybrae at Birregurra. I have found that the mixture spits like mad and a deep pan is necessary. George does not find this and recommends a wide pan that is no more than 10–12 cm high. You may, however, need to have a tea towel ready to wrap around your stirring hand to avoid burns!

A reader once wrote to me and said that she dried out her quince paste by placing the tin on the shelf under the rear window of her car. She said that after a week or two of driving about the paste had dried very satisfactorily!

8 quinces, washed, peeled
  and cored
1 cup water
juice of 1 lemon
sugar

Cut quinces into chunks and place in a large saucepan with a tight-fitting lid with water, lemon juice and a quarter of the cores and pips. Cook over moderate heat until quince is quite tender, about 30 minutes. Pass contents of saucepan through medium disc of a food mill (or use a food processor) and weigh purée. (The cores and pips will be barely noticeable and the extra pectin in the mixture hastens the cooking process.) Mix purée with three-quarters of its weight of sugar. Return to a wide-based saucepan and cook over moderate heat, stirring every few minutes, until paste leaves sides of pan and colour is a deep pinky-red. This should take 3–4 hours. At this point it will be quite hard to push the spoon through the mass.

Allow mixture to cool a little, then pour it into an oiled tray lined with greaseproof paper. (This amount of fruit will fill a lamington tin, 28 cm × 18 cm × 5 cm.) Dry mixture in a warm place for several days or overnight in an oven with the pilot light left on. Cover with greaseproof paper if you have an ant problem. When dry, wrap paste well in greaseproof paper and then in foil. It stores indefinitely in an airtight tin.

fried quince
Serve quince slices fried in oil and butter with any meat dish with a vaguely Middle Eastern flavour, say forequarter lamb chops stewed with onion, saffron, a cinnamon stick and drops of orange-flower water.

quail and quince
Fry sliced quince in a mixture of butter and oil until golden brown. Tuck under or around quail to be roasted.

poached quince

SERVES 6

6 quinces, washed and peeled
2.25 litres light Sugar Syrup
1 vanilla bean
juice of 1 lemon

Preheat oven to 150°C. Cut quinces into quarters or sixths. Cut out cores and tie them loosely in a piece of muslin. Put sugar syrup in a large enamelled cast-iron casserole with vanilla bean, lemon juice and muslin bag, then add quince. Cover tightly and bake in oven for at least 4 (and up to 8) hours until quince is deep red. Do not stir or the quince may break up. Cool and serve either on its own or as part of an autumn compote with poached pear and sliced orange. Split the vanilla bean and scrape seeds into quince syrup.

syrup Extra syrup left after poaching the quince can be refrigerated in a screw-top jar and boiled down until quite thick to glaze fruit tarts, or it can be used as is to make Eliza Acton's Quince Custard (*see* p. 612).

eliza acton's quince custard

MAKES 1 LITRE

The vanilla-scented quince syrup from Poached Quince is used to make this sweet pouring custard. Sometimes I dilute the cold custard with cream.

600 ml quince poaching syrup
  (see p. 612)
12 egg yolks, whisked
juice of 1 lemon
pouring cream (optional)

Bring syrup to simmering point, then pour onto egg yolks and mix well. Return to rinsed-out saucepan and cook gently, stirring all the time, until custard thickens. Strain into a bowl, add lemon juice and stir now and then as it cools. Dilute with cream, if you wish.

maggie's pot-roasted quinces

SERVES 6

This is one of the signature dishes developed by my good friend Maggie Beer during her days at The Pheasant Farm Restaurant in South Australia's Barossa Valley. A tray of these sticky beauties, glowing deep ruby and with bursting skins, is one of the most beautiful and opulent sights one could ever experience. Choose the rounded variety of quince at the greenish yellow stage, if possible.

6 quinces (preferably with
  stem and leaf attached),
  well washed
1.5 litres water
4 cups sugar
juice of 3 lemons

Pack quinces, water and sugar into a heavy-based non-reactive saucepan. Boil vigorously for 30 minutes until syrup thickens (large bubbles will form). Lower heat and simmer for up to 5 hours, using a simmer mat, if necessary. Turn quinces at least 4 times

---

quince sauce

Melt a spoonful of quince jelly in the pan juices of a roasted quail or squab or sautéd kidneys or liver and stir in a squeeze of lemon juice for a very simple sauce.

quince and apple or pear

Add a little thinly sliced quince to any recipe that uses apple or pear, such as a pie, crumble or steamed pudding, to add a lovely scent, tinge of pink and special tart flavour.

during cooking process to ensure they become a deep-ruby colour through to core. Add lemon juice in final minutes of cooking (this helps cut the sweetness). Serve whole quinces with a little jellied syrup and fresh cream. Or serve a piece of quince alongside a slice of Quince and Nut Cake (*see* p. 614).

maggie's pickled quinces

MAKES 2 LITRES

Maggie Beer recommends this pickle with terrines, hams, pickled pork, slow-cooked lamb or kid dishes, or smoked kangaroo.

6 quinces, washed
juice of 1 lemon
1.2 litres white-wine vinegar
3½ cups sugar
2 teaspoons cloves
2 teaspoons black peppercorns
cayenne pepper (optional)

Peel quinces, then cut into quarters and discard cores. Set aside in water acidulated with lemon juice to prevent discoloration. In a heavy-based non-reactive saucepan, bring vinegar, sugar and spices to a boil, stirring until sugar has dissolved. Add quince and simmer until just soft and turning pink (15–20 minutes). Watch that quince does not become mushy. Allow to cool. Spoon quince into clean, sterilised jars. Boil spiced vinegar for 15 minutes to reduce a little, then ladle into jars to cover fruit. Divide cloves and peppercorns evenly between jars. Seal and allow to mature for several weeks.

baked quinces
Stuff cored quinces with an equal quantity of butter and sugar mashed with dried fruit, preserved ginger or cinnamon, or push a clove through the quince skin, and stand in a baking dish. Pour in a little water and add a spoonful of quince jelly or honey and bake at 180°C for 1½ hours. Serve with thick cream.

stephanie's quince tart

SERVES 8

1 quantity Shortcrust Pastry
30 thick slices Poached
   Quince (see p. 612),
   well drained

FILLING
2 eggs
½ cup sugar
1 heaped tablespoon plain
   flour
125 g unsalted butter

Preheat oven to 200°C. Line a 24 cm loose-bottomed flan tin with pastry and bake blind at 200°C for 20 minutes. Remove from oven and reduce temperature to 180°C. Allow pastry case to cool, then remove foil. Arrange quince slices in a circle around edge, then fill in centre with remaining quince.

   To make the filling, beat eggs and sugar until thick and pale, then add flour. Melt butter and cook until a deep gold. Add butter to egg mixture and spoon over fruit in pastry case. Cook for 25 minutes or until filling has set. It will look golden brown and be a little puffed but will subside as it cools.

pears and plums This tart is also delicious made with poached, drained pears or poached blood plums.

quinces baked in honey

SERVES 3–6

This recipe was originally published in 1960 by my mother, Mary Burchett, in her cookery book Through My Kitchen Door. *The dish has been a favourite in my restaurant for many years.*

quince cream
Stir a little melted quince jelly into mascarpone to serve with a quince, apple or walnut tart.

3 quinces, washed well
80 g butter
4 tablespoons light honey
¼ cup water

Preheat oven to 150°C. Halve but do not peel quinces, then remove pips and core from each with a spoon to make a neat hollow. Select a gratin dish that will hold quince halves snugly and grease with a third of the butter. Arrange quince halves hollows uppermost. Divide remaining butter and honey between hollows and pour water gently around sides. Cover with foil and bake for at least 3 hours until quinces are soft and a rich red. (Turn quinces over after 1½ hours.) Serve hot or warm with hollows filled with honey juices and offer thick or clotted cream.

quince and nut cake

This cake can be made using walnuts, almonds or pecans, or a mixture.

375 g plain flour
2 teaspoons bicarbonate of
  soda
2 teaspoons ground cinnamon
2 teaspoons ground allspice
pinch of salt
1 cup roughly crushed nuts
2 cups Poached Quince (see
  p. 612) or quince pulp
1 cup brown sugar
2 eggs
250 g unsalted butter, melted
  and cooled
pure icing sugar (optional)

Preheat oven to 180°C, then butter a 23 cm ring tin and dust it with flour. Sift flour, bicarbonate of soda, spices and salt and stir in nuts. Combine quince and sugar in a large bowl. Whisk eggs into butter and gently stir into quince mixture. Gently stir in flour mixture and mix well. Spoon into prepared tin. Bake for 55–60 minutes or until a skewer inserted in middle comes out clean. Cool cake in tin. Unmould and scatter with icing sugar, if desired, to serve.

other recipes

moroccan tagine with quince *see* LAMB

rabbit

rabbit   The wild or European rabbit (*Oryctolagus cuniculus*) is Public Enemy Number One in Australia today. Imported from Europe in the mid-1800s to provide food, the rabbit, left to breed in the wild without sufficient predators to help redress the ecological imbalance, quickly became (and still remains) a rampant pest. Its burrowing erodes the soil and, along with its feeding habits, has left thousands of hectares denuded and countless native plants and animals extinct. It is said that the rabbit costs the Australian wool industry alone $115 million annually. The introduced virus myxomatosis decimated the rabbit population briefly in the 1950s, but rabbits have since developed immunity and their numbers have grown again to plague proportions. | It is no wonder, then, that the escape in October 1995 of the CSIRO-tested rabbit calicivirus from South Australia's Wardang Island was greeted with measured delight. Its effectiveness became very apparent as reports of dying rabbits were related daily in the newspapers. As hyperbole took over from fact, I contacted the CSIRO to learn more about the calicivirus and what it means to Australia, and especially to Australian cooks. >

rabbit
goes
with
bacon
olive oil
garlic
onions
carrots
thyme
rosemary
oregano
prunes
mushrooms
olives
chestnuts
pine nuts
almonds
mustard
wine vinegar
brandy
wine

The calicivirus occurs naturally (that is, it has *not* been genetically engineered) in 40 countries across 4 continents other than our own. It was designed for release in Australia in 1997–98 as part of a combined control programme using methods currently in use and was never seen as a 'magic bullet' for the entire rabbit population. Rabbits are effective reproducers: even when 70 per cent of the population is eradicated, rabbits can reach their original numbers in under a year. Rabbit shooters harvest a tiny 1–2 per cent of the population annually. To quote the CSIRO, 'based on 1991 figures, shooters would need to take approximately 150 million rabbits annually to begin to reduce the size of the rabbit population'. Even with the virus taking its toll, the European rabbit will be with us for some time.

The CSIRO reassured me that the rabbit calicivirus is species specific and 'that there is no danger to human health through the consumption of rabbits that have been in contact with the virus'. Vaccinated rabbits are also safe to eat, I was informed. However, the publicity associated with this virus had an immediate impact on the livelihood of rabbit shooters as the public was reluctant to buy rabbit. At the time of writing, those who love eating rabbit hope the response is temporary.

The rabbit has always had to battle for public acceptance, viruses aside. It is further despised by a generation of Australians because of its association with the suffering experienced during the Great Depression of the 1930s. Rabbit was Depression food ('bush mutton'): it was cheap and always available, and trapping rabbits for skins became a way of earning a few shillings. (My grandfather told me of how he used to lay a round of traps and by the time he had finished he could go back to the beginning, certain of finding an animal in each trap. I remember the frightening bunch of traps, with their savage jaws and blood stains, that hung from a nail in the barn.)

Rabbit is still inexpensive and can be delicious, as a new generation of food lovers is discovering.

VARIETIES AND SEASON

There are still caveats on commercial enclosed breeding of rabbits in most parts of Australia. At the time of writing the farming of rabbits is permitted in Western Australia, New South Wales and the Australian Capital Territory. The farmed rabbits are larger, have whiter flesh, are covered with a thin layer of fat and are generally more tender and juicy than their wild cousins. These rabbits are expensive and not widely available to the general buying public as rabbit farmers are concentrating on establishing restaurant and hotel business at this stage. Wild rabbit is available at all times of the year. Young rabbits (known, perhaps unfortunately, as kittens) are considered the most succulent. The breeding season, from spring to autumn, means that supplies of these can fluctuate.

SELECTION AND STORAGE

Rabbits are sold by most butchers, some poultry suppliers and in fresh food markets. They are always sold head off and skinned, so that it is difficult to tell their age. An older rabbit has worn teeth, blunt, ragged claws and tough, leathery ears. Smooth, sharp claws and tender ears are a sign of youth. We only have size and general condition to judge by. I have always found it difficult to tell a tender rabbit from a tough one, but I have certainly experienced both. It is easier to notice whether a rabbit is fresh or not. The liver should be glistening, there should be no suggestion of dryness of the flesh and the rabbit should not smell strongly. Supple, soft fat around the kidneys and in the belly cavity is a further indication of good condition.

One rabbit weighs about 800 g skinned and gutted, enough for 2 people – just! If cooking for rabbit lovers, buy extra. Rabbit is sold *whole* or jointed into *back legs*, *forelegs*, *saddle* and *fillets*. (But if you buy jointed rabbit you have no way of knowing if the back legs are from the same animal which supplied the portions of saddle. Therefore you cannot know how fresh or old your meat is. Better to choose your rabbit and either ask the butcher to portion it for you in the shop, or take it home and do it yourself.) **Boned rabbit meat** is also available in some markets. This can be used to make rabbit satays and quick stir-fries, while **minced rabbit** is useful for terrines. Rabbit **kidneys** and **liver** usually come as part of the deal when you buy a whole rabbit and are delicacies enjoyed by too few food lovers.

To store rabbit, remove all wrappings and refrigerate on a plate covered with plastic film. Use the meat within a day or two. Store the kidneys and liver on a separate plate and use within 24 hours.

PREPARATION AND COOKING

Like the meat from most wild animals, rabbit meat is lean and can be tough and dry. It presents a real challenge to the cook and many cooks fail the test! There is no need to soak rabbit overnight, as many older recipe books instruct. It is certainly in no need of having flavour leached from it. Rabbit is not at all strongly flavoured.

The back legs take a lot longer to cook than do the saddle or the forelegs, which are the most tender. For these reasons, I am not an admirer of whole roasted rabbit. If the back legs are cooked properly, the saddle will be splintery and dry. If the saddle is moist and juicy, the back legs will be underdone. Better to marinate and then roast the legs separately from the saddle. Better still to braise them. The saddle consists of the 2 fillets and the tiny under-fillets attached to the backbone and ribcage, and is covered with a fine sinew, which must be removed as it toughens and shrinks during cooking.

Wild rabbit has no covering fat. The cook must compensate for this by either wrapping the meat in fat (bacon, pancetta, pork hard back fat or, best of all, caul fat), or marinating it for 1 hour in olive oil with other flavourings such as herbs, garlic, a little lemon juice or wine, and pepper.

rabbit liver croutons
Sauté rabbit liver quickly, then spread a crouton with sorrel or spinach purée or Dijon mustard and top with the liver.

rabbit satay
Marinate small pieces of rabbit in Satay Marinade (see NUTS*), then thread onto soaked bamboo skewers and grill. Serve on a green salad with extra satay sauce.*

TO JOINT Follow the bone structure to remove both the back legs and the forelegs. Cut the saddle into 2–3 pieces for a casserole or barbecue or leave it whole for roasting. The flap of belly skin that once encased the internal organs is pretty useless and can be cut away and used to make a stock (add it to a bought carcass or use the ribcage of your own rabbit). Leave the kidneys intact on the underside of the saddle, if roasting.

TO REMOVE SINEW **Saddle** If the saddle is intact, pierce the sinew with a narrow-bladed knife and cut it away in strips, being very careful not to gouge into the flesh beneath. **Fillets** Put each fillet sinew downwards on your chopping board with the narrowest end towards you. Slip a narrow-bladed, sharp knife between the sinew and the flesh and work it towards the fattest end of the fillet using a seesawing motion.

TO PAN-FRY Boned rabbit *fillets* cook in 3–4 minutes only. Select a frying pan (not too big), heat butter to foaming and slip in your seasoned and/or marinated fillets. Seal well until golden, then turn and seal again. Remove pan from heat, cover for a minute, then slice and serve the fillet.

TO ROAST A *saddle* of rabbit, marinated in oil and herbs for 1 hour, should be browned quickly in butter and then put into a hot oven (220°C) for 5 minutes only. Remove the saddle from the oven and wrap it loosely in foil and allow to rest on a warm plate for 10 minutes. During those 10 minutes, deglaze the pan with a glass of wine and reduce it over high heat, adding a little stock, if you have any, or water or cream and any collected juices from the foil parcel. Carve each side of the saddle, that is, each fillet, away from the backbone, and slice diagonally. Retrieve the tiny underfillets from the other side. Drop the carved meat into the sauce with any garnishes (sautéd mushrooms, braised witlof or celery or turnips, cooked small onions, and so on) to warm and serve at once. *Back legs* go into the oven 30 minutes before the saddle; the *forelegs* go in 10 minutes later (20 minutes before the saddle).

TO BRAISE The *back legs* are ideal for country casseroles. Marinate them in oil and herbs, or wrap them in a veil of caul fat or a slice of thin streaky bacon. Brown the legs in butter and/or olive oil and tuck them into a casserole with vegetables (whole potatoes, onions, turnips, and small carrots or carrot chunks), garlic, and some wine and stock (chicken stock is ideal, so don't be concerned about not having rabbit stock), then cover and bake at 180°C for 1 hour or until quite tender. Serve with a puréed vegetable (potato, swede, pumpkin), which will soak up the delicious juices, and plenty of freshly chopped parsley. By adding specific garnishes to the casserole you will make classic dishes such as rabbit with prunes, and mushrooms will make some version of rabbit chasseur.

The *forelegs* can be cooked the same way, but they will take less time. Do not flood them with liquid, instead add just enough to not quite cover them. They do not need to be wrapped in fat, although little cubes of smoked bacon are excellent with any rabbit dish. Press a butter wrapper down on the forelegs, then cover and gently braise at 180°C in the oven or pot-roast on the stove using a simmer mat. Strongly flavoured herbs such as lemon thyme or oregano can be mixed with parsley for sprinkling on at the last minute.

rabbit with prunes

SERVES 4

12 prunes, stoned
4 tablespoons brandy
½ cup red wine
2 small rabbits
125 g streaky bacon, diced
30 g butter
12 pickling onions, peeled
1 tablespoon plain flour
2 cups hot chicken or rabbit
    stock
1 sprig thyme
salt
freshly ground black pepper
1 tablespoon sugar
3 tablespoons water
1 tablespoon red-wine vinegar

Soak prunes for 1 hour in brandy and red wine. Joint rabbits, reserving kidneys. Cut saddle into 2–3 pieces.

Preheat oven to 180°C. Cook bacon gently until golden in an enamelled cast-iron casserole big enough to hold rabbit. Lift out bacon and reserve. Add butter to bacon fat and brown rabbit in batches until golden brown. Transfer browned pieces to a plate until all are done. Add onions to fat and cook, turning, until coloured all over, then remove to a plate. Add flour and stir and scrape until browned, about 3 minutes. Tip in hot stock and stir vigorously to loosen all crusty bits to make the beginnings of a sauce.

Put back legs and saddle pieces into casserole with thyme, bacon, salt and pepper. Cover with buttered baking paper and then the lid and cook for 45 minutes. Add onions and forelegs and their juice, then add prunes and their soaking liquor.

Heat sugar and water in a small saucepan until a golden caramel. Add vinegar and warm until caramel has dissolved. Add to casserole and stir through. Taste and adjust seasoning. Cover casserole with buttered paper again and continue to cook until tender – at least 30 minutes, maybe longer. Serve with mashed potato. This dish reheats well. >

rabbit with pasta
Seal sliced rabbit fillet in a litle hot olive oil and add chopped witlof, shredded radicchio hearts or sliced red cabbage and toss until wilted. Grind on pepper and add a splash of red-wine vinegar or balsamic vinegar and a nut of butter and toss until the rabbit is cooked. Tip onto a dish of hot pasta and scatter with toasted pine nuts.

variations Forget the prunes and the caramel and try one of the following options instead. Add chunks of carrot, small turnips and whole blanched garlic cloves when you add the onions and forelegs. Or add a handful of stoned green olives and 1 cup diced peeled tomato when you add the onions and forelegs. Or substitute cider for the stock, or use half stock, half cider, and add 1 cup diced peeled tomato. Or roll each piece of rabbit in Dijon mustard and brown carefully before proceeding with the recipe.

mary's rabbit pie   SERVES 4

Mary was my mother and my mentor. This rabbit pie is a family heirloom, cooked wherever and whenever my family meets.

1 rabbit
2 litres Chicken Stock ✒ or
    water
1 stick celery, chopped
½ carrot, sliced
1 onion
1 piece lemon zest
1 stalk parsley
1 bay leaf
1 sprig thyme
1 teaspoon black peppercorns
100 g smoked streaky bacon,
    finely diced
200 g button mushrooms, sliced
100 g flaked almonds, toasted
1 cup freshly chopped parsley
salt
freshly ground black pepper
1 quantity Shortcrust Pastry ✒
½ cup fresh breadcrumbs

SAUCE
150 g butter
150 g plain flour
1.25 litres reserved cooking
    liquid
200 ml cream
juice of 2 lemons
salt
freshly ground black pepper

Remove kidneys and liver from rabbit and reserve. Simmer rabbit in stock with celery, carrot, onion, zest, herbs and peppercorns until back legs test tender, 1–2 hours. Allow rabbit to cool completely in stock. Remove rabbit and set strained cooking liquid aside for later use. Strip all meat from carcass and cut into small pieces. Discard bones.

Lightly sauté bacon and mushrooms and quickly sear reserved kidneys and liver. Mix rabbit meat with bacon, mushrooms, almonds and chopped kidneys and liver in a bowl. Mix in parsley and season well. Cover with plastic film.

To make the sauce, cook butter and flour over a gentle heat to make a *roux* ✒. Gradually add the reserved cooking liquid, stirring, and bring to simmering point. Add cream and lemon juice and simmer for 10 minutes on a simmer mat to prevent sauce sticking. Check for seasoning and add enough sauce to meat to make a creamy, not sloppy, filling. Allow to cool completely.

Preheat oven to 200°C. Line a 28 cm × 18 cm × 5 cm lamington tin with pastry (reserve some pastry to make a latticed top) and bake blind ✒ for 20 minutes. Remove pastry case from oven and allow to cool. Reduce oven temperature to 180°C. Spoon

---

rabbit rillettes
Make rabbit rillettes to the recipe given for Pork Rillettes (see PORK*) by adding 1 kg rabbit legs (forelegs and back legs). Be sure to discard all the rabbit bones most scrupulously when shredding the cooked meats, as tiny pieces of rabbit bone are very sharp.*

fried rabbit
Dust a jointed very young rabbit with seasoned flour and deep-fry in a heavy-based saucepan in clean olive oil at 175°C for about 10 minutes. Serve with a green salad full of plenty of freshly chopped green herbs and pass garlic mayonnaise.

filling into pastry case (it will be easier to cut squares or wedges if filling
is a maximum of 4 cm deep). Scatter top with breadcrumbs and criss-cross
strips of pastry over filling. Bake for 15–20 minutes until pastry is well
browned. Serve warm or cold with mustard, chutney or pickled fruit.
poaching This method of simmering rabbit in stock can be used if
wanting meat for sandwiches or whenever a filling is required.

rabbit baked with thyme and mustard *see* THYME

other recipes

r h u b a r b   The reputation that rhubarb (*Rheum rhaponticum*), a native of Russia, has for being good for you no doubt stems from the fact that it was only used for medicinal purposes until the eighteenth century as its roots had purgative qualities. We now know that its leaves are poisonous, containing serious quantities of oxalic acid, and it is only the coloured stalks that are eaten. (The stalks contain oxalic acid also but in harmless quantities, given the portions one usually eats.) │ Somehow I was never told that rhubarb was good for me, so I grew up loving it. I loved its beautiful rose-pink colour, its sharp and surprising flavour, and the way I could trail a spoonful of proper custard through my bowl of rhubarb and admire the patterns I made. My mother also loved rhubarb: it was simple to grow, and there were 4 ravenous children and Grandpa all ready to enthuse over her latest rhubarb creation (I remember with pleasure her yeast doughnuts filled with sweet rhubarb). I must say, however, that my father did not care for rhubarb much. >

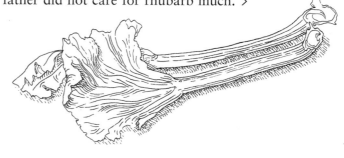

Rhubarb is closely related to wild dock and sorrel and is really a vegetable but is treated as a fruit. Its other name of 'pie plant' gives an indication of its most popular culinary use. Rhubarb purée combines well with custards and cream to make delicious and very pretty ice-creams and fools. Its sharpness can also be successful as a sauce or relish with rich meat or fish.

VARIETIES AND SEASON

Rhubarb is not sold by variety, although many growers believe the finest to be the cherry cultivar, which is grown extensively in South Australia. Rhubarb is grown in the open in Australia and is available all year, unlike in Britain and Europe where it is often forced out of season in hothouses. In winter here it grows more slowly, resulting in thinner, redder stalks. In warmer weather the stalks grow thicker and tend to be greenish red.

SELECTION AND STORAGE

Red rhubarb looks a lot more appealing and tastes sweeter than green. As red rhubarb is more readily available in winter, it makes sense to use it freely during this time. Rhubarb becomes floppy quite quickly after picking, so if the bunches in the greengrocer's have wilted the rhubarb has probably been picked for too long. Look for bunches that are crisp and upright, and prefer well-coloured stalks.

Slice off and discard the leaves before refrigerating the stalks, wrapped in plastic film or in a vegetable storage bag, in the crisper drawer for up to a week. Cooked rhubarb keeps well in a covered container in the refrigerator for 4–5 days.

PREPARATION AND COOKING

Australian growers stress that our rhubarb rarely requires stringing and is very tender. Most of my favourite rhubarb dishes start off with rhubarb purée, which sounds better than stewed rhubarb. Rhubarb has so much moisture in it that it barely needs any more added. Remove all leaves, as they are poisonous, then cut off the flat brown part from the bottom of each stalk. String the rhubarb only if the stalks are very large and green. Cut the stalks into 3 cm lengths (some pie fillings require very thin slices).

TO PURÉE Put the prepared rhubarb into a heavy-based, enamelled cast-iron saucepan with a generous strewing of sugar and a couple of spoonfuls of water, then cover tightly with a lid. Stand the saucepan over medium heat; in 5 minutes lift the lid and stir. The rhubarb will be almost ready. In a few more minutes it will have cooked to a soft purée. Blend the rhubarb in a food processor if you want

rhubarb goes with
sugar
honey
butter
apples
ginger
pastry
cinnamon
vanilla
rosewater
strawberries
plums
almonds
yoghurt
soft white cheese

rhubarb purée
Add a few drops of rosewater to rhubarb purée and serve with creamy sheep's milk yoghurt flavoured with wild honey.

rhubarb fool
Blend rhubarb purée (with or without rosewater), then chill and fold into an equal quantity of whipped cream.

a perfectly smooth preparation, or leave it as it is to enjoy with your breakfast cereal.

recipes

rhubarb sauce
Serve rhubarb purée as a surprising sauce with oily fish, such as grilled salmon.

rhubarb and apple tart
Pile sliced rhubarb and apple into a baked pastry case and add the filling used in Stephanie's Quince Tart (see QUINCES*). Bake at 190°C until set.*

rhubarb ice-cream
Stir rhubarb purée into Egg Custard and then churn in an ice-cream machine. Blend the purée first in a food processor for a perfectly smooth, evenly pink ice-cream or leave it textured for a speckled ice-cream.

rhubarb pie

SERVES 6

Lard pastry will give a softer, more cakey crust, if that is your preference.

1 quantity Shortcrust or Lard Pastry
500 g rhubarb, sliced
100 g brown sugar
1 tablespoon cornflour
3 tablespoons currants
milk
1 tablespoon castor sugar

Preheat oven to 200°C. Line a 22 cm pie plate with pastry, leaving enough for a lid. Combine rhubarb, brown sugar, cornflour and currants and pile into pie plate (the rhubarb will shrink a lot in the baking). Cut a lid from remaining pastry and cover rhubarb, pinching edges together to seal. Brush pastry with milk and scatter with castor sugar. Slash 2 slits in crust to allow steam to escape. Stand pie plate on a larger baking tray (in case any juice leaks out) and bake for 35 minutes. Allow to cool a little before cutting.

rhubarb yeast cake

SERVES 4–6

500 g rhubarb, chopped
½ cup sugar
3 tablespoons seedless raisins, sultanas or currants
4 tablespoons chopped walnuts
2 tablespoons Cognac
ground cinnamon
castor sugar

DOUGH
2 teaspoons instant dried yeast
125 g plain flour
pinch of salt
4 tablespoons milk
1 tablespoon sugar
80 g butter
1 egg

Blanch rhubarb in boiling water for 1 minute, then drain and dry well. Mix with remaining ingredients except cinnamon and castor sugar and cool.

To make the dough, mix yeast, flour and salt in a bowl. Warm milk with sugar and butter until butter has just melted. Pour liquid into a well in flour, then add egg and work to a smooth dough. Put dough into a lightly buttered bowl and set aside, covered with a tea towel, in a draught-free spot until doubled in size (about 1 hour). Knock back dough and roll out to make a 16 cm square. Put dough on a greased baking tray and place filling down centre. Using a pair of scissors, snip sides at 3 cm intervals through to filling, then fold strips alternately over filling. Cover with a clean tea towel for 30 minutes for a second rising. Bake at 180°C for 30 minutes. Allow to cool a little, then sprinkle with a mix of cinnamon and castor sugar. Serve warm with thick cream.

rhubarb and red fruit sago sauce   SERVES 6–8

Called 'rotegrütze', versions of this pudding occur all through Poland and Germany. I have included a Barossa Valley recipe made with grape juice in GRAPES AND VINE LEAVES. *I find this version ideal for a super-rich chocolate pudding. Its acidity is welcome, and the colour is heightened by the addition of raspberries.*

375 g rhubarb, cut into
   1 cm pieces
grated zest of ½ lemon
3 tablespoons water
1 vanilla bean, split
½ cup white wine
   (late-picked spätlese *or*
   a gewürztraminer)
2 tablespoons sago
100 g sugar
500 g fresh *or* frozen
   raspberries

Place rhubarb, zest, water, vanilla bean and wine in a large non-reactive saucepan and bring to simmering point. Add sago, then reduce heat and place pan on a simmer mat. Cook gently for 15 minutes, stirring from time to time or sago will stick. Add sugar and stir until it has dissolved. Carefully add raspberries and simmer for a few minutes (or just until thawed, if using frozen berries). Stir once or twice. Do not overcook at this point. Serve warm or cold.

rhubarb muffins   MAKES 12

220 g plain flour
2 teaspoons baking powder
125 g sugar
¾ cup milk *or* buttermilk
1 egg
¾ cup vegetable oil
⅔ cup finely sliced rhubarb

Preheat oven to 180°C and thoroughly grease 12 muffin tins with a little oil. Sift flour and baking powder and stir in sugar. Mix milk, egg and oil together. Make a well in centre of flour and beat in liquid. Mix in rhubarb. Spoon batter into muffin tins until two-thirds full. Bake for 20–25 minutes. Cool muffins on a wire rack. Serve slightly warm, split, with butter and jam or just jam.

rhubarb crumble
Combine rhubarb purée with an equal quantity of butter-stewed apple chunks and spoon into a buttered dish until two-thirds full and strew with Crumble Topping. Bake at 200°C for 25 minutes until the crumble is golden brown and bubbling at the edges. For a change, replace 2 tablespoons flour in the crumble topping with ground hazelnuts and use cinnamon instead of ginger.

blushing betty
Spoon Sponge Topping over 2 cups rhubarb purée and cook for 30 minutes at 200°C until golden brown to create this delicious pudding.

r i c e Every cook should be able to cook plain rice well and make a simple pilaf and know how to use leftover cooked rice. Rice is important in the cuisines of the Middle East, West Africa, Italy, Spain and the Caribbean, as well as all of Asia (including, of course, India), so the possibilities are enormous. A bowl of fragrant rice with a topping of steamed, sliced chicken breast or steamed prawns or a steamed green vegetable and a scattering of sliced spring onion, a sprinkle of soy sauce, maybe some freshly sliced ginger and a dab of chilli provides a comforting, effortless dinner for one, and reminds us, in the hustle and bustle of our lives, of the satisfaction that can be experienced from simple, good things. | The origins of rice are obscure, but we do know that it has been valued as a food crop for a very long time. Rice was cultivated in Asia as early as 3500 BC, and was introduced to the Western world about 335 BC when Alexander the Great's soldiers entered India. The Moors planted rice in Andalusia in the eighth century AD, and in the tenth century rice cultivation began in Italy. Today this starchy grain from the grass family (Graminae) is the most important food crop for most of the world's population. *The Rice Book* by Sri Owen will answer all your questions about this wonderful ingredient. >

Rice is enormously important in Asian cultures, where subtle differences of flavour, colour, fragrance and texture are taken very seriously. Rice figures largely in religious ceremonies, too, and is a symbol of prosperity and fertility. Even in the West rice is thrown at a wedding, symbolising fertility. In Japan the planting of rice is a religious experience accompanied by a blessing from a Buddhist priest. This is one of the reasons given to explain the reluctance of the Japanese to import rice: they say they could not be certain that as much care would be taken with the traditional aspects of the planting as would take place in Japan. Australia exports 10 000 tonnes of rice to Japan annually, mostly for use in food manufacturing. Rice is grown in New South Wales north of the Murray River at Echuca, and around Leeton in the Murrumbidgee Irrigation Area.

VARIETIES AND SEASON

There are more than 40 000 different varieties of rice grown throughout the world. Cultivated rice is a single species, but its subspecies and varieties are almost endless. They are most usefully divided into 3 broad groups: long-, medium- and short-grained rice. Some divide rice further into 2 broad subdivisions: the indica rices, which are long-grained and not sticky, and the japonica rices, which are short-grained with varying degrees of stickiness. To these subdivisions has been added a third – javanica, which includes long-grained rice that is somewhat sticky. (Note that wild rice is not a true rice but the seed of an American grass.)

There are many other ways to describe rice, such as by referring to what has happened to it during processing (brown rice, parboiled rice), its texture (sticky rice) or how it is intended to be used (pudding rice). It can be described by the colour of the grain (red rice, black rice) or a name that suggests its country of origin (arborio). Or it can be referred to by a brand name. But by recognising rice as either long-grained, medium-grained or short-grained, one is less likely to become confused.

rice
goes
with
lemongrass
rice vinegar
soy sauce
seaweed
ginger
seafood
pulses
chicken
saffron
milk
turmeric
garlic
fish sauce
coconut milk
cardamom
shrimp paste
chilli sauce

LONG-GRAINED When cooked, this rice looks light and fluffy and the grains remain separate. This group includes basmati rice and patna rice, both considered ideal for pilafs, biryanis and curries; jasmine or Thai fragrant rice, a delicately scented rice used a great deal in the cooking of South-East Asia; and American Carolina rice. Long-grained rice is overwhelmingly used in savoury dishes and is available with its husks as brown rice or without husks.

SHORT- AND MEDIUM-GRAINED This rice has grains that are plumper than long-grained rice when cooked and are moist and more or less sticky. Medium-grained rice is a favourite with the Chinese. It is also available as brown rice, that is, with its husks intact. Short-grained varieties are preferred in Spain for paella, in Italy for risotto and in Japan for sushi and everyday eating. The moist grains cling together and are ideal when eating with chopsticks. Each rice is different from the other, but they are all more or less short-grained. In many parts of Asia very sticky, short-grained rice (both white and black) is used to make sweet dishes.

Arborio is medium-length with a soft texture and a chalky centre. It is used specifically for making risotto. During the cooking process some of the starch from the rice is released and creates the desired creaminess. Carnaroli and Vialone are other varieties of rice used to make risotto. Short-grained rice is traditionally used in Western countries to make puddings.

The principle varieties grown in Australia are the soft-cooking short-grained japonica, and long- and medium-grained rice, including fragrant rice. Our supermarkets stock many varieties of long-, medium- and short-grained rice. But shoppers will find an even wider selection if they frequent Asian food stores and specialist European food importers.

SELECTION AND STORAGE

Asian connoisseurs recognise whether rice is fresh by its aroma. Most of us are not able to do this without long training. However, as rice is popular and stock turns over quickly in the supermarket, freshness is not really an issue. (Be wary, though, of any packet of rice you may have had in the pantry for years as it may host weevils, which love rice.) Make sure you buy the style of rice required for the dish you wish to cook (arborio for risotto, for example). Once a packet has been opened, store it in an airtight container. If you buy rice in a large sack, it is important that it be stored in a clean, dry container with a lid.

Cooked rice should be refrigerated, as harmful bacteria can grow rapidly between 4°C and 60°C. Electric rice cookers heat rice above this temperature; the container holding the rice can be removed and refrigerated if you intend to reheat the rice.

PREPARATION AND COOKING

Some cooks wash rice before cooking, others do not. Generally, packaged rice has already been washed and does not require further washing. If you buy your rice in sacks from an Asian food store, it is necessary to wash it well to remove dust, and even stones!

There is a good deal of badly cooked rice to be experienced in Australia, unless one is eating in an Asian home or restaurant. There, rice is usually cooked in an electric rice cooker, which takes the guesswork out of estimating the amount of water to use with a specific quantity of rice, which in turn varies with the variety of rice being cooked. For those households where the cooking of rice is a frequent routine, I strongly suggest acquiring an electric rice cooker. I took years to be convinced, but after hosting a dinner for 12 one evening and being able to present perfect spiced rice from the rice cooker, I was a convert!

Good rice can also be achieved without an electric rice cooker, however. There are a few rules to follow. Rice should not be cooked in masses of water like green beans and then drained at the end. It tastes wet and flabby cooked in this manner. Well-cooked rice absorbs its liquid, the grains swelling to their maximum and retaining all their flavour. Visiting Indian food writer Madhur Jaffrey charmed an audience in Melbourne recently by saying that the grains of well-cooked rice should be like brothers – close, but not too close.

It is important to get the rice-to-water ratio right when cooking rice. However, even the experts differ on how much water should be used. Remember that 1 cup raw white rice yields about 3 cups cooked rice, while 1 cup raw brown rice yields 3½–4 cups cooked. I allow 100 g raw rice per person; as leftovers can be used in so many ways I usually cook an extra 100 g. While the rule of thumb is to allow about 1½ cups water to 1 cup rice (brown rice will need a little more water, short-grained rice may need a little less), a method used worldwide always works well for me. Put the tip of your index finger on the surface of the rice in the saucepan and add water up to the first joint.

Some countries add salt when cooking rice (India, Pakistan and Sri Lanka), others do not (Malaysia, Indonesia, Thailand and Vietnam). While water is the usual cooking liquid, chicken or fish stock can be used instead for a more flavoursome rice. The rice can also be turned in oil or butter with spices before it is put into the saucepan, for a simple pilaf.

TO COOK Choose a saucepan that has a tight-fitting lid. Bring the rice, water and salt (if using) to a bubbling boil, covered, over medium heat. Turn the heat low, then sit the pan on a simmer mat, cover the rice with a doubled sheet of baking paper or a folded tea towel, ram on the lid and leave for 20 minutes. Remove the pan from the heat, uncover it to allow steam to escape and fluff the grains with a fork. Transfer the rice, using a metal spoon rather than a wooden spoon (which has a tendency to crush the grains), to a heated serving dish.
Glutinous rice Soak the rice overnight in plenty of water. Rinse it well, then cook it in a Chinese bamboo steamer over boiling water for 20–30 minutes. Let the rice rest for 5 minutes off the heat before serving. (Some cooks prefer to line the bamboo steamer with a cloth or muslin to prevent the grains of rice lodging in the bamboo slats.) Asian food stores also sell beautiful cane baskets made just for steaming glutinous rice.

recipes

rice pilaf

SERVES 4–6

This style of cooking rice can be freely adapted as the spices, flavourings and stock can be changed. A Spanish paella is a famous and very specific type of pilaf – a memorable feast of rice, tomato, saffron, chicken and seafood.

½ teaspoon saffron threads

2 tablespoons boiling water

2 tablespoons vegetable oil
  or clarified butter ✓

4 cardamom pods, crushed

I small stick cinnamon

4 cloves

10 black peppercorns

2½ cups long-grained rice

I litre hot Chicken Stock ✓

2½ teaspoons salt

2 tablespoons blanched
  slivered almonds, toasted

Soak saffron in boiling water for 10 minutes. Heat oil in a heavy-based saucepan and fry cardamom pods, cinnamon, cloves and peppercorns for 2 minutes. Add rice and fry, stirring, for 2–3 minutes. Add hot stock, salt and soaked saffron threads and their liquid. Stir well and bring to a boil quickly, then turn heat to very low, cover tightly and cook for 20 minutes. Serve garnished with toasted almonds.

turmeric If you have no saffron, use ground turmeric when frying the spices for a brilliant yellow colour. **mary's pilaf** My mother made a similar dish to this by omitting the saffron and placing a layer of fat raisins and raw cashews on top of the uncooked rice. Once the rice was cooked she forked the fruit and nuts through it and piled it in the centre of an oval meat dish and surrounded it with a simple stew of veal chunks simmered with mushrooms and red wine. I still think the combination is memorable.

lemon risotto

SERVES 6

Making risotto is not difficult, merely relentless in holding you to the stove! It is important to use arborio or carnaroli rice, which can absorb at least 3–4 times their volume in liquid. When cooked, the rice should be soft with the merest nuttiness in the centre of each grain. The rice should not be chewy or hard, but each grain must be separate.

Risotto needs constant watching and constant stirring: the process is a leisurely one. Reconstituted risotto may be acceptable but never has the creaminess and sauciness of a freshly served version. You should have to wait for risotto in a restaurant. If it appears in 5 minutes, it will not be memorable. If you are cooking for food lovers, risotto is an ideal dish to prepare with drink in hand and the conversation flowing in the kitchen around you. When it is ready, it should be rushed to the table and eaten without delay. Having mastered this basic version, turn to Italian cookbooks for interesting variations.

1 lemon
1.5 litres Chicken Stock
300 ml dry white wine
120 g unsalted butter
1 small onion, very finely
  chopped
600 g arborio rice
90 g parmesan cheese, freshly
  grated
3 tablespoons finely chopped
  fresh parsley

Juice and zest lemon. Heat stock and wine in a saucepan. In a heavy-based deep frying pan melt half the butter over gentle heat and sauté onion until softened and translucent. Add rice and raise heat to moderate. Stir to ensure rice is evenly coated with butter. Add 1 cup stock. Simmer, stirring constantly, and add 1 cup hot stock at a time as the liquid is absorbed, making sure that the rice is always just covered. After 15–20 minutes, remove risotto from heat and taste rice. It should be perfectly cooked. Add cheese, remaining butter, parsley and lemon zest and juice. Cover for 2 minutes, then transfer to a warm platter and serve at once.

green herb pilaf

SERVES 2–4

A herb pilaf is another simple dish worth building into your repertoire. It is good for lunch or supper on its own, or can be served in smaller quantities with a grilled chicken breast or escalope of veal.

1 tablespoon olive oil
40 g butter
½ cup finely chopped fresh
  parsley
2 tablespoons finely chopped
  fresh coriander leaves
2 tablespoons finely chopped
  watercress leaves
1 cup finely chopped spring
  onion (including greens)
2 handfuls baby spinach leaves,
  washed, dried and finely
  chopped
1 cup long-grained rice
1½ cups water *or* Chicken
  Stock
salt
freshly ground black pepper
freshly grated parmesan *or*
  pecorino cheese

Heat oil and half the butter in a heavy-based saucepan. Add herbs, watercress, spring onion and spinach and cook for a few minutes, stirring. Add rice and cook, stirring, until grains look shiny and are flecked with green. Add water and salt. Bring to a boil over a moderate heat, then turn heat to very low, cover pan and transfer it to a simmer mat and cook undisturbed for 20 minutes. Stir remaining butter into rice with a fork. Turn into a hot serving dish, grind over pepper and pass the cheese separately.

rice balls
Mix leftover rice pilaf or risotto with an egg or two, then form into balls, roll lightly in flour and shallow-fry in olive oil until golden and crisp. These are great for lunch with home-made tomato sauce. Tuck a cube of fresh mozzarella in the centre of each rice ball, so that the cheese melts as the rice fries, to make Italian suppli (telephone wires).

chicken congee

SERVES 6

Congee is a wonderfully soothing street food available at stalls from early in the morning until late at night in most Asian cities. It can be simple or it can be elaborate, savoury or sweet, with garnishes that include preserved duck eggs, fermented bean curd, pickles or salads of shredded chicken meat. This recipe is based on one given by Meera Freeman in The Vietnamese Cookbook. *Meera uses cracked black pepper in place of the chilli, and fish sauce instead of the soy I have suggested. Try it both ways.*

fried rice

Toss and fry 3 cups cooked rice in 2 tablespoons very hot oil in a wok until the grains are separate and lightly coloured. Sprinkle the rice with a tablespoon each of light soy sauce and mushroom soy sauce and mix evenly, then add spring onions sliced on the diagonal and toss and stir for a further minute. Add ham, egg, prawns, peas and so on, as you like.

1 x 1.6 kg chicken
1.5 litres well-flavoured
   Chicken Stock
2 tablespoons peanut oil
2 cups medium-grained rice
1 fresh chilli, seeded and very
   finely sliced
3 spring onions, sliced

DIPPING SAUCE

1 clove garlic
1 small fresh chilli, seeded
1 teaspoon sugar
1 tablespoon rice vinegar
3 tablespoons water
3 tablespoons light soy sauce
squeeze of lime juice

Poach chicken in stock for 45 minutes. Cool chicken in stock for 10 minutes then remove. Discard skin and cut breast meat into fine strips. Return stock to a boil.

To make the dipping sauce, mash garlic with chilli in a mortar and pestle and combine with remaining ingredients. Stir to dissolve sugar and set aside.

Heat oil in a wok and fry rice for a minute or so until opaque. Transfer rice to a saucepan and add boiling stock to come a good 5 cm above rice. Cover and cook gently until rice is soft and soupy, about 30 minutes (this is one time where you can let your rice get mushy!). Place some shredded chicken and a few slices of chilli and spring onion in each bowl and ladle in the soupy rice broth. Serve the sauce on the side for each person to add.

jamaican rice and 'peas'

SERVES 4–6

This delicious national dish is served at breakfast with salted fish and even curries. It can accompany any combination of meat, fish and vegetables for lunch or dinner as well. The 'peas' referred to are dried pulses. In Jamaica the variety, as I remember, was red and of the size of our black-eyed peas. As in so many cultures, the legume or pulse provides the protein that is absent in the rice, resulting in a nutritious as well as inexpensive dish.

½ cup black-eyed peas,
  soaked overnight
1 litre cold water
600 ml coconut milk
salt
freshly ground black pepper
1 teaspoon fresh thyme leaves
2 tablespoons vegetable oil
2 cloves garlic, chopped
1 fresh chilli, seeded and
  chopped
2 cups long-grained rice
2 spring onions, finely sliced

Place soaked peas in cold water and simmer until tender (about 1½ hours). Add coconut milk, salt, pepper and thyme and simmer 5 minutes. Heat oil in a saucepan, then sear garlic and chilli for 1 minute, then add rice. Turn to coat until glistening and tip in coconut milk mixture. Cover saucepan closely and simmer over lowest heat for 20 minutes until all liquid has been absorbed. Spoon onto a hot serving dish and scatter with spring onion.

mango with sticky rice   SERVES 6

A Thai dessert from Mogens Bay Esbensen's book Thai Cuisine, *this combines the silkiness of glutinous rice with the richness of mango.*

200 g glutinous rice, soaked
  overnight
400 ml coconut milk
pinch of salt
100 ml light Sugar Syrup
6 mangoes
toasted sesame seeds

Drain rice and steam, covered, for 20–30 minutes. Transfer rice to a bowl and allow to cool. Skim any thick cream from coconut milk and set aside. Add remaining coconut milk and salt to cooled rice, then stir in sugar syrup. Arrange peeled and sliced mango on each plate and add a small mound of rice. Top with a teaspoon of reserved coconut cream (if any) and sprinkle with toasted sesame seeds.

damien's toasted almond rice   SERVES 8

This creamy rice dessert is wonderful alongside a compote of poached fruit such as figs or plums. On one special occasion I scattered it with pieces of gold leaf as part of a Middle Eastern dinner.

1.4 litres milk
150 g sugar
pinch of salt
1 vanilla bean, split
240 g short-grained rice
3 cups cream, whipped
150 g flaked almonds, toasted

Bring milk to a boil with sugar, salt and vanilla bean, then tip in rice and stir until boiling. Reduce heat and simmer very gently for 30 minutes until rice is properly cooked. Allow to cool. Fold cream into rice with half the almonds. Turn into a bowl and then unmould onto a platter and decorate with remaining almonds.

english rice pudding

SERVES 4

Many people dislike this dessert, having had poorly made versions at school. I only ever had delicious rice pudding and have always loved it. I think slow-cooking is the answer. This is the sort of pudding that used to go into the oven underneath the roast on Sunday before the family left for church and would be reaching perfection on our return. Our family tradition decreed that one spooned a big dollop of plum jam on top of each portion. I have no idea why.

2 eggs

2 tablespoons sugar

2 cups milk

4 tablespoons short-grained rice, washed and drained

I bay leaf *or* few drops of pure vanilla

freshly grated nutmeg (optional)

Preheat oven to 160°C and butter a 750 ml pie dish. Lightly beat eggs with sugar and milk. Put rice in pie dish, pour over milk mixture and add bay leaf. Bake for 1½ hours until thick and creamy with a brown crust on top. Grate nutmeg over, if liked, and serve with cream.

variations Add sultanas and glacé peel to the rice, or include a small glass of brandy with the milk.

other recipes

cabbage leaves stuffed with pork, sausage and rice *see* CABBAGES AND BRUSSELS SPROUTS

janni's dolmades *see* GRAPES AND VINE LEAVES

squid stuffed with rice and currants *see* SQUID, CALAMARI, CUTTLEFISH AND OCTOPUS

rock lobsters

The spiky Australian crustacean that I and the fishing fraternity call rock lobster is also frequently called crayfish. In England the same creature is known as a spiny lobster, and as a *langouste* by the French. In Europe the word 'crayfish' refers to a freshwater crustacean (*ecrevisse*, in French), very similar or identical to our yabby. | There are similarities in appearance and flavour between our rock lobsters and the lobster of the North Atlantic, but they belong to quite different families. The most important difference in appearance is that our rock lobsters do not have the large and culinarily important front claws of the North Atlantic lobster. Our rock lobsters have rough and spiky shells; the North Atlantic lobster does not. Our rock lobsters have firmer flesh than the northern lobsters. | Rock lobsters are a $336 million industry in Australia. Sadly for local rock lobster lovers, the majority of the catch is exported live or frozen to Japan, and as frozen tails to the United States. The discarded heads are processed to become pet food and liquid fertiliser and are an important addition to salmon feed. >

**rock
lobsters
go
with**
butter
olive oil
lemons
pepper
fennel
mayonnaise
basil
tarragon
parsley
bay leaves
potatoes
cream
vermouth
tomatoes
salad leaves
melons
chillies
garlic
ginger
spring onions
coriander

For the home cook the most obvious thing about rock lobster is its exorbitant price. This was not always the case, however. At fishing ports around the coast one used to be able to buy freshly boiled 'crays' for a reasonable price. The export market has changed all this, and much commercial fishing is now handled by larger boats owned by a few huge companies and the local cray fisherman is history in many seaside towns. Today the rock lobsters that are available on the coast have frequently been caught elsewhere and have been boiled and frozen before being offered for sale.

Having given the down side, it is important to note that there still *are* some places where local fishermen catch and sell live and freshly boiled rock lobster. I have experienced this at Robe, South Australia, and at Queenscliff, Flinders and Lakes Entrance in Victoria. And good fishmongers should be able to supply you with live or cooked – but not frozen – rock lobsters. When you are staying near the ocean, or passing through a fishing town, either patronise a restaurant that offers poached or grilled green (uncooked) rock lobster or else buy a live one and deal with it yourself.

I have a fairly purist attitude to garnishing and saucing this luxurious food. I cannot bear cheese with rock lobster, nor do I think Cognac does much for it. For my digestion, most wine and cream sauces are too rich with this already very rich meat. Instead I like just enough shellfish-based butter sauce or melted butter with a few herbs added to ooze under the flesh and settle in the shell, so that each bite is flavoured but not swamped. I also like it with fresh lime or lemon wedges and a bowl of crisp watercress, or served simply with hot boiled potatoes or a softboiled-egg vinaigrette. As with all the best ingredients, simplicity is the key.

VARIETIES AND SEASON

Increasingly, conservation issues are politically important and influence decisions regarding quotas, size limits and closed seasons. The closed seasons vary in different fishing grounds. Management of this valuable industry is aimed at protecting breeding stock and controlling the harvesting. Berried females (with eggs) are prohibited in all fisheries, and there are differing regulations relating to minimum size, number of pots permitted, and so on.

There are 4 species of rock lobster to watch out for. The descriptions that follow are for live rock lobsters, since they all turn red once cooked.

Eastern Also known as the Sydney spiny or packhorse rock lobster, *Jasus verreauxi* is found from Tweed Heads, New South Wales, to Port MacDonnell in South Australia, including Bass Strait and around Tasmania. It is light-to-dark green in northern waters but reddish purple in more southern waters. It weighs 2–7 kg. **Southern** *J. edwardsii* is reddish purple and orange when from shallow waters or purple and creamy-yellow when found in deep water. It weighs 2–5 kg and has a particularly rough and spiky tail section. It is found from Coffs Harbour, New South Wales, along the Victorian and South Australian coasts to Dongara, Western Australia.

Tropical The *Panulirus* species marketed as tropical rock lobsters occur around our northern coastline, from southern Western Australia to Sydney. Of these *P. ornatus* is particularly well named, being spectacularly marked and coloured. Information about their size and weight varies. I have only experienced them in the Northern Territory, where they were smallish, weighing a little less than 1 kg. **Western** *P. cygnus* is a reddish brown to deep maroon. It weighs 1.4–2.5 kg and is found in Western Australia, from Albany to North West Cape.

SELECTION AND STORAGE

There are 2 ways of buying rock lobster: live and cooked. All rock lobsters, live or cooked, should feel heavy for their size. Rock lobsters shed their shells many times in their lifetime. Just after moulting the flesh can be watery and soft and loose within the shell. Such a rock lobster will not feel as weighty as one in its prime. The shell will turn bright red after it has been cooked, no matter what colour its shell when alive.

A *live* rock lobster is called a 'green' rock lobster, just as uncooked prawns are sold as 'green' prawns, whether or not they are green in colour. Never buy a dead green rock lobster, unless you have instructed the fishmonger to kill the creature just before you take delivery of it. Like all crustaceans, rock lobsters start to deteriorate as soon as they are taken from the sea.

A live rock lobster should be lively and when picked up its tail should flap angrily! If the tail hangs limply, do not buy it: the lobster is dead or dying, and the flesh will have lost condition. Frozen green rock lobster tails are prepared for export; they will never taste as wonderful as freshly prepared rock lobster. Never attempt to substitute a cooked rock lobster in a recipe calling for a green (live) rock lobster. It is the same thing as recooking a piece of meat – inevitably the dish will be tough and dry.

A *cooked* rock lobster will be bright red and should have its tail curled tightly against its body. If it hangs limply, it was boiled after death and the flesh will have lost condition. A freshly cooked crayfish should smell sweet with absolutely no suggestion of ammonia.

Try to time the cooking and serving of rock lobster so that you are not tempted to refrigerate it. The flesh hardens when chilled and is so much more wonderful warm or at room temperature. So – go to your fishmonger or market, buy your rock lobster and serve it as soon as you can after arriving home or at the very latest the next day.

PREPARATION AND COOKING

Preparing rock lobster requires organisation and a cooperative fishmonger. If, for example, your dish requires a green rock lobster, get your fishmonger to kill it just before you collect it, having advised him or her how you plan to prepare the dish, so that it isn't then boiled before you pick it up.

There is much debate on the most humane and efficient method of killing a live rock lobster. I wonder how much difference there is between being frozen and then plunged into boiling water, or being drowned in fresh water before being boiled or grilled. It is well documented that the meat from beef cattle and sheep will be tough unless the beasts are slaughtered in a manner that minimises stress. The same thing might apply to rock lobsters.

TO KILL

The *least* satisfactory method of killing a live rock lobster is to throw it into a large pot of boiling water. In a home kitchen the volume of water used is rarely enough to maintain the temperature required to kill the creature instantly. A crustacean that thrashes around always seems to throw off its legs and, in my opinion, the flesh toughens. The best options are to place the live rock lobster head down in a large trough of cold water, where it will drown in about 20 minutes (this is the best method if you plan to stir-fry or barbecue your rock lobster), or it can be put into cold salt water that is brought slowly to a boil. The creatures dies painlessly (it is claimed) as the temperature rises. Otherwise place the live rock lobster in the freezer for 1 hour, where it will 'go to sleep' (the cold stuns it), and then plunge it into boiling salted water or chop it into sections. Fishmongers stab the live rock lobster on the underside of the tail where the tail meets the head and split it between the eyes and then through the length of the tail section. This method is excellent, as the rock lobster dies instantly, but it is not recommended to amateur cooks. Once killed, the rock lobster will start to lose its juices in the form of oozing black liquid within an hour or so, so cook it quickly.

TO BOIL

Sea water is the ideal cooking liquid for rock lobster. After that comes salted water (400 g salt to 4 litres water) or a well-flavoured Court-bouillon✣. Never use less than 4 litres water, and double this if cooking 2 rock lobsters. Bring your chosen cooking liquid to a boil, then slip in the green rock lobster. Boil the rock lobster in your chosen cooking liquid for 8 minutes per 500 g, plus 5 minutes extra. The timing should commence from the time the water returns to a boil. Lift the cooked rock lobster out of the pot and allow it to cool for 5 minutes. Punch a small hole in the head and leave it tilted, so that any excess liquid can drain away (this step is optional). When the rock lobster is cool enough to handle, split the tail section or pull it away from the head in one piece (the latter will give you rounds of tail meat), then split the head. Remove the bony head sac, then the intestinal thread that runs through the centre of the tail. Reserve the soft brown material (green when uncooked) in the head (this is the 'mustard' or 'tomalley') to add to your sauce. Serve with your choice of accompaniments or else remove the tail meat and slice to serve as a salad, either in the shell or not as you prefer. If you have left the tail whole in order to have rounds of meat, cut away the softer undershell of the tail to remove the meat in one piece.

TO STIR-FRY OR BARBECUE Kill the rock lobster by either drowning, stabbing or freezing it, then split it in 2 lengthwise unless intending to barbecue it whole. If you halved the rock lobster, remove and discard the bony head sac and the intestinal thread. Scoop out any mustard from where the tail joins the head and reserve to add to your sauce, if desired. **To stir-fry** Cut the raw tail meat into sections by chopping or cutting across the shell. Chop the claws from the head and crack them, then chop the head section across into 2 pieces. Stir-fry with chosen seasonings for no more than 5 minutes until the shell turns slightly red, then add any sauce ingredients and cook, covered, for another 5 or so minutes until the shell turns bright red. **To barbecue** If you have split the rock lobster in half, paint the flesh liberally with olive oil or melted butter or a mixture of both. Place the rock lobster halves in a dish and cover with chopped herbs, such as bay leaves, thyme, oregano and fennel stalks, and leave at room temperature while waiting for the barbecue (20 minutes or so). Ensure that the barbecue has burned down to coals and there are no fierce flames. The rock lobster must be grilled gently to avoid it toughening. Grill the rock lobster halves shell-side down to the heat, basting the flesh frequently with the herbs and oil or butter, until shells are bright red and the flesh is still a little translucent. If grilling a whole rock lobster, turn it and grill until all sides are bright red. Rock lobster halves will take 10–15 minutes, depending on their size. A whole rock lobster will take 20–25 minutes. (A fancy variation, if using a whole rock lobster, is to punch a hole in its head and force herb butter through the hole several times during cooking.) Transfer the rock lobster halves to the marinating dish and allow to rest for a few minutes before serving, or split open the whole rock lobster, then extract the intestinal thread and head sac and spoon on oil or butter laced with herbs and grind over black pepper.

TO SERVE IN THE SHELL The meat of the rock lobster clings tenaciously to the shell. For luxurious eating, cut the cooked tail meat from the shell, then slice and return it. If serving a sauce, a little can be spooned into the empty shell, the meat returned and a little more sauce drizzled over the top.

recipes

rock lobster butter sauce

SERVES 2–4

This sauce is best served with half a freshly boiled lobster, the meat of which has been sliced away from the shell. Pour a little sauce into the shell, then replace the meat to serve. Sometimes a fishmonger may have frozen rock lobster heads, which are fine for this sauce. It is worth asking. The reduction can be made up to 2 days ahead and refrigerated.

boiled rock lobster

Split a freshly boiled rock lobster and serve it warm with a cut lemon, some melted butter, freshly ground black pepper, salad leaves for mopping in the juices, and a hunk of bread.

1 green rock lobster head section
olive oil
½ onion or 2 shallots, chopped
½ carrot, chopped
1 bay leaf
3 stalks parsley
1 tablespoon tomato paste
1 clove garlic
½ cup dry white wine
2 cups water
125 g cold unsalted butter
lemon juice
Tabasco

Chop head into small pieces. Sauté pieces in a trace of oil in a saucepan with onion, carrot, bay leaf and parsley until shells are bright red. Add tomato paste, garlic, wine and water and simmer for 30 minutes. Strain, pressing hard on shells and vegetables, and return liquid to rinsed-out pan. Boil hard until reduced to ½ cup. Whisk butter into reduction until sauce is creamy. Adjust seasoning with drops of lemon juice and Tabasco.

variations The reduction could be two-thirds white wine and a third aniseed-flavoured liqueur (pastis, ouzo or sambucca) and the sauce could be finished with diced young fennel previously blanched in lightly salted water, and maybe a little finely chopped anchovy. The reduction could also be some of the Court-bouillon used to cook the rock lobster. Add a cup of finely puréed cooked tomato before adding the butter and you will have a delicious and pretty rose–pink sauce. The reduction can also be stirred into Mayonnaise or Hollandaise Sauce.

violet oon's chilli lobster

SERVES 4

The following is based on a wonderful dish I saw demonstrated by Violet Oon in Singapore in 1994. (It is also good with crab or prawns.) It is quite spicy, so vary the quantity of chilli, if you wish. In Singapore this dish is traditionally served with slices of white bread with which you scoop up the delicious gravy.

1 x 1.5 kg green rock lobster
3 tablespoons vegetable oil
8 cloves garlic, finely chopped
(*continued next page*)

To make the sauce, mix all ingredients and set aside. Prepare rock lobster for stir-frying by chopping it into pieces, and reserve mustard. Heat wok and add oil. Add garlic

8 fresh red chillies, finely
  chopped

I teaspoon rice vinegar *or*
  fresh lime juice

I egg

I coriander plant (including
  roots), washed and finely
  chopped (about ½ cup)

4 spring onions, cut into
  6 cm pieces

SAUCE

I cup water

5 tablespoons tomato sauce

I teaspoon fermented black
  beans

I½ teaspoons cornflour

¼ teaspoon dark soy sauce

I½–3 tablespoons sugar

¼ teaspoon salt

to hot oil and stir-fry for 1 minute, then tip
in chilli and stir-fry another minute. Add
rock lobster and stir-fry for 3–4 minutes
until shells turn slightly red. Stir sauce
ingredients into wok for 2 minutes, then
add any reserved mustard. Cover, then
simmer over high heat for 5–7 minutes until
shells turn bright red. Remove lid and add
rice vinegar. Crack egg into sauce and mix
to form shreds. Add coriander and spring
onion, stir well and serve immediately.

dipping sauce
*Serve Thai-style
Dipping Sauce (see
YABBIES) with freshly
boiled rock lobster.*

**rock lobster
and basil**
*Fry basil leaves to
partner barbecued
rock lobster.*

rock lobster oil

MAKES 2 CUPS

*This oil can be made with cooked rock lobster heads but the flavour will
be less intense. Uncooked prawn heads or yabby heads can also be used.
Use the oil to flavour pasta sauces or make Mayonnaise to serve with a
rock lobster salad.*

500 g green rock lobster
  heads

I litre olive oil

I cup finely diced vegetables
  (carrot, onion, celery)

2 cloves garlic, chopped

I bay leaf

2–3 sprigs parsley

2–3 sprigs thyme

I cup dry white wine

Crush rock lobster shells using a rolling pin.
Heat ½ cup of the oil in an enamelled cast-
iron casserole and sauté shells over high
heat, stirring, for 10 minutes. Add
vegetables, garlic and herbs and sauté for a
further 10 minutes, stirring. Tip in wine and
allow to bubble fiercely for a few minutes.
Add remaining oil, then reduce heat, stir
well and simmer for 30 minutes. Turn off
heat and allow casserole to stand,
uncovered, overnight at room temperature.

Strain oil through a doubled layer of damp muslin or a very fine sieve and
bottle into sterilised glass containers. The oil will keep very well in the
refrigerator for a month.

chilli oil Add fresh chillies with the vegetables for a more piquant oil.

softboiled-egg vinaigrette

SERVES 2

This sauce is also excellent with asparagus, which is convenient as asparagus also goes well in a rock lobster salad. Double the quantities for serving 4 people.

rock lobster mayonnaise
Stir rock lobster 'mustard' through home-made Mayonnaise ✔ as an accompaniment to freshly cooked rock lobster.

1 egg
1 shallot *or* ¼ mild onion, finely chopped
1 tablespoon finely chopped fresh parsley
2 teaspoons finely chopped fresh basil *or* tarragon
1 teaspoon very finely chopped fresh chives
50 ml olive oil
salt
freshly ground black pepper
lemon juice

Boil egg for 3 minutes. In a food processor or blender, combine shallot and herbs with runny egg yolk. Add oil with motor running. Season with salt, pepper and lemon juice and fold in finely chopped egg white. Serve as soon as possible.

vermouth and rock lobster fettuccine

SERVES 4

This is one instance where I add cream to rock lobster.

1 × 1.5 kg rock lobster, freshly boiled
1 onion, finely chopped
½ cup dry vermouth
1 cup pouring cream
freshly ground black pepper *or* Tabasco
½ cup freshly chopped parsley *or* basil *and* parsley *or* chives *and* tarragon
500 g fresh fettuccine
salt
butter

Bring a large saucepan of water to a boil in readiness for cooking pasta. Cut rock lobster meat into 1 cm pieces, then cover with plastic film and set aside. Cook onion in vermouth over moderate heat until only a wet mush remains. Add cream and boil vigorously for 2–3 minutes. Season with pepper and add herbs. Toss in rock lobster and warm, off heat, for a minute or so while pasta is cooking. Drain pasta, then season and toss with a little butter and stir through rock lobster sauce. Serve with a watercress or rocket salad to follow.

other recipes

cantaloupe sauce for rock lobster or crab *see* MELONS

rosemary

'There's rosemary, that's for remembrance. Pray you, love, remember,' says Ophelia in *Hamlet*. | Rich in myth and symbolism, in early times rosemary (*Rosmarinus officinalis*) was important at weddings, funerals and banqueting festivities. It was the herb sacred to friendship, and is certainly still regarded with affection by many, especially on Remembrance Day. And those who have made the pilgrimage to Gallipoli have seen rosemary growing wild there. It was also thought to have a head-clearing effect, so students in ancient Greece wore it to improve their memory. | Rosemary is another of the herbs that originated in the Mediterranean region, and it is the cooks of Italy, southern France and Spain who use rosemary to best advantage. At roadside vans throughout the countryside in Lazio and Tuscany one is offered portions of *porchetta* – a whole pig stuffed with startling amounts of garlic and rosemary and then roasted. One is carved a portion, lean and fat and skin, which is then pressed into a crusty, unbuttered roll. A memorable lunch for a hungry traveller. >

Rosemary comes quickly to mind when one thinks of roasted meats, especially those that are spit-roasted or barbecued. Its pungent aroma fills the kitchen when one opens the oven door on rosemary-scented roast lamb. But rosemary is not only good with lamb and other meat. It also pairs well with fish, bread and beans in soups or purées, and is an essential part of a *soffritto*, the base of so many stews and braises produced in Italian and Spanish kitchens. A small amount of rosemary is added to the mixture known as *herbes de Provence*, which always includes thyme, oregano and usually savoury as well. The same finely chopped needles can be stirred into bread or pizza dough. And I especially enjoy using a compound butter of roasted garlic and roasted rosemary, which is delicious melted over grilled fish, lamb chops or baked tomatoes.

VARIETIES AND SEASON

Rosemary has leathery, needle-like leaves that are dark green on top and silver underneath. The leaves are pungently aromatic with a fragrance a little reminiscent of camphor. The small, pale-blue flowers are fragrant too. There is also a creeping variety used in cooking that is grown as a popular rockery plant (*R. prostrata*). Rosemary is evergreen, so it is available all year round.

SELECTION AND STORAGE

Almost everyone will either grow a rosemary bush, know someone who has one or else will walk past a rosemary hedge on their daily route to or from work, so buying rosemary shouldn't be necessary. Rosemary bushes become leggy and need pruning. This is the time to plan to cook something skewered with rosemary stalks. Rosemary is best used fresh, although freshly dried needles hold their fragrance for quite a long time. Avoid buying dried rosemary, which, after tasting the real thing, disappoints. Fresh rosemary keeps well in a tightly closed plastic bag in the refrigerator.

PREPARATION

When a recipe calls for chopped rosemary remember that the leaves are quite tough, so 'chopped finely' means *very* finely. Nobody enjoys biting on a hard piece of rosemary leaf. The leaves always fall off the stalks in a hot oven, so you will need to strain them out of any sauce you make with the pan juices if you add a whole piece of rosemary, as I do. The leaves don't need to be chopped, however, as they will have become very brittle.

To skewer food with rosemary, strip most of the leaves from the stem, leaving a tuft at one end, and sharpen the tip with a small knife to make skewering easier. If grilling over charcoal, the tuft of leaves may well scorch. Don't worry: this adds to the aroma! I spread the stripped leaves to dry for a day and then store them in a screw-top jar.

recipes

rosemary and garlic butter

MAKES 2 CUPS

This butter is wonderful on almost anything grilled!

10 cloves garlic
15 cm sprig fresh rosemary,
    leaves stripped
1 tablespoon olive oil
500 g softened butter
1 tablespoon freshly chopped
    parsley
salt
freshly ground black pepper

Preheat oven to 180°C. Place garlic in a small saucepan, cover with cold water and bring to a boil. Pour off water and repeat process twice, then drain. Place garlic and rosemary leaves in a small ovenproof dish with oil and bake until garlic is quite soft and rosemary is crisp (10–15 minutes). Squeeze garlic from skins and chop to a fine paste with rosemary. In a food processor, blend butter until very creamy. Add garlic and rosemary paste and parsley and process until combined. Taste for salt and pepper. Divide mixture in half and scrape each onto a sheet of baking paper and roll like a sausage, twisting the ends. Freeze until needed.

rosemary and bay leaf savoury custards

SERVES 8

These delicate custards come from Patricia Wells's book Trattoria.

375 ml milk
625 ml cream
3 tablespoons finely chopped
    fresh rosemary leaves
4 fresh bay leaves
4 large eggs
2 large egg yolks
30 g parmesan cheese, freshly
    grated
¼ teaspoon freshly grated
    nutmeg
¼ teaspoon sea salt
white pepper

Preheat oven to 160°C and butter 8 × 150 ml moulds. Bring milk and cream to boiling point. Remove from heat and add rosemary and bay leaves, then cover and allow to infuse for 10 minutes. Strain through a fine sieve into a bowl and allow to cool. Blend eggs and yolks lightly (they should be just mixed but not frothy) and stir into cooled milk mixture. Add cheese, nutmeg and salt and stir to mix. Check seasoning and add white pepper, if necessary.

Pour custard into prepared moulds and stand in a baking dish on a cloth to prevent them moving about. Pour in boiling water to come two-thirds up sides of moulds. Bake for 40–50 minutes until custards are set. Remove from oven, then remove custards from baking dish. Cool a little before serving. Turn out gently and serve with a savoury sauce, such as Fresh Tomato Sauce (*see* TOMATOES) or a mushroom or parsley sauce.
tartlets Line tartlet tins with Shortcrust Pastry and bake blind. Fill the pastry cases with custard and bake at 175°C until set, about 20 minutes. Serve warm.

rabbit with rosemary
Wrap rabbit hind legs (or quail or a baby chicken) in thickly buttered foil and tuck in a few rosemary sprigs. Season well, then seal and bake over charcoal for about 30 minutes, turning the package from time to time.

rosemary baked vegetables
Mix finely chopped rosemary with fresh breadcrumbs and strew over onions, tomatoes or pumpkin to be baked alongside meat.

rosemary roasts
Tuck a sprig of rosemary into the baking dish when roasting a leg or shoulder of lamb or a chicken or pigeon.

rosemary 'pesto'

½ cup finely chopped fresh
   rosemary
1 clove garlic, finely chopped
½ cup pine nuts
3 tablespoons extra-virgin
   olive oil
salt
freshly ground black pepper

In a food processor, blend rosemary, garlic and nuts to a smooth paste. Dribble in oil to make a spreading consistency, then season. Spread sparingly on toasted pita bread or on an uncooked or freshly baked pizza base as a simple topping and serve with olives.

soffritto

Sauté a handful each of finely chopped vegetables (celery, onion, leek, carrot) with a handful of herbs (mostly parsley, thyme and a little rosemary) in olive oil until all has softened and the vegetables have started to brown. Add meat, beans or fish to this soffritto and proceed to make a stew, as the Italian or Spanish would do.

roasted rosemary potatoes

SERVES 4

These rosemary-baked potatoes are delicious with anything at all, but especially with a pork roast or tossed with a green salad for lunch.

750 g red-skinned potatoes,
   peeled
1 tablespoon finely chopped
   fresh rosemary leaves
3 tablespoons extra-virgin
   olive oil
4 cloves garlic, unpeeled and
   lightly crushed
sea salt
freshly ground black pepper

Preheat oven to 220°C. Cut potatoes into quarters or sixths, depending on size, and rub completely dry. Combine rosemary and oil in a bowl, then drop in potato and massage well to coat. Spread potato in a single layer on a baking tray or in a gratin dish and add garlic. Bake for 45 minutes until potato is tender and golden. Season and serve at once.

fast pasta sauce with rosemary and meat juices

SERVES 2

250 g fresh fettuccine
100 g unsalted butter
2 teaspoons finely chopped
   fresh rosemary leaves
3 cloves garlic, finely chopped
½ cup strong roasting juices,
   very well reduced Chicken
   or Veal Stock ✐ or gravy left
   from a stew
freshly grated parmesan
   cheese

Boil fettuccine in plenty of salted water until it is just bite-tender. While pasta is cooking, melt butter and gently sauté rosemary and garlic until garlic is just golden. Add meat juices and simmer for a few seconds. Drain pasta, toss with sauce and offer cheese.

pizza rustica with potato and rosemary MAKES 2

Romans eat pizza bianca – pizza sprinkled with oil, sea salt and crumbled rosemary – as a morning snack. Trays of assorted pizzas emerge from ovens at lunchtime in Rome. And it is not only the children who rush to buy a portion! My favourites were the doubled sandwich of mozzarella with delicate cooked ham, and a delectable version covered with the thinnest slices of tender potatoes topped with rosemary. This is an attempt at the dish. Do not slice the potatoes until the dough is ready for shaping as they may start to discolour.

2 tablespoons polenta
3 potatoes
I quantity Pizza Dough ✎
4 tablespoons extra-virgin
    olive oil
I teaspoon finely chopped
    fresh rosemary leaves
3 x 4 cm sprigs rosemary
sea salt
freshly ground black pepper

Preheat oven to 250°C. Sprinkle 2 x 26 cm pizza trays with polenta. Slice potatoes very thinly and coat with extra-virgin olive oil. Divide dough in half. Oil your hands and work dough as thinly as possible on pizza trays, stretching, pushing and patting it. Allow dough to recover for 5 minutes, then arrange potato slices, overlapping slightly, on pizza bases, pressing them in firmly. Strip leaves from rosemary sprigs and scatter over pizza bases with chopped rosemary, sea salt and pepper. Bake for 15 minutes, then lower oven temperature to 200°C. Slip pizzas from trays and bake for a further 5 minutes, until bases are crisp. The pizzas are ready when edges are crisp and golden and potato is tender and starting to brown on top.

rosemary oil
Make rosemary oil by infusing chopped rosemary and the very best extra-virgin olive oil. Keep it in a dark place for a few days, then strain, if you like, and drizzle over a grilled lamb chop or a piece of fish.

tuna grilled with rosemary SERVES 4

4 x 180 g tuna steaks
2 tablespoons extra-virgin
    olive oil
16 sprigs fresh rosemary, each
    about the same length as
    tuna steaks
sea salt
freshly ground black pepper

Several hours before dinner, rub tuna with half the olive oil and cross-tie each steak with fine string as though you were tying a parcel. Slip 2 sprigs of rosemary under string on each side of each steak. Cover with plastic film and refrigerate for up to 6 hours.

Remove steaks from refrigerator 30 minutes before cooking. Prepare barbecue or preheat chargrill pan. Season fish and grill for 2–4 minutes each side depending on thickness of steaks (tuna is best cooked medium–rare). Snip strings and slice each steak into 2–3 pieces, or leave whole. Drizzle with remaining olive oil and serve at once. Any charred pieces of rosemary that are left add to the charm of the dish.

grilled spiced beef on rosemary skewers MAKES 10

10 woody branches rosemary,
    each 15–18 cm long
500 g lean rump steak,
    coarsely minced
½ teaspoon freshly grated
    nutmeg
½ teaspoon ground cloves
½ teaspoon ground cinnamon
salt
freshly ground black pepper
olive oil

Strip most of the leaves from rosemary branches, leaving a tuft on one end. Using a knife, whittle a point at other end of skewers. Set leaves aside. Soak skewers in water for 5–10 minutes.

Mix meat with nutmeg, cloves, cinnamon, salt and pepper, then mince again through finest hole of mincer. Transfer to food processor and process quickly to a smooth paste. Tip into a bowl. Oil your hands well, divide meat and press around each rosemary skewer. Scatter over a few reserved rosemary leaves. The meat should look oily.

Prepare barbecue or preheat chargrill pan. Grill skewers over high heat (keeping tufts away from fire if barbecuing), turning carefully once. Leave meat pink in the middle. Enjoy with Smoky Eggplant Purée (*see* EGGPLANTS) or washed salad leaves.

other recipes

roasted leg of lamb with rosemary and garlic and all the trimmings
    see LAMB
rosemary and polenta pan bread *see* CORN
slow-roasted loin of pork with garlic, rosemary and fennel *see* PORK

Sage A member of the extensive genus *Salvia*, of which my herb book claims there are 700 members, sage originated in the northern Mediterranean. I have read that along the Dalmatian coast bees feast on sage flowers and produce a very special honey. The plant has long been held in high regard as a herb – both for its culinary uses and its health-giving properties. Rosemary Hemphill, in her *Herbs for All Seasons*, says that the Romans grew sage wherever they travelled and that the herb was believed to prolong youth. Today sage is still recognised as a healing herb, earning thoroughly its genus name, which means 'health'. English cooks include sage in traditional stuffings for roast goose or duck, believing that the pungency of the herb assists the digestion of the rich meat. But the masters with sage in the kitchen are the Italians. They almost always sauté the leaves in butter or olive oil until they are crisp and sweet. Italians also often sauté sage with other herbs and vegetables in a *soffritto*, the beginnings of a stew.

VARIETIES AND SEASON

The culinary sages are perennials, although they can be badly affected by frost and their growth is pretty spindly during the winter months. The plants are best trimmed hard after flowering, and once they look woody, after a couple of years, they should be replaced. Common sage is the species we use most often when cooking, although it is also worth mentioning a couple of other species with culinary merit. The best time for sage is October–June.

Common *S. officinalis* is an attractive herb with aromatic, slightly bitter, silver–grey pebbly leaves that change colour from green to grey as they mature. **Pineapple** *S. rutilans* is a tall, handsome plant with long, raspy-textured leaves that have a strong pineapple scent. I have a border of pineapple sage in my garden and the bonfire-red flowers are delightful. Its chopped leaves add a definite pineapple flavour to salads. **Red** *S. officinalis* var. *purpurea* is a smaller plant than common sage and has deep-plum leaves with good flavour.

SELECTION AND STORAGE

The leaves of sage are mostly used fresh, and the younger the better. As the leaves get older they also become stronger in flavour. As sage is an extremely assertive flavour, prefer the smaller leaves. If storing fresh sage, enclose it in a plastic bag and refrigerate it for up to 3 days. To dry sage, pick the leaves on a dry day, just as the flowers appear. Remove any damaged leaves from the bunch and hang it to dry completely. When dried, strip the leaves and store them in an airtight container. Be careful, dried sage is very powerful. As Elizabeth David once wrote, too much sage can smell of dried blood. Certainly the older leaves do!

PREPARATION AND COOKING

I do not wash the sage leaves picked from my bush as I do not use any nasty sprays. However, I do inspect the leaves closely for insect damage, especially underneath them. Sage leaves can be chopped for use in stuffings but are mostly used whole.

TO CRISP SAGE IN BUTTER | Drop 3–5 sage leaves per person into a hot frying pan with 20 g cold butter per person and swirl over moderate heat until the butter foams and the leaves are crisp. Transfer the leaves to kitchen paper to drain, then stop the butter cooking by placing the base of the pan in cold water. Spoon the golden brown butter and the leaves over veal scaloppine, sautéed or poached brains, a fillet of fish or vegetable-filled ravioli. *Bellissimo!*

recipes

traditional sage stuffing for goose, duck or turkey

125 g breadcrumbs
60 g grated suet
grated zest of 1 lemon
4 fresh sage leaves, finely
 chopped
½ clove garlic, finely chopped
1 egg yolk
3 tablespoons milk
salt
freshly ground black pepper

Mix all ingredients together and adjust seasoning. Stuff cavity of bird just before cooking and roast according to size. Cooking time is about 1¼ hours for a well-done duck and about 2 hours for a goose, or rather a gosling, as a mature goose is too tough to eat. *See p. 216 for instructions on roasting a turkey.*

saltimbocca alla romana

SERVES 4

This is one of Italy's best-known dishes, and deservedly so. The most difficult part of the recipe will be obtaining high-quality pale veal. I suggest an Italian butcher.

8 x 100 g veal scaloppine
8 fresh sage leaves
8 paper-thin slices prosciutto
 crudo, trimmed of fat
½ cup plain flour
salt
freshly ground black pepper
100 g unsalted butter
2 tablespoons olive oil
1 cup dry white wine *or*
 dry marsala

Place a plastic bag over veal and flatten meat gently using a meat mallet or heavy tumbler. Skewer a sage leaf, a slice of ham and a piece of veal with a toothpick, then dip in seasoned flour and shake off excess. Repeat with remaining veal, ham and sage leaves.

 Heat half the butter and half the oil in a frying pan until foaming. Slip in 4 veal slices and brown for 3 minutes on each side, then transfer to a warm plate. Wipe out pan but do not wash it. Heat remaining butter and oil and cook rest of veal. Return all veal slices to pan and increase heat to full. Pour over wine and let it bubble furiously for a minute. Serve immediately.

butter and sage sauce Add extra butter and sage leaves to pan with the wine. Allow to bubble again and spoon over the meat. **lemon** Omit the ham and sage. Sauté thin slices of lemon in the frying pan before adding the floured veal. Finish with sage leaves sautéed in butter and serve with Smoky Eggplant Purée (*see* EGGPLANTS), fried artichokes or sautéed zucchini.

sage and onion
Roast thickly sliced oiled onion with sprigs of sage, covered, at 180°C for 30 minutes. Stir the juices and onion around and cook, uncovered, for a further 30 minutes. Season with freshly ground black pepper and sea salt. A few drops of red-wine or balsamic vinegar is a delicious addition.

roast potatoes with sage
Rub unpeeled small potatoes with olive oil, then sprinkle with salt and pepper. Tuck small sprigs of sage here and there among them and roast at 180°C for 1 hour until potatoes are cooked and their skins are beautifully crisp.

chicken breasts with sage

SERVES 4

4 chicken breast fillets, skinned
5 tablespoons extra-virgin olive oil
24 fresh sage leaves
4 thin slices lemon
3 tablespoons lemon juice
60 g unsalted butter
sea salt
freshly ground black pepper

Marinate chicken for 30 minutes in half the oil with sage, lemon slices and lemon juice. Remove chicken and pat dry. Strain the marinade and reserve both liquid and solids. Heat remaining oil with butter in a frying pan and cook lemon slices for a minute until browned. Remove to a warm plate. Slip chicken into pan and cook over low-to-moderate heat for 5 minutes until browned. Turn, then season and add reserved sage. Cook for 5 minutes. Remove chicken and sage to warm plate with lemon slices. Tip fat from pan and return to heat. Pour in reserved marinade, then increase heat to full and bubble for less than a minute and spoon over chicken. Serve on a green salad or with buttered pasta or sliced, steamed zucchini.

roman lamb stew

SERVES 2–3

Ask your butcher to prepare the meat for this dish for you: it needs to be on the bone for the best results.

2 cloves garlic, cut into slivers
1 shoulder spring lamb, cut into chunks on the bone
1 sprig rosemary
½ cup dry white wine
2 tomatoes, peeled, seeded and roughly chopped
salt
freshly ground black pepper
SOFFRITTO
2 tablespoons olive oil
1 carrot, finely diced
1 stick celery, finely sliced
1 good sprig sage
3–4 stalks parsley

To make the *soffritto*, heat oil in a cast-iron casserole and sauté vegetables and herbs until softened and starting to brown. Insert garlic between meat and bone in each piece of lamb. Add lamb and rosemary to casserole. Sauté and turn for 15 minutes, watching that nothing catches or burns. Add wine, tomato, salt and pepper, then reduce heat and simmer gently for 30 minutes until lamb is tender. Serve with Artichokes and Peas with Sage (*see* ARTICHOKES) for a glorious spring meal.

mixed kebabs
Skewer chunks of fresh mozzarella, thick slices of breadstick and slices of prosciutto crudo interspersed with pieces of sage leaf. Brush with olive oil and grill, turning and basting once or twice, until the cheese is melting and the bread is crusty at the edges.

bean and sage salad
Stir butter- or oil-crisped sage leaves into a warm salad of cooked dried beans with parsley and olive oil.

other recipes

artichokes and peas with sage *see* ARTICHOKES

pork sausages with sage and tomato *see* SAUSAGES

Salad greens

To experience a green salad made from leaves just gathered from a garden is to appreciate how good life can be. There is a crispness and presence about those sun-warmed leaves that is unforgettable. Turned briefly in fine olive oil with a very small amount of good wine vinegar, pepper and sea salt, such a salad will forever remain the yardstick in your taste memory. | I lust for salad – I usually serve it after meat or fish or with cheese, but often salad is the main production in my house. Then, quickly seared, grilled, boiled or sliced ingredients are added to the leaves and the whole is tossed and on a platter in no more than 20 minutes. That's what I call fast food! | I published my thoughts about creating a substantial salad in 1984 in my first book, *Stephanie's Menus for Food Lovers*. Looking back, there is little I want to change. I still decide on the background first – will it be leaves only, or will it be based on barely cooked green beans or spicy lentils or warm white beans? Then I look for some crunch from bacon fried crisp, croutons rubbed with garlic, toasted seeds or nuts, or crisp wafers of potato. >

My salad must have something substantial as its focus, be it fish (fresh or smoked), prawns, cheese, chicken, tongue or a vegetable. And then the dressing is mixed. Never forget that some ingredients contribute their own juices. The brine of the freshly opened oyster, the bacon fat from the pan or the liquid trapped inside a roasted red pepper are all added to the olive oil, that most wonderful of ingredients, always the best I can buy, accented maybe with a touch of vinegar or citrus juice and an appropriate seasoning. I add any finishing touches (freshly chopped herbs or a fine julienne of blanched orange zest) and gently tumble the salad onto a beautiful platter.

While many varieties of lettuce have been cultivated for some 5000 years, and salads of herbs and vegetables were even recorded in the Middle Ages, our experience of The Salad until recently has been limited to the iceberg lettuce with wedges of tomato or sometimes a coleslaw. But salad varieties have proliferated over the last decade and now most suburban greengrocers will have a tub of mixed small leaves (known as 'mesclun', which means 'mixed' in the language of Provence), another of baby spinach leaves and maybe a third of peppery rocket leaves. In buckets will be watercress, mizuna, coriander, dill, basil, Vietnamese mint, common mint, chives, and so on. On the shelves you will find cos and mignonette lettuces, curly endive, witlof, radicchio, butterhead lettuces, oak-leaf lettuces and, of course, iceberg lettuces, presenting a bewildering but gorgeous bank of frilly, frizzy and floppy pinks, greens, reds and browns! And those who live alone can buy a single witlof or a handful of spinach leaves and look forward to a salad without worrying about what to do with a yellowing giant iceberg.

VARIETIES AND SEASON

Salad greens can be divided into 2 groups: the lettuces (*Lactuca sativa*) and the 'others', which includes the chicories (*Cichorium intybus*) and endives (*C. endivia*), and so on. The variety is seemingly infinite. Because of the range of climatic regions in Australia a surprising number of varieties are grown somewhere all year round. A few of the best known and best flavoured are:

BUTTERHEAD LETTUCE Also known as the butter or Boston lettuce, this variety has soft leaves that are a medium green or brown-and-red tinged. It bruises easily but has a good flavour. The *mignonette* is a popular variety of butterhead lettuce and has soft crinkly leaves that are usually brownish red but can be green. Butterheads are available all year and are quite delicious dressed with some of the meat juices from a roast mixed with a little oil.

COS LETTUCE This lettuce is essential for making Caesar salad. Its long leaves are crunchy and dark green to a pale yellow–green at the centre. Also known as the romaine lettuce, cos is available all year. I particularly like little gem, a small cultivar that is very common in England but not seen in Australia.

CRESS | Watercress (*Nasturtium officinale*), the best known of the cresses, has a mustardy bite, and is often served in small bunches alongside a rich small bird. I also like watercress and cucumber tossed in sour cream. Other cresses are often included in mesclun, as the leaves tend to be hot and spicy. Cress is available all year but does not like excessive heat.

ENDIVE | A chicory, this fine, frizzy-leafed vegetable is sold as curly endive or frisée, while to the French it is *chicorée frisée*. It is slightly bitter and great with bacon or poultry livers and creamy or mustardy dressings. It is best in winter. The batavia endive has broader leaves and is crunchier than its cousin. It is sometimes called by its French name of *escarole*, although I have also heard it called *batavia* in French greengrocers.

ICEBERG LETTUCE | Also known as a crisphead lettuce, this stayer is useful for Asian dishes where one wraps minced pigeon or pork in lettuce, or for fine shredding, or for picking from the garden while still a little soft-hearted. It is available all year.

LAMB'S LETTUCE | *Valerianella locusta*, also known as mache or corn salad, is mildly flavoured and very tender when young. Snails love it! It is great combined with young beetroot leaves and is best in autumn and spring.

LOOSE-LEAF LETTUCE | This, in fact, is a group of lettuces that are also described as 'cut-and-come-again' or 'salad bowl' varieties. This refers to their usefulness in the garden: individual leaves can be picked as required from the growing plants. The most familiar of these are the *oak-leaf* varieties, while lollos and marvel of four seasons are popular cultivars. These lettuces are mild in flavour and very tender and are available all year.

RADICCHIO | One of the chicories, radicchio comes in shades of red, green, cream and variegated. There are hearted and loose-leaf varieties. Radicchio can be bitter and can take a strong dressing or be grilled or fried. It is best in winter.

ROCKET | *Eruca sativa*, also known as roquette, rugula or arugula, grows wild in the Mediterranean

garnishes can be
olives
walnuts
almonds
pine nuts
croutons
grilled polenta
bacon
toasted sesame
  seeds

salad dressings like
balsamic vinegar
olive oil
anchovies
capers
mustards
herbs
crushed spices
browned butter
roasting juices
juices from a
  marinade
pickles
sour cream
mayonnaise

region and also in my garden! It self-seeds easily and must be picked when young and tender to enjoy its unique peppery flavour. It becomes very hot when overmature. Rocket combines beautifully with mild cheeses and olives and is an essential ingredient in mesclun. It is best in spring and early summer as it bolts in very hot weather.

SORREL | Common sorrel (*Rumex acetosa*) has a lemon flavour that is quite sharp. The young leaves are good in small quantities with other leaves and are delicious in soup. Sorrel is best in spring.

WITLOF | There is endless confusion over the name of this chicory. The French call the blanched, white-tipped, pale yellow–green 'chicons' *endives*, but the Belgian name is the one adopted in this country. A mild and very crunchy vegetable, witlof (or whitlof or witloof) is available all year. It is especially delicious with goat's cheese and fresh pear. *See* WITLOF for more information.

SELECTION AND STORAGE

Choose the freshest salad greens rather than deciding on a particular variety before you go shopping. Remember, the more recently it has been picked, the better it will be. Local is best! The lettuce (or chicory or whatever) should not be a crumpled ball of broken leaves or have any signs of wilt, slimy brown patches or sunburn. Hydroponic salad greens are sold with their roots still attached. They always look perfect. Sometimes greens grown in the ground will taste better. Buy one of each, then wash and dress them separately and taste to make up your own mind.

Never store salad greens next to apples, pears, melons or bananas as these fruit release ethylene gas that will cause the vegetables to brown rapidly. To store a *whole* lettuce or similar, give it a quick rinse, remove the core, place the vegetable in a plastic container and snap on the lid. The leaves will stay crisp for several days in the refrigerator. *Loose* salad leaves should be rinsed and stored in a paper-lined plastic bag or a clean tea towel in the crisper in the refrigerator. Try to buy loose leaves as you need them as they will only store for a day.

Please do not store little jars of made-up vinaigrette! Stored dressings quickly develop horrible flavours and any herbs become grey and slimy, rather like dead flowers.

PREPARATION

All salads and herbs must be washed in plenty of water before they are served. (Varieties such as endive are notorious for being reluctant to yield every gritty particle. Be especially careful of crinkly varieties and those with tightly furled stems or leaves.) Lift the leaves from the water to a salad spinner and spin gently – not too many at once. Transfer the leaves to a dry, clean tea towel, pat them with kitchen paper and gently roll up the towel. This parcel goes into the refrigerator now for up to 1 hour. Or you can transfer the leaves from the salad spinner to a plastic bag lined with kitchen paper. However you do it, the leaves must be quite dry when dressed otherwise the oil will roll off rather than coat them and you will find a tell-tale pool of water at the bottom of the bowl with globules of oil and vinegar floating in it.

Even the best salad greens can be ruined by a clumsy dressing. I discuss the virtues of different types of oil in OLIVES AND OLIVE OIL and vinegar in VINEGAR. What oil and vinegar you use to dress your salad will depend on your budget and your taste preference. The better the oil and vinegar, the better your salad will be.

a simple dressing
SERVES 2–3

pinch of sea salt
½–1 teaspoon wine vinegar
freshly ground black pepper
1 good tablespoon best-quality
   olive oil

Sprinkle crumbled salt into a salad bowl and dissolve it in vinegar. Grind in pepper and add oil. Mix gently, then tumble in your dried greens and turn in dressing. Eat!

vegetable salad
Crisp leftover roasted vegetables in a hot oven and toss through a salad.

radicchio braised with blue cheese
SERVES 4

Many salad leaves can be braised or made into subtle soups. Here is one recipe for radicchio that has made many people happy. This full-flavoured dish can be served with a mild meat such as veal or chicken, or as a bed for grilled sausages.

1 hearted radicchio
60 g butter
freshly ground black pepper
2 teaspoons balsamic vinegar
100 g creamy blue cheese,
   thinly sliced

Discard any damaged leaves and cut radicchio into quarters or eighths, keeping core intact. Wash radicchio well and drain in a colander, then pat dry. Select a heavy-based frying pan that will hold radicchio very snugly and melt butter over moderate heat. Add radicchio, then grind over pepper and gently turn pieces in butter. After a few minutes the radicchio will wilt and shrink and turn a bronze colour. Sprinkle over vinegar, then increase heat to high and turn pieces in syrupy juices for a minute or so. Line a baking tray or chargrill pan with baking paper. Place radicchio on baking paper and spoon over any juices. Set aside until ready to serve.

Preheat oven to 220°C. Cover radicchio with cheese and bake for

lettuce soup
Make a soup by sweating lots of shredded iceberg or cos lettuce in butter with a chopped onion for 5 minutes. Dilute with Chicken Stock or water, then simmer for 15 minutes. Purée in a food processor. Reheat gently and swirl in a little cream, herb butter or separately cooked green peas.

5 minutes until bubbling. (The radicchio can also be finished under a preheated grill, but the radicchio must be hot or the cheese will burn before the radicchio is hot all the way through.) Serve immediately.

cream dressing for strongly flavoured firm salad leaves
SERVES 4

rocket salad
Add freshly shaved parmesan to a simple salad of rocket leaves.

roasting juices as dressing
Use the roasting juices when cooking meat or fish to dress your salad.

1 clove garlic, crushed
2 teaspoons Dijon mustard
2 teaspoons red-wine vinegar
3 tablespoons olive oil
2 tablespoons thick cream
freshly ground black pepper

Mix garlic to a smooth paste with mustard and vinegar in salad bowl. Whisk in oil, then cream and pepper. Add greens (witlof or cos lettuce are ideal) and turn over and over to coat thoroughly. Serve immediately.

bacon and mustard dressing for 'bitey' greens
SERVES 4

This dressing suits salad leaves with substance and bite, such as endive. Serve the salad with grilled or toasted croutons rubbed with garlic, if you like.

2 rashers smoked streaky
   bacon, cut into dice
1 tablespoon Dijon mustard
2 teaspoons red-wine vinegar
3 tablespoons olive oil
freshly ground black pepper

Gently sauté bacon in a dry frying pan until fat runs, then remove with slotted spoon. Reserve bacon fat. Whisk mustard with vinegar to an emulsion, then whisk in oil and bacon fat. Turn greens in dressing with bacon and grind over pepper to taste.

other recipes

autumn salad with red and yellow tomatoes *see* TOMATOES

chestnut and bacon salad *see* CHESTNUTS

goat's cheese on salad leaves with an anchovy dressing *see* CHEESE

jenny's caesar salad *see* EGGS

parsley salad *see* PARSLEY

pear and walnut salad *see* PEARS

potato and sorrel omelette *see* POTATOES

rocket and oregano pizza *see* OREGANO AND MARJORAM

salad of grilled lamb *see* LAMB

salade niçoise *see* BEANS, FRESH

squab pigeon and fig salad *see* QUAIL AND SQUAB PIGEONS

warm salad of roasted or grilled kangaroo *see* KANGAROO

see also OLIVES AND OLIVE OIL; SPINACH; VINEGAR; WITLOF

Sausages   Those European countries which love sausages, such as France, Italy and Germany, have an extensive range of regional specialities. Versions of many of these are made in Australia. Sausage-making was well established in China 3000 years ago, and 2000 years ago in Roman Gaul (France) sausages were depicted in bas reliefs. These have been identified as the ancestors of many traditional varieties of sausages still made in France and Italy.   The word 'sausage' comes from the Latin *salsus*, which means salt. Sausages of whatever size – fresh, cooked or dried – consist of chopped or minced meat (usually but not always pork), flavourings, and in many cases preservatives, which may mean salt or may include nitrites and nitrates, smoke flavourings and so on. Fresh sausages for frying or grilling often include additional starch or cereal. Dried and cooked sausage-manufacture can involve the specialist skills of curing, fermenting, smoking and drying. The filling is stuffed into a casing, either a natural one obtained from the intestines of animals or a synthetic one. >

**fresh
sausages
go
with**
mashed potato
mustard
tomato sauce
grilled tomato
pickles
relishes
spiced fruit

**cooked
sausages
go
with**
*mostarda di
    Cremona*
sauerkraut
dried beans
cabbages
mustard
fried apple
chestnuts
pasta

A good fresh sausage has to include a high percentage of fat to be palatable and juicy. Most fresh sausages are neither cured nor smoked, but there are exceptions. (The frankfurter is smoked and the Italian cotechino is lightly salted.) A well-made fresh sausage makes a delightful, simple and popular family meal, and, if one shops widely, a different variety could be eaten every week for at least a year. Cooked sausages may or may not be smoked and include varieties such as mortadella, blood sausage and Polish sausage. Dried sausages have always been a popular way of preserving food for the winter in the Northern Hemisphere, and pork has always been the preferred meat, both because of its availability and its high fat content. In the world's cooler northern countries it is possible to produce a moist sausage that keeps. In the drier and hotter Mediterranean regions sausages have less moisture and seasonings are more pronounced.

Since the tragic incident in South Australia in 1995 when a young girl died after eating contaminated mettwurst sausage new regulations have come into force throughout Australia. The 'Code of Hygienic Production; Uncooked Fermented Comminuted Meat Products' requires that some of the traditional methods of sausage-manufacture be replaced by methods considered to be without risk to the consumer. Starter cultures have replaced natural fermentation in the manufacture of mettwurst and salami; alternatively, natural-ferment sausages are to be cooked to an internal core temperature of 65°C. Several of the long-established firms in South Australia's Barossa Valley have gone out of business as a result of the general loss of consumer confidence in these products. There is no question that using starter cultures rather than a slow ferment and heat-treating sausages results in a loss of both distinctive flavours and texture, not to mention artisanal knowledge. I would like to believe that responsible smallgoods manufacturers could continue with traditional practices while taking proper care to follow best-practice recommendations for hygiene. There is also no question that the general public does not understand that if one is transporting food for hours on a hot Australian summer's day, either from the shops to home or from home to a picnic spot, a chiller in the boot of the car is a necessity, not a fussy accessory.

VARIETIES AND SEASON

Fresh, cooked and dried sausages are available year round. There are dozens of different types available, reflecting the rich diversity of Australia's culinary scene. Most of us are more familiar with Italian, German and Austrian-style varieties than with French-style sausages. French charcuterie is deservedly famous and there are examples of fresh boiling sausages (cervelas and saucisson de Lyon) and dried sausages (saucisson sec) worth seeking out in specialised butchers' shops in some of our capital cities. I give here a broad selection of some commonly available sausages.

BLOOD | Sold in Spanish, Italian and German butchers' or specialist shops, blood sausages may look alarming but taste delicious. The common ingredient in this cooked sausage is pig's blood, but it may also include oatmeal, bread, apples, chestnuts, onions, cream and a wide range of spices. National preferences vary as far as the texture of this sausage goes also. Italian, French and Spanish-style blood sausages are loose-textured and moist; German and English versions are more compact. This sausage is either fried or grilled whole or is cut into slices and then grilled. It has different names in different culinary traditions: black pudding in Britain, *biroldo* in Italy, *boudin noir* in France, *morcilla* in Spain and *blutwurst* in Germany.

BRATWURST | This is a German-style fresh sausage, made from a mixture of highly seasoned pork, veal and onion. It is best grilled and enjoyed with mustard. A bratwurst roll is a special treat at several stalls at Melbourne's Queen Victoria market.

BREAKFAST | Thick or thin, this fresh sausage is made from finely minced pork and usually cereal and is mildly spiced. It is generally pan-fried and served with bacon and tomatoes and maybe eggs. Breakfast sausages are increasingly diverse. They may be flavoured with tomato, curry, onion, satay spices, and so on. The meat used may include lamb, beef, venison or kangaroo, for example. The majority are still made with some pork, however. The much-loved English banger, as in 'bangers and mash', is the plump version of this sausage.

CEVAPCICI | Perhaps technically speaking a meatball, this fresh sausage is without a casing, like the cré-pinette. It is highly spiced and a speciality of the former Yugoslavia. Minced beef and/or pork and fresh herbs are formed into logs about 8 cm long. They are great grilled for breakfast or brunch, served with a bowl of chutney or hot relish and good crunchy toast.

CHORIZO | This highly spiced pork and red pepper sausage is available fresh, dried or semi-dried from Spanish shops and good delicatessens and is usually very hot. It is ideal for grilling or frying and for adding to hearty meals of cooked dried beans, chick peas or cabbage or soups, or combining with other meat in spicy stews. Air-dried chorizo is sliced and eaten raw, and there are smoked versions as well. Be sure to specify the style of chorizo you want.

COTECHINO | This large, specialised Italian fresh sausage contains a very coarse-cut mixture of lean and fat pork. *Coteca* is rind or skin in Italian, and the cotechino includes pig's skin, usually the pig's cheek for its unique gelatinous texture. These sausages are available mostly in the winter months and are boiled.

lap
cheong
goes
with
rice
stir-fried Chinese
   greens

salami
goes
with
raw fennel
sheep's milk cheese
radishes
olives
sun-dried tomatoes
pickled cucumbers

COUNTRY-STYLE PORK

This fresh sausage ought to contain a coarse-cut mixture of highly seasoned pork. The seasonings reflect English traditions (mace, sage, thyme), as opposed to Italian. It is best grilled.

CRÉPINETTE

Not quite a 'true' fresh sausage, a crépinette is sausage mixture that has been wrapped in caul fat rather than stuffed into a casing. The sausage mixture is often a highly individual combination created by an enthusiastic butcher or delicatessen owner. Looking like a little patty in a lacy casing, a crépinette requires delicate handling when grilling or frying as the thin membrane can split. Crépinettes are easy to make at home, provided you have a mincing attachment for your electric mixer or a butcher who will sell you minced pork or a mixture of pork and veal.

FRANKFURTER

A blend of pork, beef and sometimes poultry meat, true frankfurters, a cooked sausage, are smoked over wood. Nowadays the smoking is mostly applied as a paint rather than being a separate process. Regional custom decrees that frankfurters are purple–red in New South Wales, red–orange in Victoria and orange in South Australia. Frankfurters have become very bland and a mass-market commodity. They are boiled and often used in the ubiquitous hot dog, usually with mustard added. Here and there one may find a country butcher who still smokes frankfurters over wood.

ITALIAN PURE PORK

Sold as salsiccie casalinga or continental sausage, this dense fresh sausage is made of coarsely minced pure pork and is usually flavoured with garlic and peppercorns. It can be either grilled or fried. Don't confuse it with the English-influenced country-style pork sausage, a much less assertive affair.

KABANA

Also known as cabanossi, this coarsely textured thin sausage is made from highly seasoned pork and beef and is smoked and fully cooked. Some versions include hot pepper. Kabana is a popular snack food and is usually served cut into small chunks. Some people select their kabana soft and moist, others prefer a sausage that has hung for a while and become somewhat dry.

KNACKWURST This German sausage is usually sold in pairs. The sausage is coarsely textured and made from beef, veal and pork and seasoned with garlic. It is fully cooked but is usually simmered again with sauerkraut or in soups and stews.

LAP CHEONG This highly distinctive pork sausage is Chinese. It is flavoured with spices, especially star anise, and is then smoked and dried. The thin, deep reddish brown sausages include pork fat in quite big chunks and are usually sold in a bundle. Lap cheong is used in stir-fries. There is a more powerful version that includes duck liver.

MORTADELLA The pride of Italy's Bologna, this large, fully cooked sausage ought to be delicate and smooth. In Rabelais's time, this sausage included myrtle leaves (*morta* in dialect). Some versions include peppercorns, others pistachio nuts. It has one of the highest fat contents of all cooked sausages. Some Italians claim that the quality of our pork has led to inferior mortadella. It is usually sliced and served as is but it can also be added to sauces, pasta stuffings or sautés.

POLISH Kielbasa, its Polish name, is a smoked, fully cooked sausage made from beef and pork highly spiced with garlic. It is often used sliced or cut into chunks in mixed salads with cooked dried beans, spring onions, beetroots and capers.

SALAMI Salami is the supreme dried sausage. True salami is made from uncooked meat, but some sausages sold as salami are in fact fully cooked. (It is worth re-reading the introductory notes regarding recent changes in regulations that govern the manufacture of uncooked fermented sausages in Australia.) Most salami is made from fresh pork and has a coarsely ground texture with garlic as the main spice. Salami is generally cured during processing and may or may not be smoked. The types and amount of meat used; the proportion of lean to fat; how finely, coarsely or uniformly the fat appears among the lean; the choice of seasoning; and the degree of salting and drying dictate the nature of the salami. The following are a few of the styles you are likely to encounter in an Australian delicatessen. *Salami calabrese* is a hot, spicy Italian-style salami that includes chillies, red wine and red peppers and is air-dried, whereas the style of *salami casalinga* ('home-made' salami) depends on where 'home' is or was in Italy for the person who made it. *Soppressa salami*, another Italian-style salami, includes pork and beef and is highly regarded. A coarsely textured, air-dried sausage, it is tied with string to create its traditional bulging shape. *Salami csabai*, a Hungarian-style, air-

bratwurst in beer
Sauté sliced onion in oil until well softened and golden. Add a bay leaf, coarsely cracked pepper and a glass of beer, then boil hard for a few minutes. Add parboiled bratwurst sausages, then tip in another glass of beer and simmer for 15 minutes.

dried salami, is made from very finely minced pork and beef and is seasoned with cracked peppercorns and paprika. *Mettwurst* is a medium-textured, German-style salami made from pork. It is mildly seasoned and smoked and air-dried. This style of sausage has become very well known (and notorious since 1995) in South Australia's Barossa Valley, where it is still made by the descendants of the Lutherans who settled there in the 1840s. And then there are Danish-style, German-style and Polish-style salami, each with its own characteristics.

salami in antipasto
Include a selection of salami on a spring antipasto platter with crunchy radishes, olives and peeled raw broad beans.

cevapcici on peppers
Grill and skin a quantity of sweet peppers. Chop them and stew with a spoonful of red-wine vinegar and another of olive oil. Brush cevapcici with olive oil, then grill and serve on top of the stewed peppers.

WEISSWURST | A German-style fresh sausage with a high proportion of veal as well as pork, the weisswurst is very pale in colour and is mildly spiced. It is ideal grilled and served with mustard, rye bread and beer.

SELECTION AND STORAGE

Fresh sausages are on sale at all butchers' shops and most supermarkets. They should look shiny and smooth and have no unpleasant odour. Refrigerate them, freed of all shop wrappings, on a plate covered with plastic film for 2 days.

The best selection of *cooked* and *dried* sausages can be found in the specialist delicatessens located in all our fresh food markets, where stallholders are eager to offer samples. Buy a few slices of those that intrigue you and ask for the names to be written on the parcels, so that you will remember them when you are tasting at home. Cooked sausages such as knackwurst, blood sausages or frankfurters should be stored and used as fresh sausages. Others such as the fully cooked mortadella and Polish sausages can be refrigerated for up to 5 days, wrapped. They will keep better in a large piece than sliced. Dried sausages, such as lap cheong or salami, will keep well at cellar temperature (about 13°C) for several weeks if uncut. The sausage will continue to dry as it hangs. Once cut, dried sausage should be refrigerated, well wrapped in plastic film, and used within 5 days.

PREPARATION AND COOKING

Sausages require little preparation – some are grilled, others are simply sliced. For all sausages, however, remember not to carry them in a hot car for any length of time. This includes as a sandwich in a briefcase: wrap your lunch in a damp tea towel, or pack a frozen carton of juice with it, and refrigerate or eat it without undue delay when you arrive at your destination.

FRESH | It is a good idea to prick most fresh sausages with a fine skewer and to parboil them in 1 cm water for 5 minutes before grilling or frying. This allows some of the fat to escape and prevents the sausage bursting on the grill or barbecue.

Cotechino should be treated differently from the usual frying and grilling sausage. It is pricked with a fine skewer and then simmered in water very gently for 1 hour before being skinned and cut into thick slices and served with lentils or potatoes and often the Italian condiment *mostarda di Cremona*. The various **French-style boiling sausages** are cooked and served the same way.

COOKED | Some cooked sausages are always reheated, and others are sometimes. *Frankfurters* are simmered in water for 5 minutes just to heat through. *Knackwurst* can be buried in cooking sauerkraut or a bean stew for up to 1 hour without fear of collapse. *Blood sausage* is usually fried or grilled. In Bologna, cubes of **mortadella**, usually eaten as it is, are minced and added to pasta sauces and stuffings or tossed with vegetables as they stew in a little oil or butter (sliced carrot and diced mortadella is delicious). *Kabana* and **Polish sausage** are usually eaten as snacks or can be mixed into salads.

DRIED | Dried sausages are mostly for slicing and snacking. The rind of sliced dried sausage should always be peeled away before slicing to prevent choking. I find thin slices of **salami** with a few olives and a glass of wine one of the most lively ways of stimulating the taste buds. Chinese **lap cheong** lasts for weeks and should be sliced thinly and steamed for a few minutes before being added to a bowl of steamed rice or stir-fried vegetables.

crépinettes and chestnuts
SERVES 4

recipes

Look for pork crépinettes at speciality butchers or delicatessens. This goes well with crisp-cooked buttered cabbage.

1 tablespoon olive oil
20 g butter
4 pork crépinettes
2 teaspoons plain flour
100 ml marsala *or* port
1 cup Chicken *or* Veal Stock
20 blanched, peeled chestnuts
salt
freshly ground black pepper

Heat oil and melt butter in a frying pan. When foaming, slip in crépinettes, best-side down. Turn after a few minutes and brown other side. Remove gently from pan to a plate. Add flour to pan drippings and stir until a smooth paste. Gradually stir in marsala and stock. Stir until sauce is smooth. If too thick, add a spoonful of water. Drop in chestnuts and simmer, covered, for 5 minutes. Uncover, return crépinettes to pan and simmer gently until chestnuts are quite tender. Taste for seasoning.

bangers and mash
Serve slowly fried fresh pure pork sausages on a generous mound of well-seasoned creamy mashed potato.

pork sausages with sage and tomato SERVES 4

4 fresh pure pork sausages,
    parboiled

12 fresh sage leaves

2 tablespoons olive oil

3 tomatoes, peeled, seeded
    and diced

salt

freshly ground black pepper

Fry parboiled sausages and sage leaves in oil over moderate heat until sausages are well browned and sage leaves are crisp. Pour off any excess fat and tip in chopped tomato. Cook for 15 minutes until tomato has collapsed, then season and serve.

**blood sausage
and apple**
*Grill diagonally
sliced blood sausage
briefly until very
hot. Serve with a
panful of butter-
fried apple.*

polish sausage and potato salad SERVES 4

*This salad is fine made with any cooked sausage that is not too highly spiced.
I like using Polish sausage.*

4 waxy potatoes

500 g Polish sausage, skinned

2 tablespoons finely chopped
    spring onion

3 tablespoons finely chopped
    fresh parsley

2 tablespoons chopped pickled
    cucumber

1 tablespoon capers

2 tablespoons olive oil

2 teaspoons red-wine vinegar

Boil potatoes until tender. Drain and cool for a few minutes. Peel if you wish, then chop into bite-sized pieces. Cut sausage into small chunks. Toss with all other ingredients. Serve warm.

other recipes

braised stuffed trotters *see* TROTTERS

cabbage leaves stuffed with pork, sausage and rice *see* CABBAGES AND
    BRUSSELS SPROUTS

spanish potato with chorizo *see* POTATOES

Scallops

Scallops   The scallop is a hermaphrodite mollusc, its beautifully shaped fluted shell made famous by Botticelli's painting *The Birth of Venus*, where Venus is shown standing in a scallop shell rising from the sea, draped only in her long red–golden hair.   │   There are hundreds of varieties of scallops world-wide, with 3 main species being caught in Australia. The edible part of a scallop consists of the creamy-white muscle and the orange–pink or purple 'coral', which is the roe or reproductive organ. In parts of Europe and in Canada the mantle, the frilly membrane that encloses the muscle and the gut, is also eaten. In the United States and South-East Asia the coral is not eaten; scallops harvested in Australia that may be destined for the export market (such as our saucer scallops) come to market with their coral already removed.   │   Many European recipe books instruct one to cook scallops for 15 minutes. But most European scallops are considerably larger than ours, although the smaller *pétoncles* and *vanneaux*, as they are called by the French, are more similar. Some of these recipes involve poaching and then slicing the scallops and mixing them with rich mornay or cream sauces and/or mashed potato, before piling it all back into the shells and baking until browned. I wonder how much of the flavour and texture of the scallop is left after all this? >

scallops
go
with
garlic
butter
parsley
chives
thyme
tomatoes
celery
fennel
artichoke hearts
sweet peppers
shallots
leeks
spinach
cream
pasta
salad leaves
white wine
vermouth
saffron
coriander
soy sauce
ginger
lemons
limes
mussels
pipis

My advice is to stay away from recipes that tell you to poach scallops in stock and to finish the stock with cream or butter. It is easy to overcook the scallops and end up with rubber balls in sauce. And distrust *any* scallop recipe that tells you to cook them for more than 3–5 minutes.

There was shameful and thoughtless overfishing of the major scallop beds in Victoria and Tasmania during the 1970s and 1980s. Powerful dredges damaged the scallop habitats and it is only now that the beds are recovering. One positive result from this situation has been the development of scallop farms that are now producing high-quality scallops. The competition offered by the queen scallops that are hand-collected off South Australia's Eyre Peninsula has meant that consumers are now increasingly able to purchase other scallops (mainly farmed) on the half-shell. This is a wonderful way to present scallops, the shell being the perfect sauce container.

VARIETIES AND SEASON

There are times of the year when the scallop supply might be patchy. Scallops spawn to coincide with changes in water temperature – this usually occurs at the beginning of summer. Spawning scallops are not in prime condition – their coral is less bright and plump and their muscle less firm – although they are still perfectly edible. Their flavour is more spicy than sweet at this time. In addition, authorities are constantly supervising stock levels in the scallop fisheries, and beds are closed from time to time to allow stocks to recover. As more scallop farms become fully productive there will probably be a time when scallops are available throughout the year.

There are 3 main species of scallop available to Australians. Differences in flavour have a great deal to do with freshness. However, the queen scallop is more definitely flavoured than the commercial scallop. Both are sweet and delicious when freshly harvested and cooked appropriately.

COMMERCIAL From Victorian and Tasmanian fishing grounds comes *Pecten fumatus*, marketed as the commercial scallop but also known as the southern, king or Tasmanian scallop. Recognised by its typical pink–brown fluted shell, it is easily the most commonly available scallop. The commercial scallop is found around Australia's southern coast, from Shark Bay in Western Australia to Tuncurry in New South Wales.

QUEEN From the Eyre Peninsula in South Australia comes the beautiful purple-shelled *Chlamys bifrons*, which has startling purple roe. Also known as the Coffin Bay scallop, this species is marketed rather prosaically as a 'scallop'. It is hand-collected by divers, so is expensive and mostly sold direct to restaurants.

SAUCER There are 3 types of saucer scallop available commercially. From Queensland comes Ballot's saucer scallop (*Amusium balloti balloti*), also known as the Queensland or tropical scallop. A subspecies comes from Western Australia, the western saucer scallop. These scallops have thin and rather flat shells. The outer surface is smooth and polished. One half is white, while the other is striped or banded in shades of brown and/or red. There are minor differences between the saucer scallop caught in the west and the one caught in the north. The delicate saucer scallop (*A. pleuronectes*), also known as the Asian moon scallop or the sun or mud scallop, is a tiny mollusc caught in the northern waters off the Northern Territory and around Weipa off the Cape York Peninsula in Queensland. The shell is white on one side and has dark-edged, spotted rays on a dull-pink background on the other.

SELECTION AND STORAGE

Scallops are rich and often served with buttery sauces, so 6 per person is enough for a first course. If scallops are to be the main dish, I would serve 10 or, at most, 12, depending on their size.

Scallops should smell sweet without any trace of ammonia and should never be soaked in water as they absorb it. When such scallops are put in a pan they will steam rather than sear and be flabby rather than springy. Therefore, if purchasing scallops off the shell, go for those that are pale gold (not pearly-white) and don't worry if they look sticky. These are known to fishmongers as 'dry' scallops. The fat, white scallops have been soaked! Soaking increases weight and apparent size – an unacceptable practice.

Cleaned scallops sold on the half-shell are a wonderful resource. Buy scallops sold like this whenever you are lucky enough to find them. The shell is the perfect baking dish for the scallop and the perfect container for a sauce. Now and then one also sees live scallops for sale. They will need to have the mantle and gut removed. This is not very difficult but I would prefer someone else to do it for me, so ask your fishmonger.

Use fresh dry scallops within 36 hours for best results, and refrigerate them until required. Unwashed dry scallops freeze well either on the shell or loose. If on the shell, freeze them in layers with plastic film between each layer. Thaw the scallops on a thick pad of kitchen paper on a plate in the refrigerator and, as with all shellfish, use without delay.

PREPARATION AND COOKING

Scallops, whether on or off the shell, need to have their dark intestinal threads cut away, as well as any wispy traces of brownish beard (don't confuse this with the coral). Slice the thread away with a small, sharp knife and cut off the beard all in one quick operation.

Scallops take 3–5 minutes to cook, depending on size and whether they are roasted in the oven or seared in a hot pan. If you are planning to serve scallops in the shell with a sauce, make the sauce separately and spoon it while still hot over the quickly baked or grilled scallops. The scallops will overcook if you cover them with a cold sauce and reheat the sauce in the oven or under the griller. Save the shells and wash them and then dry them in a warm oven. Then you'll be ready for a day when you may not be able to buy your scallops on the half-shell.

Briefly searing scallops on a very hot, oiled solid cooking surface produces some of the best results. A heavy-based frying pan will do the job but it needs to be heavy enough to withstand full heat without buckling.

OFF THE SHELL | Place the trimmed scallops in a colander and give them a quick rinse under a strong blast of cold water, lifting and stirring as you go. Shake and then thoroughly drain the scallops on a clean cloth or a thick layer of kitchen paper. Unless you intend to poach them, transfer the scallops to a bowl, sprinkle them with a few drops of olive oil and add a few turns of the pepper mill before covering them with plastic film and refrigerating them until ready to cook.

ON THE SHELL | Lift the trimmed scallop and wipe underneath it with a clean cloth to free any trapped sand or shell particles and wipe around the shell, dipping the cloth frequently in water as you go. Try not to dislodge the scallop. Paint the scallop with a trace of oil, then grind over pepper and refrigerate, covered with plastic film, until needed.

TO SEAR | Pour a film of olive oil into a hot heavy-based frying pan and allow it a minute to heat up. Tip in the scallops and quickly separate them, so that each is sitting flat-side down. Wait 1–2 minutes while they hiss and sizzle, then turn them over for another full minute. Don't poke or move them around. Remove the scallops to a heated plate and serve as desired.

TO ROAST ON THE HALF-SHELL | Clean the scallops and their shells, leaving the scallops attached. Mix a little sambal oelek, if desired, with some olive oil. Using a pastry brush, paint each scallop lightly with the mixture. If you are not using sambal oelek, just paint them with oil and grind over pepper. Bake the scallops on their shells at 220°C for 5 minutes. Spoon on your chosen hot sauce and transfer the sauced shells to serving plates and serve immediately.

scallops on the half-shell with garlic SERVES 4

The scallops for this first course can be prepared an hour or so beforehand. I sometimes put 2 scallops in a shell, so that each guest receives 6 scallops in 3 shells, making the plates a little less crowded.

1 large onion, very finely chopped
½ cup extra-virgin olive oil
2 cloves garlic, very finely chopped
½ cup freshly chopped parsley
1 cup fresh white breadcrumbs
24 scallops on the half-shell
salt
freshly ground black pepper

Preheat oven to 180°C. Sauté onion in 1 tablespoon of the oil until quite soft and pale gold. Add garlic and sauté for 1 minute, then tip into a bowl and mix with parsley and breadcrumbs.

Clean scallops and cut each away from shell. Add scallops to breadcrumb mixture, then add remaining oil and season. Wash shells well and dry in oven. Turn oven up to 220°C. Pile scallop mixture into shells and bake for 5 minutes until it is bubbling at the edges and breadcrumbs are starting to turn golden brown. Serve with a wedge of lemon and crusty bread to wipe out the shells.

pipis and mussels Pipis that have been separately steamed open are lovely tossed with the scallops, as are small mussels. **toppings** Other things can be mixed with the oil and breadcrumbs: a little Fresh Tomato Sauce (*see* TOMATOES), a spoonful of puréed red pepper, a fine dice of sautéed red pepper and celery, a spoonful of coarsely chopped almonds, and so on. **skewers** If you do not have scallops on the half-shell but like the idea of the recipe, prepare the dish as described and then thread the scallops onto bamboo skewers or halved skewers for a cocktail party (soak the skewers in cold water for 30 minutes first). Grill for 2 minutes a side under a preheated griller on lightly oiled foil to prevent them sticking.

seared scallops
Serve seared scallops on dressed salad leaves or with wok-cooked baby bok choy or other stir-fried vegetables.

scallops and beurre blanc
Top roasted scallops on the half-shell with a little Beurre Blanc full of finely chopped fresh herbs.

linguine and scallops
Add seared scallops to linguine tossed with Fresh Tomato Sauce (see TOMATOES*).*

leek and cream stew for roasted scallops SERVES 4

This 'stew' is sufficient for 24 roasted scallops on the half-shell. You will need to time this first course carefully, so that the cooked scallops don't stand around for too long before the hot sauce is added. As the sauce is rich, it is a good idea to roast 2 scallops per shell and serve 3 shells per person, so that you use a little less cream.

2 leeks, white and palest-green
part only
50 g butter
I clove garlic, very finely
chopped
I cup cream
juice of ½ lemon
salt
freshly ground black pepper
2 tablespoons freshly chopped
parsley

Cut leeks into fine julienne about 6 cm long. Soak leek in cold water, swishing well, for 10 minutes, then drain in a colander and roll in a clean tea towel. Heat butter in a heavy-based frying pan. Add leek and garlic and cook slowly, covered, for 10 minutes until leek has softened and is tender (eat a little to test). Remove lid, increase heat and add cream. Boil until cream has bubbled up well and started to thicken, about 5 minutes. Add lemon juice to taste, then season and stir in parsley. Spoon while warm over roasted scallops on the half-shell and serve immediately.
deep-fried leek Top each shell with a tangle of deep-fried wisps of leek. The same julienne can be deep-fried at 160°C until a deep gold and crisp. Drain well on kitchen paper.

asian scallops
Add finely chopped garlic, ginger and coriander root to the frying pan when searing scallops (only do this if you are able to cook the scallops in a single batch as these flavourings tend to stick).

scallops on sticks
Offer seared scallops speared on toothpicks with Thai-style Dipping Sauce (see YABBIES) *as a pre-dinner nibble.*

scallops provençale

SERVES 4

'Provençale' is menu talk to indicate that there will be garlic, tomatoes and maybe sweet peppers in a dish. This soupy stew is a favourite at my home.

I small onion, finely chopped
2 tablespoons extra-virgin
olive oil
2 cloves garlic, finely chopped
I red pepper, seeded and
finely diced
I inner rib celery, finely diced
24 scallops, cleaned
¼ cup dry white wine
tiny pinch of ground saffron
I cup Fresh Tomato Sauce
(see p. 709)
salt
freshly ground black pepper
2 tablespoons freshly chopped
parsley

Sauté onion gently in a heavy-based frying pan in 1 tablespoon of the oil. When pale gold, add garlic, red pepper and celery. Cook over moderate heat for 5 minutes until vegetables have softened a little. Scrape into a basin and wipe out pan. Heat remaining oil until very hot. Add scallops and sear for 1 minute, then turn to sear other side. Quickly tip in wine and saffron and allow to bubble fiercely for a minute, then return vegetables to pan with tomato sauce. Bring back to boiling point, taste for salt and pepper and then serve in pasta bowls and sprinkle generously with parsley. Offer slices of hot toast alongside.

other recipes
scallops with jerusalem artichokes *see* JERUSALEM ARTICHOKES

Silver beet Once cultivated in everyone's vegetable garden, silver beet (*Beta vulgaris* var. *cicla*) has fallen out of favour in recent times. I was pleased to read in Melbourne's *Age* newspaper in January 1994 that 41 per cent of Victorians have vegetable patches, so maybe there is still a wealth of home-grown silver beet out there in the suburbs. | Silver beet is known as chard or Swiss chard in the United States and England and as *blettes* in France. Other names are leaf beet and seakale beet, which remind us that this vegetable is related to the beetroot family, although in its case the leaves have developed rather than the roots. In Australia it is known as common old silver beet, the poor relation of spinach. | While spinach is wonderful, silver beet should be valued for its own characteristics, not for its similarity to something else. After all, what about those stems! The stems are delicious and can be combined with cream and blue cheese to produce a vegetable gratin of exquisite flavour. I first tasted this gratin at the Restaurant Troisgros in Roanne, France, and since then have often served it in individual terracotta dishes to delighted customers. My favourite combination is grilled calf's liver topped with a melting slice of Parsley Butter (*see* PARSLEY) with the silverbeet gratin served alongside. >

piadina
Make piadina as the Italians do: cook a selection of leafy vegetables separately – try silverbeet leaves, turnip tops, cabbage leaves and radicchio leaves – then drain them well and sauté in oil and garlic. Toss with a rustic pasta or eat with something mild-flavoured such as a veal chop or sandwich with warm focaccia.

The large, crinkly leaves of silver beet have more texture than spinach and are better suited to being slowly braised with olive oil, where they do not collapse as spinach does. Silverbeet leaves are often used in Italy combined with fresh ricotta cheese and a generous seasoning of nutmeg as a filling for small pasta in preference to the better-known version using spinach leaves.

Silver beet is much hardier than spinach and more tolerant of hot and dry weather. It is a cut-and-come-again vegetable, which is one of the reasons for its popularity with home gardeners. To cut a few leaves of young, crisp silver beet and know that the plant will quickly resprout is riches indeed.

VARIETIES AND SEASON

Silver beet is not sold by variety, although there are some cultivars that have darker leaves (Fordhook giant or Fordhook master) and some that have lighter green leaves (lucullus). To confuse things, what is sold as *rainbow chard*, which has red, purple, orange, yellow or cream stems, is simply another form of silver beet. It is usually picked much smaller than silver beet. Silver beet and rainbow chard are available all year, although you may have to ask your greengrocer to stock rainbow chard.

SELECTION AND STORAGE

Best of all is to pick your own silver beet. Pick from the outside of the plant, breaking leaves with a downwards and sideways action. Always leave 4–5 centre stalks for quick regrowth and cut off any flower stems that appear. Once flowering is established the plant will quickly become unproductive.

However, most of us will buy our silver beet. Look for the smallest bunch, which ought also to be the youngest. It is inevitable that the leaves start to flop after picking, but they should not be withered or sunburnt or show excessive signs of insect damage. The stems should be crisp, not bendy. Rainbow chard can also be bought as a bunch and is about a quarter the size of conventional silver beet. It is sometimes picked very small and sold loose as a vegetable for stir-frying.

When you get home, cut the leaves away from the stems for more manageable storage. Store the leaves and the stems either separately or together in a vegetable storage bag in the crisper section of the refrigerator. Do not wash the silver beet or chard before storing it. Both vegetables will be fine refrigerated this way for 2–3 days.

PREPARATION AND COOKING

You will have already cut the leaves away from the stems for storage. Next, trim 1 cm from the end of each stem. Pull the strings away from the outside of the stems, using a small sharp knife, and discard. Cut each stem across into slices and wash well. Wash the leaves well (check for little snails!), then tear them into pieces or roll up each one and slice it, thickly or thinly.

TO COOK | **Stems** Blanch the stems in plenty of lightly salted water for about 10 minutes and then drain well before tossing them with olive oil or stewing them in butter or cream or tomato sauce. There will be less 'greying' of the stems if a stainless steel or other non-reactive saucepan is used. **Leaves** Either steam the leaves for 3–4 minutes until tender or place them in a saucepan with no more water than that clinging to the leaves and cook them, covered, for a few minutes until tender. Drain the cooked silver beet and toss with butter or olive oil or proceed with a specific recipe.

silverbeet frittata

SERVES 6

A perfect lunch dish, this frittata is ideal with a fresh tomato salad.

1 bunch rainbow chard or
¼ bunch silver beet
(about 400 g)
olive oil
freshly ground black pepper
½ cup freshly grated parmesan
cheese
6 eggs, lightly whisked

Separate leaves from stems unless using very young rainbow chard, which can be cooked whole. Trim stems and cut into pieces 1 cm square. Wash leaves, then roll them up and slice them. Sauté stems in a film of oil over moderate heat in a large frying pan for 5 minutes. Add leaves and cover pan until leaves wilt down, then sauté for 4 minutes. Tip contents of pan into a colander resting over a bowl and drain well. Wipe out pan with kitchen paper.

Stir pepper, cheese and drained stems and leaves into egg. Add another good film of oil to pan and stand over high heat. Wait a few minutes, then tip in egg mixture. The edges should frill and puff up at once. Lower heat to medium and cook until top is just moist. Run a flexible spatula around sides and under frittata a couple of times as it cooks to ensure it is not sticking. Slide pan under a preheated griller for a minute until top has set, then loosen sides and underneath with spatula. Place a warmed platter over pan and invert frittata. To serve, scatter with fresh herbs, if desired, and cut into thick wedges.

sautéd silver beet with olive oil, pine nuts and currants

SERVES 4

This sticky and delightful dish goes very well with simple meat dishes such as grilled or roasted chicken or a pan-fried escalope of veal. I like it piled onto grilled garlic-rubbed bread as a lunch dish or spooned into baked tartlet cases. Any leftovers can be stirred into beaten eggs to become a fancier frittata of silver beet than in the next recipe.

italian vegetable soup
Drop finely shredded silverbeet leaves into a simmering vegetable soup minutes before serving. A thread of extra-virgin olive oil drizzled into each portion will add an authentic Italian touch.

sardines and silver beet
Fry sardines in hot olive oil, then add drained, cooked silverbeet leaves. Fork together and eat as is or spoon onto spaghetti. Pine nuts are good, too.

½ bunch silver beet (12
    leaves and stems)
3 tablespoons olive oil
I small onion, finely chopped
2 cloves garlic, finely chopped
½ cup currants
½ cup toasted pine nuts

Separate silverbeet stems from leaves. Trim stems, then split them lengthwise and cut into pieces 1 cm square. Wash leaves, then roll them up and slice them. Heat half the oil in a heavy-based frying pan and sauté onion until pale gold. Add stems and garlic and sauté for 5 minutes. Add sliced leaves to pan and trickle over remaining oil. Cover pan until leaves have softened, then remove lid and stir well. Add currants and pine nuts and cook, lifting and turning, until stems are tender but leaves are still glossy and green.

gratin of silverbeet stems

SERVES 4

I like using Milawa Blue or Gippsland Blue cheese, both made from cow's milk, or Meredith Blue, a sheep's milk cheese, for this dish. Serving individual gratins is a nice touch, but this works just as well in a large dish.

I bunch silver beet (12 stems)
I cup cream
100 g soft blue cheese
freshly grated nutmeg
salt
freshly ground black pepper
2 teaspoons softened butter
½ cup fresh white
    breadcrumbs

Preheat oven to 180°C. Cut silverbeet leaves away from stems and reserve for another dish. Cut stems into 8 cm lengths that are 1 cm wide. Blanch stems for 10 minutes in a large saucepan of boiling, lightly salted water. Drain, then quickly run under cold water to stop cooking. Drain again on kitchen paper. Bring cream to a boil, then drop in cheese and lower heat. Stir gently until cheese has melted, then season with nutmeg, salt and pepper. Drop in stems and stir to mix well. Grease a gratin dish or dishes with butter and spoon in stems and sauce. Smooth top and scatter breadcrumbs over. Bake until bubbling and golden – an individual dish will need 15 minutes, a large one 25 minutes.
leaves Wash 1–2 leaves per person, then roll them up and cut into slices. Blanch for 2 minutes and drain, then stew in 1 tablespoon butter for a minute. Drain the leaves again and drop them into the finished sauce with the stems before adding the breadcrumbs.

silver beet and parsley
Sauté blanched silverbeet stems over a moderate heat with sliced garlic and a generous amount of olive oil until very tender. Toss in plenty of chopped parsley, then increase the heat for a minute and serve with pork sausages, grilled chicken or a veal chop.

silver beet on toast
Sauté drained, cooked silverbeet leaves in fruity olive oil, turning over and over for a couple of minutes, and serve on garlic-rubbed toast. Sauté ham, pancetta or smoked streaky bacon in oil before adding the greens, if you like.

Spinach

Spinach One cookbook I have read describes spinach as 'a common leaf vegetable of Persian origin'. How dismissive of a vegetable rightly prized and praised in the cookery of almost the entire world! Its silky tenderness is equally at home in Indian, Chinese, Italian, French or Middle Eastern recipes.

Spinach (*Spinacea oleracea*) is considered one of the aristocrats of the vegetable world. Its flavour is delicate and delicious, it complements without overpowering, it cooks in a few minutes, and it is delicious raw. Spinach can be temperamental to grow as it responds instantly to extremes of climate, wilting at either excessive heat or sudden frost. Torrential rain will deposit mud between the leaves, and this tendency to harbour grit and earth is its most infuriating characteristic as far as the cook is concerned.

Spinach was first cultivated by the Persians in the sixth century and is another of the vegetables introduced to Spain (and thus Europe) by the Arabs in the eleventh century. It has been popular in England since the Middle Ages, and has gone down in mythology as the energy food of the American cartoon hero Popeye. This is not surprising, since spinach is one of the most nutritious vegetables known and is an excellent source of fibre, iron and vitamins. >

A number of vegetables carry the tag 'spinach' while not actually being spinach at all. Of these, Chinese and water spinach will be familiar to those who frequent Asian food stores, while another, New Zealand spinach, should be better known to us all. Indigenous to Australia, New Zealand and the Pacific islands, New Zealand spinach (*Tetragonia tetragonoides*) grows wild and unchecked on vacant land and along sandy foreshores and coastal cliffs. It was collected by Sir Joseph Banks on his voyages to the Pacific with James Cook, and seeds collected by Banks were grown at Kew Gardens, England, in 1772. This green vegetable is being marketed as warrigal greens or warrigal cabbage by companies interested in promoting the use of indigenous and wild foods (from time to time it is encountered in fresh food markets in France, where it is sold as *tetragone*). The leaves of this matting plant are much smaller than those of true spinach. It has spreading stems 60–80 cm long, but only the tender tips are harvested. When freshly picked the leaves are sweet and tender and quite delicious.

VARIETIES AND SEASON

Spinach is known in some States as English spinach. Curly-leafed and flat-leafed varieties of spinach are available to home gardeners, but most of us have no choice and buy whatever our greengrocer has on offer. Many of us can also now buy loose baby spinach leaves. Spinach is available all year round, at least in the southern and eastern States.

SELECTION AND STORAGE

Choose spinach that looks perky and has bright-green leaves that are not too large. A good **bunch** will squeak when handled. Nowadays one often has the option of buying **loose** smaller leaves. I look closely at these to be sure that I am getting choice young spinach rather than all that can be saved from overblown or damaged bunches. **Frozen** chopped spinach is useful for emergencies or a quick soup but is no substitute for fresh. It is also very wet when thawed and needs to be drained well before use.

To store a bunch of spinach, remove the string, which may be cutting into the lower leaves, and refrigerate the spinach, unwashed, in a vegetable storage bag in the crisper and use within a few days. Only wash spinach before storing it if you know it will be eaten the next day (at the latest), otherwise the damp leaves will very quickly become slimy. To store loose leaves, refrigerate them in a vegetable storage bag, unwashed, remembering that they will not keep as well as a bunch. Use loose leaves within 2 days.

PREPARATION AND COOKING

All spinach needs to be washed well, even loose leaves. If you have bought spinach by the bunch you must wash it *extremely* well. Professional cooks and lovers of super-smooth spinach purée take the time (and it is time-consuming) to remove the central stem that runs the full length of each leaf. If the stem is left in, the purée will always be a little fibrous and stringy. When I stem a bunch of spinach, I only do the large and medium leaves and set aside the inner smaller leaves for a quick stir-fry or sauté or to eat raw.

If serving cooked young leaves reheated in butter, be careful not to serve an excessive amount of stalk. This can be quite dangerous as the stalks can cause choking. Better to trim off the bottom stalks whether or not you intend to stem the leaves.

A bunch of spinach weighs about 850 g; once stemmed it weighs about 475 g, with small leaves reserved for a salad. A generous cup of cooked, drained and squeezed spinach weighs about 275 g; when chopped this becomes a scant cup.

There are 2 schools of thought regarding the cooking of spinach: the 'plenty-of-water' school and the 'water-clinging-to-the-leaves' school. My own thinking is that where one is dealing with spinach for 2–4, the latter is the method to go for. When cooking spinach for 50, or even 10, I go for the lots-of-water approach. Without plenty of water there is too much danger of the spinach catching before it has been turned over properly.

TO REMOVE THE STEMS | Fold each leaf in half and rip the stem from the root end towards the tip of the leaf. Discard the stem and drop the pieces of leaf into a sinkful of water.

TO WASH | Remove each leaf in turn if preparing a bunch (discard any that are yellow or slimy) and swirl them in a sink full of cold water. Lift the leaves out of the sink into a basin or onto the draining board of the sink and change the water. You will see the washed-out dirt at the bottom of the sink. Repeat this washing process twice. If you are not going to cook the spinach at once, or it is destined for a salad tomorrow, spin it gently in a salad spinner, then put it in a vegetable storage bag or plastic bag lined with kitchen paper and finish with another few sheets of kitchen paper. Store it in the crisper section of the refrigerator. *Don't* store spinach like this for more than 24 hours as it will start to yellow and wilt.

TO COOK | **Without water** Transfer freshly washed spinach to a roomy saucepan (you may have to moisten spinach that has been washed and then stored) and cook with only the water clinging to the leaves. As the spinach on the bottom collapses, lift it to the top until all is wilted and bright green. This will take no more than 3–5 minutes. **With water** Plunge spinach into a large saucepan of lightly salted boiling water for 2 minutes only.

middle eastern spinach
Cook a chopped onion and 1–2 garlic cloves in olive oil until soft, then mix in chopped cooked spinach and add enough best-quality yoghurt to give a thick creamy mixture. Season with salt, cayenne pepper, lemon juice and ground roasted cumin and/or quickly sautéd mustard seeds.

creamed spinach
Stir a spoonful of thick cream into puréed spinach and let it bubble briefly. Don't forget the nutmeg.

TO COOL RAPIDLY

If you are making a roulade or gnocchi, and need cold rather than hot spinach, you can cool cooked spinach rapidly in a large bath of water with ice-cubes in it. After cooling, drain the spinach, squeeze it well and either chop it by hand or use a food processor. A food processor will not create a smooth purée if the spinach is cold, but the result will be quite satisfactory for roulades or gnocchi.

TO DRAIN

Whichever cooking method is used, the next step is to drain the spinach well. Put the spinach into a colander and use the back of a small plate to press out any remaining moisture. (In old kitchenware shops one can sometimes find a giant wooden mushroom sold as a cabbage press – such things are equally useful for spinach.)

TO PURÉE

Transfer the hot, drained spinach as fast as possible to a food processor, then add a generous amount of softened butter and process until you have a lovely green purée. Season well with salt, a trace of fresh nutmeg and some pepper. Once completed, the purée can be stored and reheated carefully either over direct heat or by steaming it in a covered container.

recipes

spinach and ricotta gnocchi

SERVES 2–4

spinach and anchovies
Sauté sliced garlic in olive oil, then stir in finely chopped cooked spinach and 1–2 finely chopped anchovies. Grind over pepper and pile onto toasted, grilled or fried rounds of bread.

Good food should never be wasted. If you have leftover cooked spinach these gnocchi are an ideal preparation. If you can only make a small number of gnocchi, serve them alongside whatever else you are having for dinner in place of potatoes or rice. The quantities I give here will feed 4 as a first course and 2 for a more substantial meal. The spinach used must be absolutely dry.

275 g ricotta cheese
400 g cooked, very well drained, finely chopped spinach (about I bunch)
3 tablespoons freshly grated parmesan cheese
3 tablespoons plain flour
2 eggs
salt
freshly ground black pepper
freshly grated nutmeg
I20 g butter
I2 fresh sage leaves

Drain ricotta in a colander for several hours. Press ricotta through a sieve into a bowl and mix in spinach, parmesan, flour, eggs and seasonings thoroughly. Taste for salt and pepper. Refrigerate mixture for several hours or overnight, covered.

Preheat oven to 160°C. Dust a board with flour and form spinach mixture into cork shapes or small balls. When gnocchi are ready sift a further layer of flour over them. Grease a gratin dish with a third of the butter and keep it warm in the oven. Bring a large, wide saucepan of lightly salted

water to a simmer. Drop in half the gnocchi, allowing plenty of room and ensuring water keeps simmering. When gnocchi rise to top they are done (about 5 minutes). Remove with a perforated spoon to gratin dish. Repeat until all gnocchi are cooked and return dish to oven.

Crisp sage leaves in half the remaining butter in a hot frying pan, then remove. Cook remaining butter until golden brown and smelling nutty. Stop it cooking by placing base of pan into cold water. Drop in sage leaves, then pour sauce over gnocchi. Serve at once, offering extra parmesan.

spinach roulade

SERVES 8

60 g butter
2 bunches spinach, cooked
   and chopped
salt
freshly ground black pepper
freshly grated nutmeg
5 eggs, separated
4 tablespoons freshly grated
   parmesan cheese
2 tablespoons freshly chopped
   parsley

FILLING
250 g flat mushrooms, evenly
   sliced
60 g butter
1 tablespoon plain flour
150 ml cream
salt
freshly ground black pepper

To make the filling, sauté mushrooms in butter over moderate heat, covered, just until juices are running. Stir in flour and cook 2 minutes. Mix in cream and bring to boiling point, stirring carefully so you do not break up mushrooms. Simmer for 2 minutes, then taste for seasoning. Allow to cool but do not refrigerate.

Preheat oven to 175°C and line a 34 cm × 24 cm Swiss-roll tin with baking paper. Melt butter in a saucepan, then add spinach and season well with salt, pepper and nutmeg and transfer to a bowl. Stir egg yolks and half the parmesan cheese into spinach mixture. Whip egg whites to firm snowy peaks with a tiny pinch of salt and lightly fold into spinach mixture, then immediately tip into prepared tin. Smooth top and bake for 12–15 minutes. The roulade should feel firm in the centre but

still springy. Run a knife around edges and turn roulade onto a clean tea towel sprinkled with remaining parmesan cheese mixed with parsley. Strip off baking paper, then quickly spread filling over roulade. Roll up using the cloth to assist, starting from the long side. Settle roulade onto a serving platter, seam-side down. Allow to cool completely before cutting into thick slices with a sharp knife.

spinach ricotta terrine with pear dressing

SERVES 8–10

You will need to tear any large leaves into smaller pieces for this terrine.

potato and spinach soup
Sweat a chopped onion, some garlic and 3 large diced potatoes in olive oil, then cover with water, add a bay leaf and simmer until potato is tender. Drop in a bunch of washed, stemmed spinach and simmer for 5 minutes. Blend in a food processor, then season soup with freshly ground black pepper, salt and a pinch of ground roasted cumin.

spinach and pear
Sauté sliced or diced ripe pear in butter and add to spinach purée or a buttery tangle of small spinach leaves.

olive oil

¼ cup freshly grated parmesan
   cheese

3 spring onions, finely chopped

2 cloves garlic, finely chopped

I bunch spinach, stemmed,
   washed and well drained

350 g ricotta cheese

8 eggs

1½ cups cream

salt

freshly ground black pepper

freshly grated nutmeg

PEAR DRESSING

2 ripe, juicy pears, peeled and
   cores removed

½ cup walnut oil

½ cup olive oil

salt

freshly ground black pepper

red-wine vinegar

spinach with garlic

Sauté sliced garlic in olive oil, then stir in a large handful of stemmed small spinach leaves until wilted. Drain, then return to the pan and add a good squeeze of lemon or orange juice, a drizzle of extra-virgin olive oil and a grinding of pepper. Scatter toasted pine nuts or slivered almonds over to serve.

Preheat oven to 180°C and oil a 1.5 litre enamelled cast-iron terrine mould. Line base with baking paper and brush it with oil. Sprinkle base and sides of terrine mould with parmesan. Heat 1 tablespoon oil in a wok or large frying pan. Sauté spring onion and garlic for 1 minute. Add spinach and toss until wilted and bright green. Purée spinach mixture in a food processor, then add ricotta and process until smooth. Blend in eggs and cream and season with salt, pepper and nutmeg. Pour mixture into mould and cover with buttered foil or baking paper.

Stand mould in a baking dish and pour in hot water to come two-thirds up its sides. Bake for 1 hour, then plunge a fine skewer into centre to test middle is firm. The skewer should come out quite clean. Allow terrine to cool in water bath for 30 minutes. Refrigerate and turn out when cold.

To make the pear dressing, purée pears in a blender (*not* a food processor) and, with the motor running, slowly add oils. Season with salt, pepper and a little vinegar. Serve slices of terrine with the sauce around it and a salad of watercress, freshly sliced pear, olives and some lightly toasted walnuts alongside.

warm spinach salad

SERVES 4

This meal takes only about 8 minutes to prepare!

4 eggs

8–12 slices pancetta *or* streaky
   bacon

4 tablespoons olive oil

I tablespoon wine vinegar

8 handfuls small spinach
   leaves, washed

salt

freshly ground black pepper

Boil eggs for 5 minutes. Sauté pancetta in a non-stick frying pan until crisp and fat is running. Remove to a plate. Whisk oil and vinegar, then tip into pan and quickly add spinach. Toss until spinach is lightly warmed but not collapsed. Turn onto warmed plates, crumble over bacon, scoop eggs onto leaves and season.

additions Add a slice of grilled sourdough bread rubbed with garlic, a handful of toasted pine nuts, cubes of cheese, olives, roasted sweet peppers, slices of smoked chicken, leftover roast lamb, or ham, and so on.

spanakopita

This filling, given here for a family-sized pie, can be used just as well to make tiny filo triangles to serve as quick savouries. When handling filo pastry, cover the unused sheets with a sheet of foil and then cover this with a damp tea towel to stop the pastry drying out.

1 onion, finely chopped

1 tablespoon olive oil

2 spring onions, very finely chopped

1 large bunch spinach, stemmed, washed, dried and finely chopped

2 tablespoons freshly chopped mint

2 tablespoons freshly chopped parsley

freshly grated nutmeg

2 eggs

125 g fetta cheese, crumbled

125 g ricotta cheese

60 g freshly grated kasseri, romana or pecorino cheese

freshly ground black pepper

120 g unsalted butter, melted

10 sheets filo pastry

Preheat oven to 180°C. Sauté onion in oil until softened. Add spring onion, spinach, herbs and nutmeg and cook, stirring, until spinach is soft and there is no liquid in pan. Tip into a colander resting over a plate and allow to cool. Beat eggs in a large bowl, then add cheeses and cooled spinach mixture. Adjust seasoning with pepper.

Select a rectangular metal baking dish 28 cm × 18 cm × 8 cm. It should be a bit smaller than half a sheet of filo. Brush dish with a little melted butter. Cut pastry sheets in half and, brushing each sheet with melted butter, settle 10 pastry layers in dish, pressing pastry up sides. Spoon in spinach mixture. Settle a further 10 buttered pastry sheets over spinach, tucking any overlap down sides. Score top of pie into squares, but do *not* cut through bottom. Bake for 1 hour until golden brown and serve warm or cold.

cheesy spinach
Bury a nugget of gruyère, raclette, fontina or taleggio cheese in mounds of seasoned cooked spinach and then arrange on bread croutons or baking paper. Top with 1 tablespoon melted butter and bake for 10 minutes at 180°C. Serve underneath or alongside grilled chops or as a light first course.

other recipes

calf's kidney with spinach *see* KIDNEYS

chick peas with spinach *see* CHICK PEAS

green herb pilaf *see* RICE

Squid, calamari, cuttlefish and octopus

Thanks to our Mediterranean migrants, squid and to a lesser extent octopus and cuttlefish have become sought-after and appreciated foods throughout Australia. What was once used only as bait now commands high prices. Much of the squid caught in northern waters is a by-product of prawn-trawling; that caught in the south is specifically targeted. | The names used for squid can be confusing: the Italian word for more than one squid is *calamari* and yet the word 'calamari' is used for specific varieties, while other varieties are known simply as squid. In the general marketplace all varieties are known as squid or calamari, without distinction. Squid, calamari and their cousins octopus and cuttlefish are all cephalopods, being molluscs without a shell. Almost all cephalopods squirt a brownish or black veil of ink to hide their escape from predators. This ink is used to colour and flavour pasta and certain seafood stews. >

Learning to love squid is not always an easy thing. I recall an afternoon 25 years ago visiting my Greek friend Melita who was preparing squid for dinner that night. I stared at her black arms in horror and at the sink full of murky grey water. She laughed at my distaste and promised me a dish of squid that would convince me. And, of course, she did, and I became a squid lover for life. Again with Melita, on holiday in Ithaca, I watched the returning fishermen bash their catch of octopus against the stony breakwater. A few hours later we enjoyed a glass of ouzo and pieces of warm octopus tentacles marinated in Ithacan oil as an apéritif before dinner. Today deep-fried calamari has converted many of the young and this dish is now absolutely mainstream and available in the nation's take-away fish-and-chip shops.

Squid and calamari must be cooked either very briefly (2–5 minutes) or for a long time. Inbetween cooking will result in the tough, rubbery texture that is what many non-squid lovers have probably experienced. Small cuttlefish are as tender as squid, but larger cuttlefish are as unyielding as octopus and need special treatment to make them tender. Cuttlefish appear on Italian menus as *seppia*, octopus as *polpo*. Marcella Hazan is insistent that it is only the ink from cuttlefish that should be used to cook with as she believes it is the only variety sweet enough. Most cooks use squid ink, however.

**squid
and
calamari
go
with**
olive oil
garlic
parsley
lemons
tomatoes
mayonnaise
balsamic vinegar
red-wine vinegar
oregano
rice
onions
soy sauce
spring onions
ginger

VARIETIES AND SEASON

SQUID AND CALAMARI | Squid and calamari come in various sizes and several varieties. Each consists of a body or hood, 2 tentacles and 8 'arms', mantle or fins, ink sac (which is embedded in the head), intestines and an internal transparent 'bone' or shield. The body, mantle and tentacles are eaten, as is the ink. The difference between calamari and squid is slight: calamari have long triangular flaps running along each side of the body, while squid have smaller pointed flaps attached only to the narrow end of the body, resembling an arrow or bishop's mitre. Both squid and calamari range in colour from pink to brown to greyish blue, and can change their colour for camouflage.

In Australia 4 species of squid and calamari are caught. You will be most familiar with the varieties caught nearest to your own market. From our northern waters come northern calamari (*Sepioteuthis lessoniana*) and mitre or Asian squid (*Loligo chinensis*), while southern calamari (*S. australis*) and arrow squid (*Nototodarus gouldi*) are found in the south. Each is marketed as either calamari or squid. One variety or another is available all year.

CUTTLEFISH | Cuttlefish (*Sepia* species) consist of a short, rounded body or hood, tentacles, ink sac (which is embedded in the body), intestines and an internal cuttlebone. Cuttlefish vary in colour but are often brownish pink with wavy markings.

Body size varies enormously from 6–20 cm. Cuttlefish have 2 tentacles and 8 'arms', and are caught as a by-product of prawn-trawling. They are prolific in New South Wales and Queensland waters.

OCTOPUS Octopus (*Octopus* species) consist of the body or head, very large and muscular tentacles and an ink sac and intestines. An octopus has no bony support. They vary in colour from brownish black to blueish grey and in size from about 50 cm long (including the tentacles) to much larger. There are also tiny varieties. Octopus have 8 tentacles and appear regularly in our markets. They are predators of rock lobsters and much of the fishing of octopus is designed to protect the valuable rock lobster catch.

SELECTION AND STORAGE

Calamari is more tender than squid and is recommended for frying, quick grilling or stir-frying. Squid is best suited for stewing and stuffing. Whether calamari or squid or cuttlefish, thin-fleshed specimens are more tender than thick-fleshed. This relates to size, so select smaller to medium-sized fish rather than the giants one sometimes sees. Rings cut from these huge bodies can be tough and look pretty unappealing. For this reason, prefer whole calamari to buying prepared rings, as often these rings have been cut from a huge fish. However, sometimes cleaned calamari and cleaned cuttlefish are offered for sale. If they smell sweet and are firm to the touch, they can be a good buy for a quick stir-fry or grill.

Fresh squid, calamari, cuttlefish and octopus should smell sweet with no trace of ammonia. Use as soon as possible after purchase, certainly within 36 hours, and do not store with the guts intact. Squid, calamari and cuttlefish absorb water, so do not leave them soaking in a bucket of water. They freeze well without significant loss of texture (freezing octopus will actually break down the texture a bit, making it more tender). If buying frozen squid, calamari, cuttlefish or octopus, either store it in the freezer or thaw it in the refrigerator and clean it as soon as possible. Freezing coagulates the ink of squid, calamari, cuttlefish and octopus. If you wish to use it, scrape the frozen granules into a small bowl and rehydrate them with a little hot water.

PREPARATION AND COOKING

Squid, calamari, cuttlefish and octopus can always be cleaned by your fishmonger, but this is also easy to do yourself with a bit of practice. I suffer from a slight allergy when handling squid in quantity and have found others on my staff with the same reaction. If you have itchy hands after cleaning squid, I suggest that next time you wear disposable gloves.

TO CLEAN **Squid and calamari** Tip the squid into a sinkful of cold water. Grasp the tentacles in a bunch in your right hand. Give a firm pull and twist and the guts and tentacles will come away together. Using a knife or scissors, cut the tentacles just below the ink sac, which is clearly visible as a purple bulge. Holding the tentacles, press the bunch away from you – the 'beak' or anus will pop out. Cut away and discard the anus, guts and ink sac (unless you wish to stew your squid in its own ink, in which case drop the ink sac into a small bowl). Rinse the tentacles in water and reserve. Now draw out the transparent cartilaginous shield from inside the body. Rinse the body under running water and strip off the purplish black membrane, dropping it into the bin as you go. Rinse the body inside and out once again and add it to the tentacles. Dry the squid or calamari well on a cloth or with kitchen paper.   **Cuttlefish** Cut open the body and remove the cuttlebone. Slip your fingers under the visible membrane, then pull it away and discard it. You have now exposed the ink sac and the guts. Detach and reserve the ink sac (if desired), then detach and discard the rest of the guts. Remove the anus from the tentacles as for squid and calamari. Under running water, rinse and strip away the coloured membrane that covers the body and the tentacles. Cuttlefish are much harder to skin than squid. If intended to be grilled, the skin can be left in place. Rinse the tentacles and body inside and out and dry well.   **Octopus** Freshly caught octopus are very tough and always tenderised. In the Greek islands, and no doubt elsewhere in the Mediterranean, the octopus is quickly killed, repeatedly bashed against the rocks (40 times, says my friend Melita) and between each bashing massaged against the rocks until it froths! Melita says that much freshly caught octopus that comes into our markets is tenderised in a small cement mixer! I have read that in Japan the octopus is placed in a bath of grated white radish (daikon) and is kneaded by hand. A meat mallet will help the home cook. There is no doubt in my mind that it is this initial tenderising that enables octopus tentacles to emerge tender and succulent from the barbecue grill after only a few minutes' cooking. Whatever method is used, the octopus flesh should no longer feel bouncy. Cut the tentacles away from the head well below the hard central beak. (If the head is larger than 20 cm it is often discarded or used for a stock.) Cut away the beak and the anal portion, then turn the body inside out. Remove all internal organs and the ink sac. Cut the suckers away from the tentacles and remove the tips of each tentacle. Strip the skin away from each tentacle under running water. This is quite hard to do. Some cooks prefer to strip the skin away after cooking. This is not feasible if the tentacles are to be grilled, so persevere. Rinse and dry well.

TO COOK IN OWN JUICE Slice prepared *squid, calamari* or *cuttlefish* into fine rings or pieces and cut the tentacles into 6 cm lengths. Put the fish, a garlic clove and ½ cup cold water into a small saucepan that has a tight-fitting lid. Place over moderate heat and cover tightly. After 3 minutes remove from the heat and stir – the fish will be starting to look pink and the water should be bubbling. Put the lid back on and cook for a further 2–3 minutes, then taste a piece. It should be deliciously tender. Tip through a strainer to discard the liquid. Transfer the fish to a bowl and pour over olive oil and lemon juice while still warm. Season. When cool, stir in lots of chopped herbs. This method is also suitable for pieces of *octopus* tentacle, but expect them to take about 30 minutes to be tender. Slice the tentacles into small pieces and season as above.

TO GRILL OR BARBECUE Clean but do not skin *calamari* or small *cuttlefish*. Leave the bodies whole or slit them open. Skin *octopus* tentacles and make small diagonal cuts along their length every 6 cm, cutting about a third through the tentacle. Pack the cleaned bodies and trimmed tentacles tightly and marinate overnight with finely sliced garlic, 1–2 bay leaves and olive oil. Next day, heat the electric griller or barbecue and lift the calamari, cuttlefish or octopus from the marinade. Drain off excess oil and then grill for several minutes each side. The skin will develop a wonderful bronze–gold colouring. When the tip of a knife slips through the body wall or the tentacle it is ready. Transfer to a warm dish, drizzle with some extra-virgin olive oil and leave to rest for 5 minutes.

TO FRY Slice prepared *squid* or *calamari* into thin rings and cut the tentacles into clusters about 4 cm long. Dip in seasoned flour or preferred batter ◿. Shake off the excess and deep-fry in plenty of clean, hot olive oil at 160°C, or shallow-fry, until golden brown. Drain well on kitchen paper.

recipes

barbecued calamari with soy sauce SERVES 4

4 small–medium calamari
  (bodies 12 cm long)
2 tablespoons brown sugar
8 spring onions, cleaned and
  cut to 10 cm long
3 tablespoons light soy sauce
1 tablespoon light vegetable
  oil
1 lime

Slit each calamari body along one side and, with a very sharp knife, score inside skin diagonally in both directions, creating a cross-hatch effect. Rub sugar into cuts and cut each body into 4 pieces. Cut tentacles into 6 cm lengths. Mix squid and spring onions in a bowl. Mix soy sauce with oil and pour over squid. Leave for 30 minutes before draining, then grill over coals (for preference) or under a hot griller. The tentacles and spring onions may be sufficiently done in 3 minutes. The other pieces may take an extra few minutes. Serve with Thai-style Dipping Sauce (*see* YABBIES) or your favourite hot relish and a squeeze of lime.

stir-fry This calamari dish can be stir-fried ✎ in a hot wok in a little extra oil rather than being grilled.

thai-inspired calamari salad

SERVES 6

A simplified and adapted version of a David Thompson recipe.

6 small calamari, cleaned and sliced into rings (include tentacles cut into clusters)
1 Granny Smith apple, unpeeled and cut into julienne
2 shallots, very finely sliced
1 tablespoon fresh coriander leaves
1 tablespoon freshly torn mint leaves
3 tablespoons peanuts

DRESSING
2 fresh chillies, seeded and finely sliced
pinch of salt
1 tablespoon palm sugar
2 tablespoons fish sauce
1 tablespoon fresh lime *or* lemon juice

Cook calamari with ½ cup cold water, covered, for 5 minutes over moderate heat until tender, then drain. Combine all salad ingredients. Mix dressing ingredients. Stir dressing through salad and serve in lettuce cups or heaped over finely shredded crisp green salad leaves.

sauce for fried squid
Serve well-drained fried squid or calamari with lemon and Mayonnaise ✎, Fresh Tomato Sauce (see TOMATOES*), Ponzu Sauce ✎ or Thai-style Dipping Sauce (see* YABBIES*).*

squid stuffed with rice and currants

SERVES 4

½ onion, finely chopped
100 ml olive oil
½ cup long-grained rice
1¼ cups water
¼ cup currants
¼ cup freshly chopped parsley
1 tablespoon freshly chopped dill
(*continued next page*)

Sauté onion in oil, then add rice and stir well. Add water and remaining ingredients except pine nuts, squid and tomato juice. Simmer very gently until rice is cooked, about 10 minutes. Stir in pine nuts, then taste for salt and pepper. Allow stuffing to cool.

Preheat oven to 180°C. Using a small spoon, stuff squid bodies and arrange snugly in an oiled baking dish, preferably

salt

freshly ground black pepper

¼ cup toasted pine nuts

8 small squid, cleaned
(bodies 12 cm long)

tomato juice

one that has a lid. Do not stuff them too tightly as the bodies will shrink in the cooking process (some stuffing will probably ooze out too). Arrange tentacles, cut into pieces, in spaces between bodies and pour over sufficient tomato juice to come two-thirds up bodies. Cover baking dish and bake for 45 minutes–1 hour, turning squid after 30 minutes. If the dish seems too juicy and squid is tender, pour juices into a pan and reduce them somewhat. If the juice is too thick, thin it with a little water.

vine leaves This stuffing can also be used to stuff vine leaves.

bbq calamari
Toss sliced barbecued calamari or cuttlefish through pasta or serve on lettuce leaves. Offer it on its own with finely sliced chilli and lemon wedges.

squid stuffed with pork and prawns   SERVES 6

6 squid, cleaned

100 g minced pork

100 g minced prawn meat

1 tablespoon freshly chopped
coriander stems, leaves
and roots

1 teaspoon fish sauce

1 egg, lightly beaten

salt

freshly ground black pepper

oil

1 onion, chopped

1 clove garlic, crushed

1½ cups white wine

1 small fresh chilli, finely
chopped (optional)

3 tomatoes, chopped

2 tablespoons freshly chopped
parsley

Preheat oven to 180°C. Mince tentacles or chop finely. Mix minced tentacles with pork, prawn meat, coriander, fish sauce and egg, then season. Stuff mixture (not too tightly) into squid bodies and secure open ends with toothpicks. Carefully place squid in a single layer in a cast-iron casserole with a little oil, onion and garlic and sauté for 2 minutes, turning. Add wine, chilli, tomato, salt and pepper. Transfer casserole to oven and bake, covered, for 45 minutes until squid can be easily pierced with the tip of a small knife. Serve scattered with fresh parsley.

squid cooked in its own ink   SERVES 4

Squid absorbs the flavours of the ingredients it is stewed with to become thick and rich.

1 kg small–medium squid,
cleaned (ink sacs reserved)

4 tablespoons olive oil

(continued next page)

Cut squid bodies into rings and tentacles into bunches 6 cm long. Heat oil in a cast-iron casserole or deep frying pan. Sauté garlic, onion, oregano and bay leaf for

3 cloves garlic, chopped

2 large onions, finely chopped

1 large sprig oregano

1 bay leaf

2 large tomatoes, peeled,
   seeded and chopped

¼ cup vermouth *or* white
   wine

2 tablespoons water

salt

freshly ground black pepper

freshly chopped parsley

5 minutes. Add tomato and vermouth and simmer for 5 minutes. Preheat oven to 180°C if using a casserole. Slit ink sacs and squeeze ink through a coarse strainer into a bowl and mix with water. Add ink and squid to casserole, then season and cover. If using a casserole, transfer to oven and cook for 45 minutes until squid is completely tender. If using a frying pan, put pan on a simmer mat and complete cooking on stove. Taste for tenderness and seasoning and scatter generously with chopped parsley. Serve with a grilled slice of sourdough bread rubbed with garlic or spread with Anchovy Butter (*see* ANCHOVIES).

speedy version After adding the squid and ink, the heat under the frying pan can be increased and the squid cooked briskly. This way the squid will be ready in less than 5 minutes. Taste and adjust seasoning and scatter with parsley. This method does not produce the rich flavours that slow cooking does, but the end result is still delicious.

other recipes

stir-fried squid and celery *see* CELERY AND CELERIAC

sweet potatoes

sweet potatoes The sweet potato (*Ipomoea batatas*) is the tuber of a trailing vine and first cousin to the spectacular (but invasive) morning glory vine. It is native to Central America and can be added to the long list of foods brought back to Europe by Columbus. It was a staple food of the Arawak Indians of Jamaica and is still much loved in the West Indies, as it is in New Zealand, where it has been since the fourteenth century, courtesy of the Polynesians. An instant hit in Spain, the sweet potato was received half-heartedly in England after a brief honeymoon period during Elizabethan times. Sweet potatoes are now grown around the world in tropical and subtropical regions, including Australia. This lumpy, heavy and rather unprepossessing vegetable has purple, buff–yellow or brown skin. (It is not to be confused with a yam or taro, both of which are staples in the Pacific islands and New Guinea and quite different species.) Apparently the leaves of the sweet potato can be eaten like spinach and can be picked while the tuber is still growing. I have never seen a sweet potato plant *in situ*, so this is a surprise still to come. Apart from everyday baked and mashed sweet potato, there are interesting ways of preparing this vegetable in the cookery of the Deep South of the United States, the Pacific islands, South-East Asia and the West Indies. >

Candied sweet potato is a traditional accompaniment to roast turkey for the American Thanksgiving dinner. Be cautious, however, of American recipes for candied or sweet potato puddings. The amounts of sugar used are often excessive. I have included a recipe for a sweet potato pudding that is the nearest I have found to the sticky, spicy dish I enjoyed so much in the 1960s in Jamaica.

I have always loved mealy, starchy food and the dry-yet-earthy flavour of sweet potato intrigues and pleases me. The brown-skinned variety has a flavour close to that of chestnuts, the purple and buff–yellow varieties are drier but much sweeter.

VARIETIES AND SEASON

In Australia we have 3 varieties of sweet potato, which are available all year, the peak season being in autumn and winter. They are sold simply as sweet potatoes, the colour of their skins being the consumer's sole guide. The **brown** sweet potato has cream-to-beige flesh that resembles a chestnut in flavour. The flesh discolours very quickly and is softer and moister than the other varieties but can also be more fibrous and is best for baking. In Australia orange-fleshed, **buff–yellow** sweet potato is often called by its Maori name of kumara. It bakes drier than the brown or purple varieties and is the one usually used for puddings or candying. The creamy-white flesh of the all-purpose **purple** sweet potato discolours quickly and is medium–dry.

SELECTION AND STORAGE

Select clean, smooth, well-shaped sweet potatoes and avoid any with black–brown spots or soft patches. Go for those that are medium-sized and avoid any that are sprouting. Store in a cool, dark, airy place, as you would potatoes, and use within a week. Do not refrigerate.

PREPARATION AND COOKING

Sweet potatoes can be baked, boiled, mashed, fried, candied or made into quick breads and puddings, to name the most common preparations. The brown and purple-skinned varieties discolour very quickly after being peeled. To delay this, drop the peeled chunks into cold water until all are prepared.

TO BAKE | Sweet potatoes keep their shape far better when baked in their skins. Slice off any wrinkled bits at each end of the tuber and scrub the skins well. Cut the tuber into large chunks and dry before rolling lightly in oil and baking at 180°C. Sweet potatoes cook faster than ordinary potatoes. A medium-sized chunk will be tender in 30 minutes.

sweet potatoes go with
butter
salt
brown sugar
maple syrup
cinnamon
nutmeg
rosemary
oregano
cream
bacon
ham
chicken
turkey
coconut milk
turmeric

sweet potato gratin
Purée baked or mashed sweet potato and mix with an egg, a little melted butter and salt and pepper and bake in a buttered gratin dish at 180°C for 20 minutes. It will puff a little and become golden brown and is delicious with grilled bratwurst sausages.

| **TO BOIL** | Boil chunks of sweet potato with the skins intact in lightly salted water for 15 minutes until tender. Drain and peel. Boiled sweet potato that is to be mashed can be prepared up to 2 days in advance and refrigerated, covered. |

| **TO MASH** | Boil, bake or steam chunks of sweet potato until tender, then peel, if necessary. Mash with a food processor or food mill. Season with butter, salt and pepper or even a little cream. Reheat in a bowl over hot water if purée has been refrigerated. |

| **TO FRY** | Cut the sweet potato into thin slices and deep-fry in clean oil at 160°C. Parboil larger chips, then drain and dry well and shallow-fry or deep-fry. |

recipes

honeyed sweet potato
Drizzle thickish slices of orange-fleshed sweet potato with honey, then pour in a little orange juice and bake at 180°C until sticky and tender, about 30 minutes.

candied sweet potato   SERVES 4

2 sweet potatoes, boiled
60 g butter
60 g brown sugar *or*
    4 tablespoons maple syrup
1 teaspoon balsamic vinegar *or*
    good red-wine vinegar

Peel sweet potato and cut into slices or chunks. Melt butter and dissolve sugar in it. Boil until mixture is bubbly, then toss sweet potato in it until syrup has largely been absorbed and sweet potato is tender. Keep heat high and sprinkle on vinegar, which will evaporate quickly. Serve at once.

sweet potato and prawn fritters   SERVES 6

These wonderful fritters can sometimes be enjoyed in Vietnamese restaurants. This recipe comes from Meera Freeman's The Vietnamese Cookbook *and serves 6 as part of an Asian meal.*

250 g sweet potatoes, peeled
100 g green prawns, shelled
    and de-veined
½ cup self-raising flour
½ cup rice flour
pinch of ground turmeric
1 teaspoon sugar
pinch of salt
1–2 cups thick coconut milk
vegetable oil

Grate sweet potatoes coarsely, then squeeze to extract as much moisture as possible and drain. Slice prawns in half lengthwise and set aside. In a large bowl, mix flours with turmeric, sugar and salt. Gradually add enough coconut milk to make a thick batter. Stir in sweet potato and prawns, mixing well to distribute prawns evenly through batter. If batter becomes too thick, add a little coconut milk. It should hold its shape when fried. Heat enough oil in a wok or frying pan to deep-fry fritters. Fry tablespoonfuls of batter, a few at a time, for 2–3 minutes on both sides or until golden brown on outside and soft on inside. Drain on kitchen paper and serve hot with soft lettuce leaves, fresh mint and Thai-style Dipping Sauce (*see* YABBIES).

sabee sabee kumala

SERVES 4–6

This recipe has been adapted from one that appears in Traditional Torres Strait Island Cooking *by Ron Edwards. 'Sabee sabee' means 'simmered in coconut milk'. In the islands most vegetables are starchy, and this dish could just as easily be made from any combination of sweet potato, ordinary potato, cassava, taro, yam or pumpkin. It would be set out with others of meat, fish and rice. The green bananas used are simply unripe bananas, a common ingredient or side dish in Africa and the West Indies as well as the Torres Strait.*

350 g sweet potato, peeled and diced
350 g pumpkin, peeled and diced
1 small onion, finely diced
pinch of salt
coconut milk
4 green bananas

Put sweet potato, pumpkin, onion and salt in a saucepan and almost cover with coconut milk. Bring to a boil, uncovered, and simmer for 10 minutes. Scoop flesh from bananas with a spoon and add to pan. Simmer until banana and vegetables are soft, about 15 minutes.

jamaican sweet potato pudding

SERVES 8

700 g sweet potatoes, peeled and grated coarsely
2/3 cup brown sugar
1½ cups coconut milk
½ teaspoon ground cinnamon
1 teaspoon ground ginger
¼ teaspoon ground or freshly grated nutmeg
few drops of pure vanilla
20 g butter, melted
½ cup seeded raisins
3 eggs

Preheat oven to 180°C and butter a 1.5 litre gratin dish. Mix all ingredients to make a batter of a dropping consistency. Spoon batter into prepared dish and bake for 1 hour. Serve with thick cream or thick coconut cream.

baked sweet potato
Toss small chunks of parboiled sweet potato with a little brown sugar, ground ginger and allspice. Season and pile into a buttered gratin dish. Slosh over dry apple cider and 1–2 tablespoons cream and bake at 180°C until tender. Serve as a side dish with pork, or with a large salad.

grilled sweet potato
Cut peeled sweet potato into 5 mm thick slices, then brush with melted butter or olive oil mixed with very finely chopped rosemary or oregano and grill under a moderate heat until blistered and tender.

sweet potato cornbread or corn pone

Corn pone is a cross between a pudding, a cake and a bread – originally it was a thin cake baked on a heated stone. There are many variations of corn pone throughout the South of the USA. Some are made with sweetened condensed milk, some with all cornmeal and some with astonishingly large amounts of butter. Such dishes are eaten as bread alongside meat or, just as often, as a sweet pudding. This version is based on a recipe in Betty Fussell's book I Hear America Cooking.

sweet potato chips

Deep-fry very thinly sliced sweet potato in hot, clean oil at 160°C and serve alongside a spicy dip, such as Guacamole (see AVOCADOS*) or Hummus (see* CHICK PEAS*).*

900 g sweet potato, boiled
   and mashed (to yield
   2 cups)
125 g unsalted butter
4 eggs, lightly beaten
½ cup brown sugar
½ teaspoon bicarbonate
   of soda
1 teaspoon salt
1 teaspoon ground cinnamon
1 cup plain yoghurt
2 cups fine polenta

Preheat oven to 180°C and butter a 20 cm square cake tin. Purée 2 cups mashed sweet potato in a food processor with all ingredients except yoghurt and polenta. Stir in yoghurt and polenta and pour into prepared tin. Bake for 45 minutes or until a fine skewer inserted in centre comes out clean. Cool a little before turning out and cutting into squares.

tarragon

tarragon A native of southern Europe, tarragon (*Artemisia* species) derives its name from the French *estragon*, in turn derived from the Latin *dracunculus*, meaning 'little dragon'. Most authorities suggest that tarragon has this name because of its supposed efficacy in curing the bites of mad dogs or other venomous creatures. | The finer of the 2 varieties available, French tarragon is one of the most aristocratic of the culinary herbs. It has a delicate and subtle aroma and flavour of aniseed that could never be mistaken for the robust and rustic aniseed character of fennel. When nibbled raw, French tarragon always has a slight tongue-numbing effect, another way of distinguishing it from its lesser relative, Russian tarragon. | French tarragon is one of the ingredients in the classic *fines herbes* mixture of chervil, chives, tarragon and parsley. But perhaps its most memorable use is with a butter-roasted or poached chicken. One can slip a sprig of the herb into the cavity of the chicken, or chop some leaves and work them with a little butter and then slip this under the breast skin of a roasting chicken, or do both. If you are simmering a chicken with carrots, onions and stock, there should be a generous sprig of tarragon in the herb bundle you add to the stock, and when you make a simple sauce from the stock it should be finished with finely chopped tarragon. >

**tarragon
goes
with**
*chicken
eggs
fish
shallots
beef
tomatoes
mayonnaise
vinegar*

**tarragon
mayonnaise**
*Add a generous
quantity of freshly
chopped tarragon
to Mayonnaise
(made with
Tarragon Vinegar,
see* VINEGAR, *if
possible) and serve
with hardboiled
eggs, poached fish
or warm boiled
potatoes.*

Some say a classic Tartare Sauce should use tarragon vinegar for the may-onnaise. Tarragon is also the essential herb used in Béarnaise Sauce. This rich butter-and-egg-yolk sauce is seen less frequently these days, but it is delicious with rare roasted or grilled beef, even if only enjoyed once a year.

VARIETIES AND SEASON

It is important to notice the differences in leaf size and flavour between French and Russian tarragon.

FRENCH | *A. dracunculus* smells and tastes delicately of aniseed. It is a perennial that dies to the ground in late autumn and reappears in spring. It rarely flowers and never sets seed, so can only be propagated by root division or cuttings. As it is very difficult to strike, it is far better to divide the roots when the plant is dormant and to plant them about a metre apart in a sunny, well-drained spot in the garden. If your plant does not return with vigorous growth in the spring it is safe to assume it does not like its new home. Is it too wet? You can count on fresh French tarragon from September–May.

RUSSIAN | *A. dracunculoides* doesn't even count as a useful herb, as far as I am concerned. It is a much larger and more vigorous plant than French tarragon, with coarser leaves and a rank flavour that reminds me of common grass. It frequently bears tiny yellow–green flowers. Russian tarragon is in no way a substitute for French tarragon. Sadly it is not uncommon to find it sold as French.

SELECTION AND STORAGE

As I have already stressed, the most important thing to watch for in selecting this herb is to ensure you have the real thing. Pinch off a leaf in the green-grocer's and do not buy until the aromatic and delicious flavour convinces you. Also note the tongue-numbing phenomenon.

Do not buy tarragon that has blackened, water-logged leaves or that looks limp or yellowing. Store it, unwashed, in a paper-lined plastic bag in the refrigerator. (The leaves quickly blacken if they are wet.) It will keep well for up to a week like this. Tarragon is not very successful dried, in my opinion. Better, I find, to have made and frozen a roll of tarragon butter and a bottle of tarragon vinegar for the winter months.

PREPARATION

French tarragon leaves are used whole or chopped. Sprigs of tarragon are used to flavour vinegar and poultry. Where it has been used in a stock or sauce it is a good idea to intensify the flavour by adding extra freshly chopped tarragon just before serving.

chicken in the pot with tarragon cream sauce

SERVES 4

1 x 1.8–2 kg corn-fed chicken
1 bay leaf
parsley stalks
1 large sprig tarragon
8 black peppercorns
Chicken Stock ✦ or water
4 carrots, peeled and cut into
    chunks
4 pickling onions
4 turnips, peeled and cut into
    chunks
4 small potatoes, washed
8 cloves garlic
1 tablespoon freshly chopped
    tarragon
1 tablespoon freshly chopped
    parsley

SAUCE

30 g butter
30 g plain flour
juice of ½ lemon
3 egg yolks
½ cup cream
salt
freshly ground black pepper

Wrap chicken in a layer of muslin to keep skin white. Place chicken breast down with herbs and peppercorns in a pot that will take all the vegetables too. Pour on stock to just cover and gently bring to simmering point. Skim, then simmer for 15 minutes. Add vegetables and garlic. Cover pot and simmer for 40 minutes. Test thickest part of thigh with a fine skewer. If juices are still pink, not clear, simmer an extra 10 minutes and then test again. When cooked, remove chicken and vegetables to a plate, cover loosely with buttered foil and keep warm. Ladle off 1 litre poaching liquid and boil rapidly to reduce by half.

To make the sauce, melt butter in a clean saucepan and add flour. Cook 3–4 minutes, stirring, until golden. Gradually stir in reduced, hot poaching liquid, ensuring sauce is smooth after each addition. Bring to a simmer, then reduce heat and simmer gently for 5 minutes. Remove from heat. While sauce is simmering, joint chicken into manageable pieces and arrange on a warmed platter with vegetables around it. Spoon over a ladleful of hot poaching liquid and scatter with half the parsley and tarragon. To finish the sauce, whisk lemon juice, egg yolks and cream together. Add ½ cup hot sauce to egg yolk mixture, then stir well and tip it back into sauce off heat. Stir to thicken. *Do not* boil sauce again or it will curdle. Taste for seasoning and stir in remaining herbs. Serve chicken and vegetables on their platter and offer sauce separately.

poaching liquid Any excess poaching liquid can be frozen for future use, used as the base for a delicious soup the next day or used to make Eggs in Tarragon Jelly (*see* below).

tarragon butter
Chop a quantity of tarragon leaves finely, then work them with unsalted butter, a squeeze of lemon juice, salt and pepper until well blended. (Add parsley, chives and chervil and a scrap of finely chopped garlic too, if you like.) Roll up in baking paper and then in doubled foil and date and freeze.

tomato and tarragon soup
Make a lovely summer soup of ripe tomatoes and Chicken Stock ✦ and flavour it with plenty of tarragon as a change from basil.

eggs in tarragon jelly

SERVES 4

Make this elegant first course when you have leftover stock from Chicken in the Pot with Tarragon Cream Sauce (see above). It is important to use very small eggs – they should be no larger than 45 g (bantam eggs are ideal). Try your local fresh food market. While egg moulds can be bought from speciality shops, small rounded tea cups can be used.

leeks with tarragon
Steam leeks until tender, then halve lengthwise and serve scattered with tarragon and parsley and sprinkled with a few drops of Tarragon Vinegar (see VINEGAR*).*

tarragon chicken
Slip a slice of tarragon butter under the breast skin of a baby chicken before roasting it for 30 minutes at 200°C.

2 egg whites
½ cup finely chopped vegetables
1 tablespoon finely chopped fresh tarragon
2 cups cold tarragon chicken stock
8 gelatine leaves
4 sprigs tarragon
4 × 5-minute boiled eggs, peeled

To clarify the stock, follow the instructions in the Basics section (*see* p. 34), using the first 4 ingredients listed here.

Soak gelatine leaves in cold water for 5 minutes, then squeeze. Drop gelatine into clarified stock and stir to mix. Put a sprig of tarragon into 4 × 150 ml moulds, then pour in stock to 1 cm deep and refrigerate until set. Rest an egg on jelly layer in each mould, then cover with more jelly. Refrigerate until set. To serve, dip each mould into hot water for a few seconds and then unmould very carefully (it's rather tricky). Surround with asparagus spears.

h a m For a change, finish off the moulds with a piece of cooked ham cut to their shape. This helps hold the eggs down and the pink glows prettily through the jelly when they are unmoulded.

flathead poached with milk and tarragon SERVES 4

4 or 8 flathead tail fillets, skinned (about 800 g)
40 g butter
4 generous sprigs tarragon
salt
white pepper
150 ml milk
1 teaspoon chopped small capers
4 tablespoons cream
2 teaspoons finely chopped fresh parsley
1 teaspoon finely chopped fresh tarragon

Preheat oven to 180°C. Butter an ovenproof dish that will hold fish snugly. Add tarragon to dish and place a piece of fish over each sprig. Season and pour milk over. Cover with buttered baking paper and bake for 10–15 minutes, depending on size of fillets. Remove fish to a warmed plate and strain cooking juices into a small saucepan. Reduce juices by half over high heat, then add capers and cream. Bring to a boil and boil hard for 3–4 minutes. Taste for seasoning and stir in parsley and chopped tarragon. Spoon over the fish and serve or allow to cool completely and serve cold.

other recipes

tarragon vinegar *see* VINEGAR

t h y m e The common thyme that many of us grow and love is an 'improved' form of the wild thyme that one encounters growing over Mediterranean hillsides. In its wild version the plant forms dense little cushions, and it is wonderful to walk on sun-crisped thyme and to pull a handful to use with the evening meal. I did this a few years ago in Provence and hope to do it again some day. My hands were scented for hours. Old herb books point out that thyme and lavender often exist side by side, and this was certainly the case on the hillsides I walked on. | Thyme has what I would describe as a 'vigorous' flavour, almost peppery in character, and is for foods that can carry strong flavours. It is one of the essential herbs in the mixture *herbes de Provence*, along with savoury, bay leaves and rosemary. It is also always included in a bouquet garni, used in stock and soup-making. Thyme is usually cooked with foods rather than being added at the end, although the new shoots of lemon thyme can be added to salads. Commercial stuffings and seasoned breadcrumbs are to be avoided as they contain excessive quantities of stale dried thyme that overpowers other ingredients.

VARIETIES AND SEASON

Thyme is another of those herbs of which there are many, many varieties. In my garden I grow lemon thyme, caraway thyme and a pretty variety called silver posy, which has the same flavour as common thyme. Thyme is a perennial and although it can become straggly and benefits from a good cutback in the winter, it is possible to pick it from my garden all year round.

CARAWAY | *Thymus herba-barona* creeps close to the ground. Its leaves are brownish green and the flowers are deep purple–pink. It is very strongly scented with caraway – in fact, it is so strongly scented that I hesitate to use it. Maybe I should try a very little in a bread.

COMMON | *T. vulgaris* has tiny, pointed grey–green leaves. Both the stems and the leaves have a delightful warm and spicy flavour. Common thyme has pink flowers.

LEMON | *T. citriodorus* has rounder, greener leaves than common thyme. The flowers are pink and the whole plant smells and tastes of lemon. It is best used at the end of cooking, so that the fresh lemon scent is not lost.

SELECTION AND STORAGE

Become familiar with the different leaf shapes and colours of common thyme and lemon thyme. I find that too often lemon thyme is offered when one asks for common thyme. Is it because a stalk of lemon thyme looks 'juicier' than the smaller, narrower common thyme? I do not believe common and lemon thyme are interchangeable. Common thyme is much tougher to handle and whereas one can recommend putting tiny shoots of lemon thyme in a salad or bowl of mixed herbs to serve with a fresh cream cheese, I would not do so with common thyme.

Thyme dries very well. Cut it just as it flowers and hang until it is quite dry. Store the entire bunch in an airtight container, or strip the leaves and store the leaves and the stalks separately. As with all dried herbs, only use them for one season. Store fresh thyme, unwashed, in a paper-lined plastic bag in the refrigerator. It will last at least a week before it starts looking bedraggled and drops its leaves.

PREPARATION

I strip the leaves from thyme to scatter over grilled foods, either before grilling (common thyme) or after grilling (lemon thyme). When using common thyme for a bouquet garni, wrap a thread around the bundle of aromatics for easy retrieval.

rabbit baked with thyme and mustard

SERVES 2

The rabbit must be young and tender for this recipe to be successful. Serve it with soft polenta or a rice pilaf.

1 handful fresh common
   thyme
1 young rabbit, jointed
2 cloves garlic, smashed
1 bay leaf
3 tablespoons olive oil
freshly ground black pepper
3 tablespoons Dijon mustard
salt

Strip leaves from thyme and reserve stalks. Put rabbit, garlic, thyme leaves, bay leaf and oil in a bowl, then grind over pepper and refrigerate, covered, overnight.

Next day, preheat oven to 180°C. Rub rabbit with mustard and put into a casserole that has a lid with garlic and thyme stalks. Dribble over oil from bowl, then cover tightly and bake for 40 minutes. Taste and adjust seasoning, if necessary.

thyme with casseroles

Tuck a good sprig of thyme into casseroles of jointed chicken, rabbit or lamb cooked with tomatoes and peppers.

roasted yabbies with thyme oil

SERVES 4

You need live yabbies for this dish. Refer to pp. 769–70 for instructions on how to kill them.

20 yabbies, freshly killed and
   chilled
freshly ground black pepper
1 tablespoon fresh thyme
   leaves
½ cup extra-virgin olive oil

Carefully split each yabby and its shell lengthwise, including head, using a heavy chef's knife. Remove intestinal thread from each half. Arrange yabby halves, flesh-side up, in a single layer on an oiled baking tray. Grind a little pepper over each and scatter with thyme. Paint flesh with oil. Leave yabbies at room temperature for up to 1 hour before cooking. Preheat oven or griller to maximum. Grill or roast yabbies for 4 minutes until flesh is just firm. Drizzle with a little more oil before serving with sea salt and a bowl of lemon wedges.

fines herbes

Add lemon thyme leaves to a fines herbes mixture to scatter over fish.

t o m a t o e s

t o m a t o e s Native to Central and South America, the tomato (*Lycopersicon esculentum*) joins the long list of foods brought back to Europe by the Spanish explorers and colonists in the early sixteenth century. The word 'tomato' is derived from its Mexican name, *tomatl*. | As the tomato is cousin to deadly nightshade, the potato and tobacco, it was regarded at first with some suspicion by the Provençals and the Italians, who found it attractive to look at and an effective deterrent against ants and mosquitoes but couldn't quite come at eating it. It was not until the late sixteenth century that the tomato became their treasured love apple, *pomme d'amour*, and golden apple, *pomodoro*. It took another 200 years for the tomato to become appreciated in northern Europe. The British remained suspicious for much longer. | The first tomatoes were probably yellow, and the wild tomato still found in Mexico and Central America resembles our cherry tomato. Today tomato varieties are legion, and probably no other ingredient has had as much written about it, latterly bemoaning the quality of the tomatoes in general commerce. >

In Australia, thanks to a significant influx of Mediterranean migrants, tomato-growing and eating has been a serious matter for many for the last 50 years. We, too, have trays of tasteless tomatoes in our supermarkets and greengrocers, but alongside these have always been sun-ripened tomatoes from Murray Bridge and the Riverland, with bulging curves or meaty globes. Backyard crops have also offered wider choice. Older varieties such as rouge de marmande and grosse lisse are still grown by some farmers alongside the less tasty, hydroponically grown, perfect product, but they say that the general public rejects the individual look of these tomatoes. Not all tasteless tomatoes are hydroponically grown, but I have not yet tasted a hydroponic tomato that compares in richness of flavour with a well-bred, sun-ripened tomato. It is up to us to reverse the trend, or we will be the losers.

Our problem is that too few of us have had the chance to do a comparative taste test of varieties. Instead, we have been led to believe that a neat row of evenly shaped round tomatoes, all uniformly red, is a better alternative to making a selection from a box of uneven, perhaps lumpy specimens, some red, some half-red and some quite green. But what is missed out on is individuality and, above all, taste. Thankfully, there is renewed interest in growing older varieties (called 'heirloom' tomatoes). Some of these are as beautiful as jewels, with glowing gold–green, striped skins or deep-red skins slashed with gold, or dark plum–red or glowing gold skins. Their flavour is a thrilling surprise – acid yet sweet – and they have tender skins and are juicy and more or less meaty, depending on character. Digger's Seeds at Dromana, Victoria, will be happy to sell you seeds of these tomatoes through their mail-order service.

My favourite breakfast in late summer and early autumn is thickly sliced tomato on hot, hard, buttered toast, sprinkled with a flake or two of sea salt and a grind of fresh pepper. This is the best time for tomatoes, whether bumpy, round, egg-shaped or miniature or yellow or red. Look out for the globular and heavy-in-the-hand beef or oxheart tomatoes – when fully ripe these are sensational. (Outside tomato season, cans of peeled or crushed tomatoes and tomato paste are excellent products to have in the pantry cupboard. They are far superior to watery, pale and rock-hard fresh tomatoes.) Wooden crates of richly red fruit are offered for trifling sums at the fresh food markets during February and March, and this is the moment for making tomato sauce or relish in quantity. This tradition is still upheld in many European households and it can be a wonderful way to catch up with an old friend. An afternoon's conversation as you core and press tomatoes leaves you both in touch with each other's lives – as well as having the bonus of jars of relish or bottles of sauce. Together with pans of concentrated tomato paste, rows of halved tomatoes drying in the sun are a common sight in the south of Italy. I once saw a movie where women

tomatoes
go
with

olive oil
sea salt
pepper
basil
wine vinegar
mild onions
garlic
toast
breadcrumbs
sweet peppers
fresh cheeses
parmesan cheese
cheddar cheese
goat's cheese
cucumber
chives
parsley
oregano
eggs
cream
sour cream
yoghurt
shellfish
fish
polenta
chillies
turmeric
ginger
mustard seeds

spread their *conserva* directly on the metal roof, where it dried very quickly in the fierce heat. The leathery paste was then scraped into jars. I wondered if the roof was clean and free of rust!

VARIETIES AND SEASON

Several of the heirloom varieties are being seen in our better fruit shops now, and enterprising growers delivered boxes of sensational striped tomatoes to me in the summer of 1995. However, it would be misleading to suggest that the average fruit shop is selling tomatoes by named variety. They are not. And where tomatoes are described by name it can be confusing, as many of the names seem to vary from State to State, even shop to shop. Sometimes it is more relevant to know where or how a tomato was grown rather than its name. Ask the advice of your greengrocer when selecting tomatoes for sauce or salad.

Having said that, heirloom varieties that have delighted me have been tigerella (red and yellow stripes), black Russian (red and dark-red stripes), colossal yellow (as the name suggests) and brandywine (a dark-red, bumpy tomato). I love rouge de marmande and have several plants in my garden, and there is a heavy egg-shaped tomato that is delicious; it is not a roma but I do not know its name. And even the smallest courtyard garden can support tomato plants in a tub. Cherry tomatoes crop prolifically and look lovely also.

Most tomatoes belong to one of 5 loosely defined groups – beef, cherry, hollow, plum and round – each of which has its specific uses. Large-fruited, thick-walled *beef* tomatoes are best for slicing into memorable tomato salads, for making bruschetta and for grilling. Small-fruited, very sweet *cherry* tomatoes are for nibbling by the handful. The tiny Tim, one of the smaller varieties, is particularly good. *Hollow* tomatoes have thick walls and hollow compartments from which the seeds are easily removed, making them an obvious choice for stuffing. The golden filler is a yellow variety. Elongated *plum* or egg tomatoes are great for making sauces (they are often referred to as paste tomatoes) and are the best variety for drying. The roma is a plum tomato. *Round* tomatoes, which are medium-sized, are for general-purpose cooking (sauces, soups and stews). The grosse lisse is a fine example.

Tomatoes are in the shops all year round. As already stated, they are best in late summer and autumn, when ripened by the sun. However, due to Australia's range of climates, reasonable to good tomatoes are grown outside in Queensland and Western Australia in autumn, winter and spring. It is worth knowing that tomatoes grown outdoors have twice the amount of vitamin C as hothouse tomatoes. Avoid glasshouse or hothouse tomatoes. I find hydroponically grown tomatoes disappointing in flavour.

SELECTION AND STORAGE

Treat with suspicion advice to buy tomatoes that are well formed, of uniform colour and free from blemishes. Some of the finest tomatoes will be half-ripened when picked and may well be lopsided or lumpy or even have a scar where they have grown pressed against a stalk. Provided a tomato variety has good flavour and has been grown with full sun, it will be a great tomato!

Select tomatoes according to when you wish to eat them and how you intend to prepare them. For eating *raw* that night in a salad, select the ripest, firmest and best beef or bumpy variety. Buy several extra tomatoes that are still a little green at the shoulders, so that you can repeat the salad a couple of days later. Greenish tomatoes will attain full colour and flavour if left for a day or so at room temperature and will both ripen and soften on your kitchen window-sill. For making *sauce* or tomato *soup*, buy richly red tomatoes (they are even better if they are softening somewhat). Tomatoes are often labelled 'for cooking' and, provided they are not split, leaking or mouldy, are a good buy. Even if you had no intention of making tomato soup for dinner, this is the day to do it!

Tomatoes should be bought in small quantities, so that they can be stored at room temperature. Only refrigerate tomatoes if you have bought a large number and sauce-making has to wait for a day or so, or if your own tomatoes have all suddenly ripened on the vine.

At the end of the season most vines will carry a good number of mature green tomatoes that will no longer ripen. They will benefit from a few days inside, where they will develop further flavour before you turn them into green tomato pickle or relish or fry them for breakfast or supper.

Dried tomatoes can either be fully dried or semi-dried. If semi-dried, they will only keep for a week or so, refrigerated. If fully dried and covered with olive oil, the tomatoes will keep for months. Commercially available fully dried tomatoes vary a lot. Some are very leathery and need to be rehydrated with a little hot water before using. Others are a delicious chewy snack straight from the jar. If you make your own you can control the dryness.

PREPARATION

No Mediterranean cook would even consider peeling or seeding a tomato intended for a salad or raw tomato sauce. And yet even the late, great Jane Grigson advised that tomatoes be peeled before adding them to a salad. This advice is only relevant if supplies are limited to tomatoes with thick and tough skins: this is not the case in Australia.

When a tomato is to cook in a sauce with other ingredients it *is* important to remove the skin and seeds; the skin otherwise ends up as tiny rolled fragments in the sauce and cooked tomato seeds are bitter. If making a tomato sauce that will be sieved later, I seed the tomatoes but leave the skins on. A food mill or sieve will trap all skin effectively and one has the bonus of its flavour and colour. There are ways to peel and seed tomatoes, each method suiting different forms of preparation.

sauce vierge for fish
Season diced ripe tomato with salt, pepper and a little wine vinegar and add a generous quantity of herbs and an even more generous quantity of barely warmed extra-virgin olive oil. Serve as a sauce with grilled fish. I like it spooned over fried eggs!

TO PEEL AND SEED | **Boiling water** This method is ideal for tomatoes that are to be added to stews or made into sauce. It is particularly useful when preparing a lot of tomatoes. Cut a cross in the bottom of the tomato and cut out the core from the stem end. Bring a saucepan of water to a boil, then dip the tomato into the water for 30 seconds and remove quickly to a bowl of cold water. Strip off the skin, then halve the tomato and squeeze it firmly into a strainer resting over a bowl. Return any tomato juice in the bowl to the sauce or soup you are making and discard the seeds. **Flame** Use this method when preparing a couple of tomatoes for a sauce or stews, but only if you have a gas flame. Cut a cross in the bottom of the tomato and cut out the core from the stem end. Spear the tomato on a long-handled fork and turn over a gas flame for a minute or so until the skin is a little blistered. Strip off the skin, then halve the tomato and squeeze the seeds into a strainer resting over a bowl. Reserve the juice and discard the seeds. **Peeler** This is the best method if raw, diced, peeled tomato is needed. Using an asparagus or ordinary vegetable peeler, cut the skin from the tomato using a loose-wristed, zigzagging motion down the tomato, following its curves. Halve the tomato and with the handle of a teaspoon scoop out the seeds and jelly from each cavity.

TO DICE | Peel the tomato with a vegetable peeler for preference, then cut in half. Cut each half horizontally into 2–3 slices, depending on the size of the tomato and how small you want the pieces to be. Cut through the stacked slices, then turn them 90 degrees and cut through the slices again to form dice.

FOR STUFFING | The inner walls of a peeled, halved tomato can be hollowed out for stuffing. Scoop out the seeds and jelly from each cavity with the handle of a teaspoon.

TO DRY | Egg-shaped tomatoes are best for drying, and can be dried in the sun or oven. Whichever method you are using, halve the tomatoes lengthwise, then remove the seeds, if desired, and sprinkle the cut surface with sea salt. When thoroughly dry, or semi-dried if that is what you prefer, layer the tomatoes with fresh basil, rosemary or thyme in sterilised containers and fill with olive oil. Press down hard to release any trapped air. Unpeeled garlic cloves, a tiny chilli or capers can be added, too, if you like. **Sun-dried** Dry the salted tomatoes on wire cake racks in full sun away from ants. For truly sun-dried tomatoes you will need 2–3 days of sunshine and the tomatoes must be brought in each evening. **Oven-dried** Heat the oven to 60°C. Put the salted halves on wire cake racks and place the racks directly on the shelves of the oven. Leave for at least 10 hours, but check after 8 hours.

fresh tomato sauce
SERVES 4

This kitchen staple can be made in a few minutes in a saucepan on top of the stove or it can take more than an hour in a moderate oven. The oven method results in a richer-flavoured sauce, the top of the stove is ideal for an instant meal of pasta. This sauce freezes beautifully.

If you leave the skins on your tomatoes as I do, you will need a food mill for passing the sauce. (For a quick sauce, dice the tomato and forget about the food mill.) If you have skinned the tomatoes, a food processor will do a fine job. Your sauce will be orange and very smooth. Mine will be more textured and red.

500 g ripe tomatoes, cored
  and seeded
1 onion, sliced
2 cloves garlic, sliced
½ cup olive oil
salt
freshly ground black pepper

Tumble tomato halves, onion and garlic with oil and put into a saucepan or spread in a baking dish into which vegetables will fit without too much extra space. Cook, tightly covered, on top of stove over a moderate heat for about 15 minutes or bake at 180°C until tomato halves have collapsed, skins are wrinkled and golden brown and juices are flowing (this should take at least 1 hour). When tomato and onion are quite soft, press everything through the coarsest disc of a food mill. Season to taste.

For a smoother sauce, pass mixture through food mill's medium disc. For a thicker sauce, reduce sauce in a pan over a simmer mat, stirring frequently. For a thinner sauce, add ½ cup red wine, water or meat stock. **herbs and spices** Add fresh herbs: basil, oregano or rosemary and/or a bay leaf. If using oregano or rosemary, strip the leaves from the stalks and cook them with the sauce. When using a bay leaf, remove it before passing the sauce through the mill. If using basil, tear or cut the leaves and stir them into the sauce after you have pressed it through the food mill. You could include a whole fresh chilli for a spicy sauce. Remove it before passing the sauce through the food mill, though. **aromatics** You can include a small amount of bacon, a carrot, some celery and/or some red or white wine from the beginning of the cooking time. As carrots and celery develop lovely sweetness after long baking, I would

tomato salad
Thickly slice fantastic tomatoes, drizzle them generously with extra-virgin olive oil and leave for an hour. Add flakes of sea salt, freshly ground black pepper and torn basil leaves and then taste the juice. If it needs further acid, add a little red-wine vinegar. A popular addition is paper-thin slices of mild onion.

have a preference for the oven-baked method if I were including them in my sauce. **other uses** Add this sauce to Beurre Blanc ✎, as much or as little as you like; whisk olive oil into it to make a tomato vinaigrette for shellfish; or use it as is to cook button mushrooms or small onions for an antipasto selection.

bruschetta
Toss sliced or chopped tomato in extra-virgin olive oil and add a few torn basil leaves. Pile onto grilled sourdough (or other good bread) that has been rubbed with a cut clove of garlic for this delicious Italian appetiser.

kathy's tomato relish   MAKES 3 LITRES

I don't know why this is a relish rather than a sauce but it tastes good! As it has no onion, it keeps well for at least a year.

1 tablespoon cloves
1 tablespoon black peppercorns
2 tablespoons whole allspice
5 kg tomatoes, roughly chopped
6 cloves garlic, finely chopped
1 tablespoon ground ginger
½ teaspoon cayenne pepper
30 g salt
600 ml white-wine vinegar
1 kg white sugar

Tie cloves, peppercorns and allspice in a square of muslin. Put all ingredients except sugar into a large stockpot. Bring to a boil and boil steadily for 1 hour, stirring from time to time. Add sugar and continue to boil, stirring every 20 minutes or so, for a further 2 hours. Remove muslin bag, pressing it well before discarding it. Pass relish through coarse disc of a food mill and, using a funnel, bottle at once into hot, sterilised ✎, dry bottles. Cap and allow to cool before storing.

green tomato relish   MAKES 1 LITRE

1.5 kg green tomatoes
2 large onions
½ teaspoon salt
1 tablespoon Dijon mustard
1 tablespoon garam masala
½ teaspoon cayenne pepper
1 teaspoon mustard seeds
pinch of ground cloves
pinch of ground turmeric
100 ml cider vinegar or white-wine vinegar
100 g white sugar
1 teaspoon cornflour

Thinly slice the tomatoes and onions, then place all ingredients except cornflour in a large stockpot. Bring to a boil, then lower heat and cook, uncovered, for 1¼ hours. Mix cornflour to a cream with a little water. Remove a ladleful of hot liquid from pot and add to cornflour. Stir, then quickly add mixture to pot, giving it a good stir, so that liquid thickens evenly. Cook for 15 minutes, then spoon into hot, sterilised ✎ jars and seal at once.

tomatoes provençale   SERVES 4

Each Provençal cook has his or her favourite version of this dish.

4 tablespoons extra-virgin
    olive oil

4 large ripe tomatoes, halved
    crosswise

salt

freshly ground black pepper

4 cloves garlic, finely chopped

4 tablespoons coarse
    breadcrumbs (sourdough or
    other good bread)

4 tablespoons freshly chopped
    parsley

Heat half the oil in a frying pan and place tomato halves cut-side down in hot oil. Sizzle for 5 minutes, then reduce heat for 10 minutes. Carefully turn tomato halves and cook a further 10 minutes. Remove tomato halves to a hot plate, then season with salt and pepper. Add remaining oil to hot pan and quickly toss garlic, breadcrumbs and parsley until breadcrumbs are a little crisp. Spoon over tomatoes and serve at once.

autumn salad with red and yellow tomatoes

SERVES 4

This salad is assembled in a few minutes, with nothing more exotic than fine tomatoes, choice green leaves, a couple of still-warm, hardboiled eggs, olives, fresh mozzarella (sold as bocconcini or milk cherries, if bite-sized) and crunchy croutons. Bocconcini cheese is sold stored in brine. Always check the 'use-by' date and never buy out-of-date cheese. It should smell sweet, not sour. The croutons are cut from yesterday's breadstick, not last week's. They can be stored for a day in either a freezer bag or a tightly closed jar. Cut your herbs at the last minute. That wonderful aroma of freshly chopped parsley starts to disappear within minutes. Keep some in a bowl in the refrigerator and smell it an hour later to see if I am telling the truth.

2 eggs

4 bocconcini or 8 milk cherries

extra-virgin olive oil

freshly ground black pepper

2 handfuls salad leaves,
    washed and dried

1 teaspoon wine vinegar

sea salt

8 breadstick slices

1 clove garlic

4 best-quality red and yellow
    tomatoes, sliced

2 tablespoons freshly chopped
    fresh herbs (parsley, basil)

16 olives

Boil eggs for 6 minutes. Tap egg shells as you lift them from hot water, then run under cold tap to peel. Remove cheese from brine and pat dry on kitchen paper. Slice cheese if large, then roll in a little oil and grind on some pepper. Dress salad leaves with vinegar, 2 tablespoons oil, salt and pepper. Brush breadstick slices lightly with oil and grill quickly. While still warm, stroke one side with cut garlic clove. Slice eggs while still warm and gently toss with all ingredients. Prefer a flat, wide platter, so that your guests don't have to brutalise the salad in order to choose a little of everything.

snapper with tomato

Put a whole snapper into an oiled baking dish and surround it with Fresh Tomato Sauce (see p. 709) and maybe some olives. Bake for 30 minutes at 200°C – cover the dish with foil for the first 20 minutes, then uncover and add freshly chopped herbs for the last 10 minutes.

baked lamb and tomato

Toss slices of leftover roast lamb or chicken with Fresh Tomato Sauce (see p. 709) and spoon into an ovenproof dish. Scatter with breadcrumbs, drizzle with a little olive oil and bake at 180°C until golden and crusty on top.

tomato soup with basil and croutons

SERVES 6

60 g butter
1 onion, sliced
1.5 kg very ripe tomatoes, seeded
1 litre Chicken Stock
2 tablespoons potato flour
salt
freshly ground black pepper
day-old breadstick, sliced
olive oil
1 clove garlic
2 tablespoons roughly chopped basil leaves

Melt butter and gently sauté onion in a large saucepan until softened. Roughly chop tomatoes. Add tomato to pan, then cover and cook gently until tomato is very soft, about 20 minutes. Pass tomato through medium disc of a food mill and return to pan. Add stock and heat to simmering point. Mix potato flour to a smooth cream with a little cold water. Stir a good ladleful of soup into potato flour mixture and return to pan. Stir until soup returns to a simmer. Cook for a further 15 minutes and adjust seasoning. Pass through finest disc of a food mill if there are too many fragments for your liking. For the smoothest texture of all, whizz it in the blender.

Grill breadstick slices brushed with oil on one side and swipe with cut garlic clove while warm. Return soup to boiling point, then ladle into bowls, scatter with basil and offer garlic croutons separately.

gazpacho

SERVES 6–8

The quality of the tomatoes, sherry vinegar and oil is what makes a splendid rather than an ordinary gazpacho. I use a meat mincer for the vegetables, but a food processor will do. The texture should be coarse but there should not be large lumps.

1.5 kg ripe tomatoes, chopped
200 g Lebanese *or* long cucumber, chopped
150 g red pepper, chopped
2 cloves garlic
100 g crustless sourdough bread
2 cups cold water
3 teaspoons salt
freshly ground black pepper or Tabasco
½ cup sherry vinegar
½ cup extra-virgin olive oil

Mince or process vegetables, garlic and bread and transfer to a large bowl. Stir in water, salt, pepper and vinegar. Refrigerate for at least 1 hour for bread to swell and flavours to blend. Just before serving, stir in oil and taste for seasoning. The soup should have quite a tang to it.

fried green tomato

Dip thickly sliced green tomato into lightly whisked egg and then polenta and fry in olive oil until golden and crunchy. Great with bacon or sausages or just as they are.

pan catalan

To make the Spanish version of bruschetta, toast or grill thick slices of good bread and rub both sides with a cut clove of garlic. Halve a ripe and juicy tomato and massage it into the bread. There should be little left of the tomato but the spent skin. Drizzle with extra-virgin olive oil and sprinkle with a little sea salt and freshly ground pepper.

tomato and mustard tart

SERVES 4

This tart can be made with either home-made or commercial puff pastry.

1 quantity Puff Pastry
1 tablespoon Dijon mustard
2 tablespoons finely chopped
    shallots
10–12 thick slices tomato,
    seeded
sea salt
freshly ground black pepper
extra-virgin olive oil
1 tablespoon chopped basil

Preheat oven to 220°C. Roll pastry out to make a 20 cm round 5 mm thick, transfer to a baking tray and prick all over with a fork. Spread pastry with mustard and bake for 10 minutes. Scatter with shallots and arrange tomato on pastry, then season and drizzle with oil. Bake for a further 10 minutes. Serve scattered with basil and accompanied by a leafy salad.

buttery tomato
Cook thickly sliced tomato quite gently in butter in a covered frying pan. Season and serve on hot toast.

other recipes

artichokes with tomato vinaigrette *see* ARTICHOKES
barbecued belly pork with tomato and maple syrup glaze *see* PORK
bocconcini, tomato and basil salad *see* BASIL
fennel and tomato fish soup *see* FENNEL
fettuccine with bug meat and roasted tomato sauce *see* BUGS
greek country salad *see* CHEESE
mexican ceviche *see* LEMONS AND LIMES
okra with tomatoes *see* OKRA
pappa al pomodoro *see* BREAD
peperonata *see* PEPPERS AND CHILLIES
pork sausages with sage and tomato *see* SAUSAGES
prawns with ginger, spring onion and tomato *see* GINGER
ratatouille *see* ZUCCHINI AND SQUASH
tripe with tomato and lots of parsley *see* TRIPE

tongue

t **o n g u e**   Young cooks have mostly never bought a tongue. Some recoil in horror when faced with the physical reality of a calf's, ox or lamb's tongue. There is absolutely no doubt what it is, whereas these cooks may not quite realise that a chop is in fact one of the ribs of a lamb! | If you can get past this prejudice you will find that tongue is delicate in flavour, soft and melting of texture when served hot and smooth and creamy when cold. Cold tongue marries particularly well with pickled cucumber, pickled walnuts, anchovies, capers and the like, and hot tongue is excellent with the rich, smooth and slightly sweet flavours of a well-made winy sauce spiked with sour cherries or raisins, for example. My speciality of Pickled Watermelon Rind (*see* MELONS) is excellent with cold tongue dishes. | The other virtues of tongue are that it is inexpensive and simple (although long) to cook. Ox or calf's tongues are ideal as main courses or as part of a selection of cold dishes. Lamb's tongue, being so much smaller, is excellent as a first course or chopped into stuffings. The memorable Italian dish *bollito misto* (literally 'mixed boil') usually includes tongue along with chicken, beef or veal brisket, a pig's head and sausage. I include a recipe for *bollito misto* in *Stephanie's Feasts and Stories* and heartily recommend the dish to all adventurous cooks. >

Pickled and pressed tongue is very much part of my family memories of Christmas, and our 'potted meat' or brawn always contained pickled tongue as well as inexpensive cuts of pork.

VARIETIES AND SEASON

Calf's tongue is the most tender; it is also the most desirable of all tongues as it has the richest flavour. *Ox* tongue is also good, but if very large it can be coarse-textured. *Lamb's* tongue is as tender as butter, but can be difficult to peel. *Pig's* tongue is available at Asian butchers, but is usually not seen in the average suburban butcher's shop. Its flavour is stronger than a calf's or lamb's tongue.

Tongue is sold fresh or pickled by the butcher. Pickled tongue is also available smoked. Tongue is available all year but because of limited demand not all butchers will have it in stock, so you may need to order it.

SELECTION AND STORAGE

An average calf's tongue will feed 2–3 for a main course and an average ox tongue will feed 4, while 2 lamb's tongues serve 1 as a first course.

Tongue is only pink if it has been pickled. 'Fresh' tongue still tastes delicious when cooked but is a grey–brown colour rather than the dramatic pink of a pickled tongue. The pickling or brining intensifies the flavour, and I prefer tongue this way. If you want a pickled tongue, you will need to order it from your butcher 2 days ahead. To be properly pickled, a piece of meat should be immersed in brine for at least 8 hours. Sometimes the meat is injected with brine more or less on demand. This is a lot less satisfactory as one is very likely to find that the brine has only started to penetrate the flesh, resulting in mottled meat.

Refrigerate tongue, freed of all wrappings, on a plate and cover with plastic film. Cook within 24 hours of purchase. A cooked, skinned tongue can be kept submerged in its poaching liquid for 2–3 days. A pressed tongue set in jelly will keep for at least a week refrigerated.

PREPARATION AND COOKING

Tongue must always be poached to be tender, even if it is to be glazed and finished on the barbecue or in the oven, and its thick skin must be removed after cooking. The skin comes away very easily while the tongue is still warm but clings tenaciously if it has been allowed to cool completely.

TO POACH AND SKIN | If pickled, rinse the tongue well and put it in a saucepan of cold water, then bring it to simmering point. Tip off this water (and with it any excess salt) and start the final cooking process.

tongue goes with

pickled cucumbers
capers
parsley
mayonnaise
fresh tomato sauce
horseradish
pickled walnuts
anchovies
garlic
sour cherries
raisins
redcurrant jelly
sweet peppers
fortified wine
mustard
onions

Put 1–2 large tongues or 6 lamb's tongues into a large saucepan with 1 sliced onion, 1 sliced carrot, ½ celery stick, 2 garlic cloves, 1 bay leaf, a sprig of thyme and a few parsley stalks. Barely cover with meat stock (veal or chicken for preference) or water, then add ¼ cup white wine, a few black peppercorns and 2 cloves. Bring to simmering point and cook very gently for at least 2 hours for lamb's tongues and up to 3 hours for a calf's or ox tongue. (It is *very important* that the water barely moves during the cooking process. If the water is allowed to boil the tongue will toughen.) Check for tenderness after 2 hours: a fine skewer must slip through the tongue without any resistance before the tongue can be deemed cooked.

Once cooked, allow the tongues to cool in the poaching liquid a little until it is possible to handle them. Remove a cooled tongue and strip off the skin, running the tongue under cold water if it is still very hot, and then trim off any gristly bits. Return the skinned tongue to the warm poaching liquid at once and continue to skin any remaining tongues. When all the tongues are skinned, lift them into a clean container. Bring the poaching liquid back to a boil and boil for 5 minutes, then taste for salt and pepper and strain over the tongues.

salsa verde

MAKES 1 CUP

pesto tongue
Spread Pesto (see BASIL) or a paste of finely chopped red pepper bound with a little olive oil on thinly sliced cooked tongue.

Thinly sliced cold tongue spread with this beautiful green sauce is a very delicious summer party dish if your guests have sophisticated palates. It also makes a good pasta sauce on its own.

1 thick slice stale bread
4 tablespoons olive oil
3 pickled cucumbers (not dill pickles)
2 cloves garlic
1 tablespoon capers
2 anchovies, chopped
1 tablespoon lemon juice
1 large handful parsley, washed, dried and finely chopped
freshly ground black pepper

Soak bread in 2 tablespoons of the oil for 30 minutes. Crumble bread and blend in a food processor very briefly. Remove to a bowl. Roughly chop cucumbers, garlic, capers and anchovies in the food processor with lemon juice, then mix into bread. Stir in parsley and remaining oil. The sauce should be very green and quite thick. Taste and adjust seasoning. Use within 24 hours to enjoy the best flavour and texture.

cumberland sauce

MAKES ⅔ CUP

If the palates of your guests are resolutely Anglo-Saxon, try cold sliced tongue with this traditional English sauce. Cumberland sauce keeps well but may need to be warmed a little if it has set too firmly in the refrigerator.

zest of 1 orange
1 teaspoon Dijon mustard
4 tablespoons redcurrant, crabapple or quince jelly
white pepper
¼ teaspoon ground ginger
½ cup port or Victorian muscat or tokay

Put zest into a small saucepan, cover with cold water and slowly bring to a boil. Strain, discard water and dry zest on kitchen paper. Put zest into a bowl with mustard, jelly and spices, then stand bowl over simmering water and stir until quite smooth. Add wine and simmer for 5 minutes. Serve cold, but not refrigerated.

pressed tongue

SERVES 8

To make this dish the tongues should be poached in stock, which is then used to set the tongue. As you may want to display your turned-out pressed tongue, the stock must be firmly jellied. To test if the poaching stock is sufficiently jellied, place a little in the refrigerator and check it after an hour. If it is liquid or wobbly you will need to add gelatine✎.

1 clove garlic, very finely chopped
1 teaspoon grated orange zest
½ cup freshly chopped parsley
1 litre well-jellied stock
3 pickled calf's tongues, poached and skinned
3 slices leg ham (5 mm thick)

Mix garlic, zest and parsley. Pour a little stock into a 1.5 litre terrine mould to film the base, then sprinkle with a little parsley mixture and refrigerate until set (about 30 minutes). Wrap each tongue in a slice of ham. Put a tongue into the terrine mould with its heel hard against one end. Place second tongue with its heel under tip of first tongue, then position third tongue with its

heel under tip of second tongue. When sliced, there should be roughly equal amounts of meat and jelly. Scatter parsley mixture over tongue and pour over stock. Keep tongues submerged by inverting the terrine lid or by covering with a double layer of foil and using light weights (tins or packets) until stock has set. Refrigerate until set, about 6 hours or overnight.

Quickly run mould under hot water, being careful not to wet jelly, and loosen sides with a knife. Turn out and slice. Offer Salsa Verde (*see* p. 716), the Italian condiment *mostarda di Cremona* or your own pickles.
variations Omit the ham. Set a layer of jelly on a wide meat platter. Arrange slices of cooked tongue on it, then glaze with more nearly-set jelly. Scatter with parsley mixture just as you set the platter on the table.

tongue in mustard cream

Mix sour cream, Dijon mustard, lots of parsley and a finely sliced spring onion or shallot and add diced cooked tongue. Serve in the crisp inner leaves of a butterhead or mignonette lettuce or surrounded by thickly sliced and oiled tomato.

tongue in tomato sauce

Toss diced cooked tongue with Fresh Tomato Sauce (see TOMATOES), *herbs and green peppercorns.*

margaret's potted tongue

MAKES 2½ CUPS

If you have leftover poached tongue you can halve these ingredients.

1 pickled tongue, poached and
   skinned
120 g softened butter
1 tablespoon Dijon mustard
2 teaspoons Worcestershire
   sauce
1 teaspoon ground ginger
¼ teaspoon freshly grated
   nutmeg
¼ teaspoon ground cloves
dash of cayenne pepper
salt

Blend tongue to a paste in a food processor, then transfer to a bowl. Process butter until smooth and very soft, then add mustard, Worcestershire sauce, spices and salt. Tip butter into bowl and mix well. (For a smoother blend without any pink flecks, return tongue to food processor and mix with butter.) Check seasoning. Spoon mixture into pots and refrigerate until firm. If sealed with a layer of clarified butter ✔, potted tongue will keep for at least a week in the refrigerator.

tongue in piquant cream

Use 8 pickled and poached lamb's tongues instead of belly pork when making Belly Pork in a Piquant Cream Sauce (see PORK*). Halve them lengthwise and warm through in a lightly oiled frying pan while crisping diced bacon.*

smoked tongue with red pepper sauce

SERVES 4

As for all pickled tongues, smoked tongue is rinsed well and brought to a simmer in a saucepan of cold water to rid it of excess salt. In this recipe the tongue does not need to be poached as well, since it is cooked in stock.

1 smoked ox tongue
1 carrot, chopped
1 onion
4 cloves
1 stick celery, sliced
3 stalks parsley
1 sprig thyme
1 bay leaf
3 cloves garlic, peeled
2 tablespoons red-wine
   vinegar
1 teaspoon mustard seeds
Veal or Chicken Stock ✔
3 red peppers, halved and
   seeded
40 g butter
2 tablespoons plain flour
1 teaspoon Dijon mustard
½ teaspoon paprika
freshly ground black pepper

Place tongue in a large saucepan with all ingredients down to and including mustard seeds and cover with stock. Bring to simmering point, then cover and cook very gently for 2½ hours. Check tongue is tender by piercing it with a skewer – there should be no resistance. If not tender, simmer a further 30 minutes and check again. Add red peppers and simmer for 30 minutes until perfectly tender. Remove peppers to a blender with onion and purée with ½ cup cooking liquid until smooth. Set aside. Strain remaining cooking liquid and set aside 1½ cups for the sauce. Remove tongue to a basin, then pour over remaining cooking liquid and allow to cool a little. Skin tongue and return to basin of cooking liquid.

   Melt butter in a saucepan, then stir in flour and cook for 2 minutes. Whisk in reserved 1½ cups cooking liquid and puréed peppers. Bring to a boil and add mustard and paprika, then taste for seasoning and grind in pepper, if necessary. Slice tongue, spoon sauce over and serve immediately.

braised tongue with madeira sauce SERVES 4–6

For this dish it is essential that the tongues be cooked in stock, preferably veal, as the braising liquid forms the basis of the sauce. If you have any preserved sour cherries or sliced home-pickled plums, the fruit can be dropped into the sauce after the butter has been added.

2 calf's *or* 1 ox tongue
  (pickled *or* fresh)
1.5 litres Veal Stock
4 shallots *or* 1 small onion,
  finely chopped
8 button mushrooms, chopped
60 g butter
1 tablespoon plain flour
½ cup white wine
½ cup Madeira, tokay *or* port

Preheat oven to 160°C. Put tongues into a baking dish that holds them quite snugly and pour over sufficient stock to cover (you may not need the entire quantity). Press buttered baking paper down onto surface, then cover tightly and cook for at least 2 hours or until tongues are tender. Remove tongues and allow to cool a little, then skin. Set tongues aside in a basin, covered with one-third of the braising juices, and keep warm while finishing the sauce.

Sauté shallots and mushrooms in half the butter for several minutes until softened. Add flour and cook for 2 minutes, stirring. Pour on both wines and bring to a boil, stirring. Bubble until liquid has reduced by three-quarters. Add remaining braising juices and bring sauce to a simmer. Alow it to simmer gently until reduced by one-third. Taste for seasoning (add any home-made pickle at this point) and whisk in the remaining butter. Remove tongues from basin and slice thickly. Arrange on a heated platter and spoon sauce over. Serve with smooth mashed potato.

warm tongue salad
Serve sliced cooked tongue tossed with warm potatoes, spring onions and olive oil as a warm salad.

tongue with hummus
Stir diced cooked tongue through Hummus (see CHICK PEAS) *and add plenty of parsley.*

t r i p e The introductory remarks I made relating to tongue could apply equally as well to tripe, I fear. Few young cooks have any knowledge of or much desire to get to know this ingredient. Only eyeballs seem to strike more terror into the hearts and minds than does tripe! Tripe also has an image problem as the word has come to mean 'rubbish' or 'nonsense', and it is associated with northern-England nostalgia – flat caps, poverty and grime. │ One doesn't even see tripe very often these days. Tripe is the lining of the 4 stomachs of cud-chewing animals. Classified as offal, it is usually sold parboiled and bleached, and has often been frozen at the abattoir. Devotees feel that the bleaching and parcooking of tripe removes much of its flavour, its hint of 'danger' as one enthusiast explained to me! It is possible to order cleaned but uncooked tripe, which then requires up to 8 hours' cooking. │ Tripe haters speak disparagingly of its slippery texture, which is just the thing tripe lovers enjoy, along with its mild flavour and ability to meld with sticky meats and other flavours to result in delicious saucy dishes. >

Uncooked tripe is used to make such classic dishes as *tripes à la mode de Caen*. Try it in Normandy would be my advice, or at the bistro Pharamond behind Les Halles in Paris. There, piping hot pieces of tripe and calf's feet in sticky, cider-flavoured meat juices with chunks of carrot and potato are brought to the table in a terracotta dish sitting over a charcoal burner. Very rustic and very delicious. It illustrates one thing about tripe: it must be served very hot! Another famous French tripe speciality is *pieds et paquets*, where lamb's trotters are braised with bacon-and-garlic-stuffed parcels of sheep's tripe. Neither of these dishes bears any resemblance to the English dish where tripe is cooked in milk with onions, probably the worst way to serve tripe in the entire world.

I have included a recipe using uncooked tripe given to me by a fine French cook, Dany Chouet, who is co-proprietor of Cleopatra Guest House in the Blue Mountains. The dish is absolutely succulent. But I suggest that beginners introduce themselves to tripe cookery by using an easier method. Tripe can be cooked, and then fried or grilled, or it can be sautéd, stewed with onions and/or tomatoes, cooked under a cheese-and-crumb crust or slow-braised in stock, wine or cider. Italians cook beautiful tripe dishes with rich tomato flavours and parmesan cheese. The Chinese, who love textured food, are good with tripe, too. One of the most delicious and lip-sticking specialities at yum cha is tripe with ginger in a golden, sticky sauce.

tripe goes with
onions
carrots
leeks
potatoes
garlic
tomatoes
cider
white wine
red-wine vinegar
bacon
parsley
bay leaves
thyme
lima beans
haricot beans

VARIETIES AND SEASON

Various types of calf's, ox, pig and sheep's tripe are eaten, with *ox* tripe being by far the most usually available. *Lamb's* tripe is thinner than that of the ox or calf, very supple and well suited to wrapping around savoury stuffings. *Sheep's* tripe is used to make haggis. *Pig's* tripe is available from Asian butchers. From whatever animal the tripe comes, it is always sold cleaned, usually bleached and usually parcooked to various degrees. It is possible to order 'green' or unbleached, uncooked tripe, which is what is required for many of the long-simmered tripe dishes of France. Unbleached, uncooked tripe is greyish brown in colour. I find it annoying that there is so much variation in the parcooking of tripe. It is therefore difficult to give cooking times and the cook must be prepared to nibble a piece of tripe to see if it is tender. Tripe is bleached by being soaked in a weak peroxide solution. Bleached, parcooked tripe is either cream-coloured or a startling snowy-white.

The 3 most commonly available varieties of ox tripe are blanket, book and honeycomb tripe. From the first stomach, the rumen, *blanket* tripe has a rough texture and varies in thickness. There is often a distinct layer of fat that can be cut away, if you like. Also known as Bible tripe, *book* tripe comes from the third stomach, the omasum. The name refers to its folds. It is the least commonly available, being difficult to clean. The lining of the second stomach – the reticulum – is accurately described as *honeycomb* tripe. This piece of tripe is shaped like a small purse and is ideal for stuffing. A fourth variety, *reed* tripe, comes from the fourth stomach, the abomasum, but I have never seen it. In Lancashire it is known as black or slut tripe!

Tripe is available all year but as it is often frozen it should be ordered well in advance, especially if uncooked tripe is required.

SELECTION AND STORAGE

Select *bleached, parcooked* tripe for tripe dishes that take about an hour to cook. *Unbleached, uncooked* tripe should be chosen for dishes that require up to 8 hours' cooking. Ask your butcher how long his or her tripe will take to cook. There is considerable variation. As there is not much interest in tripe preparation, one is frequently offered tripe that has been bleached for so long that it has a bloated and very soft texture. Do not buy tripe like this – it is likely that it will fall into rags in the sauce. Tripe should smell sweet and look firm, moist and bouncy. I like the textural interest of honeycomb tripe and the thickness of blanket tripe for dishes where the tripe will be cut into strips.

All offal deteriorates quickly, so use your tripe within 24 hours of purchase. Refrigerate tripe, freed of all wrappings, on a plate covered with plastic film. A cooked dish of tripe will last several days in the refrigerator.

PREPARATION

Don't contemplate trying to buy *uncleaned* tripe – even if you could get it, cleaning tripe is best left to the specialists. *Cleaned* tripe needs no preparation, whether it has been parcooked and bleached or not. Just make sure you know which kind you have purchased and how long it is likely to take to cook. Because tripe has no natural gelatine, *unbleached, uncooked* tripe is often cooked with pig's trotters or pork rind, which add body and stickiness to the finished sauce. This is not possible for dishes using *parcooked, bleached* tripe as the cooking time is too short. Either start cooking the trotters or pork rind first of all and add the tripe later, or choose good stock and rich vegetables to add the extra flavour and body to the tripe. Cooked tripe should still have some bite to it and not disintegrate into thin strings.

tripe with tomato and lots of parsley
SERVES 4–6

Here is my introductory tripe dish, a blend of French and Italian traditions. It can be prepared well ahead and reheated before serving. If you don't like this, you don't like tripe.

1 kg bleached, parcooked honeycomb tripe
½ cup olive oil
2 onions, finely chopped
1 carrot, peeled and diced
250 g smoked streaky bacon, finely diced
1 stick celery, finely chopped
3 cloves garlic, finely chopped
2 tablespoons red-wine vinegar
1 kg ripe tomatoes, peeled, seeded and roughly chopped
1 cup well-reduced Veal Stock
1 bay leaf
1 small fresh chilli, seeded
6 potatoes, cut in half
salt
freshly ground black pepper
½ cup freshly chopped parsley

Cut tripe into 2 cm × 6 cm strips. Heat oil in a wide saucepan and sauté onion and carrot for 5 minutes until lightly coloured. Add bacon, celery and garlic and sauté a further 5 minutes, then tip in tripe. Allow tripe to start to colour a little at edges, then increase heat to full and drizzle in vinegar. Stir until liquid has evaporated. Add tomato, stock, bay leaf and chilli and stir through tripe, then simmer gently, covered, for 30–45 minutes until tomato has broken down. The sauce should be rich in flavour and quite thick. If not, increase heat a little to reduce excess liquid. Remove from heat and set aside. Cook potato in lightly salted water. When tender, peel and drop into sauce. (The recipe can be finished to this point hours before dinner.)

To finish, transfer tripe to an ovenproof dish. Add potato and enough sauce to make the dish juicy but not sloppy. Taste for salt and pepper. The dish should be well seasoned. Reheat in an oven set at 200°C and serve absolutely bubbling and strewn with parsley.

variations To give this dish an Italian accent, cover the tomato and tripe with a layer of parmesan cheese and reheat under the griller rather than in the oven. If you like, omit the potato and add separately simmered dried beans or chick peas to the tripe and sauce before reheating it in the oven or under the griller.

hot–sour fried tripe
SERVES 4

This recipe comes from Sri Owen's Indonesian Food and Cookery *with very minor changes. The number of chillies can be reduced to suit your palate.*

15 g tamarind pulp

½ cup boiling water

1 kg bleached, parcooked tripe

5 shallots, quartered

3 cloves garlic, sliced

5 fresh chillies, halved and
seeded

1 teaspoon ground ginger

½ teaspoon ground coriander

1 teaspoon finely chopped
lemongrass

1 teaspoon brown sugar

1½ teaspoons salt

2 bay leaves

1 cup vegetable oil

Soak tamarind pulp in boiling water for 30 minutes, then squeeze pulp and press it and liquid through a coarse strainer over a bowl. Measure 4 tablespoons of this tamarind water and put into a large saucepan with all ingredients except oil. Simmer for 30 minutes or until tender, then allow tripe to cool in cooking liquid. Drain tripe, removing any pieces of chilli or herb, and cut into small squares. Heat oil in a wok and stir-fry tripe until nicely brown. Serve hot with rice.

tripe and onions

Fry thinly sliced onion in pork fat or olive oil until softened and golden brown. In a separate pan, heat a little more fat or oil and fry thinly sliced parcooked tripe until crisp at the edges. Add the onion to the tripe, stirring and lifting to mix well, and cook for 20 minutes. Increase the heat to full, then splash in a little wine vinegar (which will evaporate instantly if the pan is as hot as it should be) and add freshly ground black pepper and lots of chopped parsley.

red-cooked pig's tripe with ginger   SERVES 4–6

I have commented before on the Asian interest in texture in food. In A Guide to Chinese Eating, *Kenneth Lo says of tripe: 'when it is well-cooked it has a firm squashy layer as well as its jelly-like layer … biting into a piece should be like biting into a savoury jelly-cake'. This recipe approximates the yum cha dish I remember with so much pleasure from a visit to Hong Kong.*

500 g cleaned, uncooked
pig's tripe

1 tablespoon vegetable oil

6 slices fresh ginger, cut into
julienne

4 spring onions, cut into
6 cm pieces

3 tablespoons dark *or* standard
soy sauce

2 tablespoons rice wine

1 tablespoon sugar

pinch of salt

2 cups Chicken Stock

1 cup loosely packed
coriander leaves

Place tripe in a saucepan of water and bring to a boil. Simmer for 2 hours. Taste to see if it is nearly tender – it should still be al dente. Drain and cut into strips 3 cm wide by 6 cm long. In a heavy-based cast-iron casserole heat oil and sear ginger and spring onion. Add tripe and toss to seal, then add remaining ingredients except coriander. Cover tightly and simmer for 1 hour. The tripe should be very tender. Remove lid and increase heat to concentrate sauce, stirring to prevent ingredients catching. Tip into a heated dish and scatter with coriander. Serve with rice or steamed buns from an Asian take-away.

dany's tripe

SERVES 6

Dany reminds me that in Périgord this dish would be cooked using calf's tripe and feet. Here she uses uncooked, unbleached tripe. This dish is very similar to tripes à la mode de Caen *from Normandy.*

1.5 kg cleaned, uncooked, unbleached tripe
1 pig's trotter
1 litre dry white wine
2 cloves
1 onion
4 carrots, washed
4 large leeks, washed and split lengthwise
1 stick celery
1 bouquet garni (thyme, bay leaf, parsley stalks)
½ head garlic, skin on
1 teaspoon salt
10 white peppercorns
1 tablespoon pork *or* duck fat
2 tablespoons plain flour
3 cloves garlic, finely chopped
1 tablespoon freshly chopped parsley
3 tablespoons brandy

Soak tripe and trotter in cold water for 2 hours, changing water 2–3 times. Scrape any hairs off trotter. Place tripe and trotter in a large stockpot and cover with wine. Stick cloves into onion and add to pot with carrot, green part of leeks, celery, bouquet garni, head of garlic, salt and peppercorns. Bring to a boil and simmer, covered, slowly on top of stove or in oven set at 150°C for 6–7 hours or until tripe is tender. Allow to cool a little, then strain contents through a colander. Reserve cooking liquid but discard vegetables.

Chop white part of leeks very finely. In a heavy-based saucepan cook leek in pork fat very slowly until it softens. Stir in flour and cook for 3–4 minutes, stirring, then gradually add half the reserved cooking liquid. Let sauce come to a simmer while you remove bones from trotter and cut meat and skin into fine dice. Cut tripe into 4 cm squares. Return trotter meat and tripe to sauce. Add more reserved cooking liquid if sauce is too thick or there is not enough to cover meat. Three-quarters cover pot and simmer for 45 minutes. Check seasoning and add chopped garlic, parsley and brandy and cook for 15 minutes. Serve very hot, accompanied by lots of toast or boiled potatoes.

tablier de sapeur
Make this Lyonnaise bistro dish by dipping strips of fully cooked tripe in a sharp vinaigrette and then in egg and breadcrumbs. Fry in oil until crisp and serve as a snack with mayonnaise sharpened with herbs and pickled cucumber.

t r o p i c a l   f r u i t   In North Queensland and the Northern Territory the growing of tropical fruit is a thriving industry. A percentage of our crop is exported to South-East Asia. Australia also imports tropical fruit from South-East Asia, so it is sometimes difficult to identify a local season. With the expansion of the tropical fruit industry has come an unwelcome migrant from South-East Asia: the papaya fruit fly. In 1995 it appeared to establish itself in the rainforests of North Queensland. The fear is that as the fly attacks unripe fruit, the fruiting, seeding and germination patterns in our rainforests may be changed forever, not to mention the considerable damage the fly may do to orchard-grown fruit. A good reason to be vigilant about not bringing undeclared fruit or plants back from overseas or interstate holidays. | For most of us tropical fruit is evocative of warm nights and bare legs. Some tropical fruit have been in our fruit bowls forever. Pineapples, bananas and passionfruit have been mainstream items for as long as we can remember. Passionfruit grow happily in temperate climates, anyway. But more unusual tropical fruit have only really become a familiar sight in our greengrocers' shops since the mid-1980s. >

Thanks once again to our migrants, especially those from South-East Asia, the demand is such that regular supplies are freighted to the southern States in excellent condition. Shops displaying jackfruit, mangoes, soursops, rambutans, custard apples, fresh lychees, and so on can be found in all our capital cities, and supermarkets are including more and more tropical fruit among the apples and oranges. Those who holiday in tropical Australia and South-East Asia have the opportunity of tasting these fruit in season. It can be a memorable experience and prevents us succumbing to unripe papaya or custard apples back in more temperate climates. Most tropical fruit cannot be stored at temperatures below 13°C and in general should be enjoyed at the peak of their perfection.

At the Sunday market in Port Douglas, in Far North Queensland, farmers gather to sell a very wide range of tropical fruit. On my last visit I bought custard apples, soursops, white-and-purple star apples, carambola, rambutans, mangosteens, black sapotes and rose papaya. It was not mango season but the market was shaded by an immense mango tree and the carpet of seeds reminded me that the fruit bats are very well fed here.

The pulp of soursop and custard apple freezes perfectly and makes great ice-cream. In North Queensland, restaurants often use soursop to make a splendid daiquiri. Unripe mangoes are used to make chutneys and pickles, and the Timorese stalls selling green papaya salad at the Mindil Beach Market in Darwin are very well patronised. But mostly it is difficult to think of anything better to do with these fruit than to eat them as they are, perhaps with a squeeze of lime juice. Both rambutans with their soft hairy spines and lychees in their scarlet shells are so pretty that a bowl of them set on the table is like presenting your guests with a beautiful work of art. If you can find any, add a few mangosteens. Their dull-purple skins and solid curves make them appear as if carved by Gauguin from some dense wood.

all tropical fruit go with
lime juice
lemon juice
rum
sugar syrup
coconut

some tropical fruit go with
chillies
garlic
coriander
pork

VARIETIES AND SEASON

It would be impossible to list all the varieties of tropical fruit grown in Australia. Instead, the following are those one is most likely to find in greengrocers' shops across the country. Residents of northern Australia will have access to a far wider selection.

CARAMBOLA

Averrhoa carambola is also known as the five-cornered or star fruit. It is thought to have originated in Malaysia or Indonesia and is widely cultivated in South-East Asia, China, India and South America. The carambola is usually yellow–green and is very crisp and juicy with a delightfully refreshing flavour. While all carambolas turn waxy when ripe, some change to bright yellow or even pinky-yellow and others remain green. The 5 ribs of all varieties form a star when the fruit is cut crosswise. Carambolas are available most of the year in Australia, the peak season being October–July.

CUSTARD APPLE Native to South and Central America, the custard apple (*Annona cherimola* and *A. atemoya*) belongs to the Annonaceae family, which includes the soursop. The custard apple has a delightful fragrance and the flesh is creamy, juicy and sweet. While the flesh is the consistency of thick custard, the fruit itself bears absolutely no resemblance to an apple. Instead, it is green, heart-shaped and can be rather bumpy. Black, shiny seeds are embedded in the flesh. Custard apples are in season March–September.

LYCHEE *Litchi chinensis* is a native of subtropical China. Also known as a litchi, it is closely related to the longan (*Euphoria longan*), which is similar in flavour but without the beautiful shell of the lychee. Although lychees were introduced to Australia by Chinese miners in the late 1800s, we have only recently seen the fresh fruit in our shops. The scarlet shell of the ripe fruit, marked just like Chinese checkers, was a delightful surprise to me, accustomed up until then to the canned fruit served in too-sweet syrup in Chinese restaurants. The fresh fruit is very sweet and juicy and most refreshing at the end of a meal. Its flavour is reminiscent of a ripe, peeled muscat grape. The pearly-white flesh encloses a shiny brown seed. This seed is toxic and should never be consumed. Lychees are available November–February.

MANGO *Mangifera indica* is Australia's most important tropical fruit crop and has been cultivated in Queensland since 1840. Originally from South-East Asia or the Indian–Burmese border, where they have been cultivated for more than 4000 years, mangoes are now grown almost everywhere in the world where the climate is suitable, with India producing most of all. The Kensington pride or Bowen mango is the most common variety grown in Australia, but since 1985 more than 200 varieties have been cultivated. The skins of mangoes range in colour from green to sunset-red, while the perfumed, richly fla-voured flesh ranges from golden yellow to deep orange. The flesh of different varieties has more or less fibre, and modern cultivars have been specifically bred to reduce the fibre. All varieties have a large, flat pip in the centre that is very fibrous. Mangoes range in size from that of an egg to as big as a softball. Local mangoes are in season October–March. Imported mangoes are in the shops March–August.

MANGOSTEEN *Garcinia mangostana* is a native of the Malay Peninsula, East Indies and Philippines and is

considered very highly indeed in South-East Asia. This round fruit has a thick, smooth, leathery, purple skin in which nestle 4–8 highly scented, treacly segments. Its flavour has been likened to that of a well-ripened plum. At present mangosteens are grown in only a few of the tropical fruit orchards of North Queensland. They appear erratically January–April.

PAPAYA | *Carica papaya* originated in Central America but is now grown in most tropical and subtropical regions of the world. Although described as a tree, it is in fact a large herbaceous plant or softwood tree, like the banana. In tropical climates papaya trees grow very fast. They fruit for 2 successive years and are then cut down and replaced. Papaya and pawpaw are the same fruit, although the term 'pawpaw' is often used in Australia. It is probably best to decide on 'papaya', as there is another fruit related to the custard apple family that has the common name of 'papaw' (note the difference in spelling).

The fruit of the papaya tree is a squarish football shape and ranges in skin colour from green to yellow to pinky-red. Not all papaya flesh is yellow. Some of the most luscious varieties have rose-pink flesh. Unripe, rock-hard papaya (both yellow and pink-fleshed varieties) is also sold and is a popular ingredient in South-East Asian salads when grated or chopped. Ripe papaya has a distinctive and rich flavour, slightly oily in character. The flesh should be very juicy and soft; it lacks acidity, which is why papaya is so good with freshly squeezed lime. The fruit contains masses of grey, shiny seeds. The skin of the fruit and the leaves of the tree contain papain, an enzyme used as a meat tenderiser and to manufacture chewing gum and toothpaste. Papaya is available all year, the peak seasons being September–December and March–May.

RAMBUTAN | *Nephelium lappaceum* was originally from the Malay Peninsula but is now widely cultivated. It is sometimes called the hairy lychee, which refers to its soft, plastic-feeling red or yellow spines. Most rambutans are scarlet when ripe, like lychees, while other varieties are greenish or yellow–orange. The flavour and character of the fruit is close to that of the lychee, having the same translucent flesh, although the flesh of the rambutan is more acid. Rambutans are available December–August, with peak supplies December–March.

SOURSOP | Related to the custard apple and a native of the West Indies, *Annona muricata* can be enormous, weighing up to several kilograms. The flesh is fragrant and highly acid, a little reminiscent of a pineapple, and the fruit is very juicy. The skin is green and covered in fine hairs. Like the custard apple, the soursop has black, shiny seeds embedded in the flesh. Soursops are in season March–September.

SELECTION AND STORAGE

CARAMBOLA

Avoid fruit that has brown bruises or limp edges. Carambola will continue to ripen at room temperature. They can be used as a vegetable when green and astringent, can be added to sweet or savoury salads or can be eaten fresh like an apple. Carambola can be stored in the refrigerator for a few days when ripe.

CUSTARD APPLE AND SOURSOP

The skin of all Annonaceae is very delicate and breaks easily, so make sure you choose specimens without any soft spots or broken skin. Carry these fruit home carefully, and if they do not feel soft to the touch leave them at room temperature for a day or two until they do. The skin may develop some blackening. Once ripe, eat them straightaway as, like all tropical fruit, if left to become overripe the flesh quickly ferments. They are susceptible to cool-storage damage and if stored below 6°C the skin discolours rapidly. Most soursops are too acid to be eaten fresh without extra sugar.

LYCHEE

Lychees do not continue to ripen after harvesting. They last longer if a little of the stem remains attached. Lychees are very perishable if stored at room temperature. The lychee quickly loses its ripe, bright skin colour several days after harvesting, so colour is a reliable indicator of freshness. The colour can be maintained longer if the fruit is stored at a low temperature. Lychees will keep for a week or so in the refrigerator in a sealed plastic or vegetable storage bag.

MANGO

The ripeness of a mango cannot be judged by its colour. There are varieties that are perfectly ripe and remain bright green, just as there are varieties with a crimson blush on one cheek that might still not be ripe. An unripe mango smells and tastes like kerosene. Keep an unripe mango in a warm place for a few days until it yields a little when cradled in your hand. Totally unripe mangoes are used to make chutney, or, dried, become amchur, a spice used in some Indian dishes. When mangoes are picked a caustic sap squirts from the fruit stalk. Wear gloves to pick fruit and sunglasses to protect your eyes and hands. The mango has a short life at room temperature once fully ripe. Stored at 13°C (cellar temperature), it will keep well for several days. If mangoes are to be pulped, they can be frozen whole. The skin will blacken but the flesh remains in good condition. Fully ripe mango cheeks can be sliced, packed in freezer bags – separated by liners – and frozen. The sliced fruit will emerge with flavour intact but of a mushier texture, fine for drinks, ice-creams or sauces.

sambal

Make a fresh sambal by mixing finely diced underripe mango, freshly grated coconut, finely chopped coriander and fresh ginger, quite a bit of salt, and chilli paste or sambal oelek. Allow to stand for an hour. Serve with barbecued fish or grilled quail.

MANGOSTEEN | Fruit is picked at early maturity when it will last for several weeks, but if harvested too soon the fruit does not develop full flavour. Mangosteens harvested fully ripe will not last many days. Store the fruit in the refrigerator to delay deterioration a little.

PAPAYA | Like mango, a truly ripe papaya is sublime but a semi-ripe one is revolting, having the bitter taste of bile. Papaya continues to ripen after picking and the green skin will become heavily splashed with yellow. Ripe fruit should feel more yielding than a ripe avocado. Size bears absolutely no relationship to maturity. Most varieties of papaya vary quite considerably in size, even if from the same tree. Store papaya in the refrigerator for several days, and cover with plastic film once cut.

RAMBUTAN | Rambutans should have bright-looking spines. They are very perishable at room temperature, and in temperatures of 25°C and over will remain marketable for only 3–4 days. The storage life can be extended by refrigerating the fruit in a sealed plastic bag in the vegetable crisper for up to 10 days.

PREPARATION

CARAMBOLA | Trim away the edges of the 5 ribs before slicing the fruit.

CUSTARD APPLE AND SOURSOP | A ripe custard apple is a treat and should be enjoyed just as it is, maybe with a squirt of lime juice. Cut or break it open and serve with a small spoon or fork. Do not eat the black seeds of either fruit. Peeling and seeding these fruit may cause some skin irritation. If in doubt, wear a pair of disposable gloves. The ripe flesh of both the custard apple and soursop can be made into a purée, which in turn makes delicious ice-cream. **To purée** Slice open the fruit, then scoop the flesh into a stainless steel or nylon sieve resting over a bowl and push the flesh through using the back of a spoon. Discard the seeds. Measure the pulp and freeze it or continue with your recipe. As a rule of thumb, 500 g fruit will yield 1 cup purée.

LYCHEE | Lychees are most wonderful served as they are, glorious shells and twiggy branches too, if possible. Provide a plate for the peeled skins.

lychees and melons
Toss peeled lychees with green and orange melon balls, then squeeze over a fresh lime or drizzle with coconut jelly in syrup (available in the cool-drink section of Asian food stores).

soursop sorbet
Make soursop sorbet for 6 by sharpening 2 cups heavy Sugar Syrup with lemon juice, then mixing this into 2 cups soursop purée with a little white rum. Churn in an ice-cream machine.

MANGO

A mango has a wide but narrow pip in the middle of the fruit. To get at the fruit, stand the mango on its rounded end, narrowest side towards you. Slice off each rounded 'cheek', leaving the fibrous pip and the flesh surrounding it. This flesh is best sucked away from the stone, preferably bending over a sink. Score the flesh of each cheek through to the skin using a sharp knife and making 3–4 equally spaced cuts. Do the same from the opposite direction. You have now scored the flesh into diamonds. Bend the skin backwards and the diamonds of mango flesh will be accessible. Serve fresh mango like this for breakfast accompanied by fresh lime or to accompany sticky rice as a dessert (*see* RICE).

MANGOSTEEN

To get at the flesh of a mangosteen, one must perform a Caesarean section by cutting a circle around the thick stalk and crown of flattened leaves, which, when lifted, will reveal the segments of creamy flesh about the size and shape of a small mandarin. This is a very special fruit and should be savoured just as it is, straight from the skin.

PAPAYA

Halve the fruit and scoop out the seeds. Cut the fruit into wedges as one does for a melon or cut the flesh away from its thin skin and present it in long slices or cut into chunks. A few seeds can be crushed and sprinkled over tropical salads. They taste faintly peppery. Excess fruit is used to make jams, chutneys and pickles. For those of us who live in more temperate climates the concept of excess papaya is not something we have to worry about. Papaya leaves are used as a tenderising wrapping for tough meat that is to be barbecued.

RAMBUTAN

Serve rambutans whole, still in their spectacular skins (they are easy to peel). Offer your guests a small plate or bowl to collect the skins.

recipes

papaya and banana smoothie

SERVES 1

This could be made equally well with mango and banana.

1 cup sliced papaya
1 banana
2 teaspoons honey
½ cup crushed ice
2 cups chilled milk

Blend fruit and honey in a food processor until smooth. Gradually add ice and milk and blend until smooth and foamy. Serve immediately.

mango salsa

SERVES 2–4

1 mango, peeled and diced

2 slices red onion *or*
  2 shallots, very finely
  chopped

1 fresh red chilli, seeded and
  finely chopped

¼ cup finely chopped fresh
  mint leaves

2 tablespoons fresh lime juice

2 tablespoons olive oil

salt

freshly ground black pepper

Combine all ingredients and allow to stand for several hours before using. Great with a salad of warm duck breast or alongside grilled prawns or scallops.

tropical daiquiri
In a blender, process 45 ml white rum, 3 tablespoons soursop pulp, 15 ml white curaçao and 6 ice-cubes. Next time, try mango!

mango chutney

MAKES 1.5 LITRES

Sometimes you may find hard, unripe mangoes for sale. These are intended for making pickles. This chutney comes from Mogens Bay Esbensen's book A Taste of the Tropics.

1.5 kg green mangoes, peeled
  and sliced

50 g salt

250 g tamarind pulp

700 g brown sugar

2 cups white-wine vinegar

100 g raisins *or* sultanas

100 g freshly chopped ginger

6 dried red chillies, coarsely
  chopped

1 tablespoon whole allspice

Toss mango with salt in a stainless steel saucepan and leave for a few hours. Transfer mango to a colander and drain well. Put drained mango into a stainless steel stockpot with remaining ingredients and bring to a boil, stirring from time to time to prevent mixture sticking. Reduce to a simmer and cook for 40 minutes. Bottle into clean, dry, sterilised jars and seal. This chutney tastes best after it has matured for a month or so. It seems to keep forever.

grilled mango
Place a mango cheek per person on an oiled sheet of foil, flat-side up, and sprinkle with cinnamon or brown sugar or both (or chilli powder or freshly chopped ginger). Grill until the flesh starts to blister and brown. Serve with pork, duck or prawns.

padang sour–sharp fish

SERVES 4

This recipe is based on one from Jane Grigson and Charlotte Knox's Exotic Fruits and Vegetables. *They recommend preparing the dish one day and reheating it the next. Even better, I believe, is to eat it cold, either the day it is made or the following day.*

**papaya dipping
sauce**

*Add a couple of
tablespoons of
crushed papaya
seeds and plenty
of coarsely chopped
coriander and spring
onion with Thai-
style Dipping Sauce
(see* YABBIES*). Serve
alongside a warm or
cold seafood salad.*

**smoked chicken
and papaya**

*Arrange thinly sliced
smoked chicken
breast and ripe
papaya on a platter.
Squeeze over fresh
lime juice and
garnish with freshly
grated ginger and
torn mint leaves.
Serve with a salad
of coriander leaves
and coarsely grated
green papaya or
fresh coconut.*

4 x 180 g pieces chunky fish
   (tuna, hapuku, blue eye,
   for example)
1 teaspoon salt
2 tablespoons lemon juice
7 macadamias
2 onions, sliced
2 cloves garlic, chopped
1 level tablespoon finely
   chopped fresh chilli
2 x 5 mm slices fresh ginger
¼ teaspoon ground turmeric
4 tablespoons water
1 stalk lemongrass, bruised
3 unripe carambola, thinly
   sliced

Marinate fish in salt and lemon juice in
refrigerator for 45 minutes. In a food
processor, blend macadamias, onion, garlic,
chilli, ginger and turmeric to a paste. Put
paste, water and lemongrass into a heavy-
based frying pan large enough to hold fish
in a layer and bring to a simmer. Slip in
carambola and cook gently for 5 minutes,
stirring often. Add fish and any juices,
turning to coat with paste, and cook until
tender, about 10 minutes. Turn fish with
care, then remove pan from heat. Allow fish
to cool in pan. When cold, refrigerate. Next
day, reheat carefully using a simmer mat,
shaking the pan gently, or serve it cold
(remember to remove dish from refrigerator
30 minutes ahead to allow it to come to
room temperature).

tropical fruit salad

SERVES 6

This is the combination I use to accompany my Passionfruit Bavarois (see
PASSIONFRUIT*). When I serve it with the bavarois I cut the fruit very, very
small, so that it can be served in a passionfruit shell. If being served by itself
or alongside the Custard Apple or Soursop Bavarois (see p. 735), the fruit
can be cut to any size you wish.*

1 custard apple, peeled
2 bananas, peeled
1 mango, peeled
1 x 400 g rose papaya, peeled
3 kiwi fruit, peeled
2 passionfruit, halved
castor sugar (optional)

Cut all fruit except passionfruit into similar-
sized dice, discarding seeds, and put in a
serving bowl. Scoop passionfruit pulp into
bowl and mix well. Add sugar, if using, and
mix again. The acidity of the passionfruit
prevents the banana discolouring. Leave for
at least 30 minutes before serving.

custard apple or soursop ice-cream

SERVES 8

This ice-cream of Mogens Bay Esbensen's, from his Thai Cuisine, *is a great
favourite of mine.*

3 cups puréed custard apple
   or soursop

200 g castor sugar

2 eggs, lightly beaten

2 tablespoons fresh lime juice

2 cups cream

Mix fruit purée with sugar. Add eggs, lime juice and cream, then mix well. Churn in an ice-cream machine according to the manufacturer's instructions, then freeze. Let this ice-cream soften a little before serving.

grilled tropical fruit kebabs   SERVES 4

1 mango, peeled and cut
   into chunks

1 carambola, thickly sliced

1 papaya, peeled, seeded
   and cut into chunks

½ pineapple, peeled and
   cut into chunks

1 banana, peeled and thickly
   sliced

8 lychees, peeled and seeded

2 tablespoons dark rum

2 tablespoons honey

2 tablespoons melted butter

Arrange fruit on 4 skewers (soaked for 30 minutes, if bamboo). Mix rum with honey and spoon over fruit. Allow to stand for 30 minutes, spooning juices over once or twice. Heat griller and line tray with foil. Brush skewers with melted butter and grill until hot through and blistered on the edges. Pour remaining honey mixture and melted butter over and serve with a tropical-fruit ice-cream.

custard apple or soursop bavarois   SERVES 4

6 gelatine leaves

90 ml fresh lime juice

3 cups puréed custard apple
   or soursop

200 g pure icing sugar

300 ml cream, whipped

Soak gelatine leaves in a little cold water for 5 minutes. Heat lime juice to simmering point. Squeeze gelatine leaves, then drop into lime juice, stirring to dissolve. Stir lime juice mixture into fruit purée, then sift in a little of the icing sugar (you will need more if using soursop than if using custard apple).

Whisk mixture to blend it perfectly. Taste for sweetness and adjust, if necessary. Fold cream into purée, then pour into individual moulds or a large bowl. Refrigerate until set. Serve with a tropical fruit salad.

quick mango ice-cream

To make mango ice-cream for 4, process the flesh from 2 mangoes with the juice of a lime, then add ½ cup castor sugar. Whip 300 ml cream, fold it into the purée and churn in an ice-cream machine. Eat this ice-cream the day it is made as it becomes icy the next.

custard apple fool

Combine 1 cup custard apple purée with the juice of a lime and dark rum to taste, then whip 1 cup cream and fold it into the purée. Serve in 4 pretty glasses with crisp biscuits.

other recipes

mango with sticky rice *see* RICE

port douglas fruit salad *see* PINEAPPLES

see also BANANAS; PINEAPPLES

t r o t t e r s   I have memories of a family picnic in the Adelaide Hills in the 1950s when I was very young; I watched in amazement as my mother got right into a jellied pig's trotter. I have to admit that this wobbly, pale-beige thing with *toes* seemed an extraordinary thing to eat. Why can't I remember when I first discovered the delights for myself?   As I have already noted regarding offal and other 'fancy bits', many cooks have never eaten or even contemplated eating a trotter. Young cooks in my kitchen have confided to me that they have wondered why I am so enthusiastic about something as basic as the feet of a pig. Well, one of the reasons that trotters appeal to me is that you get two things for the price of one: a delicious and sticky salad or a hot and crunchy grill and a pot of jellied stock.   Pig's trotters are rich in gelatine and contribute richness and stickiness to any stock or stew. They can be cooked and served cold as a salad, either in their jellied juices or mixed with other things. Once cooked they can be rolled in crumbs and grilled and served with a mustardy mayonnaise, or they can be stuffed and then braised in a sauce. The Chinese love stickiness and chewing soft bones, and trotters offer both these things – they are delicious cooked with Asian flavourings. >

A speciality of Modena in northern Italy is *zampone*, a boned pig's trotter stuffed with a rich and spicy pork mince. The *zampone* is simmered in stock for several hours and is then sliced and served with lentils or becomes part of the delicious dish of mixed boiled meats called *bollito misto*.

VARIETIES AND SEASON

The trotters available in Australia are those from the back of the pig. Calf's and lamb's feet are much used in Europe. There are time-consuming processes to be gone through, however, before they can be sold legally in Australia (the scraping of hair), and as most abattoirs find this too difficult, they are virtually unobtainable.

SELECTION AND STORAGE

Trotters are sold fresh or pickled. *Pickled* trotters have a superior flavour if to be eaten cold. If the trotters are to be cooked with other meat, prefer *fresh* ones, as the pickling solution will turn the other meat pink. As with all pickled meat it is advisable to give the butcher 2 days' warning. Demand for pickled offal is never great and it is likely trotters will have to be pickled just for you. For this reason, order 3–4 at a time. Do the same when ordering fresh trotters for stocks or stews. Ask the butcher to saw them in half lengthwise (unless you want them kept whole for stuffing) and then freeze them until your next stock-making day. If your local butcher rarely has pig's trotters, head off to an Asian butcher. When you read a recipe that instructs you to add a calf's foot to the pot, substitute 2 pig's trotters. There is not a lot of meat on a trotter but it is rich and is often combined with other rich ingredients, so 1 trotter per person is sufficient.

Refrigerate pickled or fresh trotters freed of all wrappings for a maximum of 2 days. Fresh trotters can be stored in a basin of cold water with a little vinegar added to prevent them discolouring. Store pickled trotters on a plate and cover with plastic film.

PREPARATION AND COOKING

Trotters need to cook for 3–4 hours to yield all their goodness, so do not rush any operation that involves them. If you have bought pickled trotters, you will need to soak them in cold water for a few hours to rid them of any excess salt before you cook them. Before cooking trotters by any method, check them for any bristles not removed by the butcher, especially between the toes! Singe the bristles off over a gas flame or scrape them off with a sharp knife.

If you wish to make a sauce from the cooking liquid (or want better-flavoured jelly), replace the water with chicken or veal stock. After the

**trotters
go
with**
mustard
capers
pickled cucumbers
parsley
chives
spring onions
mayonnaise
shallots
white wine
cream
fresh tomato sauce
watercress
oranges
olives
leeks
potatoes

trotters have been cooked the stock will set to a firm jelly that could also be clarified.

To serve trotters in a sauce or a salad or set in jelly, it is easier for your guests to cope if the trotters have been *boned*. It is essential that the trotters are boned if they are to be stuffed or formed into small patties for grilling. Where the trotter is to be cut up, it is usually boned once it has been cooked. Trotters are boned raw to keep a better shape for stuffing, quite a difficult thing to do.

TO COOK If you wish the trotters to keep their shape and pale colour (if stuffing them later, for instance), wrap the trotter in a piece of muslin and bind it with tape or string to a flat-handled wooden spoon or a wooden ruler. If the trotters are to be crumbed, or you don't mind if they become a bit discoloured, don't worry about the muslin. If the trotters are to be cut in small pieces, don't worry about tying them to a wooden spoon either.

Put the trotters into a stockpot with 1 onion, 1 carrot, 1 stick celery, some parsley stalks, a sprig of thyme, some peppercorns and a bay leaf and barely cover with chicken or veal stock or cold water. Bring to a boil, then skim very well and lower the heat. Simmer very gently for 4 hours. Test with a fine skewer (through the muslin, if used). If it slides through easily, the trotters are cooked. If there is resistance, continue to simmer them. When cooked, allow the trotters to cool in the cooking liquid. Remove muslin, if used, and proceed with the desired preparation.

TO BONE **Raw** Make a slit down the centre of the underside of each trotter and, using a small, sharp knife, gently ease the skin away from the bones, peeling it down like a glove. Do this until you come to the smallest bones in the toes. Using a cleaver, cut right through the central bone with a sharp blow. Leave the toe bones in position. **Cooked** Split each trotter in half lengthwise, if this has not already been done by the butcher. Remove all the bones with your fingers. Drop each boned trotter into a bowl of cooking liquid to delay any discoloration until all are boned. If the trotter is to be stuffed, you might leave in the very tiniest bones at the end of the toes or the trotter may look very ragged. Cut the meat into small pieces, if needed.

recipes

caribbean pig's trotters stew

SERVES 6–8

This was a favourite party dish of my first husband, who was Jamaican. He included plenty of pig's tails as well as the feet. It cost practically nothing to make, which was important as we had no money, and he used to serve it on entirely unsuitable paper plates to a roomful of enthusiastic and noisy Jamaicans in our cold London flat.

6 pickled pig's trotters, soaked

3 pickled pig's tails, soaked and cut into 6 cm lengths

1 bay leaf

6 whole allspice, coarsely crushed

cayenne pepper

250 g chick peas or black-eyed peas

2 tablespoons lard

1 fresh red chilli, seeded and chopped

1 onion, chopped

2 tomatoes, peeled, seeded and chopped

2 fat spicy pork sausages (fresh chorizo would do), chopped

4 potatoes, peeled and halved

2 teaspoons salt

Put trotters and tails into a stockpot with bay leaf, allspice and cayenne pepper, then cover generously with water. Bring to a simmer and skim, then simmer partially covered for 1½ hours. Add chick peas and simmer for another 1½ hours, by which time all should be cooked.

Melt lard in a frying pan and fry chilli, onion, tomato and sausage. Add this to stockpot and cook for 15 minutes. Add potato and salt and simmer, uncovered, until potato is tender.

jellied trotters
Cut boned, cooked trotters into pieces, then season and add a few drops of best-quality wine vinegar, a little strained cooking liquid, lots of finely chopped shallots and parsley and some chopped capers. Pack into a rectangular gratin dish, then refrigerate. When set, cut into squares and serve on a bed of greens with sliced orange tossed with paper-thin slices of onion and black olives.

trotters with velouté sauce   SERVES 4

When making this sauce, you will need to reserve the liquid used to cook the trotters.

40 g butter

2 tablespoons plain flour

600 ml strained cooking liquid

salt

freshly ground black pepper

4 pig's trotters, cooked and boned

Melt butter in a saucepan, then stir in flour to make a *roux* and cook over gentle heat for 5 minutes, stirring. Bring cooking liquid to a simmer, then gradually whisk into *roux* and stir until it comes to a boil. Reduce heat and place pan on a simmer mat. Simmer sauce for 15 minutes, then adjust seasoning. Cut trotters into small pieces and put into a shallow gratin dish. Spoon over warm sauce and reheat in oven at 180°C. Serve with plenty of hot toast.

additions Simple additions are cream, cream and lemon juice, sliced button mushrooms cooked for 2 minutes in a little butter and water and then strained, or freshly chopped herbs. **sauce poulette** Mix 2 egg yolks with 2 tablespoons lemon juice and stir in ½ cup of the hot velouté sauce. Tip this mixture back into the sauce, then stir over a low heat until the sauce thickens but does not boil (it will curdle if it boils). Stir in 2 tablespoons freshly chopped parsley (mushrooms and cream can also be added, if desired).

braised stuffed trotters

SERVES 8

3 onions, finely chopped
olive oil
1 kg minced pork
500 g crumbled cotechino
    sausage or other uncooked
    boiling sausage
½ cup pistachios, roughly
    chopped
salt
freshly ground black pepper
8 fresh pig's trotters, boned
good Chicken or Veal Stock

Preheat oven to 180°C. Cook onion in oil over a gentle heat until soft and yellow, then combine all ingredients in a bowl except trotters and braising liquid. Stuff each trotter with mixture and squeeze skin back into its former shape. Braise stuffed trotters in enough stock to barely cover in oven for at least 3 hours, tucked tightly together in a covered baking dish split-side down, so that they cannot move around. These trotters are fantastic served with creamy mashed potato.

variations Instead of stock, braise the trotters in thin Fresh Tomato Sauce (*see* p. 709) *or* Tomato and Maple Syrup Glaze (*see* p. 567).

crumbed trotters with mustard mayonnaise

SERVES 4

I have read in Jane Grigson's classic work Charcuterie and French Pork Cookery *that in the village of Sainte-Ménéhould, most famous for these crumbed and grilled trotters, the real secret was that the trotters were cooked for 48 hours, by which time one could crunch through the soft bones as well as the crisp coating and sticky softness of the flesh.*

While for some recipes the trotters are allowed to cool in their stock, here they are removed from the liquid to cool. The trotters must be dry, otherwise the crumbs will not adhere.

4 pig's trotters, cooked
Dijon mustard
melted butter
fine breadcrumbs

Remove trotters from cooking liquid and allow to cool. Cut trotters in half lengthwise, then paint them with mustard and arrange on a plate. Cover trotters with

trotter salad
Cut cooked, boned trotters into small pieces and toss with capers, pickled cucumbers, parsley, very finely chopped shallot and 3 parts best olive oil to 1 part red-wine vinegar. Add boiled new potatoes, 1–2 anchovies or some freshly chopped orange, if desired. Serve at room temperature (if refrigerated, the trotter meat will all stick together).

plastic film and weight with a board on which you place some tins. Leave until absolutely cold.

Preheat oven to 200°C. Dip cold trotters into melted butter and coat with a good layer of breadcrumbs. Arrange on a baking tray lined with baking paper and bake until very hot, about 20 minutes. Dribble with a little more melted butter and transfer to a preheated griller to brown and crisp crumbs – watch closely that crumbs do not burn. There should be no need to turn trotters. Serve with the Mustard Mayonnaise ✐ and a lightly dressed green salad for lunch.

tartare sauce For a change, serve trotters with Tartare Sauce ✐.

chinese-style trotters with ginger and black rice vinegar
SERVES 6

This Cantonese dish is always prepared for a woman who has just given birth and is ritually shared with visitors to the household, says Bruce Cost in his book Ginger East to West. *I love it with steamed Chinese buns, either pork-filled or plain. Buy some at an Asian take-away shop and steam them hot at home in a bamboo steamer.*

1 kg fresh pig's trotters, chopped into 3–4 pieces
500 g fresh ginger, cut into 5 mm slices
2 cups black rice vinegar
½ tablespoon mushroom soy sauce
salt
½ cup finely sliced spring onion

Cover trotter pieces with cold water and bring to a boil in a stockpot. Discard water and rinse trotter pieces under running water to wash off any scum. Cover again with water and bring to a simmer, then cook for 45 minutes, covered. Add ginger, vinegar and soy sauce. Cook gently for 2 hours, uncovered. The sauce should reduce gradually. Check if trotter pieces are tender and add salt if necessary. The meat should be covered with a syrupy sauce. Serve sprinkled with spring onion.

pork jelly
Use the clarified ✐, sparkling pork jelly left from cooking trotters in umpteen ways: set trotters in a shining coating, serve it as a jellied or hot consommé, use it to fill any spaces between the filling and pastry in a warm pork pie, or set Ham and Pistachio Mousse (see HAM*).*

dany's tripe *see* TRIPE

other recipes

turnips and swedes

French food historian Maguelonne Toussaint-Samat reminded me in *The History of Food* that at school I was told (as she was) that 'in the Middle Ages the peasants lived a very wretched life. They were called villeins, and ate roots'. This was supposedly a terrible fate, and yet we still eat roots – and seeds and leaves and stalks – with enthusiasm. The real message being conveyed was of the desperate poverty experienced, and that root vegetables were easy to grow and easy to dig for. │ The turnip (*Brassica rapa*) and the closely related swede (*B. napus*) are still considered lower-class foods by many of Anglo-Saxon origin, who remember watery orange or white slush served at boarding-school dinners. However, turnips are much appreciated in many other cultures. The Japanese and cooks in the Middle East have their own methods for pickling young turnips, and the French, who have always known that turnips are delicious, understand how to complement the natural sweetness and peppery flavour of the turnip with richness from the juices of braised dishes or with plenty of butter. >

The stronger-flavoured swede, however, is still unknown in France other than as winter food for cattle. Swedes are called 'neeps' in Scotland, and a buttery purée is the famous 'bashed neeps' best known as an accompaniment to haggis. The swede is known as rutabaga in the United States, from the Swedish dialect *rotabagge*, which means ram's root. Bunches of small or immature turnips, each about the size of a large radish or a golf ball, are becoming more widely available. These are a treat and when braised or stewed in butter become a very high-class dish to serve alongside a roasted duck or leg of lamb.

The leafy tops of turnips, once well washed and lightly cooked, are also edible. They have a slight hotness and bitterness, which make them ideal when partnered with something neutral such as pasta. These tops, known as *broccoletti di rapa*, are a speciality in Rome in the spring. They can also be served simply with melted or browned butter or tossed with sautéd smoked bacon.

VARIETIES AND SEASON

Turnips and swedes vary considerably in size, shape and colour. They can be round or flattened; most turnips have white flesh, while most swedes have yellow flesh. The skins of both can be white flushed with purple or greenish purple, but most swedes have skins that are yellow–brown flushed with purple. There are also varieties of turnips that have red skins. Turnips and swedes are not sold by variety here. The main turnip grown in Australia is the purple-top white globe, while the variety of swede that dominates is the champion purple top. I would love some grower to investigate the suitability of the flattened French turnip that braises to exquisite translucence. It can be quite large but in France is sold in bunches in the spring when each turnip is about 5 cm in diameter.

Most English gardening books caution against winter turnips as being coarse of flavour and stringy. In Australia our milder climates have meant that both turnips and swedes are available all year, although the bulk of the crop is harvested in late autumn through the winter and into spring.

There is a vegetable sold in Asian food stores as white turnip, white radish, daikon or loh baak, its Chinese name. While belonging to the Brassicaceae along with the turnip or swede, it is in fact a radish. As it is often sold as a turnip, it is worth noting its characteristics here. Most varieties are long and heavy like an outsized carrot with white skin, but it can also be short and stumpy. The flesh inside is white, crisp and mild. This vegetable, perhaps best referred to as daikon, is used extensively in both Japanese cooking (where it is shredded, dipped in iced water or pickled) and in Cantonese cookery, where it is used to make turnip cake, the steamed rice-flour pudding that can be either sweet or savoury and is served at Chinese New Year.

turnips
and
swedes
go
with
butter
pepper
beef stock
chicken stock
cream
onions
spring onions
leeks
parsley
garlic
gruyère cheese
bacon
ham
sausages
duck
beef
lamb
carrots
potatoes

SELECTION AND STORAGE

Choose firm, taut turnips or swedes with springy tops. Remember that the leaves are edible, so good-looking ones are a bonus. Do not buy a turnip or swede with soft patches or that does not feel heavy for its size. Do not buy monster-sized vegetables in case they are soft in the centre or stringy. Turnips or swedes should not have a rank, coarse smell.

To store, cut the leaves from the turnips and refrigerate them unwashed in a vegetable storage bag in the crisper. Use the tops within 24 hours. *Turnips* without their leaves will refrigerate well for a week or so in the crisper. Turnips have a higher moisture content than swedes and will not keep as long. *Swedes* will keep well for 3 weeks or more in the crisper.

PREPARATION AND COOKING

Turnips and swedes need to be peeled before cooking; mature specimens need to be peeled quite thickly. Small golf-ball turnips can be cooked unpeeled, but I prefer to peel them in case there is any bitterness in the skin.

Care should be taken when cutting turnips and swedes as, like pumpkin, they are hard and the knife can slip. Place the peeled vegetable on your workbench. Hold it in place with one hand and cut with the other. (The hand holding the vegetable should be over each side of the knife, so that if the knife slips there are no fingers in the way.) Cut once from stem to bottom and then place the cut side flat on the bench before you slice the vegetable.

TO BOIL Cook peeled turnip or swede in 2 cm lightly salted water, tightly covered, until just tender (about 15 minutes). Boiled turnip is a pretty ordinary dish. It really needs to be finished with lots of butter and herbs.

TO STEAM Steaming is especially suited to small turnips, peeled or not. Golf-ball turnips will steam in about 8 minutes (test them with a fine skewer). Cubes or chunks of swede or turnip will take more or less time, depending on the size of the pieces. Finish with butter and herbs or proceed to mash.

TO MASH Boil or steam peeled turnip or swede, then mash with butter and seasonings. Pass the mash through a food mill or purée it in a food processor. A purée of turnip prepared this way will not become pasty as a potato purée does. As with parsnip, a superior mash results if the turnip or swede is boiled in stock rather than water.

pickled turnip
Sprinkle halved, peeled small turnips generously with salt and leave for 30 minutes. Rinse and dry the turnip, then cover with rice vinegar flavoured with Ponzu Sauce or Japanese soy sauce and add a little sugar to taste. Refrigerate for a few hours before using. The pickled turnip keeps for a week.

TO BRAISE | Best of all. As for all braising, butter an appropriately sized gratin or baking dish and add the peeled, cut turnip or swede. Pour in good stock to nearly cover and bake, covered, at 180°C for 45 minutes to 1 hour until the vegetables are tender. If you have too much liquid left in the dish, transfer the uncovered dish to the top of the stove and boil hard, shaking frequently, until the turnip is coated with a sticky sauce. If a shaking of sugar is added at the end with the seasonings, the cooked turnips will be glazed.

TO ROAST | For *soft, melting* turnip, tuck large chunks or whole small turnips around a chicken or leg of lamb for roasting an hour before your estimated finishing time and let them absorb the roasting juices. For *crisply roasted* turnip, roll peeled small turnips or chunks in olive oil and bake them in their own dish until tender, turning once or twice. Small turnips will take 25 minutes, while larger chunks may take 5 minutes longer.

TURNIP LEAVES | Pick over turnip tops to remove any dead leaves or stringy stalks. Wash very well and drain. Cook in plenty of lightly salted water for 3–4 minutes, then drain well. Add butter and season, or proceed with your recipe.

pickled turnips

MAKES 1.5–2 LITRES

In A New Book of Middle Eastern Food *Claudia Roden has much to say about the different methods used to pickle a wide range of foods in the Middle East. This is her recipe for pickled turnips, a classic preparation in the region. They are a delightful nibble and look very exotic as they are tinted bright pink by the beetroot.*

1 kg small white turnips, peeled
celery leaves
2–4 cloves garlic
1 raw beetroot, peeled and sliced
4–5 level tablespoons salt
1 litre water
300 ml white-wine vinegar

Wash turnips and halve or quarter them. Pack into clean, sterilised glass jars with celery leaves and garlic, adding beetroot at regular intervals. Dissolve salt in water and stir in vinegar, then pour over vegetables to cover. Seal jars tightly. Store at room temperature for 10 days, then transfer to a cool spot. This pickle is not long-lasting and should be eaten within a month.

honeyed baby turnips

Toss steamed baby turnips in a little butter melted with the same amount of honey and finish with pepper and herbs.

turnip leaves sautéd with anchovies and breadcrumbs

SERVES 2–4

2 cloves garlic, finely chopped
½ cup extra-virgin olive oil
3 anchovies, drained
½ small fresh chilli, seeded
 and very finely chopped
½ cup fresh fine breadcrumbs
3 cups washed turnip leaves
salt
freshly ground black pepper

Gently sauté garlic in half the oil. Add anchovies and chilli and stir with a wooden spoon until anchovies dissolve. Tip in breadcrumbs and fry, stirring, until golden. Set aside.

Drop turnip leaves into a large saucepan of lightly salted boiling water and cook for 3 minutes. Drain very well. Heat remaining oil in a frying pan, then add drained turnip leaves and sauté for 5 minutes, lifting and stirring. Season. Arrange on a warm serving dish and scatter with the breadcrumb and anchovy mixture.

braised and glazed turnips

SERVES 6

This is my favourite way with turnips. Braising is an interesting way of cooking vegetables, and can be achieved both in the oven (see WITLOF*) and on the stove top. It is most suited to vegetables that take some time to become tender, as it is the gradual exchange of flavours of juices to vegetable and vegetable to juices that results in the subtle and luscious flavours.*

The cooking of the turnip leaves and the final glazing of the vegetables can be delayed until you are ready to serve. The pan is removed from the heat up to 30 minutes before serving and is returned to the heat for the turnip leaves to be added, the turnips to be reheated and the glaze to be reduced.

6 large *or* 12 small turnips,
 with leaves
50 g butter
1 tablespoon olive oil
1 clove garlic, unpeeled and
 lightly crushed (optional)
1 tablespoon sugar
2 cups good stock *or* half wine
 and half water
salt
freshly ground black pepper

Remove leaves from turnips and set aside. Peel turnips, then halve or quarter if large. Heat butter and oil until sizzling in a large saucepan. Drop in garlic, if using, then add turnips, turning to coat. Sprinkle on sugar and stir until a golden caramel has formed. Meanwhile, heat stock. Pour hot stock into turnip pan, then adjust heat to a steady simmer and cover. Cook for 10 minutes, shaking pan from time to time, then check tenderness of turnips – they may require another few minutes. At this point there should still be enough liquid to come halfway up the turnips. (Lower heat and add 1 tablespoon water if this is not so.) The dish can be left, off the heat, for up to 30 minutes at this stage. >

turnip pasta sauce
Stew turnip leaves in olive oil with chopped onion and garlic, then toss through pasta and grind over black pepper.

turnip in meat juice
Stew steamed turnip for a minute in butter, then add a little leftover meat juice and bubble until the liquid has evaporated. Finish with parsley and/or chives and season.

turnip top salad
Dress drained, cooked turnip leaves with extra-virgin olive oil and a few drops of wine vinegar, or toss them in a pan with a chopped garlic clove and olive oil.

While the final cooking is taking place, plunge turnip leaves into boiling, salted water, then drain and chop roughly. When turnips are tender, remove lid and discard garlic clove, then season. Drop in turnip leaves and increase heat, shaking pan gently to distribute the wonderful sticky glaze.

bashed neeps

SERVES 4

This buttery purée is excellent with beef, so don't think you can only enjoy it with a haggis. The pinch of ginger is added on the advice of Mistress Dods, who wrote in 1837 that the ginger 'corrects the flatulent properties of this vegetable'.

3 swedes, peeled and cut
   into chunks
60 g butter
freshly ground white pepper
pinch of ground ginger

In a saucepan, boil swedes in 2 cm lightly salted water, covered, for 10–15 minutes until tender. Drain and return pan to stove to drive off any excess moisture. Mash swedes and beat in butter and seasonings. Serve very hot.

potato A purée of swedes will always be fairly fluid. You could cook some potato as well to add body.

michael's turnip dumplings

SERVES 6

These dumplings are delicious in a clear chicken consommé, as an addition to a stew of chicken or duck and vegetables, or with a poached fillet of beef.

I medium potato, cut into 6
250 g turnips, peeled and
   roughly chopped
½ onion, finely chopped
100 g butter
I teaspoon salt
2 tablespoons sugar
water
100 g fine semolina
100 g self-raising flour
white pepper
2–3 eggs, lightly beaten
extra flour
I litre Chicken Stock ✎ or
   lightly salted water

Put potato, turnip, onion, butter, salt and sugar into a saucepan and barely cover with water. Bring to a boil, uncovered. Simmer, stirring regularly, until vegetables are tender and liquid has nearly evaporated. The last few minutes are important – the pan will need a shake or two as the last spoonfuls of liquid begin to caramelise around the vegetables. Tip mixture into a food processor and quickly process until smooth. Cool a little. Add semolina, flour, pepper and just enough egg to make a cohesive mixture. Turn out onto a lightly floured work surface and knead quickly to bring dumpling mix together. Roll into marble-sized balls or gnocchi shapes (*see* POTATOES). ❯

stir-fried swede
Stir-fry finely sliced turnip or swede and carrot over high heat, then moisten with a little stock and cover for 2 minutes. Toss in herbs or other seasonings and serve alongside a veal chop, grilled liver or pork medallion.

grated turnip
Sprinkle grated turnip with salt and set aside for 30 minutes. Squeeze well and toss with butter and herbs in a frying pan or mix with lightly whisked eggs and cook as an omelette.

Bring stock to a boil in a large saucepan. Drop in some dumplings, allowing room to swell. As dumplings rise to surface (this takes a few minutes), lift them out with a perforated skimmer and drain for a moment over pot. If intended as a garnish for consommé or creamy soup, transfer at once to hot consommé or soup. Otherwise, tip into a buttered dish and put in warm oven until ready to serve. Repeat with remaining dumplings.

ah foon's turnip cake

Although more correctly considered a radish, daikon or moolah *is often referred to as a white turnip. This recipe is delicious! Lup yuk (dried pork) and lap cheong (Chinese sausage, see* SAUSAGES*) are available from Asian food stores.*

vegetable oil
1 tablespoon dried shrimp
2 tablespoons rice wine *or* dry sherry
100 g lup yuk, thinly sliced
100 g Chinese lap cheong sausage, thinly sliced
1 kg daikon, peeled
300 g rice flour
1 teaspoon salt
1 teaspoon sugar
sesame seeds
freshly chopped coriander leaves
finely sliced spring onion

Oil a 20 cm square or round cake tin and line with baking paper. Soak dried shrimp in wine for 30 minutes, then squeeze, drain and chop finely. Slice lup yuk and lap cheong thinly. Sauté slices in a little oil in a non-stick frying pan until fragrant, then tip into a large mixing bowl.

Grate daikon fairly coarsely using the shredding device on a food processor. Add to mixing bowl with flour, salt and sugar and mix together. Pack into oiled tin and cover with foil. Place tin in a bamboo steamer over a pot of boiling water, cover and steam for 1 hour. Allow to cool.

When cake is cool, turn out of tin and cut into 1 cm slices. Heat a little oil in a frying pan and fry slices over high heat, turning once. Sprinkle with sesame seeds, coriander and spring onion and serve.

variation Instead of using a cake tin, pack the mixture directly into a bamboo steamer lined with muslin. Fold muslin over top of mixtue and cover with bamboo lid. Place steamer over pot of boiling water and proceed with recipe.

other recipes

squab pigeon liver and turnip salad *see* LIVER

Veal

Obtaining quality veal has always been difficult in Australia. Veal, the meat from young calves, is very lean and tender and, because of its immaturity, has a delicate flavour. It is an ideal vehicle for well-flavoured sauces and accompaniments. | The best veal comes from calves that are fed on milk until they are slaughtered. When a calf is weaned and starts to eat grass its pale flesh begins to redden and its flavour becomes less delicate. Vealers have always been important in alpine European countries. There, calves born to ensure the necessary lactation of cows over winter months could not be fattened on snow-covered mountain pastures. They were brought inside and kept with their mothers. It follows that the cuisines of northern European countries, especially Italy and Austria, include many veal dishes. | Our cattle have access to open pasture all year and most newly born calves quickly move onto grass. What veal does reach our butcher shops varies widely in quality. There is a huge difference in texture and flavour, for example, between the meat of a newly born calf (reddish wobbly meat sold in Australia as 'bobby' veal, a term dating from the time when farmers received 'a bob' a calf) and a well-muscled calf of 12 weeks of age or thereabouts that has been fed on a milk diet, first from its mother and then on demand in an open barn. >

veal

goes

with

butter

lemons

breadcrumbs

olive oil

white wine

marsala

cream

mushrooms

tomatoes

olives

mustard

artichokes

eggplants

leeks

onions

anchovies

parsley

garlic

raw ham

parmesan cheese

spinach

sorrel

sage

rosemary

potatoes

capers

pasta

rice

The calves bred here for milk veal are not confined in small pens, as happens in some European veal farming. They move freely in open barns and have unrestricted access to milk (and sometimes grain), water and fresh air. Such veal is expensive to produce. There are not many farmers prepared to milk-feed their calves, so the demand always exceeds the supply for meat of this quality. It is fair to say that some of the demand is met by selling consumers young beef and calling it veal.

VARIETIES AND SEASON

Veal is classed by weight and age, not by quality. The Rolls-Royce of veal is produced from calves that weigh 70–90 kg and are 12–16 weeks of age. Such animals are usually of French lineage, being from breeds such as charolais and Belgian blue. There is also good-quality veal available from smaller and younger animals, somewhere from 40–70 kg and 8–12 weeks of age. Some of this veal has been fed on grass as well as milk, and its flesh is darker and correspondingly fuller flavoured. Bobby veal is still for sale, although much of it is used in the processing industries. A chop from a bobby vealer will be about the same size as a lamb chop. A chop from a calf 40 kg and upwards should be at least the size of a pork chop, and a chop from the Rolls-Royce variety will be nearly the size of a T-bone steak. The optimum time for natural veal is winter and spring. As the production of milk-fed animals increases, it is envisaged that it will be possible to have limited supplies of milk-fed veal all year round.

SELECTION AND STORAGE

Every cook needs a trustworthy butcher (and fishmonger and greengrocer). Ask your butcher if he or she can supply good-quality veal and when, and whether it is from a grass-fed or milk-fed calf. Veal should be pale pink or a pinky-red without visible fat. Because of its lack of fat care must be taken not to dry veal when cooking it. The general rule for veal is that moist cooking methods (such as braising and poaching or roasting with continual basting) are used for large pieces or joints. Thin slices from the leg or loin are succulent and can be quickly sautéd. It is important to select an appropriate cut of meat for the dish you want to cook. Do not be tempted to buy and roast a cheaper cut better suited to braising, for example.

FOR ROASTING The best cuts for roasting are from the *leg* or *loin*, the choicest parts of the hindquarter. The leg is usually divided into its various muscles, the *topside*, the *silverside* or the *round*, which is often sold as a *nut* of veal or rump. The leg and loin can be roasted bone-in or boned. The *boned shoulder* is sometimes rolled and tied for roasting, though I prefer to braise this cut.

FOR BRAISING | All the cuts from the *leg* can be successfully braised as a change from roasting. Braising is also recommended for forequarter cuts, such as the *shoulder* or *neck*, and for the *brisket* and *shank*, also known as the shin. The best (meatiest) shanks come from the hindleg, though they are usually not identified as such. Sliced shank is sold for osso buco as *shin of veal*. *Brisket*, or breast of veal as it is also known, can be boned and stuffed. The slow, moist cooking of a braise softens the connective tissue to melting tenderness and results in velvety juices. These same cuts are often boned and chopped and sold as 'pie veal' and they do make beautiful pies and casseroles.

FOR GRILLING | Choose thick *loin* or *best-end-of-neck* chops for grilling. The classic *cotoletta Milanese* is correctly a best-end-of-neck chop served on the bone.

FOR PAN-FRYING | *Scaloppine* or *escalopes* (to use the French term) are suitable for pan-frying, as are thicker *boneless cutlets* or *chops on the bone*. It is important that both you and your butcher understand each other. A scaloppine is cut on the bias from a single leg muscle. It is *not* a slice straight through a boneless leg, which will include 3 different muscles, each of which will behave differently in the pan. While not technically a scaloppine or escalope, sometimes you will be given an opened-out *tenderloin*, stripped of all silver membrane. This is very acceptable and frequently easier to obtain.

FOR POACHING | *Brisket* is ideal for poaching and is usually boned and stuffed; however, it is chopped for a classic *blanquette de veau*. A *nut* of veal or other part of the *leg* is used for the Italian speciality *vitello tonnato*. *Shank* or shin of veal can be poached also, and any miscellaneous pieces, especially bony scraps, will yield marvellous stock.

VEAL OFFAL | Veal offal is considered very special, particularly the liver and sweetbreads. Veal *sweetbreads* are fiddly to prepare and almost impossible to obtain for the home cook as they are a valuable export item, so I mention them simply in passing. Any collection of French recipes will abound in elaborate ways of dealing with sweetbreads, should you be lucky enough to find them. Calf's *liver* is readily available and is delicious quickly grilled, so that it is still pink in the middle (*see* LIVER). Calf's *kidney* is also delicious (*see* KIDNEYS). Each calf only has 2 kidneys, so they are difficult to obtain. Once you have made friends with your butcher, he or she may be able to get them for you. However, most butchers buy in already-trimmed portions and cuts of meat and there are very few left who bone out a whole carcass. Calf's **brains** are very difficult to obtain. Substitute 2 sets of lamb's brains in any recipe calling for calf's brains (*see* BRAINS).

Veal has a great deal of natural gelatine and veal **bones** make the finest stock. The demand for bones is often in excess of the supply, so it is a good idea to place a regular order with your butcher if you plan to keep a supply of good veal stock on hand.

Refrigerate all cuts of veal, freed of wrappings, on a wire rack over a plate or tray and cover with a damp cloth or plastic film to prevent the surface drying out. Use all pieces of veal within 3 days. Minced veal should be refrigerated on a plate, covered with plastic film, and used within 24 hours. Offal should be refrigerated, covered, on a separate plate and used within 24 hours. Vacuum-packed meat will keep up to 1 week in the refrigerator, but be careful that there are no tiny airholes in the bag. Any air bubbles are an indication that the product has deteriorated. Any vacuum-packed meat that is leaking should be inspected closely. If there is more than a containment odour, do not eat it.

PREPARATION AND COOKING

Veal needs protection while cooking to stop it drying out, especially when roasting. This is why braising larger cuts is so popular – moistness is assured.

TO ROAST

Caul fat is an excellent wrap for lean cuts of veal. You can also buy a chunk of **pork hard back fat** from a butcher or good delicatessen; tie thinly sliced sheets or strips of the fat to a rolled veal roast. As the meat cooks, the fat or caul melts, keeping the meat moist. Wrapping a small veal roast in **well-buttered foil** or **basting** it every 20 minutes will also keep it moist. To prepare to roast, remove any silver membrane from the joint to prevent it curling or twisting. Season and wrap the meat in caul fat, back fat or buttered foil, then roast at 180°C, allowing 30 minutes per 500 g. Baste the meat with cooking juices or stock every 20 minutes.

TO BRAISE

Sometimes extra fat is introduced when braising particularly lean cuts of veal, such as silverside, by poking small pieces of pork hard back fat into the surface of the meat. This technique is known as larding and requires a special tool known as a larding needle.

General remarks on braising are included in OXTAIL. Possible liquids to use for braising include stock (veal or chicken), wine with or without tomatoes, and, as a last resort, water, all combined with aromatic herbs and vegetables. Remember that the meat shouldn't be floating in liquid, which reduces in cooking to make a sauce. A braise can be cooked on top of the stove, on a simmer mat if necessary, or in the oven. If the latter, braise at 180°C until the meat is fork-tender. The times will vary considerably depending on the size of the piece or pieces. Expect a rolled and stuffed brisket to serve 4–6 to take 2–2½ hours.

TO GRILL | A veal chop that is 2.5–4 cm thick will need basting or to be marinated in olive oil and will be cooked through in 8–10 minutes, depending on its thickness.

TO PAN-FRY | Cut away any membrane as it will cause the veal to curl and buckle when it hits the hot fat in the pan. Do not pound the meat vigorously to flatten it as this may press out its juices. If the meat really is uneven (and it should not be from a good butcher), flatten it gently between 2 sheets of plastic film using the palm of your hand or the side of a heavy knife. Sauté veal in a mixture of oil and butter or in clarified butter ✓. The cuts recommended for sautéing are frequently protected from drying out by being dipped first in egg or melted butter and then in a coating of fine breadcrumbs. They can also be stuffed and rolled, and the range of sauces and garnishes is infinite. Cooking times vary according to the thickness: 5–8 minutes for a thin scaloppine to 8–10 minutes for a thicker cutlet or chop.

TO POACH | The preferred poaching medium is usually water with aromatic herbs and vegetables. The first stage of poaching is skimming the scum that rises to the surface as the meat starts to firm and cook. Careful skimming and maintaining the liquid at a bare shiver (the surface should not break) will guarantee the clearest broth. In many cases this broth is used as the sauce or to make a sauce. Poaching times will depend on the shape and thickness of the meat. Expect a rolled and stuffed veal brisket to take 1½ hours.

veal scaloppine

SERVES 2

The key here is to use a pan that will just hold the meat. Too big and the fat will burn, too small and the meat juices will bubble and stew the meat instead of quickly evaporating and leaving those precious brown scraps that will be the beginning of the sauce. Keep this as a special dish – it's tricky cooking for more than 2 as the meat will not be at its best if crowded in the pan or held for too long.

salt

freshly ground black pepper

2 × 150–180 g veal scaloppine

plain flour

butter

olive oil

4 thin slices lemon

1 handful fresh sage leaves

crumbed scaloppine
Dip floured veal scaloppine into seasoned whisked egg and then a mixture of two-thirds breadcrumbs and one-third freshly grated parmesan cheese. Fry in olive oil and butter for 1–2 minutes a side and serve with wedges of lemon.

Preheat oven to 150°C and put plates in to warm. Dip seasoned meat in flour and dust off excess. Heat a nut of butter and a small slosh of oil in a frying pan. Drop in lemon and brown on both sides. Remove lemon to a hot plate and slip veal into pan. Seal for 1–2 minutes, then turn and seal other side quickly. Remove veal to oven. Drop sage leaves and 20 g butter into pan and swirl around. Lift pan from heat as butter foams and leaves become crisp. Spoon sage and butter over meat and serve immediately.

rosemary and cream Caramelise lemon slices in the frying pan, then tip in the juice of a lemon or ¼ cup dry white wine and allow to sizzle and bubble. Drop in 1 teaspoon very finely chopped fresh rosemary and 2 tablespoons thick cream. Stir together and allow to bubble up. Turn cooked scaloppine in sauce and serve immediately. **marsala and mushrooms** Tip 1 cup thinly sliced mushrooms into the frying pan and stir around for a minute. Add ¼ cup marsala and allow it to bubble up, stirring gently. Stir in ¼ cup strong stock and bring to a boil. Turn the cooked scaloppine in the sauce and serve immediately. **saltimbocca** Flour and season the veal as above. Secure a sage leaf and a slice of raw ham to each scaloppine with a toothpick. Sauté ham-side down in butter and oil as above, then turn. Tip in ½ cup marsala or dry white wine and bubble for a minute, then reduce heat and simmer for 3–4 minutes until the veal is tender.

veal chops in red wine with bacon and mushrooms

SERVES 4

1 kg veal forequarter chops

salt

freshly ground black pepper

½ cup plain flour

2 tablespoons olive oil

3 thick rashers smoked streaky bacon, cut into small lardons (rind removed)

2 cloves garlic, finely chopped

½ bottle dry red wine

1 generous sprig thyme

1 bay leaf

1 cup Veal Stock ✓

250 g button mushrooms

Preheat oven to 180°C. Roll chops in seasoned flour and set aside. Gently heat oil in an enamelled cast-iron casserole and sauté bacon until fat has rendered. Remove bacon with a slotted spoon and brown the chops in remaining fat, in batches if necessary. Lift chops from casserole and set aside. Sauté garlic for 1 minute. Deglaze casserole with wine, scraping and stirring well. Return chops to casserole, settling them down into the bubbling wine. Scatter bacon into casserole, then drop in thyme and bay leaf. Add sufficient stock to barely cover meat. Cover casserole and cook in oven for 1 hour. Check that chops are nearly tender, then drop in mushrooms and cook for 30 minutes. Serve with rice or boiled small new potatoes rolled in butter and parsley.

osso buco

Ideally, osso buco is made with slices of veal shin from the hindleg, which is meatier than the foreleg. This recipe could also be made with forequarter chops, but the cooking time will probably be a little less.

4 thick *or* 8 smaller slices
   veal shin

salt

freshly ground black pepper

plain flour

50 g butter

2 tablespoons olive oil

½ cup dry white wine

250 g tomatoes, peeled and
   roughly chopped *or*
   1 x 350 g can peeled,
   chopped tomato

6 cloves garlic, coarsely
   chopped

Veal *or* Chicken Stock ✒ *or*
   water

½ quantity Gremolata (see
   p. 494)

Roll veal in seasoned flour, then brown in butter and oil in an enamelled cast-iron casserole. Arrange meat in a single layer, marrow-side uppermost. Pour over wine and allow to bubble up quite strongly. Add tomato, garlic and sufficient stock to barely cover meat (about 2 cups). Place baking paper, cut to fit, on top of liquid to protect meat and delay evaporation.

Cover casserole and simmer very gently for 45 minutes on top of stove or in oven set at 160°C. Check that meat is still just covered with sauce – if not, add a little more stock or water and replace baking paper. Cook another 45 minutes – by this time the sauce should have reduced and become thick and the meat should be quite tender. If the meat is not ready, cook a further 30 minutes. To reduce the sauce if it is too liquid, remove lid and increase heat for 5–10 minutes. To serve, transfer cooked meat very carefully to a hot serving dish or individual plates and scatter with gremolata.

bbq scaloppine

Marinate veal scaloppine in oil and freshly chopped rosemary for 10 minutes, then drain. Slap onto a hot barbecue for 2 minutes a side. Spoon over a mixture of oil and lemon juice thick with chopped herbs.

vitello tonnato

There are many versions of this classic Italian dish. It is ideal for a large gathering as it is easily doubled and can be prepared well in advance. The veal can rest in its sauce, undecorated, for 24 hours. Cover it with plastic film, however, to prevent the sauce darkening too much. If you wish to keep the platter refrigerated for a day, reserve some sauce to add as a final coating before you decorate and present the dish. Allow 30 minutes for the dish to return to room temperature.

2 x 750 g nuts of veal
4 anchovies, cut into pieces
1 onion, sliced
1 stick celery, sliced
1 carrot, sliced
3 cloves garlic, peeled
1 bay leaf
1 sprig rosemary
2 stalks parsley
1½ lemons
½ cup dry white wine
water
extra anchovies
olives
capers *or* caper berries

SAUCE

1 x 150 g can tuna in olive
   oil, drained
1 tablespoon drained capers
4 anchovies
1½ cups Mayonnaise
salt
white pepper
lemon juice (optional)

fried scaloppine
Spread veal scaloppine thinly with tapenade before dipping in egg and then in breadcrumbs and frying.

Make incisions all over veal with tip of a small knife and insert pieces of anchovy. Select a large saucepan or enamelled cast-iron casserole that will hold meat fairly snugly. Place meat in pan with vegetables, garlic and herbs, then add ½ lemon cut in half. Add wine and sufficient water to just cover meat. Simmer very gently on stove until meat is easily pierced with a fine skewer. This will take 1½–2 hours. Allow meat to cool in its strained cooking liquid, then refrigerate, preferably overnight or for up to 2 days.

To make the sauce, blend tuna, capers and anchovies to a smooth paste in a food processor, then add mayonnaise. If sauce is thicker than cream, thin it by working in a little veal cooking liquid. Adjust seasoning. It may take a few drops of lemon juice, too.

Remove veal from its cooking liquid and wipe it free of any jellied stock. Select a large meat platter and spread a thin layer of sauce on it. Slice veal thinly and arrange a layer on sauce, overlapping slices a little. Cover with more sauce, then arrange more sliced meat and more sauce. Continue until all the meat has been sliced and sauced, finishing with a layer of sauce. Thinly slice remaining lemon and decorate sauce, adding the extra anchovies, olives and capers. Serve with a leafy salad or sliced celery and hardboiled egg.

veal braised with mushrooms and wine   SERVES 4

This is the sort of cooking I wish to encourage. Ten minutes of activity and then it is all in the oven, so that you can take off your shoes, read the paper in peace and collect your thoughts after a busy day.

salt
freshly ground black pepper
1 x 750 g nut of veal *or* other
   small veal roast
2 tablespoons olive oil
50 g butter
(*continued next page*)

Preheat oven to 180°C and season veal. Heat oil and butter in an enamelled cast-iron casserole that will hold all the vegetables. Drop in rosemary and lightly crushed garlic and allow to sizzle for a minute. Seal veal well on both sides, then pour in wine. Add potatoes and stock. >

I generous sprig rosemary

2 cloves garlic, unpeeled

3 tablespoons marsala *or* port
   or ½ cup dry white wine

8 small potatoes

I cup strong Veal Stock ✓

16 button mushrooms

Tightly cover casserole and place in oven for 1 hour. Check meat is nearly tender and turn it over in the juices, then tip in mushrooms. Cover again and cook for 30 minutes. Serve with a leafy green salad.

veal brisket stuffed with olives

SERVES 4–6

Ask your butcher to bone half a brisket (also known as a breast of veal) to create a pocket for stuffing. Remember to ask for the bones, as they are perfect for making stock.

½ veal brisket, boned with
   pocket cut

I tablespoon olive oil

I thick rasher smoked streaky
   bacon, diced *or* several
   slices pancetta, chopped

I onion, diced

I stick celery, finely sliced

I carrot, diced

4 cloves garlic, peeled

½ cup marsala *or* white wine

2 tablespoons tomato paste

I cup Veal Stock ✓

I bay leaf

I large sprig thyme

STUFFING

250 g minced pork *or* half
   pork and half veal

I thick slice sourdough bread,
   crumbled (crusts removed)

½ cup stoned black olives,
   coarsely chopped

½ cup coarsely chopped
   fresh parsley

2 cloves garlic, chopped finely

salt

freshly ground black pepper

I egg

a little milk

To make the stuffing, mix all ingredients to a cohesive paste. Push stuffing into pocket in veal and even it out. Close pocket with fine metal skewers, or sew it up.

Preheat oven to 180°C. In an enamelled cast-iron casserole or a deep baking dish that will take meat snugly, heat oil and gently sauté bacon, vegetables and garlic until softened and lightly coloured. Put in veal and brown gently all over. Increase heat and pour in wine. Let wine bubble and reduce, then add tomato paste mixed with stock. Tuck in bay leaf and thyme, then cover meat with baking paper cut to fit. Put on lid (or cover tightly with a doubled layer of foil if using a baking dish) and transfer to oven for 2–2½ hours. Test meat is quite tender, then lift it out and cut into thick slices. Serve with pasta that has been tossed through the meat juices.

veal meatballs
Season 300 g minced veal with salt, pepper, herbs and 2 tablespoons Dijon mustard and mix in an egg. Roll into tiny meatballs and fry in clarified butter ✓. Scatter with chopped toasted pine nuts and serve with drinks, or toss through pasta.

Vinegar

Vinegar A popular condiment throughout Europe for thousands of years, vinegar derives its name from *vin aigre*, which in turn comes from the latin *vinum* (wine) and *acer* (sour), giving a direct clue to its character. In Roman and Byzantine times mustard was diluted with vinegar in very much the same way as mustard is made today. Verjuice, the tart juice of unripe grapes, was also used to add acidity to dishes and sauces (*see* GRAPES AND VINE LEAVES). Rice has long been used in Asian cuisines to create a range of vinegars too (*see* Basics). By the fifteenth century, salad, more or less as we know it today, was served and dressed with oil and vinegar. In *The History of Food*, Maguelonne Toussaint-Samat quotes Rabelais's list of suitable salad ingredients as including cress, hops, wild cress, asparagus and chervil. There is a famous saying that a good dressing demands a miser for the vinegar, a spendthrift for the oil and a wise man for the salt. We might also add to this that there should be as much concern about the quality of each of these ingredients as the quantity. Olive oil is dealt with in OLIVES AND OLIVE OIL, and salt is mentioned in Basics. It seems appropriate, then, to include a few paragraphs regarding the choice and use of vinegar – in this case, primarily wine or fruit vinegars.

VARIETIES AND SEASON

There is great variety in the flavours of vinegars available. Flavour is derived from the nature and quality of the base ingredient, the method of manufacture, and the herbs or fruits that can be macerated in the vinegar. There are 3 principal methods of manufacture.

ORLÉANAIS METHOD | This is the oldest vinegar-making process. Red or white wine (or sherry or other wines) is stored in partially full and loose-bunged oak barrels. In the past the wine was allowed to acetify naturally, but today most vinegar-makers add cultures of acetic acid bacteria to quickly dominate any wild micro-organisms in the wine, thus reducing the chance of these undesirable bacteria and yeast spoiling the vinegar. Usually the process takes place in less than 12 months, then the vinegar is fined (made clear), filtered and made ready for bottling. Some vinegar-makers age the vinegar in oak barrels before bottling, as this allows the vinegar and wine flavours to be made more complex and produces a softer, richer-flavoured vinegar. Vinegars made by this method are powerful and should be used judiciously. The bacteria that act on the base material form a greyish mass of *Mycoderma aceti* that is sometimes known as a vinegar 'mother'. This mother can continue to convert wine to vinegar indefinitely.

The same method of manufacture can be used to make fruit vinegars, such as cider or pear. The fruit is frozen after harvesting to facilitate extraction of the juice. The Berry Farm in the Margaret River region of Western Australia produces lovely fruit vinegars as well as excellent red-wine vinegar. Still more excellent red-wine vinegars are produced in South Australia at the Yalumba (Hill Smith label) and Coriole vineyards and at de Bortoli in Victoria. These are the vinegars I choose.

RAPID PROCESSES | Commercial vinegars are usually produced by rapid processes as the slowness of the Orléanais method results in high production costs. These rapid processes fall into 2 main categories, the trickling process and the submerged culture process. In the *trickling process*, bacteria-soaked wood shavings are soaked in an alcoholic solution made from malt or sugar cane until the liquid converts to acetic acid. The process is completed in a few days. The *submerged-culture process* involves using a high degree of aeration and mixing to promote rapid growth of the acetic acid bacteria in an alcoholic solution, thus producing the vinegar. The process can be run continuously, and completed vinegar is generally drawn off daily.

vinegar goes with
salad leaves
cucumbers
duck livers
strawberries
dill pickles
peppercorns
egg sauces
herbs
fish
olive oil

These rapid-process vinegars use the lowest-cost sources of alcohol, such as neutral cane spirit, and this results in vinegars that are very neutral in flavour. They are suitable for making pickles or relishes where plenty of other flavours will be introduced, but are not recommended to dress a salad.

BALSAMIC VINEGAR | Balsamic vinegar is a speciality vinegar from around Modena in the north of Italy. It commences with unfermented trebbiano grape juice (must), which is boiled down before the fermentation process begins. It is during this process that some of the caramel flavours that are characteristic of this vinegar are produced. The concentrated grape juice is allowed to ferment in barrels and the alcohol converts slowly to acetic acid. The young vinegar is transferred from one wooden barrel to a smaller wooden barrel over a period of years and gains complexity of flavour from the various barrels. The wood for the barrels may include chestnut, oak, mulberry, juniper and other timbers. The process lasts somewhere between 5 and 30 years. The original bulk of the grape must is vastly reduced to a powerful, slightly sweet and syrupy essence at the completion of the process. The very finest balsamic vinegars are considered as precious as the best liqueurs and are very powerful. They are also very costly. I have been offered a teaspoonful of one of these long-aged treasures by a fine Italian chef as one might be offered a digestif after an excellent dinner.

SELECTION AND STORAGE

Decide to reserve commercially made clear vinegar for pickling only. Wine vinegar is delightful, and such a little is used each time it is not extravagant to buy a good one. Aged vinegars will have developed richer, more concentrated flavours and you will need less of them. Flavoured vinegars are widely available, too. Often this means commercial vinegar flavoured with a herb or crushed fruit. Sometimes it means Orléanais vinegar flavoured with a herb or herbs. Sometimes it means fruit and vinegar preparations, such as old-fashioned raspberry vinegar cordial, intended to be further diluted (and still available at Seppeltsfield in South Australia's Barossa Valley). All vinegars will evaporate and oxidise, so keep bottles tightly closed and in a cool, dark cupboard.

PREPARATION AND COOKING

Vinegar requires no preparation other than to uncork the bottle. *Red-wine vinegars* are an essential part of my everyday salad dressing, and I use no more than 1 teaspoon of vinegar to maybe 4–5 parts extra-virgin olive oil. The *best aged vinegars* are an excellent deglazer of the frying pan. Tip in a spoonful and allow it to hiss and bubble and almost evaporate in a second. Follow with a swirl of butter or olive oil or a dash of wine or stock and you have a sauce for sautéd liver, underfillet of lamb, fillet of fish or sliced

balsamic lamb

Seal some lamb underfillets in a little olive oil in a hot frying pan, then add 1 teaspoon balsamic vinegar and roll the meat in it. Reduce the juices for 3 minutes, turning the lamb once or twice, and serve.

raspberry duck salad

Deglaze the pan with raspberry vinegar after sautéing duck livers. Add a little stock, then pour the syrupy dressing over the livers sitting on a small handful of salad leaves and grind pepper over.

zucchini. A good vinegar can also be used in cooking to accent a dish or in a marinade. Some sauces include vinegar (Béarnaise✎ depends on **tarragon vinegar** in the initial reduction). It has become very fashionable to use **balsamic vinegar** in the kitchen. It is a fantastic ingredient, but I question its appropriateness with a simple salad of green leaves. Conversely, it is a revelation tossed with sugared strawberries! And Gazpacho (*see* TOMATOES) is not the same unless the final zing comes from Spanish **sherry vinegar**.

Throughout this book vinegar is used in dressings, sauces, pickling solutions (both sweet and savoury), relishes and chutney. As vinegar supports other ingredients rather than acting on its own, I refer you to the ingredient you wish to spice, bottle or preserve for an appropriate recipe.

When pickling with vinegar the preserving agent is the acetic acid in the vinegar rather than the small amount of salt that is sometimes used to draw moisture from the fruit or vegetable to be processed, either as a preliminary brine bath or as a dry-salt rub. Dry-salting is more usual for pickles intended to be crisp, and a brine for those that are intended to be soft.

Pickling solutions can be sweet or savoury, and a specialised vinegar can impart extra flavour. Sweet pickling solutions, used for fruit such as plums, peaches, pears, quinces, and so on, are often flavoured with aromatic spices such as cloves, cinnamon, bay leaves and allspice and these preparations are often described as 'spiced fruit'. Savoury pickling solutions, for eggs, onions or shallots, cucumbers or garlic, often include fresh or dried bay leaves, fresh herbs (such as tarragon, fennel and thyme) and spices such as peppercorns. The time that the fruit or vegetable should be simmered in the vinegar solution varies considerably, and in some recipes the solution is made separately and poured hot or cold over the fruit or vegetable packed into jars.

When pickling fruit or vegetables remember that both salt and vinegar are corrosive and all pots and saucepans used should be enamelled cast-iron or stainless steel. Similarly, choose glass or glazed stoneware containers to store your pickles and ensure the lids are protected.

recipes

tarragon vinegar

This is more of an idea than a recipe and is a simple and useful one for all cooks. It evolved through a discussion with Peter Wall, winemaker from Yalumba, famous for its vinegars as well as its wines, as we prepared for a seminar on fermentation during Melbourne's 1996 Food and Wine Festival's Master Class weekend. Peter insists on summer tarragon, believing the herb's unique flavour is at its best in that season, and uses masses of it. He also removes the herb once it has done its job of flavouring the vinegar and refrigerates it for later use in stocks and sauces. Peter uses a sherry vinegar or a blend of sherry and red-wine vinegar.

balsamic pears
Add 1 teaspoon balsamic vinegar to a pan of poached pears.

good-quality vinegar
tarragon

Stuff a clean wide-necked jar or bottle with tarragon (don't skimp) and pour in vinegar. Seal. Allow to mature for up to 3 months in a cool spot, checking now and then, until the flavour is strong enough for you. Strain vinegar and decant into sterilised bottles for storing. Refrigerate the pickled tarragon in a screw-top glass jar and use in the winter months when fresh tarragon is out of season. Discard any unused vinegar 6 months after opening it.

other recipes

bread and butter zucchini pickles *see* ZUCCHINI AND SQUASH

chinese-style trotters with ginger and black rice vinegar *see* TROTTERS

green tomato relish *see* TOMATOES

kathy's tomato relish *see* TOMATOES

maggie's pickled quinces *see* QUINCES

mango chutney *see* TROPICAL FRUIT

old-fashioned raspberry vinegar *see* BERRIES AND CURRANTS

peach or nectarine chutney *see* PEACHES AND NECTARINES

persian sugar-pickled garlic *see* GARLIC

pickled cherries *see* CHERRIES

pickled cornichons *see* CUCUMBERS

pickled cumquats *see* CUMQUATS

pickled eggs *see* EGGS

pickled ginger *see* GINGER

pickled okra *see* OKRA

pickled plums *see* PLUMS AND PRUNES

pickled turnips *see* TURNIPS AND SWEDES

pickled watermelon rind *see* MELONS

pineapple and rum pickle *see* PINEAPPLE

plum sauce *see* PLUMS AND PRUNES

Witlof

Witlof I have mentioned witlof briefly in SALAD GREENS, but as it is so good as a cooked vegetable I have decided to give it its own entry. | One of the problems with this vegetable has been getting its name right. It is a member of the large chicory family and counts among its relations radicchio, another highly valued salad vegetable. In fact, witlof is simply a forced form of radicchio, both of which are forms of *Cichorium intybus*, wild chicory. Once called chicory, then Belgian endive or witloof, it now seems to be marketed in Australia exclusively as witlof. However, recipes for it may well be found under endive or chicory in European or American books. Read the recipe to find out whether a loose-leafed vegetable is being referred to (which we would call radicchio) or whether it is indeed what we know as witlof. | To achieve its pristine colour and tight-packed form, witlof is forced and blanched. The young plant is dug up and its roots and top are trimmed; it is then buried in sand and held in complete darkness at a constant temperature until the witlof spear forms. (This technique first came into being in the 1840s in Belgium.) Witlof has to be stored under purple paper at the greengrocer's to protect it from light, which turns it green and bitter. >

Once witlof was only seen during the winter months and its crisp, slightly bitter leaves were the standby in a winter salad bowl. It is still a favourite salad of mine and I like it with softer things such as slices of ripe pear or room-temperature creamy blue cheese. It goes especially well with other bitey leaves, such as watercress and rocket, and its leaf spears are useful as containers for cocktail food. And don't forget its attractions as a cooked vegetable! Witlof is particularly wonderful braised. The art of braising vegetables is one I champion at every opportunity. Like so much oven-cooking, braising has the advantage of needing little attention once one has understood the basics and prepared the dish properly.

VARIETIES AND SEASON

The more usual variety of witlof is white with tightly furled leaves, the tips that one can see being pale gold to pale green. Recently I have been able to obtain a red variety. This looks exquisite in a salad but when cooked the red turns to a less attractive shade of mud. Witlof is now available all year.

SELECTION AND STORAGE

Witlof is not a vegetable to buy many days in advance as it deteriorates quickly when exposed to light. Choose tight chicons (as each witlof is sometimes called) and avoid any where the tips or edges of the leaves are browning or loosening. For this reason, I prefer to buy my witlof individually rather than on a plastic tray, as you so often see it. One witlof per person is perfect if you are preparing a salad or a cooked dish.

Refrigerate witlof in a brown paper bag in the vegetable crisper and use it within 2 days. Better than brown paper would be to ask your greengrocer for any extra purple paper, so that you can wrap the witlof in it.

PREPARATION AND COOKING

Do not soak witlof. Instead, pull away any damaged outside leaves and wipe with a damp cloth. If preparing witlof for cooking, cut a thin slice from the root end and proceed with the recipe. To use witlof as a salad vegetable, pull away as many leaves as will come easily, then cut another slice from the base to free more of the very tightly furled inner leaves, and so on.

Some recipes instruct cooks to blanch witlof in slightly salted water until barely tender before finishing it with stock, butter or cream. An even more delicious result is achieved if the entire cooking can be done with light stock. The initial cooking will probably take 10–15 minutes, depending on the size of the witlof; the finishing (about 5 minutes) can be done at a higher temperature.

recipes

witlof in cheese sauce

4 witlof

Chicken Stock or water

4 slices leg ham (optional)

2 tablespoons Dijon mustard
   (optional)

40 g butter

1 cup milk

1 tablespoon plain flour

60 g gruyère cheese, cut
   into tiny dice

salt

freshly ground black pepper

fresh breadcrumbs

2 tablespoons freshly grated
   parmesan or crumbled
   creamy blue cheese

Preheat oven to 180°C. Simmer witlof in stock for 10 minutes. Drain very well, pressing witlof to ensure sauce will not be diluted unattractively by oozing juices. Spread each slice of ham with mustard, if using, and wrap around each witlof. Using half the butter, grease a gratin dish into which witlof will just fit neatly and arrange vegetables in dish.

Heat milk in a small saucepan. Melt remaining butter in another pan, then stir in flour and cook for 3 minutes, stirring. Gradually whisk in hot milk and stir until it reaches simmering point. Drop in gruyère and allow to soften. Taste sauce for salt and pepper and spoon over witlof. Scatter with breadcrumbs and parmesan (or dot with pieces of blue cheese). Bake for 15 minutes until golden brown and bubbling. Serve as a first course or as a light lunch with a salad.

no cheese A richer but stunning variation is to mix ¼ cup marsala into 1 cup cream with some sliced green olives and to bake the ham-covered witlof in this rather than the cheese sauce. Breadcrumbs are still a good idea.

braised witlof

Braising relies on a relatively small amount of liquid compared with the main ingredient. The liquid surrounds and nourishes the main ingredient and each gives its flavours to the other. If the cooking time is judged properly, the liquid will have become a sauce precisely at the time the main ingredient is ready. Choosing an appropriately sized dish is very important.

Because of its attractive bitterness I like to serve this dish with something that is quite bland in flavour, such as a roasted quail, or alternatively with something rather rich that can do with having its richness offset by bitterness, such as a ham hock, pig's trotter or squab pigeon.

butter

witlof

salt

freshly ground black pepper

stock

Preheat oven to 180°C. Butter a gratin dish in which the required amount of witlof will just fit. Roll witlof in melted butter, then arrange in dish and season. Pour over stock to come halfway up the witlof. Press baking

garnish for witlof
Sauté a fine dice of celery, onion, carrot and garlic until starting to brown and scatter over braised witlof with parsley.

witlof cream
Stir a little lemon juice, Dijon mustard, salt and pepper into some cream and whip it firmly. Toss finely sliced witlof and celery in this dressing, then scatter generously with chopped chives and serve with smoked eel or smoked trout.

fruit and nut witlof
Scatter a handful of sultanas and/or another of pine nuts over witlof to be braised.

paper cut to fit right down on witlof and then cover with a lid or a doubled piece of foil. Bake for 20 minutes. Remove dish from oven and turn witlof. Return to oven, uncovered and without baking paper, for a further 20 minutes. By the end of the cooking time the witlof should be tender and the sauce reduced and sticky. If the vegetables are cooked but still swimming in juice, remove them to a warm dish and boil liquid hard on stove. Return witlof to dish when only a few spoonfuls are left, just enough to give a shiny and sticky finish.

variations Scatter the witlof after the first 20 minutes with a layer of breadcrumbs or add some coarsely grated gruyère. Alternatively, use Fresh Tomato Sauce (*see* TOMATOES) in place of some of the stock at the beginning of the braising time.

grilled witlof
Halve braised witlof (or witlof that has been cooked in stock or salted water) lengthwise, then brush with olive oil and grill or barbecue until the exposed surface is a rich golden brown, 5–10 minutes.

buttered witlof

SERVES 4

This quick method of cooking witlof is the perfect accompaniment to a slice of veal.

4 witlof
4 tablespoons butter
salt
freshly ground black pepper
juice of ½ lemon
2 teaspoons freshly snipped
  chives
2 tablespoons freshly chopped
  parsley

Cut each witlof crosswise into 2–3 cm slices. Melt butter in a frying pan, then add witlof and toss to coat. Add seasoning to taste. Sauté for 4–5 minutes, then add lemon juice and stir in chives and parsley. Serve immediately.

extra richness Add 4 tablespoons rich stock when sautéing, or some thick cream before stirring in the herbs.

other recipes

pear and walnut salad *see* PEARS

Yabbies

Yabbies   Australia has many varieties of freshwater crayfish but the best known is the yabby. *Cherax destructor* is so named for its habit of burrowing to escape drought or extreme cold, often into the walls of irrigation channels or dams. The yabby is widely distributed throughout the country and lives naturally in freshwater billabongs, lakes, rivers, dams and swamps and can tolerate very high temperatures.   The French equivalent is the *écrevisse*, acclaimed as a delicacy and so appreciated that supplies are now very scarce. Crawfish are a similar and much-vaunted delicacy caught in the bayous of Louisiana, and tourists line up at New Orleans restaurants to eat these creatures (a third the size of our yabbies).   Until recently Australian gourmets largely ignored their yabbies. Catching and eating them was almost exclusively a recreational sport for country children. Thanks to the efforts of a few dedicated people, cooks are now well supplied with clean, plump yabbies, most of them farmed but some still caught in the wild in baited pots. All are purged in clean water before delivery to customers. >

yabbies
go
with
butter
olive oil
pepper
chillies
thyme
dill
spring onions
cream
parsley
bay leaves
garlic
tomatoes
saffron
fish sauce
light soy sauce
mayonnaise

Yabby-farming is not new to Australia, since most farmers have kept a few in their dams, but the new farming methods are. Wild-caught broodstock is transferred to breeding ponds, and the juveniles are transferred to grow-out ponds. The mature yabbies are supplied to restaurants and specialist retailers. Extensive culture farms are found in the Wimmera and Goulburn Valley, Victoria, and around Bordertown, South Australia, but the largest are in Western Australia's Swan Valley.

Yabbies are marketed here and overseas – the main export destinations being Hong Kong and Singapore. It is so important that we recognise our culinary resources before others do, otherwise we face soaring prices (as has happened with rock lobster) or the supply being commandeered. At the time of writing, about a third of the commercial production of freshwater crayfish is exported, but it is said that there is unlimited potential in Asian markets. Exporting produce is a good thing, as long as local supply (and the quality) is maintained at affordable prices.

VARIETIES AND SEASON

The name yabby is applied to all members of the *Cherax* species except *C. quadricarinatus*, the Queensland redclaw, and *C. tenuimanus*, the Western Australian marron. In Western Australia yabbies are known as koonacs and gilgies. The body colour of the yabby ranges from pale grey–blue to dark brown, with a mottled pattern on the outer edge of the claws. It has 2 main front claws and 8 slender legs that are of no culinary importance. The shells of yabbies turn a brilliant orange–red when cooked.

While the yabby is the subject of this section, we do have other freshwater crayfish. The Tasmanian freshwater crayfish (*Astacopsis gouldi*) is fully protected as it is an endangered species, while Victoria's now rarely seen massive Murray River crayfish (*Euastacus armatus*) is a casualty of water salinity and the introduction of the European carp to the Murray River system. The Western Australian marron, indigenous to the Margaret River region, is closely controlled, although licensed marron farming is permitted on Kangaroo Island as well as in Western Australia. Queensland's excellent redclaw is also farmed. It does not travel well and is best enjoyed in Queensland.

Yabbies are now available all year, although supplies are limited during the winter when yabbies living in natural habitats dig in for the colder months. They are at their best in spring and autumn. Yabbies usually breed in the summer and during this time the flesh can be loose. Like all crustaceans, they moult regularly and just after casting their shell the flesh is also loose. It is for these reasons that one is instructed to prefer crustaceans that feel heavy for their size. Note that berried females, that is yabbies with eggs underneath, are protected.

SELECTION AND STORAGE

If you have caught your own yabbies, store them in a bucket of cold water for 48 hours so that they can purge themselves, and place a cake rack or similar over the bucket to prevent any yabbies wandering off. If there are too many yabbies in the bucket the larger ones may attack and eat the smaller ones. If you think this might happen, divide the yabbies between 2 buckets.

Most yabbies are sold whole and *cooked*, although live ones can be found occasionally. *Live* yabbies from yabby farms are sold purged. Never buy dead uncooked yabbies as deterioration will be guaranteed. Be very critical when buying cooked yabbies – they should feel firm in your hand, be bright red and smell pleasant. Unless you are certain that they have been cooked in the last 12 hours, don't buy them. Like all crustaceans, yabbies start to deteriorate quickly when cooked. Reject any yabby smelling of ammonia. Make a friend of your fishmonger and ask his or her advice. Sometimes the yabbies might be supplied live to the fish market and be cooked on the spot. If this is the case there is not a problem. Restaurants have live yabbies delivered to the door several times a week. The yabbies go to sleep in the cold, so yabbies stored in a commercial coolroom stay very quiet and maintain top condition until they are cooked.

Allow 4–6 yabbies of average size (60 g) per person as a first course with a rich sauce; double or triple this quantity if the entire meal is to be yabbies. Cooked yabbies should be refrigerated covered with a wet cloth and must be eaten within 24 hours.

PREPARATION AND COOKING

If you have bought *freshly cooked* yabbies, remember that they should not be cooked again but used for a salad. If you are preparing live yabbies, they need to be in good condition whether you are going to serve them hot or cold. This means that the yabbies cannot be alive and screaming as they hit the hot cooking liquid. If they are, they will thrash about and struggle and, even ignoring any possible psychological trauma to the cook, the yabby flesh risks becoming pasty. As yabbies go to sleep when they are cold, chill them for an hour or so before cooking. They will slide into the cooking liquid and die instantly without suffering and without loss of condition.

Because the yabbies one buys are already purged there is not much grit in their intestines. In Europe it is common practice to extract the intestinal thread of freshwater crayfish by twisting it out of a live creature, which is held firmly while this bit of torture takes place. I am not sentimental about eating animals but I cannot condone such a barbaric practice. Such trauma frequently results in pasty yabby flesh.

TO COOK

Boiling water This method is used when the yabbies are to be cooked in a sauce, added to a soufflé or tart filling or roasted. Dip chilled live yabbies quickly into boiling water to kill them instantly, then transfer them to a bowl of water with ice in it to stop the cooking process. **Court-bouillon** This method is used when no further cooking is required. Cook chilled live yabbies in Court-bouillon for 8–10 minutes or until the shells turn bright red. When cooking yabbies in a court-bouillon, offer them still in their shells and provide really large napkins, fingerbowls and a huge platter for the debris. Don't cook too many yabbies at once if you want to enjoy them hot, as the effort of shelling them and cracking the claws takes time. Your guests will appreciate a half-time clear-up of shell, guts and hands and a fresh delivery of steaming yabbies.

TO SHELL

Pull the tail section away from the head. With the forefinger and thumb, press in the edges to loosen the shell. Peel the tail shell away, leaving the end tail piece on or not as you wish. Reserve the head to make a sauce or stock. Crack the large claws and serve, or add them to a stock or sauce preparation.

The edible meat of the yabby is almost exclusively in the tail. The big front claws have very sweet meat but it is not worth extracting the tiny quantity except for the very largest creatures. The claws and heads make sensational soup or sauce, so all is not lost.

recipes

yabbies in broth
Ladle yabbies cooked in Court-bouillon into bowls with a little of the cooking liquor.

thai-style dipping sauce
MAKES ½ CUP

This quantity is sufficient for 20–30 yabbies.

2 tablespoons palm sugar, crushed

2 tablespoons fresh lime *or* lemon juice

1 tablespoon fish sauce

2 small fresh chillies, seeded and finely chopped

Dissolve palm sugar in lime juice. Add fish sauce and chilli and mix well. This sauce can be stored for several days.
variations The proportions of lime juice, fish sauce and sugar can be varied to taste. A little tamarind water could be added too, or chopped coriander or mint leaves.

garlic and ginger dipping sauce
MAKES ½ CUP

This sauce is useful for other fish and shellfish too. The quantity is sufficient for 20–30 yabbies.

1 teaspoon vegetable oil

1 clove garlic, finely chopped

2 teaspoons finely chopped
fresh ginger

100 ml Fresh Tomato Sauce
(see p. 709)

2 teaspoons sambal oelek

1 teaspoon fish sauce

juice of 1 lemon or lime

Heat the oil in a frying pan and sear garlic
and ginger for 30 seconds until fragrant.
Stir in remaining ingredients and taste for
fish sauce and sambal oelek. Dilute with
Court-bouillon ✒ if too thick. This sauce
does not keep well, so make it when you
are ready to use it.

yabbies and sauce
*Serve freshly cooked
yabbies with
Beurre Blanc ✒,
Hollandaise Sauce ✒
or Ponzu Sauce ✒ .*

yabby salad with walnuts and potatoes   SERVES 4

*For this salad you will need to reserve the court-bouillon used to cook the
yabbies.*

28 yabbies, cooked in Court-
bouillon ✒

16–20 walnut halves

walnut oil *or* extra-virgin
olive oil

8 small yellow-fleshed
potatoes

Mayonnaise ✒

4 small handfuls mixed salad
leaves, washed and dried

2 tablespoons finely chopped
fresh parsley

1 teaspoon finely chopped
fresh dill (optional)

Select the 4 largest and most beautiful
yabbies and set aside. Remove head and
claws from remaining yabbies and set aside.
Shell tails, leaving fanned tail piece
attached. Drop shelled tail meat into a bowl
of court-bouillon used to cook yabbies, both
to wash out any vestiges of grit in intestinal
tracts and to prevent flesh hardening while
you shell the rest. Rinse all shelled tails
in court-bouillon, then transfer them to
another bowl, checking that there is no
unsightly black thread left in any yabby.
Discard this court-bouillon. Ladle some
fresh court-bouillon over yabby tails and
leave at room temperature.

Rub walnuts with oil and toast in an oven set at 180°C until golden and
crunchy. Leave at room temperature. Cook potatoes in lightly salted water
until tender, drain and slice thickly into a large bowl. Allow potato to cool
for a few minutes, then drain yabbies on kitchen paper and add to bowl.
Toss with enough mayonnaise to coat lightly. Arrange salad leaves in a
small mound on each plate. Tuck potato around salad and pile on yabby
tails. Scatter over walnuts and herbs. Place a whole yabby on each plate.
variations Forget the salad leaves and substitute boiled artichokes for
the potatoes. Spread the leaves and pile the shelled tails into the heart of
the artichoke. Or serve warm asparagus spears instead of the potatoes,
or as well as.

yabby bisque

SERVES 4

This classic shellfish bisque is a luxury dish. I don't like waste and all those heads and claws of yabbies have to be used somehow! The heads and claws can be frozen and the soup-making delayed if you don't want to have yabbies 2 days in a row. Uncooked heads and tails will give the best flavour, but cooked ones are fine to use.

yabbies on rye
Serve freshly cooked yabbies with thinly sliced rye bread and spicy relish or mayonnaise flavoured with plenty of freshly chopped dill.

2 tablespoons olive oil
40 g butter
1 small onion, finely chopped
½ carrot, sliced
1 stick celery, chopped
2 cloves garlic, sliced
1 bay leaf
3 tablespoons tomato paste
heads and claws from
   20 cooked yabbies
½ cup dry white wine
tiny pinch of powdered saffron
   (optional)
1 litre Court-bouillon
2 tablespoons ground rice or
   rice flour
salt
freshly ground black pepper

Heat half the oil and butter in a heavy-based saucepan and sauté vegetables and garlic until lightly coloured. Add bay leaf and tomato paste and stir well. Increase heat, then add remaining oil and butter and sauté yabby claws and heads over high heat for 5 minutes. Transfer contents of pan to a food processor – a bit at a time – and crush. Transfer crushed yabby shells and vegetables to pan and return it to heat. Pour in wine, stir well and add saffron (if using) and court-bouillon. Simmer for 15 minutes.

Patiently and slowly force contents of pan through coarsest disc of a food mill into a bowl. The quality of the soup will depend on the effort exerted at this step. Stir ground rice to a paste with a little soup, then stir into sieved soup. Return soup to rinsed-out pan and simmer again, stirring, for about 10 minutes. Pass soup through medium disc of food mill into a bowl. Return soup again to rinsed-out pan and adjust seasoning. It should be quite peppery. Reheat to serve. Add a teaspoonful of lightly whipped cream to each bowl, if liked.

yabby tails If you have extra yabby tails you could warm some in a little butter and a touch of cayenne pepper and put a couple in each soup plate before ladling the soup over.

yabby tail tartlets

MAKES 6

Don't be fooled by the size of these tarts – this dish is rich! As yabbies are freshwater creatures you will need to add more salt than if using prawns, for instance.

½ quantity Shortcrust Pastry ✎

3 tomatoes, peeled, seeded
and chopped

I teaspoon brandy

few drops of Tabasco

20 g butter

salt

4 egg yolks

I cup cream

I teaspoon freshly chopped
parsley

18 freshly cooked yabbies

Line 6 × 8–10 cm loose-bottomed flan tins with pastry and bake blind ✎ at 200°C for 20 minutes. Remove pastry cases from oven and reduce temperature to 180°C.

In a saucepan over gentle heat, cook tomato with brandy and Tabasco in butter until fairly dry, then season with salt and cook a minute more. Whisk egg yolks with cream. Stir tomato mixture into cream, then add parsley and taste for seasoning.

Check yabby tails for any traces of intestinal vein. Halve lengthwise and place 6 pieces in each pastry case. Place pastry cases on a baking tray and ladle tomato custard mixture over yabby tails. Bake for 10–15 minutes until golden and set. Allow to settle for 5 minutes before serving. Serve for lunch with a small salad of soft leaves on each plate.

yabbies with olive oil

Offer a jug of extra-virgin olive oil, sea salt and a pepper mill with freshly cooked yabbies.

yabbies with dill butter sauce   SERVES 4

You need to reserve the court-bouillon used to cook the yabbies to make this dish.

20 yabbies, cooked in Court-
bouillon ✎

150 g cold unsalted butter

freshly ground black pepper

3 tablespoons freshly
chopped dill

Put yabbies into a deep, heated dish. Cover with foil and keep warm. Strain 1 cup hot court-bouillon into a small saucepan and rapidly reduce by three-quarters. Over heat, whisk butter into reduction a quarter at a time. When butter is incorporated, take sauce off heat then season with pepper and stir in dill. Ladle over yabbies and serve at once. Offer soup spoons as well as fingerbowls and very capacious napkins. For a Scandinavian touch, serve small potatoes boiled in their skins and a bowl of sour cream mixed with lots of dill.

roasted yabbies with thyme oil *see* THYME   other recipes

yoghurt

Yoghurt is the best known and most available of a range of cultured fermented milk products. It is made from pasteurised milk that becomes a creamy curd when bacteria (*Lactobacillus bulgaricus* and *Streptococcus thermophilus*) are introduced. The bacteria sets (or 'clabbers') the milk into the yoghurt curd, converting most of the lactose present in whole milk to lactic acid. (This is why those who are lactose-intolerant can eat yoghurt.) Some yoghurt also contains *Lactobacillus acidophilus*.

Many health claims are made about yoghurt, particularly about its digestibility. Some say it re-establishes flora in the gut that are necessary for the digestive process. (It is suggested that in Western society the taking of antibiotics and environmental factors may have damaged our digestive systems.) In the Balkans, where yoghurt has been a staple food for thousands of years, it is claimed as one of the reasons for the longevity of its population. >

Yoghurt is also a staple throughout the Middle East, where it appears in hot and cold soups, salads, drinks and marinades for meat or as the basic liquid used in cooking a dish. It is equally important in Indian cookery. In *The Complete Asian Cookbook* Charmaine Solomon gives interesting side dishes from India that combine yoghurt with eggplant and mustard seeds, or spiced yoghurt with cucumber and coconut or just banana. I have also read that Lebanese families who emigrate usually take a *laban* (yoghurt) culture with them to their new country.

There is no such thing as a bad food! But one has to admit that people have likes and dislikes. I do not like yoghurt or crème fraîche or sour cream or fromage blanc. That is, I do not like eating these ingredients just as they are. But an apple tart baked with crème fraîche spooned over it as it cooks will develop a lovely golden glaze and taste wonderful. Fromage blanc mixed with fresh herbs and a fine paste of garlic and seasoned with salt and pepper is delicious (but I cannot eat it plain with berries). Sour cream stirred into thick pumpkin soup or borscht is just right. And although I can never enjoy yoghurt at breakfast or as a lunch dish, I do enjoy its flavour in cooking and marinades, and I love yoghurt cheese flavoured with garlic and herbs and rolled into balls. My most-recent tasting of the creamy sheep's milk yoghurt available flavoured with wild honey *almost* persuaded me to spoon it directly from the jar.

Yoghurt is simple to make at home but it appears in such profusion in supermarkets and food shops, and at such reasonable prices, that I wonder why anyone bothers.

yoghurt goes with
salt
olive oil
garlic
mint
parsley
onions
chives
paprika
roasted cumin
coriander
thyme
oregano
tamarind
cucumber
spinach
potatoes
tomatoes
eggplants
lamb
pistachios

VARIETIES AND SEASON

In general commerce yoghurt is sold as plain or flavoured. Both are further divided into low-fat and regular varieties. Flavoured yoghurts have sugar as well as flavour extracts and colouring added. They also have stabilisers such as gelatine added to guarantee a creamy, custard-like texture. There are also speciality yoghurts available made with goat's milk and sheep's milk. Both of these have a higher butterfat content than cow's milk and produce particularly creamy and silky-textured yoghurt. They also contain *Lactobacillus acidophilus*.

Yoghurt is available at all times of the year. For those who make yoghurt, the curdling or clabbering of the milk may take an hour or so longer in the colder months.

SELECTION AND STORAGE

As acidity levels continue to develop in yoghurt stored at higher temperatures, it is a good idea to check the use-by date and always to buy the freshest and coldest product. Make sure you buy plain or natural yoghurt without vanilla flavouring to use in cooking, and check that the label states clearly that *Lactobacillus bulgaricus* and *Streptococcus thermophilus* are present.

Refrigerate yoghurt at once. Store-bought yoghurt will stay fresh for 2 weeks at least at temperatures of 3–5°C. Keep the containers tightly closed, so that they do not pick up odours from other foods.

PREPARATION

Do not shake or whip yoghurt, as this breaks up the curd and causes the whey to separate out. Yoghurt will also quickly separate when heated, due to its delicate acid balance. To avoid this, either stir yoghurt into hot cooked foods at the last minute or stabilise it before using. Due to the higher fat content of goat's milk and sheep's milk yoghurt, they are able to be boiled satisfactorily with only the addition of salt. Cooks are often instructed to strain yoghurt, too, to rid it of excess whey.

TO STABILISE | Stir 1 litre yoghurt over moderate heat to liquefy it. Add 1 egg white (or 1 tablespoon cornflour mixed to a paste with a little water) and 1 teaspoon salt and mix well, then bring to a boil, stirring all the time in *one* direction only. Simmer gently for about 10 minutes until rich and creamy. Do *not* cover the yoghurt as even one drop of water will spoil it. (I would love to know why every instruction stresses to stir in one direction only. Is there a scientific reason for this or is it to protect the stirrer from the Evil Eye?)

TO DRAIN | When using yoghurt as the base for a salad or side dish, drain it in a muslin bag or muslin-lined strainer for 1 hour to rid it of excess whey. Whisk the yoghurt until creamy and add your chosen ingredients. The longer it is drained, the firmer it becomes. As 600 ml yoghurt will release 200 ml whey over 24 hours, ensure the strainer is resting over a suitably sized bowl.

recipes

labna – yoghurt cheese

MAKES 10–15

These cheese balls are delicious on garlic croutons or on opened-out pita bread with salad ingredients. Or serve them with a baked potato instead of butter. Labna can be scattered with or rolled in finely chopped herbs or ground spices or small amounts of very finely chopped spring onion. They can also be drizzled with honey and a light dusting of cinnamon. I find it a good idea not to use a glass jar as the balls are quite soft and one risks damaging them while gouging a few out.

600 ml plain yoghurt
1 teaspoon salt
garlic cloves, unpeeled and
    bruised
sprigs of rosemary
extra-virgin olive oil

Mix yoghurt with salt and drain for 2 days, refrigerated, through a doubled sheet of muslin lining a strainer resting over a large bowl. Roll mixture into small balls, then store in a flat container. Scatter in garlic and rosemary and cover with oil. Leave overnight for flavours to blend. The balls are delicious for at least 2 weeks – but I have never managed to have any left longer than this!

drained yoghurt The drained yoghurt – there should be about 1½ cups – can be slightly sweetened and used to accompany desserts. Or it can be mixed with chopped spring onion and freshly ground black pepper for a savoury topping for hot toast.

tzatziki

SERVES 4–6

A deservedly popular Middle Eastern combination, tzatziki is often served as part of a meze table, a selection of enticing small dishes designed to whet the appetite. If a thicker tzatziki is desired, drain the yoghurt for a few hours.

1 Lebanese *or* long cucumber,
    peeled and finely diced
sea salt
2 cloves garlic, finely chopped
2 cups plain yoghurt (the
    thicker and creamier the
    better)
2 tablespoons dried mint
1 tablespoon extra-virgin
    olive oil
freshly ground black pepper
sprigs of mint

Mix cucumber with salt and leave for 30 minutes. Drain cucumber and squeeze well without crushing it. In another bowl, combine garlic with yoghurt. Stir in cucumber and dried mint. Turn onto a flat dish and drizzle with oil. Grind over pepper and decorate with fresh mint.

quick yoghurt marinade for chicken or lamb

SERVES 4

This is a simple marinade for chicken or tender cuts of lamb that you can quickly skewer and grill or barbecue. If you enjoy the flavour, I urge you to consult books on Indian cookery to understand better the subtlety possible by using a variety of spices. This version is just the beginning!

yoghurt and herb spread
Blend equal quantities of unsalted butter and fetta cheese in a food processor with a generous quantity of chopped parsley, mint and coriander. Stir in enough drained yoghurt to make a spreadable mixture. Refrigerate until firm. Excellent on toast in the morning!

eggplant in yoghurt
Fold diced fried eggplant and sliced garlic into drained yoghurt, then season with pepper and garnish with chopped walnuts or lightly fried mustard seeds. Serve as a Middle Eastern salad or dip.

1 small onion, chopped

2 cloves garlic, chopped

2 slices fresh ginger, peeled
   and chopped

light vegetable oil

1 cup plain yoghurt

1 teaspoon ground turmeric

salt

chilli powder (optional)

4 chicken breasts *or* 750 g
   trimmed, cubed lamb

Soak bamboo skewers in water for 30 minutes. Fry onion, garlic and ginger in 1 tablespoon oil for 5 minutes. Stir into yoghurt and add turmeric, salt and chilli, if using. Add meat and thread on skewers and leave for 1 hour. Allow any excess marinade to drain off, then brush meat lightly with oil and grill on a barbecue or under an electric griller, turning once, for about 5 minutes a side. Serve with fresh coriander and rice.

lamb and yoghurt from a pakistani recipe

SERVES 4–6

1 kg leg *or* shoulder of lamb,
   trimmed and cubed

1 cup plain yoghurt, stabilised

1 cup puréed canned tomato
   (including juice)

1 fresh chilli, seeded and
   finely chopped

2 onions, chopped

4 slices fresh ginger, chopped

2 teaspoons ground turmeric

salt

4 cloves garlic, chopped

2 tablespoons coriander seeds,
   lightly crushed

40 g butter

½ cup coriander leaves and
   stems, coarsely chopped

½ cup parsley, coarsely
   chopped

Preheat oven to 150°C. Place lamb, yoghurt, tomato, chilli, onion, ginger and turmeric in an enamelled cast-iron casserole with a tight-fitting lid. Stir well, then cover and place in oven for 1½ hours. Test for tenderness and salt. Sauté garlic and coriander seeds in butter until fragrant, then stir into casserole. Scatter with herbs just before serving with plain or saffron rice.

raw beetroot and yoghurt salad

SERVES 6

If a thicker cream is desired, drain the yoghurt overnight.

1 bunch coriander, washed

½ bunch mint, washed

(*continued next page*)

Chop coriander (stems and leaves) to make about 1 cup. Chop mint (leaves only) to make about ½ cup. Toss beetroot with

---

cucumber raita

Add finely chopped cucumber, salt, pepper and roasted ground cumin to drained yoghurt. Serve with curries or as a dip. Swap cooked, drained spinach or finely chopped tomato and mild onion for the cucumber for a change.

sweet yoghurt cream

Drain yoghurt overnight in the refrigerator and mix with vanilla bean seeds, castor sugar and whipped cream and serve alongside something faintly Middle Eastern, such as poached quinces scattered with pomegranate seeds.

3 beetroots, trimmed, peeled
  and coarsely grated

juice of 2 lemons

salt

freshly ground black pepper

2 cups plain yoghurt
  (preferably sheep's milk)

herbs and lemon juice and season. Arrange in a ring on a platter and pile yoghurt in centre. Serve with yoghurt-marinated lamb or chicken skewers placed on the beetroot for an attractive presentation or, more simply, with substantial bread for lunch.

poached eggs with yoghurt and garlic sauce

SERVES 4

4 eggs

2 tablespoons unsalted butter

2 tablespoons freshly chopped
  parsley

freshly ground black pepper

SAUCE

3 cloves garlic, very finely
  chopped

pinch of salt

2 tablespoons freshly snipped
  chives

500 g yoghurt, drained
  overnight

To make the sauce, pound garlic and salt in a mortar and pestle until you have a smooth paste. Stir garlic paste and chives into yoghurt.

Poach eggs until just set. Lift from water and drain briefly on a folded napkin. Divide yoghurt sauce between 4 warmed plates. Slip 1 egg onto each plate, centring it on the sauce. Melt butter to sizzling in a frying pan and stir in parsley. Spoon butter and parsley over eggs and grind on pepper. Eat immediately!

sweet yoghurt and saffron pudding

SERVES 4–6

This dish was inspired by a recipe of Madhur Jaffrey's. I have served it alongside a Middle Eastern Fruit Salad (see APRICOTS) as one might have thought of cream or ice-cream (which would both be culturally inappropriate).

½ teaspoon saffron threads

1 tablespoon warmed milk

2 tablespoons castor sugar or
  more to taste

seeds from 4 cardamom pods,
  crushed

600 ml yoghurt, drained
  overnight

2 tablespoons pistachios,
  chopped

Dissolve saffron in milk and stir in sugar and cardamom seeds. Work this mixture very well into drained yoghurt until quite smooth. Pack into small pots or press into a pudding basin lined with plastic wrap. Refrigerate until ready to serve.

Serve straight from small pots or turn out from pudding basin onto a serving plate and peel of plastic wrap. Scatter pistachios over surface.

tomato and yoghurt juice

Combine equal quantities of tomato juice and still mineral water, then stir in yoghurt to taste. Add a large sprig of bruised mint and season with salt and Tabasco.

indian fruit lassi

Blend 2 cups grape juice (or apricot nectar), 1 cup plain yoghurt and ½ cup crushed ice in a food processor until creamy.

yoghurt and pistachio cake

This exotic cake is based on a recipe from Classical Turkish Cooking *by Ayla Algar. I made it after I was given a box of the very first of the Australian pistachio crop. The nuts were especially large and still covered in their glorious purple–pink coats. The cake has a tender texture and is superb with grilled figs.*

I cup fresh pistachios
150 g plain flour
¾ teaspoon bicarbonate of soda
¼ teaspoon baking powder
¼ teaspoon salt
6 eggs, separated
I cup sugar
¾ cup plain yoghurt
½ cup olive oil
½ teaspoon cream of tartar

Preheat oven to 180°C. Butter and flour a 26 cm springform tin. Rub pistachios to remove as much skin as possible, then grind finely in a food processor. Sift flour with bicarbonate of soda, baking powder and salt. In another bowl, beat egg yolks with half the sugar until pale and very thick. Mix in yoghurt and oil, then fold in flour and nuts. Beat egg whites with cream of tartar to form soft peaks, then add remaining sugar and beat to firm peaks. The whites should look shiny and not dry and granular. Gently fold egg white into batter. Pour into prepared tin and bake for 55 minutes. Cool in tin on a wire rack. Serve plain with coffee or tea or fresh fruit.

other recipes

mint and yoghurt chutney *see* MINT
stuffed bush marrow with yoghurt sauce *see* ZUCCHINI AND SQUASH

zucchini and squash

Zalong with the bush marrow, pattipan squash, choko and pumpkin, zucchini belongs to the *Cucurbita* genus, the edible gourds or squash. This family has hundreds of varieties displaying a wide range of colours, sizes and shapes. Some authorities divide the lot into summer squash (zucchini, pattipan squash and bush marrows) and winter squash (the pumpkins). I have commented further on these distinctions and the history of these vegetables in PUMPKINS. The zucchini is a variety of squash or marrow picked when small. The popularity of the zucchini represents the changes that have taken place in Australian eating over the last couple of decades. Everyone uses the Italian name for this small member of the squash family. In English cookbooks it is almost always referred to by the French term *courgette*, showing the prevalent culinary influence in that country. In Australia zucchini are available in every fruit and vegetable shop and are a popular crop in the home vegetable garden. >

There are many tall tales of zucchini and squash that have grown to monstrous proportions hidden under luxuriant leaves. If you have grown a giant and cannot find anyone to give it to, you may wish to try stuffing it. I have even heard of desperate home gardeners who wrench out too-fertile zucchini bushes in the dead of night only to find them sprouting vigorously next season from the compost heap! If your bushes are as vigorous as this it makes even more sense to eat the flowers to check their rampant reproduction.

In some of my English cookbooks I detect a faint sniff when writers speak of zucchini. One even says that they have no taste and she would prefer a bush marrow any day. All I can think is that the delectable zucchini loses flavour without hot sunshine and that she cannot have experienced the joy of a just-picked sweet zucchini cooked quickly with a splash of water and a knob of butter.

VARIETIES AND SEASON

Zucchini, pattipan squash and bush marrows, our most commonly available squash, are all forms of *Cucurbita pepo*, although they do not tend to be identified by variety in the shops. The range of climatic regions in this continent means that all varieties of zucchini and squash are available most of the time. However, the best produce is that grown close to home. In the southern and south-eastern States that still means the finest zucchini appear during spring, summer and autumn. One cannot hope to use zucchini flowers too far from the garden, as they close within hours of picking. They are definitely a fleeting delight of summer and are only at a few specialist greengrocers at the moment. In Italy bunches of zucchini flowers burst from every market stall in summer. Small pattipan squash appear mainly in summer and early autumn.

BUSH MARROWS | Long white and long green bush marrows have, respectively, white or striped green skin and can attain mammoth proportions. The smaller bush marrows, the size of a long football, are good stuffed. Bush marrows do not tend to be sold by variety.

PATTIPAN SQUASH | Also known as button squash, this small vegetable ranges in size from that of a 50 cent coin to as round as a jam jar lid and has a flattened top with scalloped edges. Pale to bright green or deep yellow sometimes touched with dark green, pattipan squash have sweet, dense flesh when young. They are not sold by variety, rather by colour.

ZUCCHINI | Zucchini can be dark green, pale green or yellow and either slender or tear-shaped. The most common variety sold is blackjack, which is slender and dark green. Newly popular is a golden variety sold to gardeners as golden zucchini hybrid. There is another zucchini that has a more pronounced swelling at the tip and is pale green and vaguely striped. In my market it is sold as white or Lebanese zucchini. It has a very fine flavour and is to be recommended to home gardeners.

SELECTION AND STORAGE

All soft-skinned squash (*zucchini* and *pattipan squash*) should have glossy, tender skins and be unblemished. Do not buy any that are soft or spongy to the touch. The seeds should be barely noticeable when you cut into the vegetable. Pattipan squash should be immature when purchased. Avoid those that are chalky-white as they are overmature and will be fibrous with pronounced seeds. Mature pattipan squash are only good for hollowing and stuffing. All soft-skinned squash should be used as soon as possible. Their flavour is delicate and diminishes with long storage and can become rank and bitter, and the flesh can become cottony. *Bush marrows* have harder skins that should still feel firm and look taut. Avoid any with sunken or withered skin or soft patches.

Refrigerate zucchini and squash in a vegetable storage bag in the crisper and eat within 2–3 days. Zucchini and squash do not like being chilled. The vegetable bag, in my view, is essential – without it the texture of these vegetables diminishes very rapidly. Store bush marrows in a basket in a cool place. Stored in the open air they should be used within 36 hours. Once cut, bush marrows must be refrigerated, the cut surface covered with plastic film, and used within 24 hours.

PREPARATION AND COOKING

Zucchini and other immature squash do not need peeling. Slice off each end and proceed with the recipe. Older recipe books often recommend salting sliced zucchini and leaving the slices to sweat for 30 minutes or so before rinsing and drying them, as one does for mature eggplant. If the zucchini you are using are as young and tender as they ought to be, I find no reason to do this. Such zucchini are delicious finely sliced and eaten raw. Never cook zucchini or squash in boiling water. They will become waterlogged and lose their delicate texture. Zucchini and squash can be steamed but I find they still taste a bit watery by this method. My preference is to use butter or oil and a *little* water.

TO COOK IN BUTTER OR OIL This is my favourite method. Rinse the zucchini or squash under the tap, then slice, halve, or leave whole, depending on their size and your inclination. Place the vegetable in a smallish saucepan without too much extra space, then

grilled zucchini
Sprinkle grilling zucchini with freshly grated parmesan cheese before cooking the second side.

zucchini flower stuffings
Stuff zucchini flowers with finely chopped bocconcini tossed with chopped anchovies; finely chopped mortadella sausage mixed with garlic, breadcrumbs, parsley, parmesan and drops of olive oil to make a paste; or very fresh ricotta cheese mixed with finely chopped spinach or silver beet and seasoned with salt, pepper and nutmeg.

drizzle over olive oil or add 20 g butter for 3–4 zucchini and pour in 1 tablespoon water. Jam on the lid and cook over a moderate heat for 3–5 minutes, depending on whether the zucchini or squash have been cut or not. Season with salt, pepper and fresh herbs. **Buttery gratings** Grate zucchini on the largest hole of a grater or use the coarsest julienne blade on your food processor. Bring a saucepan of lightly salted water to a boil. Place the zucchini in a conical sieve and immerse in the water for 30 seconds. Remove, then shake. Tip the zucchini into a wide colander and drain well, then blot with kitchen paper. Transfer the zucchini to a frying pan with melted butter and fresh herbs. Fork through to become thoroughly hot and serve at once.

TO STIR-FRY

Zucchini and squash are excellent stir-fried. Slice the vegetable, then toss in hot oil until shiny. Add a drizzle of something – water, stock or light soy sauce – and cover and cook for 2–4 minutes.

TO GRILL

Halve zucchini or squash or cut thick slices on the bias. Brush with olive oil and place under a hot griller until the surface starts to look blistered and golden. Turn for another few minutes. You can also use a chargrill pan.

Zucchini bushes produce 2 sorts of *flower*. The flower with the immature vegetable attached is the female. The more dramatic flower that appears on a long stalk from the centre of the plant is the male. It is this flower that is sold in bunches and used for fritters in Italy. The male flower has done its job of fertilising the female and is dispensable. Not so the female flower, which shrinks as the zucchini swells. Italians find the vogue for stuffing the flower attached to the immature vegetable mystifying, although they often buy zucchini still with flowers attached (a sign of youth) and cook them like that.

Inspect flowers for insects that may be hidden among the stamens, then nip out the stamens and pistil with your fingers. (Some writers suggest removing the stem and the calyx – the green cup holding the petals together. I don't, as the stem gives you something to hold onto when turning the fritter both in the batter and later in the hot oil.) Unstuffed flowers can be chopped and sautéd and added to omelettes or risotto or scattered over lightly fried zucchini slices. If stuffing the flowers, do so as soon as possible after you've picked or bought them as the petals start to close once picked. Do not delay the frying for more than an hour or so, and fry the flowers straightaway if the stuffing is wet, otherwise the petals will fall apart.

Stuffings can include fresh cheese, sausage, and so on. The stuffed flowers can be dipped into Beer Batter ✓, Cornflour Batter ✓ or a whisked egg and then breadcrumbs or polenta, for a crunchier finish.

fettuccine with zucchini

Fry thinnish rounds of zucchini in olive oil quickly but carefully until golden brown on each side. Add thinly sliced garlic and a handful of freshly chopped parsley or basil and toss with hot fettuccine. Serve sprinkled with freshly grated parmesan.

marinated zucchini

Layer grilled zucchini in a flat dish with thinly sliced garlic, chopped mint, pepper, a sprinkling of red-wine vinegar and a drizzle of olive oil on each layer and marinate for 1 hour before enjoying.

TO STUFF AND COOK ZUCCHINI FLOWERS

Place a lump of stuffing in each flower and gently fold the petals around the filling. Dip the stuffed flower in the selected batter or egg and then crumbs and shallow-fry until golden brown. Drain very well on crumpled kitchen paper and serve immediately.

bread and butter zucchini pickles

MAKES I LITRE

These quick and easy pickles are just as good if made with small pickling cucumbers. I like them in rye bread sandwiches with ham, pastrami or rare roast beef.

1 kg small zucchini, sliced on diagonal
3 onions, finely sliced
½ cup salt
3 cups white-wine vinegar
1½ cups sugar
1 tablespoon yellow mustard seeds
1 teaspoon dry mustard
2 teaspoons ground turmeric

Toss zucchini and onion with salt in a stainless steel or ceramic bowl, then cover with cold water. Leave for 1 hour, then drain in a colander. Return drained zucchini to bowl. Combine remaining ingredients in a saucepan and stir over gentle heat until sugar has dissolved. Bring to a boil and pour over drained zucchini. Leave to cool. Use at once or pack into sterilised jars and refrigerate. Use within 2 months.

zucchini chips

SERVES 4

These chips have been known to convert many a child to zucchini and are a fantastic way to use up larger zucchini. They are particularly delicious alongside a fried fillet of fish and create an interesting variation on the standard fish and chips. The fish can be dipped in the same batter. I also use this batter to coat a variety of vegetables – eggplant slices, blanched florets of cauliflower and broccoli, sticks of carrot, mushrooms, and so on. Served with a wedge of lemon and Fresh Tomato Sauce (see TOMATOES), such a selection is a favourite lunch dish. You will need to have plenty of crumpled kitchen paper ready on a tray to drain the chips.

1 medium zucchini, washed
vegetable oil for deep-frying
1 quantity Beer Batter
salt (optional)

Trim ends from unpeeled zucchini and cut lengthwise into sticks. Heat a good quantity of oil in a deep-sided saucepan to 175°C. Dip zucchini in batter, then carefully lower into oil and cook 4–5 minutes until golden brown. Drain well on kitchen paper and sprinkle with salt, if you wish.

spring vegetable salad

Cook sliced zucchini or pattipan squash, beans, asparagus, peeled broad beans, peas and sliced very young leek separately until barely tender. Drain well and spread out on a platter. Drizzle with extra-virgin olive oil and scatter with herbs while still warm. Add any special extra bits (anchovy, roasted sweet pepper, slow-cooked onion, or toasted pine nuts) and gently lift and toss to combine.

ratatouille

SERVES 6

The original French version of ratatouille results in a soft stew where the ingredients have melded and mostly lost their shape but have produced luscious juices. Some modern cooks prefer to cook each ingredient separately and combine the dish at the end, or to shorten the cooking time of their ratatouille radically and leave the vegetables crunchy. I prefer the traditional method, although I do stop the cooking once the vegetables are tender.

Ratatouille is my choice to accompany warm roast lamb on those occasions when you wish to sit with friends and enjoy a summer's evening and not rush about in the kitchen. Both the lamb and the ratatouille will be timed to be completed before your friends arrive.

3 eggplants, cut into 3 cm
    cubes
salt
½ cup olive oil
2 onions, thinly sliced
2 cloves garlic, thinly sliced
3 red peppers, seeded and cut
    into 3 cm cubes
6 small or 3 larger zucchini,
    cut into 3 cm chunks
a few coriander seeds, crushed
4 large ripe tomatoes, peeled,
    seeded and chopped
freshly ground black pepper
freshly chopped parsley or
    basil

Place eggplant on a tray and lightly sprinkle with salt. Cover with a sheet of foil and press lightly with a few tins for 1 hour. Wipe off moisture with kitchen paper and discard juices. Heat oil in an enamelled cast-iron casserole in which the finished dish can be served and sauté onion until limp and golden. Add garlic, peppers and eggplant, then cover casserole and cook gently for 40 minutes. Add zucchini, coriander seeds, tomato and a grinding of pepper and cook for a further 20 minutes until vegetables are tender. Stir in parsley and adjust seasoning.

zucchini and avocado

Toss chunks of ripe avocado with thinly sliced raw zucchini, olive oil and lemon juice and season. Pile on toast for a quick brunch.

zucchini omelette

Whisk 2 eggs, then season and stir in some chopped parsley, basil, mint or oregano. Fry sliced zucchini in olive oil until golden brown, then stir into the eggs and cook as a medium-thick omelette in hot olive oil in a heavy-based frying pan. Eat with a tomato salad for a gorgeous solo lunch.

stuffed bush marrow with yoghurt sauce

SERVES 4

This dish can also be made using larger-than-desired zucchini that have been halved lengthwise and hollowed out a little to hold some stuffing. In this case, add the scooped flesh to the stuffing. Extra-large pattipan squash can also be used: cut off a small lid, then hollow out a space for the stuffing.

The sauce includes egg white, which stabilises the yoghurt (this process is described in YOGHURT). Its piquant flavour goes well with the light spiciness of the filling.

½ cup cracked wheat

I large onion, very finely
  chopped

I tablespoon olive oil

500 g finely minced lamb *or*
  beef

½ cup coarsely chopped
  parsley *or* mint

salt

pinch of cayenne pepper

2 teaspoons ground cumin

I teaspoon ground allspice

I football-sized bush marrow,
  cut in half lengthwise

SAUCE

3 cups plain yoghurt

I egg white

3 cloves garlic, chopped

I teaspoon dried mint

salt

20 g butter

Preheat oven to 180°C. Soak cracked wheat
in water for 5 minutes, then squeeze dry.

To make the sauce, whisk yoghurt and
egg white, then simmer uncovered for
10 minutes, stirring. Mix garlic, mint and
salt and sauté in butter for 1 minute, then
stir into yoghurt mixture.

Sauté onion in oil until golden. Mix onion
with remaining ingredients except marrow
and fry a tiny ball to test seasoning. Pack
into marrow halves, then settle them in an
appropriately sized gratin dish. Pour over
sauce and bake for 45 minutes. Serve hot,
warm or cold.

zucchini salad

*Slice raw zucchini
thinly, then toss
with olive oil, salt,
pepper, lemon juice
and fresh herbs and
eat as a salad. Make
Bagna Cauda Sauce
(see* ANCHOVIES*) to
go with it as a dip.*

twice-cooked zucchini soufflés

SERVES 6

*Zucchini and cheese are made for each other. I have a twice-cooked soufflé
on my menu as a first course that customers refuse to allow me to remove.
Here is my version of it with zucchini added.*

3 zucchini, coarsely grated

80 g butter

350 ml milk

60 g plain flour

I tablespoon thick cream

I tablespoon freshly grated
  parmesan cheese

3 egg yolks

salt

freshly ground black pepper

freshly grated nutmeg
  (optional)

4 egg whites, firmly beaten

2 cups cream

Preheat oven to 180°C and butter 6 ×
150 ml soufflé dishes. In a frying pan, sauté
zucchini in 20 g of the butter for 3–5
minutes, stirring. Tip into a strainer resting
over a bowl to drain. Warm milk gently.
Melt remaining butter in zucchini pan and
stir in flour. Cook, stirring, for 5 minutes.
Gradually whisk in warm milk and stir until
sauce boils, then remove from heat. Stir in
zucchini, cream and parmesan and cool for
5 minutes.

Add egg yolks to zucchini mixture and
season to taste with salt, pepper and a scrap
of nutmeg, if desired. Fold in egg whites

and spoon mixture into prepared dishes. Bake for 15–18 minutes until firm and puffed, then remove to a draught-free spot to cool. Ease soufflés out of dishes carefully while still a little warm and arrange, well spaced, in a buttered ovenproof dish.

When ready to serve, pour ⅓ cup cream over each soufflé and bake at 180°C for 15–20 minutes until swollen and golden brown on top. Serve at once with a green salad and maybe a light home-made tomato sauce.

bibliography

Acton, Eliza. *The Best of Eliza Acton*, ed. Elizabeth Ray. Penguin Books, Harmondsworth, 1974.

Alexander, Stephanie. *Stephanie's Australia*. Allen & Unwin, Sydney, 1991.

—— *Stephanie's Feasts and Stories*. Allen & Unwin, Sydney, 1988.

—— *Stephanie's Menus for Food Lovers*. Mandarin Australia, Melbourne, 1991.

—— *Stephanie's Seasons*. Allen & Unwin, Sydney, 1993.

Algar, Ayla. *Classical Turkish Cooking*. HarperCollins, New York, 1991.

Arthur Yates & Co. Pty Ltd. *Yates Garden Guide* (centennial edn). Angus & Robertson, Sydney, 1994.

Australian Meat and Livestock Corporation. *The Executive Chefs' Guide to Australian Meat*. Sydney, n.d.

—— *Food Service Buyers Guide for Beef and Lamb*. Sydney, n.d.

Bacon, Vo. *The Fresh Fruit Cookbook*. Regency Publications, Melbourne, 1984.

—— *The Fresh Vegetable Cookbook*. Regency Publications, Melbourne, 1984.

Beer, Maggie. *Maggie's Farm*. Allen & Unwin, Sydney, 1993.

Beranbaum, Rose Levy. *The Cake Bible*. Macmillan, London, 1993.

Bertolli, Paul with Waters, Alice. *Chez Panisse Cooking*. Random House, New York, 1988.

Bissell, Frances. *Oriental Flavours*. Macmillan, London, 1990.

Blackman, Grant. *Australian Fish Cooking*. Hill of Content, Melbourne, 1978.

—— *The Great Australian Shellfish Cookbook*. Cassell Australia, Stanmore, 1979.

Boddy, Michael and Boddy, Janet. *Kitchen Talk* (vol. I, nos 1–13). The Bugle Press, via Binalong, NSW, 1989–92.

Brown, Lynda. *The Cook's Garden*. Vermilion, London, 1992.

Burchett, Mary. *Through My Kitchen Door*. Georgian House, Melbourne, 1960.

Bureau of Resource Sciences. *Australian Fisheries Resources*. Department of Primary Industries & Energy and the Fisheries Research & Development Corporation, Canberra, 1993.

—— *Marketing Names for Fish and Seafood in Australia*. Department of Primary Industries & Energy and the Fisheries Research & Development Corporation, Canberra, 1995.

Carey, Nora. *Perfect Preserves*. Stewart, Tabori & Chang, New York, 1990.

Cost, Bruce. *Ginger East to West*. Aris, Berkeley, 1984.

Coyle, L. Patrick. *The World Encyclopedia of Food*. Facts on File, New York, 1982.

Dahlen, Martha. *A Cook's Guide to Chinese Vegetables*. Odyssey, Hong Kong, 1992.

Darwin Garden Club. *Darwin Gardener's Gourmet Guide*. Darwin, 1981.

David, Elizabeth. *A Book of Mediterranean Food* (illustrated rev. edn). Dorling Kindersley, London, 1988.

—— *English Bread and Yeast Cookery*. Penguin Books, Harmondsworth, 1979.

—— *French Provincial Cooking*. Penguin Books, Harmondsworth, 1970.

—— *Summer Cooking* (rev. edn). Penguin Books, Harmondsworth, 1965.

Davidson, Alan and Knox, Charlotte. *Fruit*. Simon & Schuster, New York, 1991.

—— *Seafood*. Mitchell Beazley, London, 1989.

Di Stasio, Rinaldo, Dupleix, Jill and Durack, Terry. *Allegro al Dente*. William Heinemann, Melbourne, 1994.

Dods, Mistress Margaret. *The Cook and Housewife's Manual* (6th edn). Oliver & Boyd, Edinburgh, 1837.

Dowell, Philip and Bailey, Adrian. *The Book of Ingredients*. Mermaid Books, London, 1983.

Edwards, Ron. *Traditional Torres Strait Island Cooking*. Rams Skull Press, Kuranda, 1988.

Esbensen, Mogens Bay. *A Taste of the Tropics*. Viking O'Neil, South Yarra, 1988.

—— *Thai Cuisine*. Thomas Nelson, Melbourne, 1986.

Freeman, Meera and Nhan, Le Van. *The Vietnamese Cookbook*. Viking, Ringwood, 1995.

Fuhrer, Bruce. *A Field Companion to Australian Fungi*. Five Mile Press, Melbourne, 1985.

Fussell, Betty. *I Hear America Cooking*. Viking, New York, 1986.

Glasse, Hannah. *The Art of Cookery* (8th edn). A. Millar et al., London, 1763.

Glowinski, Louis. *The Complete Book of Fruit Growing in Australia*. Lothian Books, Melbourne, 1991.

Gray, Patience. *Honey from a Weed*. Prospect Books, London, 1986.

Gray, Rose and Rogers, Ruth. *The River Cafe Cookbook*. Ebury Press, London, 1995.

Greene, Bert. *Greene on Greens*. Doubleday, Sydney, 1984.

Grigson, Jane. *Charcuterie and French Pork Cookery*. Penguin Books, Harmondsworth, 1970.

—— *Jane Grigson's Fruit Book*. Michael Joseph, London, 1982.

—— *Jane Grigson's Vegetable Book*. Atheneum, New York, 1979.

—— *The Observer Guide to British Cookery*. Michael Joseph, London, 1984.

Grigson, Jane and Knox, Charlotte. *Exotic Fruits and Vegetables*. Jonathan Cape, London, 1986.

Halici, Nevin. *Turkish Cookbook*. Dorling Kindersley, London, 1989.

Hazan, Marcella. *Marcella's Kitchen*. Macmillan, London, 1987.

Hazen, Janet. *Garlic*. Chronicle Books, San Francisco, 1992.

Hemphill, Rosemary. *Herbs for All Seasons*. Penguin Books, Ringwood, 1990.

Hom, Ken. *The Taste of China*. Papermac, London, 1992.

Isaacs, Jennifer. *Bush Food*. Weldon, Sydney, 1987.

Jaffrey, Madhur. *Eastern Vegetarian Cooking*. Arrow Books, London, 1990.

Johns, Leslie and Stevenson, Violet. *Fruit for the Home and Garden*. Angus & Robertson, Sydney, 1985.

Kasper, Lynne Rossetto. *The Splendid Table*. William Morrow & Co., New York, 1992.

Koffmann, Pierre. *Memories of Gascony*. Octopus, London, 1990.

Kuo, Irene. *The Key to Chinese Cooking*. Thomas Nelson, Melbourne, 1977.

Larkcom, Joy. *Oriental Vegetables*. John Murray, London, 1991.

—— *The Salad Garden*. Doubleday, Sydney, 1984.

Liew, Cheong and Ho, Elizabeth. *My Food*. Allen & Unwin, Sydney, 1996.

Lin, Hsiang Ju and Lin, Tsuifeng. *Chinese Gastronomy*. Thomas Nelson, London, 1969.

Lo, Kenneth. *A Guide to Chinese Eating*. Phaidon, Oxford, 1976.

Low, Tim. *Wild Food Plants of Australia*. Angus & Robertson, Sydney, 1991.

Macquarie Dictionary of Cookery, gen. ed. Judy Jones. Macquarie Books, Sydney, 1983.

Madison, Deborah. *The Savory Way*. Bantam Books, New York, 1990.

Manfield, Christine. *Paramount Cooking*. Viking, Ringwood, 1995.

Manfredi, Stefano. *Fresh from Italy*. Hodder & Stoughton, Sydney, 1994.

McGee, Harold. *On Food and Cooking*. Collier Books, New York, 1988.

Michalak, Patricia and Peterson, Cass. *Vegetables* (Lothian Successful Organic Gardening). Lothian Books, Melbourne, 1995.

Middione, Carlo. *The Food of Southern Italy*. William Morrow & Co., New York, 1987.

Miller, Mark. *The Great Chile Book*. Ten Speed Press, Berkeley, 1991.

National Food Authority. 'Code of hygienic production; uncooked fermented comminuted meat products' – an amendment to the *Food Standards Code*. Australian Government Publishing Service, Canberra, April 1995.

New South Wales Department of Agriculture. *Home Fruit Growing*. Sydney, 1984.

New South Wales Department of Agriculture & Fisheries. *The Home Vegetable Garden* (8th edn). Sydney, 1991.

Norwak, Mary. *The Farmhouse Kitchen*. Penguin, Harmondsworth, 1979.

Owen, Sri. *Indonesian Food and Cookery*. Prospect Books, London, 1983.

—— *The Rice Book*. Doubleday, London, 1993.

Painter, Gilian. *The Herb Garden Displayed*. Hodder & Stoughton, Auckland, 1978.

Phillips, Roger and Rix, Martyn. *Vegetables* (The Garden Plant Series). Macmillan, London, 1995.

Queensland Department of Primary Industries. *Queensland Food Book*. Brisbane, 1988.

—— *Tropical Tree Fruits of Australia*. Brisbane, 1984.

Roden, Claudia. *A New Book of Middle Eastern Food*. Penguin, Harmondsworth, 1986.

Rogers, Jo. *What Food is That?* (abridged edn). Lansdowne, Sydney, 1995.

Routhier, Nicole. *The Foods of Vietnam*. Stewart, Tabori & Chang, New York, 1989.

Shaida, Margaret. *The Legendary Cuisine of Persia*. Penguin Books, Harmondsworth, 1994.

Simetti, Mary Taylor. *Pomp and Sustenance*. Knopf, New York, 1989.

Skinner, Gwen. *Simply Living*. Reed, Auckland, 1981.

Solomon, Charmaine. *The Complete Asian Cookbook* (rev. edn). Lansdowne, Sydney, 1992.

Spencer, Colin. *Vegetable Book*. Conran Octopus, London, 1995.

—— *Vegetable Pleasures*. Fourth Estate, London, 1992.

Spry, Constance and Hume, Rosemary. *The Constance Spry Cookery Book* (rev. edn). Weidenfeld & Nicolson, London, 1971.

Tankard, Glenn. *Tropical Fruit*. Viking O'Neil, South Yarra, 1987.

Thompson, David. *Classic Thai Cuisine*. Simon & Schuster Australia, Sydney, 1993.

Time-Life. *The Good Cook* series (*Beef and Veal*; *Fish and Shellfish*; *Grain, Pasta and Pulses*; *Lamb*; *Offal*; *Pork*), chief consultant Richard Olney. Time-Life, New York, 1978–81.

Toussaint-Samat, Maguelonne. *The History of Food*. Blackwell, Cambridge, USA, 1992.

Tsuji, Shizuo. *Japanese Cooking: a Simple Art*. Kodansha, Tokyo, 1981.

Visser, Margaret. *Much Depends on Dinner*. Penguin, Harmondsworth, 1986.

—— *The Rituals of Dinner*. Grove Weidenfeld, New York, 1991.

von Bremzen, Anya and Welchman, John. *Please to the Table: the Russian Cookbook*. Workman Press, New York, 1990.

Waters, Alice. *Chez Panisse Menu Cookbook*. Random House, New York, 1982.

Wells, Patricia. *Trattoria*. William Morrow & Co., New York, 1993.

list of plates

We thank the following for permission to reprint recipes:

Cantaloupe Ice-cream: Elizabeth David, French Provincial Cooking, *Penguin, Harmondsworth, and David Higham Associates, London; Coconut Milk: Charmaine Solomon*, The Complete Asian Cookbook, *Lansdowne Publishing, Sydney; Coriander Peanut Pesto: Christine Manfield*, Paramount Cooking, *Viking, Ringwood; Fettuccine with Gorgonzola: Rinaldo Di Stasio, Jill Dupleix and Terry Durack*, Allegro al Dente, *William Heinemann, Melbourne; Hot Spicy Fish, Moroccan Tagine with Quince, Claudia Roden's Middle Eastern Orange Cake, Pickled Turnips: Claudia Roden*, A New Book of Middle Eastern Food, *Penguin, Harmondsworth, and David Higham Associates, London; Hot–sour Fried Tripe: Sri Owen*, Indonesian Food and Cookery, *Prospect Books, London; Lemon Salad Based on Marcella's: Marcella Hazan*, Marcella's Kitchen, *Macmillan, London, and Alfred A. Knopf, New York; Mango Chutney: Mogens Bay Esbensen*, A Taste of the Tropics, *Viking O'Neil, Ringwood; Olive Oil and Dessert Wine Cake: Alice Waters*, Chez Panisse Menu Cookbook, *Random House, New York; and Lescher & Lescher, New York; Parsnip Croquettes: Colin Spencer*, Vegetable Pleasures, *Fourth Estate, London; Patafla from Provence: recipe Jill Norman, used by Elizabeth David in* A Book of Mediterranean Food, *Penguin, London; Pickled Cornichons: Nora Carey*, Perfect Preserves, *Stewart, Tabori & Chang, New York; Rosemary and Bay Leaf Savoury Custards: Patricia Wells*, Trattoria, *William Morrow & Co, New York; Russian Sour Cherry Soup: Anya von Bremzen and John Welchman*, Please to the Table: the Russian Cookbook, *Workman Publishing, New York; Salmoriglio – Oregano Sauce: Rose Gray and Ruth Rogers*, The River Cafe Cookbook, *Ebury Press, London; Squab Pigeon and Fig Salad: Stefano Manfredi*, Fresh from Italy, *Hodder Headline, Sydney; Sweet Potato and Prawn Fritters: Meera Freeman and Le Van Nhan*, The Vietnamese Cookbook, *Viking, Ringwood; Tung Po Pork: Ken Hom*, The Taste of China, *Papermac, London; Yam Goong – Salad of Bug Meat with Mint and Lemongrass, Mango with Sticky Rice, Custard Apple or Soursop Ice-cream, Panang Gai – Dry Chicken Curry: Mogens Bay Esbensen*, Thai Cuisine, *Viking O'Neil, Ringwood* | *Every effort has been made to trace copyright holders, and the publishers would like to hear from anyone who believes they have not been acknowledged correctly.*

index